THE DIRECTORY OF
COMMUNITY
SERVICES 2006/07

PMH

Professional, Managerial & Healthcare Publications Ltd

PO Box 100, Chichester, West Sussex PO18 8HD
Telephone: +44 (0)1243 576444 Fax: +44 (0)1243 576456
Email: info@directoryCHS.co.uk

Publishing Details

Directory of Community Health Services 2006/07

Subscriptions
The *Directory of Community Health Services* is available on sale from the publishers, price £49.95 inc p&p (NHS price £29.95). Generous discounts are available for bulk orders. For further details contact the publishers on 01243 576444.

Previous editions
Please destroy any previous editions of the *Directory of Community Nursing* you may hold, as the information in them is now out-of-date.

Next edition
The next edition of the *Directory of Community Health Services* will be published during 2007. Details of prices and advertising rates can be obtained from the Publishers (please see below).

Errors and omissions
While every effort has been made to ensure the accuracy of all information included in the *Directory of Community Health Services*, the publishers cannot accept responsibility for any errors or admissions within it.

Comments and suggestions
Comments and suggestions for improvements or additions to the *Directory* are always gratefully received and will be given careful consideration by the publishers for possible inclusion in the next edition.

Copyright and publication rights

ISBN 1-898789-45-2

Publishing
Editor: Ruth Fermor
Data Management: Bill Tate
Data Entry: Fiona Jones
Commercial Manager: Ryszard Holowenko
Editiorial Consultant: Pat Scowen MA

SOUTH TYNESIDE	ld
○○○○○○○○○○8301l 3/07	
8301	
Bertrams	18.01.07
Ret A/	£29.95
610.7343	

Professi ... td
PO Box 100, Chichester, West Sussex PO18 8HD
Telephone: +44 (0)1243 576444 Fax: +44 (0)1243 576456
Email: info@directoryCHS.co.uk

Part of the Keyways Publishing group

Essential reading for all your healthcare team

Journal of Family Health Care is published bi-monthly and is an essential companion for all health professionals working with the family.

Subscription to this respected publication is only £28.00 for one year or £60.00 for three years.

Your subscription will include *School Health, Family Health Care Bulletins* and other supplements published in conjunction with *Journal of Family Health Care*.

A subscription form is enclosed with this directory. Please complete the form and return it to ensure you receive a personal copy or subscribe online at www.KeywaysPublishing.com

Your vital link in the chain of patient care

The *Directory of Mental Health Services* provides a unique and wide ranging contact reference specifically designed to serve the mental health and learning disabilities sector, updated annually. Whether on the social worker's desk, in the CPN's office, the GP's surgery or the outpatient department, DMHS is always on call!

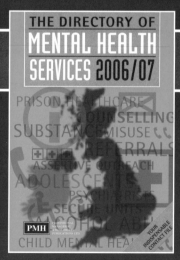

For information on these publications please telephone 01243 576444 or visit www.KeywaysPublishing.com

When you're running a busy surgery, you need equipment you can count on.

GE imagination at work

Dinamap® ProCare 400

Accurate blood pressure readings even on restless patients by measuring two heart beats. Available with SpO$_2$, temperature, printer or printerless versions and data output from RS232.

Dinamap®
ProCare 400

Dinamap® Pro 1000

Reliable Dinamap® blood pressure monitoring with SpO$_2$, ECG and IVAC® Turbo•Temp™ Dinamap® ASAP allows fast, accurate, non-invasive blood pressure monitoring.

Dinamap®
Pro 1000

TruSat™ Pulse Oximeter

The latest advancement in pulse oximeters, combining the reliable performance and usability of a table top oximeter with the rugged, lightweight features of a handheld oximeter. Also available with Trend download.

TruSat™
Pulse Oximeter

TuffSat® Pulse Oximeter

This extremely durable handheld pulse oximeter is one of the smallest oximeters available. Use Relative Perfusion Index™ to locate the strongest pulse signal on your patient.

TuffSat®
Pulse Oximeter

GE Healthcare
71 Great North Road • Hatfield • AL9 5EN

Tel: 01707 263570 • Fax: 01707 260065
www.gehealthcare.com

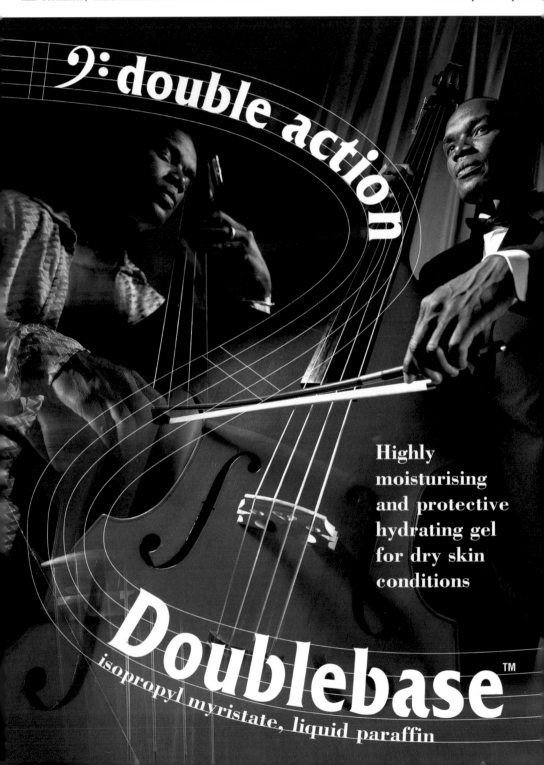

double action

Highly moisturising and protective hydrating gel for dry skin conditions

Doublebase™

isopropyl myristate, liquid paraffin

Contents

Section 1

Section 2

Contents

Section 3

Alphabetical Indexes

The Researchers and Publishers of the *Directory of Community Health Services* would like to thank all nursing and midwifery managers and their staff for their continued help in updating entries. Please inform the Publishers at any time of further changes so that these can be noted for future editions. (See form on page 1.78).

The protein gap: finding the missing piece

Protein deficiency[1] can cause severe adverse effects, so selecting a high protein supplement (Fortisip Protein) instead of a standard supplement can benefit patients.

When people are ill, protein requirements increase[2,3] while protein intake decreases[4] - leading to a protein gap.

Just 2 x 200 ml bottles of Fortisip Protein per day provide 40 g protein (equivalent to 6.5 eggs or 2 pints of milk)[5] - together with energy, vitamins and minerals, effectively filling the protein gap.

Fortisip Protein the missing piece in your patient's protein intake.

For more information or to request samples call 01225 751 098.

References: 1. Thomas B. Dietary protein and amino acids. In: Manual of Dietetic Practice. Blackwell Science: 141-45, 2001. 2. Elia M. Special nutritional problems and the use of enteral and parenteral nutrition. In: Oxford textbook of medicine. Oxford Medical Publications: 1314-26, 1996. 3. Soulsby C et al. Estimating nutritional requirements for adults. In: A pocket guide to clinical nutrition, 2004. 4. Stratton J et al. Disease-related malnutrition: an evidence-based approach to treatment. CABI Publishing 2003. McCance & Widdowson's The Composition of Foods. 6th Ed. Royal Society of Chemistry, 2002.

NUTRICIA
CLINICAL *care*
Making the difference

Milton.
kills MRSA

 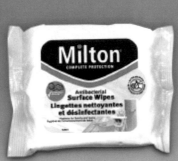  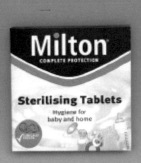

The Milton Antibacterial and Sterilising ranges are clinically proven to kill all harmful bacteria and fungi - including the superbug MRSA.

Whether you're in hospital, at home or out and about, take Milton Antibacterial Hand Gel and Milton Antibacterial Surface Wipes for complete peace of mind.

Effective and guaranteed safe for baby, Milton is the safest choice in preventing the spread of MRSA.

The Milton antibacterial range is available in the baby aisle of larger Boots stores, Tesco, Superdrug, Sainsbury's, Co-op and selected pharmacies. Visit www.milton-tm.com for more information.

Milton. Complete Protecti

From the Minister for Social Care

The world of health and social care is changing. It is changing to fit with a society that wants public services convenient to the way people live their lives now.

That means that instead of people coming to services, services go to people. More services in the community was a key aspect of our new White Paper, Our health, our care, our say. We will have more services in community hospitals, more services in schools, more services in children's centres, more services in GP surgeries and more services in people's homes.

Crucial to making this happen will be the nurses who work in the community. You will be helping ensure services put people in control, focus on prevention and provide integrated care.

Putting people in control will involve you working closely with those you care for, helping them become partners in their own care. This might be through encouraging self-care for long term conditions or helping people make use of technology to assist them in their own home.

Prevention is about taking a long term view and helping people adopt healthy lifestyles. Midwives, health visitors and school nurses in particular, are ideally placed to help ensure that children get a healthy flying start to life.

Integration will mean working closely with your colleagues in social care. The White Paper has a commitment to joint health and social care teams being in place by 2008, so you can expect to be working with social care colleagues in the near future. Together your complementary

Ivan Lewis MP Minister for Social Care

skills will mean better care for the people who use services.

These are exciting times of change, but I know this can bring extra pressures in terms of work. Colleagues and organisations can provide a huge amount of support and I hope this *Directory of Community Health Services* will help you in making the necessary contacts.

I believe community nurses are vitally important to the future of health and social care and I want to conclude by thanking you for all the wonderful work you have done, and will do.

Ivan Lewis MP

May 2006

Changes to this edition of the Directory

Structural and administrative changes continue to take place within all areas of the NHS to consolidate Primary Care as the focal point of patient care within the NHS. With the expansion of the community services the amount of data being provided within the PMH directories has increased enormously.

To accommodate this expansion the information is now being presented in two volumes. The *Directory of Community Nursing* has been renamed *Directory of Community Health Services* and retains all the key information previously included apart from the Mental Health Services.

The companion volume, our new *Directory of Mental Health Services* provides greatly extended information on this increasingly important aspect of Community care together with information on services for those with learning disabilities.

The entries for the Primary Care Trusts in this edition of the *Directory of Community Health Services* continue to reflect the current departmental structure that has evolved as the PCTs assume responsibility for an increasing range of Community Services and Community Hospitals.

How the Directory mirrors the new NHS structure

As part of the NHS reorganisation the four Health and Social Care Regions have been abolished and the 28 SHAs reduced to ten. The information for England is now shown within the ten new Strategic Health Authorities (SHAs). These are included alphabetically and the name of the relevant SHA appears in the header at the top of each page.

The new SHAs are: East Midlands, East of England, London, North East, North West, South Central, South East Coast, South West, West Midlands and finally Yorkshire & Humberside. Information for England is followed by Wales, Scotland, Northern Ireland and Offshore which includes the

Isle of Man, Jersey and Guernsey.

Wales still retains its Health Authorities, whilst Scotland has dissolved all the Acute and Primary Care Trusts. The Health Boards are responsible for health services throughout Scotland and these services are provided through their Acute and Primary Care Divisions. Within each Primary Care Division there are a number of Community Health Partnerships and these are included alphabetically within each Health Board.

Northern Ireland retains the Health and Social Service Boards. All Community Trusts then appear alphabetically under their relevant health authority.

Throughout the Directory staff are listed by department within the Trust that employs them. Where a service is shared between Trusts, the Directory has to rely on this information being provided by the Trusts concerned.

At the beginning of each SHA in section 2 there is a map showing the new Health Authority boundaries and the main towns and areas served by that Authority. There are also a number of useful alphabetical indexes at the back of the Directory.

The Primary Care Service is now responsible for virtually all Community Nursing Services but many Specialist Nurses in Secondary Care maintain a vital role in providing "seamless care" for patients. This can involve Primary Care, Secondary Care and Social Services, especially for Liaison Specialists, Discharge Facilitators and Specialist Nurses in Children's Services.

To ensure that the Directory is as complete and accurate as possible and reflects the interdependence of the services, we have, where possible, included relevant services provided by the Acute NHS Trusts even though these may not fall within the strict definition of Community Nursing Services.

Do you work in
COMMUNITY CARE?

If you care about your future, join UNISON

Decisions will soon be made that affect your job – and who employs you.

Healthcare services across the UK are changing. Under plans already announced for England, staff may end up being moved to another employer and having their jobs radically altered.

UNISON is the largest union in healthcare and we are determined to resist needless change and make sure the interests of our members are protected.

Join us - and together we can make sure employers and government listen to primary care staff.

Phone UNISON on 0845 355 0845 (local rate).
Textphone users call UNISONdirect on
0800 0 967 968
Lines open from 6am-midnight Monday-Friday
and 9am-4pm on Saturdays.

www.unison.org.uk/join

Join UNISON -
your friend at work

positively
public

A Guide to using the Directory

This latest edition of the *Directory of Community Health Services* and the new *Directory of Mental Health Services* has been formatted to conform to the new NHS structure established by the creation of the ten new Strategic Health Authorities (SHAs). In England trusts are included alphabetically within each SHA and the name of the relevant SHA appears at the top of each page. In order to maintain the user-friendly reputation of our directory the SHAs are also presented alphabetically. The departmental listings for the Primary Care Trusts have been extended to include additional specialities and should enable users to find the information they need even more rapidly.

How the Directory can help you

This Directory is an important resource in establishing and maintaining the contacts that are key to providing the continuing care of at-risk individuals and families.

The NHS is becoming an increasingly complex organisation, with Authority and Trust names and areas changing frequently and different parts of the UK having different administrative structures. The population is becoming more mobile and patients are discharged from hospital earlier making referrals to and between the community services more numerous and more complicated. Yet as the Victoria Climbie Inquiry by Lord Laming highlighted, speed, accuracy and written confirmation of referrals as well as inter-agency working are all essential in providing a safe, effective service.

Whatever part of the UK and whichever branch of the NHS you work in, you know how difficult and time-consuming it can be to find contact details for the community services. By their nature these services are likely to be dispersed over a wide area with staff operating from a variety of different offices and clinical bases. This is where the Directory can help you.

If you work in the community and have a patient or family moving to another area, you can quickly contact your opposite number to alert them to a problem or a clinical need – again, in any part of the UK.

In the boxes are some practical examples of how the Directory can help ensure seamless care.

Diana, a 79 year old from Hampshire, is in your Care of the Elderly Unit in London after collapsing at an exhibition. She lives alone and will need home support. By looking up Hampshire Social Services in the Directory and ringing the Home Care Services you are able to arrange meals and an assessment visit. The Directory also tells you which PCT covers Diana's village so you ring the community nurses to arrange removal of Diana's stitches. As a result, Diana is able to go home a day earlier than envisaged.

You are a school nurse. Two children from an asylum seeker's family are doing well at one of your schools, though one has been assessed for epilepsy. The family is about to move to Liverpool at short notice. Looking under Liverpool Social Services you ring the manager for Asylum Seekers who promises his team will contact the family and try to arrange school placements promptly through the education department. You look up the PCT and discuss the family with the school nursing service. You now have a named person to forward the assessments to and an undertaking that this will be followed up.

Rani's first baby was born at your maternity department yesterday. You discover that on discharge Rani now intends to go to her husband in Birmingham, 40 miles away. She had recently lived with her sister in your area, having left her husband because of domestic violence. You are concerned for Rani and the baby's safety. Using the Directory you phone the community midwives in Birmingham. They agree to monitor the situation and pass the information to the health visitor.

GENUS PHARMACEUTICALS

Tuberculosis Treatment Guide
& Patient Information

1st and 2nd Phase Treatments

A prescribing and treatment guide for the primary
treatment of Tuberculosis in adults.

Supporting the treatment of Tuberculosis

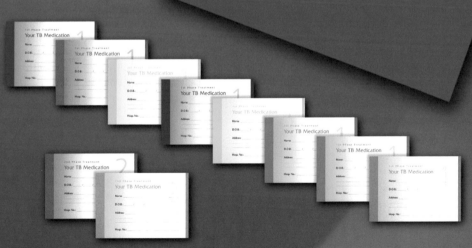

Please call Genus on **01635 568400**
for free copies of the treatment guide

A Guide to using the Directory

Kemal is a 30 year-old with recurrent bipolar disorder and a record of poor compliance with medication. His sister reports he has moved to Glasgow with a new girlfriend. You use our new Directory of Community Mental Health Services to phone community mental health services in Glasgow to find out who to speak to and where to forward the records.

Mrs G phones your PCT for help for her widowed father-in-law from Cardiff who has come to stay with her in Somerset after major surgery for bowel cancer. He is also diabetic and confused. She is nervous about dealing with his colostomy and diabetes. At home he received visits from the district nurses. Before visiting you use the Directory to phone the hospital and community services in Cardiff for further information and for records to be sent to you straightaway.

What the Directory contains

The Directory contains detailed and comprehensive information covering the whole of the UK, including the Isle of Man and the States of Jersey and Guernsey.

Entries in *Directory of Community Health Services* provide information on Community Nursing and Midwifery and include contact details for *Central Community Nursing Offices* and the following services: *District Nursing, Health Visiting, School Nursing, Child Protection, Family Planning, Community Midwifery and services for People with Learning Disabilities.*

The names of senior managers for these services are given, together with addresses and telephone numbers and, where appropriate, emergency / night / twilight numbers. Entries also provide names and contact numbers for *Clinical Nurse Specialists, Liaison Staff* and the *Administration Bases for Child Health Records.*

Entries for *Social Services Authorities* include emergency numbers, home care and meals on wheels services. Information about the Commission for Social Care Inspection is listed, as are the contact details for many useful statutory, professionals and voluntary organisations.

We also publish the *Directory of Mental Health Services* which provides information on the Mental Health Services including Senior Managers and Commissioners within the Trusts and Social Services together with information and contact details for staff and services providing care and support for Children and Adolescents, Adults, the Elderly and those with problems relating to Alcohol and Substance abuse. Services for adults and children with Learning Disabilities are also included.

HANDY TIP FOR SEARCHES

Do you know where your patient is going but not the name of the local Community Trust? Look up the name of the town in the greatly enhanced alphabetical Index of Major Towns and Villages and you will be directed to the relevant page to find the detailed information you need.

essential
healthcare

Putting the Care into Healthcare

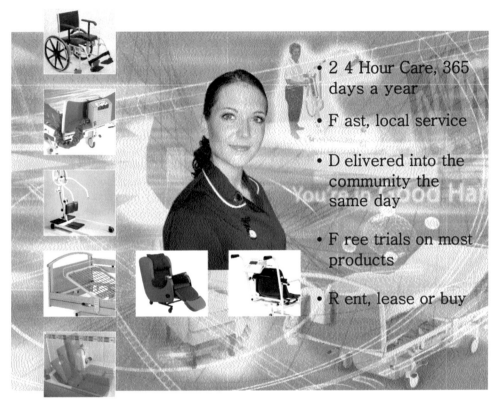

- 2 4 Hour Care, 365 days a year
- F ast, local service
- D elivered into the community the same day
- F ree trials on most products
- R ent, lease or buy

With service centres throughout the UK, Essential Healthcare can provide most products required in the care sector, direct from stock. Whether the service user is in a care home, hospital or in their own residence, Essential Healthcare will provide guidance, advice and help to achieve the highest level of care. Our experienced advisors currently work with community loan stores, nursing homes, hospices and many charitable operations, putting the care into healthcare.

Phone Today to find your nearest Local Service Centre
Essential Healthcare
Phone: 0845 344 1900
Fax: 0845 344 1901   Email: info@essential-healthcare.com

"Our Health Our Care Our Say"
A vote of confidence for community services

The Government White Paper "Our Health Our Care Our Say" published in 2006 is a welcome impetus to the development of community services and a vote of confidence in those who deliver them. Given the political pressure on successive governments to focus on hospitals and beds, that confidence has been hard won over many years and the results are quite spectacular.

The policy, professional and structural developments that have taken place over the past twenty years, which have led us to where we are now, are too numerous to mention here. The White Paper "Promoting Better Health", published in 1987, was one such development. It foreshadowed the GP 1990 Contract, and led, for instance, to the emergence of, and rapid increase in, the Practice Nursing workforce. Practice Nurses have established themselves alongside their community practitioner colleagues in District Nursing and Health Visiting as a key force in community services.

District Nurses themselves have constantly developed and expanded their roles and services to meet the demands of a population with shifting needs and expectations, as well as the changing practices in hospital care, including much earlier discharge. We have seen the ongoing development of specialist nursing services, nurse prescribing and nurse practitioners. There have been changes in the roles of school nurses and health visitors and in the delivery of community paediatrics. Alongside this we have seen wholesale change in the approach to providing support for people with learning disabilities. And health promotion, understated in the past, has moved centre stage.

In more recent years these changes have been accelerated by the National Service Frameworks and associated policy initiatives. The NSF for Older People has given significant impetus to the development of holistic assessment for older people, development of stroke services, intermediate care and the role of community rehabilitation. The NSF for Long Term Conditions and the new role of Community Matron, in turn, will drive another phase of enhanced care in the community, supported by accelerated developments in health technologies. There has been evolution in children's services, culminating in the Children's NSF and the development of Children's Trusts. 'Valuing People', the White Paper on Learning Disabilities, has consolidated expectations of the recent past and placed aspirations for these services on a different level. Alongside this there have been radical changes to the way in which social care and housing services are provided.

The new White Paper is an agenda to go further faster, with closer integration between colleagues in health and social care a pre-requisite for success. The people needed to turn the White Paper's aspirations into reality are listed in this Directory.

The Directory is used in many different ways to support local delivery of services. But it has additional potential – to link up people who have similar professional responsibilities and challenges across the country. The more we share, the quicker we learn, the more we progress and the sooner the patients and service users get the intended benefits. This implies the need to develop networks, share innovations and benchmark with others. The Directory can help us do just that.

Keith Wilson
Professor in Primary & Community Care, University of Sheffield

If the question is about ileostomy or internal pouches

...the answer is at your fingertips

Visit **www.the-ia.org.uk** or email **info@the-ia.org.uk**

- Hospital and home visiting
- Advisory services
- Lectures and demonstrations
- Equipment exhibitions
- Members meetings
- Medical research

Many years experience and over 10,000 members and branches nationwide enables ia to advise and help you and your patients with all aspects of living with an ileostomy or internal pouch.

Because we know, we care.

The Ileostomy and Internal Pouch Support Group
Peverill House, 1-5 Mill Road, Ballyclare Tel. 0800 0184724 Fax. 028 93324606*

*Supplied by MCI World Com

A whole new wardrobe for wet wrapping.

A new range of easy-to-apply washable clothing for wet wrapping in the treatment of paediatric atopic eczema.

They'll fit into your busy life...and they'll fit your kids like a glove.

completely washable
can be machine washed up to **30 times** for frequent use

continued softness
'stay-soft' fabric retains its softness, **even after repeated washing**

comfortable
2-way stretch material and stretch seams for comfort and ease of movement

convenient
ready to wear, no need to cut, tie or pin bandages together

clava

vest

mittens

tights

leggings

socks

>>> **comfi fast**®
easywrap™ suits

Available on **Drug Tariff** and **NHS Contract**

For further information please contact the Patient Care Division on **0161 785 3608**

Synergy Healthcare (UK) Limited, Patient Care Division, Lion Mill, Fitton Street, Royton, Oldham OL2 5JX. England.
Tel: 0161 624 5641 Fax: 0161 627 0902 Email: patientcare@synergyhealthcare.plc.uk

Synergy™ ╬ Healthcare

www.**synergyhealthcare**.plc.uk

SHI0486 Apr06

Strides in school nursing

These are exciting times for school nursing, which looks set to expand in numbers and influence. In England the Government has pledged to increase the NHS's 2,400 school nurses so that by 2010 there will be at least one full-time, year-round, qualified school nurse working with every cluster of primary schools and their linked secondary school[1]. This is part of a drive to improve young people's health which includes targets to reduce obesity, smoking, drug misuse and teenage pregnancy.

Having more school nurses is good news for school children, whose health receives comparatively little attention. Young people are our future and the school years are important. Today's children rarely suffer from the rickets and tuberculosis of 100 years ago but can still face difficulties at a vulnerable time in their life through, for example, asthma, eczema, epilepsy, learning and other disabilities.

Young people's mental and physical wellbeing can also be affected by factors such as anxiety about tests and exams, bullying, abuse, an unstable home life and pressure to become sexually active at an early age.

The modern school health service

Routine check-ups by school medical officers and hygiene inspections by nurses have given way to a more holistic approach. Today's school health service is largely nurse-led, with an emphasis on working with the schools, local youth services and other health and social service professionals. It offers screening and immunisation, advice for individual children, guidance for schools, child safeguarding, and fulfils a public health role for the school-aged population.

School nurses work with teachers to provide health education in the Personal, Health and Social Education curriculum. Some nurses are involved in innovations such as drop-in centres[2] where young people can consult them in confidence about a variety of topics including contraception and sexual health. School nurses visit children and parents at home to advise if necessary. They now have wider opportunities to prescribe under the extension to nurse prescribing which starts from May 2006.

School nurses and their teams provide a vital service for children with special needs in mainstream and special schools. This includes educating schools about the children's health needs so they can get the most from their education.

Finally, it is good to see the Department of Health and the Department of Education and Skills actively working together to promote school nursing. A recent joint publication[3] for head teachers, which highlights the advantages of having a school nurse and using the nurse's skills effectively, is progress indeed.

Pat Scowen MA SRN HV
Editor, *Journal of Family Health Care* and *School Health*

References
1. Government Guidance to Support School Nursing. London: Department of Health (DH) and Department for Education and Skills (DfES). See also DH Press Release 2006/0109
2. Richardson-Todd B. Sexual health services in school: a project in a multi-agency drop-in. *Journal of Family Health Care* 2006; 16(1): 17-20
3. Department for Education and Skills and Department of Health. Looking for a School Nurse? Nottingham: DfES Publications, 2006. Also www.dh.gov.uk

ordinary house, ordinary street, ordinary life principles, extraordinary concept in learning disability provision

At Innova House our philosophy is all should have an ordinary life. Our new residential Centre for Learning Disability comprises five individual purpose built houses set in a safe community based complex designed for single occupancy or small group living.

This unique approach sets new standards in learning disability provision as we optimise the potential of each service user, developing skills and building on strengths and confidence through **ordinary life principles**.

For further information, a site visit or referral please contact Tracey Ryan, Scheme Manager on 01623 626252 or e: tracey.ryan@innova-house.com 👶

t: 01623 626252
78 - 86 Forest Road, Mansfield, Nottinghamshire. NG18 4BU

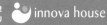

Infant Massage

Infant massage has been identified as being particularly well suited to support health professionals, such as health visitors, midwives, neonatal nurses and nursery nurses in their preventive and health promotion work with parents and infants. Because it is necessary for health professionals to consider the evidence base for infant massage, Zealey[1] conducted a systematic literature review. This found positive results in favour of facilitating infant massage in the community.

The benefits to be gained from positive touch in infancy and childhood are relevant to the goals in the Government's "Every Child Matters". This initiative, especially "What Works in Parenting Support?", emphasises the importance of improving outcomes for children and young people.

There is some evidence for a variety of physiological benefits for the infant such as strengthening the digestive and immune systems, improving skin condition, reducing anxiety and inducing more restful sleep. Mothers can benefit physically too, for example oxytocin levels are higher after a mother has massaged her baby. Massage is sometimes used for preterm infants.

Helping parent and child to bond

Infant massage can be an effective way of enhancing parent-infant interaction which is beneficial for both parents and babies. It can help with the relationship between a mother and baby as the mothers learn to understand their infant's communication. It can help mothers at risk of or suffering from postnatal depression[2]. A recent study suggests some benefit for children with autism[3].

In some parts of the world it is part of the culture for mothers to massage their children but in the UK parents may need to be taught this skill. Courses are available to train health professionals and others how to teach parents to massage (see Useful addresses, below).

Anita Epple
Qualified infant massage teacher and trainer

References
1. Zealey C *Community Practitioner* 2005; 78(3): 98-101: 98-101
2. Field T *et al. Infant Behavior and Development* 1996; 19(1): 107-112-114
3. Cullen-Powell LA *et al. Journal of Child Health Care* 2005; 9(4): 245-255

Useful addresses

The Guild of Infant and Child Massage (ww.gicm.org.uk)
Self-regulatory body for massage trainers and teachers in the UK.
Accredits courses and teachers that meet its standards.

TRAINING PROVIDERS
Two of the organisations providing training in how to teach massage are
The International Association of Infant Massage (www.iaim.net/) and
TouchLearn (www.touchlearn.co.uk).

RESEARCH
Touch Research Institutes University of Miami School of Medicine
(www.miami.edu/touch-research/)
Conduct research into the effects of massage therapy.

STRENGTHENING THE VOICE OF COMMUNITY NURSING

The Community Practitioners' and Health Visitors' Association is the UK professional body that represents health visitors, as well as school, community, district, practice and nursery nurses.

As a part of the Amicus union's growing Health Sector, the CPHVA campaigns to protect the professional status, as well as the pay and conditions of its members at a time of radical change in the NHS.

Amicus/CPHVA talks on a daily basis to key decision makers in the NHS and government to ensure that community nurses influence future policy.

To know more about Amicus/CPHVA, please visit our website www.amicus-cphva.org

To become a member contact our membership hotline: 0845 850 4242 or join on line at www.amicustheunion.org

RADICAL
PROFESSIONAL
CARING

NHS Direct

NHS Direct 0845 4647 (24 hours)
www.nhsdirect.nhs.uk

NHS Direct is a telephone service staffed by nurses, giving confidential healthcare advice and information 24 hours a day. Since it was launched in Spring 1998 it has taken more than 20 milllion calls. In April 2004 it became a new Special Health Authority but is still known simply as NHS Direct.

For just the price of a local call, NHS Direct enables you to speak directly to other experienced nurses and professional advisors about any health problems or queries. Using their skills and experience, together with a comprehensive computer system, NHS Direct can provide you with advice on what to do next.

NHS Direct also provides general information about local health services – such as late night pharmacists, out of hours dentists or support groups – or more in-depth information about a particular health condition that may be causing you problems. It can provide confidential interpreters in many languages. NHS Direct is also available on www.nhsdirect.nhs.uk.

A handy reference book, the NHS Direct self-help guide: Not feeling well? is available free of charge from most pharmacies and GP surgeries.

Headquarters
NHS Direct New Media
Strawberry Fields
Berrywood Business Village
Tollbar Way, Hedge End
Hampshire SO30 2UN
Tel: 01489 773 720
Fax: 01489 773 721
NHS Direct HQ
207 Old Street
London
EC1 V9PS
Tel: 0207 599 4200
Fax: 0207 599 4299
E-mail: 1stname.surname@nhsdirect.nhs.uk

North
Greater Manchester, Cheshire & Wirral
Ladybridge Hall
399 Chorley New Road
Bolton
BL1 5DD
Tel: 01204 498 300
Fax: 01204 599 522
North East
Sterling House
Balliol Business Park
Newcastle Upon Tyne
NE12 8EW
Tel: 0191 215 0267
Fax: 0191 270 5060
North West Coast
Lancashire Ambulance Service NHS Trust
Ambulance Headquarters
49-451 Garstang Road
Broughton
Preston
PR3 5LN
Tel: 01772 903 925
Fax: 01772 903 927

South Yorkshire and South Humber
Sheffield Childrens Hospital NHS Trust
Weston Bank
Sheffield
S10 2TH
Tel: 0114 271 7192
Fax: 0114 271 7233
Tees, East and North Yorkshire
Fairfields
Shipton Road
York
YO30 1XW
Tel: 01904 666 048
Fax: 01904 666 070
West Yorkshire
Springhill
Wakefield 41 Business Park
Brindley Way
Wakefield
WF2 0XQ
Tel: 01924 889 889
Fax: 01924 889 810

East and Midlands
Anglia
Chesterton Medical Centre
35 Union Lane
Cambridge
CB4 1PX
Tel: 01223 702 760
Fax: 01223 702 761
Bedfordshire & Hertfordshire
Ambulance & Paramedic Trust
1 Hammond Road
Bedford
MK41 0RG
Tel: 01234 275 627
Fax: 01234 355 191

NHS Direct

East Midlands
Seaton House
City Link
London Road
Nottingham
NG2 4LA
Tel: 0115 934 3200
Fax: 0115 934 3215

Essex
Essex Ambulance Service HQ
Hospital Approach
Broomfield
Chelmsford
CM1 7WS
Tel: 01245 444 488
Fax: 01245 443 611

Midlandshires
Mid Staffordshire General Hospital NHS Trust
Weston Road
Staffordshire
ST16 3SA
Tel: 01785 230 517
Fax: 01785 230 770

West Midlands
Navigation Point
Waterfront Business Park
Waterfront Way
Brierley Hill
West Midlands
DY5 1LX
Tel: 01384 246 423
Fax: 01384 475 942

London

North Central London
The Tower
St Charles Hospital
Exmoor Street
London, W10 6DZ
Tel: 0208 962 7600
Fax: 0208 962 7601

North East London
2-14 Illford Hill
Illford, Essex
IG1 2PT
Tel: 0208 924 6800
Fax: 0208 924 6868

South East London
County House
221-241 Beckenham Road
Beckenham
Kent
BR3 4UF
Tel: 0208 676 7300
Fax: 0208 676 7350

South West London (merging with SE London 2007)
Mayday University Hospital
London Road
Croydon
CR7 7YE
Tel: 0208 410 5590
Fax: 0208 410 5591

West London
Harmoni Gp Co-op
North Wing
1 Armstrong Way
Southall
Middlesex
UB2 4SA
Tel: 0208 867 1400
Fax: 0208 867 1301

South

Avon, Gloucestershire & Wiltshire
Acuma House
Axis 4/5, Woodlands
Almondsbury
Bristol
BS32 4jt
Tel: 01454 627 200
Fax: 01454 627 201

Hampshire & Isle of Wight
Strawberry Fields
Berrywood Business Village
Tollbar Way, Hedge End
Hampshire
SO30 2UN
Tel: 01489 773 700
Fax: 01489 773 701

Kent, Surrey & Sussex
Oaklands House
Coulsdon Road
Caterham
Surrey
CR3 5YA
Tel: 01634 897 360
Fax: 01634 897 390

Thames Valley and Northamptonshire
Marlborough Court
Sunrise Parkway
Linford Wood East
MK14 6DY
Tel: 01908 689 800
Fax: 01908 673 760

West Country
Abbey Court
Eagle Way
Sowton
Exeter
EX2 7HY
Tel: 01392 441 200
Fax: 01392 441 205

Social Care Inspection

England

In April 2005 new methods of inspection were introduced by the CSCI to inspect and monitor all social care providers in England. The new inspection methodology, detailed in the CSCI's 'Inspecting for Better Lives' produced in November 2004, is designed to place people who use social care services and their experiences at the heart of the way CSCI inspects and regulates care services.

The new inspections enable the public to have access to new easier-to-read reports that highlight the real experiences of the people who use those care services. Every care service user interviewed by CSCI inspectors is now given a leaflet giving them information on how to contact that inspector again in the future, should they need to, and details of the CSCI's internet site and national helpline number.

The plans set out in "Inspecting for Better Lives", come into effect over a three year period. The first of these changes came into force in April 2005, as announced. Others, such as moving towards more unannounced inspections, encouraging more whistle-blowing, conducting mystery shopping exercises, and involving service users on inspection teams, are coming on stream as plans are finalised and implemented.

1. Created by the Health and Social Care (Community Health and Standards) Act 2003, the Commission for Social Care Inspection began operations on 1 April 2004. It replaced the Social Services Inspectorate (SSI), SSI/Audit Commission Joint Review Team and National Care Standards Commission.

2. The Commission's primary aim is to improve social care by putting the needs of people who use care services first.

3. It is now the single inspectorate for social care in England, responsible for regulating and inspecting all social care providers – whether public sector or privately owned.

Wales

In Wales this service is provided by the Care Standards Inspectorate for Wales which is an operationally independent part of the National Assembly for Wales. It regulates the services through a national office, eight regional and three local offices across Wales.

The four main areas of work are registration, inspection, complaints and enforcement.

Scotland

The Scottish Commission for the Regulation of Care (the Care Commission) was established as an independent regulator set up under the Regulation of Care (Scotland) Act 2001 to regulate care services in Scotland.

The Commission regulates over 14,500 care services used by almost 230,000 people each year and of the 580 staff, 360 are directly involved in inspection services.

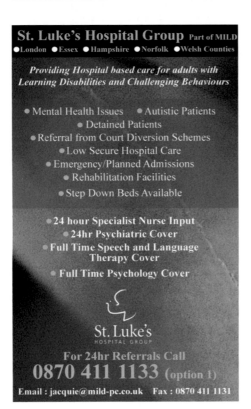

Social Care Inspection

Commission for Social Care Inspection Offices

Head Offices

London
Commission for Social Care Inspection, 33 Greycoat Street, London, SW1P 2QF, tel.: 020 7979 2000, fax.: 020 7979 2111

Newcastle
St Nicholas Building, St Nicholas Street, Newcastle upon Tyne, NE1 1NB, tel.: 0191 233 3600, fax.: 0191 233 3569

Leeds
St Paul's House, 23 Park Square (South), Leeds, LS1 2ND tel.: 0113 220 4600, fax.: 0113 220 4628

Customer Services
Tel. 0845 015 0120
Textphone: 0845 015 2255
Email: enquiries@csci.gsi.gov.uk
www.csci.org.uk

Regional Offices

East of England
East of England Regional Office
Capital Park, Fulbourn, Cambridge, CB1 5XE, tel.: 01223 771300, tel.: 01223 771300, fax.: 01223 771339

Bedford
4A Clifton House, Goldington Road, Bedford, MK40 3NF, tel.: 01234 220860, fax.: 01234 220870

Cambridgeshire & Peterborough
Po Box 796, Mortlock House, Station Road, Impington, Cambridge, CB4 9WG, tel.: 01223 266120

Norwich - Norfolk
3rd Floor, Cavell House, St Crispins Road, Norwich, NR3 1YF, tel.: 01603 598700, fax.: 01603 598746

Colchester - North Essex
Fairfax House, Causton Road, Colchester, CO1 1RJ, tel.: 01206 715630, fax.: 01206 715656

Southend - South Essex
Kingswood House, Baxter Avenue, Southend-on-Sea, SS2 6BG, tel.: 01702 236010, fax.: 01702 236056

Ipswich - Suffolk
5th Floor, St Vincent House, Cutler Street, Ipswich, IP1 1UQ, tel.: 01473 269050, fax.: 01473 269096

Welwyn Garden City – Hertfordshire
Mercury House, 1 Broadwater Road, Welwyn Garden City, Herts, AL7 3BQ, tel.: 01707 379370, fax.: 01707 379396

London
London Regional Office
3rd Floor, Finlaison House, 15-17 Furnival Street, London, EC4A 1AB, tel.: 020 7979 8051, fax.: 020 7979 8010

London Central Registration Team
3rd Floor, Caledonia House, 223 Pentonville Road, London, N1 9NG, tel.: 020 7239 0345, fax.: 020 7239 0309

Harrow - Brent & Harrow
4th Floor, Aspect Gate, 166 College Road, Harrow, Middlesex, HA1 1BH, tel.: 020 8420 0100, fax.: 020 8420 0119

Camden - Camden & Islington
Centro 4, 20-23 Mandela Street, Camden, London, NW1 0DW, tel.: 020 7255 9540, fax.: 020 7255 9560

Hammersmith - Central & South West London
(Chelsea, Hammersmith, Kensington, Westminster), 11th Floor, West Wing, 26-28 Hammersmith Grove, , London, W6 7SE, tel.: 020 8735 6370, fax.: 020 8735 6386

Croydon - Croydon & Sutton
8 th Floor, Grosvenor House, 125 High Street, Croydon, CR0 9XP, tel.: 020 8256 6430, fax.: 020 8256 6466

Ilford - North East London
(Barking, Havering, Redbridge, Waltham Forest), Ferguson House, 109-113 Cranbrook Road, Ilford, IG1 4PU, tel.: 020 8477 0960, fax.: 020 8477 0984

Southgate - North London
(Southgate, Barnet, Enfield, Haringey), 1st Floor, Solar House, 282 Chase Road, , London, N14 6HA, tel.: 020 8447 6930

Southwark – South London
Southwark Office, Ground Floor, 46 Loman Street, Southwark, SE1 0EH, tel.: 020 7803 4960, fax.: 020 7803 4996

Sidcup - South East London
River House, 1 Maidstone Road, Sidcup, DA14 5RH, tel.: 020 8308 3520, fax.: 020 8308 3556

Wimbledon - South West London
(Kingston, Merton, Richmond, Wimbledon, Wandsworth), Ground Floor, Hartfield House, 41-47 Hartfield Road, , London, SW19 3SG, tel.: 020 8254 4950, fax.: 020 8254 4960

Stratford – East London
Stratford Office, 4th Floor, Gredley House, 1-11 Broadway, Stratford, E15 4BQ, tel.: 020 8221 3360, fax.: 020 8221 3396

Ealing - West London
(Ealing, Hillingdon, Houslow), Ground Floor, 58 Uxbridge Road, Ealing, London, W5 2ST, tel.: 020 8280 0347, fax.: 020 8280 0340

North East
North East Regional Office
St Nicholas Building, St Nicholas Street, Newcastle upon Tyne, NE1 1NB, tel.: 0191 233 3300, fax.: 0191 233 3301

Darlington - County Durham & Darlington
1 Hopetown Studios, Brinkburn Road, Darlington, DL3 6DS, tel.: 01325 371720, fax.: 01325 371766

Cramlington - Northumbria
Northumbria House, Manor Walks, Cramlington, Northumberland, NE23 6UR, tel.: 01670 707900, fax.: 01670 707930

South Shields - South of Tyne
Baltic House, Port of Tyne, Tyne Dock, South Shields, NE34 9PT, tel.: 0191 497 4220, fax.: 0191 497 4256

Stockton on Tees - Tees Valley
Unit B, Advance, St Mark's Court, , Stockton-on-Tees, TS17 6QX, tel.: 01642 628960, fax.: 01642 628966

North West
North West Regional Office
11th Floor, West Point, 501 Chester Road, Old Trafford, Lancashire, M16 9HU, tel.: 0161 876 2400, fax.: 0161 876 2429

Bolton - Bolton, Bury, Rochdale & Wigan
Turton Suite, Paragon Business Park, Chorley New Road, Port Way, Bolton, BL6 6HG, tel.: 01204 676120, fax.: 01204 676166

Northwich - Cheshire, Halton & Warrington
Unit D, Off Rudheath Way, Gadbrook Park, Northwich, Cheshire, CW9 7LT, tel.: 01606 333400, fax.: 01606 333446

Penrith - Cumbria
Eamont House, Penrith 40 Business Park, Penrith, Cumbria, CA11 9BP, tel.: 01768 214730, fax.: 01768 214766

Social Care Inspection

Accrington – E. Lancs, Blackburn & Darwen
First Floor, Unit 4, Petre Road, Clayton-le-Moors, Accrington, BB5 5JB, tel.: 01254 306600, fax.: 01254 306656

Liverpool - Liverpool & Wirral
3rd Floor, Campbell Square, 10 Duke Street, Liverpool, L1 5AS, tel.: 0151 705 2000, fax.: 0151 705 2046

Knowsley - Liverpool North
2nd Floor, Burlington House, Crosby Road North, Liverpool, L22 0PF, tel.: 0151 949 9540, fax.: 0151 949 9549

Manchester, Salford & Trafford
9th Floor, Oakland House, Talbot Road, Manchester, M16 0PQ, tel.: 0161 772 1620, fax.: 0161 772 1676

Preston - North Lancashire & Blackpool
Unit 1, Tustin Court, Port Way, Preston, PR2 2YQ, tel.: 01772 730100

Ashton under Lyne - Oldham, Stockport & Tameside
2nd Floor, Heritage Wharf, Portland Place, Ashton-under-Lyne, Lancs, OL7 0QD, tel.: 0161 214 8120, fax.: 0161 214 8156

South East
South East Regional Office
4th Floor, Finlaison House, 15-17 Furnival Street, London, EC4A 1AB, tel.: 020 7979 8079, fax.: 020 7979 8091

Theale - Berkshire
1015 Arlington Business Park, Theale, Reading, RG7 4SA, tel.: 0118 903 3230

Aylesbury - Buckinghamshire
Cambridge House, 8 Bell Business Park, Smeaton Close, Aylesbury, HP19 8JR, tel.: 01296 737550, fax.: 01296 737558

Eastbourne - East Sussex
Ivy House, 3 Ivy Terrace, Eastbourne, BN21 4QT, tel.: 01323 636200, fax.: 01323 636256

Southampton - Hampshire
4th Floor, Overline House, Blechynden Terrace, Southampton, SO15 1GW, tel.: 02380 821300, fax.: 02380 821396

Newport - Isle of Wight
Ground Floor, East Wing, Mill Court, , Newport, Isle of Wight, PO30 2AA, tel.: 01983 824130, fax.: 01983 824140

Ashford - East Kent
11th Floor, International House, Dover Place, Ashford, TN23 1HU, tel.: 01233 619330, fax.: 01233 619366

Maidstone - West Kent
The Oast, Hermitage Court, Hermitage Lane, Maidstone, ME16 9NT, tel.: 01622 724950, fax.: 01622 724980

Oxford
Burgner House, 4630 Kingsgate, Cascade Way, Oxford Business Park South, Oxford, OX4 2SU, tel.: 01865 397750, fax.: 01865 397763

Eashing - Surrey
The Wharf, Abbey Mill Business Park, Eashing, Godalming, GU7 2QN, tel.: 01483 413540, fax.: 01483 413578

Worthing - West Sussex
2nd Floor, Ridgeworth House, Liverpool Gardens, Worthing, BN11 1RY, tel.: 01903 222950, fax.: 01903 222996

South West
South West Regional Office
33 Colston Avenue, Bristol, BS1 4UA, tel.: 0117 930 7110, fax.: 0117 930 7112

Bristol
(Bristol, Bath & NE Somerset, N Somerset, South Glos), 300 Aztec West, Almondsbury, Bristol, BS32 4RG, tel.: 01454 454010, fax.: 01454 454047

St Austell - Cornwall & the Isles of Scilly
John Keay House, Tregonissey Road, St Austell, PL25 4AD, tel.: 01726 624550, fax.: 01726 624596

Gloucestershire
Unit 1210 Lansdowne Court, Gloucester Business Park, Brockworth, Gloucester, GL3 4AB, tel.: 01452 632750, fax.: 01452 632782

Exeter - North Devon
Suite 1 & 7, Renslade House, Bonhay Road, Exeter, EX4 3AY, tel.: 01392 474350, fax.: 01392 474396

Poole - Dorset
Unit 4, New Fields Business Park, Stinsford Road, Poole, Dorset, BH17 0NF, tel.: 01202 662 992, fax.: 01202 662 996

Taunton - Somerset
Ground Floor, Riverside Chambers, Tangier, Castle Street, Taunton, TA1 4AL, tel.: 01823 345960, fax.: 01823 345988

Ashburton - South Devon
Unit D1, Linhay Business Park, Ashburton, Devon, TQ13 7UP, tel.: 01364 651800, fax.: 01364 651856

Chippenham - Wiltshire & Swindon
Suite C, Avonbridge House, Bath Road, Chippenham, SN15 2BB, tel.: 01249 454550, fax.: 01249 454582

East Midlands
East Midlands Regional Office
Unit 7, Interchange 25 Business Park, Bostocks Lane, Sandiacre, Nottingham, NG10 5QG, tel.: 0115 921 0950, fax.: 0115 921 0960

Derby - Derbyshire
South Point, Cardinal Square, Nottingham Road, Derby, DE1 3QT, tel.: 01332 851800, fax.: 01332 851810

Enderby - Leicestershire & Rutland
The Pavilions, 5 Smith Way, Grove Park, , Leicester, LE19 1SX, tel.: 0116 281 5900, fax.: 0116 281 5910

Lincoln - Lincolnshire
Unit A, The Point, Weaver Road, Off Whisby Road, Lincoln, LN6 3QN, tel.: 01522 699310, fax.: 01522 699356

Northampton - Northamptonshire
1st Floor, Newland House, Campbell Square, Northampton, NN1 3EB, tel.: 01604 887620, fax.: 01604 887652

Nottingham - Nottinghamshire
Edgeley House, Tottle Road, Riverside Business Park, Nottingham, NG2 1RT, tel.: 0115 934 0910

West Midlands
West Midlands Regional Office
Ladywood House, 45-56 Stephenson Street, Birmingham, B2 4UZ, tel.: 0121 600 5300, fax.: 0121 600 5335

Birmingham
Ladywood House, 45-56 Stephenson Street, Birmingham, B2 4UZ, tel.: 0121 600 5300, fax.: 0121 600 5758

Coventry
5th Floor, Coventry Point, Market Way, Coventry, CV1 1EB, tel.: 02476 500850, fax.: 02476 500875

Halesowen - Dudley & Sandwell
West Point, Mucklow Business Park, Mucklow Hill, Halesowen, West Midlands, B62 8DA, tel.: 0121 423 5410, fax.: 0121 423 5446

Hereford - Herefordshire
178 Widemarsh Street, Hereford, Herefordshire, HR4 9HN, tel.: 01432 845700, fax.: 01432 845726

Shrewsbury - Shropshire
1st Floor, Chapter House South, Abbey Lawn, Abbey Foregate, Shrewsbury, SY2 5DE, tel.: 01743 284300, fax.: 01743 284323

Stafford - Staffordshire
Dyson Court, Staffordshire Technology Park, Beaconside, Stafford, ST18 0ES, tel.: 01785 270930, fax.: 01785 270940

Leamington Spa - Warwickshire
Imperial Court, Holly Walk, Leamington Spa, CV32 4YB, tel.: 01926 436950, fax.: 01926 436951

Social Care Inspection

Wolverhampton
2nd Floor, St Davids Court, Union Street, Wolverhampton, WV1 3JE, tel.: 01902 873720, fax.: 01902 873730

Worcester - Worcestershire
The Coach House, John Comwyn Drive, Perdiswell Park, , Worcester, WR3 7NW, tel.: 01905 753910, fax.: 01905 753956

Yorkshire and the Humber
Yorkshire and Humberside Regional Office
St Paul's House 23 Park Square (South), Leeds, LS1 2ND
tel.: 0113 220 5600, fax. : 0113 220 4628

Brighouse, Calderdale, Kirklees & Wakefield
Park View House, Woodvale Office Park, Woodvale Road, Brighouse, West Yorkshire, HD6 4AB, tel.: 01484 404930, fax.: 01484 404986

Doncaster
1st Floor, Barclay Court, Heavens Walk, Doncaster, DN4 5HZ, tel.: 01302 765350, fax.: 01302 765386

Hessle - East Riding
Unit 3, Hesslewood Country Office Park, Ferriby Road, Hessle, HU13 0QF, tel.: 01482 350636, fax.: 01482 350629

Rodley - Leeds & Bradford
Aire House, Town Street, Rodley, Leeds, LS13 1HP, tel.: 0113 201 1075, fax.: 0113 201 1096

Scunthorpe
1st Floor, 3 Park Square, Laneham Street, Scunthorpe, North Lincs, DN15 6JH, tel.: 01724 749040

Sheffield & Barnsley
Ground Floor, Unit 3, Waterside Court, Bold Street, Sheffield, S9 2LR, tel.: 0114 256 4530, fax.: 0114 256 4556

York
1st Floor, Unit 4, Tribune Court, Monk's Cross, Huntington, York, YO32 9GZ, tel.: 01904 545000, fax.: 01904 545046

Wales

Care Standards Inspectorate for Wales

National Office
4/5 Charnwood Court, Heol Billingsley, Parc Nantgarw, Nantgarw, CF15 7QZ, tel.: 01443 848450, fax.: 01443 848472, www.csiw.wales.gov.uk

Regional Offices
Cardiff
1 Alexandra Gate, Ffordd Pengam, Tremorfa, Cardiff, CF24 2SA, tel.: 029 2047 8600, fax.: 029 2047 8614

Mid Wales
Government Buildings, Spa Road East, Llandrindod Wells, Powys, LD1 5HA, tel.: 01597 829319, fax.: 01597 824375

North East Wales
Broncoed House, Broncoed Business Park, Wrexham Road, Mold, Flintshire, CH7 1HP, tel.: 01352 707900, fax.: 01352 707905

North West Wales
Government Buildings, Dinerth Road, Rhos On Sea, Colwyn Bay, LL28 4UL, tel.: 01492 542580, fax.: 01492 542569

South East Wales
6th Floor, Civic Centre, Pontypool, Torfaen, NP4 6YB, tel.: 01495 761200, fax.: 01495 761239

South West Wales
Unit C, Phase 3, Tawe Business Village, Phoenix Way, Swansea Enterprise Park, Swansea, SA7 9LA, tel.: 01792 310420, fax.: 01792 313038

Vale & Valley
Units 4/5, Charnwood Court, Heol Billingsley, Parc Nantgarw, Nantgarw, CF15 7QZ, tel.: 01443 848527/28/29, fax.: 01443 848526

West Wales
Government Buildings, Picton Terrace, Carmarthen, SA31 3BT, tel.: 01267 223402, fax.: 01267 242924

Local Offices
Aberaeron
Unit 9, Aberaeron Craft Centre, Aberaeron, Ceredigion, SA46 0DX, tel.: 01545 570931, fax.:: 01545 571793

Caernarfon
Government Buildings, Penrallt, Caernarfon, Gwynedd, LL55 1EP, tel.: 01286 662300, fax.: 01286 662301

Haverfordwest
Rooms 60-65, 1st Floor, Meyler House, St Thomas Green, Haverfordwest, Pembrokeshire, SA61 1QP, tel.: 01437 769111, fax.: 01437 768388

Scotland

The Scottish Commission for the Regulation of Care – the Care Commission

National Office
Compass House, 11 Riverside Drive, Dundee, DD1 4NY, tel.: 01382 207100, fax.: 01382 207289

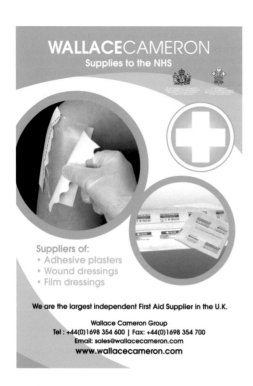
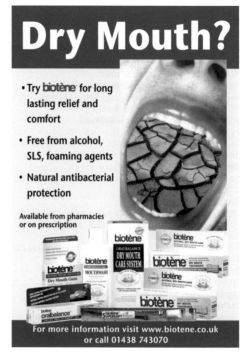

Strategic Health Authorities Reconfiguration

The Government is now implementing the structural changes that reduces the number of Strategic Health Authorities in England from 28 to 10. The following list identifies these new SHAs together with those that have been amalgamated to create them.

ENGLAND

East Midlands SHA

Leicestershire, Northampton and Rutland SHA
Lakeside House, 4 Smith Way, Grove Park, LEICESTER, LE19 1SS, Tel.: 0116 295 7500

Trent SHA
Octavia House, Interchange Business Park, SANDIACRE, NG10 5QG, Tel.: 0115 968 4444

East of England SHA

Bedfordshire and Hertfordshire SHA
c/o Tonman House, 63-77 Victoria Street, ST ALBANS, Herts, AL1 3ER, Tel.: 01727 812929,

Essex SHA
Swift House, Hedgerows Business Park, Colchester Road, CHELMSFORD, Essex, CM2 5PF, Tel.: 01245 397600

Norfolk, Suffolk and Cambridgeshire SHA
Victoria House, Capital Park, Fulborn, CAMBRIDGE, CB1 5XB, Tel.: 01223 597500, Fax.: 01223 597555

London SHA

London North Central SHA
Victory House, 170 Tottenham Court Road, LONDON, W1T 7HA, Tel.: 020 7756 2500, Fax.: 020 7756 2502

London North East SHA
Aneurin Bevan House, 81 Commercial Road, LONDON, E1 1RD, Tel.: 020 7655 6600, Fax.: 020 7655 6666

London North West SHA
Victory House, 170 Tottenham Court Road, LONDON, W1T 7HA, Tel.: 020 7756 2500

London South East SHA
1 Lower Marsh, LONDON, SE1 7NT, Tel.: 020 7716 7000, Fax.: 020 7716 7037

London South West SHA
Hartfield House, 41-47 Hartfield Road, WIMBLEDON, SW19 3RG, Tel.: 020 8545 6000,

North East SHA

County Durham and Tees Valley SHA
Teesdale House, Westpoint Road, Thornaby, STOCKTON-ON-TEES, Tel.: 01642 666700

Northumberland, Tyne and Wear SHA
Riverside House, Goldcrest Way, NEWCASTLE UPON TYNE, NE15 8NY, Tel.: 0191 210 6400

North West SHA

Cheshire and Merseyside SHA
Quayside, Wilderspool Park, Stockton Heath, WARRINGTON, WA4 6HL, Tel.: 01925 406000

Cumbria and Lancashire SHA
Preston Business Centre, Fulwood, PRESTON, PR2 8DY, Tel.: 01772 647190,

Greater Manchester SHA
Gateway House, Piccadilly South, MANCHESTER, M60 7LP, Tel.: 0161 236 9456,

South Central SHA

Hampshire and Isle of Wight SHA
Oakley Road, Millbrook, SOUTHAMPTON, S016 4GX, Tel.: 023 8072 5400

Thames Valley SHA
Jubilee House, 5510 John Smith Drive, Oxford Business Park South, COWLEY, OX4 2LH, Tel.: 01865 337000

South East Coast SHA

Kent and Medway SHA
Preston Hall, AYLESFORD, Kent, ME20 7NJ, Tel.: 01622 710161, Fax.: 01622 719802

Surrey and Sussex SHA
York House, 18-20 Massetts Road, HORLEY, RH6 7DE, Tel.: 01293 778899

South West SHA

Avon, Gloucestershire and Wiltshire SHA
Jenner House, Langley Park Estate, CHIPPENHAM, BN15 1GG, Tel.: 01249 858500

Dorset and Somerset SHA
Charter House, Watercombe Lane, YEOVIL, BA20 2SU, Tel.: 01935 384000, Fax.: 01935 384079

South West Peninsular SHA
Peninsula House, Kingsmill Road, Tamar View Industrial Estate, SALTASH, PL12 6LE, Tel.: 01752 315001, E-mail

Strategic Health Authorities Reconfiguration

West Midlands SHA

Birmingham and the Black Country SHA
St Chad's Court, 213 Hagley Road, Edgbaston,
BIRMINGHAM, B16 9RG, Tel.: 0121 695 2222

Shropshire and Staffordshire SHA
Mellor House, Corporation Street, STAFFORD,
ST16 3BR, Tel.: 01785 252233
West Midlands South SHA
Osprey House, Albert Street, REDDITCH, B97
4DE, Tel.: 01527 587500

Yorkshire and the Humber SHA

N. & E. Yorkshire and N. Lincolnshire SHA
The Innovation Centre, York Science Plc,
Innovation Way, Heslington, YORK, YO10 5DG,
Tel.: 01904 435331, Fax.: 01904 435333

South Yorkshire SHA
5 Old Fulwood Road, SHEFFIELD, S10 3TG,
Tel.: 0114 263 0300

West Yorkshire SHA
Blenheim House, West One, Duncombe Street,
LEEDS, LS1 4PL, Tel.: 0113 295 2000

WALES

Mid & West Wales
2nd Floor, St Davids Hospital, Jobswell Road,
CARMARTHEN, SA31 3YH, Tel.: 01267 225062,
Fax.: 01267 225056, E-mail:
nhs.mwro@wales.gsi.gov.uk

North Wales
Bromfield House, Queens Lane, Bromfield
Industrial Estate, MOLD, CH7 1XB, Tel.: 01352
706971, Fax.: 01352 757567, E-mail:
nhs.nwro@wales.gsi.gov.uk

South East Wales
2nd Floor, Brecon House, Mamhilad Park
Estate, PONTYPOOL, NP4 0YP, Tel.: 01495
758042, Fax.: 01495 763862, E-mail:
nhs.sero@wales.gsi.gov.uk
1stname.surname@ciosha.cornwall.nhs.uk

SCOTLAND

NHS Argyll & Clyde Services now provided by
NHS Greater Glasgow and NHS Highland

NHS Ayrshire & Arran
Head Office, Boswell House, 10 Arthur Street,
AYR, Strathclyde, KA7 1QJ, Tel.: 01292 611040,
www.show.scot.nhs.uk/aahb

NHS Borders
District Headquarters, Newstead, MELROSE,
Roxburghshire, TD6 9DB, Tel.: 01896 825500,
Fax.: 01896 823401, E-mail:
borders.scot.nhs.uk, Web Site:
www.show.scot.nhs.uk/bhb

NHS Dumfries & Galloway
Gierson House, The Crichton, Bankend Road,
DUMFRIES, DG1 4ZH, Tel.: 01387 272700,
Fax.: 01387 252375, E-mail:
initial.2nd@dghb.scot.nhs.uk, Web Site:
www.show.scot.nhs.uk/dghb

NHS Fife
Springfield House, CUPAR, Fife, KY15 5UP,
Tel.: 01334 656200, Fax.: 01334 652210, E-mail:
david.elder@fife-hb.scot.nhs.uk, Web Site:
www.show.scot.nhs.uk/fhb

NHS Forth Valley
33 Spittal Street, STIRLING, FK8 1DX, Tel.:
01786 463031, Fax.: 01786 451474, E-mail:
fvhb@dial.pipex.com, Web Site:
www.show.scot.nhs.uk

NHS Grampian
Summerfield House, 2 Eday Road, ABERDEEN,
AB15 6RE, Tel.: 01224 558565, E-mail:
neil.campbell@ghb.grampian.scot.nhs.uk

NHS Greater Glasgow
Dalin House, PO Box 15329, 350 Vincent
Street, GLASGOW, G3 8YZ, Tel.: 0141 201
4444, Fax.: 0141 201 4401, E-mail:
1stname.2ndname@gghb.scot.nhs.uk, Web
Site: www.show.scot.nhs.uk/gghb

NHS Highland
Assynt House, Beechwood Park, INVERNESS,
IV2 3HG, Tel.: 01463 717123, Fax.: 01463
235189, E-mail:
firstname.surname@hhb.scot.nhs.uk, Web Site:
www.highlandhealth.org.uk

NHS Lanarkshire
District Headquarters, 14 Beckford Street,
HAMILTON, Lanarkshire, ML3 0TA, Tel.: 01698
281313, Fax.: 01698 286950

NHS Lothian
148 Pleasance, EDINBURGH, EH8 9RS, Tel.:
0131 536 9000, Fax.: 0131 536 9009

NHS Orkney
Garden House, New Scapa Road, KIRKWALL,
Orkney, KW15 1BQ, Tel.: 01856 885400, Fax.:
01856 885411, E-mail:
1stname.2ndname@orkney-hb.scot.nhs.uk

Strategic Health Authorities Reconfiguration

NHS Shetland
Brevik House, South Road, LERWICK,
Shetland, ZE1 0TG, Tel.: 01595 696767, Fax.:
01595 696727, www.shetlandhealthboard.org

NHS Tayside
East Day Home, Kings Cross, Clepington
Road, DUNDEE, Tayside, DD3 8EA, Tel.: 01382
818479, Fax.: 01382 424003, Web Site:
www.show.scot.nhs.uk/thb

NHS Western Isles
Health Board Offices, 37 South Beach Street
STORNOWAY, Isle of Lewis, HS1 2BB, 04405,
E-mail: wihb@sol.co.uk, Web Site:
www.hebrides.com

OFFSHORE

Isle of Man Department of Health & Social Security
Crookall House, Demesne Road, DOUGLAS,
Isle of Man, IM1 3QA, Tel.: 01624 642608, Fax.:
01624 642617

States of Guernsey Board of Health
John Hendry House, Le Vanquiedor, ST
MARTIN'S, Guernsey, GY4 6UU, Tel.: 01481
725241, Fax.: 01481 235341

States of Jersey Health & Social Services
4th Floor, Peter Crill House, Gloucester Street,
ST HELIER, Jersey, JE2 3QS, Tel.: 01534
622285, Fax.: 01534 37768

NORTHERN IRELAND

Northern HSSB
County Hall, 182 Galgorm Road, BALLYMENA,
County Antrim, BT42 1QB, Tel.: 028 2565 3333,
Fax.: 028 2566 2311, E-mail:
pr@nhssb.n.i.nhs.uk,
Web Site: www.nhssb.n-i.nhs.uk

Eastern HSSB
Champion House, 12-22 Linenhall Street,
BELFAST, BT2 8BS, Tel.: 028 9032 1313,
Fax.: 028 9023 3020,
E-mail: enquiry@ehssb.n-i.nhs.uk,
Web Site: www.n-inhsuk/boards/boards.html

Southern HSSB
Tower Hill, ARMAGH, BT61 9DR, Tel.: 028 3741
0041, Fax.: 028 3741 4550, E-mail:
amandast@shssb.nhs.n-i.uk
Western HSSB
15 Gransha Park, Clooney Road,
LONDONDERRY, BT47 6TG, Tel.: 028 7186
0086, Fax.: 028 7186 0311, E-mail:
firstinitial.surname@whssb.n-i.nhs

Cancer Care 2006
The National Cancer Directory

A comprehensive review of Diagnostic Screening & Treatment Centres, Hospices, Charities & Palliative Care Services within the UK today

produced and published by
Cambridge Healthcare Publishing Ltd

www.chp.uk.net

Just
£90 per copy for
20,000+ contact details
Buy 2 copies at £75 each
or 3+ at £60 each
Charities & Hospices
may buy at £40
each

Fully updated for 2006
& Now with Cancer
Research Networks

Primary Care Trust Reconfiguration

Final proposals for the reconfiguration of the Primary Care Trust structure within England were published in May 2006. At the time of going to press these plans are still the subject of consultation but in principle are likely to be implemented in the Autumn of 2006.

The following listings show the proposed structure by new Strategic Health Authorities (SHA) which are due for implementation in July 2006.

The new PCTs are listed alphabetically within their SHA followed by the old PCTs which have been amalgamated to create them. The Area Maps at the beginning of each SHA in Section 2 of this directory show the SHA boundaries and the main towns/districts served by that Authority.

EAST MIDLANDS SHA

Bassetlaw PCT
No change

Derby City PCT
Central Derby
Greater Derby

Derbyshire County PCT
Amber Valley
Chesterfield
Derbyshire Dales & South Derbyshire
Erewash
High Peak & Dales
North Eastern Derbyshire

Leicester City Teaching PCT
Eastern Leicester Teaching
Leicester City Teaching

Leicestershire County and Rutland PCT
Charnwood & N West Leicestershire
Hinckley and Bosworth
Melton, Rutland and Harborough
South Leicestershire

Lincolnshire Teaching PCT
East Lincolnshire
Lincolnshire South West Teaching
West Lincolnshire

Northamptonshire Teaching PCT
Daventry and South Northamptonshire
Northampton Teaching
Northamptonshire Heartlands

Nottingham City PCT
No change

Nottinghamshire County Teaching PCT
Ashfield
Broxtowe and Hucknall
Gedling
Mansfield District
Newark and Sherwood
Rushcliffe

EAST OF ENGLAND SHA

Bedfordshire PCT
Bedford
Bedford Heartlands

Cambridgeshire PCT
Cambridge City
East Cambridgeshire & Fenland
Huntingdonshire
South Cambridgeshire

East and North Hertfordshire PCT
North Hertfordshire and Stevenage
Royston, Buntingford & Bishop's Stortford
South East Hertfordshire
Welwyn Hatfield

Great Yarmouth & Waveney Teaching PCT
Great Yarmouth Teaching
Waveney

Luton Teaching PCT
No change

Mid Essex PCT
Chelmsford
Maldon and South Chelmsford
Witham, Braintree & Halstead

Norfolk PCT
Broadland
North Norfolk
Norwich
Southern Norfolk
West Norfolk

North East Essex PCT
Colchester
Tendring

Peterborough PCT
North Peterborough
South Peterborough

South East Essex PCT
Castle Point & Rochford
Southend Teaching

South West Essex Teaching PCT
Basildon Teaching
Billericay, Brentwood and Wickford
Thurrock Teaching

Suffolk PCT
Central Suffolk
Ipswich
Suffolk Coastal
Suffolk West

West Essex PCT
Epping Forest
Harlow
Uttlesford

West Hertfordshire PCT
Dacorum
Hertsmere
St. Albans and Harpenden
Watford and Three Rivers

LONDON SHA

North Central London PCT
Barnet
Camden
Enfield
Haringey Teaching
Islington

Primary Care Trust Reconfiguration

North East London PCT
Barking and Dagenham
City and Hackney Teaching
Havering
Newham
Redbridge
Tower Hamlets
Waltham Forest

North West London PCT
Brent Teaching
Ealing
Hammersmith and Fulham
Harrow
Hillingdon
Hounslow
Kensington and Chelsea
Westminster

South East London PCT
Bexley Care Trust
Bromley
Greenwich Teaching
Lambeth
Lewisham
Southwark

South West London PCT
Croydon
Kingston
Richmond and Twickenham
Sutton and Merton
Wandsworth Teaching

NORTH EAST SHA

County Durham PCT
Derwentside
Durham and Chester-le-Street
Durham Dales
Easington
Sedgefield

Darlington PCT
No change

Gateshead PCT
No change

Hartlepool PCT
No change

Middlesbrough PCT
No change

Newcastle PCT
No change

Northumberland Care Trust
No change

North Tyneside PCT
No change

Redcar and Cleveland PCT
Langbaurgh

South Tyneside PCT
No change

Sunderland Teaching PCT
No change

Stockton-on-Tees Teaching PCT
North Tees

NORTH WEST

Ashton, Leigh and Wigan PCT
No change

Blackburn with Darwen Teaching PCT
No change

Blackpool PCT
No change

Bolton PCT
No change

Bury PCT
No change

Central Lancashire PCT
Chorley and South Ribble
Preston
West Lancashire

Cumbria PCT
Carlisle and District
Eden Valley
Morecambe Bay (South Lakeland)
West Cumbria

East Cheshire PCT
Central Cheshire
Eastern Cheshire

East Lancashire PCT
Burnley, Pendle and Rossendale
Hyndburn and Ribble Valley

Halton and St Helens PCT
Halton
St Helens

Knowsley PCT
No change

Liverpool PCT
Central Liverpool
North Liverpool
South Liverpool

Manchester PCT
Central Manchester
North Manchester
South Manchester

North Lancashire PCT
Fylde
Morecambe Bay (Lancaster)
Wyre

Oldham PCT
No change

Rochdale, Heywood and Middleton PCT
Heywood and Middleton
Rochdale

Salford Teaching PCT
No change

Sefton PCT
South Sefton
Southport and Formby

Stockport PCT
No change

Tameside and Glossop PCT
No change

Trafford PCT
Trafford North
Trafford South

Warrington PCT
No change

Wirral PCT
Bebington and West Wirral
Birkenhead and Wallasey

West Cheshire PCT
Cheshire West
Ellesmere Port and Neston

Primary Care Trust Reconfiguration

SOUTH CENTRAL

Berkshire East Teaching PCT
Bracknell Forest
Slough Teaching
Windsor, Ascot and
Maidenhead

Berkshire West PCT
Newbury and Community
Reading
Wokingham

Buckinghamshire PCT
Chiltern and South Bucks
Vale of Aylesbury
Wycombe

Hampshire PCT
Blackwater Valley and Hart
East Hampshire
Eastleigh and Test Valley
South
Fareham and Gosport
Mid-Hampshire
New Forest
North Hampshire

Isle of Wight Healthcare PCT
No change

Milton Keynes PCT
No change

Oxfordshire PCT
Cherwell Vale
North East Oxfordshire
Oxford City
South East Oxfordshire
South West Oxfordshire

Portsmouth City Teaching PCT
No change

Southampton City PCT
No change

SOUTH EAST COAST

Brighton & Hove City Teaching PCT
No change

East Sussex Downs and Weald PCT
Eastbourne Downs
Sussex Downs and Weald

Eastern and Coastal Kent Teaching PCT
Ashford
Canterbury and Coastal
East Kent Coastal Teaching
Shepway
Swale Teaching

Hastings and Rother PCT
Bexhill and Rother
Hastings and St Leonards

Medway Teaching PCT
No change

Surrey PCT
East Elmbridge and Mid Surrey
East Surrey
Guildford and Waverley
North Surrey
Surrey Heath and Woking

West Kent PCT
Dartford, Gravesham and Swanley
Maidstone Weald
South West Kent

West Sussex Teaching PCT
Adur, Arun and Worthing Teaching
Crawley
Horsham and Chanctonbury
Mid-Sussex
Western Sussex

SOUTH WEST

Bath and North East Somerset PCT
No change

Bournemouth and Poole Teaching PCT
Bournemouth Teaching
Poole

Bristol Teaching PCT
Bristol North Teaching
Bristol South and West Teaching

Cornwall and Isles of Scilly PCT
Central Cornwall
North and East Cornwall
West of Cornwall

Devon PCT
East Devon
Exeter
Mid Devon
North Devon
South Hams and West Devon
Teignbridge

Dorset PCT
North Dorset
South and East Dorset
South West Dorset

Gloucestershire PCT
Cheltenham and Tewkesbury
Cotswold and Vale
West Gloucestershire

North Somerset PCT
No change

Plymouth Teaching PCT
No change

South Gloucestershire PCT
No change

Somerset PCT
Mendip
Somerset Coast
South Somerset
Taunton Deane

Swindon PCT
No change

Torbay Care Trust PCT
No change

Wiltshire PCT
Kennet and North Wiltshire
South Wiltshire
West Wiltshire

WEST MIDLANDS

Birmingham East and North PCT
Eastern Birmingham
North Birmingham

Coventry Teaching PCT
No change

Dudley PCT
Dudley Beacon and Castle
Dudley South

Primary Care Trust Reconfiguration

Heart of Birmingham Teaching PCT
No change

Herefordshire PCT
No change

North Staffordshire PCT
Newcastle-under-Lyme
Staffordshire Moorlands

Sandwell
Oldbury and Smethwick
Rowley Regis and Tipton
Wednesbury and West Bromwich

Shropshire County PCT
No change

Solihull PCT
No change

South Birmingham PCT
No change

South Staffordshire PCT
Burntwood, Lichfield and Tamworth
Cannock Chase
East Staffordshire
South Western Staffordshire

Stoke on Trent Teaching PCT
North Stoke Teaching
South Stoke Teaching

Telford and Wrekin
No change

Walsall Teaching PCT
No change

Warwickshire PCT
North Warwickshire
Rugby
South Warwickshire

Wolverhampton City PCT
No change

Worcestershire PCT
Redditch and Bromsgrove
South Worcestershire
Wyre Forest

YORKSHIRE AND THE HUMBER

Barnsley PCT
No change

Bradford and Airedale Teaching PCT
Airedale
Bradford City Teaching
Bradford South and West
North Bradford

Calderdale PCT
No change

Doncaster PCT
Doncaster Central
Doncaster East
Doncaster West

East Riding of Yorkshire PCT
East Yorkshire
Yorkshire Wolds and Coast

Hull Teaching PCT
Eastern Hull Teaching
Western Hull Teaching

Kirklees PCT
Huddersfield Central
North Kirklees
South Huddersfield

Leeds PCT
East Leeds
Leeds North East
Leeds North West
Leeds West
South Leeds

North East Lincolnshire PCT
No change

North Lincolnshire PCT
No change

North Yorkshire and York PCT
Craven, Harrogate and Rural District
Hambleton and Richmondshire
Scarborough, Whitby and Ryedale
Selby and York

Rotherham PCT
No change

Sheffield PCT
North Sheffield
Sheffield South West
Sheffield West
South East Sheffield

Wakefield
Eastern Wakefield
Wakefield West

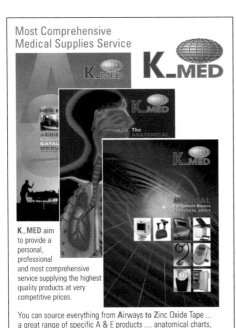

Social Services: England

The Social Services aim to provide a wide range of quality care services for both adults and children. They are there to help families in distress, in assisting adults to live independently and ensuring the safety of children. To achieve this they work closely with Health Authorities, Housing Agencies and with many voluntary and private organisations.

Specialist teams are based at local offices and in hospitals where they offer advice, assess needs and arrange services. Child Protection officers work together with the police, schools and health service to protect children who may be at risk from harm, abuse, ill treatment or neglect.

Many of the services offered by Social Services are free of charge although some such as meals on wheels and residential and day centres may have a charge which will be assessed on a clients ability to pay.

An interpreting service is usually available to assist people whose first language is not English.

Whole System Strategies
Integrated Care Consultancy

WSS is a specialist consultancy with a primary focus on care outside hospital and the hospital/community care interface, especially in the areas of elderly care, long term conditions and mental health.

Our clients include NHS and Social Services commissioners, NHS and independent sector providers of care.

Services for Commissioners:

- Whole System Reviews – system analysis, joint commissioning arrangements, integrated care delivery
- Service-specific reviews and commissioning – identifying under/over provision, achievement of standards and SLA conformance, Best Value.
- Support for developing contestability arrangements and practice based commissioning of specific services

Services for Providers:

- Service redesign – service analysis and capacity
- Organisational change
- Integrated team working – review and facilitation
- Market entry – new entrant NHS and social care practitioners, existing independent sector providers, business scoping and planning.
- Inter-sectoral partnership working

WSS also provides a specialist counselling and mentoring service for NHS managers involved in organisational change and/or seeking career development

If you are interested in learning more about what we can offer, or becoming a WSS Associate Consultant, please email us at **admin@wholesystemstrategies.co.uk** telephone us on **01302 311723** or visit our web site **www.wholesystemstrategies.co.uk**

For queries about our counselling service you may wish to use our confidential email address **counselling@wholesystemstrategies.co.uk**

Social Services: England

Barking & Dagenham
London Borough Barking & Dagenham, Civic Centre, Dagenham, Essex, RM10 7BW, tel.: 020 8592 4500 (0900-1700), fax: 020 8227 2241
Emergencies, tel.: 0208 594 8356 (1701-0900)
Ms Julia Ross, tel.: 020 8227 2332, Director
Child Protection Service Mr Chris Pelham, tel.: 0208 227 2318 ext 2318, Service Manager
Home Care Service Ms Maggie Uttley, tel.: 0208 227 2290
Meals on Wheels Apetito, tel.: 020 8227 2783

Barnet
London Borough Barnet, Barnet House, 1255 High Road, Whetstone, London, N20 0EJ, tel.: 020 8359 2000(0900-1715 Mon-Thurs - 1700 Fri)., e-mail: firstname.surname@barnet.gov.uk, web site: www.barnet.gov.uk
Emergencies, tel.: 020 8359 2000 (out of hours)
Mr Paul Fallon, Director
Ms Lynda Shanks, Executive Assistant to Director, tel.: 020 8359 5798
Asylum Seekers Ms Carolyn Greenaway, tel.: 020 8359 4207
Child Protection Service Ms Bridget Griffin, Divisional Manager, Listening to Children, tel.: 020 8359 4532
Child Protection Service Mr Phil Morris, Divisional Manager, Listening to Children, tel.: 020 8359 4532
Home Care Ms Debbie Pearson, tel.: 020 8359 3372
Housing & Supported Living Services Mr Nigel Hamilton, Head of Housing, tel.: 020 8359 6063
Meals on Wheels Ms Glynnis Joffe, tel.: 020 8359 4290

Barnsley
Barnsley Metropolitan Borough Council, Wellington House, 36 Wellington Street, Barnsley, South Yorkshire, S70 1WA, tel.: 01226 770770 (0845-1700 & -1655 thurs/fri)
Barnsley District General Hospital Social Work Department, tel.: 01226 730000 ext 2222
Childrens Disability Team, tel.: 01226 298508
Emergency Duty Team, tel.: 01226 715656 (1700-0845), e-mail: 24 hour Sat/Sun
Mrs Sandie Keene, Director
Learning Disability Team, tel.: 01226 775377
Mount Vernon Hospital Social Work Department, tel.: 01226 777843
Mrs Emma O'Grady, Communications Officer, tel.: 01226 772370
Physical & Sensory Disability Team, tel.: 01226 282025
Home Care Service Mr Paul Higginbottom, tel.: 01226 770770

Bath & North East Somerset
Bath & North East Somerset Council, PO Box 3343, Bath, BA1 2ZH, tel.: 01225 477000 (0830-1700 & -1630 Fri)
Ms Jane Ashman, Adult & Health Services, Strategic Director
Duty Officers, Adult Care Duty, tel.: 01225 396 201/231/237
Emergencies, tel.: 01454 615165 (1700-0830)
Child Protection Service Mr Maurice Lindsay, Head of Children & Family Services, tel.: 01225 396289
Home Care Service Ms Sian Walker, Group Manager, tel.: 01225 396538
Housing & Supported Living Services Ms Jane Shayler, Head of Service, tel.: 01225 396120
Housing Options/Homelessness Ms Rosemary Hester, Homelessness Manager, tel.: 01225 396296 (Admin)

Bedfordshire
Bedfordshire County Council, County Hall, Cauldwell Street, Bedford, MK42 9AP, tel.: 01234 363222 (0845-1720 Mon-Thurs, -1630 Fri), web site: www.bedfordshire.gov.uk
Asylum Seekers Ms Barbara Mallon, tel.: 01582 818039
Children's Services Mr Malcolm Newsam, Director
Home Care Service Ms Pauline Sanderson, tel.: 01582 818071
Meals on Wheels Ms Pauline Sanderson, tel.: 01582 818071

Bexley
Bexley London Borough, Adult Social Services, Hill View, Hill View Drive, Welling, Kent, DA16 3RY, e-mail: firstname.surname@bexley.gov.uk
Emergencies, tel.: 020 8303 7777/7171 (1700-0830 w'days, 24hrs w/es)
Mr Ted Hart, Committee Officer, tel.: 020 8303 7777 ext 4189
Adult Social Services Mr Simon Leftley, tel.: 020 8836 8185, Director

Birmingham
Birmingham City Council, Level 5, Louisa Ryland House, 44 Newhall Street, Birmingham, B3 3PL, tel.: 0121 303 7859 (0830-1715), web site: www.birmingham.gov.uk
Mr Peter Hay, Director
Ms Cheryl Hopkins, Transition Co-ordination & Commissioning, tel.: 0121 303 4861, Assistant Director
Outside Office Hours Emergency Duty Team, tel.: 0121 675 4806
Mr Bill Robertson, Commissioning & Adult Education, tel.: 0121 303 7859
Ms Alison Waller, Specialist Services, tel.: 0121 224 4765, Assistant Director
Mr Steve Wise, Finance & Resources, tel.: 0121 303 2108
Child Protection Service Ms Carol Douch, tel.: 0121 303 8454, Head of Service
Community Meals Head of Service, tel.: 0121 303 4104
Disability Service Ms Lesley Heale, tel.: 0121 303 4086

Social Services: England

Home Care Service Ms Sue Amour, Selly Oak Team Manager, tel.: 0121 303 5194

Home Care Service Ms Cheryl Bates, Perry Barr Team Manager, tel.: 0121 303 0799

Home Care Service Ms Doreen Colley, Hall Green Team Manager, tel.: 0121 303 0900

Home Care Service Ms Corinne Hughes, Out of Hours Team Manager, tel.: 0121 464 5001

Home Care Service Ms Lorna King, Erdington Team Manager, tel.: 0121 303 9652

Home Care Service Ms Helen Lee, HOB Team Manager Team 1, tel.: 0121 303 0576

Home Care Service Ms Frances Linn, Yardley Team Manager, tel.: 0121 303 8800

Home Care Service Ms Janneth Rodney, Sutton Team Manager, tel.: 0121 303 9253

Home Care Service Ms Lesley Smith-Woodman, Northfield Team Manager, tel.: 0121 303 5795

Home Care Service Ms Marie Southwick, HOB Team Manager Team 2, tel.: 0121 303 8221

Older People Services Mr Jon Tomlinson, tel.: 0121 464 7164

Vulnerable Adults Services Mr Berkley Broomes, tel.: 0121 303 6694

Blackburn with Darwen

Blackburn with Darwen Borough Council, Jubilee House, Jubilee Street, Blackburn, Lancs, BB1 1ET, tel.: 01254 585585, fax: 01254 587591, web site: www.blackburn.gov.uk

Mr Peter Dillon, Head of Older People's Services

Mr Tim O'Shea, Head of Mental Health Services

Mr Allan Ricketts, Community Care & Health: Adults of Working Age, Assistant Director

Mr Simon Robson, Head of Community Care

Mr Stephen Sloss, Director of Social Services

Older People Services Mr David Kerambrum, Deputy Director (Community Care & Health)

Blackpool

Blackpool Borough Council, Progress House, Clifton Road, Blackpool, FY4 4US, tel.: 01253 477666 (0845-1700 Mon-Thurs, -1630 Fri)

Mrs Seonaid Elliott, Communications Manager

Mr Steve Pullan, Director

Home Care Service Ms Christine Prestwood

Bolton

Bolton Metro, Le Mans Crescent, Civic Centre, Bolton, BL1 1SA, tel.: 01204 337210 (0900-1700), e-mail: firstname.surname@bolton.gov.uk

Asylum Seekers, tel.: 01204 335218

Child Protection, tel.: 01204 337479

Children with Disabilities, tel.: 01204 337720

Emergencies, tel.: 01204 337777 (1700-0900 & weekends)

Family Placement, tel.: 01204 337962

Family Support, tel.: 01204 337400

Homeless Families, tel.: 01204 335830

Housing & Regeneration, tel.: 01204 331008

Leaving Care, tel.: 01204 337400

Looked After Children, tel.: 01204 337400

Travellers, tel.: 01204 335264

Adult Social Services Mr John Rutherford, tel.: 01204 337200, Director

Children's Services Mrs Margaret Blenkinsop, tel.: 01204 332010, Director

Home Care/Meals on Wheels Contact HQ for appropriate District Office, tel.: 01204 337210

Bournemouth

Bournemouth Borough Council, Town Hall, Bournemouth, Dorset, BH2 6DY, tel.: 01202 451451 (0830-1715 Mon-Thurs, -1630 Fri), web site: www.bournemouth.gov.uk

Emergencies, tel.: 01202 668123 (out of hours)

Ms Judith Geddes, Interim Corporate Director, tel.: 01202 458702

Mrs Marilyn Richards, Information Officer, tel.: 01202 458861

Adult Care & Community Services Mr Peter Munns, tel.: 01202 458722, Head of Service

Children's Services Mr Kevin Jones, tel.: 01202 458704, Head of Service

Community Care Mrs Adrienne Stathakis, Interim Head, tel.: 01202 458719

Home Care/Meals on Wheels Bournemouth Care Direct, tel.: 01202 454979

Bracknell Forest

Bracknell Forest Borough Council, Time Square, Market Street, Bracknell, RG12 1JD, tel.: 01344 352000, fax: 01344 351596, e-mail: socialservices.housing@bracknell-forest.gov.uk, web site: www.bracknell-forest.gov.uk

Mr Graz Dziewulska, Head of Organisational Development

Emergency Duty Team (Social Workers), tel.: 01344 786512

Ms Margaret Gent, Head of Performance Management & Communications

Ms Lynne Lidster, Strategy & Policy/Partnership, Acting Manager

Ms Daphne Obang, Social Services & Housing, tel.: 01344 351939, Director

Mr Robert Poole, Business Manager

Ms Sandie Slater, Head of ITC

Ms Linda Wells, Sustainable Communities, Assistant Director

Adult Social Services Duty Team, tel.: 01344 351500

Community Care Mr Glyn Jones, Director

Emergencies Emergencies - Forestcare Emergency Service (24 hr), tel.: 01344 786543

Meals on Wheels Ms Lynn Bayliss, tel.: 0118 987 7061

Social Services: England

Bradford

Bradford Metropolitan District Council, Olicana House, Chapel Street, Bradford, BD1 5RE, tel.: 01274 432918 (0830-1700)
Asylum Seekers Ms Lal , Divisional Service Manager, tel.: 01274 432986
Child Protection Service Mr Paul Hill, Principal Care Manager, tel.: 01274 434361
Home Care Service Ms Pat Cole, Manager Domiciliary Care, tel.: 01274 432482
Looked After Children Mr Roger Morris, Divisional Service Manager, tel.: 01274 437077
Meals Service Ms Pat Cole, Manager Domiciliary Care, tel.: 01274 432482
Social Services Ms Kath Tunstall, tel.: 01274 432900, Director

Brent

London Borough of Brent, Mahatma Gandhi House, 34 Wembley Hill Road, Wembley, Middlesex, HA9 8AD, tel.: 020 8937 4300 (0900-1700)
Emergencies, tel.: 020 8863 5250
Ms Sandhya Thacer, PA to Director of Housing & Community Care, tel.: 020 8937 2341
Home Care/Meals on Wheels Ms Ros Howard, tel.: 020 8937 4030
Housing & Community Care Mr Martin Cheeseman, Director

Bristol

Bristol City Council, PO Box 30, Amelia Court, Pipe Lane, Bristol, BS99 7NB, tel.: 0117 922 2000 (0830-1700 Mon-Thurs, -1630 Fri), web site: www.bristol-city.gov.uk
Asylum Seekers Ms Cathy Morgan
Child Protection Service Ms Lucy Young, Planning & Development Manager, tel.: 0117 903 7778
Home Care Service Ms Cathy Morgan
Homeless Families Neighbourhood & Housing Services Department, Travellers
Looked After Children Ms Karen Gazzard
Looked After Children Ms Christine Teller
Meals on Wheels Mr John Hilton
Smoking Cessation Ms Pauline Davey, Central Support Service
Social Services & Health Ms Annie Hudson, Acting Director

Bromley

London Borough of Bromley, Civic Centre, Stockwell Close, Bromley, BR1 3UH, tel.: 020 8464 3333 (0845-1700), web site: www.bromley.gov.uk
Emergencies, tel.: 020 8464 4848 (1700-0845)
Mr Terry Rich, Director
Child Protection Service Ms Julie Daly, Q A & Commissioning, tel.: 020 8313 4610
Home Care Service Mr Richard Haines, tel.: 07780 684147
Transport & Meals Mr Brian Curle, tel.: 0208 313 4853

Buckinghamshire

Buckinghamshire County Council, County Hall, Walton Street, Aylesbury, Bucks, HP20 1YU, tel.: 01296 395000 (0900-1730, -1700 Fri)
Emergencies, tel.: 01494 817750 (out of hours)
Mrs Rita Lally, Director
Mr Kerry Stevens, tel.: 01296 382615, Head of Service
Home Care/Meals on Wheels Ms Alison Bulman, tel.: 01296 387111, Service Manager
Home Care/Meals on Wheels Ms Sarah Burke, tel.: 01494 683536, Service Manager
Home Care/Meals on Wheels Mr Simon Ternerlies, tel.: 01494 475122

Bury

Bury Metropolitan Borough Council, Castle Buildings, Market Place, Bury, BL9 0LT, tel.: 0161 253 5000 (0845-1700)
Ms Lynne Breen, Home Care Assessor Manager (South Team), tel.: 0161 253 7155
Ms Ann Grogan, Home Care Provider Manager (North Team), tel.: 0161 253 5485
Ms Eleni Ioannides, Executive Director, Children's Services
Mrs Diana Phillips, Home Care Provider Manager, tel.: 0161 253 6689
Mrs Kay Robinson, Home Care Assessor Manager (South Team), tel.: 0161 253 7157
Mrs Judith Savin, Home Care Assessor Manager (South Team), tel.: 0161 253 7051
Adult Social Services Ms Pat Horan, Executive Director
Asylum Seekers Ms Karen Young, tel.: 0161 253 6123, Team Leader
Community Services Miss Julie Owen, Service Manager
Looked After Children Ms Elizabeth Shingler, tel.: 0161 253 5497, Service Manager

Calderdale

ADULT SOCIAL CARE, Calderdale Metropolitan Borough Council, Health & Social Care Directorate, 1 Park Road, Halifax, HX1 2TU, tel.: 01422 363561 (0900-1700 Mon-Fri), web site: www.calderdale.gov.uk
Emergencies, tel.: 01422 365101 (out of hours)
Initial Response Team, Temporary tel no - office changes, tel.: 01422 353279
Looked After Children, Temporary tel no - office changes underway, tel.: 01422 363561
Adult Social Services Mr Phil Shire, Head of Service
Asylum Seekers Ms Lisa Walch, tel.: 01422 393331
Children's Services Ms Carol White, tel.: 01422 392511, Director
Home Care Service Ms Margaret Moss, tel.: 01422 363561
Meals Service Ms Helen Sutcliffe, tel.: 01422 363561

Social Services: England

Cambridgeshire
Cambridgeshire County Council, Castle Court, Shire Hall, Castle Hill, Cambridge, CB3 0AP, tel.: 08450 455201 (0800-2000 Mon-Sat), web site: www.cambridgeshire.gov.uk
Mr Paul Ainsworth, Communication Manager, tel.: 01223 718141
Out of hours, tel.: 01733 234724 (1700-0845)
Adult Social Services Ms Claire Bruin, Director
Child Protection Service Mr Peter Wilson, Audit & Practice Standards Manager, tel.: 01480 375510
Children's Services Mr Gordon Jeyes, Director
Home Care Service Ms Jane Fowler, tel.: 01353 724870
Meals on Wheels Mr Roger Abraham, tel.: 01223 712040

Camden
London Borough Camden, 79 Camden Road, London, NW1 9ES, tel.: 020 7974 6666 (0900-1700)
Ms Alessia Antonelli, PA to Director, tel.: 020 7974 3503
Emergencies, tel.: 020 72784444 (1700-0900)
Mr Neil Litherland, Director
Home Care Service Ms Pam Jones, tel.: 020 7530 5349
Meals on Wheels Mr Robert Donald, tel.: 020 7974 6684

Cheshire
Cheshire County Council, County Hall, Chester, CH1 1BW, tel.: 01244 603231 (0830-1700 Mon-Thurs, -1630 Fri)
Access Services Central (Crewe & Nantwich), tel.: 01270 505100
Access Services Central (Vale Royal), tel.: 01606 814900
Access Services East (Macclesfield & Congleton), tel.: 01625 534700
Access Services West (Chester & Ellesmere Port), tel.: 01244 603400
Emergencies, tel.: 01606 76611 (out of hours)
Mr John Weeks, Director
Community Meals Ms Cath Wright, tel.: 01606 815062

Cornwall
Cornwall County Council, Old County Hall, Station Road, Truro, Cornwall, TR1 3AY, tel.: 01872 322000, web site: www.cornwall.gov.uk
Emergencies, tel.: 01208 251300 (1715-0830)
Adult Social Services Dr Carol Tozer, Director
Home Care Service Via Local Offices

Coventry
Coventry Metropolitan District Council, Council Offices, Little Park Street, Coventry, CV1 5RS, tel.: 024 7683 3333 (0830-1700 Mon-Thurs, -1630 Fri)
Mr John Bolton, Director of Social Services & Housing
Emergencies, tel.: 024 7683 2222 (out of hours)
Home Care Service Ms Sandra Walton, tel.: 024 7668 0600

Croydon
London Borough of Croydon, Taberner House, Park Lane, Croydon, Surrey, CR9 2BA, tel.: 020 8726 6000 (0900-1700)
Care Homes Dawn Service, tel.: 020 8760 5768 x 62807
Emergencies, tel.: 020 8726 6000 (24 hours)
Ms Gloria Eveleigh, Adult Protection Co-ordinator, tel.: 020 870 5768 x 65790
Mr John Haseler, Joint Commissioning - Mental Health Services, tel.: 020 8274 6267, Manager
Mr Peter Houghton, Residential & Day Services, tel.: 020 8726 6000 x 63503, Service Manager
Ms Sharon Houlden, Substance Misuse, tel.: 020 8276 5729, Service Manager
Ms Hannah Miller, Director
Mr Simon Wadsworth, Aids/Hiv & Substance Misuse, tel.: 020 8726 6000 x 62910, Service Manager
Ms Joannah Weightman, Joint Commissioning - LD Services, tel.: 020 8726 6000 x 62134, Manager
Adult Social Services Ms Brenda Scanlan, tel.: 020 8726 6000 x 5727, Divisional Director
Asylum Seekers Adults in Need, tel.: 020 8760 5768 x 62574
Child Protection Service Ms Joan Semeonoff, Social Services, tel.: 020 8726 6000 x 62125, Manager
Home Care Service Mr Trevor Mosses, Commissioning Manager, tel.: 020 8726 6000 x 62869, e-mail: Older People/Physical Disability
Homeless Service Housing Options Team, tel.: 020 8726 6100
Meals on Wheels Ms Antoinette Nottedge-Everest, tel.: 020 8726 6000 x 62677

Cumbria
Cumbria County Council, 15 Portland Square, Carlisle, CA1 1QQ, tel.: Out of Hours 01228 526690
Mr David Alexander, Interim Head of Children's Services
Children's Services & Child Protection, tel.: 01228 607002
Customer Services - Allerdale, tel.: 01900 325325
Customer Services - Barrow, tel.: 01229 894894
Customer Services - Carlisle, tel.: 01228 607000
Customer Services - Eden, tel.: 01768 242242
Customer Services - South Lakes, tel.: 01539 773377
Customer Services -Copeland, tel.: 01946 852852
Mr John McMullon, Head of Adult Services
Adult Social Services Mrs Jill Stannard, Director
Children's Services Mrs Moira , Director

Darlington
Darlington Borough Council, Adult Social Services; Community Services, Central House, Gladstone Street, Darlington, County Durham, DL3 6JX, tel.: 01325 346200 (0830-1700 Mon-Thurs, -1630 Fri)
Mr Cliff Brown, Director
Emergencies, tel.: 01642 631123 (out of hours)

Derby City

Derby City Council, Middleton House, 27 St Mary's Gate, Derby, DE1 3NS, tel.: 01332 717777 (0830-1700), web site: www.derby.gov.uk
Mr Michael Foote, Corporate & Adult Social Services, tel.: 01332 717360, Corporate Director
Out of Hours, tel.: 01332 711250 (1700-0830)
Child Protection Service Duty Manager, tel.: 01332 717777
Children & Young People's Services Mr Andrew Flack, tel.: 01332 717118, Director
Home Care/Meals on Wheels Duty Manager, tel.: 01332 717777

Derbyshire

Derbyshire County Council, County Hall, Matlock, DE4 3AG, tel.: 01629 772225 (0830-1730)
Mr B Buckley, Director
Emergencies, tel.: 01773 728222 (1700-0900)
Home Care Service Ms Madeline Fullerton, tel.: 01629 772065

Devon

Devon County Council, County Hall, Topsham Road, Exeter, EX2 4QR, tel.: 01392 382000 (0900-1700 Mon-Thurs, -1600 Fri)
Customer Services, tel.: Freephone 0800 212783
Emergencies, tel.: 0845 600 0388 (out of hours)
Mr David Johnstone, Director
Child Protection Service East Devon Team, tel.: 01392 384444
Child Protection Service Exeter Team, tel.: 01392 384444
Child Protection Service Mid Devon Team, tel.: 01392 384100
Child Protection Service North Devon Team, tel.: 01271 388549
Child Protection Service South Hams Team, tel.: 01392 386675
Child Protection Service Teignbridge Team, tel.: 01392 384900
Child Protection Service Torridge District Team, tel.: 01237 475693
Child Protection Service West Devon Team, tel.: 01822 614121
Home Care/Meals on Wheels Care Direct, tel.: Freephone 0800 444 000
Travellers Gypsies & Travellers Liaison, tel.: 01392 381105/01884 243825

Doncaster

Doncaster Metropolitan Borough Council, PO Box 251, The Council House, Doncaster, South Yorkshire, DN1 3DA, tel.: 01302 737777 (0830-1700)
Emergencies, tel.: 01302 796000 (out of hours)
Mr Paul Evans, Neighbourhoods/Communities & Children's Services, Strategic Director
Home Care/Meals on Wheels Mr Simon Mallett, tel.: 01302 737760

Dorset

Dorset County Council Social Care & Health, County Hall, Colliton Park, Dorchester, DT1 1XJ, tel.: 01305 251000 (0840-1720 Mon-Thurs, -1600 Fri)
Emergencies, tel.: 01202 668123 (out of hours)
Mr Steve Pitt, Director
Home Care Service Community Support Centre, tel.: 01305 228448
Meals on Wheels Via Local Office (Bridport), & Adult/Childcare Referrals, tel.: 01308 422234
Meals on Wheels Via Local Office (Christchurch), & Adult/Childcare Referrals, tel.: 01202 474106
Meals on Wheels Via Local Office (North Dorset: Sturminster Newton), & Adult/Childcare Referrals, tel.: 01258 472652
Meals on Wheels Via Local Office (Purbeck: Wareham), & Adult/Childcare Referrals, tel.: 01929 553456
Meals on Wheels Via Local Office (Sherborne), & Adult/Childcare Referrals, tel.: 01935 814104/5
Meals on Wheels Via Local Office (West Dorset: Dorchester), & Adult/Childcare Referrals, tel.: 01305 251414
Meals on Wheels Via Local Office (Weymouth & Portland), & Adult/Childcare Referrals, tel.: 01305 760139
Meals on Wheels Via Local Office (Wimborne: Ferndown), & Adult/Childcare Referrals, tel.: 01202 877445

Dudley

Dudley MBC, Ednam House, St James's Road, Dudley, West Midlands, DY1 3JJ, tel.: 01384 815822 (0900-1700), e-mail: social.care@dudley.gov.uk, web site: www.dudley.gov.uk
Ms Ann Askew, Physical & Sensory, tel.: 01384 815822
Mr Richard Carter, Mental Health, tel.: 01384 815822
Emergencies, tel.: 01384 456111 (out of hours)
Mr Brian Nesbitt, Residential Services, tel.: 01384 815822
Ms Ann Parkes, Learning Disability, tel.: 01384 815822
Mrs Linda Sanders, tel.: 01384 815822, Director
Mr Gus Swanson, Information Officer, tel.: 01384 815870
Child Protection Service Mr Graham Tilby, tel.: 01384 815822
Home Care Service Ms Sue Beach, tel.: 01384 815822
Meals on Wheels Mr Mike Marshall, tel.: 01384 815822

Durham

Durham County Council, Social Services Dept, County Hall, Durham, DH1 5UG, tel.: 0191 383 3000 (0830-1700), web site: www.durham.gov.uk
Ms Christina Blythe, Youth Offending Service, tel.: 0191 383 3982, Head of Service
Emergencies, tel.: 0845 505010 (2000-0800) (1300 Sat-0800 Mon)
Mr J Gavyrot, Strategic Finance, tel.: 0191 383 3388
Ms Debbie Jones, tel.: 0191 383 3000, Acting Director
Social Care Direct, For all referrals for services, tel.: 0845 850 5010
Mr J Thornberry, OP/PDSI/MHSOP, Head of Service
Mrs L A Tickell, LD/MH/SM, Head of Service

Social Services: England

Child Protection Service Mr Carl Docking, Standards & Development Officer, tel.: 0191 383 3323

Children & Families Service Ms Gail Hopper, tel.: 0191 383 3322, Head of Service

Ealing
London Borough of Ealing, Social Services, Perceval House, 14-16 Uxbridge Road, Ealing, London, W5 2HL, tel.: 020 8825 5000 (0800-1730)
Ms Ehronda Barke, All Children & Adult Referrals, tel.: 020 8825 8000, Manager

Emergencies, tel.: 020 8825 5000 (1730-0800)

Inspectors for Residential Homes in Ealing, National Care Standards Commission, tel.: 020 8280 0347

Ms Belinda Murphy, Adult Protection, tel.: 020 8825 6228, Manager

Ms Fiona Sims, Housing & Social Services Complaints, tel.: 020 8825 8100, Manager

Social Services Customer Contact Centre, tel.: 020 8825 8000

Child Protection Service Ms Finola Culbert, tel.: 020 8825 7304, Manager

Home Care Service Ms Suzette Walrond, tel.: 020 8825 5000, e-mail: (New Referrals 020 8825 8000)

Meals on Wheels Ms Diane McSweeney, tel.: 020 8825 5000, e-mail: (New Referrals 020 8825 8000)

East Riding of Yorkshire
East Riding of Yorkshire, County Hall, Beverley, HU17 9BA, tel.: 01482 887700 (0830-1730 Mon-Thurs, -1630 Fri), fax: 01482 393009, web site: www.eastriding.gov.uk
Emergencies, tel.: 01482 880826 (1700-0830 Mon-Thurs,1700 Fri-830 Mon

Mr Andrew Williams, Director of Children, Family & Adult Services

Child Protection Service Ms Nicola Furness, Senior Information Officer, Childcare, tel.: 01482 396472

Child Protection Service Ms Sue Marson, Senior Information Officer, Childcare, tel.: 01482 396472

East Sussex
East Sussex County Council, PO Box 5, County Hall, St Anne's Crescent, Lewes, East Sussex, BN7 1SW, tel.: 01273 481000 (0800-1715 Mon-Thurs -1645 Fri)
Emergencies, tel.: 01273 481000 (out of hours)

Mr Keith Hinkley, Adult Social Care, Acting Director

Child Protection Service Ms Fiona Johnson, tel.: 01273 481289, Head of Service

Community Meals Ms Jane Carter, Contracts Manager (Catering), tel.: 01273 482513

Home Care Service Mr Shane Heber, tel.: 01424 443893, Head of Service

Enfield
London Borough of Enfield, PO Box 60, Civic Centre, Silver Street, Enfield, Middlesex, EN1 3XL, tel.: 020 8379 1000 (24hrs)

Ms Sue Collingridge, Re-enablement Team, tel.: 020 8379 8099, Service Manager

Emergencies, tel.: 020 8366 6565 (24 hours)

Mr Ray James, Community, Housing & Adult Social Services, tel.: 020 8379 4340, Assistant Director

Ms Bernie Pizzaro, Purchasing, Monitoring & Review Manager, tel.: 020 8379 2660/2845/2878

Home Care Service Ms Jenny Murtagh, Acting Home Care Team Leader, tel.: 020 8350 1113

Essex
Essex County Council, County Hall, PO Box 297, Chelmsford, CM1 1YS, tel.: 01245 492211 (0900-1730)
Emergencies, tel.: 01245 434083 (out of hours)

Ms Jenny Owen, Service Director

Home Care/Meals on Wheels Mr Ian Goode

Gateshead
Gateshead Council, Civic Centre, Regent Street, Gateshead, Tyne & Wear, NE8 1HH, tel.: 0191 433 3000 (0830-1700), web site: www.gateshead.gov.uk
Direct Payments, tel.: 0191 433 3000 ext 2425

Emergencies, tel.: 0191 433 3000 (24 hours)

Fair Access to Care - Eligibility Criteria, tel.: on website

Gateshead Charter for Long Term Care, tel.: on website

Mrs Rosemary Lockett, Head of Adult Care, tel.: 0191 433 2350

Mr Mike Routledge, Protection of Vulnerable Adults, tel.: 0191 433 3000 ext 2613, Co-ordinator

Mr Graeme Wilson, Travellers & Gypsies, tel.: 0191 433 3907

Asylum Seekers Ms Shela Close, tel.: 0191 433 2735

Child Protection Service Mr Ken Heppell, tel.: 0191 433 2374, Co-ordinator

Child Protection Service Frances Powell, tel.: 0191 433 3000, Head of Service

Home Care Service Ms Margaret Barrett, tel.: 0191 4338030

Home Care Service Mr Ken Robson, tel.: 0191 4338800

Homeless Service Ms Christine Cross, tel.: 0191 433 2629

Meals on Wheels Ms Jackie McDonnell, tel.: 0191 433 2486

Smoking Cessation Ms Maria Williams, tel.: 0191 451 6610

Gloucestershire
Community & Young People's Directorate, Shire Hall, Gloucester, GL1 2TR, tel.: 01452 425302, web site: www.gloucestershire.gov.uk
Ms Jo Davidson, Group Director Community & Young People

Emergencies, tel.: 01452 614194 (1700-0900)

Ms Margaret Sheather, Group Director - Adult Care, tel.: 01452 425102

Asylum Seekers Ms Tina Reid, Community Services Manager, tel.: 01452 427300

Child Protection Service Mr Duncan Siret, Lead Co-ordinator

Home Care Service Ms Vareta Bryan, tel.: 01453 760500

Home Care Service Mr David Dungworth, tel.: 01594 820557

Meals on Wheels Ms Julie Moore, tel.: 01452 425320

Greenwich
London Borough Greenwich, Nelson House, 50 Wellington Street, Woolwich, London, SE18 6PY, tel.: 020 8854 8888(0900-1730 Mon-Thurs, -1630 Fri), web site: www.greenwich.gov.uk
Emergencies, tel.: 020 8854 0396 (out of hours)
Mr John Nawrockyi, Director
Mr David Riley, Information Manager, tel.: 020 8921 2656
Ms Alison Vosper, Public Information & Communications Manager, tel.: 020 8921
Children & Families Service Mr Andrew O'Sullivan, tel.: 020 8921, Head of Service
Home Care/Meals on Wheels Ms Linda Gardner, Adults Contracts Manager, tel.: 020 8921 2327
Meals on Wheels Mr Mike Marriott

Hackney
London Borough Hackney, 205 Morning Lane, London, E9 6JX, tel.: 020 8356 5000 (0900-1700)
Emergencies, tel.: 020 8356 2300 (out of hours)
Ms Mary Richardson, Director
Child Protection Service Ms Rhonda Miedziolka, Principal Manager, tel.: 020 8356 5947
Home Care Service Ms Janice Wightman, tel.: 020 8356 4768
Meals on Wheels Ms Esther Karunwi, tel.: 020 8356 4830

Halton
Halton Borough Council, Municipal Building, Kingsway, Widnes, Cheshire, WA8 7QF, tel.: 0151 424 2061 (0845-1730)
Emergencies, tel.: 01606 76611
Mr Dwayne Johnson, Health & Community, Strategic Director
Child Protection Service Ms Ann Towey, Divisional Manager (Acting)
Children & Young People's Services Ms Diana Terris, Strategic Director
Home Care Service Ms Francine Coy, Runcorn, tel.: 0151 906 4848
Home Care Service Mr Damian Nolan, Widnes, tel.: 0151 424 2061
Meals on Wheels Ms Sue Wallace-Bonner, tel.: 01928 704454

Hammersmith & Fulham
London Borough Hammersmith & Fulham, 145 King Street, London, W6 9XY, tel.: 020 8748 3020 (0845-1700 Mon-Thurs, -1645 Fri)
Mr Geoff Alltimes, Director
Emergencies, tel.: 020 8748 8588 (out of hours)
Home Care Service Mr David Williams, tel.: 020 8748 3020 ext 5049, Manager

Meals on Wheels Ms Sue Beresford, tel.: 020 8748 3020 ext 5758, Manager

Hampshire
Hampshire County Council, The Castle, Winchester, S023 8UQ, tel.: 01962 847208 (0830-1700 Mon-Thurs, - 1630 Fri)
Ms Dawn Burton, County Manager Physical Disability, tel.: 01962 847257
Ms Ruth Dixon, County Manager Mental Health, tel.: 01962 847107
Ms Gill Duncan, Residential, Nursing & Day-Care, tel.: 01962 833018, Director
Emergencies, tel.: 0845 600 4555 (1700-0830)
Ms Janet Feat, Family Support, Children in Need, tel.: 01962 847183, Service Manager
Mr Mohammed Mossadaq, Equality & Diversity, tel.: 01962 845880
Mr Derek Oliver, County Manager Learning Disability, tel.: 01962 847294
Mr Vincent Oliver, County Manager, tel.: 01962 833016
Ms Rosie Peart, Child Protection Coordinator, tel.: 01962 845073
Adult Social Services Ms Ree Mattocks, Director
Children's Services Mr John Coughlan, Director
Home Care Service Ms Sally Trinder, tel.: 01962 833005

Haringey
Haringey Council, 40 Cumberland Road, Wood Green, London, N22 7SG, tel.: 020 8489 0000 (0845-1730)
Ms Janet Allen, Travellers Community Team, tel.: 020 8489 3005
Ms Anne Bristow, Director of Social Services, tel.: 020 8489 0000
Child Protection & Planning Advice, tel.: 020 8489 1192
Child Protection Referrals - East, tel.: 020 8489 5408
Child Protection Referrals - West, tel.: 020 8489 1857
Emergencies, tel.: 020 8348 3148 (24hrs)
Mr Farzad Fazilat, Asylum Team, tel.: 020 8489 4962
Ms Margaret Griffin, Homeless Families, tel.: 020 8489 4301
Homeless Families, tel.: 020 8489 4359
Ms Rachel Oakley, Looked After Children, tel.: 020 8489 3754, Service Manager
Smoking Cessation, tel.: 020 8489 4556/4
Child Protection Service Ms Teresa Walsh Jones, tel.: 020 8489 1177, Service Manager
Home Care/Meals on Wheels Ms Eva Darlow, tel.: 020 8489 4823, Service Manager

Harrow
London Borough Harrow, Civic Centre, PO Box 7, Station Road, Harrow, Middlesex, HA1 2UL, tel.: 020 8863 5611
Child & Adolescent Mental Health Service, CAMHS Co-ordinator, tel.: 020 8420 9680
Children in Need Team, tel.: 020 8863 5544
Children with Disabilities Team, tel.: 020 8863 5544

Children's Referral & Assessment Team, tel.: 020 8863 5544

Elderly Services (East), tel.: 020 8951 3811

Elderly Services (West), tel.: 020 8429 4488

Emergencies, tel.: 020 8424 0999 (out of hours)

Helpline (Community Alarm Service), tel.: 020 8861 3242

HLDT, tel.: 020 8424 1019

NPH Social Work Team, tel.: 020 8869 2594

Ms Lorraine O'Reilly, Executive Director of People First

Physical Disability & Sensory Impairment Team, tel.: 020 8424 1694

Teenage Pregnancy Co-ordinator, tel.: 020 8424 1699

Adult Social Services Ms Penny Furness-Smith, Director

Children's Services Mr Paul Clark, Director

Hartlepool

Hartlepool Borough Council, PO Box 96, Civic Centre, Hartlepool, TS24 9YW, tel.: 01429 266522 (0830-1700 Mon-Thurs, -1630 Fri)

Ms Jenette Donkin, Senior Admin Officer, tel.: 01429 523665

Ms Sandra Robinson, Acting Assistant Director, tel.: 01429 523943

Adult Care & Community Services Ms Nicola Bailey, tel.: 01429 523914, Director

Community Services Mr John Mennear, Acting Assistant Director, tel.: 01429 523943

Home Care Service Mr John Lovatt, Acting Head of Business Unit (Adults), tel.: 01429 284034

Havering

London Borough of Havering, Havering Direct, Town Hall, Main Road, Romford, Essex, RM1 3BD, tel.: 01708 432000 (0900-1700)

Emergencies, tel.: 01708 433999 (1700-0900)

Mr Robin Kelleher, Inspection Consortium, tel.: 0208 477 0960

Miss Natalia Nash, Customer Relations Officer, tel.: 01708 433038

Ms Marilyn Richards, tel.: 01708 432000, Director

Asylum Seekers Mr John Rood, tel.: 01708 432852

Child Protection Service Ms Irene Craig, Quality Assurance Manager, tel.: 01708 433016

Home Care/Meals on Wheels Ms Fiona Amber, tel.: 01708 433088

Herefordshire

Herefordshire Council, Brockington, 35 Hafod Road, Hereford, HR1 1SH, tel.: 01432 260000 (0830-1715)

Emergencies, tel.: 01905 748033 (1700-0900)

Adult Care & Community Services Mr Geoff Hughes, tel.: 01432 260695, Director

Child Protection Service Mr Steve Merrell, Childrens Service Manager (Operations), tel.: 01432 260229

Children's Services Ms Sue Fiennes, tel.: 01432 260048, Director

Home Care Service Ms Sheila Morgan, tel.: 01432 261646,

Team Manager

Meals on Wheels Ms Clare Price, tel.: 01432 267555

Hertfordshire

Hertfordshire County Council, County Hall, Pegs Lane, Hertford, SG13 8DP, tel.: 01992 555555, e-mail: hertsdirect@hertscc.gov.uk, web site: www.hertsdirect.org.uk

Mr John Harris, Children, Schools & Families, tel.: 01438 737500, Director

Adult Social Services Mr Earl Dutton, Assistant Director Elderly & Physical Disability

Adult Social Services Ms Cathy Kerr, Learning Disability & Mental Health, Assistant Director

Adult Social Services Ms Sarah Pickup, tel.: 01438 737400, Director

Child Protection Service Ms Carol Taylor, tel.: 01438 737500, Head of Service

Meals on Wheels Via District Councils

Hillingdon

London Borough of Hillingdon, Social Services & Housing, Civic Centre, High Street, Uxbridge, Middlesex, UB8 1UW, tel.: 01895 250111 (0900-1700)

Mr John Doran, Head of Performance, Finance & Commissioning, tel.: 01895 250527

Children's Services Ms Kamini Rambellas, tel.: 01895 250527, Head of Service

Social Services & Housing Mr Hugh Dunnachie, tel.: 01895 250506, Corporate Director

Hounslow

London Borough Hounslow, Housing & Community Services, Civic Centre, Lampton Road, Hounslow, Middlesex, TW3 4DN, tel.: 020 8583 3500 (0900-1700)

Emergencies, tel.: 020 8583 2222 (out of hours)

Ms Andrea Smith, PA To Director, tel.: 020 8583 3500 ext 3500

Ms Susanna White, Director

Isle of Wight

Isle of Wight Council, Adult, Housing & Community Services Directorate, 17 Fairlee Road, Newport, Isle of Wight, PO30 2EA, tel.: 01983 520600 (0830-1700 Mon-Thurs, -1630 Fri), web site: www.iwight.com

Emergencies, tel.: 01983 821105 (24 hours)

Emergencies, tel.: 01983 821105 (24 hrs)

Mr Glen Garrod, Adult & Community Services, tel.: 01983 520600, Strategic Director

Ms Sue Lightfoot, Safer Communities, tel.: 01983 814381, Service Manager

Mr Martyn Pearl, Head of Housing, tel.: 01983 823040

Ms Debbie Platt, Business Development, tel.: 01983 814381, Service Manager

Mrs Sandy Weller, Head of Adult Services, tel.: 01983 520600

Mr Graham Wilmhurst, Head of Housing, tel.: 01983 823040

ext 3061
Child Protection Service Ms Prue Grimshaw, Head of
Children's Services, tel.: 01983 821000 ext 3411
Children & Families Service Mr David Pettit, Director
Children's Services Mrs Prue Grimshaw, tel.: 01983 520600,
Acting Head
Home Care Service Ms Kim Dueck, tel.: 01983 533772
Home Care Service Mrs Kim Dueck, tel.: 01983 533772
Meals on Wheels Mrs Sandy Weller, tel.: 01983 520600

Isles of Scilly
Council of the Isles of Scilly, Health & Social Care, Park House, The Parade, St Mary's, Isles of Scilly, TR21 0LP, tel.: 01720 422148
Community Services Mr R Scaife, tel.: 01720 422148,
Director

Islington
London Borough Islington, 5 Highbury Crescent, London, N5 1RW, tel.: 020 7527 2000 ext 4103 (0900-1700
Mr Paul Curran, Director
Emergencies, tel.: 020 7527 2000 (24 hours)
Home Care Service Ms Gwen Ovshinsky (Commissioner),
tel.: 020 7527 4015
Home Care Service Ms Marilyn Richards, tel.: 020 7527
4357, Manager
Meals on Wheels Mr Chris Evans, tel.: 020 7226 6341

Kensington and Chelsea
Royal Borough of Kensington and Chelsea, Town Hall, Hornton Street, London, W8 7NX, tel.: 020 7361 2563 (0900-1700 Mon-Fri)
Ms Jean Daintith, Executive Director
Emergencies, tel.: 020 7373 2227 (out of hours)
Home Care Emergency Services, tel.: 020 7373 2227
Mr Peter West, Head of Community Care

Kent
Kent County Council, Brenchley House, 123-135 Week Street, Maidstone, Kent, ME14 1RF, tel.: 08458 247247 (24 hr), web site: www.kent.gov.uk
Emergencies, tel.: 0345 626777 (out of hours)
Adult Social Services Mr Oliver Mills, Managing Director
Home Care/Meals on Wheels Via Area Business Managers
at Area Offices or Customer Care Manager at Kent County
Council

Kingston Upon Hull
Kingston upon Hull City Council, Brunswick House, Strand Close, Beverley Road, Hull, HU2 9DB, tel.: 01482 616011/12 (0830-1700 Mon-Thurs, -1630 Fri)
Ms G Bower, Assertive Outreach Team (Mental Health), tel.:
01482 335670, Manager
Emergency Duty Team, tel.: 01482 788080 (1630-0830)
Adult Social Services Mr Alec Pearson, tel.: 01482 616005,
Head of Service

Asylum Seekers Mr Steve Ibbetson, tel.: 01482 211100,
Manager.
Children & Families Service Mr Jon Plant, tel.: 01482
616004, Head of Service
Meals on Wheels Mr Neil Bottomley, tel.: 01482 620788,
Manager

Kingston Upon Thames
Community Services Directorate, Guildhall 1, Kingston upon Thames, KT1 1EU, tel.: 020 8547 6008 (0845-1700 Mon-Thurs, -1645 Fri)
Emergencies, tel.: 020 8770 5000 (out of hours)
Ms Karen Fenwick, Senior Customer Services Officer, tel.:
020 8547 4716
Ms Lin Phillips, tel.: 020 8547 6104, Customer Services
Manager
Mr Roy Taylor, Director
Home Care Service Contact Customer Services at
Community Services Directorate
Meals on Wheels Ms Valerie Kinloch, tel.: 020 8541 5780

Kirklees
Kirklees Metropolitan Council, Oldgate House, 2 Oldgate, Huddersfield, HD1 6QF, tel.: 01484 221000 x 5330 (0845-1715 Mon-Thurs-1645 Fri)
Emergencies, tel.: 01924 326489 (out of hours)
Adult Social Services Mr Mark Weavers, tel.: 01484 225079,
Head of Service
Child Protection Service Social Services Child Protection &
Review Unit, tel.: 01924 483749
Home Care Service Ms Helen Clay, tel.: 01484 226274
Home Care Service Group Manager, tel.: 01484 226246

Knowsley
Knowsley Health & Social Care Headquarters, PO Box 23, Nutgrove Villa, Westmorland Road, Huyton, Knowsley, L36 6GA, tel.: 0151 443 4900 (0830-1700), fax: 0151 443 3670, web site: www.knowsley.gov.uk
Ms Nita Cresswell, Lead - Adults of Employment Age
Emergencies, tel.: 07659 590081 (out-of-hours)
Mrs Anita Marsland, Director
Ms Amanda Risino, Director of Service Provision
Child Protection Service Mr Bill Dawson, tel.: 0151 443
4079, Acting Service Manager
Children's Services Ms Lesley Hollinshead, Acting Strategic
Lead
Health & Social Care Mrs Anita Marsland, Chief Executive -
PCT, Executive Director
Home Care Service Mrs Diana Ralph, tel.: 0151 443 4607,
Service Manager
Home Care Service Ms Barbara Riddell, tel.: 0151 443
4605, Service Manager
Meals on Wheels Ms Jackie Culshaw, tel.: 0151 443 3608

Social Services: England

Lambeth

London Borough of Lambeth, Adult & Community Services, Phoenix House, 10 Wandsworth Road, London, SW8 2LL, tel.: 020 7926 4788, web site: www.lambeth.gov.uk
Emergencies, tel.: 020 7926 1000 (1700-0830)
Adult Care & Community Services Mr Andrew Webster, Executive Director
Home Care/Meals on Wheels Ms Carline Francis, tel.: 020 7926 5138

Lancashire

Lancashire County Council, PO Box 162, East Cliff County Offices, Preston, PR1 3EA, tel.: 01772 254868 (0845-1700), web site: www.lancashire.gov.uk
Emergencies, tel.: 0845 602 1043 (1700-0845 & B hols)
Homecare (Meals on Wheels via local offices)
Mr Richard Jones, Director

Leeds

Leeds City Council, Merrion House, 110 Merrion Centre, Leeds, LS2 8QB, tel.: 0113 247 8630 (0830-1700)
Emergencies, tel.: 0113 240 9536 (1700-0830)
Children's Services Ms Rosemary Archer, Director
Home Care Service Ms Margaret Pease, tel.: 0113 247 7971
Meals on Wheels Mrs J Gibbons, tel.: 0113 247 8585

Leicester City

Leicester City, 1 Grey Friars, Leicester, LE1 5PH, tel.: 0116 253 1191 (0830-1700 Mon-Thurs, -1630 Fri)
Mr Tony Billings, Directorate Support & Communications Officer, tel.: 0116 252 8886
Emergencies, tel.: 0116 255 1606 (out of hours)
Adult Care & Community Services Ms Sally Burton, tel.: 0116 252 8300, Corporate Director
Child Protection Service Ms Pat Nawrockyi, Independent Review, Social Care & Health, tel.: 0116 225 4723, Service Manager
Home Care Service Ms Maureen Dover, tel.: 0116 221 1517, Service Manager
Meals on Wheels Mr Yatish Shah, Contracts Officer (Community Care Services), tel.: 0116 252 8336

Leicestershire

Leicestershire County Council, County Hall, Glenfield, Leicester, LE3 8RL, tel.: 0116 232 3232 (0830-1630 Mon-Thurs, -1600 Fri)
Communications & Consultation Team, tel.: 0116 265 7404
Emergencies, tel.: 0116 255 1606 (Out of Hours)
Adult Social Services Mr John Kershaw, tel.: 0116 232 3232, Acting Director
Child Protection Service Children & Young People's Service, tel.: 0116 232 3232
Home Care/Meals on Wheels Via Local Office (Charnwood), tel.: 01509 266641
Home Care/Meals on Wheels Via Local Office

(Harborough), tel.: 01858 465331
Home Care/Meals on Wheels Via Local Office (Hinckley & Bosworth), tel.: 01455 636964
Home Care/Meals on Wheels Via Local Office (Melton), tel.: 01664 564698
Home Care/Meals on Wheels Via Local Office (NW Leics), tel.: 01530 275200
Home Care/Meals on Wheels Via Local Office (Oadby, Wigston, Blaby), tel.: 0116 278 7111
Looked After Children Children & Young People's Service, tel.: 0116 232 3232

Lewisham

London Borough Lewisham, Social Care & Health Directorate, 3rd Floor, Town Hall Chambers, Catford, London, SE6 4RY, tel.: 020 8314 8674 (0900-1700)
Emergencies, tel.: 020 8314 6000 (0900-1700)
Zena Peatfield, Executive Director
Home Care Service Via Adult Services Team (East), tel.: 020 8314 8866
Home Care Service Via Adult Services Team (North), tel.: 020 83148822
Home Care Service Via Adult Services Team (South), tel.: 020 8314 7766
Home Care Service Via Adult Services Team (West), tel.: 020 8314 7755
Meals on Wheels Mr Graham Taylor, tel.: 020 8314 8888

Lincolnshire

Lincolnshire County Council, Orchard House, Orchard Street, Lincoln, LN1 1BA, tel.: 01522 554001 (0900-1700)
Mr Matthew Bukowski, Director
Emergencies, tel.: 01529 413366 (out of hours)
Mr Joe Warner, Strategic Development (Social Inclusion), tel.: 01522 554046, Manager
Home Care/Meals on Wheels Via Local Offices

Liverpool

Liverpool City Council, Management Suite, First Floor, Millennium House, 60 Victoria Street, Liverpool, L1 6JQ, tel.: 0151 233 3000 (0830 1645)
Mr Tony Hunter, Supported Living & Community Safety, Executive Director
Adult Social Services Emergencies, tel.: 0151 233 3019
Asylum Seekers Mr Robert Pickering, Senior Manager, Supported Living in Neighbourhoods, tel.: 0151 233 3000
Child Protection/Looked After Children Mr Stuart Smith, AED - Education Support, tel.: 0151 233 3000
Children's Services Emergencies, tel.: 0151 233 3029
Home Care/Meals on Wheels Ms Sue Trafford, Senior Manager,Service Modernisation & Improvement
Homeless Families/Travellers Mr Robert Pickering, Senior Manager, Supported Living in Neighbourhoods, tel.: 0151 233 3000

Social Services: England

London City

Corporation of London (City), Milton Court, Moor Lane, London, EC2Y 9BL, tel.: 020 7332 1224 or 020 7606 3030 ex 1224 (0915-1700) Emergencies, tel.: 020 8356 2300
Ms Pam Donnellan, Director
Home Care/Meals on Wheels Miss C Richardson, tel.: 020 7332 1220

Luton

Unity House, 111 Stuart Street, Luton, Bedfordshire, LU1 5NP, tel.: 01582 546000 (0845-1720 Mon-Thurs, - 1630 Fri), web site: www.luton.gov.uk
Emergencies, tel.: 08702 385465 (via Healthcall)
Ms Maria Silver, Senior Administrative Officer, tel.: 01582 546440
Community Care Duty Desk, tel.: 01582 547659/547660
Home Care Service Duty Desk, tel.: 01582 726869
Home Care Service Ms Jill Jackson, tel.: 01582 547794
Housing & Community Care Ms Jo Cleary, Corporate Director
Meals on Wheels Duty Officer, Adult/Older Person's Services, tel.: 01582 547660/547659

Manchester

Manchester City Council, Children's Dept, PO Box 536, Town Hall Extension, Manchester, M60 2AF, tel.: 0161 255 8250 (24 hrs), web site: www.manchester.gov.uk
Contact Services, For All Services, tel.: 0161 255 8250 (24 hr)
Emergencies, tel.: 0161 255 8250 (24 hr)
Adult Social Services Ms Caroline Marsh, Director
Children's Services Ms Pauline Newman, Director

Medway

Medway Council, Health and Community Services, Municipal Buildings, Canterbury Street, Gillingham, ME7 5LA, tel.: 01634 334466 (Mon-Thurs 0830-1715, Fri 0830-1645)
Access and Information - Asylum Seekers, tel.: 01634 334466
Emergencies (1700-0900 & -1645 Fri), tel.: 0845 762 6777
Health Promotion, tel.: 01634 333010
Child Protection Service Access and Information, tel.: 01634 334466
Community Services Ms Ann Windiate, Director
Home Care Service Access and Information, tel.: 01634 334466
Homeless Service Housing Support Team, tel.: 01634 333500
Meals on Wheels Access and Information, tel.: 01634 334466

Merton

London Borough of Merton, Community & Housing, Merton Civic Centre, London Road, Morden, Surrey, SM4 5DX, tel.: 020 8545 3711 (0900-1800), fax: 020 8545 4198, web site: www.merton.gov.uk
Emergencies, tel.: 020 8770 5000 (after 1500 hrs)
Children, School & Families Ms Helen Lincoln, Head of Social Care, tel.: 020 8545 3630
Community Care Mr John Haffenden, Interim Head, tel.: 020 8545 3791
Housing & Community Care Mr Jeff Hobden, Interim Director, tel.: 020 8545 3711

Middlesbrough

Middlesbrough Council, PO Box 234, 3rd Floor Civic Centre, Middlesbrough, TS1 2XH, tel.: 01642 245432 (0830-1700 Mon-Fri)
Ms Jan Douglas, (Corporate), tel.: 01642 245432, Director
Emergencies, tel.: 01642 631163 (1700-0830) & 24hr Sat & Sun
Child Protection Service Ms Denyse Waites, tel.: 01642 300870, Service Manager
Home Care Service Ms Yvonne Morren, tel.: 01642 815076, Service Manager
Meals on Wheels Duty Team, tel.: 01642 726004

Newcastle upon Tyne

Newcastle City Council, Social Services Directorate, Civic Centre, Newcastle upon Tyne, NE1 8PA, tel.: 0191 211 6363 (0815-1630 Mon-Fri), web site: www.newcastle.gov.uk
Children's Services Referrals - Cruddas Park, tel.: 0191 277 2500
Children's Services Referrals - Sheriff Leas, tel.: 0191 286 3311
Children's Services Referrals - Walker, tel.: 0191 295 5535
Community Care Referrals - Gosforth, tel.: 0191 277 2077
Community Care Referrals - Newburn, tel.: 0191 277 2555
Emergencies (1700-0845 Mon-Fri), tel.: 0191 232 8520
Adult Social Services Ms Catherine Fitt, Director
Children's Services Ms Catherine Fitt, Executive Director
Home Care Service Mrs Chris Dugdale, tel.: 0191 211 6396
Meals on Wheels Ms Lisa Burr, tel.: 0191 277 3776

Newham

London Borough of Newham, Broadway House, 322 High Street, Stratford, London, E15 1AJ, tel.: 0208 430 2000 (0900-1700)
Out of Hours, tel.: 0208 472 9624
Adult Social Services Ms Venetta Johnston, tel.: 020 8430 2000 ext 42673, Executive Director
Child Protection/Looked After Children Ms Jackie Cook, tel.: 0208 430 2000 ext 42517, Service Manager
Children & Young People's Services Ms Pauline Maddison, tel.: 020 8430 2000 ext 42402, Executive Director
Children, Young People & Families Ms Jenny Dibsdall, tel.: 0208 430 2000 ext 42670, Head of Service
Home Care/Meals on Wheels Mr Ian Kennedy, tel.: 0208 430 2000 ext 45720, Service Manager

Social Services: England

Norfolk
Norfolk County Council, County Hall, Martineau Lane, Norwich, NR1 2SQ, tel.: 0844 800 8014 (24 hrs), web site: www.norfolk.gov.uk
Emergencies, tel.: 0844 800 8014 (24hrs)
Adult Social Services Mr H Bodmer, Director
Children's Services Ms L Christensen, Director
Home Care/Meals on Wheels Contact District Offices, tel.: 0844 800 8014

North East Lincolnshire
North East Lincolnshire Council, Fryston House, Fryston Corner, Grimsby, DN34 5BB, tel.: 01472 325500 (0830-1700)
Child Protection & Planning, tel.: 01472 325464
Emergencies, tel.: 01469 516016
Home Care/Meals on Wheels, tel.: 01472 325181
Ms Jeannette Logan, Community Services Manager, tel.: 01469 570718
Ms Sue Mason, Team Manager Hospital Social Work Team, tel.: 01472 874111 ext 7434
Ms Julie Ogley, Executive Director, Community Care
Ms Marianne Warren, Physical Disability & Sensory Impairment Team, tel.: 01472 325298, Team Manager
Children's Services Mr Andrew Samson, Executive Director

North Lincolnshire
North Lincolnshire Council, The Angel, Market Place, Brigg, North Lincolnshire, DN20 8LD, tel.: 01724 296401 (0830-1700 Mon-Thurs -1630 Fri), web site: www.northlincs.gov.uk
Out of hours, tel.: 01724 296555
Child Protection Service Ms Sue Sheriden, Team Co-ordinator, tel.: 01724 298293
Children's Services Mr Richard Stiff, tel.: 01724 296002, Director
Home Care/Meals on Wheels Ms Wendy Lawrey, tel.: 01724 298150

North Somerset
North Somerset District Council, PO Box 52, Town Hall, Weston-super-Mare, BS23 1ZY, tel.: 01934 634803 (0830-1700 Mon-Thurs, -1630 Fri)
Mrs Diane Cruickshank, PA to Director, tel.: 01934 634803
Emergencies, tel.: 01454 615046 (out of hours)
Ms Jane Smith, Director
Mr Graham Turner, Chief Executive Officer
Home Care Service Ms Emma Bowyer, tel.: 01275 882173
Meals on Wheels Ms Cheryl Kavanagh, tel.: 01275 882190

North Tyneside
North Tyneside Council, Social Services Directorate, Unicon House, Suez Street, North Shields, NE30 1BB, tel.: 0191 200 8181 (0830-1700 Mon-Thurs, -1630 Fri)
Emergencies, tel.: 0191 200 6800 (24 hrs)
Mr Paul Hanson, tel.: 0191 200 8181, Director
Adult Social Services Mr Ian Whitehead, Head of Service
Child Protection Service Ms Kath McEvoy, Child Protection Coordinator, tel.: 0191 200 8181
Home Care Service Ms Eleanor Binks, tel.: 0191 200 6050
Meals on Wheels Ms Karen Coleman, tel.: 0191 2005177

North Yorkshire
North Yorkshire, County Hall, Northallerton, DL7 8DD, tel.: 01609 532165 (0830-1700 Mon-Thurs, -1630 Fri)
Emergencies, tel.: 01904 762314 (out of hours)
Mr Derek Law, Corporate Director, tel.: 01609 532165
Mrs Tricia Richards, Support Officer to Corporate Director, tel.: 01609 532165
Child Protection Service Ms Pauline Martin, Manager, Area Child Protection Committee, tel.: 01423 855476
Home Care Service Mr Tony Campbell, tel.: 01609 532684
Housing & Supported Living Services Mr Neil Revely, Community Care - North Yorkshire, tel.: 01609 532535, Assistant Director
Meals on Wheels Customer Relations Unit, Harrogate, tel.: 01423 568099
Meals on Wheels Customer Relations Unit, Craven, tel.: 01756 793700
Meals on Wheels Customer Relations Unit, Selby, tel.: 01757 213651
Meals on Wheels Customer Relations Unit, Ripon, tel.: 01765 608636
Meals on Wheels Customer Relations Unit, Scarborough/Ryedale, tel.: 08459 501555
Meals on Wheels Customer Relations Unit, Hambleton/Richmondshire, tel.: 01609 779999

Northamptonshire
Northamptonshire County Council, County Hall, PO Box 177, Northampton, NN1 1AY, tel.: 01604 236236
Mr Mark Charters, Statutory Director, Social Services
Emergencies, tel.: 01604 626938 (out of hours)
Children & Families Service Ms Sue Richards, Director
Community Services Mr Mark Charters, Director

Northumberland
Northumberland Care Trust, Merley Croft, Loansdean, Morpeth, Northumberland, NE61 2DL, tel.: 01670 394400 (0900-1700)
Emergencies, tel.: 0845 6005252 (1700-0900)
S.T.A.R.T (Short Term Assessment and Re-enablement Team) Blyth Valley, tel.: 01670 536810
Mr C Taylor, Social Care, Director
Home Care Service Berwick, tel.: 01289 309353
Home Care Service Home Care Alnwick, tel.: 01665 606303
Home Care Service Home Care Blyth Valley, tel.: 01670 536810
Home Care Service Home Care Central, tel.: 01670 822423
Home Care Service Home Care West, tel.: 01661 839203
Home Care Service NCT, tel.: 01670 823792
Meals on Wheels Age Concern, tel.: 01670 700910
Meals on Wheels Via Area Offices or WRVS, tel.: 01670 528220

Social Services: England

Nottingham City
Nottingham City Council - Social Services, 14 Hounds Gate, Nottingham, NG1 7BE, tel.: 0115 915 5500 (0830-1650), web site: www.nottinghamcity.gov.uk
Mr David Coope, Marketing and PR Officer, tel.: 0115 915 7008
Emergencies, tel.: 0115 915 9299 (1650-0830)
Child Protection Service Ms Sue Gregory, Children & Families Services Director
Home Care Service Ms Joan Gavigan, tel.: 0115 915 1082
Meals on Wheels Mr Gareth Buckeridge, tel.: 0115 915 0461
Social Services & Health Mrs Sallyanne Johnson, Corporate Director

Nottinghamshire
Nottinghamshire County Council, West Bridgford, Nottingham, NG2 7QP, tel.: 0115 982 3823 (0830-1700 Mon-Thurs, -1630 Fri), web site: www.nottinghamshire.gov.uk
Asylum Seekers, tel.: 0845 330 4216
Director, tel.: 0115 982 3823
Emergencies, tel.: 0115 844 7333 (out of hours)
Home Care Services, tel.: 0845 045 0140
Homeless Families/Travellers, tel.: 0845 330 4216
Smoking Cessation, tel.: 0845 330 4216
Child Protection/Looked After Children Contact Centre, tel.: 0845 330 4216
Home Care/Meals on Wheels Via Local Office (Rushcliffe), tel.: 0115 914 1500
Meals on Wheels/Home Care Via Local Office (Broxtowe), tel.: 0115 917 5800
Meals on Wheels/Home Care Via Local Office (Gedling), tel.: 0115 854 6000
Meals on Wheels/Home Care Via Local Office (Mansfield & Ashfield), tel.: 01623 433433
Meals on Wheels/Home Care Via Local Office (Newark), tel.: 01636 682700
Meals on Wheels/Home Care Via Local Office (Ollerton), tel.: 01623 861340
Meals on Wheels/Home Care Via Local Office (Retford), tel.: 01777 716161
Meals on Wheels/Home Care Via Local Office (Worksop), tel.: 01909 533533

Oldham
Oldham Metropolitan Borough Council, Civic Centre, PO Box 22, West Street, Oldham, OL1 1UW, tel.: 0161 911 4750 (0840-1700 Mon-Fri), web site: www.oldham.gov.uk
Emergencies, tel.: 0161 222 6936
Adult Care & Community Services Ms Veronica Jackson, Executive Director
Children's Services Ms Teresa Broadbent, tel.: 0161 770 6578, Head of Service
Home Care Mrs Margaret Williams, tel.: 0161 222 6794
Older People Services Ms Dorothy Phillips, tel.: 0161 222 6900, Head of Service
Older People Services Ms Althea Rankin, tel.: 0161 770 8248, Head of Service

Oxfordshire
Oxfordshire County Council, Oxfordshire - Customer Service Unit (CSU), Yarnton House, Rutten Lane, Yarnton, Oxon, OX5 1LP, tel.: 01865 375515 (0830-1700 Mon-Thurs, -1600 Fri), fax: 01865 841666
Emergencies, Open Out of Hours when CSU is closed), tel.: 0800 833408 (out of hours)
Mr Charles Waddicor, Director for Social & Community Services

Peterborough
Greater Peterborough Primary Care Partnership, Integrated Adult Social Care Services, 2nd Floor, Town Hall, Bridge Street, Peterborough, PE1 1FA
Mr Brian Parrot, Director Adult Social Care

Plymouth
Plymouth Social Services, Windsor House, Tavistock Road, Plymouth, PL1 2AA, tel.: 01752 307329 (0900-1700), web site: www.plymouth.gov.uk
Ms Teresa Barrett, Domiciliary Services Manager, tel.: 01752 308692
Mrs Liz Bawn, Physical & Sensory Disabilities, tel.: 01752 305133
Emergencies (17.00 - 21.00), tel.: 01752 346984
Mr Paul Francombe, Learning Disability Manager, tel.: 01752 314390
Mr Julian Grail, Access to Care, tel.: 01752 308891
Ms Ann Haley, PA to Corp. Director (Community Services), tel.: 01752 307525
Ms Jennifer Jones, Mental Health & Substance Abuse, tel.: 01752 308959
Mrs Bronwen Lacey, Director of Children's Social Care, tel.: 01752 307463
Ms Mairead MacNeil, Children's Social Care, tel.: 01752 307346, Assistant Director
Social Inclusion Unit, tel.: 01752 304321
Mr Clive Turner, Community Services, tel.: 01752 307525, Corporate Director
Mr Gary Walbridge, Intermediate Care, tel.: 01752 308958
Child Protection Service Ms Maureen Gimley, Officer, tel.: 01752 306031
Community Meals Mr Simon Fleming, tel.: 01752 305128
Community Services Ms Pam Marsden, Adult Social Care, tel.: 01752 307344, Assistant Director
Emergencies Mr Richard Lemon, tel.: 01752 346984
Homeless Service Mr Andy Edwards, tel.: 01752 307329
Social Services Ms Verity Jones, Strategy & Performance Division, tel.: 01752 307345, Assistant Director

Poole
Borough of Poole, Civic Centre, Poole, BH15 2RU, web site: www.boroughofpoole.com
Adult Commissioning, tel.: 01202 261150

Adult Provider, tel.: 01202 261000
Children & Families, tel.: 01202 735046 (0830-1715 Mon-Thurs, -1645 Fri)
Emergencies, tel.: 01202 668123 (out of hours)
Ms Norma Lambert, PA to Policy Directors, tel.: 01202 633203
Home Care Service Mr Peter Moore, tel.: 01202 261027
Home Care Service Mr Jeff Russell, tel.: 01202 261029
Social Services Ms Jan Thurgood, Policy Director

Portsmouth
Portsmouth City Council, Civic Offices, Guildhall Square, Portsmouth, PO1 2EP, tel.: 023 9284 1174 (0830-1700 Mon-Thurs, -1600 Fri), web site: www.portsmouth.gov.uk
Adult Services (Age 18-64), tel.: 023 9220 0132
Children & Families, tel.: 023 9283 9111
Emergency Duty Service, tel.: 0845 6004555
Ms Margaret Geary, Health, Housing & Social Care, Strategic Director
Older Persons Help Desk (Age 65 & Over), tel.: 023 9289 3800
Home Care Service Mrs Sue Page, (Acting Manager), tel.: 023 9266 5713
Meals on Wheels WRVS, tel.: 023 9268 8378

Reading
Reading Borough Council, PO Box 2624, Reading, RG1 7WB, tel.: 0118 939 0900 (0900-1700), web site: www.reading.gov.uk
Emergencies, tel.: 01344 786543 (1700-0900)
Child Protection Service Ms Alison Twynam, tel.: 0118 939 0351, Service Manager
Home Care Service Ms Lynette Greenaway, tel.: 0118 939 0354
Housing & Community Care Ms Eileen Means, tel.: 0118 939 0094, Director
Meals on Wheels Mr Mike Hill, tel.: 0118 987 1486

Redbridge
London Borough Redbridge, Ley Street House, 497/499 Ley Street, Ilford, Essex, IG2 7QX, tel.: 020 8478 3020 (24 hrs)
Mr John Drew, Director of Housing & Community Services
Mr Patrick Power, Managing Director Children's Trust
Children's Services Ms Pat Reynolds, Director
Community Care Mr John Powell, Chief Officer
Home Care/Meals on Wheels Ms Nicola Parry, Principal Officer
Housing Options/Homelessness , tel.: 020 8708 4002

Redcar & Cleveland
Redcar & Cleveland Borough Council, Scafield House, Kirkleatham Street, Redcar, TS10 1SP, tel.: 01642 771500 (Mon-Thurs 0830-1700, Fri -1630)
Director, Health & Social Well Being, tel.: 01642 771673
Mrs Michelle Dickerson, Office Manager, tel.: 01642 771500

Emergencies (1700-0830 & weekends/Bank hols 24hr), tel.: 08702 402994
Ms Lynn Johnson, Head of Commissioning, tel.: 01642 771500
Mrs Jenny Lewis, Head of Children's Services, tel.: 01642 444342
Ms Barbara Shaw, Head of Children's Social Care, tel.: 01642 771500

Richmond upon Thames
London Borough Richmond upon Thames, 42 York Street, Twickenham, TW1 3BW, tel.: 020 8891 7600 (0900-1715 Mon-Thurs, 1700 Fri)
Ms Ellen Acutt, Receptionist, tel.: 0208 891 7600
Mr Brian Castle, Housing/Homelessness, tel.: 020 8891 7482/7409, Manager
Emergencies, tel.: 020 8744 2442 (1800-0800)
Mr Jeff Jerome, Social Services & Housing, Director
Asylum Seekers Mr Brian Castle, Housing Needs Manager, tel.: 020 8891 7482
Child Protection Service Mr Kieran Travers, tel.: 020 8891 7600 ext 7830, Manager
Looked After Children Mr Paul Walsh, Principal Manager, tel.: 020 8891 7679
Meals on Wheels Range George, tel.: 020 8891 7660
Smoking Cessation Ms Sue Mooney, Stop Smoking Programme Manager (Kingston&Richmond), tel.: 020 8973 3073
Travellers Ms Velia Hartland, Adviser Vulnerable Pupils & Ethnic Minority, tel.: 020 8891 7700

Rochdale
Rochdale Metropolitan Borough Council, Child & Adult Care Services HQ, PO Box 67, Municipal Offices, Smith Street, Rochdale, OL16 1YQ, tel.: 01706 865203/02 (0830-1645), web site: www.rochdale.gov.uk
Emergencies (including weekends & bank holidays), tel.: 01706 354836 (1700-0800 approx)
Mr Terry Piggott, Executive Director
Child Protection Service Ms Elaine King, tel.: 01706 925365, Manager
Children's Services Mr Steve Titcombe, tel.: 01706 925203, Head of Service
Home Care/Meals on Wheels Ms Amanda Carr, tel.: 01706 764874

Rotherham
ADULT SOCIAL CARE, Rotherham Metropolitan Borough Council, Crinoline House, Effingham Square, Rotherham, South Yorks, S65 1AW, tel.: 01709 382121 (0830-1700 or ansaphone)
Ms Lynne Hiley, Management Support Officer, tel.: 01709 823901
Adult Social Services Mr J Gomersall, Executive Director
Children's Services Ms P Allen, tel.: 01709 823905, Acting Head

Home Care/Meals on Wheels Mr John Harding, tel.: 01709 336510

Rutland
Rutland County Council, Catmose, Oakham, Rutland, LE15 6HP, tel.: 01572 722577 (0830-1700 Mon0Thurs, - 1630 Fri), web site: www.rutland.gov.uk
Emergencies, tel.: 0116 255 1606 (out of hours)
Adult Social Services Mr Colin Foster, Housing & Health, Director
Child Protection Service Mr Steven Attwood, Head of Children & Families, tel.: 01572 722577
Home Care/Meals on Wheels Ms Jean Love, tel.: 01572 758336

Salford
Salford City Council Community & Social Services, Crompton House, 100 Chorley Road, Swinton, Salford, M27 6BP, tel.: 0161 793 2240 (0830-1630), e-mail: social services@salford.gov.uk, web site: www.salford.gov.uk
Child Protection, tel.: 0161 603 4325
Emergencies, tel.: 0161 794 8888 (1630-0830)
Family Support Services, tel.: 0161 799 3608
Ms Kay George, Physical Disability & Sensory Services, tel.: 0161 607 69999/790 4402 (minicom)
Homeless Families/Asylum Seekers, tel.: 0161 607 1626
Looked After Children, tel.: 0161 603 4300
Mrs Anne Williams, tel.: 0161 793 2200, Director
Child Protection Service Head of Service (Safeguarding & Integration), tel.: 0161 603 4500
Home Care Service Ms Ann Eve, tel.: 0161 906 1500
Home Care Service Ms Janet Senior, tel.: 0161 906 1500
Meals on Wheels Ms Jean Clare, tel.: 0161 925 1367
Social Work Team Mr Brian Gathercole, Salford East Adult & Older People, tel.: 0161 831 7484
Social Work Team Ms Angela Whyte, Salford West Adult & Older People, tel.: 0161 603 4400

Sandwell
Sandwell Metropolitan Borough Council, Kingston House, 438 High Street, West Bromwich, West Midlands, B70 9LD, tel.: 0121 569 5464 (0900-1730 Mon-Thurs, - 1700 Fri)
Ms Pamela Carter, Administration, tel.: 0121 569 5448, Principal Officer
Emergencies, tel.: 0121 561 3704 (out of hours)
Ms Angela Saganowska, Executive Director
Asylum Seekers Ms Joginder Kaur, Administrator, tel.: 0121 557 8855
Asylum Seekers Ms Susan Lorimer, Administrator, tel.: 0121 557 8855
Child Protection Service Mr Phil Smith, Quality Development Manager, tel.: 0121 544 6033
Home Care Service Ms Brenda Essom (Ongoing Service), tel.: 0121 553 6644
Home Care Service Ms Ada Rose (Ongoing Service), tel.: 0121 500 4850

Home Care Service Ms Eileen Watson (Ongoing Service), tel.: 0121 422 8242
Home Care/Meals on Wheels New Adult Referrals - Oldbury, tel.: 0121 544 6029
Home Care/Meals on Wheels New Adult Referrals - Rowley, tel.: 0121 569 5604
Home Care/Meals on Wheels New Adult Referrals - Smethwick, tel.: 0121 569 5594
Home Care/Meals on Wheels New Adult Referrals - Tipton, tel.: 0121 569 5932
Home Care/Meals on Wheels New Adult Referrals - Wednesbury, tel.: 0121 505 5553
Home Care/Meals on Wheels New Adult Referrals - West Bromwich, tel.: 0121 569 5554

Sefton
Sefton Council, Merton House, Stanley Road, Bootle, Merseyside, L20 3UU, tel.: 0151 934 3737 (0900-1730 Mon-Thurs, -1615 Fri)
Mr Charlie Barker, Director
Emergencies, tel.: 0151 920 8234 (1730-0900 Mon-Fri, all weekends)
Home Care/Meals on Wheels Customer Services, tel.: 0151 934 3737

Sheffield
Sheffield City Council, Social Services Directorate, Redvers House, Union Street, Sheffield, S1 2JQ, tel.: 0114 273 4908 (Adults) /4855 (Children & Families)
Contact for their services is via their access teams
Ms Joanne Roney, Director

Shropshire
Shropshire County Council, Shropshire Community Services, Shirehall, Abbey Foregate, Shrewsbury, SY2 6ND, tel.: 01743 253729 (Mon-Thurs 0845-1700, Fri - 1600), web site: www.shropshireonline.gov.uk
Emergencies (Mon-Thurs 1645-0845. Fri-Mon 1545-0845), tel.: 01743 244197
Meals on Wheels, tel.: 01743 253788
START, tel.: 01743 255756
Children & Young People's Services Ms Liz Nicholson, tel.: 01743 254301, Corporate Director
Community Services Mr Jack Collier, tel.: 01743 253701, Corporate Director

Slough
Slough Borough Council, Town Hall, Bath Road, Slough, SL1 3UQ, tel.: 01753 552288 (0900-1645), web site: www.slough.gov.uk
Emergencies, tel.: 01344 786 543 (1600-0900)
Ms Janet Tomlinson, Strategic Director Education & Children's Services
Ms Dawn Warwick, Deputy Chief Exec Community & Cultural Services
Child Protection Service Mr Robin Crofts, (Inclusion), tel.: 01753 01753 787645 ext 7645, Assistant Director

Social Services: England

Home Care Service Mr George Howard, tel.: 01753 690 931

Meals on Wheels Ms Josie Payne, tel.: 01753 690 930

Solihull
Solihull Metropolitan Borough Council, PO Box 32, Council House, Solihull, West Midlands, B91 3QY, tel.: 0121 704 6000 (0845-1720 Mon-Thurs, -1625 Fri)
Emergencies, tel.: 0121 605 6060 (out of hours)
Adult Social Services Mr Bindi Nagra, tel.: 0121 704 6728, Service Director
Children's Services Ms Anne Plummer, Service Director
Home Care Service Mr Doug Haggart - (Homecare External), tel.: 0121 788 4489
Home Care Service Ms Sue Munbodh - (Homecare In-house), tel.: 0121 704 7165

Somerset
Somerset County Council, County Hall, Taunton, TA1 4DY, tel.: 01823 355455 (0830-1700), web site: www.somerset.gov.uk
Children/Young People/Learning, tel.: 0845 345 9122
Community Services for Adults, tel.: 0845 345 9133
Emergencies, tel.: 01458 253241 (1700-0830)
Mrs Miriam Maddison, Director of Community Services
People with Learning Disabilities - Mendip, tel.: 0174 355400
People with Learning Disabilities - Somerset Coast, tel.: 01278 455571
People with Learning Disabilities - South Somerset, tel.: 01935 470600
People with Learning Disabilities - Taunton, tel.: 01823 257908
Mrs Janet Regis, Public Information Manager, tel.: 01823 355127
Signposts - Services for Adults with Physical Disabilities & Older People, tel.: 0800 317220
Mr David Taylor, Director of Children's Services
Child Protection Service Mr Tony May, Policy Development Officer, tel.: 01823 355900

South Gloucestershire
South Gloucestershire Council, St Luke's Close, Emersons Way, Emersons Green, BS16 7AL, tel.: 01454 865922 (0830-1700)
Emergencies, tel.: 01454 615165 (out of hours)
Community Care Mr Peter Murphy, Director
Home Care Service Ms Di Longley
Meals on Wheels Ms Debbie Heath, tel.: 01454 865997

South Tyneside
South Tyneside Metropolitan Borough Council, Kelly House, Campbell Park Road, Hebburn, Tyne & Wear, NE31 2SW, tel.: 0191 427 1717 (0830-1700 Mon-Thurs, -1630 Fri), web site: www.southtyneside.info
Emergencies, tel.: 0191 456 2093 (out of hours)
Mr Jim Wilson, Director

Southampton
Southampton City Council, Civic Centre, Southampton, S014 7LY, tel.: 02380 832621 (0830-1700), web site: www.southampton.gov.uk
Adult Social Services Contact Centre, tel.: 02380 834567
Dr John Beer, Communities, Health & Care, tel.: 023 8083 2621, Executive Director
Children & Families Contact Centre, tel.: 02380 833336
Emergencies, tel.: 023 8023 3344 (1700-0830)

Mr Tim Pascoe, New Communities Project Manager, tel.: 023 8091 5444
Ms Fiona Penfold, Substance Misuse Service Delivery, tel.: 02380 717171, Manager
Child Protection Service Ms Sally Cosstick, Childrens Assessment Team, tel.: 023 8083 4604, Team Manager
Home Care/Meals on Wheels Ms Jan Brenton, tel.: 023 5091 5305
Homeless Families Homelessness Healthcare Team, tel.: 023 8033 6991

Southend-on-Sea
Southend-on-Sea Borough Council, Civic Centre, PO Box 6, Victoria Avenue, Southend on Sea, SS2 6ER, tel.: 01702 534646 (0900-1730 Mon-Thurs, -1630 Fri), web site: www.southend.gov.uk
Adults - Learning Disability, tel.: 01702 534689
Designated Complaints Officer, tel.: 01702 534638
Duty Officer, Physical Disability & Sensory Impairment, tel.: 01702 534232
Duty Officer, Occupational Therapy, tel.: 01702 442160
Emergencies, tel.: 0845 6061212 (out of hours)
Ms Jenny Fowers, Customer Services Manager, tel.: 01702 534638
Meals on Wheels, tel.: 01702 534777/534440
South East Stop Smoking Service, tel.: 01268 464511/01702 224605
Mr Phil Stepney, Director of Social Care
Child Protection Service First Contact Team, tel.: 01702 534490/534495
Children's Services Duty Desk, Children with Disabilities, tel.: 01702 534495
Home Care Service , tel.: 01702 534415
Older People Services Duty Team, tel.: 01702 534777/534440

Southwark
London Borough of Southwark, Mabel Goldwin House, 49 Grange Walk, London, SE1 3DY, tel.: 020 7525 5000 (0900-1700), web site: www.southwark.gov.uk
Emergencies, tel.: 020 7525 5000
Ms Jacquie Hibbs, Business Unit Welfare Catering Client, tel.: 020 7525 3627
Ms Carol Wilby, Finance & Admin Officer, tel.: 020 7525 3991
Child Protection Service Mr Malcolm Ward, Quality Assurance Manager

Social Services: England

Health & Community Services Mr Chris Bull, Strategic Director
Smoking Cessation Mrs Doris Gaga, Stop Smoking Counsellor

St Helens
St Helens Council, 2nd Floor, Gamble Buildings, Victoria Square, St Helens, Merseyside, WA10 1DY, tel.: 01744 456000 (0845-1715 Mon-Thurs, Fri 1700), web site: www.sthelens.gov.uk
Contact Centre, tel.: 01744 456470, e-mail: contactcentre@sthelens.gov.uk
Ms Debbie Cook, Intermediate Care, e-mail: debbiecook@sthelens.gov.uk
Customer Services Team, tel.: 01744 456276/277/278/279/695
Emergencies, tel.: 01744 22328 (1645-0845)
Ms Sue Lightup, tel.: 01744 456309, e-mail: suelighup@sthelens.gov.uk, Director
Ms Pat Oxley, Directo Payments Team, e-mail: patoxley@sthelens.gov.uk
Ms Sheila Roberts, Teenage Pregnancy, tel.: 01744 675653, e-mail: sheilaroberts@sthelens.gov.uk, Co-ordinator
Ms Amanda Stonehouse, Sure Start Plus Programme, tel.: 01744 675609, e-mail: amandastonehouse@sthelens.gov.uk, Manager
Child Protection Service Mrs Arnon Lowe, tel.: 01744 456965, Manager
Home Care/Meals on Wheels Ms Dianne Lightfoot, tel.: 01744 677740 ext 130, Service Manager

Staffordshire
Staffordshire County Council, St Chad's Place, Stafford, ST16 2LR, tel.: 01785 277088 (0830-1700 Mon-Thurs, -1630 Fri)
Emergencies, tel.: 01785 354030 (out of hours)
Ms Jane K Smith, Admin Officer, tel.: 01785 277122
Health & Social Care Mr Eric Robinson, Corporate Director
Home Care Service Ms Susan Farrier-Ray, tel.: 01785 277081
Meals on Wheels Mr Brendan Sullivan, tel.: 01785 277090

Stockport
Stockport Metropolitan Borough Council, Ponsonby House, Edward Street, Stockport, SK1 3UR, tel.: 0161 474 4609 (0830-1700), web site: www.stockport.gov.uk/social services
Ms Janet Beer, Disability Services (Adult), tel.: 0161 477 3700, Service Manager
Emergencies, tel.: 0161 718 2118 (out of hours)
Home Support Service, tel.: 0161 456 7747
Ms Maggie Kufeldt, Old Peoples Services, tel.: 0161 428 3241, Service Manager
Ms Hilary Makepeace, Old Peoples Services, tel.: 0161 427 7011, Service Manager
Mr Iain Skelton, Homecare & Old Peoples Services, tel.:

0161 456 7747, Service Manager
Mr Andrew Webb, Director
Child Protection Service Ms Charlotte Ramsden, Acting Service Manager, tel.: 0161 474 5657
Community Meals Ms Jan Royle, tel.: 0161 484 0053
Home Care Service Mr Iain Skelton, tel.: 0161 456 7747
Meals on Wheels Ms Jan Royle, tel.: 0161 484 0053

Stockton-on-Tees
Stockton on Tees Borough Council, Municipal Buildings, Church Road, Stockton-on-Tees, TS18 1YD, tel.: 01642 393939 (0830-1700 Mon-Thurs, -1630 Fri)
Ms Ann Baxter, Corporate Director Children, Educ & Social Care
Emergencies, tel.: 08702 402994 (out of hours)
Mr Rob Papworth, Performance Manager, tel.: 01642 527453
Child Protection Service Mr Neil Pocklington, tel.: 01642 527456
Home Care Service Ms Mari Rose, tel.: 01642 617617
Meals on Wheels Access Unit, tel.: 01642 415030

Stoke-on-Trent
Stoke-on-Trent City Council, Social Care, Floor 4, Civic Centre, Stoke-on-Trent, ST4 1WB, tel.: 01782 235985
Child Protection, tel.: 01782 235100
Emergencies, tel.: 01782 234234 (out of hours)
Home Care Services/Meals on Wheels, tel.: 01782 234235 or 239050
Looked After Children, tel.: 01782 235100
Adult Social Services Mr Alan Coe, tel.: 01782 235985, Assistant Director
Children & Young People's Services Ms Rhona Bradley, tel.: 01782 235985, Assistant Director

Suffolk
Suffolk County Council, Endeavour House, 8 Russell Road, Ipswich, IP1 2BX, tel.: 01473 583000
Adult Care & Community Services Mr Graham Gatehouse, Director
Children & Young People's Services Mrs Rosalina Turner, Director

Sunderland
Sunderland City Council, Adult Services, 50 Fawcett Street, Sunderland, SR1 1RF, tel.: 0191 520 5555 (0830-1715 Mon-Fri)
Emergencies, tel.: 0191 528 9110
Ms Paula James, Communications Officer, 0191 566 2689
Mr David Smith, Acting Director

Surrey
Surrey County Council, County Hall, Penrhyn Road, Kingston-Upon-Thames, Surrey, KT1 2DN, tel.: 08456 009 009 (0900-1700), fax: 020 8541 9004, web site: www.surreycc.gov.uk
Emergencies, tel.: 01483 517898 (1700-0900)

Social Services: England

Sutton
London Borough Sutton, Civic Offices, St Nicholas Way, Sutton, Surrey, SM1 1EA, tel.: 020 8770 5000 (24 hr)
Mr Ian Davey, Interim Director of Community Services
Emergencies, tel.: 020 8770 5000 (24 hr)
Asylum Seekers Mr Stephen Baker, tel.: 020 8770 5718
Home Care Service Ms Cherryl Bone, tel.: 020 8770 4103
Homeless Families Mr Paul Aston, tel.: 020 8770 5732
Meals on Wheels Ms Pam Norton, tel.: 020 8770 4542

Swindon
Swindon Borough Council, Civic Offices, Euclid Street, Swindon, SN1 2JH, tel.: 01793 463000 (0830-1700 Mon-Thurs, -1630 Fri)
Emergency Duty Service, tel.: 01793 436699
Ms Jeanette Fisher, Homecare, tel.: 01793 465824
Mr Angus Gault, Independent Reviewing Manager, tel.: 01793 466958
General Enquirires, tel.: 01793 466900
Ms Ingrid Hewson, Independent Reviewing Manager, tel.: 01793 463818
Mr Andrew Ireland, Acting Director, tel.: 01793 463419

Tameside
Tameside Metropolitan Borough Council, Council Offices, Wellington Road, Ashton under Lyne, Lancashire, OL6 6DL, tel.: 0161 342 8355, web site: www.tameside.gov.uk
Emergencies (Out of Hours), tel.: 0161 342 8355
Children & Young People's Services Ms Cheryl Eastwood, (Children), Assistant Executive Director
Children & Young People's Services Mr Ian Smith, Executive Director
Children & Young People's Services Mr Jim Taylor, (Education), Assistant Director
Social Care & Health Ms Stephanie Butterworth, (Adult Services), Assistant Executive Director
Social Care & Health Mr Huw Davies, (Housing & Community Regeneration), Assistant Executive Director
Social Care & Health Mr Colin McKinless, Executive Director

Telford & Wrekin
CHILDREN & YOUNG PEOPLE, Borough of Telford & Wrekin, Civic Offices, PO Bo 440, Telford, TF3 4WF, tel.: 01952 202100 (0900-1700)
16+ Team, Corporate Parenting, tel.: 01952 246810
Adults with Learning Disabilities Team, tel.: 01952 202600
Assessment & Case Management, tel.: 01952 641641
Disabled Children's Team, tel.: 01952 522780
Emergency Duty Team (out of office hours), tel.: 01952 676500
Family Placement Team, tel.: 01952 641641
Housing Needs & Homelessness, tel.: 01952 202983
Looked After Team, tel.: 01952 641641
Mental Health Services (Central Telford), tel.: 01952 617862
Mental Health Services (North Telford), tel.: 01952 222725
Mental Health Services (South Telford), tel.: 01952 680104
Occupational Therapy Team, tel.: 01952 202870
Physical & Sensory Disability Duty Team, tel.: 01952 202860
Safeguarding Advisory Service, tel.: 01952 250421
Safeguards Team, tel.: 01952 641641
Substance Misuse Services (North Telford), tel.: 01952 222220
Substance Misuse Services (South Telford), tel.: 01952 505571
Children & Young People's Services Mrs Christine Davies, Corporate Director
Older People Services Duty Team, tel.: 01952 202820

Thurrock
Thurrock Council, Civic Offices, New Road, Grays, Essex, RM17 6TJ, tel.: 01375 652675 (0845-1715 Mon-Thurs, -1645 Fri)
Mr Steve Beynon, Children, Education & Families, tel.: 01375 652586, Director
Emergencies, tel.: 01375 372468
Ms Jan Hurn, tel.: 01375 652856
Mrs Christine Paley, Community Well-being, Director
Child Protection Service Ms Christine Miller, Children's Quality & Performance Manager, tel.: 01375 652898
Home Care/Meals on Wheels Contact Duty Officer

Torbay
ADULT SOCIAL CARE, Torbay Care Trust, Bay House, Riviera Park, Torquay, Devon, TQ2 7TD, tel.: 01803 210500
Mrs Pat Bridle, Domiciliary Care (Torquay), tel.: 01803 402820/3, Team Leader
Ms Jane Bruce, Operational Manager - Housing, tel.: 01803 208724
Mrs Tina Butterwith, Domiciliary Care (Brixham), tel.: 01803 402826, Team Leader
Emergencies, tel.: 01803 292166 (1630-0900)
Mrs Vicky Ford, Domiciliary Care (Torquay), tel.: 01803 402820/3, Team Leader
Miss Liz-Anne Hartland, Domiciliary Care (Paignton), tel.: 01803 402829, Team Leader
Ms Jenny Jameson, Domiciliary Care (Paignton), tel.: 01803 402830, Team Leader
Adult Social Services Mrs Jain Wood, Director
Child Protection Service Mr John Edwards, Operations Manager, tel.: 01803 208563
Children's Services Ms Margaret Dennison, tel.: 01803 208400, Director
Home Care Service Mrs Jean Ford, tel.: 01803 402820
Home Care Service Mrs Jo Mitchell, tel.: 01803 402820
Meals on Wheels Ms Christine Comberg (Torquay & Paignton), tel.: 01803 313164 & 316206
Meals on Wheels Ms Leni Cox (Brixham), tel.: 01803 883864

Social Services: England

Tower Hamlets
London Borough Tower Hamlets, 62 Roman Road, Bethnal Green, London, E2 0QJ, tel.: 020 7364 5000 (0900-1730)
Emergency Duty Team, tel.: 0207 364 7000
Mr John Goldup, Director of Adult Services
Child Protection Service Ms Ann Roach, tel.: 0207 364 2162
Home Care Service Ms Christine Oates, tel.: 020 7364 2209
Looked After Children Ms Jenny Boyd
Meals on Wheels Ms Angela Elkholm, tel.: 020 7364 2176

Trafford
ADULT SOCIAL CARE, Trafford Metropolitan Borough Council, Town Hall, Talbot Road, Stretford, Manchester, M32 0YT, web site: www.trafford.gov.uk
Emergencies, tel.: 0161 912 2020 (24hrs)
Mr Chris Ferns, Commissioning (Learning Disability), tel.: 0161 912 4776, Associate Director
Ms Dorothy Houghton, Deputy Director, Education Services, tel.: 0161 912 4545
Mr Ian Thomas, Associate Director Commissioning (Learning Disabilities, tel.: 0161 912 4707
Mr Mil Vasic, Access & Assessment, tel.: 0161 912 5100, Director
Mr Andy Warrington, Head of Business Support Services, tel.: 0161 912 4769
Ms Margaret Woodhouse, Director, Education & Early Years Service, tel.: 0161 911 8606
Adult Social Services Mr David Hanley, tel.: 0161 912 4107, Head of Service
Children & Families Service Ms Katherine MacKay, tel.: 0161 912 5009, Head of Service
Children & Young People's Services Mr Chris Pratt, tel.: 0161 912 1901, Executive Director
Children, Young People & Families Ms Fiona Waddington, tel.: 0161 911 8650, Director
Community Services & Social Care Mr Mike Cooney, tel.: 0161 912 4009, Executive Director
Community Services & Social Care Ms Anne Higgins, Deputy Executive Director, tel.: 0161 912 4396
Looked After Children Mr Matthew Brazier, tel.: 0161 912 3968, Head of Service
Meals on Wheels Mr Mark Grimes, Provider Services Manager, tel.: 0161 912 1585

Wakefield
Wakefield Metropolitan District Council, 8 St John's North, Wakefield, West Yorkshire, WF1 3QA, tel.: 01924 307700 (0830-1700 Mon-Thurs -1630 Fri)
Emergencies (Social Care Direct), tel.: 01924 303456
Ms Elaine McHale, Corporate Director
Ms Linda Popplewell, Secretary to Director, tel.: 01924 307728
Child Protection Service Ms Rosie Faulkner, Business Manager, tel.: 01924 302628
Child Protection Service Ms Viv Woodhead, tel.: 01924 302628, Co-ordinator

Walsall
Walsall Metropolitan Borough Council, 1st Floor, Civic Centre, Darwall Street, Walsall, WS1 1RG, tel.: 01922 650000 (0845-1715 Mon-Thurs, -1645 Fri), web site: www.walsall.gov.uk
Child Protection Service, tel.: 01922 646640
Domiciliary Care Services, tel.: 01922 658985
Emergency Response Team, tel.: 01922 653555
Mr Dave Martin, Health Social Care & Supported Housing, Director
Meals Service, tel.: 01902 636985

Waltham Forest
London Borough Waltham Forest, Silver Birch House, Uplands Business Park, Blackhorse Lane, Walthamstow, London, E17 5SD, tel.: 020 8496 3000, web site: www.walthamforest.gov.uk
Adults First Response North Team, tel.: 020 8496 1816/7
Adults First Response South Team, tel.: 020 8496 1245
Children's First Response Team, tel.: 020 8496 2310
Emergencies, tel.: 020 8496 3000
Whipps Cross Hospital Social Work Teams, tel.: 020 8539 5522

Wandsworth
London Borough Wandsworth, Town Hall, Wandsworth High Street, London, SW18 2PU, tel.: 0208 871 6000 (0900-1700)
Emergencies, tel.: 0208 871 6000 (1800-2100)
Mr Peter B West, Director of Social Services, tel.: 0208 871 6291
Child Protection Service Mr Paul Secker, Service Manager, tel.: 0208 871 6998
Home Care Service Mr Noel Mulvihill, Acting Manager, tel.: 0208 871 7154
Meals on Wheels Ms Katrina Mackie, Contract Compliance Monitoring Officer, tel.: 0208 871 8660

Warrington
Warrington Borough Council, Bewsey Old School, Lockton Lane, Bewsey, Warrington, WA5 0BF, tel.: 01925 444400
Ms Sue Anderson, Secretary to Ms Sumner, tel.: 01925 444021
Mr John Dunkerley, Childrens Social Care & Youth Service, tel.: 01925 443900, Head of Service
Out of Hours Service, tel.: 01925 444400
Ms Angie Simpson-Adkins, Secretary to Mr Dunkerley, tel.: 01925 443907
Ms Helen Sumner, Strategic Director, Adult Social Services, tel.: 01925 444095

Warwickshire
Warwickshire County Council, PO Box 48, Shire Hall, Warwick, CV34 4RD, tel.: 01926 410410 (0900-1730)
Ms Marion Davis, Director of Social Care & Health
Emergencies, tel.: 01926 886922 (1730-0900 Mon-Fri,

Social Services: England

24hrs weekends)
Ms Julie Quinn, Secretary to Director SSD, tel.: 01926 412198
Child Protection Service Local Office (Bedworth), tel.: 024 76 643838
Child Protection Service Local Office (North Warwickshire), tel.: 01827 711101
Child Protection Service Local Office (Nuneaton), tel.: 024 76 351234
Child Protection Service Local Office (Rugby), tel.: 01788 570011
Child Protection Service Local Office (Southam), tel.: 01926 813110
Child Protection Service Local Office (Stratford), tel.: 01789 269391
Child Protection Service Local Office (Warwick), tel.: 01926 334111
Home Care/Meals on Wheels Local Office (Rugby), tel.: 01788 570011
Home Care/Meals on Wheels Local Office (Alcester), tel.: 01789 763041
Home Care/Meals on Wheels Local Office (Bedworth), tel.: 024 7664 3838
Home Care/Meals on Wheels Local Office (North Warwickshire), tel.: 01827 714861
Home Care/Meals on Wheels Local Office (Nuneaton), tel.: 024 7635 1234
Home Care/Meals on Wheels Local Office (Shipston on Stour), tel.: 01608 663522
Home Care/Meals on Wheels Local Office (Southam), tel.: 01926 813110
Home Care/Meals on Wheels Local Office (Stratford-upon-Avon), tel.: 01789 269391
Home Care/Meals on Wheels Local Office (Warwick), tel.: 01926 492481

West Berkshire
West Berkshire Council, Avonbank House, West Street, Newbury, RG14 1BZ, tel.: 01635 42400 (0830-1700 Mon-Thurs - 1630 Fri)
Emergencies, tel.: 01344 786543 (1700-0900 & weekends)
Ms Margaret Goldie, Community Care & Housing, Corporate Director
Child Protection Service Ms Linda Clifford-Hayes, tel.: 01635 503159, Co-ordinator
Children & Young People's Services Ms Margaret Goldie, Interim Corporate Director
Home Care Service Ms Frances Tippett, tel.: 01635 503385, Manager
Meals on Wheels Ms Janet Smith, tel.: 01635 519755

West Sussex
Social & Caring Services, West Sussex County Council, The Grange, Tower Street, Chichester, West Sussex, PO19 1QT, tel.: 01243 777415 (0800-1700), e-mail: socialandcaring.services@westsussex.gov.uk

Mrs Michelle Crowley, Communications Manager, tel.: 01243 777415
Emergencies, tel.: 01903 694422 (1700-0800)
General enquiries about all services, tel.: 01243 777415
Adult Social Services Mr John Dixon, Strategic Director
Children & Young People's Services Mr Robert Black, Strategic Director

Westminster
City of Westminster, Social & Community Services, PO Box 240, 64 Victoria Street, London, SW1E 6QP, tel.: 020 7641 6000 (0900-1700)
Emergencies, tel.: 020 7641 6000 (1700-0900)
Mrs Julie Jones, Director
Child Protection Service Ms Sally Trench, Head of Commissioning, Child Protection & Quality, tel.: 020 7641 7665
Home Care Service Ms Ann Cottrell, tel.: 020 7641 5790
Meals on Wheels Mr Bill Peters, tel.: 020 7402 7896

Wigan
Wigan Civic Centre, Millgate, Wigan, Lancashire, WN1 1AZ, tel.: 01942 828777 (Mon-Fri 0845-8pm, Sat 0845-1pm)
Ms Liv Birchall, Disability Resource Centre, tel.: 01942 700889
Central Duty Team, tel.: 01942 828777
Ms Karen Dunn, Public Information, tel.: 01942 827173
Mr George Ellis, Customer Relations Manager, tel.: 01942 827797
Emergencies, tel.: 0161 834 2436 (out of hours)
Mr Geoff Walby, Sensory Team, tel.: 01942 700889
Mr Bernard Walker, Director
Child Protection Service Mr Sean Atkinson, Group Manager (Acting), tel.: 01942 769763
Children & Young People's Services Mr Sean Atkinson, Group Manager (Acting), tel.: 01942 769763
Home Care Service Ms Rita Forbes, tel.: 01942 621251
Home Care Service Ms Mavis Welsh, tel.: 01942 621251
Meals on Wheels Ms Kathy Rudd, tel.: 01942 827829

Wiltshire
Wiltshire County Council, Adult & Community Services, County Hall, Bythesea Road, Trowbridge, Wiltshire, BA14 8LE, tel.: 01225 713530, web site: www.wiltshire.gov.uk
Emergencies, tel.: 0845 607 0888 (out of hours)
Dr Ray Jones, Director
Home Care Service Ms Ann Langhurst, Manager - Kennet & North Wiltshire
Home Care Service Ms Lyn Leather, Manager - West Wiltshire, tel.: 01225 785952
Home Care Service Ms Marlene Teitge, Manager - South Wiltshire, tel.: 01980 664980

Social Services: England

Windsor & Maidenhead

Royal Borough of Windsor & Maidenhead, Town Hall, St Ives Road, Maidenhead, Berks, SL6 1RF, tel.: 01628 798888 (0845-1715 Fri -1645), web site: www.rbwm.gov.uk

Mr Allan Brown, Head of Community Care & Commissioning, tel.: 01628 683701
Emergencies, tel.: 01344 786543 (out of hours)
Mr Jim Gould, Director
Mr Dave Horler, Head of Organisational Development & Support, tel.: 01628 796720
Mr Chris Thomas, Head of Housing & Residential Development, tel.: 01628 796091

Mr Ed Thompson, Joint Commissioning Manager, tel.: 01628 796671
Child Protection Service Ms Heather Andrews, Head of Children & Families, tel.: 01628 683177
Child Protection Service Ms Lorraine Campion, tel.: 01628 683210, Co-ordinator
Children & Families Service Ms Sheila Jones, tel.: 01628 683211, Service Manager
Home Care Service Ms Helen Latter, Head of Joint Intermediate Care, tel.: 01628 683702
Homeless Families Ms Jane Worley, Housing Options Manager, tel.: 01628 683673
Meals on Wheels Ms Janet Dawson, (Adult Care), tel.: 01628 683793, Service Manager

Wirral

Metropolitan Council Wirral, Social Services HQ, Westminster House, Hamilton Street, Birkenhead, Wirral, CH41 5FN, tel.: 0151 666 3650, fax: 0151 666 4747
Emergencies, tel.: 0151 652 4991 (1700-2100, 24hrs w/es & bank hols)
Mr Kevin Miller, Director
Ms Jenny Ricketts, Care Services Manager, tel.: 0151 666 3624

Wokingham

ADULT COMMUNITY CARE, Wokingham District Council, PO Box 154, Shute End, Wokingham, RG40 1WN, tel.: 0118 947 6776
Ms Trudy Eldridge, PA to Statutory Director of Social Services, tel.: 0118 974 6774
Ms Sue Kelly, Domiciliary Care Manager, tel.: 0118 974 6918
Out of Hours (17.00-09.00), tel.: 01344 786 543
Child Protection Service Mr Bob Dewing, tel.: 0118 944 5341, Co-ordinator
Children's Services Mr Mark Molloy, tel.: 0118 974 6775, Corporate Head
Community Care Ms Pat Brecknock, tel.: 0118 974 6762, Corporate Head
Looked After Children Ms Lynne Pitt, tel.: 0118 974 6880, Service Manager
Smoking Cessation Mr Ray Foan, Stop Smoking Service

Manager, Wokingham PCT, tel.: 0118 949 5193
Social Services Mr Doug Patterson, Chief Executive & Statutory Director, tel.: 0118 974 6001

Wolverhampton

Wolverhampton City Council, Civic Centre, St Peter's Square, Wolverhampton, WV1 1RT, tel.: 01902 556556 (0830-1700)
Emergencies, tel.: 01902 552999 (out of hours)
Homeless Families, tel.: 01902 554747/554807/554741/551037
Looked After Children, tel.: 01902 553001
Mr G Mason, Director

Child Protection Service Assessment & Child Protection, tel.: 01902 555392
Home Care/Meals on Wheels Via North East Sector Team for Older People, tel.: 01902 553600
Home Care/Meals on Wheels Via South East Sector Team for Older People, tel.: 01902 553635
Home Care/Meals on Wheels Via South West Sector Team for Older People, tel.: 01902 553700

Worcestershire

Worcestershire County Council, PO Box 372, County Hall, Worcester, WR5 2XE, tel.: 01905 763763 (0830-1700)
Access Centre for all new referrals, tel.: 0845 607 2000
Ms Jennie Bashforth, Director
Mr Stephen Chandler, Manager Learning Disabilities, tel.: 01905 763763
Ms Linda Cooper, Operational Support Manager, tel.: 01905 766427
Emergencies, tel.: 01905 748033 (out of hours)
Home Care Service, tel.: 01905 734210
Child Protection Service Mr Alan Ferguson, Planning & Review Unit Manager, tel.: 01905 763763
Children's Services Mrs Anne Binney, Head, tel.: 01905 763763
Meals on Wheels Ms Sandy Graham, tel.: 01905 768357
Older People Services Mr Eddie Clarke, Physical Disability & Sensory Impairment, tel.: 01905 763763

York

Community Services, City of York Council, PO Box 402, Customer Advice Centre, George Hudson Street, York, YO1 6ZE, tel.: 01904 613161 (0830-1700)
Ms J Cocker, Learning Culture & Childrens Services, tel.: 01904 555695
Emergencies, tel.: 01904 762314
Mr Bill Hodson, Director
Adult Social Services Ms Val Sutton, Acting Group Manager, Purchasing, tel.: 01904 554065
Adult Social Services Ms Ann Tidd, Group Manager, Purchasing, tel.: 01904 554155

Social Services: Wales

Blaenau Gwent

Blaenau Gwent County Borough Council, Anvil Court, Church Street, Abertillery, NP13 1DB, tel.: 01495 354680

Mr Mike Murphy, LD/Mental Health, tel.: 01495 355593, Service Manager

Mrs Angela Penwill, Provider Services, tel.: 01495 355754, Service Manager

Mrs Ruth Sinfield, First Service, Assessment & Planning, tel.: 01495 355774, Manager

Adult Social Services Mrs Liz Majer, tel.: 01495 355272, Assistant Director

Child Protection Service Mr Nigel Brown, Monitoring & Review Manager, tel.: 01495 356016

Children's Services Mr David Johnston, tel.: 01495 355067, Assistant Director

Looked After Children Mr Christopher Bradley, tel.: 01495 355795, Service Manager

Older People/Disability Services Mrs Heather Tyrrell, tel.: 01495 355594, Service Manager

Social Services Mr Phil Hodgson, Corporate Director

Bridgend

Bridgend County Borough Council, Sunnyside, Bridgend, CF31 4AR, tel.: 01656 642200 (0830-1700 Mon-Thurs, -1630 Fri)

Emergencies, tel.: 01443 849944 (out of hours)

Home Care, tel.: 01656 664517

Homeless Service, tel.: 01656 643542

Meals on Wheels, tel.: 01656 774941

Residential Homes, tel.: 01656 664517

Adult Social Services Mr Gordon Jones, (Older/Disabled People), Head of Service

Children's Services Vacant Position, tel.: 01656 642200, Assistant Director

Community Care Mr Tony Garthwaite, Executive Director

Home Care/Meals on Wheels Mr Chris Brookes-Dowsett, tel.: 01656 664517

Housing & Community Care Mr Jim McKirdle, Head of Service

Mental Health/Learning Disability Ms Sue Cooper, Adult Services (Substance Misuse), Head of Service

Caerphilly

Caerphilly County Borough Council, Hawtin Park, Gellihaf, Pontllanfraith, Blackwood, NP2 2PZ, tel.: 01443 864673 (0830-1700)

Mr Joe Howsam, Director

Home Care Service Mr Adrian Read, tel.: 01443 864554, Service Manager

Meals on Wheels Ms Sally Franks, tel.: 01443 865760

Residential Homes Ms Jean Bailey, tel.: 01495 756316, Head of Registration/Inspection

Cardiff

City & County of Cardiff, County Hall, Atlantic Wharf, Cardiff, CF10 4UW, tel.: 029 2087 2000 (0830-1700 Mon-Thurs, -1630 Fri)

Ms Neelam Bhardwaja, Corporate Director

Care Standards Inspectorate for Wales, tel.: 029 2047 8600

Child Protection Services, tel.: 029 2077 4600

Emergencies, tel.: 029 2044 8360 (out of hours)

Home Care Services, tel.: 029 2054 4850

Adult Social Services Social Care Services, tel.: 029 2052 0984

Children's Services Social Care Services, tel.: 029 2053 6400

Meals on Wheels Mr Alan Bines, tel.: 029 2056 6533, Co-ordinator

Carmarthenshire

Carmarthenshire County Council, 3 Spilman Street, Carmarthen, Carmarthenshire, SA31 1LE, tel.: 01267 228918 (0845-1700 Mon-Thurs, -1630 Fri), e-mail: socialcare@carmarthenshire.gov.uk

Mr Colin Allen, Physical Disabilities, Senior Principal Officer

Mr Bill Collins, Head of Adult Services - Social Care & Housing, tel.: 01267 228915

Emergencies, tel.: 01267 234800 (24 hours)

Mr Mark Evans, Mental Health, Senior Principal Officer

Mr Bruce McLernon, Director

Mr Robin Moulster, Learning Disabilities, Senior Principal Officer

Child Protection Service Mr Stefan Smith, Senior Principal Officer, tel.: 01267 228914 ext 2914, Senior Principal Officer

Home Care Service Ms Audrey Beyron, tel.: 01267 224262

Meals on Wheels Ms Vivian Kincaid, tel.: 01267 224261

Older People Services Senior Principal Officer, tel.: 01267 228918

Ceredigion

Cyngor Sir Ceredigion County Council, Min-Aeron, Rhiw Goch, Aberaeron, SA46 0DY, tel.: 01545 572616 (0845-1700 Mon-Thurs, -1630 Fri)

All service requests to go through the Contact Centre, tel.: 01545 574000

Contact Centre, tel.: 01545 574000

Mr A P Davies, Director

Mrs Eleri Davies, Director's Secretary, tel.: 01545 572601

Emergencies, tel.: 0845 601 5392 (1700-0900)

Meals on Wheels Ms Jane Johnson (WRVS), tel.: 01545 571883

Residential Homes Ms Angela Williams, Care Standards Inspectorate, tel.: 01267 223573, Manager

Social Services: Wales

Conwy
Conwy County Borough Council, Builder Street, Llandudno, LL30 1DA, tel.: 01492 574065 (0845-1715 Mon-Thurs, -1645 Fri)
Child Protection Service, tel.: 01492 514871
Disabled Parking Badges, tel.: 01492 871444
Emergencies, tel.: 01492 515777 (1700-0900)
Ms Bethan Jones, tel.: 01492 574061, Director
Learning Disability Services, tel.: 01492 575374
Mental Health Services, tel.: 01492 860926 & 01492 532164
Services for Older People, tel.: 01492 575600
Services for Physically Disabled & Sensorily Impaired, tel.: 01492 564840
Children & Families Service Civic Centre Annexe, Colwyn Bay, LL29 8AR, tel.: 01492 514871
Home Care/Meals on Wheels Team Manager, tel.: 01492 544277

Denbighshire
Denbighshire County Council
First Contact Team, tel.: 01824 712448
First Contact Team, tel.: 01824 706488

Flintshire
Flintshire County Council, Adult Social Care, County Hall, Mold, CH7 6NN, tel.: 01352 702642 (0830-1700), web site: www.flintshire.gov.uk
Adult Social Care, tel.: 01352 702642
Children's Services, tel.: 01352 701000
Emergencies, tel.: 01352 753403 (out of hours)
Ms Susan Lewis, tel.: 01352 752121, Director

Gwynedd
Cyngor Gwynedd Council, County Offices, Shirehall Street, Caernarfon, LL55 1SH, tel.: 01286 679975 (0900-1700 Mon-Fri)
Emergencies, tel.: 01286 675502
Mr Glyn Hughes, tel.: 01286 679227, Head of Service
Child Protection Service Ms Marian Hughes, tel.: 01286 679700, Service Manager
Home Care/Meals on Wheels Ms Catrin Rutherford, tel.: 01341 422180

Isle of Anglesey
Cyngor Sir Ynys Mon/Isle of Anglesey County Council, Swyddfa'r Sir/Council Offices, Llangefni, Ynys Mon/Anglesey, LL77 7TW, tel.: 01248 752700, fax: 01248 750107, e-mail: socialservices@anglesey.gov.uk, web site: www.anglesey.gov.uk
Llinos Edwards, Looked After Children Nurse, tel.: 01248 752702
Emergencies, tel.: 01286 675502
Byron Williams, Housing & Social Services, Director
Child Protection Service Duty Officer (Children's Services), tel.: 01248 752733/752722
Home Care/Meals on Wheels , tel.: 01248 752792

Homeless Service Mr Dylan Rees, tel.: 01248 752267, Principal Officer
Residential Homes Ms Deborah Russell, Care Standards Inspectorate for Wales, tel.: 01492 542580/01286 662300, Regional Director

Merthyr Tydfil
Merthyr Tydfil County Borough Council, Adults Families & Lifelong Learning Directorate, Ty Keir Hardie, Riverside Court, Avenue de Clichy, Merthyr Tydfil, CF47 8XE, tel.: 01685 724500 (0830-1700 Mon-Thurs, -1630 Fri), fax: 01685 384868, e-mail: adultsfamilieslifelonglearning@mertyr.gov.uk

Adult Mental Health Team, tel.: 01685 721671
Adult Services Duty Desk, tel.: 01685 724507
Adult Services General Enquiries (Reception), tel.: 01685 724500
Care Management (Older Persons), tel.: 01685 724561/724552
Commissioning Contracting & Resource Services, tel.: 01685 725062/724695
Community Care (policy/strategy), tel.: 01685 724693
Community Occupational Therapy Team, tel.: 01685 373359
Continuing Social Care (Home Care), tel.: 01685 724557 (0830-1700/fri 1630)
Continuing Social Care (Home Care) Out of Hours, tel.: 0771 293 6570 (1700-2200)
Daytime Activities Services (Day Care), tel.: 01685 721764
Disability Team Adult Services, tel.: 01685 724988
Emergencies (out of hours), tel.: 01685 724507
Financial Services, tel.: 01685 724648
Health Social Care & Well-Being Support Office, tel.: 01685 724623/726221
Home Services - Initial Response Team, tel.: 01685 373359
Home Services - Intermediate Care Team, tel.: 01685 373359
Home Services - Supported Living Team, 01685 722488
Information Officer (General), tel.: 01685 724680
Mr Giovanni Isingrini, tel.: 01685 724680, Director
Lifelong Learning & Skills Development, tel.: 01685 724602
Meals on Wheels, tel.: 01685 723466
Referral & Assessment (Older Persons), tel.: 01685 7247544
Substance Misuse (MIDAS), tel.: 01685 721991

Monmouthshire
Social & Housing Services, Monmouthshire County Council, Cwmbran, South Wales, NP44 2XH, tel.: 01633 644644 (0840-1715 Mon-Thurs, -1615 Fri)
Out of Hours, tel.: 0800 3284432
 Morley Sims, Health/Safety & Facilities Manager, tel.: 01873 735904
Community Meals Mrs Pauline Batty, tel.: 01873 882910
Home Care Service Mr Colin Richings, tel.: 01291 638922
Residential Homes Ms Mary Daisley, tel.: 01873 853706

Social Services: Wales

Neath Port Talbot

Neath Port Talbot County Borough Council, Civic Centre, Port Talbot, SA13 1PJ, tel.: 01639 763333 (0830-1700), web site: www.npt.gov.uk

Emergencies, tel.: 01639 895455 (1730-0130 Mon-Fri;0900-0130 Sat/Sun)

Mr Colin Preece, Director

Child Protection Service Mrs Liz Pearce, P.O. - Children & Young People's Services, tel.: 01639 763333

Home Care/Meals on Wheels Mrs Mair Davies, tel.: 01639 763333

Homeless Service Ms Rachel McCartney, P.O. Homelessness & Advice

Looked After Children Mr Robin Williams, P.O. - Children & Young People's Services

Newport

Newport City Council, Social Wellbeing & Housing, Civic Centre, Newport, South Wales, NP20 4UR, tel.: 01633 656656 (0830-1700 Mon-Thurs, -1630 Fri)

Home Care Service, tel.: 01633 656656

Mrs Lis House, Community Care & Adult Services, tel.: 01633 656656, Head of Service

Mr Robert Lynbeck, Head of Housing & Area Regeneration, tel.: 01633 656656

Mr Ellis Williams, tel.: 01633 656656, Director

Child Protection Service Ms Judith Corlett, tel.: 01633 656656, Service Manager

Children & Families Service Mrs Sharon Davies, tel.: 01633 656656, Head of Service

Pembrokeshire

Pembrokeshire County Council, County Hall, Haverfordwest, SA61 1TP, tel.: 01437 764551 (0900-1700 Mon-Fri)

Ms Amanda Davies, Secretary to Director, tel.: 01437 775831

Emergencies, tel.: 0845 601 5522

Ms Rosemary Griffiths, tel.: 01437 775912

Mr Jon Skone, Director

Home Care Service Ms Sue Thomson, Independent Living, tel.: 01437 776061, Customer Services Manager

Residential Homes Ms Doreen Mackin, tel.: 01348 873888, Customer Services Manager

Powys

Powys County Council, County Hall, Llandrindod Wells, Powys, LD1 5LG, tel.: 01597 826000 (0830-1700 Mon-Thurs -1630 Fri), web site: www.csd.powys.gov.uk

Care Standard Inspectorate Wales, tel.: 01597 829319

Emergencies, tel.: 08457 573818 (out of hours)

Mr Philip Robson - Group Director of Community Services, Director of Social Services

Mrs R Thomas, PA to Group Director, Community Services, tel.: 01597 826906

Child Protection Service Ms Maurice Emberson, Interim Head of Children's Services, tel.: 01597 826123

Home Care/Meals on Wheels Area: Brecon, tel.: 01874 623741

Home Care/Meals on Wheels Area: Llandrindod Wells, tel.: 01597 827102

Home Care/Meals on Wheels Area: Newtown, tel.: 01686 617521

Home Care/Meals on Wheels Area: Welshpool, tel.: 01938 552017

Home Care/Meals on Wheels Area: Ystradgynlais, tel.: 01639 844595

Home Care/Meals on Wheels Ms Ros Thomas, tel.: 01874 615923

Rhondda Cynon Taff

Rhondda Cynon Taff County Borough Council, The Pavilions, Cambrian Park, Clydach Vale, Tonypandy, CF40 2XX, tel.: 01443 424000 (0830-1700 Mon-Thurs, -1630 Fri)

Emergencies, tel.: 01443 204010 (out of hours)

Ms Sue Hetherington, Clerical Assistant, tel.: 01443 424150

Ms Christine Laird, Director

Home Care/Meals on Wheels Area: Cynon, tel.: 01685 875481

Home Care/Meals on Wheels Area: Rhondda, tel.: 01443 431513

Home Care/Meals on Wheels Area: Taff Ely, tel.: 01443 486731

Residential Homes Mrs C James, tel.: 01443 668844

Residential Homes Mrs C Lewis, tel.: 01443 668844

Residential Homes Mrs S Rees, tel.: 01443 668844, Head of Service

Residential Homes Mrs S Whitson, tel.: 01443 668844

Swansea

City & County of Swansea, County Hall, Oystermouth Road, Swansea, SA1 3SN, tel.: 01792 636000 (0830-1700 Mon-Thurs, -1630 Fri), fax: 01792 636807, web site: www.swansea.gov.uk

Emergency Duty Service, tel.: 01792 636000 (out of hours)

Ms Katrina Guntrip, Principal Officer, tel.: 01792 636659

Home Care Service Ms Julie Butt, tel.: 01792 636256

Home Care Service Mrs Julia Crawley, tel.: 01792 636433

Social Services & Housing Mr Jack Straw, Director

Torfaen

Torfaen County Borough Council, 2nd Floor, County Hall, Cwmbran, NP44 2WN, tel.: 01633 648777 (0830-1700 Mon-Thurs, -1630 Fri)

Mr Gary Birch, Director

Emergencies, tel.: Via Local Police

Asylum Seekers Mr Adrian Huckin (Housing Department), tel.: 01495 762200

Child Protection Service Mr Paul Meredith, tel.: 01633 648777, Assistant Director

Home Care Service Mrs Val Bessell, tel.: 01633 648500, Team Manager
Homeless Families Mr Adrian Huckin (Housing Department), tel.: 01495 762200
Meals on Wheels Mrs Julie Drew, tel.: 01633 648733

Vale of Glamorgan
Vale of Glamorgan County Council, Dock Office, Barry Docks, Barry, CF63 4RT, tel.: 01446 704677 (0830-1700)
Adult Community Care Services, tel.: 01446 731100
Mr James Cawley, Director of Community Services
Child Protection/Looked After Children, tel.: 01446 725202
Children & Family Services, tel.: 01446 725202
Children with Disabilities, tel.: 01446 704824
Emergencies Out of Hours, tel.: 029 2044 8360
Home Care Services/Meals on Wheels, tel.: 01446 731100
Homeless Families, tel.: 01446 709500

Wrexham
Wrexham County Borough Council, Crown Buildings, 31 Chester Street, Wrexham, LL13 8ZE, tel.: 01978 292999 (0830-1700)
Asylum Seekers, tel.: 01978 292973
Child Protection/Looked After Children, tel.: 01978 267000
Emergencies, tel.: 01978 264358 (1700-0830, 24hrs weekends)
Mr Andrew Figiel, Chief Social Services Officer
Homeless Families/Travellers, tel.: 01978 315300
Smoking Cessation, tel.: 01978 292040
Mrs Sheila Wentworth, Assistant Chief Officer Adults Services
Home Care/Meals on Wheels Ms Sue Dutton, tel.: 01978 292000, Service Manager

Social Services: Scotland

Aberdeen City

Aberdeen City Council, St Nicholas House, Broad Street, Aberdeen, AB10 1BY, tel.: 01224 522000 (0830-1700)

Mr Alan Care at Home Service, tel.: 01224 522000
Chief Social Worker, tel.: 01224 522000
Community Meals, tel.: 01224 522000
Out of Hours Social Work Team, (emergencies only), tel.: 01224 693936 (1630-0830)

Aberdeenshire

Aberdeenshire Council, Woodhill House, Westburn Road, Aberdeen, AB16 5GB, tel.: 01467 620981 (0845 606 7000)

Emergencies (Mon-Fri 1630-Midnight) (Sat/Sun 0845-Midnight), tel.: 0845 840 0070
Mr Colin Mackenzie, Director
Ms Amanda Roe, Information Manager, tel.: 01467 625567
Child Protection Service Mr Chris Booth, Head of Social Work (Child Care, tel.: 01569 763800
Home Care Service Ms Pam Bradley, tel.: 01569 768427, Manager
Home Care Service Ms Elizabeth McAtarsney, tel.: 01888 563796, Manager
Home Care Service Mr Davy Ritchie, tel.: 01346 512095, Manager
Home Care Service Ms Linda Wood, Acting Manager, tel.: 01467 628308
Meals on Wheels Ms Moira Hart (mobile 0771 489 8593, tel.: 01224 572962, Service Manager

Angus

Angus Council, Social Work & Health, St Margaret's House, Orchard Loan, Orchard Bank Business Park, Forfar, DD8 1WS, tel.: 01307 461460 (0845-1700 Mon-Fri)

Out of Hours (all day Sat/Sun & Public Holidays), tel.: 01382 436430 (1700-0845)
Dr Robert Peat, Director
Child Protection Service Mr George Bowie, tel.: 01241 435651, Service Manager
Home Care/Community Meals Ms Susan MacLean, tel.: 01307 465143, Service Manager

Argyll & Bute

Argyll & Bute Council, Community Services, Dalriada House, Lochnell Street, Lochgilphead, Argyll, PA31 8ST, tel.: 01546 602177 (0900-1700), e-mail: firstname.surname@argyll-bute.gov.uk

Mr Dougie Dunlop, Head of Children/Families (& Criminal Justice), tel.: 01546 604256
Emergencies - Standby Service for Out of Hours Emergencies, tel.: 0800 811505
Ms Sandra Greer, Head of Community Support, tel.: 01546 604391
Mr Jim Robb, Head of Integrated Care, tel.: 01369 708900
Mr Alex Taylor, Oban, Lorn and the Isles, tel.: 01631 563068, Service Manager

Service Manager, Mid Argyll, Kintyre & Islay, tel.: 01586 552659
Mr Rodger Wilson, Helensburgh and Lomond, tel.: 01436 658750, Service Manager
Child Protection Service Ms Liz Strang, tel.: 01546 604281, Co-ordinator
Community Services Mr Douglas Hendry, tel.: 01546 604244, Director
Homeless Service Ms Moira MacDonald, Community Support Development Manager, tel.: 01631 572184
Housing & Supported Living Services Mr Gordan Nash, (including Travellers/Gypies), tel.: 01546 604574
Looked After Children Mr Derek Bannon, Children's Resource Manager, tel.: 01436 677186

Borders

Scottish Borders Council, 1st Floor, Old School Building, Council Headquarters, Newtown St Boswells, Roxburghshire, TD6 0SA, tel.: 01835 825080 (0845-1700)

Emergencies, tel.: 01896 752111 (out of hours)
Ms Emma Gunter, Secretary, tel.: 01835 825080
Mr Andrew Lowe, Director
Child Protection Service Ms Gillian Nicol, tel.: 01835 825080, Co-ordinator
Children's Services Ms Ann Blackie, tel.: 01896 757230, Service Manager
Home Care Service Ms Barbara Harrison, Project Manager, tel.: 01835 825080
Home Care/Meals at Home Mr Nic Goodwin, tel.: 01835 825080, Service Manager
Homeless Families Ms Kim Suttle, Housing Advice Support & Mediationm, tel.: 01835 865189, Manager
Smoking Cessation Mr Tom Trotter, Health Improvement Officer, tel.: 01835 825080

Clackmannanshire

Clackmannanshire Council, Lime Tree House, Castle Street, Alloa, FK10 1EX, tel.: 01259 450000 (0900-1700)

Care Commission, Residental Homes Inspection, tel.: 01382 207289
Emergencies, tel.: 01786 470500 (1700-0900)
Mr David Jones, Director
Home Care Service Ms Linda Melville, tel.: 01259 211058, Service Manager
Meals on Wheels Ms Cath Arnold, tel.: 01259 219012, Team Manager
Social Services Ms Deirdre Cilliers, Chief Social Work Officer, tel.: 01259 452419

Dumfries & Galloway

Dumfries & Galloway Council, Woodbank, 30 Edinburgh Road, Dumfries, DG1 1NW, tel.: 01387 260458

Care Commission, Care Commission, tel.: 01382 207195
Emergencies, tel.: 01387 260000 (24 hours)
Ms Beth Smith, Chief Social Work Officer
Home Care/Meals on Wheels Mr Richard Blackburn, tel.: 01387 260522/260000

Social Services: Scotland

Dundee

Dundee City Council, Floor 7, Tayside House, 28 Crichton Street, Dundee, DD1 3RN, tel.: 01382 433712 (0830-1700 Mon-Fri), web site: www.dundeecity.gov.uk

Asylum Seekers, tel.: 01382 435265

Child Protection Senior Social Worker, tel.: 01382 668538

Home Care Services/Meals on Wheels, tel.: 01382 438300

Homeless Families, tel.: 01382 438300

Looked After Children, tel.: 01382 438300

Out of Hours Service, tel.: 01382 432270 (1630-0930)

Social Work Access Team, tel.: 01382 435265

Travellers, tel.: 01382 455265

Community Care Ms Laura Bannerman, tel.: 01382 438302, Manager

Older People Services Social Work First Contact Team, tel.: 01382 435106

Social Work Team Mr Alan Baird, tel.: 01382 433314, Director

East Ayrshire

East Ayrshire Council, Civic Centre, John Dickie Street, Kilmarnock, KA1 1BY, tel.: 01563 576000 (0900-1700 Mon-Thurs, -1600 Fri)

Mrs Jackie Donnelly, Executive Head of Social Work, tel.: 01563 576000

Emergencies, tel.: 0800 811505 (out of hours)

Mr Stephen Moore, Head of Social Work

Mr John Mulgrew, Director

Mr Graham Short, Executive Director of Educational & Social Service, tel.: 01563 576000

Child Protection Service Mr Bill Eadie, Children & Families, tel.: 01563 576728, Principal Officer

Home Care Service Ms Ruth Gray, tel.: 01563 555378

Home Care Service Ms Eleanor McCaffer, tel.: 01563 528011

Older People Services Mr Martin Clark, Service Unit Manager, tel.: 01563 576927

East Dunbartonshire

East Dunbartonshire Council, William Patrick Library, 2-4 West High Street, Kirkintilloch, G66 1AD, tel.: 0141 775 9000 (0900-1700 Mon-Fri), web site: www.eastdunbarton.gov.uk

Ms Sue Bruce, Chief Executive

Ms Jean Campbell, Finance Manager - Finance Planning & Commissioning, tel.: 0141 775 9000

Emergencies, tel.: 0800 811 505

Mr Tony Keogh, Head of Social Work

Mrs Freda McShane, Service Delivery Co-ordinator

Home Care/Meals on Wheels Mr David Formstone, tel.: 0141 775 9000

Meals on Wheels/Home Care Mr David Formstone, tel.: 0141 775 9000

East Lothian

East Lothian Council, 9-11 Lodge Street, Haddington, EH41 3DX, tel.: 01620 826600 (0900-1700 Mon-Thurs, -1600 Fri)

Ms Jan Cochran, Head of Community Support, tel.: 01620 827877

Emergencies, tel.: 0800 731 6969 (1700-0830)

Emergency & Out of Hours (Child Protection - Social Work), tel.: 0131 554 4301/0800 731 6969

Ms Joyce Gordon, Frozen Meals, tel.: 01620 827525

Mr Derek Phaup, Home Care/Frozen Meals, tel.: 0131 653 4313

Mr Bruce Walker, Director of Community Services, tel.: 01620 827541

Child Protection Service Children's Services Duty Social Worker (Haddington), tel.: 01620 826600

Child Protection Service Children's Services Duty Social Worker (Musselburgh), tel.: 0131 665 3711

Child Protection Service Duty Social Worker - Health, Royal Hospital for Sick Children, tel.: 0131 536 0501

Child Protection Service Mr Ronnie Hill, Regional Manager, Care Commission, tel.: 0131 653 4100

Child Protection Service Paediatrican On Call (Out of Hours) - Health, tel.: 0131 536 0000

Child Protection Service Paediatrician On Call - Health, tel.: 0131 536 8107 (0900-1700)

East Renfrewshire

East Renfrewshire Council, Council Buildings, Eastwood Park, Rouken Glen Road, Giffnock, Glasgow, G46 6UG, tel.: 0141 577 3839 (0845-1645 Mon-Thurs, -1555 Fri)

Emergencies, tel.: 0800 811 505

Mr George Hunter, Director

Home Care Service Ms Dorothy Gormlie, tel.: 0141 577 3767, Manager

Residential Homes Scottish Commission for Regulation of Care, tel.: 0141 843 4239

Edinburgh

City of Edinburgh Council, Shrubhill House, Shrub Place, Leith Walk, Edinburgh, EH7 4PD, tel.: 0131 553 8356 ext 8201, web site: www.edinburgh.gov.uk

Ms Monica Boyle, Head of Quality & Resources, tel.: 0131 553 8319

Ms Sue Brace, Head of Planning & Commissioning, tel.: 0131 553 8322

Emergencies, tel.: 0800 731 6969

Mr Peter Gabbitas, tel.: 0131 553 8201, Director

Home Care Service, tel.: 0131 553 8440

Meals on Wheels, tel.: 0131 553 8440

Child Protection Service Mr Duncan MacAulay, General Manager, tel.: 0131 553 8288

Home Care/Meals on Wheels Mr Bill King, Operations Manager (Domiciliary Care), tel.: 0131 553 8440

Social Services: Scotland

Falkirk

Falkirk Council, Brockville, Hope Street, Falkirk, FK1 5RW, tel.: 01324 506400 (0900-1700), web site: www.falkirk.gov.uk

Ms Janet Birks, Director

Emergencies, tel.: 01786 470500 (out of hours)

Ms Rosina Gorrie, Admin Co-ordinator, tel.: 01324 506525

Home Care/Meals on Wheels Mr Alec Graham, tel.: 01324 506400

Residential Homes Care Commission, tel.: 0845 6030890

Fife

Fife Council, Fife House, North Street, Glenrothes, KY7 5LT, tel.: 01592 414141, fax: 01592 413417, web site: www.fifedirect.org.uk

Emergencies, tel.: 01592 415000 (1700-0900)

Mr Stephen Moore, Head of Social Work

Child Protection Service Mr Roy MacGregor, tel.: 01334 412357, Service Manager

Child Protection Service Ms Theresa Stephenson, tel.: 01383 313308, Service Manager

Home Care Service Mr Alastair MacLeod, tel.: 01592 412014, Service Manager

Looked After Children Mr Roy MacGregor, tel.: 01334 412357, Service Manager

Looked After Children Ms Theresa Stephenson, tel.: 01383 313308, Service Manager

Meals on Wheels Ms Karen Briggs, tel.: 01592 415481, Team Leader

Glasgow

Glasgow City Council, Social Work Services, Nye Bevan House, 20 India Street, Glasgow, G2 4PF, tel.: 0141 287 8700 (0845-1645 Mon-Thurs, -1555 Fri)

Ms Margaret Ball, Information Officer, tel.: 0141 287 8729

Mr David Comley, Director

Emergencies, tel.: 0800 811505 (out of hours)

Principal Officer, Residential Services (Older People), tel.: 0141 420 5500

Asylum Seekers Project Manager, tel.: 0141 222 7300

Child Protection Service Senior Officer, tel.: 0141 420 5500

Home Care/Meals on Wheels Principal Officer Community Services, tel.: 0141 420 5500

Homeless Families Manager, tel.: 0141 287 1800

Looked After Children Principal Officer, tel.: 0141 420 5500

Highland

Highland Council, Glenurouhart Road, Inverness, IV3 5NX, tel.: 01463 702861

Ms Harriet Dempster, Director

Emergencies, tel.: 0345 697284 (1700-0900)

Ms Fiona Palin, Criminal Justice Service & Central Services, tel.: 01463 702874

Mr Ian Sutherland, CA/T, tel.: 01463 703450

Children & Families Service Ms Sandra Campbell, Head of Operations (Children), tel.: 01463 702872

Community Care Mr Jon King, Head of Operations, tel.: 01463 702876

Home Care Service Ms Sue Owen, tel.: 01463 703465

Inverclyde

Inverclyde Council, Dalrymple House, 195 Dalrymple Street, Greenock, PA15 1UN, tel.: 01475 714000 (0845-1645 Mon-Thurs, -1555 Fri)

Emergencies, tel.: 0141 357 3696 (out of hours)

Ms Yvonne Goldie, Service Manager (Strategic Services), tel.: 01475 714000 ext 4010

Mr Robert Murphy, Chief Social Work Officer

Home Care Service Organisers, tel.: 01475 714600

Midlothian

Midlothian Council, Fairfield House, 8 Lothian Road, Dalkeith, EH22 3ZH, tel.: 0131 271 7500 (0900-1700 Mon-Thurs, -1545 Fri), web site: www.midlothian.gov.uk

Emergencies, tel.: 0800 7316969 (1700-0900 Mon-Fri, 1545-0900 Fri-Mon)

Mr John Scott, Head of Children & Families & Criminal Justice

Community Care Mr Colin Anderson, Head of Service

Social Work Team Mr Malcolm McEwan, Director

Moray

Moray Council, Commerical Services Department, Council Headquarters, High Street, Elgin, IV30 1BX, tel.: 01343 563530 (0845-1700 Mon-Fri)

Emergencies, tel.: 08457 565656 (out of hours)

Mr Sandy Riddell, Director

Home Care/Meals on Wheels Mrs Susan Anderson, Domiciliary Care Manager, tel.: 01343 567839

Residential Homes Ms Irene Grant, tel.: 01343 557065, Head of Registration/Inspection

North Ayrshire

North Ayrshire Council, Elliott House, Redburn Industrial Estate, Kilwinning Road, Irvine, Ayrshire, KA12 8TB, tel.: 01294 317700 (0900-1645 Mon-Thurs, -1630 Fri)

Mrs Bernadette Docherty, Director

Emergencies, tel.: 0800 811505 (out of hours)

Children & Families Service Ms Sandra Paterson, Criminal Justice, tel.: 01294 317733, Head of Service

Community Care Mr Louis Skehal, Head of Service, tel.: 01294 317732

Home Care/Meals on Wheels Ms Denise Brown, tel.: 01294 317783, Chief Officer

Home Care/Meals on Wheels Ms Clare Devaney, tel.: 01294 317740

Residential Homes Ms Eleanor Gallacher, tel.: 01294 317742

Social Services: Scotland

North Lanarkshire
North Lanarkshire Council, Scott House, 73/77 Merry Street, Motherwell, ML1 1JE, tel.: 01698 332000 (0845-1645 Mon-Thurs, -1555 Fri)
Ms Christine Clelland, tel.: 01698 332029, Service Manager
Mr James Dickie, Director
Asylum Seekers Mr Kevin McGown, Liaison
Child Protection/Looked After Children Ms Susan Taylor, Manager
Home Care Service Ms Christine Cleland, Service Manager Homecare
Home Care Service Mr Jim Nisbet, Manager, Older People's Services
Residential Homes Mr Denis O'Donnell, Manager
Smoking Cessation Mr Joe Docherty, Senior Health & Safety Officer
Travellers Mr Kevin McGown, Liaison

Orkney
Orkney Islands Council, Community Social Services Dept, Council Offices, Kirkwall, Orkney, KW15 1NY, tel.: 01856 873535 (0900-1700), web site: www.orkney.gov.uk
Emergencies, tel.: 01856 888000 (24hrs)
Mr Harry Garland, tel.: 01856 873535, Director
Mrs Gillian Morrison, Head of Strategic Services, tel.: 01856 873535
Children & Families Service Mr Adrian Williams, Criminal Justice, tel.: 01856 873535, Assistant Director

Perth & Kinross
Perth & Kinross Council, Pullar House, 35 Kinnoull Street, Perth, PH1 5GD, tel.: 01738 476700 (0845-1700)
Emergencies, tel.: 01382 436430 (1700-0845)
Mr Ian Manson, Director
Home Care Service Ms Fiona Stewart, Service Manager
Home Care/Meals on Wheels Mr George Welsh, Service Manager
Residential Homes Mr Tim Hewett, tel.: 01738 476700, Service Manager

Renfrewshire
Renfrewshire Council, Municipal Buildings (North), Cotton Street, Paisley, PA1 1TZ, tel.: 0141 842 5167 (0845-1645)
Mr David Crawford, Director
Ms Wilma Miller, Secretary, tel.: 0141 842 5167
Community Care Ms Patricia Maclachlan, tel.: 0141 842 5164, Head of Service
Older People Services Mr Peter McCulloch, (Residential & Day Services), tel.: 0141 842 5971, Principal Officer

Shetland
Shetland Islands Council, Social Work Service, 92 St Olaf Street, Lerwick, Shetland, ZE1 0ES, tel.: 01595 744400 (0900-1700 Mon-Thurs/-1600 Fri), fax: 01595 744436, e-mail: social.work@sic.shetland.gov.uk, web site: www.shetland.gov.uk

Mr Brian Doughty, Interim Head of Social Work & CSWO, tel.: 01595 7444001
Emergencies, tel.: 01595 695611(1700-0900 Mon-Fri, 24hr Sat-Sun)
Home Care/ Meals on Wheels, tel.: 01595 744467
Mrs Ann Williamson, Fieldwork, tel.: 01595 744400, Service Manager
Child Protection Service Ms Helen Watkins, tel.: 01595 744435
Children's Services Mr Stephen Morgan, (Looked After Children), tel.: 01595 744400, Service Manager
Community Care Ms Christine Ferguson, tel.: 01595 744300, Manager

South Ayrshire
South Ayrshire Council, Holmston House, 3 Holmston Road, Ayr, KA7 3BA, tel.: 01292 612059 (0845-1645 Mon-Thurs,-1600 Fri)
Emergencies, tel.: 0800 811505 (1645-0845)
Mr Jim Hunter, Criminal Justice, tel.: 01292 612059, Manager
Mrs Jenny Thompson, tel.: 01292 612419, Acting Director
Adult Social Services Ms Annabel Sinclair, tel.: 01292 612059, Manager
Children & Families Service Ms Anne Stewart, tel.: 01292 612059, Manager
Home Care/Meals on Wheels Mr Neil Watson, tel.: 01292 612059, Service Manager
Housing & Supported Living Services Mr Ken Hamilton, Head of Regeneration & Housing, tel.: 01292 612088
Older People Services Mr Alistair Scobie, tel.: 01292 612059, Manager

South Lanarkshire
South Lanarkshire Council Offices, Almada Street, Hamilton, ML3 0AA, tel.: 01698 454444 (0845-1645 Mon-Thurs, -1615 Fri)
Emergencies, tel.: 0800 811505 (out of hours)
Ms Brenda Hutchinson, Personnel Services Manager
Mr Harry Stevenson, Social Work Resources, Executive Director
Asylum Seekers Mr Alex Davidson, Head of Adult Services
Child Protection/Looked After Children Ms Brenda Doyle, Head of Child & Family Services
Home Care/Meals on Wheels Mr Jim Wilson, Head of Older People's Services
Homeless Families/Travellers Mr Alex Davidson, Head of Adult Services

Stirling
Stirling Council, New Viewforth, Stirling, FK8 2ET, tel.: 0845 277 7000 (0900-1700), web site: www.stirling.gov.uk
Ms Marjory Booth, Scottish Commission Regulation Care Central East, tel.: 01786 406363, Locality Manager
Emergencies, tel.: 0845 277 7000 (1700-0900)

Ms Georgina McClenaghan, Administrator Community Care, tel.: 01786 442669

Ms Shiona Strachan, Care Management Services, tel.: 01786 443641, Development Manager

Child Protection Service Ms Julie Main, Co-ordinator, tel.: 01786 443493

Children & Families Service Mr Bill Eadie, Social Work, tel.: 01786 443422, Head of Service

Children's Services Mr David Jeyes, tel.: 01786 442680, Director

Community Care Ms Irene Cavanagh, Chief Social Work Office, tel.: 01786 442689

Community Services Ms Janice Hewitt, tel.: 01786 442677, Director

Home Care Service Ms Alison Jardine, tel.: 01786 471177, Development Manager

West Dunbartonshire

Council Offices, Garshake Road, Dumbarton, G82 3PU, tel.: 01389 737000 ext 7526

Emergencies, tel.: 0800 811505

Ms Beryl Middleton, Head of Quality Assurance, tel.: 0141 951 6140

Mr James Watson, Section Head - Childcare, tel.: 0141 951 6195

Meals on Wheels/Home Care Ms Lynn McKnight, Home Care Section Head, tel.: 0141 951 6166

Social Services Mr William Clark, Acting Director

West Lothian

West Lothian Community Health & Care Partnership, Strackbrock PC, 189 West Main Street, Broxburn, West Lothian, EH52 5LH, tel.: 01506 775547 (0830-1700 Mon-Thurs, -1600 Fri)

Mr Grahame Blair, Social Policy, Head of Service

Emergencies, tel.: 01506 777401/2 (1530-0830 hrs)

Children & Families Service Mr Bill Atkinson, Senior Manager, tel.: 01506 775675

Home Care Service Mr Ian Quigley, tel.: 01506 771755

Meals on Wheels Ms Jean Civil, tel.: 01506 777345

Western Isles

Comhairle nan Eilean Siar, Council Offices, Sandwick Road, Stornoway, Isle of Lewis, HS1 2BW, tel.: 01851 703773 (0900-1700) ext 330

Emergencies, tel.: 01851 701702 (1700-0900)

Mr Malcolm Smith, Director

Child Protection Service Mr Iain Macaulay, Depute Director of Social Work, tel.: 01851 703773 ext 334

Home Care Service Mr John Edward, tel.: 01851 709600

Offshore

Guernsey

Guernsey Social Care Services, D.O.K. House, Le Vauquiedor, St Andrews, Guernsey, GY6 8TW, tel.: 01481 725241 ext 4747 (0830-1645)

Mrs Sue Bourne, Community Team Manager - District Nurses, tel.: 01481 725241 ext 5254

Adult Social Services Mrs Tina Poxon, Director

Child Protection Service Mrs Jackie Gallienne, Senior Manager - Community & Maternity Services, tel.: 01481 729021

Child Protection Service Mrs Debbie Pittman, Manager Health Visiting, tel.: 01481 725241 ext 5247

Home Care Service Mrs Sue Spaven, Community Team Manager, tel.: 01481 725241 ext 4713

Meals on Wheels Mrs Janet Sherwill (WRVS - Bailiwick Organiser), tel.: 01481 247518

Residential Homes Mrs Sandra Jones, Inspector (Registration & Inspection), tel.: 01481 725241 ext 4555

Social Work Team Mrs Kay Sykes, Community Team Manager, tel.: 01481 725241 ext 3313

Isle of Man

Department of Health & Social Security, Social Services Division, Hillary House, Prospect Hill, Douglas, IM1 1EQ, tel.: 01624 686179 (0915 -1700 Mon-Thurs, -1630 Fri)

Mr David Cooke, Director

Emergencies, tel.: 01624 631212 (24 hours)

Jersey

Social Services, Maison Le Pape, The Parade, St Helier, Jersey, JE2 3PO, tel.: 01534 623526 (0830-1700)

Ms M Baudains, Directorate Manager, Social Services

Emergencies, tel.: 01534 612612 (out of hours)

Child Protection Service Duty Officer, Out of Hours Tel: 01534 612612, tel.: 01534 623500

Home Care Service Ms Karen Huchet, tel.: 01534 789950, Director

Looked After Children Duty Officer, Out of Hours Tel: 01534 612612, tel.: 01534 623500

Meals on Wheels Mrs M Becquet, tel.: 01534 851468

Residential Homes Mrs C Blackwood, tel.: 01534 623719, Head of Registration/Inspection

Social Services: Northern Ireland

Eastern (Northern Ireland)
Eastern Health & Social Services Board, Champion House, 12-22 Linenhall Street, Belfast, BT2 8BS, tel.: 02890 321 313 (0800-1700)
Mr Hugh Connor, Director
Emergencies, tel.: 028 9056 5444
Mr Peter Gibson, Deputy Director
Ms Bernie McNally (North & West Belfast Trust), Director of Social Work, tel.: 02890 327 156
Mr Stephen O'Brien (South & East Belfast Trust), Director of Social Work, tel.: 02890 565 555
Ms Marion Reynolds, Deputy Director
Mrs Kate Thompson (Down Lisburn Trust), Director of Social Work, tel.: 02892 665 181
Mr Cecil Worthington (Ulster Community & Hospitals Trust), Director of Social Work, tel.: 02891 816 666

Northern (Northern Ireland)
Northern Health & Social Services Board, County Hall, 182 Galgorm Road, Ballymena, Co Antrim, BT42 1QB, tel.: 028 2566 2218 (0900-1700), web site: www.nhssb.n-i.nhs.uk
Mr Seamus McErlean, Residential & Nursing Homes Inspection, tel.: 028 93 354848
Out of Hours Social Work Service, tel.: 028 94 468833
Mr Pat Purvis (Northern Health & Social Services Board), Smoking Cessation, tel.: 028 25 311168, Co-ordinator
Mrs Rosemary Simpson (Homefirst Community Trust), Social Work & Children's Services, tel.: 028 25 653377, Director
Adult Social Services Ms Margaret Gordon (Causeway Health & Social Services Trust), tel.: 028 276 66600, Director
Adult Social Services Mr Seamus Logan, Travellers & Asylum Seekers, tel.: 028 2531 1228, Assistant Director
Adult Social Services Mr Martin Sloan (Homefirst Community Trust), tel.: 028 25 653377, Director
Child Protection/Looked After Children Ms Rosemary Simpson (Homefirst), tel.: 028 2565 3377
Child Protection/Looked After Children Mr John Toner (Causeway), tel.: 028 2766 6600
Children's Services Mr John Toner (Causeway Health & Social Services Trust), Also Acting Director of Social Work, tel.: 028 2766 6600, Assistant Director
Home Care/Meals on Wheels Ms Margaret Gordon (Causeway), tel.: 028 2766 6600
Home Care/Meals on Wheels Mr Martin Sloan (Homefirst), tel.: 028 2565 3377
Homeless Families Northern Ireland Housing Executive, tel.: 028 2565 3399
Smoking Cessation Ms Pat Purvis, NHSSB, tel.: 028 2531 1168
Social Services Mr Kevin Keenan, tel.: 028 2531 1217, Acting Director

Southern (Northern Ireland)
Southern Health & Social Services Board, Tower Hill, Armagh, BT61 9DR, tel.: 028 3741 0041 (0900-1700)
Ms Carol Burns, Office Manager, tel.: 028 3741 4610
Emergencies, tel.: 028 8772 2821 (Dungannon)
Emergencies, tel.: 028 3833 4444 (Portadown)
Emergencies, tel.: 028 3083 5000 (Newry)
Ms Fionnuala McAndrew, Director
Home Care Service Ms Marian Corrigan, tel.: 028 3741 4612
Residential Homes Mr Malcolm Allen, tel.: 028 9056 3700, Head of Registration/Inspection

Western (Northern Ireland)
Western Health & Social Services Board, Area Board Headquarters, 15 Gransha Park, Clooney Road, Londonderry, BT47 1TG, tel.: 028 7186 0086 (0900-1700 Mon-Fri)
Prof Dominic Burke, Director
Emergencies, tel.: 028 7134 5171 (24 hours)
Home Care/Meals on Wheels Mr Noel Quigley, tel.: 028 7186 0086
Residential Homes Mrs Josephine Fee, tel.: 028 8224 5828, Manager

Updating Information for the
Directory of Community Health Services

Before a new edition of the Directory is published, questionnaires are sent to managers to update the entries. The Publishers would like to thank all nurse managers and their staff for their continued help. It would also be helpful if users would contact the Publishers at any time with any amendments, additional information or suggestions to be considered for future editions. Please do this by completing the form below.

Please use CAPITALS –

Name of PCT or NHS Trust/ other employing organisation

....

....

Contact name ....

....

Title/Position ....

Speciality (*if applicable*) ....

Office address ....

....

.... Postcode ....

Telephone number .... Extension ....

Any other relevant information/comments on the Directory

....

....

....

....

This information has been supplied by:

Name ....

Title ....

Tel No .... Fax No ....

Signature .... Date ....

Email address: ....

Please return to: PMH Publications, PO Box 100, Chichester, West Sussex PO18 8HD
Fax: 01243 576456   E-mail: rachel.langdon@pmh.uk.com

Useful Addresses & Phone Numbers

2Care - Supporting Older People and People with Mental Health Needs 11 Harwood Road London SW6 4QP, Tel.: 020 7371 0118, Website: www.2care-rsl.org.uk, E-mail: enquiries@2care-rsl.org.uk

AAA (Action Against Allergy)
PO Box 278 Twickenham TW1 4QQ, Tel.: 020 8892 2711, Website: www.actionagainstallergy.co.uk, E-mail: AAA@actionagainstallergy.freeserve.co.uk.

Abbeyfield Society
Abbeyfield House 53 Victoria Street St Albans AL1 3UW, Tel.: 01727 857536, Website: www.abbeyfield.com, E-mail: post@abbeyfield.com.

Acne Support Group
PO Box 9 Newquay TR9 6WG, Tel.: 0870 870 6263, Website: www.stopspots.org, E-mail: alison.dudley@btopenworld.com.

ACT (Association for Children with Life-threatening or Terminal Conditions and their Families)
Orchard House Orchard Lane Bristol BS1 5DT, Tel.: 0117 922 1556, Fax: 0117 930 4707, Help Line: 0845 108 2201, Website: www.act.org.uk, E-mail: info@act.org.uk.

Action Medical Research
Vincent House North Parade Horsham RH12 2DP, Tel.: 01403 210406, Fax: 01403 210541, Website: www.action.org.uk, E-mail: info@action.org.uk.

Action on Elder Abuse
Astral House 1268 London Road Norbury SW16 4ER, Tel.: 020 8765 7000, Help Line: 080 8808 8141.

Action on Smoking and Health (ASH)
102 Clifton Street London EC2A 4HW, Tel.: 020 7739 5902, Website: www.ash.org.uk, E-mail: enquiries@ash.org.uk.

Adoption UK
46 The Green South Bar Street Banbury OX16 9AB, Tel.: 01295 752240, Fax: 01295 752241, Help Line: 0870 7700 450, Website: www.adoptionuk.org, E-mail: admin@adoptionuk.org.uk.

Afasic
2nd Floor 50-52 Great Sutton Street London EC1V ODJ, Tel.: 020 7490 9410, Help Line: 0845 355 5577, Website: www.afasic.org.uk, E-mail: info@afasic.org.uk.

Age Concern England
Astral House 1268 London Road London SW16 4ER, Tel.: 0845 077 0755, Website: www.ageconcern.org.uk.

Age Concern Scotland
Causewayside House Causewayside Edinburgh EH9 1PR, Tel.: 0845 833 0200, Help Line: 0845 125 9732, Website: www.ageconcernscotland.org.uk, E-mail: enquiries@acscot.org.uk.

Al-Anon Family Groups UK & Eire
61 Great Dover Street London SE1 4YF, Tel.: 020 7403 0888, Fax: 020 7378 9910, Website: www.al-anonuk.org.uk, E-mail: alanonuk@aol.com.

Alcohol Concern
Waterbridge House 32-36 Loman Street London SE1 0EE, Tel.: 020 7928 7377, Website: www.alcoholconcern.org.uk.

Alcohol Recovery Project (ARP)
2nd Floor 7 Holyrood Street London SE1 2EL, Tel.: 020 7403 3369, Fax: 020 7357 6712, Website: www.arp-uk.org, E-mail: joyefolu@arp-uk.org.

Alcoholics Anonymous (AA)
General Service Office PO Box 1 Stonebow House Stonebow York YO1 7NJ, Tel.: 01904 644026, Fax: 01904 629091, Help Line: 0845 769 7555, Website: www.alcoholics-anonymous.org.uk.

Allergy UK
3 White Oak Square London Road Swanley BR8 7AG, Tel.: 01322 619 898, Fax: 01322 663 480, Website: www.allergyuk.org, E-mail: Peter@allergyuk.org.

Alzheimer Scotland
22 Drumsheugh Gardens Edinburgh EH3 7RN, Tel.: 0131 243 1453, Fax: 0131 243 1450, Help Line: 0808 808 3000 freeph, Website: www.alzscot.org, E-mail: alzheimer@alzscot.org.

Alzheimer's Society
Gordon House 10 Greencoat Place London SW1P 1PH, Tel.: 020 7306 0606, Fax: 020 7306 0808, Help Line: 0845 306 0898, Website: www.alzheimers.org.uk, E-mail: info@alzheimers.org.uk.

Amalgamated School Nurses' Association (ASNA)
c/o General Secretary - Sheila Munks 4 First Avenue Colwick Nottingham NG4 2DX, Tel.: 0115 912 0062.

Anaphylaxis Campaign
PO Box 275 Farnborough GU14 6SX, Tel.: 01252 542029, Fax: 01252 377140, Website: www.anaphylaxis.org.uk, E-mail: info@anaphylaxis.org.uk.

APEC (Action on Pre-eclampsia)
84-88 Pinner Road Harrow HA1 4HZ, Tel.: 020 8863 3271, Fax: 020 8424 0653, Help Line: 020 8427 4217, Website: www.apec.org.uk, E-mail: mikerich@apec.org.uk.

Arthritis Care
18 Stephenson Way London NW1 2HD, Tel.: 020 7380 6500, Fax: 020 7380 6505, Help Line: 0808 800 4050, Website: www.arthritiscare.org.uk, E-mail: helplines@arthritiscare.org.uk.

Arthritis Research Campaign (arc)
St Mary's Gate Chesterfield S41 7TD, Tel.: 01246 558033, Fax: 01246 558007, Website: www.arc.org.uk, E-mail: info@arc.org.uk.

Association for Continence Advice
Fitwise Management Ltd Drumcrass Hall Bathgate EH48 4JT, Tel.: 01506 811077, Fax: 01506 811477, Website: www.aca.uk.com, E-mail: info@fitwise.co.uk.

Association for Improvements in the Maternity Services (AIMS)
5 Port Hall Road Brighton BN1 5PD, Tel.: 020 8723 4356, Help Line: 01753 652781, Website: www.aims.org.

Association for Post Natal Illness
145 Dawes Road London SW6 7EB, Tel.: 020 7386 0868, Fax: 020 7386 8885, Website: www.apni.org, E-mail: info@apni.org.

Association for Spina Bifida and Hydrocephalus (ASBAH)
Asbah House 42 Park Road Peterborough PE1 2UQ, Tel.: 01733 555 988, Fax: 01733 555985, Website: www.asbah.org, E-mail: info@asbah.org.

Association of Breastfeeding Mothers
PO Box 207 Bridgwater TA6 7YT, Tel.: 0870 401 7711, Website: www.abm.me.uk, E-mail: info@abm.me.uk.

Association of Childrens Hospices
1st Floor, Canningford House 38 Victoria Street Bristol BS1 6BY, Tel.: 0117 989 7820, Fax: 0117 929 1999, Website: www.childhospice.org.uk, E-mail: info@childhospice.org.uk.

Association of Disabled Professionals (ADP)
BCM ADP London WC1N 3XX, Tel.: 01204 431638, Fax: 01204 431638, Website: www.adp.org.uk, E-mail: adp.admin@ntlworld.com.

Association of Medical Secretaries, Practice Managers, Administrators & Receptionists (AMSPAR)
c/o Chief Executive - Tom Brownlie Tavistock House North Tavistock Square London WC1H 9LN, Tel.: 020 7387 6005, Fax: 020 7388 2648, Website: www.amspar.com, E-mail: info@amspar.co.uk.

Association of Nurses in Substance Abuse (ANSA)
37 Star Street Ware SG12 7AA, Tel.: 0870 241 3503, Fax: 01920 462 730, Website: www.ansa.uk.net, E-mail: ansa@profbriefings.co.uk.

Association of Optometrists (AOP)
61 Southwark Street London SE1 0HL, Tel.: 020 7261 9661, Website: www.aop.org.uk.

Association of Radical Midwives
16 Wytham Street Oxford OX1 4SU, Tel.: 01865 248159, Fax: 01865 248159, Website: www.radmid.demon.co.uk, E-mail: sarahmontagu@postmaster.co.uk.

Association of the British Pharmaceutical Industry (ABPI)
12 Whitehall London SW1A 2DY, Tel.: 020 7930 3477, Fax: 020 7747 1411, Website: www.abpi.org.uk, E-mail: abpi@abpi.org.uk.

Association of Young People with Myalgic Encephalopathy (AYME)
PO Box 5766 Milton Keynes MK10 1AQ, Tel.: 08451 232389, Website: www.ayme.org.uk, E-mail: info@ayme.org.uk
Admin Tel No 01908 379737.

Asthma UK
Summit House 70 Wilson Street London EC2A 2DB, Tel.: 020 7786 4900, Help Line: 0845 701 0203, Website: www.asthma.org.uk, E-mail: email via website.

Ataxia UK
Winchester House Kennington Park Cranmer Road London SW9 6EJ, Tel.: 020 7582 1444, Fax: 020 7582 9444, Help Line: 0845 644 0606, Website: www.ataxia.org.uk, E-mail: enquiries@ataxia.org.uk.

BackCare - the charity for healthier backs
16 Elmtree Road Teddington TW11 8ST, Tel.: 020 8977 5474, Fax: 020 8943 5318, Help Line: 08709 500 275, Website: www.backcare.org.uk, E-mail: info@backcare.org.uk.
Leading national charity (with network of local branches) to help people manage and prevent back pain by providing advice, promoting self help, encouraging debate and funding scientific research; runs a telephone helpline and publishes a range of books and leaflets including "The Guide to the Handling of Patients" and "Safer Handling in the Community" and "Carers' Guide".

Barnardo's
Barkingside, Tanners Lane, Ilford IG6 1QG, Tel.: 020 8550 8822.

BASE
c/o 2 Lllys Aneurin Garden Village Gorseinon Swansea SA4 4HW, Tel.: 0845 1300 675, Fax: 0845 2800 104, Website: www.base.org.uk, E-mail: enquiries@base.org.uk.

BDF Newlife
Hemlock Way Cannock WS11 7GF, Tel.: 01543 462 777, Fax: 01543 468 999, Help Line: 08700 707 020, Website: www.bdfnewlife.co.uk, E-mail: info@bdfnewlife.co.uk.

BIBIC - The British Institute for Brain Injured Children
Knowle Hall Bridgwater TA7 8PJ, Tel.: 01278 684060, Fax: 01278 685573, Website: www.bibic.org.uk, E-mail: info@bibic.org.uk.

Useful Addresses & Phone Numbers

BLISS
68 South Lambeth Road London SW8 1RL, Tel.: 0870 7700 337, Fax: 0870 7700 338, Help Line: 0500 618140, Website: www.bliss.org.uk, E-mail: nicolem@bliss.org.uk.

Blood Pressure Association
60 Cranmer Terrace London SW17 0QS, Tel.: 020 8772 4994, Fax: 020 8772 4999, Website: www.bpassoc.org.uk, E-mail: info@bpassoc.org.uk.

bpas (formerly British Pregnancy Advisory Service)
bpas Head Office 4th Floor, Amec House Timothy's Bridge Road Stratford-upon-Avon CV37 9BF, Tel.: 0870 365 5050, Fax: 0870 365 5051, Website: www.bpas.org, E-mail: info@bpas.org.

Brain & Spine Foundation
7 Winchester House Kennington Park Cranmer Road London SW9 6EJ, Tel.: 020 7793 5900, Fax: 020 7793 5939, Help Line: 0808 808 1000, Website: www.brainandspine.org.uk, E-mail: info@brainandspine.org.uk.

Brain Tumour UK
PO Box 94 Cumbria CA28 7WZ, Tel.: 0845 4500 386, Website: www.braintumouruk.org.uk, E-mail: info@braintumouruk.org.uk.

BREAK
Davison House 1 Montague Road Sheringham NR26 8WN, Tel.: 01263 822161, Fax: 01263 822181, Website: www.break-charity.org, E-mail: office@break-charity.org.

Breast Cancer Care
Kiln House 210 New Kings Road London SW6 4NZ, Tel.: 020 7384 2984, Fax: 020 7384 3387, Help Line: 0808 800 6000, Website: www.breastcancercare.org.uk, E-mail: info@breastcancercare.org.uk.

British Acupuncture Council (BAcC)
63 Jeddo Road London W12 9HQ, Tel.: 020 8735 0400, Website: www.acupuncture.org.uk, E-mail: info@acupuncture.org.uk.

British Agency for Adoption & Fostering (BAAF)
Saffron House 6-10 Kirly Street London EC1N 8TS, Tel.: 0207 421 2600, Fax: 0207 421 2601, Website: www.baaf.org.uk, E-mail: mail@baaf.org.uk.

British Association for Counselling and Psychotherapy (BACP)
BACP House 35-37 Albert Street Rugby CV21 2SG, Tel.: 0870 443 5252, Fax: 0870 443 5161, Website: www.bacp.co.uk, E-mail: bacp@bacp.co.uk.

British Association for Service to the Elderly (BASE)
119 Hassell Street Newcastle-under-Lyme ST5 1AX, Tel.: 01782 661033, Fax: 01782 661033, Website: www.base.org.uk, E-mail: enquiries@base.org.uk.

British Association for the Study & Prevention of Child Abuse & Neglect (BASPCAN)
17 Priory Street York YO1 6ET, Tel.: 01904 613605, Fax: 01904 642239, Website: www.baspcan.org.uk, E-mail: baspcan@baspcan.org.uk.

British Association of Dermatologists
4 Fitzroy Square London W1T 5HQ, Tel.: 020 7383 0266, Fax: 020 7388 5263, Website: www.bad.org.uk, E-mail: admin@bad.org.uk.

British Association of Skin Camouflage
Head Office PO Box 202 Macclesfield SK11 6FP, Tel.: 01625 871129, Website: www.skin-camouflage.net, E-mail: basc9@hotmail.com.

British Colostomy Association
15 Station Road Reading RG1 1LG, Tel.: 0118 939 1537, Fax: 0118 956 9095, Help Line: 0800 328 4257, Website: www.bcass.org.uk, E-mail: sue@bcass.org.uk.

British Dental Association (BDA)
64 Wimpole Street London W1G 8YS, Tel.: 020 7935 0875, Website: www.bda.org, E-mail: info@bda.org.

British Dental Health Foundation
Smile House 2 East Union Street Rugby CV22 6AJ, Tel.: 0870 770 4000, Fax: 0870 770 4010, Website: www.dentalhealth.org.uk, E-mail: mail@dentalhealth.org.uk.

British Dermatological Nursing Group
4 Fitzroy Square London W1T 5HQ, Tel.: 020 7383 0266, Website: www.bdng.org.uk, E-mail: bdng@bad.org.uk.

British Geriatrics Society
Marjorie Warren House 31 St John's Square London EC1M 4DN, Tel.: 020 7608 1369, Fax: 020 7608 1041, Website: www.bgs.org.uk, E-mail: Info@bgs.org.uk.

British Heart Foundation
14 Fitzhardinge Street London W1H 6DH, Tel.: 020 7725 0658, Website: www.bhf.org.uk, E-mail: internet@bhf.org.uk.

British Herbal Medicine Association (BHMA)
1 Wickham Road Boscombe Bournemouth BH7 6JX, Tel.: 01202 433691, Fax: 01202 417079, Website: www.bhma.info, E-mail: secretary@bhma.info.

British Homeopathic Association (BHA)
Hahnemann House 29 Park Street West Luton LU1 3BE, Tel.: 0870 444 3950, Fax: 0870 444 3960, Website: www.trusthomeopathy.org, E-mail: info@trusthomeopathy.org.

British Institute of Learning Disabilities (BILD)
Campion House Green Street Kidderminster DY10 1JL, Tel.: 01562 723010, Fax: 01562 723029, Website: www.bild.org.uk, E-mail: enquiries@bild.org.uk.

British Kidney Patient Association (BKPA)
Bordon GU35 9JZ, Tel.: 01420 472021/2, Fax: 01420 475831, Website: www.britishkidney-pa.co.uk.

British Liver Trust
2 Southampton Road Ringwood Hampshire BH24 1HY, Tel.: 0870 7708028, Website: www.britishlivertrust.org.uk, E-mail: info@britishliverturst.org.uk.

British Lung Foundation
73-75 Goswell Road London EC1V 7ER, Tel.: 020 7688 5555, Fax: 020 7688 5556, Website: www.lunguk.org, E-mail: enquires@blf.uk.org.

British Medical Association (BMA)
BMA House Tavistock Square London WC1H 9JP, Tel.: 020 7387 4499, Website: www.bma.org.uk, E-mail: email via website.

British Naturopathic Association (BNA)
Goswell House 2 Goswell Road Street BA16 0JG, Tel.: 01458 840072, Fax: 08707 456985, Help Line: 08707 456984, Website: www.naturopaths.org.uk, E-mail: admin@naturopaths.org.uk.

British Nutrition Foundation (BNF)
High Holborn House 52-54 High Holborn London WC1V 6RQ, Tel.: 020 7404 6504, Website: www.nutrition.org.uk, E-mail: postbox@nutrition.org.uk.

British Organ Donor Society (BODY)
Balsham CB1 6DL, Tel.: 01223 893636, Website: www.argonet.co.uk/body, E-mail: body@argonet.co.uk.

British Polio Fellowship (BPF)
Ground Floor, Unit A Eagle Office Centre The Runway South Ruislip HA4 6SE, Help Line: 0800 0180586, Website: www.britishpolio.org.uk, E-mail: info@britishpolio.org.uk.

British Retinitis Pigmentosa Society (BRPS)
PO Box 350 Buckingham MK18 1GZ, Tel.: 01280 821334, Fax: 01280 815900, Help Line: 0845 123 2354, Website: www.brps.org.uk, E-mail: info@brps.org.uk.

British Society for Music Therapy (BSMT)
61 Church Hill Road East Barnet EN4 8SY, Tel.: 020 8441 6226, Fax: 020 8441 4118, Website: www.bsmt.org, E-mail: info@bsmt.org.

British Society of Clinical Hypnosis
125 Queensgate Bridlington YO16 7JQ, Tel.: 01262 403103, Website: www.bsch.org.uk, E-mail: sec@bsch.org.uk.

British Tinnitus Association (BTA)
Ground Floor Unit 5, Acorn Business Park Woodseats Close Sheffield S8 0TB, Fax: 0114 258 2279, Help Line: 0800 018 0527, E-mail: info@tinnitus.org.uk.

Brittle Bone Society
30 Guthrie Street Dundee DD1 5BS, Tel.: 01382 204446, Fax: 01382 206771, Help Line: 0800 028 2459, E-mail: bbs@brittlebone.org.

Brook Advisory Centres
Brook Central 421 Highgate Studios 53-79 Highgate Road London NW5 1TL, Tel.: 020 7284 6040, Help Line: 0800 018 5023, Website: www.brook.org.uk, E-mail: admin@brookcentres.org.uk.

Camphill Village Trust
Delrow House Hilfield Lane Aldenham Watford WD25 8DJ, Tel.: 01923 856006.

Cancer Care Society
11 The Cornmarket Romsey SO51 8GB, Tel.: 01794 830300, Fax: 01794 518133, Website: www.cancercaresoc.demon.co.uk, E-mail: info@cancercaresoc.demon.co.uk.

Cancer Research UK
PO Box 123 Lincoln's Inn Fields London WC2A 3PX, Tel.: 020 7061 8355, Help Line: 0800 226 237, Website: www.cancerresearchuk.org, E-mail: cancer.info@cancer.org.uk.

CancerBACUP
3 Bath Place Rivington Street London EC2A 3JR, Tel.: 0207 696 9003, Fax: 0207 769 69002, Help Line: 0808 800 1234, Website: cancerbacup.org.uk, E-mail: info@cancerbacup.org.uk.

CancerBACUP (Scotland)
3rd Floor Cranston House 104-114 Argyle Street Glasgow G2 8BW, Tel.: 0141 223 7676, Help Line: 0808 800 1234, Website: www.cancerbacup.org.uk.

Capability Scotland
Advice Service Capability Scotland (ASCS) 11 Ellersly Road Edinburgh EH12 6HY, Tel.: 0131 313 5510, Fax: 0131 346 1681, Website: www.capability-scotland.org.uk, E-mail: ascs@capability-scotland.org.uk.

Cardiomyopathy Association
40 The Metro Centre Tolpits Lane Watford WD18 9SB, Tel.: 01923 249977, Fax: 01923 249987, Website: www.cardiomyopathy.org, E-mail: info@cardiomyopathy.org.
The Cardiomyopathy Association provides support, advice and information for individuals and families suffering from Cardiomyopathy. The Association works to raise awareness amongst health professionals, educational institutions and the general public. It publishes information material, including booklets, videos, posters and CD Roms and runs an annual programme of regional awareness meetings.

Useful Addresses & Phone Numbers

CARE (Cottage and Rural Enterprises Ltd)
9 Weir Road Kibworth LE8 0LQ, Tel.: 0116 279 3225, Fax: 0116 796 384, Website: www.care-ltd.co.uk, E-mail: info@care-ltd.co.uk.

Care Programme Approach Association (CPAA)
c/o CPAA Administrator Walton Hospital Whitecotes Lane Chesterfield S40 3HW, Tel.: 01246 515975, Fax: 01246 515976, Website: www.cpaa.org.uk, E-mail: cpa.association@chesterfieldpct.nhs.uk.
Acting as a managed network, collecting, analysing and disseminating information on CPA to members; giving relevant support to all involved in the operation of CPA and care management; developing and influencing the provision of relevant training to all involved in the operation of CPA and care management; developing/sharing good practice regionally and nationally.

CAREconfidential
Tel.: 01256 817683, Help Line: 0800 028 2228, Website: www.careconfidential.com, E-mail: admin@careconfidential.com.

Carers UK
20-25 Glasshouse Yard London EC1A 4JT, Tel.: 020 7490 8818, Help Line: 0808 808 7777, Website: www.carersuk.org, E-mail: info@carersuk.org.

Catholic Children's Society (Westminster)
73 St Charles Square London W10 6EJ, Tel.: 020 8969 5305, Fax: 020 8960 1464, Website: www.cathchild.org.uk, E-mail: jrichards@cathchild.org.uk.

Challenging Behaviour Foundation
c/o Friends Meeting House Northgate Rochester ME1 1LS, Tel.: 01634 838739, Fax: 01634 828588, E-mail: karen@thecbf.org.uk.

Changing Faces
33-37 University Street London WC1E 6JN, Tel.: 0845 4500275, Website: www.changingfaces.org.uk.

Chartered Society of Physiotherapy (CSP)
Enquiry Handling Unit 14 Bedford Row London WC1R 4ED, Tel.: 020 7306 6666, Fax: 020 7306 6611, Website: www.csp.org.uk, E-mail: enquiries@csp.org.uk.

Child Accident Prevention Trust
4th Floor, Cloister Court 22-26 Farringdon Lane London EC1R 3AJ, Tel.: 020 7608 3828, Website: www.capt.org.uk, E-mail: safe@capt.org.uk.

Child Growth Foundation (CGF)
2 Mayfield Avenue Chiswick London W4 1PW, Tel.: 020 8995 0257, Help Line: 020 8994 7625, Website: www.heightmatters.org.uk & www.factsoflife.org.uk.

Child Health Records Department SSAFA Forces Help
HQ British Forces Germany Health Service British Forces Health Complex BFPO 40, Tel.: 0049 2161 908 2351.

Child Poverty Action Group (CPAG)
94 White Lion Street London N1 9PF, Tel.: 020 7837 7979, Fax: 020 7837 6414, Website: www.cpag.org.uk.

ChildLine
45 Folgate Street London E1 6BRT, Tel.: 0207 650 3200, Help Line: 0800 1111 (24 hrs), Website: www.childline.org.uk, E-mail: kholden@childline.org.uk.

Children's Liver Disease Foundation
36 Great Charles Street Birmingham B3 3JY, Tel.: 0121 212 3839.

Cleft Lip and Palate Association (CLAPA)
1st Floor, Green Man Tower 332B Goswell Road London EC1V 7LQ, Tel.: 0207 833 4883, Fax: 0207 431 8881, Website: www.clapa.com, E-mail: info@clapa.com.

CLIC Sargent
Griffin House 161 Hammersmith Road London W6 8SG, Tel.: 0208 752 2800, Fax: 0208 752 2806, Help Line: 0800 197 0068, Website: www.clicsargent.org.uk, E-mail: info@clicsargent.org.uk.

Coeliac UK
Suite A-D Octagon Court High Wycombe HP11 2HS, Tel.: 01494 437278, Fax: 01494 474349, Help Line: 0870 4448804, Website: www.coeliac.co.uk, E-mail: helpline@coeliac.co.uk.

Community Practitioners' & Health Visitors' Association
33-37 Moreland Street London EC1V 8HA, Tel.: 020 7505 3000, Website: www.amicus-cphva.org.

Contact a Family
209-211 City Road London EC1V 1JN, Tel.: 020 7608 8700, Fax: 020 7608 8701, Help Line: 0808 808 3555, Website: www.cafamily.org.uk, E-mail: info@cafamily.org.uk.

Continence Foundation
307 Hatton Square 16 Baldwins Gardens London EC1N 7RJ, Tel.: 020 7404 6875, Fax: 020 7404 6876, Help Line: 0845 3450165, Website: www.continence-foundation.org.uk, E-mail: continence-help@dial.pipex.com.

Counsel and Care
Twyman House 16 Bonny Street London NW1 9PG, Tel.: 020 7241 8555.

Couple Counselling Scotland
18 York Place Edinburgh EH1 3EP, Tel.: 0845 119 6088, Fax: 0845 119 6089, Website: www.couplecounselling.org, E-mail: enquiries@couplecounselling.org.

Useful Addresses & Phone Numbers

Crossroads Caring for Carers
Information & Communications Department 3rd Floor 49 Charles Street Cardiff CF10 2GD, Tel.: 0845 450 0350, Fax: 029 2022 2311, Website: www.crossroads.org.uk, E-mail: communications@crossroads.org.uk.

Cystic Fibrosis Trust
11 London Road Bromley BR1 1BY, Tel.: 020 8464 7211, Website: www.cftrust.org.uk, E-mail: enquiries@cftrust.org.uk.

DEBRA
Debra House 13 Wellington Business Park Duke's Ride Crowthorne RG45 6LS, Tel.: 01344 771961, Fax: 01344 762661, Website: www.debra.org.uk, E-mail: debra@debra.org.uk.

Department for Education and Employment (DFEE)
Sanctuary Buildings Great Smith Street London SW1P 3BT, Tel.: 0870 000 2288, Website: www.dfes.gov.uk, E-mail: info@dfes.gsi.gov.uk.

Department of Health
Head of Knowledge Management, Complaints & Public Enquiries Customer Service Directorate, Richmond House 79 Whitehall London SW1A 2NS, Tel.: 020 7210 3000, Fax: 020 7210 5525, Help Line: 020 7210 4850, E-mail: dh@dhmail.gov.uk.

Department of Health, Social Services and Public Safety, N Ireland
Castle Buildings Upper Newtownards Road Belfast BT4 3SJ, Tel.: 028 9052 0000, Website: www.dhsspsni.gov.uk.

Depression Alliance (DA)
35 Westminster Bridge Road London SE1 7JB, Help Line: 0845 123 2320, Website: www.depressionalliance.org, E-mail: information@depressionalliance.org.

Diabetes UK
10 Parkway Camden London NW1 7AA, Tel.: 020 7424 1000, Help Line: 0845 120 2960, Website: www.diabetes.org.uk, E-mail: info@diabetes.org.uk.

DIAL UK - The Disability Helpline
St Catherine's Tickhill Road Doncaster DN4 8QN, Tel.: 01302 310 123, Fax: 01302 310 404, Website: www.dialuk.org.uk, E-mail: enquiries@dialuk.org.uk.

Disability Alliance
Universal House 88-94 Wentworth Street London E1 7SA, Tel.: 020 7247 8776, Fax: 020 7247 8765, Website: www.disabilityalliance.org, E-mail: office.da@dial.pipex.com.

Disabled Drivers' Association
National Headquarters Ashwellthorpe Norwich NR16 1EX, Tel.: 0870 770 3333, Fax: 01508 488173, Website: www.dda.org.uk, E-mail: hq@dda.org.uk.

Disabled Living Foundation (DLF)
380-384 Harrow Road London W9 2HU, Tel.: 020 7289 6111, Help Line: 0845 130 9177, Website: www.dlf.org.uk, E-mail: dlfinfo@dlf.org.uk.

Disabled Student Services
The Open University Hammerwood Gate Kents Hill Milton Keynes MK7 6AA, Tel.: 01908 653745, Website: www.open.ac.uk/disability, E-mail: osd-wh@open.ac.uk.

Down's Heart Group
PO Box 4260 Dunstable LU6 2ZT, Tel.: 0845 166 8061, Fax: 0845 166 8061, Website: www.dhg.org.uk, E-mail: info@dhg.org.uk.

Down's Syndrome Association
The Langdon Down Centre 2A Langdon Park Teddington TW11 9PS, Tel.: 0845 2300372, Website: www.downssyndrome.org.uk, E-mail: info@downs-syndrome.org.uk.

Drugaid
16 Clive Street Caerphilly CF83 1GE, Tel.: 029 2086 8675, Website: www.drugaidcymru.com, E-mail: office@drugaidcymru.com.

DrugScope
32-36 Loman Street London SE1 0EE, Tel.: 0870 774 3682, Fax: 020 7922 1771, Website: www.drugscope.org.uk, E-mail: info@drugscope.org.uk.

Eating Disorders Association (EDA)
Wensum House 103 Prince of Wales Road Norwich NR1 1DW, Tel.: 0870 770 3256, Fax: 01603 664915, Help Line: 0845 634 1414, Website: www.edauk.com, E-mail: info@edauk.com.

Education for Health
The Athenaeum 10 Church Street Warwick CV34 4AB, Tel.: 01926 493313, Fax: 01926 493224, Website: www.educationforhealth.org.uk, E-mail: enquiries@educationforhealth.org.uk.

ENABLE Scotland
6th Floor 7 Buchanan Street Glasgow G1 3HL, Tel.: 0141 226 4541, Help Line: 0141 226 4541, Website: www.enable.org.uk, E-mail: enable@enable.org.uk.

Epilepsy Action
New Anstey House Gate Way Drive Yeadon Leeds LS19 7XY, Tel.: 0113 210 8800, Fax: 0113 391 0300, Help Line: 0808 800 5050, Website: www.epilepsy.org.uk, E-mail: epilepsy@epilepsy.org.uk.

Epilepsy Nurses Association (ESNA)
Cornwall Partnership NHS Trust, West Resource Centre The Kernow Building, Wilson Way, Pool Redruth TR15 3QE, Tel.: 0207 815 5984, Website: www.esnaonline.org.uk, E-mail: somersjc@sbu.ac.uk.

Useful Addresses & Phone Numbers

Epilepsy Scotland
48 Govan Road Glasgow G51 1JL, Tel.: 0141 427 4911,
Help Line: 0808 800 2200, Website:
www.epilepsyscotland.org.uk, E-mail:
enquiries@epilepsyscotland.org.uk.

ERIC (Education and Resources for Improving Childhood Continence)
34 Old School House Britannia Road Kingswood Bristol
BS15 8DB, Tel.: 0117 960 3060, Help Line: 0845 370 8008,
Website: www.eric.org.uk/www.trusteric.org, E-mail:
info@eric.org.uk.

Ex-Services Mental Welfare Society
Tyrwhitt House Oak Lawn Road Leatherhead KT22 0BX,
Tel.: 01372 841680, Website: wstso1@combatstress.org.uk.

Ex-Services Mental Welfare Society or Combat Stress
Hollybush House Hollybush By Ayr KA6 7EA, Tel.: 01292
560322.

Family Fund
PO Box 50 York YO1 9ZX, Help Line: 0845 130 45 42,
Website: www.familyfund.org.uk, E-mail:
adh@familyfund.org.uk.

Fellowship of Depressives Anonymous (FDA)
Box FDA Self Help Nottingham Ormiston House 32-36
Pelham Street NG1 2EG, Tel.: 0870 774 4320, Fax: 0870
774 4319, Website: www.depressionanon.co.uk, E-mail:
fdainfo@hotmail.co.uk.

Foresight-Preconception
178 Hawthorn Road West Bognor PO21 2UY, Tel.: 01243
868001, Fax: 01243 868180, Website: www.foresight-
preconception.org.uk.

Foundation for the Study of Infant Deaths
Artillery House 11-19 Artillery Row London SW1P 1RT, Tel.:
020 7222 8001, Fax: 020 7222 8002, Help Line: 020 7233
2090, Website: www.sids.org.uk/fsid, E-mail:
fsid@sids.org.uk.

fpa (Family Planning Association)
2-12 Pentonville Road London N1 9FP, Tel.: 020 7837
5432, Fax: 020 7837 3034, Help Line: 0845 310 1334,
Website: www.fpa.org.uk.

Fragile X Society
Rood End House 6 Stortford Road Great Dunmow CM6
1DA, Tel.: 01371 875100, Fax: 01371 859915, Website:
www.fragilex.org.uk, E-mail: info@fragilex.org.uk.

Frederick Andrew Convalescent Trust
Andrew and Co St Swithins Square Lincoln LN2 1HB, Tel.:
01522 512123, Website: www.fact-online.co.uk, E-mail:
karen.armitage@andrew-felicity.solicitors.co.uk.

Gamblers Anonymous
Tel.: 08700 50 8880 24 hours a day,
Website: www.gamblersanonymous.org.uk.

Gardening for Disabled Trust
Petteridge Place Brenchley TN12 7PQ, 01892 722 030.

General Chiropractic Council
44 Wicklow Street LONDON WC1X 9HL, Tel.: 020 7713
5155, Fax: 020 7713 5844, Website: www.gcc-uk.org, E-
mail: enquiries@gcc-uk.org.

General Council and Register of Naturopaths (GCRN)
Goswell House 2 Goswell Road Street BA16 0JG, Tel.:
08707 456984, Fax: 08707 456985, Help Line: 08707
456984, Website: www.naturopathy.org.uk, E-mail:
admin@naturopathy.org.uk.

General Hypnotherapy Register
PO Box 204 Lymington SO41 6WP, Tel.: 01590 683770,
Website: www.general-hypnotherapy-register.com, E-mail:
info@general-hypnotherapy-register.com.

General Medical Council (GMC)
Regent's Place 350 Euston Road London NW1 3JN, Tel.:
0845 357 8001, Website: www.gmc-uk.org, E-mail:
gmc@gmc-uk.org.

Gingerbread (Association for One Parent Families)
307 Borough High Street London SE1 1JH, Help Line: 0800
018 4318.

Glencraft
The Royal Aberdeen Workshops For The Blind & Disabled
132 Wellington Road Aberdeen AB12 3LQ, Tel.: 01224
873366, Fax: 01224 894659, Website: www.glencraft.co.uk,
E-mail: info@glencraft.co.uk.

Guideposts Trust Ltd
Two Rivers Station Lane Witney OX28 4BH, Tel.: 01993
772886, Website: guidepoststrust.org.uk, E-mail:
gpt@guidepoststrust.org.uk.

Haemochromatosis Society
Hollybush House Hadley Green Road Barnet EN5 5PR,
Tel.: 020 8449 1363, Fax: 020 8449 1363, Website:
www.haemochromatosis.org.uk, E-mail:
info@haemochromatosis.org.uk.

Haemophilia Society
1st Floor Petersham House 57a Halton Gardens London
EC1N 8JG, Tel.: 02078 311 020, Fax: 0207 405 4824,
Website: www.haemophilia.org.uk, E-mail:
info@haemophilia.org.uk.

**Halliwick Association of Swimming Therapy (Halliwick
AST)** c/o Hon Sec, Eric Dilley ADKC Centre, Whitstable
House Silchester Road London W10 6SB, Tel.: 020 8968
7609, Website: www.halliwick.org.uk.

Useful Addresses & Phone Numbers

Havens Hospices
Fair Havens Hospice & Little Havens Children's Hospice Administration & Appeals, Stuart House 47 Second Avenue Westcliff on Sea SS0 8HX, Tel.: 01702 220 350, Fax: 01702 220 351, Website: www.havenshospices.org.uk, E-mail: stuarthouse@havenshospices.org.uk.

Headway - the brain injury association
4 King Edward Court King Edward Street Nottingham NG1 1EW, Tel.: 0115 924 0800, Fax: 0115 958 4446, Help Line: 0808 800 2244, Website: www.headway.org.uk, E-mail: enquiries@headway.org.uk.

Health & Safety Executive (HSE)
Enquiry Services Team Room 001, Magdalen House Stanley Precinct Bootle L20 3QZ, Tel.: 0845 3450055, Fax: 02920 853260, E-mail: hseinformationservices@natbrit.com.

Health Professions Council (HPC)
Park House 184 Kennington Park Road London SE11 4BU, Tel.: 020 7582 0866, Fax: 020 7820 9684, Website: www.hpc-uk.org, E-mail: info@hpc-uk.org.

Health Promotion Library
National Assembly for Wales Ffynnon-las, Ty Glas Avenue Llanishen Cardiff CF4 5DZ, Tel.: 02920 681 239, Website: cmo.wales.gov.uk, E-mail: hplibrary@wales.gsi.gov.uk.

Health Scotland
Woodburn House Canaan Lane Edinburgh EH10 4SG, Tel.: 0131 536 5500, Website: www.healthscotland.com, E-mail: publications@health.scot.nhs.uk.

Health Service Commissioner (Ombudsman)
Millbank Tower Millbank London SW1P 4QP, Tel.: 0845 015 4033, Fax: 020 7217 4000, Website: www.ombudsman.org.uk, E-mail: phso.enquiries@ombudsman.org.uk.

Hearing Concern
95 Grays Inn Road London WC1X 8TX, Tel.: 0845 0744 600, Fax: 0207 440 9872, Website: www.hearingconcern.org.uk, E-mail: info@hearingconcern.org.uk.

Help the Aged
207-221 Pentonville Road London N1 9UZ, Tel.: 020 7278 1114, Fax: 020 7278 1116, Website: www.helptheaged.org.uk.

Herpes Viruses Association
41 North Road London N7 9DP, Tel.: 020 7607 9661, Help Line: 0845 123 2305, Website: www.herpes.org.uk, E-mail: info@herpes.org.uk.

Hospice Information Service at St Christopher's
St Christopher's Hospice 51-59 Lawrie Park Road Sydenham London SE26 6DZ, Tel.: 020 8768 4500, Website: www.stchristophers.org.uk, E-mail: info@stchristophers.org.uk.

Huntington's Disease Association
Down Stream Building 1 London Bridge London SE1 9BG, Tel.: 0207 0221 950, E-mail: info@hda.org.uk.

Hyperactive Children's Support Group (HACSG)
71 Whyke Lane Chichester PO19 7PD, Tel.: 01243 539966, Fax: 01243 539966, Website: www.hacsg.org.uk.

I CAN
4 Dyer's Buildings Holborn London EC1N 2QP, Tel.: 0845 225 4071, Fax: 0845 225 4072, Website: www.ican.org.uk.

ia The Ileostomy and Internal Pouch Support Group
Peverill House 1-5 Mill Road Ballyclare BT39 9DR, Tel.: 028 9334 4043, Fax: 028 9332 4606, Help Line: 0800 0184724, Website: www.the-ig.org.uk, E-mail: info@the-ia.org.uk.

Incontact
United House North Road London N7 9DP, Tel.: 0870 770 3246, Website: www.incontact.org, E-mail: info@incontact.org.

Independent Age - Royal United Kingdom Beneficent Association (Rukba)
6 Avonmore Road London W14 8RL, Tel.: 020 7605 4200, Fax: 020 7605 4201, Website: www.independentage.org.uk, E-mail: charity@independentage.org.uk.

Infertility Network UK
Charter House 43 St Leonards Road Bexhill on Sea TN40 1JA, Tel.: 08701 188088, Fax: 01424 731858, Website: www.infertilitynetworkuk.com, E-mail: admin@infertilitynetworkuk.com.

Institute for Complementary Medicine (ICM)
PO Box 194 London SE16 7QZ, Tel.: 020 7237 5165, Website: www.I-c-m.org.uk.

International Glaucoma Association (IGA)
Woodcote House 15 Highpoint Business Villlage Henwood Ashford TN24 8DH, Tel.: 0870 6091870 / 71, Website: www.glaucoma-association.com, E-mail: info@iga.org.uk. *The IGA telephone helpline offers information and emotional support (9.30 am to 5.00 pm Monday to Friday). Free information leaflets and posters are available singularly or in quantity for display and distribution. Other publications include members' newsletters and 'Glaucoma Forum' magazine for medical professionals. We also have an informative website.*

Useful Addresses & Phone Numbers

Jewish Deaf Association (JDA)
Julius Newman House Woodside Park Road, Off High Road North Finchley London N12 8RP, Tel.: 020 8446 0502, Fax: 0208 445 7451, Website: www.jewishdeaf.org.uk, E-mail: jda@dircon.co.uk.

Joint Committee of the Order of St John and the British Red Cross Society
5th Floor 22-26 Albert Embankment London SE1 7TJ, Tel.: 020 7735 9800.

Kidney Research UK
Kings Chambers Priestgate Peterborough PE1 1FG, Tel.: 01733 704650, Fax: 01733 704699, Help Line: 0845 300 1499, Website: www.kidneyresearchuk.org, E-mail: info@kidneyresearchuk.org.

King's Fund
11-13 Cavendish Square London W1G 0AN, Tel.: 020 7307 2400, Fax: 020 7307 2801, Website: www.kingsfund.org.uk, E-mail: information@kingsfund.org.uk.

La Leche League (Great Britain) - Breastfeeding Help & Information (LLLGB)
PO Box 29 West Bridgford Nottingham NG2 7NP, Help Line: 0845 120 2918, Website: www.laleche.org.uk.

Leonard Cheshire
30 Millbank London SW1P 4QD, Tel.: 020 7802 8200, Fax: 020 7802 8250, Website: www.leonard-cheshire.org, E-mail: info@london.leonard-cheshire.org.uk.

Let's Face It
72 Victoria Avenue Westgate-on-Sea CT8 8BH, Tel.: 01843 833724, Website: www.lets-face-it.org.uk, E-mail: chrisletsfaceit@aol.com & Julia@Julia21.wanadoo.co.uk.

Leukaemia Care
One Birch Court Blackpole East Worcester WR3 8SG, Tel.: 01905 755977, Fax: 01905 755166, Help Line: 0800 1696680, Website: www.leukaemiacare.org.uk, E-mail: info@leukaemiacare.org.uk.

Leukaemia Research Fund
43 Great Ormond Street London WC1N 3JJ, Tel.: 020 7405 0101, Website: www.lrf.org.uk, E-mail: info@lrf.org.uk.

Life
Life House Newbold Terrace Leamington Spa CV32 4EA, Tel.: 01926 421587/311667, Fax: 01926 336497, Help Line: 0800-849-4545, Website: www.lifecharity.org.uk, E-mail: info@lifecharity.org.uk.

Listening Books
12 Lant Street London SE1 1QH, Tel.: 020 7407 9417, Fax: 020 7403 1377, Website: www.listening-books.org.uk, E-mail: info@listening-books.org.uk.

Lymphoedema Support Network
St Luke's Crypt Sydney Street London SW3 6NH, Tel.: 020 7351 4480, Fax: 020 7349 9809, Website: www.lymphoedema.org/lsn, E-mail: adminlsn@lymphoedema.freeserve.co.uk.

Lymphoma Association
PO Box 386 Aylesbury HP20 2GA, Tel.: 01296 619400, Fax: 01296 619414, Help Line: 0808 808 5555, Website: www.lymphoma.org.uk, E-mail: information@lymphoma.org.uk.

Macmillan Cancer Relief
89 Albert Embankment London SE1 7UQ, Tel.: 020 7840 7840, Fax: 020 7840 7841, Help Line: 0808 808 2020, Website: www.macmillan.org.uk, E-mail: media@macmillan.org.uk.

Macular Disease Society
PO Box 1870 Andover SP10 9AD, Tel.: 01264 350 551, Fax: 01264 350 558, Help Line: 0845 241 2041, Website: www.maculardisease.org, E-mail: info@maculardisease.org.

Marfan Association UK
Rochester House 5 Aldershot Road Fleet GU51 3NG, Tel.: 01252 810472, Fax: 01252 810473, Website: www.marfan.org.uk, E-mail: marfan@tinyonline.co.uk.

Margaret Blackwood Housing Association
Craigievar House 77 Craigmount Brae Edinburgh EH12 8XF, Tel.: 0131 317 7227, Fax: 0131 317 7294, Website: www.mbha.org.uk, E-mail: info@mbha.org.uk.
Housing association providing specially designed and adapted houses, flats, supported accommodation and flexible, individually-tailored support services for disabled people and their families in community settings in Scotland. 1500 houses are located in 84 schemes throughout mainland Scotland.

Marie Curie Cancer Care
89 Albert Embankment London SE1 7TP, Tel.: 020 7599 7777, Fax: 020 7599 7788, Website: www.mariecurie.org.uk, E-mail: info@mariecurie.org.uk.

Marie Stopes International
153-157 Cleveland Street London W1T 6QW, Tel.: 020 7574 7355, Website: www.mariestopes.org.uk, E-mail: services@mariestopes.org.uk.

Marriage Care
Clitherow House 1 Blythe Mews Blythe Road London W14 0NW, Tel.: 020 7371 1341, Help Line: 0845 660 6000, Website: www.marriagecare.org.uk, E-mail: Angela@marriagecare.org.uk.

Useful Addresses & Phone Numbers

MDF Bi Polar Organisation (was Manic Depression Fellowship)
21 St George's Road London SE1 6ES, Tel.: 020 7793 2600, Fax: 020 7793 2639, Website: www.mdf.org.uk, E-mail: mdf@mdf.org.uk.

MedicAlert Foundation
1 Bridge Wharf 156 Caledonian Road London N1 9UU, Help Line: 0800 581420, Website: www.medicalert.org.uk, E-mail: info@medicalert.org.uk.

Mencap (Royal Society for Mentally Handicapped Children and Adults)
4 Swan Courtyard Coventry Road Birmingham B26 1BU, Tel.: 020 7454 0454, Help Line: 0808 808 1111, Website: www.mencap.org.uk / www.askmencap.info, E-mail: information@mencap.org.uk.

Meniere's Society
The Rookery Surrey Hills Business Park Wotton Dorking RH5 6QT, Tel.: 01306 876883, Help Line: 0845 120 2975.

Meningitis Research Foundation
Midland Way Thornbury Bristol BS35 2BS, Tel.: 01454 281811, Fax: 01454 281094, Help Line: 080 8800 3344 -24 hr, Website: www.meningitis.org..

Meningitis Trust
Fern House Bath Road Stroud GL5 3TJ, Tel.: 01453 768000, Help Line: 0845 6000 800, Website: www.meningitis-trust.org, E-mail: info@meningitis-trust.org.

Mental Health Foundation incorporating The Foundation for People with Learning Disabilities
9th Floor, Sea Containers House 20 Upper Ground London SE1 9QB, Tel.: 0207 803 1100, Fax: 0207 803 1111, Website: www.mentalhealth.org.uk, E-mail: mhf@mhf.org.uk.

Mental Health Nurses Association
Cals Meyn Grove Lane Hinton Chippenham SN14 8HF, Tel.: 07860 702303, Website: www.amicus-mhna.org, E-mail: Brian.Rogers@amicustheunion.org.

Metropolitan Society for the Blind
Lantern House 102 Bermondsey Street London SE1 3UB, Tel.: 020 7403 6184, Fax: 020 7234 0708, Website: www.msb.gb.com, E-mail: enquiries@msb.gb.com.

Mind Cymru (National Association for Mental Health)
3rd Floor Quebec House, Castlebridge Cowbridge Road East Cardiff CF11 9AB, Tel.: 029 2039 5123 Admin, Fax: 029 2034 6585, Help Line: 0845 7660163, Website: www.mind.org.uk, E-mail: info@mind.org.uk.

Mobility Information Service (MIS)
20 Burton Close Dawley Telford TF4 2BX, Tel.: 01743 340269, Website: www.mis.org, E-mail: mis@nmcuk.freeserve.co.uk.

Mobilise Organisation – The Disabled Drivers' Motor Club
Cottingham Way Thrapston NN14 4PL, Tel.: 01832 734724, Website: ddmc.org.uk.

Motability
Goodman House Station Approach Harlow CM20 2ET, Tel.: 0845 456 4566, Fax: 01279 632000, Website: www.motability.co.uk.

Motor Neurone Disease Association
PO Box 246 Northampton NN1 2PR, Tel.: 01604 250505, Fax: 01604 624726, Help Line: 08457 626262, Website: www.mndassociation.org, E-mail: care@mndassociation.org.

Multiple Births Foundation
Hammersmith House, Level 4 Queen Charlotte's & Chelsea Hospital Du Cane Road London W12 0HS, Tel.: 020 8383 3519, Fax: 020 8383 3041, Website: www.multiplebirths.org.uk, E-mail: mbf@hhnt.nhs.uk.

Multiple Sclerosis National Therapy Centres
Bradbury House 155 Barkers Lane Bedford MK41 9RX, Tel.: 01234 325781, Website: www.ms-selfhelp.org.

Multiple Sclerosis Resource Centre (MSRC)
7 Peartree Business Centre Peartree Road Stanway Colchester CO3 0JN, Tel.: 01206 505444, Help Line: 0800 783 0518, Website: www.msrc.co.uk, E-mail: info@msrc.co.uk.

Multiple Sclerosis Society of Great Britiain and Northern Ireland (MS Society)
MS National Centre 372 Edgware Road London NW2 6ND, Tel.: 020 8438 0700, Fax: 020 8438 0878, Help Line: 0808 800 8000, Website: www.mssociety.org.uk, E-mail: webinfoenquiries@mssociety.org.uk.

Multiple Sclerosis Society Scotland
Ratho Park 88 Glasgow Road Ratho Station Edinburgh EH28 8PP, Tel.: 0131 335 4050, Fax: 0131 335 4051, Website: www.mssocietyscotland.org.uk, E-mail: admin@mssocietyscotland.org.uk.

Multiple Sclerosis Trust
Spirella Building Bridge Road Letchworth Garden City SG6 4ET, Tel.: 01462 476700, Fax: 01462 476710, Website: www.mstrust.org.uk, E-mail: info@mstrust.org.uk.

Muscular Dystrophy Campaign
7-11 Prescott Place London SW4 6BS, Tel.: 020 7720 8055, Website: www.muscular-dystrophy.org, E-mail: info@muscular-dystrophy.org.

Myositis Support Group
146 Newtown Road Woolston Southampton SO19 9HR, Tel.: 02380 449708, Fax: 02380 396402, Website: www.myositis.org.uk.

THE DIRECTORY OF
COMMUNITY HEALTH
SERVICES 2006/07

Formerly Directory of Community Nursing

ORDER FORM

PROFESSIONAL,
MANAGERIAL
& HEALTHCARE
PUBLICATIONS LTD

YOUR INDISPENSABLE CONTACT FILE

The contact directory for community practitioners

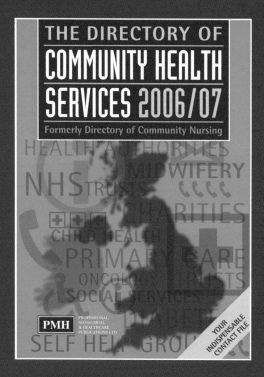

THE DIRECTORY OF
**COMMUNITY HEALTH
SERVICES 2006/07**
Formerly Directory of Community Nursing

HEALTH AUTHORITIES
MIDWIFERY
NHS TRUSTS
CHARITIES
CHILD HEALTH
PRIMARY CARE
ONCOLOGY TRUSTS
SOCIAL SERVICES
DIABETES
SELF HELP GROUPS

PMH PROFESSIONAL, MANAGERIAL & HEALTHCARE PUBLICATIONS LTD

YOUR INDISPENSABLE CONTACT FILE

Completely updated and revised, the *Directory of Community Health Services* 2006/07 (formerly *Directory of Community Nursing*) gives you the essential contact details to make a referral, transfer or discharge. With this unique reference book you can quickly liaise with community nursing staff, midwifery and social services anywhere in the UK.

The town index with this year's Directory covers around 4,000 towns and villages, and also identifies the PCT which serves them.

The Directory gives you the names of nursing and midwifery managers and the addresses and telephone numbers (including emergency out-of-hours contacts) for key community services throughout the UK. These include:

- **District Nursing**
- **Health Visiting** (Child Health Records Administration Bases including Child Protection and Child Health)
- **Community Midwifery**
- **School Nursing**
- **Family Planning**
- **Community Nursing Services for Learning Disabilities**

Your vital link in the chain of patient care

In this edition you will find:

- Extended indexing covering around 4,000 towns and villages
- Loan equipment departments and pharmacy services
- User-friendly format including improvements suggested by you, the users.
- Maps showing new Strategic Health Authorities
- PCT and Social Care Trust changes
- Information on service providers – "which Trust provides what"
- Contact details for practitioners' administrative bases <u>and</u> places of work, where these are different
- Social Services and Social Service Departments, including emergency numbers, home care and meals on wheels
- Names and addresses of useful statutory, professional and voluntary organisations

Managers –

The Directory is an essential tool for all your staff, saving time and helping to avoid damaging delays in referrals and discharges.

Ease your budget by organising bulk orders! Major savings available, bringing down the single copy price to as little as £19.95 – a saving of 33%!!

Generous discounts for NHS bulk orders –

Copies of the Directory are available from the Publishers at the prices shown below, which include postage and packing, assuming a single delivery address for multiple orders.

To order, just complete the form overleaf and return to the Publishers.

Pre-Pub Offer Deadline 23 June

No. of copies	1-9	10+	Pre-Pub
Unit price (£) for NHS and booksellers	£29.95	£19.95	£16.95
The pre-publication offer applies to orders of 10+ copies only			
Unit price (£) for non-NHS orders	£49.95	£34.95	£27.95
The pre-publication offer applies to orders of 10+ copies only			

Your order form

Please send .... copies at £.......... each of ***Directory of Community Health Services***

Name...

Job description/Title ....

Delivery address ....

....

....

.... Postcode..........................

Please provide your e-mail address: ....

Daytime Telephone No...

Order Ref No.................................... Fax No:.............................

I enclose a cheque for the sum of £............... made payable to PMH Publications

Credit Card Payments

Please debit my Visa/Mastercard/Delta (please delete as appropriate)

No. ☐☐☐☐ ☐☐☐☐ ☐☐☐☐ ☐☐☐☐ Security code ☐☐☐

Expiry date ☐☐ / ☐☐

for the sum of £ ....

Name and address of credit card holder (if different to above) ....

....

....

....

.... Postcode ....

If you would like to be invoiced
please enclose an official purchase order

Signature..

Date..

From time to time PMH Publications and other companies may wish to send details of other products and offers to you.
If you do not wish to receive these communications, please tick box ☐

Please return to: PMH Publications, PO Box 100, Chichester, West Sussex PO18 8HD
Tel: +44(0)1243 576444   Fax: +44(0)1243 576456

Useful Addresses & Phone Numbers

Myotonic Dystrophy Support Group
35a Carlton Hill Carlton NG4 1BG, Tel.: 0115 987 5869, Help Line: 0115 987 0080, Website: www.mdsguk.org, E-mail: mdsg@tesco.net.

N. Ireland Assoc for Mental Health
Beacon House 80 University Street Belfast BT7 1HE, Tel.: 028 9032 8474, Fax: 028 9023 4940, Website: www.niamh.co.uk, E-mail: info@niamh.co.uk.

NASPCS (Charity for Incontinent and Stoma Children)
51 Anderson Drive Valley View Park Darvel KA17 0DE, Tel.: 01560 322024, Website: www.naspcs.co.uk, E-mail: john@stoma.freeserve.co.uk.

National Association for Colitis and Crohn's Disease
4 Beaumont House Sutton Road St Albans AL1 5HH, Tel.: 01727 830038, Fax: 01727 862550, Help Line: 0845 130 2233, Website: www.nacc.org.uk, E-mail: nacc@nacc.org.uk.

National Association for the Relief of Paget's Disease (NARPD)
323 Manchester Road Walkden Worsley Manchester M28 3HH, Tel.: 0161 799 4646, Fax: 0161 799 6511, Website: www.paget.org.uk, E-mail: director@paget.org.uk.

National Association of Health Workers for Travellers
Balsall Heath HC Edward Road Balsall Heath Birmingham B12 9LB, Tel.: 0121 446 2300, Fax: 0121 446 5936, E-mail: joanne.davis@hobtpct.nhs.uk.

National Association of Laryngectomy Clubs (NALC)
Lower Ground Floor 152 Buckingham Palace Road Victoria London SW1W 9TR, Tel.: 020 7730 8585, Fax: 020 7730 8584, Website: www.nalc.ik.com.

National Association of Widows
48 Queens Road Coventry CV1 3EH, Tel.: 024 7663 4848, Website: www.nawidows.org.uk, E-mail: office@nawidows.org.uk.

National Cancer Alliance
PO Box 579 Oxford OX4 1LB, Tel.: 01865 793566, Website: www.nationalcanceralliance.co.uk, E-mail: nationalcanceralliance@btinternet.com.

National Childbirth Trust (NCT)
Alexandra House Oldham Terrace Acton London W3 6NH, Tel.: 0870 444 8707, Fax: 0870 770 3237, Website: www.nct.org.uk.

National Consumer Council (NCC)
20 Grosvenor Gardens London SW1W 0DH, Tel.: 020 7730 3469, Fax: 020 7730 0191, Website: www.ncc.org.uk, E-mail: info@ncc.org.uk.

National Council for Palliative Care
189-194 York Way London N7 9AS, Tel.: 020 7697 1520, Fax: 020 7697 1530, Website: www.ncpc.org.uk, E-mail: enquiries@ncpc.org.uk.

National Eczema Society
Hill House Highgate Hill London N19 5NA, Tel.: 020 7281 3553, Help Line: 0870 241 3604, Website: www.eczema.org, E-mail: helpline@eczema.org.

National Kidney Federation
6 Stanley Street Worksop S81 7HX, Tel.: 01909 487795, Fax: 01909 481723, Help Line: 0845 601 0209, Website: www.kidney.org.uk, E-mail: nkf@kidney.org.uk.

National Osteoporosis Society
Camerton Bath BA2 0PJ, Tel.: 01761 471771, Fax: 01761 471104, Help Line: 0845 450 0230, Website: www.nos.org.uk.

National Phobics Society
Zion CRC 339 Stretford Road Hulme Manchester M15 4ZY, Tel.: 0870 122 2325, Fax: 0161 227 9862, Website: www.phobics-society.org.uk, E-mail: nationalphobic@btconnect.com.

National Society for Epilepsy
Chesham Lane Chalfont St Peter SL9 0RJ, Tel.: 01494 601 300, Fax: 01494 871 927, Website: www.epilepsynse.org.uk.

National Society for Phenylketonuria (UK) Ltd (NSPKU)
Contact: Lucy Welch, Administrator PO Box 26642 London N14 4ZF, Tel.: 0845 603 9136, Website: www.nspku.org, E-mail: info@nspku.org.

National Society for the Prevention of Cruelty to Children (NSPCC)
Weston House 42 Curtain Road London EC2A 3NH, Tel.: 020 7825 2500, Fax: 020 7825 2525, Help Line: 0808 800 5000, Website: www.nspcc.org.uk, E-mail: help@nspcc.org.uk.

NCH
85 Highbury Park London N5 1UD, Tel.: 020 704 7000, Fax: 020 7226 2537, Website: www.nch.org.uk.

Neonatal Nurses Association
PO Box 8708 Nottingham NG2 7BJ, Tel.: 0115 941 7224.

Neuroblastoma Society
Tel.: 01371 876254, Website: www.nsoc.co.uk, E-mail: nsoc@ukonline.co.uk.

Neurofibromatosis Association
Quayside House 38 High Street Kingston on Thames KT1 1HL, Tel.: 020 8439 1234, Fax: 020 8439 1200, Help Line: 0845 602 4173, Website: www.nfauk.org, E-mail: nfa@zetnet.co.uk.

Useful Addresses & Phone Numbers

Northern Ireland Practice & Education Council for Nursing & Midwifery (NIPEC)
c/o Mr E N Thom, Head of Corporate Services Centre House 79 Chichester Street Belfast BT1 4JE, Tel.: 028 9023 8152, Fax: 028 9033 3298, Website: www.nipec.n-i.nhs.uk, E-mail: enquiries@nipec.n-i.nhs.uk.

OEDA, the Occupational and Environmental Diseases Association
PO Box 26 Enfield EN1 2NT, Tel.: 020 8360 8490.

One Parent Families
National Office 255 Kentish Town Road London NW5 2LX, Tel.: 0800 018 5026, Fax: 020 7482 4851, Website: www.oneparentfamilies.org.uk, E-mail: info@oneparentfamilies.org.uk.

OVACOME
Elizabeth Garrett Anderson Hospital Huntley Street London WC1E 6DH, Tel.: 0207 380 9589, Website: www.ovacome.org.uk, E-mail: ovacome@ovacome.org.uk.

Papworth Trust
Papworth Everard Cambridge CB3 8RG, Tel.: 01480 830341, Fax: 01480 830781, Website: www.papworth.org.uk, E-mail: info@papworth.org.uk.

Parentline Plus
520 Highgate Studios 53-79 Highgate Road London NW5 1TL, Tel.: 020 7284 5500, Fax: 020 7284 5501, Help Line: 0808 800 2222, Website: www.parentlineplus.org.uk, E-mail: parentsupport@parentlineplus.org.uk.

Parents for Children (PFC)
253-254 Upper Street London N1 1RY, Tel.: 020 7288 4320, Fax: 020 7288 4327, Website: www.parentsforchildren.org.uk, E-mail: info@parentsforchildren.org.uk.

Parkinson's Disease Society
215 Vauxhall Bridge Road London SW1V 1EJ, Tel.: 020 7931 8080, Help Line: 0808 800 0303, Website: www.parkinsons.org.uk, E-mail: enquiries@parkinsons.org.uk.

Phoenix House Charity and Social Landlord
3rd Floor Asra House 1 Long Lane London SE1 4PG, Tel.: 020 7234 9756, Fax: 020 7234 9770, Website: www.pheonixhouse.org.uk, E-mail: info@phoenixhouse.org.uk.

Physically Disabled and Able Bodied (PHAB)
Sumit House Wandle Road Croydon CR0 1DF, Tel.: 020 8667 9443.

Portland College for People with Disabilities
Nottingham Road Mansfield NG18 4TJ, Tel.: 01623 499111, Fax: 01623 499134, Website: www.portland.org.uk, E-mail: gbird@portland.org.uk.

Psoriasis Association (PA)
7 Milton Street Northampton NN2 7JG, Tel.: 01604 711129, Fax: 01604 792894, Help Line: 08456 760 076, Website: www.psoriasis-association.org.uk, E-mail: mail@psoriasis.demon.co.uk.

Psychiatric Rehabilitation Association
The Groupwork Centre Bayford Mews Bayford Street London E8 3SF, Tel.: 020 8985 3570, Website: www.pra-london.co.uk, E-mail: ppra528898@aol.com.

Public Services Ombudsman for Wales
1 Ffordd yr hen gae Pencoed Bridgend CF35 5LJ, Tel.: 0845 601 0987, Fax: 01656 641199, www.ombudsman-wales.org.uk, E-mail: ask@ombudsman-wales.org.uk.

Queen Elizabeth's Foundation for Disabled People
Leatherhead Court Leatherhead KT22 0BN, Tel.: 01372 841100, Website: www.qef.org.uk, E-mail: info@qef.org.uk.

QUIT
211 Old Street London EC1V 9NR, Tel.: 020 7251 1551, Fax: 020 7251 1661, Help Line: 0800 002 200, Website: www.quit.org.uk, E-mail: stopsmoking@quit.org.uk.

RADAR (Royal Association for Disability and Rehabilitation) 12 City Forum 250 City Road London EC1V 8AF, Tel.: 020 7250 3222, Fax: 020 7250 0212, Website: www.radar.org.uk, E-mail: radar@radar.org.uk.

Raynaud's and Scleroderma Association Trust
112 Crewe Road Alsager ST7 2JA, Tel.: 01270 872776, Fax: 01270 883556, Help Line: 0800 917 2494, Website: www.raynauds.org.uk, E-mail: info@raynauds.org.uk.

RCN Cancer Nursing Society
Royal College of Nursing 20 Cavendish Square London W1M 0AB, Tel.: 020 7647 3835, Website: www.rcn.org.

RCN Community and PHC Nursing
Royal College of Nursing 20 Cavendish Square London W1G 0RN, Tel.: 0207 647 3740, Website: www.rcn.org.uk. *The RCN provides an enormous range of services, relevant to nurses working in the community. They span from professional forum activities and newsletters, specialist journals, expert advice and information, publications, conferences, opportunities for continuing professional development - including leadership to newly developed websites and specialist chat rooms.*

RCN Community Children's Nurses Forum
Royal College of Nursing 20 Cavendish Square London W1G 0RN, Tel.: 020 7647 3753, Website: www.rcn.org.uk. *Expert body within RCN concerned with promotion of good practice, management and teaching of children's nursing. The RCN Community Children's Nurses Forum organises professional activities for its members and provides an expert resource to both RCN members and external organisations.*

Useful Addresses & Phone Numbers

RCN Diabetes Nursing Forum
Royal College of Nursing 20 Cavendish Square London W1M 0AB, Tel.: 020 7409 3333, E-mail: sarahobuk@yahoo.co.uk.
The Forum aims to represent diabetes nursing in all its forms, and promote excellent practice in diabetes nursing care. The Forum holds an annual conference and a twice yearly newsletter is published. The Forum advises the RCN on issues relating to diabetes nursing and represents it on many national commitees and working groups.
RCN Direct
Tel.: 0845 7726100.

RCN Gerontological Nursing Programme
c/o Pauline Ford (Director) Royal College of Nursing 20 Cavendish Square London W1M 0AB, Tel.: 020 7647 3742, Website: www.rcn.org.uk.
The Gerontological Nursing Programme brings together all the RCN's work on nursing and older people and integrates policy, education, research and practice development activities. The programme works in partnership with the RCN's membership led specialist Forums for nursing and older people and the RCN's Policy Unit.

RCN Mental Health Nursing Forums
c/o Ian Hulatt, Mental Health Adviser or Sandra Hall, Forum Organiser Royal College of Nursing, 20 Cavendish Square London W1G 0RN, Tel.: 020 7647 3741, E-mail: Ian.Hulatt@rcn.org.uk.

Real Nappy Association
PO Box 3704 London SE26 4RX, Website: www.realnappy.com, E-mail: contact@realnappy.com.

Red Lion Group
c/o Stoma Care Dept Northwick Park Hospital Watford Road Harrow HA1 3UJ, Tel.: 020 8235 4126, Fax: 020 8235 4111.

Registered Nursing Home Association (RNHA, Blue Cross)
15 Highfield Road Edgbaston Birmingham B15 3DU, Tel.: 0121 454 2511, Fax: 0121 454 0932, Website: www.rnha.co.uk, E-mail: info@rnha.co.uk.

Relate
Herbert Gray College Little Church Street Rugby CV21 3AP, Tel.: 0845 456 1310, Website: www.relate.org.uk, E-mail: enquiries@relate.org.uk.

Re-Solv (The Society for the Prevention of Solvent and Volatile Substance Abuse)
30a High Street Stone ST15 8AW, Tel.: 01785 817885, Fax: 01785 813205, Website: www.re-solv.org, E-mail: information@re-solv.org.

Rethink - Severe Mental Illness
Tel.: 0845 456 0455, Help Line: 020 8974 6814, Website: www.rethink.org, E-mail: info@rethink.org.

Rett Syndrome Association UK
113 Friern Barnet Road London N11 3EU, Tel.: 0870 770 3266, Fax: 0870 770 3265, Website: www.rettsyndrome.org.uk, E-mail: info@rettsyndrome.org.uk.

Richmond Fellowship
80 Holloway Road Highbury London N7 6JG, Tel.: 020 7697 3300, Fax: 020 7697 3301, Website: www.richmondfellowship.org.uk, E-mail: annie.miller@richmondfellowship.org.uk.

Riding for the Disabled Association (RDA)
Lavinia Norfolk House Avenue R National Agricultural Centre Stoneleigh Park CV8 2LY, Tel.: 0845 658 1082, Fax: 0845 658 1083, Website: www.rda.org.uk.

Royal Air Forces Association
117 1/2 Loughborough Road Leicester LE4 5ND, Tel.: 0116 268 8754, Website: www.rafa.org.uk.

Royal Association for Deaf people (RAD)
RAD Centre Walsingham Road Colchester CO2 7BP, Tel.: 01206 509509, Fax: 01206 769755, Website: www.royaldeaf.org.uk, E-mail: info@royaldeaf.org.uk.

Royal College of General Practitioners (RCGP)
14 Princes Gate Hyde Park London SW7 1PU, Tel.: 020 7581 3232, Fax: 020 7225 3047, Website: www.rcgp.org.uk, E-mail: info@rcgp.org.uk.

Royal College of Midwives (RCM)
15 Mansfield Street London W1G 9NH, Tel.: 020 7312 3535, Fax: 020 7312 3536, Website: www.rcm.org.uk, E-mail: info@rcm.org.uk.

Royal Hospital for Neuro-disability
West Hill Putney London SW15 3SW, Tel.: 020 8780 4500, Fax: 020 8780 4501, Website: www.neuro-disability.org.uk, E-mail: info@rhn.org.uk.

Royal National Institute of the Blind (RNIB)
105 Judd Street London WC1H 9NE, Tel.: 020 7388 1266, Fax: 020 7388 2034, Help Line: 0845 766 9999, Website: www.rnib.org.uk, E-mail: helpline@rnib.org.uk.

Royal Society for the Prevention of Accidents (RoSPA)
Edgbaston Park 353 Bristol Road Birmingham B5 7ST, Tel.: 0121 248 2000, Fax: 0121 248 2001, Website: www.rospa.com, E-mail: help@rospa.com.

Samaritans
The Upper Mill Kingston Road Ewell KT17 2AF, Tel.: 020 8394 8300, Fax: 020 8394 8301, Help Line: 0845 790 9090, Website: www.samaritans.org.uk, E-mail: admin@samaritans.org.

Useful Addresses & Phone Numbers

SANDS Stillbirth and Neonatal Death Society
28 Portland Place London W1B 1LY, Tel.: 020 7436 7940, Fax: 020 7436 3715, Help Line: 020 7436 5881, Website: www.uk-sands.org, E-mail: support@uk-sands.org.

SANELINE
1st Floor, Cityside House 40 Alder Street London E1 1EE, Tel.: 020 7375 1002, Fax: 020 7375 2162, Help Line: 0845 767 8000, Website: www.sane.org.uk.

Sargent Cancer Care for Children
Griffin House 161 Hammersmith Road London W6 8SG, Tel.: 020 8752 2800, Website: www.sargent.org, E-mail: care@sargent.org.

Schizophrenia Association of Great Britain (SAGB)
International Schizophrenia Centre Bryn Hyfryd The Crescent Bangor LL57 2AG, Tel.: 01248 354048, Fax: 01248 353659, Website: www.sagb.co.uk, E-mail: info@sagb.co.uk.

Scoliosis Association (UK)
2 Ivebury Court 323-327 Latimer Road London W10 6RA, Tel.: 020 8964 5343, Fax: 020 8964 5343, Help Line: 020 8964 1166, Website: www.sauk.org.uk, E-mail: sauk@sauk.org.uk.

Scottish Association for Mental Health (SAMH)
Cumbrae House 15 Carlton Court Glasgow G5 9JP, Tel.: 0141 568 7000, Fax: 0141 568 7001, Website: www.samh.org.uk, E-mail: enquire@samh.org.uk.

Scottish Council on Deafness (SCoD)
Central Chambers, Suite 62 93 Hope Street Glasgow G2 6LD, Tel.: 0141 248 2474, Fax: 0141 248 2479, Website: www.scod.org.uk, E-mail: admin@scod.org.uk.

Scottish Health Visitors Association (SHVA)/Section of UNISON
Douglas House 60 Belford Road Edinburgh EH4 3UQ, Tel.: 0870 7777 006, Fax: 0131 220 6389.

Scottish National Institution for the War Blinded
PO Box 500 Gillespie Crescent Edinburgh EH10 4HZ, Tel.: 0131 229 1456, Website: www.royalblind.org, E-mail: enquiries.warblinded@royalblind.org.

Scottish Public Services Ombudsman
4 Melville Street Edinburgh EH3 7NS, Tel.: 0870 011 5378, Fax: 0870 011 5379, Website: www.scottishombudsman.org.uk, E-mail: enquiries@scottishombudsman.org.uk.

Scottish Society for Autism
Hilton House Alloa Business Park Whins Road Alloa FK10 3SA, Tel.: 01259 720044, Fax: 01259 720051, Website: www.autism-in-scotland.org.uk, E-mail: autism@autism-in-scotland.org.uk.

Scottish Spina Bifida Association (SSBA)
190 Queensferry Road Edinburgh EH4 2BW, Tel.: 0131 332 0743, Fax: 0131 343 3651, Help Line: 08459 111112, Website: www.ssba.org.uk, E-mail: mail@ssba.org.uk.

Sense
11-13 Clifton Terrace Finsbury Park London N4 3SR, Tel.: 020 7272 7774, Fax: 020 7272 6012, Website: www.sense.org.uk, E-mail: enquiries@sense.org.uk.

Sexual Dysfunction Association
Windmill Place Business Centre 2-4 Windmill Lane Southall UB2 4NJ, Tel.: 0870 774 3573, Fax: 0870 774 3572, Help Line: 0870 7743571, Website: www.sda.uk.net, E-mail: info@sda.uk.net.

Shelter (National Campaign for Homeless People)
88 Old Street London EC1V 9HU, Tel.: 020 7505 2056, Website: www.shelter.org.uk.

Shingles Support Society
41 North Road London N7 9DP, Tel.: 020 7607 9661, Help Line: 0845 123 2305, Website: www.herpes.org.uk/shingles.htm, E-mail: info@herpes.org.uk.

Sickle Cell Society
54 Station Road Harlesden London NW10 4UA, Tel.: 020 8961 7795, Fax: 0208 961 8346, Website: www.sicklecellsociety.org, E-mail: info@sicklecellsociety.org.

Soldiers, Sailors, Airmen & Families Association - Forces Help (SSAFA)
Community Health Service, Child Health Record Dept Contact: Mrs Anne Baird, Senior Child Health Records Administrator, HQ BFG Health Service, British Forces Health Complex, BFPO 40, Tel.: 0049 2161 908 2351
Nurse Advisor, Child Protection: Mrs Ann Coles, address as above, Tel.: 0049 2161 908 2429
General Enquiries Community Health Issues Contact: Mrs Sally McFerran, Assistant Director Clinical Governance Overseas Commands. Tel.: 020 7463 9250/253

Sons of Divine Providence
13 Lower Teddington Road Hampton Wick Kingston-on-Thames KT1 4EU, Tel.: 020 8977 5130, Fax: 020 8977 0105, Website: www.sonsofdivineprovidence.org, E-mail: mhealy@sons-ofdevine.org.

Speakability
1 Royal Street London SE1 7LL, Tel.: 020 7261 9572, Fax: 020 7928 9542, Help Line: 080 8808 9572, Website: www.speakability.org.uk, E-mail: speakability@speakability.org.uk.

Useful Addresses & Phone Numbers

Spinal Injuries Association (Paraplegics & Tetraplegics)
Acorn House 387-391 Midsummer Boulevard Milton Keynes MK9 3HP, Tel.: 0845 678 6633, Fax: 01908 608492, Help Line: 0800 980 0501, Website: www.spinal.co.uk, E-mail: sia@spinal.co.uk.

Spinal Injuries Scotland
Festival Business Centre 150 Brand Street Glasgow G51 1DH, Tel.: 0141 314 0056, Help Line: 0141 314 0057, Website: www.sisonline.org, E-mail: kristin@sisonline.org.

St Christopher's Hospice
51-59 Lawrie Park Road Sydenham London SE26 6DZ, Tel.: 020 8768 4500, Fax: 020 8659 8680, Website: www.stchristophers.org.uk, E-mail: info@stchristophers.org.uk.

St Dunstan's
12-14 Harcourt Street London W1H 4HD, Tel.: 020 7723 5021, Fax: 020 7262 6199, Website: www.st-dunstans.org.uk, E-mail: enquiries@st-dunstans.org.uk.

St John Ambulance (Order of St John)
27 St John's Lane London EC1M 4BU, Tel.: 0207 324 4000, Fax: 0207 324 4001, Website: www.sja.org.uk, E-mail: pr@nhq.sja.org.uk.

Talking Newspaper Association of the UK
National Recording Centre Heathfield TN21 8DB, Tel.: 01435 866102.

Tamba (Twins and Multiple Births Association)
2 The Willows Gardner Road Guildford GU1 4PG, Tel.: 0870 770 3305, Fax: 0870 770 3303, Website: www.tamba.org.uk, E-mail: enquiries@tamba.org.uk.
Supports families with twins, triplets or more and professionals concerned with their care. Network of local Twins Clubs. Specialist support groups for families with triplets or more, special needs, one parent families, infertility support, bereavement. Publications. Tamba Twinline: Tel. 0800 138 0509 (1000-1300 and 1900-2200 everyday) (Parents helpline).

Tamworth PND Support Group
Midwifery Office, Glascote Health Centre Caledonian Glascote Tamworth B77 4DE, Tel.: 01827 288495, E-mail: jillbeckett@hotmail.com.
This group was formed in February 1997 and takes referrals from Health Visitors, Midwives, GP's, Social Services and Voluntary Services. Its facilitated by a multi-disciplinary group - Midwife, Health Visitor and a Community Mental Health Nurse. It meets each week and have a focus of discussion ie PND, Birth Experiences, Mothers & Bonding etc. Creche provided.

Teenage Cancer Trust
38 Warren Street London W1T 6AE, Tel.: 020 7387 1000, Fax: 020 7387 6000, Website: www.teenagecancertrust.org, E-mail: tct@teenagecancertrust.org.

Telephones for the Blind Fund
7 Huntersfield Close Reigate RH2 0DX, Tel.: 01737 248032.

The British Dietetic Association
5th Floor Charles House 148/9 Great Charles Street Birmingham B3 3HT, Tel.: 0121 200 8080, Fax: 0121 200 8081, Website: www.bda.uk.com, E-mail: info@bda.uk.com.

The British Pain Society
21 Portland Place London W1B 1PY, Tel.: 020 7631 8870, Fax: 020 7323 2015, Website: www.britishpainsociety.org, E-mail: info@britishpainsociety.org.

The British Stammering Association
15 Old Ford Road London E2 9PJ, Tel.: 020 8983 1003, Fax: 020 8983 3591, Help Line: 0845 603 2001, Website: www.stammering.org, E-mail: info@stammering.org (Helpline Scotland 08453 303800).

The Child Bereavement Trust
Aston House High Street West Wycombe HP14 3AG, Tel.: 01494 446648, Fax: 01494 440057, Help Line: 0845 357 1000, Website: www.childbereavement.org.uk, E-mail: enquiries@childbereavement.org.uk.

The Children's Society
Edward Rudolf House Margery Street London WC1X 0JL, Tel.: 020 7841 4400, Fax: 020 7841 4416, Website: www.childrenssociety.org.uk, E-mail: supporteraction@childrenssociety.org.uk.

The Children's Trust
Tadworth Court Tadworth KT20 5RU, Tel.: 01737 365000, Fax: 01737 365001, Website: www.thechildrenstrust.org.uk, E-mail: enquiries@thechildrenstrust.org.uk.
Outreach home care, part of The Children's Trust, provides a nursing and care service in response to the needs of families and children with disabilities and complex needs. Provided in children's own homes or other community settings.

The Cry-sis Helpline
BM Crysis London WC1N 3XX, Tel.: 08451 228 669, Website: www.cry-sis.org.uk, E-mail: info@cry-sis.org.uk.

The Disabilities Trust (formerly Disabled Housing Trust) (TDT)
32 Market Place Burgess Hill RH15 9NP, Tel.: 01444 239123, Fax: 01444 244978, Website: www.disabilities-trust.org.uk, E-mail: info@disabilities-trust.org.uk.

The Disabled Photographers' Society
PO Box 130 Richmond TW10 6XQ, Website: www.dps-uk.org.uk, E-mail: enquiries@dps-uk.org.uk.

The Dystonia Society
1st Floor, Camelford House 89 Albert Embankment London SE1 7TP, Tel.: 0845 458 6211, Fax: 0845 458 6311, Help Line: 0845 458 6322, Website: www.dystonia.org.uk.

Useful Addresses & Phone Numbers

The Eyecare Trust
PO Box 131 Market Rasen LN8 5TS, Tel.: 0845 1295001,
Fax: 0845 129 5002, Website: www.eye-care.org.uk, E-mail:
info@eyecaretrust.org.uk.

The Fostering Network
87 Blackfriars Road London SE1 8HA, Tel.: 020 7620 6400,
Fax: 020 7620 6401, Help Line: 0800 040 7675, Website:
www.fostering.net, E-mail: info@fostering.net.

The Horder Centre
St John's Road Crowborough TN6 1XP, Tel.: 01892
665577, Fax: 01892 662142, Website:
www.hordercentre.co.uk, E-mail: arthritis@horder.co.uk.

The Jessie May Trust
35 Old School House Kingswood Foundation Estate,
Britannia Road, Kingswood Bristol BS15 8DB, Tel.: 0117
961 6840, Fax: 0117 960 7783, Help Line: 0117 958 2172,
Website: www.jessiemaytrust.org.uk, E-mail:
info@jessiemaytrust.org.uk.

The ME Association
4 Top Angel Buckingham Industrial Park Buckingham MK18
1TH, Fax: 01280 821602, Help Line: 0870 444 1835, E-
mail: meconnect@meassociation.org.uk.

The Migraine Trust
55-56 Russell Square London WC1B 4HP, Tel.: 020 7436
1336, Website: www.migrainetrust.org, E-mail:
info@migrainetrust.org.

The Miscarriage Association
c/o Clayton Hospital Northgate Wakefield WF1 3JS, Tel.:
01924 200799, Fax: 01924 298834, Website:
www.miscarriageassociation.org.uk, E-mail:
info@miscarriageassociation.org.uk.

The National Deaf Children's Society (NDCS)
15 Dufferin Street London EC1Y 8UR, Tel.: 020 74908656,
Fax: 020 7251 5020, Help Line: 0808 800 8880, Website:
www.ndcs.org.uk, E-mail: helpline@ndcs.org.uk.

The Patients Association
PO Box 935 Harrow HA1 3YJ, Help Line: 0845 608 4455,
Website: www.patients-association.com, E-mail:
mailbox@patients-association.com.

The Queen's Nursing Institute
3 Albemarle Way London EC1V 4RQ, Tel.: 020 7490 4227,
Fax: 020 7490 1269, Website: www.qni.org.uk, E-mail:
peggy.garrett@qni.org.uk.

The Royal British Legion HQ
48 Pall Mall London SW1Y 5JY, Tel.: 0845 772 5725, Fax:
0207 973 7399, Website: www.britishlegion.org.uk.

The Royal British Legion Scotland
New Haig House Logie Green Road Edinburgh EH7 4HR,
Tel.: 0131 557 2782, Fax: 0131 557 5819, Website:
www.rblscotland.org, E-mail: admin@rblscotland.org.

The Royal National Institute for Deaf People (RNID)
19-23 Featherstone Street London EC1Y 8SL, Tel.: 0808
808 0123, Fax: 020 7296 8199, Website: www.rnid.org.uk,
E-mail: informationline@rnid.org.uk.

The Royal Society for the Promotion of Health
38A St George's Drive London SW1V 4BH, Tel.: 020 7630
0121, Fax: 020 7976 6847, Website: www.rsph.org, E-mail:
rshealth@rshealth.org.uk.

The Salvation Army
101 Newington Causeway London SE1 6BN, Tel.: 020 7367
4500, Fax: 020 7367 4728, Website:
www.salvationarmy.org.uk, E-mail:
press.office@salvationarmy.org.uk.

The Schizophrenia Association of Great Britain
Bryn Hyfryd, The Crescent Bangor LL57 2AG, Tel.: 01248
354048, Fax: 01248 354048, Website: www.sagb.co.uk, E-
mail: info@sagb.co.uk.

**The Sequal Trust (formerly Special Equipment and Aids
for Living)**
3 Ploughmans Corner Wharf Road Ellesmere SY12 0EJ,
Tel.: 01691 624222, Fax: 01691 624222, Website:
www.the-sequal-trust.org.uk, E-mail:
thesequaltrust@freeuk.com.

The Shaftesbury Society
16 Kingston Road London SW19 1JZ, Tel.: 0845 3306 033,
Fax: 020 8239 5580, Website: www.shaftesburysociety.org,
E-mail: info@shaftesburysociety.org.

The Stroke Association
Stroke House 240 City Road London EC1V 2PR, Tel.: 020
7566 0300, Help Line: 0845 303 3100, Website:
www.stroke.org.uk, E-mail:
informationservice@stroke.org.uk.

The Terrence Higgins Trust
314-320 Grays Inn Road London WC1X 8DP, Tel.: 020
7812 1600, Fax: 020 7812 1601, Help Line: 0845 1221 200,
Website: www.tht.org.uk, E-mail: info@tht.org.uk.

The Vegan Society
Donald Watson House 7 Battle Road St Leonards-on-Sea
TN37 7AA, Tel.: 01424 427393, Fax: 01424 717064,
Website: www.vegansociety.com, E-mail:
info@vegansociety.com.

Thomas Pocklington Trust
5 Castle Row Horticultural Place Chiswick W4 4JQ, Tel.:
020 8995 0880, Fax: 020 8987 9965, E-mail:
johnb@pocklington-trust.org.uk.

Useful Addresses & Phone Numbers

Together - Working for Wellbeing
1st Floor, Lincoln House 296-302 High Holborn London
WC1V 7JH, Tel.: 020 7061 3400, Fax: 020 7061 3401,
Website: www.together-uk.org, E-mail: contactus@together-uk.org.

Tuberous Sclerosis Association
PO Box 12979 Barnt Green Birmingham B45 5AN, Tel.:
0121 445 6970, Fax: 0121 445 6970, Website:
www.tuberous-sclerosis.org, E-mail: support@tuberous-sclerosis.org.

UK Thalassaemia Society
19 The Broadway Southgate Circus London N14 6PH, Tel.:
020 8882 0011, Fax: 020 8882 8618, Website:
www.ukts.org, E-mail: office@ukts.org.

UKC (UK Coalition of People Living with HIV and AIDS)
250 Kennington Lane London SE11 5RD, Tel.: 020 7564
2180, Fax: 020 7564 2140, Website: www.ukcoalition.org,
E-mail: reception@ukcoalition.org.

Ulster Cancer Foundation (Cancer Information Helpline)
40/42 Eglantine Avenue Belfast BT9 6DX, Tel.: 028 9066
3281, Help Line: 0800 783 3339, Website:
www.ulstercancer.org, E-mail: info@ulster-cancer.org.

Unique - the Rare Chromosome Disorder Support Group
PO Box 2189 Caterham CR3 5GN, Tel.: 01883 330766,
Fax: 01883 330766, Website: www.rarechromo.org, E-mail:
info@rarechromo.org.

Urostomy Association
Central Office 18 Foxglove Avenue Uttoxeter ST14 8UN,
Tel.: 0870 7707931, Fax: 0870 7707932, Website:
www.uagbi.org, E-mail: info.ua@classmail.co.uk
08452 412159.

Victim Support
National Office Cranmer House 39 Brixton Road London
SW9 6DZ, Tel.: 020 7735 9166, Fax: 020 7582 5712, Help
Line: 0845 30 30 900, Website: www.victimsupport.org.uk,
E-mail: contact@victimsupport.org.uk.

Vitalise
12 City Forum 250 City Road London EC1V 8AF, Tel.: 0845
345 1970, Fax: 0845 345 1978, Website:
www.vitalise.org.uk, E-mail: info@vitalise.org.uk.

Wales Council for the Blind
3rd Floor Shand House 20 Newport Road Cardiff CF24
0DB, Tel.: 029 2047 3954, Website: www.wcb-ccd.org.uk,
E-mail: staff@wcb-ccd.org.uk.

WellBeing of Women funding vital health research
27 Sussex Place Regent's Park London NW1 4SP, Tel.: 020
7772 6400, Fax: 020 7724 7725, Website:
www.wellbeingofwomen.org.uk, E-mail:
wellbeingofwomen@rcog.org.uk.

Williams Syndrome Foundation
161 High Street Tonbridge TN9 1BX, Tel.: 01732 365152,
Fax: 01732 360178, Website: www.williams-syndrome.org.uk, E-mail: John.Nelson-wsfoundation@btinternet.com.

World Cancer Research Fund (WCRF UK)
19 Harley Street London W1G 9QJ, Tel.: 020 7343 4200,
Fax: 020 7343 4201, Website: www.wcrf-uk.org.

Wound Care Society
PO Box 170 Huntingdon PE29 1PL, Tel.: 01480 434401,
Website: www.woundcaresociety.org, E-mail:
woundcare.society@btinternet.com.

WRVS
Garden House Milton Hill Steventon Abingdon OX13 6AD,
Tel.: 01235 442900, Fax: 01235 861166, Website:
www.wrvs.org.uk, E-mail: enquiries@wrvs.org.uk.

Directory of Community Health Services 2006/07

ORDER FORM

Note: payment with order please, unless enclosing an official order

Please send..........copy/copies at £...............each of the *Directory of Community Health Services 2006/07,* (see below for quantity discounts).

No of copies	1 - 9	10+
Unit prices (£) for NHS health professionals, booksellers, charities	29.95	19.95
Unit price (£) for others	49.95	34.95

Name..

Job description/Title...

Place of work..

Delivery address...

....

....

....Postcode.....................................

Daytime Telephone No...

Email Address...

Order Ref No...................................... Fax No:.....................................

I enclose a cheque for the sum of £..................made payable to **PMH Publications**

Credit Card Payments

Please debit my Visa/Mastercard/Delta (please delete as applicable)

Card No. _ _ _ _   _ _ _ _   _ _ _ _   _ _ _ _   Security code. _ _ _

Expiry date _ _ / _ _   for the sum of £...........................

Name and address of credit card holder (if different to above)

....

....Postcode.....................................

OR: I HAVE ENCLOSED AN OFFICIAL PURCHASE ORDER – PLEASE INVOICE ME ☐

Signature.. Date...

From time to time PMH Publications and other companies may wish to send details of other products and offers to you. If you do not wish to receive these communications, please tick box ☐

Section 2

Section 3

Alphabetical Indexes

Changes to this Edition of the Directory

Structural and administrative changes continue to take place within all areas of the NHS to consolidate Primary Care as the focal point of patient care within the NHS. With the expansion of the community services the amount of data being provided within the PMH directories has increased enormously.

To accommodate this expansion the information is now being presented in two volumes. The Directory of Community Nursing has been renamed The Directory of Community Health Services and retains all the key information previously included apart from the Mental Health Services.

The companion volume, our new Directory of Mental Health Services, provides greatly extended information on this increasingly important aspect of community care together with information on services for those with learning disabilities.

The entries for the Primary Care Trusts in this edition of the Directory of Community Health Services continue to reflect the current departmental structure that has evolved as the PCTs assume responsibility for an increasing range of Community Services and Community Hospitals.

How the Directory mirrors the new NHS structure

As part of the NHS reorganisation the 4 Health and Social Care Regions have been abolished and the 28 SHAs reduced to ten. The information for England is now shown within the 10 new Strategic Health Authorities (SHAs). These are included alphabetically and the name of the relevant SHA appears in the header at the top of each page.

The new SHAs are:- East Midlands, East of England, London, North East, North West, South Central, South East Coast, South West, West Midlands and finally Yorkshire & Humberside. Information for England is followed by Wales, Scotland, Northern Ireland and Offshore which
includes the Isle of Man, Jersey and Guernsey.

Wales still retains its Health Authorities, whilst Scotland has dissolved all the Acute and Primary Care Trusts. The Health Boards are responsible for health services throughout Scotland and these services are provided through their Acute and Primary Care Divisions. Within each Primary Care Division there are a number of Community Health Partnerships and these are included alphabetically within each Health Board

Northern Ireland retains the Health and Social Service Boards. All Community Trusts then appear alphabetically under their relevant health authority.

Throughout the Directory staff are listed by department within the Trust that employs them. Where a service is shared between Trusts, the Directory has to rely on this information being provided by the Trusts concerned.

At the beginning of each SHA in section 2 there is a map showing the new Health Authority boundaries and the main towns and areas served by that Authority. There are also a number of useful alphabetical indexes at the back of the Directory.

The Primary Care Service is now responsible for virtually all Community Nursing Services but many Specialist Nurses in Secondary Care maintain a vital role in providing "seamless care" for patients. This can involve Primary Care, Secondary Care and Social Services, especially for Liaison Specialists, Discharge Facilitators and Specialist Nurses in Children's Services.

To ensure that the Directory is as compete and accurate as possible and reflects the interdependence of the services, we have, where possible, included relevant services provided by the Acute NHS Trusts even though these may not fall within the strict definition of Community Nursing Services.

East Midlands Strategic Health Authority

with major towns and
Primary Care Trust boundaries
Pop: 4,279,707

Yorkshire &
The Humber

Retford

Chesterfield

Lincoln

Bakewell

Sutton in Ashfield

Mansfield

Newark

Arnold

Sleaford

Belper

Nottingham

Boston

Ilkeston

West Bridgford

Derby

Burton on Trent

Melton Mowbray

Loughborough

Stamford

Leicester

West Midlands

Market Bosworth

East of England

Wellingborough

Daventry

Northampton

South Central

East Midlands Strategic Health Authority

Amber Valley Primary Care Trust

Trust Headquarters, Meadow Suite
Babington Hospital, Derby Road
BELPER
DE56 1WH
Tel.: 01773 525099

Admin & Senior Management
Ms B Harris, Lead Nurse, Tel.: 01773 525099
Ms W Lawrence, Chief Executive, Tel.: 01773 525090
Mr C Rowlands, Director for Community & Primary Care Services, Trust Headquarters, Babington Hospital, Tel.: 01773 525099

Child Health
Child Health Department, Derwent Shared Services NHS Trust, Child Health, 4th Floor Laurie House, Colyear St, Derby, DE1 1LJ, Tel.: 01332 868816/17/18/19
Ms C Clemson, Divisional Manager, Children's Services, Tel.: 01332 362221 ext 3516
Ms K Groves, Lead Clinician, Children's Services, Wilderslowe, 121 Osmaston Road, Derby, DE1 2GA, Tel.: 01332 363371

Child Health Records
Child Health Records, Child Health Department, Derwent Shared Services NHS Trust, 4th Floor Laurie House, Colyear Street, Derby, DE1 1LJ, Tel.: 01332 868816/17/18/19

Child Protection/Safeguarding Children
Mrs L Hopwell, Co-ordinator, Looked After Children Department, Wilderslowe, 121 Osmaston Road, Derby, DE1 2GA, Tel.: 01332 363371
Ms P Newcombe, Named Nurse, Child Protection, Wilderslowe, 121 Osmaston Road, Derby, DE1 2GA, Tel.: 01332 363371

Clinical Leads (NSF)
Ms A Wright, Clinical Lead, CHD, Diabetes,
Ms B Harris, Clinical Lead, Cancer,
Mr C Rowlands, Clinical Lead, Care of the Elderly,
Ms J Wheeldon, Clinical Lead, Children,

Community Nursing Services
Mr C Short, Manager, Babington Hospital, Tel.: 01773 525030
Ms J Wheeldon, Manager, Babington Hospital, Tel.: 01773 525030

District Nursing
Daytime, Evening & Night Services, Tel.: 01332 366717
Mr C Short, Manager, Babington Hospital, Tel.: 01773 525030
Weekend Service, (0900-1630 hrs), Tel.: 01332 366717
Ms J Wheeldon, Manager, Babington Hospital, Tel.: 01773 525030

Family Planning Services
Ms V Todd, Co-ordinator, Wilderslowe, 121 Osmaston Road, Derby, DE1 2GA, Tel.: 01332 332766

Liaison Services
Liaison Services, Tel.: 01332 366717

School Nursing
Mr C Short, Manager, Babington Hospital, Tel.: 01773 525030
Ms J Wheeldon, Manager, Babington Hospital, Tel.: 01773 525030

Smoking Cessation
Ms S Devine,

Specialist Nursing Services
Ms G Telford, Community Nurse, Chemotherapy, Derbyshire Royal Infirmary, Tel.: 01332 347141
Ms A Goodhead, Tissue Viability, Derbyshire Royal Infirmary, Tel.: 01332 347141

The Homeless/Travellers & Asylum Seekers
Ms S A Coope, General Manager, - East, Babington Hospital, Tel.: 01773 525030
Mr C Short, General Manager, - West, Babington Hospital, Tel.: 01773 525030

Ashfield & Mansfield District Primary Care Trusts

Trust Headquarters, Ransom Hall
Ransom Wood Business Park, Southwell Rd West
Rainworth, MANSFIELD
Nottinghamshire
NG21 0ER
Tel.: 01623 414114

Admin & Senior Management
Ms L Boxall, Assistant Director, Community Nursing Services, Integrated management structure so all staff cover both Ashfield & Mansfield PCTs, Tel.: 01623 414114 ext 4529
Mr E de Gilbert, Chief Executive, Integrated management structure so all staff cover both Ashfield & Mansfield PCTs, Tel.: 01623 414114
Mrs J James, Director, Operational Services (Children & Young People), Integrated management structure so all staff cover both Ashfield & Mansfield PCTs, Tel.: 01623 414114 x 6937
Mr G Stokes, General Manager, Community Childrens Services, Integrated management structure so all staff cover both Ashfield & Mansfield PCTs, Tel.: 01623 414114 x4590
Mrs R Trainor, Director of Operational Services (Adult Services), Ransom Hall, Tel.: 01623 414114 ext 4610

Child Health
Mrs V Briscoe, Head of Child Health/School Nurses - Mansfield District PCT, St John Street Health Centre, Tel.: 01623 784358
Ms F Moir, Manager, Child Health Services - Mansfield District PCT, Mansfield Community Hospital, Tel.: 01623 785176
Ms J Wain, Head of Child Health/School Nurses - Ashfield PCT, Oates Hill Health Centre, Tel.: 01623 557136

Child Health Records
Ms F Moir, Centralised & Child Health Services Dept, Mansfield Community Hospital, Stockwell Gate, Mansfield, NG18 5QJ, Tel.: 01623 785170

Child Protection/Safeguarding Children
Ms C Staley, Team Leader Vunerable Children's Services, Mansfield Community Hospital, Stockwell Gate, Mansfield, NG18 5QJ, Tel.: 01623 785165
Ms M Marriott, Named & Designated Nurse, Child Protection, Mansfield Community Hospital, Stockwell Gate, Mansfield, NG18 5QJ, Tel.: 01623 785165

Clinical Leads (NSF)
Dr C Kenny, Clinical Lead, CHD & Diabetes, Ransom Hall, Tel.: 01623 414114 ext 4511
Dr C Kenny, Clinical Lead, Cancer, Ransom Hall, Tel.: 01623 414114 ext 4511
Mrs K Fradley, Clinical Lead, Care of the Elderly, Ransom Hall, Tel.: 01623 414114 ext 4618

Community Matrons
Ms E Alder, Long Term Conditions - Mansfield District PCT, Community Matron, St John Street Health Centre, Mansfield, NG18 1RH, Tel.: 01623 784301
Ms L Ashmore, Long Term Conditions Ashfield PCT, Community Matron, Ashfield Community Hospital, Tel.: 01623 784785
Ms M Hoyland, Long Term Conditions Ashfield PCT, Community Matron, Ashfield Community Hospital, Tel.: 01623 784733
Ms M Wilson, Long Term Conditions - Mansfield District PCT, Community Matron, St John Street Health Centre, Mansfield, NG18 1RH, Tel.: 01623 784301

Community Nursing Services
Ms S Appleton, Team Leader, Community Nursing Services - Ashfield PCT, Kirkby-in-Ashfield Health Centre, Tel.: 01623 752686
Ms J Baldwin, Team Leader, Community Nursing Services - Mansfield District PCT, Mansfield Community Hospital, Tel.: 01623 785091

Ms A Hunter, Team Leader, Community Nursing Services - Mansfield District PCT, Oak Tree Lane Health Centre, Jubilee Way South, Mansfield, NG18 3SF, Tel.: 01623 651261

Ms S Musgrove, Team Leader, Community Nursing Services - Mansfield District PCT, Oak Tree Lane Health Centre, Jubilee Way South, Mansfield, NG18 3SF, Tel.: 01623 651261

Mrs J Polkey, Team Leader, Community Nursing Services - Ashfield PCT, Oates Hill Health Centre, Tel.: 01623 557136

District Nursing

Ms R Trainor, Director of Operational Services (Adults)/Lead Nurse, Ransom Hall, Southwell Road West, Rainworth, Mansfield, NG21 0ER, Tel.: 01623 414114

Family Planning Services

Ms J Kochanowski, Team Leader, Family Planning Services, St John Street Health Centre, Tel.: 01623 784347

Health Visitors

Mrs V Briscoe, Head of Health Visitors - Mansfield District PCT, St John Street Health Centre, Tel.: 01623 784358

Ms W van Alderwegan, Paediatric Liaison Health Visitor/CONI, Children's Centre, King's Mill Hospital, Mansfield Road, Sutton in Ashfield, NG17 4JL, Tel.: 01623 785019

Ms J Wain, Head of HVs - Ashfield PCT, Kirkby Bungalows, 72 Portland Street, Kirkby in Ashfield, Tel.: 01623 751984 x 22

School Nursing

Mrs V Briscoe, Head of Child Health/School Nurses - Mansfield District PCT, St John Street Health Centre, Tel.: 01623 784347

Ms J Wain, Head of Child Health/School Nurses - Ashfield PCT, 72 Portland Street, Tel.: 01623 557136

Specialist Nursing Services

Ms J Dudley, British Heart Foundation Nurse, Ransom Hall, Tel.: 01623 414114

Ms L Tucker, Young Physically Disabled, Link Nurse, Chatsworth Rehabilitation Centre, Mansfield Community Hospital, Tel.: 01623 785150

Ms A Wilson, British Heart Foundation Nurse, Ransom Hall, Tel.: 01623 414114

Ms F Saunders, Senior Advisor, Continence, Ashfield Community Hospital, Tel.: 01623 784785

Ms S Thompson, Coronary Heart Disease Facilitator, Coronary Care, St John Street Health Centre, Tel.: 01623 784335

Ms D Johnson, Nurse, Infection Control, Oak Tree Lane Health Centre, Tel.: 01623 651261

Ms J Wright, Advisor, Senior Nurse, Infection Control, Oak Tree Lane Health Centre, Tel.: 01623 651261

Ms V Rose, Nurse Consultant, Intermediate Care, St Johns Street Health Centre, Tel.: 01623 784339

Ms J Grendon, Macmillan Nurse, Lung Cancer, John Eastwood Hospice, Tel.: 01623 622626

Ms E Blinko, Hospital & Community Nurse, Macmillan, Newark Hospital, Tel.: 01636 685881

Mr J Brodrick, Hospital & Community, Nurse, Macmillan, Newark Hospital, Tel.: 01636 685881

Ms P Grundy, Community Nurse, Macmillan, John Eastwood Hospice, Tel.: 01623 622626

Mr T Reid, Public Health, Macmillan, Ransom Hall, Tel.: 01623 622626

Ms L Sargeant, Hospital Support Team Nurse, Macmillan, John Eastwood Hospice, Tel.: 01623 622626

Ms J Thraves, Community Nurse, Macmillan, John Eastwood Hospice, Tel.: 01623 622626

Ms S Turton, Hospital Support Team Nurse, Macmillan, John Eastwood Hospice, Tel.: 01623 622626

Ms V White, Hospital & Community Nurse, Macmillan, Newark Hospital, Tel.: 01636 685881

Ms J Bolus, Specialist Nurse, Osteoporosis, Mansfield Community Hospital, Tel.: 01623 785024

Ms R Langrick, Nurse, Tissue Viability, Oak Tree Lane Health Centre, Tel.: 01623 651261

Bassetlaw Primary Care Trust

Trust Headquarters, Retford Hospital
North Road, RETFORD
Notts, DN22 7XF
Tel.: 01777 274400
Fax.: 01777 710535

Child Health

Mrs J Fennell, Senior Nurse, Retford Hospital, North Road, Retford, DN22 7XF, Tel.: 01777 274400

Paediatric Nursing Service, Retford Hospital, North Road, Retford, DN22 7XF, Tel.: 01777 274400

Child Health Records

Mrs C Burkitt, Administration Manager, Retford Hospital, North Road, Retford, Notts, DN22 7XF, Tel.: 01777 274400

Records Storage, Randall Park Resource Centre, Randall Way, Retford, Tel.: 01777 869 074

Child Protection/Safeguarding Children

Mrs C Burke, Designated Nurse, Child Protection, Barrowby House, Bassetlaw District General Hospital, Kilton, Worksop, S81 0BD, Tel.: 01909 500990 ext 2514

Clinical Leads (NSF)

Dr P Foster, Clinical Lead, CHD, Cancer,

Mrs L Clark, Clinical Lead, Diabetic Care,

Mrs J Walker, Clinical Lead, Older People,

Community Matrons

Mrs C Higgins, Community Matron, Manton Clinic, Pelham Street, Worsop, Tel.: 01909 472022

Ms S Jones, Community Matron, Retford Hospital, North Road, Retford, DN22 7XF, Tel.: 01909 274400

Mrs S Pollard, Community Matron, Carlton Surgery, Long Lane, Carlton, in Lindrick, Tel.: 01909 732933

Community Nursing Services

Mrs J Cotton, Deputy Director of Community Services, Retford Hospital, North Road, Retford, DN22 7XF, Tel.: 01777 274400

Single Point of Access, Retford Hospital, North Road, Retford, DN22 7XF, Tel.: 01777 274422

District Nursing

Mrs J Cotton, Deputy Director of Community Services, Retford Hospital, North Road, Retford, DN22 7XF, Tel.: 01777 274400

Family Planning Services

Mrs J Fennell, Senior Nurse, Retford Hospital, North Road, Retford, DN22 7XF, Tel.: 01777 274400

Health Visitors

Mrs J Cotton, Deputy Director of Community Services, Retford Hospital, North Road, Retford, DN22 7XF, Tel.: 01777 274400

HIV/AIDS

Ms J Fennell, Retford Hospital, Tel.: 01777 274400 ext 4489

Liaison Services

Mrs M Beecher, Community Liaison Specialist, Social Work Dept, Bassetlaw District General Hospital, Kilton, Worksop, S81 0BD,

Pharmacy

Mr B Wilson, Advisor, Retford Hospital, North Road, Retford, Notts, DN22 7XF, Tel.: 01777 274400 ext 4415

Smoking Cessation

Ms C Rice, Retford Hospital, North Road, Retford, DN22 7XF, Tel.: 01777 274410

Specialist Nursing Services

Mrs K Darlington, Advisor, Continence, Retford Hospital, North Road, Retford, DN22 7XF, Tel.: 01777 274400 ext 4497

Mrs T Bainbridge, Nurse Advisor, Diabetes, Retford Hospital, North Road, Retford, DN22 7XF, Tel.: 01777 274400 ext 4576

Mrs C Forman, Nurse, Infection Control, Tuxford Clinic, Newark Road, Tuxford, NG22 0NA, Tel.: 01777 871664

Mrs M Rainford, Nurse, Infection Control, Diabetes, Tuxford Clinic, Newark Road, Tuxford, NG22 0NA, Tel.: 01777 871664

Mrs J Boswell, Nurse, Macmillan, Retford Hospital, North Road, Retford, DN22 7XF, Tel.: 01777 274400

East Midlands Strategic Health Authority

Mrs L Jones, Nurse, Macmillan, Retford Hospital, North Road, Retford, DN22 7XF, Tel.: 01777 274400

Mrs M Lester, Nurse, Tissue Viability, Bassetlaw Hospital, Kilton, Worksop, S81 0BD, Tel.: 01909 500990 ext 2901

Broxtowe and Huckwall Primary Care Trust

Trust Headquarters, Priory Court
Derby Road,
NOTTINGHAM, NG9 2TA
Tel.: 0115 875 4900

Admin & Senior Management
Ms E McGuirk, Chief Executive, Tel.: 0115 875 4925
Ms B Reed, Patient/Primary Care Manager, Tel.: 0115 875 4942
Ms J Webber, Director of Community Services, Tel.: 0115 875 4919

Child Health
Ms S Dryden, Children with Disabilities, Children's Centre, City Hospital Campus, Hucknall Road, Nottingham, NG5 1PB, Tel.: 0115 962 7658
Mr A Perks, Child Health/School Nurses, Priory Court, Derby Road, Nottingham, NG9 2TA,
Dr L Polnay, Child Health, Radford Health Centre, Ilkeston Road, Radford, Nottingham, Tel.: 0115 942 0360

Child Health Records
Ms S Dryden, Child Health Records, Children's Centre, Nottingham City Hospital Campus, Hucknall Road, Nottingham, NG5 1PB, Information Services, Linden House, 261 Beechdale Road, Aspley, Nottingham, NG8 3EY, Tel.: 0115 942 6000 ext 48728

Child Protection/Safeguarding Children
Ms J Dickens, Child Protection, Children's Centre, Nottingham City Hospital Campus, Hucknall Road, Nottingham, NG5 1PB, Tel.: 0115 962 7658
Ms V Simmner, Named Nurse, Child Protection, Children's Centre, Nottingham City Hospital Campus, Hucknall Rd, Nottingham, NG5 1PB,

Clinical Leads (NSF)
Ms J Copping, Clinical Lead, CHD & Diabetes,
Ms L Davidson, Clinical Lead, CHD & Diabetes,
Mr N Thompson, Clinical Lead, Cancer,
Mr A Perks, Clinical Lead, Care of the Elderly,

District Nursing
Mr A Perks, District Nurses, Priory Court, Derby Road, Nottingham, NG9 2TA,
Ms B Reed, Patient/Primary Care Manager, Tel.: 0115 875 4942
Ms J Webber, Director of Community Services, Tel.: 0115 875 4919

Family Planning Services
Ms J Parker, Lead Nurse, Victoria Health Centre, Glasshouse Street, Nottingham, NG1 3LW, Tel.: 0115 948 0500

Health Visitors
Mr A Perks, Priory Court, Derby Road, Nottingham, NG9 2TA,

Other Services
Ms K Hughes, Health Shop, Broad Street, Nottingham, Tel.: 0115 947 5474

School Nursing
Mr A Perks, School Nursing, Priory Court, Derby Road, Nottingham, NG9 2TA,
Ms S Spanswick, Adviser School Nursing, Eastwood Health Centre, Nottingham Road, Eastwood, Notts, NG16 3GL, Tel.: 01773 712218

Specialist Nursing Services
Ms S Brown, Continence, Continence Advisory Service, Ropewalk House, The Ropewalk, Nottingham, Tel.: 0115 948 5511
Ms S Taj, Asian Worker, Diabetic Care, Dietetics Dept, Linden House, Tel.: 0115 942 6000
Ms M Wilson, Huntington's Disease, Sherwood Rise Clinic, 29 Nottingham Road, Sherwood, Nottingham, Tel.: 0115 969 2277
Ms F Lewis, Infection Control, Sherwood Health Centre, Tel.: 0115 956 8898

Ms L Bradbury, Macmillan, Hayward House, City Hospital, Tel.: 0115 969 1169
Ms H Coxon, Macmillan, Hayward House, City Hospital, Tel.: 0115 969 1169
Ms A Hallsworth, Macmillan, Hayward House, City Hospital, Tel.: 0115 969 1169
Ms C Halsall, Macmillan, Hayward House, City Hospital, Tel.: 0115 969 1169
Ms L Phillips, Macmillan, Hayward House, City Hospital, Tel.: 0115 969 1169
Ms P Wakefield, Macmillan, Hayward House, City Hospital, Tel.: 0115 969 1169
Ms C Guilford, Nurse Specialist, Primary Care, Portland Medical Practice, The Health Centre, Curtis Street, Hucknall, Nottingham, NG15 7JE,
Ms G Bailey-Holgate, Sickle Cell & Thalassaemia, Mary Potter Hostel, Mary Potter Health Centre, Gregory Boulevard, Nottingham, NG7 7HY, Tel.: 0115 942 0330
Ms S Pankhurst, Tissue Viability, Sherwood Health Centre, Tel.: 0115 956 8898

The Homeless/Travellers & Asylum Seekers
Homeless Team, Sherwood Rise Clinic, Tel.: 0115 969 2277

Central Derby Primary Care Trust

Trust Headquarters, Derwent Court
1 Stuart Street
DERBY, DE1 2FZ
Tel.: 01332 203102

Admin & Senior Management
Mr G English, Chief Executive,

Child Health
Child Health Department, Derwent Shared Services NHS Trust, Child Health, 4th Floor Laurie House, Colyear St, Derby, DE1 1LJ, Tel.: 01332 868816/17/18/19

Child Health Records
Child Health Records, Child Health Department, Derwent Shared Services NHS Trust, 4th Floor Laurie House, Colyear Street, Derby, DE1 1LJ, Tel.: 01332 868816/17/18/19

Child Protection/Safeguarding Children
Child Protection Unit, Wilderslowe, 121 Osmaston Road, Derby, DE1 2GD, Tel.: 01332 363371
Mrs L Hopwell, Co-ordinator, Looked After Children Department, Wilderslowe, 121 Osmaston Road, Derby, DE1 2GA, Tel.: 01332 363371
Ms T Ndili, Named Nurse, Child Protection,
Ms M Saunders, Designated Nurse for whole of Southern Derbyshire, Child Protection, Wilderslowe, 121 Osmaston Road, Derby, DE1 2GD, Tel.: 01332 363371
Dr J Tresidder, Designated Doctor for whole of Southern Derbyshire, Child Protection, Wilderslowe, 121 Osmaston Road, Derby, DE1 2GD, Tel.: 01332 363371

Clinical Leads (NSF)
Dr P Marks, Clinical Lead, Cancer,
Dr P Wood, Clinical Lead, CHD,
Dr M Browne, Clinical Lead, Diabetic Care,
Dr L Elliott, Clinical Lead, Older People,

HIV/AIDS
Ms M Dawson, Babington Hospital, Tel.: 01773 824171

Specialist Nursing Services
Ms R Dutton, Continence, Home Loans Store, Manor Parkway, Derby, Tel.: 01332 267976
Ms H Daly, Diabetic Care, Derbyshire Royal Infirmary, London Road, Derby, DE1 2QY, Tel.: 01332 254610
Ms C Evans, Infection Control, Health & Safety Services, Babington Hospital, Tel.: 01773 824171
Mrs M Campbell, Macmillan, Macmillan Unit, London Road, Derby, Tel.: 01332 254906

Ms E Evans, Stoma Care, Liaison Office, 123/5 Osmaston Road, Derby, Tel.: 01332 366717
Ms S Woodcock, Stoma Care, Liaison Office, 123/5 Osmaston Road, Derby, Tel.: 01332 366717

Charnwood & N W Leicestershire Primary Care Trust
Trust Headquarters
Woodgate, LOUGHBOROUGH
LE11 2TZ
Tel.: 01509 567700

Admin & Senior Management
Ms A Barrett, Director of Quality & Professional Practice,
Mr A Clarke, Chief Executive,
Clinical Leads (NSF)
Dr P Mulka, Clinical Lead, Cancer,

Chesterfield & North Derbyshire Royal Hospital NHS Trust
Trust Headquarters
Chesterfield & North Derbyshire Royal Hospital, Calow
CHESTERFIELD
S44 5BL
Tel.: 01246 277271

Admin & Senior Management
Mr R Clarke, Director of Nursing & Clinical Dev, Chesterfield & N Derbyshire Royal Hospital, Calow, Chesterfield, S44 5BL, Tel.: 01246 277271 ext 2426
Ms S McDermott, Deputy Director of Nursing & Clinical Dev, Chesterfield & N Derbyshire Royal Hospital, Calow, Chesterfield, S44 5BL, Tel.: 01246 277271 ext 3151
Mr E Morton, Chief Executive, Chesterfield & N Derbyshire Royal Hospital, Calow, Chesterfield, S44 5BL, Tel.: 01246 277271 ext 2144
Child Health
Ms L Chambers, Community Paediatric Team Leader (Continence), Child, Adolescent & Family Therapy Services, Marsden Street Clinic, Chesterfield, S40 1JY, Tel.: 01246 514412
Child, Adolescent & Family Therapy Services, Edmund Street Clinic, Chesterfield, S44 8TD, Tel.: 01246 451252
Child, Adolescent & Family Therapy Services, Buxton Health Centre, New Spring House, Bath Road, Buxton, SK17 6NN, Tel.: 01298 72445
Mr N Palfreyman, Service Manager, (Acting), Marsden Street Clinic, Chesterfield, S40 1JY, Tel.: 01246 297751
Ms H Parkes, Community Paediatric Team Leader (Oncology),
Child Health Records
Child Health Records, Saltergate Health Centre, Saltergate, Chesterfield, S40 1SX, Tel.: 01246 514426
Child Protection/Safeguarding Children
Ms K Bennett, Child Protection, Saltergate Health Centre, Saltergate, Chesterfield, S40 1SX, Tel.: 01246 514405 ext 2954
Ms J Bizley, Child Protection, Saltergate Health Centre, Saltergate, Chesterfield, S40 1SX, Tel.: 01246 514405 ext 2954
Ms L Hughes, Senior Nurse Advisor, Child Protection, Saltergate Health Centre, Saltergate, Chesterfield, S40 1SX, Tel.: 01246 514405 ext 2954
Ms K Lush, Child Protection, Saltergate Health Centre, Saltergate, Chesterfield, S40 1SX, Tel.: 01246 514405 ext 2954
Community Midwifery
Community Midwifery Office, Tel.: 01246 512577
Emergencies, Tel.: 01246 200666
Miss S Smith, Head of Midwifery, Scarsdale Wing, Chesterfield & North Derbyshire Royal Hospital, Tel.: 01246 512505
Liaison Services
Ms G Hesketh, Community Liaison, Chesterfield & N Derbyshire Royal Hospital, Calow, Chesterfield, S44 5BL, Tel.: 01246 552622

Ms S Mace, Paediatric Liaison Health Visitor, Chesterfield & N Derbyshire Royal Hospital, Calow, Chesterfield, S44 5BL, Tel.: 01246 277271 ext 2513
Ms P Perry, Neonatal Midwifery, Chesterfield & N Derbyshire Royal Hospital, Calow, Chesterfield, S44 5BL, Tel.: 01246 277271 ext 2516
Ms J Sambrook, Paediatric Liaison (Cardio, Respirat, CF), CDC, Saltergate, Chesterfield, S40 1SX, Tel.: 01246 552955 ext 4561
School Nursing
Ms M Bound, Lead Professional School Nurse, Saltergate Health Centre, Saltergate, Chesterfield, S40 1SX, Tel.: 01246 514409
Mrs H Guildford, Lead Professional School Nurse, Saltergate Health Centre, Saltergate, Chesterfield, S40 1SX, Tel.: 01246 514409

Chesterfield Primary Care Trust
Trust Headquarters, Scarsdale
Nightingale Close, off Newbold Road
CHESTERFIELD, Derbyshire, S41 7PF
Tel.: 01246 231255

Admin & Senior Management
Ms A Dray, Chief Executive, Scarsdale, Nightingale Close, off Newbold Road, Chesterfield, Derbyshire, S41 7PF,
Ms K Martin, Acting Director of Nursing & Clinical Quality, Walton Hospital, Whitecotes Lane, Chesterfield S41 7PF,
Child Protection/Safeguarding Children
Ms C Hill, Safeguarding Children, Named Nurse, Child Protection, Saltergate Health Centre, Chesterfield, Tel.: 01246 514405
Clinical Leads (NSF)
Dr R Mee, Clinical Lead, CHD & Diabetes, The Surgery, Scarsdale Road, Whittington Moor, Chesterfield, S41 8NA,
Dr D Black, Clinical Lead Cancer, Scarsdale, Nightingale Close, off Newbold Road, Chesterfield, Derbyshire, S41 7PF,
Community Matrons
Ms V Longden, Community Matron, Holywell House, Holywell Street, Chesterfield, S41 7SD, Tel.: 01246 273075
Ms F Mossman, Community Matron, Brimington Surgery, Church Street, Brimington, Chesterfield, S43 1JG, Tel.: 01246 273224
Ms A Thickett, Community Matron, Avenue House Surgery, 109 Saltergate, Chesterfield, S40 1LE, Tel.: 01246 556967
Ms L Yates, Avondale Surgery, 5 Avondale Road, Chesterfield, S40 4TF, Tel.: 01246 232946
District Nursing
Ms A Baker, Community Services Manager, Community Nursing Office, Walton Hospital, Whitecotes Lane, Chesterfield, S40 3HW, District Nurses, Walton Hospital, Whitecotes Lane, Chesterfield, S40 3HW, Tel.: 01246 515639
Ms C Payne, Primary Care Services Manager, Walton Hospital, Whitecotes Lane, Chesterfield, S40 3HW, Tel.: 01246 515639
Health Visitors
Health Visitors, Walton Hospital, Tel.: 01246 515639
Learning Disabilities
Ms A Gibbins, Manager, Ash Green, Ashgate Road, Chesterfield, S42 7JE,

Daventry & South Northants Primary Care Trust
Trust Headquarters, Nene House
Drayton Fields Industrial Estate
DAVENTRY
Northants, NN11 5EA
Tel.: 01327 705610

Admin & Senior Management
Ms S Buckingham, Director of Nursing & Professional Development,
Dr K Herbert, Chief Executive,
Child Protection/Safeguarding Children
Ms J Forrester, Child Protection, Nene House, Drayton Fields Industrial Estate, Daventry, NN11 5EA, Tel.: 01327 708108

East Midlands Strategic Health Authority

Clinical Leads (NSF)
Dr M Davies, Clinical Lead, Cancer,
Dr J Shribman, Clinical Lead, CHD,
Dr A Craig, Clinical Lead, Diabetic Care,
Ms L Woods, Clinical Lead, Older People,
Specialist Nursing Services
Ms T Longhurst, Continence, Brixworth Clinic,
Ms J Phillips, Services Manager, Palliative Care, Cynthia Spencer
Hospice, Northampton, Tel.: 01604 678033

Derby Hospitals (Foundation) NHS Trust
Trust Headquarters, Derby City General Hospital
Uttoxeter Road
DERBY
DE22 3NE
Tel.: 01332 340131

Admin & Senior Management
Ms K Fawcett, Director of Nursing, Derby Hospitals (Foundation)
NHS Trust, Derby City General Hospital, Uttoxeter Road, Derby,
DE22 3NE, Tel.: 01332 340131

Derbyshire Dales & South Derbyshire Primary Care Trust
Trust Headquarters, Park Hill
Hilton Road
EGGINTON
Derbyshire
DE65 6GU
Tel.: 01283 731300
Fax.: 01283 731301

Admin & Senior Management
Ms N Ennis, Chief Executive, Parkhill, Hilton Road, Egginton,
Derbyshire, DE65 6GU, Tel.: 01283 731300
Ms J Pendleton, Director of Patient Services, Parkhill, Hilton Road,
Egginton, Derbyshire, DE65 6GU, Tel.: 01283 731300
Child Health
Child Health Department, Derwent Shared Services, 4th Floor,
Laurie House, Colyear St, Derby, DE1 1LJ, Tel.: 01332 626300
Child Health Records
Child Health Department, Derwent Shared Services, 4th Floor,
Laurie House, Colyear Street, Derby, DE1 1LJ, Tel.: 01332 626300
Child Protection/Safeguarding Children
Ms A Robinson, Named Nurse, Child Protection, Wilderslowe, 121
Osmaston Road, Derby, DE1 2GD, Tel.: 01332 363371
Ms D Cook, Named Nurse, Looked After Children, Repton Health
Centre, Askew Grove, Repton, Derbyshire, DE65 6SH, Tel.: 01283
703407
Mrs L Hopwell, Co-ordinator, Looked After Children, Wilderslowe,
121 Osmaston Road, Derby, DE1 2GA, Tel.: 01332 363371
Ms J Murray, Named Nurse, Looked After Children, Repton Health
Centre, Askew Grove, Repton, Derbyshire, DE65 6SH, Tel.: 01283
703407
Clinical Leads (NSF)
Ms J Mellor, Clinical Lead, Cancer,
Dr J Titterton, Clinical Lead, CHD, - Diabetes,
Community Matrons
Ms K Elliott, Community Matron, Long Term Conditions, - Cancer,
Repton Health Centre, Askew Grove, Repton, Derbyshire, DE65
6SH, Tel.: 01283 703407
Ms A Heeley, Community Matron, Long Term Conditions, - Cancer,
Repton Health Centre, Askew Grove, Repton, Derbyshire, DE65
6SH, Tel.: 01283 703407
Ms M Miles, Community Matron, Long Term Conditions, - Cancer,
Repton Health Centre, Askew Grove, Repton, Derbyshire, DE65
6SH, Tel.: 01283 703407

Ms L Ratcliffe, Community Matron, Long Term Conditions, - Cancer,
Repton Health Centre, Askew Grove, Repton, Derbyshire, DE65
6SH, Tel.: 01283 703407
District Nursing
Ms S Allen, Team Leader, Repton Health Centre, Askew Grove,
Repton, Derbyshire, DE65 6SH, Tel.: 01283 703407
Ms A Wilson, Team Leader, Repton Health Centre, Askew Grove,
Repton, Derbyshire, DE65 6SH, Tel.: 01283 703407
Equipment Loan Services
ICES for Derby City, NRS, Tel.: 0845 1204768
ICES for Derbyshire County, Mediquip, Tel.: 01773 604426
Wheelchair & Incontinence Services, Manor Stores, Off Uttoxeter
Road, Derby, DE22 3NB, Tel.: 01332 267973
Health Visitors
Ms J Fairfield, Team Leader, Repton Health Centre, Askew Grove,
Repton, Derbyshire, DE65 6SH, Tel.: 01283 703407
Ms G Levick, Team Leader, Wirksworth Health Centre, Hannage
Way, Wirksworth, Derbyshire, DE4 4JG, Tel.: 01629 823721
Liaison Services
Liaison Services, Wilderslowe, 121 Osmaston Road, Derby, DE1,
Pharmacy
Ms J Titterton, Park Hill, Hilton Road, Egginton, Derbyshire, DE65
6GU, Tel.: 01283 731300
School Nursing
Ms J Fairfield, Team Leader, Repton Health Centre, Askew Grove,
Repton, Derbyshire, DE65 6SH, Tel.: 01283 703407
Ms G Levick, Team Leader, Wirksworth Health Centre, Hannage
Way, Wirksworth, Derbyshire, DE4 4JG, Tel.: 01629 823721
Specialist Nursing Services
Ms D Roscoe, Liaison Nurse, Cardiac Rehabilitation, Park Hill, Hilton
Road, Egginton, Derbyshire, DE65 6GU, Tel.: 01283 731300
Ms J Russell, Nurse, COPD, Repton Health Centre, Askew Grove,
Repton, Derbyshire, DE65 6SH, Tel.: 01283 703407
Ms S Towey, Nurse, COPD, Repton Health Centre, Askew Grove,
Repton, Derbyshire, DE65 6SH, Tel.: 01283 703407
Ms J Carr, Nurse, Infection Control, Repton Health Centre, Askew
Grove, Repton, Derbyshire, DE65 6SH, Tel.: 01283 703407

Derbyshire Mental Health Services NHS Trust
Trust Headquarters, Bramble House
Kingsway Hospital, Kingsway
DERBY
Derbyshire
DE22 3LZ
Tel.: 01332 623737

Learning Disabilities
Amber Valley Team, Tel.: 01773 828644
Derby City (East) Team, Tel.: 01332 293474
Derby City (North) Team, Tel.: 01332 717777
Derby City (South Team), Tel.: 01332 717000
Derbyshire Dales (South) Team, Tel.: 01629 825400
Erewash Team, Tel.: 0115 909 8679
Ms C Gilby, Acting Associate Director of Learning Disabilities, Aston
Hall Hospital, Aston upon Trent, Derbyshire, DE72 2AL, Tel.: 01332
792414/794247
South Derbyshire Team, Tel.: 01283 238085

East Lincolnshire Primary Care Trust
Trust Headquarters, Boston West Business Park
Sleaford Road
BOSTON
PE21 8EG
Tel.: 01205 318000

Admin & Senior Management
Ms J Froggatt, Chief Executive,

East Midlands Strategic Health Authority

Child Health Records
Ms V Holmes, Lincolnshire South West PCT, c/o Orchard House, Sleaford,
Clinical Leads (NSF)
Dr R North, Clinical Lead, Child Protection,
Dr I Harkess, Clinical Lead, Children,
Dr D Bailey, Clinical Lead, Diabetic Care,
District Nursing
Ms L Johnson, Community Senior Nurse - District Nursing, c/o Spaldiney Health Centre,
Ms V Raies, Community Senior Nurse - District Nursing, c/o ELPCT, BBC West Street, Boston, PE21 8QR,
Ms L Simpson, Head of Community Nursing, Boston West Business Park, Sleaford Road, Boston, PE21 8EG, Tel.: 01205 318000
Health Visitors
Ms C Dunnington, Community Senior Nurse - Health Visitors,
Ms E Marshall, Community Senior Nurse - Health Visitors,
Ms S McKown, Community Senior Nurse - Health Visitors,
Ms S Shaw, Community Senior Nurse - Health Visitors,
Specialist Nursing Services
Ms J Coupland, The New Surgery, Wragby,
Mr C Smith, Cardiac Rehabilitation, Lindsey Suite, Louth County Hospital, Tel.: 01507 600100
Ms M Johnstone, Project Lead, Intermediate Care, Louth County Hospital,
Ms L Bray, Palliative Care, Health Centre, 78 Victoria Road, Mablethorpe, Tel.: 01507 473250/479843

Eastern Leicester Primary Care Trust

Trust Headquarters, Mansion House
41 Guildhall Lane
LEICESTER
LE1 5FR
Tel.: 0116 295 1400

Admin & Senior Management
Miss C Clifton, Chief Executive,
Ms A Hogarth, Acting Director of Patient Services,
Child Health
Ms E Bretney-Dextor, Enkalon House, 3rd Floor, 92 Regent Road, Leicester, Tel.: 0116 295 1585
Child Health Records
Child Health Department, Bridge Park Road, Thurmaston, Leicester, LE4 8PQ, Tel.: 0116 225 2525
Child Protection/Safeguarding Children
Ms A Hogarth, Lead - Child Protection, Enkalon House, 3rd Floor, 92 Regent Road, Leicester, Tel.: 0116 295 1585
Ms J Lane, Child Protection, Enkalon House, 3rd Floor, 92 Regent Road, Leicester, Tel.: 0116 295 1589
Clinical Leads (NSF)
Dr T McMullen, Clinical Lead, CHD
Dr P Copson, Clinical Lead, Cancer,
Dr V Jaranji, Clinical Lead, Children,
Dr M Wheatley, Clinical Lead, Diabetic Care,
Dr E Yardley, Clinical Lead, Older People,
Community Nursing Services
Ms N Stott, Enkalon House, 3rd Floor, 92 Regent Road, Leicester, Tel.: 0116 295 1584
District Nursing
Ms E Bretney-Dextor, Neighbourhood Co-ordinator, Prince Philip House, St Matthews Health Centre, Malabar Road, Leicester, LE1 2NZ, Tel.: 0116 224 4600
Ms C Carter, Neighbourhood Co-ordinator, Enkalon House, 3rd Floor, 92 Regent Road, Leicester, Tel.: 0116 295 1582
Charnwood Health Centre, 1 Spinney Hill Road, Leicester, LE5 3GH, Tel.: 0116 253 8031

Prince Philip House, St Matthews Health Centre, Malabar Road, Leicester, LE1 2NZ, Tel.: 0116 224 4600
Rushey Mead Health Centre, Gleneagles Avenue, Leicester, LE4 7ZX, Tel.: 0116 266 9631
St Peters Health Centre, Sparkenhoe Street, Leicester, LE2 0TA, Tel.: 0116 253 1941
Ms N Stott, Neighbourhood Co-ordinator, St Peters Health Centre, Sparkenhoe Street, Leicester, LE2 0TA, Tel.: 0116 253 1941
Uppingham Road Health Centre, 131 Uppingham Road, Leicester, LE5 4BP, Tel.: 0116 276 4545
Specialist Nursing Services
Ms V Jivanji, Sickle Cell & Thalassaemia, Charnwood Health Centre, Tel.: 0116 253 8031
The Homeless/Travellers & Asylum Seekers
Ms J Gray, Consultant Nurse - Homeless Service, Tel.: 0116 295 4631
Ms H Rhodes, Consultant Nurse - Assist Service, Tel.: 0116 295 4631

Erewash Primary Care Trust

Trust Headquarters, Toll Bar House
Derby Road
ILKESTON
Derbyshire
DE7 5FE
Tel.: 0115 931 6100
Fax.: 0115 931 6101

Admin & Senior Management
Ms V Jablonski, Director of Nursing & Quality,
Child Health
Child Health Department, Derwent Shared Services NHS Trust, Child Health, 4th Floor Laurie House, Colyear St, Derby, DE1 1LJ, Tel.: 01332 868816/17/18/19
Ms M Sharpe, Assistant Director of Clinical Services (Community), Toll Bar House, Derby Road, Ilkeston, Derbyshire, DE7 5FE, Tel.: 0115 931 6100
Child Health Records
Child Health Records, Child Health Department, Derwent Shared Services NHS Trust, 4th Floor Laurie House, Colyear Street, Derby, DE1 1LJ, Tel.: 01332 868816/17/18/19
Child Protection/Safeguarding Children
Mrs H Gulliford, Looked After Children, Named Nurse, Ilkeston Health Centre, White Lion Square, Ilkeston, Derbyshire, DE75 7EF, Tel.: 0115 9305599
Mrs L Hopwell, Co-ordinator, Looked After Children Department, Wilderslowe, 121 Osmaston Road, Derby, DE1 2GA, Tel.: 01332 363371
Ms M Racioppi, Named Nurse, Child Protection, Wilderslowe, Osmaston Road, Derby, Tel.: 01332 363371
Clinical Leads (NSF)
Ms V Jablonski, Clinical Lead, Older People & Children's,
Ms G Greensmith, Clinical Lead, Cancer,
Dr J Ashcroft, Clinical Lead, CHD,
Mr D Muir, Clinical Lead, Diabetic Care,
Community Nursing Services
Mr R Carroll, Director, Primary Care & Community Services, Ilkeston Health Centre, South Street, Ilkeston, Derbyshire, DE7 5PZ, Tel.: 0115 951 2300
Mrs V Jablonski, Director of Clinical Services, Toll Bar House, Derby Road, Ilkeston, Derbyshire, DE7 5FE, Tel.: 0115 931 6100
District Nursing
Mr R Carroll, Director, Primary Care & Community Services (District Nurses), Ilkeston Health Centre, South Street, Ilkeston, Derbyshire, DE7 5PZ, Tel.: 0115 951 2300
Ms V Jablonski, Director of Clinical Services, Toll Bar House, Derby Road, Ilkeston, Derbyshire, DE7 5FE, Tel.: 0115 931 6100

East Midlands Strategic Health Authority

Family Planning Services
Dr Abrahan, Consultant, c/o Wilderslowe, Osmaston Road, Derby,
Tel.: 01332 363371

Health Visitors
Ms M Sharpe, Service Manager, Children's Services (Health
Visitors), Long Eaton Health Centre, Midland, Tel.: 0115 946 1200

Liaison Services
Liaison Services, Tel.: 01332 366717

Specialist Nursing Services
Mr D Muir, Lead, Diabetic Care, Ilkeston Community Hospital,
Heanor Road, Ilkeston, Derbyshire, DE7 8LN, Tel.: 0115 930 5522
Ms G Renshaw, Haematosis Nurse, Haematology, Highfields
Medical Centre, 86 College Street, Long Eaton, Nottingham, NG10
4NP, Tel.: 0115 973 4502
Ms C Waterfield, Haematosis Nurse, Haematology, Highfields
Medical Centre, 86 College Street, Long Eaton, Nottingham, NG10
4NP, Tel.: 0115 973 4502
Ms L Palframan, Home Support, Intensive Care, Ilkeston Community
Hospital, Heanor Road, Ilkeston, Derbyshire, DE7 8LN, Tel.: 0115
930 5522

Walk In Centres
Ilkeston Health Centre, South Street, Ilkeston, Derbyshire, DE7 5PZ,
Tel.: 0115 930 5599
Long Eaton Health Centre, Midland Street, Long Eaton,
Nottinghamshire, NG10 1NY, Tel.: 0115 946 1200

Gedling Primary Care Trust

Trust Headquarters, Byron Court
Brookfield Road, Arnold
NOTTINGHAM, NG5 7ER
Tel.: 0115 993 1444

Admin & Senior Management
Ms L Winstanley, Chief Executive, Byron Court, Brookfield Road,
Arnold, Nottingham, NG5 7ER, Tel.: 0115 993 1444

Child Health
Ms G Smith, Senior Manager, Primary Care (Children & Young
People), Park House Health & Social Care Centre, 61 Burton Road,
Carlton, Nottingham, NG4 3DQ, Tel.: 0115 961 7616

Child Health Records
Health Records Manager, Nottingham Health Informatics Service,
Linden House, 261 Beechdale Road, Aspley, Nottingham, NG8 3EY,
Tel.: 0115 942 6000

Child Protection/Safeguarding Children
Ms K Pell, Named Nurse, Child Protection,

Clinical Leads (NSF)
Mrs T Gaskill, Director of Primary Care, Park House Health & Social
Care Centre, 61 Burton Road, Carlton, Nottingham, NG4 3DQ, Tel.:
0115 961 7616
Dr M Corcoran, Clinical Lead, Cancer, Byron Court, Brookfield Road,
Arnold, Nottingham, NG5 7ER, Tel.: 0115 993 1431
Dr M Corcoran, Clinical Lead, Diabetic Care, Byron Court, Brookfield
Road, Arnold, Nottingham, NG5 7ER, Tel.: 0115 993 1431

Community Matrons
Ms J Brocklehurst, Senior Manager, Primary Care (Adults), Park
House Health & Social Care Centre, 61 Burton Road, Carlton,
Nottingham, NG4 3DQ, Tel.: 0115 961 7616

District Nursing
Ms J Brocklehurst, Senior Manager, Park House Health & Social
Care Centre, 61 Burton Road, Carlton, Nottingham, NG4 3DQ, Tel.:
0115 961 7616

Health Visitors
Ms G Smith, Senior Manager, Primary Care (Children & Young
People), Park House Health & Social Care Centre, 61 Burton Road,
Carlton, Nottingham, NG4 3DQ, Tel.: 0115 961 7616

Other Services
Ms S Marston, Park House Health & Social Care Centre, 61 Burton
Road, Carlton, Nottingham, NG4 3DQ, Tel.: 0115 961 7616

Pharmacy
Ms J Swan, Senior Manager, Primary Care (Pharmacy & Planning),
Byron Court, Brookfield Road, Arnold, Nottingham, NG5 6LN,

School Nursing
Ms R Woods, School Nurse Co-ordinator, Calverton Clinic, St
Wilfrid's Square, Calverton, Nottingham, NG14 6FP, Tel.: 0115
9652610

The Homeless/Travellers & Asylum Seekers
Podiatry Service provided for the Homeless,

Greater Derby Primary Care Trust

Trust Headquarters, Derwent Court
1 Stuart Street
DERBY, DE1 2FZ
Tel.: 01332 224000

Admin & Senior Management
Ms L Elliott, Lead Clinician,
Mr D Hathaway, Chief Executive,
Ms T Thompson, Director of Patient Care Services,

Child Health
Child Health Department, Derwent Shared Services NHS Trust,
Child Health, 4th Floor Laurie House, Colyear St, Derby, DE1 1LJ,
Tel.: 01332 868816/17/18/19

Child Health Records
Child Health Records, Child Health Department, Derwent Shared
Services NHS Trust, 4th Floor Laurie House, Colyear Street, Derby,
DE1 1LJ, Tel.: 01332 868816/17/18/19

Child Protection/Safeguarding Children
Mrs L Hopwell, Co-ordinator, Looked After Children Department,
Wilderslowe, 121 Osmaston Road, Derby, DE1 2GA, Tel.: 01332
363371
Mrs R Walker, Looked After Children, Named Nurse, Sinfin Moor
Health Centre, Sinfin District Centre, Arleston Lane, Sinfin, Derby,
DE24 3DF, Tel.: 01332 764012
Ms A Nyatanga, Named Nurse, Child Protection, Wilderslowe, 121
Osmaston Road, Derby, DE1 2GD, Tel.: 01332 363371

Clinical Leads (NSF)
Dr P Marks, Clinical Lead, Cancer,
Dr P Wood, Clinical Lead, CHD,
Dr M Browne, Clinical Lead, Diabetic Care,
Dr L Elliott, Clinical Lead, Older People,

District Nursing
District Nurses, All based at GPs throughout area,

Health Visitors
Health Visitors, All based at GPs throughout area,

Liaison Services
Mr C Anderson, Liaison, Sister, 123/5 Osmaston Road, Derby, Tel.:
01332 366717
Ms G Ashley, Liaison, Sister, 123/5 Osmaston Road, Derby, Tel.:
01332 366717
Ms E Morris, Liaison, Sister, 123/5 Osmaston Road, Derby, Tel.:
01332 366717
Ms L Palfreman, Liaison, Sister, 123/5 Osmaston Road, Derby, Tel.:
01332 366717
Ms D Stanley Smith, Liaison, Sister, 123/5 Osmaston Road, Derby,
Tel.: 01332 366717

Specialist Nursing Services
Ms A Bradbrook, Nurse, Assessment, Derby City General Hospital,
Uttoxeter Road, Derby, Tel.: 01332 340131 ext 6968
Ms H Joolia, Nurse, Assessment, Derby City General Hospital,
Uttoxeter Road, Derby, Tel.: 01332 340131 ext 6968
Ms J Townes, Nurse, Assessment, Derby City General Hospital,
Uttoxeter Road, Derby, Tel.: 01332 340131 ext 6968
Ms R Dutton, Continence, Home Loans Store, Manor Parkway,
Derby, Tel.: 01332 267976
Ms F Kinghorn, Continence, Home Loans Store, Manor Parkway,
Derby, Tel.: 01332 267976

East Midlands Strategic Health Authority

Ms K Dale, Co-ordinator, Intermediate Care, 123/5 Osmaston Road, Tel.: 01332 299983
Ms S Cliff, Dietetic Adviser, Nutrition, Aston Hall Hospital, Weston Road, Aston upon Trent, Derby, Tel.: 01332 792412
Ms R Cornes, Older People, 123/5 Osmaston Road, Derby, Tel.: 01332 299983

High Peak and Dales Primary Care Trust
Trust Headquarters, Newholme Hospital
Baslow Road
BAKEWELL
Derbyshire
DE45 1AD
Tel.: 01629 817892
Fax.: 01629 817960

Admin & Senior Management
Dr B Laurence, Director of Public Health, Newholme Hospital, Tel.: 01629 817937
Mr N Swanwick, Chief Executive,
Child Health Records
Mrs J Thompson, Assistant Director Support Services, Buxton Hospital, London Road, Buxton, SK17 9NJ, Tel.: 01298 212227
Child Protection/Safeguarding Children
Mrs A Ledger, Director of Practice & Professional Development, Newholme Hospital, Tel.: 01629 817967
Clinical Leads (NSF)
Mr P Carney, Clinical Lead, Cancer, Head of Finance & Commissioning,
Dr B Laurence, Clinical Lead, Children, Director of Public Health,
Dr B Laurence, Clinical Lead, Diabetes, Director of Public Health,
Mrs A Ledger, Clinical Lead, Long Term Conditions, Director of Practice & Professional Development,
Mr T Broadley, Clinical Lead, Older People, Director of Primary & Community Care Services,
Community Matrons
Mr P Murphy, Matron, Newholme Hospital, Baslow Road, Bakewell, DE45 1AD, Tel.: 01629 817856
Ms K Sherlock, Matron, Whitworth Hospital, 330 Bakewell Road, Darley Dale, Matlock, DE4 2JD, Tel.: 01629 580211
Ms H Worsley, Cavendish Hospital, Manchester Road, Buxton, SK17 6TE, Tel.: 01298 212273
District Nursing
Mr T Broadley, Director of Primary & Community Care Services, Newholme Hospital, Tel.: 01629 817890
Equipment Loan Services
Mrs E Price, Assistant Director of Rehabilitation Services, Whitworth Hospital, 330 Bakewell Road, Darley Dale, Matlock, DE4 2JD, Tel.: 01629 593032
Family Planning Services
Ms P Jackson, Contraception & Sexual Health, Lead Nurse, Saltergate Health Centre, Saltergate, Chesterfield, S40 1SX, Tel.: 01629 514700
Health Visitors
Mr T Broadley, Director of Primary & Community Care Services, Newholme Hospital, Tel.: 01629 817890
Pharmacy
Ms H Tomlinson, Newholme Hospital, Tel.: 01629 817930

Hinckley & Bosworth Primary Care Trust
Trust Headquarters, Swan House Business Centre
The Park
MARKET BOSWORTH
Warks
CV13 0LJ
Tel.: 01455 293200
Fax.: 01455 290700

Admin & Senior Management
Mr C Blackler, Chief Executive, Tel.: 01455 293200
Mrs N Dymond, Director of Nursing & Quality Improvement, Tel.: 01455 293200
Dr D Jackson, Clinical Governor, Tel.: 01455 293200
Mrs D Postle, Head of Nursing, Tel.: 01455 293200

Kettering General Hospital NHS Trust
Trust Headquarters, Kettering General Hospital
Rothwell Road
KETTERING
Northamptonshire
NN16 8UZ
Tel.: 01536 492000
Fax.: 01536 493767

Child Protection/Safeguarding Children
Ms C Grundy, Child Protection, Stockburn Memorial Home, Tel.: 01536 410360
Community Midwifery
Community Midwives, Tel.: 01536 492899
Ms E Kennedy, Head of Midwifery & Gynaecology, Rockingham Wing, Kettering General Hospial NHS Trust, Rothwell Road, Kettering, NN16 8UZ, Tel.: 01536 492895
Ms B Norman, Senior Clinical Midwife, Kettering General Hospial NHS Trust, Rothwell Road, Kettering, NN16 8UZ, Tel.: 01536 492889
HIV/AIDS
Warren Hill House, Kettering General Hospital, Tel.: 01536 493593/493594
Learning Disabilities
Mrs A McCarthy, Special Needs Specialist,
Liaison Services
Ms F Defrais, Kettering General Hospital, Tel.: 01536 493305/493554

Leicester City West Primary Care Trust
Trust Headquarters, Ground Floor
Mansion House, 41 Guildhall Lane
LEICESTER
LE1 5FR
Tel.: 0116 295 1100

Admin & Senior Management
Ms M Ashton, Director of Nursing, Research & Development, 4th Floor Humberstone House, 81-83 Humberstone Gate, Leicester, LE1 1WB, Tel.: 0116 295 8453
Mr M Darby, Director of Clinical Services,
Mr R McMahon, Chief Executive, Ground Floor, Mansion House, 41 Guildhall Lane, Leicester, LE1 5FR, Tel.: 0116 295 1100
Child Health Records
Child Health Department, Bridge Park Plaza, Bridge Park Road, Thurmaston, Leicester, LE4 8PQ, Tel.: 0116 225 2525
Child Protection/Safeguarding Children
Mr A Spanswick, Named Nurse, Child Protection, Bridge Park Plaza, Bridge Park Road, Thurmaston, Leics, LE4 8PQ, Tel.: 0116 225 3926
Clinical Leads (NSF)
Dr T Paterson, Clinical Lead, Cancer,
Dr M Ashton, Clinical Lead, CHD,
Dr M Tolofari, Clinical Lead, Children,
Dr D Talbot, Clinical Lead, Diabetic Care,
District Nursing
Beaumont Leys Health Centre, 1 Littlewood Close, Beaumont Leys, Leicester, LE4 0QR,
New Parks Health Centre, St Oswald Road, Leicester, LE3 6RT,
Pasley Road Health Centre, Pasley Road, Eyres Monsell, Leicester, LE2 9BU,

East Midlands Strategic Health Authority

Westcotes Health Centre, Fosse Road South, Leicester, LE3 0LP,
Winstanley Drive Health Centre, 138 Winstanley Drive, Leicester,
LE3 1PB,
Other Services
Ms L Wilkins, Primary Care, Nurse Advisor,

Leicestershire Partnership NHS Trust
Trust Headquarters, George Hine House
Gipsy Lane
LEICESTER, LE5 0TD
Tel.: 0116 225 6000

Learning Disabilities
Ms C Cunningham-Hill, Assistant Director, Mansion House, Leicester
Frith Hospital, Groby Road, Leicester, LE3 9QF, Tel.: 0116 225 5200
Ms G Gates, Nurse Advisor, Leicester Frith Hospital, Groby Road,
Leicester, LE3 9QF, Tel.: 0116 225 5205
Ms H McCabe, Team Manager, City,
Ms P Ostell, Team Manager, North Leicestershire,
Ms A Porter, Team Manager, South Leicestershire,

Lincolnshire Partnership NHS Trust
Trust Headquarters, Cross O Cliff Court
Bracebridge Heath
LINCOLN
Lincolnshire
LN4 2HN
Tel.: 01522 513355

Learning Disabilities
Boston, 1 Corktree Crescent, London Road, Boston, PE21 7EH, Tel.:
01205 367604
Bourne/Stamford, Chartwell House, Pinfold Road, Bourne, PE10
9HT, Tel.: 01778 426645
Grantham, 40 Westgate, Grantham, NG31 6LY, Tel.: 01476 578318
Lincoln, Orchard House, Orchard Street, Lincoln, Tel.: 01522 554156
Louth, Tel.: 01507 601957
Skegness, 40 Algitha Road, Skegness, Tel.: 01754 765206
Sleaford, Council Offices, Kesteven Street, Sleaford, NG34 7EB,
Tel.: 01529 414144
Spalding, Health Clinic, Beechfield Gardens, Holland Road Clinic,
Spalding, PE11 1UH, Tel.: 01775 711551
West Lindsey, Market Rasen Team, Health Clinic, Gordon Fields,
Market Rasen, LN8 3AD, Tel.: 01673 844544
West Lindsey, John Coupland Hospital, Ropery Road,
Gainsborough, DN21 2GJ, Tel.: 01427 816557

Lincolnshire South West Primary Care Trust
Trust Headquarters, Orchard House
South Rauceby
SLEAFORD
NG34 8PP
Tel.: 01529 416000

Admin & Senior Management
Mr D Bray, Chief Executive,
Mr D Dunham, General Manager, Orchard House, South Rauceby,
Sleaford, NG34 8PP,
Ms S Savage, Director of Community Sevices,
Child Health Records
Ms V Holmes, Child Health Supervisor, Orchard House, South
Rauceby, Sleaford, NG34 8PP, Tel.: 01529 416000
Child Protection/Safeguarding Children
Miss C Smith, Designated Nurse/Child Protection Department
Manager, Orchard House, South Rauceby, Sleaford, NG34 8PP,
Tel.: 07919 046562
Clinical Leads (NSF)
Dr J Glencross, Clinical Lead, CHD & Diabetes,
Dr S Glencross, Clinical Lead, Cancer,

Community Nursing Services
Ms S Savage, Director of Primary & Community Services, Orchard
House, South Rauceby, Sleaford, NG34 8PP, Tel.: 01529 416089
District Nursing
Mrs J Jollands, Manager, District Nursing, Orchard House, South
Rauceby, Sleaford, NG34 8PP, Tel.: 01529 416000
Health Visitors
Mrs J Jollands, Manager, Health Visiting, Orchard House, South
Rauceby, Sleaford, NG34 8PP, Tel.: 01529 416000
School Nursing
Mrs J Jollands, Manager, School Nursing/Child Health, Orchard
House, South Rauceby, Sleaford, NG34 8PP, Tel.: 01529 416000
Specialist Nursing Services
Ms M Smith, Advisor, Continence, Springfield Park, Springfield
Road, Grantham, Tel.: 01476 590285
Ms M Beswick, Podiatry, Orchard House, South Rauceby, Sleaford,
NG34 8PP, Tel.: 01529 416063
Ms H Field, Tissue Viability, Springfield Park, Springfield Road,
Grantham, Tel.: 01476 590416

Melton, Rutland & Harborough Primary Care Trust
Trust Headquarters, PERA Innovation Park
Nottingham Road
MELTON MOWBRAY
Leicestershire
LE13 0RH
Tel.: 01664 855000
Fax.: 01664 855001

Admin & Senior Management
Mrs D Murphy, Director of Nursing & Clinical Governance, Tel.:
01664 855006
Mrs W Saviour, Chief Executive,
Child Health Records
Childrens Services, Bridge Park Plaza, Bridge Park Road,
Thurmaston, Leicester, LE4 8PQ, Tel.: 0116 225 2525
Child Protection/Safeguarding Children
Ms C Silcott, Named Nurse, Child Protection, Market Harborough
District Hospital, Coventry Road, Market Harborough, Leics, LE16
9DD, Tel.: 01858 418197
Clinical Leads (NSF)
Dr K Allen, Clinical Lead, Cancer,
Dr P Rathbone, Clinical Lead, CHD,
Dr S Wooding, Clinical Lead, Older People,
Community Nursing Services
Mrs K Baxter, Melton and Syston, Senior Nurse, St Mary's Hospital,
Thorpe Road, Melton Mowbray, Leics, LE13 1SJ, Tel.: 01664
854806
Mrs N Beacher, Market Harborough, Senior Nurse, Market
Harborough District Hospital, Coventry Road, Market Harborough,
Leics, LE16 9DD, Tel.: 01858 418106
Ms R Sylvester, Rutland, Senior Nurse, Rutland Memorial Hospital,
Cold Overton Road, Oakham, Rutland, LE15 6NT, Tel.: 01572
722008
District Nursing
District Nurses, Rutland, Rutland Memorial Hospital, Cold Overton
Road, Oakham, Rutland, LE15 6NT, Tel.: 01572 722552
District Nurses, Syston, Syston Health Centre, Melton Road, Syston,
Leics, LE7 2EQ, Tel.: 0116 2640964
District Nurses, Market Harborough, Market Harborough District
Hospital, Coventry Road, Market Harborough, Leics, LE16 9DD, Tel.:
01858 410500
District Nurses, Kibworth, Kibworth Health Centre, Smeeton Road,
Kibworth, Leics, LE8 0LG, Tel.: 0116 2791239
District Nurses, Melton, St Mary's Hospital, Thorpe Road, Melton
Mowbray, Leics, LE13 1SJ, Tel.: 01664 854800

East Midlands Strategic Health Authority

Family Planning Services
Family Planning, Market Harborough - Tuesdays 7-9pm, Market Harborough District Hospital, Coventry Road, Market Harborough, Leics, LE16 9DD, Tel.: 01858 410240
Family Planning, Rutland - Tuesdays 6-8pm, Rutland Memorial Hospital, Cold Overton Road, Oakham, Rutland, LE15 6NT, Tel.: 01572 722070
Family Planning, Melton & Syston - Wednesdays 6-8pm, St Mary's Hospital, Thorpe Road, Melton Mowbray, Leics, LE13 1SJ, Tel.: 01664 854800
Health Visitors
Health Visitors, Melton, St Mary's Hospital, Thorpe Road, Melton Mowbray, Leics, LE13 1SJ, Tel.: 01664 854800
Health Visitors, Rutland, Rutland Memorial Hospital, Cold Overton Road, Oakham, Rutland, LE15 6NT, Tel.: 01572 722552
Health Visitors, Syston, Syston Health Centre, Melton Road, Syston, Leics, LE7 2EQ, Tel.: 0116 2640964
Health Visitors, Market Harborough, Market Harborough District Hospital, Coventry Road, Market Harborough, Leics, LE16 9DD, Tel.: 01858 410500
School Nursing
School Nurses, Market Harborough, Market Harborough District Hospital, Coventry Road, Market Harborough, Leics, LE16 9DD, Tel.: 01858 410500
School Nurses, Melton & Syston, St Mary's Hospital, Thorpe Road, Melton Mowbray, Leics, LE13 1SJ, Tel.: 01664 854800
School Nurses, Rutland, Rutland Memorial Hospital, Cold Overton Road, Oakham, Rutland, LE15 6NT, Tel.: 01572 722552
The Homeless/Travellers & Asylum Seekers
Health Visitors, New Parks Health Centre, Leicester, Tel.: 0116 2958750

Newark & Sherwood Primary Care Trust

Trust Headquarters, 65 Northgate
NEWARK
NG24 1HD
Tel.: 01636 700238

Admin & Senior Management
Ms B Dempster, Director of Operations & Strategy, Tel.: 01636 670619
Mr D Sharp, Chief Executive,
Child Health Records
Centralised & Child Health Services Department, Mansfield Community Hospital, Stockwell Gate, Mansfield, NG18 5QJ, Tel.: 01623 785170
Child Protection/Safeguarding Children
Ms J Bizley, North Notts Consultant Nurse, Mansfield Community Hospital, Tel.: 01623 785165/785179
Ms C Williams, Child Protection, Newark HC, 21 Lombard Street, Newark, Notts, Tel.: 01636 704693
Clinical Leads (NSF)
Dr P Jones, Clinical Lead, Cancer,
Dr V Pollard, Clinical Lead, CHD,
Community Matrons
Ms C Corringham, Community Matron, Edwinstowe HC, High Street, Edwinstowe, Notts, Tel.: 01636 825851
Ms J Dennis, Community Matron, Southwell MC, Ropewalk, Southwell, Notts, Tel.: 01636 817931
Ms G Goodwin, Team Leader, Community Matron, Hawtonville Clinic, St Mary's Gardens, Newark, Notts, Tel.: 01636 703500
Ms Z Read, Community Matron, Newark Health Centre, 21 Lombard Street, Newark, Notts, Tel.: 01636 703255
Ms L Sinclair, Community Matron,
District Nursing
Ms S Briggs, Locality Manager, Newark Clinic, 21 Lombard Street, Newark, NG24 1XQ, Tel.: 01636 703255

Ms M Coates, Evening Service - District Nurses, Newark HC, 21 Lombard Street, Newark, Notts, Tel.: 01636 704693
Ms C Lobo, Team Leader, District Nurses, Newark HC, 21 Lombard Street, Newark, Notts, Tel.: 01636 704693
Ms L Penford, Team Leader, District Nurses, Southwell MC, Ropewalk, Southwell, Notts, Tel.: 01636 817938
Equipment Loan Services
ICES (from Feb 02),
Health Visitors
Ms J Dickinson, Older People, Health Visitor,
Ms T Durrani, Team Leader, Health Visitors, Rainworth HC, Warsop Lane, Rainworth, Notts, Tel.: 01623 793966
Ms W Van Alderwegen, Paediatric Health Visitor/CONI, Tel.: 01623 785019
Ms S Wiseman, Team Leader, Health Visitors, Fountain MC, Sherwood Avenue, Newark, Tel.: 01636 704693
Liaison Services
Ms M Gannon, Intermediate Care Co-ordinator,
Ms L Sitton Kent, Intermediate Care Co-ordinator,
Pharmacy
Ms C Quinn, Pharmacy, Newark & Sherwood PCT HQ, 65 Northgate, Newark, Notts, Tel.: 01636 700238
School Nursing
Ms T Durrani, Rainworth HC, Warsop Lane, Rainworth, Notts, Tel.: 01623 793966
Ms S Wiseman, Fountain MC, Sherwood Avenue, Newark, Tel.: 01636 704693
Specialist Nursing Services
Ms G Bacon, King's Mill Centre, Sutton in Ashfield, Tel.: 01623 622515 ext 3390
Ms A Jones, Determining Nurse - FNC, Social Service Offices, 65 Northgate, Newark, Tel.: 01636 654654
Ms F Saunders, Continence, Ashfield Community Hospital, Kirkby, Notts, Tel.: 01623 784785
Ms M Maddison, Co-ordinator, Continuing Care, St John Street Health Centre, Mansfield, Tel.: 01623 622541
Ms D Warrington, Co-ordinator, Continuing Care, St John Street Health Centre, Mansfield, Tel.: 01623 622541
Ms S Bird, Infection Control, Southwell MC, Ropewalk, Southwell, Notts, Tel.: 01636 817938
Ms L Woolmer, Manager, Palliative Care, John Eastwood Hospice, Sutton in Ashfield, Tel.: 01623 622626
Ms L McNamara, Parkinson's Disease, Mansfield Community Hospital, Tel.: 01623 785127
Ms H Lamont, Rehab Physio, Pulmonary Disorder, Hawtonville Clinic, St Mary's Gardens, Newark, Notts, Tel.: 01636 703500
Ms K McEwan, COPD, Nurse Specialist, Respiratory, Hawtonville Clinic, St Mary's Gardens, Newark, Notts, Tel.: 01636 703500
Ms R Langrick, Tissue Viability, Oak Tree Lane Health Centre, Mansfield, Tel.: 01623 651261
The Homeless/Travellers & Asylum Seekers
Ms F Fish, Health Visitor, Edwinstowe Health Centre, High Street, Edwinstowe, Notts, Tel.: 01623 822063
Ms E Whylie, Lombard Street Surgery, Lombard Street, Newark, Notts, Tel.: 01636 702363

North Eastern Derbyshire Primary Care Trust

Trust Headquarters, St Mary's Court
St Mary's Gate
CHESTERFIELD
S41 7TD
Tel.: 01246 551158
Fax.: 01246 544620

Admin & Senior Management
Ms S Hubbard, Senior Nurse Primary Care, St Mary's Court, St Mary's Gate, Chesterfield, S41 7TD, Tel.: 01246 551158

East Midlands Strategic Health Authority

Dr M McShane, Chief Executive, Block C, St Mary's Court, St Mary's Gate, Chesterfield, S41 7TD, Tel.: 01246 551158

Mrs S Moody, Director of Patient Services, Block C, St Mary's Court, St Mary's Gate, Chesterfield, S41 7TD, Tel.: 01246 551158

Mrs T Owen, Director of Quality Improvement & Executive Nurse, Block C, St Mary's Court, St Mary's Gate, Chesterfield, S41 7TD, Tel.: 01246 551158

Ms V Roberts, Senior Nurse - Primary Care, St Mary's Court, St Mary's Gate, Chesterfield, S41 7TD, Tel.: 01246 551158

Child Protection/Safeguarding Children

Ms C Webster, Child Protection, Saltergate Clinic, Chesterfield,

Clinical Leads (NSF)

Mrs A Hayes, Clinical Lead, CHD, St Mary's Court,

Community Matrons

Ms T Goldsmith, Community Matron, Bolsover Clinic, Unit 15, Bolsover Business Park, Woodhouse Lane, Bolsover, S44 6BD, Tel.: 01246 823146

Ms T Mansell, Community Matron, Bolsover Clinic, Unit 15, Bolsover Business Park, Woodhouse Lane, Bolsover, S44 6BD, Tel.: 01246 823146

Ms H Morrison, Community Matron, Bolsover Clinic, Unit 15, Bolsover Business Park, Woodhouse Lane, Bolsover, S44 6BD, Tel.: 01246 823146

Ms W Rayner, Community Matron, Bolsover Clinic, Unit 15, Bolsover Business Park, Woodhouse Lane, Bolsover, S44 6BD, Tel.: 01246 823146

Ms M Scaise, Community Matron, Bolsover Clinic, Unit 15, Bolsover Business Park, Woodhouse Lane, Bolsover, S44 6BD, Tel.: 01246 823146

Ms P Taylor, Community Matron, Bolsover Clinic, Unit 15, Bolsover Business Park, Woodhouse Lane, Bolsover, S44 6BD, Tel.: 01246 823146

Health Visitors

Mr S Randolph, Health Visitor for Older People, Whitwell Health Centre, The Square, Whitwell, Nr Worksop, Notts, Tel.: 01909 720851

Other Services

Mrs R Sowerby, Primary Care Manager - Provider Services,

School Nursing

Ms J Duly, Saltergate Clinic, Saltergate, Chesterfield, S40 1SX,

Specialist Nursing Services

Ms J Brown, Nurse Specialist, Continence, Walton Hospital, Whitecotes Lane, Walton, Chesterfield, Tel.: 01246 515151

Mr P McCarthy, Nurse Specialist, Diabetes, Chesterfield PCT, Scarsdale, Newbold Road, Chesterfield, Tel.: 01246 231255

Ms M O'Connor, Nurse Specialist, Infection Control, Walton Hospital, Whitecotes Lane, Walton, Chesterfield, Tel.: 01246 515151

Ms J Bennett, Nurse Specialist, Stroke Care, Walton Hospital, Whitecotes Lane, Walton, Chesterfield, Tel.: 01246 515151

Ms B Craven, Nurse Specialist, Tissue Viability, Walton Hospital, Whitecotes Lane, Walton, Chesterfield, Tel.: 01246 515151

Northampton General Hospital NHS Trust

Trust Headquarters, Northampton General Hospital
Billing Road, NORTHAMPTON, NN1 5BD
Tel.: 01604 634700
Fax.: 01604 544630

Acute Specialist Nursing Services

Ms K Grey, Labour Ward, Tel.: 01604 634700

Ms C Lockyer, Midwife Development, Tel.: 01604 634700

Ms J Matthew, Community In-patient Physio, Tel.: 01604 634700

Ms P Massey, A&E, Tel.: 01604 634700

Ms M Ward, Acute Pain, Tel.: 01604 634700

Ms S Ireson, Nurse, Breast Care, Tel.: 01604 634700

Ms N Clifford, Chest Nurse, Cardiac, Tel.: 01604 634700

Ms J Mason, Service Manager Cardiac, Eleanor Ward, Tel.: 01604 634700

Ms K Noy, Chest Nurse, Cardiac, Tel.: 01604 634700

Ms S Hargreaves, Nurse Practitioner, Colorectal, Tel.: 01604 634700

Ms C Sombach, Nurse Practitioner, Colorectal, Tel.: 01604 634700

Ms V Beedle, Colposcopy, Tel.: 01604 634700

Ms P Slinn, Restart Programme, COPD, Tel.: 01604 634700

Ms M Burt, Nurse, Critical Care, Tel.: 01604 634700

Ms P Woolacot, Clinical Nurse Specialist, Dermatology, Tel.: 01604 634700

Ms J Anfield, Diabetic Care, Tel.: 01604 545822

Ms E Richardson, Nurse, Diabetic Care, Tel.: 01604 634700

Ms I Eirkson, Nurse, Epilepsy, - Paediatrics, Tel.: 01604 634700

Ms S Belson, Nurse, Fertility, Tel.: 01604 634700

Ms N Phelan, Genetics, Tel.: 01604 544659

Ms C Campbell, Clinical Nurse Specialist, Gynae/Oncology, Tel.: 01604 634700

Ms D Johnson, Nurse Specialist, Gynaecology, - Urology, Tel.: 01604 634700

Ms S Rose, Pre-op Assessment, Gynaecology, Tel.: 01604 634700

Ms G Smith, Gynaecology, Tel.: 01604 634700

Ms S Wilde, Gynaecology, Tel.: 01604 634700

Ms A Steele, Nurse, Haematology, Tel.: 01604 634700

Ms L Davies, Infection Control, Tel.: 01604 634700

Ms J Dilley, Outreach Nurse, ITU, Tel.: 01604 634700

Ms A Hicks, Maxillofacial, Tel.: 01604 634700

Ms K Franklin, Neurology, Tel.: 01604 634700

Ms M Goodwin, Neurology, Tel.: 01604 634700

Ms F Masters, Sister, Nutrition, Tel.: 01604 634700

Ms S Kells, Macmillan Nurse, Oncology, Tel.: 01604 634700

Ms L Wells, Macmillan Nurse, Oncology, Tel.: 01604 634700

Ms L Sangster, Orthopaedics, - Trauma, Tel.: 01604 634700

Ms D Sweeney, Orthopaedics, - Trauma, Tel.: 01604 634700

Ms J Burditt, Community, Paediatrics, Tel.: 01604 634700

Community Sisters, Paediatrics, Tel.: 01604 545517

Ms J Melvin, Macmillan, Clinical Nurse Specialist, Palliative Care, Tel.: 01604 634700

Ms M Coe, Facilitator, Practice Development, Tel.: 01604 634700

Ms J Taylor, Head of Therapy, Radiology, Tel.: 01604 634700

Ms A Howes, CCU, Rehabilitation, Tel.: 01604 634700

Ms S Ward, CCU, Rehabilitation, Tel.: 01604 634700

Ms M Jeffrey, Development, Research, Tel.: 01604 634700

Ms S Marsh, Development, Research, Tel.: 01604 634700

Ms J Woodward, Midwife, Research, Tel.: 01604 634700

Ms C Warlow, Services Manager, Resuscitation Training, Tel.: 01604 634700

Ms A Bardill, Stoma Care, Tel.: 01604 545570

Ms A Rashwan, Stoma Care, Tel.: 01604 634700

Ms B Finch, Urodynamics, Tel.: 01604 634700

Ms P Ferrar, Macmillan Nurse, Urology/Oncology, Tel.: 01604 634700

Ms L Earby, Nurse, Vascular, Tel.: 01604 634700

Admin & Senior Management

Ms L Anderson, Deputy Director Patient & Nursing Services, Northampton General Hospital, Billing Road, Northampton, NN1 5BD, Tel.: 01604 545759

Ms J Rumsey, Director Patient & Nursing Services, Northampton General Hospital, Billing Road, Northampton, NN1 5BD, Tel.: 01604 545752

Child Health

Child Health Services, Northampton General Hospital, Cliftonville, Northam, Tel.: 01604 634700

Child Health Records

Ms S Collier, Child Health Records, Northampton General Hospital, Cliftonville, Northam, Tel.: 01604 544596

Child Protection/Safeguarding Children

Ms S Leatherland, Senior Nurse, Child Protection, Northampton General Hospital, Billing Road, Northampton, NN1 5BD, Tel.: 01604 544984

East Midlands Strategic Health Authority

Community Midwifery
Mrs K Grey, Specialist Midwife, Northampton General Hospital, Cliftonville, Northampton, NN1 5BD, Tel.: 01604 545265
Mrs J Hayley, Assistant Director, Head of Midwifery/Gynaecology, Barratt Maternity Home, Northampton General Hospital, Tel.: 01604 634225

Health Visitors
Ms A Rampley, Liaison Paediatric Health Visitor, c/o Disney Ward, Northampton General Hospital, Cliftonville, NN1 5BD, Tel.: 01604 544673

Learning Disabilities
Ms L Cockerill, Learning Disabilities, 37 Camelot Way, Duston, Northampton,

Other Services
Ms R Young, Medical Admissions Unit, Tel.: 01604 634700

School Nursing
Ms W Irons, Liaison School Nurse, c/o Disney Ward, Northampton General Hospital, Cliftonville, NN1 5BD, Tel.: 01604 544292

Northampton Primary Care Trust

Trust Headquarters, Highfield
Cliftonville Road
NORTHAMPTON
NN5 5DN
Tel.: 01604 615000
Fax.: 01604 615261/615010

Admin & Senior Management
Ms M Burrows, Chief Executive,
Ms A Hillery, Director of Community Development, Sunnyside, Cliftonville, Northampton General Hospital, Tel.: 01604 232337
Mr A Howard, Director of Integrated Care & Operations, Tel.: 01604 615307

Child Health Records
See Northampton General Hospital NHS Trust,

Child Protection/Safeguarding Children
Mrs F Dale, Designated Nurse, Child Protection, Camp Hill Clinic, Hunsbury Hill Road, Northampton, NN4 9UW, Tel.: 01604 666513

Clinical Leads (NSF)
Dr K Sood, Clinical Lead, CHD & Older People,
Dr M Barrowclough, Clinical Lead, Diabetic Care,

District Nursing
Ms K Abel, Senior Manager, Primary Care, Weston Favell Health Centre, Billing Brook Road, Northampton, NN3 4DW, Tel.: 01604 412130
Ms D Wooton, Community Evening Nursing Service, Kent House, Princess Marina Hospital, Upton, Northampton, NN5 6UH, Tel.: 01604 595216

Family Planning Services
Mrs G Black, Senior Nurse, St Giles Clinic, St Giles Street, Northampton, Tel.: 01604 620673
Dr F Mason, Clinical Director, St Giles Clinic, St Giles Street, Northampton, Tel.: 01604 620673

Liaison Services
Mrs H Anderson, Community Liaison, Billing House, Northampton General Hospital, Cliftonville, Northampton, NN1 5BD, Tel.: 01604 545568/545569
Mrs E Stock, Community Liaison, Billing House, Northampton General Hospital, Cliftonville, Northampton, NN1 5BD, Tel.: 01604 545568/545569

School Nursing
Ms V McDonald, School Nurse Manager, c/o Child Health Directorate, Northampton General Hospital, Billing Road, Northampton, NN1 5BD, Tel.: 01604 544605

Specialist Nursing Services
Disability Service, Cedar House, Manfield Campus, Kettering Road, Northampton, NN3 1AD, Tel.: 01604 499652

Ms F Llewellyn, Nurse Practitioner, Weston Favell Health Centre, Billing Brook Road, Northampton, NN3 4DW, Tel.: 01604 412130
Ms E Nesbitt, Macmillan, Danetre Hospital, Tel.: 01327 312267
Nurses, Macmillan, Cynthia Spencer House, Manfield Campus, Tel.: 01604 670671
Ms M Rogers, Macmillan, Danetre Hospital, Tel.: 01327 312160
Mrs E Clarke, Macmillan, Radiotherapy, Northampton General Hospital, Cliftonville, Northampton, NN1 5BD, Tel.: 01604 545228
Ms R Barlow, Community Team Manager, Rehabilitation, Highfield, Cliftonville Road, Northampton, NN5 5DN, Tel.: 01604 615262/615304
Ms E Penn, Clinical Nurse Specialist, Tissue Viability, Kent House, Princess Marina Hospital, Upton, Northampton, NN5 6UH, Tel.: 01604 752323
Ms E Musgrove, Wound Care, Kent House, Princess Marina Hospital, Tel.: 01604 752323

The Homeless/Travellers & Asylum Seekers
Ms V Dumbleton, Travellers & Homeless, Health Visitor, Maple Healthcare Project, St Michael's Church Office, Perry Street, Northampton, NN1 4HL, Tel.: 01604 250969
Ms V Dumbleton, Travellers, Whitefields Surgery, Hunsbury Hill Road, Camphill, Northampton, NN4 9, Tel.: 01604 666513

Northamptonshire Healthcare NHS Trust

Trust Headquarters, York House
Isebrook Hospital
WELLINGBOROUGH
NN8 1LP
Tel.: 01933 440099

Admin & Senior Management
Ms H Smart, Director of Nursing,

Clinical Leads (NSF)
Ms E N Griffiths, Clinical Lead, Cancer,

Community Midwifery
Community Midwifery Services Direct Lines, Tel.: 01536 494078/79
Mrs C Ginns, Community Midwifery Matron, Tel.: 01536 493359/492896
Miss E Kennedy, Head of Midwifery, Rockingham Wing, Kettering General Hospital, Rothwell Road, Kettering, NN16 8UZ, Tel.: 01536 492895/493689
Midwifery Services between 9.15 - 10 am, Tel.: 01933 440099

Northamptonshire Heartlands Primary Care Trust

Trust Headquarters, Bevan House
Kettering Parkway, Venture Park
KETTERING
NN15 6XR
Tel.: 01536 480300

Admin & Senior Management
Mrs R Patrick, Professional Head of Nursing, Tel.: 01536 494247
Ms D Smith, Executive Nurse/Deputy Director of Clinical Services, Nene House, Isebrook Hospital, Wellingborough, NN8 1LP, Tel.: 01536 494247

Child Health
Community Children's Nurse, Kettering General Hospital,

Child Health Records
Ms S Toyer,

Child Protection/Safeguarding Children
Ms A Nichols,

Clinical Leads (NSF)
Dr J Hughes, Clinical Lead, CHD & Cancer,
Dr T Morley, Clinical Lead, Diabetic Care,

Community Nursing Services
Ms I Hanlon,

East Midlands Strategic Health Authority

District Nursing
Ms L Bone, District Nurse,
Ms M Earl, District Nurse,
Ms J Jenkins, District Nurse,
Ms M Law, District Nurse,
Ms J Putnins, District Nurse,
Family Planning Services
Family Planning Services, (0830-1630), Tel.: 01536 492220
Health Visitors
Ms S Everett, Health Visitor,
Ms J Garside, Health Visitor,
Ms S Large, Health Visitor,
School Nursing
Ms S Toyer, Childrens Services (School Nurse), St Marys Hospital, Kettering,
Smoking Cessation
Ms S Bedfield,
Specialist Nursing Services
Ms H Lunt, CHD, Willowbrook Health Centre, Corby,
Ms G Rolfe, Dermatology, Albany House Medical Centre, Wellingborough,
Ms L Burgess, Diabetic Care, Kettering General Hospital,
Ms D Quinn, Multiple Sclerosis, Rectory Road Health Clinic, Rushden,
Mr R Glasspool, Parkinson's Disease, Rectory Road Health Clinic, Rushden,
Ms L Lancaster, Stoma Care, Kettering General Hospital,

Nottingham City Primary Care Trust

Trust Headquarters, Standard Court,
The Ropewalk, Park Row
NOTTINGHAM
NG1 6GN
Tel.: 0115 9123344

Admin & Senior Management
Mrs K Frankland, Locality General Manager, Sherwood Health Centre, Elmswood Gardens, Mansfield Road, Nottingham, NG5 4AD, Tel.: 0115 969 1777
Mr P Hunt, Locality General Manager, Meadows Health Centre, 1 Bridgeway Centre, Meadows, Nottingham, NG2 2JG, Tel.: 0115 986 1831
Mrs S Kirkwood, Locality General Manager, Wollaton Vale Health Centre, Wollaton Vale, Nottingham, NG8 2GR, Tel.: 0115 928 8861
Ms S Millbank, Chief Executive,
Mrs S Parker, Locality General Manager, Bulwell Health Centre, Main Street, Bulwell, Nottingham, NG6 8QJ, Tel.: 0115 977 0022
Mrs S Pickett, Locality General Manager, Meadows Health Centre, 1 Bridgeway Centre, Meadows, Nottingham, NG2 2JG, Tel.: 0115 986 1831
Mrs M Richardson, Locality General Manager, Meadows Health Centre, 1 Bridgeway Centre, Meadows, Nottingham, NG2 2JG, Tel.: 0115 986 1831
Ms J Sheard, Executive Nursing & Provisioning Director, Bulwell Health Centre, Main Street, Bulwell, Nottingham, NG6 8QJ, Tel.: 0115 875 9442
Mr R Simmons, Locality General Manager, Strelley Health Centre, Strelley Road, Strelley, Nottingham, NG8 6LN, Tel.: 0115 929 6911
Mr C Todd, Locality General Manager, Sherwood Rise Health Centre, Nottingham Road, Nottingham, Tel.: 0115 919 2550
Child Health
Ms K Frankland, Locality General Manager, Sherwood Health Centre, Elmswood Gardens, Mansfield Road, Nottingham, NG5 4AD, Tel.: 0115 969 1777
Child Health Records
Miss S Curtis, Child Health Records, Linden House, 261 Beechdale Road, Aspley, Nottingham, NG8 3EY, Tel.: 0115 942 8728

Child Protection/Safeguarding Children
Ms C Brown, Child Protection, Children's Centre, City Hospital Campus, Hucknall Road, Nottingham, NG5 1PB, Tel.: 0115 962 7658
Ms J Dickens, Child Protection, Children's Centre, City Hospital Campus, Hucknall Road, Nottingham, NG5 1PB, Tel.: 0115 962 7658
Ms S Morrell, Child Protection, Children's Centre, City Hospital Campus, Hucknall Road, Nottingham, NG5 1PB, Tel.: 0115 962 7658
Ms J O'Daly, Child Protection, Children's Centre, City Hospital Campus, Hucknall Road, Nottingham, NG5 1PB, Tel.: 0115 962 7658
Clinical Leads (NSF)
Mr R Simmons, Clinical Lead, CHD & Diabetes,
Ms S Kirkwood, Clinical Lead, Cancer,
Ms C Jordan, Clinical Lead, Care of the Elderly,
Ms K Frankland, Clinical Lead, Children,
Community Midwifery
Mrs L Jones, Head of Midwifery, Old Basford Health Centre, 1 Bailey Street, Old Basford, Nottingham, NG6 0HD, Tel.: 0115 942 0323
District Nursing
Ms L Colton, District Nurse Clinical Lead, John Ryle Health Centre, Southchurch Drive, Clifton, Nottingham, NG11 8AB, Tel.: 0115 940 5298
Ms J Hunt, District Nurse Clinical Lead, Wollaton Vale Health Centre, Wollaton Vale, Nottingham, NG8 2GR, Tel.: 0115 928 7793
Ms T Keane, District Nurse Clinical Lead, Radford Health Centre, Ilkeston Road, Radford, Nottingham, NG7 3GW, Tel.: 0115 942 0360
Ms D Kelly, District Nurse Clinical Lead, Bestwood Health Centre, Pedmore Valley, Bestwood Park Estate, Nottingham, NG5 5NN, Tel.: 0115 920 8799
Ms J McFarland, District Nurse Clinical Lead, Sneinton Health Centre, Beaumont Street, Nottingham, NG2 4PJ, Tel.: 0115 948 0488
Ms T Norris, District Nurse Clinical Lead, Derby Road Health Centre, 336 Derby Road, Nottingham, NG7 1QG, Tel.: 0115 978 8587
Ms E Self, District Nurse Clinical Lead, Meadows Health Centre, 1 Bridgeway Centre, Meadows, Nottingham, NG2 2JG, Tel.: 0115 986 1831
Equipment Loan Services
Ms S Bailey, ICES Partnership Manager, Acorn Annexe, Acorn Day Centre, Dalkeith Terrace, Hyson Green, Nottingham, NG7 5JG, Tel.: 0115 975 5651
Family Planning Services
Ms J Parker, Contraception & Sexual Health Services, Victoria Health Centre, Glasshouse Street, Nottingham, NG1 3LW, Tel.: 0115 948 0500
Health Visitors
Ms J Harrison, Health Visitor Clinical Lead, Meadows Health Centre, 1 Bridgeway Centre, Meadows, Nottingham, NG2 2JG, Tel.: 0115 986 1831
Ms K Kerslake, Health Visitor Clinical Lead, Sherwood Rise Health Centre, Nottingham Road, Nottingham, NG7 7AD, Tel.: 0115 919 2550
Ms J Moran, Health Visitor Clinical Lead, Strelley Health Centre, Strelley Road, Strelley, Nottingham, NG8 6LN, Tel.: 0115 929 6911
Ms R North, Health Visitor Clinical Lead, Sneinton Health Centre, Beaumont Street, Sneinton, Nottingham, NG2 4PJ, Tel.: 0115 948 0488
Ms S Roberts, Health Visitor Clinical Lead, Hucknall Road Medical Centre, Kibworth Close, Nottingham, NG5 1NA, Tel.: 0115 960 6652
Ms L Watson, Health Visitor Clinical Lead, Meadows Health Centre, 1 Bridgeway Centre, Meadows, Nottingham, NG2 2JG, Tel.: 0115 986 1831
Ms A Wilson, Health Visitor Clinical Lead, Bulwell Health Centre, Main Street, Bulwell, Nottingham, NG6 8QJ, Tel.: 0115 977 0022

East Midlands Strategic Health Authority

Other Services

Ms A Bancroft, Health Shop, Broad Street, Hockley, Nottingham, Tel.: 0115 947 5474

Ms H Coombes, Manager of Prison Health Services, HMP Nottingham Prison, Perry Road, Nottingham,

Ms H McCloughry, Rehabilitation & Intermediate Care Services, Mary Potter Hostel, Gregory Boulevard, Nottingham, NG7 7HY, Tel.: 0115 928 8861

Ms M Richardson, Manager, Interpreting Services, Meadows Health Centre, 1 Bridgeway, Meadows, Nottingham, NG7 2JG, Tel.: 0115 986 1831

Ms H Storer, Dietetic Service, Linden House, 261 Beechdale Road, Bilborough, Nottingham, NG8 3EY, Tel.: 0115 942 6000

Pharmacy

Ms M Bassi, Prescribing Advisor, Standard Court, Park Row, Nottingham, NG1 6GN, Tel.: 0115 912 3344

Ms T Behrendt, Prescribing Advisor, Standard Court, Park Row, Nottingham, NG1 6GN, Tel.: 0115 912 3344

School Nursing

Ms S Munks, Clinical Lead School Nurse, Wollaton Vale Health Centre, Wollaton Vale, Nottingham, NG8 2GR, Tel.: 0115 287 793

Ms J Simmonds, Clinical Lead School Nurse, Sherwood Rise Health Centre, Nottingham Road, Nottingham, NG7 7AD, Tel.: 0115 919 2550

Specialist Nursing Services

Ms S Harrop, Phlebotomy Co-ordinator, Old Basford Health Centre, 1 Bailey Street, Basford, Nottingham,

Ms S Brown, Continence, Ropewalk, The Ropewalk, Nottingham, Tel.: 0115 948 5534

Ms G Peck, Specialist Nurse, Diabetic Care, St Anns Health Centre, St Anns Well Road, Nottingham, Tel.: 0115 948 0560

Ms F Branton, Nurse, Infection Control, Sherwood Health Centre, Elmswood Gardens, Sherwood, Nottingham, NG5 4AD, Tel.: 0115 969 2277

Ms M Bates, (May Scheme), Macmillan, Wollaton Vale Health Centre, Wollaton Vale, Wollaton, Nottingham, NG8 2GR, Tel.: 0115 928 8861

Ms C Halsall, Nurse, Macmillan, Hayward House, City Hospital Campus, Hucknall Road, Nottingham, Tel.: 0115 969 1169

Ms J Bloomfield, Sickle Cell & Thalassaemia, Mary Potter Hostel, Gregory Boulevard, Hyson Garden, Nottingham, NG7 7HY, Tel.: 0115 942 0330

Ms S Pankhurst, Nurse, Tissue Viability, Sherwood Health Centre, Elmswood Gardens, Sherwood, Nottingham, NG5 4AD, Tel.: 0115 969 2277

The Homeless/Travellers & Asylum Seekers

Ms A Farnsworth, Specialist Nursing Traveller Team, Bulwell Health Centre, Main Street, Bulwell, Nottingham, NG6 8QJ, Tel.: 0115 977 0022

Ms S Regel, The Homeless/Travellers/Refugees, Sherwood Rise Health Centre, Nottingham Road, Nottingham, NG7 7AD, Tel.: 0115 919 2550

Walk In Centres

Ms A Simpson, Walk in Centre, London Road, Seaton House, City Link, Nottingham, NG2 4LA, Tel.: 0115 844 0212

Nottingham University Hospital NHS Trust

Nottingham City Hospital
Hucknall Road
NOTTINGHAM
NG5 1PB
Tel.: 0115 969 1169

Acute Specialist Nursing Services

Ms C Bill, Advanced Disease, Specialist Nurse, Breast Care, Tel.: ext 46827

Ms K Hassell, Advanced Disease, Specialist Nurse, Breast Care, Tel.: ext 45278

Ms L Jackson, Nurse Practitioner, Breast Care, Tel.: ext 34031

Ms K Mullinger, Nurse Practitioner, Breast Care, Tel.: ext 34350

Ms J O'Sullivan, Primary Disease, Specialist Nurse, Breast Care, Tel.: ext 39056

Ms R Owers, Nurse Practitioner, Breast Care, Tel.: ext 39053

Ms H Richardson, Primary Disease, Clinical Nurse Specialist, Breast Care, Tel.: ext 46827

Ms N Scot, Family History, Clinical Nurse Specialist, Breast Care, Tel.: ext 46869

Ms J Stewart, Primary Disease, Senior Nurse, Breast Care, Tel.: ext 46990

Ms L Winterbottom, Advanced Disease, Macmillan Nurse, Breast Care, Tel.: ext 46827

Ms K Allsop, Rapid Access Pain Clinic Nurse, Cardiology, Tel.: ext 46213

Ms J Burton, Clinical Trials Coordinator, Cardiology, Tel.: ext 34612

Mr P Ellis, Pre Admissions Co-ordinator, Cardiology, Tel.: ext 34979

Ms D Falcon-Long, Clinical Trials Coordinator, Cardiology,

Ms M Gadsby, Pre admissions clinic Nurse, Cardiology, Tel.: ext 46236

Ms C Smeathers, Rapid Access Pain Clinic Nurse, Cardiology, Tel.: ext 46232

Ms K Casement, Nurse Specialist, Cleft Lip & Palate, Tel.: ext 46184

Ms V Martin, Nurse Consultant, Cleft Lip & Palate, Tel.: ext 46184

Ms H McEachran Hill, Nurse Specialist, Cleft Lip & Palate, Tel.: ext 46184

Ms N Smith, Nurse Specialist, Cleft Lip & Palate, Tel.: ext 46184

Ms C Stone, Nurse Specialist, Cleft Lip & Palate, Tel.: ext 46184

Ms A Foster, Clinical Nurse Specialist, Continence, - Adults, Tel.: ext 34996

Ms A Brown, Child & Family Nurse Therapist, COPD, - Paediatrics, Tel.:

Ms A Dinning, Outreach Nurse, Critical Care, Tel.: ext 46070

Ms A Horner, Outreach Nurse, Critical Care, Tel.: ext 46111

Ms G Hudson, Outreach Nurse, Critical Care, Tel.: ext 46671

Ms C West, Clinical Governance, Critical Care, Tel.: ext 34214

Ms K Cuttell, Specialist Nurse, Diabetes, - Paediatrics, Tel.: ext 47515

Ms G Francis, Clinical Nurse Specialist, Diabetes, - Adults, Tel.: ext 46818

Ms L Houghton, Clinical Nurse Specialist, Diabetes, - Adults, Tel.: ext 46621

Ms C Soar, Clinical Nurse Specialist, Diabetes, - Adults, Tel.: ext 37921

Ms H Sowter, Clinical Nurse Specialist, Diabetes, - Adults, Tel.: ext 37922

Ms M Miles, Nurse Counsellor, Genetics, Tel.: ext 34437

Ms A Pilkington, Nurse Counsellor, Genetics, Tel.: ext 34437

Ms K Seitz, Nurse Counsellor, Genetics, Tel.: ext 34599

Ms H Westmoreland, Nurse Counsellor, Genetics, Tel.: ext 34437

Ms F Richardson, Lymphoma, Clinical Nurse Specialist, Haematology, Tel.: ext 34683

Ms L Watson, Bone Marrow Transplant, Co-ordinator, Haematology, Tel.: ext 45702

Ms J Dudley, Specialist Nurse, Heart Failure, Tel.: ext 34000

Ms A Holliday, Clinical Nurse Specialist, Infectious Diseases,

Ms J Blunt, Specialist Nurse, Pain Management, Tel.: 9202674

Ms G Harvey, Specialist Nurse, Pain Management, Tel.: ext 47345

Mr J Millard, Specialist Nurse, Pain Management, Tel.: ext 46803

Ms C Morrison, Specialist Nurse, Pain Management, Tel.: ext 46803

Ms A Nixon, Specialist Nurse, Pain Management, Tel.: ext 34035

Ms M Orpen, Specialist Nurse, Pain Management, Tel.: ext 46803

Ms A Baker, Sister, Rehabilitation, Tel.: ext 46618

Ms A Boswell, Transplant, Research Nurse, Renal, Tel.: ext 45023

Mr R Bowen, Donor Transplant Coordinator, Renal, Tel.: ext 46076

Ms S Broome, Nurse Practitioner, Renal, Tel.: ext 49768

Ms M Fish, Nurse Practitioner, Renal, Tel.: ext 49768

Ms A Frankton, Liver Donor Coordinator, Renal, Tel.: ext 39405

Ms T Friend, Donor Transplant Coordinator, Renal, Tel.: ext 45171

Ms L Fullerton, Anaemia Nurse, Renal, Tel.: ext 47202
Mr B Harvey, Paediatric Acute Dialysis Specialist, Renal, Tel.: ext 46448
Ms K Helm, Paediatric Transplant Sister, Renal, Tel.: ext 46608
Ms W Spooner, CAPD Manager, Renal, Tel.: ext 46137
Ms C Taggert, Research Nurse, Renal,
Ms J Dale, C.F., Nurse Specialist, Respiratory, - Paediatrics, Tel.: ext 46471
Ms D Foster, Specialist Nurse, Respiratory, - Paediatrics,
Ms J Mighton, Specialist Nurse, Respiratory, - Paediatrics,
Ms S Day, Clinical Nurse Specialist, Stoma Care, Tel.: ext 46736
Ms L Alexander, Nurse Practitioner, Thoracic, - Surgical, Tel.: ext 46101
Ms S Yates, Clinical Nurse Specialist, Tissue Viability,
Ms G McMonnies, Clinical Nurse Specialist, Urology, - Paediatrics, Tel.: ext 46626
Ms E Pacey, Clinical Nurse Specialist, Urology, - Adults, Tel.: ext 34082
Ms C Rhodes, Clinical Nurse Specialist, Urology, - Paediatrics, Tel.: ext 46626

Community Midwifery
Ms J Fagan, Senior Midwife Projects - Maternity Unit, Tel.: 47178
Ms A Godfrey, Midwife/Antenatal Screening Co-ordinator, Tel.: 47408
Ms S Goodley, Continuing Care Coordinator Neonatal Unit - Midwifery, Tel.: 46208

Liaison Services
Ms H Kirkham, Lower Limb Amputee Clinic, Liaison Nurse, Mobility Centre, Tel.: 47539
Ms M Perry, Lower Limb Amputee Clinic, Liaison Sister, Mobility Centre, Tel.: 47539

Queen's Medical Centre
NOTTINGHAM
NG7 2UH
Tel.: 0115 924 9924

Acute Specialist Nursing Services
Mr S Davidson, Nurse Specialist, Anti-Coagulation,
Mr J Waterall, Outreach, Nurse Specialist, Cardiac,
Mr M Melville, Nurse Specialist, Cardiac Rehabilitation,
Ms W Bee, Rapid Access, Nurse Specialist, Chest,
Ms J Wragg, Nurse Specialist, Colposcopy,
Ms W Berridge, Nurse Specialist, COPD,
Ms F Branch, Nurse Consultant, Critical Care,
Ms C Gradwell, Nurse Specialist, Dermatology,
Ms S Lawton, Nurse Consultant, Dermatology,
Ms P Clarke, Nurse Specialist, Diabetes,
Ms J Thompson, Nurse Specialist, DVT,
Ms B Pick, Nurse Specialist, Endoscopy,
Mr S Chalkley, Nurse Specialist, Epilepsy,
Ms C Hayes, Nurse Specialist, Epilepsy,
Ms A Massingham, Nurse Specialist, Haemophilia,
Ms R Kempson, Community Interface, Nurse Specialist, HCE,
Mr G Proctor, Interface, Nurse Specialist, HCE,
Ms S Stringer, Nurse Specialist, Head & Neck, - Cancer,
Ms D Pearce, Nurse Specialist, Heart Failure,
Ms P Powell, Nurse Specialist, Immunology, - Allergy,
Ms R Wheldon, Nurse Specialist, Immunology, - Deficiency,
Mr A Mierkalns, Nurse Specialist, Liver,
Ms L Heath, Nurse Specialist, Lung Cancer,
Ms J Meyerowitz, Nurse Specialist, Menopause,
Ms F Barnett, Nurse Specialist, Multiple Sclerosis,
Ms M Botsie, Nurse Specialist, Multiple Sclerosis,
Ms K Smith, Nurse Specialist, Multiple Sclerosis,
Ms S Adams, Nurse Specialist, Neuro-oncology,
Ms J Wright, Nurse Specialist, Neuro-oncology,
Ms J King, Nurse Specialist, Occulo Plastics,

Ms S Kordula, Nurse Specialist, Osteoporosis,
Ms L Marshall, Nurse Specialist, Osteoporosis,
Ms M Baker, Nurse Specialist, Pain Management,
Ms S Berrisford, Nurse Specialist, Pain Management,
Ms A Cavan, Nurse Specialist, Pain Management,
Ms J Conners, Nurse Specialist, Pain Management,
Mr I Nash, Nurse Specialist, Pain Management,
Ms T Towell, Nurse Consultant, Pain Management,
Ms S MacDonald-Preston, Nurse Specialist, Palliative Care,
Ms S Spencer, Nurse Specialist, Palliative Care,
Ms K Anderton, Nurse Specialist, Parkinson's Disease,
Ms J Morgan, Nurse Specialist, Respiratory,
Mr G Eyre, Nurse Specialist, Resuscitation,
Ms A Muir, Nurse Specialist, Rheumatology,
Ms G Godsall, Nurse Specialist, Skin Cancer,
Ms J Watts, Nurse Specialist, Stoma Care,
Ms S Pankhurst, Nurse Specialist, Tissue Viability,
Ms A Rich, Nurse Specialist, Vascular, - Ulcers,

Admin & Senior Management
Mr P Daly, Assistant Director of Nursing - Practice Development, C Floor, South Block, Queen's Medical Centre,
Ms F Dobson, Head of Continuing Professional Development, C Floor, South Block, Queen's Medical Centre,
Ms S Gavin, Assistant Director of Nursing - Surgical Division, Queen's Medical Centre,
Ms F McQuire, Head of Nursing & Midwifery Workforce Development, C Floor, South Block, Queen's Medical Centre,
Mr C Ovington, Director of Nursing, C Floor, South Block, Queen's Medical Centre,
Ms L Towell, Assistant Director of Nursing - Women & Children's Division, Queen's Medical Centre,
Mr P Walmsley, Assistant Director of Nursing - Medical Division, Queen's Medical Centre,
Ms T Walsh, Recruitment & Retention, Senior Nurse, C Floor, South Block, Queen's Medical Centre,
Ms M Clarke, Head, Infection Control, C Floor, South Block, Queen's Medical Centre,
Ms N Vaughan, Head, Infection Control, C Floor, South Block, Queen's Medical Centre,

Child Health
Ms N Gibbons, Gastro (Children),
Ms L Hutchinson, Rheumatology (Children),
Ms J Masterman, Head Nurse/Matron Children's Surgery,
Ms M Parr, Oncology (Children),
Ms J Savory, Pain Control (Children),
Ms F Simpson, Head Nurse/Matron Children's Medicine,
Ms A Swarbrick, Respiratory (Children),
Ms B Waldron, Epilepsy (Children),
Ms A Wright, Bowel (Children),

Child Protection/Safeguarding Children
Ms K Newham, Child Protection,

Community Midwifery
Ms L Gustard, Head of Midwifery,
Ms C Litherland, Neonatal Unit,
Ms A Walton, Early Pregnancy,

Discharge Co-ordinators
Ms G Rooker, Queen's Medical Centre,

Liaison Services
Mr M Holmes, Alcohol Liaison, Nurse Specialist,

Matrons/Modern Matrons
Mr G Marsh, Nights, Head Nurse/Matron,
Ms M Mercer, Head Nurse/Matron, Critical Care,
Ms K Bywater Pinto, Head Nurse/Matron, Dermatology,
Ms J Keogh, Head Nurse/Matron, Emergency Care,
Ms M Bentley, Head Nurse/Matron, ENT Surgery,
Ms J Barker, Head Nurse/Matron, General Surgery,
Ms J Golding, Head Nurse/Matron, Gynaecology,
Ms S Wright, Head Nurse/Matron, Gynaecology,

East Midlands Strategic Health Authority

Ms D Gill, Specialities, Head Nurse/Matron, Medical,
Mr A Harper, Acute HCE, Head Nurse/Matron, Medical,
Ms C Swinscoe, Head Nurse/Matron, Medical Admissions,
Ms C Maling, Neurosciences, Head Nurse/Matron, Neurosurgery,
Ms A Watts, Head Nurse/Matron, Ophthalmology,
Ms S Wade, Head Nurse/Matron, Orthopaedics, - Surgical,
Ms G Rooker, HCE, Head Nurse/Matron, Rehabilitation,
Mr J Murray, Cardio, Head Nurse/Matron, Respiratory,
Ms K Shacklock, Head Nurse/Matron, Spinal Injuries,
Ms S Dennis, Head Nurse/Matron, Trauma, - Surgical,

Nottinghamshire Healthcare NHS Trust

Trust Headquarters, The Resource
Duncan Macmillan House, Porchester Road
NOTTINGHAM
NG3 6AA
Tel.: 0115 969 1300

Learning Disabilities

Ms D Carr, CPN, Dept of LD, Highbury Hospital, Bulwell, Nottingham, NG6 9DR, Tel.: 0115 9770000 ext 47868
Mrs C Cheetham, Directorate General Manager, 70 Portland Street, Kirkby in Ashfield, Notts, NG17 7AG, Tel.: 01623 785477
Ms P Hubbard, Nurse Manager, Learning Disability, Hillside House, Bassetlaw Hospital, S81 0BD, Tel.: 01909 502855
Learning Disability Team, The Hurst, Cheapside, Worksop, S80 2JD, Tel.: 01909 530205
Mansfield & Ashfield Team, 68 Portland Street, Kirkby in Ashfield, NG17 7AB, Tel.: 01623 785454
Newark & Sherwood, Byron House, Newark Hospital, Boundary Road, Newark, NG24 4DE, Tel.: 01636 685925/7
Mrs S A Redhead, Team Leader, 70 Portland Street, Kirkby in Ashfield, Notts, NG17 7AG, Tel.: 01623 785489
Mrs H Scott, Executive Director, Duncan Macmillan House, Porchester Road, Nottingham, NG3 6AA, Tel.: 0115 969 1300

Rushcliffe Primary Care Trust

Trust Headquarters, Easthorpe House
165 Loughborough Road, Ruddington
NOTTINGHAM
NG11 6LQ
Tel.: 0115 956 0300
Fax.: 0115 956 0302

Admin & Senior Management

Ms V Bailey, Director of Health Improvement & Planning, Easthorpe House, 165 Loughborough Road, Ruddington, Nottingham, NG11 6LQ,
Mr M Morgan, Chief Executive,

Child Health

Ms L Owen-Jones, Co-ordinator, West Bridgford Health Centre, Musters Road, West Bridgford, Nottingham, NG2 7PX, Tel.: 0115 945 5066
Ms J Cloke, Liaison, Paediatrics, Queen's Medical Centre, Derby Road, Nottingham, Tel.: 0115 924 9924 ext 43417

Child Health Records

Info Services, Linden House, 261 Beechdale Road, Aspley, Nottingham, NG8 3EY, Tel.: 0115 942 6000 ext 48728

Child Protection/Safeguarding Children

Ms J Dickens, Child Protection, Children's Centre, City Hospital Campus, Hucknall Road, Nottingham, NG5 1PB, Tel.: 0115 962 7658
Ms R Lindsey, Child Protection, Children's Centre, City Hospital Campus, Hucknall Road, Nottingham, NG5 1PB, Tel.: 0115 962 7658

Clinical Leads (NSF)

Dr M Jephcote, Clinical Lead, Cancer,
Dr J Griffiths, Clinical Lead, CHD,
Dr G Derbyshire, Clinical Lead, Diabetic Care,

District Nursing

Ms R Bush, Clinical Locality Manager, Cotgrave Health Centre, Candleby Lane, Cotgrave, Nottingham, NG12 3JQ, Tel.: 0115 989 3421
District Nurse Referrals, (0830-1700 Mon-Fri), Wollaton Vale Health Centre, Tel.: 0115 928 7719
Out of Hours District Nurse Referrals, Ambulance Control, Tel.: 0115 929 9338

Family Planning Services

Family Planning Service, Victoria Health Centre, Glasshouse Street, Nottingham, NG1 3LW, Tel.: 0115 948 0500

Specialist Nursing Services

Ms S Brown, Continence, Ropewalk House, The Ropewalk, Nottingham, Tel.: 0115 948 5511
Ms F Lewis, Infection Control, Sherwood Health Centre, Tel.: 0115 956 8898
Ms S Reed, Community, Rehabilitation, Mary Potter Hostel, Gregory Boulevard, Nottingham, NG7 7HY, Tel.: 0115 978 4561
Ms S Pankhurst, Tissue Viability, Sherwood Health Centre, Tel.: 0115 956 8898

The Homeless/Travellers & Asylum Seekers

Homeless Team, Sherwood Rise Clinic, Tel.: 0115 969 2277

Sherwood Forest Hospitals NHS Trust

Trust Headquarters, Kings Mill Hospital
Mansfield Road
SUTTON-IN-ASHFIELD
Nottinghamshire
NG17 4JL
Tel.: 01623 622515
Fax: 01623 621770

Acute Specialist Nursing Services

Ms C Holditch, Specialist Nurse, Acute Pain,
Ms J Taphouse, Specialist Nurse, Acute Pain, Tel.: x 4047
Ms G Clarke, Specialist Nurse, Breast Care, Tel.: x 3884
Ms L Salmon, Specialist Nurse, Breast Care, Tel.: x 3884
Ms J Hayes, Specialist Nurse, Cardiac, Tel.: x 6308
Ms M Parkin, Specialist Nurse, Cardiac, Tel.: x 6308
Ms C Roe, Research Nurse, Cardiac, Tel.: x 4071
Ms H Tuffee, Specialist Nurse, Cardiac, Tel.: x 6308
Ms J Douglas, Specialist Nurse, Cardiac Rehabilitation, Tel.: x 3734
Ms B Ross, Specialist Nurse, Chronic Pain, Tel.: x 6151
Ms S Costello, Specialist Nurse, Colorectal, Tel.: x 3881
Ms S Godber, Specialist Nurse, Colorectal, Tel.: x 3881
Ms M Pashley, Acting, Specialist Nurse, Colorectal, Tel.: x 3881
Ms S Carr, Advisor, Continence, Tel.: x 4732
Ms J Godling, Advisor, Specialist Nurse, Continence, Tel.: x 4732
Mrs R Wint, Advisor, Specialist Nurse, Continence, Tel.: x 3543
Ms L Stradz, Specialist Nurse, Dermatology, Tel.: x 3115
Mrs P Bushby, Senior, Specialist Nurse, Diabetes, Tel.: x 3536
Mrs K Earnshaw, Specialist Nurse, Diabetes, Tel.: x 3531
Ms E Emmerson, Specialist Nurse, Diabetes, Tel.: x 3531
Ms H Marsh, Specialist Nurse, Diabetes, - Paediatrics, Tel.: x 3531
Ms K Ward, Specialist Nurse, Diabetes, Tel.: x 3531
Ms B Flynn, Specialist Nurse, Discharges, Tel.: x 3299
Ms K Pritchard, Specialist Nurse, Gastroenterology, Tel.: x 4277
Ms S Goralik, Specialist Nurse, Gynae/Oncology, Tel.: x 3073
Ms S Maloney, Nurse Practitioner, Gynaecology, Tel.: x 3073
Mrs M Greaney, Specialist Nurse, Haematology, Tel.: x 3081
Ms A Beal, Specialist Nurse, Heart Failure, Tel.: x 4196
Ms M Curtis, Specialist Nurse, Lung Cancer, Tel.: x 3332
Ms J Morley, Specialist Nurse, Lung Cancer, Tel.: x 3896
Ms S Smith, Specialist Nurse, Oncology, Tel.: x 3061
Ms R Jackson, Specialist Nurse, Orthopaedics, Tel.: x 4104
Ms J Bolus, Specialist Nurse, Osteoporosis, Tel.: x 5124
Ms S Hancock, (Ambulatory) (R/Hood), Specialist Nurse, Paediatrics, Tel.: x 3021

Ms L Macnamara, Specialist Nurse, Parkinson's Disease, Tel.: x 5127

Mr D Henstock, Drug & Alcohol, Specialist Nurse, Rehabilitation, Tel.: x 3935

Ms B Barlow, Specialist Nurse, Respiratory, - Paediatrics, Tel.: x 3905

Mrs D Reynolds, Specialist Nurse, Respiratory, Tel.: x 3541

Ms G Burbage, Specialist Nurse, Rheumatology, Tel.: x 3655

Ms A Mee, Specialist Nurse, Rheumatology, Tel.: x 3655

Ms H Burke, Specialist Nurse, Stoma Care, Tel.: x 3390

Ms T Birchall, Specialist Nurse, Tissue Viability, - Vascular, Tel.: x 3091

Ms L Thorpe, Specialist Nurse, Trauma & Orthopaedics, Tel.: x 4118

Ms J Lewis, Specialist Nurse, Upper GI, Tel.: x 3851

Ms P Kirby, Lead, Specialist Nurse, Vascular, Tel.: x 3091

Ms H McMillian, Outreach, Specialist Nurse, Vascular, Tel.: x 3091

Ms H Byrne, Specialist Nurse, X Ray, Tel.: x 4065

Child Protection/Safeguarding Children

Ms J Bradford, Vulnerable Children, Specialist Nurse,

Ms S Spanswick, Advisor, Named Nurse, Safeguarding Children, Tel.: 01623 622515 ext 3256

Community Midwifery

Mrs M Curtis, Midwifery Co-ordinator, Kings Mill Hospital, Tel.: 01623 622515 ext 3766

Mrs A Greenwood, Senior Midwife & Supervisor of Midwives - Newark & Sherwood Community, Newark Hospital, Boundary Road, Newark, NG24 4DE, Tel.: 01633 685601

Mrs J Matthews, Midwifery Co-ordinator, Kings Mill Hospital, Tel.: 01623 622515 ext 3766

Mr S Mehigan, Midwifery Co-ordinator - Mansfield Community, Kings Mill Hospital, Tel.: 01623 622515 ext 6225

Mrs J Savage, Head of Midwifery Services, Kings Mill Hospital, Tel.: 01623 622515 ext 3976

Mrs J Shaw, Midwifery Co-ordinator - Ashfield Community, Kings Mill Hospital, Tel.: 01623 622515 ext 6225

Ms D Thompson, Infant Feeding Advisor Specialist Midwife, Tel.: ext 3746

Mrs A Whitham, Midwifery & Gynaecology Manager, Chestnut House, Kings Mill Hospital, Tel.: 01623 622515 ext 3970

Discharge Co-ordinators

Ms B Flynn, Senior Nurse, Tel.: 01623 622515 x 3299

Ms Y Hudson, Specialist Nurse, Tel.: 01623 622515 x 6319

Ms C Whetton, Senior Nurse, Tel.: 01623 622515 x 6343

South Leicestershire Primary Care Trust

Trust Headquarters, The Rosings
Forest Road, Narborough
LEICESTER
LE9 5EQ
Tel.: 0116 286 3178

Admin & Senior Management

Mrs J Dowling, Head of Service Delivery, Tel.: 0116 286 3458

Child Protection/Safeguarding Children

Mrs M Waugh, Named Nurse, Child Protection,

Community Nursing Services

Ms J North, Service Manager, The Rosings, Forest Road, Narborough, Leicester, LE9 5EQ, Tel.: 0116 286 1884

HIV/AIDS

Mr L Pringle, HIV, Sexual Health, George Hine House, Towers Hospital, Gipsy Lane, Leicester, LE5 0TD, Tel.: 0116 225 6000

Specialist Nursing Services

Miss A O'Donnell, Community Education Facilitator,

Mr C Rushby, Community Education Facilitator,

Ms C Cawood, Advisor, Continence, George Hine House, Towers Hospital, Gipsy Lane, Leicester, LE5 0TD, Tel.: 0116 225 6000

Mrs R Lawson, Lead Nurse, Continuing Care,

Mrs J Leonard, Clinical Nurse Specialist, Diabetic Care,

Mrs J Fisher, Specialist Nurse, Heart Failure,

Mrs P Copson, Palliative Care, George Hine House, Towers Hospital, Gipsy Lane, Leicester, LE5 0TD, Tel.: 0116 225 6000

Mr K Charity, Tissue Viability, Tel.: 0116 225 5480

Mrs C Wheatley, Tissue Viability, Cropston Ward,

Southern Derbyshire Acute Hospitals NHS Trust

Trust Headquarters, Derby City General Hospital
Uttoxeter Road
DERBY
DE22 3NE
Tel.: 01332 340131
Fax.: 01332 290552

Child Health

Ms V Bennett, Paediatric Surgical Liaison Sister, Derbyshire Children's Hospital, Tel.: 01332 340131 ext 6807

Ms N Brett, Paediatric Medical Liaison Sister, Derbyshire Children's Hospital, Tel.: 01332 340131 ext 6807

Ms H Burgess, Paediatric Medical Liaison Sister, Derbyshire Children's Hospital, Tel.: 01332 340131 ext 6807

Ms A Denness, Paediatric Surgical Liaison Sister, Derbyshire Children's Hospital, Tel.: 01332 340131 ext 6807

Ms S Doherty, Paediatric Diabetes, Diabetes Centre, Derbyshire Royal Infirmary, Tel.: 01332 347141 ext 4610

Ms R Fulwell, Paediatric Emergency Liaison, Children's Hospital & Derbyshire Royal Infirmary, Tel.: 01332 347141 ext 6969

Ms M Mahon, Paediatric Diabetes, Diabetes Centre, Derbyshire Royal Infirmary, Tel.: 01332 347141 ext 4610

Ms J O'Neil, Paediatric Diabetes, Diabetes Centre, Derbyshire Royal Infirmary, Tel.: 01332 347141 ext 4610

Ms R Salloway, Paediatric Medical Liaison Sister, Derbyshire Children's Hospital, Tel.: 01332 340131 ext 6807

Ms R Wheway, Paediatric Medical Liaison Sister, Derbyshire Children's Hospital, Tel.: 01332 340131 ext 6807

Community Midwifery

Mrs S Appleby, Head of Midwifery Services Southern Derbyshire, Tel.: 01332 625625

Mrs H Boniface, Directorate Midwifery Manager (Primary Care), Tel.: 07799337570

The United Lincolnshire Hospitals NHS Trust

Trust Headquarters, Grantham & District Hospital
101 Manthorpe Road
GRANTHAM
NG31 8DG
Tel.: 01476 565232

Acute Specialist Nursing Services

Ms N Holvey, TOPS Counsellor, Lincoln County Hospital, Tel.: 01522 512512 ext 3118

Ms J Rivers, Training Officer, Pilgrim Hospital, Tel.: 01205 364801

Ms M Shobrook, Step up/Step down, Lincoln County Hospital, Tel.: 01522 512512

Ms B Maplethorpe, Acute Pain, Lincoln County Hospital, Tel.: ext 2117

Ms A D'Allorzo, Advanced Neonatal, Lincoln County Hospital, Tel.: 01522 512512

Ms S Edley, Advanced Neonatal, Lincoln County Hospital, Tel.: 01522 512512

Ms E Miles, Advanced Neonatal, Lincoln County Hospital, Tel.: 01522 512512

Ms R Williams, Advanced Neonatal, Lincoln County Hospital, Tel.: 01522 512512

Ms J Coen, Anaesthetics, Pilgrim Hospital, Tel.: 01205 364801

Ms K Pettit, Asthma, Pilgrim Hospital, Tel.: 01205 364801ext 3347

Ms M Wilkinson, Asthma, Pilgrim Hospital, Tel.: 01205 364801

Ms M Dixon, Breast Care, Grantham & District Hospital, Tel.: 01476 565232 ext 4764

Ms L Fisher, Breast Care, - Oncology, Pilgrim Hospital, Tel.: 01205 364801

Ms J Hinchcliffe, Macmillan, Breast Care, Lincoln County Hospital, Tel.: 01522 512512 ext 3790

Ms A McPherson, Liaison, Cardiac, Pilgrim Hospital, Tel.: 01205 364801 ext 3282

Ms A Charman, Cardiac Assessment, Grantham & District Hospital, Tel.: 01476 565232

Mr D Proctor, Cardiac Assessment, Pilgrim Hospital, Tel.: 01205 364801

Ms J Rennie-Lovely, Cardiac Assessment, Pilgrim Hospital, Tel.: 01205 364801

Mr J Williams, Cardiac Assessment, Pilgrim Hospital, Tel.: 01205 364801

Ms M Willoughby, Cardiac Assessment, Pilgrim Hospital, Tel.: 01205 364801

Ms A Bunn, Cardiac Rehabilitation, Louth County Hospital, Tel.: 01507 600100

Ms A Forbes, Cardiac Rehabilitation, Pilgrim Hospital, Tel.: 01205 364801

Ms C Laventure, Co-ordinator, Cardiac Rehabilitation, Grantham & District Hospital, Tel.: 01476 565232

Ms M Ward, Cardiac Rehabilitation, Pilgrim Hospital, Tel.: 01205 364801

Ms K Warris, Cardiac Rehabilitation, Lincoln County Hospital, Tel.: 01522 512512 ext 3114

Ms J Bridges, Colorectal, Pilgrim Hospital, Tel.: 01205 364801

Ms K Carteledge, Colorectal, Lincoln County Hospital, Tel.: 01522 512512

Ms J Fitzgerald, Colorectal, Lincoln County Hospital, Tel.: 01522 512512 ext 3776

Ms B Lee, Colorectal, Grantham & District Hospital, Tel.: 01476 565232 ext 4822

Ms A Nettleton, Advisor, Colorectal, Pilgrim Hospital, Tel.: 01205 364801

Ms S Nightingale, Colorectal, Pilgrim Hospital, Tel.: 01205 364801 ext 3466

Ms D Pycock, Colorectal, Pilgrim Hospital, Tel.: 01205 364801

Ms J shewan, Clinical Nurse Specialist, Colorectal, Lincoln County Hospital, Tel.: 01522 512512

Ms A Stuart-Stamp, Colorectal, Grantham & District Hospital, Tel.: 01476 565232 ext 4822

Mrs A Netherton, Continence, Pilgrim Hospital, Tel.: 01205 364801 ext 3545

Mr N Fox, Outreach, Critical Care, Pilgrim Hospital, Tel.: 01205 364801

Ms C Hay, Critical Care, Grantham & District Hospital, Tel.: 01476 565232

Ms D McHale, Critical Care, Lincoln County Hospital, Tel.: 01522 512512

Ms N Newton, Critical Care, Lincoln County Hospital, Tel.: 01522 512512

Ms L Ruigrok, Outreach, Critical Care, Pilgrim Hospital, Tel.: 01205 364801

Ms K Radley, Dermatology, Pilgrim Hospital, Tel.: 01205 364801

Ms K Shepherd, Dermatology, Lincoln County Hospital, Tel.: 01522 512512 ext 3712

Ms C Addison, Diabetic Care, Pilgrim Hospital, Tel.: 01205 364801 ext 2695

Ms D Clark, Diabetic Care, Grantham & District Hospital, Tel.: 01476 565232 ext 4815

Ms V Dobson, Diabetic Care, Louth County Hospital, Tel.: 01507 600100 ext 349

Ms J Jessop, Diabetic Care,Pilgrim Hospital, Tel.: 01205 364801 ext 2695

Ms A Prest, Diabetic Care, Pilgrim Hospital, Tel.: 01205 364801 ext 2695

Ms M Snell, Diabetic Care, Lincoln County Hospital, Tel.: 01522 512512 ext 3074

Ms P Taylor, Diabetic Care, Louth County Hospital, Tel.: 01507 600100 ext 349

Ms R Nicholls, Specialist Nurse, ENT Surgery, Pilgrim Hospital, Tel.: 01205 364801

Ms S Snook, Genetics, Lincoln County Hospital, Tel.: 01522 512512 ext 2311

Ms S Palmer, Gynae/Oncology, Pilgrim Hospital, Tel.: 01205 364801

Ms V Shoulder, Gynae/Oncology, Lincoln County Hospital, Tel.: 01522 512512 ext 3118

Ms H Watkins, Gynae/Oncology, Lincoln County Hospital, Tel.: 01522 512512

Ms K Blythe, Macmillan, Haematology, Grantham & District Hospital, Tel.: 01476 565232 ext 4628

Ms B Moses, Clinical Nurse Specialist, Haematology, Grantham & District Hospital, Tel.: 01476 565232

Mr A Palmer, Macmillan, Haematology, Lincoln County Hospital, Tel.: 01522 512512 ext 3729

Ms A Whyatt, Haemophilia, - Haematology, Lincoln County Hospital, Tel.: 01522 512512

Ms A Gladwin, Heart Failure, Pilgrim Hospital, Tel.: 01205 364801

Ms J Scrafton, Heart Failure, Lincoln County Hospital, Tel.: 01522 512512

Mr M Cole, Infection Control, Grantham & District Hospital, Tel.: 01476 565232 ext 4581

Ms M Fairless-Clarkson, Infection Control, Louth County Hospital, Tel.: ext 1242

Mr A Hurry, Infection Control, Grantham & District Hospital, Tel.: ext 4581

Ms C Hutson, Infection Control, Lincoln County Hospital, Tel.: 01522 512512 ext 3152

Ms M Matthews, Infection Control, Lincoln County Hospital, Tel.: ext 3152

Ms S Silvester, Infection Control, Pilgrim Hospital, Tel.: ext 3336

Ms S Silvester, Infection Control, Pilgrim Hospital, Tel.: 01205 364801

Ms S Smirthwaite, Infection Control, Lincoln County Hospital, Tel.: ext 3152

Ms J Douglass, Macmillan, Lung Cancer, Lincoln County Hospital, Tel.: 01522 512512 ext 3041

Ms G Wibberley, Lung Cancer, Lincoln County Hospital, Tel.: 01522 512512

Ms L Carter, Macmillan, Pilgrim Hospital, Tel.: 01205 364801 ext 3542

Ms M Coy, Macmillan, Grantham & District Hospital, Tel.: 01476 565232 ext 4627

Ms C Gasson, Macmillan, Grantham & District Hospital, Tel.: 01476 565232

Ms E Graves, Macmillan, Pilgrim Hospital, Tel.: 01205 364801 ext 3543

Ms K Howard, Macmillan, Grantham & District Hospital, Tel.: 01476 565232

Mr M Laycock, Macmillan, Grantham & District Hospital, Tel.: 01476 565232 ext 4588

Ms S Lewis, Macmillan, Grantham & District Hospital, Tel.: 01476 565232 ext 4664

Ms A Pilkington, Macmillan, Grantham & District Hospital, Tel.: 01476 565232

Ms M Quigg, Macmillan, Pilgrim Hospital, Tel.: 01205 364801 ext 3544

Ms M Wright, Macmillan, Pilgrim Hospital, Tel.: 01205 364801 ext 3541

Ms J Beer, Clinical Nurse Specialist, Oncology, Lincoln County Hospital, Tel.: 01522 512512

East Midlands Strategic Health Authority

Ms R Martinelli, Orthopaedics, Grantham & District Hospital, Tel.: 01476 565232 ext 4849

Ms E Osbourne, Orthopaedics, Grantham & District Hospital, Tel.: 01476 565232 ext 4849

Ms K Flippance, Physical Disability, Lincoln County Hospital, Tel.: 01522 577215

Ms S Robbins-Cherry, Physical Disability, Lincoln County Hospital, Tel.: 01522 577025

Ms D Wilkinson, Physical Disability, Lincoln County Hospital, Tel.: 01522 577215

Mr T Vine, Practice Development, Lincoln County Hospital, Tel.: 01522 512512

MS D Ward, Practice Development, Lincoln County Hospital, Tel.: 01522 512512

Ms C Swann, Respiratory, Lincoln County Hospital, Tel.: 01522 512512 ext 2750

Ms J Wildman, Respiratory, Grantham & District Hospital, Tel.: 01476 565232

Mr I Wilson, Officer, Resuscitation Training, Lincoln County Hospital, Tel.: 01522 512512

Ms N Bartholomew, Rheumatology, Lincoln County Hospital, Tel.: 01522 512512 ext 3143

Ms J Gordon, Rheumatology, Lincoln County Hospital, Tel.: 01522 512512 ext 3143

Mr M Collier, Tissue Viability, Pilgrim Hospital, Tel.: 01205 364801

Mr L Hecht, Tissue Viability, Lincoln County Hospital, Tel.: 01522 512512 ext 3115

Ms K McErlain, Co-ordinator, Trauma, Lincoln County Hospital, Tel.: 01522 512512

Ms H Noorpuri, Co-ordinator, Trauma, Pilgrim Hospital, Tel.: 01205 364801

Ms L Gilbert, Urology, Pilgrim Hospital, Tel.: 01205 364801

Ms P Keightley, Clinical Nurse Specialist, Urology, Lincoln County Hospital, Tel.: 01522 512512

Mr S Whitehead, Clinical Nurse Specialist, Urology, Lincoln County Hospital, Tel.: 01522 512512

Mr D Wiles, Urology, Grantham & District Hospital, Tel.: 01476 565232 ext 4348

Admin & Senior Management

Mrs L A Higginbottom, c/o Facilities, Lincoln County Hospital, Lincoln, LN2 5QY, Tel.: 01522 573328

Ms S Skelton, Director of Nursing & Midwife, Grantham & District Hospital, 101 Manthorpe Road, Grantham, NG31 8DG, Tel.: 01476 565232

Child Health

Ms B Bailey, Childrens Diabetes Nurse, Lincoln County Hospital, Tel.: ext 3423

Ms S Beresford, Community Children, Grantham & District Hospital, Tel.: 01476 565232 ext 4457

Ms J Dixon, Community Children, Lincoln County Hospital, Tel.: 01522 512512

Ms K Harness, Child Diabetes, Pilgrim Hospital, Tel.: 01205 364801 ext 2568

Lead Community Childrens Nurse, Lincoln County Hospital, Tel.: ext 3784

Ms P Leitch, Paediatric Support, Lincoln County Hospital, Tel.: 01522 512512 ext 3335/378

Ms H Lythgoe, Childrens Macmillan Nurse, Grantham & District Hospital, Tel.: ext 4259

Ms H Lythgoe, Paediatric Macmillan, Lincoln County Hospital, Tel.: 01522 512512

Ms H Rostron, Macmillan, Community Children, Lincoln County Hospital, Tel.: 01522 512512

Ms B Simmons, Childrens Diabetes Nurse, Grantham & District Hospital, Tel.: ext 4284

Ms E Thomas, Child Diabetes, Pilgrim Hospital, Tel.: 01205 364801 ext 2568

Ms O Thomas, Child Diabetes, Pilgrim Hospital, Tel.: 01205 364801 ext 2568

Ms T Wilson, Children Bereavement Co-ordinator, All Sites, Tel.: 07900 246496

Ms S Woods, Child Respiratory, Grantham & District Hospital, Tel.: 01476 565232 ext 4457

Community Midwifery

Mrs P Appleby, Head of Midwifery, Pilgrim Hospital, Sibsey Road, Boston, Lincolnshire, PE21 9QS, Tel.: 01205 364801 ext 2425

Boston Office, Pilgrim Hospital, Sibsey Road, Boston, Lincolnshire, PE21 9QS, Tel.: 01205 364801 ext 2415/242

Ms B Clark, Professional Development Midwife, Lincoln County Hospital, Tel.: 01522 512512

Community Managers Office, Lincoln County Hospital, Greetwell Road, Lincoln, LN2 5QY, Tel.: 01522 573772

Ms L Hrabowenskyj, Head of Midwifery, Lincoln County Hospital, Greetwell Road, Lincoln, LN2 5QY, Tel.: 01522 572398

Liaison Services

Ms E Angove, Discharge Liaison, Pilgrim Hospital, Sibsey Road, Boston, PE21 9QS, Tel.: 01205 364801 ext 2667

Ms A Bunn, Discharge Liaison, Louth County Hospital, High Holme Road, Louth, LN11 0EU, Tel.: 01507 600100

Ms P Davis, Discharge Liaison, Pilgrim Hospital, Sibsey Road, Boston, PE21 9QS, Tel.: 01205 364801 ext 2667

Ms A Hauton, Discharge Liaison, Lincoln County Hospital, Greetwell Road, Lincoln, LN2 5QS, Tel.: 01522 577215

Mr C Melynczenko, Discharge Liaison, Lincoln County Hospital, Greetwell Road, Lincoln, LN2 5QS, Tel.: 01522 577215

Ms A Thorpe, Discharge Liaison, Lincoln County Hospital, Greetwell Road, Lincoln, LN2 5QS, Tel.: 01522 577215

Smoking Cessation

Ms C Warne, Smoking Cessation, Lincoln County Hospital, Tel.: 01522 512512

University Hospitals of Leicester NHS Trust

Trust Headquarters, Gwendolen House
Gwendolen Road
LEICESTER
LE5 4QF
Tel.: 0116 249 0490
Fax.: 0116 258 4666

Community Midwifery

Mrs P Bates, Head of Midwifery, Kensington Building, Leicester Royal Infirmary, LE1 5WW, Tel.: 0116 258 6416

Community Midwifery Office, Leicester General Hospital, Gwendolen Road, Leicester, LE5 4PW, Tel.: 0116 258 4834

Emergencies, Delivery Suite, Leicester General Hospital, Gwendolen Road, Leicester, LE5 4PW, Tel.: 0116 258 8310

Mrs S Holligan, Community Manager, Leicester General Hospital, Gwendolen Road, Leicester, LE5 4PW, Tel.: 0116 258 6087

Health Visitors

Ms S Coker, Liaison Paediatric Health Visitor, Knighton Street Offices, Leicester Royal Infirmary, Leicester, LE1 5WW, Tel.: 0116 258 6161/5130

West Lincolnshire Primary Care Trust

Trust Headquarters, Cross O'Cliff
Bracebridge Heath
LINCOLN
LN4 2HN
Tel.: 01522 513355
Fax.: 01522 540706

Admin & Senior Management

Mr E Butterworth, Director of Quality & Development,

Ms S Miles, Head of Community Nursing Services, 1 St Anne's Close, Lincoln, LN2 5RB, Tel.: 01522 512999

Mr T Rideout, Chief Executive,

Child Health Records
Child Health Records, Child Health Department, 92 Newland, Lincoln, LN1 1YA, Tel.: 01522 514814

Child Protection/Safeguarding Children
Ms J Gilbert, Named Nurse, Child Protection, Moore House, Child & Family Service, 10/11 Lindum Terrace, Lincoln, Tel.: 01522 513875

Clinical Leads (NSF)
Dr M Overton, Clinical Lead, Children,
Dr M Fallon, Clinical Lead, Cancer,
Dr N Siriwardena, Clinical Lead, CHD,
Ms J Beecham, Clinical Lead, Diabetic Care, Health Centre, Moor Lane, North Hyneham, LN6 9BA, Tel.: 01522 682823
Dr H Barczak, Clinical Lead, Older People,

Community Matrons
Ms L Harrison, Long Term Conditions, Community Matron, Old Health Centre, 2 Highfield Road, Saxilby, Lincoln, LN1 2QP, Tel.: 01522 504560
Ms R Gavin, Community Matron, Heart Failure, Old Health Centre, 2 Highfield Road, Saxilby, Lincoln, LN1 2QP, Tel.: 01522 504560
Ms J Trueman, Community Matron, Respiratory, Old Health Centre, 2 Highfield Road, Saxilby, Lincoln, LN1 2QP, Tel.: 01522 504560
Ms S Parsons, Community Matron, Stroke Care, Old Health Centre, 2 Highfield Road, Saxilby, Lincoln, LN1 2QP, Tel.: 01522 504560

Community Nursing Services
Ms S Miles, Head of Primary Care Services, 1 St Anne's Close, Lincoln, LN2 5RB, Tel.: 01522 512999

District Nursing
Ms D Rigby, Professional Lead District Nursing, 1 St Anne's Close, Lincoln, LN2 5RB, Tel.: 01522 512999

Health Visitors
Ms S Kershaw, Professional Lead Health Visiting, 1 St Anne's Close, Lincoln, LN2 5RB, Tel.: 01522 512999
Ms S Milton, Children with Disabilities, Health Visitor, Moore House, Lindum Terrace, Lincoln, LN2 5RT, Tel.: 01522 513875

Liaison Services
Ms A Burlis, Intermediate Care, West Wing, Lincoln Hospital, LN2 5QY, Tel.: 01522 787599

Other Services
Ms K Wilding, Out of Hours Emergency Service, Tel.: 01522 548201

School Nursing
Ms J Wood, Professional Lead School Nursing, Tel.: 01522 512999

Specialist Nursing Services
Ms D Ramm, Continence, 1 St Anne's Close, Lincoln, LN2 5RB, Tel.: 01522 512999
Ms W Coffey, Head of Services, Older People, John Coupland Hospital, Ropery Road, Gainsborough, DN21 2TJ, Tel.: 01427 816500
Ms C Carr, Palliative Care, 1 St Anne's Close, Lincoln, LN2 5RB, Tel.: 01522 545230
Ms M Leggett, Palliative Care, 1 St Anne's Close, Lincoln, LN2 5RB, Tel.: 01522 545230
Ms L Wilkinson, Palliative Care, 1 St Anne's Close, Lincoln, LN2 5RB, Tel.: 01522 545230
Ms P Pirrie, Tissue Viability, John Coupland Hospital, Gainsborough, Tel.: 01427 816504

East of England Strategic Health Authority

with major towns and Primary Care Trust boundaries
Pop: 5,491,293

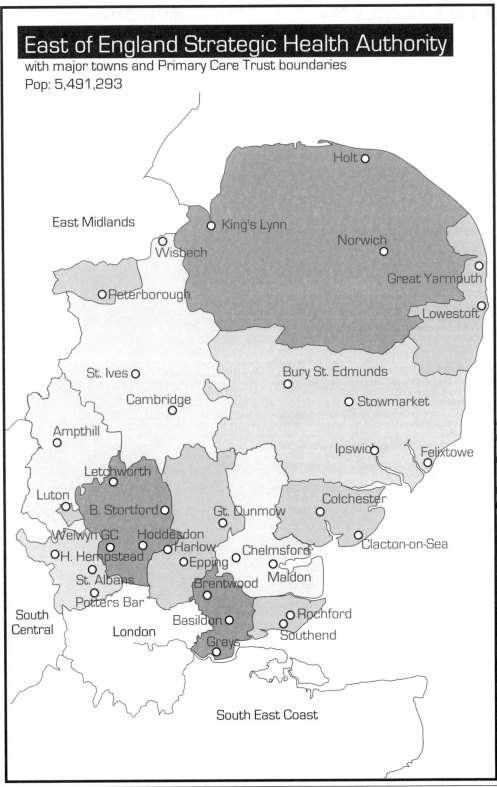

East Midlands

Holt O

King's Lynn O

Wisbech O

Norwich O

Great Yarmouth O

O Peterborough

Lowestoft O

St. Ives O

Bury St. Edmunds
O

Cambridge
O

Stowmarket O

Ampthill
O

Ipswich O

Felixtowe O

Letchworth
O

Luton
O

B. Stortford O

Gt. Dunmow
O

Colchester
O

Welwyn GC
O

Hoddesdon
O

Harlow O

Chelmsford O

Clacton-on-Sea

O H. Hempstead

Epping O

St. Albans
O

Brentwood

Maldon O

Potters Bar
O

South
Central

Basildon O

Rochford O

London

Grays

Southend

South East Coast

East of England Strategic Health Authority

Basildon & Thurrock University Hospitals NHS Foundation Trust
Maternity Unit, Basildon Hospital
Nethermayne
BASILDON
Essex
SS16 5NL
Tel.: 01268 533911
Fax.: 01268 593601

Community Midwifery
Mrs L Cook, General Manager, Obstetrics & Gynaecology, Head of Midwifery, Tel.: 01268 593266
Emergencies, Tel.: 01268 533911 ext 3553

Basildon Primary Care Trust
Trust Headquarters, Phoenix Court
Christopher Martin Road
BASILDON
Essex
SS14 3HG
Tel.: 01268 705000
Fax.: 01268 705100

Admin & Senior Management
Mr P McSweeney, Director, Integrated Care & Board Nurse, Phoenix Court, Christopher Martin Road, Basildon, Essex, SS14 3HG, Tel.: 01268 705162
Ms G Mills, Associate Director, Integrated Care Children & Therapies, Phoenix Court, Christopher Martin Road, Basildon, Essex, SS14 3HG, Tel.: 01268 705112
Ms M-A Munford, Chief Executive, Phoenix Court, Christopher Martin Road, Basildon, Essex, SS14 3HG, Tel.: 01268 705121

Child Protection/Safeguarding Children
Ms B Coates, Named Nurse, Child Protection, Phoenix Court, Christopher Martin Road, Basildon, Essex, SS14 3HG, Tel.: 01268 705181

Clinical Leads (NSF)
Dr G Chajed, Clinical Lead, CHD,

Community Matrons
Community Matrons Team, F Block, Nurses Campus, Basildon Hospital, Nethermayne, Basildon, SS16 5NL, Tel.: 01268 593369

District Nursing
Ms R Albon, Locality Matron, West Basildon, Phoenix Court, Christopher Martin Road, Basildon, Essex, SS14 3HG, Tel.: 01268 705000
Ms L Bartlett, Locality Matron, North Basildon, Phoenix Court, Christopher Martin Road, Basildon, Essex, SS14 3HG, Tel.: 01268 705000
District Nurse Liaison, Block F, Nurses Campus, Basildon Hospital, Nethermayne, Basildon, SS16 5NL, Tel.: 01268 593469
Ms C Greenwood, Locality Matron, North Basildon, Phoenix Court, Christopher Martin Road, Basildon, Essex, SS14 3HG, Tel.: 01268 705000
Ms M Hollins, Locality Matron, East Basildon, Phoenix Court, Christopher Martin Road, Basildon, Essex, SS14 3HG, Tel.: 01268 705000
Ms G Newby, Locality Matron, South Basildon, Phoenix Court, Christopher Martin Road, Basildon, Essex, SS14 3HG, Tel.: 01268 705000

Health Visitors
Ms R Albon, Locality Matron, West Basildon, Phoenix Court, Christopher Martin Road, Basildon, Essex, SS14 3HG, Tel.: 01268 705000

Ms L Bartlett, Locality Matron, North Basildon, Phoenix Court, Christopher Martin Road, Basildon, Essex, SS14 3HG, Tel.: 01268 705000
Ms C Greenwood, Locality Matron, North Basildon, Phoenix Court, Christopher Martin Road, Basildon, Essex, SS14 3HG, Tel.: 01268 705000
Ms M Hollins, Locality Matron, East Basildon, Phoenix Court, Christopher Martin Road, Basildon, Essex, SS14 3HG, Tel.: 01268 705000
Ms G Newby, Locality Matron, South Basildon, Phoenix Court, Christopher Martin Road, Basildon, Essex, SS14 3HG, Tel.: 01268 705000

School Nursing
School Nursing, Phoenix Court, Christopher Martin Road, Basildon, Essex, SS14 3HG, Tel.: 01268 705000

Specialist Nursing Services
Continence Advisory Service, 3rd Floor, Phoenix House, Christopher Martin Road, Basildon, Essex, SS14 3EZ, Tel.: 01268 448500
Ms B Brook, Diabetes Intermediate Care Manager, Diabetes, Diabetes Care Centre, Orsett Hospital, Rowley Road, Orsett, RM16 3EU, Tel.: 01268 592238
Ms C Watson, Nurse, Infection Control, Phoenix Court, Christopher Martin Road, Basildon, Essex, SS14 3HG, Tel.: 01268 705000

Bedford Hospital NHS Trust
Trust Headquarters, South Wing
Kempston Road
BEDFORD
MK42 9DJ
Tel.: 01234 355122

Acute Specialist Nursing Services
Ms L Curson, Back Care Advisor, Back Care Advisor, Britiannia House, Tel.: 01234 355122 ext 2107
Ms S Florey, Surgical Nurse Facilitator, Pre-Operative Assessment, 2nd Floor, Tel.: 01234 355122 ext 5467
Ms S Frampton, Clinical Nurse Lead, Cardiology Dept, Simon Whitbread House, Tel.: 01234 355122 ext 2289
Ms K Hopkinson, Manual Handling Trainer, Back Care Advisor Dept, Britannia House, Tel.: 01234 355122 ext 2107
Ms M Moore, Clinical Specialist, Delivery Suite, Tel.: 01234 795812 ext 5812
Ms S Cope, Clinical Nurse Specialist, Anti-Coagulation, - Haematology, Anticoagulation & Haematology Clinic, Tel.: 01234 355122 ext 5938
Ms C Watson, Nurse, Anti-Coagulation, - Haematology, Haematology/Anticoagulant Clinic, Bedford Hospital, Tel.: 01234 355122 xt 5938
Ms G Shingler, Specialist Nurse Counsellor/Lymphoedema Specialist Nurse, Breast Care, Breast Care Dept, Primrose Oncology Unit, Bedford Hospital, Tel.: 01234 792057
Ms E Wiggins, Specialist Nurse, Breast Care, Primrose Centre, Bedford Hospital, Tel.: 01234 355122 ext 5268
Ms H Phillips, Cardiac Support Nurse/Heart Failure Nurse Specialist, Cardiac, Cardiology Dept, Simon Whitbread House, Bedford Hospital, Tel.: 01234 792618 ext 2487
Ms E Church, Research Nurse, Clinical Trials, Primrose Oncology Centre, Bedford Hospital, Tel.: 01234 795924 ext 2683
Ms A Britchford, Specialist Nurse, Colorectal, - Urology, Urodynamic Clinic, Simon Whitbread House, Bedford Hospital, Tel.: 01234 355122 ext 2541
Ms J Cottam, Specialist Nurse, Colorectal, - Stoma, Colorectal Nursing Service, Bedford Hospital, Tel.: 01234 355122 ext 2887
Ms K Richards, Nurse, Colorectal, Colorectal Nursing Service, Tel.: 01234 355122 ext 2887
Ms J Brown, Specialist Nurse, Diabetic Care, - Paediatrics, North Bedfordshire Diabetes Centre, Tel.: 01234 795916

Ms L Cowley, Specialist Nurse, Diabetic Care, Diabetes Centre, Rye Close, Tel.: 01234 792312 ext 2973

Ms J de Souza, Specialist Nurse, Diabetic Care, Diabetes Centre, Rye Close, Tel.: 01234 792314 ext 2969

Ms J Pledger, Nurse Consultant, Diabetic Care, The Diabetes Centre, Rye Close, Tel.: 01234 792297 ext 2970

Ms P Newell, ENT/OMF Specialist Nurse, ENT Surgery, ENT Outpatient Dept, Simon Whitebread House, Bedford Hospital, Tel.: 01234 355122 ext 5693

Ms J Magee, Nurse, Infection Control, Bedford Hospital, Tel.: 01234 355122 ext 5248

Ms A Deary, Unit Manager, Oncology, Bedford Hospital, Tel.: 01234 355122 ext 2332

Ms L Newton, Nurse Practitioner, Orthopaedics, - Trauma, Orthopaedic OPD, Tel.: 01234 355122 ext 4026

Ms B Cootes, Specialist Nurse, Pain Management, Critical Care/Anaesthetics, Bedford Hospital, Tel.: 01234 355122 ext 5984

Ms D Boustred-Blake, Specialist Nurse, Parkinson's Disease, Gilbert Hitchcock, Annexe 21, Kimbolten Road, Bedford, MK40 2AW, Tel.: 01234 310118

Mr S Langham, Nurse Specialist, Respiratory, Elizabeth Ward, Tel.: 01234 355122 ext 5409

Ms C Smith, Respiratory, - Paediatrics, c/o Riverbank Ward, Cygnet Wing, Bedford Hospital, Tel.: 01234 795740 ext 5392

Ms S Collins, Service Manager, Resuscitation Training, Accident & Emergency Dept, Tel.: 01234 355122 ext 2304

Ms H Lindsay-Clerk, Paediatric Oncology, Sister, Rheumatology, Tel.: 01234 355122 ext 5394

Ms A Smith, Acting, Nurse, Tissue Viability, Britannia House, Ground Floor, Bedford Hospital, Tel.: 01234 355122 ext 5867

Ms S Vitellaro, Nurse, Tissue Viability, Britannia House, Ground Floor, Tel.: 01234 355122 ext 5867

Ms M Daly, Clinical Nurse Specialist, Urology, - Oncology, Primrose Centre, Tel.: 01234 355122 ext 5507

Ms N Smith, Clinical Nurse Specialist, Urology, - Oncology, Primrose Centre, Tel.: 01234 355122 ext 5507

Admin & Senior Management
Ms J Halliday, Director of Nursing & Patient Services, Bedford Hospital (South Wing), Kempston Road, Bedford, MK42 9DJ, Tel.: 01234 792292

Child Health Records
Ms H Ramsden, Manager, Medical Records, Tel.: 01234 355122 ext 2884

Child Protection/Safeguarding Children
Ms H Hughes, Named Nurse, Child Protection, Bedford Hospital, Tel.: 01234 355122 ext 5949

Community Midwifery
Emergencies, Bedford Hospital, Kempston Road, Bedford, MK42 9DJ, Tel.: 01234 795805

Miss N Gallagher, Head of Midwifery, Bedford Hospital, Kempston Road, Bedford, MK42 9DJ, Tel.: 01234 795981

Ms S Whiterod, Midwifery Manager, Bedford Hospital, Kempston Road, Bedford, MK42 9DJ, Tel.: 01234 355122 ext 5577

Discharge Co-ordinators
Ms A Lee, Discharge Co-ordinator, Tel.: 01234 355122 ext 2684

Equipment Loan Services
Ms V Kilgar, Head Occupational Therapist, Bedford Hospital, Tel.: 01234 355122 ext 5856

Family Planning Services
Ms G Fletcher, Manager, Bridge House, Bedford Hospital, Tel.: 01234 355122 ext 2416

HIV/AIDS
Ms G Fletcher, Sexual Health Speciality Nurse, Department Manager, Bridge House, Bedford Hospital, Tel.: 01234 792146 ext 2416

Matrons/Modern Matrons
Mr B Ahmed, Theatre, Modern Matron, Bedford Hospital, Tel.: 01234 355122 ext 2351

Ms F Bertasius, Critical Care, Modern Matron, Bedford Hospital, Tel.: 01234 355122 ext 5559

Ms D Fllisher, Medicine, Modern Matron, Bedford Hospital, Tel.: 01234 355122 ext 5695

Ms N Gallagher, Midwifery, Modern Matron, Bedford Hospital, Tel.: 01234 355122 ext 5797

Ms C Groome, Paediatrics, Modern Matron, Bedford Hospital, Tel.: 01234 355122 ext 5724

Ms S Hartnett, Medicine, Modern Matron, Bedford Hospital, Tel.: 01234 355122 ext 5695

Mr P Raynor, A & E, Modern Matron, Bedford Hospital, Tel.: 01234 355122 ext 2651

Ms J Rowling, Surgery - Short Stay, Modern Matron, Bedford Hospital, Tel.: 01234 355122 ext 5342

Ms K Shade, Site Manager, Modern Matron, Bedford Hospital, Tel.: 01234 355122 ext 5455

Ms S Shipton, Surgery, Modern Matron, Bedford Hospital, Tel.: 01234 355122 ext 2036

Ms A Showell, Medicine - Elderly, Modern Matron, Bedford Hospital, Tel.: 01234 355122 ext 5695

Bedford Primary Care Trust

Trust Headquarters, Gilbert Hitchcock
21 Kimbolton Road
BEDFORD
MK40 2AW
Tel.: 01234 795714

Admin & Senior Management
Ms M Stockham, Chief Executive,

Mrs D Warren, Assistant Director Clinical Development, Tel.: 01234 315882

Mr D White, Director of Care, Tel.: 01234 795773

Child Health Records
Ms D Buchanan, Admin Manager, Bedford Heights, Manton Lane, Bedford, MK41 7PA, Tel.: 01234 310165

Child Protection/Safeguarding Children
Ms M Taylor, Child Protection Lead, Bedford PCT, Gilbert Hitchcock House, Tel.: 01234 795793

Clinical Leads (NSF)
Mr D White, Clinical Lead, Care of the Elderly,

Ms L Lomax, Clinical Lead, CHD,

Ms K Taylor, Clinical Lead, Diabetic Care,

District Nursing
Ms S Metcalf, District Nursing Service Manager, Bedford PCT, Gilbert Hitchcock Annexe, 21 Kimbolton Road, Bedford, MK40 2AW, Tel.: 01234 315870

Equipment Loan Services
Mr B Stevens, Assistant Director Adult & Elderly Services, Bedford PCT, Gilbert Hitchcock House, Tel.: 01234 795714 ext 3909

Health Visitors
Ms A Richards, Health Visiting Lead, Bedford PCT, Gilbert Hitchcock House, Tel.: 01234 795793

Liaison Services
Ms C Mann, Community Discharge Planning, Bedford Hospital, Kempston Road, Bedford,

Pharmacy
Ms S Khatri, PCT Pharmaceutical Advisor, Bedford PCT, Gilbert Hitchcock House, Tel.: 01234 795772

Ms J Smith, PCT Pharmaceutical Advisor, Bedford PCT, Gilbert Hitchcock House, Tel.: 01234 795772

School Nursing
Ms C Thomas, School Nursing Lead Nurse, Bedford PCT, Gilbert Hitchcock House, Tel.: 01234 792617

Specialist Nursing Services
Ms S Nichols, Senior Nurse, Gladys Ibbett Day Hospice,

Ms C Saunders, Non-Medical Prescribing Lead for Bedfordshire, Bedford PCT, Gilbert Hiltchcock Annexe, Tel.: 01234 315873

Ms B Spencer, Practice Nurse Facilitator, Bedford PCT Headquarters, Tel.: 01234 315884

Ms L Lomax, Lead Nurse, COPD, Bedford PCT Headquarters, Tel.: 01234 315884

Ms K Taylor, Specialist Community Nurse, Diabetic Care, Bedford PCT Headquarters, Tel.: 01234 315884

Mrs J Sherwood, Nurse, Infection Control, Tel.: 01234 315889

Ms L Barton, Macmillan, Gladys Ibbett House, 3 Linden Road, Bedford, MK40 2DD, Tel.: 01234 310005

Ms S Lee, Macmillan, Gladys Ibbett House, 3 Linden Road, Bedford, MK40 2DD, Tel.: 01234 310005

Ms C Rubini, Macmillan, Gladys Ibbett House, 3 Linden Road, Bedford, MK40 2DD, Tel.: 01234 310005

Ms H Sharpe, Macmillan, Gladys Ibbett House, 3 Linden Road, Bedford, MK40 2DD, Tel.: 01234 310005

Mrs D Blake, Parkinson's Disease, Gilbert Hitchcock House Annexe, 21 Kimbolton Road, Bedford, MK40 2AW, Tel.: 01234 310118

Mrs J Desouza, Specialist Nurse, Prison Health Care, Bedford Prison,

Ms C Mason, Nurse Specialist, TB, Ombesley House, Bedford Hospital, Tel.: 01234 355122

Ms D Freshwater, Specialist Nurse, Wound Care, Bedford PCT, Gilbert Hitchcock Annexe, Tel.: 01234 315872

The Homeless/Travellers & Asylum Seekers
Ms D Webb, Healthy Living & Partnership Manager, Bedford PCT, Gilbert Hitchcock House, Tel.: 01234 792047

Bedfordshire and Luton Community NHS Trust

Trust Headquarters, Charter House
Alma Street
LUTON
LU1 2PJ
Tel.: 01582 700171
Fax: 01582 700151

Learning Disabilities
Beech Close Resource Centre, Beech Close, Dunstable, LU6 3SD, Tel.: 01582 666080

Mrs N Leslie, Community Learning Disability Nursing, Clinical Nurse Specialist, Twinwoods Health Resource, Milton Road, Clapham, Bedford, Bedfordshire, MK41 6AT, Tel.: 01234 310569

Twinwoods Health Resource Centre, Milton Road, Clapham, Bedford, Bedfordshire, MK41 6AT, Tel.: 01234 310589

Bedfordshire Heartlands Primary Care Trust

Trust Headquarters, 1 & 2 Doolittle Mill
Froghall Road
AMPTHILL
Bedfordshire
MK4 2NX
Tel.: 01525 631153

Admin & Senior Management
Ms W Atkins, Facilities & Admin Manager (Community), Tel.: 01525 636921

Ms P Barber, Head of Facilities & Admin (Community), Tel.: 01525 636919

Ms L Gudgin, Professional Lead, Practice Nursing, Tel.: 01525 631303

Ms J Jefferies, Continence Service Manager, Tel.: 01525 751159

Ms S Jordan, Associate District Director, Tel.: 01525 636822

Ms M Moran, Associate Director, Community Nursing Services, 1 & 2 Doolittle Mill, Froghall Road, Ampthill, Beds, MK4 2NX, Tel.: 01525 636818

Ms S Reavey, Director of Nursing & Patient Services, 1 & 2 Doolittle Mill, Froghall Road, Ampthill, Beds, MK4 2NX, Tel.: 01525 631321

Ms M Wallace, Professional Lead, Training & Dev, Tel.: 01525 631169

Ms S Wingrove, Intermediate Care Services Manager, 1 & 2 Doolittle Mill, Froghall Road, Ampthill, Beds, MK4 2NX, Tel.: 01525 636804

Child Health Records
Pre-School, South Bedfordshire, Liverpool Road Health Centre, 9 Mersey Place, Luton, LU1 1HH, Tel.: 01582 700206

Pre-School, North & Mid Bedfordshire, Bedford Heights, Manton Lane, Bedford, MK41 7PA, Tel.: 01234 310166

School Age, North & Mid Bedfordshire, Bedford Heights, Manton Lane, Bedford, MK41 7PA, Tel.: 01234 310165

School Age, South Bedfordshire, Liverpool Road Health Centre, 9 Mersey Place, Luton, LU1 1HH, Tel.: 01582 700216

Child Protection/Safeguarding Children
Mrs H Hughes, Designated Nurse, Safeguarding Children, c/o Flitwick Clinic, Highlands, Flitwick, Tel.: 01525 719896

Ms R Kind, Named Nurse, Safeguarding Children, 1 & 2 Doolittle Mill, Froghall Road, Ampthill, Beds, MK4 2NX, Tel.: 01525 636923

District Nursing
Ms C Calver, Clinical Support Manager, 1& 2 Doolittle Mill, Froghall Road, Ampthill, Beds, MK45 2NX, Tel.: 01525 631305

Health Visitors
Ms L Finlay, Clinical Support Manager, Leighton Buzzard Health Centre, Bassett Road, Leighton Buzzard, Beds, Tel.: 01525 631304

Other Services
Ms H Hardy, Senior Manager Counselling Services, Tel.: 01525 636807

Ms B Herrera, Continuing Health Care/NHS Funded Nursing Care Co-ordinator, Tel.: 01525 636911

Specialist Nursing Services
Mrs S Gebhard, Practice Placement Lead, Tel.: 01525 636991

Ms J Goll, Matron, Biggleswade Hospital 01767 224907/Steppingley Hospital 01525 631171,

Ms L Bonner, Bladder/Bowel Dysfunction, Nurse Consultant, Continence, Tel.: 01525 751132

Ms A White, Community Nurse, Infection Control, Tel.: 01525 636974

Ms C Clarke, Specialist Nurse, IV Therapy, Tel.: 01525 636925

Community Service, Macmillan, Steppingley Hospital, Tel.: 01525 631177

Billericay, Brentwood & Wickford Primary Care Trust

Trust Headquarters, High Wood Hospital
Ongar Road
BRENTWOOD
Essex
CM15 9DY
Tel.: 01277 302516

Admin & Senior Management
Ms J Evans, Head of Clinical Services, Adult & Older People, Tel.: 01277 302250

Mr H Perry, Chief Executive,

Child Health Records
Mr S McArthur, Highwood Hospital, Geary Drive, Brentwood, Essex, CM15 9DY, Tel.: 01708 465000

Child Protection/Safeguarding Children
Mr S McArthur, Highwood Hospital, Geary Drive, Brentwood, Essex, CM15 9DY, Tel.: 01708 465000

Community Matrons
Ms S Moore, Community Matron, Highwood Hospital, Geary Drive, Brentwood, Essex, CM15 9DY, Tel.: 01708 465000

District Nursing
MS W Chen, Highwood Hospital, Geary Drive, Brentwood, Essex, CM15 9DY, Tel.: 01708 465000

Ms J Evans, Highwood Hospital, Geary Drive, Brentwood, Essex, CM15 9DY, Tel.: 01708 465000

East of England Strategic Health Authority

Equipment Loan Services
Essex Equipment Services,
Health Visitors
Mr S McArthur, Highwood Hospital, Geary Drive, Brentwood, Essex, CM15 9DY, Tel.: 01708 465000
Learning Disabilities
Mr G Sumner, Tel.: 01708 465000
Liaison Services
Ms W Thompson, Older People's Liaison, Admin Offices, High Wood Hospital, Tel.: 01277 302306
School Nursing
Mr S McArthur, Highwood Hospital, Geary Drive, Brentwood, Essex, CM15 9DY, Tel.: 01708 465000
Specialist Nursing Services
Ms L Jobson, Elderly Integrated Care Pathway Manager, Admin Offices, High Wood Hospital, Tel.: 01277 302306
Ms L Sparks, Elderly Integrated Care Pathway Manager, Admin Offices, High Wood Hospital, Tel.: 01277 302306
Ms S Moore, Nurse Specialist, Diabetes, Tel.: 01708 465000
Ms S Moore, Nurse Specialist, Parkinson's Disease, Tel.: 01708 465000
The Homeless/Travellers & Asylum Seekers
Ms K Abbott, Highwood Hospital, Geary Drive, Brentwood, Essex, CM15 9DY, Tel.: 01708 465000

Broadland Primary Care Trust

Trust Headquarters, Sapphire House
Roundtree Way
NORWICH
NR7 8SS
Tel.: 01603 481600

Admin & Senior Management
Ms M Carson, Director of Clinical Services & Quality,
Mr M Taylor, Chief Executive,
Child Health
Ms J Whiting, Broadland PCT, Sapphire House,
Child Protection/Safeguarding Children
Ms J Whiting, Broadland PCT, Sapphire House,
Clinical Leads (NSF)
Mr D Olley, Clinical Lead, Care of the Elderly,
Community Matrons
Ms V Aldridge,
Community Nursing Services
Mrs E Bailey,
Mr P Pacey, Head of Community Services, Tel.: 01603 481600
District Nursing
Ms J Valle, Broadland PCT, Sapphire House,
Specialist Nursing Services
Ms J Vincent, Co-ordinator, Palliative Care, Sapphire House, Tel.: 01603 481600
Walk In Centres
Norwich Walk-In Centre, Dussindale, Pound Lane, Norwich, NR7 0RS,

Cambridge City Primary Care Trust

Trust Headquarters, Heron Court
Ida Darwin, Fulbourn
CAMBRIDGE
CB1 5EE
Tel.: 01223 884008
Fax.: 01223 885728

Admin & Senior Management
Mr N Beverley, Acting Chief Executive, Heron Court, Ida Darwin, Fulbourn, Cambridge, CB1 5EE, Tel.: 01223 885718
Mrs S Bremner, Director of Primary & Community Services, Heron Court, Ida Darwin, Fulbourn, Cambridge, CB1 5EE, Tel.: 01223 884050

Mr G Nice, Director of Nursing & Quality Performance, Heron Court, Ida Darwin, Fulbourn, Cambridge, CB1 5EE, Tel.: 01223 884273
Child Health
Ms J Acornley, Team Leader, Children with Palliative Care Needs, Diana Nursing Team, Block 9, Ida Darwin, Fulbourn, Cambridge, CB1 5EE, Tel.: 01223 884335
Ms J Galway, Assistant Director - Childrens Services, Block 13, Ida Darwin, Fulbourn, Cambridge, CB1 5EE, Tel.: 01223 884033
Ms R Moxon, Children with Disabilities Team Leader, Douglas House, 18 Trumpington Street, Cambridge, CB2 2AH, Tel.: 01223 568808
Dr D Vickers, Medical Director of Children's Services, Block 13, Ida Darwin, Fulbourn, Cambridge, CB1 5EE, Tel.: 01223 884167
Child Health Records
Ms G Skews, Child Health Dept, Ida Darwin, Fulbourn, Cambridge, CB1 5EE, Tel.: 01223 884186
Ms J Wright, Child Health Dept, Ida Darwin, Fulbourn, Cambridge, CB1 5EE, Tel.: 01223 884184
Child Protection/Safeguarding Children
Ms R Cox, Named Nurse, Child Protection, Block 13, Ida Darwin, Fulbourn, Cambridge, Tel.: 01223 884151
Clinical Leads (NSF)
Mr T Dutton, Deputy Chief Executive/NSF Lead, Heron Court, Fulbourn, Cambridge, CB1 5EE, Tel.: 01223 885740
Mr M Jarman-Howe, Long Term Conditions, Heron Court, Fulbourn, Cambridge, CB1 5EE, Tel.: 01223 884454
Community Nursing Services
Ms M Appleby, Assistant Director (Interface), Primary Care & Community Services, Nightingale Court, Ida Darwin, Fulbourn, Cambridge, CB1 5EE, Tel.: 01223 884329
Ms K Caley, Assistant Director (City), Primary Care & Community Services, Nightingale Court, Ida Darwin, Fulbourn, CB1 5EE, Tel.: 01223 885744
Mr G Nice, Director of Nursing & Quality Performance, Heron Court, Ida Darwin, Fulbourn, CB1 5EE, Tel.: 01223 884273
Mrs C Welton, Assistant Director (South), Primary Care & Community Services, Nightingale Court, Ida Darwin, Fulbourn, CB1 5EE, Tel.: 01223 885799
District Nursing
Ms K Caley, Assistant Director (City), Primary Care & Community Services, Nightingale Court, Ida Darwin, Fulbourn, CB1 5EE, Tel.: 01223 885744
Equipment Loan Services
Mr S Gilbert, Discharge Planning Team, 28 Long Road, Cambridge, Tel.: 01223 714400
Joint Equipment Services, Anglia Support Services, Tel.: 01223 726212
Smoking Cessation
Dr D Gregson, Director of Public Health, Nightingale Court, Ida Darwin, Fulbourn, Cambridge, Tel.: 01223 885843
Specialist Nursing Services
Ms J Dowse, Specialist Nurse, Continence, Princess of Wales Hospital, Lynn Road, Ely, Cambs, CB6 1DN, Tel.: 01353 652145
Ms R Wright, Specialist Nurse, Diabetic Care, Brookfields Hospital, Mill Road, Cambridge, CB1 3DF, Tel.: 01223 723004
Mr C Sharp, Specialist Nurse, Infection Control, Kingfisher House, Kingfisher Way, Hinchingbrooke Business Park, Huntingdon, PE29 6FH, Tel.: 01480 398620
Ms L Moth, Nurse, Macmillan, Arthur Rank House, Brookfields, Mill Road, Cambridge, CB1 3DF, Tel.: 01223 723137
Ms A Pope, Nurse, Macmillan, Arthur Rank House, Brookfields, Mill Road, Cambridge, CB1 3DF, Tel.: 01223 723137
Ms S Roberts, Nurse, Macmillan, Arthur Rank House, Brookfields, Mill Road, Cambridge, CB1 3DF, Tel.: 01223 723137
Ms W Williams, Nurse, Macmillan, Arthur Rank House, Brookfields, Mill Road, Cambridge, CB1 3DF, Tel.: 01223 723137
Ms M Stratford, Matron, Palliative Care, Arthur Rank House, Brookfields, Mill Road, Cambridge, CB1 3DF, Tel.: 01223 723110

East of England Strategic Health Authority

Ms J Young, Specialist Nurse, Parkinson's Disease, Brookfields Hospital, Mill Road, Cambridge, CB1 3DF, Tel.: 01223 723018

Ms A Perrin, Specialist Nurse, Tissue Viability, Brookfields Hospital, Mill Road, Cambridge, CB1 3DF, Tel.: 01223 723019

The Homeless/Travellers & Asylum Seekers

Mr K Reynolds, Strategic Lead - Community Living, Nightingale Court, Ida Darwin, Fulbourn, Cambridge, Tel.: 01223 884331

Cambridge University Hospitals NHS Foundation Trust

Trust Headquarters
Hills Road
CAMBRIDGE
CB2 2QQ
Tel.: 01223 245151

Acute Specialist Nursing Services

Ms S Kinna, Acute Pain, Dept Anaesthesia, Box 93, Addenbrooke's Hospital, Tel.: 01223 217795

Ms R Sapsford, Acute Pain, Dept Anaesthesia, Box 93, Addenbrooke's Hospital, Tel.: 01223 217795

Ms L Lydon, Allergy, Clinic 2a, Box 20, Addenbrooke's Hospital, Tel.: 01223 216977

Ms K Burnet, Breast Care, Box 97, Addenbrooke's Hospital, Tel.: 01223 217627

Ms D Chapman, Breast Care, Box 97, Addenbrooke's Hospital, Tel.: 01223 217627

Ms H Harte, Breast Care, Box 97, Addenbrooke's Hospital, Tel.: 01223 217627

Ms L Newbery, Breast Care, Box 97, Addenbrooke's Hospital, Tel.: 01223 217627

Ms J Rowley, Breast Care, Box 97, Addenbrooke's Hospital, Tel.: 01223 217627

Ms P Willcocks, Breast Care, Box 97, Addenbrooke's Hospital, Tel.: 01223 217627

Ms G Simon, Chronic Pain, Box 215, Addenbrooke's Hospital, Tel.: 01223 216993

Nurse, Continence, Box 10, Addenbrooke's Hospital, Tel.: 01223 217465

Ms M Collins, Endocrinology, - Diabetes, Box 49, Addenbrooke's Hospital, Tel.: 01223 596096

Ms J Reynolds, Endocrinology, - Diabetes, Box 49, Addenbrooke's Hospital, Tel.: 01223 586095

Ms R Wright, Endocrinology, - Diabetes, Box 49, Addenbrooke's Hospital, Tel.: 01223 723004

Ms Q Tuffnell, Endoscopy, Box 219, Addenbrooke's Hospital, Tel.: 01223 216515

Ms A Nightingale, Gastroenterology, Box 133, Addenbrooke's Hospital, Tel.: 01223 257212

Ms H Burton, Genetics, Box 134, Addenbrooke's Hospital, Tel.: 01223 216446

Ms S Downing, Genetics, Box 134, Addenbrooke's Hospital, Tel.: 01223 216446

Ms S Everest, Genetics, Box 134, Addenbrooke's Hospital, Tel.: 01223 216446

Ms A Kershaw, Genetics, Box 134, Addenbrooke's Hospital, Tel.: 01223 216446

Ms A Middleton, Genetics, Box 134, Addenbrooke's Hospital, Tel.: 01223 216446

Ms S Robathan, Genetics, Box 134, Addenbrooke's Hospital, Tel.: 01223 216446

Ms V Wiles, Genetics, Box 134, Addenbrooke's Hospital, Tel.: 01223 216446

Ms L Putt, Immunology, Clinic 2a, Box 40, Addenbrooke's Hospital, Tel.: 01223 216431

Ms R Brooks, Infection Control, Box 89, Addenbrooke's Hospital, Tel.: 01223 217497

Ms L Fitzgibbon, Infection Control, Box 89, Addenbrooke's Hospital, Tel.: 01223 217497

Ms C Trundle, Infection Control, Box 89, Addenbrooke's Hospital, Tel.: 01223 217497

Ms D O'Donovan, Infectious Diseases, Box 25, Addenbrooke's Hospital, Tel.: 01223 217314

Ms A Dowsett, Neuro-oncology, Box 181, Addenbrooke's Hospital, Tel.: 01223 214485

Ms G Jenner, Neuro-oncology, Box 181, Addenbrooke's Hospital, Tel.: 01223 214485

Ms A LeFebvre, Neuro-oncology, Box 181, Addenbrooke's Hospital, Tel.: 01223 214485

Ms C Parsons, Neuro-oncology, Box 181, Addenbrooke's Hospital, Tel.: 01223 214485

Mr H Taylor, Neuro-oncology, Box 181, Addenbrooke's Hospital, Tel.: 01223 214485

Ms S Cottee, Clinical, Nutrition, Box 201A, Addenbrooke's Hospital, Tel.: 01223 216037

Ms T Edgeway, Clinical, Nutrition, Box 201A, Addenbrooke's Hospital, Tel.: 01223 216037

Ms L Russell, Clinical, Nutrition, Box 201A, Addenbrooke's Hospital, Tel.: 01223 216037

Ms N Turnball, Clinical, Nutrition, Box 201A, Addenbrooke's Hospital, Tel.: 01223 216037

Ms C Alban-Jones, Macmillan, Palliative Care, Oncology Dept, Box 193, Addenbrooke's Hospital, Tel.: 01223 274404

Ms L Baker, Macmillan, Palliative Care, Oncology Dept, Box 193, Addenbrooke's Hospital, Tel.: 01223 274404

Ms E Bruce, Macmillan, Palliative Care, Oncology Dept, Box 193, Addenbrooke's Hospital, Tel.: 01223 274404

Ms J Gibbons, Macmillan, Palliative Care, Oncology Dept, Box 193, Addenbrooke's Hospital, Tel.: 01223 274404

Ms C Tiffen, Macmillan, Palliative Care, Oncology Dept, Box 193, Addenbrooke's Hospital, Tel.: 01223 274404

Ms S Perrot, Respiratory, Clinic 2a, Box 40, Addenbrooke's Hospital, Tel.: 01223 216647

Ms E Reid, Respiratory, Clinic 2a, Box 40, Addenbrooke's Hospital, Tel.: 01223 216647

Ms I Debirham, Rheumatology, Box 44, Addenbrooke's Hospital, Tel.: 01223 217398

Ms J Isaacson, Rheumatology, Box 44, Addenbrooke's Hospital, Tel.: 01223 217398

Ms S Skingle, Rheumatology, Box 44, Addenbrooke's Hospital, Tel.: 01223 217398

Ms K Bennett, Stoma Care, - Coloproctology, Box 207, Addenbrooke's Hospital, Tel.: 01223 216505

Ms V Coleman, Stoma Care, - Coloproctology, Box 207, Addenbrooke's Hospital, Tel.: 01223 216505

Ms K Goodwin, Stoma Care, - Coloproctology, Box 207, Addenbrooke's Hospital, Tel.: 01223 216505

Ms J Perkins, Stoma Care, - Coloproctology, Box 207, Addenbrooke's Hospital, Tel.: 01223 216505

Ms M Waller, Stoma Care, - Coloproctology, Box 207, Addenbrooke's Hospital, Tel.: 01223 216505

Ms S Wilkinson, Stoma Care, - Coloproctology, Box 207, Addenbrooke's Hospital, Tel.: 01223 216505

Ms E Harris, TB, Clinic 2a, Box 40, Addenbrooke's Hospital, Tel.: 01223 216431

Ms S Davies, Tissue Viability, Box 135, Addenbrooke's Hospital, Tel.: 01223 216033/723019

Ms A-M Perrin, Tissue Viability, Box 135, Addenbrooke's Hospital, Tel.: 01223 216033/723019

Ms C Young, Tissue Viability, Box 135, Addenbrooke's Hospital, Tel.: 01223 216033/723019

Ms T Pendreigh, Bone Marrow Co-ordinator, Transplant, Camilla Ward, Box 193, Addenbrooke's Hospital, Tel.: 01223 217224

East of England Strategic Health Authority

Admin & Senior Management
Ms M Berry, Chief Nurse, Management Offices, Addenbrooke's Hospital, Hills Road, Cambridge, CB2 2QQ, Tel.: 01223 217875
Child Health
Ms J Pool, Paediatric Asthma, Children's Services, Box 45, Addenbrooke's Hospital, Tel.: 01223 216585
Community Midwifery
Ms S Bowman, Clinical Services Manager, Delivery Unit & Theatres, Tel.: 01223 217008
Community Midwifery Services, Rosie Hospital, Robinson Way, Cambridge, CB2 2SW,
Ms C Edmund, Clinical Services Manager, Community & Antenatal, Tel.: 01223 217658
Ms K Evans, Clinical Services Manager, Inpatients, Tel.: 01223 217756
Head of Midwifery/Operations Manager, Women's Services, Rosie Hospital Community Services, Rosie Hospital, Addenbrooke's Hospital, Hills Road, Cambridge, CB2 2QQ,
HIV/AIDS
Ms F Wilson, HIV, Clinic 1a, Box 38, Addenbrooke's Hospital, Tel.: 01223 217766
Liaison Services
Ms E Boismier, Liaison Discharge Planning, Box 195, Addenbrooke's Hospital, Tel.: 01223 714436
Ms J Middleton, Liaison Discharge Planning, DME Level 1, Box 135, Addenbrooke's Hospital, Tel.: 01223 274625
Ms S Page, Liaison Discharge Planning, DME Level 1, Box 135, Addenbrooke's Hospital, Tel.: 01223 274625
Ms E Tidbury, Liaison Discharge Planning, DME Level 1, Box 135, Addenbrooke's Hospital, Tel.: 01223 274625
Ms K Wilson, Liaison Discharge Planning, DME Level 1, Box 135, Addenbrooke's Hospital, Tel.: 01223 274625

Cambridgeshire & Peterborough Mental Health Partnership NHS Trust

Trust Headquarters, Kingfisher House
Kingfisher Way, Hinchingbrooke Business Park
HUNTINGDON
PE29 6FH
Tel.: 01480 398500

Learning Disabilities
Cambridge City Team, Tel.: 01223 885761
Mr P Craik, Acting, Services Manager, Gloucester Centre, Morpeth Close, Orton Longueville, Peterborough, PE2 6JU, Tel.: 01733 363100
East Cambridgeshire Team, Tel.: 01353 652240
Emergencies, Community Unit, Primrose Lane, Huntingdon, PE29 1WG, Tel.: 01480 416416
Mr G Hunt, Assistant Lead Commissioner (Health), Community Unit, Primrose Lane, Huntingdon, PE29 1WG, Tel.: 01480 415266
Miss L Nairn, Lead Clinician, S.A.L.D. Block 11, Ida Darwin Hospital, Tel.: 01223 884078
Mr B Sheridan, Nurse Manager, Park View Resource Centre, Birch Tree Close, London Road, King's Lynn, PE30 5QD, Tel.: 01553 613613 ext 5503
South Cambridgeshire Team, Tel.: 01223 884071
Mr C Wong, Director, Learning Disability Service, 53 Thorpe Road, Peterborough, Cambridgeshire, PE3 6AN,

Castle Point & Rochford Primary Care Trust

Trust Headquarters
12 Castle Road
RAYLEIGH
Essex
SS6 7QF
Tel.: 01268 464500

Admin & Senior Management
H Brown, Director of Integrated Care (Interim) & Strategic Planning, 12 Castle Road, Rayleigh, Essex, SS6 7QF, Tel.: 01268 464500
Mr M McCann, Chief Executive,
Child Health
Mrs S Farr, Head of Childrens Service, 12 Castle Road, Rayleigh, Essex, SS6 7QF, Tel.: 01268 464598
Mr J Pugh, Paediatric Community Nursing Team Manager, 2nd Floor, Suffolk House, Baxter Avenue, Southend-on-Sea, Essex, SS2 6HZ, Tel.: 01702 313690
Child Health Records
Mr P Gladman, Deputy Child Health Manager, Suffolk House, Baxter Avenue, Southend-on-Sea, SS2 6HZ, Tel.: 01702 313581
Ms S McCarthy, Information Project Manager, Community House, Room F27, Union Lane, Rochford, Essex, SS4 1RB, Tel.: 01702 578012
Child Protection/Safeguarding Children
Mrs G Parker, Named Nurse, Child Protection, 12 Castle Road, Rayleigh, Essex, SS6 7QF, Tel.: 01268 464614
Clinical Leads (NSF)
Dr M Lester, GP Lead, Prescribing, The Hollies, 41 Rectory Road, Hadleigh, Essex, SS7 2NA, Tel.: 01702 558147
Dr J Nicholls, GP Lead, Clinical Governance, Church View Surgery, Burley House, 15-17 High Street, Rayleigh, Essex, SS6 7DY, Tel.: 01702 774477
Dr M Mujahid, GP Lead, Cancer, 1a Oak Road, Canvey Island, Essex, SS8 7AX, Tel.: 01268 692211
Dr C Kothari, GP Lead, CHD, Southwell House, Back Lane, Rochford, Essex, SS4 1AY, Tel.: 01702 545241
Dr G Kittle, GP Lead, Child Protection, Church View Surgery, Burley House, 15-17 High Street, Rayleigh, Essex, SS6 7DY, Tel.: 01702 774477
Dr C Lewis, GP Lead, Diabetic Care, Audley Mills Surgery, 57 Eastwood Road, Rayleigh, Essex, SS6 7JF, Tel.: 01268 774981
Community Matrons
Ms K Ambrose, Community Matron, Mapline House, 14 Bull Lane, Rayleigh, Tel.: 01268 775650
Ms L Chiesa, Community Matron, Gt Wakering Health Centre, High Street, Gt. Wakering, Essex, Tel.: 01702 577802
Ms B Piper, Community Matron, Thundersley Clinic, 8 Kenneth Road, Thundersley, Essex, Tel.: 01268 366820
Community Nursing Services
H Brown, Director of Integrated Care (Interim) & Strategic Planning, 12 Castle Road, Rayleigh, Essex, SS6 7QF, Tel.: 01268 464500
Mrs S Farr, Head of Childrens Service, 12 Castle Road, Rayleigh, Essex, SS6 7QF, Tel.: 01268 464598
Ms C Hanna, Head of Adult Services, 12 Castle Road, Rayleigh, Essex, SS6 7QF, Tel.: 01268 464556
District Nursing
Ms C Hanna, Head of Adult Services - District Nursing, 12 Castle Road, Rayleigh, Essex, SS6 7QF, Tel.: 01268 464556
Ms J Myles, Modern Matron for District Nursing, Canvey Health Centre, Third Avenue, Canvey Island, Essex, SS8 9SU, Tel.: 01268 366450
Family Planning Services
Ms K Payne, Contraception & Sexual Health Service Manager, Kingsley Ward Centre, Family Plan Clinic, Warior House, 42-82 Southchurch Rd, SouthendonSea, SS1 2LZ, Tel.: 01702 577035
Health Visitors
Mrs S Farr, Head of Childrens Service - Health Visiting, 12 Castle Road, Rayleigh, SS6 7QF, Tel.: 01268 464598
Liaison Services
Mrs J Blackaby, Liaison Nurse for Care Homes, Burley House, 15-17 High Street, Rayleigh, Essex, SS6 7DY, Tel.: 01702 343599
Mrs J Keam-George, District Nurse Liaison Administrator, Churchfield House, Southend General Hospital, Prittlewell Chase, Westcliff on Sea, Essex, SS0 0RY, Tel.: 01702 435599

East of England Strategic Health Authority

Mrs K Law, Liaison Nurse for Care Homes, Burley House, 15-17 High Street, Rayleigh, Essex, SS6 7DY, Tel.: 01702 361230
Other Services
Ms T Broderick, Intermediate Care Lead, 12 Castle Road, Rayleigh, Essex, SS6 7QF, Tel.: 01268 464529
Ms K Chapman, Falls Co-ordinator, Burley House, 15-17 High Street, Rayleigh, Essex, SS6 7DY, Tel.: 01268 361230
Ms D Payne, Project Lead for Special Needs, Rayleigh Clinic, Eastwood Road, Rayleigh, Essex, SS0 7JP, Tel.: 01268 366610
Pharmacy
Mr S Nice, Director of Pharmacy, Southend General Hospital, Prittlewell Chase, Westcliff on Sea, Essex, SS0 0RY, Tel.: 01702 221091
Smoking Cessation
South Essex Stop Smoking Services, Mapline House, 14 Bull Lane, Rayleigh, Essex, Tel.: 01268 464511
Specialist Nursing Services
Ms A Davis, Asthma, - Allergy, Rayleigh Clinic, Eastwood Road, Rayleigh, Essex, SS6 7JP, Tel.: 01268 366616
Ms K Banham, Nurse Specialist, Continence, 3rd Floor Phoenix Court, Christopher Martin Rd, Basildon, Essex, SS14 3EZ, Tel.: 01268 448500
Ms A Hodgkins, Clinical Nurse Specialist, Diabetic Care, 212A London Road, Hadleigh, Essex, SS7 2PD, Tel.: 01702 554105
Ms S Brill, Nurse, Infection Control, Health Protection Agency, 8 Collingwood Road, Witham, Essex, CM8 2TT, Tel.: 01376 302282
Ms C Doyle, Team Manager, Macmillan, Fair Haven's Hospice, Chalkwell Avenue, Westcliff on Sea, Essex, SS0 8HN, Tel.: 01702 332487
Ms M Stapleton, Team Manager, Macmillan, 3rd Floor Phoenix Court, Christopher Martin Rd, Basildon, Essex, SS14 3EZ, Tel.: 01268 448522
Ms A Brown, Nurse Specialist, Tissue Viability, Rayleigh Clinic, Eastwood Road, Rayleigh, Essex, SS6 7JP, Tel.: 01268 366600
Ms K Fox, Nurse Specialist, Tissue Viability, Rayleigh Clinic, Eastwood Road, Rayleigh, Essex, SS6 7JP, Tel.: 01268 366600
Ms P Ross, Nurse Specialist, Tissue Viability, Rayleigh Clinic, Eastwood Road, Rayleigh, Essex, SS6 7JP, Tel.: 01268 366600

Central Suffolk Primary Care Trust

Trust Headquarters, Stow Lodge Centre
Chilton Way
STOWMARKET
IP14 1SZ
Tel.: 01449 616346

Admin & Senior Management
Mrs S Baker, Associate Director, Hartismere Lodge, Castleton Way, Eye, Suffolk, IP23 7BH, Tel.: 01379 873 750
Mr H Brown, Chief Executive,
Child Health
Child Health Department, Child Health Centre, Hospital Road, Bury St Edmunds, IP33 1ND, Tel.: 01284 775000
Mrs D Cordle, Head of Children & Family Services, St Helens House, Foxhall Road, Ipswich, Suffolk, Tel.: 01473 275 547
Ms L Searle, Children's Service Manager, Tel.: 01284 775077
Child Health Records
Child Health Department, Transfer of Records: Bury & W Suffolk Borders, Child Health Centre, Hospital Road, Bury St Edmunds, IP33 1ND, Tel.: 01284 775000
Ms W Longhurst, Admin,
Other Areas, Child Health Department, 1st Floor, St Clements Hospital, Foxhall Road, Ipswich, IP3 8LS,
South Waveney, Lowestoft Hospital, Tennyson Road, Lowestoft, NR32 1PT, Tel.: 01502 587311
Ms J Yates, Team Leader, Computer Information, Tel.: 01473 329211

Child Protection/Safeguarding Children
Ms J Scott, Designated Nurse, Child Protection, Endeavour House, Ipswich, Suffolk, Tel.: 01473 264 356
Clinical Leads (NSF)
Dr J Herman, Clinical Lead, Cancer,
Dr J Collier, Clinical Lead, CHD, Tel.: 01449 614 024
Dr D Egan, Clinical Lead, Diabetic Care,
Dr J Smith, Clinical Lead, Older People, Tel.: 01379 873 754
Community Nursing Services
Mrs J Fooks-Bale, Head of Community Services, Hartismere Lodge, Castleton Way, Eye, Suffolk, IP23 7BH, Tel.: 01379 873 755
District Nursing
Ms S Baker, Co-ordinator, Hartismere Lodge, Castleton Way, Eye, IP23 7BH, Tel.: 01379 873135
Mrs D Cordle, Head of Children & Family Services, St Helens House, Foxhall Road, Ipswich, Suffolk, Tel.: 01473 275 547
Mrs J Fooks-Bale, District Nurses, Hartismere Lodge, Castleton Way, Eye, Suffolk, IP23 7BH, Tel.: 01379 873 755
Equipment Loan Services
Mr B Hale, Community Equipment Services Manager, Ransomes Europark, Ipswich, Tel.: 01473 721167
Other Services
Mr A Winterbone, Manager, Independent Living Services, Chantry Clinic, Ipswich, Tel.: 01473 603645
Specialist Nursing Services
Mr A Winterbone, Independent Living, Services Manager, Chantry Clinic, Hawthorn Drive, Ipswich, IP2 0QY, Tel.: 01473 603645
Mr J Cuckow, Rehabilitation, Cardiac, Chantry Clinic, Hawthorn Drive, Ipswich, IP2 0QY, Tel.: 01473 686371
Ms S Baker, Manager, Continence, Hartismere Lodge, Castleton Way, Eye, IP23 7BH, Tel.: 01379 873135
Ms S Carter, Advisor, Continence, Hartismere Lodge, Castleton Way, Eye, Suffolk, IP23 7BH, Tel.: 01379 873 762
Ms S Nairn, Advisor, Continence, Hartismere Lodge, Castleton Way, Eye, Suffolk, IP23 7BH, Tel.: 01379 873 762
Ms N Chatters, Diabetic Care, - Adults, West Suffolk Hospital, Tel.: 01284 713311
Ms L Cole, Diabetic Care, - Adults, West Suffolk Hospital, Tel.: 01284 713311
Ms S Griggs, Diabetic Care, - Adults, West Suffolk Hospital, Tel.: 01284 713311
Ms M Hunt, Diabetic Care, - Adults, West Suffolk Hospital, Tel.: 01284 713311
Ms A Hood, Team Leader, Macmillan, St Helen's House, 571 Foxhall Road, Ipswich, IP3 8LX, Tel.: 01473 274060
Ms N McGreavy, Support, Neurology, Thingoe House, Cotton Lane, Bury St Edmunds, IP33 1YJ, Tel.: 01284 702544
Ms S Wright, Support, Neurology, Thingoe House, Cotton Lane, Bury St Edmunds, IP33 1YJ, Tel.: 01284 702544
Ms D Cooper, Stoma Care, Whitton Clinic, Meredith Road, Ipswich, IP1 6ED, Tel.: 01473 461821
Ms S Skingley, Stoma Care, Whitton Clinic, Meredith Road, Ipswich, IP1 6ED, Tel.: 01473 461821

Chelmsford Primary Care Trust

Trust Headquarters, Wood House
St John's Hospital, Wood Street
CHELMSFORD, CM2 9BG
Tel.: 01245 295000

Admin & Senior Management
Mr M Halliday, Chief Executive, Wood House, St John's Hospital, Wood Street, Chelmsford, CM2 9BG, Tel.: 01245 295000
Clinical Leads (NSF)
Ms J Maxwell, Clinical Lead, Cancer,
District Nursing
Ms J Goodwin, Primary Care Co-ordinator, Wood House, St John's Hospital, Wood Street, Chelmsford, CM2 9BG, Tel.: 01245 295000

East of England Strategic Health Authority

Colchester Primary Care Trust

Trust Headquarters, Health Offices
Turner Road
COLCHESTER
CO4 5JR
Tel.: 01206 288500

Admin & Senior Management
Ms R McHearne, Education, Training & Specialist Nursing, Nurse Manager, Central Clinic, East Lodge Court, High Street, Colchester, CO1 1UJ, Tel.: 01206 744056
Mr B Osborne, Chief Executive,
Ms K Smith, Acting Director of Nursing & Quality, Trust Headquarters, Health Offices, Turner Road, Colchester, C04 5JR, Tel.: 01206 288500

Child Health
Ms S Willis, Modern Matron HV & SN, Central Clinic, East Lodge Court, High Street, Colchester, CO1 1UJ, Tel.: 01206 744038

Child Health Records
Ms P Holmes, Admin, Central Clinic, East Lodge Court, High Street, Colchester, CO1 1UJ, Tel.: 01206 579411

Child Protection/Safeguarding Children
Child Protection, Provided by Essex Rivers NHS Trust,
Ms J M Young, Children & Families Manager, Colchester PCT, Health Offices, Turner Road, Colchester, CO4 5JR, Tel.: 01206 288539
Ms W Van Houtteghem, Named Nurse, Child Protection, Central Clinic, East Lodge Court, High Street, Colchester, CO1 1UJ, Tel.: 01206 744051

Clinical Leads (NSF)
Ms L Mahon-Daly, Clinical Lead, Cancer, 122 Shrub End Road, Colchester, CO3 4RY, Tel.: 01206 573605
Ms P Turner, Clinical Lead, Care of the Elderly, Colchester PCT, Health Offices, Turner Road, Colchester, CO4 5JR, Tel.: 01206 288552
Mr M Gogarty, Clinical Lead, CHD, Colchester PCT, Health Offices, Turner Road, Colchester, CO4 5JR, Tel.: 01206 288590

Community Nursing Services
Ms S Willis, Modern Matron HV & SN, Central Clinic, East Lodge Court, High Street, Colchester, CO1 1UJ, Tel.: 01206 744038

District Nursing
Ms W Tankard, Modern Matron District Nursing, Trust Headquarters, Health Offices, Turner Road, Colchester, C04 5JR, Tel.: 01206 744124

Family Planning Services
Ms C Marfleet, Essex Rivers Healthcare Trust, Colchester General Hospital, Turner Road, Colchester, Tel.: 01206 472398

Health Visitors
Ms H Bohr, Children with Special Needs, Health Visitor, East Lodge Court, Tel.: 01206 744035

Learning Disabilities
Braintree, Witham, Halstead Service (Team), Tel.: 01376 308900
Chelmsford Services (Team), Tel.: 01245 544300
Colchester Services (Team), Health House, Grange Way, Colchester, CO2 8GU, Tel.: 01206 747726
Epping Service (Team), Tel.: 01279 827303
Ms F Gerrie, Director of Learning Disability Services, Heath House, Whitehall Industrial Estate, Colchester, Tel.: 01206 747712
Maldon Service (Team), Tel.: 01621 725900
Tendring Services (Team), Tel.: 01255 201936

Liaison Services
Ms R Manning, Essex Rivers NHS Trust, Gainsborough Wing, Colchester General Hospital, Turner Road, Colchester, Tel.: 01206 747474

Pharmacy
Ms M Tompkins, Head of Medicines Management, Colchester PCT, Health Offices, Turner Road, Colchester, CO4 5JR, Tel.: 01206 288556

Smoking Cessation
Ms S White, Stop Smoking Co-ordinator, Cornerstone, 5-7 Sir Isaacs Walk, Colchester, CO1 1AQ, Tel.: 01206 574256

Specialist Nursing Services
Ms L Archer, Nurse, Cardiology, 659-622 The Crescent, Colchester Business Park, Colchester, Tel.: 01206 288226
Ms J Joslin, Nurse Facilitator, Diabetic Care, Cornerstone, 5-7 Sir Isaacs Walk, Colchester, CO1 1AG, Tel.: 01206 574256
Ms S Nicol, Nurse Facilitator, Diabetic Care, Cornerstone, 5-7 Sir Isaacs Walk, Colchester, CO1 1AG, Tel.: 01206 574256
Ms A Jones, Co-ordinator, Intermediate Care, Central Clinic, East Lodge Court, High Street, Colchester, CO1 1UJ, Tel.: 01206 744079
Ms P Holt, Nurse, Occupational Health, Essex County Hospital, Lexden Road, Colchester, Tel.: 01206 851436
Ms D Cook, Nurse, Primary Care, - Oncology, Monkwick Clinic, Queen Elizabeth Way, Monkwick, Colchester, CO2 8LT, Tel.: 01206 747100
Ms L Jongepier, Team Leader, Chronic Obstructive, Pulmonary Disorder, Hythe Clinic, Ventura Drive, The Hythe, Colchester, CO1 2FG, Tel.: 01206 745604
Ms D Rampton, Team Leader, Chronic Obstructive, Pulmonary Disorder, Hythe Clinic, Ventura Drive, The Hythe, Colchester, CO1 2FG, Tel.: 01206 745604

The Homeless/Travellers & Asylum Seekers
Ms E Bishton, Partnership Support Manager (Public Health Directorate), Colchester PCT, The Crescent, 659-662 Colchester Business Park, Colchester, Tel.: 01206 288210

Dacorum Primary Care Trust

Trust Headquarters, Isbister Centre
Chaulden House Gardens
HEMEL HEMPSTEAD
Herts
HP1 2BW
Tel.: 01442 840950

Admin & Senior Management
Ms C Hawkins, Director of Nursing,
Ms T Horn, Chief Executive,

Child Health
Provided by Hertfordshire Partnership Trust,

Child Health Records
Child Health Provided by Hertfordshire Partnership Trust,

Child Protection/Safeguarding Children
Ms S Appleton, Professional Lead, Tel.: 01442 255404
Ms C Gayle, Named Nurse, Unit 1, The Old School House, George Street, Hemel Hempstead, Herts, HP2 5UJ, Tel.: 01442 236875

Clinical Leads (NSF)
Dr J Chapman, Clinical Lead, Chronic Disease,
Dr J Kearney, Clinical Lead, Cancer,
Dr C Pelley, Clinical Lead, Children,
Dr L Hill, Clinical Lead, Older People,

Community Nursing Services
Ms A Clare, Associate Director, Civic Centre, Marlowes, Hemel Hempstead, HP1 1UU, Tel.: 01442 405633

District Nursing
Ms A Clare, Associate Director, Civic Centre, Marlowes, Hemel Hempstead, HP1 1UU, Tel.: 01442 405633

Family Planning Services
Via Hertfordshire Partnership Trust,

Health Visitors
Ms S Geraghty, Health Visitor - Liaison, Hemel Hempstead General Hospital, Hillfield Road, Hemel Hempstead, HP2 4AD, Tel.: 01442 213141

Liaison Services
Ms S Geraghty, Liaison, Health Visitor, Hemel Hempstead General Hospital, Hillfield Road, Hemel Hempstead, HP2 4AD, Tel.: 01442 213141

East of England Strategic Health Authority

Other Services
Ms B Hall, Nurse Lead, Watford General Hospital, Vicarage Road, Watford, WD1 8UB, Tel.: 01923 217167
Nurse Lead, Hospital at Home Services, Hemel Hempstead Hospital, Hillfield Road, Hemel Hempstead, HP2 4AD, Tel.: 01442 28774
Specialist Nursing Services
Ms S Norman, Nurse Lead,
Out of Hours Nursing (W Herts), Harpenden Memorial Hospital, AL5 4TA, Tel.: 01582 462458
Ms T Cooper, Lead Nurse, Palliative Care, Unit 1, The Old School House, George Street, Hemel Hempstead, Herts, HP2 5UJ, Tel.: 01442 218414
The Homeless/Travellers & Asylum Seekers
Ms W Chiu, Travellers, Health Visitor, Tel.: 01442 266509

East & North Hertfordshire NHS Trust
Trust Headquarters, Lister Hospital
Coreys Mill Lane
STEVENAGE
Hertfordshire
SG1 4AB
Tel.: 01438 314333

Child Health
Children's Community Team, The Mulberry Bush Unit for Children & Teenagers, Lister Hospital, Tel.: 01438 314333 ext 4012
Children's Community Team, Mezzanine Floor, QE11 Hospital, Howlands, Welwyn Garden City, Herts, AL7 4HQ,
Child Protection/Safeguarding Children
Dr D Croft, Consultant Community Paediatrician, Child Development Centre, Danestrete, Stevenage, Herts, SG1 1HB, Tel.: 01438 314333 ext 2455
Ms M Emson, Named Nurse, Child Protection, The Mulberry Bush Unit for Children & Teenagers, Lister Hospital, Tel.: 01438 784717
Community Midwifery
Emergencies, Queen Elizabeth II Hospital, Howlands, Welwyn Garden City, AL7 4HQ, Tel.: 01707 328111 or bleep 523
Miss A Hewitt, Head of Midwifery, Queen Elizabeth II Hospital, Howlands, Welwyn Garden City, AL7 4HQ, Tel.: 01707 328111 ext 4398
Outpatient Services, Queen Elizabeth II Hospital, Howlands, Welwyn Garden City, AL7 4HQ, Tel.: 01707 328111 ext 4609
Mrs M Tiplady, Head of Midwifery, Lister Hospital, Coreys Mill Lane, Stevenage, Hertfordshire, SG1 4AB, Tel.: 01438 314333 ext 5601/2
Ms S Yeap, Senior Clinical Midwife, Queen Elizabeth II Hospital, Howlands, Welwyn Garden City, AL7 4HQ, Tel.: 01707 328111 ext 4316
Health Visitors
Ms R Bradford, Special Needs Health Visitor, Bowling Road Health Centre, Ware, Herts, Tel.: 01920 462388
Ms T Ivison, Special Needs Health Visitor, Bowling Road Health Centre, Ware, Herts, Tel.: 01920 462388
Ms B Morrison, Liaison Health Visitor - 01707 328111 ext 4364, QE11 Hospital, Howlands, Welwyn Garden City, Herts, AL7 4HQ, Tel.: 01707 365379
Liaison Services
Ms B Morrison, Liaison Health Visitor - 01707 328111 ext 4364, QE11 Hospital, Howlands, Welwyn Garden City, Herts, AL7 4HQ, Tel.: 01707 365379

East Cambridge & Fenland Primary Care Trust
Trust Headquarters, Fenland View
Alexandra Road
WISBECH
Cambridgeshire
PE13 1HQ
Tel.: 01945 469400

Admin & Senior Management
Ms A Bradford, Chief Executive, (Acting),
Child Health Records
Mrs J Garratt, Admin Manager, Child Health Admin Dept, Eastgate Ward, Peterborough District Hospital, PE3 6DA, Tel.: 01733 874905
Clinical Leads (NSF)
Dr A Chandler, Clinical Lead, Cancer,
Dr A Wordsworth, Clinical Lead, Diabetic Care,
Dr C Nicholl, Clinical Lead, Older People,
Community Nursing Services
Ms K Meetterhauser, Community, Nurse Manager,
Ms L Randall, Community, Nurse Manager,
District Nursing
Doddington Community Hospital, Benwick Road, Doddington, March, PE15 0UG, Tel.: 01354 644299
Princess of Wales Hospital, Ely, Tel.: 01353 652000
Other Services
Central Hall Headquarters, (East Cambridgeshire Area), 52-54 Market Street, Ely, CB7 4LS, Tel.: 01353 654200
Fenland View Headquarters, (Fenland Area), Alexandra Road, Wisbech, PE13 1HQ, Tel.: 01945 469400
Ms M Risino, Manager, Community & Primary Care Services (Fenland), Doddington Community Hospital, Tel.: 01354 644299
Ms J Round, Manager, Community & Primary Care Services (East Cambs), Princess of Wales Hospital, Ely, Tel.: 01353 652000

Epping Forest Primary Care Trust
Trust Headquarters, Hawthorn Lodge
St Margaret's Hospital, The Plain
EPPING
CM16 6TN
Tel.: 01992 902010

Admin & Senior Management
Ms B Meadows, Director of Primary Care, Birchwood House, St Margaret's Hospital, Epping, Essex, CM16 6TN, Tel.: 01279 827319
Mrs J Minihane, Lead Nurse, Tel.: 01279 827027
Mrs C O'Connell, Director of Primary Care, Birchwood House, St Margaret's Hospital, Epping, Essex, CM16 6TN, Tel.: 01279 827319
Ms L Steer, Associate Director, Clinical Governance, Tel.: 01279 827476
Child Health
Mrs T Smith, Locality Clinical Development Manager, Primary Care, Birchwood House, St Margaret's Hospital, Epping, Essex, CM16 6TN, Tel.: 01278 827571
Child Health Records
Ms A Goodyear, Manager, Child Health Information Dept, Latton Bush Centre, Southern Way, Harlow, CM18 7BL, Tel.: 01279 698800
Child Protection/Safeguarding Children
Ms C Allen, Named Nurse, Child Protection, Birchwood House, St Margaret's Hospital, Epping, Essex, CM16 6TN, Tel.: 01279 827475
Ms S McClymont, Lead, Child Protection, Addison House, Hamstel Road, Harlow, CM20 1EP, Tel.: 01279 694940
Clinical Leads (NSF)
Mr M Sodha, Clinical Lead, Cancer,
Community Nursing Services
Ms B Meadows, Director of Primary Care, Birchwood House, St Margaret's Hospital, Epping, Essex, CM16 6TN, Tel.: 01279 827319
Mrs C O'Connell, Director of Primary Care, Birchwood House, St Margaret's Hospital, Epping, Essex, CM16 6TN, Tel.: 01279 827319
District Nursing
Ms B Meadows, Director of Primary Care, Birchwood House, St Margaret's Hospital, Epping, Essex, CM16 6TN, Tel.: 01279 827319
Mrs C O'Connell, Director of Primary Care, Birchwood House, St Margaret's Hospital, Epping, Essex, CM16 6TN, Tel.: 01279 827319
Family Planning Services
Hosted by neighbouring acute trust,

East of England Strategic Health Authority

HIV/AIDS
Mr T Skeate, Action for Men - AIDS/HIV/STD, Health, Planning & Development, St Margaret's Hospital, Epping, Essex, CM16 6TN,
Liaison Services
Ms F Richards, Liaison, Paediatrics, Tel.: 01279 694943
Other Services
Ms S Burge, Business Manager, Discharge co-ordinators, Older Peoples Services, St Margaret's Hospital, Epping, Essex, CM16 6TN,
Pharmacy
Ms N Garrett, Nurse Prescribing Lead,
Smoking Cessation
Ms A Cowie, Associate Director Public Health, Tel.: 01279 827476
Specialist Nursing Services
Ms G Mehta, Locality Clinical Development Manager, Primary Care, St Margaret's Hospital, Epping, Essex, CM16 6TN,
Ms R McKenzie, Specialist Nurse, Continence, Independent Living Centre, Bishop's Stortford, Herts, Tel.: 01279 444455
Ms P Mitchell, NHS Funded Nursing, Dev Lead for Nursing & Residential Care Homes, Continuing Care, Older Peoples Services, St Margaret's Hospital, Epping, Essex, CM16 6TN,
Ms J Reay, Nurse, Macmillan, Macmillan Nurse, Hamstel House, Princess Alexandra Hospital, Harlow, Essex,
Mrs J Minihane, Director, Lead Nurse, Older People, Older Peoples Services, St Margaret's Hospital, Epping, Essex, CM16 6TN, Tel.: 01279 827857
Ms A Cowie, Associate Director, Public Health, Health, Planning & Development, St Margaret's Hospital, Epping, Essex, CM16 6TN,
Ms C Malone, Specialist Nurse, Tissue Viability, - Wound Care, Specialist Services, Hawthorn Lodge, St Margaret's Hospital, Epping, Essex, CM16 6TN,
The Homeless/Travellers & Asylum Seekers
Ms A Cowie, Assistant Director Public Health, Birchwood House, St Margaret's Hospital, Epping, Essex, CM16 6TN,

Essex Rivers Health Care NHS Trust

Trust Headquarters, Colchester General Hospital
Turner Road
COLCHESTER
Essex
CO4 5JL
Tel.: 01206 747474
Fax.: 01206 854877

Acute Specialist Nursing Services
Mrs V Bradbury, Cytotoxics Specialist Practitioner, Tel.: 01206 744540
Ms E Garnish, Non-Invasive Ventilation, Clinical Nurse Specialist, Tel.: 01206 742687
Mrs J Hendricks, Laparoscopic Nurse Practitioner, Tel.: 0795 2120225
Ms T Lacey, Audit Surveillance Nurse, Tel.: 01206 744265
Mrs S Meekingsl, Cytotoxics Specialist Practitioner, Tel.: 01206 744540
Mrs C Wiseman, Disability, Clinical Nurse Specialist, Tel.: 01206 742160
Miss K Rooke, Research Sister, Clinical Nurse Specialist, Breast Care, Tel.: 01206 744734
Mrs L Keating, Clinical Nurse Specialist, Cardiac Rehabilitation, Tel.: 01206 742794
Ms J Payne, Clinical Nurse Specialist, Cardiac Rehabilitation, Tel.: 01206 742794
Mr C Campbell, Clinical Nurse Specialist, Chemotherapy, Tel.: 01206 744540
Ms J Malyan, Clinical Nurse Specialist, Chemotherapy, Inpatient Cytotoxic Care, Tel.: Bleep 922
Mrs S Parr, Clinical Nurse Specialist, Chemotherapy, Inpatient Cytotoxic Care, Tel.: Bleep 871

Ms V Scott, Clinical Nurse Specialist, Chemotherapy, Tel.: 01206 744540
Mr J Turton, Clinical Nurse Specialist, Chest Pain, Tel.: 01206 742794
Mrs E Jeffries, Support Nurse, Colorectal, Tel.: 01206 742356
Mrs B Coward, Clinical Nurse Specialist, Continence, Tel.: 01206 742338
Mrs S Robertson, Clinical Nurse Specialist, Dermatology, Tel.: 01206 744435
Mrs M Bancroft, Clinical Nurse Specialist, Diabetic Care, Tel.: 01206 742159
Ms C Hoy, Clinical Nurse Specialist, Diabetic Care, Tel.: 01206 742159
Mrs S Newman, Clinical Nurse Specialist, Diabetic Care, - Paediatrics, Tel.: 07659 114094
Mrs H Thompson, Clinical Nurse Specialist, Diabetic Care, Tel.: 01206 742076
Ms K Turner, Clinical Nurse Specialist, Diabetic Care, Tel.: 01206 742076
Mrs H Drudge-Coates, Clinical Nurse Specialist, DVT, Tel.: 01206 742098
Mrs A Wordley, Nurse Consultant, GI, Tel.: 01206 742413
Ms S Quartly, GU Medicine, Tel.: 01206 744559
Ms L Golding, Support Nurse, Haematology, Tel.: 01206 742190
Ms S Hunter, Support Nurse, Haematology, Tel.: 01206 742190
Ms J Tonkin, Nurse Consultant, Haemotology, Tel.: 01206 742414
Ms S Philpott, Clinical Nurse Specialist, Head & Neck, - Oncology, Tel.: 01206 744783
Mrs S Merrell, Co-ordinator, Head Injury, - Medicine, Tel.: 01206 742692
Mrs H Dakin, Senior Nurse, Infection Control, Tel.: 01206 744265
Mrs M Purslow, Clinical Nurse Specialist, Leg Ulcers, - Dermatology, Tel.: 01206 744435
Ms A Brown, Lung Cancer, Tel.: 01206 744620
Ms S Anderson, Clinical Nurse Specialist, Multiple Sclerosis, Tel.: 01206 742160
Mrs A Fenning, Support Nurse, Pain Management,
Mrs L Halls, Sister, Pain Management,
Mrs B Johnston, Inpatients, Macmillan Nurse, Palliative Care, Tel.: 01206 747480/4018
Mr C Lockyer, Inpatients, Macmillan Nurse, Palliative Care, Tel.: 01206 747480/4018
Ms L Villanuea, Parkinson's Disease, Tel.: 01206 742521
Mrs N Brownlie, Project Nurse, Renal, Tel.: 01206 288280
Mr A Bennell, Clinical Nurse Specialist, Respiratory, 01206 744111
Miss K Welham, Clinical Nurse Spec., Respiratory, 01206 744111
Mrs J Lozano, Clinical Nurse Specialist, Rheumatology, Tel.: 01206 742279
Mrs S Hewitson, Support Nurse, Stoma Care, Tel.: 01206 742009
Mrs F Horan, Clinical Nurse Specialist, Stoma Care, Tel.: 01206 742009
Mrs S Mills, Clinical Nurse Specialist, Stoma Care, Tel.: 01206 742009
Ms M Keating, Clinical Nurse Specialist, Stroke Care, Tel.: 01206 742462
Ms S Shaw, PDN, Tissue Viability, Tel.: 01206 742452
Ms Y French, Clinical Nurse Specialist, Upper GI, 01206 744272
Mrs L Powell, Clinical Nurse Specialist, Urology, - Oncology, Tel.: 01206 742964
Mrs E Rayner, Clinical Nurse Specialist, Vascular, Tel.: 01206 744273
Child Protection/Safeguarding Children
Mrs G Edwards, Named Nurse for ERHT, Child Protection, Colchester General Hospital, Turner Road, Colchester, Essex, CO4 5JL, Tel.: 01206 742267
Mrs L Greenall, Designated Nurse Safeguarding Children, Primary Care Centre, Turner Road, Colchester, CO4 5JL, Tel.: 01206 744009

Mrs K Moss, Named Nurse Safeguarding Children, Colchester General Hospital, Turner Road, Colchester, Essex, CO4 5JL, Tel.: 01206 742267

Community Midwifery
Constable Wing, Colchester General Hospital, Turner Road, Colchester, Essex, CO4 5JL, Tel.: 01206 742369
Emergencies, Clacton & District Hospital, Tower Road, Clacton-on-Sea, Essex, CO15 1LH, Tel.: 01255 421235
Emergencies, Harwich & District Hospital, 419 Main Road, Dovercourt, Harwich, Essex, CO12 4EX, Tel.: 01255 503700
Emergencies, Colchester General Hospital, Turner Road, Colchester, Essex, CO4 5JL, Tel.: 01206 845240
Mrs A Ferris, Head of Midwifery/Divisional Manager, Colchester General Hospital, Turner Road, Colchester, Essex, CO4 5JL, Tel.: 01206 742481
Midwifery - Clacton, 01255 201600, Clacton & District Hospital, Tower Road, Clacton-on-Sea, Essex, CO15 1LH, Tel.: 01206 747474 ext 1600
Midwifery - Harwich, 01255 201224, Harwich & District Hospital, 419 Main Road, Dovercourt, Harwich, Essex, CO12 4EX, Tel.: 01206 747474 ext 1224

Equipment Loan Services
Ms M Paget, Colchester Community Equipment Services, Colchester General Hospital, Turner Road, Colchester, Essex, CO4 5JL, Tel.: 01206 742758

Family Planning Services
Ms N Leeds, Family Planning Services, Greenstead Clinic, St Edmunds Centre, Tamarisk Way, Colchester, Essex, CO4 3GW, Tel.: 01206 747815
Dr C Marfleet, Consultant Women's Reproductive Health, Colchester General Hospital, Turner Road, Colchester, Essex, CO4 5JL, Tel.: 01206 742977
Ms A Ratcliff, Family Planning Services, Greenstead Clinic, St Edmunds Centre, Tamarisk Way, Colchester, Essex, CO4 3GW, Tel.: 01206 747815

Health Visitors
Mrs V Petrakos, Paediatric Liaison Health Visitor, Colchester General Hospital, Turner Road, Colchester, Essex, CO4 5JL, Tel.: 01206 744290

Liaison Services
Mrs K Bird, TB Liaison Nurse, Chest Unit Office, Tel.: 01206 742864
Mrs T Leppard, Blood Transfusion Liaison, Tel.: 01206 742709
Ms H Mee, Liaison Services, Colchester General Hospital, Turner Road, Colchester, Essex, CO4 5JL, Tel.: 01206 742258

The Homeless/Travellers & Asylum Seekers
Ms H Mee, Liaison Services, Colchester General Hospital, Turner Road, Colchester, Essex, CO4 5JL, Tel.: 01206 742258

Great Yarmouth Primary Care Trust

Trust Headquarters,
Astley Cooper House
Estcourt Road
GREAT YARMOUTH
Norfolk, NR30 4JH
Tel.: 01493 856156

Admin & Senior Management
Mr M Stonard, Chief Executive,

Child Health Records
Child Health Dept, 1st Floor St Clement's Hospital, Foxhall Road, Ipswich, IP3 8LS,
Ms J Yates, Team Leader, Computer Information, Tel.: 01473 329211

Child Protection/Safeguarding Children
Ms S Herbert, Child Protection, Children's Centre, Newberry Clinic, Lowestoft Road, Gorieston, Great Yarmouth, NR31 6SQ, Tel.: 01493 442322/661443

Clinical Leads (NSF)
Dr M Hardman, Clinical Lead, Cancer,
Dr A Allan, Clinical Lead, Diabetes,
Dr A Penn, Clinical Lead, CHD,
Dr A Cousins, Clinical Lead, Older People,

District Nursing
Ms M Hardman, Head of District Nursing, Trust Headquarters, Tel.: 01493 856156 ext 32

Health Visitors
Mrs C Driver, Head of Health Visitors, Trust Headquarters, Tel.: 01493 856156 ext 33

Greater Peterborough Primary Care Partnership

Trust Headquarters, Town Hall
Bridge Street
PETERBOROUGH
PE1 1FA
Tel.: 01733 758500

Admin & Senior Management
Mrs J Dodds, Assistant Director Nursing, Town Hall, Bridge Street, Peterborough, PE1 1FA, Tel.: 01733 758585
Mrs H Smith, Director of Clinical Services, Town Hall, Bridge Street, Peterborough, PE1 1FA, Tel.: 01733 882137
Mr C Town, Chief Executive, Tel.: 01733 758460

Child Health
Ms Y Burdock, Clinical Development Manager, City Health Cllinic, Wellington Street, Peterborough, PE1 5DU, Tel.: 01733 466668
Ms H Forty, Children's Community Nurse, Peterborough District Hospital, Tel.: 01733 874896

Child Health Records
Mrs J Garratt, Admin Manager - Child Health Dept, Child Health Dept, Peterborough District Hospitals Trust, Thorpe Road, Peterborough, PE3 6DA, Tel.: 01733 874905

Child Protection/Safeguarding Children
Ms S Hackney, Looked After Children, Designated Nurse, Child Health, Eastgate, Peterborough District Hospital, Thorpe Road, Peterborough, PE3 6DA, Tel.: 01733 74911
Mrs K Bush, Named Nurse, Child Protection, City Health Clinic, Wellington Street, Peterborough, PE1 5DU, Tel.: 01733 466669
Ms H Herron, Designated Nurse, Child Protection, City Health Clinic, Wellington Street, Peterborough, PE1 5DU, Tel.: 01733 466669

Clinical Leads (NSF)
Dr K Wishart, Clinical Lead, Clinical Audit, c/o Trust Headquarters,
Dr P Hartropp, Clinical Lead, Cancer, Yaxley Group Practice, Lansdowne Road, Yaxley, PE7 3JL, Tel.: 01733 240478
Dr K Prasad, Clinical Lead, Care of the Elderly, Westwood Clinic, Wicken Way, Westwood, PE3 7JW, Tel.: 01733 265560
Dr M Caskey, Clinical Lead, CHD, Park Medical Centre, 164 Park Road, PE1 2UF, Tel.: 01733 552801
Dr J Roland, Clinical Lead, Diabetic Care, PHT, Edith Carvell Hospital, Bretton Gate, Peterborough, Tel.: 01733 874000

Community Nursing Services
Ms N Ayres, Service Manager, City Health Cllinic, Wellington Street, Peterborough, PE1 5DU, Tel.: 01733 466633

District Nursing
Ms N Ayres, Service Manager, City Health Cllinic, Wellington Street, Peterborough, PE1 5DU, Tel.: 01733 466633
Mrs H Smith, Director of Clinical Services, Town Hall, Bridge Street, Peterborough, PE1 1FA, Tel.: 01733 758510

Family Planning Services
Mrs J Dodds, Assistant Director Nursing, Town Hall, Bridge Street, Peterborough, PE1 1FA, Tel.: 01733 758585

Learning Disabilities
Ms K Inskip, Assistant Director, Adult Disability, Town Hall, Bridge Street, Peterborough, PE1 1FA, Tel.: 01733 758570

East of England Strategic Health Authority

Liaison Services
Mr C Cooper, Team Leader, Transfer of Care Team, Peterborough Hospitals Trust, Thorpe Road, Peterborough, Tel.: 01773 874000
Liaison Services, Peterborough District Hospital, Thorpe Road, Peterborough, Tel.: 01733 874000
Mrs H Thorpe, TB Liaison, Peterborough District Hospital, Thorpe Road, Peterborough,
Pharmacy
Ms V Shaw, Chief Pharmacist, Tel.: 01733 758553
Smoking Cessation
Ms J Beever, Smoking Cessation Co-ordinator, St Johns, Thorpe Road, Peterborough, PE3 6JG, Tel.: 01733 882288
Specialist Nursing Services
Mrs P Rowley, Continuing ECH, Bretten Gate, Peterborough, Tel.: 01733 874000
Mrs H Thorpe, Poplar Avenue, Dogsthorpe, Peterborough, Tel.: 01733 874756
Mrs D Beales, CHD, City Health Clinic, Wellington Street, Peterborough, Tel.: 01733 466601
Ms A Edwards, Coronary Heart Disease, City Health Clinic, Tel.: 01733 466653
Mrs G Nixon, Diabetic Care, 10 Thistlemoor Road, Peterborough,
Mrs A Lilley, Intermediate Care,
Ms C Noble, Parkinson's Disease, - Neuro, Tern House, Gloucester Centre,, Tel.: 01733 363100
Mrs J McAllister, Respiratory, City Health Clinic, Wellington Street, Peterborough, Tel.: 01733 466615

Harlow Primary Care Trust
Trust Headquarters,
16th Floor
Terminus House
HARLOW
Essex
CM20 1XE
Tel.: 01279 694747

Admin & Senior Management
Ms R Cutts, Director of Nursing, 16th Floor, Terminus House, Harlow, Essex, CM20 1XE, Tel.: 01279 694768
Child Health
Ms J Edmondson, Immunisation Team Under Fives, Latton Bush Centre, Southern Way, Harlow, CM18 7BL, Tel.: 01279 698808
Ms M Fletcher, New Birth Team, Latton Bush Centre, Southern Way, Harlow, CM18 7BL, Tel.: 01279 698805
Ms A Goodyear, Manager, Child Health Information Dept, Latton Bush Centre, Southern Way, Harlow, CM18 7BL, Tel.: 01279 698800
Ms S Norris, Assistant Manager Child Health Info Dept, Latton Bush Centre, Southern Way, Harlow, CM18 7BL, Tel.: 01279 698801
Ms C Pears, Immunisation Team Under Fives, Latton Bush Centre, Southern Way, Harlow, CM18 7BL, Tel.: 01279 698807
Ms P Priest, Immunisation Team Under Fives, Latton Bush Centre, Southern Way, Harlow, CM18 7BL, Tel.: 01279 698809
Ms Y Rains, Newbirth Team, Latton Bush Centre, Southern Way, Harlow, CM18 7BL,
Ms M Seers, Newbirth Team, Latton Bush Centre, Southern Way, Harlow, CM18 7BL,
Ms G Wright, Childrens Services Manager, Terminus House, Harlow, Essex, CM20 1XE, Tel.: 01279 694765
Child Health Records
Ms G Wright, Childrens Services Manager, Terminus House, Harlow, Essex, CM20 1XE, Tel.: 01279 694765
Child Protection/Safeguarding Children
Ms S McClymont, Lead Nurse, Child Protection, Addison House, Hamstel Road, Harlow, Essex, CM20 1EP, Tel.: 01279 694940
Dr R Rajari, Named Doctor, Child Protection,

Clinical Leads (NSF)
Mrs R Cutts, Clinical Lead, Diabetes
Mrs P Hercules, Clinical Lead, Older People,
Community Nursing Services
Mr S Bailey, Locality Manager, Terminus House, Harlow, Essex, CM20 1XE, Tel.: 01279 694734
Mrs J Jones, Community Matron, Barbara Castle Health Centre, Broadley Road, Harlow, Essex, CM19 5RL, Tel.: 01279 416931
Mrs H Vander Puize, Locality Manager, Terminus House, Harlow, Essex, CM20 1XE, Tel.: 01279 694706
Other Services
Ms P Gurton, Associate Director of Integrated Services, Harlow PCT, Terminus House, Harlow, Essex, CM20 1XE, Tel.: 01279 694718
Ms S Radford, Cancer Information, Addison House, Hamstel Road, Harlow, Essex, CM20 1DS, Tel.: 01279 698674
School Nursing
Ms A Ginn, School Team/Community Information, Latton Bush Centre, Southern Way, Harlow, CM18 7BL, Tel.: 01279 698803
Ms T Helsey, School Team/Community Information, Latton Bush Centre, Southern Way, Harlow, CM18 7BL, Tel.: 01279 698804
Ms M Mason, School Team/Community Information, Latton Bush Centre, Southern Way, Harlow, CM18 7BL, Tel.: 01279 698802
Ms H Ottley, Team Leader, School Nursing, Lister House Community Clinic, Staple Tye, Harlow, Essex, CM18 7LS, Tel.: 01279 698669
Smoking Cessation
Ms A Cowie, Associate Director, Public Health, 16th Floor, Terminus House, Harlow, Essex, CM20 1XE, Tel.: 01279 694727
Specialist Nursing Services
Ms C Wells, Falls Co-ordinator, Leah Manning Centre, Tel.: 01279 698600
Ms C Woods, Lead Nurse, Harlow WIC, Wych Elm, Harlow, Essex, CM20 1QP, Tel.: 01279 694775
Mrs M Hanbury, Lead Nurse, Cancer, Terminus House, Harlow, Essex, CM20 1XE, Tel.: 01279 694768
Ms L Skidmore, Nurse Specialist, Cardiology, Keats Community Clinic, Bush Fair, Harlow, Essex, CM18 6LY, Tel.: 01279 698613
Ms B Wood, Team Leader, Intermediate Care, Leah Manning, Harlow, Essex,
Mr A Hughes, Case Manager, Older People, Lister House Community Clinic, Staple Tye, Harlow, Essex, CM18 7LS, Tel.: 01279 698669
Ms J Allen, Nurse Specialist, Parkinson's Disease, Keats Community Clinic, Bush Fair, Harlow, Essex, CM18 6LY, Tel.: 01279 698609
Mr R Gulrazani, Nurse Specialist, Respiratory, Keats Community Clinic, Bush Fair, Harlow, Essex, CM18 6LY, Tel.: 01279 698611
Ms M Jackson, Lead Nurse, Information Centre, Young People, Occasio House, Playhourse Square, Harlow, Essex, CM2 1AP, Tel.: 01279 625735

Hertfordshire Partnership NHS Trust
Trust Headquarters
99 Waverley Road
ST ALBANS, Hertfordshire
AL3 5TL
Tel.: 01727 811888

Learning Disabilities
Mr P Absolom, Team Manager, Letchworth Social Services, Old Grammar School, Broadway, Letchworth, Herts, SG6 3QG, Tel.: 01462 480663
Ms D Aremu, Team Manager, Letchworth Social Services, Old Grammar School, Broadway, Letchworth, Herts, SG6 3QG, Tel.: 01462 480663
Berkhamsted & Hemel Hempstead Team, Greenhills, Tenzing Road, Hemel Hempstead, HP2 4HS, Tel.: 01442 388700
Mrs R Fallon-Williams, Assistant Director, 3rd Floor, St Peters House, 2 Bricket Road, St Albans, Herts, AL1 3JW, Tel.: 01727 829817

East of England Strategic Health Authority

Harpenden & St Albans Team, St Peters House, 2 Bricket Road, St Albans, Herts, AL1 3JW, Tel.: 01727 829489

Mr B Seewoolall, Community Nurse Manager, 305 Ware Road, Hailey, Hertford, SG13 7PG, Tel.: 01992 444411

Ms H Swain, Lead Nurse, 3rd Floor, St Peters House, 2 Bricket Road, St Albans, Herts, AL1 3JW, Tel.: 01727 829800

Tertiary Services, Harperbury Hospital, Harper Lane, Shenley, Radlett, WD7 9HQ, Tel.: 01923 854961

Three Rivers Team, Shepherd Centre, Middleton Road, Mill End, Rickmansworth, WD3 2JF, Tel.: 01923 766908

Watford & Hertsmere Teams, Nascot Lawn, 92a Langley Road, Watford, WD1 3PJ, Tel.: 01923 238476

Mr G Wiseman, Team Manager, Danestrete Centre, Southgate, Stevenage, Herts, SG1 1HB, Tel.: 01438 314333 ext 2511

Ms R Wong, Team Manager, Danestrete Centre, Southgate, Stevenage, Herts, SG1 1HB, Tel.: 01438 314333 ext 2511

Mr H Yeoh, Team Manager, Letchworth Social Services, Old Grammar School, Broadway, Letchworth, Herts, SG6 3QG, Tel.: 01462 480663

Hertsmere Primary Care Trust

Trust Headquarters, Barry House
High Street
POTTERS BAR
Hertfordshire
EN6 5AS
Tel.: 01707 647586

Admin & Senior Management
Ms J Clark, Chief Executive, Barry House, High Street, Potters Bar, Herts, EN6 5AS, Tel.: 01707 622 939

Mrs M Roach, Director of Nursing, Potters Bar Community Hospital, Barnet Road, Hertfordshire, EN6 2RY, Tel.: 01707 654758

Child Protection/Safeguarding Children
Ms S Dixon, Named Nurse, Child Protection, Elstree Way Clinic, Tel.: 0208 953 3321/3241

Clinical Leads (NSF)
Dr J Bonnet, Clinical Lead, Cancer,
Dr M Edwards, Clinical Lead, CHD,
Dr P Gledstone, Clinical Lead, Children,
Dr M Roach, Clinical Lead, Older People,

District Nursing
Borehamwood, District Nursing Service, Elstree Way Clinic, Borehamwood, WD6 1JT, Tel.: 0208 953 3321/3241

Potters Bar, District Nursing Service, Potters Bar Community Hospital, Tel.: 01707 662624

Health Visitors
Borehamwood, Health Visitor Services, Elstree Way Clinic, Borehamwood, WD6 1JT, Tel.: 0208 953 3321/3241

Hinchingbrooke Health Care NHS Trust

Trust Headquarters, Hinchingbrooke Hospital
Hinchingbrooke Park
HUNTINGDON
Cambridgshire
PE29 6NT
Tel.: 01480 416416
Fax.: 01480 416561

Community Midwifery
Day Assessment Unit, Tel.: 01480 363564

Ms J Driver, Senior Clinical Midwifery Manager Clinical Risk, Emergencies, Tel.: ext 6245

Mrs C Griffiths, Head of Midwifery & Women's Services, Hinchingbrooke Hospital, Tel.: 01480 363688

Ms V Lister, Senior Clinical Midwifery Manager, Midwifery Unit, Tel.: 01480 416243

Mr C Nixon, Senior Clinical Midwifery Manager Delivery Suite/Postnatal Ward,

Huntingdonshire Primary Care Trust

Trust Headquarters, The Priory
Priory Road, ST IVES
Cambridgeshire, PE27 5BB
Tel.: 01480 308 221

Admin & Senior Management
Ms J Dullaghan, Director of Nursing & Clinical Services, The Priory, Priory Road, St Ives, Cambridgeshire, PE27 5BB, Tel.: 01480 308214

Mr P Wightman, Acting Chief Executive,

Child Health
Mrs J Hoare, Head of Children's Services, South Buillding, Primrose Lane, Huntingdon, Cambs, PE29 1WG, Tel.: 01480 415204

Child Health Records
Child Health Records, Community Unit, Primrose Lane, Huntingdon, PE29 1WG, Tel.: 01480 415221

Mrs J Hoare, Manager, South Building, Primrose Lane, Huntingdon, PE29 1WG, Tel.: 01480 415204

Child Protection/Safeguarding Children
Ms B Cannon, Child Protection, Community Unit, Primrose Lane, Huntingdon, Cambridgeshire, PE29 1WG, Tel.: 01480 415105

Clinical Leads (NSF)
Dr I Williams, Clinical Lead, Cancer,
Dr A Aggarwal, Clinical Lead, CHD,
Dr P Harding, Clinical Lead, CHD,
Dr M Moore, Clinical Lead, Diabetic Care,
Dr B Boyle, Clinical Lead, Older People,

Community Nursing Services
Community Nursing, Newtown Centre, Nursery Road, Huntingdon, PE29 3RS, Tel.: 01480 415280

Family Planning Services
Dr F McCullough, Manager, Hinchingbrooke Hospital, Hinchingbrooke Park, Huntingdon, PE29 6NT, Tel.: 01480 416416 ext 6243

Health Visitors
Ms F Curran, Health Visiting, South Building, Primrose Lane, Huntingdon, Cambridgeshire, PE29 1WG, Tel.: 01480 415107

HIV/AIDS
Ms M Worral, Newtown Centre, Nursery Road, Huntingdon, Cambs, PE29 3RS, Tel.: 01480 415333

Liaison Services
Liaison Services, Hinchingbrooke Hospital, 01480 416416 bleep 361

School Nursing
Mrs F Curran, Manager, School Nursing, South Building, Primrose Lane, Huntingdon, Cambridgeshire, PE29 1WG,

Smoking Cessation
Ms J Walsh, Ramsey Road Clinic, St Ives, Cambs, Tel.: 01480 300080

Specialist Nursing Services
Ms S Jones, Anti-Coagulation, Hinchingbrooke Hospital, Tel.: 01480 416416 bleep 310

Ms L Taylor, Breast Care, Hinchingbrooke Hospital, Tel.: 01480 416416 ext 3500

Ms G Pascoe, Continence, Hinchingbrooke Hospital, Tel.: 01480 416416 ext 6734

Ms C Brown, Haematology, Hinchingbrooke Hospital, Tel.: 01480 416416

Ms T Sage, Haematology, Hinchingbrooke Hospital, Tel.: 01480 416416

Team, Intermediate Care, Hinchingbrooke Hospital, Tel.: 01480 416091

Ms H Prior, Community Services Manager, Macmillan, Hinchingbrooke Hospital, Tel.: 01480 416416 ext 6103

Ms D Lightfoot, Respiratory, Hinchingbrooke Hospital, Tel.: 01480 416416 ext 6682

Ms S Haseler, Stoma Care, Hinchingbrooke Hospital, Tel.: 01480 416735

East of England Strategic Health Authority

Ipswich Hospital NHS Trust
Trust Headquarters, Ipswich Hospital
Heath Road
IPSWICH
Suffolk
IP4 5PD
Tel.: 01473 712233
Fax.: 01473 703400

Acute Specialist Nursing Services
Ms A Hallett, Complementary Therapies, Onc & Haem Dept, Tel.: ext 6903
Ms K Scott, Moving & Handling Advisor, Erica Training Centre, Tel.: ext 6379
Ms J Shanks, X-Ray Dept, Tel.: ext 5375
Ms A Bloomfield, A&E, Tel.: ext 1044
Mr S Christie, A&E, Tel.: ext 1035
Ms S Knight, A&E, Tel.: ext 1035
Ms T Evans, Nurse Specialist, Acute Pain, Pain Management Unit, Tel.: ext 1010
Ms K Street, Acute Pain, Pain Management Unit, Tel.: ext 5193
Ms K Hamilton, Theatres, Anaesthetics, Training Office, South Theatres, Tel.: ext 1134
MS B Marshall, Asthma, Clinic H, OPD, Tel.: ext 5748
Ms S Boreham, Breast Care, Tel.: ext 5300
Ms J Calcluth, Nurse Specialist, Breast Care, Breast Care Office, Tel.: ext 5300
Ms H Clarke, Nurse Specialist, Breast Care, Breast Care Office, Tel.: ext 5300
Ms K Collingridge, Nurse Specialist, Breast Care, Breast Care Office, Tel.: ext 5300
Ms H Gray, Breast Care, Tel.: ext 5300
Ms S Cuckow, Rapid Access Chest Pain, Cardiology, Clinic G, Tel.: ext 5782
Ms C Pond, Rapid Access Chest Pain, Cardiology, Clinic G, Tel.: ext 5782
Ms K Hind, Coloproctology, Surgical Directorate, South Finance Suite, Tel.: ext 6805
Ms H Sewell, Coloproctology, Surgical Directorate, South Finance Suite, Tel.: ext 6805
Ms K Gould, Colorectal, Tel.: ext 1865
Ms V Reid, Colorectal, Tel.: ext 1865
Ms W Russell, Vascular, Colorectal, Tel.: ext 1865
Ms L Carpenter, Critical Care, General & Special Surgery Offices, Tel.: ext 6252
Ms S Chatterton, Critical Care, General & Special Surgery Offices, Tel.: ext 6252
Ms J Sumpton, Critical Care, General & Special Surgery Offices, Tel.: ext 6252
Ms R Yale, Nurse Specialist, Critical Care, General & Special Surgery Offices, Tel.: ext 6252
Ms M Brown, Dermatology, Tel.: ext 6717
Ms J Peters, Dermatology, Tel.: ext 6386
Ms D Cox, Diabetic Care, Diabetes Centre, Tel.: ext 6190
Mr J Hassler-Hurst, Paediatric Community Link Lead, Diabetic Care, Tel.: ext 6189
Ms S Mitchell, Community Link Lead, Diabetic Care, Tel.: ext 6190
Ms A Scott, Diabetic Care, Diabetes Centre, Tel.: ext 6192
Ms A Scott, Diabetic Care, - Adults, Tel.: ext 6192
Ms C Wadham, Diabetic Care, - Paediatrics, Ipswich Hospital, Tel.: ext 6189
Ms M Lanyon, Endocrinology, Endocrine Unit, Tel.: ext 6604
Ms J Bartle, ENT Surgery, Clinic E, OPD, Tel.: ext 5145
Ms M Peachey, Epilepsy, Clinical Neurology, Tel.: ext 6046
Ms A Garnham, Gynae/Oncology, Tel.: ext 6788
Ms S Hadwen, Gynaecology, Tel.: ext 5661

Ms P Russell, Gynaecology, Tel.: ext 5661
Ms L Milton, Head & Neck, - Cancer, ENT OPD, Tel.: ext 5145
Ms L Taylor, Infection Control, Pathology Lab, Tel.: ext 5485
Ms S Deas, Intermediate Care, Rapid Response Office, North Corridor, Tel.: ext 6259
Mr R Goodrum, Nurse Specialist, ITU, Critical Care Services, ITU, Tel.: ext 1320
Ms S Allen, Specialist, IV Therapy, Tel.: ext 1233
Ms L Parrish, IV Therapy, IV Therapy, Tel.: ext 6954
Ms L Collins, Emergency, Medicine, Tel.: ext 1165
Mr C Boyes, Multiple Sclerosis, Neurology Portacabin, Tel.: ext 6091
Ms L Cartmel, Nephrology, Tel.: ext 6732
Ms D Bromley, Nutrition, Medical Directorate, Tel.: ext 6218
Ms L Jankowski, Older People, - Medicine, Orford Ward, Tel.: ext 6139
Ms G Bailey, Oncology, Tel.: ext 6387
Ms R Hockney, Oncology, Tel.: ext 6037
Ms G Reid, Oncology, Tel.: ext 6037
Ms J Walkeden, Ophthalmology, Tel.: ext 5827
Mr F Grimshaw, Orthopaedics, - Trauma, Tel.: ext 1360
Ms C Howard, Orthopaedics, - Trauma, Capel Day Room, Tel.: ext 1360
Ms S Hunnibell, Orthopaedics, Pain Management Unit, Tel.: ext 1360
Ms F Last, Orthopaedics, - Trauma, Tel.: ext 1360
Ms S Stephenson, Orthopaedics, - Trauma, Capel Day Room, Tel.: ext 1295
Ms H Vernau, Orthopaedics, Brantham Ward, Tel.: ext 1360
Ms N Goodwin, Palliative Care, Wolveston Wing, Tel.: ext 6932
Ms L Spurling, Palliative Care, Wolveston Wing, Tel.: ext 6932
Ms H Williams, Parkinson's Disease, Tel.: ext 6243
Ms S Kaznica, Pathology, - Blood Transfusion, Tel.: ext 5391
Ms K Richards, Respiratory, - Paediatrics, Tel.: ext 1196
Ms M Purnell, Officer, Resuscitation Training, Office PGME, Tel.: ext 1212
Ms R Brett, Rheumatology, Out-Patients Dept, Tel.: ext 5315
Ms G Rose, Rheumatology, Out-Patients Dept, Tel.: ext 5315
Ms S Power, Stoma Care, Tel.: ext 5301
Ms S Stopher, Stoma Care, Tel.: ext 5301
Ms A Woolgar, Stoma Care, Tel.: ext 5301
Ms G Stansfield, Tissue Viability, CTU, Tel.: ext 1019
Ms S King, Upper GI, Tel.: ext 1865
Mr K Rengert, Nurse Specialist, Upper GI, General Surgery, Tel.: ext 1865
Ms M Lynch, Urology, Tel.: ext 1862
Ms K Mowle, Urology, Tel.: ext 1374
Ms J Smith, Urology, Tel.: ext 1374
Mr C Garlick, Urology/Oncology, Somersham Ward, Tel.: ext 6903

Child Health
Ms M Sakanovic, Paediatric Oncology, Tel.: ext 1380
Ms S Birkett, Paediatric, Respiratory, Children's OPD, Tel.: ext 1381

Community Midwifery
Mrs C Colbourne, Head of Midwifery, Obstetrics & Gynae, Ipswich Hospital, Heath Road, Ipswich, Suffolk, IP4 5PD, Tel.: 01473 703000
Emergencies, Ask for Senior Midwife, Tel.: 01473 712233
Gilchrist Maternity Unit, Tel.: 01379 870600
Mrs M Head, Midwifery Manager, Ipswich Hospital, Heath Road, Ipswich, Suffolk, IP4 5PD, Tel.: 01473 703005

HIV/AIDS
Ms K Morris, HIV/Palliative Care, Infectious Diseases, Pinewood Surg, Shepard Drive, Ipswich, IP8 3SL, Tel.: 01473 692616

Liaison Services
Hospital Community Liaison Team, Ipswich Hospital, Heath Road, Ipswich, IP4 5PD, Tel.: 01473 702363
Ms F Yule, Liaison, Psychiatric, Tel.: ext 5688

Smoking Cessation
Ms H Andrews, Tel.: ext 6314/5

East of England Strategic Health Authority

Ipswich Primary Care Trust

Trust Headquarters, 2nd Floor
St Clements Main Building, Foxhall Road
IPSWICH, Suffolk
IP3 8LS
Tel.: 01473 329500
Fax.: 01473 329050

Admin & Senior Management
Ms C Taylor Brown, Chief Executive, Tel.: 01473 329532
Child Health
Ms N Clemo, Children's Services, Tel.: 01449 776581
Child Health Records
Ms J Bilotta, Clinical Co-ordinator, Health Visiting, 2nd Floor St
Clements, Foxhall Road, Ipswich, IP3 8LS, Tel.: 01473 329519
Child Protection/Safeguarding Children
Ms J Bilotta, Clinical Co-ordinator, Health Visiting, 2nd Floor St
Clements, Foxhall Road, Ipswich, IP3 8LS, Tel.: 01473 329519
Clinical Leads (NSF)
Mrs A Hood, Clinical Lead, Cancer,
Dr J Collier, Clinical Lead, CHD,
Dr O Powell, Clinical Lead, Diabetic Care,
Dr A Taylor, Clinical Lead, Older People,
Community Nursing Services
Ms C Rhind, Service Manager, 2nd Floor St Clements, Foxhall Road,
Ipswich, IP3 8LS, Tel.: 01473 329512
District Nursing
Mr J Such, Director of Health & Social Care,
Mr T Ward, Director, Health Improvements,
Health Visitors
Ms J Bilotta, Clinical Co-ordinator, Health Visiting, 2nd Floor St
Clements, Foxhall Road, Ipswich, IP3 8LS, Tel.: 01473 329519
Liaison Services
Community Liaison Team, Ipswich Hospital NHS Trust, Heath Road,
Ipswich, Tel.: 01473 702363
Other Services
Ms S Barron, General Practice Nurse Facilitator, 2nd Floor St
Clements, Foxhall Road, Ipswich, IP3 8LS, Tel.: 01473 329563
Ms D Godbold, Head of Intermediate Care Services, Hartismere
Hospital, Suffolk, Tel.: 01379 873759
Ms S Stallabrass, Community Refugee Team Co-ordinator, 70-74 St
Helen Street, Ipswich, IP4 2LA, Tel.: 01473 341750
The Homeless/Travellers & Asylum Seekers
Ms K Cubitt, Allington House, Woodbridge Road, Ipswich, Tel.:
01473 275258

James Paget Healthcare NHS Trust

Trust Headquarters, James Paget Hospital
Lowestoft Road
GORLESTON
Great Yarmouth
NR31 6LA
Tel.: 01493 452452
Fax.: 01493 452078

Acute Specialist Nursing Services
Mrs M Butt, Clinical Nurse Specialist, Tel.: 01493 453261
Mrs B Inyang, Clinical Nurse Specialist, Tel.: 01493 453261
Mrs V Sawden, Clinical Nurse Specialist, Tel.: 01493 453261
Mr T Charity, Nurse Practitioner, Advanced, Tel.: 01493 453683
Ms A Andrzejewski, Nurse Specialist, Anti-Coagulation, Tel.: 01493
453213
Ms J Foster, Nurse Specialist, Anti-Coagulation, Tel.: 01493 453213
Ms S Simpson, Nurse Specialist, Anti-Coagulation, Tel.: 01493
453213
Mrs V Amanat, Breast Care, Tel.: 01493 452447
Mrs J Shreeve, Nurse Specialist, Cardiac Rehabilitation, Tel.: 01493
452547
Ms M Seehra, Continence, Tel.: 01493 3511

Mrs K Peat, Nurse Specialist, Dermatology, Tel.: 01493 453545
Mrs J Ramsay, Nurse Specialist, Dermatology, Tel.: 01493 453545
Mrs C Allen, Nurse Specialist, Diabetes, Tel.: 01493 453373
Mr F Grinnell, Nurse Specialist, Diabetes, Tel.: 01493 453373
Miss J Jennings, Nurse Specialist, Diabetes, Tel.: 01493 453373
Mr C Allen, Health Visitor, Diabetic Care, Tel.: 01493 453373
Mr F Grinell, Diabetic Care,
Mrs S Plume, Liaison, Discharges, Patient Progress Manager, Tel.:
01493 453650
Mrs L Mileham, Nurse Practitioner, Emergency Care, Tel.: 01493
452364
Ms D Currie, Sub-fertility, Nurse Specialist, Fertility, Tel.: 01493
452366
Ms R Thompson, Nurse Specialist, Gynae/Oncology, Tel.: 01493
452367
Ms R Conway, Nurse Specialist, Haematology, Tel.: 01493 452869
Ms D Smith, Tracheostomy, Head & Neck, Tel.: 01493 453146
Ms L Hawtin, Infection Control, Tel.: 01493 452168
Mr R Furness, Lung Cancer, Tel.: 01493 452047
Ms L Cutting, Nurse Practitioner, Oncology, Tel.: 01493 452869
Mrs J Aitchison, Ophthalmology, Tel.: 01493 452452
Mr M Ludford, Charge Nurse, Outreach, Tel.: 01493 453261
Ms J Austin, Nurse Consultant, Pain Management, Tel.: 01493
452077
Ms S Ives, Nurse Specialist, Pain Management, Tel.: 01493 453141
Ms C Martin, Nurse Specialist, Pain Management, Tel.: 01493
453354
Ms A Baxter Pownall, Nurse Specialist, Palliative Care, Tel.: 01493
453439
Miss J Beales, Nurse Specialist, Palliative Care, Tel.: 01493 453439
Ms D Berrisford, Nurse Specialist, Palliative Care, Tel.: 01493
452084
Ms E Crowe, Nurse Specialist, Palliative Care, Tel.: 01493 453439
Mrs M Crump, Nurse Specialist, Palliative Care, Tel.: 01493 452084
Ms S Fish, Nurse Specialist, Palliative Care, Tel.: 01493 452084
Ms J Fuller, Nurse Specialist, Palliative Care, Tel.: 01493 453439
Mrs G Gibbs, Nurse Specialist, Palliative Care, Tel.: 01493 452084
Ms K Nobes, Team Leader, Palliative Care, Tel.: 01493 452804
Ms J Philpott, Nurse Specialist, Palliative Care, Tel.: 01493 453439
Ms M Whitehouse, Nurse Specialist, Palliative Care, Tel.: 01493
453439
Ms H Matthews, Respiratory, Tel.: 01493 453423
Ms S Bruce Leggett, Support Nurse, Rheumatology, Tel.: 01493
452869
Ms M Jordan, Stoma Care, - Colorectal, Tel.: 01493 452427
Ms A Fenn, Nurse Specialist, Urology/Oncology, Tel.: 01493 452510
Admin & Senior Management
Mr N Coveney, Director of Nursing & Patient Care, Lowestoft Road,
Gorleston, Great Yarmouth, Norfolk, NR31 6LA, Tel.: 01493 452759
Child Health
Children's Community Nursing Team, Tel.: 01493 453175
Ms S Herbert, Clinical Community Paediatric Manager, Children's
Centre, Newberry Clinic, Lowestoft Road, Gorleston, Great
Yarmouth, NR31 6JQ, Tel.: 01493 442322/661443
Mr F O'Driscoll, Divisional Manager, James Paget Hospital,
Lowestoft Road, Gorleston, Greater Yarmouth, NR31 6LA, Tel.:
01493 452231
Child Health Records
Child Health Records, c/o Child Health Dept, St Clements Hospital,
Ipswich, Tel.: 01473 329209
Child Protection/Safeguarding Children
Ms S Herbert, Child Protection, Children's Centre, Newberry Clinic,
Lowestoft Road, Gorleston, Great Yarmouth, NR31 6JQ, Tel.: 01493
442322/661443
Community Midwifery
Emergencies, Ask for Senior Midwife, Tel.: 01493 452480
Maternity Department, Tel.: 01493 452212
Ms J Pearman, Head of Midwifery Services, Tel.: 01493 452592

East of England Strategic Health Authority

Family Planning Services
Managed by Lowestoft/Waveney PCT,
HIV/AIDS
Ms J Gee, STD/HIV Health Advisers, James Paget Hospital, Tel.: 01493 452747
Mr P Nicholls, STD/HIV Health Advisers, James Paget Hospital, Tel.: 01493 452747
Learning Disabilities
Managed by Norfolk Mental Health,
Liaison Services
Managed by Great Yarmouth PCT,
School Nursing
Ms D Deavin, Team Leader, School Nurses, Tel.: 01493 337917
Ms I Haysom, Lead for School Nurses,
Smoking Cessation
Managed by Great Yarmouth PCT,
The Homeless/Travellers & Asylum Seekers
Managed by Great Yarmouth PCT,

King's Lynn & Wisbech Hospitals NHS Trust

Trust Headquarters, Queen Elizabeth Hospital
Gayton Road
KING'S LYNN
Norfolk, PE30 4ET
Tel.: 01553 613613
Fax.: 01553 613700

Acute Specialist Nursing Services
Ms H Gallagher, Medical Device Nurse,
Ms E Peters, Clinical Placement Facilitator,
Ms M Pomeroy, Cadet Nurse Co-ordinator,
Ms K Willis, Anti-Coagulation,
Mrs A Holford, Breast Care,
Mrs S Edwards, Nurse, Cancer, - Prostate,
Ms C Blake, Nurse, Cardiac Rehabilitation,
Ms K Sidell, Cardiac Rehabilitation,
Ms M Steward, Colorectal,
Mr A Billington, Clinical Educator, Critical Care,
Ms L Goodall, Dermatology,
Ms I Bane, Diabetic Care,
Ms A R Bunkle, Diabetic Care,
Ms S Thompsett, Diabetic Care,
Ms A Mills, Health Adviser, G.U.M,
Ms C Atterbry, Transfusion Medicine, Haematology,
Mrs L Grimmer, Haematology,
Ms J Miller, Haematology,
Ms A Rodriguez, Haematology,
Ms E Hardy, Infection Control,
Mrs I Barrett, Macmillan,
Mrs S Dale, Macmillan,
Ms M Gore, Macmillan,
Mrs J Havercroft, Macmillan,
Mrs R Vivian, Macmillan,
Ms T Beckett, Trials, Oncology,
Mrs B Perryman, Sister, Oncology,
Ms D Campbell, Specialist Nurse, Ophthalmology,
Miss A Cole, Ophthalmology,
Miss S Earl, Ophthalmology,
Mrs S King, Ophthalmology,
Ms S Tabor, Specialist Nurse, Ophthalmology,
Ms J Allen, Orthopaedics,
Ms L Heighton, Specialist Nurse, Pain Management,
Mrs C Kent, Specialist Nurse, Respiratory,
Mr C Pidgeon, Resuscitation Training,
Ms D Bond, Specialist Nurse, Rheumatology,
Ms S Sisson, Specialist Nurse, Rheumatology,
Mrs G Skipper, Stoma Care,
Ms S Hoare, Urology,

Admin & Senior Management
Miss J Miller, Head of Nursing, Surgical Directorate, Queen Elizabeth Hospital, Gayton Road, King's Lynn, Norfolk, PE30 4ET,
Mrs C Roberts, Head of Nursing, Medical Directorate, Queen Elizabeth Hospital, Gayton Road, King's Lynn, Norfolk, PE30 4ET,
Child Protection/Safeguarding Children
Mrs W Steward-Brown, Child Protection, Tel.: 01553 613613 bleep 1225
Community Midwifery
Ms A Compton, Community Midwifery Manager, Women & Children's Directorate, Queen Elizabeth Hospital, Tel.: 01553 613537
Ms B James, Head of Midwifery & Nursing, Women & Children's Directorate, Queen Elizabeth Hospital, Tel.: 01553 613537
Liaison Services
Team Leader, Liaison Elderly, Tel.: 01553 613613 ext 3813

Luton & Dunstable Hospital NHS Trust

Trust Headquarters, Luton & Dunstable Hospital
Lewsey Road
LUTON
Bedfordshire
LU4 0DZ
Tel.: 0845 127 0127
Fax.: 01582 492130

Acute Specialist Nursing Services
Ms J Chalkley, Macmillan, Breast Care,
Ms L Josiah, Colorectal, Luton & Dunstable Hospital,
Ms S McIntosh, Colorectal, Luton & Dunstable Hospital,
Ms J Fisher, Diabetic Care, Diabetes Information Centre, Tel.: 01582 497152
Ms D Morrison, Diabetic Care, Paediatric, Diabetes Information Centre, Tel.: 01582 497152
Ms S Tomkins, Diabetic Care, Diabetes Information Centre, Tel.: 01582 497152
Ms S White, Diabetic Care, Diabetes Information Centre, Tel.: 01582 497152
Ms S Fox, Infection Control, Tel.: bleep 152
Ms M McCarron, Palliative Care, Tel.: bleep 269
Ms H Gillanders, Stoma Care, Luton & Dunstable Hospital, Tel.: bleep 056
Child Protection/Safeguarding Children
Ms M McIntrye, Maternity, Lewsey Road, Luton, LU4 0DZ, Tel.: 01582 497023
Ms T Sciver, Maternity, Lewsey Road, Luton, LU4 0DZ, Tel.: 01582 497023
Community Midwifery
Ms S
Ms S Carrertt, Sure Start Midwife, Luton & Dunstable Hospital, Tel.: 07715 510 481
Ms F Forsythe, Sure Start Midwife, Luton & Dunstable Hospital, Tel.: 07715 510 481
Mrs H Lucas, Head of Midwifery, Tel.: 01582 497582 bleep 251
Mrs M McIntyre, Community Midwifery Manager, Tel.: 01582 497023bleep 051
Mrs S Moffatt, General Manager, Women & Children's Services, Tel.: 01582 497024
Mrs T Scivier, Community Midwifery Manager, Tel.: 01582 497023bleep 051
Ms J Simmonds, Infant Feeding Advisor, Luton & Dunstable Hospital, Tel.: 01582 718045
Mrs B Stacey, Director of Nursing & Midwifery, Luton & Dunstable Hospital NHS Trust, Lewsey Road, Luton, LU4 0DZ, Tel.: 01582 497012
HIV/AIDS
Ms S O'Driscoll, HIV Specialist Midwife, Luton & Dunstable Hospital, Tel.: 01582 497586

East of England Strategic Health Authority

Luton Primary Care Trust

Trust Headquarters, Nightingale House
94 Inkerman Street
LUTON
LU1 1JD
Tel.: 01582 528840
Fax.: 01582 528841

Child Protection/Safeguarding Children
Ms S Steffens, Child Protection, Gooseberry Hill Clinic, 62 Gooseberry Hill, Luton, Beds, LU3 2LB, Tel.: 01582 707464
Clinical Leads (NSF)
Dr W Matta, Clinical Lead, CHD,
Dr P Singer, Clinical Lead, Diabetic Care,
Community Matrons
Ms C White, Clinical Lead, Advanced Primary Practitioners, The Atrim, Unit 2, Burrs Place, off Park Street West, Luton, Beds, LU1 3BE, Tel.: 01582 557181
District Nursing
Mrs R Taylor, District Nursing, Community Services Manager, Nightingale House, 94 Inkerman Street, Luton, LU1 1JD, Tel.: 01582 708338
Family Planning Services
Family Planning Services, The Lodge, 4 Geroge Street West, Luton, Beds, Tel.: 01582 511000
Health Visitors
Mrs R Taylor, Health Visitors, Community Services Manager, Nightingale House, 94 Inkerman Street, Luton, LU1 1JD, Tel.: 01582 708338
School Nursing
Child Health Department, Liverpool Road Health Centre, 9 Mersey Place, Luton, Beds, LU1 1PP, Tel.: 01582 708100
Specialist Nursing Services
Ms M Scarlett, Haemoglobinopathy Nurse Specialist, Britannic House, 18-20 Dunstable Road, Luton, Tel.: 01582 708308
Ms D Chalkley, Nurse, TB, Liverpool Road Health Centre, Mersey Place, Liverpool Road, LU1 3HH, Tel.: 01582 708191
The Homeless/Travellers & Asylum Seekers
Ms C Woodmansey, Healthcare for Homeless, Asylum Seekers & Travellers Team, Health Visitor, The Lodge, 4 George Street West, Luton, Beds, Tel.: 01582 511000

Maldon & South Chelmsford Primary Care Trust

Trust Headquarters, 1st Floor, Admin Block
St Peter's Hospital, 32a Spital Road
MALDON
CM9 6EG
Tel.: 01621 727300

Admin & Senior Management
Mr J Collins, Director of Primary & Community Services/Director of Nursing, Tel.: 01621 727368
Mr M Harrison, Chief Executive,
Child Health
Ms K Clibbens, Safeguarding Children, Nurse Consultant, Child Health Services, Unit 12, Atlantic Square, Station Road, Witham, CM8 2TL, Tel.: 01376 302643
Ms V Waldon, Director of Specialist Services, St Peter's Hospital, Tel.: 01621 727320
Child Health Records
Mr P Booth, Manager, Unit 12 Atlantic Square, Station Road, Witham, CM8 2TL, Tel.: 01376 302619
Child Protection/Safeguarding Children
Ms K Clibbens, Nurse Consultant, Child Protection, Child Health Services, Unit 12, Atlantic Square, Station Road, Witham, CM8 2TL, Tel.: 01376 302643

Clinical Leads (NSF)
Dr N Cooper, Clinical Lead, Cancer,
Dr J Williams, Clinical Lead, CHD, Tel.: 01245 225522
Dr M Haeger, Clinical Lead, Diabetic Care,
Dr J Williams, Clinical Lead, Diabetic Care,
Dr S Chatten, Clinical Lead, Older People,
District Nursing
Ms C Jones, Intermediate/Community Services Manager (District Nurses), Villa 3, St Peter's Hospital, Tel.: 01621 727378
Family Planning Services
Ms S Scales, Moulsham Lodge Clinic, Tel.: 01245 318766
HIV/AIDS
Mr C Quinn, Cuton Hall Lane, Springfield, Chelmsford, CM2 5PX, Tel.: 01245 318400
Liaison Services
Ms S Carey, Liaison, Community Care Reception, Broomfield Hospital, Court Road, Chelmsford, CM1 7ET, Tel.: 01245 514488/318863
Specialist Nursing Services
Ms J Crozier, Matron, St Peters Hospital, Tel.: 01621 727296
Mr M Hampshire, Health Adviser, ILA Essex, Whitelands, Terling Road, Hatfield Peverel, CM3 2AQ, Tel.: 01245 380888
Ms J Hunt, Matron, St Peters Hospital, Tel.: 01621 727300
Ms J Miranda, Continence, Cuton Hall Lane, Springfield, Chelmsford, CM2 5PX, Tel.: 01245 318400
Ms J MacLaughlam, Nurse Specialist, Diabetic Care, St Peters Hospital,
Ms J McLaughlan, Nurse Specialist, Diabetic Care, ARU, St Peters Hospital, Tel.: 01621 727300
Ms L Allen, Nurse, Infection Control, Witham, Tel.: 01376 302282

Mid Essex Hospital Services NHS Trust

Trust Headquarters, Broomfield Court
Puddingwood Lane, Broomfield
CHELMSFORD
Essex
CM1 7WE
Tel.: 01245 440761
Fax.: 01245 514675

Acute Specialist Nursing Services
Ms K Bartholomew, Practice Educatior/Supervisor Midwifery, APU Maternity, Tel.: 01376 558553
Ms A Smith, Maternity, Matron, Labour Ward, St John's, Tel.: 01245 513004
Ms S Thomas, Prosthetics, Nurse Specialist, Tel.: 01245 516493
Ms E Peall, Emergency Services, Matron, A&E, Tel.: 01245 515103
Ms L Mustard, Nurse Specialist, Acute Pain, Level 4 DSU, Tel.: 01245 516034
Ms K Tighe, Nurse Specialist, Acute Pain, Level 4 DSU, Tel.: 01245 516034
Ms T Dearson, Nurse Specialist, Breast Care, Tel.: 01245 513551
Ms C Ollenbuttel, Nurse Specialist, Breast Care, Tel.: 01245 513551
Ms K Rooke, Research, Nurse Specialist, Breast Care, Tel.: 01245 513343
Ms H Stubbings, Nurse Specialist, Breast Care, Tel.: 01245 513551
Ms L Cohen, Specialist, Cardiac Rehabilitation, Cardiac Unit, Tel.: 01245 516376
Ms A Karabardak, Revascularisation Specialist Nurse, Cardiac Rehabilitation, Tel.: 01245 516376
Ms T Corby, Emergency Care, Clinical Nurse Specialist, Children, Sunshine Ward, Tel.: 01245 513263
Ms C Newman, Matron, Children, Sunshine Ward, St John's, Tel.: 01245 513124
Ms K Mackrodt, Nurse Specialist, Chronic Pain, Level 4, Tel.: 01245 514068
Ms R Lake, Nurse Specialist, Cleft Lip & Palate, Tel.: 01245 516029

East of England Strategic Health Authority

Ms M Butler, Nurse Specialist, Coloproctology, Level 2 Coloprotology, Tel.: 01245 514465

Ms G Wheeler, Nurse Endoscopist, Colorectal, Tel.: 01245 514280

Ms D Currie, Nurse Specialist, Continence, Galbraith House, Tel.: 01245 516810

Ms S Lucas, Matron, Critical Care, Theatres, Tel.: 01245 514271

Ms K Boyden, Nurse Specialist, Dermatology, South Wing 3, Tel.: 01245 514295

Ms S Haylett, Nurse Specialist, Dermatology, Tel.: 01245 514295

Ms S Arun, Nurse Specialist, Diabetic Care, - Paediatrics, Tel.: 01245 513461

Ms M Bardle, Nurse Specialist, Diabetic Care, Diabetes Centre, Tel.: 01245 514388

Ms H Hynes, Nurse Specialist, Diabetic Care, Tel.: 01245 514388

Ms L Joslin, Nurse Specialist, Diabetic Care, Diabetes Centre, Tel.: 01245 514747

Ms J Young, Nurse Specialist, Diabetic Care, Tel.: 01245 514748

Ms M Roberts, Nurse, Endoscopy, Tel.: 01245 514280

Ms J Wright, Nurse, Endoscopy, Tel.: 01245 514280

Ms E Ray, Aural Care, Nurse Specialist, ENT Surgery, St John's, Tel.: 01245 513100

Ms L Smart, Matron, General Surgery, Tel.: 01245 514480

Ms F Munson, Nurse Specialist, Gynae/Oncology, St John's, Tel.: 01245 510344

Ms J Torble, Nurse Specialist, Gynae/Oncology, Tel.: 01245 513044

Ms H Willis, Matron, Gynaecology, St John's, Tel.: 01245 513004

Ms M Collard, Nurse Specialist, Haematology, B11, Tel.: 01245 516681

Ms A Wisbey, Matron, Head & Neck, Ward J5, St John's, Tel.: 01245 513114

Ms G Abrahall, Senior, Nurse Specialist, ITU, East Wing, Tel.: 01245 514055

Ms L Butler, Nurse Specialist, Lung Cancer, EEG Corridor, Tel.: 01245 516244

Ms J Gillam, Nurse Specialist, Macmillan, Galbraith House, Tel.: 01245 514503

Ms V Leah, Nurse Consultant, Medicine, - Acute, B15, Tel.: 01245 515043

Mr J Watkins, Matron, Medicine, - Acute, EEG Corridor, Tel.: 01245 514514

Ms J Kempster, Nurse Specialist, Multiple Sclerosis, Galbraith House, Tel.: 01245 516829

Ms J Foley, Clinical Nurse Specialist, Neurology, Tel.: 01245 514438

Ms R Frost, Matron, Rehab, Older People, Therapy Services, Tel.: 01245 515214

Ms H Bridle, Research, Nurse Specialist, Oncology, Tel.: 01245 514768

Ms T Camburn, Research, Lead Nurse, Oncology, Tel.: 01245 516599

Mr M Riddleston, Macmillan, Lead Nurse, Oncology, Galbraith House, Tel.: 01245 514575

Ms L Villers, Macmillan, Clinical Nurse Specialist, Oncology, Galbraith House, Tel.: 01245 514575

Ms J Francis, Matron, Orthopaedics, B24, Tel.: 01245 516331

Ms J Gillam, Macmillan, Nurse Specialist, Palliative Care, Galbraith House, Tel.: 01245 514503

Ms I Richmond, Nurse Specialist, Palliative Care, Tel.: 01245 514503

Ms H Wright, Macmillan, Clinical Nurse Specialist, Palliative Care, Galbraith House, Tel.: 01245 514503

Ms A Gazzard, Matron, Plastic Surgery, St Andrews, B27, Tel.: 01245 516300

Ms A Armstrong, Nurse Consultant, Renal, Renal Unit, Tel.: 01245 516787

Ms E Brown, Anaemia Management, Nurse Specialist, Renal, Tel.: 01246 514208

Ms C Grinsted, Clinical Nurse Manager, Renal, Renal Unit, Tel.: 01245 514204

Ms S Lal, Pre-dialysis, Nurse Specialist, Renal, Tel.: 01245 514208

Ms C Morgan, Nurse Consultant, Renal, Tel.: 01245 514204

Ms L Whitehouse, Research, Nurse Specialist, Renal, Tel.: 01247 514208

Ms L Hill, Nurse Specialist, Rheumatology, South Wing 3, Tel.: 01245 514193

Ms K Sandlin, Nurse Specialist, Stoma Care, Tel.: 01245 514465

Ms N Saunders, Nurse Specialist, Stoma Care, Level 2, Tel.: 01245 514465

Ms J Blackwell, Nurse Specialist, Stroke Care, B20, Tel.: 01245 516087

Ms A Richardson, Nurse Specialist, Thrombolysis, Tel.: 01245 516693

Ms F Robinson, Nurse Specialist, Thrombolysis, Cardiac, Tel.: 01245 516693

Ms M Galvin, Clinical Nurse Specialist, Tissue Viability, Tel.: 01245 516748

Ms K Moore, Nurse Endoscopist, Upper GI, Tel.: 01245 514280

Ms J Cook, Nurse Specialist, Urology, B9, Tel.: 01245 514760

Ms J Long, Nurse Specialist, Urology, Tel.: 01245 514760

Ms A Lewis, Nurse Specialist, Urology/Oncology, Tel.: 01245 514499

Ms M Galley, Nurse Specialist, Vascular, Level 3, South Wing, Tel.: 01245 514308

Admin & Senior Management

Mrs T Dowdeswell, Deputy, Director of Nursing, Galbraith House, Tel.: 01245 516535

Mrs S Gooch, Director of Nursing, Corporate Office, Broomfield Court, Tel.: 01245 514452

Ms G Partridge, Deputy, Director of Nursing, Galbraith House, Tel.: 01245 516535

Child Protection/Safeguarding Children

Ms K Kandola, Nurse Specialist, Child Protection, Broomfield Court Annexe, Tel.: 01245 514728

Community Midwifery

Ms C Bromwich, Midwifery Manager, St John's Hospital, Wood Street, Chelmsford, Essex, CM2 9BG, Tel.: 01245 513039

Ms C Bromwich, Clinical Co-ordinator, William J Courtauld Hospital, London Road, Braintree, Essex, CM7 2LJ, Tel.: 01376 558553

Ms C Bromwich, Clinical Co-ordinator, St Peter's Hospital, Spital Road, Maldon, Essex, CM9 6EG, Tel.: 01621 875305/6

Ms D Cobie, G Grade/Supervisor Midwife, Labour Ward, St John's, Tel.: 01621 513057

Mrs M J Freeman, Head of Midwifery/General Manager for Obstetrics & Gynae, St John's Hospital, Wood Street, Chelmsford, Essex, CM2 9BG, Tel.: 01245 513138

Ms Y Roder, Midwifery Manager, St John's, Tel.: 01246 513039

Ms A Smith, Matron - Maternity Services, St John's Hospital, Wood Street, Chelmsford, Essex, CM2 9BG, Tel.: 01245 513043

Ms J Troy, Midwifery Manager, St John's, Tel.: 01246 513039

District Nursing

Mrs Pinborough, District Nurse Liaison, Broomfield Hospital, Chelmsford, Essex, CM1 7ET,

HIV/AIDS

Mr G Sheriff, GUM Clinical Advisor, GUM Clinic, St John's, Tel.: 01245 513382

Learning Disabilities

Ms A Taylor, LD Hospital Liaison Nurse Specialist, Galbraith House, Tel.: 01245 516810

Norfolk & Norwich University Hospital NHS Trust

Trust Headquarters, Norfolk & Norwich Univ Hospital
Colney Lane
NORWICH
Norfolk
NR4 7UY
Tel.: 01603 286286

East of England Strategic Health Authority

Child Health
Ms A Betteridge, Child Respiratory, Jenny Lind Children's Dept, Norfolk & Norwich University Hospital, Tel.: 01603 287851
Ms R Larkins, Child Oncology, Jenny Lind Children's Dept, Norfolk & Norwich University Hospital, Tel.: 01603 287852
Ms J Shirtliffe, Child Surgical, Jenny Lind Children's Dept, Norfolk & Norwich University Hospital, Tel.: 01603 286320
Ms G Ward, Child Diabetes, Jenny Lind Children's Dept, Norfolk & Norwich University Hospital, Tel.: 01603 287504
Ms L Yaxley, Child Diabetes, Jenny Lind Children's Dept, Norfolk & Norwich University Hospital, Tel.: 01603 287504

Community Midwifery
Miss G Moore, Midwifery Manager, Level 3, West Block, Norfolk & Norwich University Hospital, Tel.: 01603 287239
Transfer of Mothers, Tel.: 01603 286559
Transfer of Mothers - Out of Hours, Tel.: 01603 481222

Learning Disabilities
Ms M Burchell, Special Needs Specialist,

North Herts & Stevenage Primary Care Trust
Trust Headquarters, Solutions House
Dunhams Lane
LETCHWORTH GARDEN CITY
SG6 1BE
Tel.: 01462 708470
Fax.: 01462 708471

Child Health Records
Mrs C Harrison, Child & School Health Support Officer, Bedford Road Health Centre, Hitching, SG5 1HF, Tel.: 01438 781322

Child Protection/Safeguarding Children
Ms C Mitchell, Named Nurse, Child Protection, Bedford Road Health Centre, Hitchin, Herts, SG5 1HF, Tel.: 01438 781311

Clinical Leads (NSF)
Dr T Kostick, Clinical Lead, Cancer,
Dr J Stevenson, Clinical Lead, CHD,
Dr M Slattery, Clinical Lead, Diabetic Care,

Community Nursing Services
Mrs J Linskill, Director of Nursing, Children & Older People Services, Solutions House, Dunhams Lane, Letchworth Garden City, SG6 1BE, Tel.: 01462 708478

District Nursing
Mrs J Lawson, Manager, Bedford Road Health Centre, Hitchin, SG5 1HF, Tel.: 01438 781314
Mrs L Rotchell, Manager, Mindenhall Court, 17 High Street, Stevenage, SG1 3HS, Tel.: 01438 791970

Family Planning Services
Family Planning Service, Provided by South East Herts PCT, Parkway Health Centre, Birdcroft Road, Welwyn Garden City, AL8 6JE, Tel.: 01707 386877

Health Visitors
Ms C Slater, Community Nurse Manager, Mindenhall Court, Stevenage, Tel.: 01438 791970
Ms J Walton, Community Nurse Manager, Bedford Road, Hitchin, Tel.: 01438 781311

Liaison Services
Ms M Gray, Intermediate Care & Community Liaison, Lister Hospital, Stevenage, Herts, Tel.: 01438 781036
Paediatric Liaison Nurse, Lister Hospital, Stevenage, Herts, Tel.: 01438 781232

School Nursing
Ms C Slater, Community Nurse Manager, Mindenhall Court, Stevenage, Tel.: 01438 791970
Ms J Walton, Community Nurse Manager, Bedford Road, Hitchin, Tel.: 01438 781311

Specialist Nursing Services
Ms E Eden, Nurse, Cardiac Rehabilitation, Park Drive Health Centre, Tel.: 01462 892274

Ms E Wright, Nurse, Cardiac Rehabilitation, Park Drive Health Centre, Tel.: 01462 892274
Ms A Winder, Continence, Park Drive Health Centre, Baldock, Tel.: 01462 491353
Nursing Services, Dermatology, Gregan's House, Bedford Road, Hitchin, Tel.: 01462 427036
Ms M Hayes, Diabetic Care, Gregan's House, Bedford Road, Hitchin, Tel.: 01462 427038
Ms H Tilbe, Leg Ulcers, Stanmore Road Health Centre, Stevenage, SG1 3QA, Tel.: 01438 311531
Team, Macmillan, Park Drive Health Centre, Baldock, SG7 6EN, Tel.: 01462 896086
Ms C Reynolds, Nurse, Multiple Sclerosis, Gregan's House, Bedford Road, Hitchin, Tel.: 01462 427038
Ms J Holt, Assistant Director Services, Older People, Tel.: 01462 708491
Ms P Gordon, TB, Lister Hospital, Tel.: 01438 781582

North Norfolk Primary Care Trust
Trust Headquarters, Kelling Hospital
High Kelling
HOLT
NR25 6QA
Tel.: 01263 710611

Admin & Senior Management
Mrs P Ambrozevich, Director of Health Services & Nursing, Kelling Hospital, Tel.: 01263 710611
Ms D Clarke, Chief Executive,

Child Protection/Safeguarding Children
Ms H Riseborough, Team Leader, Health Visiting, Kelling Hospital, Tel.: 01263 713333

Clinical Leads (NSF)
Ms C Haddow, Clinical Lead, Cancer,

Community Nursing Services
Ms P Ambrozevich, Director of Health Services & Nursing, Tel.: 01263 710611
Ms S Kenyon, Community Hospitals Manager, Kelling Hospital, Tel.: 01263 713333

District Nursing
Ms C Haddow, Team Leader, District Nursing, Kelling Hospital, Tel.: 01263 713333

Health Visitors
Ms H Riseborough, Team Leader, Health Visiting, Kelling Hospital, Tel.: 01263 713333

Pharmacy
Ms C Walton, Prescribing Advisor, Kelling Hospital, Tel.: 01263 710611

Smoking Cessation
Ms L Hillman, Director of Public Health, Kelling Hospital, Tel.: 01263 710611

Norwich Primary Care Trust
Trust Headquarters, St Andrew's House
St Andrew's Business Park, Thorpe St Andrew
NORWICH
Norfolk, NR7 0HT
Tel.: 01603 307000

Admin & Senior Management
Ms J Archer, Assistant Director of Quality & Nursing (LD & Prison Service), St Andrew's House, St Andrew's Business Park, Thorpe St Andrew, Norwich, NR7 0HT, Tel.: 01603 307279
Mrs K Branson, Director of Quality & Nursing, St Andrew's House, St Andrew's Business Park, Thorpe St Andrew, Norwich, NR7 0HT, Tel.: 01603 307135
Mrs S Glenn, Assistant Director of Quality & Clinical Practice, St Andrew's House, St Andrew's Business Park, Thorpe St Andrew, Norwich, NR7 0HT, Tel.: 01603 307186

East of England Strategic Health Authority

Child Health
Ms J Dawson, Adult Nurse, Epilepsy, Lawson Road Health Centre, Norwich, NR3 4LE, Tel.: 01603 428103
Ms S Tyler, Child Nurse, Epilepsy, Lawson Road Health Centre, Norwich, NR3 4LE, Tel.: 01603 428103
Child Health Records
Child Health Records, St Andrew's House, Tel.: 01603 307000
Child Protection/Safeguarding Children
Ms J Black, Child Protection, Colman Road Health Centre, Norwich, NR4 7HG, Tel.: 01603 508929
Clinical Leads (NSF)
Ms M Ayers, Clinical Lead, Cancer,
Dr T Hadley, Clinical Lead, Older People,
District Nursing
District Nursing Referrals,
Medicom, Tel.: 01603 481234
Health Visitors
Ms L Everett, Paediatric Liaison Health Visitor, 40 Upton Road, Norwich, NR4 7PA, Tel.: 01603 506535
Health Visitors, HV/TL, Norwich Community Hospital, Bowthorpe Road, Norwich, Tel.: 01603 776776
Learning Disabilities
Ms J Archer, Assistant Director of Quality & Nursing (LD & Prison Service), St Andrew's House, St Andrew's Business Park, Thorpe St Andrew, Norwich, NR7 0HT, Tel.: 01603 307279
Ms D Elleray, Learning Difficulties - Children, Lawson Road Health Centre, Norwich, NR3 4LE, Tel.: 01603 428103
Mr J Gwynn, Team Leader, City Team, Norwich Community Hospital, Bowthrope Road, Norwich, NR2 3TU, Tel.: 01603 281781
School Nursing
School Health/Nursing Service, Trust Headquarters, St Andrew's House, Tel.: 01603 307390
Specialist Nursing Services
Ms M Low, Continence, Norwich Community Hospital, Tel.: 01603 776751
Specialist Nurse, Infection Control, Norwich Community Hospital, Tel.: 01603 776757
Ms J Hadley, Respiratory, Norwich Community Hospital, Tel.: 01603 776750
The Homeless/Travellers & Asylum Seekers
Ms J Mosley, Travellers, Health Visitor, Adelaide Street Health Centre, Norwich, NR2 4JL, Tel.: 07786 707368

Papworth (Foundation) NHS Trust
Trust Headquarters, Papworth Everard
CAMBRIDGE
CB3 8RE
Tel.: 01480 830541
Fax.: 01480 831315

Admin & Senior Management
Mr N Davis, Director of Nursing, Papworth (Foundation) NHS Trust, Papworth Everard, Cambridge, CB3 8RE, Tel.: 01480 830541

Peterborough & Stamford Hospitals NHS Foundation Trust
Trust Headquarters, Edith Cavell Hospital
Bretton Gate
PETERBOROUGH
Cambridgshire
PE3 9GZ
Tel.: 01733 874000
Fax.: 01733 874001

Child Protection/Safeguarding Children
Ms R Mease, Named Nurse, Child Protection, c/o Amazon Ward, PD Hospital, Thorpe Road, Peterborough, PE3 6DA, Tel.: 01733 874910

Community Midwifery
Ms C Carter, Professional Lead for Head of Midwifery, Community Midwives Voicemail, Peterborough Maternity Unit, Alderman's Drive, Peterborough, Cambridgshire, PE3 6BP, Tel.: 01733 874585
Ms J Doran, Matron Outpatient Maternity Services, Peterborough Maternity Unit, Alderman's Drive, Peterborough, Cambridgshire, PE3 6BP, Tel.: 01733 874985
Ms J Porter, Head of Midwifery, AGM Women & Child Service Unit, Peterborough Maternity Unit, Alderman's Drive, Peterborough, Cambridgshire, PE3 6BP, Tel.: 01733 874562
Mrs M Renton, General Manager, Women & Child & Head of Midwifery, Peterborough Maternity Unit, Alderman's Drive, Peterborough, Cambridgshire, PE3 6BP, Tel.: 01733 875878
Matrons/Modern Matrons
Ms C Carter, Inpatient Maternity Services, Matron, Maternity Unit, Alderans Drive, Peterborough, PE3 6BP, Tel.: 01733 874091
Ms J Doran, Outpatient Services, Matron, Tel.: 01733 874985
Ms S Hartley, Childrens Services, Matron, Amazon Ward, PD Hospital, Thorpe Road, Peterborough, PE3 6DA, Tel.: 01733 874188

Princess Alexandra Hospital NHS Trust
Trust Headquarters, Princess Alexandra Hospital
Hamstel Road
HARLOW
Essex
CM20 1QX
Tel.: 01279 444455
Fax.: 01279 429371

Child Health
Ms S Barron, Community Children (General, Respiratory, CF), Hamstel House, Princess Alexandra Hospital, Tel.: 01279 827175
Ms S Clarke, Community Children (General, Oncology), Hamstel House, Princess Alexandra Hospital, Tel.: 01279 827175
Ms J Dunlea, Team Leader, Community Children, Hamstel House, Princess Alexandra Hospital, Hamstel Road, Harlow, Essex, CM20 1QX, Tel.: 01279 827175
Ms J Priest, Community Children (General, Diabetes), Hamstel House, Princess Alexandra Hospital, Tel.: 01279 827175
Ms C Sadlers, Community Children (Neonatal), Hamstel House, Princess Alexandra Hospital, Tel.: 01279 827175
Child Protection/Safeguarding Children
Ms S McClymont, Specialist, Child Protection, 2nd Floor, Addison House, Hamstel Road, Harlow, CM20 1EP, Tel.: 01279 694940
Community Midwifery
Mrs W Matthews, Head of Midwifery, Maternity Department, Princess Alexandra Hospital, Tel.: 01279 827104
Mrs A Peacock, Community Midwife Manager, Tel.: 01279 444455 ext 2942
Liaison Services
Ms F Richards, Liaison, Paediatrics, Addison House, Hamstel Road, Harlow, CM20 1EP, Tel.: 01279 694943

Royston, Buntingford & Bishops Stortford Primary Care Trust
Trust Headquarters, Herts & Essex Hospital
Haymeads Lane
BISHOPS STORTFORD
CM23 5JH
Tel.: 01279 827228

Admin & Senior Management
Mrs M Brierley, Director of Operations/Nursing Leadership, Tel.: 01274 827307
Child Health
Ms K Bilsby, Nursing & Clinical Services Manager,
Ms D Hubbard, Nursing & Clinical Services Manager,

East of England Strategic Health Authority

Ms K Shrimpton, Nursing & Clinical Services Manager,
Ms H Stephenson, Nursing & Clinical Services Manager,
Ms J Wilson, Nursing & Clinical Services Manager,

Child Health Records

Mr P Hancock, Manager, Bishop's Stortford, Charter House,
Parkway, Welwyn Garden City, AL4 6JL, Tel.: 01707 390855
Mrs C Harrison, Manager, Royston, Bedford Road Health Centre,
Hitchin, SG5 1HF, Tel.: 01438 781322
Ms J Sulston, Manager, Buntingford, Ambulance HQ, Ascot Lane,
Welwyn Garden City, AL7 4HL, Tel.: 01707 328111

Child Protection/Safeguarding Children

Ms A Aslett, Named Nurse, Child Protection, Royston Health Centre,
Melbourn Street, Royston, SG8 7BS, Tel.: 01763 257984
Ms S Thompson, Named Nurse, Child Protection, Royston Health
Centre, Melbourn Street, Royston, SG8 7BS, Tel.: 01763 257974

Clinical Leads (NSF)

Dr P Keller, Clinical Lead, CHD & Diabetes, Tel.: 01279 827228
Dr M Hardwick, Clinical Lead, Cancer, Tel.: 01279 827228

Community Nursing Services

Ms K Bilsby, Nursing & Clinical Services Manager,
Ms D Hubbard, Nursing & Clinical Services Manager,
Ms K Shrimpton, Nursing & Clinical Services Manager,
Ms H Stephenson, Nursing & Clinical Services Manager,
Ms J Wilson, Nursing & Clinical Services Manager,

District Nursing

Ms K Bilsby, Nursing & Clinical Services Manager,
Ms D Hubbard, Nursing & Clinical Services Manager,
Ms K Shrimpton, Nursing & Clinical Services Manager,
Ms H Stephenson, Nursing & Clinical Services Manager,
Ms J Wilson, Nursing & Clinical Services Manager,

Health Visitors

Ms K Bilsby, Nursing & Clinical Services Manager,
Ms D Hubbard, Nursing & Clinical Services Manager,
Ms K Shrimpton, Nursing & Clinical Services Manager,
Ms H Stephenson, Nursing & Clinical Services Manager,
Ms J Wilson, Nursing & Clinical Services Manager,

Liaison Services

Ms K Hamblin, PALS Co-ordinator,

South Cambridgeshire Primary Care Trust

Trust Headquarters, Heron Court
Ida Darwin, Fulbourn
CAMBRIDGE
CB1 5EE
Tel.: 01223 885706

Admin & Senior Management

Mr N Beverley, Acting Chief Executive, Heron Court, Ida Darwin,
Fulbourn, Cambridge, CB1 5EE, Tel.: 01223 885718
Mrs S Bremner, Director of Primary & Community Services, Heron
Court, Ida Darwin, Fulbourn, Cambridge, CB1 5EE, Tel.: 01223
884050
Mr G Nice, Director of Nursing & Quality Performance, Heron Court,
Ida Darwin, Fulbourn, Cambridge, CB1 5EE, Tel.: 01223 884273

Child Health

Ms J Acornley, Team Leader, Children with Palliative Care Needs,
Diana Nursing Team, Block 9, Ida Darwin, Fulbourn, Cambridge,
CB1 5EE, Tel.: 01223 884335
Ms J Galway, Assistant Director - Childrens Services, Block 13, Ida
Darwin, Fulbourn, Cambridge, CB1 5EE, Tel.: 01223 884033
Ms R Moxon, Children with Disabilities Team Leader, Douglas
House, 18 Trumpington Street, Cambridge, CB2 2AH, Tel.: 01223
568808
Dr D Vickers, Medical Director of Children's Services, Block 13, Ida
Darwin, Fulbourn, Cambridge, CB1 5EE, Tel.: 01223 884167

Child Health Records

Ms G Skews, Child Health Dept, Ida Darwin, Fulbourn, Cambridge,
CB1 5EE, Tel.: 01223 884186

Ms J Wright, Child Health Dept, Ida Darwin, Fulbourn, Cambridge,
CB1 5EE, Tel.: 01223 884184

Child Protection/Safeguarding Children

Ms R Cox, Named Nurse, Child Protection, Block 13, Ida Darwin,
Fulbourn, Cambridge, Tel.: 01223 884151

Clinical Leads (NSF)

Mr T Dutton, Deputy Chief Executive/NSF Lead, Heron Court,
Fulbourn, Cambridge, CB1 5EE, Tel.: 01223 885740
Mr M Jarman-Howe, Long Term Conditions, Heron Court, Fulbourn,
Cambridge, CB1 5EE, Tel.: 01223 884454

Community Nursing Services

Ms M Appleby, Assistant Director (Interface), Primary Care &
Community Services, Nightingale Court, Ida Darwin, Fulbourn,
Cambridge, CB1 5EE, Tel.: 01223 884329
Ms K Caley, Assistant Director (City), Primary Care & Community
Services, Nightingale Court, Ida Darwin, Fulbourn, CB1 5EE, Tel.:
01223 885744
Mr G Nice, Director of Nursing & Quality Performance, Heron Court,
Ida Darwin, Fulbourn, CB1 5EE, Tel.: 01223 884273
Mrs C Welton, Assistant Director (South), Primary Care &
Community Services, Nightingale Court, Ida Darwin, Fulbourn, CB1
5EE, Tel.: 01223 885799

District Nursing

Ms M Appleby, Assistant Director (Interface), Primary Care &
Community Services, Nightingale Court, Ida Darwin, Fulbourn,
Cambridge, CB1 5EE, Tel.: 01223 884329
Ms K Caley, Assistant Director (City), Primary Care & Community
Services, Nightingale Court, Ida Darwin, Fulbourn, CB1 5EE, Tel.:
01223 885744
Mr G Nice, Director of Nursing & Quality Performance, Heron Court,
Ida Darwin, Fulbourn, CB1 5EE, Tel.: 01223 884273
Mrs C Welton, Assistant Director (South), Primary Care &
Community Services, Nightingale Court, Ida Darwin, Fulbourn, CB1
5EE, Tel.: 01223 885799

Equipment Loan Services

Mr S Gilbert, Discharge Planning Team, 28 Long Road, Cambridge,
Tel.: 01223 714400
Joint Equipment Services, Anglia Support Services, Tel.: 01223
726212

Smoking Cessation

Dr D Gregson, Director of Public Health, Nightingale Court, Ida
Darwin, Fulbourn, Cambridge, Tel.: 01223 885843

Specialist Nursing Services

Ms J Dowse, Specialist Nurse, Continence, Princess of Wales
Hospital, Lynn Road, Ely, Cambs, CB6 1DN, Tel.: 01353 652145
Ms R Wright, Specialist Nurse, Diabetic Care, Brookfields Hospital,
Mill Road, Cambridge, CB1 3DF, Tel.: 01223 723004
Mr C Sharp, Specialist Nurse, Infection Control, Kingfisher House,
Kingfisher Way, Hinchingbrooke Business Park, Huntingdon, PE29
6FH, Tel.: 01480 398620
Ms L Moth, Nurse, Macmillan, Arthur Rank House, Brookfields, Mill
Road, Cambridge, CB1 3DF, Tel.: 01223 723137
Ms A Pope, Nurse, Macmillan, Arthur Rank House, Brookfields, Mill
Road, Cambridge, CB1 3DF, Tel.: 01223 723137
Ms S Roberts, Nurse, Macmillan, Arthur Rank House, Brookfields,
Mill Road, Cambridge, CB1 3DF, Tel.: 01223 723137
Ms W Williams, Nurse, Macmillan, Arthur Rank House, Brookfields,
Mill Road, Cambridge, CB1 3DF, Tel.: 01223 723137
Ms M Stratford, Matron, Palliative Care, Arthur Rank House,
Brookfields, Mill Road, Cambridge, CB1 3DF, Tel.: 01223 723110
Ms J Young, Specialist Nurse, Parkinson's Disease, Brookfields
Hospital, Mill Road, Cambridge, CB1 3DF, Tel.: 01223 723018
Ms A Perrin, Specialist Nurse, Tissue Viability, Brookfields Hospital,
Mill Road, Cambridge, CB1 3DF, Tel.: 01223 723019

The Homeless/Travellers & Asylum Seekers

Mr K Reynolds, Strategic Lead - Community Living, Nightingale
Court, Ida Darwin, Fulbourn, Cambridge, Tel.: 01223 884331

East of England Strategic Health Authority

South East Hertfordshire Primary Care Trust

Trust Headquarters, 1-4 Limes Court
Conduit Lane
HODDESDON
EN11 8EP
Tel.: 01992 706120

Admin & Senior Management
Mr V McCabe, Chief Executive,
Dr M Perkin, Public Health Director,
Child Health
Hertford County Hospital, North Road, Hertford, Tel.: 01707 369148
Hoddesdon, Hoddesdon Health Clinic, High Road, Hoddesdon,
EN11 8BE, Tel.: 01992 471818
Waltham Cross, Stanhope Road Surgery, Stanhope Road, Waltham
Cross, EN8 7DJ, Tel.: 01992 621613
Child Health Records
QE2 Hospital, Howlands, Welwyn Garden City, Herts, AL7 4HQ,
Tel.: 01707 328111
Child Protection/Safeguarding Children
Mr G McCabe, Named Doctor Child Protection, Wallace House
Surgery, 11 St Andrew Street, Hertford, SG14 1HZ, Tel.: 01992
557600
Ms S Thompson, Named Nurse, Child Protection, Hoddesdon Health
Clinic, High Road, Hoddesdon, Herts, Tel.: 01992 474669
Clinical Leads (NSF)
Mr S Malusky, Clinical Lead, CHD, Diabetes,
Ms A Southworth, Clinical Lead, Older People,
Community Nursing Services
Ms C Donaldson, Head of Nursing & Clinical Services, Hoddesdon
Health Clinic, High Road, Hoddesdon, EN11 8BE, Tel.: 01992
471818
District Nursing
Bowling Road District Nursing Team, Bowling Road, Ware, Herts,
Tel.: 01920 462388
Hertford County Hospital District Nursing Team, North Road,
Hertford, Tel.: 01707 369148
Hoddesdon District Nursing Team, Hoddesdon Health Clinic, High
Road, Hoddesdon, EN11 8BE, Tel.: 01992 471818
Waltham Cross District Nursing Team, Stanhope Road Surgery,
Stanhope Road, Waltham Cross, EN8 7DJ, Tel.: 01992 621613
Family Planning Services
Dr B Bean, Parkway Health Clinic, Birdcroft Road, Welwyn Garden
City, Herts, Tel.: 01707 386860
Health Visitors
Bowling Road HV Team, Bowling Road, Ware, Herts, Tel.: 01920
462388
Hertford County Hospital HV Team, North Road, Hertford, Tel.:
01707 369148
Hoddesdon HV Team, Hoddesdon Health Clinic, High Road,
Hoddesdon, EN11 8BE, Tel.: 01992 471818
Waltham Cross HV Team, Stanhope Road Surgery, Stanhope Road,
Waltham Cross, EN8 7DJ, Tel.: 01992 621613
Pharmacy
Ms H Gray, 1-4 Limes Court, Conduit Lane, Hoddesdon, Herts,
EN11 8EP, Tel.: 01992 706120

South Essex Partnership NHS Trust

Trust Headquarters, Dunton Court
Aston Road
LAINDON
Essex
SS15 6NX
Tel.: 01375 364650

Learning Disabilities
Mr T Colgrave, Modern Matron, 1 Heath Close, Billericay, Essex,
CM12 9NW, Tel.: 01277 631968

Ms D Cook, Director, Dunton Court, Aston Road, Laindon, Essex,
SS15 6NX, Tel.: 01375 364632
Mr J Cronin, Assistant Director, 1 Heath Close, Billericay, Essex,
CM12 9NW, Tel.: 01277 631968

Southend Hospital NHS Trust

Trust Headquarters, Southend Hospital
Prittlewell Chase
WESTCLIFF-ON-SEA
Essex, SS0 0RY
Tel.: 01702 435555
Fax.: 01702 221109

Community Midwifery
Ms V Harris, Community Midwifery Manager, Tel.: 01702 435555 ext
2245
Out of hours, Tel.: ext 2883/2888
Miss D Ryan, Director of Midwifery Services, Tel.: 01702 221193

Southend Primary Care Trust

Trust Headquarters, Harcourt House
Harcourt Avenue
SOUTHEND
Essex
SS2 6HE
Tel.: 01702 224600

Admin & Senior Management
Ms J Garbutt, Chief Executive,
Mr M Hennessy, Director of Primary Care & Executive Nurse,
Mrs K Paul, Associate Director, Integrated Services, Tel.: 01702
534611
Child Health
Ms Y Campen, Head of Children & Young Peoples Services (School
Nurses), Southend PCT, Harcourt House, Harcourt Avenue,
Southend on Sea, SS2 6HE, Tel.: 01702 226614
Child Protection/Safeguarding Children
Ms C White, Named Nurse, Child Protection, Warrior House, 42-82
Southchurch Road, Southend on Sea, SS1 2LZ, Tel.: 01702 577013
Clinical Leads (NSF)
Dr T Dickens, Clinical Lead, Cancer,
Dr B Houston, Clinical Lead, CHD,
Dr M Kent, Clinical Lead, Diabetic Care,
Community Nursing Services
Ms K Paul, Associate Director, Integrated Services, Southend
Borough Council, Social Care, Civic Centre, Victoria Avenue,
Southend on Sea, Essex, Tel.: 01702 534611
District Nursing
Ms Y Campen, Head of Children & Young Peoples Services,
Harcourt House, Harcourt Avenue, Southend on Sea, SS2 6HE, Tel.:
01702 226614
Ms K Paul, Adult Services Manager (District Nurses), Harcourt
House, Harcourt Avenue, Southend on Sea, SS2 6HE, Tel.: 01702
224600
Liaison Services
Mr D A Smith, Operation Lead for District Nursing, Westcliff Clinic,
415 Westborough Road, Westcliff on Sea, SS0 9TN, Tel.: 01702
577370
Specialist Nursing Services
Ms R Rothman, Post Natal Depression, Thorpedene Clinic,
Delaware Road, Shoeburyness, SS3 9NW, Tel.: 01702 578800
Ms S Bailey, Nurse Consultant, Intermediate Care, Harcourt House,
Harcourt Avenue, Southend on Sea, SS2 6HE, Tel.: 01702 224600
The Homeless/Travellers & Asylum Seekers
Ms J Lashly, Homeless Team, Health Visitor, Thorpedene Clinic,
Delaware Road, Shoeburyness, SS3 9NW, Tel.: 01702 578800
Mr O Mingard, Homeless, Women's Refuge, Travelling Families,
Thorpedene Clinic, Delaware Road, Shoeburyness, SS3 9NW, Tel.:
01702 578804

East of England Strategic Health Authority

Southern Norfolk Primary Care Trust

Trust Headquarters, The Courtyard
Ketteringham Hall
WYMONDHAM
Norfolk
NR18 9RS
Tel.: 01603 813820
Fax.: 01603 813865

Admin & Senior Management
Ms W Hardicker, Assistant Director of Modernisation, The Courtyard, Ketteringham Hall, Wymondham, Norfolk, NR18 9RS,
Mr C Humphris, Chief Executive, Tel.: 01603 813821
Mrs V MacQueen, Director of Nursing & Children's Services, The Courtyard, Ketteringham Hall, Wymondham, Norfolk, NR18 9RS, Tel.: 01603 813854
Child Health Records
Child Health Records, Eastern Support Services, St Andrew's House, Northside, St Andrew's Business Park, Thorpe St Andrew, Norwich, NR7 0HT, Tel.: 01603 307000
Child Protection/Safeguarding Children
Ms J Evans, Named Nurse, Child Protection, Tel.: 01953 606201
Clinical Leads (NSF)
Mrs K Griffiths, The Courtyard, Ketteringham Hall, Wymondham, Norfolk, NR18 9RS, Tel.: 01603 813820
Mrs H Mills, The Courtyard, Ketteringham Hall, Wymondham, Norfolk, NR18 9RS, Tel.: 01603 813820
Dr N Thomson, Clinical Lead, Diabetes & CHD, The Health Centre, Mount Street, DISS, IP22 3QG, Tel.: 01379 642021
Dr J Battersby, Clinical Lead, CHD, Diabetes, Cancer, The Courtyard, Ketteringham Hall, Wymondham, Norfolk, NR18 9RS, Tel.: 01603 813820
District Nursing
Ms S Stockton, Prof Lead for District Nursing, Tel.: 01508 521051
Family Planning Services
Dr J Battersby, Director of Public Health, Tel.: 01603 813845
Health Visitors
Mrs M Graves, Assistant Director of Children's Services, Tel.: 01842 756441
Learning Disabilities
South Norfolk Community LD Team, Wymondham Health Centre, 18 Bridewell Street, Wymondham, NR18 0AR, Tel.: 01953 604637
Pharmacy
Mr C Daly, Head of Prescribing, Tel.: 077989 25316
School Nursing
Mrs M Graves, Assistant Director of Children's Services, Tel.: 01842 756441
Smoking Cessation
Dr J Battersby, Director of Public Health, Tel.: 01603 813845
The Homeless/Travellers & Asylum Seekers
Dr J Battersby, Director of Public Health, Tel.: 01603 813845

St Albans & Harpenden Primary Care Trust

Trust Headquarters
99 Waverley Road
ST ALBANS
AL3 5TL
Tel.: 01727 831219

Admin & Senior Management
Ms J Clark, Chief Executive,
Ms H Moulder, Deputy Chief Executive, 99 Waverley Road, St Albans, Herts, AL3 5TL, Tel.: 01727 732266
Child Health
Ms E Fisher, Associate Director for Children & Young People, Principal Health Centre, Civic Close, St Albans, AL1 3LA, Tel.: 01727 830130

Child Protection/Safeguarding Children
Ms C Gayle, Principle Health Centre, Civic Close, St Albans, AL13 3LA, Tel.: 01727 830130
Clinical Leads (NSF)
Dr P Sawyer, Clinical Lead, Cancer,
Dr M Allen, Clinical Lead, CHD,
Dr T Haseler, Clinical Lead, Diabetic Care,
Dr B Covell, Clinical Lead, Older People,
Community Nursing Services
Mr R Ferris, Director of Nursing & Services, 99 Waverly Road, St Albans, Herts, AL3 5TL, Tel.: 01727 732266
District Nursing
Mrs G Broderick, Assistant Director Primary Care Nursing, (First Contact/Long Term Conditions), Harpenden Memorial Hospital, Carlton Road, Harpenden, AL5 4TA, Tel.: 01582 460429
Ms D Dyne, Associate Director for Community Hospitals,
Ms E Fisher, Associate Director for Children & Young People, Principal Health Centre, Civic Close, St Albans, AL1 3LA, Tel.: 01727 830130
Pharmacy
Ms M Whittick, Head of Prescribing, 99 Waverley Road, St Albans, Herts, AL3 5TL, Tel.: 01727 732282
Smoking Cessation
Mr R Trevillion, 99 Waverley Road, St Albans, Herts, AL3 5TL, Tel.: 01727 732257
Specialist Nursing Services
Ms J Ward, Team Leader, Respiratory, St Albans City Hospital, Normandy Road, St Albans, AL3 5PN, Tel.: 01727 897834
The Homeless/Travellers & Asylum Seekers
Ms M Sklar, Homeless, Principle Health Centre, Civic Close, St Albans, AL1 3LA, Tel.: 01727 830130

Suffolk Coastal Primary Care Trust

Trust Headquarters, Bartlet Hospital Annexe
Undercliff Road East
FELIXSTOWE
IP11 7LT
Tel.: 01394 458900

Admin & Senior Management
Ms A Selby, Chief Executive,
Ms A Taylor, Director of Primary & Community Services,
Clinical Leads (NSF)
Mr B Webb, Clinical Lead, Cancer, Bartlet Hospital Annexe, Undercliff Roadeast, Felixstowe, IP11 7LT, Tel.: 01394 458921
Ms A Taylor, Clinical Lead, Care of the Elderly, Bartlet Hospital Annexe, Undercliff Roadeast, Felixstowe, IP11 7LT, Tel.: 01394 458909
Mr B Webb, Clinical Lead, CHD, Bartlet Hospital Annexe, Undercliff Roadeast, Felixstowe, IP11 7LT, Tel.: 01394 458921
Dr G Taylor, Clinical Lead, Diabetic Care, 7 Little St John Street, Woodbridge, IP12 1EE, Tel.: 01394 382046
District Nursing
Ms N Parkinson, Clinical Services Manager, District Nurses, Felixstowe General Hospital, Felixstowe, IP11 7HJ, Tel.: 01394 458835
Health Visitors
Ms T Wright, Health Visiting Clinical Co-ordinator, Woodbridge Clinic, Pytches Road, Woodbridge, IP12 1EP, Tel.: 01394 389249

Suffolk Mental Health Partnership NHS Trust

Trust Headquarters, Suffolk House
Foxhall Road
IPSWICH
Suffolk
IP3 8NN
Tel.: 01473 329600

East of England Strategic Health Authority

Learning Disabilities

Mr A Brown, Clinical Manager - LD West, Stourmead House, Stourmead Close, Kedington, Haverhill, Suffolk, CB9 7PA, Tel.: 01440 715900

Mr D Clark, Head of Specialist Healthcare - LD, Resource Centre, Walker Close, Foxhall Road, Ipswich, Suffolk, IP3 8LY, Tel.: 01473 275417

Mrs P Clarke, Clinical Manager - LD Central, Resource Centre, Walker Close, Foxhall Road, Ipswich, Suffolk, IP3 8LY, Tel.: 01473 275440

Mr J Cullum, Clinical Manager - LD North, Lothingland Community Unit, 1 Airey Close, Union Lane, Oulton, Lowestoft, Suffolk, NR32 3JQ, Tel.: 01502 560111

Mrs J Mayhew, Community Nursing Lead - LD Central, Resource Centre, Walker Close, Foxhall Road, Ipswich, Suffolk, IP3 8LY, Tel.: 01473 275440

Mrs C Scott-Molloy, Community Nursing Lead - LD West, Stourmead House, Stourmead Close, Kedington, Haverhill, Suffolk, CB9 7PA, Tel.: 01440 715900

Mrs I Wentworth-Wood, Community Nursing Lead - LD North, A12 Industries Spec Nursing Tm, Carlton Park Ind Estate, Ronald Lane, Saxmundham, Suffolk, IP17 1NL, Tel.: 01728 604313

Suffolk West Primary Care Trust

Trust Headquarters, Thingoe House
Cotton Lane
BURY ST EDMUNDS
IP33 1YJ
Tel.: 01284 829600

Admin & Senior Management
Ms S Hayter, Assistant Director of Clinical Services, Tel.: 01284 829671

Mr M Stonard, Chief Executive,

Mr J Williams, Director of Clinical Services & Learning, Thingoe House, Cotton Lane, Bury St Edmunds, IP33 1YJ, Tel.: 01284 829665

Child Health Records
Senior Clark, Medical Records Officer, Tel.: 01284 775063

Child Protection/Safeguarding Children
Ms J Scott, Designated Nurse, Child Protection, Tel.: 01473 275214

Clinical Leads (NSF)
Dr A Hutton, Clinical Lead, CHD,

Community Matrons
Ms S Burns, Community Matron,

Ms C Ryan, Community Matron,

District Nursing
Ms P Chappell, Head of Nursing, Tel.: 01284 829609

Ms S Coupe, District Nurse,

Ms A Keighley, District Nurse,

Ms F Whitfield, District Nurse,

Equipment Loan Services
Suffolk Central Primary Care Trust,

Family Planning Services
Dr F Reader, Service Lead, Tel.: 01473 428001

Health Visitors
Mrs J Hayes, Head of Children & Family Service, Tel.: 01284 829600

Ms V Haynes, Health Visitor,

Ms J Nevin, Health Visitor,

Ms A Raven, Health Visitor,

School Nursing
Ms H East, School Nurse Team Leader, Tel.: 01284 775078

Specialist Nursing Services
Ms L Hartley, Specialist Nurse, Diabetic Care, Tel.: 01284 712832

Ms J Harris, Specialist Nurse, Infection Control, Tel.: 01284 829668

Ms N McGreavy, Community, Nurse Specialist, Neurology, Tel.: 01284 748848

Tendring Primary Care Trust

Trust Headquarters, Kennedy House
Kennedy Way
CLACTON-ON-SEA
CO15 4AB
Tel.: 01255 206060

Admin & Senior Management
Mr D Cohen, Assistant Director of Operations, Tel.: 01255 206046

Ms L Woodcock, Director of Nursing & Community Services,

Child Health
Ms D Peggs, Children's Services Manager, Kennedy House, Kennedy Way, Clacton on Sea, Essex, CO15 4AB, Tel.: 01255 206245

Child Health Records
Ms S Lucus, Colchester Primary Care Trust, Colchester PCT, Central Clinic, East Hill, Colchester, Essex, CO1 1UJ, Tel.: 01206 744082

Child Protection/Safeguarding Children
Ms C Macgregor, Clinical Lead, Child Protection, Carnarvon House, Carnarvon Road, Clacton on Sea, Essex, CO15 6QD, Tel.: 01255 206227

Named Nurse, Child Protection, Carnarvon House, Carnarvon Road, Clacton on Sea, Essex, CO15 6QD, Tel.: 01255 206003

Clinical Leads (NSF)
Ms I Ross, Clinical Lead, Cancer, 268 High Street, Dovercourt, Essex, Tel.: 01255 201209

Ms L Parker, Clinical Lead, Care of the Elderly, Seaview, Clacton Hospital, Tower Road, Clacton on Sea, Essex, CO15 1LH, Tel.: 01255 201739

Ms P Parker, Clinical Lead, CHD, Colchester PCT, The Health Office, Turner Rd, Colchester, Essex, CO4 5JR, Tel.: 01206 288500

Ms M O'Brien, Clinical Lead, Continence, Clacton Hospital, Tower Road, Clacton on Sea, Essex, CO15 1LH, Tel.: 01255 201734

Ms S Smyth, Clinical Lead, Diabetic Care, Kennedy House, Kennedy Way, Clacton on Sea, Essex, CO15 4AB, Tel.: 01255 206229

Ms V Lynch, Clinical Lead, Urology, Kennedy House, Kennedy Way, Clacton on Sea, Essex, CO15 4AB, Tel.: 01255 206230

Community Matrons
Mr J Douglas, Clacton Hospital, Tower Road, Clacton on Sea, Essex, CO15 1LH, Tel.: 01255 201502

Community Midwifery
Ms E Cattermole, Head of Midwifery, Clacton Hospital, Tower Road, Clacton on Sea, Essex, CO15 1LH, Tel.: 01255 201686

Community Nursing Services
Ms L Parker, Head of Community Nursing, Seaview, Clacton Hospital, Tower Road, Clacton on Sea, Essex, CO15 1LH, Tel.: 01255 201739

District Nursing
Ms L Parker, Head of District Nurses, Seaview, Clacton Hospital, Tower Road, Clacton on Sea, Essex, CO15 1LH, Tel.: 01255 201739

Equipment Loan Services
Mr G Raynor, Support Service Manager, Essex Equipment Services, Catalyst House, Severalls Ind Estate, Colchester, Essex, CO4 4QC, Tel.: 01206 518888

Family Planning Services
Ms K Ramkhelawon, Assistant Director of Public Health, Kennedy House, Kennedy Way, Clacton on Sea, Essex, CO15 4AB, Tel.: 01255 206074

Health Visitors
Ms D Peggs, Children's Services Manager (Health Visitors), Kennedy House, Kennedy Way, Clacton on Sea, Essex, CO15 4AB, Tel.: 01255 206245

Learning Disabilities
Mr P Ainsworth, Director of Modernisation & Commissioning, Kennedy House, Kennedy Way, Clacton on Sea, Essex, CO15 4AB, Tel.: 01255 206230

East of England Strategic Health Authority

Liaison Services
Ms S Bacon, Corporate Communications Manager, Kennedy House, Kennedy Way, Clacton on Sea, Essex, CO15 4AB, Tel.: 01255 206241
Mr M Cable, Head of Corporate Services, Kennedy House, Kennedy Way, Clacton on Sea, Essex, CO15 4AB, Tel.: 01255 206091
Pharmacy
Mr P Breame, Head of Medicines Management, Kennedy House, Kennedy Way, Clacton on Sea, Essex, CO15 4AB, Tel.: 01255 206085
Specialist Nursing Services
Ms K Clark, Residential Homes, Nurse Specialist, Clacton Hospital, Tower Road, Clacton on Sea, Essex, CO15 1LH, Tel.: 01255 201748
Mr J Mills, Collaborative Care, Nurse Specialist, Clacton Hospital, Tower Road, Clacton on Sea, Essex, CO15 1LH, Tel.: 01255 201565
Ms L Booth, Nurse Specialist, Continuing Care, Clacton Hospital, Tower Road, Clacton on Sea, Essex, CO15 1LH, Tel.: 01255 201736
Ms M Lazenby, Nurse Specialist, Tissue Viability, Carnarvon House, Carnarvon Road, Clacton on Sea, Essex, CO15 6QD, Tel.: 01255 206201
The Homeless/Travellers & Asylum Seekers
Ms L Parker, Lead Person, Seaview, Clacton Hospital, Tower Road, Clacton on Sea, Essex, CO15 1LH, Tel.: 01255 201739

Thurrock Primary Care Trust

Trust Headquarters, PO Box 83
Civic Offices, New Road
GRAYS
Essex
RM17 6FD
Tel.: 01375 406400
Fax.: 01375 406400

Admin & Senior Management
Mrs S Adams-O'Shea, Deputy Chief Executive, Director of Nursing & Clinical Governance,
Mrs J Hunter, Chief Executive,
Child Health Records
Ms L Lovell, Manager, Block F, Nurses Campus, Basildon Hospital, Nethermayne, Basildon, SS16 5NL, Tel.: 01268 533911 ext 3254
Child Protection/Safeguarding Children
Mrs M Low, Looked After Children, Designated Nurse, South Ockendon Health Centre, Darenth Lane, South Ockendon, Essex, RM15 5LP, Tel.: 01708 852205
Dr J Moore, Named Doctor for Child Protection, Laindon Health Centre, Laindon, Basildon, Essex, SS15 5TR,
Mrs M Stephens, Named Nurse, Child Protection, South Ockendon Health Centre, Darenth Lane, South Ockendon, Essex, RM15 5LP, Tel.: 01708 852205
Clinical Leads (NSF)
Dr A Bose, Clinical Lead, Cancer,
Dr E Shehadeh, Clinical Lead, CHD,
Dr R Mohiile, Clinical Lead, Diabetes,
Mrs Z Deaton, Clinical Lead, Older People,
Community Nursing Services
Ms T Greatrex, Community Rehabilitation Manager, Modern Matron, Tel.: 01375 364609
District Nursing
Ms P Arthur, Community District Nursing Matron, South Ockendon Health Centre, Darenth Lane, South Ockendon, Essex, RM15 5LP, Tel.: 01708 853295
Mrs P Arthur, District Nursing, Modern Matron, Gifford House, Thurrock Community Hospital, Long Lane, Grays, RM16 2PC, Tel.: 01375 364449
Mrs J Gardener, District Nursing, Modern Matron, Gifford House, Thurrock Community Hospital, Long Lane, Grays, RM16 2PC, Tel.: 01375 364449

Family Planning Services
Ms I Whitwell, Co-ordinator, Tel.: 01268 592350
Ms M Williams, Co-ordinator, Teenage Pregnancy, Tel.: 01375 406437
Mr C Willis, Service Manager, Young Peoples Advisory, Tel.: 01268 592396
Health Visitors
Mrs C Butler, Health Visiting, Modern Matron, South Ockendon Health Centre, Darenth Lane, South Ockendon, Essex, RM15 5LP, Tel.: 01708 853295
Paediatric Health Visitor, Block F, Nurses Campus, Tel.: 01268 598033
HIV/AIDS
Ms L Lambertini, Community Nursing Service, GUM Dept, Orsett Hospital, Rowley Road, Orsett, Grays, Essex, RM16 3EU, Tel.: 01268 592363
Liaison Services
Ms J Forge, Liaison, Health Visitor,
Liaison Services District Nurses, Block H, Nurses Campus, Basildon Hospital, Tel.: 01268 533911 ext 3469
School Nursing
Mrs M Pollington, School Health, Modern Matron, South Ockendon Health Centre, Darenth Lane, South Ockendon, Essex, RM15 51P, Tel.: 01708 853295
Smoking Cessation
Ms J Menzies, Specialist Smoking Co-ordinator, Tel.: 01375 406400
Specialist Nursing Services
Ms M Burnley, Nurse Practitioner, Purfleet Care Centre, Tank Hill Road, Purfleet, Tel.: 01708 864834
Mr M Redman, Lead Nurse, Residential Care Homes, Gifford House, Thurrock Hospital, Long Lane, Grays, Essex, Tel.: 01375 364435
Ms C Suppiah, Community Development, Nurse Specialist, Target Centre, Tilbury, Calcutta Road, Tilbury, Tel.: 01375 858512
Ms A Murgan, Associate Director, Intermediate Services, Intermediate Care, Gifford House, Thurrock Hospital, Long Lane, Grays, Essex, RM16 2PX, Tel.: 01375 364429
The Homeless/Travellers & Asylum Seekers
Grays Health Centre, Brooke Road, Grays, Essex, RM17 5BY, Tel.: 01375 393236
Ms T Kearney, Lead Nurse, Tel.: 01375 397470
Nurse Led PMS Pilot - Acorns, c/o Queensgate Centre, Orsett Road, Grays, RM17 5DF,

Uttlesford Primary Care Trust

Trust Headquarters, John Tasker House
56 New Street
DUNMOW
Essex
CM6 1BH
Tel.: 01371 878295

Admin & Senior Management
Mrs M Walker, Chief Executive,
Child Health Records
Ms A Goodyear, Manager, Child Health Information Dept, Latton Bush Centre, Southern Way, Harlow, CM18 7BL, Tel.: 01279 698800
Child Protection/Safeguarding Children
Ms S McClymont, Child Protection, 2nd Floor, Addison House, Hamstel House, Harlow, CM20 1EP, Tel.: 01279 694940
Clinical Leads (NSF)
Dr G Pritchard, Clinical Lead, Cancer,
Dr C Paul, Clinical Lead, CHD,
Dr J Hockey, Clinical Lead, Diabetic Care,
Dr C Richardson, Clinical Lead, Older People,
District Nursing
Ms G Walker, Community Services Manager, District Nurses, Saffron Walden Community Hospital, Radwinter Road, Saffron Walden, CB11 3HY, Tel.: 01799 562900

East of England Strategic Health Authority

Health Visitors
Ms G Walker, Community Services Manager, Health Visitors, Saffron Walden Community Hospital, Radwinter Road, Saffron Walden, CB11 3HY, Tel.: 01799 562900

Liaison Services
Ms F Richards, Paediatrics Liaison, Tel.: 01279 694943

School Nursing
Ms G Walker, Community Services Manager, School Nurses, Saffron Walden Community Hospital, Radwinter Road, Saffron Walden, CB11 3HY, Tel.: 01799 562900

Watford & Three Rivers Primary Care Trust

Trust Headquarters, Royalty House
10 King Street
WATFORD
Herts, WD18 0BW
Tel.: 01923 281600

Admin & Senior Management
Ms F Cox, Chief Executive,

Child Protection/Safeguarding Children
Ms M Hemley, Named Nurse, Child Protection, Skidmore Way Clinic, Skidmore Way, Rickmansworth, WD3 1SZ, Tel.: 01923 775065

Clinical Leads (NSF)
Dr J King, Clinical Lead, Cancer,
Dr R Jones, Clinical Lead, CHD,
Dr S McCann, Clinical Lead, Diabetic Care,
Dr A Wall, Clinical Lead, Older People,

Community Nursing Services
Ms A Jones, Director of Nursing & Intermediate Care, 1a High Street, Rickmansworth, Hertfordshire, WD3 1ET, Tel.: 01923 713050

District Nursing
Ms A Jones, Director of Nursing & Intermediate Care, 1a High Street, Rickmansworth, Hertfordshire, WD3 1ET, Tel.: 01923 713050

Health Visitors
Mrs F Evershed, Paediatric Liaison Health Visitor, Hornets Ward, Watford General Hospital, Vicarage Road, Watford, Herts, WD18 0HB, Tel.: 01923 244366 ext 3604

Waveney Primary Care Trust

Trust Headquarters
1 Common Lane North
BECCLES
Suffolk
NR34 9BN
Tel.: 01502 719500
Fax.: 01502 719874

Admin & Senior Management
Mr A Evans, Chief Executive, 1 Common Lane North, Beccles, Suffolk, NR34 9BN, Tel.: 01502 533733
Ms A McCreadie, Director of Services, Tel.: 01502 719597

Child Health Records
Dr J Mawer, Consultant Community Paediatrician, Lowestoft Hospital, Tel.: 01502 527 584

Clinical Leads (NSF)
Mrs L Clarke, Clinical Lead, Intermediate Care & Rehabilitation, Lowestoft Hospital, Tel.: 01502 719592
Ms C Craig, Clinical Lead, Adult & Older People, Lowestoft Hospital, Tel.: 01502 719593
Mrs S Mummery, Clinical Lead, Child & Family Services, Lowestoft Hospital, Tel.: 01502 719593
Dr G Mohan, Clinical Lead, CHD, Lowestoft Hospital, Tel.: 01502 719500
Ms N Sawkins, Clinical Lead, Palliative Care, Lowestoft Hospital, Tel.: 01502 719500

District Nursing
Ms D Burke, District Nurses Team Leader, 5 Police Station Road, Lowestoft, NR32 1NY, Tel.: 01502 532662

Mrs S Macnab, District Nurses Team Leader, Beccles Hospital, St Mary's Road, Beccles, Suffolk, NR34 9NQ, Tel.: 01502 719800

Family Planning Services
Mrs I Haysom, 6 Regent Road, Lowestoft, Suffolk, NR32 1PA, Tel.: 01502 532656

Health Visitors
Mrs S Mummery, Health Visitors - Head of Child & Family Services, 1 Common Lane North, Beccles, Suffolk, NR34 9BN, Tel.: 01502 719500

School Nursing
Mrs S Mummery, School Nurses - Head of Child & Family Services, 1 Common Lane North, Beccles, Suffolk, NR34 9BN, Tel.: 01502 719500

Specialist Nursing Services
Ms S Roberts, Senior Practice Nurse, Beccles Surgery, Tel.: 01502 589 151

Welwyn & Hatfield Primary Care Trust

Trust Headquarters, Charter House
Parkway
WELWYN GARDEN CITY
Herts, AL8 6JL
Tel.: 01707 361204
Fax.: 01707 361286

Child Health Records
Manager, Child Health Information System, Charter House, Parkway, Welwyn Garden City, AL8 6JL, Tel.: 01707 361204

Child Protection/Safeguarding Children
Ms L Alleyne, Designated Nurse for Looked After Children/Care Leavers, Parkway Health Clinic, Birdcroft Road, Welwyn Garden City, Herts, AL8 6ER, Tel.: 01707 386870
Care Leavers Nurse, Parkway Health Clinic, Birdcroft Road, Welwyn Garden City, Herts, AL8 6ER, Tel.: 01707 386889
Specialist Nurse, Looked After Children, Parkway Health Clinic, Birdcroft Road, Welwyn Garden City, Herts, AL8 6ER, Tel.: 01707 386870

District Nursing
Director of Nursing & Provider Services, Queensway Health Clinic, Queensway, Hatfield, AL10 0LF, Tel.: 01707 264577

Family Planning Services
Manager, Parkway Health Clinic, Tel.: 01707 386877

Liaison Services
Ms J Ng, District Nurse Liaison, QE11 Hospital, Howlands, Welwyn Garden City, Tel.: 01707 365039
Mr S Richards, District Nurse Liaison, QE11 Hospital, Howlands, Welwyn Garden City, Tel.: 01707 365039

School Nursing
School Health/Nursing Service, Parkway Health Clinic, Birdcroft Road, Welwyn Garden City, AL8 6JL, Tel.: 01707 324541

Smoking Cessation
Smoking Cessation, Charter House, Parkway WGC,

Specialist Nursing Services
Ms C Wilson, Site Manager, QVM Hospital & Danesbury Community Hospitals, Welwyn, Herts, Tel.: 01707 365292
Ms K Alwright, Continence, Parkway Health Clinic, Birdcroft Road, Welwyn Garden City, AL8 6JE, Tel.: 01707 386878
Ms K Hill, Clinical Nurse Manager, Intermediate Care, QVM Hospital, Welwyn, Herts, Tel.: 01707 280366
Ms B Trowbridge, Lymphoedema, Queensway Health Clinic, Queensway, Hatfield, AL10 0LF, Tel.: 01707 280353

West Herts Hospitals NHS Trust

Trust Headquarters, Hemel Hempstead Hospital
Hillfield Road
HEMEL HEMPSTEAD
HP2 4AD
Tel.: 01442 213141

East of England Strategic Health Authority

Child Protection/Safeguarding Children
Ms B Lynch, Designated Nurse, Child Protection, St Nicholas Ward, Hemel Hempstead Hospital, Tel.: 01442 287884
Community Midwifery
Ms S Axam, Manager, Obstetrics & Gynaecological, Hemel Hempstead General Hospital, Hillfield Road, Hemel Hempstead, HP2 4AD, Tel.: 01442 287790
Ms F Burt, Manager, Obstetrics & Gynaecological (Acting Manager), Watford General Hospital, Vicarage Road, Watford, WD1 8HB, Tel.: 01923 217181
Ms K Proctor, General Manager, Head of Midwifery, Based at Watford Maternity Unit, Watford General Hospital, Vicarage Road, Watford, WD1 8HB, Tel.: 01923 244366
Liaison Services
Ms N Young, Discharge Facilitator, Hemel Hempstead General Hospital, Hillfield Road, Hemel Hempstead, HP2 4AD, Tel.: 01442 287027

West Norfolk Primary CareTrust

Trust Headquarters, St James
Extons Road
KING'S LYNN
Norfolk, PE30 5NU
Tel.: 01553 816200

Admin & Senior Management
Ms H Daniels, Chief Executive,
Ms S Gurr, Director of Community Services,
Ms S Hall, Intermediate Care, Senior Nurse Manager,
Ms A Hoscrop, Head of Nursing & Senior Nurse Manager,
Ms D Thurston, Childrens Services/Public Health, Senior Nurse Manager, St James, Extons Road, King's Lynn, Norfolk, PE30 5NU, Tel.: 01553 816348
Child Health Records
Child Health Records, Child Health Department, St James, Extons Road, King's Lynn, Norfolk, PE30 5NU, Tel.: 01553 816364
Child Protection/Safeguarding Children
Ms K Crome, Child Protection, St James, Extons Road, King's Lynn, Norfolk, PE30 5NU, Tel.: 01553 816234
Clinical Leads (NSF)
Dr A Burgess, Clinical Lead, Cancer,
Dr I Mack, Clinical Lead, CHD,
District Nursing
District Nurses, St James, Extons Road, King's Lynn, Norfolk, PE30 5NU, Tel.: 01553 816200
Family Planning Services
Ms S Williams, Sexual Health & Family Planning, St James, Extons Road, King's Lynn, Norfolk, PE30 5NU, Tel.: 01553 816382
Health Visitors
Health Visitors, St James, Extons Road, King's Lynn, Norfolk, PE30 5NU, Tel.: 01553 816200
Ms R Monk, Specialist Health Visitor for Child Development Centre, CAST Office, QEH, Kings Lynn, Norfolk, PE30 5ET, Tel.: 01553 613987
Liaison Services
Ms S Hall, Discharge Liaison Sr Speciality - Care of the Elderlly/Falls, CAST Office, QEH, Kings Lynn, Norfolk, PE30 5ET, Tel.: 01553 613813
Ms K Jones, Clinical Lead, Enhanced Community Palliative Care Discharge Liaison Sr, CAST Office, QEH, Kings Lynn, Norfolk, PE30 5ET, Tel.: 01553 613813
Ms M Reilly, Discharge Liaison Sister, CAST Office, QEH, Kings Lynn, Norfolk, PE30 5ET, Tel.: 01553 613813
Ms A Thatcher, Discharge Liaison Team Leader Sr, Marie Curie, CAST Office, QEH, Kings Lynn, Norfolk, PE30 5ET, Tel.: 01553 613813
Ms J Whitear, Discharge Liaison Sr Speciality - Orthopaedics, CAST Office, QEH, Kings Lynn, Norfolk, PE30 5ET, Tel.: 01553 613813

Other Services
Ms I Bane, Diabetes Specialist, Queen Elizabeth Hospital, Gayton Road, Kings Lynn, PE30 4ET, Tel.: 01553 613494
Ms C Lobo, Public Health, St James, Extons Road, King's Lynn, Norfolk, PE30 5NU, Tel.: 01553 816200
Ms J Widdowson, Diabetes Facilitator, St James, Extons Road, King's Lynn, Norfolk, PE30 5NU, Tel.: 01553 816226
Specialist Nursing Services
Ms J Rogerson, Continence, St James, Extons Road, King's Lynn, Norfolk, PE30 5NU, Tel.: 01553 816381
Ms K Jarrald, Nurse Specialist, COPD, Pentney Ward Office, Queen Elizabeth Hospital, King's Lynn, Norfolk, PE30 4ET, Tel.: 01553 613099
Ms S Oughton, Nurse Specialist, COPD, Pentney Ward Office, Queen Elizabeth Hospital, King's Lynn, Norfolk, PE30 4ET, Tel.: 01553 613099
Ms J White, Nurse Specialist, COPD, Pentney Ward Office, Queen Elizabeth Hospital, King's Lynn, Norfolk, PE30 4ET, Tel.: 01553 613099
Ms J Bradshaw, Multiple Sclerosis, St James, Extons Road, King's Lynn, Norfolk, PE30 5NU, Tel.: 01553 816375
Ms S Barton, Rehabilitation, - Neuro, St James, Extons Road, King's Lynn, Norfolk, PE30 5NU, Tel.: 01553 816375

West Suffolk Hospitals NHS Trust

Trust Headquarters, Hardwick Lane
BURY ST EDMUNDS
Suffolk
IP33 2QZ
Tel.: 01284 713000
Fax.: 01284 701993

Child Health
Ms J Plumb, Tel.: 01284 713612
Ms J Sharp, Tel.: 01284 713612
Community Midwifery
Ms P Davis, Head of Midwifery/General Manager, Maternity Unit, West Suffolk Hospital, Tel.: 01284 713220
Maternity Unit, Tel.: 01284 713253
Ms J Palmer, Community Midwifery Manager, Tel.: 01284 713153
Liaison Services
Ms G Bush, Liaison General, Elderly & Paediatric, West Suffolk Hospital, Hardwick Lane, Bury St Edmunds, Suffolk, IP33 2QZ, Tel.: 01284 713474/713369
Ms J Downes, Liaison Team Leader, West Suffolk Hospital, Hardwick Lane, Bury St Edmunds, Suffolk, IP33 2QZ, Tel.: 01284 713474/713369
Ms H Grimsdell, Liaison General, Elderly & Paediatric, West Suffolk Hospital, Hardwick Lane, Bury St Edmunds, Suffolk, IP33 2QZ, Tel.: 01284 713474/713369
Ms J Harper, Liaison General, Elderly & Paediatric, West Suffolk Hospital, Hardwick Lane, Bury St Edmunds, Suffolk, IP33 2QZ, Tel.: 01284 713474/713369
Ms K Marsh, Liaison General, Elderly & Paediatric, West Suffolk Hospital, Hardwick Lane, Bury St Edmunds, Suffolk, IP33 2QZ, Tel.: 01284 713474/713369

Witham, Braintree & Halstead Care Trust

Trust Headquarters, Warwick House
Market Square
BRAINTREE
Essex
CM7 3HQ
Tel.: 01376 331549

Admin & Senior Management
Ms R Boyce, Director of Nursing, Witham, Braintree, Halstead Care Trust HQ, Warwick House, Market Place, Brainree, CM7 3HQ, Tel.: 01376 331549

Child Health

Ms S St Pierre, Associate Director Childrens Services, Warwick House, Market Square, Braintree, Essex, CM7 3HQ, Tel.: 01376 333700/703

Child Health Records

Mr P Booth, Witham & Braintree Child Health Records, Unit 12, Atlantic Square, Station Road, Witham, Tel.: 01376 302619

Ms P Holmes, East Lodge Court, Colchester, CO1 1UJ, Tel.: 01206 579411

Child Protection/Safeguarding Children

Mrs P Emery, Named Nurse, Child Protection, Witham, Braintree & Halstead Care Trust, Tel.: 01376 302769

Community Nursing Services

Mrs M Lancaster, Nursing Services Manager, Kestral House, Hedgerows Business Park, Springfield, Chelmsford, Tel.: 01245 398750

District Nursing

Mrs M Lancaster, Nursing Services Manager, Kestral House, Hedgerows Business Park, Springfield, Chelmsford, Tel.: 01245 398750

Equipment Loan Services

Essex Community Equipment Store, Catalyst House,

Family Planning Services

Family Planning, through Maldon & South Chelmsford PCT, St Peters Hospital, 32A Spital Road, Maldon, CM9 6EG, Tel.: 01621 854344

Health Visitors

Ms P Jackson, Warwick House, Tel.: 01376 331549

Ms S St Pierre, Health Visitors Manager, Warwick House, Tel.: 01376 331549

Liaison Services

Liaison Services Halstead, Colchester General Hospital, Turner Road, Colchester, Tel.: 01206 747474

Liaison Services Witham & Braintree, Through Mid Essex Hospitals, Broomfield Hospital, Hospital Road, Chelmsford, CM1 7ET, Tel.: 01245 440761

Specialist Nursing Services

Ms C Turner, Continence, 42 London Road, Braintree,

Ms I Doherty, COPD, Broomfield Hospital, Broomfield Court, Hospital Road, Chelmsford, CM1 7ET, Tel.: 01245 440761

Mrs L Jewsbury, Services Manager, Diabetic Care,

Ms J Shields, Infection Control, Warwick House, Market Place, Braintree, CM7 3HQ, Tel.: 01376 331549

Ms C Claeys, Palliative Care, Kestral House, Hedgerows Business Park, Springfield, Chelmsford, Tel.: 01245 398770

Ms L Grothier, Tissue Viability, Kestral House, Hedgerows Business Park, Springfield, Chelmsford, Tel.: 01245 398770

London Strategic Health Authority

with major towns and Primary Care Trust boundaries

Pop: 7,428,590

East of England

Enfield

Barnet

Harrow

Tottenham

Walthamstowe

Hampstead

Ilford

Hornchurch

Wembley

Mile End

City

Newham

Barking

Hillingdon

Southall

Westminster

Chelsea

Greenwich

Hounslow

Lambeth

Bexley

Fulham

Lewisham

Teddington

Surbiton

Bromley

Sutton

Croydon

South East Coast

London Strategic Health Authority

London Strategic Health Authority

Barking & Dagenham Primary Care Trust
Trust Headquarters, Clock House
East Street
BARKING
Essex
IG11 8EY
Tel.: 020 8591 9595

Admin & Senior Management
Ms H Aerst, Chief Executive,
Director of Child & Family Services & Nursing, The Willows', St George's Hospital, 117 Suttons Lane, Hornchurch, RM12 6RS, Tel.: 01708 465445
Child Health
Ms V Hanson, Service Manager, The Willows, St George's Hospital, 117 Suttons Lane, Hornchurch, RM12 6RS, Tel.: 01708 465039
Ms D Tedder, Child Development Team Co-ordinator, Orchard View, St George's Hospital, Tel.: 01708 465265
Child Health Records
Programme Manager, The Willows, St George's Hospital, 117 Suttons Lane, Hornchurch, RM12 6RS, Tel.: 01708 465426
Child Protection/Safeguarding Children
Ms S Hanson, Nurse Specialist, The Willows, St George's Hospital, 117 Suttons Lane, Hornchurch, RM12 6RS, Tel.: 01708 455497
Ms E Doherty, Designated Nurse, Child Protection, The Willows, St George's Hospital, 117 Suttons Lane, Hornchurch, RM12 6RS, Tel.: 01708 465497
Clinical Leads (NSF)
Ms J Ross, Clinical Lead, Cancer,
District Nursing
District Nurses, Annie Prendergast Clinic, Ashton Gardens, Chadwell Heath, Romford, RM6 6RT, Tel.: 020 8918 0500
Health Visitors
Health Visitors, Annie Prendergast Clinic, Ashton Gardens, Chadwell Heath, Romford, RM6 6RT, Tel.: 020 8918 0500
Ms A Jones, Liaison Paediatric, Health Visitor, The Willows, St George's Hospital, 117 Suttons Lane, Hornchurch, RM12 6RS, Tel.: 01708 465497
Learning Disabilities
Mr C Martin, Service Manager, Social Services, Civic Centre, Dagenham, RM10 13W, Tel.: 0208 592 4500
Ms C Mortimer, Manager, 27 Woodward Road, Dagenham, RM9 4SJ, Tel.: 020 8595 1667
Mr P Valoo, Lead Nurse, Tel.: 0208 270 6586
Specialist Nursing Services
Ms J Loader, Strategic Lead Older People's Services, Tel.: 020 8918 0517

Barking, Havering & Redbridge Hospitals NHS Trust
Trust Headquarters, Harold Wood Hospital
Gubbins Lane
ROMFORD
RM3 0BE
Tel.: 01708 345533

Child Health
Ms C Clarke, Oncology Macmillan (Children), Oldchurch Hospital, Waterloo Road, Romford, RM7 0BE, Tel.: 01708 708289
Ms D Harvey-Coggans, Diabetes (Children), Oldchurch Hospital, Waterloo Road, Romford, RM7 0BE, Tel.: 01708 708289
Ms C Mummery, Children's Home Care Team Co-ordinator, Oldchurch Hospital, Waterloo Road, Romford, RM7 0BE, Tel.: 01708 708289

Community Midwifery
Discharges, King George Hospital, Barley Lane, Goodmayes, Ilford, Essex, IG3 8YB, Tel.: 020 8970 8245
Mrs L Imber, Maternity Resource Manager (Matron) for Community & ANC, Harold Wood Hospital, Gubbins Lane, Harold Wood, Romford, Essex, RM3 0BE, Tel.: 01708 708122
Mrs L Thomas, Head of Midwifery/Director of Women's & Children Services, Harold Wood Hospital, Gubbins Lane, Harold Wood, Romford, Essex, RM3 0BE, Tel.: 01708 345533
Mrs L Thomas, Head of Midwifery, King George Hospital, Barley Lane, Goodmayes, Ilford, Essex, IG3 8YB, Tel.: 020 8970 8198
Liaison Services
Ms M Linney, Discharge Co-ordinator (Oldchurch, Harold Wood, Barking & King George's Hospitals), Harold Wood Hospital, Romford, RM3 0BE, Tel.: 020 8924 6204
Ms J Morrison Harris, Discharge Co-ordinator (Oldchurch, Harold Wood, Barking & King George's Hospitals), Harold Wood Hospital, Romford, RM3 0BE, Tel.: 020 8924 6204

Barnet & Chase Farm Hospitals NHS Trust
Trust Headquarters, The Ridgeway
ENFIELD
EN2 8JL
Tel.: 0845 111 4000

Child Protection/Safeguarding Children
Ms J Pickersgill, Lead Midwife, Child Protection, Edgware Birth Centre, Edgware Community Hospital, Edgware, Middlesex, HA8,
Community Midwifery
Mrs C Bagan, Barnet - Senior Midwifery Manager, Outpatients & Community Services, Community Midwifery Office, Ground Floor, Thames House, Barnet Hospital, Tel.: 020 8216 5414
Mrs C Bagan, Chase Farm - Senior Midwifery Manager, Outpatients & Community Services, Midwifery Manage Office, 2nd Floor, Womens & Childrens Unit, Chase Farm Hosp, The Ridgeway, EN2 8JL, Tel.: 0845 111 1298
Chase Farm Midwifery Services, Chase Farm Hospital, The Ridgeway, Enfield, Middlesex, EN2 8JL, Tel.: 0845 111 4000
Ms B Dale, Specialist Midwife Antenatal Education/Infant Feeding, c/o Wellhouse Centre, Level 2, Barnet Hospital, Wellhouse Lane, Barnet, EN5 3DJ, Tel.: 0208 216 5136
Head of Midwifery - Barnet Site, Ground Floor, Thames House, Barnet Hospital, Wellhouse Lane, EN5 3DJ, Tel.: 0208 216 5415/5417
Head of Midwifery - Chase Farm Site, Midwifery Manage Office, 2nd Floor, Womens & Childrens Unit, Chase Farm Hosp, The Ridgeway, EN2 8JL, Tel.: 020 845 111 1247/1289
Out of hours, Chase Farm Hospital, The Ridgeway, Enfield, Middlesex, EN2 8JL, Tel.: 020 8375 1100
Ms L Pitblado, Chase Farm - Senior Clinical Midwife, Community, Midwifery Manage Office, 2nd Floor, Womens & Childrens Unit, Chase Farm Hosp, The Ridgeway, EN2 8JL, Tel.: 0845 111 1439
Ms L Pitblado, Barnet - Senior Clinical Midwife, Community, Community Midwifery Office, Ground Floor, Thames House, Barnet Hospital, Tel.: 020 8216 5414
Ms C Rogers, Consultant Midwife, Chase Farm Maternity Unit, 1st Floor, The Ridgeway Birth Centre, Chase Farm Hospital, Tel.: 0208 111 4000 ext 1439
The Ridgeway Birth Centre, Chase Farm Hospital, The Ridgeway, Enfield, Middlesex, EN2 8JL, Tel.: 0845 111 4000
Ms C Trembath, Specialist Midwife for Midwife Led Care, Delivery Suite, Chase Farm Maternity Unit, Chase Farm Hospital, Tel.: 0208 111 4000
Ms R Villar, Specialist Midwife for Midwife Led Care, Delivery Suite, Chase Farm Maternity Unit, Chase Farm Hospital, Tel.: 0208 111 4000

Liaison Services

Ms J Hale, Discharge Co-ordinator, Bed Bureau, Barnet General Hospital, Wellhouse Lane, Barnet, EN5 3DJ, Tel.: 020 8216 4000

Ms J Jeffryes, Chase Farm Hospital, Tel.: 0208 375 4000 ext 2146

Ms G MacDonald, Discharge Co-ordinator, Bed Bureau, Barnet General Hospital, Wellhouse Lane, Barnet, EN5 3DJ, Tel.: 020 8216 4000

Ms R O'Connell, Discharge Co-ordinator, Bed Bureau, Barnet General Hospital, Wellhouse Lane, Barnet, EN5 3DJ, Tel.: 020 8216 4000

Smoking Cessation

Ms S Ash, Smoking Cessation Midwife for Barnet Services, c/o Wellhouse Wavens Centre, Barnet Hospital, Wellhouse Lane, Barnet, EN5 3DJ,

Barnet Primary Care Trust

Trust Headquarters, 3rd Floor, Westgate House
Edgware Community Hospital, Burnt Oak Broadway
EDGWARE
Middlesex
HA8 0AD
Tel.: 020 8952 2381
Fax.: 020 8937 7727

Admin & Senior Management

Ms A Blair, Director of Primary Care, Westgate House, Edgware Community Hospital, Burnt Oak Broadway, Edgware, Middlesex, HA8 0AD, Tel.: 020 8937 7631

Mr A Burnett, Director of Public Health/Health Improvement, Westgate House, Edgware Community Hospital, Burnt Oak Broadway, Edgware, Middlesex, HA8 0AD, Tel.: 020 8937 7690

Ms L Cardell, Director of Communications, Westgate House, Edgware Community Hospital, Burnt Oak Broadway, Edgware, Middlesex, HA8 0AD, Tel.: 020 8937 7643

Mr D Carter, Director of Finance, Westgate House, Edgware Community Hospital, Burnt Oak Broadway, Edgware, Middlesex, HA8 0AD, Tel.: 020 8937 7660

Mrs A Edgington, Director of Nursing, Hyde House, The Hyde, Edgware Road, Edgware, Middlesex, NW9 6QQ, Tel.: 020 8201 4822

Mr C Halloran, Director of Operations & Community Services, Westgate House, Edgware Community Hospital, Burnt Oak Broadway, Edgware, Middlesex, HA8 0AD, Tel.: 020 8732 6421

Mr T Hellings, Director of Partnerships & Workforce, Westgate House, Edgware Community Hospital, Burnt Oak Broadway, Edgware, Middlesex, HA8 0AD, Tel.: 020 8937 7655

Mr C Hollwey, Chief Executive, Westgate House, Edgware Community Hospital, Burnt Oak Broadway, Edgware, Middlesex, HA8 0AD, Tel.: 020 8937 7647

Mr S Huddleston, Director of IM&T, Westgate House, Edgware Community Hospital, Burnt Oak Broadway, Edgware, Middlesex, HA8 0AD, Tel.: 020 8732 6826

Mr N McElduff, Director of Estates, Facilities & Procurement, Westgate Annex, Edgware Community Hospital, Burnt Oak Broadway, Edgware, Middlesex, HA8 0AD, Tel.: 020 8732 6250

Mr D Wright, Director of Commissioning & Planning, Westgate House, Edgware Community Hospital, Burnt Oak Broadway, Edgware, Middlesex, HA8 0AD, Tel.: 020 8937 7613

Child Health Records

Child Health Records, Edgware Community Hospital, Burnt Oak Broadway, Edgware, Middlesex, HA8 0AD, Tel.: 020 8952 2381

Child Protection/Safeguarding Children

Ms J Mace, Head of Children's Health, Westgate House, Edgware Community Hospital, Burnt Oak Broadway, Edgware, Middlesex, HA8 0AD, Tel.: 020 8937 7651

Ms S Lai, Named Nurse, Child Protection, 1 Wellhouse Lane, Barnet, Herts, EN5 3DJ, Tel.: 020 8441 2371

Ms S McGovern, Designated Nurse, Child Protection, 1 Wellhouse Lane, Barnet, Herts, EN5 3DJ, Tel.: 020 8441 2371

Clinical Leads (NSF)

Dr C Stephens, Clinical Lead, Cancer,

Dr A Robinson, Clinical Lead, Older People,

Community Nursing Services

Ms J Ayyildiz, Community Services Dev Manager West Locality, Westgate House, Edgware Community Hospital,

Ms A Mount, Community Services Development Manager South Locality, Oak Lane Clinic, Oak Lane, London, N2 8LT, Tel.: 0208 349 7000

Ms V Stimpson, Community Services Manager North Locality, Bullimore House, Finchley Memorial Hospital, Tel.: 0208 349 6479

District Nursing

District Nurses & Health Visitors, Edgware Community Hospital, Burnt Oak Broadway, Edgware, Middlesex, HA8 0AD, Tel.: 020 8952 2381

Emergencies/Night, Tel.: 020 8952 2381

Ms S Masterson, Clinical Manager (Older People & Adults) West Locality, Grahame Park Health Centre, The Concourse, Grahame Park Way, Colindale, NW9 5XT,

Ms E E Mills, Clinical Manager (Children & Families) North Locality, East Barnet Health Centre, 149 East Barnet Road, Barnet, EN4 8QN,

Ms L Yilma, Clinical Manager (Children & Familes) West Locality, Mill Hill Clinic, Hartley Avenue, Mill Hill,

Equipment Loan Services

Red Cross, Unit 10, Brunswick Industrial Estate, Waterfall Road, London, N11 1JL,

Family Planning Services

Ms K Bushel, Sexual Health Manager, 1 Wellhouse Lane, Barnet, EN5 3DH, Tel.: 0208 447 0603

HIV/AIDS

Ms C Tuile, HIV Nurse Specialist, 1 Wellhouse Lane, Barnet, EN5 3DH, Tel.: 0208 447 0603

Learning Disabilities

Mrs A Pointu, Nurse Consultant (Learning Disabilities), Barnet Learning Disabilities Service, 313 Ballards Lane, London, N12 8LY, Tel.: 020 8492 5454

Liaison Services

Ms B Tomkin, PALS Co-ordinator, Patient Advice & Liaison Service, Advice Centre, Edgware Community Hospital, Tel.: 0208 937 7173

Other Services

Ms B Carolan, General Manager, Finchley Memorial Hospital, Granville Road, Finchley, London, N12 0JE, Tel.: 020 8349 6300

Ms B Persaud, General Manager, Edgware Community Hospital, Burnt Oak Broadway, Edgware, Middlesex, HA8 0AD, Tel.: 020 8952 2381

Pharmacy

Ms K Spooner, Community Pharmacy Services Advisor, Edgware Community Hospital, Tel.: 020 8937 7173

School Nursing

School Health/Nursing Service, Edgware Community Hospital, Burnt Oak Broadway, Edgware, Middlesex, HA8 0AD, Tel.: 020 8952 2381

Specialist Nursing Services

Ms M Gehamri, Residential Home Nurse, 1 Wellhouse Lane, Barnet, EN5 3DH, Tel.: 0208 447 0603

Ms G Hazlett, Advisor, Continence, Finchley Memorial Hospital, Granville Road, Finchley, N12 0JE, Tel.: 0208 349 6431

Ms M Holliday, Nurse Manager, Continuing Care, Oak Lane Clinic, Oak Lane, London, N2 8LT,

Ms B Nash, Nurse Manager, Continuing Care, Oak Lane Clinic, Oak Lane, London, N2 8LT,

Ms M Roy, Nurse Manager, Continuing Care, Oak Lane Clinic, Oak Lane, London, N2 8LT,

Ms H Maitland, Nurse Specialist, Stoma Care, Finchley Memorial Hospital, Granville Road, Finchley, N12 0JE, Tel.: 0208 349 6439

Ms J Flynn, Nurse Specialist, Tissue Viability, East Barnet Health Centre, East Barnet Road, Barnet, EN4 8QZ,

London Strategic Health Authority

The Homeless/Travellers & Asylum Seekers
Ms C McCullagh, 36B Woodhouse Road, N12 0RG, Tel.: 0208 446 8400

Walk In Centres
Ms P Bowman, Edgware Walk-in Centre, Edgware Community Hospital,
Ms K Jewson, Finchley Walk-in-Centre, Finchley Memorial Hospital, Tel.: 0208 349 6337

Barts and The London NHS Trust

Trust Headquarters, 5th Floor
Alexandra House, Royal London Hospital
WHITECHAPEL
London
E1 1BB
Tel.: 020 7377 7000
Fax.: 020 7377 7413

Acute Specialist Nursing Services
Ms J Butler, Heart Failure - Pager No 07659 110576, Education Block, Tel.: 020 8983 2239
Ms A Mahon, Peritoneal Dialysis - Pager No 07659 120487, CAPD Unit, King George, V Block, St Bartholemew's Hospital, Tel.: 020 7601 8282
Ms F McCormack, Drugs & Alcohol Misuse, The Royal London Hospital, Tel.: 020 7377 7000
Ms A Cain, Continence, c/o Phyllis Friend Ward, The Royal London Hospital, Tel.: 020 7377 7000 ext 3994
Ms R Russell, Clinical Nurse Specialist, Continence, c/o Phyllis Friend Ward, The Royal London Hospital, Tel.: 020 7377 7000 ext 3994
Ms K Bonner, Asthma, COPD, 1st Floor, Education Block, The London Chest Hospital, Bonner Road, London, E2 9JX, Tel.: 020 7377 7000 ext 2408
Mr M Butler, Clinical Nurse Specialist, Cystic Fibrosis, Room 1, 1st Floor, Education Centre, The London Chest Hospital, Tel.: 020 7377 7000 ex 16 2442
Ms E Figueira, Diabetic Care, 4th Floor, Alexandra House, The Royal London Hospital, Tel.: 020 7377 7000 ext 2609
Mr M Cocksedge, TB, Ground Floor, Nurses Home, The London Chest Hospital, Bonner Road, London, E2 9JX, Tel.: 020 7377 7000 ext 2296

Admin & Senior Management
Ms K Fenton, Director of Nursing & Quality, Royal London Hospital, 5th Floor, Alexandra House, Whitechapel, London, E1 1BB, Tel.: 020 7377 7010

Child Health
Ms L Collyer, Paediatric Cystic Fibrosis - Bleep 1081, Pager No 07659 143374, 2nd Floor, Fielden House, The Royal London Hospital, Tel.: 020 7377 7000 ext 3939
Ms K Davies, Paediatric Endocrinology, 1st Floor, David Hughes Building, The Royal London Hospital, Tel.: 020 7377 7000 ext 6307
Ms S Higginson, Infant Care, Breastfeeding - Pager No 07659 115911, 3rd Floor, Fielden House, The Royal London Hospital, Tel.: 020 7377 7000 ext 3948
Ms S Hotchkin, Surgical, Stoma Care - Pager No 07659 115908, 1st Floor, Eva Luckes House, The Royal London Hospital, Tel.: 020 7377 7000
Ms E Jacobson, Retinoblastoma, 1st Floor, Eva Luckes House, The Royal London Hospital, Tel.: 07786 138974
Ms P Kane, Paediatric Respiratory - Bleep 1095, Pager No 07659 143623, 2nd Floor, Fielden House, The Royal London Hospital, Tel.: 020 7377 7000 ext 3944
Ms M Kersjes, Paediatric Pain Management, 1st Floor, David Hughes Building, The Royal London Hospital, Tel.: 020 7377 7000 ext 3985

Mr J Khair, Nutrition - bleep 0044, Pager No 07659 125902, 2nd Floor, David Hughes Building, The Royal London Hospital, Tel.: 020 7943 1354
Ms H Maciver, Surgical, Stoma Care - Pager No 07659 115908, 1st Floor, Eva Luckes House, The Royal London Hospital, Tel.: 020 7377 7000
Ms K Newell, Paediatric Haematology - Bleep 1048, Pager No 07659 152645, 2nd Floor, Fielden House, The Royal London Hospital, Tel.: 020 7377 7000 ext 3942
Ms H Roberts, Child & Family Health - Pager No 08700 555500 825658, 2nd Floor, Fielden House, The Royal London Hospital, Tel.: 020 7377 7000 ext 3133
Ms A Tate, Bereavement, c/o Goldsmith Ward, The Royal London Hospital, Tel.: 020 7377 7000 ext 3425
Ms C Wyatt, Paediatric Diabetes - Pager No 07659 191030, 2nd Floor, Fielden House, The Royal London Hospital, Tel.: 020 7377 7000 ext 3938
Ms J Robinson, Paediatric Dermatology - Bleep 1096, Pager No 07659 152646, Dermatology, 2nd Floor, Fielden House, The Royal London Hospital, Tel.: 020 7377 7000 ext 3946
Ms A Cox, Oncology Macmillan - Pager No 07659 113661, Oncology, 1st Floor, Luckes House, The Royal London Hospital, Tel.: 020 7377 7000 ext 3945
Ms M Crisp, Oncology - Pager No 07659 108878, Oncology, 1st Floor, Luckes House, The Royal London Hospital, Tel.: 020 7377 7000 ext 3943

Community Midwifery
Mrs R Akoto-Appiah, Midwife Project Manager, Royal London Hospital, Whitechapel Road, Whitechapel, London, E1 1BB, Tel.: 020 7377 7000 ext 3470
Mrs M Buckley, Head of Maternity Services, Royal London Hospital, Whitechapel Road, Whitechapel, London, E1 1BB, Tel.: 020 7377 7000 ext 7173
Community Admin Manager, Royal London Hospital, Whitechapel Road, Whitechapel, London, E1 1BB, Tel.: 020 7377 7000 ext 7658
Community Team Midwives, Globe & St Stephen's, Royal London Hospital, Whitechapel Road, Whitechapel, London, E1 1BB, Tel.: Pager No 809439
Community Team Midwives, Tower & Hessel, Royal London Hospital, Whitechapel Road, Whitechapel, London, E1 1BB, Tel.: Pager No 816943
Community Team Midwives, Spitalfields & Bethnal Green, Royal London Hospital, Whitechapel Road, Whitechapel, London, E1 1BB, Tel.: Pager No 816058
Community Team Midwives, Island & Limehouse, Royal London Hospital, Whitechapel Road, Whitechapel, London, E1 1BB, Tel.: Pager No 816623
Community Team Midwives, St Paul's & Stepney Gardens, Royal London Hospital, Whitechapel Road, Whitechapel, London, E1 1BB, Tel.: Pager No 813001
Mrs T Lawton, Manager, Labour Ward, Royal London Hospital, Whitechapel Road, Whitechapel, London, E1 1BB, Tel.: 020 7377 7000 ext 2555
Mrs D McEneaney, Community Midwifery Manager, Royal London Hospital, Whitechapel Road, Whitechapel, London, E1 1BB, Tel.: 020 7377 7000 ext 2764
Postnatal Discharges, Royal London Hospital, Whitechapel Road, Whitechapel, London, E1 1BB, Tel.: fax 020 7377 7459
Ms T Ryan, Inpatient Services Manager, Royal London Hospital, Whitechapel Road, Whitechapel, London, E1 1BB, Tel.: 020 7377 7000 ext 2473

Liaison Services
Ms E Onyejiaku, Paediatric Health Visitor (Pager No 07659 152573), Clinical NS Secs Office, 2nd Floor, Fielden House, Royal London Hospital, Stepney Way, E1 1BB, Tel.: 020 7377 7000 ext 3949
Paediatric Continuing Care Team, Clinical NS Secs Office, 2nd Floor, Fielden House, Royal London Hospital, Stepney Way, E1 1BB, Tel.: 020 7377 7193/7769

London Strategic Health Authority

Bexley Care Trust

Trust Headquarters
221 Erith Road
BEXLEYHEATH
Kent, DA7 6HZ
Tel.: 020 8298 6000

Admin & Senior Management
Senior Management, Trust HQ, 221 Erith Road, Bexleyheath, Kent, DA7 6HZ, Tel.: 020 8298 6000
Child Health
Children's Nursing Teams, Tel.: 020 8298 6040
Dr S Sivakumar, Lead Community Paediatric Clinician, Tel.: 020 8298 6000
Child Health Records
Administration, Trust Headquarters, Tel.: 020 8298 6000
Child Protection/Safeguarding Children
Child Protection Advisor, Tel.: 020 8298 6079
Designated Nurse, Looked After Children, Tel.: 01322 356358
Dr M Mather, Designated Doctor Looked After Children, Tel.: 020 8298 6000
Clinical Leads (NSF)
Dr A Barnett, Clinical Lead, Cancer,
Dr A Barnett, Clinical Lead, Diabetic Care,
Dr H Patrick, Clinical Lead, Older People,
Community Nursing Services
Director of Quality Improvement & Nursing, Tel.: 020 8298 6000
District Nursing
Ms K Gore, Lead Locality Nurse, North Bexley, Tel.: 01322 357894
Ms A Neave, Lead Locality Nurse, Frognal, Tel.: 020 8298 6137
Ms M Schwencke, Out of Hours Twilight/Night Service, Tel.: 020 8298 6000
Ms K Wardle, Lead Locality Nurse, Clocktower, Tel.: 020 8298 6137
Family Planning Services
Lead Sexual Health Nurse, Lakeside Health Centre, Tel.: 020 8320 5564
Sexual Health Services, Trust Headquarters, Tel.: 020 8298 6000
Health Visitors
Ms L Bates, Lead Locality Nurse, Health Visitors, Clocktower, Tel.: 020 8298 6137
Mr P Gannon, Lead Locality Nurse, Health Visitors, North Bexley, Tel.: 01322 357894
Ms K Gunasekara, Lead Locality Nurse, Health Visitors, North Bexley, Tel.: 01322 357894
Ms M Hawes-Gatt, Lead Locality Nurse, Health Visitors, Frognal, Tel.: 020 8298 6137
Parenting Lead Health Visitor, Tel.: 020 8303 0439
HIV/AIDS
HIV Nurse, 245 Broadway Clinic, Bexleyheath, Tel.: 020 8304 3760
Liaison Services
District Nurses Liaison Sister, Queen Mary's Hospital, Frognal Avenue, Sidcup, DA14 6LT, Tel.: 020 8302 2678 ext 4077
Liaison Health Visitor, Tel.: 020 8302 2678 ext 4223
School Nursing
Ms L Bates, Lead Locality Nurse, School Health Advisor, Clocktower, Tel.: 020 8298 6137
Mr P Gannon, Lead Locality Nurse, School Health Advisor, North Bexley, Tel.: 01322 357894
Ms K Gunasekara, Lead Locality Nurse, School Health Advisor, North Bexley, Tel.: 01322 357894
Ms M Hawes-Gatt, Lead Locality Nurse, School Health Advisor, Frognal, Tel.: 020 8298 6137
School Health/Nursing Service, Trust Headquarters, Tel.: 020 8298 6000
Specialist Nursing Services
Ellenor Foundation, Tel.: 020 8302 2678 ext 3014
Heart Nurse, Chronic Disease Management, Tel.: 01322 357951
Advisor, Continence, Tel.: via 020 8298 1669/1662

Nurse, Diabetes, Tel.: 01322 553876
Lead, Infection Control, Tel.: 020 8298 6000
Community Team, Rehabilitation, Bostal House, Goldie Leigh Hospital, Lodge Hill, Abbey Wood, London, SE2 0AY, Tel.: 020 8319 7146
Nurse, Stoma Care, Tel.: 020 8302 2678 ext 3282
Nurse Specialist, TB, 245 The Broadway, Bexleyheath, Kent, Tel.: 020 8304 3967
Nurse, Tissue Viability, Erith Health Centre, 50 Pier Road, Erith, Kent, Tel.: 01322 336661

Brent Teaching Primary Care Trust

Trust Headquarters
116 Chaplin Road
WEMBLEY
Middlesex, HA0 4UZ
Tel.: 020 8795 6000

Admin & Senior Management
Ms P Atkinson, Director of Nursing, Quality & Clinical Governance, Wembley Centre for Health & Care, 116 Chaplin Road, Wembley, HA0 4UZ, Tel.: 0208 795 6767
Ms D Breen, Assistant Director - Southern Localities, Willesden Community Hospital, Harlesden Road, London, NW10 3RY, Tel.: 0208 451 8298
Mr R Goodyer, Specialist Services Manager, Wembley Centre for Health & Care, Wembley, HA0 4UZ, Tel.: 020 8795 6000
Ms L Greenhill, Assistant Director - Northern Localities, Wembley Centre for Health & Care, 116 Chaplin Road, Wembley, HA0 4UZ, Tel.: 0208 795 6105
Mr A Parker, Acting Chief Executive, Wembley Centre for Health & Care, 116 Chaplin Road, Wembley, HA0 4UZ, Tel.: 0208 795 6485
Child Health
Ms Y Arnold, Community Children Nurses, c/o Barnaby Bear Ward, Central Middlesex Hospital, Acton Lane, Park Royal, London, NW10 7NS, Tel.: 0208 453 2125
Child Health Records
Ms D Ellis, Child Health Computing Manager, Wembley Centre for Health & Care, Barham House, 116 Chaplin Road, Wembley, HA0 4UZ, Tel.: 0208 795 6321
Child Protection/Safeguarding Children
Ms P Bell, Designated Nurse for Looked After Children, Wembley Centre for Health & Care, 116 Chaplin Road, Wembley, HA0 4UZ, Tel.: 0208 795 6342
Ms J McLeary, Child Protection Advisor, Wembley Centre for Health & Care, Barham House, 116 Chaplin Road, Wembley, HA0 4UZ, Tel.: 0208 795 6397
Ms L Reid, Child Protection Advisor, Wembley Centre for Health & Care, Barham House, 116 Chaplin Road, Wembley, HA0 4UZ, Tel.: 0208 795 6389
Ms L Rejoinan, Child Protection Advisor, Wembley Centre for Health & Care, Barham House, 116 Chaplin Road, Wembley, HA0 4UZ, Tel.: 0208 795 6397
Ms B Halford, Designated Nurse, Child Protection, Wembley Centre for Health & Care, Barham House, 116 Chaplin Road, Wembley, HA0 4UZ, Tel.: 0208 795 6396
Clinical Leads (NSF)
Ms M McLennan, Clinical Lead, CHD & Respiratory, Tel.: 0208 795 7488
Ms G Jones, Clinical Lead, Cancer, Tel.: 0208 795 6654
Ms P Singh, Clinical Lead, Care of the Elderly, Tel.: 0208 795 7472/6154
Ms S Mansurali, Clinical Lead, Children,
Ms L Sevak, Clinical Lead, Diabetic Care, Tel.: 0208 795 6155
Community Nursing Services
Ms P Atkinson, Director of Nursing, Quality & Clinical Governance, Wembley Centre for Health & Care, 116 Chaplin Road, Wembley, HA0 4UZ, Tel.: 0208 795 6767

London Strategic Health Authority

District Nursing
Ms T Coyne, Professional Facilitator - District Nursing, Wembley Centre for Health & Care, 116 Chaplin Road, Wembley, HA0 4UZ, Tel.: 0208 795 7456
Ms U Fernandez, Professional Facilitator - District Nursing, Wembley Centre for Health & Care, 116 Chaplin Road, Wembley, HA0 4UZ, Tel.: 0208 795 7455

Family Planning Services
Ms J Chandler, Nurse Manager, Pound Lane Clinic, Pound Lane, London, NW10 2HH, Tel.: 0208 459 5116

Health Visitors
Ms R George, Professional Facilitator - Health Visiting, Wembley Centre for Health & Care, 116 Chaplin Road, Wembley, HA0 4UZ, Tel.: 0208 795 6008

HIV/AIDS
Mr M Jowata, HIV, Wembley Centre for Health & Care, 116 Chaplin Road, Wembley, HA0 4UZ, Tel.: 0208 795 6115

Liaison Services
Ms J Butchard, Special Needs Co-ordinator CDT, Wembley Centre for Health & Care, Barham House, 116 Chaplin Road, Wembley, HA0 4UZ, Tel.: 0208 795 6338
Ms M Yates, Professional Facilitator for Practice Nurses, Wembley Centre for Health & Care, 116 Chaplin Road, Wembley, HA0 4UZ, Tel.: 0208 795 6097

Other Services
Mr P Laffey, Willesden Hospital for Physical Disabilities & Older People's Services, Willesden Hospital, Harlesden Road, Willesden, London, NW10 3RY, Tel.: 0208 459 1292
Ms J Matthews, Kingsbury Hospital for Learning Disabilities, Kingsbury Hospital, Honeypot Lane, Kingsbury, London, NW9 9QY, Tel.: 0208 8451

Pharmacy
Ms H Patel, Pharmacy, Wembley Centre for Health & Care, 116 Chaplin Road, Wembley, HA0 4UZ, Tel.: 0208 795 6162
Ms R Rajyaguru, Pharmacy, Wembley Centre for Health & Care, 116 Chaplin Road, Wembley, HA0 4UZ, Tel.: 0208 795 6162

School Nursing
Ms C Bellringer, Professional Facilitator - School Nursing, Wembley Centre for Health & Care, 116 Chaplin Road, Wembley, HA0 4UZ, Tel.: 0208 795 6800

Smoking Cessation
Ms S Sidhu, Acting Smoking Cessation Co-ordinator, Unit 61, The Designworks, Park Parade, Harlesden, London, NW10 4HT, Tel.: 0208 965 2269

Specialist Nursing Services
Ms G Conway, Continence, Wembley Centre for Health & Care, Barham House, 116 Chaplin Road, Wembley, HA0 4UZ, Tel.: 0208 795 6455
Ms S Chahal, Coronary Heart Disease, Coronary Care, Chalkhill Health Centre, Chalkhill Road, Wembley, HA9 9BQ, Tel.: 0208 904 0911
Ms C Mohamed, Coronary Heart Disease, Coronary Care, Chalkhill Health Centre, Chalkhill Road, Wembley, HA9 9BQ, Tel.: 0208 904 0911
Ms L Savek, Diabetic Care, Wembley Centre for Health & Care, 116 Chaplin Road, Wembley, HA0 4UZ, Tel.: 0208 795 6155
Ms L Leaver, Infection Control, Chalkhill Health Centre, Chalkhill Road, Wembley, HA9 9BQ, Tel.: 0208 904 0911
Mr T Wong, Infection Control, Chalkhill Health Centre, Chalkhill Road, Wembley, HA9 9BQ, Tel.: 0208 904 0911
Ms C Sarabay, Palliative Care, Pembride Unit, St Charles Hospital, Exmoor Street, London, W10 6DZ, Tel.: 0208 962 4417
Ms J Parry, Stoma Care, Central Middlesex Hospital, Acton Lane, Park Royal, London, NW10 7NS, Tel.: 0208 965 5733
Nurse, Tissue Viability, Chalkhill Health Centre, Chalkhill Road, Wembley, HA9 9BQ, Tel.: 0208 904 0911

The Homeless/Travellers & Asylum Seekers
Ms L Hunt, Refugees, Wembley Centre for Health & Care, 116 Chaplin Road, Wembley, HA0 4UZ, Tel.: 0208 795 6318
Ms J Wilson, Specialist School Nurse for Homeless Team, Craven Park Health Centre, Shakespeare Crescent, London, NW10 8XW, Tel.: 0208 965 0151

Bromley Hospitals NHS Trust

Trust Headquarters, Princess Royal Univ Hospital
Farnborough Common
ORPINGTON
Kent
BR6 8ND
Tel.: 01689 863000

Community Midwifery
Ms M Brown, Clinical Midwifery Specialist, Community Midwifery, Princess Royal University Hospital, Farnborough Common, Orpington, Kent, BR6 8ND, Tel.: 01689 864827
Ms A Canning, Divisional Head/Head of Midwifery Services, Maternity Admin I, Level 3 South Wing, Princess Royal University Hospital, Tel.: 01689 864887
L/Ward, Princess Royal University Hospital, Farnborough Common, Orpington, Kent, BR6 8ND, Tel.: 01689 864839
Out of hours, Princess Royal University Hospital, Farnborough Common, Orpington, Kent, BR6 8ND, Tel.: 01689 864831

Bromley Primary Care Trust

Trust Headquarters, Bassetts House
Broadwater Gardens, Farnborough
ORPINGTON
Kent, BR6 7UA
Tel.: 01689 853339
Fax: 01689 855662

Child Health
Ms F Pendleton, 14 Ashtree Close, Farnborough, Orpington, Kent, BR6 7UA, Tel.: 01689 880716
Ms K Plumb, Head of Nursing Children, Adolescents & Young People, 14 Ashtree Close, Farnborough, Orpington, Kent, BR6 7UA, Tel.: 01689 880891

Child Health Records
Mr C Marvin, School Health Administrator, CRC, Phoenix Centre, 40 Masons Hill, Bromley, Kent, BR2 9JG,
Over 5s, School Health Dept, Willows Clinic, Red Hill, Chislehurst, BR7 6DA, Tel.: 020 8467 1631
Under 5s, Information Dept, Bassetts House, Tel.: 01689 853339

Child Protection/Safeguarding Children
Ms J Fairfax, Child Protection Team, Bassetts House, Broadwater Gardens, Farnborough, Orpington, Kent, BR6 7UA, Tel.: 01689 853339

Clinical Leads (NSF)
Mr G Burchell, Clinical Lead, Clinical Services & Care Environment, 14 Ashtree Close, Tel.: 01689 880704
Mr C Mulcair, Clinical Lead, Service Development Manager, 14 Ashtree Close, Tel.: 01689 880717
Dr N Lemic, Clinical Lead, Cancer,
Mrs S Southon, Clinical Lead, Older People,

Community Nursing Services
Ms K Bott, Associate Director of Nursing, Bassetts House, Broadwater Gardens, Farnborough, Orpington, Kent, BR6 7UA, Tel.: 01689 853339
Ms C Jones, Executive Nurse, Bassetts House, Broadwater Gardens, Farnborough, Orpington, Kent, BR6 7UA, Tel.: 01689 853339

District Nursing
Ms M Mulholland, Head of Nursing (Adults), Bassetts House, Broadwater Gardens, Farnborough, Orpington, Kent, BR6 7UA, Tel.: 01689 880719

London Strategic Health Authority

Family Planning Services
Ms Y Hopper, Beckenham Clinic, 14 The Crescent, Beckenham, BR3 1DU,
Health Visitors
Ms C Gibson, Specialist Health Visitor for Special Needs 0-19 years, Phoenix Children's Resource Centre, 40 Masons Hill, Bromley, BR2 9JG, Tel.: 020 8466 9988
Paediatric Health Visitor, Phoenix Children's Resource Centre, 40 Masons Hill, Bromley, BR2 9JG, Tel.: 020 8464 7578
Ms L Torpey, Liaison, Health Visitor, Phoenix Children's Resource Centre, 40 Masons Hill, Bromley, BR2 9JG, Tel.: 020 8466 9988
HIV/AIDS
Ms S Barber, HIV Care Services, GU Clinic, Beckenham Hospital, 379 Croydon Road, Beckenham, BR3 3PR, Tel.: 020 8289 6647
Learning Disabilities
Ms R Povey, Deputy Team Manager, Community LD Team, Bassetts Centre, Acorn Way, Starts Hill Road, Farnborough, Orpington, BR6 7WF, Tel.: 01689 853388
Liaison Services
Ms Y Holcroft, Nursing Home Liaison, The Willows Clinic, Red Hill Chislehurst, BR7 6DA, Tel.: 0208 467 1631
Ms J Pasfield, Assistant Clinical Service Manager/Head of Nursing Older People, Orpington Locality, 4 Ashtree Close, c/o Bassetts House, Broadwater Gardens, Farnborough, Orpington, Tel.: 01689 863967
Other Services
Ms M Faulkner, Care Co-ordination for Older People, 55 Chislehurst Road, Orpington, Kent, BR6 0DF, Tel.: 01689 878442
Heart Failure Nurse Team, Summit House, 1st Floor, Glebe Way, West Wickham, Kent, Tel.: 020 8776 3683
Mr A Mowatt, Bromley Alcohol Services (BAS), 171a High Street, Beckenham, Kent, BR3 1AH, Tel.: 020 8663 6883
Ms G Fiumicelli, Co-ordinator, CHD, Summit House, First Floor, Glebe Way, West Wickham, Kent, Tel.: 020 8776 3680
Ms M Nuttall, Co-ordinator, Screening Project Manager, CHD, Summit House, First Floor, Glebe Way, West Wickham, Kent, Tel.: 020 8776 3680
Ms E Dias, Infection Control, Bassetts House, Broadwater Gardens, Farnborough, Orpington, Kent, BR6 7UA, Tel.: 01689 853339
Specialist Nursing Services
Mrs L Burgess, Specialist Nurse, Breast Care, Princess Royal University Hospital, Farnborough Common, Orpington, Kent, BR6 8ND, Tel.: 01689 863175
Ms R Comey, Continence, Princess Plain Clinic, Bromley, BR2 8LD, Tel.: 0208 462 1255
Ms J Sullivan, Continence, Princess Plain Clinic, Bromley, BR2 8LD, Tel.: 0208 462 1255
Ms M Tipson, Specialist Nurse, Diabetic Care, Orpington Hospital, Sevenoaks Road, Orpington, Kent, Tel.: 01689 866065
Ms Y Cho, Co-ordinator, CARTs, Intermediate Care, Bassetts House, Broadwater Gardens, Farnborough, Orpington, Kent, BR6 7UA, Tel.: 01689 853339
Ms G Dunwoody, Tissue Viability, The Willows Clinic, Red Hill, Chislehurst, Tel.: 0208 467 1631
The Homeless/Travellers & Asylum Seekers
Ms S Mather, Primary Care Refugee Project, Health Development Unit, Beckenham Hospital, 379 Croydon Road, Beckenham, Kent, BR3 3QL,

Camden & Islington Mental Health & Social Care NHS Trust
2nd Floor East Wing
St Pancras Hospital
LONDON
NW1 0PE
Tel.: 020 7530 3000

Learning Disabilities
Ms J Hanson, Manager (Camden), Bedford House, 125-133 Camden High Street, London, NW1, Tel.: 020 7974 3737
Mr B Stephens, Manager (Islington), 1 Lowther Road, London, N7 8SL, Tel.: 020 7527 6600

Camden Primary Care Trust
Trust Headquarters, St Pancras Hospital
4 St Pancras Way
LONDON
NW1 0PE
Tel.: 020 7530 3500
Fax.: 020 7530 3104

Admin & Senior Management
Dr A Kessel, Public Health Director, Tel.: 020 7530 3500 ext 5433
Mr R Larkman, Chief Executive,
Ms C Townsend, Director of Specialist Community Services, Executive Office, 4th Floor, East Wing, St Pancras Hospital, St Pancras Way, London, NW1 0PE, Tel.: 020 7530 3070
Child Health
Child Health Information Service, Fax: 020 7530 3836, Crowndale Health Centre, 59 Crowndale Road, London, NW1 1TN, Tel.: 020 7530 3853/3837/3845
Ms N Jirira, Change Implementation Manager, Children & Families, Tel.: 020 7530 2550
Ms F Moorhouse, Advanced Practitioner, Children & Families, Tel.: 020 7530 4300
Ms J Myers, Child Health, St Pancras Hospital, Tel.: 020 7530 5467
Child Health Records
Ms C Brothwood, The Royal Free Hospital, Pond Street, London, NW3 2QG, Tel.: 020 7830 2440
Child Health Information Service, Fax: 020 7530 3836, Crowndale Health Centre, 59 Crowndale Road, London, NW1 1TN, Tel.: 020 7530 3853/3837/3845
Child Protection/Safeguarding Children
Ms S Lynch, St Pancras Hospital, Tel.: 020 7530 3202/3203/4723
Ms J Myers, Specialist Nurse, Child Protection, St Pancras Hospital, Tel.: 020 7530 5467
Clinical Leads (NSF)
Ms M Bisset, Clinical Lead, Cancer,
Dr S Luttrell, Clinical Lead, Care of the Elderly, Tel.: 020 7530 3284
Dr K Hoffman, Clinical Lead, CHD, Tel.: 020 7530 3330
Dr K Hoffman, Clinical Lead, Diabetic Care, Tel.: 020 7530 3330
Community Nursing Services
Ms V Manning, St Pancras Hospital, Tel.: 0207 530 3300
District Nursing
Belsize Priory Health Centre, 208 Belsize Road, NW6 4DJ, Tel.: 020 7530 2600
Crowndale Health Centre, 56 Crowndale Road, NW1 1TU, Tel.: 020 7530 3800
Gospel Oak Clinic, Lismore Circus, NW5 4QF, Tel.: 020 7530 4600
Ms J Gough, Public Health (District Nurses), St Pancras Hospital, Hunter Street Health Centre, London, WC1 1BN, Tel.: 020 7530 4300
Kentish Town Health Centre, 2 Bartholomew Road, NW5, Tel.: 020 7530 4700
Solent Road Centre, NW6 1TP, Tel.: 020 7530 2550
St Albans Clinic, St Albans Road, NW5, Tel.: 020 7530 4800
Equipment Loan Services
Managed by Camden Social Services & Huntley National Care,
Family Planning Services
Ms N Penny, St Pancras Hospital, Tel.: 020 7530 5011
Health Visitors
Ms J Fraser, Special Needs Child (Camden), Health Visitor, Greenland Road, Children's Centre, 4 Greeland Road, NW1 0AS, Tel.: 020 7530 4820
Ms J Gough, Public Health (Health Visitors), St Pancras Hospital,

London Strategic Health Authority

HIV/AIDS
Mr K Miles, AIDS/HIV/STD, Nurse Specialist,
Liaison Services
Ms A Lloyd, UCLH Paediatric Liaison, Tel.: 020 7387 9300 ext 5171
Specialist Nursing Services
Ms J Joseph, Practice Educators, St Pancras Hospital, Tel.: 020 7530 3960
Ms R Haffenden, Respiratory/Cardio Vascular/Diabetes, Asthma, St Pancras Hospital, Tel.: 0207 530 2668
Ms M Wells, Nurse Specialist, Continence, - Stoma, St Pancras Hospital, Tel.: 020 7530 3316
Ms M Davies, Nurse Consultant, Dermatology, 3rd Floor, Bedford House, 125-133 Camden High Street, London, NW1 7JR, Tel.: 0207 685 5805
Ms R Davis, Nurse Consultant, Dermatology, 3rd Floor, Bedford House, 125-133 Camden High Street, London, NW1 7JR, Tel.: 0207 685 5805
Ms J Greening, Nurse Specialist, Elderly Care, St Pancras Hospital, Tel.: 020 7530 3795
Ms M Bisset, Nurse Specialist, Palliative Care, St Pancras Hospital, Tel.: 020 7530 3585
Ms S Kiernan, Nurse Specialist, Tissue Viability, St Pancras Hospital, Tel.: 020 7530 3585
The Homeless/Travellers & Asylum Seekers
Ms E Dirken, Homeless People, PCHP, St Pancras Hospital, Tel.: 020 7530 3444
Ms M Doherty, Homeless People, PCHP, St Pancras Hospital, Tel.: 020 7530 3444
Ms M Garnes, Homeless People, Kings Cross Primary Care Health Centre, 264 Pentonville Road, N1 9JY, Tel.: 020 7530 5770
Mrs L Ibison, Specialist Practitioner, Homeless Families, Tel.: 020 7530 4700
Ms V Manning, Homeless/Travellers/Refugees, St Pancras Hospital, Tel.: 020 7530 3300
Mr C Miller, Homeless People, PCHP, St Pancras Hospital, Tel.: 020 7530 3444
Walk In Centres
Commuter Walk-in Centre, (Under Development), Kings Cross, Mortimer Market Centre, Mortimer Market, off Capper Street, London, WC1E 6AU,

Chelsea & Westminster Healthcare NHS Trust
Trust Headquarters, Chelsea & Westminster Hospital
369 Fulham Road
LONDON
SW10 9NH
Tel.: 020 8746 8000

Community Midwifery
Ms M Cronin, Head of Midwifery & Gynaecology, Tel.: 020 8846 7900
Discharges, Tel.: 020 8746 8800 Voice Mail
Ms M Griffin, Community Midwifery Manager, Tel.: 020 8846 7854
Ms L Ronnie, Clinical Nurse Leader,

City & Hackney Teaching Primary Care Trust
Trust Headquarters, St Leonard's
Nuttall Street
LONDON, N1 5LZ
Tel.: 020 7683 4000
Fax.: 020 7739 8455

Admin & Senior Management
Mrs M Clarke CBE, Director of Quality & Service Improvement (Nurse Director), Tel.: 020 7682 2755
Mr S Gilvin, Director of Primary Care & Adult Community Nursing, St Leonard's, Nuttall Street, London, N1 5LZ, Tel.: 020 7683 4137

Mr S Rowlands, Director of Specialist Community Health Services, St Leonard's, Nuttall Street, London, N1 5LZ, Tel.: 020 7683 4149
Child Health
Mrs N Kline, Lead Nurse Child & Adolescent Services, Tel.: 020 7683 4146
Ms M Smikle, Service Development Manager, Tel.: 020 7683 4314
Child Health Records
Ms M Agu, Operations Manager, St Leonard's, Nuttall Street, London, N1 5LZ, Tel.: 020 7683 4456
Child Protection/Safeguarding Children
Ms J Barker, Nurse Consultant, St Leonard's, Nuttall Street, London, N1 5LZ, Tel.: 020 7683 4315
Ms A Scully, Tel.: 020 7683 4288
Ms I Williecarr, Tel.: 020 7683 4317
Clinical Leads (NSF)
Mr D Sloan, Director of Health Improvement, St Leonard's, Nuttall Street, London, N1 5LZ, Tel.: 020 7683 4249
District Nursing
Ms K Gordon, Modernisation Nurse Manager - District Nurses South, Lower Clapton Health Centre, Tel.: 020 8919 5004
Ms A Lancaster-Parsad, Modernisation Nurse Manager - District Nurses North, Fountayne Road Health Centre, Tel.: 020 7683 4837
Ms S Mason, Modern Matron - District Nursing, Lower Clapton Health Centre, Tel.: 020 8919 5000
Ms S Powell, Modern Matron - District Nursing, Fountayne Road Health Centre, Tel.: 020 7683 4837
Ms B Syms, Modern Matron - District Nursing, Fountayne Road Health Centre, Tel.: 020 7683 4837
Family Planning Services
Ms J Wales, Clinical Nurse Manager, St Leonards, Nuttall Street, London, N1 5LZ, Tel.: 020 7683 4494
Health Visitors
Ms S Baldwin, Modern Matron - Health Visiting, Somerford Grove Health Centre, Tel.: 020 7241 9708
Ms E Blackman, Modernisation Nurse Manager - Health Visitors South, Rushton Medical Centre, Tel.: 020 7739 4840
Ms P Chung, Modernisation Nurse Manager - Health Visitors North, Barton House Health Centre, Tel.: 020 7683 4954
Ms T Gage, Modern Matron - Health Visiting, St Leonard's, Tel.: 020 7683 4474
Ms F Mkandawire, Modern Matron - Health Visiting, Fountayne Road Health Centre, Tel.: 020 7682 4837
Ms G Rooney, Modern Matron - Health Visiting, Rushton Street Medical Centre, Tel.: 020 7739 4840
HIV/AIDS
Ms R Constable, Team Leader, HIV, St Leonard's, Tel.: 020 7683 4300
Learning Disabilities
Ms M Huskisson, Community Team Manager, St Leonard's, Nuttall Street, London, N1 5LZ, Tel.: 020 7683 4338
Ms E Zengerink, Nurse Consultant, St Leonard's, Nuttall Street, London, N1 5LZ, Tel.: 020 7683 4261
Specialist Nursing Services
Ms L Flack, Continence, St Leonard's, Tel.: 020 7683 4253
Ms M Macey, Nurse Specialist, COPD, St Leonard's, Tel.: 020 7682 4000
Ms R Scott, Nurse Specialist, Heart Failure, St Leonard's, Tel.: 020 7682 4000
Ms H Barklem, Nurse, Palliative Care, St Joseph's Hospice, Mare Street, Hackney, E8, Tel.: 020 8525 5000
Ms N Marsh, Nurse, Practice Development, St Leonard's, Tel.: 020 7683 4000
Ms G Crosby, Tissue Viability, St Leonard's, Tel.: 020 7683 4000
The Homeless/Travellers & Asylum Seekers
Health Worker for Travellers, Lower Clapton Health Centre, Tel.: 020 8919 5000
Refuges & Asylum Seekers, The Sanctuary Practice (PMS), John Scott Health Centre, Green Lanes, N4 2NU, Tel.: 020 7683 4766

London Strategic Health Authority

Croydon Primary Care Trust

Trust Headquarters, Knollys House
17 Addiscombe Road
CROYDON
Surrey, CR0 6SR
Tel.: 020 8274 6000

Admin & Senior Management
Ms C Taylor, Chief Executive,
Child Health
Ms J Ardley, Team Leader, Child Hospital at Home, Morland Road Clinic, Tel.: 020 8656 6722
Ms S Wates, Special Needs Children, Morland Road Clinic, Tel.: 020 8656 6722
Child Health Records
Ms S Clarke, Child Health Dept, 12-18 Lennard Road, Tel.: 020 8274 6353
Child Protection/Safeguarding Children
Ms B Ladbury, Child Protection, Mayday Hospital, Energy Room, London Road, Thornton Heath, CR7 7YE, Tel.: 020 8401 3162
Clinical Leads (NSF)
Mr A Brzezicki, Clinical Lead, Cancer,
Community Nursing Services
Ms M Ioannou, Director of Quality Nursing AHPs, Knolly's House, 17 Addiscombe Road, Croydon, Surrey, CR0 6SR, Tel.: 020 8274 6000
Ms C Power, Services Information Officer - One-Stop Information Point, Lennard Road, Tel.: 020 8274 6333
District Nursing
Ms P Leigh, Clinical Lead for District Nurses, Tel.: 020 8274 6229
Equipment Loan Services
Access Ability Centre, 28 Bollogne Road, Croydon, CR0 2QT, Tel.: 020 8664 8860
Family Planning Services
Dr A Elliman, NHS Walk-In Centre, Tel.: 020 8666 0368
Family Planning Service, 45 High Street, Croydon, CR0 1QD, Tel.: 020 8666 0368
Health Visitors
Ms M Jones, Clinical Lead for Health Visitors, Tel.: 020 8274 6234
HIV/AIDS
Ms J Baverstock, Child with HIV/AIDS, Morland Road Clinic, 6 Morland Road, Addiscombe, Croydon, CR0 6NA, Tel.: 020 8656 6722
MS C Grogan, Dept of GU Medicine, Mayday Hospital, Tel.: 020 8401 3002/3006
Liaison Services
Ms M Kanninen, A & E Liaison, Mayday University Hospital, London Road, Thornton Heath, CR7 7YE, Tel.: 020 8401 3658
Ms S Kirchin, Children's Liaison, Mayday University Hospital, London Road, Thornton Heath, CR7 7YE, Tel.: 020 8401 4192
Ms E McGill, Liaison, Hospital District Nurse, Mayday University Hospital, London Road, Thornton Heath, CR7 7YE, Tel.: 020 8401 3147
Ms S Parry, Community Nursing Liaison, Mayday University Hospital, London Road, Thornton Heath, CR7 7YE, Tel.: 020 8401 3147
Pharmacy
Ms E Callaghan, Chief Pharmacist, Knollys House, Tel.: 020 8274 6220
School Nursing
Ms L Dell, Head of School Nursing, Knolly's House, Tel.: 020 8274 6109
Specialist Nursing Services
Ms P Robinson, LTC, Nurse Consultant, Windsor House, 1270 London Road, Norbury, London, SW16 4DH, Tel.: 0208 765 1491
Mrs V Chambers, Senior Community Nurse, Cardiac, 12-18 Lennard Road, Croydon, CR9 2RS, Tel.: 020 8274 6426
Ms T Turner, Continence, Parkway Health Centre, Parkway, New Addington, Croydon, CR0 0JA, Tel.: 01689 842554

Ms M Prentice, Diabetic Care, 12-18 Lennard Road, Croydon, CR9 2RS, Tel.: 020 8274 6332
Ms M Brice, BNF, Nurse Consultant, Heart Failure, Windsor House, 1270 London Road, Norbury, London, SW16 4DH, Tel.: 0208 765 1491
Ms A Bentley, Team Leader, Community Service, Intermediate Care, Morland Lodge, 1st Floor, 4 Morland Road, Croydon, CR0 6NA, Tel.: 020 8662 1026
Ms J Coleman, Palliative Care, Mayday Hospital, Tel.: 020 8401 3000 ext 4906
Mr M Cooper, Palliative Care, Mayday Hospital, Tel.: 020 8401 3000 ext 4906
Ms A Diffley, Palliative Care, Mayday Hospital, Tel.: 020 8401 3000 ext 4906
Ms S Carter, Tissue Viability, 12-18 Lennard Road, Croydon, CR9 2RS, Tel.: 020 8274 6449
The Homeless/Travellers & Asylum Seekers
Ms J Foster, Young Persons Health Advisor, 12-18 Lennard Road, Croydon, Surrey, CR9 2RS, Tel.: 020 8274 6437
Ms J Francois, Team Leader, Homeless Health Team, 12-18 Lennard Road, Croydon, Surrey, CR9 2RS, Tel.: 020 8274 6346
Walk In Centres
Croydon NHS Walk-In Centre, 45 High Street, Croydon, CR0 1QD, Tel.: 020 8666 0555

Ealing Hospital NHS Trust

Trust Headquarters, Ealing Hospital
Uxbridge Road
SOUTHALL
Middlesex, UB1 3HW
Tel.: 020 8967 5000

Acute Specialist Nursing Services
Ms S Ramrachia, Breast Care, Ealing Hospital, Tel.: 020 8967 5693
Ms J Harvey, Diabetic Care, Ealing Hospital, Tel.: 020 8967 5519
Ms A Hetreed, Diabetic Care, Ealing Hospital, Tel.: 020 8967 5519
Ms T Honey, Diabetic Care, Ealing Hospital, Tel.: 020 8967 5519
Ms R Kapoor, Diabetic Care, Ealing Hospital, Tel.: 020 8967 5519
Community Midwifery
Community Midwifery Manager, Tel.: 020 8967 5586
Ms M McLoughlin, Assistant Director of Nursing/Head of Midwifery & Paediatrics, Tel.: 020 8967 5589
Ms R Patterson, Community Midwifery Manager,
Discharge Co-ordinators
Ms S Saylick, Discharge Co-ordinator, Ealing Hospital,
Liaison Services
Ms H Hoade, Community Liaison Sister, Intermediate Care Service, Level 3, Ealing Hospital, Gen Wing, Uxbridge Road, Southall, UB1 3HW, Tel.: 020 8967 5576/5400
Ms S Saulick, Discharge Liaison Nurse, Intermediate Care Service, Level 3, Ealing Hospital, Gen Wing, Uxbridge Road, Southall, UB1 3HW, Tel.: 020 8967 5576
Ms A Skenderian, Discharge Liaison Facilitator, Ealing Hospital, Tel.: 020 8967 5576

Ealing Primary Care Trust

Trust Headquarters
1 Armstrong Way
SOUTHALL
Middlesex, UB2 4SA
Tel.: 020 8893 0303
Fax.: 020 8893 0398

Admin & Senior Management
Mr R Creighton, Chief Executive,
Ms M Saunders, Chair,
Child Health
Child Health Department, Mattock Lane Clinic, 78 Mattock Lane, Ealing, W13 9NZ, Tel.: 020 8383 5757

London Strategic Health Authority

Child Health Records
Child Health Records, Mattock Lane Clinic, 78 Mattock Lane, W13 9NZ, Tel.: 020 8383 5757
Child Health Records, Thelma Golding Centre, 92 Bath Road, Hounslow, Middlesex, TW3 3EL, Tel.: 020 8630 3359

Child Protection/Safeguarding Children
Ms I Owusli-Ansah, P/T HV Child Protection Advisor, Oldfield Family Practice, 285 Greenford Road, Greenford, Tel.: 020 8578 1914
Ms C Adams, Designated Nurse, Child Protection, Windmill Lodge, Uxbridge Road, Southall, Middlesex, UB1 3EU, Tel.: 020 8354 8980
Ms L Fairclough, Advisor, Child Protection, Acton Health Centre, 35-61 Church Road, Acton, W3 8QE, Tel.: 020 8383 8742
Ms P Wear, Named Nurse, Child Protection, Windmill Lodge, Uxbridge Road, Southall, Middlesex, UB1 3EU, Tel.: 020 8354 8863

Clinical Leads (NSF)
Dr P Randev, Clinical Lead, Cancer, Tel.: 01494 817 665

Health Visitors
Ms S Masters, Specialist Health Visitor for Children with special needs, Ealing Child Development Team, Windmill Lodge, Uxbridge Road, Southall, Middlesex, UB1 3EU, Tel.: 020 8354 8404
Ms V Moody, Specialist Health Visitor for Children with special needs, Ealing Child Development Team, Windmill Lodge, Uxbridge Road, Southall, Middlesex, UB1 3EU, Tel.: 020 8354 8404

Liaison Services
Seconded Post, Tel.: 020 8967 5433

Specialist Nursing Services
Ms S Mensah, Haemoglobinopathies, Windmill Lodge, Uxbridge Road, Southall, Middlesex, UB1 3EU, Tel.: 020 8354 8022
Ms S King, Advisor, Continence, Brentford Health Centre, Boston Manor Road, Brentford, Middlesex, TW8 8DS, Tel.: 020 8630 3838

Enfield Primary Care Trust

Trust Headquarters, Holbrook House
Cockfosters Road
BARNET
Hertfordshire, EN4 0DR
Tel.: 0208 272 5500
Fax.: 0208 272 5700

Admin & Senior Management
Ms K Leach, Director of Nursing, Holbrook House, Cockfosters Road, Barnet, Hertfordshire, EN4 0DR, Tel.: 0208 272 5548

Child Health Records
Child Health Records, Holbrook House, Cockfosters Road, Barnet, Hertfordshire, EN4 0DR, Tel.: 0208 272 5500

Child Protection/Safeguarding Children
Ms J Anyaegbunham, Named Nurse, Child Protection, The Laurels Clinic, 110 Barrowell Green, London, N21 3AY, Tel.: 0208 886 2584
Ms L Carmi, Designated Nurse, Child Protection, The Laurels Clinic, 110 Barrowell Green, London, N21 3AY, Tel.: 0208 886 2584

Clinical Leads (NSF)
Dr L Wise, Clinical Lead, Older People,
Dr P Barnes, Clinical Lead, Cancer & Diabetes, Cancer,

District Nursing
Ms M Andrews, Locality Manager, Enfield North, Moorfield Road, Enfield, EN3 6PS, Tel.: 0208 804 7530
Ms K Lewis, Locality Manager, Southgate, N11,N13,N14,N21, Cockfosters, Laurels Clinic, Barrowell Gardens, N21 3AY, Tel.: 0208 882 6532
Out of Hours, Twilight, Night, Tel.: 0208 366 6600

Family Planning Services
Reproductive & Sexual Health, Wenlock House, Tel.: 0208 362 7630

Health Visitors
Ms S Finnie, Paediatric Liaison Health Visitor/CONI, Room 11, Ante-natal Clinic, Chase Farm Hospital, The Ridgeway, Enfield, Middx, EN2 8JL, Tel.: 0208 375 1275

Ms S Lai, Paediatric Liaison Health Visitor/CONI, Room 37 Old Nurses Home, North Middlesex Hospital, Edmonton, N18 1QX, Tel.: 0208 887 4010
Ms M Murrill, Health Visitor, Central Clinic, 5 Pleuna Road, Edmonton, N9 0BU, Tel.: 0208 803 0653

HIV/AIDS
Palliative Care Team, (HIV), Flat 7, St Michael's Site, Tel.: 0208 367 4099

Learning Disabilities
Ms S Hebbes, Manager, Cumbria Village, Chase Farm Hospital Site, The Rigeway, Enfield, EN2 8JL, Tel.: 0208 375 1341

Liaison Services
Ms A Cope, Co-ordinator, Intermediate Care Team & Community Liaison, Magnolia Unit, Tel.: 0208 342 2166

Specialist Nursing Services
Ms S Conroy, Continence, The Laurels Clinic, Barrowell Green, London, N21 3AY, Tel.: 0208 447 8106
Ms M Dooley, Continence, Cedar House, Tel.: 0208 366 6600 ext 4939
Ms L Mossey, Continence, The Laurels Clinic, Barrowell Green, London, N21 3AY, Tel.: 0208 447 8106
Team, (Macmillan, Lymphoedema), Palliative Care, Flat 7, St Michael's Site, Tel.: 0208 367 4099
Ms C Challis, TB, Public Health, Chest Clinic, North Middlesex Hospital, Tel.: 0208 887 2332
Ms J White, TB, Public Health, Chest Clinic, North Middlesex Hospital, Tel.: 0208 887 2332

Epsom & St. Helier NHS Trust

Trust Headquarters, St Helier Hospital
Wrythe Lane
CARSHALTON
Surrey, SM5 1AA
Tel.: 020 8296 2000
Fax.: 020 8641 9391

Acute Specialist Nursing Services
Ms M Miller, Breast Care, Epsom General Hospital, Tel.: 01372 735735 ext 5131
Nurses, Cardiac, Epsom General Hospital, Tel.: 01372 735347
Ms W Dudley, Dermatology, St Helier Hospital, Bleep 589, Tel.: 020 8296 2000
Ms M Booth, Diabetic Care, St Helier Hospital, Bleep 697, Tel.: 020 8296 2000 ext 2563
Ms H Henderson, Diabetic Care, Epsom General Hospital, Tel.: 01372 735735 ext 5444
Ms L O'Donoghue, Diabetic Care, Epsom General Hospital, Tel.: 01372 735735 ext 5444
Ms S Patel, Diabetic Care, Epsom General Hospital, Tel.: 01372 735308 bleep 452
Ms M Rudrum, Diabetic Care, Epsom General Hospital, Tel.: 01372 735735 ext 5444
Ms P Stugnell, Diabetic Care, St Helier Hospital, Bleep 697, Tel.: 020 8296 2000 ext 2563
Mr D Shaw, GU Medicine, St Helier Hospital, Tel.: 020 8296 2000 ext 2543
Ms A Higgins, Haematology, St Helier Hospital, Tel.: 020 8296 2000 ext 2815
Ms J Short, Haematology, St Helier Hospital, Tel.: 020 8296 2000 ext 2815
Ms H Weekes, Haematology, St Helier Hospital, Tel.: 020 8296 2000 ext 2815
Ms G Hickman, Infection Control, St Helier Hospital, Tel.: 020 8296 2000 bleep 753
Ms P Hart, HDU, ITU, St Helier Hospital, Tel.: 020 8296 2000 ext 2171

London Strategic Health Authority

Ms P Battell, Macmillan, St Helier Hospital, Tel.: 020 8296 2000 ext 3199

Ms C Maylin, Macmillan, St Helier Hospital, Tel.: 020 8296 2000 ext 3199

Ms L Reed, Macmillan, St Helier Hospital, Tel.: 020 8296 2000 ext 3199

Ms S Wemyss, Macmillan, St Helier Hospital, Tel.: 020 8296 2000 ext 3199

Ms J Doran, Community, Specialist, Paediatrics, Epsom General Hospital, Tel.: 01372 735735 ext 5265

Ms D Gohill, Nurse Practitioner, Paediatrics, Epsom General Hospital, Tel.: 01372 735735 bleep 555

Ms G Day, Pain Management, St Helier Hospital, Tel.: 020 8296 2000 bleep 580

Ms B O'Keeffe, Pain Management, St Helier Hospital, Tel.: 020 8296 2000 bleep 440

Ms S Clelland, Palliative Care, Epsom General Hospital, Tel.: 01372 735735 ext 6425

Discharges, Respiratory, Epsom General Hospital, Tel.: 01372 735735

Ms P MacDonald, Respiratory, St Helier Hospital, Tel.: 020 8296 2000 ext 3117

Ms H Parnell, Respiratory, St Helier Hospital, Tel.: 020 8296 2000 ext 3514

Mr D Salisbury, Respiratory, St Helier Hospital, Tel.: 020 8296 2000 ext 3117

Ms J Dunwoody, Rheumatology, St Helier Hospital, Tel.: 020 8296 2000 bleep 811

Ms V Dodson, Stoma Care, St Helier Hospital, Bleep 547, Tel.: 020 8296 2000 ext 2640

Ms S Woodward, Stoma Care, - Colorectal, Epsom General Hospital, Tel.: 01372 735232

Mrs P Beldon, Tissue Viability, Epsom General Hospital, Tel.: 01372 735735 ext 5177

Ms W Naish, Urology, Epsom General Hospital, Tel.: 01372 735299

Ms J Pinfield, Urology, St Helier Hospital, Tel.: 020 8296 2000 ext 2809

Ms S Sowton, Urology/Oncology, Epsom General Hospital, Tel.: 01372 735199

Admin & Senior Management

Director of Nursing & Clinical Development, St Helier Hospital, Wrythe Lane, Carshalton, Surrey, SM5 1AA, Tel.: 01372 735204

Child Health

Ms T Hatcher, Paediatric Cystic Fibrosis, Queens Mary's Hospital, Wrythe Lane, Carshalton, SM5 1AA, Tel.: 020 8296 3071

Ms L McGraw, Paediatric Cystic Fibrosis, Queens Mary's Hospital, Wrythe Lane, Carshalton, SM5 1AA, Tel.: 020 8296 2000 ext 3076

Ms M Phillips, Paediatric Home Care Sister, Queens Mary's Hospital, Wrythe Lane, Carshalton, SM5 1AA, Tel.: 020 8296 2000 ext 3075

Ms G Ramsammy-Westmaas, Paediatric Home Care Leader, Queens Mary's Hospital, Wrythe Lane, Carshalton, SM5 1AA, Tel.: 020 8296 2000 ext 3070

Ms A Ryley, Paediatric Asthma, Queens Mary's Hospital, Wrythe Lane, Carshalton, SM5 1AA, Tel.: 020 8296 2000 ext 3077

Community Midwifery

Community Midwives, Women's Health Unit, St Helier Hospital, Wrythe Lane, Carshalton, Surrey, SM5 1AA, Tel.: 020 8296 2990

Mrs A Johnston, Clinical Midwifery Manager, Epsom General Hospital, Dorking Road, Epsom, Surrey, KT18 7EG, Tel.: 01372 735735 ext 6401

Mrs S Morris De Lassalle, Clinical Midwifery Manager, Women's Health Unit, St Helier Hospital, Wrythe Lane, Carshalton, Surrey, SM5 1AA, Tel.: 0208 296 2990

Mrs M Wheeler, Head of Midwifery, Epsom General Hospital, Dorking Road, Epsom, Surrey, KT18 7EG, Tel.: 01372 735735

Mrs M Wheeler, Director of Midwifery Services, Women's Health Unit, St Helier Hospital, Wrythe Lane, Carshalton, Surrey, SM5 1AA, Tel.: 020 8296 2908

Liaison Services

Ms Davison, Discharge Planning, Epsom General Hospital, Dorking Road, Epsom, Surrey, KT18 7EG, Tel.: 01372 735314

Great Ormond Street Hospital for Children NHS Trust

Great Ormond Street Hospital for Children
Great Ormond Street, Bloomsbury
LONDON
WC1N 3JH
Tel.: 020 7405 9200
Fax.: 020 7829 8643

Acute Specialist Nursing Services

Ms N Bennett-Rees, Clinical Nurse Specialist, Bone Marrow Transplant (BMT), Tel.: ext 8820/bleep 0418

Ms M Finch, Clinical Nurse Specialist, Bone Marrow Transplant (BMT), Host Defence, Tel.: ext 0216/bleep 0487

Ms N Hewit, Clinical Nurse Specialist, Bone Marrow Transplant (BMT), Tel.: ext 8584/bleep 0575

Ms C Noctor, Clinical Nurse Specialist, Cardiac, Tel.: ext 8828/bleep 0617

Ms C Carter, Inherited Disease, Clinical Nurse Specialist, Cardio vascular, Tel.: ext 5305

Ms S-J Mead-Regan, Clinical Nurse Specialist, Cardio vascular, Tel.: ext 5305/bleep 1050

Ms C Carter, Advanced, Nurse Practitioner, Cardiothoracic, Tel.: ext 5305

Ms H Dawkins, Specialist Nurse, Cardiothoracic, - Transplantation, Tel.: ext 8829

Ms F Molloy, Advanced, Nurse Practitioner, CCU, Tel.: ext 5708

Ms J Hughes, Clinical Nurse Specialist, Cleft,

Ms S Wright, Clinical Nurse Specialist, Cleft Lip & Palate, Tel.: ext 7949

Ms B Farren, Clinical Nurse Specialist, Clinical Genetics, Tel.: ext 2177

Ms D Coulson, Cardiorespiratory, Clinical Nurse Specialist, Critical Care, Tel.: ext 5646/bleep 1007

Ms C Dawson, Clinical Nurse Specialist, Cystic Fibrosis, Tel.: ext 8813

Ms D Sheehan, Clinical Nurse Specialist, Cystic Fibrosis, Tel.: ext 2328/bleep 0581

Ms L Foster, Clinical Nurse Specialist, Dermatology, Tel.: ext 0068

Mr A Green, Clinical Research Co-ordinator, Dermatology, Tel.: ext 7805/bleep 0508

Ms H Kennedy, Clinical Nurse Specialist, Dermatology, Birthmarks, Tel.: ext 1113

Ms J Linward, Clinical Nurse Specialist, Dermatology, Birth Mark Unit, Tel.: ext 5132

Ms J Stevens, Clinical Nurse Specialist, Dermatology, Tel.: ext 0400/bleep 0359

Ms J Turner, Specialist Nurse, Dermatology, Tel.: ext 0014

Ms S Turner, Clinical Nurse Specialist, Dermatology, Tel.: ext 0068

Ms R Mayers, Clinical Nurse Specialist, Endocrine Surgery, - Adolescent, Tel.: ext 7995/bleep 0110

Ms S Bryan, Clinical Nurse Specialist, Endocrinology, - Paediatrics, Tel.: ext 7995 bleep 0110

Ms S Langham, Clinical Nurse Specialist, Endocrinology, Tel.: ext 8214

Ms L Walsh, Gastro, Nurse Practitioner, Endocrinology,

Ms S Ward, Clinical Nurse Specialist, Endocrinology, Tel.: ext 8214

Ms A Kennett, Clinical Nurse Specialist, ENT Surgery, Maxillofacial & Dental Surgery, Tel.: ext 8825

Ms F Chard, Clinical Nurse Specialist, Epilepsy, Complex,

Ms S Hannan, Clinical Nurse Specialist, Epilepsy, - Surgical, Tel.: ext 5824

Ms J Brind, Clinical Nurse Specialist, Gastroenterology, Tel.: ext 8304/bleep 0921

Ms K Baker, Clinical Nurse Specialist, Haematology, Tel.: ext 7990/bleep 0687

Ms A Barry, Nurse Practitioner, Haematology-Oncology, Tel.: ext 5060

Ms K Bravery, Nurse Practitioner, Haematology-Oncology, Tel.: ext 5723/bleep 0118

Ms A Ho, Specialist Nurse, Haematology-Oncology, Tel.: ext 8810

Ms M Cantwell, Specialist Nurse, Haemodialysis, Tel.: ext 5311/bleep 0400

Ms A Phillott, Clinical Nurse Specialist, Haemophilia, Tel.: ext 8846/bleep 1032

Ms C Gilbert, Clinical Nurse Specialist, Hypoglycaemia, Tel.: ext 0360/bleep 1016

Ms K Fiske, IG Therapy, Specialist Nurse, Immunology, Tel.: ext 5024

Ms J Gaspar, Clinical Nurse Specialist, Immunology, Tel.: ext 5024

Ms L Henderson, Specialist Nurse, Immunology, Tel.: ext 5024/0486

Ms W Mills, Clinical Nurse Specialist, Immunology, Tel.: ext 5024/bleep 0620

Ms A Tulloch, Specialist Nurse, Immunology, Tel.: ext 8556

Ms S MacQueen, Clinical Lead, Clinical Nurse Specialist, Infection Control, Tel.: ext 5284

Ms D Bardell, Clinical Nurse Specialist, Infectious Diseases, Tel.: ext 5284

Ms J Flynn, Clinical Nurse Specialist, Infectious Diseases, Tel.: ext 8266/bleep 0906

Ms J Lawley, Clinical Nurse Specialist, Infectious Diseases, Tel.: ext 8555/bleep 0730

Ms K Berry, Specialist Nurse, IV Therapy, Tel.: ext 0049/bleep 0366

Ms L Mills, Clinical Nurse Specialist, IV Therapy, Tel.: ext 0049

Ms R Lowe, Clinical Nurse Specialist, Leukaemia, Tel.: ext 8833

Ms J Parnell, Psychological, Clinical Nurse Specialist, Medicine, Tel.: ext 5467

Ms N Finnegan, Clinical Nurse Specialist, Metabolic Medicine, Tel.: ext 0366/bleep 2091

Ms M McSweeney, Clinical Nurse Specialist, Metabolic Medicine, Tel.: ext 1037

Ms N Mumford, Clinical Nurse Specialist, Metabolic Medicine, Tel.: ext 5769

Ms L Wright, Dialysis Unit, Clinical Nurse Specialist, Nephro-urology, Tel.: ext 5129

Ms F Blackwell, Clinical Nurse Specialist, Neurology,

Ms C Mostyn, Clinical Nurse Specialist, Neurology, Tel.: ext 5051/bleep 0211

Mr S Lazarus, Clinical Nurse Specialist, Neuro-oncology,

Ms B Ward, Clinical Nurse Specialist, Neuro-oncology, Tel.: ext 5199

Ms M Reynolds, Clinical Nurse Specialist, Neurosciences, (Hydrocephalus), Tel.: ext 0286

Ms S Gettings, Clinical Nurse Specialist, Nutrition, Tel.: ext 8679

Ms R Orton, Clinical Nurse Specialist, Nutrition, Tel.: ext 8304/bleep 0673

Ms P Cosgrove, Clinical Nurse Specialist, Orthopaedics, Tel.: ext 8132/bleep 0711

Ms Z Cherrett, Craniofacial, Specialist Nurse, Paediatrics,

Mr M Clements, CATS Team, Nurse Practitioner, Paediatrics,

Ms J Cooke, Tracheostomy Care Surgery, Clinical Nurse Specialist, Paediatrics, Tel.: ext 8257/bleep 0712

Ms J Denyer, Epidermolysis Bullosa, Clinical Nurse Specialist, Paediatrics, Tel.: ext 0068/bleep 0693

Ms H Fletcher, Symptom Care Team, Specialist Nurse, Paediatrics,

Ms L Hackett, IPPD (Private Patients), Clinical Nurse Specialist, Paediatrics, Tel.: ext 5114/bleep 0483

Ms K Hammond, CATS, Specialist Nurse, Paediatrics, Tel.: ext 4855

Ms R Higson, CATS, Specialist Nurse, Paediatrics, Tel.: ext 4855

Mr D Leverett, Clinical Nurse Specialist, Paediatrics, (UCH/GOSH)-Leucopheresis, Tel.: 020 7387 9300 x 8255

Ms V Milovanovic, Perioperative, Specialist Nurse, Paediatrics, Tel.: ext 7969/bleep 0339

Mr M O'Brien, Occupational Therapy, Clinical Nurse Specialist, Paediatrics, Tel.: ext 5929/bleep 0982

Ms L Shields, Advanced, Nurse Practitioner, Paediatrics, Children's Acute Transport Service (CATS), Tel.: ext 4855

Ms C Wenden, Symptom Care Team, Clinical Nurse Specialist, Paediatrics, Tel.: ext 8678

Ms A White, Craniofacial, Clinical Nurse Specialist, Paediatrics, Tel.: ext 0674

Ms J Xu-Bayford, Gene Therapy, Clinical Nurse Specialist, Paediatrics, Tel.: ext 8821

Ms T Boggs, Clinical Nurse Specialist, Pain Management, Tel.: ext 5940

Ms L Bruce, Clinical Nurse Specialist, Pain Management, Tel.: ext 5940/bleep 0422

Ms K Hunt, Clinical Nurse Specialist, Pain Management, Tel.: ext 5940

Ms R Hall, Clinical Nurse Specialist, Plastic Surgery, Tel.: ext 8537

Ms Y Flynn, Hypertension, Clinical Nurse Specialist, Pulmonary Disorder, Tel.: ext 1007/bleep 0863

Ms T Kleidon, Interventional, Clinical Nurse Specialist, Radiology, Tel.: ext 7856/bleep 0426

Ms L Ridley, Clinical Nurse Specialist, Radiology, Interventional, Tel.: ext 0491

Ms S Bradley, Clinical Nurse Specialist, Renal, Tel.: ext 8815

Ms T Calvert, Clinical Nurse Specialist, Renal, Tel.: ext 5353/bleep 0742

Ms C Jennings, Clinical Nurse Specialist, Renal, - Transplantation,

Ms J Pullen, Specialist Nurse, Renal, - Transplantation, Tel.: ext 8815

Ms P Livermore, Nurse Practitioner, Rheumatology, Tel.: ext 8484/bleep 0533

Ms R McGowan, Clinical Nurse Specialist, Rheumatology, Tel.: ext 5826/blee 0416

Ms H Johnson, Clinical Nurse Specialist, Stoma Care, Tel.: ext 5695/bleep 0609

Ms M Comac, Clinical Nurse Specialist, Symptom Care, - Paediatrics, Tel.: ext 8678

Ms J Hemsley, Clinical Nurse Specialist, Symptom Care, - Paediatrics, Tel.: ext 8678

Ms M Scanes, Live Donor Co-ordinator, Clinical Nurse Specialist, Transplant, Tel.: ext 8172/bleep 0400

Ms N Shaw, Cardiothoracic, Sister, Transplant, Tel.: ext 8828

Ms B Carr, Clinical Nurse Specialist, Urology, - Paediatrics, Tel.: ext 5916 bleep 0260

Ms L Healiss, Clinical Nurse Specialist, Urology, - Paediatrics, Tel.: bleep 0260

Ms K Ryan, Clinical Nurse Specialist, Urology, - Paediatrics, Tel.: ext 7863

Ms K Walder, Clinical Nurse Specialist, Vascular, (Vasculitis), Tel.: ext 0062/bleep 0907

Admin & Senior Management

Ms E Brennan, Nurse Consultant, Renal Transplant & Medicine, Tel.: ext 5102/bleep 0043

Mr C Caldwell, Assistant Chief Nurse, Acute Medical Services (AMS) & Staff Development, Tel.: ext 8336/bleep 0201

Ms S Chapman, Clinical Site Practitioner, Nurse Consultant, Tel.: ext 8465/bleep 0005

Ms J Ellis, Chief Nurse, Tel.: ext 8604

Ms A Gregorowski, Nurse Consultant, Adolescent Medicine, Tel.: ext 5150

Ms K Halford, Assistant Chief Nurse, Anaesthetics & Surgical Services (DASS) & Practice Development, Tel.: ext 5576/bleep 0403

Ms C Joyce, Assistant Chief Nurse, Nursing & Workforce Development, Tel.: ext 5581

Ms C Twomey, Assistant Chief Nurse, Cardio Respiratory & Critical Care (CRACC) & Advanced Nursing Practice, Tel.: ext 8019

Ms J Williss, Deputy Chief Nurse, Tel.: ext 8361

London Strategic Health Authority

Ms K Khair, Nurse Consultant, Haematology, Tel.: ext 8846/bleep 0610

Ms L May, Nurse Consultant, Neurology, Tel.: ext 8826/bleep 2058

Child Protection/Safeguarding Children

Ms L Cooke, Named Nurse, Child Protection, Tel.: ext 5126/bleep 0650

Ms G Earl, Nurse Consultant, Child Protection, Tel.: ext 7834/bleep 0860

HIV/AIDS

Ms M Clapson, HIV/AIDS, Clinical Nurse Specialist, Tel.: ext 8231/bleep 0261

Liaison Services

Ms J Jacob, Liaison Nurse, Cardiac, CRACC, Tel.: ext 8382

Ms C Noctor, Liaison Nurse, Cardiac, CRIC, Tel.: ext 8828

Ms M Goodwin, Cardiac, Liaison Nurse, Cardiothoracic, Tel.: ext 5909

Ms N Laing, Liaison Sister, Family Health, PICU, Tel.: ext 8808/bleep 0678

Ms E Rose, Support Worker, Family Health, NICU, Tel.: ext 8812

Ms A Scales, Liaison Sister, Family Health, PICU, Tel.: ext 8808/8683

Ms P Shroff, Liaison Nurse, Family Health, PICU, Tel.: ext 8808

Ms H Waddington, Liaison Nurse, Family Health, CRACC, Tel.: ext 8812

Ms M Wallis, Nurse Advisor, Neonatal, Tel.: ext 0439/bleep 0697

Ms M Craig, Community Link Team Leader, Ophthalmology, Tel.: ext 0487

Ms L Howlett, Spinal, Liaison Nurse, Orthopaedics, Tel.: ext 8238/8807

Ms S Penney, Liaison Nurse, Rheumatology, Tel.: ext 5826

Matrons/Modern Matrons

Ms N Stephens, Modern Matron, Anaesthetics, Theatres, Tel.: ext 5894/bleep 1005

Ms S Cullen, Acting, Modern Matron, Cardiac, Critical Care, Tel.: ext 8828

Ms T Norris, Modern Matron, Cleft, Tel.: ext 1004/bleep 0808

Ms Z Wilks, Modern Matron, Gastroenterology, Endocrinology, Metabolic Medicine, Adolescent Med, Outpatients, Genetics, Tel.: ext 5080/bleep 0387

Ms K De Wet, Modern Matron, General Surgery, Neo-natal Surgery, Orthopaedics & Spinal, Tel.: ext 8477/bleep 2035

Ms J Bayliss, Modern Matron, Haematology-Oncology, Pallative Care, Tel.: ext 0076/bleep 437

Ms W Pearson, Modern Matron, Intensive Care, - Paediatrics, (PICU), Tel.: ext 8809

Ms C Stopp, Modern Matron, Intensive Care, Neo Natal (NICU), Tel.: ext 8812

Ms L Pilgrim, Modern Matron, Nephro-urology, Tel.: ext 8814

Ms J Robinson, Modern Matron, Neurosciences, Tel.: ext 0467/0289

Ms H Hatter, Ladybird & Angio, Modern Matron, Paediatrics, Tel.: ext 8829/0203

Ms B Norman, Acute General, Modern Matron, Paediatrics, North Middlesex Hospital, Tel.: 020 8887 4099 ext 3099

Ms C Wray, Acute General, Modern Matron, Paediatrics, North Middlesex Hospital, Tel.: bleep 164

Ms M Ferguson, Modern Matron, Respiratory, Transitional Care Unit (TCU), Tel.: ext 5402/bleep 0984

Ms A Philps, Modern Matron, Rheumatology, Bone Marrow Transplant, Infectious Diseases, Dermatology, Tel.: ext 0497/bleep 0904

Other Services

Ms I Dodkins, Extra Corporal Membrane Oxygenation Co-ordinator, Tel.: ext 8652

Mr D Fisher, Counsellor Renal Unit, Tel.: ext 8153

Ms M O'Callaghan, Extra Corporal Membrane Oxygenation Co-ordinator, Tel.: ext 8180/0679

Ms E Polke, Retrieval Co-ordinator - CATS, Tel.: ext 4856

Ms M Porritt, Extra Corporal Membrane Oxygenation Co-ordinator, Tel.: ext 8652

Mr M Shaw, Extra Corporal Membrane Oxygenation Co-ordinator, Tel.: ext 8652

Ms S Simpson, Resuscitation Services Manager, Tel.: ext 8197

Ms L Smith, Extra Corporal Membrane Oxygenation Co-ordinator, Tel.: ext 8400

Mr P Yearley, Ward Manager, Mildred Creak Unit, Tel.: ext 5565

Ms C Walsh, Theatres Co-ordinator, Haematology-Oncology, Tel.: ext 0573/bleep 0419

Greenwich Teaching Primary Care Trust

Trust Headquarters
31-37 Greenwich Park Street
GREENWICH
SE10 9LR
Tel.: 020 8293 6700
Fax.: 020 8269 0787

Admin & Senior Management

Ms J Bell, Director of Intermediate Care & Older People Services, Highpoint House, Tel.: 020 8836 4637

Mr J Burden, Director of Primary Care, Highpoint House, Shookers Hill, London, SE18 3RZ, Tel.: 0208 836 4611

Ms A Burn, Director of Organisational Dev & Support, 31-37 Greenwich Park Street, Greenwich, SE10 9LR, Tel.: 020 8293 6774

Mr G Elvy, Director of Finance, 31-37 Greenwich Park Street, Greenwich, SE10 9LR, Tel.: 020 8293 6735

Dr D Holt, Director of Public Health, 31-37 Greenwich Park Street, Greenwich, SE10 9LR, Tel.: 020 8293 6717

Ms S Jones, Director of Services for Young People & Children, Highpoint House, Tel.: 020 8836 4608

Dr J May, PEC Chair, 31-37 Greenwich Park Street, Greenwich, SE10 9LR, Tel.: 020 8293 6700

Mr K May, Chairman, 31-37 Greenwich Park Street, Greenwich, SE10 9LR, Tel.: 020 8293 6700

Ms A O'Brien, Director of Modernisation, Highpoint House, Tel.: 020 8836 4616

PCT Lead Nurse, 31-37 Greenwich Park Street, Greenwich, SE10 9LR, Tel.: 020 8293 6717

Ms J Schofield, Chief Executive, 31-37 Greenwich Park Street, Greenwich, SE10 9LR, Tel.: 020 8293 6700

Child Health

Dr D Clow, Consultant Paediatrician, Market Street Clinic, 16/20 Market Street, Woolwich, SE18 6QR, Tel.: 020 8855 2697

Ms W Faulknall, Community Children's Nursing Team, Queen Elizabeth Hospital, Stadium Road, Woolwich, SE18 4QH, Tel.: 020 8836 5275

Ms R Matthews, Looked After Children, Market Street Clinic, Tel.: 020 8317 9415

Dr P W D Meerstadt, Consultant Community Paediatrician, Child Development Centre, 3 Wensley Close, Eltham, SE9 5AB, Tel.: 020 8850 8165

Child Health Records

Ms J Reid, Information Manager, Memorial Hospital, Shooters Hill, Woolwich, SE18 3RZ, Tel.: 020 8836 6385

Child Protection/Safeguarding Children

Ms L Kennard, Designated Nurse, Adhikaar Centre, 93 Tudway Road, Kidbrooke, SE3 9YB, Tel.: 020 8319 3430

Ms P Wren, Named Nurse, Adhikaar Centre, 93 Tudway Road, Kidbrooke, SE3 9YB, Tel.: 020 8319 3430

Clinical Leads (NSF)

Mr J Burden, Clinical Lead, Cancer, Highpoint House, Tel.: 020 8836 4611

Ms J Bell, Clinical Lead, Care of the Elderly, Highpoint House, Tel.: 020 8836 4637

London Strategic Health Authority

Dr T Dyke, Clinical Lead, CHD, 31-37 Greenwich Park Street, Tel.: 020 8293 6711

Dr T Dyke, Clinical Lead, Diabetic Care, 31-37 Greenwich Park Street, Tel.: 020 8293 6711

Dr T Challacombe, Clinical Lead, PEC Member - Vanbrugh Group Practice 2000, MH, Vanbrugh Hill Health Centre, Vanbrugh Hill, Greenwich, SE10 9HQ, Tel.: 020 8312 6090

District Nursing

Ms J Balcombe, Associate Nurse - Arsenal Locality, Market Street Clinic, 16/20 Market Street, Woolwich, SE18 6QR, Tel.: 020 8317 9415

Ms G Ekpo-Daniels, Associate Nurse - Meridian Locality, Millennium Village Health Centre, School Bank Road, Greenwich, SE10 5QN, Tel.: 020 8312 8757

Out of Hours - Emergencies/District Nurses, Tel.: Weekend & Bank Holidays 020 8854 8888, Twilight (Evening Service) 020 8856 5237, Ms L Stenning, Associate Nurse - Eltham Locality, Manor Brook Medical Centre, 117 Brook Lane, Blackheath, SE3 0EN, Tel.: 020 8856 6582

Family Planning Services

Ms F Dickson, Lead Nurse Family Planning, Market Street Clinic, Tel.: 020 8317 9415

Health Visitors

Ms G Hall, Sickle Cell & Thalassaemia, Health Visitor, Galllions Reach Health Centre, Bentham Road, Thamesmead, London, SE28 8BE, Tel.: 020 8311 4798

Ms E Infinnw, Sickle Cell & Thalassaemia, Health Visitor, Galllions Reach Health Centre, Bentham Road, Thamesmead, London, SE28 8BE, Tel.: 020 8311 4798

Ms S Morton, Health Visitor, Child Development Centre, Bungalow 3, Wensley Close, Eltham, SE9 5AB, Tel.: 020 8859 2065

Learning Disabilities

Ms C Morris, Manager, Wensley Close, Eltham, SE9 5AB, Tel.: 020 8294 1883

Liaison Services

Ms K Cooke, Maternity Liaison Health Visitor, Queen Elizabeth Hospital, Tel.: 020 8836 5387

Ms G Tew, Maternity Liaison Health Visitor, Queen Elizabeth Hospital, Tel.: 020 8836 4889

Other Services

Prison Health Services - PCT Lead, Langley Gifford, Highpoint House, Memorial Hospital, Tel.: 020 8836 4224

School Nursing

Ms J Hyde, Head of School Nursing, Passey Place Centre, 32a Passey Place, Eltham, SE9 5DQ, Tel.: 020 8859 4609

Smoking Cessation

Mr I Ojo, 1 Hyde Vale, Tel.: 020 8694 7328

Specialist Nursing Services

Ms L Phillips, Continuing Care, Specialist Nurse, Cardiac, Millenium Village Health Centre, Tel.: 020 8312 8737

Ms B William, Specialist Nurse, CHD, Millenium Village Health Centre, Tel.: 020 8312 8738

Ms L Kehinde, Nurse, Continence, Memorial Hospital, Tel.: 0208 836 6389

Ms A Stennett, Specialist Nurse, Diabetic Care, Millenium Village Health Centre, Tel.: 020 8312 8737

Ms G Orrell, Nurse, Infection Control, 31-37 Greenwich Park Street, Tel.: 020 8293 6779

Ms G Orrell, Nurse, Infection Control,

Ms V McClinton, COPD, Specialist Nurse, Respiratory, Millenium Village Health Centre, Tel.: 020 8312 8740

Ms S Brooks, Specialist Nurse, TB, Fairfield Centre, Fairfield Grove, Charlton, SE7 8TX, Tel.: 020 8305 3040

The Homeless/Travellers & Asylum Seekers

Ms M Cusick, Travellers, Health Visitor, St Mark's Medical Centre, Tel.: 020 8317 3297

Ms H Foot, Homeless, Health Visitor, Market Street Clinic, Tel.: 020 8317 9415

Guy's & St. Thomas' NHS Foundation Trust

Guy's Hospital
St Thomas' Street
LONDON
SE1 9RT
Tel.: 020 7188 7188

Acute Specialist Nursing Services

Ms G Gembarska, ENT Preassessment, 14th Floor, Guy's Tower, Guy's Hospital, Tel.: 020 7188 0798

Mr T Grant, ENT Preassessment, 14th Floor, Guy's Tower, Guy's Hospital, Tel.: 020 7188 0798

Ms U Kirwan, Hypertension, Clinical Nurse Specialist, Acute Medicine, 4th Floor, New Guy's House, Guy's Hospital, Tel.: 020 7188 3170

Ms M Bailey, Pre-dialysis, Clinical Nurse Specialist, Anaemia, Tel.: 020 7188 7542

Ms F Coldstream, Pre-dialysis, Nurse Consultant, Anaemia, Tel.: 020 7188 5694

Ms S Cox, Pre-dialysis, Nurse Consultant, Anaemia, Tel.: 020 7188 5694

Ms R Burch, Clinical Nurse Specialist, Breast Care, Tel.: 020 7188 0668

Ms R Burch, Clinical Nurse Specialist, Breast Care, 11th Floor, North Wing, St Thomas's Hospital, Tel.: 020 7188 0868

Ms T Flannery, Liaison, Clinical Nurse Specialist, Cardiac, Tel.: 020 7188 0982

Ms C Screeche-powell, Liaison, Clinical Nurse Specialist, Cardiac, Tel.: 020 7188 0982

Ms J Sanders, Clinical Nurse Specialist, Cardiac Rehabilitation, Tel.: 020 7188 0946

Ms A Woodward, Clinical Nurse Specialist, Cardiac Rehabilitation, Tel.: 020 7188 0946

Ms J Cavanagh, Clinical Nurse Manager, Cardiology, Tel.: 020 7188 1005

Mr N Webb, Non invasive, Clinical Nurse Manager, Cardiology, Tel.: bleep 2536

Mr R Lee, CCU, Clinical Nurse Manager, Cardiothoracic,

Ms R Cummings, Disease, Clinical Nurse Specialist, Colorectal, 1st Floor, North Wing, St Thomas's Hospital, Tel.: 020 7188 2564/6485

Ms F Hibberts, Benign, Clinical Nurse Specialist, Colorectal, 1st Floor, North Wing, St Thomas's Hospital, Tel.: 020 7188 2568

Ms V Ratcliff, Clinical Nurse Specialist, Continuing Care, - Cardiac, Tel.: 020 7188 0946

Ms T Garibaldinos, Contact Clinic/Photoperesis, Clinical Nurse Specialist, Dermatology, Dowling Day Unit, 1st Floor, Block 7, South Wing, Tel.: 020 7188 6386/6290

Mr I Gosling, IV Therapy Unit, Clinical Nurse Specialist, Dermatology, Dermatology Dept, 3rd Floor, Block 7, South Wing, Tel.: 020 7188 6309

Ms T Hung, Macmillan, Clinical Nurse Specialist, Dermatology, Dermatology Outpatient Dept, 1st Floor, Block 7, South Wing, Tel.: 020 7188 6384

Ms L Hunter, Outpatient Clinic, Clinical Nurse Specialist, Dermatology, Dermatology Outpatient Dept, 1st Floor, Block 7, South Wing, Tel.: 020 7188 6440 bleep 0118

Ms G Ogden, Laser Therapy, Clinical Nurse Specialist, Dermatology, Dermatology Dept, 3rd Floor, Block 7, South Wing, Tel.: 020 7188 6284 Page 881893

Ms J Smithson, Laser Therapy, Clinical Nurse Specialist, Dermatology, Dermatology Dept, 3rd Floor, Block 7, South Wing, Tel.: 020 7188 6283 Page 824731

Ms E Symmons, Laser, Biopsy, Keloid Services, Nurse Practitioner, Dermatology, Dermatology Dept, 3rd Floor, Block 7, South Wing, Tel.: 020 7188 6309

Ms S Burmiston, Clinical Nurse Specialist, Diabetes, 3rd Floor Lambeth Wing, St Thomas' Hospital, Lambeth Palace Road, London, SE1 7EH, Tel.: 020 7188 6284

Ms P Gilby, Clinical Nurse Specialist, Diabetes, 3rd Floor Lambeth Wing, St Thomas' Hospital, Lambeth Palace Road, London, SE1 7EH, Tel.: 020 7188 1934

Ms J Kidd, Clinical Nurse Specialist, Diabetes, 3rd Floor Lambeth Wing, St Thomas' Hospital, Lambeth Palace Road, London, SE1 7EH, Tel.: 020 7188 1934

Ms Z Mcmahon, Lipid, Clinical Nurse Specialist, Diabetes, 3rd Floor Lambeth Wing, St Thomas' Hospital, Lambeth Palace Road, London, SE1 7EH, Tel.: 020 7188 1261

Ms S Pender, Clinical Nurse Specialist, Diabetes, 3rd Floor Lambeth Wing, St Thomas' Hospital, Lambeth Palace Road, London, SE1 7EH, Tel.: 020 7188 1934

Ms J Cluckie, Stroke (OPAL), Clinical Nurse Specialist, Elderly Care, Mark Ward, 9th Floor, North Wing, St Thomas's Hospital, Tel.: 020 7188 2887

Ms L Breen, Clinical Nurse Specialist, Endocrinology, 3rd Floor Lambeth Wing, St Thomas' Hospital, Lambeth Palace Road, London, SE1 7EH, Tel.: 020 7188 1971

Ms L Doig, Clinical Nurse Specialist, Endoscopy, 1st Floor, College House, St Thomas's Hospital, Tel.: 020 7188 2493

Ms J Hirst, Clinical Nurse Specialist, Gastroenterology, 1st Floor, College House, St Thomas's Hospital, Tel.: 020 7188 2487

Ms M Lyons, Bio-feedback, Clinical Nurse Specialist, GI, 1st Floor, North Wing, St Thomas's Hospital, Tel.: 020 7188 4192

Ms A Mengstu, Ulcer Care, Clinical Nurse Specialist, GI, 1st Floor, North Wing, St Thomas's Hospital,

Ms M Small, Nutrition Support, Clinical Nurse Specialist, GI, 3rd Floor, Lambeth Wing, St Thomas's Hospital, Tel.: 020 7188 2009

Ms V Bevan, Clinical Nurse Specialist, Haematology, Tel.: 020 7188 2755

Ms K Lambe, Clinical Nurse Specialist, Haematology, Tel.: 020 7188 9333

Ms L Bishop, Nurse Consultant, Haematology-Oncology, Tel.: 020 7188 1431

Ms L Dunn, Clinical Nurse Manager, Haemophilia, Tel.: 020 7188 2792

Ms J Mitchell, Community, Clinical Nurse Specialist, Haemophilia, Tel.: 020 7188 2771

Ms J Stanley, Community, Clinical Nurse Specialist, Haemophilia, Tel.: 020 7188 2790

Ms E Coady, Nurse Consultant, Heart Failure, - Cardiac, Tel.: 020 7188 2045

Ms C Hazeldine, Acute Medicine, Clinical Nurse Specialist, Heart Failure, 2nd Floor, Block 6, South Wing, St Thomas's Hospital, Tel.: 020 7188 5671

Ms F Hodson, Clinical Nurse Specialist, Heart Failure, Tel.: 020 7188 9196

Ms S Moore, Clinical Nurse Specialist, Lung Care, Tel.: 020 7188 4739

Ms D Lord, Senior Nurse, Palliative Care, Tel.: 020 7188 4747

Ms L Burnapp, Living donars, Nurse Consultant, Renal, Tel.: 020 7188 5688

Ms S Clovis, Clinical Nurse Specialist, Renal, - Prostate, Tel.: 020 7188 7339

Ms S Clovis, Prostate, Clinical Nurse Specialist, Renal, Tel.: 020 7188 7339

Ms S Frame, CAPD Community, Clinical Nurse Specialist, Renal, Tel.: 020 7188 5676

Ms G Githens-Mazer, Clinical Nurse Specialist, Renal, - Anaemia, Tel.: 020 7188 5697

Ms I Gordon, Living Donors, Clinical Nurse Specialist, Renal, Tel.: 020 7188 5705

Ms T Jegede, Out-patients, Clinical Nurse Manager, Renal, - Urology, Tel.: 020 7188 9091

Ms C Kerr, Outpatients, Clinical Nurse Specialist, Renal, Tel.: 020 7188 5679

Ms S Mien Cohen, Diabetic, Clinical Nurse Specialist, Renal, Tel.: 020 7188 5684

Ms D Mndle, Haemodialysis, Clinical Nurse Manager, Renal, Tel.: 020 7188 0863

Ms J Murray, In-patients, Clinical Nurse Manager, Renal, - Urology, Tel.: 020 7188 5968

Ms N Nichols, Brachy Therapy, Clinical Nurse Specialist, Renal, Tel.: 020 7188 7339

Ms J Aquinos, Chest Department, Clinical Nurse Specialist, Respiratory, 1st Floor, Lambeth Wing, St Thomas's Hospital, Tel.: 020 7188 5823

Ms C Eames, Chest Department, Clinical Nurse Specialist, Respiratory, 1st Floor, Lambeth Wing, St Thomas's Hospital, Tel.: 020 7188 5823

Ms J Managan, Chest Department, Clinical Nurse Specialist, Respiratory, 1st Floor, Lambeth Wing, St Thomas's Hospital, Tel.: 020 7188 5823

Ms A Quinn, Chest Department, Clinical Nurse Specialist, Respiratory, 1st Floor, Lambeth Wing, St Thomas's Hospital, Tel.: 020 7188 5823

Ms E Waring, Sexual Dysfunction, Clinical Nurse Specialist, Sexual Health, - Cardiac, Tel.: 020 7188 0727

Mr N Westerdale, Clinical Nurse Specialist, Sickle Cell, Tel.: 020 7188 4227

Ms N Crawley, Clinical Nurse Specialist, Stoma Care, Ground Floor, Lambeth Wing, St Thomas's Hospital, Tel.: 020 7188 4192

Ms R Davenport, Clinical Nurse Specialist, Stoma Care, Ground Floor, Lambeth Wing, St Thomas's Hospital, Tel.: 020 7188 4192

Ms M Northover, Clinical Nurse Specialist, Stoma Care, Ground Floor, Lambeth Wing, St Thomas's Hospital, Tel.: 020 7188 4192

Ms E Shields, Clinical Nurse Specialist, Stoma Care, Ground Floor, Lambeth Wing, St Thomas's Hospital, Tel.: 020 7188 4192

Ms J Beaven, PDN, Clinical Nurse Specialist, Surgery, 15th Floor, Guy's Tower, Guy's Hospital, Tel.: 020 7188 6498

Mr J Cross, Orthopaedic Preassessment, Clinical Nurse Specialist, Surgery, 1st Floor Thomas Guy House, Guy's Hospital, Tel.: 020 7188 4479

Ms G DeLuca, Tissue Viability, Clinical Nurse Specialist, Surgery, 5th Floor Thomas Guy House, Guy's Hospital, Tel.: 020 7188 2518

Ms P Feast, Macmillan Head & Neck, Clinical Nurse Specialist, Surgery, 14th Floor, Guy's Tower, Guy's Hospital, Tel.: 020 7188 0802

Ms H Lavis, Orthopaedic Preassessment, Clinical Nurse Specialist, Surgery, 1st Floor Thomas Guy House, Guy's Hospital, Tel.: 020 7188 7690

Ms S Michie, Hand Trauma, Clinical Nurse Specialist, Surgery, Alan Apley Ward, 11th Floor N Wing, St Thomas's Hospital, Tel.: 020 7188 7628

Ms S Patt, Plastics Preassessment, Clinical Nurse Specialist, Surgery, Alan Apley Ward, 11th Floor N Wing, St Thomas's Hospital, Tel.: 020 7188 7267

Ms H Prince, Plastics Dressings Clinic, Clinical Nurse Specialist, Surgery, Alan Apley Ward, 11th Floor N Wing, St Thomas's Hospital, Tel.: 020 7188 7628

Ms S Masterson, Acute Medicine, Clinical Nurse Specialist, Tissue Viability, 5th Floor, Thomas Guy House, Guy's Hospital, Tel.: 020 7188 2518

Ms H O'Sullivan, Clinical Nurse Specialist, Transplant, Tel.: 020 7188 5715

Ms J Atkinson, Clinical Nurse Specialist, Upper GI, 11th Floor, North Wing, St Thomas's Hospital, Tel.: 020 7188 2673

Ms D Sherlaw, Clinical Nurse Specialist, Upper GI, 11th Floor, North Wing, St Thomas's Hospital, Tel.: 020 7188 2673

Ms C Underwood, Clinical Nurse Specialist, Upper GI, 11th Floor, North Wing, St Thomas's Hospital, Tel.: 020 7188 2673

Ms M Carmichael, Research, Clinical Nurse Specialist, Vascular, 1st Floor, North Wing, St Thomas's Hospital,

Child Health

Ms C Alexander, NICU, Clinical Nurse Manager, Tel.: 020 718 84038

Ms L Ferguson, PICU, Clinical Nurse Manager, Tel.: 020 718 84599

London Strategic Health Authority

Ms D Parker, Cardiac & Neuro - savannagh, Clinical Nurse Manager, Tel.: 020 718 84553

Ms A Philips, NICU, Clinical Nurse Manager, Tel.: 020 718 84039

Ms P Rasmussen, Chronic Renal Failure, Clinical Nurse Specialist, - Paediatrics, Tel.: 020 718 84590

Ms D Saunders, General Paediatrics, Clinical Nurse Manager, Tel.: 020 718 82473

Ms J Searle, Clinical Nurse Specialist, Asthma, Tel.: 020 718 84613

Ms G Hollins, Motility, Clinical Nurse Specialist, Bowel, Tel.: 020 718 84617

Ms K Chou, Outreach, Clinical Nurse Specialist, Cardiac, Tel.: 020 718 84546

Ms D Duggan, Outreach, Clinical Nurse Specialist, Cardiac, Tel.: 020 718 84546

Ms P Kenney, Outreach, Clinical Nurse Specialist, Cardiac, Tel.: 020 718 84546

Ms E Simmonds, Outreach, Clinical Nurse Specialist, Cardiac, Tel.: 020 718 84546

Ms M Cook, Fetal Counsellor, Clinical Nurse Specialist, Cardiology, Tel.: 020 718 84538

Ms A Lai, Fetal, Clinical Nurse Specialist, Cardiology, Tel.: 020 718 82308

Ms S Rollings, Fetal, Clinical Nurse Specialist, Cardiology, Tel.: 020 718 82308

Ms V Isaacs, Clinical Nurse Specialist, Cleft, Tel.: 020 718 89336

Ms E Southby, Clinical Nurse Specialist, Cleft, Tel.: 020 718 81319

Ms E Watermouth, Clinical Nurse Specialist, Cleft, Tel.: 020 718 86217

Ms A Lashwood, PGD, Clinical Nurse Specialist, Clinical Genetics, Tel.: 020 718 81379

Ms A Oboko, Clinical Nurse Specialist, Diabetes, - Paediatrics, Tel.: 020 718 84614

Ms R Cross, Liaison, Clinical Nurse Specialist, Family Health, Tel.: 020 718 84621

Ms C Campion, Community, Clinical Nurse Specialist, Genetics, Tel.: 020 718 81385

Ms R Taylor, Nurse Practitioner, Neonatal, Tel.: 020 718 88847

Ms E Rigby, Outreach, Clinical Nurse Specialist, Nephrology, - Paediatrics, Tel.: 020 718 84592

Ms D Clarke, Outreach, Clinical Nurse Specialist, Neurology, Tel.: 020 718 85944

Ms R Kelly, Neuropsych newcomen, Clinical Nurse Specialist, Neurology, Tel.: 020 718 84647

Ms K Pratt, Neuropsych newcomen, Clinical Nurse Specialist, Neurology, Tel.: 020 718 84667

Ms J Braganza, Clinical Nurse Specialist, Paediatrics, Tel.: 020 718 86092

Ms J Gick, Metabolic Outreach, Clinical Nurse Specialist, Paediatrics, Tel.: 020 718 80855

Ms D Komarony, Metabolic Outreach, Clinical Nurse Specialist, Paediatrics, Tel.: 020 718 80855

Ms E Stachan, Nurse Consultant, Paediatrics, Tel.: 020 718 86092

Ms E Appleby, Clinical Nurse Specialist, Sickle Cell, Tel.: 020 718 89432

Ms S Whetstone, Clinical Nurse Specialist, Surgical, Tel.: 020 718 86094

Ms G Walsh, Clinical Nurse Specialist, Transplant, - Paediatrics, Tel.: 020 718 84590

Ms J McKenzie, Clinical Nurse Specialist, Urology, Tel.: 020 718 84592

Community Midwifery

Ms B Ackerman, Consultant Midwife, Tel.: 020 7188 6864

Ms M Bakhtiari, Senior Community Midwifery Manager, Tel.: 020 7188 3651

Ms L Coleman, Teenphase Plus Practice Leader (midwives), Tel.: 07984 721562

Ms A Denga, Assisted Conception, Nurse Practitioner, Tel.: 020 7188 0503

Ms K Druery, CMS, CEMACH Co-ordinator, Tel.: 020 7188 5152

Ms J Dunkley-Bent, Consultant Midwife Public Health/Joint Head of Midwifery, Tel.: 020 7188 6860

Ms H Fawcett, Midwifery Manager, Tel.: 020 7188 7531

Ms D Hamilton Fairley, Service Delivery Manager, Tel.: 020 7188 6870

Ms E Hunter, Clinical Midwife Manager, Birth Centre, Tel.: 020 7188 7531

Ms G Joyce, Lead Child Protection Midwife/Clinical Midwife Manager, Tel.: 020 7188 2316

Ms T Majekodunmi, Private Midwifery (Lansdell Suite), Tel.: 07939 564671

Ms M McDonald, Service Delivery Manager, Tel.: 020 7188 6870

Ms R Metzer, Assisted Conception, Nurse Practitioner, Tel.: 020 7188 0503

Ms C Momoh, CMS, FGM, Tel.: 020 7188 6872

Ms L Mulhair, Consultant Midwife, Tel.: 020 7188 3653

Ms F Oduegwu, Practice Development Midwife Community, Tel.: 020 7188 3654

Ms M Owenbo, Assisted Conception, Nurse Practitioner, Tel.: 020 7188 0503

Prof L Page, Joint Head of Midwifery & Women's Nursing Services, Tel.: 020 7188 6875

Ms M Randhawa, Senior Midwife, Post Natal Lead, Tel.: 020 7188 6861

Ms K Rantawal, Reproductive Medicine, Clinical Nurse Specialist, Tel.: 020 7188 3682

Ms C Rozette, Fetal Midwifery, Tel.: 020 7188 7321

Ms R Thorn, Assisted Conception, Nurse Practitioner, Tel.: 020 7188 0503

Ms A Ugen, Community Midwifery Manager, Tel.: 020 7188 7836

Ms J Sim, Clinical Nurse Specialist, Gynae/Oncology, Tel.: 020 7188 2707

Ms K Gale, Emergency, Clinical Nurse Specialist, Gynaecology, Tel.: 020 7188 2173

Ms D Holloway, Nurse Consultant, Gynaecology, Tel.: 020 7188 3023

Ms S Ojakova, Clinical Nurse Specialist, Gynaecology, Tel.: 020 7188 3692

Discharge Co-ordinators

Ms J Chester, Discharge Process Manager, South Wing, Block 5, St Thomas's Hospital, Tel.: 020 7188 6135

Ms V Clarke, Elderly Care & Stroke Unit, South Wing, Block 5, St Thomas's Hospital, Tel.: 020 7188 6136

Ms S Cundasamy, Renal, Urology & S urgery (Orthopaedics), Guy's Hospital, Tel.: 020 7188 7961

Ms C Mason, General Medicine, South Wing, Block 5, St Thomas's Hospital, Tel.: 020 7188 6137

Mr D Mbang, Oncology, Surgery (ENT) & Cardiology, Guy's Hospital, Tel.: 020 7188 7962

Ms A-M McNulty-Howard, CDU, Acute Admissions Wards & Cardiology, East Wing, St Thomas's Hospital, Tel.: 020 7188 6123

Ms H Sanchez, Surgery (Plastics, Vascular & General), North Wing, St Thomas's Hospital, Tel.: 020 7188 6122

HIV/AIDS

Ms K Colborn, GUM, Nurse Practitioner, 2nd Floor Thomas Guy House, Guy's Hospital, Tel.: 020 7188 2655

Matrons/Modern Matrons

Ms G Babic-Illman, POPs, Modern Matron, Elderly Care, Ground Floor, Thomas Guy House, Guy's Hospital, Tel.: 020 7188 2092

Ms C Igbedioh, Continence, Modern Matron, Elderly Care, Ground Floor, Thomas Guy House, Guy's Hospital, Tel.: 020 7188 2093/2083

Ms S O'Neill, OPAL, Modern Matron, Elderly Care, 9th Floor, North Wing, St Thomas's Hospital, Tel.: 020 7188 2887

London Strategic Health Authority

Hammersmith & Fulham Primary Care Trust

Trust Headquarters, Parsons Green Centre
5-7 Parsons Green
LONDON
SW6 4UL
Tel.: 020 8846 6767

Admin & Senior Management
Mr C Butler, Chief Executive,
Child Health
Ms L Street, Child Health Information, Tel.: 020 8846 7969
Child Health Records
Ms L Street, Tel.: 020 8846 7969
Child Protection/Safeguarding Children
Ms L Jones, Designated Nurse, Child Protection, Children's Social
Services, Sawley Road, London, W12 0NZ, Tel.: 020 8753 1699
Community Midwifery
Midwifery, Parsons Green Centre, London, SW6 4UL, Tel.: 020 8846
6767
Community Nursing Services
Community Nursing Services, Parsons Green Centre, 5-7 Parsons
Green, London, SW6 4UL, Tel.: 020 8846 6767
District Nursing
District Nurses, Parsons Green Centre, 5-7 Parsons Green, London,
SW6 4UL, Tel.: 020 8846 6767
Family Planning Services
Family Planning Services, Parsons Green Centre, Tel.: 020 8846
6767
Family Planning Services, Milson Road Health Centre, London, W14
0LJ, Tel.: 020 7602 2723
Health Visitors
Health Visitors, Parsons Green Centre, 5-7 Parsons Green, London,
SW6 4UL, Tel.: 020 8846 6767
Learning Disabilities
Ms A Stuart, Head of Learning Disabilities, Stamford Brook Centre,
14-16 Stamford Brook Avenue, W6 8RB, Tel.: 020 8383 6464
Pharmacy
Pharmacy, Parsons Green Centre, London, SW6 4UL, Tel.: 020
8846 6767
School Nursing
School Health/Nursing Service, Parsons Green Centre, 5-7 Parsons
Green, London, SW6 4UL, Tel.: 020 8846 6767
Specialist Nursing Services
Haemoglobinopathy, Richford Gate, Tel.: 020 8237 2980
Night Nursing, Joan Bartlett Nursing Home, 1 Beatrice Place,
Marloes Road, W8 5LP, Tel.: 020 8846 6006
Ms L Batiste, Infection Control, Surgery, 1 Hammersmith Bridge
Road, W6 9DU, Tel.: 020 8748 8513
Nurses, Rehabilitation, Parsons Green Centre, Tel.: 020 8846 6841
Nursing, Respiratory, Charing Cross Hospital, Tel.: 020 8846 7044
Nursing, Sickle Cell & Thalassaemia, Richford Gate Primary Care
Centre, W6 7HY, Tel.: 020 8237 2980
Ms C McCrudden, TB, - Respiratory, OPD, Hammersmith Hospital,
Du Cane Road, W12 0HS, Tel.: 020 8383 3074
Nursing, TB, Charing Cross Hospital, W6 8RF, Tel.: 020 8883 8805
Nursing, Tissue Viability, Violet Melchett Clinic, SW3 5RR, Tel.: 020
8846 6544
The Homeless/Travellers & Asylum Seekers
Ms A Danks, White City Health Centre, W12 7PH, Tel.: 020 8846
6464
Walk In Centres
Charing Cross Walk-in Centre, Charing Cross Hospital, Fulham
Palace Road, London, W6 8RF, Tel.: 020 8383 0904
Parsons Green Walk-in Centre, 5-7 Parsons Green, London, SW6
4UL, Tel.: 020 8846 6758

Hammersmith Hospitals NHS Trust

Trust Headquarters, Hammersmith Hospital
Du Cane Road, East Acton
LONDON
W12 0HS
Tel.: 020 8383 1000

Admin & Senior Management
Mr J Clark, Acting Assistant Director of Nursing, 2nd Floor Education
Centre, Charing Cross Hospital, Fulham Palace Road, London, W6
8RF, Tel.: 020 8846 7665
Mr D Foster, Director of Nursing, Hammersmith Hospital, Du Cane
Road, East Acton, London, W12 0HS, Tel.: 020 8237 2019
Community Midwifery
Mrs M Elliott, General Manager, Director of Midwifery Services,
Hammersmith Hospital, Du Cane Road, East Acton, London, W12
0HS, Tel.: 0208 383 5094
Ms L Spires, Senior Midwife, Queen Charlottes & Chelsea Hospital,
150 Du Cane Road, East Acton, London, W12 0HS, Tel.: 020 8383
4743
Liaison Services
Ms J Dufour, Discharge Liaison Team Manager, 9E04, Charing
Cross Hospital, Tel.: 020 8846 1432 bleep 1432
Ms T McCaffrey, Hammersmith & Acton Hospitals Discharge Liaison,
Hammersmith Hospital, Tel.: 020 8383 4572 bleep 4572

Haringey Teaching Primary Care Trust

Trust Headquarters, Block B1
St Ann's Hospital, St Ann's Road
TOTTENHAM
London
N15 3TH
Tel.: 020 8442 6000

Admin & Senior Management
Prof H Hally, Director of Nursing, St Ann's Hospital, Block B1, Tel.:
020 8442 6293
Ms H Moth, Admin Manager, The Laurels Healthy Living Centre, 256
St Ann's Road, Tottenham, London, N15 3TH,
Child Health Records
Child Health Dept, Block G1, St Ann's Hospital, Tel.: 020 8442 6600
Child Protection/Safeguarding Children
Mr D Cole, Safeguarding Children's Team, Nurse Consultant, St
Ann's Hospital, Tel.: 020 8442 6987
Clinical Leads (NSF)
Dr G Taylor, Clinical Lead, Cancer,
Dr G Taylor, Clinical Lead, CHD,
Dr J Elias, Clinical Lead, Children,
Dr M Daniels, Clinical Lead, Diabetes,
District Nursing
Adult Services, Home & Hospital, Tel.: 020 8442 6578
Family Planning Services
Ms B Neary, Sexual Health, St Ann's Hospital, Tel.: 020 8442 6512
Ms E Volkman, Family Planning, St Ann's Hospital, Tel.: 020 8442
6813
Health Visitors
Ms P Loizou, Under 5s Services, Crouch End Health Centre, Tel.:
020 8341 2045
HIV/AIDS
Ms B Politz, Burgoyne Road Clinic, 58 Burgoyne Road, Haringay, N4
1AE, Tel.: 020 8340 5215
Learning Disabilities
Mr J Rowe, St Georges Ind Estate, Unit 5, White Hart Lane, N22
5QL, Tel.: 020 8489 1384
Liaison Services
Miss M Griew, Paediatric Liaison Nurse, Room 37 Old Nurses Home,
North Middlesex Hospital, Edmonton, N18 1QX, Tel.: 020 8887 4010

London Strategic Health Authority

Ms S Hall, Paediatric Liaison Specialist Nurse, Lordship Lane, Tel.: 020 8808 1748

Other Services
Mrs P Miller, Admin Manager, Burgoyne Road Clinic, 58 Burgoyne Road, Haringay, N4 1AE, Tel.: 020 8340 5215

School Nursing
Ms S Russell, School Services, G1 St Ann's Hospital, Tel.: 020 8442 6866

Specialist Nursing Services
Ms P Millard, Professional Development, Adults & Older People's Services, St Ann's Hospital, Tel.: 020 8442 6423
Ms J Grant, Professional Development, Surestart, Children, St Ann's Hospital, Tel.: 020 8442 6088
Ms R McKnight, Specialist Nurse, Continence, Bounds Green, Tel.: 020 8889 0961
Ms E Ransom, Specialist Nurse, Diabetes, Lordship Lane, Tel.: 020 8808 1748
Team, Palliative Care, St Ann's Hospital, Tel.: 020 8442 6000
Ms S Dart, Specialist Nurse, TB, St Ann's Hospital, Tel.: 020 8442 6000
Ms P Gatto, Specialist Nurse, Tissue Viability, Burgoyne Road, Tel.: 020 8340 5215

The Homeless/Travellers & Asylum Seekers
Ms T Murray, Homeless/Refugee, Stuart Crescent, Tel.: 020 8889 5641

Harrow Primary Care Trust

Trust Headquarters, Grace House
Harrovian Business Village, Bessborough Rd
HARROW
Middlesex
HA1 3EX
Tel.: 020 8422 6644

Admin & Senior Management
Ms G Gordon, Director of Provider Services, Tel.: 020 8422 6644
Mr A Morgan, Chief Executive, Tel.: 020 8422 6644

Child Protection/Safeguarding Children
Ms J Riddell-Heaney, Harrovian Business Village, Bessborough Road, Harrow, HA1 3EX, Tel.: 020 8422 6644

Clinical Leads (NSF)
Dr A Kelshiker, Clinical Lead, CHD,
Dr K Walton, Clinical Lead, Diabetes,
Dr D Cohen, Clinical Lead, Older People,

Community Nursing Services
Mrs H Baker, Head of Primary Care Nursing, Belmont Health Centre, 516 Kenton Lane, Kenton, HA3 7LT, Tel.: 020 8861 2516

District Nursing
Based on Six Sites across Harrow, Contact Primary Care Office, Belmont Health Centre, 516 Kenton Lane, Kenton, Middlesex, HA3 7LT, Tel.: 020 8861 2516

Health Visitors
Health Visiting Teams, Based on Six Sites across Harrow (Contact Primary Care Office), Belmont Health Centre, 516 Kenton Lane, Kenton, Middlesex, HA3 7LT, Tel.: 020 8861 2516
Ms R Stephens, Lead Nurse, Health Visitors, Caryl Thomas Clinic, Headstone Drive, Wealdstone, Middlesex, HA1 4UQ, Tel.: 020 8427 4484

HIV/AIDS
HIV/AIDS, Northolt Road Clinic, Northolt Road, South Harrow, HA2 8EQ, Tel.: 020 8864 9539

Learning Disabilities
Ms C Mak, Senior Nurse Manager, PO Box 161, 4th Floor, Civic Centre, Harrow, HA1 2AY, Tel.: 0208 424 1019

Other Services
Healthcare & Rehabilitation Team (H.A.R.T.), Northwick Park Hospital, Watford Road, Harrow, Middlesex, HA1 3UJ, Tel.: 020 8869 3654

Specialist Nursing Services
Ms D Hannah, Consultant Nurse Team Lead, CHD, Caryl Thomas Clinic, Headstone Drive, Wealdstone, Middlesex, HA1 4UQ, Tel.: 020 8427 4484
Mr M Nutt, Chemotherapy, Caryl Thomas Clinic, Headstone Drive, Wealdstone, Middlesex, HA1 4UQ, Tel.: 020 8427 4484
Ms A McRoberts, Continence, Caryl Thomas Clinic, Headstone Drive, Wealdstone, Middlesex, HA1 4UQ, Tel.: 020 8427 4484
Ms M Wain, Team Leader, Diabetic Care, Caryl Thomas Clinic, Headstone Drive, Wealdstone, Middlesex, HA1 4UQ, Tel.: 020 8427 4484
Ms J Grove, Infection Control, Harrovian Business Village, Bessborough Road, Harrow, Middlesex, HA1 3EX, Tel.: 020 8422 6644
Ms K Scannel, IV Therapy, Caryl Thomas Clinic, Headstone Drive, Wealdstone, Middlesex, HA1 4UQ, Tel.: 020 8427 4484
Ms M Kelly, Team Leader, Community, Palliative Care, St Lukes Hospice, Kenton Grange, Kenton Road, Harrow, HA3 0YG, Tel.: 020 8382 8000
Ms C Peak, Tissue Viability, Caryl Thomas Clinic, Headstone Drive, Wealdstone, Middlesex, HA1 4UQ, Tel.: 020 8427 4484

The Homeless/Travellers & Asylum Seekers
Ms A Hooper, Caryl Thomas Clinic, Headstone Drive, Wealdstone, Middlesex, HA1 4UQ, Tel.: 020 8427 4484
Ms H Pool, Caryl Thomas Clinic, Headstone Drive, Wealdstone, Middlesex, HA1 4UQ, Tel.: 020 8427 4484

Havering Primary Care Trust

Trust Headquarters, St George's Hospital
Suttons Lane
HORNCHURCH
Essex, RM12 6RS
Tel.: 01708 465000

Admin & Senior Management
Mrs T Berry, Director Operations, Nursing & Estates, Tel.: 01708 465305
Clinical Governance Lead, Suttons View, St George's Hospital,
Mr S East, Director of Finance,
Mr R Evans, Director Project Lead,
Dr J Harvey, Director of Public Health,
Mr R McCormack, Chief Executive, Tel.: 01708 465302
Mr J McCormick, Director HR & Organisational Development,
Ms C O'Reilly, Director of Commissioning,
Mr N Smillie, Director of Primary Care,
Mr J Tobin, Head of Older People's Services, The Willows, St George's Hospital, Tel.: 01708 465615

Child Protection/Safeguarding Children
Ms A Jones, Nurse Consultant, Child Protection, Admin Block, St George's Hospital, 117 Suttons Lane, Hornchurch, Essex, RM12 6RS, Tel.: 01708 465000 ext 4976

Clinical Leads (NSF)
Dr J V Mannakka, Medical Director,

Community Matrons
Ms S Jordon, The Willows, St George's Hospital, 117 Suttons Lane, Hornchurch, RM12 6RS, Tel.: 01708 465000

District Nursing
Ms D Chetty, Hornchurch Locality Office, St George's Hospital, 117 Suttons Lane, Hornchurch, RM12 6RS, Tel.: 01708 465000
Ms B Maryon, Suttons View, St George's Hospital, Hornchurch, Essex,

Equipment Loan Services
Mr G Bushell, St George's Hospital,

Family Planning Services
Ms J Kavanagh, The Willows, St George's Hospital, Suttons Lane, Hornchurch, Essex, RM12 6RS,
Ms S Kelsey, Contraception, Romford Clinic, Romford, Tel.: 01708 797600

London Strategic Health Authority

Health Visitors
Ms L O'Sullivan, Suttons View, St George's Hospital, Suttons Lane, Hornchurch, Essex, RM12 6RS, Tel.: 01708 465518
HIV/AIDS
Ms J Kavanagh, Julia Engwell Health Centre, Woodward Road, Dagenham, Tel.: 020 8276 7218
Learning Disabilities
Mrs J Legg, Team Manager, The Hermitage, Billet Lane, Hornchurch, RM11 1XL, Tel.: 01708 433446
Mr B Yu, Team Leader, The Hermitage, Billet Lane, Hornchurch, RM11 1XL, Tel.: 01708 433446
School Nursing
Ms S Ferris, Hornchurch Locality Office, St George's Hospital, 117 Suttons Lane, Hornchurch, RM12 6RS, Tel.: 01708 465000
Specialist Nursing Services
Ms E Edmonds, Motor Neuron, Disablement Services Centre, Harold Wood Hospital, Gubbins Lane, Harold Wood, Tel.: 01708 796200
Ms P Dooher, Breast Care, Woodlands, St George's Hospital, Tel.: 01708 465570
Ms S Sperring, Continence, Meadow View, St George's Hospital, Tel.: 01708 465142
Ms J Blewitt, Community, Manager, Diabetic Care, Woodlands, St George's Hospital, Tel.: 01708 465131
Ms E Ross, Epilepsy, Oldchurch Hospital, Oldchurch Road, Romford, Tel.: 01708 516018
Mr K Hampton, Infection Control,
Mr K Turner, Parkinson's Disease, Disablement Services Centre, Harold Wood Hospital, Gubbins Lane, Harold Wood, Tel.: 01708 796229
Ms L Brown, Team Leader, Respiratory, Woodlands, St George's Hospital, Tel.: 01708 465436
Ms J Stevens, Leg Ulcer, Tissue Viability, Elm Park Clinic, Tel.: 01708 796078

Hillingdon Hospital NHS Trust

Trust Headquarters, Hillingdon Hospital
Pield Heath Road
UXBRIDGE
Middlesex, UB8 3NN
Tel.: 01895 238282
Fax.: 01895 811687

Community Midwifery
Mrs S Dauncey, Head of Midwifery, Tel.: 01895 279476
Emergencies, Labour Ward, Tel.: 01895 279441
Maternity Unit, Tel.: 01895 279472
Ms G Morgan, Special Needs Specialist,

Hillingdon Primary Care Trust

Trust Headquarters, Kirk House
97-109 High Street
YIEWSLEY
Middlesex, UB7 7HJ
Tel.: 01895 452000
Fax.: 01895 452108

Admin & Senior Management
Ms S Clarke, Director of Operational Services & Nursing, Kirk House, Tel.: 01895 452086
Ms J Pearcey, Head of Organisational Development, Kirk House, Tel.: 01895 452060
Child Health
Community Paediatric Team, Child Development Centre, The Furze, Hillingdon Hospital, Uxbridge, Middx, UB8 3NN, Tel.: 01895 279227
Ms G Crowley, Team Leader, North Hillingdon, Eastcote Health Centre, Tel.: 020 8868 1166
Ms S James, Team Leader, Uxbridge & West Drayton, Laurel Lodge Clinic, Tel.: 01895 252681

Ms E Tabony, Team Leader, Hayes & Harlington, Minet Clinic, Tel.: 020 8573 2634
Child Health Records
Mr D Riddick, Child Health System Manager, Laurel Lodge Clinic, Tel.: 01895 813286/234624
Child Protection/Safeguarding Children
Ms T Chisholm, Health Co-ordinator, Looked After Children, Tel.: 01895 452000 ext 3007
Ms J Armstrong, Named Nurse, Child Protection, Kirk House, Tel.: 01895 452114
Ms L Crawshaw, Named Nurse, Child Protection, Kirk House, Tel.: 01895 452000 ext 3014
Ms J Reid, Lead/Designated Nurse, Child Protection, Kirk House, Tel.: 01895 452119
Clinical Leads (NSF)
Ms E Bunker, Clinical Lead, Cancer,
Community Nursing Services
Ms L Crown, Locality Nurse Manager - Uxbridge & West Drayton, Laurel Lodge Clinic, Harlington Road, Hillingdon, UB8 3HD, Tel.: 01895 811474
Ms S Elvin, Locality Nurse Manager - North Hillingdon, Eastcote Health Centre, Abbotsbury Gardens, Eastcote, HA5 1TG, Tel.: 020 8868 1166
Ms C Shermer, Locality Nurse Manager - Hayes & Harlington, Laurel Lodge Clinic, Harlington Road, Hillingdon, UB8 3HD, Tel.: 01895 811474
Family Planning Services
Mr K Thomason, Manager, Uxbridge Health Centre, Chippendale Way, Uxbridge, UB8 1QJ, Tel.: 01895 252461
Learning Disabilities
Nurse Manager, CTPLD, London Borough of Hillingdon, Civic Centre, Uxbridge, UB8 1UW, Tel.: 01895 250695
Specialist Nursing Services
Ms Z Berry, PMS Practice, Nurse Practitioner, The Orchard Practice, 70 Station Road, Hayes, UB3 4DF, Tel.: 0208 756 3940
Care Group Lead Nurses, Kirk House, Tel.: 01895 452121
Ms R Charter, Nurse Prescribing Lead, Kirk House, Tel.: 0796 1032380
Ms J Cook, HOPE (Health Opportunities Promotion & Education), Nurse Practitioner, The Orchard Practice, 70 Station Road, Hayes, UB3 4DF, Tel.: 0208 756 3940
Ms B North, Nurse, Continence, Laurel Lodge Clinic, Harlington Road, Hillingdon, UB8 3HD, Tel.: 01895 811474
Team, Diabetic Care, Diabeticare Unit, Hillingdon Hospital, Tel.: 01895 238282
Mr B Nunkoo, Nurse, Infection Control, Kirk House, Tel.: 01895 452000 ext 3012
Ms S Confavreux, Nurse Consultant, Intermediate Care, Northwood & Pinner Hospital, Pinner Road, Northwood, HA6 1TH, Tel.: 01923 833765
Team, Palliative Care, The Furze, Hillingdon Hospital, Uxbridge, UB8 3NN, Tel.: 01895 279412
Ms J-A Sharp, Nurse Consultant, Primary Care, Dr Thomas & Partners, The Cedar Brook Practice, 11 Kingshill Close, Hayes, Middx, UB4 8DD, Tel.: 07986 604520
Ms P Tsangarides, Health Visitor, TB, Kirk House, Tel.: 01895 452077
Ms L Ovens, Nurse, Tissue Viability, Northwood & Pinner Hospital, Pinner Road, Northwood, HA6 1TH, Tel.: 01923 824182/3/4

Homerton University Hospital NHS Foundation Trust

Trust Headquarters, Homerton University Hospital
Homerton Row, Homerton
LONDON, E9 6SR
Tel.: 020 8510 5555
Fax.: 020 8510 7608

London Strategic Health Authority

Admin & Senior Management
Ms F Jones, Community & Social Care Co-ordinator, Homerton Hospital, Tel.: 020 8510 5014/5555
Child Health
Ms T Foster, Paediatric Liaison Nurse Specialist, Starlight Children's Outpatients, Homerton Hospital, Homerton Row, London, E9 6SR, Tel.: 020 8510 5120
Child Protection/Safeguarding Children
Ms J Barker, Child Protection, St Leonard's, Tel.: 020 7301 3315
Ms A Bridges, Named Midwife, Child Protection, Homerton, Tel.: 020 8510 7226
Dr N Lessof, Named Consultant, Child Protection, Homerton, Tel.: 020 8510 7873
Ms T Luckett, Named Nurse, Child Protection, Homerton, Tel.: 020 8510 7231
Community Midwifery
Miss A Bridges, Head of Midwifery, Homerton University Hospital, Homerton Row, Homerton, London, E9 6SR, Tel.: 020 8510 7226
Discharges, Homerton University Hospital, Homerton Row, Homerton, London, E9 6SR, Tel.: 020 8510 7404
Miss J Douglas, Maternity Matron, Homerton University Hospital, Homerton Row, Homerton, London, E9 6SR, Tel.: 020 8510 5767
Emergencies, Homerton University Hospital, Homerton Row, Homerton, London, E9 6SR, Tel.: 020 8510 7354/7352
Miss B Scantlebury, Clinical Midwifery Manager, Homerton University Hospital, Homerton Row, Homerton, London, E9 6SR, Tel.: 020 8510 5768
Supervisor of Midwives, Homerton University Hospital, Homerton Row, Homerton, London, E9 6SR, Tel.: Bleep via switchboard
Mrs V Valdez, Clinical Midwifery Manager - Community Teams, Homerton University Hospital, Homerton Row, Homerton, London, E9 6SR, Tel.: 020 8510 7404
HIV/AIDS
Ms R Constable, HIV Team, Tel.: 020 7301 3300
Liaison Services
Ms J Kincaid, Discharge Liaison, Homerton Hospital, Tel.: 020 8510 7194/5555
The Homeless/Travellers & Asylum Seekers
Ms L Dodge, Health Workers for Travellers, Lower Clapton Health Centre, Tel.: 020 8919 5000

Hounslow Primary Care Trust
Trust Headquarters, Phoenix Court
531 Staines Road
HOUNSLOW
Middlesex, TW4 5DP
Tel.: 020 8321 2396

Admin & Senior Management
Ms S Jeffers, Director of Nursing & Clinical Governance, Phoenix Court, 531 Staines Road, Hounslow, Middlesex, TW4 5DP, Tel.: 020 8321 2020
Child Health
Ms J Baldwin, Bedfont Clinic, Imperial Road, Bedfont, Middlesex, TW14 8AG, Tel.: 020 8321 3893
Dr D Lessing, Consultant Paediatrician - Community, Thelma Golding Health Centre, 92 Bath Road, Hounslow, Middlesex, TW3 3EL, Tel.: 020 8321 2427
Child Health Records
Child Health Records, Thelma Golding Centre, 92 Bath Road, Hounslow, Middlesex, TW3 3EL, Tel.: 020 8321 2445
Child Protection/Safeguarding Children
Ms S Hunt, Designated Nurse, Child Protection, Thelma Golding Health Centre, 92 Bath Road, Hounslow, Middlesex, TW3 3EL, Tel.: 020 8321 2426
Clinical Leads (NSF)
Dr Burbidge, Clinical Lead, Cancer, Phoenix Court, 531 Staines Road, Hounslow, Middlesex, TW4 5DP,

Dr Garcha, Clinical Lead, CHD, Phoenix Court, 531 Staines Road, Hounslow, Middlesex, TW4 5DP,
Dr Mendel, Clinical Lead, Diabetic Care, Phoenix Court, 531 Staines Road, Hounslow, Middlesex, TW4 5DP,
Community Nursing Services
Ms S Jeffers, Director of Nursing & Clinical Governance, Phoenix Court, 531 Staines Road, Hounslow, Middlesex, TW4 5DP, Tel.: 020 8321 2020
District Nursing
Referrals, Heston, Hounslow, Tel.: 020 8321 2326
Referrals, Feltham, Hanworth, Bedfont, Tel.: 020 8321 3757
Referrals, Brentford, Chiswick, Isleworth, Tel.: 020 8321 3800
Family Planning Services
Ms A Wyatt, Family Planning Manager, Thelma Golding Centre, 92 Bath Road, Hounslow, Middlesex, TW3 3EL, Tel.: 020 8321 2303
Learning Disabilities
Ms S Harvey, Nurse Consultant, 68a Bath Road, Hounslow, Middlesex, TW3 3EQ, Tel.: 020 8321 3597
Pharmacy
Ms J Cree, Chief Pharmacist, Phoenix Court, 531 Staines Road, Hounslow, Middlesex, TW4 5DP, Tel.: 020 8321 2489
Smoking Cessation
Mr D McArdle, Smoking Cessation Manager, Thelma Golding Health Centre, 92 Bath Road, Hounslow, Middlesex, TW3 3EL, Tel.: 020 8321 2321

Islington Primary Care Trust
Trust Headquarters
338-346 Goswell Road
LONDON
EC1V 7LQ
Tel.: 0207 527 1000
Fax.: 0207 527 1001

Admin & Senior Management
Ms H Pettersen, Director of Services, 338-346 Goswell Road, London, EC1V 7LQ, Tel.: 0207 527 1079
Ms J Roberts, Medical Director, 338-346 Goswell Road, London, EC1V 7LQ, Tel.: 0207 527 1070
Ms S Timms, Director of Nursing, Prof. Development & Children's Services, Tel.: 0207 527 1075
Ms R Tyndall, Chief Executive, 338-346 Goswell Road, London, EC1V 7LQ, Tel.: 0207 527 1081
Child Health
Ms M Johnson, Community Children's Nursing Service, 338-346 Goswell Road, London, EC1V 7LQ, Tel.: 0207 527 1415
Mrs G Reed, Children's Audiology Service, Northern Health Centre, Tel.: 0207 445 8221
Child Health Records
Child Health Dept, 592 Holloway Road, London, N7 6LB, Tel.: 020 7530 2010/1/2
Child Protection/Safeguarding Children
Ms J Chapman, Clinical Service Manager, Child Protection, 338-346 Goswell Road, London, EC1V 7LQ/email: firstname.surname@nhs.net, Tel.: 0207 527 1058
Ms E Merrin, Team Leader, Designated & Named Nurse, Child Protection, Hornsey Rise Health Centre, Hornsey Rise, London, N19 3YU, Tel.: 0207 530 2426
Named & Designated Doctor, Child Protection, Northern Health Centre, Tel.: 0207 445 8240
Community Nursing Services
Ms S Braddell-Smith, Information on District Nursing, 338-346 Goswell Road, London, EC1V 7LQ/email: firstname.surname@nhs.net, Tel.: 0207 527 1419
Ms J Chapman, Assistant Director of Nursing, 338-346 Goswell Road, London, EC1V 7LQ/email: firstname.surname@nhs.net, Tel.: 0207 527 1058

London Strategic Health Authority

Ms S Page, Information on Health Visiting, 338-346 Goswell Road, London, EC1V 7LQ, Tel.: 0207 527 1061

Ms S Timms, Director of Nursing, 338-346 Goswell Road, London, EC1V 7LQ, Tel.: 0207 527 1075

Ms J Williams, Assistant Director of Nursing, 338-346 Goswell Road, London, EC1V 7LQ/email: firstname.surname@nhs.net, Tel.: 0207 527 1062

District Nursing

City Road Medical Centre, 192-196 City Road, London, EC1V 2QH, Tel.: 0207 530 2750

Finsbury Health Centre, Pine Street, London, EC1R 0JH, Tel.: 0207 530 4200

Goodinge Health Centre, Goodinge Close, North Road, London, N7 9EW, Tel.: 020 7530 4900

Highbury Grange Health Centre, 1-5 Highbury Grange, London, N5 2QB, Tel.: 0207 530 2888

Hornsey Rise Health Centre, Hornsey Rise, London, N19 3YU, Tel.: 0207 530 2400

Killick Street Health Centre, 75 Killick Street, London N1 9RH, Tel.: 0207 427 2753

Northern Health Centre, 580 Holloway Road, London, N7 6LB, Tel.: 0207 445 8000

River Place Health Centre, Essex Road, London, N1 2DE,

Family Planning Services

Ms T Proctor, Senior Nurse - Sexual & Reproductive Health Care - Contraception, Margaret Pyke Centre, 73 Charlotte Street, W1T 4PL, Tel.: 0207 530 3600/3623

Health Visitors

Ms O Allu, Senior Practitioner NV, Central Islington, Highbury Grange Health Centre, Tel.: 020 7530 2888

Health Visitors, Highbury Grange Health Centre, 1-5 Highbury Grange, London, N5 2QB, Tel.: 0207 530 2888

Health Visitors, Bingfield Health Centre, 8 Bingfield Street, London, N1 2AL, Tel.: 0207 527 1610

Health Visitors, Finsbury Health Centre, Pine Street, London, EC1R 0JH, Tel.: 0207 530 4200

Health Visitors, Hornsey Rise Health Centre, Hornsey Rise, London, N19 3YU, Tel.: 0207 530 2400

Health Visitors, Northern Health Centre, 580 Holloway Road, London, N7 6LB, Tel.: 0207 445 8000

Health Visitors, Goodinge Health Centre, North Road, London, N7 9EW, Tel.: 0207 530 4900

Health Visitors, Hanley Road Medical Centre, 51 Hanley Road, London, N4 3DU, Tel.: 0207 527 1510

Health Visitors, River Place Health Centre, Essex Road, London, N1 2DE, Tel.: 0207 530 2900

Mr S Page, 4th Floor, 338-346 Goswell Road, London, EC1V 7LQ, Tel.: 0207 527 1061

Ms E Phillips, Islington Child Development Team, Health Visitor, Northern Health Centre, Tel.: 0207 445 8243

Ms L Rowlinson, Senior Practitioner NV, South Islington, River Place Health Centre, Tel.: 020 7530 2900

Ms J Carroll, Liaison, Health Visitor, Paediatrics, Paediatric ODP, St Mary's Wing, Whittington Hospital, Highgate Hill, N19 5NF, Tel.: 0207 288 5472

School Nursing

Ms L Baptiste, Senior School Health/Nursing Practitioner, Tel.: 0207 530 4903

Ms S Raynor, Children's Services & School Nursing, 338-356 Goswell Road, Tel.: 0207 527 1056

School Health/Nursing, A Block, St Pancras Hospital, Tel.: 0207 530 3984

School Health/Nursing, Goodinge Health Centre, Tel.: 0207 530 4930

Smoking Cessation

Ms S Kayikci, Smoking Cessation Co-ordinator, Trust Headquarters, Tel.: 0207 527 1236

Specialist Nursing Services

Ms L Bennett, Haemoglobinopathy, Northern Health Centre, Tel.: 0207 445 8035

Ms M Garnes, Senior Practitioner - Practice Nursing, Trust Headquarters, Tel.: 0207 527 1213

Ms N Letchimanan, Professional Nurse Advisor - Practice Nursing, Tel.: 0207 527 1178

Ms L Valcarcel, Practice Nurse Women's Health, Tel.: 0207 527 1199

Mr J Fernandez, Specialist Nurse, Alcohol, Tel.: 0207 527 1188

Ms R Barton, Women's Health (Whittington), Continence, Tel.: 0207 288 3473

Ms M Hammond, Senior Practitioner, Continence, Tel.: 0207 530 3310

Ms G Fabris, Physiotherapist, COPD, Tel.: 0207 527 1202

Ms C Tully, Lead Nurse, COPD, Tel.: 0207 527 1217

Ms I Mayer, Lead Nurse, Diabetes, Tel.: 0207 527 1176

Ms D Van Rensburg, Specialist Nurse, Diabetes, Tel.: 0207 527 1198

Ms B Wright, Specialist Nurse, Diabetes, Tel.: 0207 527 1198

Ms K Dowle, Nurse, Heart Failure, Tel.: 0207 527 1211

Mr M Moeller, Nurse, Heart Failure, Tel.: 0207 527 1211

Ms G Hearne, Team Leader, Long Term Conditions, Tel.: 0207 527 1173

Ms P Mattin, Clinical Services Manager, Long Term Conditions, 338-346 Goswell Road, London, EC1V 7LQ, Tel.: 0207 527 1214

Ms M Bissett, Nurse Consultant, Palliative Care, 1st Floor, Woolfson Building, 48 Riding House, Middlesex Hospital, Tel.: 0207 530 6200

Ms S Hutton, Clinical Services Manager, Palliative Care, 1st Floor, Woolfson Building, Middlesex Hospital, Tel.: 0207 530 6200

Ms A Goodburn, Nurse Specialist, TB, UCLH, Tel.: 0207 636 8333 ext 4868

Ms M Mamdani, TB, Whittington Hospital, Tel.: 0207 288 5248

Ms S Kiernan, Nurse Consultant, Tissue Viability, St Pancras Hospital, Tel.: 0207 530 3585

Kensington & Chelsea Primary Care Trust

Trust Headquarters, Courtfield House
St Charles Hospital, Exmoor Street
LONDON
W10 6DZ
Tel.: 0208 969 2488

Admin & Senior Management

Mr P Haigh, Chief Executive,

Child Health

Ms L Blythe, Children with Disabilities, Disability Team, 36B Oxford Gardens, London, W10 5UQ,

Ms D Ellis, Child Health Manager, Child Health Dept, Courtfield House, St Charles Hospital, Exmoor Street, London, W10 6DZ, Tel.: 0208 962 4506

Ms E Welch, Team Leader, Community Childrens Nursing, World's End Health Centre, 529 Kings Road, London, SW10 0UD,

Child Health Records

Ms D Ellis, Child Health Manager (School Records), Child Health Dept, Courtfield House, St Charles Hospital, Exmoor Street, London, W10 6DZ, Tel.: 0208 962 4506

Child Protection/Safeguarding Children

Ms R Daley, Designated Nurse, Courtfield House, St Charles Hospital, Exmoor Street, London, W10 6DZ,

Ms S Donovan, Named Nurse, Courtfield House, St Charles Hospital, Exmoor Street, London, W10 6DZ,

Ms M Jameson, Looked After Children, CRT & FRP, 2A Wallingford Avenue, London, W10 6QB,

Mr G Thornton, Designated Nurse, Looked After Children, Community Child Health, The Medical Centre, 7E Woodfield Road, London, W9, Tel.: 020 7266 8774

London Strategic Health Authority

Clinical Leads (NSF)
Dr B Crede, Clinical Lead, CHD & Diabetes,
Dr J Holden, Clinical Lead, Cancer,
Dr G Morris, Clinical Lead, Older People,

Community Nursing Services
Ms J Clegg, Director of Nursing, Courtfield House, St Charles Hospital, Exmoor Street, London, W10 6DZ, Tel.: 0208 962 4498

District Nursing
Mr P Ebenezer, Continuing Care Lead (Adult Services), Kensington & Chelsea PCT, 125 Old Brompton Road, 2nd Floor, London, SW7 3RP, Tel.: 0208 846 6677
Ms R Thompson, Kensington & Chelsea PCT, 125 Old Brompton Road, 2nd Floor, London, SW7 3RP, Tel.: 0208 846 6677

Family Planning Services
Ms C Morgan, Westside Women's Services, Raymede Centre, St Charles Hospital, Exmoor Street, London, W10 6DZ, Tel.: 0208 969 2488

Health Visitors
Ms M Buckell, Children's Services - Health Visitors/School Nurses, Courtfield House, St Charles Hospital, Exmoor Street, London, W10 6DZ, Tel.: 0208 962 4046

HIV/AIDS
Ms M Makaru, 57 Charles Hospital, Exmoor Street, London, W10 6DZ,

Learning Disabilities
Mr M Gierke, Learning Disability, 20 Kingsbridge Road, London, W10 6PU,

Smoking Cessation
Mr M Mbogo, Lisson Grove Health Centre, Gate Forth Street, London, NW8 8EG, Tel.: 0800 328 8537

Specialist Nursing Services
Ms H Oliver, Continence, Colville Health Centre, Kensington Park Road, London, W11 1PA, Tel.: 0207 221 2650
Ms M Clay, Nurse Consultant, Older People, St Charles Hospital, Exmoor Street, London, W10 6DZ, Tel.: 0208 962 4498
Ms H Charles, Tissue Viability, St Charles Family Centre, St Charles Hospital, Exmoor Street, London, W10 6DZ, Tel.: 0208 969 2488

The Homeless/Travellers & Asylum Seekers
Mr E O'Toole, Health Support Team, The Medical Centre, 76 Woodfield Road, London, W9 6DZ, Tel.: 0207 286 5111

King's College Hospital NHS Trust
Trust Headquarters, King's College Hospital
Denmark Hill, Camberwell
LONDON, SE5 9RS
Tel.: 020 7737 4000

Community Midwifery
Community Midwives Office, 4th Floor Golden Jubilee Wing, King's College Hospital, Tel.: 020 7346 3548
Community Midwives Office, 4th Floor Golden Jubilee Wing, King's College Hospital, Tel.: 0207 346 3548
Out of hours, Weekends & Bank Holidays - Labour Ward, 0207 346 3222 & 0207 737 4000,
Mrs C Warwick, General Manager, Community Midwives Office, 4th Floor Golden Jubilee Wing, King's College Hospital, Tel.: 020 7346 3500
Ms J Yearwood, Community Midwifery Manager, King's College Hospital, Denmark Hill, Camberwell, London, SE5 9RS, Tel.: 020 7346 3547

Kingston Hospital NHS Trust
Trust Headquarters, Kingston Hospital
Galsworthy Road
KINGSTON UPON THAMES
Surrey, KT2 7QB
Tel.: 020 8546 7711
Fax.: 020 8547 2182

Child Health Records
Child Health Records, Elm House, 84 Ewell Road, Surbiton, Surrey, KT6 6EX,

Community Midwifery
Mrs S Byford, Lead Midwife Community Services, Maternity Unit, Kingston Hospital NHS Trust, Galsworthy Road, Kingston upon Thames, KT2 7QB, Tel.: 0208 546 7711 ext 3281
Mrs M Davies, Head of Maternity & Gynaecology, Maternity Unit, Kingston Hospital NHS Trust, Galsworthy Road, Kingston upon Thames, KT2 7QB, Tel.: 0208 546 7711 ext 2370

Health Visitors
Ms A Boatman, Liaison Health Visitor Paediatrics, Kingston Hospital, Tel.: 020 8934 3413

Kingston Primary Care Trust
Trust Headquarters, Hollyfield House
22 Hollyfield Road
SURBITON
Surrey
KT5 9AL
Tel.: 020 8339 8000
Fax.: 020 8339 8100

Admin & Senior Management
Mrs J Colvin, Locality Manager, Elmside, 1 Oakhill, Surbiton, Surrey, Tel.: 020 8547 6850
Mrs A Filkin, Locality Manager, Acre Road Clinic, 204 Acre Road, Kingston, Tel.: 020 8547 6012
Miss A Ludlum, Associate Director of Practice Development, Hollyfield House, 22 Hollyfield Road, Surbiton, Surrey, KT5 9AL, Tel.: 0208 339 8064
Mrs B Sands, Locality Manager, Newent House Annex, 8-10 Brown's Road, Surbiton, Tel.: 020 8547 6845
Ms R Stewart, Locality Manager, Roselands Clinic, 163 Kingston Road, New Malden, Surrey, Tel.: 020 8547 6049
Mrs J Willett
Willett, Director of Nursing, Hollyfield House, 22 Hollyfield Road, Surbiton, Surrey, KT5 9AL, Tel.: 0208 339 8005

Child Health
Ms C Catlow, Associate Director of Children & Family Services, Hawks Road Clinic, Hawks Road, Kingston, Tel.: 020 8546 1115

Child Protection/Safeguarding Children
Ms C Catlow, Associate Director of Children & Family Services/Designated Nurse, Hawks Road Clinic, Tel.: 020 8546 1115
Ms S Patience, Named Nurse, Child Protection, Hawks Road Clinic, Tel.: 020 8546 1115

Clinical Leads (NSF)
Dr P Moore, Clinical Lead, CHd & Diabetes, 22 Hollyfield Road, Surbiton, Surrey,
Mrs J Willett, Clinical Lead, Older People, 22 Hollyfield Road, Surbiton, Surrey,

District Nursing
Mrs J Maskell, Associate Director of Health & Social Care Teams (District Nurses), Hollyfield House, 22 Hollyfield Road, Surbiton, Surrey, KT5 9AL, Tel.: 020 8547 6113

Equipment Loan Services
Mrs J Sherlock, Associate Director - Operational Support Services, 22 Hollyfield Road, Surbiton, Surrey, KT5 9AL, Tel.: 020 8339 8115

Family Planning Services
Ms C Catlow, Associate Director of Children & Family Services, Hawks Road Clinic, Tel.: 020 8546 1115
Ms E Kennedy, Lead Nurse for Sexual Health, Hawks Road Clinic, Tel.: 020 8546 1115

Health Visitors
Ms C Catlow, Associate Director of Children & Family Services (Health Visitors), Hawks Road Clinic, Hawks Road, Kingston, Tel.: 020 8546 1115

London Strategic Health Authority

Mrs S Derby, Lead Health Visitor, Hawks Road Clinic, Hawks Road, Kingston, Tel.: 020 8546 1115

HIV/AIDS
Mr D Thompson, HIV/AIDS Nurse, 22 Hollyfield Road, Surbiton, Tel.: 020 8339 8081

Learning Disabilities
Mr D Bungaroo, Community Nurse Manager - Kingston, Crescent Resource Centre, Cocks Crescent, Blagdon Road, New Malden, KT3 4TA, Tel.: 020 8547 6558
Mr N Morrow, Deputy PLD Manager, 22 Hollyfield Road, Surbiton, KT5 9AL, Tel.: 020 8339 8063
Mr J Power, Associate Director for Learning Disability Services, 22 Hollyfield Road, Surbiton, KT5 9AL, Tel.: 020 8339 8065

Liaison Services
Ms K Crandon, Intermediate Care Teams, Tolworth Hospital, Red Lion Road, Tolworth, KT6 7QT, Tel.: 020 8274 7087
Mrs M Lax, Intermediate Care Manager, Tolworth Hospital, Red Lion Road, Tolworth, KT6 7QT, Tel.: 020 8274 7080

Other Services
Mr J Power, Associate Director Services for PLD, Hollyfield House, 22 Hollyfield Road, Surbiton, Surrey, KT5 9AL, Tel.: 020 8339 8065

Pharmacy
Mrs P Taylor, Director of Service Transformation & Programme Management, 22 Hollyfield Road, Surbiton, Surrey, KT5 9AL, Tel.: 020 8339 8193

Specialist Nursing Services
Ms K Appleton, Co-ordinator, Clinical Placements, Tel.: 020 8339 8062
Mrs J Watkins, Practice Development Nurse, 22 Hollyfield Road, Surbiton, Tel.: 020 8339 8031
Ms R Gilbert, Continence, Surbiton Hospital, Ewell Road, Surbiton, KT6 6EZ, Tel.: 020 8399 4154/7111
Ms Y Hart, Continence, Surbiton Hospital, Ewell Road, Surbiton, KT6 6EZ, Tel.: 020 8399 4154/7111
Ms C Cooper, Nurse, Infection Control, 22 Hollyfield Road, Surbiton, KT5 9AL, Tel.: 020 8339 8182
Ms N Siron, Nurse, Infection Control, 22 Hollyfield Road, Surbiton, KT5 9AL, Tel.: 020 8339 8182
Integrated Team, Palliative Care, c/o Princess Alice Hospice,
Ms J Evans, Nurse, Practice Development, Tel.: 020 8339 8061
Ms W Glencross, Nurse, Tissue Viability, Hollyfield Road, Tel.: 020 8339 8132

Walk In Centres
Walk In Centres, Hook Clinic, Roselands Clinic, Oakhill Clinic, Hawks Road Clinic, Manor Drive Clinic,

Lambeth Primary Care Trust

Trust Headquarters, 1 Lower Marsh
Waterloo
LONDON
SE1 7NT
Tel.: 020 7716 7100

Admin & Senior Management
Mr K Barton, Chief Executive,

Child Health
Ms F Stirling, Child with Special Needs- Mary Sheridan Centre for Child Health, Wooden Spoon House, 5 Dugard Way, off Renfrew Road, Kennington, SE11 4TH, Tel.: 020 7414 1400

Child Health Records
Child Health Records, Reay House, 108 Landor Road, Stockwell, SW9 9NT, Tel.: 020 7411 6115
Ms P Hinds, Administration, Reay House, 108 Landor Road, Stockwell, SW9 9NT, Tel.: 020 7411 6115 ext 6357
Mr K Jackson, Administration, Reay House, 108 Landor Road, Stockwell, SW9 9NT, Tel.: 020 7411 6115 ext 6324

Child Protection/Safeguarding Children
Ms A Williams-McKoy, Mary Sheridan Centre for Child Health, Child Protection, Wooden Spoon House, 5 Dugard Way, off Renfrew Road, Kennington, SE11 4TH, Tel.: 020 7414 1400

Clinical Leads (NSF)
Dr S Masters, Clinical Lead, Cancer & CHD,
Dr S Cottingham, Clinical Lead, Cancer,
Dr S Cottingham, Clinical Lead, CHD,
Dr M Williamson, Clinical Lead, Children,
Dr M King, Clinical Lead, Diabetic Care,
Dr L Clegg, Clinical Lead, Older People,

District Nursing
Contact MCW Records at Elizabeth Blackwell House, Wardalls Grove, Avonley Road, SE14 5ER, Tel.: 020 7346 5415
Evening Service District Nurses, Tel.: 020 7411 6120

HIV/AIDS
Ms C Wallace, 108 Landor Road, Tel.: 020 7411 6105

Liaison Services
Ms C Ominiyi, Community Liaison Nurse (Guys' & St Thomas Hospitals), Block 5 - Ground Floor, South Wing, St Thomas' Hospital, Lambeth Palace Road, London, SE1 7EH, Tel.: 020 7188 6158
Mr J Thorogood, Liaison, Health Visitor, Guy's & St Thomas', New Salomons Clinic, Guy's Hospital, Tel.: 020 7955 4068
Ms J Vessey, Liaison, Health Visitor, 1st Floor, A&E Dept, Kings College Hospital, Denmark Hill, SE5 9RS, Tel.: 020 7346 3947

Specialist Nursing Services
Ms E Campbell, Palliative Care, bleep LHC 141, Tel.: 020 7587 3939

Lewisham Primary Care Trust

Trust Headquarters, Cantilever House
Eltham Road, Lee
LONDON
SE12 8RN
Tel.: 020 7206 3200
Fax.: 020 7206 3201

Admin & Senior Management
Ms L Hadfield, Chief Executive, Cantilever House, Eltham Road, Lee, London, SE12 8RN, Tel.: 020 7206 3200

Child Health Records
Ms M Hill, Child Health Records, Ivy House, Bradgate Road, Catford, London, SE6 2TT, Tel.: 020 8613 9213

Child Protection/Safeguarding Children
Ms S Williams, Child Protection, Ivy House, Bradgate Road, Catford, London, SE6 2TT, Tel.: 020 8613 9216

Clinical Leads (NSF)
Dr G Russell, Clinical Lead, Older People, Director of Commissioning, Cantilever House,
Dr C Watts, Clinical Lead, CHD & Diabetes, Cantilever House,
Dr C Watts, Clinical Lead, Cancer, Cantilever House,

District Nursing
Ms M Davies, Deputy Director, District Nurses, Leegate House, Burnt Ash Road, Lee, London, SE12 8RG, Tel.: 020 8218 3524
Ms C Smith, District Nursing Emergencies/Night, Lee Health Centre, 2 Handen Road, London, SE12 8NP, Tel.: 020 7771 4856

Health Visitors
Ms S Fun Yapp, Neighbourhood Nurse Leader, Honor Oak Health Centre, 20 Turnham Road, Brockley, London, SE4 2LA,
Ms J Shepherd, Associate Director, Children & Young People's Services, Leegate House, Burnt Ash Road, Lee, London, SE12 8RN, Tel.: 020 218 3526

HIV/AIDS
Ms C Wallace, Manager, Masters House, Dugard Way, Kennington, London, SE11 4TH, Tel.: 020 7840 5220

Learning Disabilities
Ms A Keens, Townley Road Clinic, 121 Townley Road, East Dulwich, London, SE22 8SW, Tel.: 020 8698 6788

London Strategic Health Authority

Liaison Services
Patient Advice & Liaison Services, Lewisham Hospital, The Owen Centre, University Hospital Lewisham, Lewisham, London, SE13 6LH, Tel.: 020 8676 7415
Patient Advice & Liaison Services, Lewisham PCT, Cantilever House, Eltham Road, Lee, London, SE12 8RN, Tel.: 0800 587 7027
Specialist Nursing Services
Mrs M Noleley-Barton, Marvels Lane Health Centre, 37 Marvels Lane, Grove Park, London, SE12 9PN, Tel.: 020 7771 4347

Mayday Healthcare NHS Trust
Trust Headquarters, Mayday University Hospital
530 London Road
CROYDON
CR7 7YE
Tel.: 020 8401 3000
Fax.: 020 8665 7293

Acute Specialist Nursing Services
All Specialist Nursing contactable via main switch board,
Child Protection/Safeguarding Children
Child Protection Administration, Tel.: 020 8401 3894
Child Protection Fax, Tel.: 020 8401 3989
Child Protection Manager, Tel.: 020 8401 3162
Community Midwifery
Clinical Midwifery Manager, Tel.: 020 8401 3183
Clinical Midwifery Manager, Tel.: 020 8401 3000 ext 4443
Community Midwifery Manager, Tel.: 020 8401 3163
Head of Midwifery Office, Tel.: 020 8401 3000 ext 3159
PA to Head of Midwifery, Tel.: 020 8401 3159
Liaison Services
GP Nurse Liaison Service, Tel.: 020 8401 3462

Moorfields Foundation NHS Trust
Trust Headquarters, 162 City Road
LONDON
EC1V 2PD
Tel.: 020 7253 3411
Fax.: 020 7253 4696

Admin & Senior Management
Ms S Fisher, Director of Nursing, Moorfields (Foundation) NHS Trust, 162 City Road, London, EC1V 2PD, Tel.: 020 7253 3411

Newham Healthcare NHS Trust
Trust Headquarters, Newham General Hospital
Glen Road, Plaistow
LONDON
E13 8SL
Tel.: 020 7476 4000

Acute Specialist Nursing Services
Ms R Ramoutar-Seepaul, Lead Nurse, COPD, The Shrewsbury Centre, Shrewsbury Road, Forest Gate, E7 8QP, Tel.: 020 8586 5221
Ms M Hardy, Nurse Specialist, Heart Failure, Newham General Hospital, Tel.: 020 7476 4000
Ms L Luddington, Nurse Specialist, Heart Failure, Newham General Hospital, Tel.: 020 7476 4000
Ms H Kilvington, Early Discharge Service (Reds), Respiratory, The Shrewsbury Centre, Shrewsbury Road, Forest Gate, E7 8QP, Tel.: 020 8586 5221
Ms J Ndongwe, Early Discharge Service (Reds), Respiratory, The Shrewsbury Centre, Shrewsbury Road, Forest Gate, E7 8QP, Tel.: 020 8586 5221
Ms J Opoku-Asamoah, Early Discharge Service (Reds), Respiratory, The Shrewsbury Centre, Shrewsbury Road, Forest Gate, E7 8QP, Tel.: 020 8586 5221

Mr M van Orsouw, Nurse Practitioner, Vascular, Newham General/St Andrews Hospital, Glen Road, Plaistow, E13 8SL, Tel.: 0207 4764000 bleep 197
Community Midwifery
Ms S Cerclay, Infant Feeding Specialist Midwife, Newham General Hospital, Tel.: 0207363 8694 pager 813256
Miss H Moyo, Midwifery Manager, Tel.: 020 7363 8697

Newham Primary Care Trust
Trust Headquarters, Sydenham Building
Plaistow Hospital, Samson Street
LONDON
E13 9EH
Tel.: 020 8586 6200

Admin & Senior Management
Mr G Soutar, Deputy Director of Nursing, Plaistow Hospital, Samson Street, London, E13 9EH, Tel.: 0208 586 6400 ext 6405
Ms W Thomas, Director of Nursing, Plaistow Hospital, Samson Street, London, E13 9EH, Tel.: 020 8586 6358
Child Health
Child Development, West Ham Clinic, 84 West Ham Lane, Stratford, E15 4PT, Tel.: 020 8250 7361
Ms K Rudd, Roald Dahl PaediatricNurse for Epilepsy, York House, Tel.: 020 7445 7817
Ms J Scotland, Team Leader, Community Children's, Plaistow Hospital, Samson Street, Tel.: 020 8586 5518
Child Health Records
Lister II, Plaistow Hospital, Tel.: 020 8586 6415
Child Protection/Safeguarding Children
Mrs A Morgan, Nurse Consultant for Vulnerable Children, Plaistow Hospital, Samson Street, E13 9EH, Tel.: 020 8586 6411
Mrs K Read, Looked After Children, Nurse Specialist, Plaistow Hospital, Samson Street, E13 9EH, Tel.: 020 8586 6466
Mrs M Alexander, Liaison Health Visitor, Child Protection, Plaistow Hospital, Samson Street, E13 9EH, Tel.: 0208 586 6467
Mrs S Nichols, Named Nurse, Child Protection, Plaistow Hospital, Samson Street, E13 9EH, Tel.: 020 8586 6410
Clinical Leads (NSF)
Dr E Abiola, Clinical Lead, Cancer,
Dr P Gopinathan, Clinical Lead, Cancer,
Dr P Chandra, Clinical Lead, CHD,
Dr C Davison, Clinical Lead, Diabetic Care,
Community Nursing Services
Ms J Glasgow, Area Service Manager - Community Nursing & Health Visiting, Royal Docks Medical Centre, 19 East Ham Manor Way, E6 4NA, Tel.: 020 7445 7121
Ms H Page, Area Service Manager - Community Nursing & Health Visiting, Lord Lister Health Centre, 121 Woodgrange Road, Forest Gate, E7 0EP, Tel.: 020 8250 7200
Ms K Sidhu, Area Service Manager - Community Nursing & Health Visiting, The Centre Manor Park, 30 Church Road, Manor Park, London, E12 6AQ, Tel.: 020 8553 7425
Ms J Smith, Area Service Manager - Community Nursing & Health Visiting, Appleby Health Centre, 63 Appleby Road, E16 1LQ, Tel.: 020 7445 7087
Family Planning Services
Dr S Abbott, Service Manager, Shrewsbury Road Health Centre, Shrewsbury Road, Forest Gate, E7 8QP, Tel.: 020 8586 5148
HIV/AIDS
Dr S Abbott, Service Manager, Shrewsbury Road Health Centre, Shrewsbury Road, Forest Gate, E7 8QP, Tel.: 020 8586 5148
Learning Disabilities
Ms H Tinney, Nurse Manager, NCTPLD, Units 7-8 Stratford Office Village, 4 Romford Road, E15 4EA, Tel.: 020 8250 7500

London Strategic Health Authority

Liaison Services
Ms C Flowers, Liaison, Paediatrics, Tel.: 020 7445 7147
Mrs G Whitfield, Community Liaison Specialist, St Andrews Hospital, Devons Road, Bow, E3 3NT, Tel.: 020 7363 8238
Mrs P Williams, Community Liaison Specialist, Plaistow Hospital, Samson Street, E13 9EH, Tel.: 020 8586 5527

School Nursing
Ms S Rolfe, Head of School Nursing, Lister II Ward, Plaistow Hospital, Samson Street, E13 9EH, Tel.: 020 8586 6409

Specialist Nursing Services
Ms S Reid, New Entrants Service, Shrewsbury Road Health Centre, Forest Gate, E7, Tel.: 020 8586 5162
Ms T Kitto, Cardiac Rehabilitation, The Centre Manor Park, 30 Church Road, Manor Park, London, E12 6AQ, Tel.: 020 8553 7400
Ms M Eneberi, Continence, Plaistow Day Hospital, Samson Street, E13 9EH, Tel.: 020 8586 6230
Ms J Chapman, Team Leader, Specialist Nurse, Diabetic Care, Shrewsbury Health Centre, Tel.: 020 8586 5240
Ms W Graviles-Kwan, Specialist Nurse, Diabetic Care, Shrewsbury Health Centre, Tel.: 020 8586 5240
Ms N Hilton, Specialist Nurse, Diabetic Care, Shrewsbury Health Centre, Tel.: 020 8586 5240
Ms A McDonald, Specialist Nurse, Diabetic Care, Shrewsbury Health Centre, Tel.: 020 8586 5240
Ms R McHugh, Specialist Nurse, Diabetic Care, Shrewsbury Health Centre, Tel.: 020 8586 5240
Ms J O'Garro, Specialist Nurse, Diabetic Care, Shrewsbury Health Centre, Tel.: 020 8586 5240
Ms T O'Shea, Specialist Nurse, Diabetic Care, Shrewsbury Health Centre, Tel.: 020 8586 5240
Ms A Simler, Specialist Nurse, Diabetic Care, Shrewsbury Health Centre, Tel.: 020 8586 5240
Ms R Smeed, Specialist Nurse, Diabetic Care, Shrewsbury Health Centre, Tel.: 020 8586 5240
Ms B Burton, Sickle Cell & Thalassaemia, Plaistow Hospital, Tel.: 020 8586 6262
Ms A Beasley, Tissue Viability, 4th Floor Francis House, 760-762 Barking Road, Plaistow, E13, Tel.: 020 8271 1315
Ms C Dowsett, Tissue Viability, 4th Floor Francis House, 760-762 Barking Road, Plaistow, E13, Tel.: 020 8271 1315
Ms E Flaherty, Tissue Viability, 4th Floor Francis House, 760-762 Barking Road, Plaistow, E13, Tel.: 020 8271 1315

North Middlesex University Hospitals NHS Trust

Trust Headquarters, Sterling Way
Edmonton
LONDON
N18 1QX
Tel.: 0208 887 2000
Fax.: 0208 887 4219

Acute Specialist Nursing Services
Ms T Lee, Lead Nurse, A&E, North Middlesex University Hospital, Tel.: 0208 887 2880
Ms L Andrews, Clinical Nurse Specialist, Breast Care, North Middlesex University Hospital, Tel.: 0208 887 4203
Ms V Nangle, Clinical Nurse Specialist, Cardiac Rehabilitation, North Middlesex University Hospital, Tel.: 0208 887 4618
Ms K Earwicker, Clinical Nurse Specialist, Chemotherapy, North Middlesex University Hospital, Tel.: 0208 887 4383
Ms S Williams, Clinical Nurse Specialist, Colorectal, North Middlesex University Hospital, Tel.: 0208 887 2978
Ms G Lamptey, Clinical Nurse Specialist, Diabetes, North Middlesex University Hospital, Tel.: 0208 887 4257
Ms P Ling Fields, Clinical Nurse Specialist, Diabetes, North Middlesex University Hospital, Tel.: 0208 887 4238

Ms O O'Grady, Clinical Nurse Specialist, Diabetes, North Middlesex University Hospital, Tel.: 0208 887 2351
Ms J Quaine, Clinical Nurse Specialist, Diabetes, North Middlesex University Hospital, Tel.: 0208 887 2351
Ms F Sourie, Clinical Nurse Specialist, Fertility, North Middlesex University Hospital, Tel.: 0208 887 2620
Ms B Carvalho, Clinical Nurse Specialist, Gynaecology, North Middlesex University Hospital, Tel.: 0208 887 2985
Ms M Muli, Clinical Nurse Specialist, Haemoglobinopathy, George Marsh Centre, St Ann's Hospital, Tel.: 0208 442 6230
Ms J O'Connor, Clinical Nurse Specialist, Infection Control, North Middlesex University Hospital, Tel.: 0208 887 2383
Ms E Foody, Clinical Nurse Specialist, Lung Care, North Middlesex University Hospital, Tel.: 0208 887 2429
Ms R Vieira-Moreno, Clinical Nurse Specialist, Lung Care, North Middlesex University Hospital, Tel.: 0208 887 2475
Ms L Hurl, Research, Clinical Nurse Specialist, Oncology, North Middlesex University Hospital, Tel.: 0208 887 4356
Ms J Sterlini, Clinical Nurse Specialist, Oncology, North Middlesex University Hospital, Tel.: 0208 887 2687
Ms J Sharp, Clinical Nurse Specialist, Palliative Care, North Middlesex University Hospital, Tel.: 0208 887 2475
Ms C Thomas, Clinical Nurse Specialist, Palliative Care, North Middlesex University Hospital, Tel.: 0208 887 2475
Ms N Roheemun, Nurse Specialist, Sickle Cell, George Marsh Centre, St Ann's Hospital, Tel.: 07736 792439
Ms C Phillippou, Clinical Nurse Specialist, Upper GI, North Middlesex University Hospital, Tel.: 0208 887 2900
Ms R Dadswell, Clinical Nurse Specialist, Urology, North Middlesex University Hospital, Tel.: 0208 887 2440
Ms J Burke, Clinical Nurse Specialist, Urology/Oncology, North Middlesex University Hospital, Tel.: 0208 887 2483
Ms D Wright, Clinical Nurse Specialist, Urology/Oncology, North Middlesex University Hospital, Tel.: 0208 887 2629
Ms S Tutty, Clinical Nurse Specialist, Vascular, North Middlesex University Hospital, Tel.: 0208 887 4257

Admin & Senior Management
Mr M Bird, Senior Divisional Nurse - Medicine & Medicine for Elderly, North Middlesex University Hospital, Tel.: 0208 887 4116
Ms M Clarke, Senior Divisional Nurse - Emergency & Medical, North Middlesex University Hospital, Tel.: 0208 887 2368
Ms M Deckon, Senior Divisional Nurse - Specialist Medical, North Middlesex University Hospital, Tel.: 0208 887 4548
Ms L Donegan, Senior Divisional Nurse - Anaesthetics, Surgery & Women's, North Middlesex University Hospital, Tel.: 0208 887 4658
Ms A Garbutt, Senior Divisional Nurse - Diagnostics & Ambulatory Care, North Middlesex University Hospital, Tel.: 0208 887 4226
Ms B Norman, Senior Divisional Nurse - Paediatrics, North Middlesex University Hospital, Tel.: 0208 887 4099

Child Health Records
Ms G Cancello, Haringey PCT, St Ann's Hospital, Tel.: 0208 442 6600
Child Health Records, Enfield PCT, Holbrook House, Tel.: 0208 370 2500
Ms P Loizou, Haringey PCT, Crouch End Hill Health Centre, Tel.: 0208 341 2045

Child Protection/Safeguarding Children
Dr P Kapila, Named Doctor, Child Protection, North Middlesex University Hospital, Tel.: 0208 887 4009
Ms C Keating, Nurse, Child Protection, North Middlesex University Hospital, Tel.: 0208 887 2560
Ms S McFarlane, Named Nurse, Child Protection, North Middlesex University Hospital, Tel.: 0208 887 4099
Ms F Panel-Coates, Director of Nursing, Child Protection, North Middlesex University Hospital, Tel.: 0208 887 4276

Community Midwifery
Ms M Hicks, Bereavement Midwife, North Middlesex University Hospital, Tel.: 0208 887 4157

London Strategic Health Authority

Mrs K Patel, Head of Midwifery, North Middlesex University Hospital, Tel.: 0208 887 2494

Mrs M Satterthwaite, Community Midwifery Manager, North Middlesex University Hospital, Tel.: 0208 887 4157

Discharge Co-ordinators

Ms P Bain, Discharge Co-ordinator, North Middlesex University Hospital, Tel.: 0208 887 2833

Ms J Collins, Discharge Co-ordinator, North Middlesex University Hospital, Tel.: 0208 887 2355

Ms H Joyce, First Response Team Nurse Co-ordinator, North Middlesex University Hospital, Tel.: 0208 887 2355

Ms J Kincaid, GM Site Operations, North Middlesex University Hospital, Tel.: 0208 887 4401

Family Planning Services

Dr Christopher, Family Planning Services, St Ann's Hospital, Tel.: 0208 442 6810

HIV/AIDS

Ms A Volney-George, HIV, Clinical Nurse Specialist, North Middlesex University Hospital, Tel.: 0208 887 4547

Ms F Young, HIV, Clinical Nurse Specialist, North Middlesex University Hospital, Tel.: 0208 887 4544

Other Services

Drop in centre for sickle cell advice, George Marsh Centre, St Ann's Hospital, Tel.: 0208 442 6230

Home Pain Control Team (sickle cell), George Marsh Centre, St Ann's Hospital,

Paediatric Liaison Health Visitors

Ms M Griew, North Middlesex University Hospital, Tel.: 0208 887 4010

Ms M Hamilton, North Middlesex University Hospital, Tel.: 0208 887 4010

Oxleas NHS Trust

Trust Headquarters, Pinewood House
Pinewood Place
DARTFORD
Kent, DA2 7WG
Tel.: 01322 625700

Learning Disabilities

Ms S Burchell, Consultant Nurse, Heathview, Goldie Leigh, Lodge Hill, Abbey Wood, Tel.: 0208 319 7156

Community Team, 132-134 Powis Street, Woolwich, SE18 6NL, Tel.: 0208 921 2733

Mrs A Gordon, Community Nurse Manager, Erith Centre, Park Crescent, Erith, DA8 2EE, Tel.: 01322 356152

Ms S Scarlett, Acting, Community Nurse Manager, Tel.: 0208 921 2736

Service Manager, Heathview, Goldie Leigh, Lodge Hill, Abbey Wood, Tel.: 0208 319 7103

Mr S Whitmore, Director of Learning Disabilities & Child & Adolescent MH, Pinewood House, Pinewood Lane Dartford, DA2 7WG, Tel.: 01322 625719

Queen Elizabeth Hospital NHS Trust

Trust Headquarters, Queen Elizabeth Hospital
Stadium Road, Woolwich
LONDON, SE18 4QH
Tel.: 020 8836 6000

Child Protection/Safeguarding Children

Ms H Jakeway, Lead Nurse, Safeguarding Children, Safari Ward, QEH NHS Trust, Stadium Road, Woolwich, London, SE18 4QH, Tel.: 0208 836 5370

Community Midwifery

Discharges, Transfers, Fax 020 8836 4786, Tel.: 020 8836 4876

Mrs H Jones, Manager - Community Services, Tel.: 020 8836 4790

Out of hours, Tel.: Bleep 254

Ms A Shasha, Head of Midwifery, Tel.: 020 8836 4506

Queen Mary's Sidcup NHS Trust

Trust Headquarters, Queen Mary's Hospital
Frognal Avenue
SIDCUP
Kent
DA14 6LT
Tel.: 020 8302 2678
Fax.: 020 8308 3052

Community Midwifery

Ms L Chapman, Community Midwifery Clerk (10.30-13.30), Community Midwifery Office, Queen Mary's Hospital, Tel.: 0208 302 2678 x 4013/4286

Community Midwifery Office - Out of Hours, Tel.: 0208 302 2678 bleep 793

Ms J Dyer, Safeguarding Childrens Nurse, Named Nurse, Tel.: 020 8302 2678 ext 4748

Mrs N Henry, Clinical Midwifery Manager, Queen Mary's Hospital, Tel.: 0208 302 2678 ext 4895

Mrs N Henry, Clinical Midwifery Manager, Tel.: 020 8302 2678 ext 4895

Mrs A Jommo, Postnatal Clinical Midwifery Manager, Tel.: 020 8302 2678 ext 4309

Ms S Murrant, Community Midwifery Clerk (10.30-13.30), Community Midwifery Office, Queen Mary's Hospital, Tel.: 0208 302 2678 x 4013/4286

Mrs L Samuels-Walrond, Associate Director, Head of Midwifery, Tel.: 0208 302 2678 x 4326

Ms E Ward, Postnatal Ward, Tel.: 0208 302 2678 x 4640/4173

Redbridge Primary Care Trust

Trust Headquarters, Becketts House
2-14 Ilford Hill
ILFORD
Essex
IG1 2QX
Tel.: 0208 478 5151

Admin & Senior Management

Ms Y Jeremiah, Lead Nurse - Strategic Leadership, Becketts House, 2-14 Ilford Hill, Ilford, Essex, IG1 2QX, Tel.: 0208 478 5151

Ms K Mathews, Assistant Director Primary Care Transformation, Becketts House, Tel.: 0208 926 5278

Ms T Sawtell, Director of Primary Care & Community Management, Becketts House, Tel.: 0208 478 5151

Ms D Searle, Lead Nurse, Nurse Development, Becketts House, Tel.: 0208 478 5151

Child Health

Childrens Community Nursing Team, Redbridge Childrens Centre, Kenwood Gardens Clinic, Kenwood Gardens, Grants Hill, Ilford, Essex, IG2, Tel.: 0208 924 6117

Ms D Lamb, Nurse Co-ordinator Children & Families - West Locality, South Woodford Health Centre, 114 High Road South, Woodford, E18 2QS, Tel.: 020 8491 1806

Ms M Marsh, Nurse Co-ordinator Children & Families - South Locality, 7th Floor, Becketts House, 2-14 Ilford Hill, Ilford, Essex, IG1 2QX, Tel.: 020 8926 5136

Mrs E Powell, Child Health Department Manager, Alexander Suite, Goodmayes Hospital, Barley Lane, Goodmayes, Essex, IG3 8XJ, Tel.: 020 8970 5712

Ms J Smith, Head of Childrens Services, Becketts House, 2-14 Ilford Hill, Ilford, Essex, IG1 2QX, Tel.: 0208 478 5151

Ms C Webb, Nurse Co-ordinator Children & Families - North Central Locality, Newbury Park Health Centre, 40 Perrymans Farm Road, Newbury Park, Ilford, Essex, IG2 7LE, Tel.: 020 8491 1556

Child Health Records

Child Health Records, Alexander Suite, Goodmayes Hospital, Barley Lane, Goodmayes, IG3 8XJ, Tel.: 020 8970 4250

London Strategic Health Authority

Child Protection/Safeguarding Children
Ms Y Davies, Assistant Director of Safeguarding Children, Becketts House, Tel.: 0208 478 5151
Ms D Xavier-Anatole, Safeguarding Children, Named Nurse, Alexander Suite, Goodmayes Hospital, Barley Lane, Goodmayes, Ilford, Essex, IG3 8XJ, Tel.: 0208 970 5808/4099

Community Matrons
Ms S Neilson, Community Matron, Long Term Conditions, Diabetes Centre, Tel.: 0208 822 4054

District Nursing
Evening/Night District Nurses, Tel.: 0208 924 6513
Ms P Keating, Professional Development Nurse - Leadership, 40 Perrymans Farm Road, Newbury Park, Essex, IG2 7LE, Tel.: 020 491 1556
Ms C Lucas, Professional Development Nurse - Clinical Practice, South Woodford Health Centre, 114 High Road, South Woodford, E18 2QS, Tel.: 020 8491 3333

Family Planning Services
John Telford Clinic, 45-59 Cleveland Road, Ilford, IG1 1EE, Tel.: 0208 491 2117/8

Health Visitors
Ms C Arakelian, Paediatric Liaison Health Visitor/CONI Co-ordinator, Alexander Suite, Goodmayes Hospital, Barley Lane, Goodmayes, Essex, IG3 8XJ, Tel.: 020 8970 4216

HIV/AIDS
Ms C Duggan, Hainault Health Centre, Tel.: 020 8491 3383

Learning Disabilities
Ms J Jay, Service Manager, Integrated Teams, Redbridge & Waltham Forest Learning Disabilities, Tel.: 0208 496 1831

Other Services
Ms A Archer, Assistant Director for Older Peoples Services, Becketts House, 2-14 Ilford Hill, Ilford, Essex, IG1 2QX, Tel.: 020 8478 5151
Ms M Palmer, PALS, South Woodford Health Centre, Tel.: 0800 0926 995
Podiatry, Lavender Ward, Goodmayes Hospital, Barley Lane, Goodmayes, Essex, Tel.: 020 8924 6191

School Nursing
Ms A Hadassi, School Nursing, Hainault Health Centre, Tel.: 0208 491 1557

Specialist Nursing Services
Ms J Li, Continence, Goodmayes Hospital, Barley Lane, Goodmayes, IG3 8XJ, Tel.: 020 8970 5760
Nurses, Diabetes, Diabetes Centre, Tel.: 020 8491 1570
Ms A Malambo, Nurse Specialist, Infection Control, Becketts House, Tel.: 0208 478 5151 ext 5142
Ms L Crisp, Macmillan, Hainault Health Centre, Tel.: 020 8924 6170
Nurses, Tissue Viability, Hainault Health Centre, Tel.: 020 8491 3395

Walk In Centres
NHS Walk in Centre, (10am-7pm daily), 201-205 Cranbrook Road, Ilford, Essex, Tel.: 0208 924 6633

Richmond & Twickenham Primary Care Trust

Trust Headquarters, Thames House
180 High Street
TEDDINGTON
Middlesex
TW11 8HU
Tel.: 0208 973 3000
Fax.: 0208 973 3001

Admin & Senior Management
Ms J Mager, Chief Executive, Tel.: 0208 973 3550
Ms L Yeo, Director of Clinical Services & Nursing, Tel.: 0208 973 3128

Child Health Records
Ms M Leigh, Richmond Royal, Kewfoot Road, Richmond, TW9 2TE, Tel.: 0208 614 7426

Child Protection/Safeguarding Children
Ms L Doherty, Named Nurse, Child Protection, Thames House, 180 High Street, Teddington, Middlesex, TW11 8HU, Tel.: 0208 973 3497
Ms C Keys-Shaw, Designated Nurse, Child Protection, Thames House, 180 High Street, Teddington, Middlesex, TW11 8HU, Tel.: 0208 973 3127
Ms S Muldowney, Named Nurse, Child Protection, Thames House, 180 High Street, Teddington, Middlesex, TW11 8HU, Tel.: 0208 973 3498

Clinical Leads (NSF)
Ms C Pennycook, Clinical Lead, Cancer,
Dr P Gibson, Clinical Lead, CHD,
Dr M Harper, Clinical Lead, Children,
Dr A Pallachi, Clinical Lead, Diabetic Care,

District Nursing
Ms J Nicoli-Jones, Team Leader, Sheen Lane Health Centre, 70 Sheen Lane, London, SW14 8LP, Tel.: 0208 878 7561
Out of Hours Emergencies - District Nurses, Via Careline, Tel.: 0208 744 9414

Equipment Loan Services
Ms A Stratten, AD Adults and Older People, Thames House, 180 High Street, Teddington, Middlesex, TW11 8HU, Tel.: 0208 973 3130

Family Planning Services
Ms A Versey, Team Leader, Family Planning, Thames House, 180 High Street, Teddington, Middlesex, TW11 8HU, Tel.: 0208 973 3133

Health Visitors
Ms T Roe, Team Leader, Health Visiting, Hampton Clinic, Tangley Park Road, Hampton Nurserylands, Hampton, TW12 3YH, Tel.: 0208 973 3450
Ms L Watson, Special Needs Health Visitor, Teddington Clinic, 18 Queens Road, Teddington, TW11 0LR, Tel.: 0208 977 8131

HIV/AIDS
Ms A Hoile, Sheen Lane Health Centre, Sheen Lane, Sheen, SW14 8LP, Tel.: 0208 878 7561

Pharmacy
Ms D Adams, Chief Pharmacist, Thames House, 180 High Street, Teddington, Middlesex, TW11 8HU, Tel.: 0208 973 3125

School Nursing
Ms L Hagan, Team Leader, School Health/Nursing Service, St John's Health Centre, Oak Lane, Twickenham, TW1 3PA, Tel.: 0208 891 8130

Specialist Nursing Services
Ms C Hart, Kingston Hospital, Galsworthy Road, Kingston u Thames, KT2 7QB, Tel.: 0208 546 7711 ext 2077
Ms J Morrison, Breast Care, Kingston Hospital, Galsworthy Road, Kingston u Thames, KT2 7QB, Tel.: 0208 546 7711
Ms N Snuggs, Breast Care, Kingston Hospital, Galsworthy Road, Kingston u Thames, KT2 7QB, Tel.: 0208 546 7711
Mr S Carlton, Community Nursing Team Leader, Children, Ham Clinic, Ashburnham Road, Ham, TW10 7NF, Tel.: 0208 973 3500
Ms K Normington, Advisor, Continence, Teddington Memorial Hospital, Hampton Road, Teddington, TW11 0JL, Tel.: 0208 714 4086
Ms T Staines, Advisor, Continence, Teddington Memorial Hospital, Hampton Road, Teddington, TW11 0JL, Tel.: 0208 714 4093
Ms L Scott, Facilitator, Diabetes, Thames House, 180 High Street, Teddington, Middlesex, TW11 8HU, Tel.: 0208 973 3092
Ms S Henderson, Nurse, Infection Control, Thames House, 180 High Street, Teddington, Middlesex, TW11 8HU, Tel.: 0208 973 3000
Ms L Nazarko, Nurse Consultant, Older People, Teddington Memorial Hospital, Hampton Road, Teddington, TW11 0JL, Tel.: 0208 714 4000
Ms V Flick, Stoma Care, Kingston Hospital, Galsworthy Road, Kingston u Thames, KT2 7QB, Tel.: 0208 546 7711 ext 2251

Walk In Centres
Mrs L Coghill, Walk In Centre, Nurse Consultant, Teddington Memorial Hospital, Hampton Road, Teddington, TW11 0JL, Tel.: 0208 714 4000

London Strategic Health Authority

Royal Brompton & Harefield NHS Trust

Trust Headquarters, Royal Brompton Hospital
Sydney Street
LONDON
SW3 6NP
Tel.: 020 7352 8121
Fax.: 020 7351 8790

Acute Specialist Nursing Services
Ms K Dick, Home Care, Nurse, Cystic Fibrosis,
Ms A Fgerns, Home Care, Nurse, Cystic Fibrosis,
Ms J Francis, Nurse, Cystic Fibrosis,
Mrs P Stringer, Cystic Fibrosis,
Mrs L Biggart, Nurse, Respiratory, Royal Brompton Hospital,
Ms P Hall, Nurse, Respiratory, Royal Brompton Hospital,
Admin & Senior Management
Ms R Bulger, PA to Director of Nursing & Quality, Tel.: 020 7351 8690
Dr C Shuldham, Director of Nursing & Quality, Royal Brompton Hospital,
Liaison Services
Ms M Jiggins, Children's Cardiac Liaison Team Nurse, Royal Brompton Hospital,
Ms V Johansen, Children's Cardiac Liaison Team Nurse, Royal Brompton Hospital,
Ms M McLaughlin, Children's Cardiac Liaison Team Nurse, Sub Speciality in Fetal Cardiology,
Ms J Park, Cardiac Home Care Team Nurse,
Ms B Persaud Rai, Cardiac Home Care Nurse,
Mrs E Peters, Cardiac Home Care Team Nurse,
Ms C Renwick, Children's Cardiac Liaison Team Nurse, Royal Brompton Hospital,
Mr P Walters, Cardiac Home Care Team Nurse,

Royal Free Hampstead NHS Trust

Trust Headquarters, Royal Free Hospital
Pond Street, Hampstead
LONDON
NW3 2QG
Tel.: 020 7794 0500

Admin & Senior Management
Ms C Holroyd, Nurse Director, Royal Free Hospital, Pond Street, London, NW3 2QG, Tel.: 020 7830 2900
Ms R Ouzia, Women & Children's Services,
Child Health
Ms N Kho, Senior Nurse for Child Health, Royal Free Hampstead NHS Trust,
Child Health Records
Crowndale Health Centre, Tel.: 020 7530 3853
Child Protection/Safeguarding Children
Ms H Swarbuck, School Nurse Co-ordinator, Senior Nurse, Child Protection, Royal Free Hospital, Tel.: 020 7380 5828
Community Midwifery
Mrs S Ashton May, Lead Midwife - In-hospital Services, Tel.: Bleep 443
Discharges - Community Midwives, Tel.: 020 7830 2568
Discharges - Community Receptionist, Fax 020 7830 2752,
Ms S Harririan, Lead Midwife - Day Services, Tel.: bleep 931
Labour Ward, Tel.: 0207 794 0500 ext 6256
Prof L Page, Head of Midwifery,
Ms J Walderman, Baby Feeding Advisor, Tel.: 0207 974 0500 Bleep 174
Liaison Services
Ms S Behan, Liaison A&E & Paediatrics, Child Health Department, Tel.: 020 7830 2895
Ms M Noone, Discharge Facilitator, 8th Floor, Royal Free Hospital, Tel.: 020 7830 2087

Royal Marsden NHS Trust

Trust Headquarters, 203 Fulham Road
South Kensington
LONDON
SW3 6JJ
Tel.: 0207 352 8171

Admin & Senior Management
Dr D Weir-Hughes, Director of Nursing, Royal Marsden NHS Trust, 203 Fulham Road, South Kensington, London, SW3 6JJ, Tel.: 0207 352 8171

Royal National Orthopaedic NHS Trust

Trust Headquarters, Brockley Hill
STANMORE
Middlesex
HA7 4LP
Tel.: 020 8954 2300
Fax.: 020 8954 9133

Admin & Senior Management
Mr A Palmer, Director of Nursing, Royal National Orthopaedic NHS Trust, Brockley Hill, Stanmore, Middlesex, HA7 4LP, Tel.: 020 8954 2300

South London & Maudsley NHS Trust

Trust Headquarters, 9th Floor, Tower Building
11 York Road
LONDON
SE1 7NX
Tel.: 020 7919 2362

Learning Disabilities
Ms H Charalambous, Team, Co-ordinator, 340 Brixton Road, London, SW9 7AA, Tel.: 020 7411 2960
Lambeth Borough Lead, 340 Brixton Road, London, SW9 7AA, Tel.: 020 7411 2960

Southwark Primary Care Trust

Trust Headquarters, 6th Floor
Mabel Goldwyn House, 49 Grange Walk
LONDON
SE1 3DY
Tel.: 020 7525 0400

Admin & Senior Management
Mr C Bull, Chief Executive, Tel.: 020 7525 3793
Child Health Records
Child Health Records, Elizabeth Blackwell House, Wardalls Grove, Avonley Road, London, SE14 5ER, Tel.: 020 7635 5555
Child Protection/Safeguarding Children
Ms S Mummery, Child Protection, Sheldon Centre, St Giles Road, Camberwell, SE5 7RN, Tel.: 020 7771 3400
Clinical Leads (NSF)
Ms M Jones, Clinical Lead, Cancer,
Community Nursing Services
Community Nursing Services, Elizabeth Blackwell House, Wardalls Grove, Avonley Road, London, SE14 5ER, Tel.: 020 7635 5555
District Nursing
District Nurses, Elizabeth Blackwell House, Wardalls Grove, Avonley Road, London, SE14 5ER, Tel.: 020 7635 5555
Emergencies/Night, Tel.: 020 7403 7771
Health Visitors
Health Visitors, Elizabeth Blackwell House, Wardalls Grove, Avonley Road, London, SE14 5ER, Tel.: 020 7635 5555
Ms J Prescott, Specialist Needs Health Visitor, Sheldon Centre, Tel.: 020 7771 3400

London Strategic Health Authority

HIV/AIDS
Ms C Wallace, Manager, MMRU, Wardalls Gardens, Avonley Road, New Cross, SE14 5ER, Tel.: 020 7771 5423
Learning Disabilities
Ms A Keens, Manager, 19-21 Brownhill Road, London, SE6 2HG, Tel.: 020 8698 6788
Ms D Kinnair, Director of Nursing, Tel.: 020 7525 0407
Ms S Maguire, Director, Trust Support Southwark, 1 Barry Parade, Peckham Rye, SE22 0JA, Tel.: 020 8693 6909
Liaison Services
Ms C Ominiyi, Adult Liaison Team, 3rd Floor, Hunts House, Guy's Hospital, SE1 9RT, Tel.: 020 7955 3646
Mr J Thorogood, Liaison Health Visitor Guy's, New Salomons Clinic, Guy's Hospital, Tel.: 020 7955 4068
Ms J Vessey, Liaison Kings College Hospital, 1st Floor, A&E Dept, Kings College Hospital, Denmark Hill, SE5 9RS, Tel.: 020 7346 3947
Specialist Nursing Services
Ms P Gillard, Diabetic Care, King's Diabetes Centre, Mapother House, De Crespigny Park, SE5 9RS, Tel.: 020 7346 3119
Ms J Sharpe, Diabetic Care, Diabetes Centre, 3rd Floor, Thomas Guy House, Guy's Hospital, Tel.: 020 7955 4863
Ms J Turowska, Diabetic Care, King's Diabetes Centre, Mapother House, De Crespigny Park, SE5 9RS, Tel.: 020 7346 3119
Support Team, Terminal Care, Guy's Hospital, Tel.: 020 7955 5000 ext 3223

St George's Healthcare NHS Trust

Trust Headquarters, St George's Hospital
Blackshaw Road, Tooting
LONDON, SW17 0QT
Tel.: 020 8672 1255
Fax.: 020 8672 5304

Acute Specialist Nursing Services
Ms S Lowndes, Clinical Nurse Specialist, Breast Care, Breast Clinic, Tel.: 020 8725 1589 bleep 6782
Ms D Dawson, Nurse Consultant, Critical Care, St James Wing, Tel.: 020 8725 3129
Ms C Stanley, Clinical Nurse Specialist, Dermatology, Outpatients, Tel.: 020 8725 2504 bleep 7160
Ms A Walton, Clinical Nurse Specialist, Diabetes, Thomas Addison Unit, Tel.: 020 8725 1429
Ms M Synnott-Wells, Specialist Nurse, Epilepsy, Atkinson Morley Wing, Tel.: 020 8725 4110
Ms R Law, Specialist Nurse, Infection Control, Jenner Wing, Tel.: 020 8725 5728 bleep 6798
Ms S Ellis, Nurse Consultant, Lymphoedema, Dermatology Unit, Tel.: 020 8725 1025
Ms H Jarman, Nurse Consultant, Medicine/Emergency Care, A&E, Tel.: 020 8725 1999
Mr C Way, Paediatric HDU, Nurse Consultant, Paediatrics, Intensive Care Unit, Tel.: 020 8725 2946
Ms T Glynn, Senior Nurse, Palliative Care, Clare House, Tel.: 020 8725 3311
Ms J Holden, Plastics & Reconstructive, Clinical Nurse Specialist, Plastic Surgery, Tel.: 020 8725 4710
Ms S Prigmore, Nurse Consultant, Respiratory, Chest Clinic, Tel.: 020 8725 1275
Ms C Rudoni, Clinical Nurse Specialist, Stoma Care, Tel.: 020 8725 3916 bleep 6260
Dr K Gebhardt, Pressure Prevention, Clinical Nurse Specialist, Ulcers, Tel.: 020 8725 2230
Ms S Murray, Nurse Consultant, Vascular, Tel.: 020 8725 3189 bleep 7385
Child Health
Ms A Walker, Community Childrens Nurse Manager, St George's Hospital, Tel.: 020 8725 2272

Ms H Woolford, School Health Ages 5-19, Child Health Dept, Clare House, St George's Hospital, Blackshaw Road, Tooting, London, SW17 0QT, Tel.: 020 8725 3757
Child Health Records
Ms R Meadows, Assistant Director of Nursing, Tel.: 020 8725 2076
Child Protection/Safeguarding Children
Ms R Meadows, Assistant Director of Nursing, Tel.: 020 8725 2076
Community Midwifery
Community Midwives Offices, Fax 020 8725 1975, Tel.: 020 8725 2535/6
Ms A Hellew, Director of Midwifery & General Manager for Children & Women, Tel.: 020 8725 3638
Ms L Stephens, Midwifery, Nurse Consultant, Lanesborough Wing, St George's Hospital, Tel.: 020 8725 2195
Ms R von dem Bussche, Lead Midwife Community, Tel.: 020 8725 0333
Equipment Loan Services
Ms S Piper, Equipment Library, Tel.: 0208 725 3133
Health Visitors
Ms P Bennett, Paediatric Liaison Health Visitor, Tel.: 0208 725 1286 bleep 6088
HIV/AIDS
Ms S Donaghy, Paediatric HIV/AIDS, Nurse Consultant, Nicholls Ward, Tel.: 020 8725 2096
Ms H Pritchitt, Sexual Health & HIV, Clinical Nurse Specialist, GUM Clinic, Tel.: 020 8725 2690

St. Mary's Hospital, Paddington NHS Trust

Trust Headquarters, St Mary's Hospital
Praed Street
Paddington
LONDON
W2 1NY
Tel.: 020 7886 6666
Fax.: 020 7886 6200

Child Protection/Safeguarding Children
Mr J Dunne, Child Protection, Dept of Paediatrics, 6th Floor, QEQM Wing, St Mary's Hospital, South Wharf Road, London, W2 1NY, Tel.: 0207 886 7958
Community Midwifery
Community Midwives Office, (24 hour voicemail), Fax 020 7886 2166, Tel.: 020 7886 1158
Miss F Han, Acute Services Manager, Midwifery Administration, St Mary's Hospital, Tel.: 020 7886 6763
Mrs L Pacanowski, Head of Midwifery, Midwifery Administration, St Mary's Hospital, Tel.: 020 7886 1037
Mrs E Younger, Primary Care Manager, Midwifery Administration, St Mary's Hospital, Tel.: 020 7886 6763
Health Visitors
Miss R Marriage, Liaison Paediatric Health Visitor, Children's A&E Dept, St Mary's Hospital, Tel.: 020 7886 3758
Liaison Services
Ms R Campbell, Adult Discharge Planning, St Mary's Hospital, Tel.: 020 7886 1286

Sutton & Merton Primary Care Trust

Trust Headquarters, Hamilton Wing
Nelson Hospital, Kingston Road
RAYNES PARK
Surrey
SW20 8DB
Tel.: 020 8251 1111

Admin & Senior Management
Mrs P Rossor, Director of Nursing, Executive Director of Service Delivery Sutton, Main Admin, Orchard Hill, Fountain Drive, Carshalton, Surrey, SM5 4NN, Tel.: 020 8770 8000

Ms C Schumacher, Assistant Director of Nursing, The Nelson Hospital, Kingston Road, Raynes Park, London, SW20 8DB, Tel.: 020 8251 1111

Ms C Taylor, Chief Executive, The Nelson Hospital, Kingston Road, Raynes Park, London, SW20 8DB, Tel.: 020 8251 1111

Child Health

Ms H Cook, Merton - Partnership Manager, Tel.: 020 8545 4497

Ms A Howers, Specialist Manager - Child & Family Services, Orchard Hill, Fountain Drive, Carshalton, SM5 4NR, Tel.: 020 8770 8363

Child Health Records

Child Health Department, Orchard Hill, Fountain Drive, Carshalton, SM5 4NR, Tel.: 020 8770 8000

Child Protection/Safeguarding Children

Ms L Ross, Looked After Children - Sutton, Designated Nurse, London Borough of Sutton Social Services, The Lodge, Honeywood Walk, Carshalton, SM5 3PD, Tel.: 020 8770 6591

Ms E Tanda, Looked After Children - Merton, Designated Nurse, London Borough of Merton Social Services, Worsfold House, Church Road, Mitcham, CR4 3BA, Tel.: 020 8545 4278

Dr B Ogeah, Designated Doctor, Child Protection, Orchard Hill, Fountain Drive, Carshalton, SM5 4NR, Tel.: 020 8770 8000

Ms C Stratton, Designated Nurse, Child Protection, The Wilson Hospital, Cranmer Road, Mitcham, CR4 4TP, Tel.: 020 8687 4543

Clinical Leads (NSF)

Ms J Moody, Clinical Lead, Cancer,

Dr V Gnanapragasam, Clinical Lead, CHD,

Dr J Tyrrell, Clinical Lead, Diabetic Care,

Dr C Elliott, Clinical Lead, Older People,

District Nursing

Ms T Collis, Operations Manager, Sutton, Orchard Hill, Fountain Drive, Carshalton, SM5 4NR, Tel.: 020 8770 8362

Ms J Mountford, Operations Manager, Sutton, Main Admin, Orchard Hill, Fountain Drive, Carshalton, Surrey, SM5 4NN, Tel.: 020 8770 8000

Out of Hours, Tel.: 020 8540 8892

Ms S Simpson, Operations Manager, West Merton, The Nelson Hospital, Kingston Road, Raynes Park, London, SW20 8DB, Tel.: 020 8251 0160

Ms L Wallder, Operations Manager, East Merton, The Wilson Hospital, Cranmer Road, Mitcham, CR4 4TP, Tel.: 020 8687 4690

Mrs J Wylde, Night Nursing Facilitator 020 8540 6405, Morden Road Clinic, Morden, Tel.: 020 8540 8892

Learning Disabilities

Ms H Cook, Merton - Partnership Manager, Tel.: 020 8545 4497

Ms A Daniels, Director Learning Disability Service, Orchard Hill, Fountain Drive, Carshalton, Surrey, SM5 4NR, Tel.: 020 8770 8000

Mr K Dattani Pitt, Sutton - Service Manager, Tel.: 020 8770 4332

Ms J Kinnear, Associate Director of Nursing for Learning Disabilities, Orchard Hill, Fountain Drive, Carshalton, Surrey, SM5 4NR, Tel.: 020 8770 8000

Merton Community Learning Disability Team, Russel Road, Wimbledon, Tel.: 020 8545 4520

Sutton Community Learning Disability Team, Mint House, Wallington, Tel.: 020 8770 4981

Liaison Services

Ms H Cook, Merton - Partnership Manager, Tel.: 020 8545 4497

Hospital Liaison, London Borough of Sutton, Intermediate Care Practitioner Team, Tel.: 020 8647 5534

Hospital Liaison, London Borough of Merton, Intermediate Care Practitioner Team, Tel.: 020 8642 2421

Specialist Nursing Services

Ms S Rickard, Head of Partnerships, The Nelson Hospital, Kingston Road, Raynes Park, London, SW20 8DB, Tel.: 020 8251 1111

Referral Contact Number, Intermediate Care, Tel.: 020 8789 6611

The Lewisham Hospital NHS Trust

Trust Headquarters, Univ Hospital Lewisham
Lewisham High Street, Lewisham
LONDON
SE13 6LH
Tel.: 020 8333 3000

Admin & Senior Management

Ms V Rhodes, Director of Nursing, Trust HQ, Univ Hospital Lewisham, Lewisham High Street, Lewisham, London, SE13 6LH,

Community Midwifery

Ms P Esson, Acting Head of Midwifery, Community Midwives Office, University Hospital Lewisham, Tel.: 020 8333 3101

Ms A Jones, Divisional Nurse Manager, Women's & Children's Services, University Hospital Lewisham, Tel.: 020 8333 3131

Women's Health Centre, Tel.: 020 8333 3104

The North West London Hospitals NHS Trust

Trust Headquarters, Northwick Park Hospital
Watford Road
HARROW
Middlesex
HA1 3UJ
Tel.: 020 8864 3232
Fax.: 020 8869 2009

Acute Specialist Nursing Services

Nurses, Breast Care, Northwick Park, Tel.: 0208 864 3232 x2510

Ms E Finlay, Community, Nurse Manager, Children, Northwick Park Hospital, Tel.: 0208 869 3914

Nurses, Continence, Northwick Park, Tel.: 0208 864 3232 x4167

Ms N Wheatley, Paediatric, Nurse Practitioner, Emergency Care, Central Middx Hospital, Tel.: 0208 453 2039

Nurses, Genetics, Northwick Park, Tel.: 0208 864 3232 x2769

Nurses, Infection Control, Northwick Park, Tel.: 0208 864 3232 x3663

Nurses, Macmillan, Northwick Park, Tel.: 0208 864 3232 x2546

Nurses, Tissue Viability, Northwick Park, Tel.: 0208 864 3232 x2494

Admin & Senior Management

Ms E Robb, Director of Nursing, Northwick Park Hospital, Watford Road, Harrow, Middlesex, HA1 3UJ, Tel.: 020 8869 2006

Child Health Records

Child Health Unit, Northwick Park Hospital, Tel.: 020 8869 2383

Child Protection/Safeguarding Children

Ms M Zurbrugg, Lead Nurse, Safeguarding Children, Tel.: 0208 8692379

Community Midwifery

Community Midwifery Manager, Northwick Park Hospital, Watford Road, Harrow, Middlesex, HA1 3UJ, Tel.: 020 8869 2871/2

Community Midwives, Central Middlesex Hospital, Acton Lane, Park Royal, Acton, London, NW10 7NS, Tel.: 020 8453 2466

Emergencies, Central Middlesex Hospital, Acton Lane, Park Royal, Acton, London, NW10 7NS, Tel.: 020 8453 2063

Ms C Mannion, Director of Midwifery Services, Northwick Park Hospital, Watford Road, Harrow, Middlesex, HA1 3UJ, Tel.: 020 8869 2885/6

Ms C Mannion, Director of Midwifery Services, Central Middlesex Hospital, Acton Lane, Park Royal, Acton, London, NW10 7NS, Tel.: 020 8453 2110

Maternity Unit, Northwick Park Hospital, Watford Road, Harrow, Middlesex, HA1 3UJ, Tel.: 020 8869 2871/2890

Senior Midwife, Central Middlesex Hospital, Acton Lane, Park Royal, Acton, London, NW10 7NS, Tel.: 020 8453 2102

Family Planning Services

Family Planning Services, Caryl Thomas Clinic, Headstone Drive, Wealdstone, HA1 4UQ, Tel.: 020 8863 7004

London Strategic Health Authority

Health Visitors
Ms H Legg, Liaison Health Visitor, Rainbow Childrens Centre, Central Middx Hospital, Acton Lane, London, NW10 7NS, Tel.: 0208 453 2779
Ms L Nkwocha, Liaison Health Visitor, Rainbow Childrens Centre, Central Middx Hospital, Acton Lane, London, NW10 7NS, Tel.: 0208 453 2779
HIV/AIDS
Ms M Le Prevost, Paediatric HIV Specialist, Northwick Park Hospital, Tel.: 0208 869 3914
Liaison Services
Discharge Liaison, Northwick Park Hospital, Watford Road, Harrow, Middlesex, HA1 3UJ, Tel.: 020 8864 3232
School Nursing
Ms A Hourihan, School Nurse Manager, Northwick Park Hospital, Tel.: 020 8869 2378

Tower Hamlets Primary Care Trust
Trust Headquarters, Mile End Hospital
Bancroft Road
LONDON
E1 4DG
Tel.: 0208 223 8900
Fax.: 0208 223 8907

Admin & Senior Management
Ms C Alexander, Director of Nursing & Therapies,
Mrs Z Bampoe, Associate Director, Nursing & Therapies,
Mrs A Williams, Chief Executive,
Child Health
Child Development Team, Wellington Way Health Centre, 1A Wellington Way, London, E3 4NE, Tel.: 0208 980 0531
Ms B Inal, Community Children's Nursing Team, Tel.: 0208 980 3510
Ms K Wynne, Community Children's Nursing Team, 3rd Floor, John Harrison House, Philpot Street, London, E1 2DR, Tel.: 0207 377 7215
Child Health Records
Ms L Mattis, Child Health Department, Block 2, Ground Floor, Mile End Hospital, Bancroft Road, London, E1 4DG, Tel.: 0208 223 8899
Child Protection/Safeguarding Children
Ms D Fowler, PA Secretary for Child Protection, Block Two, Ground Floor, Mile End Hospital, Bancroft Road, London, E1 4DG, Tel.: 020 8223 8879
Mr R Mills, Vulnerable Children, Nurse Consultant, Block Two, Ground Floor, Mile End Hospital, Bancroft Road, London, E1 4DG, Tel.: 020 8223 8200
Ms L Sheridan, Clinical Nurse Specialist, Child Protection, Block Two, Ground Floor, Mile End Hospital, Bancroft Road, London, E1 4DG, Tel.: 020 8223 8879
Clinical Leads (NSF)
Mr S Varley, Associate Director of Children's Services, Brooks Ward, Mile End Hospital, Bancroft Road, London, E1 4DG, Tel.: 0208 223 8353
Ms S White, Associate Director of Older People's Services, Bancroft Unit, Mile End Hospital, Bancroft Road, London, E1 4DG, Tel.: 0208 223 8838
Community Nursing Services
Community Nursing Services, (Managed by Child Health Records), 2nd Floor Burdett House, Mile End Hospital, Bancroft Road, London, E1 4DG, Tel.: 0208 223 8896
District Nursing Referrals, Tel.: 0208 223 8871
Emergencies, Tel.: 0208 223 8201
Manager, Tel.: 0208 223 7880
Family Planning Services
Mr P Young, Head of Family Planning Services, Sylvia Pankhurst Centre, Mile End Hospital, Bancroft Road, London, E1 4DG, Tel.: 0208 223 8007/8898

Health Visitors
Health Visitors, 2nd Floor Burdett House, Mile End Hospital, Bancroft Road, London, E1 4DG, Tel.: 0208223 8092/8093/8095/97
HIV/AIDS
Ms J Murat, Sylvia Pankhurst Centre, Mile End Hospital, Bancroft Road, London, E1 4DG, Tel.: 0208 223 8072
Learning Disabilities
Community Nursing Team, 130A Sewardstone Road, London, E2 9HN, Tel.: 0208 981 7425
Mr J Fagan, Clinical Nurse Specialist, Tel.: 0207 364 2034
School Nursing
Ms K Clackson, Locality Manager, School Health/Nursing Services, Newby Place Health Centre, 21 Newby Place, London, E14 0EY, Tel.: 0207 515 8893
Specialist Nursing Services
Specialist Nursing Service, Continence, Emily Graham Building, Mile End Hospital, Bancroft Road, London, E1 4DG, Tel.: 0208 223 8887/8371
Ms R Driver, Lead Nurse, Diabetes, 2nd Floor Main Building, Mile End Hospital, Bancroft Road, London, E1 4DG, Tel.: 0208 223 4147
Ms V Escudier, Clinical Nurse Specialist, Diabetes, 2nd Floor Main Building, Mile End Hospital, Bancroft Road, London, E1 4DG, Tel.: 0208 223 8836/8768
Ms J Reid, Clinical Nurse Specialist, Diabetes, 2nd Floor Main Building, Mile End Hospital, Bancroft Road, London, E1 4DG, Tel.: 0208 223 8836/8768
Ms C Wilson, Clinical Nurse Specialist, Diabetes, 2nd Floor Main Building, Mile End Hospital, Bancroft Road, London, E1 4DG, Tel.: 0208 223 8836/8768
Ms K Khambhaita, Clinical Nurse Specialist, Infection Control, 2nd Floor Burdett House, Mile End Hospital, Bancroft Road, London, E1 4DG, Tel.: 0208 223 8009/8225/8743
Ms J Lucas, Clinical Nurse Specialist, Infection Control, 2nd Floor Burdett House, Mile End Hospital, Bancroft Road, London, E1 4DG, Tel.: 0208 223 8009/8225/8743
Ms M Shalloe, Lead Nurse, Infection Control, 2nd Floor Burdett House, Mile End Hospital, Bancroft Road, London, E1 4DG, Tel.: 0208 223 8437
Ms J Wells, Clinical Nurse Specialist, Infection Control, 2nd Floor Burdett House, Mile End Hospital, Bancroft Road, London, E1 4DG, Tel.: 0208 223 8009/8225/8743
Ms J Akushie, Clinical Nurse Specialist, Tissue Viability, Block 2, Ground Floor, Mile End Hospital, Bancroft Road, London, E1 4DG, Tel.: 0208 223 8873/8331
Ms A Hopkins, Lead Nurse, Tissue Viability, Block 2, Ground Floor, Mile End Hospital, Bancroft Road, London, E1 4DG, Tel.: 0208 223 8873/8331
Ms F Worboys, Lead Nurse, Tissue Viability, Block 2, Ground Floor, Mile End Hospital, Bancroft Road, London, E1 4DG, Tel.: 0208 223 8873/8331

University College London Hospitals NHS Foundation Trust
Trust Headquarters, 2nd Floor Central
250 Euston Road
LONDON
NW1 2PG
Tel.: 0845 1555 000

Acute Specialist Nursing Services
Ms M Seth-Ward, Clinical Nurse Specialist, Acute Pain, University College Hospital, Podium 3, 3rd Floor, 235 Euston Road, London, NW1 3BU, Tel.: 0845 1555 000 x 73369
Ms D Colbeck, Clinical Nurse Specialist, Chronic Pain, National Hospital for Neurology & Neurosurgery, Queen Square, London, WC1N 3BG, Tel.: 0207 837 3611 x 3301

London Strategic Health Authority

Ms S Corker, Clinical Nurse Specialist, Chronic Pain, National Hospital for Neurology & Neurosurgery, Queen Square, London, WC1N 3BG, Tel.: 0207 837 3611 x 3301

Ms C Haslam, Nurse Specialist, Continence, National Hospital for Neurology & Neurosurgery, Queen Square, London, WC1N 3BG, Tel.: 0207 829 8713

Ms R Leaver, Lecturer, Practitioner, Continence, Urinary Diversion, Univ College Hospital, Tower Level 7, 235 Euston Road, London, NW1 3BU, Tel.: 0845 1555 000 x70700

Ms J Koay, Clinical Nurse Specialist, Diabetes, 3rd Floor Central, Euston Road, London, NW1 2PG, Tel.: 020 7380 9347

Ms S Olive, Clinical Nurse Specialist, Diabetes, 3rd Floor Central, Euston Road, London, NW1 2PG, Tel.: 020 7380 9347

Ms A Papworth, Clinical Nurse Specialist, Diabetes, 3rd Floor Central, Euston Road, London, NW1 2PG, Tel.: 020 7380 9347

Ms C Cook, Nurse, Infection Control, Dept of Microbiology, National Hospital for Neurology & Neurosurgery, Queen Square, London, WC1N 3BG, Tel.: 0207 837 3611 x3825

Ms P Folan, Lead Nurse, Infection Control, Dept of Microbiology, Windeyer Building, 46 Cleveland Street, London, W1T 4JF, Tel.: 0845 1555 000 x 8036

Ms L Buckley, Intrathecal Baclofen, Clinical Nurse Specialist, Neurology & Neurosurgery, National Hospital for Neurology & Neurosurgery, Queen Square, London, WC1N 3BG, Tel.: 0207 837 3611 x3439

Ms M Buckley, Behavioural Therapy, Clinical Nurse Specialist, Neurology & Neurosurgery, National Hospital for Neurology & Neurosurgery, Queen Square, London, WC1N 3BG, Tel.: 0207 837 3611 x3403/3135

Ms J Copeman, Neurorehab Clinical Nurse Leader, Neurology & Neurosurgery, National Hospital for Neurology & Neurosurgery, Queen Square, London, WC1N 3BG, Tel.: 0207 837 3611 x 3167

Mr A Davidson, Behavioural Therapy, Clinical Nurse Specialist, Neurology & Neurosurgery, National Hospital for Neurology & Neurosurgery, Queen Square, London, WC1N 3BG, Tel.: 0207 837 3611 x3403/3135

Ms L Jarrett, Intrathecal Baclofen, Clinical Nurse Specialist, Neurology & Neurosurgery, National Hospital for Neurology & Neurosurgery, Queen Square, London, WC1N 3BG, Tel.: 0207 837 3611 x3439

Ms R Kukkastenvehmas, Counselling & Diagnosis in Dementia, Clinical Nurse Specialist, Neurology & Neurosurgery, National Hospital for Neurology & Neurosurgery, Queen Square, London, WC1N 3BG, Tel.: 0207 676 2086

Mr S Andrews, Paediatric, Charge Nurse, Oncology, University College Hospital, Tower Level 11, 235 Euston Road, London, NW1 3BU, Tel.: 0845 1555 000 x 71115

Ms K Eaton, Nurse Consultant, Oncology, 3rd Floor Central, 250 Euston Road, London, NW1 2PG, Tel.: 0845 1555 000 x4183

Ms L Hart, Paediatric, Nurse, Respiratory, 1st Floor, 250 Euston Road, London, NW1 2PG, Tel.: 0845 1555 000 x3705

Ms M Schofield, Paediatric, Nurse, Respiratory, 1st Floor, 250 Euston Road, London, NW1 2PG, Tel.: 0845 1555 000 x3705

Ms S Fell, Clinical Nurse Specialist, Stoma Care, - Urology, 2nd Floor, Maple House, Rosenheim Wing, Ground Floor, 25 Grafton Way, London, WC1E 5DB, Tel.: 0845 1555 000 x 3966

Ms S Fillingham, Clinical Nurse Specialist, Stoma Care, - Urology, 2nd Floor, Maple House, Rosenheim Wing, Ground Floor, 25 Grafton Way, London, WC1E 5DB, Tel.: 0845 1555 000 x 3966

Ms L MacInnes, Colorectal Surgery, Nurse Specialist, Stoma Care, 2nd Floor, Maple House, Rosenheim Wing, Ground Floor, 25 Grafton Way, London, WC1E 5DB, Tel.: 020 7380 9182

Ms J Parker, Clinical Nurse Specialist, Stoma Care, - Urology, 2nd Floor, Maple House, Rosenheim Wing, Ground Floor, 25 Grafton Way, London, WC1E 5DB, Tel.: 0845 1555 000 x 3966

Ms S Lewis, Nurse, Tissue Viability, Wound Care, 2nd Floor Central, 250 Euston Road, London, NW1 2PG, Tel.: 0845 1555 000 x 4551

Admin & Senior Management
Ms L Boden, Chief Nurse, 2nd Floor Central, 250 Euston Road, London, NW1 2PG, Tel.: 020 7380 9854

Child Protection/Safeguarding Children
Ms S Jenkins, Advisor, Child Protection, University College Hospital, Tower Level 11, Team Room, 235 Euston Road, London, NW1 3BU, Tel.: 0845 1555 000 x71100

Community Midwifery
Ms J Hughes, Midwifery Lead, Elizabeth Garrett, Anderson & Obstetric Hospital, 1st Floor, Huntley Street, London, WC1E 6DH, Tel.: 0845 1555 000 x 8732

Ms A McCrae, Liaison Services Midwife/Community Midwife, Elizabeth Garrett, Anderson & Obstetric Hospital, 1st Floor, Huntley Street, London, WC1E 6DH, Tel.: 0845 1555 000 x 5238

Health Visitors
Ms A Lloyd, Paediatric Liaison Health Visitor, University College Hospital, Tower Level 11, Team Room, 235 Euston Road, London, NW1 3BU, Tel.: 0845 1555 000 x 71100

HIV/AIDS
Mr M Bruce, HIV/AIDS, Charge Nurse, University College Hospital, Tower Level 8, 235 Euston Road, London, NW1 3BU, Tel.: 0845 1555 000 ext 70832

Other Services
Ms K Eaton, Supportive Care, Nurse/Midwife Consultant, Cancer, 3rd Floor Central, 250 Euston Road, London, NW1 2PG, Tel.: 0845 1555 000 x 4183

Ms P Corrigan, Nurse/Midwife Consultant, Cardiac, The Heart Hospital, 16-18 Westmoreland Street, London, W1G 8PH, Tel.: 020 7573 8888 x 6047

Ms S Adam, Nurse/Midwife Consultant, Critical Care, University College Hospital, Tower Level 3, 235 Euston Road, London, NW1 3BU, Tel.: 0845 1555 000 x 73360

Ms K Judd, Young Onset Dementia, Nurse/Midwife Consultant, Dementia, National Hospital for Neurology & Neurosurgery, Queens Square, London, WC1N 3BG, Tel.: 020 7837 3611 x 3540

Ms R Davis, Nurse/Midwife Consultant, Dermatology, 3rd Floor Central, 250 Euston Road, London, NW1 2PG, Tel.: 0845 1555 000 x 4811

Ms L Kamps, Nurse/Midwife Consultant, Diabetes, 3rd Floor Central, 250 Euston Road, London, NW1 2PG, Tel.: 020 7380 9347

Ms A Jeanes, Nurse/Midwife Consultant, Infection Control, The Windeyer Institute of Medical Sciences, 46 Cleveland Street, London, W1T 4JF, Tel.: 0845 1555 000 x 8036

Ms A Osbourne, Nurse/Midwife Consultant, Midwifery, Elizabeth Garrett Anderson & Obstetric Hospital, Huntley Street, London, WC1E 6DH, Tel.: 0845 1555 000 x 2647

Ms Y Richens, Nurse/Midwife Consultant, Midwifery, Elizabeth Garrett Anderson & Obstetric Hospital, Huntley Street, London, WC1E 6DH, Tel.: 0845 155 000 x 2581

Ms B Porter, Nurse/Midwife Consultant, Multiple Sclerosis, National Hospital for Neurology & Neurosurgery, Queens Square, London, WC1N 3BG, Tel.: 020 7829 8798

Ms F Greenall, Nurse/Midwife Consultant, Neonatal, Elizabeth Garrett Anderson & Obstetric Hospital, Huntley Street, London, WC1E 6DH, Tel.: 0845 155 000 x 8680

Mr J Webster, Nurse/Midwife Consultant, Older People, 2nd Floor, Maple House, Rosenheim Building, 25 Grafton Way, London, WC1E 6DB, Tel.: 0845 1555 000 x 3871

Waltham Forest Primary Care Trust

Trust Headquarters, Hurst Road Health Centre
36a Hurst Road, Walthamstow
LONDON
E17 3BL
Tel.: 0208 928 2300
Fax.: 0208 928 2307

London Strategic Health Authority

Child Health

Children's Community Team, Tel.: 020 8535 6738
Children's Home Care Team, Azalea Ward, Tel.: 020 8539 5522
Children's Services, Azalea Ward, Tel.: 020 8539 5522
Ms J Newton, Specialist Children's Services, Senior Nurse Manager, Azalea Ward, Tel.: 020 8539 5522

Child Health Records

Ms K Cutter, Manager, Community Children Services, Azalea Ward, Whipps Cross Hospital, Tel.: 0208 539 5522

Child Protection/Safeguarding Children

Ms V Brandon, Child Protection, Child Health Dept, Azalea Ward, Whipps Cross Hospital, Tel.: 020 8539 5522
Ms J Shaw, Nurse Consultant, Child Protection, 4th Floor, Kirkdale House, 7 Kirkdale Road, Leytonstone, London, E11 1HP, Tel.: 020 8928 2421
Dr C Sloczynska, Designated Paediatrician, Child Protection, Azalea Ward, Whipps Cross Hospital, Tel.: 0208 535 6705/539 5522

Clinical Leads (NSF)

Dr M Huddart, Clinical Lead, Cancer,
Dr D Kapoor, Clinical Lead, CHD,
Dr R McHardy, Clinical Lead, Children,
Dr J Da'Prato, Clinical Lead, Diabetic Care,
Dr C Britt, Clinical Lead, Older People,

District Nursing

Ms M Claydon, Locality Nurse Manager (Walthamstow), Hurst Road Health Centre, Tel.: 020 8928 2329
Evening - District Nurses, (1900-2300), Tel.: 020 8345 6789
Ms H Kershaw, Locality Nurse Manager (Chingford), Chingford Health Centre, Tel.: 020 8928 7009
Mr I McQuarrie, Team Leader, Leyton & Leytonstone District Nurses, Langthorne Health Centre, 13 Langthorne Road, Leytonstone, E11 4XH, Tel.: 020 8558 7821
Ms J Mitchell, Locality Nurse Manager (Leyton/Leytonstone), 4th Floor, Kirkdale House, Leytonstone, Tel.: 020 8928 2415
Mrs C Monksfield, Team Leader, District Nurses - Leyton & Leytonstone, Langthorne Health Centre, 13 Langthorne Road, Leytonstone, E11 4XH, Tel.: 020 8558 7821
Ms J Oshungbure, Team Leader, District Nurses - Walthamstow, Forest Road Medical Centre, Walthamstow, E17, Tel.: 020 8928 8123
Ms M Sinclair, Team Leader, Walthamstow South District Nurses, Comely Bank Clinic, 46 Ravenswood Road, Walthamstow, E17 9LY, Tel.: 020 8521 8742
Ms P Withers, Team Leader, District Nurses - Chingford, Chingford Health Centre, Tel.: 020 9529 8655

Family Planning Services

Family Planning Service, Hurst Road Health Centre, Walthamstow, E17 3BL, Tel.: 020 8520 8513
Ms R Heed, Service Manager, Women & Sexual Health, Hurst Road Health Centre, Walthamstow, E17, Tel.: 0208 928 2317
Ms L Leitch-Devlin, Cervical Cytology, Clinical Nurse Specialist, Tel.: 020 8539 5522 ext 5104
Ms S Stirling, Teenage Pregnancies, Clinical Nurse Specialist,

Health Visitors

Ms A Barnes, Team Leader, Health Visitors, Chingford Health Centre, Tel.: 020 8529 8655
Ms S Edwards, Health Visisitor/ Immunisation Facilitator, Comley Bank Clinic, Thorpe Coombes Hospital, Tel.: 020 8928 2500
Ms T McLeary, Team Leader, Walthamstow South Health Visitors, Comely Bank Clinic, Tel.: 020 8521 8742
Ms N Wilson, Team Leader, Walthamstow North Health Visitors, St James Health Centre, St James Street, Walthamstow, E17 7PJ, Tel.: 020 8520 0921

HIV/AIDS

Ms R Brown, Langthorne Health Centre, Langthorne Road, Leytonstone, E11 4HX, Tel.: 020 8558 7821
Ms K Gardner, Manager, Children with HIV, Paediatrics, Azalea Ward, Whipps Cross Hospital, Tel.: 0208 539 5522

School Nursing

Ms T Chatergoon, School Nurse Team Leader, Azalea Ward, Whipps Cross Hospital, Tel.: 020 8539 5522
School Health/Nursing Service, Azalea Ward, Whipps Cross Hospital, Tel.: 020 8539 5522 ext 5110

Specialist Nursing Services

Ms B Nicholls, Patient Review, Specialist Nurse, Assessment, Chingford Health Centre, Chingford, Tel.: 020 8529 8655
Ms A Nettleship, Specialist Nurse, Asthma, Forest Road Medical Centre, Walthamstow, E17, Tel.: 020 8928 8125
Ms P Glynn, Co-ordinator, Care of the Elderly, Chingford Health Centre, Chingford, Tel.: 020 8529 8655
Ms J Dakin, Continence, B7 Ward, Whipps Cross Hospital, Tel.: 020 8539 5522 ext 5204
Ms D Flanagan, Head of Nursing, Continuing Care, Chingford Health Centre, Chingford, Tel.: 020 8529 8655
Ms S Jowata, Diabetic Care, Langthorne Health Centre, Tel.: 020 8558 7821
Mrs S Kholil, Diabetic Care, Langthorne Health Centre, Leytonstone, Tel.: 020 8558 7821
Ms L McCauley, Leg Ulcers, Hurst Road Health Centre, Walthamstow, E17, Tel.: 020 8928 2377
Nurses, Macmillan, Margaret Centre, Whipps Cross Hospital, Tel.: 020 8539 5522
Ms K Lewis, Community Nurse, Paediatrics, Azalea Ward, Whipps Cross Hospital, Tel.: 020 8539 5522
Ms C Harewood, Sickle Cell & Thalassaemia, St James Health Centre, St James Street, Walthamstow, E17 7PJ, Tel.: 020 8520 0921
Ms T Evans, Nurse Specialist, Tissue Viability, Hurst Road Health Centre, Walthamstow, E17, Tel.: 020 8928 2374

Wandsworth Primary Care Trust

Trust Headquarters
2nd Floor Teak Tower
Springfield Hospital
61 Glenburnie Road
LONDON, SW17 7DJ
Tel.: 020 8682 6170

Admin & Senior Management

Ms D Caulfeild-Stoker, Director of Nursing, Queen Mary's Hospital, Roehampton Lane, SW15 5PN, Tel.: 020 8355 2603
Ms V Cotterill, Deputy Chief Executive/Director of Primary Care, 1 Belleville Road, Battersea, SW11 6QS, Tel.: 020 7585 2293
Ms H Walley, Chief Executive,

Child Health

Ms J Abili, Manager, Child Health Dept, Unit 1, 218-220 Garratt Lane, London, SW18 4EA, Tel.: 020 8877 6311
Ms A Bandali, Child Health Dept, Unit 1, 218-220 Garratt Lane, London, SW18 4EA, Tel.: 020 8877 6311
Ms L Caulfield, Child Health Dept, Unit 1, 218-220 Garratt Lane, London, SW18 4EA, Tel.: 020 8877 6315
Ms L Irons, Child Health Dept, Unit 1, 218-220 Garratt Lane, London, SW18 4EA, Tel.: 020 8877 6314
Ms L Sibley, Child Health Dept, Unit 1, 218-220 Garratt Lane, London, SW18 4EA, Tel.: 020 8877 6312
Ms V Stansbury, Child Health Dept, Unit 1, 218-220 Garratt Lane, London, SW18 4EA, Tel.: 020 8877 6318
Ms C Whittle, Child Health Dept, Unit 1, 218-220 Garratt Lane, London, SW18 4EA, Tel.: 020 8877 6316

Child Protection/Safeguarding Children

Ms M Morgan, Designated Nurse, Child Protection, Unit 1, 218-220 Garratt Lane, London, SW18 4EA, Tel.: 020 8877 6310

Clinical Leads (NSF)

Ms S Hammond, Clinical Lead, Cancer,
Dr S Reeves, Clinical Lead, Older People,

London Strategic Health Authority

District Nursing
Balham, Tooting, Wandsworth, Balham Health Centre, 120 Bedford Hill, SW12 9HP, Tel.: 020 8700 0400
Battersea, Bendon Valley House, 218-220 Garratt Lane, SW18 4EA, Tel.: 020 7441 0900
Ms A Benincasa, Locality Association Director, Joan Bicknell Centre, Springfield Hospital, Tel.: 020 8700 0572
Ms K Gaunt, Locality Association Director, Joan Bicknell Centre, Springfield Hospital, Tel.: 020 8700 0572
Out of hours, Healthcall, Tel.: 020 8256 6340

Learning Disabilities
Mr M Abel, Service Manager, Tel.: 020 8871 7419
Ms H Cook, Community, Wandsworth & Roehampton, Services Manager, Joan Bicknell Centre, Springfield University Hospital, Burntwood Lane, SW17 7DJ, Tel.: 020 8700 0450

Liaison Services
Ms P Bennett, Liaison, Health Visitor A&E, Tel.: 020 8725 1286

Other Services
Ms S Sulaiman, Haemoglobinopathies Counsellor, Balham health Centre, Tel.: 020 8700 0616

Specialist Nursing Services
Ms H Young, Continence, St Christopher Clinic, Wheeler Court, Plough Road, Battersea, SW11 2AY, Tel.: 020 7441 0788
Team, Physical Disability, St John's Therapy Centre, 162 St John's Hill, SW11 1SP, Tel.: 020 8700 0187

The Homeless/Travellers & Asylum Seekers
Ms L Williamson, Homeless, Health Visitor, Balham Health Centre, Tel.: 020 8700 0623

West Middlesex University Hospitals NHS Trust

Trust Headquarters
West Middlesex Univ Hospital
Twickenham Road
ISLEWORTH
Middlesex
TW7 6AF
Tel.: 020 8560 2121

Acute Specialist Nursing Services
Ms R Seerkisson, Specialist Nurse, Acute Pain, Bleep 037, Tel.: 0208 321 6038
Ms J Brown, Nurse Specialist, Anti-Coagulation, Bleep 448, Tel.: 0208 321 2506
Ms J Rishraj, Senior, Nurse Specialist, Anti-Coagulation, Bleep 448, Tel.: 0208 321 6953
Ms N Cedeno, Macmillan Nurse, Breast Care, Bleep 023, Tel.: 0208 321 6786
Ms N Cedeno, Macmillan, Specialist Nurse, Breast Care, Bleep 023, Tel.: 0208 321 6786
Ms H Ricard, Macmillan Nurse, Breast Care, Bleep 023, Tel.: 0208 321 5885
Ms H Ricard, Macmillan, Specialist Nurse, Breast Care, Bleep 023, Tel.: 0208 321 5885
Ms C Shotter, Specialist Nurse, Cardiology, Bleep 064, Tel.: 0208 321 5285
Ms C Coughley, Specialist Nurse, CHD, Tel.: 0208 321 6842
Ms E Chandler, Macmillan, Solid Tumour, Nurse Specialist, Chemotherapy, Tel.: 0208 321 6264
Ms A Kaba, Rapdi Access, Sister, Chest Pain, Bleep 069, Tel.: 0208 321 6932
Ms L Armistead, Specialist Nurse, Clinical Imaging, Tel.: 0208 321 5985/5507
Ms C Dawson, Acting Lead Cancer Nurse, Nurse Specialist, Colorectal, Bleep 010, Tel.: 0208 321 5892
Mr P Eardley, Charge Nurse, Coronary Care, - Acute, Bleep 094, Tel.: 0208 321 5544
Ms L McGovern, Specialist Nurse, Dermatology, Bleep 380, Tel.: 0208 321 5544

Ms J Edwards, Paediatric, Nurse Specialist, Diabetic Care, Tel.: 0208 321 5381
Ms J Fourneaux, Specialist Nurse, Diabetic Care, Tel.: 0208 321 6114
Ms C Gunpot, Specialist Nurse, Diabetic Care, Tel.: 0208 321 6114
Ms M How, Specialist Nurse, Diabetic Care, Tel.: 0208 321 6114
Ms G Anderson, Nurse Specialist, ENT Surgery, Bleep 076,
Ms L McEvoy, Specialist Nurse, Gastroenterology, Bleep 041, Tel.: 0208 321 6139
Ms A Nienhaus, Specialist Nurse, GU Medicine, Tel.: 0208 321 6171
Ms L Felix, Lead Nurse, Gynae/Oncology, - Colposcopy, Tel.: 0208 321 6043
Ms M Chawda, Specialist Nurse, Gynaecology, Bleep 370, Tel.: 0208 321 5435
Mr E O'Reilly, Specialist Nurse, Haematology, Tel.: 0208 321 6264
Ms J Archibald, Nurse Specialist, Infection Control, Bleep 097, Tel.: 0208 321 5785
Ms L Gargee, Specialist Nurse, Infection Control, Bleep 095, Tel.: 0208 321 5785
Ms L Woodward-Stammers, HPCT, Nurse, Infection Control, Tel.: 0208 321 5785
Ms J Poynter, Specialist Nurse, Older People, Tel.: 0208 321 6512
Ms T Henry, Macmillan, Clinical Nurse Specialist, Palliative Care, - Cancer, Bleep 018 - 403, Tel.: 0208 321 6822
Ms D Home, Nurse Consultant, Rheumatology, Bleep 440, Tel.: 0208 321 5754
Ms S Firth, Specialist Nurse, Stoma Care, Bleep 009, Tel.: 0208 321 5822
Ms T Virgin-Elliston, Specialist Nurse, Stoma Care, Bleep 386, Tel.: 0208 321 5822
Mr A Wynne, Specialist Nurse, Stroke Care, Bleep 413, Tel.: 0208 321 5937
Mr S Moore, Specialist Nurse, TB, Tel.: 0208 321 5891/5240
Ms E Eismark, Nurse Specialist, Tissue Viability, Tel.: 0208 321 6103
Ms M Chituku, Nurse Practitioner, Transfusion, Bleep 030, Tel.: 0208 321 6787
Ms J Ahluwalia, Specialist Nurse, Urology, Bleep 044, Tel.: 0208 321 5080

Admin & Senior Management
Mrs Y Franks, Director of Nursing & Midwifery, Trust Management Office, West Middlesex Univ Hospital, Tel.: 0208 321 5599

Child Health
Ms H Sibley, Head of Clinical Services (Nursing), Children's Out-patient, 3rd Floor East Wing, West Middlesex University Hospital, Tel.: 0208 321 6210

Child Health Records
Ms H Sibley, Head of Clinical Services, Children's Out-patient, 3rd Floor East Wing, West Middlesex University Hospital, Tel.: 0208 321 6210

Child Protection/Safeguarding Children
Ms S Hunt, Lead, Child Protection, Houslow PCT, Thelma Golding Health Centre, 92 Bath Road, TW3 3EL, Tel.: 0208 321 2426

Community Midwifery
Ms N Harper, Senior Midwife, Maternity Services, Tel.: 0208 321 6878/5947
Ms S Koay, Advanced Neonatal Nurse Practioner/Senior Nurse, SCBU, Tel.: 0208 321 5944/5945
Ms T Neville, Associate Director of Midwifery & Quality, QMMU, West Middlesex University Hospital, Tel.: 0208 321 2580

Equipment Loan Services
Ms J Hunt, Head of Occupational Therapy, O' Block, West Middlesex Univ Hospital, Tel.: 0208 321 5133

Family Planning Services
Ms H Hall, Head of Clinical Services, Womens Sves & Sexual Health, GUM Clinic, West Middlesex University Hospital, Tel.: 0208 321 5796 bleep 256

London Strategic Health Authority

Learning Disabilities
Ms S Harvey, Consultant Nurse, Learning Disabilities, West Middlesex University Hospital, Tel.: 0208 321 5937
Liaison Services
Ms K Goodwin, Liaison Health Visitor, Children's Out-patient, 3rd Floor East Wing, West Middlesex University Hospital, Tel.: 0208 321 5379 bleep 260
Matrons/Modern Matrons
Ms D Williams, Modern Matron, A&E, Tel.: 0208 321 5594/5816/5730
Ms S Stevenson-Shand, Modern Matron, Critical Care, Tel.: 0208 321 5341/5833
Ms D Govinden, Modern Matron, Endoscopy, Tel.: 0208 321 6016/5460
Ms C Santafianos, Modern Matron, Older People, Tel.: 0208 321 6785
Ms D Matthews, Modern Matron, Outpatients, Tel.: 0208 321 5717
Starlight Children's Services, Modern Matron, Paediatrics, Tel.: 0208 321 5362/6862
Ms A Lloyd, Modern Matron, Surgery, - Orthopaedic, Tel.: 0208 321 6535/6534
Ms J Henry, Modern Matron, Theatres, Tel.: 0208 321 5819/5812
Other Services
Ms B Foulkes, Senior Occupational Health Advisor, Tel.: 0208 321 6077
Mr J Johnson, Patient Involvement Manager - PALS Team, Trust Management Office, Twickenham Road, Isleworth, TW7 6AF,
Ms S Keles, Senior Occupational Health Advisor, Tel.: 0208 321 5048
Ms A Mitchell, Occupational Health Manager, Tel.: 0208 321 5046
Smoking Cessation
Mr A Taylor, Manager, Hounslow PCT, Thelma Golding Health Centre, 92 Bath Road, Hounslow, TW3 3EL, Tel.: 0208 321 2321
The Homeless/Travellers & Asylum Seekers
Ms S Yusuff, Team Leader, Brookwood Health Centre, Brookwood Road, TW4 3HD, Tel.: 0208 630 1102

Westminster Primary Care Trust

Trust Headquarters, 15 Marylebone Road
LONDON, NW1 5JD
Tel.: 020 7150 8000

Admin & Senior Management
Ms A Duncan, Director of Nursing & Quality, 15 Marylebone Road, London, NW1 5DJ, Tel.: 020 7150 8026
Child Health
Ms K Adams, Community Children's Nursing Team, Lisson Grove Health Centre, Tel.: 020 7479 8766
Miss M Green, Community Children's Nurse, The Medical Centre, 7e Woodfield Road, London, W9 3XZ, Tel.: 020 8451 8573
Ms S Manuel, Children with Disability (Victoria Area), Chelsea & Westminster Hospital, Tel.: 0208 846 6488
Ms D Turner, Children with Disabilities, Nurse Specialist, St Mary's Hospital, Tel.: 0207 886 1450
Child Health Records
Ms D Ellis, Brent PCT, Barham House, Wembley Centre for Health & Care, Fairview Avenue, Wembley, Middx, Tel.: 020 8795 6321
Parsons Green Centre, (Victoria/Pimlico Area), Tel.: 020 8846 6767
Child Protection/Safeguarding Children
Ms A Hamilton, Named Nurse, Child Protection, Westminster PCT, Mezzanine Floor, Care First, 215 Lisson Grove, London, NW8 8LF, Tel.: 020 7641 6775
Ms S Sunderland, Designated Nurse, Child Protection, Westminster PCT, Mezzanine Floor, Care First, 215 Lisson Grove, London, NW8 8LF, Tel.: 020 7641 6774
Ms J White, Advisor, Child Protection, Westminster PCT, Mezzanine Floor, Care First, 215 Lisson Grove, London, NW8 8LF, Tel.: 020 8451 8536

Ms C Nicholls, Designated Nurse, Looked After Children, Community Child Health, The Medical Centre, 7E Woodfield Road, London, W9 3XZ, Tel.: 020 7266 8781
Clinical Leads (NSF)
Dr M Guy, Clinical Lead, All NSFs, Cancer,
District Nursing
District/Community Nursing Services, Victoria/Pimlico, South Westminster Centre, 82 Vincent Square, SW1P 2PF, Tel.: 020 8746 5757
District/Community Nursing Services, Marlebone, St Johns Wood, Lisson Grove Health Centre, Gateforth Street, NW8 7BT, Tel.: 020 7724 2391
District/Community Nursing Services, Soho/Westend, 29-30 Soho Square W1V 5DH, Tel.: 020 7534 6500
District/Community Nursing Services, Queens Park Health Centre, Dart Street, W10 4LD, Tel.: 020 8968 8899
Family Planning Services
Mr C Morgan, Westside Contraceptive Services, Parsons Green Health Centre, 5-7 Parsons Green, Fulham, SW6 4UL, Tel.: 020 8846 6767
Learning Disabilities
Care First, (Westminster Community Learning Disability), 4 Frampton Street, London, NW8 8LF, Tel.: 020 7641 6602
Other Services
Ms A Soliman, Modern Matron Nursing Homes, Garside House Nursing Home, 131 Regency Street, London, SW1P 4AH, Tel.: 020 7237 2468
Pharmacy
Community Services Pharmacist, 15 Marylebone Road, London, NW1 5JD, Tel.: 020 7150 8102
Smoking Cessation
Lisson Grove Health Centre, Gateforth Street, London, NW8 8EG, Tel.: 020 7479 8826
Specialist Nursing Services
Ms J Walker, Professional Development Nurse - Women's Health, 15 Marylebone Road, London, NW1 5DJ, Tel.: 020 7150 8048
Ms J Edwards, Community, Lead Nurse, CHD, 15 Marylebone Road, London, NW1 5DJ, Tel.: 020 7150 8051
Ms H Oliver, Continence, Colville Health Centre, 51 Kensington Park Road, W11 1PA, Tel.: 020 7221 3609
Ms A Allaw, Nurse Specialist, Diabetic Care, Westminster Diabetes Centre, 4b Maida Vale, London, W9 1SP, Tel.: 020 7316 1214
Ms S Robinson, Nurse Specialist, Diabetic Care, Westminster Diabetes Centre, 4b Maida Vale, London, W9 1SP, Tel.: 020 7316 1216
Ms J Hill, Infection Control, 125 Old Brompton Road, SW7 3RP, Tel.: 020 8383 6202
Ms E Cronin, Clinical Nurse Specialist, Stoma Care, St mary's Hospital, Praed Street, London, W2 1NY, Tel.: 020 7725 1306
Ms M Jerome, Nurse, Stoma Care, Chelsea & Westminster Hospital, 369 Fulham Road, Fulham, London, SW10, Tel.: 020 8746 5911
Ms H Charles, Tissue Viability, St Charles Hospital, Exmoor Street, W10 6DZ, Tel.: 020 8962 4467
The Homeless/Travellers & Asylum Seekers
Health Support Team, Lisson Grove Health Centre, Gateforth Street, London, NW8 8EG, Tel.: 020 7479 8805

Whipps Cross University Hospital NHS Trust
Trust Headquarters, Whipps Cross Univ Hospital
Whipps Cross Road
Leytonstone, LONDON
E11 1NR
Tel.: 020 8539 5522
Fax.: 020 8558 8115

Admin & Senior Management
Ms E Sills, Director of Nursing, Whipps Cross Road, Leytonstone, London, E11 1NR, Tel.: 020 8535 6878

London Strategic Health Authority

Community Midwifery

Ms C Falvey-Browne, Head of Midwifery Delivery Suite, Maternity Unit, Whipps Cross Hospital, Whipps Cross Road, Leytonstone, E11 1NR,

Ms P John, Head of Midwifery Community, Maternity Unit, Whipps Cross Hospital, Whipps Cross Road, Leytonstone, E11 1NR, Tel.: 0208 558 0234

Ms S Trayling, Head of Midwifery Inpatients, Maternity Unit, Whipps Cross Hospital, Whipps Cross Road, Leytonstone, E11 1NR,

Mrs M Wren, Director of Midwifery, Maternity Unit, Whipps Cross Hospital, Whipps Cross Road, Leytonstone, E11 1NR, Tel.: 0208 539 5522

Liaison Services

Ms R Howard, Discharge Co-ordinator, Patient Activity Team, Bank Area, Whipps Cross Univ Hospital, Tel.: 020 8535 6446

Whittington Hospital NHS Trust

Trust Headquarters, Whittington Hospital
Highgate Hill, Highgate
LONDON
N19 5NF
Tel.: 020 7272 3070
Fax.: 020 7288 5550

Admin & Senior Management

Ms D Wheeler, Director of Nursing, Whittington Hospital, Tel.: 020 7272 3070

Community Midwifery

Mrs R Basri, Labour Ward, Midwifery Manager, Whittington Hospital, Highgate Hill, Highgate, London, N19 5NF, Tel.: 020 7288 5163

Maternity Unit, Whittington Hospital, Highgate Hill, Highgate, London, N19 5NF, Tel.: 020 7288 3482

Ms S Tai, Acting Head of Midwifery, Whittington Hospital, Highgate Hill, Highgate, London, N19 5NF, Tel.: 020 7288 5499

Mrs L van Lessen, Community Midwifery Manager, Whittington Hospital, Highgate Hill, Highgate, London, N19 5NF, Tel.: 020 7288 3391

Health Visitors

Ms J Carroll, Liaison, Health Visitor, Paediatrics, Whittington Hospital, Tel.: 0207 288 5472

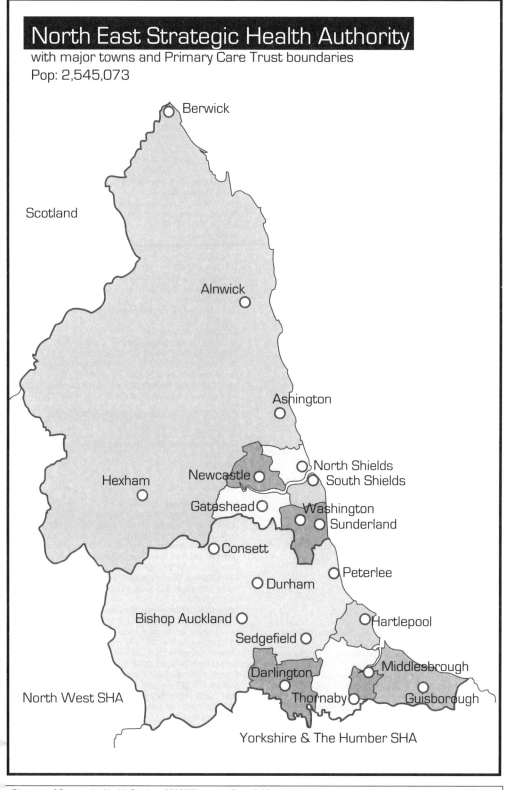

North East Strategic Health Authority

with major towns and Primary Care Trust boundaries
Pop: 2,545,073

Berwick

Scotland

Alnwick

Ashington

North Shields

South Shields

Hexham

Newcastle

Gateshead

Washington

Sunderland

Consett

Durham

Peterlee

Bishop Auckland

Hartlepool

Sedgefield

Darlington

Middlesbrough

North West SHA

Thornaby

Guisborough

Yorkshire & The Humber SHA

North East Strategic Health Authority

North East Strategic Health Authority

City Hospitals Sunderland NHS Foundation Trust

Trust Headquarters, Sunderland Royal Hospital
Kayll Road
SUNDERLAND
Tyne & Wear
SR4 7TP
Tel.: 0191 565 6256
Fax.: 0191 569 6242

Child Health
Ms C Hagland, Specialist Child Diabetes, Sunderland Royal Hospital, Tel.: 0191 565 6256 ext 42290
Ms C Hopkinson, Paediatric Community Nurse, Sunderland Royal Hospital, Tel.: 0191 565 6256 ext 41236
Ms M Linsley, Paediatric Epilepsy, Sunderland Royal Hospital, Tel.: 0191 565 6256 ext 49805
Ms T Maltby, Paediatric Community Nurse, Sunderland Royal Hospital, Tel.: 0191 565 6256 ext 41236
Ms L Wilson, Support Child Diabetes, Sunderland Royal Hospital, Tel.: 0191 565 6256 ext 42290
Ms K Coxall, Practice Development Nurse, Paediatrics, Sunderland Royal Hospital, Tel.: 0191 5656256
Mrs P Palmer, Matron, Paediatrics, Sunderland Royal Hospital, Tel.: 0191 565 6256 ext 40004

Child Health Records
School Health Records, Admin Support Manager, Children's Centre,

Child Protection/Safeguarding Children
Ms M Craig, Senior Nurse, Child Protection, The Portacabin, The Childrens Centre, Durham Road, Sunderland, SR3 4AF, Tel.: 0191 565 6256 ext 45227

Community Midwifery
Ms S Hardy, Senior Midwife, Sunderland Royal Hospital, Kayll Road, Sunderland, Tyne & Wear, SR4 7TP, Tel.: 0191 565 6256 ext 41777

Family Planning Services
Family Planning Services, Sunderland Royal Hospital, Kayll Road, Sunderland, SR4 7TP, Tel.: 0191 565 6256

Liaison Services
Ms T Laidler, Paediatric Liaison, Sunderland Royal Hospital, Tel.: 0191 565 ext 42419

School Nursing
Children's Services, School Nursing, Children's Centre, Durham Road, Sunderland, SR3 4AF, Tel.: 0191 565 6256

County Durham & Darlington Acute Hospitals NHS Trust

Trust Headquarters, Univ Hosp of North Durham
North Road
DURHAM, DH1 5TW
Tel.: 0191 333 2333

Child Health
Mrs A Bowes, Manager - Outreach Team, Paediatric Unit, Bishop Auckland General Hospital, Tel.: 01388 455616
Ms C Dixon, Manager - Specialist Health Visiting, Priory Court CDC, Annfield Plain, Stanley, Tel.: 01207 214905
Ms D Dodds, Special Needs Children, Chester le Street Health Centre, Newcastle Road, Chester-Le-Street, DH3 3UR, Tel.: 0191 333 3896
Ms K Lawther, Team Leader - Homecare Team, Shotley Bridge Hospital, Tel.: 01207 214320

Child Protection/Safeguarding Children
Mr P Burleton, Specialist Health Visitor, Child Protection, Chester le Street Health Centre, Newcastle Road, Chester-Le-Street, DH3 3UR, Tel.: 0191 333 3878

Ms N Reid, Senior Nurse, Child Protection, Chester le Street Health Centre, Newcastle Road, Chester-Le-Street, DH3 3UR, Tel.: 0191 333 3899

Community Midwifery
Mrs D Bunford, Head of Midwifery, Darlington Memorial Hospital, Hollyhurst Road, Darllington, Co. Durham, DL3 6HX, Tel.: 01325 743098
Maternity Department, Bishop Auckland Hospital, Cockton Hill Road, Bishop Auckland, Co Durham, DL14 6AD, Tel.: 01388 454000 ext 5410
Midwifery Dept, University Hospital of Durham, North Road, Durham, Co. Durham, DH1 5TW, Tel.: 0191 333 2339
Ms S Miller, Head of Midwifery, University Hospital of Durham, North Road, Durham, Co. Durham, DH1 5TW, Tel.: 0191 333 2109

Family Planning Services
Mrs M Sullivan, Assistant Head of Nursing, Family Planning Services, Framwellgate Moor Clinic, 29d Front Street, Durham, DH1 5EE, Tel.: 0191 382 6881

Health Visitors
Ms P Forster, Special Needs Health Visitor Children, Chester le Street Health Centre, Newcastle Road, Chester-Le-Street, DH3 3UR, Tel.: 0191 333 3896
Ms J Wade, Specialist Health Visitor for Pre-School Children, CDC Harewood House, Darllington, Tel.: 01325 254572

Liaison Services
Liaison Nurses, University Hospital of North Durham, Tel.: 0191 333 2668

Specialist Nursing Services
Mr C Kirby, Paediatric, Nurse Specialist, Diabetes, Ward 21, Darlington Memorial Hospital, Tel.: 01325 743401
Mrs T Laing, Paediatric, Nurse Specialist, Diabetes, Children's Ward, Bishop Auckland General Hospital, Tel.: 01388 455093
Mrs M Ridley, Lead Paediatric, Nurse Specialist, Diabetes, Treetops Ward, University Hospital of North Durham, Tel.: 0191 3332770

County Durham & Darlington Priority Services NHS Trust

Trust Headquarters, Earls House Hospital
Lanchester Road
DURHAM
DH1 5RD
Tel.: 0191 333 6262

Learning Disabilities
Mr J Ashdown, Head, Learning Disabilities Adults - Darlington, Upperthorpe, 90 Woodlands Road, Darlington, Tel.: 01325 355440
Ms M Collinson, Team Manager, Children, Sniperley House, Earls House, Lanchester Road, Durham, DH1 5RD, Tel.: 0191 333 6575
Darlington Children's Team, Upperthorpe, 90 Woodlands Road, Darlington, Tel.: 01325 555955
Mr P G Davison, General Manager, Children's Service, Sniperley House, Earls House, Lanchester Road, Durham, DH1 5RD, Tel.: 0191 333 6260
Derwentside Children's Team, The Lodge, South Moor Hospital, Stanley, Co. Durham, DH9 6DS, Tel.: 01207 214816
Mr T Dredge, Team Manager, Adults - Easington, Caroline House, St John's Square, Seaham, SR7 0JR, Tel.: 0191 5136038
Durham & Chester le Street Children's Team, Avenue House, North Road Durham, Tel.: 0191 3333457
Easington Children's Team, Caroline House, St John's Square, Seaham, SR7 0JR, Tel.: 0191 5136050
Mrs C Harper, Team Manager, Adults - Wear Valley & The Dales, Willington Health Centre, Chapel Street, Willington, Co. Durham, Tel.: 01388 646163
Ms T Joisce, Team Manager, Adults - Durham & Chester le Street, Hopper House, North Road, Durham, Tel.: 0191 383 1010
Sedgefield Children's Team, Green Lane, Spennymoor, Co. Durham, DL16 6JQ, Tel.: 01388 424200

North East Strategic Health Authority

Ms C Thompson, Team Manager, Adults - Derwentside, Ashdole House, Derwentside Magistrates Court, Consett, Co Durham, Tel.: 01207 584200

Mrs L Tickell, Operations Manager, Learning Disabilities Adults/Community, Priory House, Abbey Road, Durham, Tel.: 01913 835151

Wear Valley & The Dales, 6 Kensington, Cockton Hill Road, Bishop Auckland, Co. Durham, DL14 9HX, Tel.: 01388 602107

Mr R Wilson, Team Manager, Adults - Sedgefield, Social Services Department, Council Offices, Green Lane, Spennymoor, DL16 6JQ, Tel.: 01388 42400

Darlington Primary Care Trust

Trust Headquarters, Doctor Piper House
King Street
DARLINGTON
DL3 6JL
Tel.: 01325 364271
Fax.: 01325 746112

Admin & Senior Management
Mrs L Bailes, Head of Nursing, Doctor Piper House, King Street, Darlington, DL3 6JL, Tel.: 01325 746139
Mr C Morris, Chief Executive, Doctor Piper House, King Street, Darlington, DL3 6JL, Tel.: 01325 364271

Child Health
Mrs L Wheatley, Childrens Service Project Lead, Doctor Piper House, King Street, Darlington, DL3 6JL, Tel.: 01325 746160

Child Protection/Safeguarding Children
Mrs J Ralphs, Child Protection, Park Place Health Centre, Park Place, Darlington, DL1 5LW, Tel.: 01325 484904
Mrs G Worland, Child Protection, Park Place Health Centre, Park Place, Darlington, DL1 5LW, Tel.: 01325 484904

Community Nursing Services
Mrs L Bailes, Head of Nursing, Doctor Piper House, King Street, Darlington, DL3 6JL, Tel.: 01325 746139

District Nursing
Mrs J Storey, Clinical Lead, Doctor Piper House, King Street, Darlington, DL3 6JL, Tel.: 01325 746226

Family Planning Services
Dr J Mather, Family Planning Lead, Escomb Road Health Centre, Bishop Auckland, Co. Durham, Tel.: 01388 254305

Health Visitors
Mrs L Oliver, Clinical Lead, Doctor Piper House, King Street, Darlington, DL3 6JL, Tel.: 01325 746225

HIV/AIDS
Mr T Holmes, HIV Prevention Specialist, Doctor Piper House, King Street, Darlington, DL3 6JL, Tel.: 01325 746141

Other Services
Mrs J Finn, Firthmoor Partnership, Maidendale House, Burnside Road, Darlington, DL1 5SU, Tel.: 01325 362833
Mrs J Gilbert, Sure Start Lead, Sure Start Wave 5, Mount Pleasant Primary School, Newton Lane, Darlington, DL3 9HE, Tel.: 01325 488176
Mrs A Jones, Continuing Care Lead, Doctor Piper House, King Street, Darlington, DL3 6JL, Tel.: 01325 746180
Mr M Matthews, Sure Start Lead, Sure Start Wave 3, 2 McNay Street, Darlington, DL3 6SW, Tel.: 01325 487718

School Nursing
Mrs L Oliver, Clinical Lead, Doctor Piper House, King Street, Darlington, DL3 6JL, Tel.: 01325 746225

Smoking Cessation
Mr D Brown, Senior Adviser, Doctor Piper House, King Street, Darlington, DL3 6JL, Tel.: 01325 746131

Specialist Nursing Services
Mrs B Johnson, Immediate Care Services Lead, Hundens Rehabilitation Unit, Hundens Lane, Darlington, DL1 1DT, Tel.: 01325 489009

Mrs B Conway, Lead, CHD, Doctor Piper House, King Street, Darlington, DL3 6JL, Tel.: 01325 746187
Mrs J Roberts, Continence, Doctor Piper House, King Street, Darlington, DL3 6JL,
Mrs C Allison, Clinical Nurse Specialist, Macmillan, Butterwick Hospice, Macmillan House, Woodhouse Lane, Bishop Auckland, DL14 6JU, Tel.: 01388 607301
Mrs K Gilson, Clinical Nurse Specialist, Macmillan, Butterwick Hospice, Macmillan House, Woodhouse Lane, Bishop Auckland, DL14 6JU, Tel.: 01388 607301
Mrs M McKie, Clinical Nurse Specialist, Macmillan, Butterwick Hospice, Macmillan House, Woodhouse Lane, Bishop Auckland, DL14 6JU, Tel.: 01388 607301
Mrs B Myers, Clinical Nurse Specialist, Macmillan, Butterwick Hospice, Macmillan House, Woodhouse Lane, Bishop Auckland, DL14 6JU, Tel.: 01388 607301
Mrs J Sayer, Clinical Nurse Specialist, Macmillan, Butterwick Hospice, Macmillan House, Woodhouse Lane, Bishop Auckland, DL14 6JU, Tel.: 01388 607301
Mrs J Walker, Clinical Nurse Specialist, Macmillan, Butterwick Hospice, Macmillan House, Woodhouse Lane, Bishop Auckland, DL14 6JU, Tel.: 01388 607301
Mrs S Jackson, Lead, Osteoporosis, Doctor Piper House, King Street, Darlington, DL3 6JL, Tel.: 01325 746234

The Homeless/Travellers & Asylum Seekers
Mrs F Deehan, Carmel Medical Practice, Nunnery Lane, Darlington, DL3 8SQ, Tel.: 01325 380837

Derwentside Primary Care Trust

Trust Headquarters, The Greenhouse
Amos Drive, Greencroft Industrial Estate
ANNFIELD PLAIN
County Durham
DH9 7XP
Tel.: 01207 523600
Fax.: 01207 523601

Admin & Senior Management
Ms K Dimmick, Assistant Director of Patient Services & Professional Development, The Greenhouse, Amos Drive, Greencroft Ind Estate, Annfield Plain, County Durham, DH9 7XP, Tel.: 01207 523600
Dr A Low, Director of Health Improvement/Director of Public Health, The Greenhouse, Amos Drive, Greencroft Ind Estate, Annfield Plain, County Durham, DH9 7XP, Tel.: 01207 523600
Ms B Peppin, Director of Primary Care & Modernisation, The Greenhouse, Amos Drive, Greencroft Ind Estate, Annfield Plain, County Durham, DH9 7XP, Tel.: 01207 523600
Mr M Powell, Head of Organsiation Development, Unit 33F, No 1 Industrial Estate,
Ms H Tucker, Director of Patient Services, Clinical Governance & Nursing, The Greenhouse, Amos Drive, Greencroft Ind Estate, Annfield Plain, County Durham, DH9 7XP, Tel.: 01207 523606
Mr I Williamson, Director of Finance & Commissioning, The Greenhouse, Amos Drive, Greencroft Ind Estate, Annfield Plain, County Durham, DH9 7XP, Tel.: 01207 523600

Child Health
Ms M Malone, Children's Services Lead, Queens Road Therapy Centre,

Child Protection/Safeguarding Children
Ms M Baister, Senior Nurse, Child Protection, Chester-le-Street Health Centre,

Community Matrons
Ms A Morgan, Community Matron, South Moor Hospital,
Ms C Siddall, Community Matron, South Moor Hospital,

District Nursing
Ms J Luke, Acting Modern Matron - District Nursing, South Moor Hospital,

North East Strategic Health Authority

Health Visitors
Ms C Wotherspoon, Modern Matron Health Visiting, Queens Road Therapy Centre,
Other Services
Ms J Murray, Integrated Intermediate Services Manager, Overnight Palliative Care & Twilight Nursing,
Ms L Teasdale, Community Health Development Worker, (Stanley Green Corridor),
School Nursing
Ms K Camsell, Modern Matron School Nursing, Queens Road Therapy Centre,
Specialist Nursing Services
Ms J Armstrong, Lead Nurse, Infection Control,

Durham & Chester Le Street Primary Care Trust

Trust Headquarters, John Snow House
Durham University Science Park
DURHAM CITY
DH1 3YG
Tel.: 0191 301 1300

Admin & Senior Management
Mrs L Preston, Deputy Director of Community Care, John Snow House, Durham Univ Science Park, Durham City, DH1 3YG, Tel.: 0191 3011 300
Ms L Templey, Director of Primary & Community Care,
Mr A Young, Chief Executive,
Child Health Records
Child Health Records, Chester le Street Community Hospital, Front Street, Chester-le-Street, County Durham, DH3 3AT,
Clinical Leads (NSF)
Dr B Key, Clinical Lead, Older People, John Snow House, Durham Univ Science Park, Durham City, DH1 3YG,
Dr G Gammelin, Clinical Lead, CHD, John Snow House, Durham Univ Science Park, Durham City, DH1 3YG,
Dr T Cresswell, Clinical Lead, Children, - Cancer, John Snow House, Durham Univ Science Park, Durham City, DH1 3YG,
Dr E Holmes, Clinical Lead, Diabetic Care, John Snow House, Durham Univ Science Park, Durham City, DH1 3YG,
Community Matrons
Ms L Marshall, Community Matron, St Margarets Health Centre, Durham City, Tel.: 0191 384 3895
Community Midwifery
Ms S Miller, Midwifery, Managed through County Durham & Darlington Acute Hospitals Trust,
District Nursing
Mrs S Hood, Childrens Services Manager, Chester le Street Community Hospital, Chester le Street, DH3 3AT,
Mrs D Wilkie, Clinical Lead, Chester le Street Community Hospital, Chester le Street, DH3 3AT, Tel.: 0191 387 6524
Equipment Loan Services
Mr P Allison, Home Equipment Loan Services, Tel.: 01388 812812
Family Planning Services
Ms A Richardson, Family Planning Services PA/Secretaries, Tel.: 0191 382 6881
Mrs M Sullivan, Head of Service, Framwellgate Moor Clinic, 29d Front Street, Framwellgate Moor, Durham, DH1 5EE,
Health Visitors
Ms M Lowery, Clinical Lead Health Visiting, Tel.: 0191 387 6529
Other Services
Mrs S Lawson, Falls Co-ordinator, John Snow House, Tel.: 0191 3011 300
Pharmacy
Mrs S Kebbell, PCT Pharmacutical Advisor, John Snow House,
School Nursing
Ms R Earl, Clinical Lead, School Nursing, Chester-le-street Community Hospital,

Specialist Nursing Services
Ms S Aunglers, Continence, Chester-le-Street Community Hospital, Front Street, Chester-le-Street, Co. Durham, DH3 3AT,
Ms C Kell, Continence, Chester-le-Street Community Hospital, Front Street, Chester-le-Street, Co. Durham, DH3 3AT,
Ms P Dailey, Heart Disease, Coronary Care, Framwellgate Moor Clinic, 29d Front Street, Framwellgate Moor, Durham, DH1 5EE,
Ms A Oliver, Heart Disease, Coronary Care, Framwellgate Moor Clinic, 29d Front Street, Framwellgate Moor, Durham, DH1 5EE,
Ms B Storey, Heart Disease, Coronary Care, Framwellgate Moor Clinic, 29d Front Street, Framwellgate Moor, Durham, DH1 5EE,
Ms K Butterfield, Diabetic Care, Framwellgate Moor Clinic, 29d Front Street, Framwellgate Moor, Durham, DH1 5EE,
Ms K Murray, Diabetic Care, Framwellgate Moor Clinic, 29d Front Street, Framwellgate Moor, Durham, DH1 5EE,
Ms P Mantri, Epilepsy, Framwellgate Moor Clinic, 29d Front Street, Framwellgate Moor, Durham, DH1 5EE,
Ms D Elliott, Osteoporosis, John Snow House, Durham University Science Park, Durham City, DH1 3YG,

Durham Dales Primary Care Trust
Trust headquarters, Henson Close
South Church Enterprise Park
BISHOP AUCKLAND
County Durham
DL14 6WA
Tel.: 01388 458835

Admin & Senior Management
Mrs C Haworth, Director of Nursing & Patient Services, Henson Close, South Church Enterprise Park, Bishop Auckland, County Durham, DL14 6WA, Tel.: 01388 458835 ext 2791
Child Health Records
Ms J Clarke, Child Health Systems Supervisor, Escomb Road Annexe, Escomb Road, Bishop Auckland, DL14 6AB, Tel.: 01388 455790
Child Protection/Safeguarding Children
Ms J Ward, Senior Nurse, Child Protection, Escomb Road Annexe, Escomb Road, Bishop Auckland, DL14 6AB, Tel.: 01388 455777
Community Matrons
Ms J Armour, Community Matron, Henson Close, South Church Enterprise Park, Bishop Auckland, County Durham, DL14 6WA, Tel.: 01388 458835
Ms J Church, Community Matron, Henson Close, South Church Enterprise Park, Bishop Auckland, County Durham, DL14 6WA, Tel.: 01388 458835
Ms C Gibson, Community Matron, Henson Close, South Church Enterprise Park, Bishop Auckland, County Durham, DL14 6WA, Tel.: 01388 458835
Ms B Staddon, Community Matron, Henson Close, South Church Enterprise Park, Bishop Auckland, County Durham, DL14 6WA, Tel.: 01388 458835
Community Nursing Services
Ms J Dixon, Assistant Director of Nursing & Patient Services - Children, Henson Close, South Church Enterprise Park, Bishop Auckland, County Durham, DL14 6 WA, Tel.: 01388 458835 ext 2792
Mr K Haggerty, Assistant Director of Nursing & Patient Services - Adults, Henson Close, South Church Enterprise Park, Bishop Auckland, County Durham, DL14 6 WA, Tel.: 01388 458835 ext 2793
Ms C Haworth, Director of Nursing & Patient Services, Henson Close, South Church Enterprise Park, Bishop Auckland, County Durham, DL14 6 WA, Tel.: 01388 458835 ext 2791
District Nursing
Mr K Haggerty, Assistant Director of Nursing & Patient Services - Adult, Henson Close, South Church Enterprise Park, Bishop Auckland, County Durham, DL14 6WA, Tel.: 01388 458835 ext 2793

North East Strategic Health Authority

Family Planning Services
Dr J Mather, Family Planning Consultant, Escomb Road Annexe, Escomb Road, Bishop Auckland, DL14 6AB, Tel.: 01388 455705

Health Visitors
Ms J Dixon, Assistant Director of Nursing & Patient Services - Children, Henson Close, South Church Enterprise Park, Bishop Auckland, County Durham, DL14 6WA, Tel.: 01388 458835 ext 2792

Liaison Services
Ms V Mortimer, Liaison Services - Senior Nurses - Acute Trust, Escomb Road Annexe, Escomb Road, Bishop Auckland, DL14 6AB, Tel.: 01388 455776

Other Services
Ms J Skinner, Consultant in Palliative Care, Butterwick Hospice, Woodhouse Lane, Bishop Auckland, DL14 6JU, Tel.: 01388 603003

Pharmacy
Ms Y Maule, Pharmaceutical Advisor, Henson Close, South Church Enterprise Park, Bishop Auckland, County Durham, DL14 6 WA, Tel.: 01388 458835 ext 2865
Mr A Sinclair, Head of Pharmacy, Henson Close, South Church Enterprise Park, Bishop Auckland, County Durham, DL14 6 WA, Tel.: 01388 458835 ext 2867

School Nursing
Ms J Birtley, Modern Matron, Escomb Road Annexe, Escomb Road, Bishop Auckland, DL14 6AB, Tel.: 01388 455 807

Smoking Cessation
Ms D Hull, Smoking Cessation Advisor, Henson Close, South Church Enterprise Park, Bishop Auckland, County Durham, DL14 6WA, Tel.: 01388 458835 ext 2896

Specialist Nursing Services
Ms T Foster, Heart Disease Prevention & Management, Henson Close, South Church Enterprise Park, Bishop Auckland, County Durham, DL14 6WA, Tel.: 01388 458835 ext 2806
Ms C Levie, Specialist Nurse, CHD, Henson Close, South Church Enterprise Park, Bishop Auckland, County Durham, DL14 6WA, Tel.: 01388 458835 ext 2811
Ms C Poole, Assistant Specialist Nurse, CHD, Henson Close, South Church Enterprise Park, Bishop Auckland, County Durham, DL14 6WA, Tel.: 01388 458835 ext 2808
Ms H Trivedi, Nurse, CHD, Henson Close, South Church Enterprise Park, Bishop Auckland, County Durham, DL14 6WA, Tel.: 01388 458835 ext 2807
Ms P Munro, Advisor, Continence, Henson Close, South Church Enterprise Park, Bishop Auckland, County Durham, DL14 6WA, Tel.: 01388 458835
Ms S Goat, Co-ordinator, Continuing Care, Henson Close, South Church Enterprise Park, Bishop Auckland, County Durham, DL14 6WA, Tel.: 01388 458835 ext 2795
Ms P Crawley, BHF Nurse, Heart Failure, Henson Close, South Church Enterprise Park, Bishop Auckland, County Durham, DL14 6WA, Tel.: 01388 458835 ext 2805
Nurses, Macmillan, Butterwick Hospice, Woodhouse Lane, Bishop Auckland, DL14 6JU, Tel.: 01388 607301
Ms B Wingrove, Specialist Nurse, Multiple Sclerosis, Henson Close, South Church Enterprise Park, Bishop Auckland, County Durham, DL14 6WA, Tel.: 01388 458835 ext 2753
Ms S Ruddick, Specialist Nurse, Osteoporosis, Henson Close, South Church Enterprise Park, Bishop Auckland, County Durham, DL14 6WA, Tel.: 01388 458835 ext 2810

Easington Primary Care Trust

Trust Headquarters, Health Partnership Centre
Fern Court, Bracken Hill Business Park
PETERLEE
Co Durham
SR8 2RR
Tel.: 0191 587 4800
Fax.: 0191 587 4878

Admin & Senior Management
Ms W Baker, Director of Service Integration,
Dr R Bolas, Chief Executive, Tel.: 0191 587 4800
Mr J Corrigan, Director of Finance,
Mrs A Everden, Director of Primary Care & Clinical Governance,
Miss S Foster, Head of Older People, Physical & Learning Disabilities (Adult),
Mrs S Haywood, Director of Corporate Services,
Ms A Lynch, Director of Public Health,
Ms H Maughan, Head of Nursing Services,
Mrs P Smith, Deputy Head of Nursing Services,

Child Health
Mr M Armitage, Head of Children Services & Substance Misuse,

Child Health Records
Child Health Records, Peterlee Health Centre, Bede Way, Peterlee, Co Durham, SR8 1AD, Tel.: 0191 5862273

Child Protection/Safeguarding Children
Child Protection, Peterlee Health Centre, Bede Way, Peterlee, Co Durham, SR8 1AD, Tel.: 0191 5181844

Clinical Leads (NSF)
Dr R W Armstrong, Clinical Lead, Cancer,
Dr J Leigh, Clinical Lead, Children,
Dr B Hawes, Clinical Lead, Diabetic Care,

Community Matrons
Community Matron, Arbroath House, Seaside Lane, Easington, Peterlee, SR8 3PE, Tel.: 0191 5270410

District Nursing
CHD Lead Nurse, Health Partnership Centre, Fern Court, Bracken Hill Business Park, Peterlee, Co. Durham, SR8 2RR, Tel.: 0191 5876000
Lead Nurses for District Nursing, Health Partnership Centre, Fern Court, Bracken Hill Business Park, Peterlee, Co. Durham, SR8 2RR, Tel.: 0191 5876000

Family Planning Services
Family Planning Service, Peterlee Health Centre, Bede Way, Peterlee, Co Durham, SR8 1AD, Tel.: 0191 5862273
Young Peoples Family Planning Service, Peterlee Health Centre, Bede Way, Peterlee, Co Durham, SR8 1AD, Tel.: 0191 5862273
Young Persons Family Planning Clinic, Seaham Clinic, St Johns Square, Seaham, Tel.: 07770 271138

Health Visitors
Lead Nurses for Health Visiting, Health Partnership Centre, Fern Court, Bracken Hill Business Park, Peterlee, Co. Durham, SR8 2RR, Tel.: 0191 5876000

Liaison Services
Ms V Atkinson, Liaison, Discharge, Sister, Ward 1, University Hospital of Hartlepool, Holdforth Rd, Hartlepool, TS24 9AH, Tel.: 01429 266654
Ms S Larkin, Co-ordinator, Older People Continuing Care, Health Partnership Centre, Fern Court, Bracken Hill Business Park, Peterlee, Co. Durham, SR8 2RR, Tel.: 0191 587 4800
Rapid Response, Team Co-ordinator, Grampian House, Grampian Drive, Peterlee, Co. Durham, SR8 2LR, Tel.: 0191 5185137

School Nursing
Lead Nurses for District Nursing, Health Partnership Centre, Fern Court, Bracken Hill Business Park, Peterlee, Co. Durham, SR8 2RR, Tel.: 0191 5876000
School Nursing, Peterlee Health Centre, Bede Way, Peterlee, Co Durham, SR8 1AD, Tel.: 0191 5862273

Specialist Nursing Services
Mrs C Murch, Lead Nurse, Palliative Care, Cancer, Tel.: 0191 5862426
Mrs J Lawson, Advisor, Continence, Health Partnership Centre, Fern Court, Bracken Hill Business Park, Peterlee, Co. Durham, SR8 2RR, Tel.: 0191 5876000
Carers Scheme, Macmillan, Peterlee Community Hospital, O'Neill Drive, Peterlee, Co Durham, Tel.: 0191 586 2426

North East Strategic Health Authority

Nurse Specialists, Macmillan, Peterlee Community Hospital, O'Neill Drive, Peterlee, Co Durham, Tel.: 0191 5862426

Mr R Buckland, Nurse, Tissue Viability, Health Partnership Centre, Fern Court, Bracken Hill Business Park, Peterlee, Co. Durham, SR8 2RR, Tel.: 0191 5876000

Gateshead Health NHS Foundation Trust

Trust Headquarters, Queen Elizabeth Hospital
Sheriff Hill
GATESHEAD
NE9 6SX
Tel.: 0191 482 0000

Community Midwifery
Mrs C Dunn, Service Manager, Head of Midwifery, Maternity Unit, Queen Elizabeth Hospital, Tel.: 0191 445 2138

Maternity Unit, Queen Elizabeth Hospital, Tel.: 0191 445 2763

Ms E Turner, Senior Midwife, Maternity Unit, Queen Elizabeth Hospital, Tel.: 0191 445 2147

Learning Disabilities
Mrs E Alderson, Clinical Nurse Leader, Kingfisher House, Kingsway North, Team Valley Trading Estate, Gateshead, NE11 0JQ, Tel.: 0191 445 6702

Gateshead Primary Care Trust

Trust Headquarters, Team View
5th Avenue Business Park, Team Valley
GATESHEAD
NE11 0NB
Tel.: 0191 491 5713

Admin & Senior Management
Mr B Smith, Chief Executive,

Child Health
Ms L Hubbucks, Looked After Children Nurse, Kingfisher House, Kingsway North, Team Valley Trading Estate, Gateshead, NE11 0JQ, Tel.: 0191 445 6733

Mrs A Ryder, Team Leader, Children's Community Nursing, Low Fell Clinic, Beaconlough Road, Low Fell, Gateshead, NE9 6TD, Tel.: 0191 443 6917

Child Health Records
Bensham Hospital, Saltwell Road, Gateshead, NE8 4YL, Tel.: 0191 445 5246

Child Protection/Safeguarding Children
Ms M Lilburn, Senior Nurse, Child Protection, Dunston Hill Hospital, Whickham Highway, Gateshead, NE11 9QT, Tel.: 0191 445 6441

Clinical Leads (NSF)
Mr C Piercy, Clinical Lead, Children,
Dr M Lambert, Clinical Lead, CHD & Diabetes, Cancer,
Ms C Brown, Clinical Lead, Older People,

Community Nursing Services
Ms K Dilley, Assistant Director of Nursing, Dunston Hill Hospital, Whickham, Gateshead, NE11 9QT, Tel.: 0191 445 6476

Ms D Horsley, Locality Matron, Low Fell Clinic, Beacon Lough Road, Low Fell, Gateshead, NE9 9TD, Tel.: 0191 443 6900

Ms M Johnson, Locality Matron, Dunston Health Centre, Dunston Bank, Gateshead, Tel.: 0191 460 5249

Ms L Johnstone, Locality Matron, Grassbanks Health Centre, Wirralshir, Leam Lane Estate, Gateshead, Tel.: 0191 443 6925

Ms P Liston, Locality Matron, Low Fell Clinic, Beacon Lough Road, Low Fell, Gateshead, NE9 9TD, Tel.: 0191 443 6900

Ms J Taylor, Locality Matron, Briarwood Sector Base, Whitmore Road, Blaydon, Tel.: 0191 414 1421

District Nursing
1 Oxford Terrace, Gateshead, NE8 1RQ, Tel.: 0191 477 2169

Beacon View Medical Practice, Beacon Cough Road, Low Fell, Gateshead, NE9,

Birtley Nursing Dev Unit, Durham Road, Birtley, Co Durham, DH3 2TQ, Tel.: 0191 492 3303

Evening/Night, Walk in Centre, Bensham Hospital, Saltwell Road, Gateshead, NE8 4YL,

Felling Health Centre, Stephenson Terrace, Felling, Gateshead, NE10 9QA, Tel.: 0191 438 1971

Gateshead Health Centre, Prince Consort Road, Gateshead, NE8 1NB, Tel.: 0191 443 6820

Ryton Clinic, Grange Road, Ryton, NE40 3PL, Tel.: 0191 413 2211

Teams Family Centre, Northumberland Street, Teams, Gateshead, NE8 2PN, Tel.: 0191 477 3940

Whickham Health Centre, Rectory Lane, Whickham, Newcastle upon Tyne, NE16 0PD, Tel.: 0191 488 6777

Winlaton Clinic, Hood Square, Winlaton, NE21 6AY, Tel.: 0191 414 2071

Family Planning Services
Dr S Field, Clinical Lead, 13 Walker Terrace, Gateshead, Tel.: 0191 490 2520

Health Visitors
1 Oxford Terrace, Gateshead, NE8 1RQ, Tel.: 0191 477 2169

Bensham Clinic, Liddle Terrace, Gateshead, NE8 1YN, Tel.: 0191 477 2177

Bewick Road Surgery, 10 Bewick Road, Gateshead, NE8 4DP, Tel.: 0191 477 2296

Birtley Nursing Dev Unit, Durham Road, Birtley, Co Durham, DH3 2TQ, Tel.: 0191 492 3303

Briarwood Sector Base, Whitmore Road, Blaydon, NE21 4AN, Tel.: 0191 414 1421

Dunston Health Centre, Dunston Bank, Dunston, Gateshead, NE11 9PY, Tel.: 0191 460 5249

Gateshead Health Centre, Prince Consort Road, Gateshead, NE8 1NB, Tel.: 0191 443 6820

Grassbanks Health Centre, Leam Lane Estate, Gateshead, NE10 8DX, Tel.: 0191 443 6925

Low Fell Clinic, Beacon Lough Road, Low Fell, Gateshead, NE9 6TD, Tel.: 0191 487 0681

Ryton Clinic, Grange Road, Ryton, NE40 3PL, Tel.: 0191 413 2211

Teams Family Centre, Northumberland Street, Teams, Gateshead, NE8 2PN, Tel.: 0191 477 3940

Whickham Health Centre, Rectory Lane, Whickham, Newcastle upon Tyne, NE16 0PD, Tel.: 0191 488 6777

HIV/AIDS
Ms N Brown, 13 Walker Terrace, Gateshead, Tel.: 0191 490 1699

Liaison Services
Ms K Ingleby, Specialist Health Visitor, Children with Additional Needs, Low Fell Clinic, Tel.: 0191 443 6908

School Nursing
School Health Advisors, Wrekenton Health Centre, Springwell Road, Wrekenton, Gateshead, NE9 7AD, Tel.: 0191 495 8503

School Health Advisors, Bensham Hospital, Gateshead, Tel.: 0191 445 5253

Specialist Nursing Services
Ms C Giffin, Continence, Whickham Health Centre, Tel.: 0191 488 6777

Clinic, Leg Ulcers, Carr Hill Clinic, Carr Hill, Gateshead, NE9 5LS, Tel.: 0191 477 1912

Nurses, Macmillan, Dunston Hill Hospital, Whickham Highway, Gateshead, NE11 9QT, Tel.: 0191 445 6435

Ms C Egglestone, Stoma Care, Queen Elizabeth Hospital, Gateshead, NE9 6SX, Tel.: 0191 445 3150

Ms T Pinchbeck, Stoma Care, Queen Elizabeth Hospital, Gateshead, NE9 6SX, Tel.: 0191 445 3153

Ms H Wilson, Stoma Care, Queen Elizabeth Hospital, Gateshead, NE9 6SX, Tel.: 0191 445 3152

The Homeless/Travellers & Asylum Seekers
Ms R Andrew, Refugee/Asylum Seekers Health Visitor, Civic Centre, Regent Street, Gateshead, Tel.: 0191 433 8225

North East Strategic Health Authority

Hartlepool Primary Care Trust
Trust Headquarters, Mandale House
Harbour Walk, The Marina
HARTLEPOOL, TS24 0UX
Tel.: 01429 285079

Admin & Senior Management
Mrs L Watson, Director of Nursing & Operations, Hartlepool PCT, Mandale House, Harbour Walk, Hartlepool, TS26 9LE, Tel.: 01429 285079
Child Health
Mrs P Hunter, Senior Clinical Nurse (Modern Matron) - Children & Young People, The Health Centre, Caroline Street, Hartlepool, TS26 9LE, Tel.: 01429 267901ext 4189
Child Health Records
Ms S Pearson, Medical Records Officer, The Health Centre, Caroline Street, Hartlepool, TS26 9LE, Tel.: 01429 267901
Child Protection/Safeguarding Children
Ms A Brock, Senior Clinical Nurse, Child Protection, The Health Centre, Caroline Street, Hartlepool, TS26 9LE, Tel.: 01429 267901ext 4135
Ms A Jackson, Senior Clinical Nurse, Child Protection, The Health Centre, Caroline Street, Hartlepool, TS26 9LE, Tel.: 01429 267901ext 4135
Clinical Leads (NSF)
Ms S Judge, Clinical Lead, Adults, The Health Centre, Caroline Street, Hartlepool, TS26 9LE, Tel.: 01429 267901ext 4132
Ms A Turner, Clinical Lead, CHD, McKenzie House, Kendal Road, Hartlepool, Tel.: 01429 285366
Dr L Johnson, Clinical Lead, Diabetic Care,
Community Nursing Services
Ms S Judge, Senior Clinical Nurse (Modern Matron), Adults, The Health Centre, Caroline Street, Hartlepool, TS26 9LE, Tel.: 01429 267901ext 4132
District Nursing
Ms S Judge, Senior Clinical Nurse District Nurses, (Modern Matron) - Home Nursing, Older People, The Health Centre, Caroline Street, Hartlepool, TS26 9LE, Tel.: 01429 267901ext 4132
Family Planning Services
Mrs P Hunter, Senior Clinical Nurse (Modern Matron) Children & Young People, The Health Centre, Caroline Street, Hartlepool, TS26 9LE, Tel.: 01429 267901ext 4189
Health Visitors
Ms P Hunter, Senior Clinical Nurse (Modern Matron) Children & Young People, The Health Centre, Caroline Street, Hartlepool, TS26 9LE, Tel.: 01429 267901ext 4180
Learning Disabilities
Ms L Johnson, Director of Planning, Hartlepool PCT, Mandale House, Harbour Walk, Hartlepool, TS26 9LE,
Liaison Services
Ms K Darwin, Discharge Liaison Sister, University Hospital of Hartlepool, Holdforth Rd, Hartlepool, TS24 9AH, Tel.: 01429 266654
Pharmacy
Ms K Geddes, Prescribing Advisor, Hartlepool PCT, Mandale House, Harbour Walk, Hartlepool, TS24 0UX,
Smoking Cessation
Mr P Price, Acting Director of Public Health, Hartlepool PCT, Mandale House, Harbour Walk, Hartlepool, TS26 9LE,
Specialist Nursing Services
Mr J Black, Specialist Nurse, The Health Centre, Caroline Street, Hartlepool, TS26 9LE,
Ms S Burke, Specialist Nurse, The Health Centre, Caroline Street, Hartlepool, TS26 9LE,
Ms C Walton, Specialist Nurse, The Health Centre, Caroline Street, Hartlepool, TS26 9LE,
Ms A Turner, Coronary Heart Disease, Lead Nurse, Coronary Heart Disease, McKenzie House, Kendal Road, Hartlepool, Tel.: 01429 285366

Ms L Rosen, Nurse, Macmillan, The Health Centre, Caroline Street, Hartlepool, TS26 9LE,

Langbaurgh Primary Care Trust
Trust Headquarters, Langbaurgh House
Bow Street
GUISBOROUGH
Cleveland, TS14 7AA
Tel.: 01287 284400

Admin & Senior Management
Mr J Chadwick, Chief Executive,
Child Protection/Safeguarding Children
Ms G Halls, Designated Nurse, Looked After Children, (Redcar & Cleveland L.A.), Seafield House, Kirkleatham Street, Redcar, TS10 1SP, Tel.: 01642 771500
Clinical Leads (NSF)
Dr R Rigby, Clinical Lead, CHD & Diabetes,
District Nursing
District Nurses, Langbaurgh House, Bow Street, Guisborough, Cleveland, TS14 7AA,
Mr M Gilligan, Head of Operational Services & Prof Affairs,
Health Visitors
Health Visitors, Langbaurgh House, Bow Street, Guisborough, Cleveland, TS14 7AA,
Specialist Nursing Services
Mrs A Webb, Continence, Redcar Health Centre, Tel.: 01642 516379
Ms S Young, Palliative Care, Guisborough General Hospital, Northgate, Guisborough, TS14 6HZ, Tel.: 01287 284000
Ms J Morrisroe, Stoma Care, Redcar Health Centre, Tel.: 01642 516379
Ms C Younger, Stoma Care, Redcar Health Centre, Tel.: 01642 516379
Mrs A Peevor, Wound Care, Guisborough General Hospital, Northgate, Guisborough, TS14 6HZ, Tel.: 01287 284014

Middlesbrough Primary Care Trust
Trust Headquarters, 18 High Force Road
Riverside Park
MIDDLESBROUGH
TS2 1RH
Tel.: 01642 352370

Admin & Senior Management
Mrs B Hill, Director of Clinical Services, 18 High Force Road, Middlesbrough, TS2 1RH, Tel.: 01642 352370
Mr C McLeod, Chief Executive,
Child Health Records
Mrs C Bowen, Head of School Nursing, Poole House, Stokesley, Cleveland, Tel.: 01642 304145
Clinical Leads (NSF)
Dr S Greaves, Clinical Lead, Cancer,
Dr P McNiece, Clinical Lead, CHD,
Dr J Allison, Clinical Lead, Diabetic Care,
Dr L Wallace, Clinical Lead, Older People,
District Nursing
Mrs M Larkin, Community Nursing Services Manager (Health Visiting), Poole House, Stokesley Road, Middlesbrough, Tel.: 01642 304094
Ms B Paterson, Head of District Nursing, West Acklam Clinic, Birtley Avenue, Acklam, Middlesbrough, TS5 8LA, Tel.: 01642 513568
Family Planning Services
Dr D Beere, Consultant in Contraception & Reproductive Health, South Bank Health Shop,
School Nursing
Mrs C Bowen, Head of School Nursing, Poole House, Stokesley, Cleveland, Tel.: 01642 304145

North East Strategic Health Authority

Newcastle Primary Care Trust

Trust Headquarters
Benfield Road
NEWCASTLE UPON TYNE
NE6 4PF
Tel.: 0191 219 6000
Fax.: 0191 219 6066

Admin & Senior Management
Ms V Morris, Head of Specialist Services,
Ms J Prendergast, Head of Generalist Service,
Ms S Sengupta, Director of Health Improvement,
Child Health
Mr N Davison,
Child Protection/Safeguarding Children
Ms P Askell, Child Protection, Arthur's Hill Clinic, Douglas Terrace, Newcastle upon Tyne, NE4 6BT, Tel.: 0191 219 5205
Clinical Leads (NSF)
Dr R Cummings, Clinical Lead, Cancer,
Dr W Carr, Clinical Lead, CHD,
Dr G Wilkes, Clinical Lead, Older People,
District Nursing
Assistant General Manager, North, Gosforth Health Centre, Church Road, Gosforth, Newcastle upon Tyne, NE3 1TX, Tel.: 0191 210 6624
Mrs Y Birkett, Assistant General Manager, Geoffrey Rhodes Centre, Algernon Road, Newcastle upon Tyne, NE6 2UZ, Tel.: 0191 219 4641
Mrs R Burn, Community Nurse Leader, Geoffrey Rhodes Centre, Algernon Road, Newcastle upon Tyne, NE6 2UZ, Tel.: 0191 219 4641
Ms G Johnson, Assistant General Manager, West, Arthur's Hill Clinic, Douglas Terrace, Newcastle upon Tyne, NE4 6BT, Tel.: 0191 219 5190
Out of hours, Tel.: 0191 284 7272
Ms S Patterson, Community Nurse Leader, Arthur's Hill Clinic, Douglas Terrace, Newcastle upon Tyne, NE4 6BT, Tel.: 0191 219 5190
Family Planning Services
Dr D Mansour, Head of Service, Graingerville Clinic, Newcastle General Hospital, Tel.: 0191 219 5239
Ms S Rutherford, Community Nurse Leader, Graingerville Clinic, Newcastle General Hospital, Tel.: 0191 219 5239
HIV/AIDS
Ms P Handy, GUM, Senior Nurse, GUM Dept, Newcastle General Hospital, Tel.: 0191 273 666 ext 22855
Dr R Pattman, GUM Dept, Newcastle General Hospital, Tel.: 0191 273 666 ext 22855
Liaison Services
Ms A Giblin, Intermediate Care Development Co-ordinator, 2nd Floor, Physio Block, Newcastle General Hospital, Tel.: 0191 256 3033
Specialist Nursing Services
Ms S Horsfield, Breast Care, Victoria Wing, RVI, Tel.: 0191 282 0206/7/8
Mrs C Giffin, Continence, Tel.: 0191 219 5188
Ms D Kyne, Community Nurse Leader, Diabetic Care, Diabetes Centre, Newcastle General Hospital, Tel.: 0191 273 6666 ext 22521
Miss M Casey, Macmillan, Tel.: 0191 226 1315
Ms C Harrison, Lead Nurse, Occupational Health, Weston Court, Newcastle General Hospital, Tel.: 0191 272 1898
Miss L Brown, Stoma Care, Tel.: 0191 219 5188
The Homeless/Travellers & Asylum Seekers
Ms L Bray, Homeless, Health Visitor, Hill Court, Pitt Street, Newcastle upon Tyne, NE4 5SX, Tel.: 0191232 0476
Ms S Donnelly, Refugee, Asylum Seekers, Health Visitor, 2 Jesmond Road West, Newcastle upon Tyne, NE2 4PQ, Tel.: 0191 245 7319

Newcastle Upon Tyne Hospitals NHS Trust

Trust Headquarters, Freeman Hospital
High Heaton
NEWCASTLE UPON TYNE
Tyne & Wear
NE7 7DN
Tel.: 0191 233 6161

Child Protection/Safeguarding Children
Ms P Askell, Designated Nurse, Child Protection, CP Nurse Unit, Arthur's Hill Clinic, Douglas Terrace, Newcastle upon Tyne, NE4 6BT, Tel.: 0191 219 5205
Ms J Clarke, Named Nurse, Child Protection, Royal Victoria Infirmary, Queen Victoria Road, Newcastle upon Tyne, NE1 4LP, Tel.: 0191 282 0589
Community Midwifery
Community Midwifery Office, Royal Victoria Infirmary, Queen Victoria Road, Newcastle upon Tyne, Tyne & Wear, NE1 4LP, Tel.: 0191 2825711
Delivery Suite, Royal Victoria Infirmary, Queen Victoria Road, Newcastle upon Tyne, Tyne & Wear, NE1 4LP, Tel.: 0191 282 5719
Mrs J Farrell, Midwifery Manager, Community Services, Royal Victoria Infirmary, Queen Victoria Road, Newcastle upon Tyne, Tyne & Wear, NE1 4LP, Tel.: 0191 282 5711
Mrs J Herve, Head of Midwifery/Directorate Manager, Royal Victoria Infirmary, Queen Victoria Road, Newcastle upon Tyne, Tyne & Wear, NE1 4LP, Tel.: 0191 282 5711
Ms A Southern, Community Midwifery Office, Royal Victoria Infirmary, Queen Victoria Road, Newcastle upon Tyne, Tyne & Wear, NE1 4LP, Tel.: 0191 282 5711

North Tees & Hartlepool NHS Trust

Trust Headquarters, Univ Hosp of Hartlepool
Holdforth Road
HARTLEPOOL
Cleveland
TS24 9AH
Tel.: 01429 266654
Fax.: 01429 235389

Acute Specialist Nursing Services
Ms J Etherington, University Hospital of Hartlepool, Tel.: 01429 266654
Ms K Oram, Matron, A&E, University Hospital of North Tees, Tel.: 01429 522546
Ms S Cotton, Nurse, Breast Care, Breast Unit, North Tees Hospital, Tel.: 01642 624371
Ms G Croft, Nurse, Breast Care, Breast Unit, North Tees Hospital, Tel.: 01642 624371
Ms V Cross, Nurse, Breast Care, Breast Unit, North Tees Hospital, Tel.: 01642 624371
Ms J Harley, Breast Care, University Hospital of North Tees, Tel.: 01642 624371
Ms K Milburn, Macmillan Nurse, Breast Care, Hartlepool General Hospital, Tel.: 01429 522327
Mrs G Bowler, Nurse Endoscopist, Colorectal, IDA, University Hospital of North Tees, Tel.: 01429 266654 ext 4981
Ms L Hurst, Nurse Endoscopist, Colorectal, North Tees, Tel.: 01642 62438
Ms A Lee, Nurse Endoscopist, Colorectal, IBD, University Hospital of North Tees, Tel.: 01429 266654 ext 2335
Ms T Pugh, Stoma Care Advisor, Colorectal, Stoma Therapy Dept, Univ Hospital of Hartlepool, Tel.: 01429 522335
Ms N Robinson, Colorectal, University Hospital of North Tees, Tel.: 01642 624399
Ms G Trainer, Nurse Specialist, Colorectal, Stoma Therapy Dept, Univ Hospital of Hartlepool, Tel.: 01429 522335

Mr G Waddup, Colorectal, University Hospital of North Tees, Tel.: 01642 624399

Ms L Buglass, COPD, Hartlepool Hospital, Tel.: 01429 26665 ext 2040

Ms C Docherty, COPD, North Tees Hospital, Tel.: 01642 617617 ext 4395

Ms L Huitson, COPD, University Hospital of Hartlepool, Tel.: 01429 266654

Ms S Stych, COPD, University Hospital of North Tees, Tel.: 01642 617617

Ms B Day, Liaison, Diabetic Care, - Paediatrics, University Hospital of North Tees, Tel.: 01642 617617 ext 4151

Ms M Dobson, Diabetic Care, University Hospital of North Tees, Tel.: 01642 624110/624519

Ms L Doughty, Diabetic Care, University Hospital of Hartlepool, Tel.: 01429 266654

Ms G Dryden, Diabetic Care, University Hospital of Hartlepool, Tel.: 01429 266654

Ms C Robinson, Diabetic Care, University Hospital of North Tees, Tel.: 01642 624110/624519

Ms M Robinson, Diabetic Care, - Endocrine, University Hospital of North Tees, Tel.: 01642 617617 ext 4618

Mrs L Wharton, Infection Control, University Hospital of North Tees, Tel.: 01642 617617

Ms T Craig, Macmillan, Lung Cancer, University Hospital of North Tees, Tel.: 01642 624112

Ms T Fitzpatrick, Macmillan, Lung Cancer, University Hospital of North Tees, Tel.: 01642 624112

Ms J Harrison, Macmillan, University Hospital of North Tees, Tel.: 01642 624112

Ms M Lockey, Macmillan, University Hospital of North Tees, Tel.: 01642 624112

Ms C Murch, Macmillan, Peterlee Community Hospital, Tel.: 0191 586 2903

Ms P Ramaswany, Macmillan, University Hospital of North Tees, Tel.: 01642 624112

Ms M Roberts, Macmillan, University Hospital of Hartlepool, Tel.: 01429 266654

Ms L Rosen, Macmillan, University Hospital of Hartlepool, Tel.: 01429 266654

Ms M Wilson, Macmillan, Peterlee Community Hospital, Tel.: 0191 586 2903

Ms W Anderson, Oncology, - Haematology, University Hospital of North Tees, Tel.: 01642 617617

Ms M Elliot, Oncology, - Haematology, University Hospital of North Tees, Tel.: 01642 617617

Ms R Livingston, Oncology, - Haematology, University Hospital of Hartlepool, Tel.: 01429 266654

Ms L Smith, Oncology, - Haematology, University Hospital of Hartlepool, Tel.: 01429 266654

Mrs W Bradshaw, Homeward, Orthopaedics, University Hospital of North Tees, Tel.: 01429 522560

Mrs J Grosvenor, Homeward, Orthopaedics, University Hospital of North Tees, Tel.: 01642 624551

Ms J Branthwaite, Respiratory, North Tees Hospital, Tel.: 01642 617617 ext 4417

Ms E Moore, Respiratory, University Hospital of North Tees, Tel.: 01642 617617

Mr S Brett, Rheumatology, University Hospital of Hartlepool, Tel.: 01429 266654

Ms J Robinson, Rheumatology, University Hospital of Hartlepool, Tel.: 01429 266654

Ms J Porter, Nurse Endoscopist, Upper GI, North Tees, Tel.: 01642 62438

Mrs J Simpson, Clinical Nurse Specialist, Upper GI, University Hospital of North Tees, Tel.: 01642 617617

Ms S Brennan, Urology, University Hospital of North Tees, Tel.: 01642 623222

Mr P Clark, Urology, University Hospital of Hartlepool, Tel.: 01642 623222

Ms K Kilburn, Urology, University Hospital of North Tees, Tel.: 01642 623222

Ms A Riordon, Urology, University Hospital of Hartlepool, Tel.: 01642 623222

Child Health

Ms P King, Community Paediatrician Hartlepool, University Hospital of Hartlepool, Tel.: 01429 266654

Ms L Nicholson, Community Paediatrician North Tees Cystic Fibrosis, University Hospital of Hartlepool, Tel.: 01642 617617

Ms D Osborne, Community Paediatrician North Tees, University Hospital of Hartlepool, Tel.: 01642 617617

Mr M Telford, Community Paediatrician North Tees Life Threatening Diseases, University Hospital of Hartlepool, Tel.: 01642 617617

Ms L Wilson, Community Paediatrician Hartlepool, University Hospital of Hartlepool, Tel.: 01429 266654

Child Health Records

North Tees, University Hospital of North Tees, Tel.: 01642 617617 ext 4144

Child Protection/Safeguarding Children

Ms C Atherton, Hartlepool, Caroline Street Health Centre, Hartlepool, TS26 9LE, Tel.: 01429 267901

Ms A Jackson, Hartlepool, Caroline Street Health Centre, Hartlepool, TS26 9LE, Tel.: 01429 267901

Ms L Dobson, North Tees, Child Protection, Lawson Street Health Centre, Stockton on Tees, TS18 1HU, Tel.: 01642 416101

Mr M Robinson, North Tees, Child Protection, Lawson Street Health Centre, Stockton on Tees, TS18 1HU, Tel.: 01642 416101

Community Midwifery

Ms J Mackie, Head of Midwifery,

Ms J L Stout, North Tees, Hartlepool & East Durham, Community Midwifery Manager, Tel.: 01429 266654

Family Planning Services

Ms S Crinion, Health Advisor Sexual Health, Hartlepool, Tel.: 01429 5225

Ms T Lait-Huzzard, Health Advisor Sexual Health, North Tees, Tel.: 01642 62417

Health Visitors

Ms E M Brunini, Health Visitor Special Needs, Peterlee Community Hospital, Tel.: 0191 586 3474

HIV/AIDS

Mr T Gristwood, HP - AIDS/HIV, University Hospital of North Tees, Tel.: 01642624190

Mr T Walsh, HP/Trainer - AIDS/HIV, East Durham & Houghall Community College, Burnhope Way, Peterlee, SR8 1NU, Tel.: 0191 586 6681

Liaison Services

Ms J Stephenson, Paediatric Liaison Hartlepool, University Hospital of Hartlepool, Tel.: 01429 266654

Other Services

Ms C Sara, Sure Start, Peterlee Health Centre, Tel.: 0191 586 2273

North Tees Primary Care Trust

Trust Headquarters, Tower House
Teesdale South, Thornaby Place, Thornaby
STOCKTON ON TEES
TS17 6SE
Tel.: 01642 352297

Admin & Senior Management

Ms A Moore, Director of Operational Services & Nursing, Tel.: 01642 352178

Ms C Willis, Chief Executive, Tel.: 01642 352297

Clinical Leads (NSF)

Ms I Ablett Spence, Clinical Lead, Cancer, Tel.: 01642 352345

Dr T Roberts, Clinical Lead, CHD,

Ms R Hill, Clinical Lead, Older People, - Diabetes,

North East Strategic Health Authority

District Nursing
Ms I Ablett Spence, Tel.: 01642 352345
Liaison Services
Ms A Bright, In Reach Nurse, University Hospital of North Tees, Hardwick, Stockton on Tees, TS19 8PE, Tel.: 01642 617617 ex 4693/4107
Ms M Cambage, Rapid Response Team, University Hospital of North Tees, Hardwick, Stockton on Tees, TS19 8PE, Tel.: 01642 624108
Ms D Ewbank, Rapid Response Team, University Hospital of North Tees, Hardwick, Stockton on Tees, TS19 8PE, Tel.: 01642 624108
Ms B Johnson, In Reach Nurse, University Hospital of North Tees, Hardwick, Stockton on Tees, TS19 8PE, Tel.: 01642 617617 ex 4693/4107
Specialist Nursing Services
Ms M Marshall, Continence, University Hospital of North Tees, Tel.: 01642 617617 ext 4697

North Tyneside Primary Care Trust

Trust Headquarters, Equinox House
Silver Fox Way, Cobalt Business Park
NEWCASTLE UPON TYNE
NE27 0QJ
Tel.: 0191 219 9292

Admin & Senior Management
Mr W Charlton, Head of Community Health Development, Equinox House, Cobalt Business Park, Newcastle upon Tyne, NE27 0QJ, Tel.: 0191 291 9353
Mrs J Chatterjee, Assistant Director of Urgent Care, Equinox House, Cobalt Business Park, Newcastle upon Tyne, NE27 0QJ, Tel.: 0191 291 9354
Mr P Cusack, Assistant Director, Longterm Conditions, Equinox House, Cobalt Business Park, Newcastle upon Tyne, NE27 0QJ, Tel.: 0191 291 9353
Mrs L Dixon, Chief Operating Officer/Director of Nursing, Equinox House, Cobalt Business Park, Newcastle upon Tyne, NE27 0QJ, Tel.: 0191 219 9313
Ms V Gilroy, Planning Partnership Manager, Equinox House, Cobalt Business Park, Newcastle upon Tyne, NE27 0QJ, 0191 291 9355
Ms S Tiplady, Commissioning Manager, Older People & Physical Disability,
Mrs L Young-Murphy, Deputy Director of Nursing, Equinox House, Cobalt Business Park, Newcastle upon Tyne, NE27 0QJ, Tel.: 0191 291 9352
Child Health
Ms C Dawson, Health Dev & Commissioning Manager, Tel.: 0191 291 9398
Mrs L Young-Murphy, Deputy Director of Nursing, Equinox House, Cobalt Business Park, Newcastle upon Tyne, NE27 0QJ, Tel.: 0191 291 9352
Child Health Records
Mr J McClen, Records Manager, Equinox House, Cobalt Business Park, Newcastle upon Tyne, NE27 0QJ, Tel.: 0191 291 9349
Child Protection/Safeguarding Children
Ms S Hogarth, Senior Nurse, Child Protection, Albion Road Clinic, Albion Road, North Shields, NE29 0HG, Tel.: 0191 2196679
Community Matrons
Mr P Cusack, Tel.: 0191 291 9447
Community Midwifery
Ms C Dawson, Health Dev & Commissioning Manager, Tel.: 0191 291 9398
Community Nursing Services
Ms A Dawson, PA to Lyn Dixon, Director of Nursing, Equinox House, Cobalt Business Park, Newcastle upon Tyne, NE27 0QJ, Tel.: 0191 291 9358
Mrs L Dixon, Chief Operating Officer/Director of Nursing, Equinox House, Cobalt Business Park, Newcastle upon Tyne, NE27 0QJ, Tel.: 0191 219 9313

Mrs L Young-Murphy, Deputy Director of Nursing, Equinox House, Cobalt Business Park, Newcastle upon Tyne, NE27 0QJ, Tel.: 0191 291 9352
District Nursing
Ms T Davis, Clinical Nurse Lead for Urgent Care, Equinox House, Cobalt Business Park, Newcastle upon Tyne, NE27 0QJ, Tel.: 0191 291 9356
Ms T Davis, Clinical Nurse Lead - Out of Hours Nursing, Equinox House, Cobalt Business Park, Newcastle upon Tyne, NE27 0QJ, Tel.: 0191 291 9423
Ms J Kelly, Clinical Nurse Lead for Planned Care & Long Term Conditions, Equinox House, Cobalt Business Park, Newcastle upon Tyne, NE27 0QJ, Tel.: 0191 291 9422
Ms H McIlveen, One to One Centre (GUM), Hawkeys Lane, North Shields, Tel.: 0191 219 6610
Ms K Taylor, Clinical Nurse Lead for Nursing & Care Governance, Equinox House, Cobalt Business Park, Newcastle upon Tyne, NE27 0QJ, Tel.: 0191 291 9383
Ms L Young-Murphy, Deputy Director of Nursing, Equinox House, Silver Fox Way, Cobalt Business Park, Newcastle Upon Tyne, NE27 0QJ, Tel.: 0191 291 9352
Equipment Loan Services
Ms J Chatterjee, Tel.: 0191 291 9354
Family Planning Services
Ms H McIlveen, Head of Family Planning, One to One Centre, Hawkeys Lane, North Shields, NE29 0SF, Tel.: 0191 219 6642
Health Visitors
Ms C Coxon, Health Visitor/Health Co-ordinator, Sure Start Unit, 3rd Floor, White Swan Centre, Citadel Killingworth, NE12 6SS, Tel.: 0191 200 8244
Ms L Young-Murphy, Deputy Director of Nursing, Equinox House, Silver Fox Way, Cobalt Business Park, Newcastle Upon Tyne, NE27 0QJ, Tel.: 0191 291 9352
Learning Disabilities
Ms D Holmes, Disability Manager, North Tyneside Council, Great Lime Road, Forest Hall, Newcastle upon Tyne,
Ms J Welsh, Senior Nurse, Community LD Team, Parkside House, Elton Street, Wallsend, Tyne & Wear, NE28 8QU, Tel.: 0191 200 1077
Liaison Services
Ms D Scott, Liaison Nursing Sister - Caring for Cancer at Home, Sir GB Hunter Memorial Hospital, Tel.: 0191 200 5947
Other Services
Ms J Brown, Co-ordinator, Sure Start Howdon, 11a Howdon Lane, Howdon, Wallsend, NE28 0AL, Tel.: 0191 200 6666
Pharmacy
Mr C Edwards, Pharmaceutical Officer, Equinox House, Cobalt Business Park, Newcastle upon Tyne, NE27 0QJ, Tel.: 0191 291 9390
School Nursing
Ms L Young-Murphy, Deputy Director of Nursing, Equinox House, Silver Fox Way, Cobalt Business Park, Newcastle Upon Tyne, NE27 0QJ, Tel.: 0191 291 9352
Smoking Cessation
Ms J Logie, Arthurs Hill Clinic, Douglas Terrace, Newcastle, NE4 6BT, Tel.: 0191 219 5111
Specialist Nursing Services
Ms D Moss, Funded Nursing Care Determination Team, Sir GB Hunter Memorial Hospital, Tel.: 0191 220 5967
Mr M Osborne, Long Term Care, Specialist Nurse, Whitley Bay Older Persons Team, Suite 8, Albion House, Sidney Street, North Shields, NE29 0DW, Tel.: 0191 219 5917
Ms L English, Nurse Co-ordinator, Community, Cardiology, Sir GB Hunter Memorial Hospital, The Green, Wallsend, Tel.: 0191 220 2206
Ms L Freeman, Specialist Nurse, Continence, Sir GB Hunter Memorial Hospital, The Green, Wallsend, Tel.: 0191 220 5937

North East Strategic Health Authority

Ms M Oswald, Specialist Nurse, Continence, Sir GB Hunter Memorial Hospital, The Green, Wallsend, Tel.: 0191 220 5937
Ms V Blacklock, Facilitated Nurse, Discharges, The Cedars, Morwick Road, North Shields, Tel.: 0191 296 2589
Ms C McManis, Specialist Nurse, Infection Control, Equinox House, Cobalt Business Park, Newcastle upon Tyne, NE27 0QJ, Tel.: 0191 291 9457
Ms J Lee, Specialist Nurse, Stoma Care, Sir GB Hunter Memorial Hospital, The Green, Wallsend, Tel.: 0191 220 5918
Ms O Morris, Specialist Nurse, Stoma Care, Sir GB Hunter Memorial Hospital, The Green, Wallsend, Tel.: 0191 220 5918
Ms J Dunn, Specialist Nurse, Tissue Viability, Sir GB Hunter Memorial Hospital, The Green, Wallsend, Tel.: 0191 220 5991
Ms C Hodgeson, Specialist Nurse, Tissue Viability, Sir GB Hunter Memorial Hospital, The Green, Wallsend, Tel.: 0191 220 5991
The Homeless/Travellers & Asylum Seekers
Ms L Young-Murphy, Deputy Director of Nursing, Equinox House, Cobalt Business Park, Newcastle upon Tyne, NE27 0QJ, Tel.: 0191 291 9352

Northgate & Prudhoe NHS Trust
Trust Headquarters
Northgate Hospital
MORPETH
Northumberland, NE61 3BP
Tel.: 01670 394000

Learning Disabilities
Ms M Allan, Director of Nursing, Northgate Hospital, Morpeth, Northumberland, NE61 3BP, Tel.: 01670 394060
Mrs J Campbell, Newcastle, Clinical Nurse Manager, Community Team, Sanderson Centre, North Avenue, Gosforth, Newcastle upon Tyne, NE3 4DT, Tel.: 0191 219 6800
Mrs M Hunter, Head of Service - Newcastle, Community Team, Sanderson Centre, North Avenue, Gosforth, Newcastle upon Tyne, NE3 4DT, Tel.: 0191 219 6800

Northumberland Care Trust
Trust Headquarters, Merley Croft
Loansdean
MORPETH
NE61 2DL
Tel.: 01670 394400

Admin & Senior Management
Ms L Ions, Chief Executive,
Child Health
Ms J Bolam, Children's Community Nursing Services Manager, Child Health Centre, John Street, Ashington, Tel.: 01670 395706
Child Protection/Safeguarding Children
Mrs K Fletcher, Senior Nurse, Child Protection, Cramlington Health Centre, Forum Way, Cramlington, NE23 6QN, Tel.: 01670 712238 ext 145
Community Nursing Services
West Locality, Tanners Burn House, Hexham Business Park, Burn Lane, Hexham, NE46 3RU, Tel.: 01434 656200
District Nursing
Ms A Arter, Deputy General Manager - Blyth & Central, Northumberland Child Health Centre, John Street, Ashington, NE 63 0SE, Tel.: 01670 395706
Emergencies - Tynedale, Tel.: 01434 655655
Emergencies/Night, North Northumberland, or 01289 307484, Tel.: 01665 626700
Emergencies/Night, Blyth & Central, Tel.: 0191 273 4470
Ms L Hardy, Community, North Northumberland, Manager, Alnwick Infirmary, Alnwick, NE66 2NS, Tel.: 01665 626700
Ms L Hardy, Community Manager - Tynedale, Hexham General Hospital, Corbridge Road, Hexham, NE46 1QJ, Tel.: 01434 655655
Nights - Tynedale, Tel.: 0191 273 4470

Other Services
Mr D Parkin, Director of Social Care & Planning, Northumberland Care Trust, County Hall, Morpeth, NE61 2EF, Tel.: 01670 533877

Northumbria Health Care NHS Trust
Trust Headquarters, North Tyneside General Hospital
Rake Lane
NORTH SHIELDS
Tyne & Wear
NE29 8NE
Tel.: 0191 259 6660

Child Health
Ms J Bolam, Community Paediatrician, Child Health Centre, John Street, Ashington, Tel.: 0191219 6682/01670 395706
Children's Community Nursing, Albion Road Resource Centre, Tel.: 0191 219 6658
Ms R Chilvers, General Manager, Albion Road Clinic, Albion Road, North Shields, Tyne & Wear, NE29 0HG, Tel.: 0191 219 6651
Ms A Raine, Child & Family Psych (North Tyneside), Tel.: 0191 219 6661
Child Health Records
Ms S Bell, Computer Co-ordinator (North Tyneside), Albion Road Clinic, Tel.: 0191 219 6654
Ms K Cameron, Computer Co-ordinator (Northumberland), Northumberland Child Health Centre, John Street, Ashington, NE63 0SE, Tel.: 01670 856162
Child Protection/Safeguarding Children
Ms K Fletcher, Northumberland, Child Protection, Cramlington Health Centre, Forum Way, Cramlington, NE23 6QN, Tel.: 01670 712238
Ms S Hogarth, North Tyneside, Child Protection, Albion Road Clinic, Tel.: 0191 219 6679
Community Midwifery
Ms M Archbold, Senior Midwife, Alnwick Infirmary, Alnwick, Northumberland, NE66 2NS, Tel.: 01665 602376
Ms L Hedley, Senior Midwife, Berwick Infirmary, Berwick-upon-Tweed, Northumberland, TD15 1LT, Tel.: 01289 307484
Ms J McNichol, Head of Midwifery, Maternity Unit, Hexham General Hospital, Corbridge Road, Hexham, Northumberland, NE46 1QJ, Tel.: 01434 655655
Ms J McNichol, Head of Midwifery, North Tyneside General Hospital, Rake Lane, North Shields, Tyne & Wear, NE29 8NH, Tel.: 0191 259 6660
Mrs S Shaftoe, Head of Midwifery, Wansbeck General Hospital, Woodhorn Lane, Ashington, NE63 9JJ, Tel.: 01670 521212
HIV/AIDS
Ms H McIlveen, Sexual Health/HIV Adviser, Itol Centre, Hawkey's Lane, North Shields, NE29 0SF, Tel.: 0191 259 2519
Learning Disabilities
Mr S Gallagher, Team, Co-ordinator, Parkside House, Elton Street, Wallsend, Newcastle upon Tyne, NE28 8QU, Tel.: 0191 200 6500

Sedgefield Primary Care Trust
Trust Headquarters, Merrington House
Merrington Lane
SPENNYMOOR
DL16 7UT
Tel.: 0191 301 3820

Admin & Senior Management
Mr N Porter, Chief Executive,
Child Health
Mrs G Reeves, Team Leader, Health Centre, Bishop's Close, Spennymoor, DL16 6ED, Tel.: 01388 815711
Child Health Records
Ms J Clarke, Supervisor, Health Centre, Escomb Road, Tel.: 01388 452807/452803

North East Strategic Health Authority

Clinical Leads (NSF)
Dr A Long, Clinical Lead, Cancer,
Dr P Jones, Clinical Lead, CHD,
Dr A Sensier, Clinical Lead, Diabetic Care,
Dr R McKinty, Clinical Lead, Older People,
Community Nursing Services
Ms K Vasey, Head of Nursing & Community Services, Sedgefield
Community Hospital, Sedgefield, Stockton-on-Tees, TS21 3EE, Tel.:
01740 626641
District Nursing
Ms K Vasey, Head of Nursing & Community Services, Sedgefield
Community Hospital, Sedgefield, Stockton-on-Tees, TS21 3EE, Tel.:
01740 626641

South of Tyne & Wearside Mental Health NHS Trust

Trust Headquarters,
Cherry Knowle Hospital
RYHOPE
Sunderland
SR2 0NB
Tel.: 0191 565 6256

Learning Disabilities
Ms H Barker, Clinical Nurse Manager, 2nd Floor, Monkwearmouth
Hospital, Newcastle Road, Sunderland, SR5 1NB, Tel.: 0191 565
6256 ext 48318
Ms J-A Carter, Service Manager/Modern Matron, Dept of Learning
Disabilities, Monkwearmouth Hospital, Newcastle Road, Sunderland,
SR5 1NB, Tel.: 0191 5656256 ext 48316
Mrs J Wilson, Director, Knowle Court, Cherry Knowle Hospital,
Ryhope, Sunderland Tyne & Wear, SR2 0LY, Tel.: 0191 565 6256

South Tees Hospitals NHS Trust

Trust Headquarters, James Cook University Hospital
Marton Road
MIDDLESBROUGH
TS4 3BW
Tel.: 01642 850850

Acute Specialist Nursing Services
Ms L Turnbull, Nurse Prescribing Advisor, Bedale Health Centre,
Tel.: 01677 425111
Ms J Curtiss, Breast Care, Friarage Hospital, Tel.: 01609 779911 ext
3903
Ms C McGee, Continence, Stokesley Health Centre, Tel.: 01642
713134
Mrs C MacArthur, Diabetic Care, Friarage Hospital, Tel.: 01609
764810
Ms S Smith, Diabetic Care, Friary Clinic, Queens Road, Richmond,
DL10 4UJ, Tel.: 01748 822122
Ms J Lawn, Haematology, Friarage Hospital, Tel.: 01609 779911
Mr A Collyer, Infection Control, Friarage Hospital, Tel.: 01609
779911
Miss C Ward, Macmillan, Friarage Hospital, Tel.: 01609 763915
Mr C Ward, Nurse Consultant, Palliative Care, Rutson CH, Tel.:
01609 762001
Ms J Parrington, Nurse, Respiratory, Resp Dept, Friarage Hospital,
Tel.: 01609 764582
Ms J Thirkell, Stoma Care, Friarage Hospital, Tel.: 01609 764606
Child Health
Ms M Dunn, Paediatrics, Tel.: 01609 779911/764202
Child Protection/Safeguarding Children
Ms S Roughton, Child Protection, Rutson Community Hosptal, High
Street, Northallerton, Tel.: 01609 764839
Community Midwifery
Ms K Branch, Screening Co-ordinator for Maternity Services, James
Cook Univ Hospital, Tel.: ext 3784

Ms A Holt, Consultant Midwife, James Cook Univ Hospital,
Mrs C Murrish, Community Midwifery Co-ordinator, James Cook
University Hospital, Marton Road, Middlesbrough, TS4 3BW, Tel.:
01642 854880
Ms A Skillcorn, Community Midwifery Team Leader, Friarage
Hospital, East Road, Northallerton, North Yorkshire, DL6 1JG, Tel.:
01609 763084
Ms J Smith, Deputy Maternity Services Manager, Friarage Hospital,
East Road, Northallerton, North Yorkshire, DL6 1JG, Tel.: 01609
763078
Mrs F Toller, Maternity Services Manager, Head of Midwifery, James
Cook University Hospital, Marton Road, Middlesbrough, TS4 3BW,
Tel.: 01642 282728
Community Nursing Services
Ms M Tate, Community Nurse Manager, Friarage Hospital, Tel.:
01609 779911ext 3130
Learning Disabilities
Community Resource Team, Rutson Hospital, Northallerton, DL7
8EN, Tel.: 01609 762139
Ms R Critchley, General Manager, Friarage Hospital, Northallerton,
North Yorkshire, DL6 1JG, Tel.: 01609 763095
Mr D Hendy, Nurse Advisor, Front Offices, Rutson CH, Tel.: 01609
763926
Ms B Wilson, Nurse Advisor, Front Offices, Rutson CH, Tel.: 01609
763926
Other Services
Mr D Emson, Drugs & Alcohol, Rutson Hospital, Northallerton, DL7
8EN, Tel.: 01609 764105
School Nursing
Ms R Wigin, School Nurse Advisor, Zetland House Clinic, Tel.:
01609 764102
Smoking Cessation
Ms P Marshall, Smoking Cessation, Trust HQ,

South Tyneside Health Care NHS Trust

Trust Headquarters, South Tyneside District Hospital
Harton Wing, Harton Lane
SOUTH SHIELDS
Tyne & Wear
NE34 0PL
Tel.: 0191 454 8888

Acute Specialist Nursing Services
Ms D Cresswell, Macmillan, Nurse Specialist, Lung Cancer,
Ms K Pattison, Lead Cancer Nurse, Palliative Care,
Ms V Raine, Nurse Specialist, Palliative Care,
Ms D Townsley, Nurse Specialist, Palliative Care,
Mr J Youll, Nurse Specialist, Palliative Care,
Mrs A Bell, Nurse Specialist, Stoma Care,
Community Midwifery
Mrs B Boddy, Delivery Suite Co-ordinator, Tel.: 0191 2024190
Mr D Curry, Operational Lead Women's Services/Head of Midwifery,
Tel.: 0191 454 8888 ext 4057
Ms A Hill, Community Midwifery Services Co-ordinator, Tel.: 0191
454 8888 ext 2488/9
Out of hours, Tel.: 0191 454 8888 ext 2487
Ms J Stonehouse, Senior, Midwife, Ward 22, Tel.: 0191 454 8888 ext
2477
Ms A Wolfe, Senior, Antenatal Services, Midwife, Tel.: 0191 454
8888 ext 2459
Learning Disabilities
Emergencies, Tel.: 0191 451 6275
Learning Disability Team, Balgownie House, Bedeburn Road,
Jarrow, NE32 5BH, Tel.: 0191 483 5560
Mrs T Peters, Assistant Service Manager, c/o Monkton Hall Hospital,
Jarrow, Tyne & Wear, NE32 5PY, Tel.: 0191 4516283

North East Strategic Health Authority

South Tyneside Primary Care Trust

Trust Headquarters, Ingham House
Horsley Hill Road
SOUTH SHIELDS
Tyne & Wear, NE33 3DP
Tel.: 0191 401 4500

Admin & Senior Management
Mr R McLaughlan, Chief Executive, South Tyneside PCT, Ingham House, Horsley Hill Road, South Shields, NE33 3DP,
Mrs J Old, Head of Community Services, South Tyneside PCT, Ingham House, Horsley Hill Road, South Shields, NE33 3DP,

Child Health
Ms S Hunter, Palmer Community Hospital, Wear Street, Jarrow, NE32 3UX, Tel.: 0191 451 6050
Mrs S Culling, Nurse, Paediatrics, Stanhope Parade Health Centre, Tel.: 0191 451 6167
Mrs G Marriner, Nurse, Paediatrics, Stanhope Parade Health Centre, Tel.: 0191 451 6167

Child Health Records
Ms L Baglin, Manager, Parkdale Suite, Harton Wing, South Tyneside District Hospital, Tel.: 0191 454 8888 ext 2820-5

Child Protection/Safeguarding Children
Ms C Drummond, Child Protection, Palmer Community Hospital, Wear Street, Jarrow, NE32 3UX, Tel.: 0191 451 6055

Clinical Leads (NSF)
Dr J Gallagher, Clinical Lead, Sexual Health, Stanhope Parade Centre, Stanhope Parade, South Shields, NE33 4HX,
Dr F Al-Durrah, Clinical Lead, Cancer, Trust Headquarters, Ingham House,
Dr N Kelly, Clinical Lead, CHD,
Dr R McEwan, Clinical Lead, Children, Trust Headquarters, Ingham House,
Dr C Bradshaw, Clinical Lead, Diabetic Care, Marsden Road Health Centre, South Shields, NE34 6RE,
Dr L Holmes, Clinical Lead, Older People,

Community Nursing Services
Ms G Holdsworth, Primary Care Manager, Monkton Hall Hospital, Monkton Lane, Jarrow, Tyne& Wear, NE32 5NN, Tel.: 0191 451 6280
Ms M Jeffrey, Primary Care Manager, (Acting), Monkton Hall Hospital, Monkton Lane, Jarrow, Tyne& Wear, NE32 5NN, Tel.: 0191 451 6291
Mrs E Wharton, Primary Care Manager, Monkton Hall Hospital, Monkton Lane, Jarrow, Tyne& Wear, NE32 5NN, Tel.: 0191 451 6291

District Nursing
Boker Lane Health Centre, District Nurses, East Boldon, NE36 0RY, Tel.: 0191 554 3200
Evening/24 hr Service, Perth Green (Message Taking Facility), Tel.: 0191 423 4613
Hebburn Health Centre, District Nurses, Hebburn, NE31 2SP, Tel.: 0191 451 6200
Marsden Road Health Centre, District Nurses, South Shields, NE34 6RE, Tel.: 0191 4516560
Monkton Hospital, District Nurses, Jarrow, Tel.: 0191 451 6275
Stanhope Parade Health Centre, District Nurses, Gordon Street, South Shields, NE33 4GA, Tel.: 0191 451 6100
Tedco, District Nurses, Tedco Business Park, St Hilda's South Shields,
Westoe Road, District Nurses, South Shields, Tel.: 0191 451 6722

Family Planning Services
Dr J Gallagher, Stanhope Parade Health Centre, Tel.: 0191 451 6469

Health Visitors
Ms J Bennett, TB Control & Asylum Seekers, Health Visitor, Palmer Community Hospital, Wear Street, Jarrow, NE32 3UX, Tel.: 0191 451 6033

Boker Lane Health Centre, Health Visitors, East Boldon, NE36 0RY, Tel.: 0191 554 3200
Ms A Fearon, Children with Special Needs, Health Visitor, Palmer Community Hospital, Tel.: 0191 451 6056
Flagg Court Health Visitors, Glasgow Road, Jarrow, Tel.: 0191 451 6330
Hebburn Health Centre, Health Visitors, Hebburn, NE31 2SP, Tel.: 0191 451 6200
Hedworth Field Clinic, Health Visitors, Tel.: 0191 554 3282
Marsden Road Health Centre, Health Visitors, South Shields, NE34 6RE, Tel.: 0191 4516560
Stanhope Parade Health Centre, Health Visitors, Gordon Street, South Shields, NE33 4GA, Tel.: 0191 451 6100
Westoe Road, Health Visitors, South Shields, Tel.: 0191 451 6722

Liaison Services
Ms T Cox, Rapid Response Nurse, Perth Green House,
Ms S Harvey, Discharge Liaison Community Nurse, Perth Green House,
Ms M Samuels, Discharge Liaison Community Nurse, Perth Green House,
Ms N Sherrif, Rapid Response Nurse, Perth Green House,

Other Services
Ms S Clark, Nurse Assessor, Continuing Care, Hebburn Health Centre, Tel.: 0191 451 6231
Ms D Clayton, Continence Advisor, Monkton Hospital, Tel.: 0191 451 6305

Smoking Cessation
Ms M Williams, Advisor, Hebburn Hospital, Tel.: 0191 451 6605

Specialist Nursing Services
Mrs D Clayton, Continence, Stanhope Parade Health Centre, Tel.: 0191 451 6469
Specialist Nurses, Diabetic Care, Upper Parkdale, South Tyneside District Hospital, Tel.: 0191 454 8888
Community Nurses, Macmillan, St Claire's Hospice, Primrose Hill, Jarrow, Tel.: 0191 451 6389
Ms D Gibbons, Respiratory, South Tyneside District Hospital, Tel.: 0191 454 8888
Ms A Bell, Nurse, Stoma Care, South Tyneside District Hospital, Tel.: 0191 454 8888

The Homeless/Travellers & Asylum Seekers
Ms J Bennett, Asylum Seekers & TB Control, Health Visitor, Palmer Community Hospital, Wear Street, Jarrow, NE32 3UX, Tel.: 0191 451 6033

Sunderland Teaching Primary Care Trust

Trust Headquarters
Durham Road
SUNDERLAND
Tyne & Wear
SR3 4AF
Tel.: 0191 565 6256

Admin & Senior Management
Ms J Akehurst, Assistant Director of Nursing, Unit 30a Business & Innovation Centre, Sunderland Enterprise Park, Wearfield, Sunderland, SR5 2TA, Tel.: 0191 516 6300
Mrs B Atkinson, Director of Nursing & Community Nursing Services, Unit 30a Business & Innovation Centre, Sunderland Enterprise Park, Wearfield, Sunderland, SR5 2TA, Tel.: 0191 516 6300

Child Health Records
Ms J Old, Manager, Pallion Health Centre, Hylton Road, Sunderland, SR4 7XF, Tel.: 0191 565 6256 ext 45427

Child Protection/Safeguarding Children
Ms M Craig, City Hospitals Sunderland/Sunderland TPCT, Designated Nurse,
Ms J Fletcher, Specialist Nurse, Looked After Children, Sunderland Teaching PCT, Childrens Centre, Durham Road, Sunderland,

North East Strategic Health Authority

Clinical Leads (NSF)
Dr J Hollis, Clinical Lead, Cancer,
Dr P Wortley, Clinical Lead, CHD,
Dr I Gilmour, Clinical Lead, Children,
Dr L Glass, Clinical Lead, Older People,

Community Nursing Services
Ms B Atkinson, Director of Nursing & Community Nursing Services, Unit 30a Business & Innovation Centre, Sunderland Enterprise Park, Wearfield, Sunderland, SR5 2TA, Tel.: 0191 516 6300

District Nursing
Ms L Holmes, Manager, Galleries Health Centre, The Galleries, Washington, Sunderland, NE38 7NQ, Tel.: 0191 417 4929
Ms J Murray, Manager, Unit 30a, Business & Innovation Centre, Sunderland Enterprise Park, Wearfield, Sunderland, Tel.: 0191 516 6300
Ms J Old, Manager, Pallion Health Centre, Hylton Road, Sunderland, SR4 7XF, Tel.: 0191 565 6256 ext 45427

Health Visitors
Ms M Lax, Specialist, Health Visitor, Hendon Health Centre, Hendon, Sunderland,

Liaison Services
Ms C Chapman, Liaison Service Officer & Patient Advice, Tel.: 0191 565 6256 ext 45298
Ms R Green, Community Liaison Officer, Drug Action Team, Based at Ryhope, Tel.: 0191 569 9517 ext 43171
Ms G White, Liaison Service Officer & Patient Advice, Tel.: 0191 565 6256 ext 45212

Other Services
Ms D Spraggon, Manager, Answers Health Information Shop, Tel.: 0191 510 3133
Ms M Taylor, Drug Action Team Co-ordinator, Based at Ryhope, Tel.: 0191 569 9517 ext 43172

Specialist Nursing Services
Ms C Elliott, Bangladeshi, Specialist Nurse,
Ms A Humphries, Specialist Nurse,
Nurse Practioners, Sunderland Teaching PCT, Durham Road, Sunderland, Tel.: 0191 5656256
Ms C Donkin, Nurse Specialist, CHD, Sunderland TPCT, North Office, 30A Hylton Riverside Park, Sunderland, Tel.: 0191 516 6300
Ms P Sinclair, Nurse Specialist, CHD, Sunderland TPCT, North Office, 30A Hylton Riverside Park, Sunderland, Tel.: 0191 516 6300
Ms J Dryden, Nurse Specialist, Continence, Pallion Health Centre, Hylton Road, Sunderland, SR4 7XF, Tel.: 0191 5656256 ext 49148
Ms K Walton, Nurse Specialist, Continence, Pallion Health Centre, Hylton Road, Sunderland, SR4 7XF, Tel.: 0191 5656256 ext 49148
Ms M Kennedy, Lead Community Nurse, Dermatology, Tel.: 0191 516 6300
Ms J Jackson, Nurse Specialist, Diabetic Care, Pallion Health Centre, Hylton Road, Sunderland, SR4 7XF, Tel.: 0191 5656256 ext 45488
Ms J Oliver, Nurse Specialist, Heart Failure, Pallion Health Centre, Hylton Road, Sunderland, SR4 7XF, Tel.: 0191 5656256 ext 45490
Ms J Newby, Overnight Nurse (Community), Palliative Care, Tel.: 0191 565 6256
Ms G Nicholson, Hospital & Community, Nurse Specialist, Palliative Care, Tel.: 0191 565 6256 ext 48304
Nurses/Specialist Nurses, Palliative Care, St Benedicts Hospice, Newcastle Road, Monkwearmouth, Sunderland,
Ms L Richardson, Overnight Nurse (Community), Palliative Care, Tel.: 0191 565 6256 ext 48301
Ms S Thompson, Overnight Nurse (Community), Palliative Care, Tel.: 0191 565 6256 ext 48301
Ms S Ansah, Nurse Practitioner, Public Health, Sunderland Teaching PCT, Durham Road, Sunderland, Tel.: 0191 5656256
Ms H Downes, Nurse, Respiratory, Pallion Health Centre, Hylton Road, Sunderland, SR4 7XF, Tel.: 0191 5656256 ext 45433
Ms S Haggerty, Nurse Specialist, Respiratory, Pallion Health Centre, Hylton Road, Sunderland, SR4 7XF, Tel.: 0191 5656256 ext 45433

Tees & North East Yorkshire NHS Trust
Trust Headquarters, Flatts Lane Centre
Flatts Lane
NORMANBY
Middlesbrough
TS6 0SZ
Tel.: 01642 288288

Child Health Records
Child Health Records, West Lane Hospital, Acklam Road, Middlesbrough, TS5 4EE, Tel.: 01642 813144

Child Protection/Safeguarding Children
Mrs P Smith, Child Protection, West Lane Hospital, Tel.: 01642 824939
Mrs M Walker, Child Protection, West Lane Hospital, Tel.: 01642 824925

Learning Disabilities
Mr I Aisbitt, Service Manager, 5 Bankfields Court, Normanby, Middlesbrough, TS6 0NP, Tel.: 01642 283700
Ms J Auton, Adult Team - Hartlepool, Senior Nurse, Hart Lodge, Jones Road, Hartlepool, TS24 9BD, Tel.: 01429 285022
Mr M Bass, Head of Service - Hartlepool, Hart Lodge, Jones Road, Hartlepool, TS24 9BD, Tel.: 01429 285022
Ms J Brewis, Senior Nurse - Children, 163 Durham Road, Stockton-on-Tees, TS19 0EA, Tel.: 01642 415107
Mrs T Davison, General Manager, Stockton Integrated Services, 163 Durham Road, Stockton-on-Tees, TS19 0EA, Tel.: 01642 391411
Mr C Graham, Head of Care Management, 163 Durham Road, Stockton-on-Tees, TS19 0EA, Tel.: 01642 391412
Ms J Hall, Senior Nurse, Hart Lodge, Jones Road, Hartlepool, TS24 9BD, Tel.: 01429 285022
Mr P Newton, Director, Flatts Lane Centre, Flatts Lane, Normanby, TS6 0SZ, Tel.: 01642 283447
Mr D Williams, Head of Resources, 163 Durham Road, Stockton on Tees, TS19 0EA, Tel.: 01642 391412

North West Strategic Health Authority

with major towns and Primary Care Trust boundaries
Pop: 6,827,170

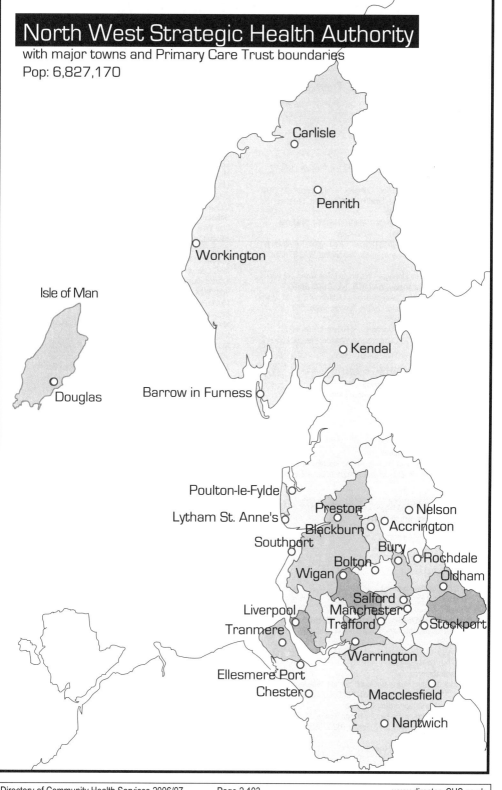

Carlisle

Penrith

Workington

Isle of Man

Kendal

Douglas

Barrow in Furness

Poulton-le-Fylde

Lytham St. Anne's

Preston

Nelson

Blackburn

Accrington

Southport

Bury

Rochdale

Bolton

Wigan

Oldham

Salford

Liverpool

Manchester

Tranmere

Trafford

Stockport

Warrington

Ellesmere Port

Chester

Macclesfield

Nantwich

North West Strategic Health Authority

North West Strategic Health Authority

5 Borough Partnership NHS Trust
Trust Headquarters, Hollins Park
Hollins Lane, Winwick
WARRINGTON
WA2 8WA
Tel.: 01925 664001

Learning Disabilities
Mr I Arthur, Director, 23 Cumber Lane, Whiston, Prescot, L35 2YZ, Tel.: 0151 426 5885
Mrs L Austin, Generic, Transition, Complex Need Services, Co-ordinator, 196A Newton Road, Lowton, Nr Warrington, Cheshire, WA3 2AQ, Tel.: 01942 513885
Ms R Chapman, General Manager, Whelley Hospital, Bradshaw Street, Wigan, WN1 3XD, Tel.: 01942 244000
Mrs K Green, Assistant Borough Director - Warrington, Fairhaven & The Alders, 12 Birch Avenue, Winwick, Warrington, WA2 9TN, Tel.: 01925 575904
Mrs C Lynch, Assistant Manager - Warrington, The Alders, 12 Birch Avenue, Winwick, Warrington, WA2 9TN, Tel.: 01925 575904
Mrs S McComb, Adult & Children's Teams- Additional Support, Co-ordinator, 196A Newton Road, Lowton, Nr Warrington, Cheshire, WA3 2AQ, Tel.: 01942 513885
Mr K McWha, Acting Nurse Manager - St Helens & Knowsley Borough, Willis House, 23 Cumber Lane, Whiston, Prescot, L35 2YZ, Tel.: 0151 426 5885

Aintree Hospital NHS Trust
Trust Headquarters, Aintree House
University Hospital Aintree, Longmoor Lane
LIVERPOOL
L9 7AL
Tel.: 0151 525 5980
Fax.: 0151 525 6086

Admin & Senior Management
Ms S Ferguson, Director of Nursing, Aintree Hospital NHS Trust, Aintree House, Univ Hospital Aintree, Longmoor Lane, Liverpool, L9 7AL,

Ashton, Leigh & Wigan Primary Care Trust
Trust Headquarters, Bryan House
61 Standishgate
WIGAN
Lancs
WN1 1AH
Tel.: 01942 772711

Admin & Senior Management
Mr P Rowe, Chief Executive,
Child Health
Ms P Fairhurst, Child Health, Senior Nurse, Child Health Directorate, Royal Albert Edward Infirmary, Wigan Lane, Wigan, WN1 2NN, Tel.: 01942 822031
Ms M Worsley, Child Epilepsy, Paediatric OPD, Royal Albert Edward Infirmary, Tel.: 01942 244000
Child Health Records
Mrs P Richards, Child Health Computer Section, Whelley Hospital, Bradshaw Street, Whelley, Wigan, WN1 3XD, Tel.: 01942 822689
Child Protection/Safeguarding Children
Ms P Lord, Child Protection, Hindley Health Centre, 17 Liverpool Road, Hindley, Wigan, WN2 3HQ, Tel.: 01942 775589
Clinical Leads (NSF)
Ms J Atherton, Clinical Lead, Cancer,

Community Nursing Services
Mrs L Batteson, Clinical Development Service Manager, Beech Hill Clinic, Beech Hall Street, Wigan, WN6 7HX, Tel.: 01942 775358
Mr B Gillespie, Operations Manager, Ashton Clinic, Queens Road, Ashton in Makerfield, Wigan, WN4 8LB, Tel.: 01942 775307
Ms A Plested, GM PC Directorate, Whelley Hospital, Bradshaw Street, Whelley, Wigan, WN1 3XD, Tel.: 01942 822653
Health Visitors
Ms P Dent, Asthma, Health Visitor, Beech Hill Clinic, Tel.: 01942 775372
Ms J Eaton, Asthma, Health Visitor, College Street Health Centre, Leigh, WN7 2RF, Tel.: 01942 775470
Liaison Services
Mrs J Elsey, Midwife, Tel.: 01695 632855
Liaison Health Visitors, Tel.: 01942 822007
Liaison Sisters - Leigh, Tel.: 01942 670222
Liaison Sisters - Wigan, Tel.: 01942 822007
School Nursing
Mr J Ward, General Manager, School Health/Nursing Service, Child Health Directorate, Billinge Hospital, Upholland Road, Billinge, Wigan, WN5 7ET, Tel.: 01695 646254
Specialist Nursing Services
Mr C Campbell, Aspull Clinic, Tel.: 01942 831169
Communicable Diseases, Pemberton Clinic, Sherwood Drive, Wigan, WN5 9QX, Tel.: 01942 214260
Mrs M Bunting, Counsellor, Breast Care, Royal Albert Edward Infirmary, Tel.: 01942 244000
Ms R Moran, Continence, Standish Clinic, High Street, Standish, Wigan, WN6 8EW, Tel.: 01257 501340
Ms P Phair, Diabetic Care, Diabetes Centre, Royal Albert Edward Infirmary, Tel.: 01942 822188
Ms L Barkuss Jones, Infection Control, Royal Albert Edward Infirmary, Tel.: 01942 822035
Ms S Harrison, Macmillan, Royal Albert Edward Infirmary, Tel.: 01942 822009
Ms J Irvine, Macmillan, Leigh Infirmary, The Avenue, Leigh, WN7 1HS, Tel.: 01942 264369
Ms L McLaughlen, Respiratory, College Street Health Centre, Leigh, WN7 2RF, Tel.: 01942 775469
Ms Y Chantler, Stoma Care, - Colorectal, Cancer Care Unit, Royal Albert Edward Infirmary, Tel.: 01942 822034

Bebington & West Wirral Primary Care Trust
Trust Headquarters, 3 Port Causeway
Bromborough
WIRRAL
CH62 4NH
Tel.: 0151 645 5300

Admin & Senior Management
Ms A Cooke, Chief Executive,
Child Protection/Safeguarding Children
Ms J Pinnington, Child Protection, Vulnerable Adults, Child Development Centre, Clatterbridge Hospital, Clatterbridge Road, Bebington, CH63 4JY, Tel.: 0151 334 4000
Ms H Stuart, Child Protection, Vulnerable Adults, Child Development Centre, Clatterbridge Hospital, Clatterbridge Road, Bebington, CH63 4JY, Tel.: 0151 334 4000
Clinical Leads (NSF)
Dr J O'Connor, Clinical Lead, Cancer,
Dr D Jones, Clinical Lead, CHD,
Dr F Sayle, Clinical Lead, Diabetic Care,
District Nursing
Ms S Christie, Operational Nurse Manager, CN Office, Oxton Clinic, 40 Balls Road, Prenton, CH43 5RE, Tel.: 0151 652 7388
Ms P Williams, Senior Nurse Continuing Care, CN Office, Oxton Clinic, 40 Balls Road, Prenton, CH43 5RE, Tel.: 0151 652 7388

North West Strategic Health Authority

Birkenhead & Wallasey Primary Care Trust
Trust Headquarters, Admin Block
St Catherine's Hospital, Church Road
BIRKENHEAD
Wirral
CH42 0LQ
Tel.: 0151 651 0011

Admin & Senior Management
Ms K Doran, Chief Executive,

Child Health
Ms C Kalayi, Assistant Directorate Manager, Tel.: 0151 482 7866
Ms P Neilson, Facilitator, Tel.: 0151 334 4000 ext 5234
Ms P Riding, Manager, Children's Services, Tel.: 0151 482 7868
Wirral Services for Child Health, Tel.: 0151 334 4000

Child Health Records
Child Health Computer Section, Clatterbridge Hospital, Clatterbridge Road, Bebington, Wirral, CH63 4JY,

Child Protection/Safeguarding Children
Ms B Chapman, Looked After Children Nurse, Social Services, Conway Building, Conway Street, Birkenhead, CH41 6LA, Tel.: 0151 666 4642
Ms J Pinnington, Strategic Development Lead for Training, Child Development Centre, Clatterbridge Hospital, Tel.: 0151 334 4000 ext 5247
Ms A Powell, Looked After Children Nurse, Social Services, Conway Building, Conway Street, Birkenhead, CH41 6LA, Tel.: 0151 666 4642
Mr M Hackett, Named Nurse, Child Protection, Oxton Clinic, 40 Balls Road, Oxton, Prenton, CH43 5RE, Tel.: 0151 652 7388
Ms H Heeley, Named Nurse, Child Protection, Oxton Clinic, 40 Balls Road, Oxton, Prenton, CH43 5RE, Tel.: 0151 652 7388
Mrs M Lesage, Named Nurse, Child Protection, Oxton Clinic, 40 Balls Road, Oxton, Prenton, CH43 5RE, Tel.: 0151 652 7388
Ms H Stuart, Designated Nurse, Child Protection, Child Development Centre, Clatterbridge Hospital, Tel.: 0151 334 4000 ext 5246

Clinical Leads (NSF)
Ms C Maddaford, Clinical Lead, Children & Care of Older People, St Catherine's Hospital, Church Road, Birkenhead, Wirral, CH42 0LQ, Tel.: 0151 651 0011
Dr A Mantgani, Clinical Lead, CHD & Diabetes, St Catherine's Hospital, Church Road, Birkenhead, Wirral, CH42 0LQ, Tel.: 0151 651 0011
Dr M Freeman, Clinical Lead, Cancer, Victoria Park Medical Centre, Bedford Avenue, Rock Ferry, CH42 4QJ, Tel.: 0151 645 8384

Community Matrons
Ms F Johnston, c/o Oxton Clinic, 40 Balls Road, Oxton, Wirral, CH43 5RE,
Mr N Powell, c/o Oxton Clinic, 40 Balls Road, Oxton, Wirral, CH43 5RE,
Ms M Pugh, c/o Oxton Clinic, 40 Balls Road, Oxton, Wirral, CH43 5RE,

Community Nursing Services
Mr A Cooper, Assistant Community Nurse Manager (Birkenhead), Tel.: 0151 651 3917
Ms S Fairclough, Community Nurse Manager (Wallasey), Oxton Clinic, 40 Balls Road, Oxton, Prenton, CH43 5RE, Tel.: 0151 652 7388
Ms V Harrison, Assistant Community Nurse Manager (Wallasey), Oxton Clinic, 40 Balls Road, Oxton, Prenton, CH43 5RE, Tel.: 0151 652 7388
Ms S Hillhouse, Deputy Director of Nursing & Quality, Oxton Clinic, St Catherine's Hospital, Church Road, Birkenhead, CH42 0LQ, Tel.: 0151 651 3968
Ms A McGlory, Professional Development & Improvement Specialist Nurse, Oxton Clinic, 40 Balls Road, Oxton, Prenton, CH43 5RE, Tel.: 0151 652 7388
Out of Hours District Nursing, Tel.: 0151 678 8496
Ms S Quinn, Community Nurse Manager (Birkenhead), Oxton Clinic, 40 Balls Road, Oxton, Prenton, CH43 5RE, Tel.: 0151 652 7388

Family Planning Services
Well Women Centre, 1st Floor, Devonshire Centre, St Catherine's Hospital, Church Road, Birkenhead, Wirral, CH42 0LQ, Tel.: 0151 604 7290

Health Visitors
Ms M O'Neill, Professional Development Nurse (Health Visiting), Tel.: 0151 651 0011 ext 260

Liaison Services
Ms J Cleary, Community/Hospital Paediatric Liaison/Continence, Health Visitor, Arrowe Park Hospital, Upton, Wirral, CH49 5PE, Tel.: 0151 678 5111 ext 2098
Mr M Grindley, Community/Hospital Liaison, District Nurse, Arrowe Park Hospital, Upton, Wirral, CH49 5PE, Tel.: 0151 678 5111 ext 2789
Ms J Hampton, Community/Hospital Liaison, District Nurse, Clatterbridge Hospital, Clatterbridge Road, Bebington, Wirral, CH63 4JY, Tel.: 0151 334 4000 ext 4331
Ms D McCormick, Community/Hospital Liaison, District Nurse, Clatterbridge Hospital, Clatterbridge Road, Bebington, Wirral, CH63 4JY, Tel.: 0151 334 4000

Other Services
Mr P Edwards, Community Services Business Manager, Admin Block, St Catherine's Hospital, Church Road, Birkenhead, Wirral, CH42 0LQ, Tel.: 0151 651 3897

Pharmacy
Mrs J Simms, Associate Director of Medicines Management, Admin Block, St Catherine's Hospital, Church Road, Birkenhead, Wirral, CH42 0LQ, Tel.: 0151 651 0011 ext 402

School Nursing
Wirral School Nursing Service, Tel.: 0151 334 4000

Smoking Cessation
Mrs C Corvers, Manager of Health Improvement Services (inc Smoking Cessation), 49 Hamilton Square, Birkenhead, CH41 5AR, Tel.: 0151 647 0211

Specialist Nursing Services
Ms J Evans, Services Manager, Continence, 3 Port Causeway, Bromborough, Wirral, CH62 4TG, Tel.: 0151 643 5434
Ms F Sayle, Nurse Specialist (Birkenhead), Diabetes, Preston Clinic, Prenton Village Road, Birkenhead, CH43 0TF, Tel.: 0151 608 4808
Ms A Murphy, Infection Control, 3 Port Causeway, Bromborough, Wirral, CH62 4TG, Tel.: 0151 643 5401
Ms C Bordley, Nurse, Macmillan, Eastham Clinic, Eastham Rake, Eastham, CH62 9AN, Tel.: 0151 328 0481
Ms S Croft, Nurse, Macmillan, Eastham Clinic, Eastham Rake, Eastham, CH62 9AN, Tel.: 0151 328 0481
Mr S Parry, Nurse, Macmillan, Eastham Clinic, Eastham Rake, Eastham, CH62 9AN, Tel.: 0151 328 0481
Ms A Williams, Nurse, Macmillan, Eastham Clinic, Eastham Rake, Eastham, CH62 9AN, Tel.: 0151 328 0481
Ms S Wong, Nurse, Macmillan, Eastham Clinic, Eastham Rake, Eastham, CH62 9AN, Tel.: 0151 328 0481
Ms N Browning, Nurse Practitioner, Older People, Parkfield Medical Centre, Sefton Road, New Ferry, CH62 5HS, Tel.: 0151 643 8188
Ms D Byrne, Nurse Practitioner, Older People, Field Road Health Centre, Field Road, New Brighton, CH45 5JP, Tel.: 0151 691 2181
Ms E Ennis, Nurse Practitioner, Older People, Parkfield Medical Centre, Sefton Road, New Ferry, CH62 5HS, Tel.: 0151 643 8188
Ms A Huggins, Nurse Practitioner, Older People, Parkfield Medical Centre, Sefton Road, New Ferry, CH62 5HS, Tel.: 0151 643 8188
Ms M Hughes, Nurse Specialist, Tissue Viability, 3 Port Causeway, Bromborough, Wirral, CH62 4TG, Tel.: 0151 643 5324
Mr I Mansell, Nurse Specialist, Tissue Viability, 3 Port Causeway, Bromborough, Wirral, CH62 4TG, Tel.: 0151 643 5323

North West Strategic Health Authority

Walk In Centres
NHS Walk-In Centre, Arrowe Park Hospital Site, Arrowe Park Road, Upton, Wirral, CH49 5PE, Tel.: 0151 488 3706
NHS Walk-In Centre, Victoria Central Hospital, Mill Lane, Wallasey, wirral, CH44 5UF, Tel.: 0151 604 7296

Blackburn and Darwen Primary Care Trust

Trust Headquarters, Guide Business Centre
School Lane
BLACKBURN
Lancashire
BB1 2QH
Tel.: 01254 267000

Admin & Senior Management
Mrs C Rae, Director of Primary Care, Guide Business Centre, School Lane, Guide, Tel.: 01254 267000
Ms J Thomas, Deputy Director of Primary Care, Guide Business Centre, School Lane, Guide,
Child Health Records
Mr C Pegler, Cobham House, Haslingden Road, Blackburn, Lancashire, BB1 2EE,
Child Protection/Safeguarding Children
Ms D Victoratos, Designated & Named Nurse, Child Protection, Larkhill Health Centre, Mount Pleasant, Blackburn, Lancashire, Tel.: 01254 263611
Clinical Leads (NSF)
Dr H Leydon, Clinical Lead, Cancer, Montague Health Centre, Oakenhurst Road, Blackburn, BB2 1PP, Tel.: 01254 263631
Dr M Dervan, Clinical Lead, Diabetic Care,
Dr I Timson, Clinical Lead, Older People,
Community Nursing Services
Ms A Barnish, Darwen - Strategic Manager, Darwen Health Centre, James Street West, Darwen, BB3 1PY,
Mrs K Jackson, North - Service Development Manager, Larkhill Health Centre, Mount Pleasant, Blackburn, Lancashire, BB1 5BJ, Tel.: 01254 263611
Ms A Rutter, East - Strategic Manager, Larkhill Health Centre, Mount Pleasant, Blackburn, Lancashire, Tel.: 01254 263611
Family Planning Services
Ms S Cullen, Larkhill Health Centre, Mount Pleasant, Blackburn, Lancashire, Tel.: 01254 263611
Health Visitors
Ms C Gorman, Service Development Manager, Darwen Health Centre, James Street West, Darwen, BB3 1PY,
Pharmacy
Ms S Reddy, Pharmaceutical Advisor, Guide Business Centre, School Lane, Guide, Tel.: 01254 267000
School Nursing
Ms A Atkin, Service Development Manager, Larkhill Health Centre, Mount Pleasant, Blackburn, BB1 5BJ, Tel.: 01254 263631
Specialist Nursing Services
Mrs J McHugh, Lead Nurse, Free Nursing Care, Livesey Clinic, Cherry Tree Lane, Blackburn, BB2 5NX,
Ms K Roberts, Nurse, Infection Control, Livesey Clinic, Cherry Tree Lane, Blackburn, BB2 5NX, Tel.: 01254 263611
The Homeless/Travellers & Asylum Seekers
Ms L Watson, Asylum Seekers Health Worker, Larkhill Health Centre, Mount Pleasant, Blackburn, Lancashire, Tel.: 01254 263611

Blackpool Primary Care Trust

Trust Headquarters, Blackpool Stadium
Seasiders Way
BLACKPOOL, F41 6JX
Tel.: 01253 651200

Admin & Senior Management
Ms W Swift, Chief Executive, Blackpool Stadium, Seasider's Way, Blackpool, F41 6JX, Tel.: 01253 651201

Child Health Records
Information Manager, Child Health Dept, Wesham Park Hospital, Tel.: 01253 306388
Child Protection/Safeguarding Children
Dr C Turner, Blackpool Stadium, Seasider's Way, Blackpool, F41 6JX, Tel.: 01253 651262
Community Nursing Services
Mrs E O'Neill, Director of Clinical Services & Standards, Blackpool Stadium, Seasider's Way, Blackpool, F41 6JX, Tel.: 01253 651261
District Nursing
Emergencies BVH Switchboard, Tel.: 01253 300000
Mrs B Hargreaves, Head of Nursing, Blackpool Stadium, Seasider's Way, Blackpool, F41 6JX, Tel.: 01253 651686
Night Nursing Service, Fax 01253 396431, Tel.: 01253 398160
Rapid Response Bleep, Tel.: 07693 253646
Rapid Response Mobile, Tel.: 07710 645985
Temporary Residents, Tel.: 01253 651685
Twilight Ansaphone, Fax 01253 396431, Tel.: 01253 398160
Family Planning Services
Ms G Hunt, Head of Sexual Health Services, Community Nursing Team, 18a Queen Street, Blackpool, FY1 1PD, Tel.: 01253 651927
Health Visitors
Emergencies BVH Switchboard, Tel.: 01253 300000
Ms B Etheridge, Paediatric Health Visitor Liaison, Victoria Hospital, Blackpool, Tel.: 01253 306680
Mrs B Hargreaves, Head of Nursing, Blackpool Stadium, Seasider's Way, Blackpool, F41 6JX, Tel.: 01253 651686
Night Nursing Service, Fax 01253 396431, Tel.: 01253 398160
Rapid Response Bleep, Tel.: 07693 253646
Rapid Response Mobile, Tel.: 07710 645985
Temporary Residents, Tel.: 01253 651685
Twilight Ansaphone, Fax 01253 396431, Tel.: 01253 398160
HIV/AIDS
Ms S Potts, Clinical Nurse Lead, Tel.: 01253 306559
Specialist Nursing Services
Home Care Advisory Team, c/o Trinity Hospice, Low Moor Road, Bispham, Blackpool, Tel.: 01253 358881
Mr F Booth, Continence, Windmill Mews, Blackpool, Tel.: 01253 655282
Nurse, Macmillan, Tel.: 01253 303670
Ms G Broadbent, Nurse, Tissue Viability, Victoria Hospital, Blackpool, Tel.: 01253 300000
The Homeless/Travellers & Asylum Seekers
Ms P Greenhill, Health Visitor, Health Team for the Homeless, Social Services Area Office, South King Street, Blackpool, FY1 4TR, Tel.: 01253 476805/6/7
Ms A Redican, Health Visitor, Health Teamfor the Homeless, Social Services Area Office, South King Street, Blackpool, FY1 4TR, Tel.: 01253 476805/6/7

Blackpool, Fylde and Wyre Hospitals NHS Trust

Whinney Heys Road
BLACKPOOL
Lancashire, FY3 8NR
Tel.: 01253 300000
Fax.: 01253 306873

Acute Specialist Nursing Services
Ms K Baird, Homeward, Nurse Practitioner, Victoria Hospital, Blackpool, Tel.: ext 5600 or bleep 859
Ms K Clowes, Medical, Victoria Hospital, Blackpool, Tel.: ext 6809
Ms L Morrison, SCBU, Clinical Nurse Specialist, Victoria Hospital, Blackpool, Tel.: ext 3636
Ms L Smith, Thrombolysis Service, Lead Nurse, Victoria Hospital, Blackpool, Tel.: bleep 832
Ms M Ageli, Practice Development, Nurse Ward 4, A&E, - Orthopaedic, Victoria Hospital, Blackpool, Tel.: ext 6133

Ms H Clarke, Nurse Practitioner, A&E, Victoria Hospital, Blackpool, Tel.: ext 3513

Ms E Larraine Patterson, Paediatric, Specialist Nurse, A&E, Victoria Hospital, Blackpool, Tel.: ext 6731

Ms J Lemon, Nurse Practitioner, A&E, Victoria Hospital, Blackpool, Tel.: ext 3513

Ms T Moreland, Nurse Practitioner, A&E, Victoria Hospital, Blackpool, Tel.: ext 3513

Ms S Riley, Practice Development, Ward 4, Nurse, A&E, - Orthopaedic, Victoria Hospital, Blackpool, Tel.: ext 3513

Ms L Robinson, Nurse Practitioner, A&E, Victoria Hospital, Blackpool, Tel.: ext 3513

Ms F Duncan, Anaesth/Theatres, Acute Pain, Victoria Hospital, Blackpool, Tel.: ext 4568 or bleep 434

Ms J Marshall, Anaesth/Theatres, Acute Pain, Victoria Hospital, Blackpool, Tel.: bleep 495

Ms P Vernon, Anaesth/Theatres, Acute Pain, Victoria Hospital, Blackpool, Tel.: bleep 403

Ms L Bracegirdle, Specialist Nurse, Breast Care, Victoria Hospital, Blackpool, Tel.: ext 4183 or bleep 431

Ms S Guilfoyle, Specialist Nurse, Breast Care, Victoria Hospital, Blackpool, Tel.: ext 6882 or bleep 135

Ms D Tysver-Robinson, Specialist Nurse, Breast Care, Victoria Hospital, Blackpool, Tel.: ext 3493 or bleep 533

Ms C Turner, Lead Nurse, Cancer, Victoria Hospital, Blackpool, Tel.: ext 7004 or bleep 327

Ms J Crook, Lead Nurse, Cardiac Rehabilitation, Victoria Hospital, Blackpool, Tel.: ext 6813 or bleep 142

Mr B Mcalee, Cardiothoracic, Victoria Hospital, Blackpool, Tel.: ext 5607

Ms H Lambert, Anaesth/Theatres, Chronic Pain, Victoria Hospital, Blackpool, Tel.: ext 3599

Ms D Proctor, Specialist Nurse, Colorectal, Victoria Hospital, Blackpool, Tel.: ext 3694 or bleep 804

Ms J Sheridan, Specialist Nurse, Colorectal, Victoria Hospital, Blackpool, Tel.: ext 6620 or bleep 069

Ms G Towers, Specialist Nurse, Colorectal, Victoria Hospital, Blackpool, Tel.: ext 4725 or bleep 069

Ms A Grasby, Nurse Practitioner, Dermatology, Victoria Hospital, Blackpool, Tel.: ext 6527

Ms J Bellis, Nurse Specialist, Diabetic Care, Victoria Hospital, Blackpool, Tel.: ext 3486

Ms A Carruthers, Nurse Specialist, Diabetic Care, Victoria Hospital, Blackpool, Tel.: ext 3486 or bleep 375

Ms E Duffield, Nurse Specialist, Diabetic Care, Victoria Hospital, Blackpool, Tel.: ext 3486 or bleep 065

Ms C Gornall, Nurse Specialist, Diabetic Care, Victoria Hospital, Blackpool, Tel.: ext 3486

Ms N Grundy, Nurse Specialist, Diabetic Care, Victoria Hospital, Blackpool, Tel.: ext 3486 or bleep 396

Ms L Gunniss, Nurse Practitioner, DVT, Victoria Hospital, Blackpool, Tel.: ext 5595 or bleep 287

Ms E Cawley, Nurse Practitioner, General Surgery, Victoria Hospital, Blackpool, Tel.: ext 2223 or bleep 894

Ms K Haigh, Nurse Practitioner, General Surgery, Victoria Hospital, Blackpool, Tel.: ext 2225 or bleep 454

Ms J Robinson, Nurse Practitioner, General Surgery, Victoria Hospital, Blackpool, Tel.: ext 2221 or bleep 810

Ms L Cole, Nurse Specialist, Gynaecology, - Oncology, Victoria Hospital, Blackpool, Tel.: ext 4736 or bleep 844

Ms D Inott, Nurse Practitioner, Gynaecology, Victoria Hospital, Blackpool, Tel.: ext 5517 or bleep 125

Ms S Morcos, Nurse Practitioner, Gynaecology, Victoria Hospital, Blackpool, Tel.: ext 5517 or bleep 067

Ms J Lickiss, Infection Control, Victoria Hospital, Blackpool, Tel.: ext 2120

Ms K Roberts, Infection Control, Victoria Hospital, Blackpool, Tel.: ext 2120

Ms D Denby, Nurse Specialist, Lung Cancer, Victoria Hospital, Blackpool, Tel.: ext 5578

Ms S Dickinson, Nurse Endoscopist, Medicine, Victoria Hospital, Blackpool, Tel.: ext 3708 or 3709

Ms R Bracewell, Medical/Cancer Research Network, Oncology, Victoria Hospital, Blackpool, Tel.: ext 5649

Mr M Coxhead, Co-ordinator, Orthopaedics, - Trauma, Victoria Hospital, Blackpool, Tel.: ext 2048 or bleep 599

Ms F Goodall, Acting Homeward, Nurse Practitioner, Orthopaedics, Victoria Hospital, Blackpool, Tel.: ext 5600 or bleep 848

Ms L Thompson, Nurse Practitioner, Orthopaedics, Victoria Hospital, Blackpool, Tel.: ext 7027 or bleep 583

Ms H Veevers, Nurse Specialist, Osteoporosis, Victoria Hospital, Blackpool, Tel.: ext 6102

Ms M Boland, Bereavement Councillor, Paediatrics, Victoria Hospital, Blackpool, Tel.: ext 6713

Ms H Moran, Palliative Care, Victoria Hospital, Blackpool, Tel.: bleep 778

Ms S Eccles, Pathology, Victoria Hospital, Blackpool, Tel.: ext 2120

Ms S Maudsley, Pathology, Victoria Hospital, Blackpool, Tel.: ext 2051

Mr S Croft, Nurse, Practice Development, Victoria Hospital, Blackpool, Tel.: ext 4433

Ms P Berry, Nurse Specialist, Respiratory, Victoria Hospital, Blackpool, Tel.: bleep 842

Ms G Ledger, Nurse Practitioner, Respiratory, Victoria Hospital, Blackpool, Tel.: ext 6973 or bleep 410

Ms J Meikle, Nurse, Respiratory, Victoria Hospital, Blackpool, Tel.: ext 3418/3419

Ms J Parkinson, Nurse Specialist, Respiratory, Victoria Hospital, Blackpool, Tel.: bleep 843

Ms M Chalk, Officer, Resuscitation Training, Victoria Hospital, Blackpool, Tel.: ext 6968

Ms G Noblett, Officer, Resuscitation Training, Victoria Hospital, Blackpool, Tel.: ext 6968

Ms J Booth, Nurse Practitioner, Rheumatology, Victoria Hospital, Blackpool, Tel.: ext 6109

Ms A Stewart, Nurse Specialist, Stroke Care, Victoria Hospital, Blackpool, Tel.: bleep 820

Mr S Colton, Surgical Services, Victoria Hospital, Blackpool, Tel.: ext 5603

Ms G Broadbent, Tissue Viability, Victoria Hospital, Blackpool, Tel.: ext 6712 or bleep 524

Ms L Jones, Tissue Viability, Victoria Hospital, Blackpool, Tel.: ext 6712 or bleep 347

Ms L Darling, Nurse Specialist, Upper GI, Victoria Hospital, Blackpool, Tel.: ext 5501 or bleep 809

Ms D Lonican, Nurse Practitioner, Urology, Victoria Hospital, Blackpool, Tel.: ext 6943 or bleep 455

Mr G Prunty, Nurse Practitioner, Urology, Victoria Hospital, Blackpool, Tel.: ext 6943 or bleep 565

Ms K Simm, Nurse Practitioner, Urology, Victoria Hospital, Blackpool, Tel.: ext 6943

Admin & Senior Management

Mrs M Sunderland, Director of Nursing & Quality, Trust HQ, Whinney Heys Road, Blackpool, Lancashire, FY3 8NR, Tel.: 01253 300000

Child Protection/Safeguarding Children

Ms T Few, Child Protection, Blackpool Victoria Hospital, Tel.: 01253 300000

Community Midwifery

Ms S Ashton, Midwifery Community Team (Blackpool), Victoria Hospital, Blackpool, Tel.: ext 6842

Ms P Canning, Midwifery Ante Natal Clinic, Victoria Hospital, Blackpool, Tel.: ext 3639 or bleep 093

Ms J Chapman, Midwifery Community Team (Green), Victoria Hospital, Blackpool, Tel.: 651545

Ms K Charles, Midwifery Community Team (White), Victoria Hospital, Blackpool, Tel.: 726844

North West Strategic Health Authority

Community Midwifery, Victoria Hospital, Blackpool, Tel.: 01253 303623

Ms J Grundy, Midwifery Community Team (Gold), Victoria Hospital, Blackpool, Tel.: 306068

Mrs R Hartley, Clinical Midwifery Leader for Community, Victoria Hospital, Blackpool, Tel.: 01253 305608

Mrs B Herring, Directorate Manager, Head of Midwifery, Women's Unit, Whinney Heys Road, Blackpool, FY3 8NR, Tel.: 01253 303623

Ms J Hibbert, Midwifery Ward C, Victoria Hospital, Blackpool, Tel.: ext 6833

Ms M Johnston, Midwifery Community Team (Blackpool), Victoria Hospital, Blackpool, Tel.: ext 6742

Ms M Murray, Midwifery & Gynae (Bereavement Support), Victoria Hospital, Blackpool, Tel.: 01253 300000 ext 6877

Ms J Scholes, Midwifery Community Team (Yellow), Victoria Hospital, Blackpool, Tel.: 821457

Ms E Shaw, Midwifery Community Team (Blackpool), Victoria Hospital, Blackpool, Tel.: ext 6842

Ms J Smith, Midwifery Ward D, Victoria Hospital, Blackpool, Tel.: ext 6822

Ms A Stephens, Midwifery Community Team (Silver), Victoria Hospital, Blackpool, Tel.: 01772 684000

Ms C Tiffin, Midwifery Community Team (Blackpool), Victoria Hospital, Blackpool, Tel.: ext 6842

Ms P Williams, Midwifery Delivery Suite, Victoria Hospital, Blackpool, Tel.: ext 3618

Ms M Murray, Bereavement Support Nurse Midwifery, Gynaecology, Victoria Hospital, Blackpool, Tel.: ext 6877 or bleep 483

Liaison Services

District Nurse Liaison, Blackpool Vistoria Hospital, Whinney Heys Road, Blackpool, FY3 8NR, Tel.: 01253 303612

Health Visitor Liaison, Womens Unit, Blackpool Vistoria Hospital, Whinney Heys Road, Blackpool, FY3 8NR, Tel.: 01253 306680

Bolton Hospitals NHS Trust

Trust Headquarters, Royal Bolton Hospital
Minerva Road, Farnworth
BOLTON
Lancashire, BL4 0JR
Tel.: 01204 390390

Admin & Senior Management
Mrs S Holland, Head of Nursing Service, Royal Bolton Hospital, Tel.: 01204 390725

Child Health
Children's Community Nursing Team, Childrens Outpatients, Royal Bolton Hospital, Bolton, BL4 0JR, Tel.: 01204 390667

Ms A Jones, Paediatric, Nurse, Asthma, Childrens Outpatients, Royal Bolton Hospital, Tel.: 01204 390667

Ms S Bennett, Paediatric, Nurse, Diabetic Care, Childrens Outpatients, Royal Bolton Hospital, Tel.: 01204 390667

Ms Y Brennand, Paediatric, Childrens Respiratory Nurse, Nurse, Respiratory, Childrens Outpatients, Royal Bolton Hospital, Tel.: 01204 390667

Community Midwifery
Beech Team (M5 Ward), Royal Bolton Hospital, Tel.: 01204 390558
Cedar Team (M4 Ward), Royal Bolton Hospital, Tel.: 01204 390631
Mrs G Naylor, Directorate Manager/Head of Midwifery & Nursing, Royal Bolton Hospital, Tel.: 01204 390757
Neonatal Unit, Royal Bolton Hospital, Tel.: 01204 390748
Oak Team (M2 Ward), Royal Bolton Hospital, Tel.: 01204 390612

Bolton Primary Care Trust

Trust Headquarters, St Peter's House
Silverwell Street
BOLTON, Greater Manchester
BL1 1PP
Tel.: 01204 377000

Admin & Senior Management
Ms H Clarke, Assistant Director of Nursing, Great Lever Health Centre, Rupert Street, Bolton, Tel.: 01204 907740

Ms M Cropper, Director of Service Provision, Great Lever Health Centre, Rupert Street, Bolton, Tel.: 01204 377040

Ms H Dobrowolska, Assistant Chief Executive, St Peter's House, Silverwell Street, Bolton, BL1 1PP,

Ms J Edwards, Assistant Director Adult Services, Great Lever Health Centre, Rupert Street, Bolton,

Mrs C Higgins, Assistant Director Older People's Services, Great Lever Health Centre, Rupert Street, Bolton,

Ms W Pickard, Deputy Director of Service Provision, St Peter's House, Silverwell Street, Bolton, BL1 1PP,

Ms K Rowlands, Assistant Director, Children's Services, Great Lever Health Centre, Rupert Street, Bolton,

Dr K Snee, Chief Executive, St Peter's House, Silverwell Street, Bolton, BL1 1PP,

Child Health Records
Ms J Flitcroft, General Administration, Acresfield House, 3rd Floor, Crompton Place, Exchange Street, Bolton, BL1 1RS, Tel.: 01204 377085

Child Protection/Safeguarding Children
Ms F Farnworth, Named Nurse, Child Protection, Avondale Health Centre, Avondale Street, Bolton, BL1 4JP, Tel.: 01204 846762

Ms P Jones, Designated Nurse, Child Protection, Avondale Health Centre, Avondale Street, Bolton, BL1 4JP, Tel.: 01204 492331 ext 238

Clinical Leads (NSF)
Mr T McKay, Programme Manager, Older People's NSF, St Peters House, Silverwell Street, Bolton, BL1 1PP,

Ms A Gillespie, Lead Nurse, Cancer, Blackrod Health Centre, Church Street, Blackrod, BL6 5EQ,

Ms L Burnett, Programme Manager, CHD, St Peters House, Silverwell Street, Bolton, BL1 1PP,

Ms L Burnett, Programme Manager, Diabetic Care, St Peters House, Silverwell Street, Bolton, BL1 1PP,

District Nursing
Ms J Rushton, Head of Clinical Services, Egerton/Dunscar Health Centre, Darwen Street, Bromley Cross, Bolton, BL7 9RG,

Equipment Loan Services
Ms A Smith, Integrated Community Equipment Stores Manager, Crescent House,

Family Planning Services
Ms R Hewart, Sexual Health, Specialist Nurse, Dept of Sexual Health, Royal Bolton Hospital, Minerva Road, Farnworth,

Ms J Young, Acting Sexual Health Services Manager, Lever Chambers Centre for Health, Ashburner Street, Bolton, Tel.: 01204 360000

Health Visitors
Ms N Holliday, Head of Clinical Services, Pikes Lane Centre, Deane Road, Bolton, BL3 5HP,

Learning Disabilities
Miss D A Royle, Joint Disability Team Manager, Falcon View, Cotton Street, Bolton, Tel.: 01204 337500

Liaison Services
Mr J Nuttall, Clerical Officer, Discharge Planning, Royal Bolton Hospital, Minerva Road, Farnworth, Bolton, BL4 0JR, Tel.: 01204 390355/390535

Ms S Nuttall, RNCC Lead Nurse, Great Lever Health Centre, Rupert Street, Bolton,

Other Services
Ms L Nutter, Intermediate Care Services Manager, c/o Darley Court, Shepherd Cross Street, Halliwell, BL1 3EJ, Tel.: 01204 337084

Pharmacy
Ms K Gibson, Clinical Effectiveness Pharmacist, St Peter's House, Silverwell Street, Bolton, BL1 1PP,

Mr A White, Clinical Effectiveness Pharmacist, St Peter's House, Silverwell Street, Bolton, BL1 1PP,

North West Strategic Health Authority

Smoking Cessation
Mr A Butterworth, Service Manager, Smoking Cessation, Great Lever Health Centre, Rupert Street, Bolton,
Specialist Nursing Services
Rapid Response Team, Darley Court, Shepherd Cross Street, Halliwell, BL1 3EJ, Tel.: 01204 337084
Ms O Cropley, Continence, Lever Chambers, Ashburner Street, Bolton, BL1 1SQ, Tel.: 01204 360029
Ms L German, Continence, Lever Chambers, Ashburner Street, Bolton, BL1 1SQ, Tel.: 01204 360029
Mrs G Griffiths, Continence, Lever Chambers, Ashburner Street, Bolton, BL1 1SQ, Tel.: 01204 360029
Ms J Herbert, Continence, Lever Chambers, Ashburner Street, Bolton, BL1 1SQ, Tel.: 01204 360029
Ms P Sumner, Continence, Lever Chambers, Ashburner Street, Bolton, BL1 1SQ, Tel.: 01204 360029
Ms V Burns, Nurse Specialist, Dermatology, Lever Chambers, Ashburner Street,
Ms J Pennington, Nurse Consultant, Diabetic Care, Diabetes Centre, Chorley Street, Bolton,
Ms A Lloyd, Nurse Consultant, Elderly Care, Minerva Day Unit, Royal Bolton Hospital, Minerva Road, Farnworth,
Ms E Hawkins, Nurse, Epilepsy, Horwich Clinic, Jones Street, Horwich, BL6 7AJ, Tel.: 01204 696341
Ms J Liddell, Nurse, Epilepsy, Horwich Clinic, Jones Street, Horwich, BL6 7AJ, Tel.: 01204 696341
Ms K Gough, Infection Control, Great Lever Health Centre, Rupert Street, Bolton,
Mrs W Shuell, Nurse, Macmillan, Bolton Hospice, Bolton, Tel.: 01204 364546
Ms A Wilkinson, Nurse, Macmillan, Bolton Hospice, Bolton,
Mr G Munslow, Communicable Diseases Nurse, Emergency Planning Lead, Public Health, St Peter's House, Silverwell Street, Bolton, BL1 1PP,
Ms L Craddock, Nurse Specialist, Rheumatology, Lever Chambers, Ashburner Street, Bolton, BL1 1SQ, Tel.: 01204 360029
Ms E Greenhalgh, Spinal Injuries, Blackrod Heath Centre, Church Street, Blackrod, BL6 5EQ, Tel.: 01204 699229
Mrs K Irvin, (Bowel Management), Nurse Specialist, Stoma Care, Lever Chambers, Ashburner Street, Bolton, BL1 1SQ, Tel.: 01204 360029
Mrs J Ashton, Nurse Consultant, Tissue Viability, Lever Chambers, Ashburner Street, Bolton, BL1 1SQ, Tel.: 01204 360000
Ms N Morton, Nurse, Tissue Viability, Lever Chambers, Ashburner Street, Bolton, BL1 1SQ, Tel.: 01204 360000
The Homeless/Travellers & Asylum Seekers
Ms C Fay, Asylum Seeker Nurse, 2-16 Mayor Street, Bolton, BL3 5HT,
Ms J Mwamba, Asylum Seeker Nurse, 2-16 Mayor Street, Bolton, BL3 5HT,
Walk In Centres
Lever Chambers Walk-in Centre, Ashburner Street, Bolton, Tel.: 01204 360000

Burnley Pendle & Rossendale Primary Care Trust

Trust Headquarters, 31/33 Kenyon Road
Lomeshaye Estate
NELSON
Lancashire
BB9 5SZ
Tel.: 01282 619909

Admin & Senior Management
Mr C Dixon, Director of Finance,
Dr E Friedman, Director of Public Health,
Ms C Galaska, Director of Service Development,
Dr J Haworth, Director of Health Standards,

Mr S Hayton, Head of Operations & Business Planning, 31/33/ Kenyon Road, Lomeshaye Estate, Nelson, Lancs, BB9 5SZ, Tel.: 01282 610296
Ms C Logan, Director of Service Provision,
Mr D Peat, Chief Executive,
Ms O Scarborough, Head of Professional Development, 31/33/ Kenyon Road, Lomeshaye Estate, Nelson, Lancs, BB9 5SZ, Tel.: 01282 610295
Child Health Records
Pre-School, Primary Care Informatics Unit, Cobham House, Haslingden Road, Blackburn, Tel.: 01254 269306
School Health, St Nicholas Health Centre, Saunder Bank, Burnley, Lancs, Tel.: 01282 668030
Child Protection/Safeguarding Children
Ms J Magee, Lead Nurse, 31/33/ Kenyon Road, Lomeshaye Estate, Nelson, Lancs, BB9 5SZ, Tel.: 01282 610281
Clinical Leads (NSF)
Dr D Deacon, Clinical Lead, Cancer,
Dr M McDevitt, Clinical Lead, CHD,
Dr J Ormrod, Clinical Lead, CHD,
Dr T McKenzie, Clinical Lead, Diabetic Care,
Dr P Rishton, Clinical Lead, Older People,
Community Nursing Services
Mrs C Davies, Professional Manager, 31/33/ Kenyon Road, Lomeshaye Estate, Nelson, Lancs, BB9 5SZ, Tel.: 01282 610276
Night Nursing Service, Tel.: 01282 442503
Out of Hours Ansaphones, Burnley/Pendle, Tel.: 01282 442503
Out of Hours Ansaphones, Rossendale, Tel.: 01706 708755
District Nursing
Mrs C Davies, Professional Manager - District/Practice Nursing, 31/33/ Kenyon Road, Lomeshaye Estate, Nelson, Lancs, BB9 5SZ, Tel.: 01282 610276
Family Planning Services
Mrs J Rutter, Co-ordinator, 31/33/ Kenyon Road, Lomeshaye Estate, Nelson, Lancs, BB9 5SZ, Tel.: 01282 610275
Health Visitors
Mrs V Sibson, Professional Manager - Health Visiting Service, 31/33/ Kenyon Road, Lomeshaye Estate, Nelson, Lancs, BB9 5SZ, Tel.: 01282 610332
HIV/AIDS
Ms M Bramwell, Burnley General Hospital, Tel.: 01282 474031
Ms B Gilbert, Burnley General Hospital, Tel.: 01282 474031
Learning Disabilities
Community Learning Disability Offices, 31/33 Kenyon Road, Laneshaye Estate, Nelson, Lancs, BB9 5SZ, Tel.: 01282 610248
Mrs C Lobley, Manager, Supported Living Service, Tel.: 01282 662490
Mrs D O'Brien, Manager, Community Support Services, Tel.: 01282 602088
Mr D Whalley, Service Manager, Learning Disability, 31/33 Kenyon Road, Laneshaye Estate, Nelson, Lancs, BB9 5SZ, Tel.: 01282 610248
School Nursing
Mrs J Rutter, Professional Manager - School Nursing Service, 31/33/ Kenyon Road, Lomeshaye Estate, Nelson, Lancs, BB9 5SZ, Tel.: 01282 610275
Smoking Cessation
Ms C Donnelly, Tel.: 01282 607002
Specialist Nursing Services
Enteral Tube Feeding, c/o Dietetics Dept, Burnley General Hospital, Tel.: 01282 4250721
Mr D Sowerby, Specialist Practitioner- Nursing/Residential Homes, Rawtenstall Health Centre, Bacup Road, Rawtenstall, Tel.: 01706 708723
Transfer of Care Service, Rossendale, Tel.: 01706 233130
Transfer of Care Services, Burnley/Pendle, Tel.: 01282 474794/5
Ms T Cain, Breast Care, Burnley General Hospital, Tel.: 01282 474779

North West Strategic Health Authority

Mrs C Farmer, Breast Care, Burnley General Hospital, Tel.: 01282 474779

Mrs M Whitaker, Breast Care, Burnley General Hospital, Tel.: 01282 474779

Ms D Sanderson, Advisor, Continence, Brierfield Health Centre, Arthur Street, Brierfield, Nelson, Tel.: 01282 698227

Ms B Ward, Nurse, Continence, Brierfield Health Centre, Arthur Street, Brierfield, Nelson, Tel.: 01282 698227

Mrs S Greenwood, Diabetic Care, Burnley General Hospital, Tel.: 01282 474795

Mrs K Guilfoyle, Diabetic Care, Burnley General Hospital, Tel.: 01282 474795

Mrs A Shirreff, Diabetic Care, Burnley General Hospital, Tel.: 01282 474795

Ms K Payton, Lead Nurse, Leg Ulcers, Rawtenstall Health Centre, Bacup Road, Rawtenstall, Tel.: 01706 708736

Mr A Lord, Lung Cancer, Nelson Health Centre, Tel.: 01282 690131

Macmillan, Culpan House, Burnley General Hospital, Tel.: 01282 474850

Ms S Synowerskyj, Lead Nurse, Transfer of Care Service, Older People, 31/33/ Kenyon Road, Lomeshaye Estate, Nelson, Lancs, BB9 5SZ, Tel.: 01282 610241

Mrs B Lubomski, Respiratory, Nelson Health Centre, Tel.: 01282 690131

Ms D Woodruff, Stoma Care, Burnley General Hospital, Tel.: 01282 474261

The Homeless/Travellers & Asylum Seekers
Ms C Hopwood, Health Visitor, Kiddrow Lane Health Centre, Kiddrow Lane, Burnley, Tel.: 01282 435311

Bury Primary Care Trust

Trust Headquarters
21 Silver Street
BURY
Greater Manchester
BL9 0EN
Tel.: 0161 762 3100

Admin & Senior Management
Ms A Coates, Acting Deputy Chief Executive,

Mr S Mills, Acting Chief Executive, 21 Silver Street, Bury, Lancs, BL9 0EN, Tel.: 0161 762 3100

Child Health
Child Health, Talbot Grove, Bury, Lancs, BL9 6PH, Tel.: 0161 293 5524

Ms M Woodhouse, Associate Director, Children's Healthcare Services/Lead Nurse Childrens, 21 Silver Street, Bury, Greater Manchester, BL9 0EN,

Child Health Records
Ms B Ashton, Manager, Talbot Grove, Bury, Lancs, BL9 6PH, Tel.: 0161 293 5513

Ms M Woodhouse, Associate Director, Children's Healthcare Services, 21 Silver Street, Bury, Greater Manchester, BL9 0EN,

Child Protection/Safeguarding Children
R Greenway, Looked After Children, Designated Nurse,

Ms M Woodhouse, Associate Director, Children's Healthcare Services/Lead Nurse Childrens, 21 Silver Street, Bury, Greater Manchester, BL9 0EN,

Mrs S Crorkan, Designated Nurse, Child Protection,

Clinical Leads (NSF)
Ms M Woodhouse, Associate Director, Children's Healthcare Services - Policy Lead, 21 Silver Street, Bury, Greater Manchester, BL9 0EN,

Ms E Rispin, Clinical Lead, CHD, Cancer,

Ms J Hall, Clinical Lead, Older People,

Community Nursing Services
Ms H Leyden, Nursing Development Director, Carne House, Parsons Lane, BL9 0JT,

Ms J Stewart, Service Director, Respite, Sunnybank Clinic, Tel.: 0161 766 3044

Ms M Woodhouse, Associate Director, Children's Healthcare Services/Lead Nurse Childrens, 21 Silver Street, Bury, Lancs, BL9 0EN, Tel.: 0161 762 3100

District Nursing
Evening Service, Tel.: 0161 764 8621

Ms M Howarth, Professional Lead Nurse, Adults,

Ms H Leyden, Nurse Development Director,

Palliative Care Night Service, Tel.: 0161 763 4242

Equipment Loan Services
Ms H Leyden, Nursing Development Director,

Family Planning Services
Ms M Woodhouse, Associate Director, Children's Healthcare Services, 21 Silver Street, Bury, Greater Manchester, BL9 0EN, Tel.: 0161 762 3095

Health Visitors
Ms S Adamson, Professional Lead Nurse, Health Visiting,

Learning Disabilities
Ms J Stewart, Service Director, Learning Disabilities/Respite, Sunnybank Clinic, Bury, Tel.: 0161 766 3044

Liaison Services
Mr R Allen, Primary Care Diabetic, Nurse, Ramsbottom Health Centre, Tel.: 01706 824294

Ms P Hartney, Community Diabetic, Nurse Specialist, Fairfield General Hospital, Rochdale Road, Bury, Lancs, BL9 7TD, Tel.: 0161 778 2688/2689

Ms B Jones, Discharge, Liaison Nurse, Fairfield General Hospital, Rochdale Road, Bury, Lancs, BL9 7TD, Tel.: 0161 778 2680/2681

Pharmacy
Mr A Martin,

School Nursing
Ms W Thompson, Professional Lead Nurse, School Nursing,

Specialist Nursing Services
Ms J Fraser, Falls Nurse, Fairfield General Hospital,

Ms M Letherland, Nurse Specialist, Breast Care, Fairfield General Hospital, Tel.: 0161 778 3288

Ms S Cowley, Nurse, Cardiac, Bardoc, Parsons Lane, Bury,

Ms N Patel, Nurse, Cardiac, Bardoc, Parsons Lane, Bury, Tel.: 0161 762 4242

Mr R Allen, Nurse Co-ordinator, Diabetic Care, Ramsbottom Health Centre,

Ms P Hartney, Nurse, Diabetic Care, Fairfield General Hospital,

Ms J Forsyth, Nurse, Macmillan, Bealeys Community Hospital, Tel.: 0161 723 0471/2

Ms J Moody, Nurse, Macmillan, Bealeys Community Hospital, Tel.: 0161 723 0471/2

Calderstones NHS Trust

Trust Headquarters, Calderstones Hospital
Mitton Road, Whalley
CLITHEROE
BB7 9PE
Tel.: 01254 822121
Fax.: 01254 823023

Admin & Senior Management
Mrs C Whalley, Director of Nursing, Calderstones NHS Trust, Calderstones Hospital, Mitton Road, Whalley, Clitheroe, BB7 9PE,

Cardiothoracic Centre (Liverpool) NHS Trust

Trust Headquarters,
Thomas Drive
LIVERPOOL
L14 3PE
Tel.: 0151 228 1616
Fax.: 0151 220 8573

North West Strategic Health Authority

Admin & Senior Management
Ms J Walters, Director of Nursing, Cardiothroacic Centre, Thomas Drive, Liverpool, L14 3PE, Tel.: 0151 228 1616

Carlisle & District Primary Care Trust
4 Wavell Drive
Rosehill, CARLISLE, CA1 2SE
Tel.: 01228 602727

Admin & Senior Management
Mrs E Crooks, Senior Clinical Manager, The Coppice, The Carleton Clinic, Carlisle, Cumbria, CA1 3SX, Tel.: 01228 603527/603581
Mrs K Douglas, Senior Clinical Manager, Intermediate Care, Granville House, Cumberland Infirmary, Carlisle, Cumbria, Tel.: 01228 814488
Mrs C Duncan, Senior Clinical Manager, The Coppice, The Carleton Clinic, Carlisle, Cumbria, CA1 3SX, Tel.: 01228 603527/603581
Mrs C Fell, Senior Clinical Manager, The Coppice, The Carleton Clinic, Carlisle, Cumbria, CA1 3SX, Tel.: 01228 603527/603581
Ms U Robertson, Modern Matron, Wigton Community Hospital, Cross Lane, Wigton, Cumbria, CA7 9DD, Tel.: 016973 66601
Child Health
Mrs C Duncan, Senior Clinical Manager, The Coppice, The Carleton Clinic, Carlisle, Cumbria, CA1 3SX, Tel.: 01228 603504
Child Health Records
Ms A Millican, Child Health Services Manager, Central Clinic, Carlisle, Cumbria, CA1 1HP, Tel.: 01228 603428
Child Protection/Safeguarding Children
Ms L Davison, Senior Nurse, Child Protection, Central Clinic, Carlisle, Cumbria, CA1 1HP, Tel.: 01228 603244
Community Nursing Services
Mrs E Crooks, Senior Clinical Manager, The Coppice, The Carleton Clinic, Carlisle, Cumbria, CA1 3SX, Tel.: 01228 603527
Mrs C Fell, Senior Clinical Manager, The Coppice, The Carleton Clinic, Carlisle, Cumbria, CA1 3SX, Tel.: 01228 603527
District Nursing
Mrs C Duncan, Senior Clinical Manager, The Coppice, The Carleton Clinic, Carlisle, Cumbria, CA1 3SX, Tel.: 01228 603504
Family Planning Services
Mrs C Duncan, Senior Clinical Manager, The Coppice, The Carleton Clinic, Carlisle, Cumbria, CA1 3SX, Tel.: 01228 603504
Liaison Services
Ms J Dixon, Paediatric Diabetic Liaison Nurse, Childrens OPD, Cumberland Infirmary, Tel.: 01228 814432
Specialist Nursing Services
Mrs S Beeton, Nurse Specialist, Continence, Central Clinic, Victoria Place, Carlisle,
Mrs C Mullin, Nurse Specialist, Cystic Fibrosis, Childrens Ward, Cumberland Infirmary, Carlisle, CA2 7HY, Tel.: 01228 523444
Mr P Weaving, Nurse Specialist, Infection Control, Cumberland Infirmary, Carlisle, Tel.: 01228 523444
Mrs M Ross, Nurse, Macmillan, Central Clinic, Victoria Place, Carlisle,

Central Cheshire Primary Care Trust
Trust Headquarters, The Barony
Barony Road
NANTWICH
CW5 5QU
Tel.: 01270 415300

Admin & Senior Management
Mr M Pyrah, Chief Executive,
Child Health
Ms L Champion, Paediatric Sister, Leighton Hospital, Tel.: 01270 612075
Mrs J Hunt, Special Needs Child, Frederick House, Princes Court, Beam Heath Way, Barony Employment Park, Nantwich, CW5 6RF, Tel.: 01270 415445

Child Health Records
Child Health Records, The Barony, Barony Road, Nantwich, CW5 5QU, Tel.: 01270 415300
Ms A Mitchell, Information Manager, Tel.: 01270 415335
Child Protection/Safeguarding Children
Ms D Jones, Designated Nurse for Safeguarding Children & Young People, Trust Headquarters, Tel.: 01270 415302
Clinical Leads (NSF)
Dr J Northall, Clinical Lead, Older People,
Dr J Branson, Clinical Lead, Cancer,
Dr L Risk, Clinical Lead, Diabetic Care,
District Nursing
Ms S Daly, GP Out of Hours, Tel.: 01270 275423
Ms F Field, Acting Director of Operational Services, Tel.: 01270 415318
Ms Y Lochhead, Head of Nursing, Tel.: 01270 415469
Liaison Services
Ms J Buckley, Specialist Nurse Paediatric Liaison, Leighton Hospital, Middlewich Road, Crewe, CW1 4QI, Tel.: 01270 612075
Ms S Gaskell, Specialist Nurse Paediatric Liaison, Leighton Hospital, Middlewich Road, Crewe, CW1 4QI, Tel.: 01270 612075
Ms L Procter, Community, Sister, Leighton Hospital, Middlewich Road, Crewe, CW1 4QJ, Tel.: 01270 612308
Specialist Nursing Services
Mrs P Brookfield, Continence, Frederick House, Princes Court, Beam Heath Way, Barony Employment Park, Nantwich, CW5 6RF, Tel.: 01270 415408
Mrs P Wild, Continence, Frederick House, Princes Court, Beam Heath Way, Barony Employment Park, Nantwich, CW5 6RF, Tel.: 01270 415436
Mr S Davies, Diabetic Care, Frederick House, Princes Court, Beam Heath Way, Barony Employment Park, Nantwich, CW5 6RF, Tel.: 01270 623833
Ms J James, Diabetic Care, Frederick House, Princes Court, Beam Heath Way, Barony Employment Park, Nantwich, CW5 6RF, Tel.: 01270 623833
Ms C Cadwalader, Infection Control, Leighton Hospital, Tel.: 01270 255141 ext 2190
Ms K Egan, Infection Control, Leighton Hosp, 01270 255141 x 2190
Nurses, Macmillan, The Hospice, Grosvenor House, Queensway, Winsford, Tel.: 01606 862112
Ms C Dean, Respiratory, Frederick House, Princes Court, Beam Heath Way, Barony Employment Park, Nantwich, CW5 6RF, Tel.: 01270 415437
Mrs A Rickards, Stoma Care, Leighton Hospital, Tel.: 01270 255141 ext 2308/244
Mrs J Woodcock, Stoma Care, Leighton Hospital, Tel.: 01270 255141 x 2308/2443
Mrs S Walsh, Tissue Viability, Frederick House, Princes Court, Beam Heath Way, Barony Employment Park, Nantwich, CW5 6RF, Tel.: 01270 415438
The Homeless/Travellers & Asylum Seekers
Mrs M Gill, Travellers, Health Visitor, Middlewich Clinic, Salinae, Lewin Street, Middlewich, CW10 9TG, Tel.: 01606 832165

Central Liverpool Primary Care Trust
Trust Headquarters,Arthouse,
1 Arthouse Square,
61-19 Seel Street
LIVERPOOL, L1 4AZ
Tel.: 0151 296 7000

Admin & Senior Management
Mr D Campbell, Chief Executive,
Ms M Cody, Acting Lead Nurse, 125 Ullet Road, Liverpool, L17 2AB, Tel.: 0151 222 7415
Child Protection/Safeguarding Children
Mrs L. Rodgers Designated Nurse, Regatta Place, Summers Road

North West Strategic Health Authority

Brunswick Business Park, Liverpool L3 4BL Tel:.0151 285 4671/0
Mrs T Jones, Named Nurse Safeguarding Children, Regatta Place,
Summers Rd, Brunswick Business Park, Liverpool L3 4BL Tel: 0151
285 4666/4670
Safeguarding Children Specialist Nurses, Sue Darley, Regatta Place,
Summers Road, Liverpool L3 4BL Tel.:0151 285 4659/4661

Central Manchester & Manchester Children's University Hospitals NHS Trust
Trust Headquarters, Cobbett House
Manchester Royal Infirmary, Oxford Road
MANCHESTER
M13 9WL
Tel.: 0161 276 1234

Child Protection/Safeguarding Children
Miss S C Lynch, Named Nurse, Child Protection, c/o Antenatal
Clinic, St Mary's Hospital, Hathersage Road, Whitworth Park,
Manchester, M13 0JH, Tel.: 0161 276 6623
Community Midwifery
Mrs K Connolly, Head of Midwifery, Sixth Floor, St Mary's Hospital,
Hathersage Road, Whitworth Park, Manchester, M13 0JH, Tel.: 0161
276 6291
Miss S C Lynch, Lead Midwife/Modern Matron Community &
Antenatal Services, St Mary's Hospital, Hathersage Road, Whitworth
Park, Manchester, M13 0JH, Tel.: 0161 276 6623

Central Manchester Primary Care Trust
Trust Headquarters, Mauldeth House
Mauldeth Road West, Chorlton
MANCHESTER
M21 7RL
Tel.: 0161 958 4000

Admin & Senior Management
Ms J Royle, Director of Operations, Tel.: 0161 958 4048
Child Health
Ms J Anderton, Paediatric Asthma Nurse, Rusholme Health Centre,
Walmer Street, M14 5NP, Tel.: 0161 225 1100
Ms L Comer, Community Children's Team - Diabetes, Brunswich
Health Centre, Hartfield Close, Brunswick Street, M13 9TP, Tel.:
0161 273 1663/276 2214
Ms A Jackson, Associate Director, Children's Service Development,
Mauldeth House, Nell Lane, Chorlton, Manchester, Tel.: 0161 958
4010
Ms P Keating, Community Children's Team, Nurse Manager,
Brunswich Health Centre, Hartfield Close, Brunswick Street, M13
9TP, Tel.: 0161 273 1663/276 2214
Mr M Kellaway, Deputy Director Community Services, Mauldeth
House, Nell Lane, Chorlton, Manchester, Tel.: 0161 958 4163
Ms J McGrogan, Community Children's Team - Home Ventilation,
Brunswick Health Centre, Hartfield Close, Brunswick Street, M13
9TP, Tel.: 0161 273 1663/276 2214
Child Health Records
Ms J Scott, Manager, Mauldeth House, Nell Lane, Chorlton,
Manchester, Tel.: 0161 958 4089
Child Protection/Safeguarding Children
Mrs P Dickinson, Senior Nurse, Moss Side Health Centre, Monton
Street, Manchester, M14 4GP, Tel.: 0161 226 5031
Mrs A Kubiak, Senior Nurse, Moss Side Health Centre, Monton
Street, Manchester, M14 4GP, Tel.: 0161 958 4000
Clinical Leads (NSF)
Mrs C Matthewson, Clinical Lead, Cancer,
Community Nursing Services
Mrs R Goodwin, Deputy Director Operations/Lead Nurse, Mauldeth
House, Nell Lane, Chorlton, Manchester, Tel.: 0161 958 4124
District Nursing
Ms G Acreman, Clinical Lead, District Nursing,

Health Visitors
Ms M Basu, Clinical Lead, Health Visiting,
Learning Disabilities
Mr M Burton, Head Learning Disabilities, Mauldeth House, Mauldeth
Road West, Manchester, M21 7RL, Tel.: 0161 958 4014/4050
Central, Chapman Place, Chapman Street, Gorton, M18 8UA, Tel.:
0161 223 9901
Mrs M Donlon, Practice Adviser - Nursing, Oakwood Resource
Centre, 177 Longley Lane, Northenden, Manchester, M22 4HY, Tel.:
0161 998 7424
North, Resource Centre, Beech Mount, Harpurhey, Manchester, M9
5XS, Tel.: 0161 205 1364
South, Oakwood Resource Unit, 177 Longley Lane, Northenden,
Tel.: 0161 998 7424
West, Chorlton Social Services, 102 Manchester Road,
Chorlton,M21 1PQ, Tel.: 0161 881 0911
Liaison Services
Ms P Bessell, Royal Infirmary Liaison, District Nurse, Ward SM8, St
Mary's Hospital, Oxford Road, Manchester, Tel.: 0161 276 4314
Ms E Lowth, Royal Infirmary Liaison, District Nurse, 1 Lorne Street,
MRI, Oxford Road, Manchester, M13 9WL, Tel.: 0161 276 4512
Other Services
Ms J Hogan, Lead Clinician, Cancer, Moss Side Health Centre, Tel.:
0161 226 5031
Ms S Webster, Lead Clinician, Infection Control,
Specialist Nursing Services
Ms K Welsh, Vulnerable Families, Nurse Consultant, Mauldeth
House, Nell Lane, Chorlton, Manchester, Tel.: 0161 958 4000
Mrs J Corbett, Continence, Longsight Health Centre, 526-528
Stockport Road, Longsight, M13 0RR, Tel.: 0161 248 1230
Mrs K Forshaw, Continence, Longsight Health Centre, 526-528
Stockport Road, Longsight, M13 0RR, Tel.: 0161 248 1230
Mrs B Starkey, Lead Nurse, Continuing Care, Mauldeth House, Nell
Lane, Chorlton, Manchester, Tel.: 0161 861 2282
Ms N Neild, Nurse Specialist, Dermatology, Levenshulme Health
Centre, Tel.: 0161 861 2300
Ms L Benson, Nurse, Infection Control,
Ms J Carson, Nurse, Macmillan, Moss Side Health Centre, Tel.: 0161
226 5031
Ms S Sutherland, Nurse, Tissue Viability, Levenshulme Health
Centre, Tel.: 0161 861 2300
The Homeless/Travellers & Asylum Seekers
Health Visitor, Homeless Families, Chorlton Health Centre, Nicolas
Road, M21 9NJ, Tel.: 0161 861 8888

Cheshire & Wirral Partnership NHS Trust
Trust Headquarters, West Cheshire Hospital
Countess of Chester Health Park, Liverpool Road
CHESTER
CH2 1BQ
Tel.: 01244 364368

Learning Disabilities
Mr P Joyce, Clinical Services Manager, Central Cheshire Locality,
Stalbridge Road Clinic, Stalbridge Road, Crewe, CW2 7LP, Tel.:
01270 654400
Mr R Kingdon, Acting Clinical Services Manager East Cheshire
Locality, Rosemount, Chester Road, Macclesfield, SK11 8QA, Tel.:
01625 663631
Mr A Moss, Clinical Services Manager, Wirral Locality, Ashton House
Hospital, Columbia Road, Oxton, Birkenhead, Wirral, L43 6TJ, Tel.:
0151 653 9660
Mr A Styring, Acting Director Learning Disabilities, Head of CAMHS,
West Cheshire Hospital, Countess of Chester Health Park, Liverpool
Road, Chester, CH2 1UL, Tel.: 01244 852322
Ms S Vernon, Clinical Services Manager, West Cheshire Locality,
Ashton House Hospital, Columbia Road, Oxton, Birkenhead, Wirral,
L43 6TJ, Tel.: 0151 653 9660

North West Strategic Health Authority

Cheshire West Primary Care Trust

Trust Headquarters, 1829 Building
Countess of Chester Health Park, Liverpool Road
CHESTER
CH2 1UL
Tel.: 01244 650300

Admin & Senior Management
Ms S Dilks, Head of Service Delivery & Development Nursing, 1829
Building, Countess of Chester Health Park, Chester, CH2 1UL, Tel.:
01244 650 392
Mr G Taylor, Chief Executive,
Ms G Walton, Director, Primary Care & Clinical Services,
Child Health
Ms S Dilks, Head of Service Delivery & Development Nursing, 1829
Building, Countess of Chester Health Park, Chester, CH2 1UL, Tel.:
01244 650 392
Child Health Records
Ms L Lewandowski, School Health Records, Moston Lodge
Children's Centre, Countess of Chester Health Park,
Child Protection/Safeguarding Children
Mrs T Rees, Moston Lodge, Countess of Chester Health Park,
Liverpool Road, Chester, CH2 1UL, Tel.: 01244 364831
Clinical Leads (NSF)
Dr T Saunders, Clinical Lead, Diabetes,
Dr P Milner, Clinical Lead, Cancer,
Dr C Holme, Clinical Lead, CHD,
Dr S Birnie, Clinical Lead, Older People,
District Nursing
Ms S Dilks, Head of Service Delivery & Development Nursing, 1829
Building, Countess of Chester Health Park, Chester, CH2 1UL, Tel.:
1244 650 392
District Nurses, Moston Lodge, Countess of Chester Health Park,
Liverpool Road, Chester, CH2 1UL, Tel.: 01244 364830
Family Planning Services
Ms S Lister,
Health Visitors
Health Visitors, Moston Lodge, Countess of Chester Health Park,
Liverpool Road, Chester, CH2 1UL, Tel.: 01244 364830
Other Services
Ms L Jackman, Facilitator, Primary Care,
Ms S Ridsdale, Facilitator, Primary Care,
Specialist Nursing Services
Mr P O'Brien, Continence, Moston Lodge, Countess of Chester
Health Park, Liverpool Road, Chester, CH2 1UL, Tel.: 01244 364740
Miss F Crowther, Macmillan, Hospice of the Good Shepherd, Gordon
Lane, Backford, Chester, CH2 4DG, Tel.: 01244 851170
Mrs H Westwell, Macmillan, Hospice of the Good Shepherd, Gordon
Lane, Backford, Chester, CH2 4DG, Tel.: 01244 851170
The Homeless/Travellers & Asylum Seekers
Ms A Bates, Moston Lodge, Countess of Chester Health Park,
Liverpool Road, Chester, CH2 1UL,

Chorley & South Ribble NHS Trust

Trust Headquarters, Chorley & South Ribble District Hospital
Preston Road
CHORLEY
PR7 1PP
Tel.: 01257 261222

Admin & Senior Management
Ms S Reed, Director of Nursing, Chorley & South Ribble NHS Trust,
Preston Road, Chorley, PR7 1PP, Tel.: 01257 261222
Clinical Leads (NSF)
Dr Sule, Clinical Lead, Cancer,

Chorley & South Ribble Primary Care Trust

Jubilee House
Lancashire Business Park, Centurion Way
LEYLAND, Lancashire
PR26 6TR
Tel.: 01772 644400
Fax.: 01772 227030

Admin & Senior Management
Mrs P Derbyshire, Director of Nursing, & Clinical Services, Jubilee
House, Lancashire Business Park, Centurion Way, Leyland,
Lancashire, PR26 6TR, Tel.: 01257 245400
Child Health Records
Ms T Atkins, Section Head - Child Health Dept, Jubilee House,
Lancashire Enterprise Business Park, Centurion Way, Farington,
Leyland, PR26 6TR, Tel.: 01772 644446
Child Health Department, Jubilee House, Lancashire Enterprise
Business Park, Centurion Way, Farington, Leyland, PR26 6TR, Tel.:
01772 644445/6/7
Child Protection/Safeguarding Children
Mrs H Duncan, Designated/Named Nurse, Safeguarding Children,
Jubilee House, Lancashire Business Park, Centurion Way, Leyland,
Lancashire, PR26 6TR, Tel.: 01772 644525
Clinical Leads (NSF)
Dr T Cockeram, Clinical Lead, Children,
Dr S Ward, Clinical Lead, Older People,
Equipment Loan Services
Ms A Gaskell, Assistant Director, Older People, Jubilee House,
Lancashire Business Park, Centurion Way, Leyland, Lancashire,
PR26 6TR, Tel.: 01772 644400
Family Planning Services
Ms M Simpkin, Jubilee House, Lancashire Business Park, Centurion
Way, Leyland, Lancashire, PR26 6TR, Tel.: 01772 644400
Health Visitors
Mrs N Leach, Assistant Director, Children & Young People, Jubilee
House, Lancashire Business Park, Centurion Way, Leyland,
Lancashire, PR26 6TR, Tel.: 01772 644400
HIV/AIDS
Ms M Simpkin, Jubilee House, Lancashire Business Park, Centurion
Way, Leyland, Lancashire, PR26 6TR, Tel.: 01772 644400
Learning Disabilities
Mrs L Moorhouse, Assistant Director, Adults, Jubilee House,
Lancashire Business Park, Centurion Way, Leyland, Lancashire,
PR26 6TR, Tel.: 01772 644400
School Nursing
Mrs N Leach, Assistant Director, Children & Young People, Jubilee
House, Lancashire Business Park, Centurion Way, Leyland,
Lancashire, PR26 6TR, Tel.: 01772 644400
Specialist Nursing Services
Mr T Burns, Behavioural Therapist Nurse,
Mr I Pomfret, Continence, The Lodge, Chorley Hospital, Preston
Road, Chorley, PR7 1PP, Tel.: 01257 245412
Mr J Allin, Epilepsy, Tel.: 01772 644130
Ms L Newsham, Infection Control,
Ms S Aspin, Tissue Viability, Tel.: 01772 644740
Ms C Landon, Blood Borne, Viruses, The Lodge, Chorley Hospital,
Preston Road, Chorley, PR7 1PP,

Christie Hospital NHS Trust

Trust Headquarters, 550 Wilmslow Road
Withington
MANCHESTER, M20 4BX
Tel.: 0161 446 3000
Fax.: 0161 446 3977

Admin & Senior Management
Ms A Norman, Director of Nursing, Christie Hospital NHS Trust, 550
Wilmslow Road, Withington, Manchester, M20 4BX, Tel.: 0161 446
3000

North West Strategic Health Authority

Clatterbridge Centre for Oncology NHS Trust
Trust Headquarters, Clatterbridge Road
Bebbington
WIRRAL
Cheshire, CH63 4JY
Tel.: 0151 334 1155

Admin & Senior Management
Ms H Porter, Director of Patient Services & Quality, Clatterbridge Centre for Oncology NHS Trust, Clatterbridge Rd, Bebbington, Wirral, Cheshire, CH634JY, Tel.: 0151 334 1155

Countess of Chester Hospital NHS Trust
Trust Headquarters, Countess of Chester Health Park
Liverpool Road
CHESTER
CH2 1UL
Tel.: 01244 365000

Admin & Senior Management
Miss C Healey, Head of Midwifery & Nursing - Women's & Children's Services, Women's & Children's Directorate, Longhouse, Liverpool Rd, Chester, CH2 1UL, Tel.: 01244 366399
Mrs S Hoyle, Directorate Manager, Women & Childrens Services, Women's & Children's Directorate, Longhouse, Liverpool Rd, Chester, CH2 1UL, Tel.: 01244 366399

Child Health
Ms U Downie, Community Children's Nurse (lead in Cystic Fibrosis, Asthma & Eczema), Countess of Chester Hospital NHS Trust, Children's Unit, Liverpool Road, Chester, CH2 1UL, Tel.: 01244 365000 ext 5254
Ms J Gratten, Community Children's Nurse (lead in Oncology & Palliative Care), Countess of Chester Hospital NHS Trust, Children's Unit, Liverpool Road, Chester, CH2 1UL, Tel.: 01244 365000 ext 5254
Mr P Langride, Community Children's Nurse (lead in Diabetes & Epilepsy), Countess of Chester Hospital NHS Trust, Children's Unit, Liverpool Road, Chester, CH2 1UL, Tel.: 01244 365000 ext 5254

Child Health Records
Ms L Lewandowski, Child Health Community & School Health Supervisor, Children's Centre, Moston Lodge, Countess of Chester Health Park, Tel.: 01244 364801

Child Protection/Safeguarding Children
Ms A Murphy, Named Nurse, Child Protection, Women's & Childrens Directorate, Longhouse, Liverpool Road, Chester, CH2 1UL, Tel.: 01244 366418
Ms T Rees, Designated Nurse, Child Protection, Children's Centre, Moston Lodge, Countess of Chester Health Park, Tel.: 01244 364831
Ms J Shenton, Lead, Midwife, Child Protection, Countess of Chester Hospital NHS Trust, Liverpool Road, Chester, CH2 1UL, Tel.: 01244 365625

Community Midwifery
Antenatal Clinic, Tel.: 01244 365106
Ms J Beech, Infant Feeding & Parent Education Co-ordinator, Tel.: 01244 365401
Blacon Sure Start Midwives, Tel.: 01244 398644
Community Midwives Office, Tel.: 01244 365166
Ms M Ellen Dean, Infant Feeding & Parent Education Co-ordinator, Tel.: 01244 365401
Ellesmere Port Sure Start Midwife, Tel.: 0151 355 2168
Emergencies - Central Labour Suite, Tel.: 01244 365026/8
Miss C Healey, Head of Midwifery & Nursing - Women's & Children's Services, Women & Childrens Directorate Offices, Longhouse, Chester, CH2 1UL, Tel.: 01244 366399
Ms M Littler, Midwife - Quality Manager Community Midwifery, Tel.: 01244 365011/365166
Ms D Sandiford, Teenage Pregnancy Midwife, Tel.: 01244 365830

Community Nursing Services
Community Midwives, Countess of Chester Hospital NHS Trust, Liverpool Road, Chester, CH2 1UL, Tel.: 01244 365166

Other Services
Ms L Chappell, Community Children's Care Package's Manager, Countess of Chester Hospital NHS Trust, Children's Unit, Liverpool Road, Chester, CH2 1UL, Tel.: 01244 365054

East Cheshire NHS Trust
Trust Headquarters, Macclesfield District General Hospital
Victoria Road
MACCLESFIELD, Cheshire
SK10 3BL
Tel.: 01625 421000

Acute Specialist Nursing Services
Ms H Cooper, I.C.U., Nurse Consultant, Macclesfield District General Hospital, Tel.: ext 1398/1032
Ms J Crowther, Advanced Neo-Natal, Nurse Practitioner, Macclesfield District General Hospital, Tel.: ext 1148
Ms J Davenport, Nurse Practitioner, Bollington Clinic,
Ms J Dean, Medical, Nurse Practitioner, Macclesfield District General Hospital, Tel.: bleep 3405
Ms L Duncan, Day Suite, Nurse Practitioner, Macclesfield District General Hospital,
Ms C Hughes, Peri Operative Sp. Practitioner, Macclesfield District General Hospital, Tel.: ext 1791
Ms H John, Nurse Development Manager, Macclesfield District General Hospital, Tel.: 508345
Ms D Pearson, Nurse, Acute Pain, Macclesfield District General Hospital, Tel.: bleep 3402
Ms J Taylor, Nurse Specialist, Asthma, Macclesfield District General Hospital, Tel.: ext 1855
Ms N Davies, Nurse Specialist, Breast Care, Macclesfield District General Hospital, Tel.: ext 3079
Ms C Gwatkin, Nurse Specialist, Breast Care, Macclesfield District General Hospital, Tel.: ext 1650
Ms D Hamer, Nurse Specialist, Breast Care, Macclesfield District General Hospital, Tel.: ext 1976
Ms K Buckley, Lead Manager, Nurse, Cancer, Macclesfield District General Hospital, Tel.: ext 3771
Ms P Spray, Sister, Cardiac Rehabilitation, Macclesfield District General Hospital, Tel.: bleep 3376
Ms J Walker, Nurse Clinician, Cardiology, Macclesfield District General Hospital, Tel.: ext 3068
Ms J Bailey, Nurse Specialist, Chemotherapy, Macclesfield District General Hospital, Tel.: ext 3203
Ms M Jepson, Nurse Specialist, Chemotherapy, Macclesfield District General Hospital, Tel.: ext 1003
Ms T Kelly, Nurse Specialist, Chemotherapy, Macclesfield District General Hospital, Tel.: ext 3203
Ms A Perks, Nurse Specialist, Colorectal, Macclesfield District General Hospital, Tel.: ext 1598
Ms S Blades, Advisor, Continence, Macclesfield District General Hospital, Tel.: 01625 665553
Ms T Cohen, Advisor, Continence, Eastern Cheshire PCT, Park Green Offices, Tel.: 01625 665552
Ms L Walwyn, Advisor, Continence, Macclesfield District General Hospital, Tel.: 01625 665554
Ms V Williams, Advisor, Continence, Macclesfield District General Hospital, Tel.: 01625 665553
Ms M Jennings, Senior, Nurse Specialist, Diabetic Care, Macclesfield District General Hospital, Tel.: ext 1744
Ms C Chasty, Liaison,Discharges, Macclesfield District General Hos
Ms K Slater, Liaison Nurse, Discharges, Macclesfield District General Hospital,
Ms R Donnelly, Nurse, Endoscopist, Macclesfield District General Hospital, Tel.: ext 1040

North West Strategic Health Authority

Ms C Pickles, Nurse Specialist, Epilepsy, Macclesfield District General Hospital, Tel.: ext 1190

Mrs L Nelson, Specialist Nurse, Gastroenterology, Macclesfield District General Hospital, Tel.: ext 3266

Ms M Allen, Specialist Nurse, GI, Macclesfield District General Hospital, Tel.: ext 1044

Ms K Howlen, Nurse Specialist, Gynae/Oncology, Macclesfield District General Hospital, Tel.: ext 1518

Ms J Best, Specialist Nurse, Infection Control, Macclesfield District General Hospital, Tel.: ext 1597

Ms C McGinley, Nurse Specialist, Infection Control, Macclesfield District General Hospital, Tel.: ext 1769

Ms A Swaine, Specialist Nurse, Infection Control, Macclesfield District General Hospital, Tel.: ext 1597 bleep 3034

Ms L Bowden, Nurse Co-ordinator, Intermediate Care, Macclesfield District General Hospital,

Ms E Hunt, Nurse Co-ordinator, Intermediate Care, Macclesfield District General Hospital,

Ms J Mellville, Nurse Co-ordinator, Intermediate Care, Macclesfield District General Hospital,

Ms J Wheelton, Nurse Co-ordinator, Intermediate Care, Macclesfield District General Hospital,

Ms A Burgoyne, Specialist Nurse, Lung Cancer, Macclesfield District General Hospital, Tel.: ext 1997

Ms L Creech, Macmillan Nurse, Lung Cancer, Macclesfield District General Hospital, Tel.: ext 1997

Ms C Pearce, Nurse, Macmillan, Macclesfield District General Hospital, Tel.: ext 1188

Ms C Pollard, Nurse, Macmillan, Macclesfield District General Hospital, Tel.: ext 3176

Ms K White, Nurse, Macmillan, Macclesfield District General Hospital, Tel.: ext 1860

Ms H Crewe, Specialist Nurse, Neurology, Macclesfield District General Hospital,

Ms C Gaskell, Research, Nurse, Oncology, Macclesfield District General Hospital, Tel.: ext 3115

Ms C Cowburn, Nurse Specialist, Ophthalmology, Macclesfield District General Hospital,

Ms J Lane, Nurse Specialist, Ophthalmology, Macclesfield District General Hospital, Tel.: ext 1413

Mrs J Webster, Specialist Nurse, Palliative Care, Macclesfield District General Hospital, Tel.: ext 3177

Mr M Smith, Practice Nurse Facilitator, Macclesfield District General Hospital, Tel.: ext 1981

Ms J Ellis, Nurse Advisor, Psychiatric, Macclesfield District General Hospital, Tel.: ext 1982

Ms E Stanmore, Clinical Manager, Rapid Response, Macclesfield District General Hospital, Tel.: ext 3077

Ms J Bayliss, Nurse, Respiratory, Macclesfield District General Hospital, Tel.: ext 1705

Ms A Graham, Nurse Specialist, Respiratory, Macclesfield District General Hospital, Tel.: ext 1705

Ms E Meecham, Nurse Specialist, Rheumatology, Macclesfield District General Hospital, Tel.: ext 1978

Ms L Butler, Service Co-ordinator, Stroke Care, Macclesfield District General Hospital, Tel.: ext 1499

Ms R Peacock, Practitioner, Surgical Services, Macclesfield District General Hospital, Tel.: ext 1275

Ms G Benn, Nurse, Tissue Viability, Macclesfield District General Hospital, Tel.: ext 1253

Ms H Miller, Nurse, Tissue Viability, Macclesfield District General Hospital, Tel.: ext 1253

Admin & Senior Management

Mrs B Salisbury, Director of Nursing & Operations, Trust HQ, Macclesfield District General Hospital, Victoria Road, Macclesfield, SK10 3BL, Tel.: 01625 421000

Child Health

Ms R Leggett, Child & Adolescent Services, Macclesfield District General Hospital, Tel.: 01625 421000

Child Protection/Safeguarding Children

Ms M McGrathy, Child Protection, Alderley Building, Macclesfield District General Hospital, Victoria Road, Macclesfield, SK10 3BL, Tel.: 01625 421000

Community Midwifery

Fully Integrated Midwifery Service, Provided by GP Attached Midwifery Group Practices, Tel.: 01625 661153

Mrs G Hopps, Head of Midwifery & Women Services, Maternity Unit, East Cheshire NHS Trust, Victoria Road, Macclesfield, SK10 3BL, Tel.: 01625 661146

Ms L Perry, Senior Midwife for Midwifery Teams, Tel.: 01625 661151

Liaison Services

Mr C Tuson, Discharge Liaison Nurse, Macclesfield District General Hospital, Tel.: 01625 421000 bleep 3443

Ms A Williamson, Community Discharge Liaison Nurse, Macclesfield District General Hospital, Tel.: 01625 421000 ext 1909

Other Services

Ms Y Awenat, Rehab/Dept of Health Research Fellow, Nurse Consultant, Macclesfield District General Hospital, Tel.: ext 1658

Ms M Black, Residential Homes Team, Macclesfield District General Hospital, Tel.: ext 1982

Ms E Churchman, NHS Funded Nursing Care, Alderley Building, Macclesfield District General Hospital, Tel.: ext 1502

Ms D Donovan, Long Term Care Manager, Macclesfield District General Hospital,

Ms M Glaser, NHS Funded Nursing Care, Alderley Building, ext 1502

Ms C Hardy, Residential Homes Team, Macclesfield District General Hospital, Tel.: ext 1866

Ms P Sinclair, Rehab Link Team, Macclesfield District General Hospital, Tel.: ext 1284

East Lancashire Hospitals NHS Trust

Trust Headquarters, Burnley General Hospital
Casterton Avenue
BURNLEY, BB10 2PQ
Tel.: 01282 425071

Child Protection/Safeguarding Children

Ms C Hindle, Midwife, Named Nurse, Child Protection, c/o Children's OPD, Edith Watson Unit, Burnley, BB10 2PQ,

Liaison Services

Ms L Maddran, Liaison Drug Midwife, Edith Watson Unit, Burnley, BB10 2PQ, Tel.: 01282 474210

Eastern Cheshire Primary Care Trust

Trust Headquarters, Winterton House
Winterton Way
MACCLESFIELD
Cheshire, SK11 0LP
Tel.: 01625 508300

Admin & Senior Management

Mrs M R Malkin, Lead Nurse/Locality Manager, Tel.: 01625 508300

Mr G Raphael, Acting Chief Executive,

Child Health

Mrs M R Malkin, Lead Nurse/Locality Manager, 32 Park Green, PCT Offices, 2nd Floor, Macclesfield, SK11 7NA, Tel.: 01625 508300

Child Health Records

Over 5s, School Health Department, Macclesfield District General Hospital, Tel.: 01625 661752

Under 5s, Child Health Department, Macclesfield District General Hospital, Tel.: 01625 661784

North West Strategic Health Authority

Child Protection/Safeguarding Children
Mrs M McGrath, Designated Senior Nurse, Child Protection, Macclesfield District General Hosp, Macclesfield, Cheshire, SK10 3BL, Tel.: 01625 661491

Clinical Leads (NSF)
Dr D Arthur, Strategic Development Lead, Cancer, Winterton House, Winterton Way, Macclesfield, SK11 0LP,
Ms B Bailey, Strategic Development Lead, Care of the Elderly, Winterton House, Winterton Way, Macclesfield, SK11 0LP,
Ms J Wood, Strategic Development Lead, CHD, - Diabetes, Winterton House, Winterton Way, Macclesfield, SK11 0LP,
Ms J Hawkes, Strategic Development Lead, Children, Winterton House, Winterton Way, Macclesfield, SK11 0LP,

Community Matrons
Ms L Bowden, Community Matron, 32 Park Green, PCT Offices, Macclesfield, Cheshire, SK11 7NA, Tel.: 01625 665580
Ms S Hambleton, Community Matron, 32 Park Green, PCT Offices, Macclesfield, Cheshire, SK11 7NA, Tel.: 01625 665580
Ms M Manley, Community Matron, 32 Park Green, PCT Offices, Macclesfield, Cheshire, SK11 7NA, Tel.: 01625 665580
Ms C Walker, Community Matron, 32 Park Green, PCT Offices, Macclesfield, Cheshire, SK11 7NA, Tel.: 01625 665580

Community Midwifery
Mrs G Hopps, Winterton House, Winterton Way, Macclesfield, SK11 0LP, Tel.: 01625 421000

Community Nursing Services
Mrs M R Malkin, Lead Nurse/Locality Manager, Winterton House, Winterton Way, Macclesfield, Cheshire, SK11 0LP, Tel.: 01625 508300

District Nursing
Mrs M R Malkin, Lead Nurse, Winterton House, Winterton Way, Macclesfield, SK11 0LP, Tel.: 01625 508300

Equipment Loan Services
Mrs A Burns, Tel.: 01625 508300

Family Planning Services
Mr G Timson, Director of Operations, Winterton House, Winterton Way, Macclesfield, SK11 0LP, Tel.: 01625 508300
Mrs J Worrall, Winterton House, Winterton Way, Macclesfield, SK11 0LP, Tel.: 01625 421000

Health Visitors
Mrs M R Malkin, Lead Nurse, Winterton House, Winterton Way, Macclesfield, SK11 0LP, Tel.: 01625 508300

Liaison Services
Mr D Bailey, Discharge Liaison, Macclesfield District General Hospital, Tel.: 01625 661658
Mr N Bailey, Liaison, Criminal Justice, Tel.: 01625 421000 ext 3012
Ms E Burgess, Paediatric, Health Visitor, Macclesfield District General Hospital, Victoria Road, Macclesfield, SK10 3BL, Tel.: 01625 661012
Ms C Chasty, Discharge Liaison, Macclesfield District General Hospital, Tel.: 01625 661658
Ms L Naull, Discharge Liaison, Macclesfield District General Hospital, Victoria Road, Macclesfield, SK10 3BL,
Ms P Sinclair, Liaison Sister - General/Elderly, Macclesfield District General Hospital, Tel.: 01625 661440
Ms K Slater, Discharge Liaison, Macclesfield District General Hospital, Tel.: 01625 661658
Ms A Williamson, Tel.: 01625 421000 ext 1909

Other Services
Ms M Black, Residential Homes Team, Macclesfield District General Hospital, Victoria Road, Macclesfield, SK10 3BL, Tel.: 01625 421000 ext 1982
Ms W Brennan, Forensic Outreach, Macclesfield District General Hospital, Tel.: 01625 421000 ext 3012
Ms S Burrows, NHS Funded Nursing Care, Macclesfield District General Hospital, Tel.: 01625 421000 ext 1502
Ms E Churchman, NHS Funded Nursing Care, Macclesfield District General Hospital, Tel.: 01625 421000 ext 1502

Continuing Healthcare, Macclesfield District General Hospital, Tel.: 01625 421000
Ms C Hardy, Residential Homes Team, Macclesfield District General Hospital, Tel.: 01625 421000 ext 1982
Ms A Kelly, Primary Nurse Development Facilitator, Macclesfield District General Hospital, Tel.: 01625 421000 ext 1032
Ms C Mitchell, Residential Homes Team, Macclesfield District General Hospital, Tel.: 01625 421000 ext 1982
Ms J Nairn, Nurse Advisor Social Services, Macclesfield District General Hospital, Tel.: 01625 534858
Ms L Naul, Residential Homes Team, Macclesfield District General Hospital, Tel.: 01625 421000 ext 1982
Ms G Rooney, Rehab Link Team, Macclesfield District General Hospital, Tel.: 01625 421000
Ms E Smith, Rehab Project Co-ordinator, Macclesfield District General Hospital, Tel.: 01625 421000 ext 3137
Ms P Spray, Cardiac Rehab Team, Macclesfield District General Hospital, Tel.: 01625 421000
Ms E Stanmore, Rehab Project Co-ordinator, Macclesfield District General Hospital, Tel.: 01625 421000 ext 3137
Ms L Tronconi, Renal Dialysis, Macclesfield District General Hospital, Tel.: 01625 421000 ext 1855
Ms K Vernon, Community Neurology, Macclesfield District General Hospital, Tel.: 01625 421000 ext 1191
Ms M Webster, Intermediate Care, Macclesfield District General Hospital, Tel.: 01625 421000

Pharmacy
Mr C Gidman, 32 Park Green, PCT Offices, Maccalesfield, SK11 7NA,

School Nursing
Mrs M R Malkin, Lead Nurse, Winterton House, Winterton Way, Macclesfield, SK11 0LP, Tel.: 01625 508300

Specialist Nursing Services
Ms T Cohen, Continence, Macclesfield District General Hospital, Tel.: 01625 665555
Mrs S Green, Continence, Macclesfield District General Hospital, Tel.: 01625 665555
Ms J Bailey, Gynae/Oncology, Macclesfield District General Hospital, Tel.: 01625 421000 ext 3203
Ms L Tyler, TB, Sanders Square Clinic, Tel.: 01625 423800

Eden Valley Primary Care Trust

Trust Headquarters
8 Tynefield Drive
PENRITH, Cumbria
CA11 8JA
Tel.: 01768 245317
Fax.: 01768 245318

Child Health
Mrs G Riley, Senior Clinical Nurse, Eden Valley PCT HQ, 8 Tynefield Drive, Penrith, CA11 8JA, Tel.: 01768 245208

Child Health Records
Ms A Milican, Child Health Manager, Central Clinic, 50 Victoria Place, Carlisle, CA1 1HN, Tel.: 01228 603428

Child Protection/Safeguarding Children
Ms L Davison, Designated Nurse, Child Protection, Central Clinic, 50 Victoria Place, Carlisle, CA1 1HN, Tel.: 01228 603200/603244

Community Nursing Services
Miss H Burton, Director of Primary & Community Care Development Eden Valey PCT HQ, 8 Tynefield Drive, Penrith, CA11 8JA, Tel.: 01768 245329

District Nursing
Mrs G Riley, Senior Clinical Nurse, Eden Valley PCT HQ, 8 Tynefield Drive, Penrith, CA11 8JA, Tel.: 01768 245208

Family Planning Services
Ms S Lightfoot, Family Planning Manager, Central Clinic, 50 Victoria Place, Carlisle, CA1 1HN, Tel.: 01228 603200

North West Strategic Health Authority

Learning Disabilities
Mr P Robertson, Director of Learning Disabilities, Carlton Clinic, Carlisle, CA1 3SX, Tel.: 01228 602552

Other Services
Dr R Walker, Clinical Governance - Medical Director Health Services, 4 Wavell Drive, Rosehill, Carlisle, CA1 2SE, Tel.: 01228 602732

Pharmacy
Ms G Johnson, Pharmaceutical Advisor, Eden Valley PCT, 8 Tynefield Drive, Penrith, Cumbria, CA11 8JA, Tel.: 01768 245368

Specialist Nursing Services
Mrs A George, Nurse, CHD, Trust Headquarters, 8 Tynefield Drive, Penrith, Cumbria, CA11 8JA, Tel.: 01768 245317
Mr P Weaving, Nurse, Infection Control, Cumberland Infirmary, Carlisle, Tel.: 01228 523444
Mrs J Ferguson, Manager, Palliative Care, Palliative Care Offices, Workington Hospital, Workington, Tel.: 01900 602244 ext 2025

Ellesmere Port & Neston Primary Care Trust

Trust Headquarters
7-9 Civic Way
ELLESMERE PORT
CH65 0AX
Tel.: 0151 373 4900

Admin & Senior Management
Ms J Harvey, Chief Executive, 7-9 Civic Way, Ellesmere Port, CH65 0AX, Tel.: 0151 373 4900
Mr B Stamp, Director, Clinical Services & Quality, 7-9 Civic Way, Ellesmere Port, CH65 0AX, Tel.: 9151 373 4900

Child Health Records
Ms B Blundell, Upton Clinic, Weston Grove, Upton, Chester, CH2 1QJ, Tel.: 01244 381366
Ms A Venables, Upton Clinic, Weston Grove, Upton, Chester, CH2 1QJ, Tel.: 01244 381366

Child Protection/Safeguarding Children
Mrs T Rees, Child Protection, Moston Lodge, Countess of Chester Health Park, Liverpool Road, Chester, CH2 1UL, Tel.: 01244 364831

Clinical Leads (NSF)
Dr G Redmayne, Clinical Lead, Cancer,
Dr S Jeffery, Clinical Lead, CHD,
Dr D Smith, Clinical Lead, Diabetic Care,
Dr C Hiles, Clinical Lead, Older People,

District Nursing
Mrs L Spall, Facilitator, Primary Care, Stanney Lane Clinic, Stanney Lane, Ellesmere Port, L65 9AH, Tel.: 0151 355 2186

Specialist Nursing Services
Ms P O'Brien, Continence, Moston Lodge, Countess of Chester Health Park, Liverpool Road, Chester, CH2 1UL, Tel.: 01244 364740
Miss F Crowther, Macmillan, Hospice of the Good Shepherd, Gordon Lane, Backford, Chester, CH2 4DG, Tel.: 01244 851170
Mrs H Westwell, Macmillan, Hospice of the Good Shepherd, Gordon Lane, Backford, Chester, CH2 4DG, Tel.: 01244 851170

Fylde Primary Care Trust

Trust Headquarters
Derby Road, Wesham
KIRKHAM
PR4 3AL
Tel.: 01253 306305

Admin & Senior Management
Ms L Cawdell, Associate Director of Nursing, Tel.: 01253 306318
Ms J Goulding, Chief Executive, Fylde PCT, Derby Road, Wesham, Kirkham, PR4 3AL, Tel.: 01253 306305
Mr K Spencer, Director of Operations - Clinical & Operational Services, Fylde PCT, Derby Road, Wesham, Kirkham, PR4 3AL, Tel.: 01253 306557

Child Health
Child Health, Child Health Dept, Wesham Headquarters, Derby Road, Wesham, Tel.: 01253 306388

Child Health Records
Child Health Records, Fylde Trust HQ, Derby Road, Wesham Kirkham, PR4 3AL, Tel.: 01253 306305

Child Protection/Safeguarding Children
Mrs A Marquis-Carr, Named Nurse, Tel.: 01253 651267
Mrs C Turner, Designated Nurse, Tel.: 01253 651262

Clinical Leads (NSF)
Dr R Thorpe, Clinical Lead, Cancer,
Mrs C Isherwood, Clinical Lead, Care of the Elderly,
Dr M Reid, Clinical Lead, CHD,
Dr K McLennan, Clinical Lead, Diabetic Care,

Community Matrons
Ms J Cairns, St Annes Clinic, Tel.: 01253 651410
Ms C Hay Thorntwaite, Freckleton Health Centre, Tel.: 01253 657221
Ms J Jackson, St Annes Clinic, Tel.: 01253 651410
Ms S Killeen, Kirkgate Centre,
Ms M Walker, St Annes Clinic, Tel.: 01253 651410

Community Nursing Services
Mrs L Edwell, Head of Adult Nursing Services, Fylde Trust HQ, Derby Road, Wesham Kirkham, PR4 3AL, Tel.: 01253 651564
Mrs S Greenwood, Head of Children & Family Services, Fylde Trust HQ, Derby Road, Wesham Kirkham, PR4 3AL, Tel.: 01253 651567
Mrs C A Isherwood, Assistant Director Clinical Services, Fylde Trust HQ, Derby Road, Wesham Kirkham, PR4 3AL, Tel.: 01253 651562

HIV/AIDS
Ms S Potts, HIV/Aids, Tel.: 01253 303236

Learning Disabilities
Mrs D Robinson, Integrated Service Manager (LD), Tel.: 01253 888735

Liaison Services
Ms B Etheridge, Paediatric Health Visitor Liaison, Victoria Hospital, Whinney Heys Road, Blackpool, Tel.: 01253 306680
Health Visitor Liaison, Womens Unit, Victoria Hospital, Whinney Heys Road, Blackpool, Tel.: 01253 306680

Other Services
Homecare Advisory Team, Trinity Hospice, Tel.: 01253 358881

Pharmacy
Mr G Atkinson, Director of Modernisation & Pharmacy, Fylde Trust HQ, Derby Road, Wesham Kirkham, PR4 3AL, Tel.: 01253 306305

Specialist Nursing Services
Ms C Turner, Breast Care, Victoria Hospital, Blackpool, Tel.: 01253 300000
Ms J Sheridan, Colorectal, Victoria Hospital, Blackpool, Tel.: 01253 300000
Mr F Booth, Head, Continence, Windmill Mews, Whitegate Drive, Blackpool, Tel.: 01253 655282
Mrs S Wignall, Paediatric, Continence, Windmill Mews, Whitegate Drive, Blackpool, Tel.: 01253 655311
Ms J Bellis, Diabetic Care, - Adults, Victoria Hospital, Blackpool, Tel.: 01253 300000
Ms K Bierne, Paediatric, Diabetic Care, Tel.: 01253 303312
Ms S Singleton, Paediatric, Diabetic Care, Tel.: 01253 303312
Ms T Cross, Infection Control, Fylde PCT, Derby Road, Wesham, Tel.: 01253 306328
Mr R Cardwell, Specialist Health Visitor, TB, Bispham Clinic, Devonshire Road, Blackpool, Tel.: 01253 352203
Ms G Broadbent, Tissue Viability, Tel.: 01253 300000

Halton Primary Care Trust

Trust Headquarters, Victoria House
The Holloway
RUNCORN, Cheshire
WA7 4TH
Tel.: 01928 790404

North West Strategic Health Authority

Admin & Senior Management
Ms H Dover, Director of Health & Social Care/Lead Nurse, Victoria House, Holloway, Runcorn, WA7 4TH, Tel.: 01928 593651
Child Health
Mrs D Roberts, School & Young People Services Manager, Highfield Clinic, Highfield Road, Widnes, Cheshire, WA8 7DJ, Tel.: 0151 420 4691
Child Health Records
Ms K Worthington, Pre-School Services Manager, Kingsway Health Centre, Widnes, WA8 7QE, Tel.: 0151 424 3055
Child Protection/Safeguarding Children
Mr C Whelan, Senior Nurse, Child Protection, Kingsway Health Centre, Kingsway, Widnes, WA8 7QE, Tel.: 0151 495 1579
Clinical Leads (NSF)
Ms H Smith, Head of Adult Services, Victoria House, Holloway, Runcorn, WA7 4TH, Tel.: 01928 593684
Mrs L Spooner, Professional Development Manager, Victoria House, Holloway, Runcorn, WA7 4TH, Tel.: 01928 593640
Community Midwifery
Mrs C Casey-Hardman, Head of Midwifery, Highfield Hopsital, Highfield Road, Widnes, WA8 7DQ, Tel.: 0151 424 2103
Community Nursing Services
Mr Malley, Community Services Manager, Victoria House, Holloway, Runcorn, WA7 4TH, Tel.: 01928 593692
Ms H Smith, Head of Adult Services, Victoria House, Holloway, Runcorn, WA7 4TH, Tel.: 01928 593684
Ms K Worthington, Pre-School Services Manager, Kingsway Health Centre, Widnes, WA8 7QE, Tel.: 0151 424 3055
District Nursing
Mr N Malley, Community Services Manager, Victoria House, Holloway, Runcorn, WA7 4TH, Tel.: 01928 593692
Ms K Worthington, Pre-School Services Manager, Kingsway Health Centre, Widnes, WA8 7QE, Tel.: 0151 424 3055
Family Planning Services
Mrs D Roberts, Family Planning Services, Highfleld Clinic, Highfield Road, Widnes, WA8 7DJ, Tel.: 0151 420 4691
Learning Disabilities
Lead Nurse, Learning Disabilities, The Bridges Learning Centre, Crow Wood Health Park, Crow Wood Lane, Widnes, WA8 3LZ, Tel.: 0151 420 7619
Liaison Services
Mr N Malley, Community Nurse Manager, Victoria House, Holloway, Runcorn, WA7 4TH, Tel.: 01928 593692
Pharmacy
Ms N Hayes, Pharmaceutical Advisor, Victoria House, Holloway, Runcorn, WA7 4TH, Tel.: 01928 790404
School Nursing
Mrs D Roberts, School & Young People Services Manager, Highfield Clinic, Highfield Road, Widnes, Cheshire, WA8 7DJ, Tel.: 0151 420 4691
Smoking Cessation
Mrs L Spooner, Professional Development Manager, Victoria House, Holloway, Runcorn, WA7 4TH, Tel.: 01928 593640

Heywood & Middleton Primary Care Trust

Trust Headquarters, London House
Oldham Road
MIDDLETON
M24 1AY
Tel.: 0161 643 6900

Admin & Senior Management
Mrs K Hurley, Associate Director of Clinical Services, Tel.: 0161 655 1590
Ms C Pollard, Director of Clinical Services, Tel.: 0161 655 1590
Mr K Surgeon, Chief Executive,

Child Health
Ms B Yarwood, Clinical Leader Children & Young People, Langley Clinic, Borrowdale Road, Tel.: 0161 251 8338
Child Health Records
Child Health Dept, Telegraph House, 3rd Floor, Tel.: 01706 652891
Child Protection/Safeguarding Children
Ms P Fraser, Named Nurse, Child Protection, Ings Lane Clinic, Phoenix Street, Rochdale, OL12 7DW, Tel.: 01706 702197
Ms L Mirabitur, Designated Nurse, Child Protection, Ings Lane Clinic, Phoenix Street, Rochdale, OL12 7DW, Tel.: 01706 702197
Clinical Leads (NSF)
Ms J Challender, Clinical Lead, Cancer,
Liaison Services
Mrs J Reid, Liaison, Paediatric, Thor Med/TB, Health Visitor, Tel.: 01706 757178
Mrs E T Thompson, Liaison, Paediatric, Thor Med/TB, Health Visitor, Tel.: 01706 757178
Other Services
Ms J Hany, Clinical Leader Public Health, Langley Clinic, Borrowdale Road, Tel.: 0161 251 8339
Ms E Stanton, Clinical Leader Older People Services, Langley Clinic, Borrowdale Road, Tel.: 0161 251 8336
Specialist Nursing Services
Mr S Pinnington, Clinical Nurse Specialist, Langley Clinic, Borrowdale Road, Langley, Middleton, M24 1AY, Tel.: 0161 251 8320
Mrs L Walsh, Clinical Nurse Specialist, Langley Clinic, Borrowdale Road, Langley, Middleton, M24 1AY, Tel.: 0161 251 8320
Mrs B Willis, Clinical Nurse Specialist, Langley Clinic, Borrowdale Road, Langley, Middleton, M24 1AY, Tel.: 0161 251 8320
Mrs B Wragg, Clinical Nurse Specialist, Langley Clinic, Borrowdale Road, Langley, Middleton, M24 1AY, Tel.: 0161 251 8320
Mrs V Orr, CHD, Yorkshire Street Surgery, Rochdale, Tel.: 01706 702089
Mrs J Ridley, CHD, Yorkshire Street Surgery, Rochdale, Tel.: 01706 702089
Mrs M Chadwick, Nurse Specialist, Continence, Darnhill Clinic, Tel.: 01706 702203/2/1
Ms L Connolly, Nurse Specialist, Continence, Darnhill Clinic, Tel.: 01706 702203
Ms C Grange, Nurse Specialist, Continence, Darnhill Clinic, Tel.: 01706 702203
Ms R Crowther, Discharge, Lead Nurse, Continuing Care, St James Place, Rochdale, Tel.: 01706 708021
Mrs A Blood, Specialist Team, Diabetic Care, Birch Hill Hospital, Tel.: 01706 754043/754042
Mrs S Greenwood, Diabetic Care, Birch Hill Hospital, Tel.: 01706 754043/754042
Mrs K Roberts, Diabetic Care, Birch Hill Hospital, Tel.: 01706 754043/754042
Mrs K Saleem, Diabetic Care, Birch Hill Hospital, Tel.: 01706 754043/754042
Ms J Bagshaw, Nurse, Epilepsy, Taylor Street Clinic, Tel.: 01706 702240
Mr P Lavin, Co-ordinator, Intermediate Care, Tudor Court, Heywood, Tel.: 01706 694530
Mrs J Sedgwick, Lead Cancer Nurse, Palliative Care, Langley Clinic, Borrowdale Road, Langley, Middleton, M24 1AY, Tel.: 0161 251 8320
Ms J Charlton, Nurse Specialist, Stoma Care, Darnhill Clinic, Tel.: 01706 702208
Mrs S Fisher, Nurse, Tissue Viability, Whitworth Clinic, Brenbar Crescent, Whitworth, OL12 9JP, Tel.: 01706 855200

North West Strategic Health Authority

Hyndburn & Ribble Valley Primary Care Trust
Trust Headquarters, Red Rose Court
Clayton Business Park, Clayton-le-Moors
ACCRINGTON
Lancs
BB5 5JR
Tel.: 01254 380400

Admin & Senior Management
Mrs E Dean, Assistant Director of Service Provision (Operational Services), Accrington Victoria Community Hospital, Haywood Road, Accrington, Lancashire, BB5 6AS, Tel.: 01254 358010
Mrs B Hilton, Director of Service Provision, PCT Headquarters, Red Rose Court, Clayton Business Park, Clayton-le-Moors, Accrington, BB5 5JR, Tel.: 01254 380400
Mr D McDonough, Assistant Director of Service Provision, Clitheroe Health Centre, Railway View Road, Clitheroe, BB7 2JG, Tel.: 01200 425171

Child Health
Ms L Maguire, Modern Matron, Great Harwood, Tel.: 01254 886155
Ms E McGladdery, Modern Matron, Ribble Valley, Tel.: 01200 421827
Ms L Moore, Acting Modern Matron, Great Harwood, Tel.: 01254 886155
Mrs B Taylor, Modern Matron, Accrington, Tel.: 01254 358030

Child Health Records
Child Health Records, Red Rose Court, Clayton Business Park, Clayton-le-Moors, Accrington, BB5 5JR, Tel.: 01254 380400

Child Protection/Safeguarding Children
Child Protection, Hyndburn Locality Offices, Accrington Victoria Hospital, Accrington, BB5 6AS, Tel.: 01254 359049

Clinical Leads (NSF)
Mrs L Stevenson, Clinical Lead, Cancer, East Lancashire Hospice, Tel.: 01254 342806
Mrs B Waddell, Clinical Lead, Care of the Elderly, Tel.: 01200 420669
Dr C Ward, Clinical Lead, CHD, Trust Headquarters, Tel.: 01254 380400
Mrs S Watson, Clinical Lead, Children, Trust Headquarters, Tel.: 01254 380400
Dr A Crowther, Clinical Lead, Diabetic Care, Trust Headquarters, Tel.: 01254 380400

Community Nursing Services
Mrs E Dean, Assistant Director of Service Provision (Operational Services), Accrington Victoria Community Hospital, Haywood Road, Accrington, Lancashire, BB5 6AS, Tel.: 01254 358010

District Nursing
Ms L Maguire, Modern Matron, Great Harwood, Tel.: 01254 886155
Ms E McGladdery, Modern Matron, Ribble Valley, Tel.: 01200 421827
Ms L Moore, Acting Modern Matron, Great Harwood, Tel.: 01254 886155
Mrs B Taylor, Modern Matron, Accrington, Tel.: 01254 358030

Equipment Loan Services
Mrs L Bracken, Park Lee Hospital, Park Lee Road, Blackburn, Tel.: 01254 342800

Learning Disabilities
Mr M Corrighan, Assistant Director of Service Provision, Bridge House, Whalley Banks, Blackburn, Lancashire, BB2 1NT, Tel.: 01254 695698

Liaison Services
Mrs C Evans, Liaison & Hospital at Home, Queens Park Hospital, Haslingden Road, Blackburn, Lancs, Tel.: 01254 294917

Pharmacy
Mrs L Rogan, Trust Headquarters, Tel.: 01254 380400

Smoking Cessation
Mrs N Parkes, Smoking Cessation, Accrington Victoria Community Hospital, Accrington, BB5 6AS, Tel.: 01254 294727

Specialist Nursing Services
Mrs R Trainer, Specialist, Continence, Accrington Victoria Community Hospital, Accrington, BB5 6AS, Tel.: 01254 359129
Mrs B Waddell, Nurse Consultant, Older People, Clitheroe Community Hospital, Tel.: 01200 420669
Mrs L Stevenson, Manager, Palliative Care, East Lancashire Hospice, Park Lee Road, Blackburn, Tel.: 01254 342806

Knowsley Primary Care Trust
Trust Headquarters, Nutgrove Villa
PO Box 23, Westmoreland Road
HUYTON
Merseyside
L36 6GA
Tel.: 0151 443 4900

Admin & Senior Management
Ms B Celik, Nursing Services Manager, Beech House, Park Road, L34 3LN, Tel.: 0151 426 8703
Mrs Chalmers, Case Management Project Lead, Poplar House, Poplar Bank, Huyton, L36 9US, Tel.: 0151 443 2873
Ms A Marsland, Chief Executive, Nutgrove Villa, Westmorland Road, Huyton, L36 6GA, Tel.: 0151 443 4900
Mrs E Sage, Head of Nursing, Beech House, Prescot, L34 3LN, Tel.: 0151 426 8703

Child Health Records
Child Health Records, Prescot Clinic, Park Road, Merseyside, L34 3LN, Tel.: 0151 289 0904

Child Protection/Safeguarding Children
Ms J Powell, Cllinical Lead for Looked after Children, Quality Assurance Unit, 45 William Roberts Avenue, Westvale, Kirkby, Knowsley, L32 0UQ, Tel.: 0151 443 4108
Mrs T Drew, Designated Nurse, Child Protection, Quality Assurance Unit, 45 William Roberts Avenue, Kirkby, L32 0UQ, 0151 443 4216
Ms A Jennings, Named Nurse, Child Protection, 45 William Roberts Avenue, Kirkby, L32 0UQ,

Clinical Leads (NSF)
Mrs L Bacon, Clinical Lead, Health Visiting, Prescot Locality Centre, 16 Park Road, Prescot, L34 3LR, Tel.: 0151 477 4788
Mrs B Carr, Clinical Lead, Health Visiting, Prescot Locality Centre, 16 Park Road, Prescot, L34 3LR, Tel.: 0151 477 4772
Mrs K Jones, Clinical Lead, Specialist Nursing, Prescot Locality Centre, 16 Park Road, Prescot, L34 3LR, Tel.: 0151 477 4775
Ms J Lawrenson, Clinical Lead, District Nursing (Acting), Prescot Locality Centre, 16 Park Road, Prescot, L34 3LR, Tel.: 0151 477 4789
Mrs P Thomas, Clinical Lead, School Nursing, Prescot Locality Centre, 16 Park Road, Prescot, L34 3LR, Tel.: 0151 477 4809
Dr L Gaulton, Clinical Lead, CHD, Diabetes,

Community Nursing Services
Mrs R Green, Out of Hours Team Leader, Henley House, Delph Lane, Whiston, Prescot, L35 7JE,
Ms J Lambe, Out of Hours Team Leader, Henley House, Delph Lane, Whiston, Prescot, L35 7JE,
Mrs R McKiernan, Out of Hours Team Leader, Henley House, Delph Lane, Whiston, Prescot, L35 7JE,
Ms M Stoddern, Out of Hours Team Leader, Henley House, Delph Lane, Whiston, Prescot, L35 7JE,

Health Visitors
Mrs L Dowling, Health Visitor for Children with Disability,
Ms K Hornshaw, Accident Prevention, Health Visitor, Poplar House, Poplar Bank, Huyton, L36 9US, Tel.: 0151 443 2875
Mrs C Williams, Drugs Health Visitor (Knowsley), Stockbridge Village Health Centre, Waterpark Drive, Stockbridge Village, Tel.: 0151 449 3950

North West Strategic Health Authority

Learning Disabilities
Mrs J Lee, 16 Park Road, Prescot, L34 3LR, Tel.: 0151 477 4778
Liaison Services
Mrs M Mackenzie, District Nurse Hospital/Community & Team
Leader Elderly, Henley House, Delph Lane, Whiston, Prescot, L35
7JE, Tel.: 0151 290 2030
Mr R F Waddington, Team Leader, Whiston Family Centre, Old
Colliery Road, Whiston, Merseyside, L35 3SX, Tel.: 0151 292 0104
Smoking Cessation
Mrs C Williams, Drugs Health Visitor (Knowsley), Stockbridge Village
Health Centre, Waterpark Drive, Stockbridge Village, Tel.: 0151 449
3950
Specialist Nursing Services
Mrs P Jones, Nurse Immunisation Co-ordinator/Nurse Prescribing
Lead, Prescot Locality Centre, 16 Park Road, Prescot, L34 3LR, Tel.:
0151 477 4789
Mr G Hirons, Nurse, Infection Control, Whiston Health Centre, Old
Colliery Road, Whiston, L35 3SX, Tel.: 0151 292 3519
Mrs G Harthen, Team Leader, Macmillan, Willowbrook Hospice,
Portico Lane, L34 2QT, Tel.: 0151 431 0156
Ms Z Keating, Macmillan, Clinical Nurse Specialist, Palliative Care,
Willowbrook Hospice, Portico Lane, L34 2QT, Tel.: 0151 431 0156
Mrs H Mack, Macmillan, Clinical Nurse Specialist, Palliative Care,
Willowbrook Hospice, Portico Lane, L34 2QT, Tel.: 0151 431 0156
Ms J Parr, Macmillan, Clinical Nurse Specialist, Palliative Care,
Willowbrook Hospice, Portico Lane, L34 2QT, Tel.: 0151 431 0156
Mr G Prince, Macmillan, Clinical Nurse Specialist, Palliative Care,
Willowbrook Hospice, Portico Lane, L34 2QT, Tel.: 0151 431 0156
Ms A Watson, Macmillan, Clinical Nurse Specialist, Palliative Care,
Willowbrook Hospice, Portico Lane, L34 2QT, Tel.: 0151 431 0156

Lancashire Care NHS Trust

Trust Headquarters, Sceptre Point
Sceptre Way, Walton Summit, Bamber Bridge
PRESTON
PR5 6AW
Tel.: 01772 695360

Learning Disabilities
Community Service Team - Central Lancs, 93 Garstang Road,
Preston, PR1 1LD, Tel.: 01772 401200
Ms D Langford, Head of Service, Central Lancs, 19 Stanleyfield
Road, Preston, PR1 1QL, Tel.: 01772 401127
Southport & Formby, Patterson Unit, Hesketh Centre, 51/55 Albert
Road, Southport, PR9 0LT, Tel.: 01704 383029
Supported Living Service, Central Lancs, 19 Stanleyfield Road,
Preston, PR1 1QL, Tel.: 01772 401135
West Lancashire, Greetby Buildings, Derby Street, Ormskirk, L39
2BP, Tel.: 01695 585845
Other Services
Ms N Armitage, Assistant Network Director - Fylde Coast, Substance
Misuse,
Ms D Bretherton, Assistant Network Director- Central & West
Lancashire, Substance Misuse,
Community Alcohol Team Preston, Preston CAT, 8-9 Fox Street,
Preston, PR1 3RG, Tel.: 01772 561300
Ms J Dunn, Team Manager, West Lancashire Criminal Justice Team,
75 Westgate, Sandy Lane, Skelmersdale, WN8 8LP, Tel.: 01695
50740
Ms J Dunn, Team Manager, West Lancashire Community Drug &
Alcohol Team, 75 Westgate, Sandy Lane, Skelmersdale, WN8 8LP,
Tel.: 01695 50740
Ms S Eames, Team Manager, Blackburn with Darwen, Hyndburn &
Ribble Valley, Community Drug & Alcohol Team, Reid House, 61-63
Preston New Road, Blackburn, Lancs, BB2 6AY, Tel.: 01254 225000
Ms A Grimshaw, Team Manager, Substance Misuse - Preston
Community Drug Team, Appley House, Appleby Street, Preston,
PR1 1HX, Tel.: 01772 406923

Ms K Hall, Assistant Network Director - Burnley, Pendle &
Rossendale, Substance Misuse,
Homeless Team & Smile YPS, & Criminal Justice Team Preston, 5
Camden Place, Winckley Square, Preston, PR7 2SJ, Tel.: 01772
556979
Ms L Hopkins, Assistant Network Director - Blackburn with Darwen,
Hyndburn & Ribble Valley, Substance Misuse,
Mr C Lee, Team Manager, Blackburn with Darwen, Hyndburn &
Ribble Valley, Criminal Justice Team, 28 Penny Street, Blackburn,
BB2 6AY,
Ms A Macintosh, Team Manager, Blackpool & Fylde Community
Drug & Alcohol Teams, Hope House, 162 Whitegate Drive,
Blackpool, FY3 9HG, Tel.: 01253 699884
Ms A Macintosh, Team Manager, Blackpool & Fylde Criminal Justice
& Needle Exchange Service, Hope House, 162 Whitegate Drive,
Blackpool, FY3 9HG, Tel.: 01253 699884
Ms M O'Neill, Team Manager, Chorley & South Ribble Community
Drug Team, 14 West Street, Chorley, PR7 2SJ, Tel.: 01257 230452
Ms M O'Neill, Team Manager, Chorley & South Ribble Criminal
Justice Team, 14 West Street, Chorley, PR7 2SJ, Tel.: 01257
230452
Ms D Rapley, Team Manager, Burnley Commulnity Drug Team &
Criminal Justice Team, 60-62 Westgate, Burnley, BB1 1RY, Tel.:
01282 432345
Mr H Thistlethwaite, Team Manager, Leyland Community Drug &
Alcohol Team, 6 Golden Hill Lane, Leyland, PR25 3NP, Tel.: 01772
773540
Mr H Thistlethwaite, Team Manager, Leyland Criminal Justice
Service, 6 Golden Hill Lane, Leyland, PR25 3NP, Tel.: 01772
773540
Ms C Wickham, Team Manager, Pendle & Rossendale Substance
Misuse Service, 60-62 Westgate, Burnley, BB1 1RY, Tel.: 01282
432345

Lancashire Teaching Hospitals NHS Trust

Trust Headquarters, Royal Preston Hospital
Sharoe Green Lane North
FULWOOD
PR2 9HT
Tel.: 01772 716565

Community Midwifery
Action Line, Chorley & South Ribble District General Hospital,
Preston Road, Chorley, PR7 1PP, Tel.: 01257 245193
Mrs C Bell, Director of Midwifery Services, Sharoe Green Hospital,
Sharoe Green, Fulwood, Preston, Lancashire, PR1 4DU, Tel.: 01772
524395
Emergencies, Sharoe Green Hospital, Sharoe Green, Fulwood,
Preston, Lancashire, PR1 4DU, Tel.: 01772 524495
Mrs L Holding, Clinical Manager, Women's Health, Chorley & South
Ribble District General Hospital, Preston Road, Chorley, PR7 1PP,
Tel.: 01257 245120
Messages, Chorley & South Ribble District General Hospital, Preston
Road, Chorley, PR7 1PP, Tel.: 01257 245109
Mr C Porter, Clinical Manager, Sharoe Green Hospital, Sharoe
Green, Fulwood, Preston, Lancashire, PR1 4DU, Tel.: 01772 524219

Liverpool Women's Hospital NHS Trust

Trust Headquarters, Crown Street
LIVERPOOL
L8 7SS
Tel.: 0151 708 9988
Fax.: 0151 702 4028

Admin & Senior Management
Mr R Dunmor, Deputy Directorate Manager Obstetric, Liverpool
Women's Hospital,

North West Strategic Health Authority

Child Protection/Safeguarding Children
Ms C O'Keeffe, Specialist Midwife/Lead, Child Protection, Antenatal Clinic Area, Liverpool Women's Hospital, Crown Street, L8 7SS, Tel.: 0151 702 4367

Community Midwifery
Mr D Akeju, Specialist Midwife - Haemoglobinopathy, Community Office Antenatal Area, Liverpool Women's Hospital, Crown Street, L8 7SS, Tel.: 0151 702 4175

Centre for Women's Health, Aintree Centre for Women's Health, Lower Lane, Aintree, Liverpool, L9 7AL, Tel.: 0151 529 3754

Emergencies, Aintree Centre for Women's Health, Lower Lane, Aintree, Liverpool, L9 7AL, Tel.: 0151 529 3425

Emergencies, Liverpool Women's Hospital, Crown Street, Liverpool, L8 7SS, Tel.: 0151 708 9988

Mrs C Finnegan, Obstetrics Manager, Liverpool Women's Hospital, Crown Street, Liverpool, L8 7SS, Tel.: 0151 702 4325

Ms C O'Keeffe, Drug Liaison Midwife, Antenatal Clinic Area, Liverpool Women's Hospital, Crown Street, L8 7SS, Tel.: 0151 702 4367

Mrs S Shannon, Deputy Director of Nursing & Midwifery, Liverpool Women's Hospital, Crown Street, Liverpool, L8 7SS, 0151 702 4030

Ms S Thompson, Specialist Midwife - Teenage Pregnancies, Xray Dept, Liverpool Women's Hospital, Crown Street, L8 7SS, Tel.: 0151 702 4223

Ms C Umbers, Acting Services Manager, Aintree Centre for Women's Health, Lower Lane, Aintree, Liverpool, L9 7AL, Tel.: 0151 529 3301

Ms L Wood, Specialist Midwife - Specialist Clinics, Xray Dept, Liverpool Women's Hospital, Crown Street, L8 7SS, 0151 702 4223

Family Planning Services
Ms C Farrel, Mersey Region Group, Family Planning Training, Liverpool Women's Hospital, Crown Street, L8 7SS, Tel.: 0151 702 4102

Liaison Services
Patient Advice & Liaison Manager, Ground Floor, Liverpool Women's Hospital, Crown Street, Liverpool, L8 7SS, Tel.: 0151 702 4353

Other Services
Ms B Webster, Infection Control Officer, Liverpool Women's Hospital, Crown Street, L8 7SS, Tel.: 0151 702 4014

Mersey Care NHS Trust

Trust Headquarters, Hamilton House
24 Pall Mall
LIVERPOOL
L3 6AL
Tel.: 0151 250 3000

Learning Disabilities
Mr M Barwood, Director of Nursing, Ashworth Hospital, Parkbourn, Maghull, L31 1DL, Tel.: 0151 473 0303

Mrs I Byrne-Watts, Service Manager, Learning Disabilities Directorate, Olive Mount Mansion, Old Mill Lane, Liverpool, L15 8LW, Tel.: 0151 737 4800

Mid Cheshire Hospitals NHS Trust

Trust Headquarters, Leighton Hospital
Middlewich Road, Leighton
CREWE
Cheshire
CW1 4QJ
Tel.: 01270 255141
Fax.: 01270 587696

Acute Specialist Nursing Services
Ms J Baker, Macmillan Nurse, Breast Care, Leighton Hospital,
Ms M Buttle, Macmillan Nurse, Breast Care, Leighton Hospital,
Mrs J Murray, Macmillan Nurse, Breast Care, Leighton Hospital,

Ms A Dye, Specialist Nurse, Dermatology, Leighton Hospital, Tel.: 01270 612542

Ms N Lawson, Specialist Nurse, Dermatology, Leighton Hospital, Tel.: 01270 612542

Ms K Yardley, Community Liaison Manager, Elderly Care, Leighton Hospital, Tel.: 01270 255141ext 3025

Ms K Egan, SVCS Manager, Lead Nurse, Infection Control, Leighton Hospital, Tel.: 01270 613149

Ms R Lea, Liaison & Development Nurse, Infection Control, Leigton Hospital, Tel.: 01270 613149

Ms A Proctor, Clinical Nurse Specialist, Infection Control, Leighton Hospital, Tel.: 01270 613149

Mrs S Walsh, Specialist Nurse, Tissue Viability, - Wound Care, Leighton Hospital, Tel.: 01270 612041

Ms D Owen, Specialist Nurse, Urology, Leighton Hospital, Tel.: 01270 255141

Child Health Records
Ms K Baker, Directorate Manager, Paediatrics, Leighton Hospital, Tel.: 01270 255141 ext 2292

Child Protection/Safeguarding Children
Ms S Gardner, Child Protection, Leighton Hospital, Tel.: 01270 255141

Ms K Baker, Directorate Manager, Paediatrics, Leighton Hospital, Tel.: 01270 255141 ext 2292

Community Midwifery
Mrs D Bailey, Directorate Manager/Head of Midwifery, Mid Cheshire Women's Health Unit, Leighton Hospital, Tel.: 01270 612145

Emergencies, Mid Cheshire Women's Health Unit, Leighton Hospital, Tel.: ext 2144

Mrs B Pennington, Director of Nursing, Leighton Hospital, Middlewich Road, Crewe, CW1 4QJ, Tel.: 01270 612352

Mrs S Taylor, Deputy Head of Midwifery, Mid Cheshire Women's Health Unit, Leighton Hospital, Tel.: 01270 612182

Women's Health Unit, Referrals, Mid Cheshire Women's Health Unit, Leighton Hospital, Tel.: 01270 612282

Discharge Co-ordinators
Ms K Yardley,

Equipment Loan Services
Mr C Cadwallader, Director of Estates & Facilities, Leighton Hospital, Tel.: 01270 612300

Liaison Services
Ms K Yardley,

Matrons/Modern Matrons
Ms M Morgan, Victoria Infirmary, Modern Matron, Victoria Infirmary, Tel.: 01606 564000

Mr J David, Modern Matron, A&E, Leighton Hospital, Tel.: 01270 255141

Ms H Nutuns, Modern Matron, Head & Neck, Leighton Hospital, Tel.: 01270 255141

Ms P Pordes, Modern Matron, Medicine, Leighton Hospital, Tel.: 01270 255141

Ms D Owen, Modern Matron, Obstetrics & Gynae, Leighton Hospital, Tel.: 01270 255141

Ms S Taylor, Modern Matron, Obstetrics & Gynae, Leighton Hospital, Tel.: 01270 255141

Ms S Banks, Modern Matron, Orthopaedics, Leighton Hospital, Tel.: 01270 255141

Ms L Jones, Modern Matron, Paediatrics, Leighton Hospital, Tel.: 01270 255141

Ms C Leech, Modern Matron, Surgical, Leighton Hospital, Tel.: 01270 255141

Ms S Mann, Modern Matron, Treatment Centre, Leighton Hospital, Tel.: 01270 255141

Paediatric Liaison Health Visitors
Ms K Baker, Directorate Manager, Paediatrics, Leighton Hospital, Tel.: 01270 255141 ext 2292

North West Strategic Health Authority

Morecambe Bay Hospitals NHS Trust
Trust Headquarters, Westmorland General Hospital
Burton Road
KENDAL, Cumbria
LA9 7RG
Tel.: 01539 795366

Acute Specialist Nursing Services
Ms D Macaulay, CAPD, Specialist Nurse, Furness General Hospital, Tel.: 01229 870870

Ms S Willis, CAPD, Specialist Nurse, Furness General Hospital, Tel.: 01229 870870

Ms L Jolly, Specialist Nurse, Acute Pain, Royal Lancaster Infirmary, Tel.: 01524 65944

Ms V Guy, Specialist Nurse, Anti-Coagulation, Royal Lancaster Infirmary, Tel.: 01524 65944

Ms K Lynn, Specialist Nurse, Anti-Coagulation, Royal Lancaster Infirmary, Tel.: 01524 65944

Ms L Troughton, Pre-Op Nurse Practitioners, Assessment, Furness General Hospital, Tel.: 01229 870870

Ms C Brearley, Macmillan, Nurse Specialist, Breast Care, Royal Lancaster Infirmary, Tel.: 01524 65944

Ms L Calvert, Macmillan, Nurse Specialist, Breast Care, Furness General Hospital, Tel.: 01229 870870

Ms J Eltherington, Macmillan, Nurse Specialist, Breast Care, Royal Lancaster Infirmary, Tel.: 01524 65944

Ms C Fox, Macmillan, Nurse Specialist, Breast Care, Westmorland General Hospital, Tel.: 01539 732288

Ms M Turner, Macmillan, Nurse Specialist, Breast Care, Royal Lancaster Infirmary, Tel.: 01524 65944

Ms J Whitton, Macmillan, Nurse Specialist, Breast Care, Furness General Hospital, Tel.: 01229 870870

Ms J Bates, Clinical Trials, Cancer, Royal Lancaster Infirmary, Tel.: 01524 65944

Ms C Tibke, Clinical Trials, Cancer, Royal Lancaster Infirmary, Tel.: 01524 65944

Ms S Bullock, Specialist Nurse, Cardiac Rehabilitation, Royal Lancaster Infirmary, Tel.: 01524 65944

Ms A Hicks, Specialist Nurse, Cardiac Rehabilitation, Furness General Hospital, Tel.: 01229 870870

Ms Y Horne, Specialist Nurse, Cardiac Rehabilitation, Furness General Hospital, Tel.: 01229 870870

Ms G Impey, Specialist Nurse, Cardiac Rehabilitation, Westmorland General Hospital, Tel.: 01539 732288

Ms H Preston, Specialist Nurse, Cardiac Rehabilitation, Royal Lancaster Infirmary, Tel.: 01524 65944

Ms S Tudor Beard, Specialist Nurse, Cardiac Rehabilitation, Furness General Hospital, Tel.: 01229 870870

Ms C Hughes, Specialist Nurse, Chronic Pain, Royal Lancaster Infirmary, Tel.: 01524 65944

Ms E Jenta, Surgical Practitioner, Colorectal, Royal Lancaster Infirmary, Tel.: 01524 65944

Ms C Pennington, Surgical Practitioner, Colorectal, Royal Lancaster Infirmary, Tel.: 01524 65944

Ms L Pickles, Specialist Nurse, Colorectal, Royal Lancaster Infirmary, Tel.: 01524 65944

Ms J Scothern, Specialist Nurse, Colorectal, Royal Lancaster Infirmary, Tel.: 01524 65944

Ms S Thompson, Specialist Nurse, Colorectal, Furness General Hospital, Tel.: 01229 870870

Ms B Allton, Clinical Nurse Specialist, Gynae/Oncology, Royal Lancaster Infirmary, Tel.: 01524 65944

Ms S Askew, Nurse Specialist, Infection Control, Furness General Hospital, Tel.: 01229 870870

Ms L Dodrell, I, Nurse Specialist, Infection Control, Royal Lancaster Infirmary, Tel.: 01524 65944

Ms S Pratt, Nurse Specialist, Infection Control, Westmorland General Hospital, Tel.: 01539 732288

Ms D Coman, Specialist, Lung Cancer, Royal Lancaster Infirmary, Tel.: 01524 65944

Ms C Palmer, Specialist, Lung Cancer, Furness General Hospital, Tel.: 01229 870870

Ms M Smith, Specialist Nurse, Lymphoedema, Furness General Hospital, Tel.: 01229 870870

Ms H Williams, Specialist Nurse, Lymphoedema, Royal Lancaster Infirmary, Tel.: 01524 65944

Ms P Brier, Surgical Practitioner, Orthopaedics, Royal Lancaster Infirmary, Tel.: 01524 65944

Ms J Denney, Macmillan, Nurse Specialist, Palliative Care, Westmorland General Hospital, Tel.: 01539 732288

Mr G Kenyon, Macmillan, Palliative Care, Royal Lancaster Infirmary, Tel.: 01524 65944

Ms J Turner, Macmillan, Specialist Nurse, Palliative Care, Furness General Hospital, Tel.: 01229 870870

Ms J Wharton, Macmillan, Specialist Nurse, Palliative Care, Furness General Hospital, Tel.: 01229 870870

Ms J Wilde, Macmillan, Palliative Care, Royal Lancaster Infirmary, Tel.: 01524 65944

Ms E Briggs, Day Hospital, Parkinson's Disease, Furness General Hospital, Tel.: 01229 870870

Ms C Jarvis, Parkinson's Disease, Royal Lancaster Infirmary, Tel.: 01524 65944

Ms A Stainton, Parkinson's Disease, Westmorland General Hospital, Tel.: 01539 732288

Ms A Calvert, Nurse, Respiratory, Westmorland General Hospital, Tel.: 01539 732288

Ms S Jewell, Nurse, Respiratory, Furness General Hospital, Tel.: 01229 870870

Ms J Moorhouse, Nurse, Respiratory, Royal Lancaster Infirmary, Tel.: 01524 65944

Ms L Baelson, Resuscitation Training, Royal Lancaster Infirmary, Tel.: 01524 65944

Mr B Geldart, Resuscitation Training, Royal Lancaster Infirmary, Tel.: 01524 65944

Mr C Hendry, Resuscitation Training, Westmorland General Hospital, Tel.: 01539 732288

Ms A Craig, Specialist Nurse, Rheumatology, Royal Lancaster Infirmary, Tel.: 01524 65944

Ms B Moffat, Specialist Nurse, Rheumatology, Furness General Hospital, Tel.: 01229 870870

Ms G Roketsky, Specialist Nurse, Rheumatology, Furness General Hospital, Tel.: 01229 870870

Ms C Spinks, Specialist, Transfusion, Royal Lancaster Infirmary, Tel.: 01524 65944

Ms E Jones, Clinical Nurse Specialist, Upper GI, Royal Lancaster Infirmary, Tel.: 01524 65944

Mr S Douglas, Clinical Nurse Specialist, Urology, - Cancer, RLI/Westmorland General Hospital, Tel.: 01539 732288

Ms M Monaghan, Nurse Specialist, Urology, Royal Lancaster Infirmary, Tel.: 01524 65944

Ms C Winder, Clinical Nurse Specialist, Urology/Oncology, Furness General Hospital, Tel.: 01229 870870

Ms D Wilson, Surgical Practitioner, Vascular, Cross Bay, Tel.: 01524 65944

Admin & Senior Management
Ms A Buchanan, Director of Nursing & Midwifery, Westmorland General Hospital, Burton Road, Kendal, LA9 7RG, Tel.: 01539 795366

Child Health
Ms J Dalton, Paediatric Diabetes Specialist Nurse, Westmorland General Hospital, Tel.: 01539 732288

Ms H Dring, Paediatric Diabetes, Royal Lancaster Infirmary, Tel.: 01524 65944

Ms L Ryan, Paediatric Nurse Practitioner, Royal Lancaster Infirmary, Tel.: 01524 65944

North West Strategic Health Authority

Ms L Shannon, Royal Lancaster Infirmary, Ashton Road, Lancaster, LA1 4RP, Tel.: 01524 65944

Ms A West, Paediatric Diabetes, Furness General Hospital, Tel.: 01229 870870

Ms H Winkfield, Paediatric Community Specialist Nurse, Furness General Hospital, Tel.: 01229 870870

Ms C Wolstenholme, Paediatric Community Specialist Nurse, Furness General Hospital, Tel.: 01229 870870

Child Health Records

Ms L Shannon, Royal Lancaster Infirmary, Ashton Road, Lancaster, LA1 4RP, Tel.: 01524 65944

Child Protection/Safeguarding Children

Ms L Shannon, Royal Lancaster Infirmary, Ashton Road, Lancaster, LA1 4RP, Tel.: 01524 65944

Community Midwifery

Miss D Fish, Head of Midwifery, Royal Lancaster Infirmary, Ashton Road, Lancaster, LA1 4RP, Tel.: 01229 870870

Helme Chase Maternity Unit, Westmorland General Hospital, Burton Road, Kendal, Cumbria, LA9 7RG, Tel.: ext 5374

Ms S Knowles, Matron, Community Midwifery, Westmorland General Hospital, Burton Road, Kendal, Cumbria, LA9 7RG, Tel.: 01539 795375

Ms J McGullion, Matron, Community Midwifery, Royal Lancaster Infirmary, Ashton Road, Lancaster, LA1 4RP,

Mrs A Oxley, Matron, Helme Chase Maternity Unit, Westmorland General Hospital, Burton Road, Kendal, Cumbria, LA9 7RG, Tel.: 01539 795375

Mrs J Pinkney, Matron, Community Midwifery, Furness General Hospital, Dalton Lane, Barrow-in-Furness, Cumbria, LA14 4LF, Tel.: 01229 870870

Women's Unit, Royal Lancaster Infirmary, Ashton Road, Lancaster, LA1 4RP, Tel.: 01524 583850

Morecambe Bay Primary Care Trust

Trust Headquarters, Tenterfield
Brigsteer Road
KENDAL
Cumbria
LA9 5EA
Tel.: 01539 735565

Admin & Senior Management

Mrs C Burdon, Senior Nurse, Tenterfield, Brigsteer Road, Kendal, Cumbria, LA9 5EA, Tel.: 01539 797893

Mrs A Ridgway, Director of Young People's Health, Nursing & Clinical Governance, Tenterfield, Brigsteer Road, Kendal, Cumbria, LA9 5EA, Tel.: 01539 797801

Child Health

Mrs E Donaldson, Community Children's Nurse, Flaxmans Court, Westmorland General Hospital, Tel.: 01539 795908

Ms L Read, Community Children's Nurse, Queen victoria Centre, Morecambe, LA4 1NN, Tel.: 01524 405727

Mrs A Ridgway, Director of Young People's Health, Nursing & Clinical Governance, Tenterfield, Brigsteer Road, Kendal, Cumbria, LA9 5EA, Tel.: 01539 797801

Child Health Records

Mr M Saul, Head of Information Services, Tenterfield, Brigsteer Road, Kendal, Cumbria, LA9 5EA, Tel.: 01539 797842

Child Protection/Safeguarding Children

Ms L Cameron, Looked After Children (Barrow & South Lakeland), Senior Nurse, Fairfield Clinic, 2 Fairfield Lane, Barrow, Cumbria, Tel.: 01229 434158

Ms R France, Looked After Children (Lancaster & Morecambe), Senior Nurse, Longlands Child Dev Centre, Westbourne Drive, Lancaster, LA1 5EE, Tel.: 01524 34331

Ms A Kopcke, Designated/Named Nurse (Lancaster), Ross Children's Centre, Euston Road, Morecambe, LA4 5LE, Tel.: 01524 424445

Ms M Lackey, Designated Nurse South Cumbria (Barrow - Kendal Area), Named Nurse, Ulverston Community Health Centre, Stanley Street, Ulverston, Cumbria, LA12 7BT, Tel.: 01229 484088

Community Nursing Services

Mrs C McCann, Head of Primary & Community Care (Lancaster), Community Offices, Slyne Road, Lancaster, Tel.: 01524 381820

Mrs P Wilson, Head of Primary & Community Care (South Cumbria), Tenterfield, Brigsteer Road, Kendal. Cumbria, LA9 5EA, Tel.: 01539 797898

District Nursing

Mrs A Middleton, Nursing Services Manager (South Lakes), Tel.: 01539 797895

Mrs D Smith, Nursing Services Manager (Barrow), College House, 1st Floor, Howard Street, Barrow, Tel.: 01229 401075

Mrs G Speight, Nursing Services Manager (Lancaster), Community Offices, Slyne Road, Lancaster, Tel.: 01524 386107

Health Visitors

Mrs S Cooper, Health Visiting Services Manager (South Cumbria), College House, 1st Floor, Howard Street, Barrow, Tel.: 01229 401074

Mrs E Cross, Child Development Centre, Health Visitor, Longlands Child Development Centre, Tel.: 01524 34331

Paediatric Liaison - Lancaster Area, (Health Visitors & School Nursing), Ryelands House Clinic, Ryelands Park, Owen Road, Lancaster, LA1 2LN, Tel.: 01524 35933

Mrs M Williams, Health Visiting Services Manager (Lancaster), Ryelands House, Ryelands Park, Owen Road, Lancaster, LA1 2LG, Tel.: 01524 35933

Learning Disabilities

Behaviour Intention Team (South Cumbria), Coniston House, 25 New Market Street, Ulverston, LA12 7LQ, Tel.: 01229 589300/10/11

Behaviour Intervention Team (Lancaster), The Knoll, Westbourne Road, Lancaster, LA1 5EF, Tel.: 01524 585793

Community Health Team (Barrow), College House, Howard Street, Barrow in Furness, Cumbria, LA14 1NB, Tel.: 01229 401100/096/097/098

Community Health Team (Kendal), Austen Suite, County Buildings, Busher Walk, Kendal, Cumbria, LA9 4RQ, Tel.: 01539 816070/2/4

Community Health Team (Lancaster), The Knoll, Westbourne Road, Lancaster, LA1 5EF, Tel.: 01524 585792

Community Health Team (Ulverston), Coniston House, 25 New Market Street, Ulverston, Cumbria, LA12 7LQ, Tel.: 01229 589301/4/5

Mr D Hemmings, Service Manager, Mobile 0780 88 999 36, Coniston House, 25 New Market Street, Ulverston, Cumbria, LA12 7LQ, Tel.: 01229 589313

Mr P Morgan, Service Manager, Mobile 07887 651247, 622 Alston House, Whitecross, Lancaster, LA1 4XQ, Tel.: 01524 541622

Mr J Rasmussen, Service Manager, Mobile 07990 595281, 622 Alston House, Whitecross, Lancaster, LA1 4XQ, Tel.: 01524 541634

Liaison Services

Ms D Bingley, Community Liaison Services - South Lakes, Westmorland General Hospital, Tel.: 01539 795296

Mrs C Ellwood, Community Liaison Services - Lancaster, Royal Lancaster Infirmary, Ashton Road, Lancaster, LA1 4RP, Tel.: 01524 583600

Mrs J Horrocks, Community Liaison Services - Lancaster, Royal Lancaster Infirmary, Ashton Road, Lancaster, LA1 4RP, Tel.: 01524 583600

Paediatric Liaison - Lancaster Area, (Health Visitors & School Nursing), Ryelands House Clinic, Ryelands Park, Owen Road, Lancaster, LA1 2LN, Tel.: 01524 35933

Ms A Taylor, Community Liaison Services - Barrow, Furness General Hospital, Barrow-in-Furness, LA14 4LF, Tel.: 01229 491119

Other Services

Drug & Alcohol Services, Community Team, Kinta House, Helme Close, Kendal, Cumbria, Tel.: 01539 732059

Drug & Alcohol Services, Community Team, Lower Priory Hall, China Street, Lancaster, Lancashire, Tel.: 01524 846106

Mrs M Holland, Adult Palliative Care Co-ordinator, Tenterfield, Brigsteer Road, Kendal, Cumbria, LA9 5EA, Tel.: 01539 797838

Ms B Hoyle, Practice Placement Facilitator, Education Centre, Westmorland General Hospital, Burton Road, Kendal, Cumbria, Tel.: 01539 795442

Mr K Murphy, Head of Drug & Alcohol Services, Inpatient & Community, The Old Fire Station, Abbey Road, Barrow in Furness, Cumbria, LA14 1XH, Tel.: 01229 814515

Smoking Cessation

Mrs A Davies, Slyne Road, Lancaster, Tel.: 01524 386136

Specialist Nursing Services

Ms Y Horne, Specialist Nurse, Cardiac Rehabilitation, 2 Fairfield Lane, Barrow-in-Furness, Cumbria, Tel.: 01229 615627

Post Vacant, Specialist Nurse, Colorectal, Ryelands Clinic, Ryelands Park, Slyne Road, Lancaster, Lancashire, Tel.: 01524 848357

Mrs J Scothern, Specialist Nurse, Colorectal, Ryelands Clinic, Ryelands Park, Slyne Road, Lancaster, Lancashire, Tel.: 01524 35933

Mrs K Hilton, Specialist Nurse, Continence, Queen Victoria Centre, Thornton Road, Morecambe, Lancashire, Tel.: 01524 405717

Mrs L Howard-Thornton, Team Leader, Specialist Nurse, Continence, Queen Victoria Centre, Thornton Road, Morecambe, Lancashire, Tel.: 01524 405729

Mr J Robinson, Specialist Nurse, Continence, Queen Victoria Centre, Thornton Road, Morecambe, Lancashire, Tel.: 01524 405719

Mrs L Schofield, Specialist Nurse, Continence, Station House Surgery, Station Road, Kendal, Tel.: 01539 738649

Mrs P Weston, Specialist Nurse, Continence, Station House Surgery, Station Road, Kendal, Tel.: 01539 738649

Mrs A Wilson, Specialist Nurse, Continence, 2 Fairfield Lane, Barrow-in-Furness, Cumbria, Tel.: 01229 615628

Mrs S Gibson, Specialist Nurse, Diabetic Care, Blackhall Unit, Westmorland General Hospital, Burton Road, Kendal, Cumbria, Tel.: 01539 727564

Mrs Z Hill, Specialist Nurse, Diabetic Care, Queen Victoria Centre, Thornton Road, Morecambe, Lancashire, Tel.: 01524 405728

Post Vacant, Specialist Nurse, Diabetic Care, Furness General Hospital, Dalton Lane, Barrow-in-Furness, Tel.: 01229 491220

Mrs D Sanderson, Specialist Nurse, Diabetic Care, Queen Victoria Centre, Thornton Road, Morecambe, Lancashire, Tel.: 01524 405728

Mrs S Walker, Specialist Nurse, Diabetic Care, Furness General Hospital, Dalton Lane, Barrow-in-Furness, Tel.: 01229 491220

Mr N Brown, Specialist Nurse, Macmillan, 2 Fairfield Lane, Barrow-in-Furness, Cumbria, Tel.: 01229 615613

Mrs E Hemingway, Specialist Nurse, Macmillan, St John's Hospice, Lancaster Road, Lancaster, Lancashire, Tel.: 01524 847257

Mrs J Kerr, Specialist Nurse, Macmillan, Weavers Court, Westmorland General Hospital, Burton Road, Kendal, Tel.: 01539 738650

Mrs C McCann, Specialist Nurse, Macmillan, St John's Hospice, Lancaster Road, Lancaster, Lancashire, Tel.: 01524 847257

Post Vacant, Specialist Nurse, Macmillan, St John's Hospice, Lancaster Road, Lancaster, Lancashire, Tel.: 01524 847257

Ms S Rafferty, Specialist Nurse, Macmillan, 2 Fairfield Lane, Barrow-in-Furness, Cumbria, Tel.: 01229 615625

Mrs D Rostron, Specialist Nurse, Macmillan, 2 Fairfield Lane, Barrow-in-Furness, Cumbria, Tel.: 01229 615613

Mrs J Wilson, Specialist Nurse, Macmillan, Weavers Court, Westmorland General Hospital, Burton Road, Kendal, Tel.: 01539 738650

Mrs M Harrison, Specialist Nurse, Respiratory, 2 Fairfield Lane, Barrow-in-Furness, Cumbria, Tel.: 01229 615601

Mrs J Till, Specialist Nurse, Respiratory, Flaxman's Court, Westmorland General Hospital, Burton Road, Kendal, Tel.: 01539 729043

Mrs M Monaghan, Specialist Nurse, Urodynamics, Royal Lancaster Infirmary, Ashton Road, Lancaster, Lancashire, Tel.: 01524 583034

North Cheshire Hospitals NHS Trust

Trust Headquarters, Warrington Hospital
Lovely Lane
WARRINGTON, Cheshire
WA5 1QG
Tel.: 01925 635911
Fax.: 01925 662048

Acute Specialist Nursing Services

Ms J Neton, Emergency Care, Tel.: 01925 635911 x5183

Ms A Howard, Gynaecology, Tel.: 01925 635911 x2781

Ms J Brookes, Medicine/Elderly Care, Warrington Hospital, Tel.: 01925 635911 x2330

Mr A Murphy, Surgery, Tel.: 01925 635911 x2677

Ms C Jones, Trauma & Orthopaedics, Tel.: 01925 635911 x2922

Child Health

Ms J Scott, Senior Nurse Manager, Tel.: 01925 635911

Child Protection/Safeguarding Children

Ms N Richardson, Tel.: 01925 635911

Community Midwifery

Ms M Hudson, Head of Midwifery, Warrington Hospital, Lovely Lane, Warrington, Cheshire, WA5 1QG, Tel.: 01925 635911

Discharge Co-ordinators

Ms J Harvey, Warrington Hospital, Tel.: 01925 635911 x2774

Ms G Melander, Halton Hospital, Tel.: 01925 635911 x3380

North Cumbria Acute Services NHS Trust

West Cumberland Hospital
Hensingham
WHITEHAVEN
CA28 8JG
Tel.: 01946 693181

Acute Specialist Nursing Services

Ms B Bainess, Bereavement Midwife, Maternity, West Cumberland Hospital, Tel.: 01946 693181

Ms I Burns, Infant Feeding Advisor, Maternity, West Cumberland Hospital, Tel.: 01946 693181 ext 3260

Child Protection/Safeguarding Children

Ms L Musgrave, Named Midwife, Child Protection, Tel.: 07867 553483

Community Midwifery

Mrs Anne Musgrave, Head of Midwifery & Community Midwifery Manager - North Cumbria, West Cumberland Hospital, Hensingham, Whitehaven, CA28 8JG, Tel.: 01946 693181 ext 4253

North Cumbria Mental Health & Learning Disabilities NHS Trust

The Carleton Clinic
Cumwhinton Drive
CARLISLE, Cumbria
CA1 3SX
Tel.: 01228 602000

Learning Disabilities

Mr J Comber, Lead Nurse in Learning Disabilities, Upper Rowanwood, Carleton Clinic, Carlisle, Cumbria, CA1 3SX, Tel.: 01228 602609

Prof D Dagnam, Clinical Director in Learning Disabilities, Thirlemere Suite, Thirlemere Buildings, Lakes Road, Derwent Howe, Workington, CA14 3YP, Tel.: 01900 606440

Ms F Dixon, Locality Manager, Thirlemere Suite, Thirlemere Buildings, Lakes Road, Derwent Howe, Workington, CA14 3YP, Tel.: 01900 606440

Mr J Gray, Co-ordinator, Eden, Health Centre, Bridge Lane, Penrith, CA11 7NX, Tel.: 01768 245271

North West Strategic Health Authority

North Liverpool Primary Care Trust
Trust Headquarters, Cottage 2
Newhall Campus, Longmoor Lane
LIVERPOOL, L10 1LD
Tel.: 0151 293 1900

Admin & Senior Management
Ms J Forrest, Chief Executive,
Ms K Wallace, Manager, Operational Services,
Child Health
Mrs C Burns, Clinical Director,
Child Protection/Safeguarding Children
Ms L Rodgers, Designated Nurse, Regatta Place, Summers Rd
Brunswick Business Park, Liverpool L3 4BL 0151 285 4671 /4670
Mrs T Jones Named Nurse Safeguarding Children, Regatta Place,
Summers Rd, Brunswick Business Park, Liverpool L3 4BL Tel.: 0151
285 4666 /4670
Safeguarding Children Specialist Nurses, Jeanette Scott, Regatta
Place, Summers Road, Liverpool L3 4BL Tel.: 0151 285 4672/4661
Community Nursing Services
Ms S Carney, Community Nurse Manager,
School Nursing
Citywide Service, School Health/Nursing Service, Cottage 7, Newhall
Campus, Longmoor Lane, Liverpool, L10 1LD,

North Manchester Primary Care Trust
Trust Headquarters, Newton Silk Mill
2nd Floor, Holyoak Street, Newton Heath
MANCHESTER
M40 1HA
Tel.: 0161 219 9400

Admin & Senior Management
Ms Y Casson, Associate Director, Facilities & Sexual Health, Newton
Silk Mill, Ground Floor, Holyoak Street, Newton Heath, Manchester,
M40 1HA, Tel.: 0161 219 9470
Mr J Harrop, Director of Operation, Newton Silk Mill, 2nd Floor,
Holyoak Street, Newton Heath, Manchester, M40 1HA, Tel.: 0161
219 9400
Mr A Johnstone, Director of Finance, 2nd Floor, Newton Silk Mill,
Ground Floor, Holyoak Street, Newton Heath, Manchester, M40
1HA, Tel.: 0161 219 9402
Mr D King, Chief Executive, Newton Silk Mill, 2nd Floor, Holyoak
Street, Newton Heath, Manchester, M40 1HA, Tel.: 0161 219 9400
Mrs D Lyon, Head of Nursing, Newton Silk Mill, Ground Floor,
Holyoak Street, Newton Heath, Manchester, M40 1HA, Tel.: 0161
219 9470
Ms C Pearson, Associate Director, Nursing, Newton Silk Mill, Ground
Floor, Holyoak Street, Newton Heath, Manchester, M40 1HA, Tel.:
0161 219 9470
Mr M Philp, Associate Director, Intermediate Care & AHP's, Newton
Silk Mill, Ground Floor, Holyoak Street, Newton Heath, Manchester,
M40 1HA, Tel.: 0161 219 9470
Ms J Purcell, Director of Health Development, 2nd Floor, Newton Silk
Mill, Ground Floor, Holyoak Street, Newton Heath, Manchester, M40
1HA, Tel.: 0161 219 9407
Ms E Roaf, Director of Public Health, Newton Silk Mill, 2nd Floor,
Holyoak Street, Newton Heath, Manchester, M40 1HA, Tel.: 0161
219 9400
Child Health Records
Ms J Scott, Child Health Manager, Mauldeth House, Mauldeth Road
West, Manchester, M21 7RL, Tel.: 0161 958 4089
Child Protection/Safeguarding Children
Ms C Craig, Senior Nurse, Child Protection, Clayton Health Centre,
89 North Road, Clayton, Manchester, M11 4EJ, Tel.: 0161 231 1151
Ms D Jennings, Senior Nurse, Child Protection, Clayton Health
Centre, 89 North Road, Clayton, Manchester, M11 4EJ, Tel.: 0161
231 1151

Clinical Leads (NSF)
Ms A Conway, Clinical Lead, Practice Nursing, Harpurhey Health
Centre, 1 Church Lane, Harpurhey, Manchester, M9 4BE, Tel.: 0161
205 5063
Mrs C Graham, Clinical Lead, Support Nurse, CHD, Newton Silk Mill,
Silk House, Holyoak Street, Newton Heath, Manchester, M40 1HA,
Tel.: 0161 219 9460
Ms A Hall, Clinical Lead, Elderly Care - Intermediate
Care/Supporting Discharges, Lead Nurse, North Manchester
General Hospital, Delauneys Road, Crumpsall, M8 6RL, Tel.: 0161
720 2932
Ms S Ware, Clinical Lead, Cancer, Victoria Mill, 10 Lower Vickers
Street, Miles Platting, Manchester, M40 7JL, Tel.: 0161 205 6111
District Nursing
Ms S L Kerwin, Clinical Lead, District Nursing, Cornerstone
Resource Centre, 2 Graham Street, Beswick, Manchester, M11 3AA,
Health Visitors
Ms F Branton, Clinical Lead, Health Visiting, Crumpsall Clinic,
Humphrey Street, Crumpsall, Manchester, M8 9JS, Tel.: 0161 720
7808
School Nursing
Ms L Waine, Clinical Lead, School Nurses, Plant Hill Clinic, Plant Hill
Road, Blackley, Manchester, M9 8LX, Tel.: 0161 740 8004
Specialist Nursing Services
Ms J Wall, Advisor, Continence, Newton Heath Health Centre, 2 Old
Church Street, Newton Heath, Manchester, M40 2JF, Tel.: 0161 684
9696
Ms M Barlow, Nurse, Macmillan, Victoria Mill, 10 Lower Vickers
Street, Miles Platting, Manchester, M40 7JL,
Ms L Hine, Nurse, Macmillan, Victoria Mill, 10 Lower Vickers Street,
Miles Platting, Manchester, M40 7JL,
Ms L Madden, Nurse, Macmillan, Victoria Mill, 10 Lower Vickers
Street, Miles Platting, Manchester, M40 7JL,
Ms M Proudman, Tissue Viability, Cornerstone Resource Centre, 2
Graham Street, Beswick, Manchester, M11 3AA,

Oldham Primary Care Trust
Trust Headquarters, Ellen House
Waddington Street
OLDHAM
OL9 6EE
Tel.: 0161 622 6500
Fax.: 0161 622 6512

Admin & Senior Management
Mrs S Dixon, Director Clinical Services, Oldham PCT, Ellen House,
Waddington Street, Oldham, OL9 6EE, Tel.: 0161 622 6513
Child Health
Ms J Payne, Manager Child Health - Admin, Oldham PCT, Ellen
House, Waddington Street, Oldham, OL9 6EE, Tel.: 0161 622 6500
Child Health Records
Ms J Payne, Manager, Oldham PCT, Ellen House, Waddington
Street, Oldham, OL9 6EE, Tel.: 0161 622 6500
Child Protection/Safeguarding Children
Ms E Godina, Named Nurse, Child Protection, Ellen House,
Waddington Street, Oldham, OL9 6EE, Tel.: 0161 622 6542
Clinical Leads (NSF)
Dr A Nye, Clinical Lead, Drugs & Alcohol,
Dr I Watson, Clinical Lead, Cancer,
Dr I Milnes, Clinical Lead, CHD,
Dr R Orr, Clinical Lead, Diabetic Care,
Dr A Kumar, Clinical Lead, Older People,
District Nursing
Ms S Schofield, Clinical Lead, District Nurse, Tel.: 0161 622 6633
Family Planning Services
Ms A Wadsworth, Manager, Oldham PCT, Ellen House, Waddington
Street, Oldham, OL9 6EE, Tel.: 0161 622 6500

North West Strategic Health Authority

Health Visitors
Ms M Forshaw, Clinical Lead, Health Visitor, Tel.: 0161 622 6608
Paediatric Liaison Health Visitor, Chalmers Keddie Building, Royal
Oldham Hospital, Rochdale Road, Oldham, OL1 2JH, Tel.: 0161 627
8753

HIV/AIDS
Ms S Russell, HIV Counsellor, Booth Street Centre, Oldham, Tel.:
0161 627 5071

Learning Disabilities
Ms D Mills, Clinical Lead, Woodfield Centre, Netherfield Close, Off
Manchester Road, Werneth, Oldham, OL8 4ET, Tel.: 0161 627 1749
Mr J Ryan, Head, Adults Learning Disability, Broadway House,
Broadway, Chadderton, Oldham, OL9 8RW, Tel.: 0161 911 3868

Liaison Services
Ms J Higgins, Manager, PALS, Block D, Brunswick Square, Union
Street, Oldham, O41 1DE, Tel.: 0161 624 6251
Ms A Shaw, Co-ordinator, Transfer of Care, Social Work Dept, Royal
Oldham Hospital, Tel.: 0161 627 8344

Other Services
Ms S Cosgrove, Co-ordinator, Continuing Health Care, Social Work
Dept, Royal Oldham Hospital, Tel.: 0161 627 8342
Ms D Hardy, Co-ordinator, Continuing Health Care, Social Work
Dept, Royal Oldham Hospital, Tel.: 0161 627 8342

School Nursing
Ms J Kershaw, Co-ordinator, School Nurses, Ellen House,
Waddington Street, Oldham, OL9 6EE, Tel.: 0161 622 6500

Smoking Cessation
Ms K Hastie, Office 1, Southlink Business Park, Oldham, OL4 1DR,
Tel.: 0161 621 5937

Specialist Nursing Services
Respiratory Care, Asthma, Chest Clinic, Royal Oldham Hospital,
Tel.: 0161 627 8526
Ms M Fox, Breast Care, Royal Oldham Hospital, Tel.: 0161 627 8459
Ms M Goulden, Breast Care, Royal Oldham Hospital, Tel.: 0161 627
8459
Ms S Martin, Breast Care, Royal Oldham Hospital, Tel.: 0161 627
8459
Ms M Mellor, Continence, Chadderton Town Health Centre, Tel.:
0161 909 8172/8165
Mr A Larkin, Nurse Consultant, Critical Care, Chalmers Keddie
Building, Tel.: 0161 624 0420
Ms J Byrom, Diabetic Care, Royal Oldham Hospital, Tel.: 0161 627
8268
Ms S Doherty, Diabetic Care, Royal Oldham Hospital, Tel.: 0161 627
8268
Nurses, Macmillan, Dr Kershaw's Hospice, Turf Lane, Royton,
Oldham, Tel.: 0161 627 4246
Mrs H Wrench, Stoma Care, Tel.: 0161 627 8419
Mrs J Berry, TB, - Respiratory, Chest Clinic, Royal Oldham Hospital,
Tel.: 0161 627 8526
Ms J Harker, Tissue Viability, Tel.: 0161 627 8701

Pennine Acute Hospitals NHS Trust
Trust Headquarters, Westhulme Avenue
OLDHAM
OL1 2PN
Tel.: 0161 624 0420

Child Protection/Safeguarding Children
Mrs L Ingoe, Lead Nurse, Child Protection, Royal Oldham Hospital,
Rochdale Road, OL1 2JH, Tel.: 0161 624 0420

Community Midwifery
Mrs D Brears, Associate Director, Women & Children's Divison,
Rochdale Infirmary, Whitehall Street, Rochdale, Lancashire, OL12
9QB, Tel.: 01706 517578
Mrs D Chadderton, Senior Midwife, Royal Oldham Hospital,
Rochdale Road, Oldham, Lancashire, OL1 2JH, Tel.: 0161 652 5811

Mrs V Devine, Senior Midwife, Fairfield General Hospital, Rochdale
Old Road, Bury, Lancashire, BL9 7TD, Tel.: 0161 778 3734
Emergencies, Fairfield General Hospital, Rochdale Old Road, Bury,
Lancashire, BL9 7TD, Tel.: 0161 705 3812
Mrs C J Trinick, Head of Midwifery, Fairfield General Hospital,
Rochdale Old Road, Bury, BL9 7TD, Tel.: 0161 778 3710

Pennine Care NHS Trust
Trust Headquarters, Tameside General Hospital
Fountain Street
ASHTON-UNDER-LYNE
Lancashire
OL6 9RW
Tel.: 0161 331 5151

Learning Disabilities
Mr R Cafiero, Service Manager, Ralph Williams Clinic, Stevenson
Square, Smallbridge, Rochdale, OL12 9SA, Tel.: 01706 702100
Specialty Services - Community, Byron Terrace, Grandidge Street,
Rochdale, Ol11 3SA, Tel.: 01706 702184
Specialty Services - Respite, Byron Terrace, Grandidge Street,
Rochdale, Ol11 3SA, Tel.: 01706 702181

Preston Primary Care Trust
Trust Headquarters, Preston Business Centre
Watling Street Road, Fulwood
PRESTON
Lancs
PR2 8DY
Tel.: 01772 645500

Admin & Senior Management
Ms G Ashworth, Director Clinical Services, Preston Business Centre,
Watling Street Road, Fulwood, Preston, PR2 8DY, Tel.: 01772
645514
Mr T Boxer, Director of Finance,
Ms J Hewitt, Chief Executive, Tel.: 01772 645505
Ms D Hounslea, Director of Modernisation,
Mr M Kindle, Director of Corporate Planning,
Ms M Morris, Director of Public Health,
Ms S Rigg, Director of Primary Care,

Child Health
Ms S Welch, Head of Children's Services, Preston Business Centre,
Tel.: 01772 645656/57

Child Health Records
Child Health Records, Willows Child Dev Centre, Pedders Lane,
Ashton, Preston, PR2 2TR, Tel.: 01772 401450

Child Protection/Safeguarding Children
Ms C Randall, Willows Child Development Centre, Tel.: 01772
401471

Clinical Leads (NSF)
Ms S Welch, Clinical Lead, Childrens, Preston Business Centre,
Watling Street Road, Fulwood, Preston, PR2 8DY, Tel.: 01772
645656
Ms G Ashworth, Clinical Lead, Cancer, Preston Business Centre,
Watling Street Road, Fulwood, Preston, PR2 8DY, Tel.: 01772
645514
Dr Fletcher, Clinical Lead, Care of the Elderly, Ribbleton Medical
Centre, Tel.: 01772 792512
Ms G Ashworth, Clinical Lead, CHD, Preston Business Centre,
Watling Street Road, Fulwood, Preston, PR2 8DY, Tel.: 01772
645514
Dr Fletcher, Clinical Lead, Ribbleton Medical Centre, Tel.: 01772
792512

Community Nursing Services
Ms E Bourne, Head of Community Nursing & Nurse Prescribing,
Preston Business Centre, Tel.: 01772 645656/57
Ms S Welch, Head of Community Nursing & Children's, Preston
Business Centre, Tel.: 01772 645656/57

North West Strategic Health Authority

Family Planning Services
Mrs M Simpkin, Chorley & South Ribble PCT, Jubilee House, Lancashire Enterprise Business Pk, Centurion Way, Leyland, PR26 6TR,
Health Visitors
Ms M Heaton, Special Needs, Health Visitor, Willows Child Development Centre, Tel.: 01772 401540
Ms S Pidgeon, Special Needs, Health Visitor, Willows Child Development Centre, Tel.: 01772 401540
Ms F Rowlands, Paediatric - Liaison, Health Visitor, Royal Preston Hospital, Sharoe Green Lane North, Fulwood, Preston, PR2 9HT, Tel.: 01772 522446
Ms S Cannon, Health Visitor, TB, Tel.: 01772 645617
Ms L Forde, Health Visitor, TB, Tel.: 01772 645617
Learning Disabilities
Ms D Langford, Head of Service, 19 Stanleyfield Road, Preston, Lancashire, Tel.: 01772 401120
Learning Disability Service, 19 Stanleyfield Road, Preston, Lancashire,,
Learning Disability Service, 93 Garstang Road, Preston, Lancashire,
Supported Living Service, 19 Stanleyfield Road, Preston, Lancashire,
Specialist Nursing Services
Ms J Whitewood, Advisor, Continence, Brookfield Clinic, Croasdale Avenue, Preston, PR2 6UB, Tel.: 01772 401812
Mrs A Graham, Diabetic Care, LASCA, Tel.: 01772 524303
Ms S Radcliff, Infection Control, Tel.: 01772 645625
Ms A Watson, Infection Control, Tel.: 01772 645625
Ms S Martin, Wound Care, Fulwood Clinic, Tel.: 01772 401321
The Homeless/Travellers & Asylum Seekers
Ms R Cowell, Homeless Team, 5 Camden Place, Winckley Square, Preston, PR1 3JL,

Rochdale Primary Care Trust
Trust Headquarters, Telegraph House
Baillie Street
ROCHDALE
OL16 1JA
Tel.: 01706 652800
Fax.: 01706 652823

Admin & Senior Management
Mr T Purt, Chief Executive,
Child Health
Mr E Cobby, Associate Director of Operational Services & Facilities Management, 3rd Floor, Telegraph House, Baillie Street, Rochdale, OL16 1JA, Tel.: 01706 652811
Child Health Records
Child Health Dept, 3rd Floor, Telegraph House, Baillie Street, Rochdale, OL16 1JA, Tel.: 01706 652891
Child Protection/Safeguarding Children
Ms P Fraser, Named Nurse, Child Protection, Ings Lane Clinic, Phoenix Street, Rochdale, OL12 7DW, Tel.: 01706 702197
Ms L Mirabitur, Designated Nurse, Child Protection, Ings Lane Clinic, Phoenix Street, Rochdale, OL12 7DW, Tel.: 01706 702197
Clinical Leads (NSF)
Dr S Will, Clinical Lead, CHD, Cancer,
Dr I Babbar, Clinical Lead, Children,
Dr D Mansfield, Clinical Lead, Diabetic Care,
Dr S Rothery, Clinical Lead, Long Term Conditions,
HIV/AIDS
Mrs C Hayes, Aids Co-ordinator, Health Promotion Unit, Penn Street Clinic, Rochdale, OL16 1HX, Tel.: 01706 517610
Liaison Services
Ms P Beresford, Liaison Paediatric, Thor Med/TB District Nurse, Tel.: 01706 702124
Ms G Dobson, Liaison Paediatric, Thor Med/TB District Nurse, Tel.: 01706 702124

Mrs J Reid, Liaison Paediatric, Thor Med/TB Health Visitor, Tel.: 01706 517178
Mrs E T Thompson, Liaison Paediatric, Thor Med/TB Health Visitor, Tel.: 01706 517178
Specialist Nursing Services
Mrs J Farrell, Asthma, Milnrow Health Centre, Stonefield Street, Milnrow, Rochdale, OL16 4HZ, Tel.: 01706 651967
Mrs L Smith, Asthma, Milnrow Health Centre, Stonefield Street, Milnrow, Rochdale, OL16 4HZ, Tel.: 01706 651967
Mrs J Ridley, CHD, Yorkshire Street Surgery, Rochdale, Tel.: 01706 702089
Mrs M Chadwick, Advisor, Continence, Darn Hill Clinic, Argyle Parade, Heywood, OL10 3RY, Tel.: 01706 757694
Ms C Grange, Specialist Nurse, Continence, Darn Hill Clinic, Argyle Parade, Heywood, OL10 3RY, Tel.: 01706 702202
Mrs R Crowther, Discharge Lead, Continuing Care, Review & Assessment Team, 2 St James Place, 160-166 Yorkshire Street, Rochdale, OL16 2DL, Tel.: 01706 708021
Mrs A Bood, Diabetes, Birch Hill Hospital, Rochdale, OL12 9QB, Tel.: 01706 754043/754095
Mrs S Doherty, Diabetes, Birch Hill Hospital, Rochdale, OL12 9QB, Tel.: 01706 754043/754095
Mrs S Greenwood, Diabetes, Birch Hill Hospital, Rochdale, OL12 9QB, Tel.: 01706 754043/754095
Mrs C O'Connor, Diabetes, - Paediatrics, Baillie Street Health Centre, Baillie Street, Rochdale, Tel.: 01706 517638
Mrs K Roberts, Diabetes, Birch Hill Hospital, Rochdale, OL12 9QB, Tel.: 01706 754043/754095
Mrs K Saleem, Diabetes, Birch Hill Hospital, Rochdale, OL12 9QB, Tel.: 01706 754043/754095
Ms J Bagshaw, Specialist Nurse, Epilepsy, Taylor Street Clinic, Taylor Street, Heywood, OL10 1EF, Tel.: 01706 702240
Mrs G Fisher, Palliative Care, Langley Clinic, Borrowdale Road, Middleton, M24 5QG, Tel.: 0161 251 8339
Mr S Pinnington, Palliative Care, Langley Clinic, Borrowdale Road, Middleton, M24 5QG, Tel.: 0161 251 8339
Mrs J Sedgewick, Clinical Lead, Palliative Care, Langley Clinic, Borrowdale Road, Middleton, M24 5QG, Tel.: 0161 251 8339
Miss L Walsh, Palliative Care, Langley Clinic, Borrowdale Road, Middleton, M24 5QG, Tel.: 0161 251 8339
Mrs B Willis, Palliative Care, Langley Clinic, Borrowdale Road, Middleton, M24 5QG, Tel.: 0161 251 8339
Mrs B D Wragg, Palliative Care, Langley Clinic, Borrowdale Road, Middleton, M24 5QG, Tel.: 0161 251 8339
Mrs J Charlton, Stoma Care, Darn Hill Clinic, Argyle Parade, Heywood, OL10 3RY, Tel.: 01706 702208
Mrs S Fisher, Nurse Advisor, Tissue Viability, Whitworth Clinic, Brenbar Crescent, Off Tong Lane, Whitworth, OL12 8BB, Tel.: 01706 855200

Royal Liverpool & Broadgreen University Hospitals NHS Trust
Trust Headquarters, Prescot Street
LIVERPOOL
L7 8XP
Tel.: 0151 706 2000
Fax.: 0151 706 5806

Admin & Senior Management
Ms J Galvani, Director of Nursing, Royal Liverpool & Broadgreen Univ NHS Trust, Prescot Street, Liverpool, L7 8XP, Tel.: 0151 706 2000

Royal Liverpool Children's NHS Trust
Trust Headquarters, Alder Hey
Eaton Road, LIVERPOOL
L12 2AP
Tel.: 0151 228 4811

North West Strategic Health Authority

Acute Specialist Nursing Services
Mrs M Ambler, Advanced, Nurse Practitioner, Eaton House, Tel.: ext 2327
Ms M Ambler, Advanced, Nurse Practitioner, PICU/HDU, ext 2723
Mr A Darbyshire, PICU, Nurse Consultant, Tel.: ext 2006
Ms C Gorst, Laser, Nurse Specialist, Tel.: ext 2402
Ms J Grogan, Craniofacial, Nurse Specialist, Tel.: ext 3520
Ms G Harrison, BPD, Nurse Specialist, Tel.: ext 2625
Ms R Hill, Advanced, Nurse Practitioner, PICU/HDU, Tel.: ext 2241
Ms P Holt, Advanced, Nurse Practitioner, PICU/HDU, Tel.: ext 2241
Miss C Lydon, Chronic Fatigue, Nurse Specialist, Tel.: ext 2273
Ms G Sefton, Advanced, Nurse Practitioner, PICU/HDU, Tel.: ext 2241
Mrs L Smith, Haemoglobinopathies, Nurse Specialist, Tel.: ext 2079
Ms L Tume, Advanced PICU, Nurse Practitioner, Tel.: ext 2656
Ms M Wright, Advanced, Nurse Practitioner, OUI,
Ms K Williams, Advanced, Nurse Practitioner, A&E, Tel.: ext 2543
Ms E Kelly, Nurse Specialist, Asthma, Tel.: ext 2936
Ms V Worrall, Nurse Specialist, Asthma, Tel.: ext 2087
Ms J Smith, Clinical Nurse Specialist, Audiology, Tel.: ext 2943
Ms A Howarth, Liaison, Nurse Specialist, Cardiac, Tel.: ext 2291
Ms G McBurney, Liaison, Nurse Specialist, Cardiac, Tel.: ext 2291
Ms M Murray, Liaison, Nurse Specialist, Cardiac, Tel.: ext 2291
Ms H McClements, Clinical Nurse Specialist, Cleft Lip & Palate, Tel.: ext 2224
Ms E Burrows, Advanced Nurse Practitioner, Cystic Fibrosis, Tel.: ext 2978
Ms J Cottrell, Nurse Specialist, Cystic Fibrosis, Tel.: ext 2297
Ms J Edmunds, Nurse Specialist, Diabetic Care, Tel.: ext 2748
Miss C Hurley, Nurse Specialist, Diabetic Care, Tel.: ext 2738
Ms S Kerr, Nurse Specialist, Diabetic Care, Tel.: ext 2738
Mr P Laing, Nurse Specialist, Endocrine Surgery, Tel.: ext 2534
Mrs Z Yung, Associate Nurse, Endocrinology, Tel.: ext 2534
Ms A Flynn, Nurse Specialist, ENT Surgery, Tel.: ext 3757
Ms L Beeston, Nurse Specialist, Epilepsy, Tel.: ext 2927
Ms A Sweeney, Nurse Specialist, Epilepsy, Tel.: ext 2927
Ms K Crook, Clinical Nurse Specialist, Gastroenterology, ext 2191
Ms T Irvine, Nurse Specialist, Gastroenterology, Tel.: ext 3725
Ms C Benfield, Nurse Specialist, Haematology, Tel.: ext 2079
Ms N Mackett, Nurse Specialist, Haematology, Tel.: ext 2079
Ms S Lowe, Nurse Consultant, Infection Control, Tel.: ext 2485
Miss C Benson, Associate Nurse, Immunology, Infectious Diseases, Tel.: ext 2079
Ms H Dunning, Nurse, Macmillan, Tel.: ext 3788
Ms P Garrett, Nurse, Macmillan, Tel.: ext 2408
Ms J Rigg, Nurse, Macmillan, Tel.: ext 2408
Ms M Williams, Nurse, Macmillan, Tel.: ext 2408
Ms A Birch, Nurse Specialist, Nephrology, Tel.: ext 2428
Ms D Williams, Advanced, Nurse Practitioner, Neurosurgery, Tel.: ext 2018
Ms M Hopkins, Advanced, Nurse Practitioner, Oncology, Tel.: ext 3784
Ms K Selwood, Advanced, Nurse Practitioner, Oncology, Tel.: ext 2799
Ms J Vickers, Nurse Consultant, Oncology, Tel.: ext 2408
Ms R Davies, Nurse Specialist, Orthopaedics, Tel.: ext 2014
Ms J Craske, Nurse Specialist, Pain Management, Tel.: ext 2003
Ms F Dooley, Nurse Specialist, Pain Management, Tel.: ext 2003
Ms E McArthur, Nurse Specialist, Pain Management, Tel.: ext 2003
Mr T Stokes, Clinical Nurse Specialist, Psychiatric, Community, Tel.: 0151 285 6500
Ms C Doyle, Advanced, Nurse Practitioner, Respiratory, Tel.: ext 3081
Ms J Kelly, Nurse Specialist, Rheumatology, Tel.: ext 2273
Ms P Coldicutt, Nurse Specialist, Stoma Care, Tel.: ext 3683
Ms H Webster, Bone Marrow, Nurse Specialist, Transplant, Tel.: ext 2183

Ms C Sanders, Nurse Specialist, Urology, Tel.: ext 2852
Admin & Senior Management
Ms R Burke, Director of Nursing, Royal Liverpool Childrens, Tel.: 0151 252 5572
Mr R Cooke, Chief Nurse, Royal Liverpool Childrens, Tel.: 0151 228 4811
Mrs J M Prescott, Care Group Manager, Royal Liverpool Children's NHS Trust - Alder Hey, Eaton Road, Liverpool, L12 2AP, Tel.: 0151 252 5500
Child Health
Community Child Health , Alder Hey Children's Hospital, Eaton Road, Liverpool, L12 2AP, Tel.: 0151 252 5500
Ms J Greer, Senior Children's Community Sister, Community Paediatric Nursing Team, Mulberry House, Alder Hey, Liverpool, L12 2AP, Tel.: 0151 293 3593
Ms S Kavanagh, Senior Children's Community Sister, Community Paediatric Nursing Team, Mulberry House, Alder Hey, Liverpool, L12 2AP, Tel.: 0151 293 3593
Ms C Langford, Senior Children's Community Sister, Community Paediatric Nursing Team, Mulberry House, Alder Hey, Liverpool, L12 2AP, Tel.: 0151 293 3593
Ms J Rowland, Senior Children's Community Sister, Community Paediatric Nursing Team, Mulberry House, Alder Hey, Liverpool, L12 2AP, Tel.: 0151 293 3593
Child Protection/Safeguarding Children
Ms J Knowles, Named Nurse, Child Protection, Community Child Health, Mulberry House, Eaton Road, Liverpool, L12 2AP, Tel.: 0151 228 4811 ext 2973
Community Nursing Services
Ms J Griffin, Senior Community Nurse, Youth Offending Team, Tel.: 0151 225 6232
Learning Disabilities
Ms J Locke,
Ms K Mpetha,
Liaison Services
District Nurse Liaison, Tel.: 0151 252 5200
Matrons/Modern Matrons
Ms K Corrin, Royal Liverpool Children's NHS Trust, Tel.: 0151 252 5133
Ms M Mercer, Royal Liverpool Children's NHS Trust, Tel.: 0151 252 5681
Mr P O'Connor, Royal Liverpool Children's NHS Trust, Tel.: 0151 252 5151
Ms D Topping, Royal Liverpool Children's NHS Trust, 0151 252 5130

Salford Primary Care Trust
Trust Headquarters
St James's House
Pendleton Way
SALFORD
Greater Manchester
M6 5FW
Tel.: 0161 743 2020

Admin & Senior Management
Ms E Robinson, Chief Executive,
Child Health
Ms C Allen, Team Leader, Diana Children's Community Nursing Services, Sandringham House, Windsor Street, Salford, M5 4DG, Tel.: 0161 212 4248/4249/4217
Ms M Burney, Team Leader, Diana Children's Community Nursing Services, Sandringham House, Windsor Street, Salford, M5 4DG, Tel.: 0161 212 4248/4249/4217
Child Health, St James's House, Pendleton Way, Salford, Greater Manchester, M6 5FW, Tel.: 0161 212 4800
Mrs L Cooper, Children with Challenging Behaviour, Sandringham House, Windsor Street, Salford, M5 4DG, Tel.: 0161 212 4218

North West Strategic Health Authority

Ms J Doxey, Team Leader, Diana Children's Community Nursing Services, Sandringham House, Windsor Street, Salford, M5 4DG, Tel.: 0161 212 4248/4249/4217

Ms C Drysdale, Clinical Lead, Diana Children's Community Nursing Services, Sandringham House, Windsor Street, Salford, M5 4DG, Tel.: 0161 212 4216

Ms S Petch, Team Leader, Diana Children's Community Nursing Services, Sandringham House, Windsor Street, Salford, M5 4DG, Tel.: 0161 212 4248/4249/4217

Mr T Plant, Children with Challenging Behaviour, Sandringham House, Windsor Street, Salford, M5 4DG, Tel.: 0161 212 4218

Child Health Records
Child Health Records, St James's House, Pendleton Way, Salford, Greater Manchester, M6 5FW, Tel.: 0161 212 4800

Child Protection/Safeguarding Children
Ms J Rollinson, Designated Nurse, Child Protection,

Clinical Leads (NSF)
Ms H Compston, Clinical Lead, Cancer,

District Nursing
Ms M Robinson, Professional Lead District Nursing, Sandringham House, Windsor Street, Salford, M5 4DG, Tel.: 0161 212 4159

Health Visitors
Ms K Whitehead, Professional Lead Health Visitor, Sandringham House, Windsor Street, Salford, M5 4DG, Tel.: 0161 212 4450

HIV/AIDS
Ms L Pilkington, HIV Support Team, Sandringham House, Tel.: 0161 212 4171

Learning Disabilities
Ms A Hardman, Facilitator, Sandringham House, Castle Courts, Windsor Street, Salford, Manchester, M5 4DG, Tel.: 0161 212 4000

Mrs D Rodger, Head of Service, Sandringham House, Castle Courts, Windsor Street, Salford, Manchester, M5 4DG, Tel.: 0161 212 4000

Liaison Services
District Nursing Liaison, Salford Royal Hospital, Stott Lane, Tel.: 0161 787 5582/4302/4581

Ms L McGahey, District Nurse, Hope & Ladywell Hospital, Tel.: 0161 787 5582/4302/4581

Ms O'Keefe, District Nurse, Hope & Ladywell Hospital, Tel.: 0161 787 5582/4302/4581

Ms E Sate, District Nurse, Hope & Ladywell Hospital, Tel.: 0161 787 5582/4302/4581

Other Services
Ms C Fentem, Community Macmillan/Specialist Palliative Care, St Ann's Hospice, Peel Lane, Little Hulton, Worsley, Manchester, M28 0FE, Tel.: 0161 702 8181

Mr R Gene, Community Macmillan/Specialist Palliative Care, St Ann's Hospice, Peel Lane, Little Hulton, Worsley, Manchester, M28 0FE, Tel.: 0161 702 8181

Ms G Longton, Community Macmillan/Specialist Palliative Care, St Ann's Hospice, Peel Lane, Little Hulton, Worsley, Manchester, M28 0FE, Tel.: 0161 702 8181

Miss P Lynch, Nursing Home Registration, Sandringham House, Tel.: 0161 212 4000

Ms B Quinn, Community Macmillan/Specialist Palliative Care, St Ann's Hospice, Peel Lane, Little Hulton, Worsley, Manchester, M28 0FE, Tel.: 0161 702 8181

School Nursing
Ms T Doyle, Professional Lead School Health, Sandringham House, Windsor Street, Salford, M5 4DG, Tel.: 0161 212 4170

Specialist Nursing Services
Mrs M Cuffwright, Health Visitor, Asthma, Sandringham House, Tel.: 0161 212 4000

Mrs E Paisley, Chest, Sandringham House, Tel.: 0161 212 4000

Mrs L Hudson, Continence, Eccles Health Centre, Tel.: 0161 789 5135

Ms A Taylor, Leg Ulcers, - Wound Care, The Willows, Lords Avenue, Salford, M5 2HH, Tel.: 0161 737 0330

Salford Royal Hospitals NHS Trust

Trust Headquarters, Hope Hospital
Stott Lane, Salford
MANCHESTER
M6 8HD
Tel.: 0161 789 7373
Fax.: 0161 206 5974

Child Protection/Safeguarding Children
Ms A Tomlinson, Matron - Public Health Lead, Hope Hospital, Tel.: 0161 206 5300

Community Midwifery
Birth Centre Hope Hospital, Tel.: 0161 206 5264

Ms D Carter, Head of Midwifery, Hope Hospital, Tel.: 0161 206 5257

Community Discharges to Salford Area, Tel.: 0161 206 5264

Ms A Tomlinson, Matron - Public Health Lead, Hope Hospital, Tel.: 0161 206 5300

South Liverpool Primary Care Trust

Trust Headquarters, Pavilion 6
The Matchworks, Speke Road
GARSTON
L19 2PH
Tel.: 0151 234 1000

Admin & Senior Management
Ms C Wall, Chief Executive, Acting, Tel.: 0151 291 7359

Child Protection/Safeguarding Children
Ms L Rodgers, Designated Nurse, Regatta Place, Summers Rd, Brunswick Business Park, Liverpool, L3 4BL Tel.: 0151 285 4671/0

Mrs T Jones, Named Nurse Safeguarding Children, Regatta Place, Summers Rd, Brunswick Business Park, Liverpool L3 4BL Tel.: 0151 285 4666 /4670

Safeguarding Children Specialist Nurses, Nerys Edwards, Regatta Place, Summers Road, Liverpool L3 4BL Tel.: 0151 285 4663/4661

Community Nursing Services
Ms M Cowell, Locality Manager, Wavertree Family Health Clinic, 57 Prince Alfred Road, Liverpool, L15 5BG, Tel.: 0151 234 1000

Health Visitors
Ms J Haughton, Paediatric Liaison, Health Visitor, A & E Dept, Aintree Hospital, Tel.: 0151 529 2518

South Manchester Primary Care Trust

Trust Headquarters, 1st Floor, Home 4,
Withington Hospital, Nell Lane
MANCHESTER
M20 2LR
Tel.: 0161 611 3300

Admin & Senior Management
Dr A Mercer, Chief Executive, Southmoor House, Southmoor Road, Wythenshawe,

Child Protection/Safeguarding Children
Ms G Crossley, Senior Nurse, Child Protection, Withington Hospital, Nell Lane, West Didsbury, Tel.: 0161 611 3559

Clinical Leads (NSF)
Dr L Batey, Clinical Lead, Cancer,
Dr K Shearer, Clinical Lead, CHD,
Dr R Thornton, Clinical Lead, Older People,

Community Nursing Services
Mr R Desir, Cluster Director/Executive Lead for Nursing, Withington Community Hospital, Nell Lane, West Didsbury, Tel.: 0161 217 3303

District Nursing
Ms M Karasu, Clinical Lead, District Nurses, Northenden Group Practice, 489 Palatine Road, Manchester, Tel.: 0161 945 3625

Ms S Lake, Clinical Lead, District Nurses, Burnage Healthcare Practice, 347 Burnage Lane, Manchester, Tel.: 0161 443 0600

North West Strategic Health Authority

Health Visitors
Ms K Watton, Clinical Lead, Health Visitors, Baguley Healthcare Centre, Tel.: 0161 998 9700
Ms H Witherington, Clinical Lead, Health Visitors, Wythenshawe Health Care Centre, 1 Stancliffe Road, Wythenshawe, Tel.: 0161 946 9437
Liaison Services
Ms J Bundy, Withington & Wythenshawe Hospitals District Nurse Liaison Sister, Social Work Dept, Wythenshawe Hospital, Southmoor Road, Wythenshawe, M23 9LT, Tel.: 0161 291 2271
Ms M Leckey, Regional District Nurse Oncology Liaison, Christie Hospital, Wilmslow Road, Withington, M20 4BX, Tel.: 0161 446 3775/6
Ms H Peperday, Withington & Wythenshawe Hospitals District Nurse Liaison Sister, Social Work Dept, Wythenshawe Hospital, Southmoor Road, Wythenshawe, M23 9LT, Tel.: 0161 291 2271
Ms A Tongue, Withington & Wythenshawe Hospitals District Nurse Liaison Sister, Social Work Dept, Wythenshawe Hospital, Southmoor Road, Wythenshawe, M23 9LT, Tel.: 0161 291 2271
School Nursing
Ms J Moldauer, Clinical Lead, Northenden Group Practice, 489 Palatine Road, Manchester, Tel.: 0161 945 3624
Specialist Nursing Services
Mrs L Batey, Stroke, CHD, Wythenshawe Health Centre, Tel.: 0161 946 9425
Mr G Wilson, Continence, Wythenshawe Health Centre, Tel.: 0161 946 9400
Ms L Rowen, Dermatology, Buccleauch Lodge, Elizabeth Singer Road, Withington, Tel.: 0161 611 3773
Mrs M Armstrong, Diabetic Care, Diabetes Centre, Wythenshawe Hospital, Southmoor Road, Wythenshawe, M23 9LT, Tel.: 0161 945 8203
Mr F Burton, Diabetic Care, Diabetes Centre, Wythenshawe Hospital, Southmoor Road, Wythenshawe, M23 9LT, 0161 945 8203
Ms M Findlay, Diabetic Care, Diabetes Centre, Wythenshawe Hospital, Southmoor Road, Wythenshawe, M23 9LT, Tel.: 0161 945 8203
Mrs J Price, Diabetic Care, Diabetes Centre, Wythenshawe Hospital, Southmoor Road, Wythenshawe, M23 9LT, Tel.: 0161 945 8203
Ms M McIvor, Stoma Care, Withington Clinic, 535 Wilmslow Road, Manchester, M20 4BA, Tel.: 0161 445 5001
Ms D Woolley, Stoma Care, Withington Clinic, 535 Wilmslow Road, Manchester, M20 4BA, Tel.: 0161 445 5001

South Manchester University Hospitals NHS Trust

Trust Headquarters, Wythenshawe Hospital
Southmoor Road, Wythenshaw
MANCHESTER
M23 9LT
Tel.: 0161 998 7070

Child Protection/Safeguarding Children
Ms A Sullivan, Vulnerable Families, Child Protection, Tel.: 0161 291 2811
Community Midwifery
Mrs S Blantern, Out Patient Services Manager & Community Manager, Maternity Unit, Wythenshawe Hospital, Southmoor Road, Wythenshaw, Manchester, M23 9LT, Tel.: 0161 291 2809
Ms R Davies, Head of Women's Services, Maternity Unit, Wythenshawe Hospital, Southmoor Road, Wythenshaw, Manchester, M23 9LT, Tel.: 0161 291 2810
Ms C Navin, Bereavement Support Midwife, Tel.: 0161 291 2930
Family Planning Services
Ms D Roney, Teenage Pregnancy, Midwife, Tel.: 0161 291 2813
Other Services
Ms K Cooper, Sure Start, Tel.: 0161 291 2813
Ms C Hale, Sure Start, Tel.: 0161 291 2813

South Sefton Primary Care Trust

Trust Headquarters, 3rd Floor Burlington House
Crosby Road North, Waterloo
LIVERPOOL
L22 0QB
Tel.: 0151 920 5056
Fax.: 0151 949 0646

Admin & Senior Management
Miss A Shaw, Director of Health Services, Burlington House, Tel.: 0151 478 1212
Ms J Snoddon, Assistant Director of Health Services, Burlington House, Tel.: 0151 920 5056 ext 225
Child Health Records
Netherton Health Centre, Magdalen Square, Netherton, L30 5FP, Tel.: 0151 521 4000
Child Protection/Safeguarding Children
Mrs S Gunson, Safeguarding Children Specialist Nurse (School Age Children), Thornton Clinic, Tel.: 0151 924 4473
A Shaw, Safeguarding Children Specialist Nurse (Pre School Children) Thornton Clinic Tel.: 0151 932 9568
Clinical Leads (NSF)
Dr C Birt, Clinical Lead, CHD & Diabetes, Burlington House,
Community Matrons
Ms C Lewis, Community Matron, Litherland Town Hall Health Centre, Hatton Hill Road, Litherland, Merseyside, L21 9JN, Tel.: 0151 475 4007/8
Ms V Stevens, Community Matron, Litherland Town Hall Health Centre, Hatton Hill Road, Litherland, Merseyside, L21 9JN, Tel.: 0151 475 4007/8
Community Nursing Services
Ms J Snoddon, Assistant Director of Health Services, Burlington House, Tel.: 0151 920 5056 ext 225
District Nursing
Ms A Birmingham, Service Manager, District Nurses, Burlington House, Tel.: 0151 920 5056
Evening/Night, Litherland Town Hall Health Centre, Hatton Hill Road, Litherland, Merseyside, L21 9JN, Tel.: 0151 475 4007/8
Family Planning Services
Bootle Health Centre, Tel.: 0151 933 6606
Health Visitors
Ms S Dalby, Service Manager, Health Visiting, Burlington House, Tel.: 0151 920 5056
Liaison Services
Liaison/Tracker, University Hospital Aintree, Tel.: 0151 529 5133/4
Pharmacy
Pharmacy Department, Burlington House, Crosby Road North, Waterloo, L22 0QB, Tel.: 0151 920 5056
School Nursing
Ms S Dalby, Service Manager, School Nurses, Burlington House, Tel.: 0151 933 6606
Smoking Cessation
Ms C Fraiser, Co-ordinator, Litherland Town Hall Health Centre, Hatton Hill Road, Litherland, Merseyside, L21 9JN, Tel.: 0151 475 4007/8
Specialist Nursing Services
Ms J O'Connor, ACTRITIE -Acute Triage Rapid Intervention, Chest, Aintree Hospital, Tel.: 0151 529 2514
Ms S Moorcroft, Specialist Nurse, Dermatology, Bootle Health Centre, Park Street, Bootle, L20 3RF, Tel.: 0151 933 6060
Ms M Daly, Specialist Nurse, Diabetes, Litherland Town Hall Health Centre, Hatton Hill Road, Litherland, Merseyside, L21 9JN, Tel.: 0151 475 4007/8
Mr G Williams, Specialist Nurse, Infection Control, Burlington House, Tel.: 0151 920 5056
Ms B Broad, Nurse, Macmillan, Litherland Town Hall Health Centre, Hatton Hill Road, Litherland, Merseyside, L21 9JN, Tel.: 0151 475 4007/8

North West Strategic Health Authority

Ms K Brownley, Nurse, Macmillan, Litherland Town Hall Health Centre, Hatton Hill Road, Litherland, Merseyside, L21 9JN, Tel.: 0151 475 4007/8

Ms G Kenny, Nurse, Macmillan, Litherland Town Hall Health Centre, Hatton Hill Road, Litherland, Merseyside, L21 9JN, Tel.: 0151 475 4007/8

The Homeless/Travellers & Asylum Seekers
Ms S Weights, Refugees, Health Visitor, Bootle Health Centre, Tel.: 0151 933 6606

Walk In Centres
Walk In Centre, Litherland Town Hall Health Centre, Hatton Hill Road, Litherland, Merseyside, L21 9JN, Tel.: 0151 475 4007/8

Southport & Formby Primary Care Trust
Trust Headquarters, 5 Curzon Road
SOUTHPORT
Merseyside
PR8 6LW
Tel.: 01704 387000

Admin & Senior Management
Ms G Dolan, Chief Executive, Trust Headquarters, 5 Curzon Road, Southport, Merseyside, PR8 6LW, Tel.: 01704 387000

Ms A Lumley, Clinical Development Coordinator, 5 Curzon Road, Southport, Merseyside, PR8 6LW, Tel.: 01704 387085

Mrs A J Power, Head of Nursing, 5 Curzon Road, Southport, Merseyside, PR8 6LW, Tel.: 01704 387015

Child Health
Ms W Murphy, Head of Children's Services, 5 Curzon Road, Southport, Merseyside, PR8 6LW, Tel.: 01704 387015

Child Health Records
Over 5's, School Med Dept, Children's Centre, 52 Hoghton Street, Southport, PR9 0PN, Tel.: 01704 547471 ext 3722

Under 5's, Child Health Dept, 5 Curzon Road, Southport, Merseyside, PR8 6LW, Tel.: 01704 387000

Child Protection/Safeguarding Children
Ms K Wright, Named Nurse, Child Protection, 2 Church Street, Southport, Tel.: 01704 383055

Clinical Leads (NSF)
Mrs G Hamblin, Clinical Lead, Cancer,

Ms J Chorley, Clinical Lead, Care of the Elderly,

Ms W Murphy, NSF Young People, Maternity Services, Children,

Community Nursing Services
Ms W Murphy, Head of Children's Services, Tel.: 01704 387000

Mrs A J Power, Head of Nursing (Adults), 5 Curzon Road, Southport, Merseyside, PR8 6LW, Tel.: 01704 387015

District Nursing
Mrs A J Power, Head of Nursing, 5 Curzon Road, Southport, Merseyside, PR8 6LW, Tel.: 01704 387015

Family Planning Services
2 Church Street Clinic, Tel.: 01704 383723

Liaison Services
Mrs S Buckley, Discharge Planning Team, Southport General Infirmary, Pilkington Road, Southport, Tel.: 01704 547471 ex 3640/3639

Specialist Nursing Services
Ms J Storer, Respiratory/Asthma, Nurse Specialist, Asthma, - Respiratory, Lincoln House Clinic, Tel.: 01704 878484

Ms V Quinney, Nurse Specialist, Continence, Poulton Road Clinic, Southport, Tel.: 01704 383205

Ms K Hampson, Nurse Practitioner, Diabetic Care, Gordon House, Leicester Street, Southport, PR9 0BG,

Ms S Houghton, Nurse Practitioner, Diabetic Care, Gordon House, Leicester Street, Southport, PR9 0BG,

Mrs D Jamnes, Nurse Specialist, Diabetic Care, Salus Centre, Southport District General Hospital, Tel.: 01704 547471 ext 4394

Ms V Hindley, Nurse Specialist, Lymphoedema, 2 Church Street, Southport, Tel.: 01704 383723

Nurse Specialists, Palliative Care, Umbrella House, Southport District General Hospital,

Mrs S Miller, Nurse Specialist, Stoma Care, Poulton Road Clinic, Southport, Tel.: 01704 383207

Ms D Oates, Nurse Specialist, Tissue Viability, - Ulcers, Churchtown Clinic, Cambridge Street, Southport, Tel.: 01704 507235

The Homeless/Travellers & Asylum Seekers
Ms L Hough, Ainsdale Clinic,

Ms W Murphy, Head Children's Services,

Southport & Ormskirk NHS Trust
Trust Headquarters, Town Lane
SOUTHPORT
PR8 6PN
Tel.: 01704 547471

Admin & Senior Management
Mr E Chew, Director of Nursing, Southport & Ormskirk NHS Trust, Town Lane, Southport, PR8 6PN,

Community Midwifery
Community Midwives Office, Team Base, Postnatal Ward, Level 3, Ormskirk District General Hospital, Wigan Rd, Ormskirk, L39 2AZ, Tel.: 01695 656668

Community Midwives Office, c/o Midwifery Led Unit, Southport District General Hospital, Town Lane, Southport, PR8 6PN, Tel.: 01704 704698

Mrs L Eastham, Ormskirk & Southport Sites, Head of Midwifery, Ormskirk & District General Hospital, Wigan Road, Ormskirk, L39 2AZ, Tel.: 01695 656664

St Helens Primary Care Trust
Trust Headquarters
Cowley Hill Lane
ST HELENS
Merseyside
WA10 2AP
Tel.: 01744 457221

Admin & Senior Management
Mrs R Burke-Sharples, Chief Executive,

Mrs N Giubertoni, Chair,

Mrs K Howell, Chief of Operations & Director of Performance,

Ms F Johnstone, Director of Public Health,

Mr M Treharne, Deputy Chief Executive & Director of Finance,

Child Health
Mrs J McDonald, Director of Child & Family Services/Designated Nurse Child Protection, St Helens PCT, The Elms, Cowley Hill Lane, St Helens, WA10 2AP, Tel.: 01744 601098

Child Health Records
Health Informatics, The Hollies, Cowley Hill Lane, St Helens, Merseyside, WA10 2AP, Tel.: 01744 697204

Child Protection/Safeguarding Children
Mrs J McDonald, Director of Child & Family Services/Designated Nurse for Child Protection, St Helens PCT, The Elms, Cowley Hill Lane, St Helens, WA10 2AP, Tel.: 01744 601098

Community Matrons
Ms A Booth, Community Matron, St Helens PCT,

Mrs W Burton, Community Matron, St Helens PCT,

Ms S Jackson, Community Matron, St Helens PCT,

Community Nursing Services
Alexandra Park, 1st Floor Court Block, Prescot Road, St Helens, WA10 3TT,

Mrs J Pickett, Head of Adult Nursing Services,

District Nursing
Mrs A McHale, Nurse Lead District Nursing, Alexandra Park, 1st Floor Court Block, Prescot Road, St Helens, WA10 3TT, Tel.: 01744 620370

North West Strategic Health Authority

Family Planning Services
Dr L Kingsley, Director of Family Planning & Reproductive Health, Alexandra Park, 1st Floor Court Block, Prescot Road, St Helens, WA10 3TT, Tel.: 01744 620364

Health Visitors
Mrs R Polding, Public Health Specialist (Children & Families), The Elms, Cowley Hill Lane, St Helens, Merseyside, WA10, Tel.: 01744 601098

Learning Disabilities
Mrs J East, St Helens Borough Director - 5 Boroughs Partnership Trust, c/o The Eccleston Centre, St Helens Hospital, Marshalls Cross Road, St Helens, WA9 3DA, Tel.: 01744 458424
Learning Disabilities, Willis House, 23 Cumber Lane, Whiston, L35 2YZ,

Liaison Services
District Nurse Liaison, Henley House, Whiston Hospital, Warrington Road, Prescot, Merseyside, L35 5DR, Tel.: 0151 290 2030

Other Services
Mr J Ball, Consultant Cardiologist, Whiston Hospital, Warrington Road, Prescot, Merseyside, L35 5DR, Tel.: 0151 426 1600
Mr N Dyer, Assistant Director Health & Social Care for Older People, St Helens Council, Gamble Buildings, Victoria Square, St Helens, Tel.: 01744 456311
Health Improvement Services, St Helens PCT, The Hollies, Cowley Hill Lane, St Helens, WA10 2AP, Tel.: 01744 697240
Mrs T Slevin, Acting Team Leader, Healthy Heart Service, Alexandra Park, 1st Floor Court Block, Prescot Road, St Helens, WA10 3TT, Tel.: 01744 620350
Ms M Barnes, Nurse Consultant, Care of the Elderly, Whiston Hospital, Warrington Road, Prescot, Merseyside, L35 5DR, Tel.: 0151 426 1600
Ms C Lamb, Acting Service Manager, Care of the Elderly, Blackbrook Local Office, 47 Blackbrook Road, St Helens, WA9 3JN, Tel.: 01744 677719
Dr K Beeby, CHD, Fingerpost Surgery, 117 Higher Parr Street, St Helens, WA9 1AG, Tel.: 01744 21867
Ms S Forster, Public Health Specialist, Diabetic Care, St Helens PCT, Cowley Hill Lane, St Helens, WA10 2AP, Tel.: 01744 457245
Mr E DeSai, Specialist, Public Health, St Helens PCT, Cowley Lane, St Helens, WA10 2AP, Tel.: 01744 457245

Pharmacy
Mrs M Geoghegan, Head of Medicines Management, St Helens PCT, The Gables, Cowley Hill Lane, St Helens, WA10 2AP, Tel.: 01744 457249

School Nursing
Mrs L Brownlow, Nurse Lead School Nursing, The Elms, Cowley Hill Lane, St Helens, Merseyside, Tel.: 01744 601098

Specialist Nursing Services
Ms K Morris, Paediatric Services, Continence, Alexandra Park, 1st Floor Court Block, Prescot Road, St Helens, WA10 3TT,
Ms G Poland, Adult Services, Continence, Alexandra Park, 1st Floor Court Block, Prescot Road, St Helens, WA10 3TT,
Nurses, Macmillan, Willowbrook Hospice, Portico Lane, Prescot, Merseyside, L34 1QT, Tel.: 0151 431 0156
Ms C Welding, Nurse, Tissue Viability, Lingholme Health Centre, Atherton Street, St Helens, WA10 2HT, Tel.: 01744 611501

The Homeless/Travellers & Asylum Seekers
Ms C Mortimore, Lead Nurse, Homelessness Team, St Helens PCT, The Gables, Cowley Hill Lane, St Helens, Merseyside, WA10 2AP, Tel.: 01744 457278

St. Helen's & Knowsley Hospitals NHS Trust

Trust Headquarters, Whiston Hospital
Warrington Road
PRESCOT
Merseyside, L35 5DR
Tel.: 0151 426 1600
Fax.: 0151 430 1720

Child Protection/Safeguarding Children
Mr M Falackerley, Named Nurse, Child Protection,
Mrs L Spakousicas, Named Midwife, Child Protection,

Community Midwifery
Miss T Bogle, Senior Manager/Modern Matron, Whiston Hospital, Tel.: 0151 430 1518
Mrs L Moore, Head of Midwifery, Whiston Hospital, Tel.: 0151 430 1524
Mrs S Nicholson, Community Midwifery Secretary, Tel.: 0151 430 1492
Mrs L Spakouskas, Community Midwifery Manager, Tel.: 0151 430 1510

Stockport Learning Disability Partnership

Learning Disability Partnership
Oak House, 2 Gatley Road
CHEADLE
Cheshire
SK8 1PY
Tel.: 0161 491 4376

Learning Disabilities
Ms M Benson, Clinical Nurse Specialist, Oak House, 2 Gatley Road, Cheadle, Cheshire, SK8 1P, Tel.: 0161 491 4376
Mr M Corrigan, Head of Service, Oak House, 2 Gatley Road, Cheadle, Cheshire, SK8 1PY, Tel.: 0161 491 4376

Stockport NHS Foundation Trust

Trust Headquarters, Stepping Hill Hospital
Poplar Grove
STOCKPORT
Cheshire
SK2 7JE
Tel.: 0161 483 1010

Community Midwifery
Maternity Unit, Tel.: ext 5510
Operational Manager, Womens Unit, Stepping Hill Hospital, Stockport, SK2 7NY, Tel.: 0161 419 5288
Mrs A Ramsay, Divisional General Manager/Head of Midwifery, Womens Unit, Stepping Hill Hospital, Stockport, SK2 7NY, Tel.: 0161 419 5500/5559

Stockport Primary Care Trust

Trust Headquarters, 7th Floor
Regent House, Heaton Lane
STOCKPORT
SK4 1BS
Tel.: 0161 426 5000

Admin & Senior Management
Mrs G Frome, Director of Clinical Services, 3rd Floor, Regent House, Heaton Lane, Stockport, SK4 1BS, Tel.: 0161 426 5523

Child Health Records
Child Health Records, 8th Floor, Regent House, Heaton Lane, Stockport, SK4 1BS, Tel.: 0161 426 5000
School Health Records, 253 London Road, Hazel Grove, Stockport, SK7 4PW, Tel.: 0161 612 4217

Child Protection/Safeguarding Children
Ms L Reason, Senior Nurse, Child Protection, Redwood Unit, 2nd Floor, Tree House, Stepping Hill Hospital, Poplar Grove, Stockport, SK2 7JE, Tel.: 0161 419 2020

Community Nursing Services
Ms J Ankrett, Head of Community Nursing, 3rd Floor, Regent House, Heaton Lane, Stockport, SK4 1BS, Tel.: 0161 426 5000

Family Planning Services
Ms B Swann, The Gallery, Cherry Tree Hospital, Tel.: 0161 419 4847
Ms B Swann, Nurse Consultant, 3rd Floor, Regent House, Heaton Lane, Stockport, SK4 1BS, Tel.: 0161 426 5000

North West Strategic Health Authority

Liaison Services

Mrs C Morris, Adult Liaison, Stepping Hill Hospital, Tel.: 0161 483 1010

Mrs P Ratcliff, Children's Liaison, Stepping Hill Hospital, Tel.: 0161 483 1010

School Nursing

Mrs L Leach, Professional Development Unit (School Nursing), 6th Floor Regent House, Heaton Lane, Stockport, SK4 1BS, Tel.: 0161 426 5000

Specialist Nursing Services

Active Case Management, 9th Floor Regent House, Heaton Lane, Stockport, SK4 1BS, Tel.: 0161 426 5000

CFS/ME, 9th Floor Regent House, Heaton Lane, Stockport, SK4 1BS, Tel.: 0161 426 5000

Service, Continence, Unit 2, Kennedy Way, Green Lane, Didsbury, Tel.: 0161 426 5000

Nurses, COPD, Kingsgate House, Wellington Road North, Stockport, SK4 1LW, Tel.: 0161 426 5000

Nurses, Dermatology, Kingsgate House, Wellington Road North, Stockport, SK4 1LW, Tel.: 0161 426 5000

Nurses, Diabetic Care, Kingsgate House, Wellington Road North, Stockport, SK4 1LW, Tel.: 0161 426 5000

Nurses, Heart Failure, Kingsgate House, Wellington Road North, Stockport, SK4 1LW, Tel.: 0161 426 5000

Nurses, Macmillan, Hazel Grove Clinic, 253 London Road, Hazel Grove, Stockport, SK7 4PW, Tel.: 0161 612 4200

Team, Palliative Care, Hazel Grove Clinic, 253 London Road, Hazel Grove, SK7 4PW, Tel.: 0161 612 4200

Dr D Waterman, Consultant, Palliative Care, Hazel Grove Clinic, 253 London Road, Hazel Grove, SK7 4PW, Tel.: 0161 612 4200

Nurses, Tissue Viability, Unit 2, Kennedy Way, Green Lane, Didsbury, Tel.: 0161 426 5000

Tameside & Glossop Acute Services NHS Trust

Trust Headquarters, Tameside General Hospital
Fountain Street
ASHTON-UNDER-LYNE
Lancashire, OL6 9RW
Tel.: 0161 331 6000

Community Midwifery

Miss A Bickerdyke, Head of Midwifery, Maternity Unit, Charlesworth Building, Fountain Street, Ashton-under-Lyne, OL6 9RW, Tel.: 0161 331 6152

Mrs C M Pearce, Deputy Head of Midwifery, Tel.: 0161 331 6159

Learning Disabilities

Ms S Butterworth, Manager, LD Service Headquarters, 4 Crowthorn Road, Ashton-under-Lyne, OL7 0DH, Tel.: 0161 330 5892

Mr D Fidler, Directorate Manager, LD Service Headquarters, 4 Crowthorn Road, Ashton-under-Lyne, OL7 0DH, Tel.: 0161 330 5892

Tameside & Glossop Primary Care Trust

Trust Headquarters, New Century House
Progress Way, Windmill Lane
DENTON, H34 2GP
Tel.: 0161 304 5300

Admin & Senior Management

Ms T Sloan, Acting Chief Executive,

Child Health

Ms T Joseph-McSween, Team Leader, Child Health, New Century House, Progress Way, Windmill Lane, Denton, H34 2GP, Tel.: 0161 304 5477

Child Health Records

Child Health Records, Tel: 0161 304 5472/5473/5474/5475/5476, New Century House, Progress Way, Windmill Lane, Denton, H34 GP,

Child Protection/Safeguarding Children

Ms E Fiveash, Designated Nurse, Child Protection, Selbourne House, Union Street, Hyde, SK14 1NG, Tel.: 0161 304 5428

Ms M Harding, Named Nurse, Child Protection, Tameside & Glossop PCT, New Century House, Windmill Lane, Denton, H34 2GP, Tel.: 0161 304 5300

Clinical Leads (NSF)

Dr K Patel, Clinical Lead, CHD,

Ms K Holden, Clinical Lead, Children, Selbourne House, Tel.: 0161 368 4242

Dr P Joyce, Clinical Lead, Diabetic Care, Churchgate Surgery, Denton,

Dr S T E Bradshaw, Clinical Lead, Older People,

Community Nursing Services

Ms L Batteson, Director of Nursing & Operations, Tel.: 0161 304 5421

District Nursing

Ms L Adie, Acting Head of Adult Services,

Family Planning Services

Ms V Redfern, Selbourne House, Union Street, Hyde, SK14 1NG,

Health Visitors

Mrs K Cross, Paediatrics Liaison, Health Visitor, Paediatric Unit, Tameside General Hospital, Fountain Street, Ashton-under-Lyne, OL6 9RW, Tel.: 0161 331 5032

Ms J Horan, Operational Head for Health Visitors,

Ms T Wood, Head of Child & Family Services,

HIV/AIDS

Ms C Bailey, Co-ordinator, Crickets Lane Clinic, Crickets Lane, Ashton-u-Lyne, OL6 6NG, Tel.: 0161 339 9400 ext 304

Learning Disabilities

Ms C Symons, Unit Manager, Learning Disability Headquarters, Frederick House, Dunkirk Lane, Hyde, SK14 4QD, Tel.: 0161 342 5225

Liaison Services

Ms S Metcalf, Liaison, General/Elderly/Ortho, District Nurse, Tameside General Hospital, Tel.: 0161 331 5184

Other Services

Shire Hill Intermediate Care Unit, Bute Street, Glossop, Derbyshire, SK13 9PZ,

Specialist Nursing Services

Ms B Murphy, Diabetic Care, Selbourne House, Tel.: 0161 330 5266

Ms C Saunders, Nurse, Infection Control, Guide Lane Clinic, Audenshaw, Manchester, M34 5HY, Tel.: 0161 330 7637

Mrs M E Hayes, Macmillan, Ann Street Health Centre, Denton, Manchester, M34 2AS, Tel.: 0161 320 7000

Mrs I Yates, Wound Care, Guide Lane Clinic, Audenshaw, Manchester, M34 5HY, Tel.: 0161 330 7637

Trafford Healthcare NHS Trust

Trust Headquarters, Trafford General Hospital
Moorside Road, Davyhulme
MANCHESTER
M41 5SL
Tel.: 0161 748 4022
Fax.: 0161 746 8556

Acute Specialist Nursing Services

Ms N Robinson Greig, Breast Care, Tel.: 0161 746 2462 bleep 121

Ms S Walsh, Colorectal, Tel.: 0161 746 2323

Ms T Bercik, Diabetic Care, Tel.: 0161 746 2458

Ms L Hopewell, Diabetic Care, Tel.: 0161 746 2458

Ms D Morrison, Diabetic Care, Tel.: 0161 746 2458

Ms N Rushton, Diabetic Care, Tel.: 0161 746 2458

Ms L Skipper, Infection Control, Tel.: 0161 746 2430

Ms N Webster, Rehabilitation, - Elderly Care, Tel.: 0161 746 2892

Ms G Mates, Respiratory, Tel.: 0161 746 2428

Ms J Hayes, Rheumatology, Tel.: 0161 746 2162

Ms F Murtaugh, Urology, Tel.: 0161 746 2975

North West Strategic Health Authority

Admin & Senior Management
Ms P Jones, Director of Nursing, Trafford Healthcare NHS Trust, Moorside Road, Davyhulme, Manchester, M41 5SL, Tel.: 0161 746 2208

Child Protection/Safeguarding Children
Ms L Lloyd, Designated/Named Nurse, Seymour Grove Health Centre, Tel.: 0161 872 5672 ext 217

Community Midwifery
Community Midwifery Office, Tel.: 0161 746 8354
Mrs R Connor, Head of Midwifery, Trafford General Hospital, Tel.: 0161 746 2132
Mrs C Ellison, Community Midwifery Manager, Tel.: 0161 746 2129
Emergencies - out of hours, Tel.: 0161 748 5542

Family Planning Services
Ms A Mather, Sexual Health, Tel.: 0161 746 2621
Ms S Williams, Senior Nurse Well Adults/FP, Tel.: 0161 746 2027

Health Visitors
Ms J Freeman, Liaison - Health Visitors, Trafford General Hospital, Moorside Road, Davyhulme, Manchester, M41 5SL, Tel.: 0161 748 4022 ext 2366
Ms C Snowdon, Liaison - Health Visitors, Trafford General Hospital, Moorside Road, Davyhulme, Manchester, M41 5SL, Tel.: 0161 748 4022 ext 2366

Liaison Services
Ms B Bradburn, Liaison - General Acute, Trafford General Hospital, Moorside Road, Davyhulme, Manchester, M41 5SL, Tel.: 0161 748 4022 ext 2347/8
Ms J Freeman, Liaison - Health Visitors, Trafford General Hospital, Moorside Road, Davyhulme, Manchester, M41 5SL, Tel.: 0161 748 4022 ext 2366
Ms C Snowdon, Liaison - Health Visitors, Trafford General Hospital, Moorside Road, Davyhulme, Manchester, M41 5SL, Tel.: 0161 748 4022 ext 2366
Ms C Tynan, Liaison - Elderly, Trafford General Hospital, Moorside Road, Davyhulme, Manchester, M41 5SL, Tel.: 0161 748 4022 ext 2349
Ms P Urbaniak, Liaison - Elderly, Trafford General Hospital, Moorside Road, Davyhulme, Manchester, M41 5SL, Tel.: 0161 748 4022 ext 2349

Trafford North Primary Care Trust

Trust Headquarters, Oakland House
Talbot Road
Manchester
M16 0PQ
Tel.: 0161 873 9500
Fax.: 0161 873 9501

Admin & Senior Management
Mrs J Musgrove, Head of Nursing, Oakland House, Talbot Road, Manchester, M16 0PQ, Tel.: 0161 873 9500
Mr T Riley, Chief Executive,
Ms D Robson, Clinical Nurse Manager, Oakland House, Talbot Road, Manchester, M16 0PQ, Tel.: 0161 873 3060
Ms J Trainor, Clinical Nurse Manager, Tel.: 0161 873 6043

Child Health
Child Health/School Nurses/Child Records/Child Protection, Trafford Healthcare Trust,

Child Health Records
Child Health Records, Community Information Dept, Trafford General Hospital, Moorside Road, Urmston, Manchester, M41 5SL, Tel.: 0161 748 4022

Clinical Leads (NSF)
Ms L Davies, Clinical Lead, Coronary Heart Disease,
Ms H Thomas, Clinical Lead, Cancer,
Mr D McNally, Clinical Lead, Older People,

Community Midwifery
Midwifery, Trafford Healthcare Trust,

District Nursing
Cornhill Clinic, Cornhill Road, Urmston, Manchester, Tel.: 0161 748 2820
Delamere Centre, Delamere Avenue, Stretford, Manchester, Tel.: 0161 864 0300
Mitford Street Clinic, Mitford Street, Stretford, Manchester, Tel.: 0161 865 6569
Partington Health Centre, Central Road, Partington, Manchester, M31 4FL, Tel.: 0161 775 1521
Seymour Grove Health Centre, Seymour Grove, Manchester, M16 0LW, Tel.: 0161 872 5672
Woodsend Clinic, Woodsend Crescent Road, Flixton, Manchester, Tel.: 0161 746 7283

Equipment Loan Services
Ms P Roberts, One Stop Resource Centre, Dare Road, Sale, Manchester,

Health Visitors
Ms L Butler, Liaison, Health Visitor, Tel.: 0161 748 4022 xt 2366
Ms J Freeman, Liaison, Health Visitor, Tel.: 0161 748 4022 xt 2366
Mrs A Greene, Health Visitor for the Elderly, North Trafford Combined Care Centre, Seymour Grove, Tel.: 0161 860 2701
Mrs M Pearson, Health Visitor for the Elderly, North Trafford Combined Care Centre, Seymour Grove, Tel.: 0161 860 2701

Learning Disabilities
Ms A Johnson, Sale Waterside, Manchester,

Liaison Services
Ms M Martin, General Liaison, Tel.: 0161 748 4022 xt 2347/8/9
Mrs C Peach, General Liaison, Tel.: 0161 746 2347/8/9
Ms C Tynan, General Liaison, Tel.: 0161 748 4022 xt 2347/8/9
Ms P Urbaniak, General Liaison, Tel.: 0161 748 4022 xt 2347/8/9
Mrs K Whittle, General Liaison, Tel.: 0161 746 2347/8/9

Other Services
In Patient Respite Unit, North Trafford Combined Care Centre, Seymour Grove, Tel.: 0161 860 2700
Pre & Post Natal Care Team, Cornhill Clinic, Cornhill Road, Davyhulme, Manchester, Tel.: 0161 748 2820

Pharmacy
Ms L Nathan, Prescribing Advisor, Tel.: 0161 873 9500

Specialist Nursing Services
Ms D Walsh, Team Manager, Community Phlebotomy Service, Mitford Street Clinic, Stretford,
Ms D Dooley, Advisor, Continence, Delamere Centre, Delamere Avenue, Stretford, Manchester, Tel.: 0161 864 0300
Ms C Hilton, Advisor, Continence, Delamere Centre, Delamere Avenue, Stretford, Manchester, Tel.: 0161 864 0300
Ms C Maguire, Advisor, Continence, Delamere Centre, Delamere Avenue, Stretford, Manchester, Tel.: 0161 864 0300
Ms D McNicoll, Advisor, Continence, Delamere Centre, Delamere Avenue, Stretford, Manchester, Tel.: 0161 864 0300
Tier 2 Diabetes Service Trafford PCT's, Diabetes, 3rd Floor, Oakland House, Talbot Road, Old Trafford, M16 0PQ,
Ms J Christian, Neuro-rehabilitation Community Team, Neurology, Seymour Unit, Trafford General Hospital,

Trafford South Primary Care Trust

Trust Headquarters, Oaklands House
Washway Road
SALE, M33 6FS
Tel.: 0161 968 3700

Admin & Senior Management
Ms C Nolan, Chief Operating Officer, Provider Unit, Tel.: 0161 968 3700
Dr T Riley, Chief Executive, Oaklands House, Washway Road, Sale, M33 6FS, Tel.: 0161 873 9500

Child Health
Dr A John, Community Paediatrician, Seymour Grove Health Centre, Tel.: 0161 872 5672

North West Strategic Health Authority

Child Protection/Safeguarding Children
Ms L Lloyd, Designated Nurse, Child Protection, Seymour Grove Health Centre, Tel.: 0161 872 5672
Clinical Leads (NSF)
Ms H Thomas, Cancer, Oaklands House, Washway Road, Sale, M33 6FS, Tel.: 0161 968 3700
Ms S Burden, Care of the Elderly, Conway Road Health Centre, Tel.: 0161 962 4132
Mr A Howard, CHD, Oaklands House, Washway Road, Sale, M33 6FS, Tel.: 0161 873 9500
Mr R Burton, Diabetic Care, Oaklands House, Washway Road, Sale, M33 6FS, Tel.: 0161 968 3700
Community Nursing Services
Ms J Musgrove, Oaklands House, Washway Road, Sale, M33 6NS, Tel.: 0161 968 3700
Ms C Throssel, Community Information, Trafford General Hospital, Moorside Road, Davyhulme, Manchester, M41 58L, 0161 748 4022
District Nursing
Care of Clinical Nurse Managers, Oaklands House, Washway Road, Sale, M33 6NS, Tel.: 0161 968 3700
Mr B McCabe, Evening/Overnight District Nursing Service, Chapel Road Clinic, Tel.: 0161 973 1329
Learning Disabilities
Ms P West,
Liaison Services
These are provided by Trafford North PCT,
Other Services
Ms D Finch, Bereavement Co-ordinator, Diane Finch Macmillan Centre, Tel.: 0161 748 4022
Ms S Williams, Well Adult Services, Trafford General Hospital, Moorside Road, Davyhulme, M41 58L, Tel.: 0161 748 4022
Pharmacy
Ms L Nathan, Trafford North PCT, Oaklands House, Washway Road, Sale, M33 6FS, Tel.: 0161 873 9500
School Nursing
Mrs Y Macareth, School Health, Seymour Grove Health Centre, Tel.: 0161 872 5672
Smoking Cessation
Ms E Kinnisburgh, Health Promotion, Poel House, Albert Street, Eccles, M30 0NJ, Tel.: 0161 787 0116
Specialist Nursing Services
Mr R Gee, ICP Facilitators, Care of Dying, Trafford General Hospital, Tel.: 0161 748 4022
Mr A Walton, Clinical Placement Development Manager, Oaklands House, Tel.: 0161 968 3700
Mrs D McNicholl, Continence, Delamere Centre, Tel.: 0161 864 0300
Ms M Biesty, Nurse, Macmillan, Trafford General Hospital, Tel.: 0161 748 4022
Ms A M Cobb, Nurse, Macmillan, Trafford General Hospital, Tel.: 0161 748 4022
Ms M Ferguson, Nurse, Macmillan, Bodmin Road Clinic, Sale, Tel.: 0161 973 1127
Ms J Murphy, Nurse, Macmillan, Trafford General Hospital, Tel.: 0161 748 4022
Ms K O'Connor, Nurse, Macmillan, Bodmin Road Clinic, Sale, Tel.: 0161 973 1127
Miss E West, Nurse, Macmillan, Bodmin Road Clinic, Sale, Tel.: 0161 973 1127
Mr K Kristofferson, Tissue Viability, Oaklands House, 0161 968 3700

Walton Centre for Neurology & Neurosurgery
Trust Headquarters, The Walton Centre
Lower Lane, Fazakerley
LIVERPOOL, L9 7LJ
Tel.: 0151 525 3611
Fax.: 0151 529 5500

Acute Specialist Nursing Services
Ms M Enis, OT, Tel.: 0151 529 3611
Ms N Grundy, MND, Nurse, Tel.: 0151 529 3611
Ms G Medley, Nurse Clinician, Tel.: 0151 529 3611
Ms J Poston, Nurse Clinician, Tel.: 0151 529 3611
Ms P Crofton, Outreach, Nurse Consultant, Critical Care, Tel.: 0151 529 3611
Ms G Hart, Nurse, Epilepsy, Tel.: 0151 529 3611
Ms S Lewis, Nurse, Epilepsy, Tel.: 0151 529 3611
Ms J McGee, Nurse, Epilepsy, Tel.: 0151 529 3611
Ms J Winterbottom, Nurse, Epilepsy, Tel.: 0151 529 3611
Ms R Bulloch, Nurse, Movement Disorder, Tel.: 0151 529 3611
Ms J Parsons, Nurse, Movement Disorder, Tel.: 0151 529 3611
Ms A Sinnott, Surgical, Nurse, Movement Disorder, 0151 529 3611
Mr A Jones, Nurse, Multiple Sclerosis, Tel.: 0151 529 3611
Ms H Leggett, Nurse, Multiple Sclerosis, Tel.: 0151 529 3611
Ms F Lynch, Nurse, Multiple Sclerosis, Tel.: 0151 529 3611
Ms K Mutch, Nurse, Multiple Sclerosis, Tel.: 0151 529 3611
Ms K Vernon, Nurse, Multiple Sclerosis, Tel.: 0151 529 3611
Ms J Mellor, Nurse, Neuro-oncology, Tel.: 0151 529 3611
Ms H Parton, Nurse, Neuro-oncology, Tel.: 0151 529 3611
Ms S Barnett, Physio, Pain Management, Tel.: 0151 529 3611
Ms J Craig, Physio, Pain Management, Tel.: 0151 529 3611
Ms C Haslam, Nurse, Pain Management, Tel.: 0151 529 3611
Ms K MacIver, Nurse, Pain Management, Tel.: 0151 529 3611
Ms S Faulds, Nurse, Tissue Viability, - Infection Control, Tel.: 0151 529 3611
Ms P Kane, Nurse, Tissue Viability, - Infection Control, Tel.: 0151 529 3611
Admin & Senior Management
Mr D Melia, Director of Nursing, The Walton Centre for Neurology & Neurosurgery, Lower Lane, Fazakerley, Liverpool, L9 7LJ, Tel.: 0151 529 5631
Child Protection/Safeguarding Children
Ms P Ellery, Child Protection, Tel.: 0151 529 5757

Warrington Primary Care Trust
Trust Headquarters, Millennium House
930-932 Birchwood Boulevard
Birchwood
WARRINGTON
WA3 7QN
Tel.: 01925 843600
Fax.: 01925 843601

Admin & Senior Management
Ms M Butler, Assistant Director of Modernisation,
Mrs A Cooke, Chief Executive,
Child Health
Ms J Harrison, Paediatric Continence, Tel.: 01925 241415
Ms J Sampson, Senior, Nurse Manager, Child Health Unit, Guardian House, Guardian Street, Warrington, WA5 1TP, Tel.: 01925 405733
Ms J Spratley, Assistant Director of Operations, Child Health Unit, Guardian House, Guardian Street, Warrington, WA5 1TP, Tel.: 01925 405714
Child Health Records
Child Health Records, Child Health Unit, Guardian House, Guardian Street, Warrington, WA5 1TP, Tel.: 01925 405700
Child Protection/Safeguarding Children
Mrs C M Fisher, Child Protection, Child Health Unit, Guardian House, Guardian Street, Warrington, WA5 1TP, Tel.: 01925 405727
Clinical Leads (NSF)
Mrs M Ibbotson, Clinical Lead, Cancer,
Community Nursing Services
Mrs A Clayton, Senior Nurse Manager, Grappenhall Clinic, Springfield Avenue, Grappenhall, Warrington, WA4 2NW, Tel.: 01925 217222

North West Strategic Health Authority

District Nursing
Mrs A Clayton, Senior Nurse Manager, Grappenhall Clinic,
Springfield Avenue, Grappenhall, Warrington, WA4 2NW, Tel.:
01925 217222
Health Visitors
Mrs C M Lawson, Paediatric Liaison Health Visitor, Warrington
Hospital, Lovely Lane, Warrington, WA5 1QG, Tel.: 01925 636693
Liaison Services
Ms G Edwards, Community Discharge Facilitator, Tel.: 01925
662496
Specialist Nursing Services
Ms C Denny, Cardiac Rehabilitation, Tel.: 01925 213347
Ms D Duane, Cardiac Rehabilitation, Tel.: 01925 213347
Ms A Leyland, Cardiac Rehabilitation, Tel.: 01925 213347
Ms A Ward, Cardiac Rehabilitation, Tel.: 01925 213347
Ms A Middleton, Continence, Tel.: 01925 751310
Ms P Pemberton, Continence, Tel.: 01925 751310
Mr L Prashar, Continence, Tel.: 01925 751310
Ms S Holt, Infection Control, Tel.: 01925 843600
Ms S Cox, Macmillan, Tel.: 01925 217211
Ms J Ellam, Macmillan, Tel.: 01925 217211
Ms C Harrison, Macmillan, Tel.: 01925 217211
Ms E McEntree, Macmillan, Tel.: 01925 217211
Ms J Shaw, Stoma Care, Tel.: 01925 662103
The Homeless/Travellers & Asylum Seekers
Ms S Craggs, Health Visitor, Garven Place Clinic, Sankey Street,
Warrington, WA1 1GP, Tel.: 01925 644206

West Cumbria Primary Care Trust

Anne Burrow Thomas Health Centre
South William Street
WORKINGTON
Cumbria
CA14 2EW
Tel.: 01900 324220

Admin & Senior Management
Ms N Carruthers, Professional Development Lead, Tel.: 01900
324250
Child Health
Flatt Walks Health Centre, Tel.: 01946 695551 ext 260
Child Health Records
Flatt Walks Health Centre, Tel.: 01946 695551 ext 260
Child Protection/Safeguarding Children
Mrs D Bertram, Child Protection, Workington Community Hospital,
Tel.: 01900 602244 ext 161
District Nursing
Mrs K Burton, Tel.: 01900 324258
Family Planning Services
Ms C Duncan, Tel.: 01228 602000
Health Visitors
Ms L Mason-Lodge, Tel.: 01900 705000
Liaison Services
Ms L Dixon, Liaison, Sister, West Cumberland Hospital, Tel.: 01946
693181 ext 3529
Other Services
Ms I Burns, Breast Feeding Adviser, West Cumberland Hospital,
Tel.: 01946 693181
Ms J Fraser, Health Adviser, Workington Community Hospital, Tel.:
01900 602244 ext 2091
Miss S McClemens, Community Rehab Team Co-ordinator, West
Cumberland Hospital, Tel.: 01946 693181
Specialist Nursing Services
Ms J Johnston, Breast Care, West Cumberland Hospital, Tel.: 01946
693181
Mrs W Colley, Continence, Flatt Walks Health Centre, Tel.: 01946
692173 ext 244

Ms E Breslin, Diabetic Care, West Cumberland Hospital, Tel.: 01946
693181
Ms F Kelly, Infection Control, West Cumberland Hospital, Tel.: 01946
693181
Ms A Walker, Leg Ulcers, West Cumberland Hospital, Tel.: 01946
693181
Ms A Walker, Leg Ulcers, West Cumberland Hospital, Tel.: 01946
693181
Ms L Hewitt, Macmillan, Palliative Care, Working Community
Hospital, Tel.: 01900 602244 ext 2030
Ms A Wear, Stoma Care, West Cumberland Hospital, Tel.: 01946
693181

West Lancashire Primary Care Trust

Trust Headquarters, Ormskirk & District General Hospital
Wigan Road
ORMSKIRK
Lancashire
L39 2JW
Tel.: 01695 598073

Admin & Senior Management
Mr A Horne, Chief Executive, Tel.: 01695 598073
Mrs L Melia, Acting Associate Director Service Provision, West
Lancs PCT, Ormskirk & District Hospital,
Child Health
Mrs L Braley, Head of Children's Services, Tel.: 01695 598144
Ms B Gray, Child Development Centre Co-ordinator, Tel.: 01695
598402
Child Health Records
Information Services, Child Health Section, Trust HQ, Ormskirk &
District General Hospital, Tel.: 01695 598116
Child Protection/Safeguarding Children
Mrs M Coll, Senior Nurse, Child Protection, Ormskirk & District
General Hospital, Tel.: 01695 598109
Clinical Leads (NSF)
Ms G Hamblin, Clinical Lead, Cancer,
Clinical Lead, Care of the Elderly, Tel.: 01695 598270
Mr D Mullen, Clinical Lead, GP, CHD, Tel.: 01257 463126
Ms M Kirwan, Clinical Lead, Diabetic Care,
District Nursing
Ms G Wallace, Executive/Lead Nurse/Community Services Manager
Tel.: 01695 598123
Family Planning Services
Ms L Dobson, Family Planning, Lead Nurse, Tel.: 01695 598123
Health Visitors
Ms M Gleave, Liaison, Paediatric, Health Visitor, Tel.: 01695 598402
HIV/AIDS
GUM Clinic, Acacia House, Tel.: 01695 656971
Learning Disabilities
Community Team, Greetby Buildings, Derby Street, Ormskirk, L39
2BP, Tel.: 01695 585845
Mr R Whittaker, Service Manager, Learning Disability, Trust
Headquarters, Ormskirk & District General Hospital, Wigan Road,
Ormskirk, Lancashire, L39 2JW, Tel.: 01695 598118
Liaison Services
Elderly Liaison Nurse, Tel.: 01695 598270
Ms S Speers, Discharge Co-ordinator, Ormskirk & District General
Hospital, Tel.: 01695 598271
Pharmacy
Ms E Johnstone, Medicines Manager, Tel.: 01695 598247
Specialist Nursing Services
Ms S McDonald, Continence, Ormskirk & District General Hospital,
Tel.: 01695 598454
Ms E Power, Diabetic Care, Ormskirk & District General Hospital,
Tel.: 01695598426
Mr B Townsend, Diabetic Care, Ormskirk & District General Hospital
Tel.: 01695598426

North West Strategic Health Authority

Ms T McLoughlin, Palliative Care, Ormskirk & District General Hospital, Tel.: 01695 598440

Ms C Wilcox, Palliative Care, Ormskirk & District General Hospital, Tel.: 01695 598440

Ms F Rattigan, Stoma Care, Tel.: 01695 656206

The Homeless/Travellers & Asylum Seekers

Ms C Snape, Travelling Families, Health Visitor, Hants Lane Clinic, Ormskirk, L39 1PX, Tel.: 01695 573526

Wirral Hospital NHS Trust

Trust Headquarters, Arrowe Park Hospital
Arrowe Park Road, Upton
WIRRAL
Merseyside
CH49 5PE
Tel.: 0151 678 5111
Fax.: 0151 604 7148

Community Midwifery

Duchess of Westminster Wing, Tel.: 0151 604 7466

Emergencies - out of hours, Tel.: 0151 678 5111 ext 2404

Ms S Hillhouse, Midwifery Manager, Tel.: 0151 678 5111 ext 2444

Ms P Lightfoot, Head of Women's Services, Tel.: 0151 678 5111 ext 2439

Team Midwifery Service, Tel.: 0151 678 5111 ext 2428

Liaison Services

Ms J Cleary, Paediatric Liaison Health Visitor, 1st Floor, Arrowe Park Hospital, Arrowe Park Road, Upton, Wirral, CH49 5PE, Tel.: 0151 604 7096

Wrightington Wigan & Leigh NHS Trust

Trust Headquarters, The Elms
Royal Albert Edward Infirmary, Wigan Lane
WIGAN
Lancashire
WN1 2NN
Tel.: 01942 244000

Acute Specialist Nursing Services

Mrs C Henshall, Antenatal Screening Co-ordinator, Antenatal Clinic, Area 5, Leigh Infirmary, Tel.: 01942 264242

Ms J Jones, Antenatal Screening Co-ordinator, Antenatal Clinic, Thomas Linacre Centre, Tel.: 01942 775700

Ms M Concannon, Sister, Acute Pain, - Palliative Care, Royal Albert Edward Infirmary, Tel.: 01942 822365

Ms S Downs, Sister, Chronic Pain, Royal Albert Edward Infirmary, Tel.: 01942 822365

Mrs J Gaskill, Nurse Specialist, Gynae/Oncology, Ward 2, Leigh Infirmary, Tel.: 01942 264694

Ms C Cameron, Nurse Practitioner, Head & Neck, Old Audiology Dept, Royal Albert Edward Infirmary, Tel.: 01942 24400 ext 3144

Mrs L Broome, Nurse Practitioner, Ophthalmology, Christopher Home Eye Unit, Royal Albert Edward Infirmary, Tel.: 01942 823277

Ms M Caufield, Clinical Nurse Specialist, Stoma Care, - Colorectal, Royal Albert Edward Infirmary, Tel.: 01942 674418

Ms Y Chantler, Clinical Nurse Specialist, Stoma Care, - Colorectal, Royal Albert Edward Infirmary, Tel.: 01942 674418

Ms N Fairclough, Clinical Nurse Specialist, Stoma Care, - Colorectal, Royal Albert Edward Infirmary, Tel.: 01942 674418

Ms S Fowler, Specialist Nurse, Urology, Royal Albert Edward Infirmary, Tel.: 01942 822370 or bleep 601

Ms F Sexton, Clinical Nurse Specialist, Urology, Royal Albert Edward Infirmary, Tel.: 01942 822370

Community Midwifery

Ms C Grundy, Drug & Alcohol Liaison Midwife, Antenatal Clinic, Thomas Linacre Centre, Parsons Walk, Wigan, Tel.: 0786 7558791

Mrs A Mundy, Senior Midwife - Community, Royal Albert Edward Infirmary, Tel.: 01942 778570

Wyre Primary Care Trust

Trust Headquarters, Derby Road
Wesham
PRESTON
PR4 3AL
Tel.: 01253 306305

Admin & Senior Management

Mrs R Roberts, Director of Clinical Services, Wyre PCT, Derby Road, Wesham, Preston, PR4 3AL, Tel.: 01253 306305

Mr D Soper, Chief Executive, Wyre PCT, Derby Road, Wesham, Preston, PR4 3AL, Tel.: 01253 306305

Child Health

Mrs C Williams, Primary Care Nurse Manager (Children & Families), Clinical Services, Cavendish House, Clarke Street, Poulton Ind Estate, Poulton-le-Fylde, FY6 8JW, Tel.: 01253 651060

Child Protection/Safeguarding Children

Ms J Abbotts, Named Nurse, Child Protection, Tel.: 01253 651266

Community Nursing Services

Mrs L Atcheson, Primary Care Nurse Manager (Adult), Clinical Services, Cavendish House, Clarke Street, Poulton Ind Estate, Poulton-le-Fylde, FY6 8JW, Tel.: 01253 651060

Ms S Scott, Assistant Director of Nursing, Clinical Services, Cavendish House, Clarke Street, Poulton Ind Estate, Poulton-le-Fylde, FY6 8JW, Tel.: 01253 651060

South Central Strategic Health Authority

with major towns and Primary Care Trust boundaries
Pop: 3,922,301

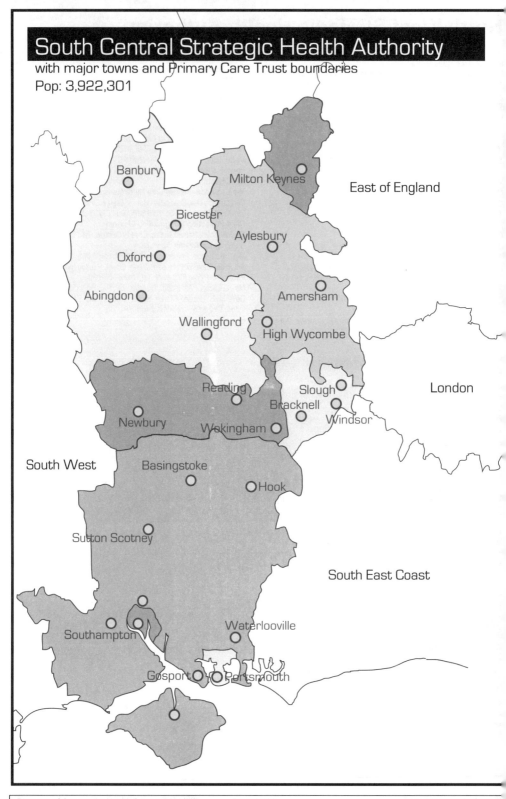

Banbury

Milton Keynes

East of England

Bicester

Aylesbury

Oxford

Abingdon

Amersham

Wallingford

High Wycombe

Reading

Slough

London

Bracknell

Newbury

Wokingham

Windsor

South West

Basingstoke

Hook

South East Coast

Sutton Scotney

Southampton

Waterlooville

Gosport

Portsmouth

South Central Strategic Health Authority

South Central Strategic Health Authority

Berkshire Healthcare NHS Trust

Trust Headquarters, Churchill House
51-52 Turing Drive
BRACKNELL
Berkshire
RG12 7FR
Tel.: 01344 422722

Learning Disabilities
Ms E Bowden, Manager, Wokingham & South Oxon Overlap, Tel.: 01491 572544
Bracknell Team, 51-52 Turing Drive, Bracknell, Berks, RG12 7FR, Tel.: 01344 422722
Ms L Kerfoot, Single Manager - Windsor & Maidenhead, Social Services, 4 Marlow Road, Maidenhead, Berks, SL6 7YR, Tel.: 01628 670117
Mr K Lewis, Director, Modernisation & Performance, Church Hill House, 51-52 Turing Drive, Bracknell, Berks, RG12 7FR, Tel.: 01344 823227
Ms T Mynett, Acting Manager, Slough, Town Hall, Bath Road, Slough, Berks, SL1 3UQ, Tel.: 01344 823255
Newbury Team, Newbury Day Centre, Newtown Road, Newbury, RG14 7EB, Tel.: 01635 41879/45075
Reading Team, Abbey Mill House, Abbey Square, Reading, RG1 3BH, Tel.: 0118 957 6266
Ms C Traynor, Manager, Reading, 25 Erleigh Road, Reading, RG1 5LR, Tel.: 0118 929 6461
Wokingham Team, Wellington House, Wellington Road, Wokingham, RG40 2AG, Tel.: 0118 974 6888/6832

Blackwater Valley & Hart Primary Care Trust

Trust Headquarters, Winchfield Lodge
Old Potbridge Road, Winchfield
HOOK
Hants
RG27 8BT
Tel.: 01252 849000
Fax.: 01252 849001

Admin & Senior Management
Mrs H Clanchy, Director of Primary & Community Care,
Ms D Glenn, Chief Executive,
Ms R Hopkins, Primary Care Manager, Fleet Hospital, Church Road, Fleet, Tel.: 01483 782753
Mrs S Price, Head of Managed Care,
Ms B Prynne, Primary Care Manager, Fleet Hospital, Church Road, Fleet, Tel.: 01483 782712

Child Health
Ms K Cridland, Frimley Children's Centre, Church Road, Frimley, Camberley, Surrey, GU16 5AD, Tel.: 01483 782800

Child Health Records
Ms G Saunders, The Jarvis Centre, Stoughton Road, Guildford, Surrey, GU1 1LJ, Tel.: 01483 783141

Child Protection/Safeguarding Children
Mrs S Mitchell, Named Nurse, Child Protection, Camberley Health Centre, 159 Frimley Road, Camberley, Surrey, GU15 2PZ, Tel.: 01276 25099

Clinical Leads (NSF)
Dr R Lawrence, Clinical Lead, CHD, The Border Practice, Blackwater Way, Aldershot, Hants, GU12 4DN, Tel.: 01252 332431
Mrs C Paterson, Clinical Lead, Diabetic Care, Camberley Health Centre, 159 Frimley Road, Camberley, Surrey, GU15 2PZ, Tel.: 01276 20101

District Nursing
Ms H Corner, Rushmoor Locality, Fleet Hospital, Church Road, Fleet, GU51 4PE, Tel.: 01483 782742
Ms T Stevens, Hart Locality, Fleet Hospital, Church Road, Fleet, Hampshire, GU51 4PE, Tel.: 01483 782772

Learning Disabilities
Mr N Buchanan, Winchfield Lodge, Old Potbridge Road, Winchfield, Hook, Hants, RG27 8BT, Tel.: 01252 849033

Liaison Services
Ms S Downing, Frimley Park Hospital, Portsmouth Road, Frimley, Camberley, Surrey, Tel.: 01276 604604

Pharmacy
Ms D Dunford, Head of Medicines Management, Harness House, Aldermaston Road, Basingstoke, Hants, RG24 9NB, Tel.: 01256 312255

Bracknell Forest Primary Care Trust

Trust Headquarters, Church Hill House
51-52 Turing Drive
BRACKNELL
Berkshire
RG12 7FR
Tel.: 01344 422722
Fax.: 01344 867990

Admin & Senior Management
Ms A Owen, Director of Nursing & Clinical Services, Church Hill House, 51-52 Turing Drive, Bracknell, RG12 7FR, Tel.: 01344 823331

Child Health
Mrs D Mitchell, Skimped Hill Health Centre, Skimped Hill Lane, Bracknell, RG12 1LH, Tel.: 01344 458116

Child Health Records
Ms L Coyne, Upton Hospital, Albert Street, Slough, SL1 2BJ, Tel.: 01753 635035

Child Protection/Safeguarding Children
Ms J Fraser, Specialist Nurse for Vulnerable Children, Skimped Hill Health Centre, Skimped Hill Lane, Bracknell, RG12 1LH, Tel.: 01344 458116
Ms S Hickson, Looked After Children's Nurse, Skimped Hill Health Centre, Skimped Hill Lane, Bracknell, RG12 1LH, Tel.: 01344 458136

Clinical Leads (NSF)
Dr A Sachdev, Clinical Lead, Cancer, Ringmead Practice, Birch Hill Medical Centre, Leppington, Birch Hill, RG12 7WW, Tel.: 01344 456535
Dr G Kassianos, Clinical Lead, CHD, Church Hill House, 51-52 Turing Drive, Bracknell, RG12 7FR, Tel.: 01344 823226
Ms S Stanton, Clinical Lead, Diabetic Care, Church Hill House, 51-52 Turing Drive, Bracknell, RG12 7FR, Tel.: 01344 823226

Community Nursing Services
Ms L Botting, Head of Nursing, Church Hill House, 51-52 Turing Drive, Bracknell, RG12 7FR, Tel.: 01344 823217

District Nursing
Ms L Botting, Head of Nursing, Church Hill House, 51-52 Turing Drive, Bracknell, RG12 7FR, Tel.: 01344 823217

Family Planning Services
Family Planning Services, Garden Clinic, Upton Hospital, Albert Street, Slough, SL1 2BJ, Tel.: 01753 635605

Health Visitors
Mrs D Daly, Children & Young People's Services Manager, Church Hill House, 51-52 Turing Drive, Bracknell, RG12 7FR, Tel.: 01344 823033

Learning Disabilities
Ms Z Johnstone, Bracknell Forest Borough Council, Time Square, Market Square, Bracknell, RG12 1JD, Tel.: 01344 311737

Liaison Services
Mr G Theobald, (PALS Manager), Church Hill House, 51-52 Turing Drive, Bracknell, RG12 7FR, Tel.: 01344 823262

Pharmacy
Ms E Mitchell, Church Hill House, 51-52 Turing Drive, Bracknell, RG12 7FR, Tel.: 01344 823233

Smoking Cessation
Ms J Reaper, Church Hill House, 51-52 Turing Drive, Bracknell, RG12 7FR, Tel.: 01344 823267

Specialist Nursing Services
Ms J Brogan, Modernisation Manager Long Term Conditions, Church Hill House, 51-52 Turing Drive, Bracknell, RG12 7FR, Tel.: 01344 823256

Ms J Beane, Intermediate Care, Nurse Specialist, Older People, Bracknell Forest Borough Council, Time Square, Market Street, Bracknell, RG12 1JD, Tel.: 01344 351450

Buckinghamshire Hospitals NHS Trust

Trust Headquarters, Amersham Hospital
Whielden Street
AMERSHAM, Buckinghamshire
HP7 0JD
Tel.: 01494 434411

Acute Specialist Nursing Services
Ms H Haywood, Ward Manager Sister, Amersham Hospital, Tel.: 01494 734633

Ms J Jones, Equipment Nurse, Stoke Mandeville Hospital, Tel.: 01296 315366

Ms H Hillson, Nurse, Breast Care, High Wycombe Hospital, Tel.: 01494 425099

Ms C Macey, Nurse, Breast Care, High Wycombe Hospital, Tel.: 01494 425099

Ms L McGhie, Nurse, Breast Care, Stoke Mandeville Hospital, Tel.: 01296 315127

Ms T Stammers, Senior Nurse, Breast Care, Stoke Mandeville Hospital, Tel.: 01296 315101

Ms D Symonds, Clinical Nurse Specialist, Breast Care, - Cancer, Wycombe Hospital, Tel.: 01494 426228

Mr R Heartvelt, Nurse Specialist, Cardiac Rehabilitation, Stoke Mandeville Hospital, Tel.: 01296 315179

Ms J Mullin, Clinical Nurse Specialist, Chemotherapy, - Cancer, Wycombe Hospital, Tel.: 01494 426238

Ms A Richards, Clinical Nurse Specialist, Chemotherapy, - Haematology, Stoke Mandeville Hospital, Tel.: 01296 315101

Ms S Clayton, Clinical Nurse Specialist, Colorectal, - Cancer, Wycombe Hospital, Tel.: 01494 426236

Ms R Radley, Nurse, Colorectal, - Stoma, Stoke Mandeville Hospital, Tel.: 01296 315101

Ms M Wood, Nurse, Colorectal, - Stoma, Stoke Mandeville Hospital, Tel.: 01296 315101

Ms K Huber, Head Nurse (Matron), Critical Care, Wycombe Hospital/Stoke Mandeville Hospital, Tel.: 01494 426457/01296 315618

Ms B Evans, Senior, Staff Nurse, Cystic Fibrosis, Wycombe Hospital, Tel.: 01494 425506

Ms M Lawlor, Photodermatology Lead Sister, Dermatology, Amersham Hospital, Tel.: 01494 734693

Ms S Wybrow, Clinical Nurse Specialist, Diabetes, Stoke Mandeville Hospital, Tel.: 01296 315530

Ms P Cook, Link Nurse, Diabetic Care, Stoke Mandeville Hospital, Tel.: 01296 315600

Mrs K Gallop, Head Nurse, Emergency Care, Stoke Mandeville Hospital,

Ms F Lis, Clinical Nurse Specialist, Gynae/Oncology, Wycombe Hospital, Tel.: 01494 526161

Ms G Wells, Nurse Practitioner, Gynae/Oncology, Stoke Mandeville Hospital, Tel.: 01296 315101

Ms L Wilks, Clinical Nurse Specialist, Haematology, - Cancer, Wycombe Hospital, Tel.: 01494 526161

Ms S Barton, Specialist Nurse, Head Injury, Amersham Hospital, Tel.: 01494 734631

Ms R Gallagher, Head Nurse, Infection Control, Stoke Mandeville Hospital, Tel.: 01296 315337

Ms C Greaves, Head Nurse, Infection Control, Wycombe Hospital, Tel.: 01494 525456

Ms F Simpson, Sister, Infection Control, Stoke Mandeville Hospital, Tel.: 01296 315337

Ms R Bryson, Clinical Nurse Specialist, Intensive Care, Wycombe Hospital, Tel.: 01494 425580

Ms J Mowforth, Clinical Nurse Specialist, Lung Cancer, Wycombe Hospital, Tel.: 01494 426231

Ms M Wyatt, Nurse, Lung Cancer, Stoke Mandeville Hospital, Tel.: 01296 315101

Ms A Homer, Hospital Nurse, Macmillan, Stoke Mandeville Hospital, Tel.: 01296 315126

Ms S Smee, Head Nurse, Medicine, (Specialist Medicine) Amersham Hospital, Tel.: 01494 734721

Mrs A Banks, Head Nurse, Medicine/Elderly Care, Wycombe Hospital,

Mrs A Collins, Head Nurse, Medicine/Emergency Care, Wycombe Hospital,

Ms E Wolfenden, Specialist, Multiple Sclerosis, Amersham Hospital, Tel.: 01494 734312

Mrs A Brandon, Head Nurse, Orthopaedics, Wycombe Hospital,

Mrs E Taylor, Senior Nurse, Pain Management, Stoke Mandeville Hospital, Tel.: 01296 315600

Clinical Nurse Specialist, Palliative Care, - Cancer, Wycombe Hospital, Tel.: 01494 526161

Ms M Park, Head Nurse (Matron), Rehabilitation, Medicine for Older People, Stoke Mandeville Hospital, Tel.: 01296 315253

Ms J Hall, Nurse, Research, Stoke Manderville Hospital, Tel.: 01296 315690

Ms K Beavil, Specialist Nurse, Rheumatology, Amersham Hospital, Tel.: 01494 734119

Ms C Bufton, Specialist Nurse, Rheumatology, Stoke Manderville Hospital, Tel.: 01296 315690

Ms D Green, Head Nurse, Spinal Injuries, Stoke Mandeville Hospital,

Mrs A Walker, Head Nurse, Surgery, Stoke Mandeville Hospital,

Ms H Cox, Link Nurse, Transplant, Stoke Mandeville Hospital, Tel.: 01296 315600

Ms H Baker, Clinical Nurse Specialist, Urology/Oncology, Wycombe Hospital,

Ms J Kearney, Clinical Nurse Specialist, Urology/Oncology, Stoke Mandeville Hospital, Tel.: 01296 315101

Admin & Senior Management
Mrs F Coogan, Deputy Director of Nursing, Stoke Manderville Hospital, Mandeville Road, Aylesbury, Bucks, HP21 8AL, Tel.: 01296 315108

Child Health
Ms D Challis, Administrator for Community Paediatrics, Wycombe General Hospital, Tel.: 01494 426676

Ms P Collins, Liaison Neonatal, Wycombe General Hospital, Queen Victoria Road, High Wycombe, HP11 2TT, Tel.: 01494 425126

Ms B Murfitt, Diabetes Paediatric Specialist Sister, Wycombe Hospital, Tel.: 01494 425658

Child Protection/Safeguarding Children
Ms T Bratby, Lead Midwife, Wycombe Hospital, Tel.: 01494 425537

Ms A Rozwadowski, Specialist Nurse Looked After Children, Tel.: 01494 734291

Ms J Davies, Child Protection, Amersham Hospital, Tel.: 01494 734809

Ms K Johns, Named Nurse, Child Protection, Wycombe General Hospital, Tel.: 01494 426504

Ms T Payne, Named Midwife, Child Protection, Stoke Mandeville Hospital, Tel.: 01296 316127

South Central Strategic Health Authority

Ms G Rennie, Named Nurse, Child Protection, Stoke Mandeville Hospital, Tel.: 01296 315142

Community Midwifery
Emmergencies, Wycombe Hospital, Queen Alexandra Road, High Wycombe, Bucks, HP11 2TT, Tel.: 01494 425513 or 425520
Mrs C Eves, Associate Director of Nursing/Head of Midwifery, Stoke Mandeville Hospital, Mandeville Road, Aylesbury, Bucks, HP21 8AL, Tel.: 01296 316142
Mrs J Martyr, Head Midwife for Community Women's Services (Matron), Wycombe Hospital, Queen Alexandra Road, High Wycombe, Bucks, HP11 2TT, Tel.: 01494 425537
Midwifery Unit, Wycombe Hospital, Queen Alexandra Road, High Wycombe, Bucks, HP11 2TT, Tel.: 01494 425172/3
Mrs T Payne, Head Midwife for Community Women's Services (Matron), Stoke Mandeville Hospital, Mandeville Road, Aylesbury, Bucks, HP21 8AL, Tel.: 01296 316143

Discharge Co-ordinators
Ms A Barnett, Stoke Mandeville Hospital, Tel.: 01296 315000
Ms J Barnett, Wycombe Hospital, Tel.: 01494 26161
Ms C Emmott, Stoke Mandeville Hospital, Tel.: 01296 315000
Ms L Ives, Wycombe Hospital, Tel.: 01494 26161
Ms G Kirkby, Stoke Mandeville Hospital, Tel.: 01296 315000
Ms M Lancaster, Stoke Mandeville Hospital, Tel.: 01296 315000
Ms T Leeson, Wycombe Hospital, Tel.: 01494 26161
Ms K Lockey, Wycombe Hospital, Tel.: 01494 26161

District Nursing
Ms B Ainley, Nurse Manager - High Wycombe, Lane End, Stokenchurch, Oakridge Centre, Desborough Road, High Wycombe, HP11 2QR, Tel.: 01494 426950
Ms A Barrett, Specialist Nurse District Nurses, Tel.: 01753 8888835
Ms S Buttfield, Prof Adviser District Nurse - Beaconsfield, Burnham, Denham, Farnham Common, Iver, Stoke Poges, Chalfonts & Gerrards X Health Clinic, Hampden Road, Chalfont St Peter, Gerrards X, SL9 9DR, Tel.: 01753 888835

Health Visitors
Ms S Butler, Professional Lead Health Visitor/Nurse Manager - Amersham, Chesham, Gt Missenden, Amersham Health Centre, Chiltern Avenue, Amersham, HP6 5AH, Tel.: 01494 722111
Ms H Dean, Specialist Nurse Health Visitor, Tel.: 01494 734043

HIV/AIDS
Ms S Alcock, Aids/HIV/STD Midwife, Stoke Mandeville Hospital, Tel.: 01296 316120
Mr W McKenna, HIV/Aids, Clinical Nurse Specialist, Wycombe General Hospital, Tel.: 01494 425485

Liaison Services
Ms A Barnett, Discharge Liaison, Stoke Mandeville Hospital, Tel.: 01296 316653
Mr G Clements, Discharge Liaison (NSIC), Stoke Mandeville Hospital, Tel.: 01296 315830
Mr C Clifford, Discharge Liaison Nurse, Florence Nightingale House, Stoke Mandeville Hospital, Tel.: 01296 315000
Ms P Collins, Liaison Neonatal, Wycombe General Hospital, Queen Victoria Road, High Wycombe, HP11 2TT, Tel.: 01494 425126
Ms H Dunne, Community Liaison Service for Spinal Injury, Stoke Mandeville Hospital, Tel.: 01296 315829
Ms C Emmott, Discharge Liaison, Stoke Mandeville Hospital, Tel.: 01296 316653
Ms L Icke, Community Discharge Co-ordinator (Page via 01494 526161), Wycombe General Hospital, Queen Victoria Road, High Wycombe, HP11 2TT, Tel.: 01494 736326
Ms M Lancaster, Discharge Liaison Nurse, Stoke Mandeville Hospital, Tel.: 01296 526161
Ms G Rennie, Team Leader, Community Nursing Team, Stoke Mandeville Hospital, Tel.: 01296 315142
Ms D Smith, Liaison Paediatric Health Visitor, Castlefield Health Clinic, Chiltern Avenue, Castlefield, High Wycombe, HP12 3UR, Tel.: 01494 527665

Ms J Stables, Discharge Liaison Nurse, Wycombe General Hospital, Tel.: 01296 526161

Buckinghamshire Mental Health NHS Trust
Trust Headquarters, Manor House
Bierton Road
AYLESBURY
Bucks
HP20 1EG
Tel.: 01296 393363

Learning Disabilities
Ms A Bussey, Director of Nursing, Manor House, Bierton Road, Aylesbury, Bucks, HP20 1EG, Tel.: 01296 504789
Mrs D Cater, Senior Manager, Buckinghamshire Learning Disability Service, 309 Cressex Road, High Wycombe, Bucks, HP12 4QG, Tel.: 01494 426832
Mr S Mitchelmore, Executive Manager for Learning Disability Services, Buckinghamshire County Council, County Hall, Walton Street, Aylesbury, Bucks, HP20 1YU, Tel.: 01296 382504

Chiltern & South Bucks Primary Care Trust
Trust Headquarters, Unit 2&3
Lacemaker Court, London Road
OLD AMERSHAM
Buckinghamshire
HP7 0HS
Tel.: 01494 606606

Admin & Senior Management
Mrs S Butler, Assistant Director of Nursing, Professional Advisor Health Visiting, Lacemaker Court, Amersham, Tel.: 01494 606689
Mrs S Buttfield, Assistant Director of Nursing, Professional Advisor District Nursing, Lacemaker Court, Amersham, Tel.: 01494 606684
Mr B Johnson, Chief Executive, Lacemaker Court, Amersham, HP7 0JD, Tel.: 01494 606609
Mrs D Raven, Director of Nursing & Community Services, Lacemaker Court, Amersham, Tel.: 01494 606692

Child Health Records
Community Office, Amersham Hospital, Whielden Street, Amersham, Bucks, HP7 0JD,

Child Protection/Safeguarding Children
Mrs J Davies, Designated Nurse, Child Protection, Community Office, Amersham Hospital, Tel.: 01494 734809
Ms D Hartrick, Named Nurse, Child Protection, Community Office, Amersham Hospital, Tel.: 01494 734809
Ms S Terry, Liaison Paediatric Health Visitor, Named Nurse, Child Protection, Community Office, Amersham Hospital, Tel.: 01494 734809

Community Matrons
Ms A Fabre, Community Matron, Sherwood House, Stones Courtyard, High Street, Chesham, HP5 1DE, Tel.: 01494 784493
Ms D Stiff, Community Matron, Threeways Surgery, 84 Rogers Lane, Stoke Poges, Bucks, Tel.: 01753 644253

District Nursing
Ms A Barrett, Practice Development, Facilitator District Nursing, Community Office, Amersham Hospital, Tel.: 01494 734807
Mrs S Boddy, Lacemaker Court, Amersham, Tel.: 01494 606691
Mrs S Buttfield, Assistant Director of Nursing, Professional Advisor District Nursing, Lacemaker Court, Amersham, Tel.: 01494 606684

Equipment Loan Services
Mr B Donnelly, Head of Service & Development - Mid & South Bucks, Community Equipment Loans Service, Amersham Hospital, Tel.: 01494 734810

Family Planning Services
Ms F Wylde, Nurse Co-ordinator, Family Planning, c/o Outpatients Dept, Wycombe Hospital,

South Central Strategic Health Authority

Health Visitors
Mrs S Butler, Assistant Director of Nursing, Professional Advisor Health Visiting, Lacemaker Court, Amersham, Tel.: 01494 606689
Ms A Reypert, Practice Development Facilitator Health Visiting, Community Office, Amersham Hospital, Tel.: 01494 734043
Ms S Terry, Paediatric Liaison Health Visitor, Community Office, Amersham Hospital, Tel.: 01494 734809
Liaison Services
Mrs S Edmondson, Community Discharge Liaison Nurse, Chalfonts & Gerrards Cross Hospital, Tel.: 01753 883821
Ms S Terry, Paediatric Liaison Health Visitor, Community Office, Amersham Hospital, Tel.: 01494 734809
School Nursing
Mrs G Jeavons, School Nurse Co-ordinator, Wye Valley Surgery, 2 Desborough Avenue, High Wycombe, Tel.: 01494 512687
Specialist Nursing Services
Ms C Mowbray, Specialist Nurse, Back Care, Community Office, Amersham Hospital, Tel.: 01494 734441
Ms G Strong, Community, Specialist Nurse, Cardiac, Community Office, Amersham Hospital, Tel.: 01494 734291
Mrs S Hill, Advisor, Continence, Marlow Health Clinic, Glade Road, Marlow, Tel.: 01628 487439
Ms N Thompson, Advisor, Continence, Marlow Health Clinic, Glade Road, Marlow, Tel.: 01628 487439
Ms N Davies, Specialist Nurse, IV Therapy, Chalfonts & Gerrards Cross Hospital, Hampden Road, Chalfont St Peter, Bucks, SL9 9DR, Tel.: 01753 883821
Macmillan Nurses, Palliative Care, Rectory Meadow Surgery, School Lane, Old Amersham, Tel.: 01494 727680
Macmillan Nurses, Palliative Care, Marlow Health Clinic, Glade Road, Marlow, Tel.: 01628 473759
Mrs S Knight, Specialist Nurse, Wound Care, Chalfonts & Gerrards Cross Hospital, Hampden Road, Chalfont St Peter, Bucks, SL9 9DR, Tel.: 01753 883821

Admin & Senior Management
Ms A Kelly, Director of Nursing & Children & Family Services, 8 Sterne Road, Tatchbury Mount, Calmore, Southampton, SO40 2RZ, Tel.: 02380 874353
Mr J Richards, Chief Executive, Tel.: 02380 874272
Child Health
Ms A Kelly, Director of Children & Family Services, 8 Sterne Road, Tatchbury Mount, Calmore, Southampton, SO40 2RZ, Tel.: 02380 874353
Ms C Messenger, Deputy Director of Children & Family Services, 8 Sterne Road, Tatchbury Mount, Calmore, Southampton, SO40 2RZ, Tel.: 02380 874295
Child Protection/Safeguarding Children
Ms D Perriment, Named Nurse, Child Protection, 8 Sterne Road, Tatchbury Mount, Calmore, Southampton, SO40 2RZ, Tel.: 02380 874165
Mrs J Satterly, Head of Safeguarding Children's Team, Designated Nurse, Child Protection, 8 Sterne Road, Tatchbury Mount, Calmore, Southampton, SO40 2RZ, Tel.: 02380 874173
District Nursing
Community Nursing Office for District Nursing Services, Eastleigh Health Centre, Newtown Road, Eastleigh, Hants, SO50 9AG, Tel.: 02380 610961 x 250
Mrs C Edwards, Head of District Nursing, Eastleigh Health Centre, Newtown Road, Eastleigh, SO50 9AG, Tel.: 02380 610961
Health Visitors
Ms J Medd, Head of Health Visiting Services, Eastleigh Health Centre, Newtown Road, Eastleigh, SO50 9AG, Tel.: 02380 610961
Other Services
Ms K Cubbon, Romsey Hospital Manager, Romsey Hospital, Winchester Road, Romsey, S051 8ZA, Tel.: 01794 834702
School Nursing
Ms G Taylor, Head of School Nursing Services, Eastleigh Health Centre, Newtown Road, Eastleigh, SO50 9AG, Tel.: 02380 610961

East Hampshire Primary Care Trust

Trust Headquarters, Raebarn House
Hulbert Road
WATERLOOVILLE
PO7 7GP
Tel.: 023 9224 8800

Admin & Senior Management
Mr T Horne, Chief Executive,
Child Health Records
Pre-School Records, Portsmouth Healthcare Trust,
School Health Records, Dunsbury Way Clinic, Havant, PO9 5BG, Tel.: 023 9248 2154
Child Protection/Safeguarding Children
Ms D Rose, Designated Nurse, Child Protection, Battenburg Avenue Clinic, Battenburg Avenue, North End, Portsmouth, PO2 0TA, Tel.: 023 9242 8802
Community Midwifery
Mrs G Edwards, Community Maternity Manager - Petersfield Hospital, Havant Health Centre, Civic Centre Road, Havant, PO9 2AZ, Tel.: 02392 344217
District Nursing
Ms J Goodall, Service Manager, Civic Offices, Civic Centre Road, Havant, PO9 2AX, Tel.: 023 9235 0010

Eastleigh & Test Valley South Primary Care Trust

Trust Headquarters, 8 Sterne Road
Calmore
SOUTHAMPTON
Hants
SO40 2RZ
Tel.: 02380 874270

Fareham & Gosport Primary Care Trust

Headquarters, Unit 180 Fareham Reach
166 Fareham Road
GOSPORT
PO13 0FH
Tel.: 01329 233447

Child Health
Mrs E Emms, Head of Children's Services, Unit 180 Fareham Reach, 166 Fareham Road, Gosport, PO13 0FH, Tel.: 01329 229420
Child Health Records
Island & Portsmouth ICT Services, St James Hospital, Locksway Road, Portsmouth, PO4 8LD, Tel.: 023 9289 4356
Child Protection/Safeguarding Children
Ms L Batty, Named Nurse, Child Protection, Gosport Health Centre, Bury Road, Gosport, PO12 3PW, Tel.: 023 9258 4201
Clinical Leads (NSF)
Dr R Roope, Clinical Lead, Cancer,
Dr G du Feu, Clinical Lead, CHD,
Dr C Kelly, Clinical Lead, Diabetic Care,
Mrs F Smart, Clinical Lead, Older People,
District Nursing
Ms K Barraclough, Modern Matron District Nursing, Gosport Health Centre, Bury Road, Gosport, PO12 3PW, Tel.: 023 9258 4201
Ms L Batty, Clinical Manager, Health Visiting (Gosport), Gosport Health Centre, Bury Road, Gosport, PO12 3PW, Tel.: 023 9258 4201
Ms S Blackburn, Clinical Manager, Health Visiting (Fareham), 6 The Potteries, Wickham Road, Fareham, PO16 7ET, Tel.: 01329 316406
Ms M Gleadall, Clinical Team Manager, Gosport Health Centre, Bury Road, Gosport, PO12 3PW, Tel.: 023 9258 4201
Ms B Gray, Service Manager, Nursing, The Potteries, St Christopher's Hospital, 52 Wickham Road, Fareham, Hants, Tel.: 01329 822269/316434

South Central Strategic Health Authority

Ms L Taylor, Clinical Manager, Health Visiting (Gosport) - Childrens, Gosport Health Centre, Bury Road, Gosport, PO12 3PW, Tel.: 023 9258 4201

Learning Disabilities

Fareham & Gosport Team, 6 The Potteries, Wickham Road, Fareham, PO16 7ET, Tel.: 01329 312854

Havant & Petersfield Team, Raebarn House, Hulbert Road, Waterlooville, PO7 7GP, Tel.: 023 9226 6277

Mr G Kearney, Community Services Manager, 6 The Potteries, Wickham Road, Fareham, PO16 7ET, Tel.: 01329 312854

Portsmouth Team, PO Box 107, Southsea, PO4 8NG, Tel.: 0239273 4175

Mrs D Wilson, Director, 6 The Potteries, Wickham Road, Fareham, PO16 7ET, Tel.: 01329 312854

Specialist Nursing Services

Ms M Houghton, Nurse, Continence, Unit 180 Fareham Reach, 166 Fareham Road, Gosport, PO13 0FH, Tel.: 01329 229462

Ms T Bee, Leg Ulcers, Unit 180 Fareham Reach, 166 Fareham Road, Gosport, PO13 0FH, Tel.: 01329 229462

Ms L Shaw, Nurse, Parkinson's Disease, Dolpainday Hospital, Tel.: 02392 584201

Heatherwood & Wexham Park Hospitals NHS Trust

Trust Headquarters, Wexham Park Hospital
Wexham Park, Wexham
SLOUGH
SL2 4HL
Tel.: 01753 633000

Acute Specialist Nursing Services

Ms K East, Lead Biomedical Scientist, Wexham Park, Haematology, Tel.: 01753 633415

Ms S Skowronski, Specialist Nurse, Acute Pain, Wexham Park, Anaesthetics, Tel.: 01753 634435

Ms R Crow, Specialist Nurse, Anti-Coagulation, Tel.: 01753 633964

Ms I Bowring, Macmillan Nurse, Breast Care, Tel.: 01753 636281

Ms M Ferguson, Macmillan Nurse, Breast Care, King Edward VII, Parapet, St Leonard's Road, Windsor, SL4, Tel.: 01753 860441

Ms M Fryer, Macmillan Nurse, Breast Care, King Edward VII, Parapet, St Leonard's Road, Windsor, SL4, Tel.: 01753 860441

Ms A M Penez, Macmillan Nurse, Breast Care, Tel.: 01753 636281

Ms J Ramm, Genetics, Nurse, Breast Care, Tel.: 01753 636705

Ms E Clarke, Senior, Specialist Nurse, Cardiac, Wexham Park, Cardiac Rehab, Tel.: 01753 634684

Ms S Clarke, Senior, Specialist Nurse, Cardiac, Wexham Park, Cardiac Rehab, Tel.: 01753 633000

Ms T Smith, Specialist Nurse, Chest, King Edward VII, Chest Clinic, St Leonard's Road, Windsor, SL4, Tel.: 01753 860441

Ms K Greatrex, Sister, Chronic Pain, Wexham Park, Theatres, Tel.: 01753 634435

Ms R Thomas, Nurse, Colorectal, Wexham Park, Surgery, Tel.: 01753 633587

Ms S Tripp, Nurse, Colorectal, Wexham Park, Surgery, Tel.: 01753 633587

Ms J Follett, Nurse Specialist, COPD, Wexham Park, Tel.: 01753 634272

Ms S Brooks, Specialist Nurse, Dermatology, Wexham Park, Dermatology, Tel.: 01753 634330

Mr A Linkcater, Nurse Specialist, Epilepsy,

Ms J Cutter, Specialist Nurse, GI, Wexham Park, GI Unit, Tel.: 01753 633000

Ms R Bliss, Specialist Nurse, Haematology, Wexham Park, Ward 9E, Tel.: 01753 633152

Ms J Wyeth, Nurse, Infection Control, Wexham Park, Microbiology, Tel.: 01753 633456

Ms M Coward, Sister, IV Therapy, Wexham Park, Orthopedics, Tel.: 01753 634197

Ms C Low, Sister, IV Therapy, Wexham Park, Orthopedics, Tel.: 01753 634197

Ms A Rivera-Vewez, Macmillan, Nurse Specialist, Lymphoedema, King Edward VII, Tel.: 01753 636733

Ms M Milne, Nurse Consultant, Macmillan, King Edward VII, Parapet, St Leonard's Road, Windsor, Tel.: 01753 860441

Ms L Shephard, Clinical Nurse Specialist, Macmillan, Wexham Park, Medicine, Tel.: 01344 623333

Ms M Holloway, Sister, Pain Management, Wexham Park, Anaesthetics, Tel.: 01753 634435

Ms D Vincent Scott, Nurse Specialist, Parkinson's Disease, Heatherwood, Tel.: ext 7706

Ms K Final, Specialist Nurse, Rheumatology, Heatherwood, Medicine, Tel.: 01344 623333

Ms N Kennedy, Specialist Nurse, Rheumatology, Wexham Park, Medicine, Tel.: 01753 633167

Ms J Trott, Specialist Nurse, Serology, Wexham Park, Medicine, Tel.: 01753 633096

Ms L Ferris, Nurse, Stoma Care, Heatherwood, Surgery, London Road, Ascot, SL5, Tel.: 01344 623333

Ms E White, Specialist Nurse, Stroke Care, Wexham Park, Medicine, Tel.: 01753 633125

Ms L O'Flynne, Nurse, Tissue Viability, St Mark's Outpatients, Watford Road, Harrow, HA1, Tel.: 020 8235 4000

Admin & Senior Management

Ms S Loader, Director of Nursing, Wexham Park Hospital, Tel.: 01753 633565

Ms K Proctor, Director of Midwifery/Deputy Director of Nursing, Maternity Dept, Wexham Park Hospital, Tel.: 01753 634572

Child Protection/Safeguarding Children

Ms C Dorman, Children Services Manager, Tel.: 01753 634609

Community Midwifery

Ms A Anderson, Community Midwifery Manager, Heatherwood & Wexham Park Hospital, Wexham Park, Wexham, Slough, SL2 4HL, Tel.: 01753 634517

Discharges, Wexham Park Hospital, Wexham Park, Wexham, Slough, SL2 4HL, Tel.: 01753 634563

Discharges, Messages, Heatherwood Hospital, London Road, Ascot, Berkshire, SL5 8AA, Tel.: 01344 877069

Non-Urgent Messages, Wexham Park Hospital, Wexham Park, Wexham, Slough, SL2 4HL, Tel.: 01753 634561

Mrs K Proctor, Director of Midwifery Services, Wexham Park Hospital, Wexham Park, Wexham, Slough, SL2 4HL, Tel.: 01753 633000

Ms O Stewart, Support for Vulnerable Women Midwifery, Tel.: 07789 868267

Liaison Services

Ms L Haslett, Patient Liaison Manager, Wexham Park Hospital, Tel.: 01753 633365

Ms G Thomson, Liaison Midwife, Teenage Pregnancy, Tel.: 07798 732274

Ms R Galloway, Liaison, Midwife, Substance Misuse, Tel.: 07747 025421

Isle of Wight Healthcare NHS Trust

Trust Headquarters, St Mary's Hospital
Parkhurst Road
NEWPORT
Isle of Wight
PO30 5TG
Tel.: 01983 524081

Acute Specialist Nursing Services

Mr S Wibberley, Nurse Specialist, Acute Pain,

Ms J Greenham, Advisor, Back Care,

Ms M Budgen, Clinical Nurse Specialist, Breast Care,

Ms J Light, Clinical Nurse Specialist, Breast Care,

Ms M Seymor, Clinical Nurse Specialist, Breast Care,

South Central Strategic Health Authority

Ms D Clarke, Clinical Nurse Specialist, Cardiology,
Ms M Murphy, Clinical Nurse Specialist, Chemotherapy,
Ms M Eriksson, Practitioner, Clinical Trials,
Ms J Hanks, Clinical Nurse Specialist, Colorectal,
Ms A Rawsthorn, Clinical Nurse Specialist, Continence,
Ms J Apsley, Nurse Specialist, Diabetes, - Paediatrics,
Ms D Hogan, Clinical Nurse Specialist, Diabetes,
Mr P Holdich, Facilitator, PCT, Diabetes,
Ms L Whittingstall, Clinical Nurse Specialist, Diabetes,
Ms P Wilson, Clinical Nurse Specialist, Diabetes,
Ms A Cantelo, Nurse Endoscopist, Endoscopy,
Ms J Taylor, Nurse Specialist, Endoscopy,
Ms F Young, Nurse Specialist, G.U.M,
Ms J Cross, Nurse Specialist, Gynaecology,
Ms A Cameron-Smith, Clinical Nurse Specialist, Health Promotion,
Ms P Greenhalgh, Surveillance, Nurse, Infection Control,
Ms M Ould, Nurse, Infection Control,
Ms J Tait, Nurse Specialist, Infection Control,
Ms K Byrne, Co-ordinator, Intermediate Care,
Ms B Behmer, Clinical Nurse Specialist, Macmillan,
Ms D curless, Clinical Nurse Specialist, Macmillan,
Mr J Pugh, Clinical Nurse Specialist, Macmillan,
Ms A Tavener, Clinical Nurse Specialist, Macmillan,
Ms P Taylor, Clinical Nurse Specialist, Macmillan,
Ms E Morey, Nurse, Multiple Sclerosis,
Ms C Burtwell, Nurse Practitioner, Neonatal, - Advanced,
Ms T Norton, Clinical, Nurse, Nutrition,
Ms J Cherian, Nurse Practitioner, Occupational Health,
Ms D Eccleston, Senior, Nurse Practitioner, Occupational Health,
Ms M Hall, Nurse, Occupational Health,
Ms S Porter, Senior, Nurse Practitioner, Occupational Health,
Ms J Burr, Nurse Specialist, Ophthalmology,
Ms C Eldridge, Nurse Specialist, Ophthalmology,
Ms J Collier, Clinical Nurse Specialist, Orthopaedics,
Ms C Sandell, Clinical Nurse Specialist, Orthopaedics,
Ms C Brenton, Specialist Nurse, Osteoporosis,
Ms J George, Community, Specialist, Palliative Care,
Ms S Ward, Nurse Specialist, Parkinson's Disease,
Ms C Ward, Nurse Facilitator, Primary Care,
Ms H O'Kell, Nurse Practitioner, Radiology,
Ms S Keaney, Clinical Nurse Specialist, Respiratory,
Ms A Snow, Clinical Nurse Specialist, Respiratory,
Ms E Healey, Nurse Specialist, Rheumatology,
Ms J Ward, Co-ordinator, Sexual Health,
Ms A Coates, Nurse Specialist, Stoma Care,
Ms L Webb, Clinical Nurse Specialist, Stoma Care, - Colorectal,
Ms J Johnson, Nurse Specialist, Stroke Care,
Ms U Sinclair, Liaison Nurse, Stroke Care,
Ms K Turner, Emergency, Nurse Practitioner, Surgical,
Ms A Price, Training, Co-ordinator, Theatres,
Ms J Morris, Nurse Specialist, Upper GI,
Mr P Gilliam, Nurse Specialist, Urology,
Ms J Perry, Clinical Nurse Specialist, Urology,

Child Protection/Safeguarding Children
Ms J Dowdall, Modern Matron, Child Protection, St Mary's Hospital, Tel.: 01983 534351
Community Midwifery
Emergencies, St Mary's Hospital, Tel.: 01983 524081 ext 4334
Ms G Kennett, Head of Women's Services, St Mary's Hospital, Tel.: 01983 524081 ext 4357
Mrs K Walker, Senior Midwife, St Mary's Hospital, Tel.: 01983 524081 ext 4516
Family Planning Services
Maternity Department, St Mary's Hospital, Tel.: 01983 554876
Matrons/Modern Matrons
Ms D Collins, Modern Matron, Medicine, St Mary's Hospital, Tel.: 01983 552057

Ms L Turner, Modern Matron, Older People, St Mary's Hospital, Tel.: 01983 552022
Ms L Harris, Modern Matron, Surgery, St Mary's Hospital, Tel.: 01983 534921
Paediatric Liaison Health Visitors
Ms J Johnston, Modern Matron, St Mary's Hospital, Tel.: 01983 534947

Isle of Wight Primary Care Trust
Whitecroft
Sandy Lane
NEWPORT
Isle of Wight
PO30 3ED
Tel.: 01983 535455
Fax.: 01983 822142

Admin & Senior Management
Mr D Crawley, Chief Executive, Tel.: 01983 535400
Child Protection/Safeguarding Children
Ms J Cusden, Director of Nursing & Service Provision, Whitecroft, Sandy Lane, Newport, Isle of Wight, PO30 3ED, Tel.: 01983 535465
Clinical Leads (NSF)
Dr P Bingham, Clinical Lead, Cancer,
Dr D Isaac, Clinical Lead, Cancer,
Dr P Randall, Clinical Lead, CHD,
Dr J Moore, Clinical Lead, Diabetic Care,
Dr G Thompson, Clinical Lead, Older People,
District Nursing
Ms P McCamley, Clinical Lead, District Nurses, Tel.: 01983 535443
Other Services
Mr O Kearney, Clinical Services Dev Manager, Service Provision, Island Doctors on Call (IDOC), Personal Dental Services & Multi Professional Triage Team, Tel.: 01983 535407
Pharmacy
Mr P Jeram, Medication Review Pharmacist, Tel.: 01983 535411
Specialist Nursing Services
Mrs A Rawsthorn, Co-ordinator, Continence, Tel.: 01983 535438
Mr P Holdich, Nurse Facilitator, Diabetic Care, Tel.: 01983 535434
Ms P McCamley, Marie Curie, Macmillan, Tel.: 01983 535443
Ms S Ward, Nurse Specialist, Parkinson's Disease, Tel.: 01983 535433

Mid Hampshire Primary Care Trust
Trust Headquarters, Unit 3 Tidbury Farm
Bullington Cross
SUTTON SCOTNEY
Hampshire
SO21 3QQ
Tel.: 01962 763940

Child Health
Ms A Aldridge, Child Health Dept, Highcroft, Romsey Road, Winchester, S022 5DH, Tel.: 01962 863511
Child Health Records
Child Health Info Dept, Highcroft, Romsey Road, Winchester, S022 5DH, Tel.: 01962 863511
Child Protection/Safeguarding Children
Ms N Black, Designated Nurse for Looked After Children, Trust Headquarters, Tel.: 01962 763997
Mrs B Derwent, Named Nurse, Child Protection, Trust Headquarters, Tel.: 01264 835247
Clinical Leads (NSF)
Dr S Watters, Clinical Lead, CHD,
Community Nursing Services
Ms K Ashton, Director of Primary & Community Care, Unit 3 Tidbury Farm, Bullington Cross, Sutton Scotney, Hampshire, SO21 3QQ, Tel.: 01962 763970

South Central Strategic Health Authority

District Nursing
Ms L Edwards, Practice Development Manager - District Nurses, Queens Road Offices, Royal Hampshire County Hospital, Tel.: 01962 825409
Ms J Monteque-Brown, Practice Development Manager - District Nurses, Queens Road Offices, Royal Hampshire County Hospital, Tel.: 01962 825409
Family Planning Services
Ms M Barber, Royal Hampshire County Hospital, Tel.: 01962 824608
Health Visitors
Ms S Wilkes, Practice Development Manager - Health Visitors, Unit 3 Tidbury Farm, Bullington Cross, Sutton Scotney, SO21 3QQ, Tel.: 01962 763964
Liaison Services
Discharge Support & Liaison, Royal Hampshire County Hospital, Tel.: 01962 824212
Ms R Newman, Manager, Intermediate Care, Trust Headquarters, Tel.: 01962 763978
Smoking Cessation
Ms N Warriner, Tel.: 01962 863511 x3677
Specialist Nursing Services
Ms L Atherton, Practice Nursing Lead Nurse & PEC Nurse, Unit 3 Tidbury Farm, Bullington Cross, Sutton Scotney, Hampshire, SO21 3QQ, Tel.: 01962 763985
The Homeless/Travellers & Asylum Seekers
Ms J Stepney, Primary Care Nurse, Trinity Centre, Winchester, Tel.: 01962 622221

Milton Keynes General NHS Trust

Trust Headquarters, Milton Keynes General Hospital
Standing Way, Eaglestone
MILTON KEYNES
Buckinghamshire
MK6 5LD
Tel.: 01908 660033
Fax.: 01908 669348

Acute Specialist Nursing Services
Ms N Vigurs, Community, Sister, Milton Keynes General Hospital, Tel.: 01908 243878
Ms J Murray, Nurse Specialist, Diabetic Care, Milton Keynes General Hospital, Tel.: 01908 243878
Ms T James, Nurse Specialist, Respiratory, Milton Keynes General Hospital, Tel.: 01908 243002
Community Midwifery
Ms E Anderson, Community Midwifery Sec., Tel.: 01908 243935
Ms S Brister, Community Neonatal Sister, Tel.: 01908 660033 ext 2101
Mrs S Cole, Head of Midwifery, Milton Keynes General Hospital, Tel.: 01908 243457
Mrs A Gillard, Divisional Personal Assistant, Milton Keynes General Hospital, Tel.: 01908 243155
Miss M Plummer, Modern Matron Ward Area, Milton Keynes General Hospital, Tel.: 01908 243116 Bleep 1128
Mrs M Thomas, Modern Matron Delivery Suite, Milton Keynes General Hospital, Tel.: 01908 660033 ext 2199
Mrs E Valentine, Modern Matron Community - Bleep 3116, Milton Keynes General Hospital, Tel.: 01908 660033 ext 5220
Women & Children's Fax Number, Tel.: 01908 243614

Milton Keynes Primary Care Trust

Trust Headquarters, The Hospital Campus
Standing Way, Eaglestone
MILTON KEYNES
Buckinghamshire
MK6 5NG
Tel.: 01908 243933

Admin & Senior Management
Ms R Westman, Acting Director Primary Care Services/Chief Nurse, Trust Headquarters, Hospital Campus, Standing Way, Milton Keynes, MK6 5NG, Tel.: 01908 243933
Child Health
Ms L Hayward, Co-ordinator, Paediatric Palliative Care Team, Tel.: 01908 660033 ext 3195
Ms E Lamb, Child Health Manager, Tel.: 01908 243514
Child Health Records
Child Health Records, Trust Headquarters,
Child Protection/Safeguarding Children
Ms J Wilkinson, Child Protection, Stantonbury Health Centre, Tel.: 01908 222223 ext 206
Clinical Leads (NSF)
Dr M Wyke, Clinical Lead, Cancer,
Mr M Mahendran, Clinical Lead, CHD,
Ms M Hartley, Clinical Lead, Diabetic Care, Shipley Court, Marshend Road, Newport Pagnell, Bucks, Tel.: 01908 500097
District Nursing
Ms S McCready, Locality Manager, District Nurse Lead, Neath Hill Health Centre, 1 Tower Hill, Neath Hill, MK14 6JY, Tel.: 01908 230525
Family Planning Services
Mrs C Thompson, Acting Senior Manager, Neath Hill Health Centre, Tel.: 01908 230525
Health Visitors
Ms C Thompson, Locality Manager,
Learning Disabilities
Mr M Chew, Director of Learning Disabilities, Trust Headquarters, Tel.: 01908 243933
Liaison Services
District Nursing Liaison/Discharge Co-ordinator, Hospital Social Work Dept, Milton Keynes General Hospital, Tel.: 01908 609791/243449
Pharmacy
Ms J Corbett, Pharmacy Lead/Chief Pharmacist, Trust Headquarters, Tel.: 01908 243933 ext 3650
School Nursing
Ms C Thompson, Senior Manager - School Nursing,
Smoking Cessation
Ms R Flower, Health Inequalities Manager,
Specialist Nursing Services
Mr R Taylor, Continence, Neath Hill Health Centre, 1 Tower Crescent, Neath Hill, Milton Keynes, MK14 6JY, Tel.: 01908 230525
Mrs M Healy, Nurse Specialist, TB, - Respiratory, Neath Hill Health Centre, 1 Tower Crescent, Neath Hill, Milton Keynes, MK14 6JY, Tel.: 01908 230525

New Forest Primary Care Trust

Trust Headquarters, 8 Sterne Road
Tatchbury Mount, Calmore
SOUTHAMPTON, SO40 2RZ
Tel.: 023 8087 4270
Fax.: 023 8087 4275

Admin & Senior Management
Ms D Foster, Director of Adults & Older People's Services, 8 Sterne Road, Tatchbury Mount, Calmore, Southampton, SO40 2RZ, Tel.: 023 8087 4270
Ms A Kelly, Director of Services, Children & Families, 8 Sterne Road, Tatchbury Mount, Calmore, Southampton, SO40 2RZ, Tel.: 023 8087 4270
Mr J Richards, Chief Executive, 8-9 Sterne Road, Tatchbury Mount, Calmore, Southampton, SO40 2RZ, Tel.: 023 8087 4270
Child Health
Ms E Martin, Lead Manager, Child & Family Services, Ashurst Hospital, Lyndhurst Road, Ashurst, Southampton, SO40 7AR, Tel.: 023 8029 3043

Child Health Records

Central Health Clinic, East Park Terrace, Southampton, SO14 0YL, Tel.: 023 8090 2565/2535

Child Protection/Safeguarding Children

Mrs J Satterly, Designated Nurse, Safeguarding Children, 4 Sterne Road, Tatchbury Mount, Calmore, Southampton, Hampshire, SO40 2RZ, Tel.: 023 8087 4173

Clinical Leads (NSF)

Mrs R Mehan, Clinical Lead, CHD,

Mrs C Messanger, Clinical Lead, Children,

Mrs R Mehan, Clinical Lead, Diabetes,

Mrs A Horsman, Clinical Lead, Older People,

District Nursing

Ms N Eastwood, Deputy Head of Services - District Nursing, Hythe Hospital, Beauleiu Road, Hythe, Southampton, SO45 4ZB, Tel.: 023 8042 3224

Ms C Edwards, Head of Service for District Nursing, Hythe Hospital,

Family Planning Services

This service is run by Southampton City PCT,

Health Visitors

Ms N Eastwood, Deputy Head of Services, Hythe Hospital, Beauleiu Road, Hythe, Southampton, SO45 4ZB, Tel.: 023 8042 3224

Miss E Martin, Locality Manager, Health Visitors, Ashurst Hospital, Lyndhurst Road, Ashurst, Southampton, SO40 7AR, Tel.: 023 8029 3043

Learning Disabilities

This service is run by Hampshire Partnership NHS Trust,

Liaison Services

Ms S Lancaster, Bed Manager - Liaison Services, Graham Unit, Lymington Infirmary, East Hill, Lymington, Hampshire, SO41 9ZJ,

Pharmacy

Mr B Curwain, Head of Primary Care/Chief Pharmacist, Fenwick Hospital, Pikes Hill, Lyndhurst, Hampshire, Tel.: 02380 286406

Smoking Cessation

Mr B Curwain, Head of Primary Care/Chief Pharmacist, Fenwick Hospital, Pikes Hill, Lyndhurst, Hampshire, Tel.: 02380 286406

Newbury & Community Primary Care Trust

**Trust Headquarters, Avonbank House
Northcroft Wing, West Street
NEWBURY
Berkshire
RG14 1BZ**
Tel.: 01635 42400

Admin & Senior Management

Ms J Bartlett, Interim Area Director, West Berkshire, Avonbank House, Northcroft Wing, West Street, Newbury, Berkshire, RG14 1BZ, Tel.: 01635 503302

Ms S Timson, Interim Director of Clinical Standards, 57-59 Bath Road, Reading, RG30 2BA,

Mrs R Wyatt, Community Nurse Manager, West Berkshire Community Hospital, Benham Hill, Thatcham, Berks, RG18 3AS, Tel.: 01635 273581

Child Health

Ms N Baker, West Berkshire Community Hospital, Tel.: 01635 273384

Ms M Chipman, Berkshire Community Hospital, Tel.: 01635 273384

Ms T Davies, Berkshire Community Hospital, Tel.: 01635 273384

Ms P Gooch, Berkshire Community Hospital, Tel.: 01635 273384

Ms J Lee, Berkshire Community Hospital, Tel.: 01635 273384

Ms S Moon, Berkshire Community Hospital, Tel.: 01635 273384

Ms V O'Doherty, Berkshire Community Hospital, Tel.: 01635 273384

Ms H Straszewski, Berkshire Community Hospital, Tel.: 01635 273384

Child Health Records

Child Health, Thames Valley Primary Care Agency, 7/9 Cremyll Road, Reading, RG1 8NQ, Tel.: 01189 183440

Child Protection/Safeguarding Children

Mrs H Rickard, Designated Nurse Looked After Children, Named Nurse, Child Protection, Avonbank House, West Street, Newbury, RG14 1BZ,

Ms J Selim, Designated Nurse, Child Protection, 3 Craven Road, Reading, RG1 5LF, Tel.: 0118 931 5800

Clinical Leads (NSF)

Dr M Thomas, Clinical Lead, Cancer,

Dr C Latham, Clinical Lead, CHD,

Dr G Vevers, Clinical Lead, Older People,

Community Midwifery

Midwives Base, West Berkshire Community Hospital, Benham Hill, London Road, Newbury, RG18 2AS, Tel.: 01635 273386

Community Nursing Services

Ms G Gleeson, Community Children's Services Coordinator, West Berkshire Community Hospital, Benham Hill, London Road, Thatcham, RG18 3AS, Tel.: 01635 273582

Ms R Wyatt, Community Nurse Manager, West Berkshire Community Hospital, Benham Hill, London Road, Thatcham, RG18 3AS, Tel.: 01635 273581

District Nursing

Mrs R Barbour, District Nurse, Woolton Hill Surgery, Trade Street, Woolton Hill, RG20 9UL, Tel.: 01635 254188

Ms R Barbour, District Nurse, Kintbury Surgery, Newbury Street, Kintbury, RG17 9UX, Tel.: 01488 657954

Mrs C Bridger, District Nurse, The Downlands Practice, East Lane, Chieveley, RG20 8UY, Tel.: 01625 248406

Mrs G Collins, District Nurse, The Falkland Surgery, Monks Lane, Newbury, RG14 7DF, Tel.: 01635 279985

Mrs R Erahdun, District Nurse, The Surgery, High Street, Compton, RG16 0NJ, Tel.: 01635 248406

Mrs A Haines, District Nurse, Chapel Row Surgery, The Avenue, Bucklebury, RG7 6NS, Tel.: 0118 9714186

Mrs M Hennessey, District Nurse, 2a The Croft, Hungerford, RG17 0HY, Tel.: 01488 687808

Mrs D Holdway, District Nurse, Lambourn Surgery, Bockhampton Road, Lambourn, RG17 8PS, Tel.: 01488 72937

Mrs C Irlam, District Nurse, Eastfield House Surgery, St Johns Road, Newbury, RG14 7LW, Tel.: 01635 524717

Mrs L McAdam, Co-ordinator, District Nurse, hatcham Medical Practice, Bath Road, Thatcham, RG18 3HD, Tel.: 01635 861278

Mrs S Mees, District Nurse, St Marys Surgery, St Mary's Road, Newbury, RG14 1EQ, Tel.: 01635 37767

Mrs A Sharkey, District Nurse, Northcroft Surgery, Northcroft Lane, Newbury, RG14 1BU, Tel.: 01635 48965

Health Visitors

Mrs G Beach, Health Visitor, Thatcham Medical Practice, Bath Road, Thatcham, RG18 3HD, Tel.: 01635 295444

Mrs S Carrington, Health Visitor, Kintbury Surgery, Newbury Street, Kintbury, RG17 9UX, Tel.: 01488 658294

Mrs A Clare, Health Visitor, 2a The Croft, Hungerford, RG17 0HY, Tel.: 01488 687812

Mrs H Cobb, Health Visitor, The Falkland Surgery, Monks Lane, Newbury, RG14 7DF, Tel.: 01635 279980

Mrs A Cox, Health Visitor, Thatcham Medical Practice, Bath Road, Thatcham, RG18 3HD, Tel.: 01635 295444

Ms A Downlands, Health Visitor, The Surgery, High Street, Compton, RG16 0NJ, Tel.: 01635 578576

Mrs H Hastings, Health Visitor, Burdwood Surgery, Wheelers Green Way, Thatcham, Tel.: 01635 873490

Mrs J Hewett, Health Visitor, Thatcham Medical Practice, Bath Road, Thatcham, RG18 3HD, Tel.: 01635 295444

Ms P James, Health Visitor, St Marys Surgery, St Mary's Road, Newbury, RG14 1EQ, Tel.: 01635 42214

Mrs M Jenkins, Health Visitor, Burdwood Surgery, Wheelers Green Way, Thatcham, Tel.: 01635 868006

Mrs S Knight, Health Visitor, The Downlands Practice, East Lane, Chieveley, RG20 8UY, Tel.: 01625 248501

South Central Strategic Health Authority

Mrs L Lawrence, Health Visitor, The Falkland Surgery, Monks Lane, Newbury, RG14 7DF, Tel.: 01635 279980

Mrs K Lewis, Health Visitor, Burdwood Surgery, Wheelers Green Way, Thatcham, Tel.: 01635 873490

Mrs H Lockyear, Health Visitor, Thatcham Medical Practice, Bath Road, Thatcham, RG18 3HD, Tel.: 01635 295444

Mrs C Meyer, Health Visitor, Chapel Row Surgery, The Avenue, Bucklebury, RG7 6NS, Tel.: 0118 9714186

Mrs R Pavlou, Health Visitor, St Marys Surgery, St Mary's Road, Newbury, RG14 1EQ, Tel.: 01635 42214

Mrs A Roberts, Health Visitors, Staff Nurse, Thatcham Medical Practice, Bath Road, Thatcham, RG18 3HD, Tel.: 01635 295444

Mrs K Robinson, Health Visitor, Northcroft Surgery, Northcroft Lane, Newbury, RG14 1BU, Tel.: 01635 41143

Mrs G Ross, Health Visitor, Lambourn Surgery, Bockhampton Road, Lambourn, RG17 8PS, Tel.: 01488 72115

Mrs C Traynor, Health Visitor, Northcroft Surgery, Northcroft Lane, Newbury, RG14 1BU, Tel.: 01635 41143

Mrs M Vickers, Health Visitor, Eastfield House Surgery, St Johns Road, Newbury, RG14 7LW, Tel.: 01635 43114

Mrs H Wooster, Health Visitor, The Downlands Practice, East Lane, Chieveley, RG20 8UY, Tel.: 01625 248501

Liaison Services

Ms J McCulloch, PALS Manager, West Berkshire Community Hospital, Benham Hill, London Road, Newbury, RG18 3AS, Tel.: 01635 273325

Pharmacy

Ms L King, Pharmacy Services Co-ordinator, West Berkshire Community Hospital, Benham Hill, London Road, Thatcham, Berks, RG18 3AS, Tel.: 01635 273580

Specialist Nursing Services

Ms R Crowder, Professional Development Nurses, 57-59 Bath Road, Reading, RG30 2BA, Tel.: 0118 962 2895

Mrs P Prynn, Advisor, Continence, Wokingham Hospital, Tel.: 0118 949 5000

Ms J Grimes, Diabetic Care, Diabetes Centre, Melrose House West, London Road, Reading, RG1 5BS, Tel.: 0118 987 7478

Mrs L Seaby, Nurse Specialist, IV Therapy, West Berkshire Community Hospital, Tel.: 01635 273575

Nurses, Macmillan, Charles Clore Centre, 214 Newton Road, Newbury, RG14 7EE, Tel.: 01635 550233

Mrs L Omerod, Macmillan, Charles Clore Centre, 214 Newton Road, Newbury, RG14 7EE, Tel.: 01635 550233

North Hampshire Hospitals NHS Trust

Trust Headquarters, North Hampshire Hospital
Aldermaston Road
BASINGSTOKE
Hampshire
RG24 9NA
Tel.: 01256 473202

Acute Specialist Nursing Services

Ms S Alves, Psydomytoma, Clinical Nurse Specialist, C Floor, North Hampshire Hospital, Tel.: 01256 473202 x 3104

Ms M Bosworth, Opthalmology, Clinical Nurse Specialist, Old Day Surgery Unit, North Hampshire Hospital, Tel.: 01256 473202 x 3572

Ms C Maddock, Nurse, Acute Pain, B Floor, North Hampshire Hospital, Tel.: 01256 473202 x 3527

Ms E Sandy-Lee Alexis, Nurse, Acute Pain, B Floor, North Hampshire Hospital, Tel.: 01256 473202 x 3527

Ms J Tambellini, Nurse, Acute Pain, B Floor, North Hampshire Hospital, Tel.: 01256 473202 x 3527

Ms A Brember, Senior, Clinical Nurse Specialist, Breast Care, C Floor, North Hampshire Hospital, Tel.: 01256 473202 x 3123

Ms C Cahill, Clinical Nurse Specialist, Breast Care, - Lymphoedema, C Floor, North Hampshire Hospital, Tel.: 01256 473202 x 3126

Ms J Palmer, Clinical Nurse Specialist, Breast Care, C Floor, North Hampshire Hospital, Tel.: 01256 473202 x 3126

Ms T Patterson, Clinical Nurse Specialist, Breast Care, C Floor, North Hampshire Hospital, Tel.: 01256 473202 x 3126

Ms S Goddard, Lead Nurse, Cancer, C Floor, North Hampshire Hospital, Tel.: 01256 473202 x 3420

Ms P Nettleton, Clinical Nurse Specialist, Chemotherapy, F Floor, North Hampshire Hospital, Tel.: 01256 473202 x 4839

Ms N Summers, Clinical Nurse Specialist, Colorectal, C Floor, North Hampshire Hospital, Tel.: 01256 473202 x 4807

Ms A Bath, Clinical Nurse Specialist, Colposcopy, Sherborne Building, North Hampshire Hospital, Tel.: 01256 473202 x 3682

Ms T Bond, Clinical Nurse Specialist, Dermatology, OPD, North Hampshire Hospital, Tel.: 01256 473202 x 3268

Ms O Harrison, Nurse Specialist, Diabetes, Adult Medicine, North Hampshire Hospital, Tel.: 01256 313613

Mr B Armstrong, Nurse Consultant, Emergency Care, North Hampshire Hospital Trust, Tel.: 01256 473202 x 3006

Ms H Rush, Lead Nurse, Emergency Care, North Hampshire Hospital Trust, Tel.: 01256 473202 x 4982

Ms J Moody, Clinical Nurse Specialist, Gynaecology, - Urological, Sherborne Building, North Hampshire Hospital, Tel.: 01256 473202 ext 3821

Ms L Lloyd, Clinical Nurse Specialist, Haematology, F Floor, North Hampshire Hospital, Tel.: 01256 473202 x 4839

Ms S Paterson, Nurse, Heart Failure, Adult Medicine, North Hampshire Hospital, Tel.: 01256 313656

Ms A Bartley, Nurse, IBD, Adult Medicine, North Hampshire Hospital, Tel.: 01256 486778

Ms J Prosser, Nurse, IBD, - Hepatitis, Adult Medicine, North Hampshire Hospital, Tel.: 01256 486778

Ms H Gray, Nurse, Infection Control, North Hampshire Hospital, Tel.: 01256 473202 x 3734

Ms A Simpson, Clinical Nurse Specialist, Liver, C Floor, North Hampshire Hospital, Tel.: 01256 473202 x 3079

Ms B King, Iron Deficiency & Carcinoid, Nurse, Medicine, Adult Medicine, North Hampshire Hospital, Tel.: 01256 313032

Ms J Metcalf, Nurse Consultant, Older People, North Hampshire Hospital Trust, Tel.: 01256 473202 x 3624

Ms M Emmett, Macmillan Nurse, Palliative Care, EHC, F Floor, North Hampshire Hospital, Tel.: 01256 473202 x 4729

Ms C Mackenzie, Macmillan Nurse, Palliative Care, EHC, F Floor, North Hampshire Hospital, Tel.: 01256 473202 x 4729

Ms M Miles, Macmillan Nurse, Palliative Care, EHC, F Floor, North Hampshire Hospital, Tel.: 01256 473202 x 4729

Ms H Sinkinson, Macmillan Nurse, Palliative Care, EHC, F Floor, North Hampshire Hospital, Tel.: 01256 473202 x 4729

Ms L Bennett, Nurse Specialist, Respiratory, Adult Medicine, North Hampshire Hospital, Tel.: 01256 313641

Ms E Maltby, Clinical Nurse Specialist, Stoma Care, C Floor, North Hampshire Hospital, Tel.: 01256 473202 x 3565

Ms E Shaw, Clinical Nurse Specialist, Stoma Care, C Floor, North Hampshire Hospital, Tel.: 01256 473202 x 3565

Ms M Topping, Nurse Specialist, Stroke care, - Brain Injury, Adult Medicine, North Hampshire Hospital, Tel.: 01256 313631

Ms P Aslet, Senior, Clinical Nurse Specialist, Urology, C Floor, North Hampshire Hospital, Tel.: 01256 313515 bleep 2359

Ms T Campbell, Clinical Nurse Specialist, Urology, C Floor, North Hampshire Hospital, Tel.: 01256 473202 x 3515

Child Health

Children's Services/School Health, G Floor, North Hampshire Hospital, Tel.: 01256 473202

Ms A Day, Community Children's Nurse, North Hampshire Hospital, Tel.: 01256 313693

Ms W Green, Community Children's Nurse, North Hampshire Hospital, Tel.: 01256 313693

Ms P Le Flufy, Acute & Ambulatory Services Manager, G Floor, North Hampshire Hospital, Tel.: 01256 313700

South Central Strategic Health Authority

Ms J Roberts, Community Children's Nurse, North Hampshire Hospital, Tel.: 01256 313693

Ms L Urwin, Community Children's Nurse (Sec), North Hampshire Hospital, Tel.: 01256 313693

Ms C Wadeson, Community Children's Nurse, North Hampshire Hospital, Tel.: 01256 313693

Mr C Wilgar, Community Children's Nurse (Diabetes), North Hampshire Hospital, Tel.: 01256 313693

Child Health Records

Mrs A Kelly, Manager, Child Health Records, G Floor North Hampshire Hospital, Tel.: 01256 313086

Child Protection/Safeguarding Children

Mrs C Newman, Designated Nurse for Looked After Children, Tel.: 01256 313394

Community Midwifery

Ms M Beattie, Clinical Midwifery Manager Maternity, North Hampshire Hospital, Tel.: x 4456

Mrs W Cotterell, Clinical Midwifery Manager, Tel.: 01256 314785

Ms W Cotterill, Clinical Midwifery Manager Midwifery, North Hampshire Hospital, Tel.: x 4785

Ms C James, Head of Midwifery, North Hampshire Hospital, Tel.: 01256 313329

Health Visitors

Ms C Ward, Liaison Paediatric Health Visitor, North Hampshire Hospital, Tel.: 01256 313129

HIV/AIDS

Mr S Day, HIV, North Hampshire Hospital, Tel.: 01256 313260

Learning Disabilities

Ms D Childs, Senior Nurse - Children with Learning Disabilities, Erdesley House, Cliddesden Court, Cliddesden Road, Basingstoke, Hampshire, RG21 8UQ, Tel.: 01256 356586

Matrons/Modern Matrons

Ms K Barton, DTC, Modern Matron, DTC, North Hampshire Hospital, Tel.: 01256 473202 x 4301

Ms L Cunningham, Modern Matron, Critical Care, C Floor, North Hampshire Hospital, Tel.: 01256 473202 x 3562

Ms P Dominey, Matron, Elderly Care, F Floor, North Hampshire Hospital Trust, Tel.: 01256 473202 bleep 1196

Ms J Cairns, Matron, Medicine, - Adults, E Floor, North Hampshire Hospital Trust, Tel.: 01256 473202 x 3624

Ms N Potter, Matron, Orthopaedics, D Floor, North Hampshire Hospital Trust, Tel.: 01256 473202 x 3183

Ms J Dean, Modern Matron, Surgery, C Floor, North Hampshire Hospital, Tel.: 01256 473202 x 3758

Ms K Rooney, Modern Matron, Theatres, Main Theatres, North Hampshire Hospital, Tel.: 01256 473202 x 3447

School Nursing

Mrs C Warner, Professional Lead, School Health Nursing, Material & Child Health Div, G Floor, North Hampshire Hospital, Tel.: 01256 313086

North Hampshire Primary Care Trust

Trust Headquarters, Harness House
Aldermaston Road
BASINGSTOKE
Hampshire
RG24 9NB
Tel.: 01256 332288

Admin & Senior Management

Mrs H Clanchy, Director of Primary & Community Care, Winchfield Lodge, Old Potbridge Road, Winchfield, Hants, RG27 8BT, Tel.: 01256 312261

Child Health

Part of North Hampshire Hospital Trust,

Child Health Records

Child Health Dept, c/o North Hampshire Hospital Trust,

Child Protection/Safeguarding Children

Ms V Elliott, Fairway House, Aldermaston Road, Basingstoke, RG24 9RH, Tel.: 01256 376465

Clinical Leads (NSF)

Dr A-M May, Clinical Lead, CHD,

Community Matrons

Ms S Garland, Community Matron, Alton Community Hospital, Chawton Park Road, Alton, Hants, GU34 1RJ,

Community Nursing Services

Mrs S Ferrett, Locality Manager, Basingstoke (South), Fairway House, Aldermaston Road, Basingstoke, RG24 9RH, Tel.: 01256 376558

Ms S Miller, Head of Community Services, Harness House, Aldermaston Road, Basingstoke, Hants, RG24 9NB, Tel.: 01256 312318

Ms P Read, Locality Manager, Basingstoke (North), Fairway House, Aldermaston Road, Basingstoke, RG24 9RH, Tel.: 01256 376559

District Nursing

Mr S Coopey, Professional Lead, District Nurse, Fairway House, Tel.: 01256 376470

Family Planning Services

Dr A Britton, Clinical Lead, Contraception & Sexual Health Service (cash), Tel.: 01256 354095

Ms J Corbett, Programme Lead, Harness House, Aldermaston Road, Basingstoke, Hants, RG24 9NB, Tel.: 01256 312337

Health Visitors

Mrs S Ferrett, Locality Manager, Basingstoke (South), Fairway House, Aldermaston Road, Basingstoke, RG24 9RH, Tel.: 01256 376558

Ms P Read, Locality Manager, Basingstoke (North), Fairway House, Aldermaston Road, Basingstoke, RG24 9RH, Tel.: 01256 376559

Liaison Services

Ms C Ward, Paediatric Liaison Health Visitor, G Floor, NHHT,

Other Services

Ms V Bayliss, Continence Services, Parklands Hospital, Aldermaston Road, Basingstoke, Tel.: 01256 817718

Mr R Cooper, Leg Ulcer Specialist, Shakespear House, Shakespear Road, Basingstoke, Hants, RG2,

Ms S Harris, Co-ordinator/South, Community Intensive Support Service, Tel.: 01420 592847

Ms P Heyfron, Day Care Services, T.O.A.D, Alliston Way, South Ham, Basingstoke, Hants, Tel.: 01256 330891

Ms K Kersley, Manager, St Michael's Hospice Community Nursing Service, St Michael's Hospice, Aldermaston Road, Basingstoke, Tel.: 01256 844744

Ms S Wood, Co-ordinator/Basingstoke, Community Intensive Support Service, Tel.: 07767 408766

Smoking Cessation

Ms C Moran, Co-ordinator, NHPCT, Harness House, Tel.: 01256 312341

Specialist Nursing Services

Mrs S Feretti, Twilight/Community Nursing - Bank, Fairway House, Aldermaston Road, Basingstoke, RG24 9RH, Tel.: 01256 376558

North Oxfordshire Primary Care Trust Partnership

Trust Headquarters, Indigo House
Banbury Business Park, Aynho Road, Adderbury
BANBURY
Oxon
OX17 3NS
Tel.: 01295 814100
Fax.: 01295 814191

Admin & Senior Management

Ms J Bell, Head of Children & Family Services, Indigo House, Banbury Business Park, Aynho Road, Adderbury, Banbury, Oxon, OX17 3NS, Tel.: 01295 814125

South Central Strategic Health Authority

Mrs H Knott, Director of Clinical Services, Indigo House, Banbury Business Park, Aynho Road, Adderbury, Banbury, Oxon, OX17 3NS, Tel.: 01295 814152

Mr N Webb, Joint Chief Executive, Indigo House, Banbury Business Park, Aynho Road, Adderbury, Banbury, Oxon, OX17 3NS, Tel.: 01295 814109

Child Health
Mrs A Jones, Co-ordinator, Primary Care, Astral House, Granville Way, Bicester, OX26 4JT, Tel.: 01869 604040

Child Health Records
Ms M Hetherington, Admin, Bourton House, 18 Thorney Leys Park, Witney, OX28 4GJ, Tel.: 01993 209561

Child Protection/Safeguarding Children
Ms J Bell, Head of Children & Family Services, Indigo House, Banbury Business Park, Aynho Road, Adderbury, Banbury, Oxon, OX17 3NS, Tel.: 01295 814125

Ms J Phipps, Named Nurse, Child Protection, Indigo House, Banbury Business Park, Aynho Road, Adderbury, Banbury, Oxon, OX17 3NS, Tel.: 01295 814100

Clinical Leads (NSF)
Dr D Hannon, Clinical Lead, Cancer,

Dr D Evans, Clinical Lead, CHD,

Dr D Evans, Clinical Lead, Diabetic Care,

Mr J Coombes, Clinical Lead, Older People, Tel.: 01295 814186

Community Nursing Services
Mrs A Jones, Primary Care Facilitator, Indigo House, Banbury Business Park, Aynho Road, Adderbury, Banbury, Oxon, OX17 3NS, Tel.: 01295 814148

District Nursing
Ms M Fitzgerald, Practice Facilitator, Indigo House, Banbury Business Park, Aynho Road, Adderbury, Banbury, Oxon, OX17 3NS, Tel.: 01295 814100

Mrs A Jones, Practice Facilitator, Indigo House, Banbury Business Park, Aynho Road, Adderbury, Banbury, Oxon, OX17 3NS, Tel.: 01295 814148

Health Visitors
Ms J Morley, Practice Facilitator, Indigo House, Banbury Business Park, Aynho Road, Adderbury, Banbury, Oxon, OX17 3NS, Tel.: 01295 814100

Liaison Services
Ms F Goddard, Nurse Manager, Community Liaison, Room 3708, Level 3, The John Radcliffe, Headley Way, Headington, Oxford, OX3 9DU, Tel.: 01865 220266/851051

School Nursing
Ms P Nicklin, Team Leader, Orchard Health Centre, Core Road, Banbury, Oxon, OX16 2ES, Tel.: 01295 819100

Smoking Cessation
Dr L Stirzaker, Director of Public Health, Indigo House, Banbury Business Park, Aynho Road, Adderbury, Banbury, Oxon, OX17 3NS, Tel.: 01295 814189

Nuffield Orthopaedic Centre NHS Trust
Trust Headquarters, Windmill Road
HEADINGTON
Oxfordshire, OX3 7LD
Tel.: 01865 741155

Admin & Senior Management
Ms J Fowler, Director of Nursing, Nuffield Orthopaedic Centre, Windmill Road, Headington, Oxfordshire, OX3 7LD, Tel.: 01865 741155

Oxford City Primary Care Trust
Trust Headquarters, Richards Buildings
Old Road Campus, Headington
OXFORD
OX3 7LG
Tel.: 01865 226900

Child Health
Ms E Glanville, Childrens Services Manager,

Child Health Records
Ms M Hetherington, Admin, Bourton House, 18 Thorney Leys Park, Witney, OX28 4GJ, Tel.: 01993 209561

Child Protection/Safeguarding Children
Ms J Bell, Child Protection, Cherwell Vale PCT Offices, Oxford Road, Banbury, OX16 9GE, Tel.: 01295 819537

Clinical Leads (NSF)
Dr R Stevens, Clinical Lead, Cancer,

Dr H Merriman, Clinical Lead, CHD,

Dr M Wilkinson, Clinical Lead, Diabetic Care,

District Nursing
East Oxford Health Centre,

Ms R Ferris, Patch Manager, Tel.: 01865 456602

Ms C Fickling, Patch Manager, Tel.: 01865 456612

Ms J Smith, Patch Manager, Tel.: 01865 456604

Family Planning Services
Ms J Bullock, County-wide service, Senior Nurse Manager, Alec Turnbull Clinic, East Oxford Health Centre, Tel.: 01865 456665

Liaison Services
Ms F Goddard, Nurse Manager, Community Liaison, Room 3708, Level 3, The John Radcliffe, Headley Way, Headington, Oxford, OX3 9DU, Tel.: 01865 220266/851051

Oxford Radcliffe Hospitals NHS Trust
Trust Headquarters, John Radcliffe Hospital
Headley Way, Headington
OXFORD, OX3 9DU
Tel.: 01865 741166

Child Protection/Safeguarding Children
Ms J Bell, Child Protection, Cherwell Vale PCT Offices, Oxford Road, Banbury, OX16 9GE, Tel.: 01295 819537

Community Midwifery
Ms F Barnsley, Chipping Norton Midwifery Unit, Tel.: 01608 641682

Ms P Green, Community Midwifery Lead - Oxford City, Tel.: 01865 221696

Ms S Hillier, Wantage Midwifery Unit, Tel.: 01235 764343

Ms Y Jones, Banbury Midwifery Unit, Tel.: 01295 229462

Mrs J Knowles, Head of Midwifery Services, Level 4, Women's Centre, Oxford Radcliffe Hospitals NHS Trust, Oxford, OX3 9DU, Tel.: 01865 220406/221696

Ms R Wright, Wallingford Midwifery Unit, Tel.: 01491 826037

Oxfordshire Learning Disabilities NHS Trust
Trust Headquarters, Slade House
Horspath Driftway
HEADINGTON
Oxford, OX3 7JH
Tel.: 01865 747455

Learning Disabilities
Cherwell, Redlands Centre, Neithrop Avenue, Banbury, OX16 7NT, Tel.: 01295 257727

Oxford City, Wadham Court, Edgeway Road, Oxford, OX3 0HD, Tel.: 01865 721433

Mr J Turnbull, Director of Nursing/Patient Services, Slade House, Horspath Driftway, Headington, Oxford, OX3 7JH, Tel.: 01865 228109

Vale & South, Abbey Centre, Audlett Drive, Abingdon, Tel.: 01235 557900

Portsmouth City Primary Care Trust
Trust Headquarters, Trust Central Office
St James Hospital, Locksway Road
PORTSMOUTH
PO4 8LD
Tel.: 023928 22444

South Central Strategic Health Authority

Admin & Senior Management
Ms S Clark, Chief Executive,
Child Health Records
Pre School, Portsmouth Healthcare NHS Trust,
School Health, Northern Parade Clinic, Tel.: 023 9266 2378
Child Protection/Safeguarding Children
Ms D Rose, Designated Nurse, Battenburg Avenue Clinic,
Battenburg Avenue, North End, Portsmouth, PO2 0TA, Tel.: 023
9242 8802
Mr C Atkins, Named Nurse, Child Protection, Somerstown Health
Centre, Blackfriars Close, Somerstown, Portsmouth, Tel.: 023 9285
1180
Clinical Leads (NSF)
Mr C Lewis, Clinical Lead, Cancer,
Community Matrons
Ms J Chalwin, Service Manager, Community Matrons, 4th Floor,
Kingsway House, 130 Elm Grove, Southsea, PO5 1LR, Tel.: 023
9243 4900 ext 244
District Nursing
Ms J Chalwin, Service Manager, District Nursing/Intermediate
Care/Palliative Care, 4th Floor, Kingsway House, 130 Elm Grove,
Southsea, PO5 1LR, Tel.: 023 9243 4900 ext 244
Health Visitors
Ms A MacNaughton, Associate Director, Community Paediatric
Health Visitors/SN/CAMHS, Trust Headquarters, Tel.: 023 9289
4353
School Nursing
School Nursing Dept, Northern Parade Clinic, Doyle Avenue,
Portsmouth, PO2 9NF, Tel.: 023 9266 2378

Portsmouth Hospitals NHS Trust
Trust Headquarters, Delacourt House
Southwick Hill Road
PORTSMOUTH
PO6 3LY
Tel.: 023 9228 6000

Admin & Senior Management
Ms G Byrne, Director of Nursing, Portsmouth Hospitals NHS Trust,
Delacourt House, Southwick Hill Road, Portsmouth, PO6 3LY, Tel.:
023 9228 6000
Child Protection/Safeguarding Children
Ms P Aspinall, Child Protection, St Mary's Hospital, Tel.: 023 9228
6000 ext 3544
Ms T Scarborough, Child Protection, St Mary's Hospital, Tel.: 023
9228 6000 ext 3544
Community Midwifery
Ms M Forrester, East Hants PCT, Community Midwifery Manager,
Grange Ward, Petersfield Hospital, Swan Street, Petersfield, Hants,
GU32 3LB, Tel.: 023 9234 4217
Ms D Hill, Portsea PCT, Community Midwifery Manager, Mary Rose
Maternity Centre, St Mary's Maternity Hospital, Tel.: 023 92 286000
ext 3561
Mrs D Ockenden, Head of Midwifery, St Mary's Maternity Hospital,
Milton Road, Portsmouth, PO3 6AD, Tel.: 023 9228 6000 ext 3649
Ms J Parker-Wisdom, Fareham & Gosport PCT, Community
Midwifery Manager, Blackbrook Maternity Home, 31 Blackbrook
House Drive, Fareham, Hants, PO14 1PA, Tel.: 01329 232275
Ms J Parker-Wisdom, Fareham & Gosport PCT, Community
Midwifery Manager, Blake Maternity Ward, Gosport War Memorial
Hospital, Annes Hill Road, Gosport, Hants, PO12 3PW, Tel.: 023 92
523650
Liaison Services
Ms J Angus, Liaison Lead Discharge Planning Co-ordinator, St
Mary's Hospital, Milton Road, Portsmouth, PO3 6AD, Tel.: 023 9228
6000 ext 2378

Reading Primary Care Trust
Trust Headquarters
57-59 Bath Road
READING, RG30 2BA
Tel.: 0118 950 3094

Admin & Senior Management
Ms J Fitzgerald, Chief Executive,
Ms S Tinson, Director of Quality, Standards & Workforce,
Ms H Waddams, Director of Clinical Services,
Child Health
Ms L Champion, New Born Hearing Screening Clerk, 7-9 Cremyll
Road, Reading, RG1 8NQ, Tel.: 0118 918 3424
Child Health Department, 7-9 Cremyll Road, Reading, RG1 8NQ,
Tel.: 0118 918 3300
Ms A Houghton, Registration - Child Health Dept, 7-9 Cremyll Road,
Reading, RG1 8NQ, Tel.: 0118 918 3430
Ms J Smith, Immunisation Information, 7-9 Cremyll Road, Reading,
RG1 8NQ, Tel.: 0118 918 3420
Specialist Child Community Team, Royal Berkshire & Battle
Hospitals NHS Trust, London Road, Reading, RG1 5AN, Tel.: 0118
987 5111
Ms W Vince, Administration Manager - Child Health Dept, 7-9
Cremyll Road, Reading, RG1 8NQ, Tel.: 0118 918 3440
Ms S Wilson, Appointments - Child Health Dept, 7-9 Cremyll Road,
Reading, RG1 8NQ, Tel.: 0118 918 3422
Child Health Records
Child Health Records, 3 Craven Road, Reading, RG1 5LF, Tel.:
0118 986 2277
Child Protection/Safeguarding Children
Mrs T Colenso-Wright, Named Nurse, Child Protection, 3 Craven
Road, Reading, RG1 5LF, Tel.: 0118 931 5800/5816
Mrs J Selim, Designated Nurse, Child Protection, 3 Craven Road,
Reading, RG1 5LF, Tel.: 0118 931 5800/5828
Clinical Leads (NSF)
Ms S Tinson, Clinical Lead, Cancer,
Dr R Croft, Clinical Lead, CHD,
Ms M Alford, Clinical Lead, Diabetic Care,
Ms H Waddams, Clinical Lead, Older People,
District Nursing
Deputy Head of Adult Services, 57/59 Bath Road, Reading, RG30
2BA, Tel.: 0118 2950
Head of Children's Services, Whitley Health & Social Services
Centre, 268 Northumberland Avenue, Reading, RG2 7PJ, Tel.: 0118
931 2111
Nurse Facilitator, 25 Erleigh Rd, Reading, RG1 5LR, 0118 929 6443
HIV/AIDS
HIV/AIDS, Duchess of Kent House, Tel.: 0118 958 9195
Liaison Services
Liaison Discharge Facilitators, Wokingham Hospital, Barkham Road,
Wokingham, Tel.: 0118 949 5000
Liaison Discharge Facilitators, Royal Berks & Battle Hospitals NHS
Trust, Royal Berkshire Hospital, London Road, Reading, RG1 5AN,
Tel.: 0118 987 5111
Specialist Nursing Services
Ms R Crowder, Professional Development Nurse, 57-59 Bath Road,
Reading, RG30 2BA, Tel.: 0118 982 2895
Ms M Woods, Professional Development Nurse, 57-59 Bath Road,
Reading, RG30 2BA, Tel.: 0118 982 2895
Nurses, Diabetic Care, Melrose Clinic, London Road, Reading, Tel.:
0118 987 7478
Nurses, Infection Control, 57-59 Bath Road, Reading, RG30 2BA,
Tel.: 0118 982 2840
Nurses, Macmillan, Duchess of Kent House, Liebenrood Road,
Reading, Tel.: 0118 955 0492
The Homeless/Travellers & Asylum Seekers
Health Visitor for Homeless, Whitley Health & Social Services
Centre, Tel.: 0118 931 2111

Royal Berkshire & Battle Hospitals NHS Trust

Trust Headquarters, Royal Berkshire Hospital
London Road, READING
Berkshire, RG1 5AN
Tel.: 0118 987 5111

Acute Specialist Nursing Services
Ms L Buttery, Breast Care, Royal Berkshire Hospital, Tel.: 0118 987 420
Ms R Haji, Breast Care, Royal Berkshire Hospital, Tel.: 0118 987 598
Ms R Richmond, Dermatology, Royal Berkshire Hospital, Tel.: 0118 987 8209
Ms C Malloch, Diabetic Care, Royal Berkshire Hospital, Tel.: 0118 987 7478
Mr N Sophal, Diabetic Care, Royal Berkshire Hospital, Tel.: 0118 987 7478
Ms S Bellars, Infection Control, Royal Berkshire Hospital, Tel.: 0118 987 7114
Ms L Jones, Infection Control, Royal Berkshire Hospital, Tel.: 0118 987 7114
Ms S Duke, Palliative Care,Royal Berkshire Hospital, 0118 987 7891
Ms M Bell, Respiratory Medicine, Royal Berkshire Hospital, Tel.: 118 987 7159
Ms G Tomsett, Stoma Care, Royal Berkshire Hospital, Tel.: 0118 987 7640
Admin & Senior Management
Ms G Valentine, Assistant Director of Nursing, Tel.: 0118 987 7786
Child Health
Community Children's Nursing Team, Children's Outpatients, Royal Berks Hospital, London Road, Reading, RG1 5AN, Tel.: 0118 987 532
Child Protection/Safeguarding Children
Ms H Kelly, Named Nurse, Child Protection, Royal Berkshire Hospital,
Ms A Stock, Named Midwife, Child Protection, Maternity Unit, Royal Berkshire Hospital,
Family Planning Services
Mrs J Burnett, Head of Family Planning Services, 7 Craven Road, Reading,
HIV/AIDS
Mr J Masters, HIV, Nurse Specialist, Royal Berkshire Hospital,
Liaison Services
Outreach Neonatal Liaison Service, Neonatal Unit, Royal Berkshire Hospital, Tel.: 0118 9878046
Mrs T White, Patient Co-ordination Manager, Royal Berkshire Hospital, Tel.: 0118 9878156
Smoking Cessation
Mrs L Webb, Midwife, Royal Berkshire Hospital,

Slough Primary Care Trust

Trust Headquarters, Beech House
Upton Hospital, Albert Street
SLOUGH, SL1 2BJ
Tel.: 01753 821441

Admin & Senior Management
Ms S Choe, Director of Primary Care, Tel.: 01753 635697
Mr K Pitchford, Acting Chief Executive,
Child Health
Ms D Dhillon, Senior Nurse, Fir Tree House, Tel.: 01753 821441
Child Health Records
Child Health Records, Fir Tree House, Upton Hospital, Slough, SL1 3BL, Tel.: 01753 821441
Child Protection/Safeguarding Children
Ms C Cupid, Child Protection, Osborne Street Clinic, Tel.: 01753 635635

Clinical Leads (NSF)
Dr D Sinclair, Clinical Lead, CHD & Diabetes,
Ms S Lund, Clinical Lead, Cancer,
Ms C Cupid, Clinical Lead, Children,
Dr R Clark, Clinical Lead, Older People,
District Nursing
District Nurses, Tel.: 01753 635635
Family Planning Services
Ms S Mehigan, Sexual Health, Garden Clinic, Upton Hospital, Tel.: 01753 635000
Ms C Roche, Acting Service Manager - Family Planning, Garden Clinic, Upton Hospital, Tel.: 01753 635000
Health Visitors
Health Visitors, Tel.: 01753 635635
Specialist Nursing Services
Ms P Neale, Practice Nurse Facilitator, Trust Headquarters, Tel.: 01753 635181
Ms E Cunningham, Leg Ulcers, Herschel Medical Centre, 45 Osborne Street, Slough, SL1 1TT, Tel.: 01753 572768
The Homeless/Travellers & Asylum Seekers
Ms P Illingworth, Homeless, Refugees, Osborne Street Clinic, Tel.: 01753 635635
Ms S Patrick, Walk-in Centre, Slough Walk-in Centre, Upton Hospital, Tel.: 01753 635505

South East Oxfordshire Primary Care Trust

Trust Headquarters, Wallingford Community Hospital
Reading Road
WALLINGFORD, OX10 9DU
Tel.: 01491 208570

Admin & Senior Management
Ms H Dover, Director of Community Services,
Ms A Kirkpatrick, Chief Executive,
Child Health
Ms C Fickling, Clinical Lead Children's Specialist, East Oxford Health Centre, Manzil Way, Cowley Rd, Oxford, OX4 1XD, 01865 456612
Child Health Records
Ms M Hetherington, Admin, Bourton House, 18 Thorney Leys Park, Witney, OX28 4GJ, Tel.: 01993 209561
Child Protection/Safeguarding Children
Ms J Bell, Child Protection, Cherwell Vale PCT Offices, Oxford Road, Banbury, OX16 9GE, Tel.: 01295 819537
Clinical Leads (NSF)
Dr V Messenger, Clinical Lead, CHD & Diabetes,
Ms J Bradlow, Clinical Lead, Cancer,
Dr J Bradlow, Clinical Lead, Children,
Dr C Periton, Clinical Lead, Older People,
District Nursing
Mr T Mellin, Acting Community Services Manager, Townlands Community Hospital, York Rd, Henley-on-Thames, 01491 572544
Health Visitors
Ms L Bixby, Paediatric Liaison Health Visitor, Accident Prevention, Level 1, A&E, The John Radcliffe, Tel.: 01865 221789
HIV/AIDS
Ms V Mowlam, HIV/AIDS, East Oxford Health Centre, Tel.: 01865 456613
Liaison Services
Ms F Goddard, Community Liaison Nurse Manager & Single Point of Access, Room 3708, Level 3, The John Radcliffe, Headley Way, Headington, Oxford, OX3 9DU, Tel.: 01865 220266/851051
Specialist Nursing Services
Ms A Bardsley, Continence, Witney Community Hospital, Tel.: 01993 209434
Ms M McLoughlin, Infection Control, OHA, Old Road, Headington, OX3 7LG, Tel.: 01865 226854
Ms J Kayley, Community, IV Therapy, East Oxford Health Centre, Tel.: 01865 456614

South Central Strategic Health Authority

South West Oxfordshire Primary Care Trust
Trust Headquarters, 1st Floor Admin Block
Abingdon Community Hospital
Marcham Road
ABINGDON, OX14 1AG
Tel.: 01235 205555

Admin & Senior Management
Ms M Wicks, Chief Executive,
Child Health
Ms C Fickling, Clinical Lead Children's Specialist, East Oxford Health
Centre, Tel.: 01865 456612
Child Health Records
Ms M Hetherington, Admin, Bourton House, 18 Thorney Leys Park,
Witney, OX28 4GJ, Tel.: 01993 209561
Child Protection/Safeguarding Children
Ms J Bell, Child Protection, Cherwell Vale PCT Offices, Oxford Road,
Banbury, OX16 9GE, Tel.: 01295 819537
Clinical Leads (NSF)
Mr M Drury, Clinical Lead, Cancer,
Dr J Bradlow, Clinical Lead, Children,
Dr V Messenger, Clinical Lead, Diabetic Care,
Dr K Wood, Clinical Lead, Older People,
District Nursing
Ms D Perkins, Patient/Primary Care Manager, Wantage Health
Centre, Tel.: 01235 205802
Ms J Smith, Lead, District Nurse, East Oxford Health Centre, Cowley
Road, Oxford, OX4 1XD, Tel.: 01865 456604
Health Visitors
Ms L Brooks, Lead, Health Visitor, Orchard Health Centre, Banbury,
Tel.: 01295 819103
Liaison Services
Ms F Goddard, Nurse Manager Community Liaison, Room 3708,
Level 3, The John Radcliffe, Headley Way, Headington, Oxford, OX3
9DU, Tel.: 01865 220266/851051
Specialist Nursing Services
Ms J Moreton, Immunisation Co-ordinator, Tel.: 01865 226852
Ms A Bardsley, Continence, Witney Community Hospital, Welch
Way, Witney, OX28 7JJ, Tel.: 01993 209434
Ms C Pullen, Infection Control, Dept of Public Health & Health Policy,
OHA, Old Road, Headington, OX3 7LG, Tel.: 01865 226854

Southampton City Primary Care Trust
Trust Headquarters, Western Community Hospital
William Macleod Way
Millbrook
SOUTHAMPTON
SO16 4XE
Tel.: 023 8029 6904

Child Health
Ms S Ramsey, Head of Child & Family Services, Central Health
Clinic, East Park Terrace, Southampton, Tel.: 023 8090 2500
Ms B Smith, Paediatric Diabetes, G Level, Southampton General
Hospital, Tel.: 023 8079 6893

Child Health Records
Child Health Records, Central Health Clinic, Tel.: 023 8090
2565/2535
Child Protection/Safeguarding Children
Ms S Ramsey, Head of Child & Family Services, Central Health
Clinic, East Park Terrace, Southampton, Tel.: 023 8090 2500
Ms N Smith, Named Nurse, Child Protection, Bitterne Health Centre,
18 Commercial Street, Southampton, SO18 6BT, Tel.: 023 80426
327
Ms L Voss, Named Nurse, Child Protection, Bitterne Health Centre,
18 Commercial Street, Southampton, SO18 6BT, Tel.: 023 80426
327

Clinical Leads (NSF)
Dr S Townsend, Clinical Lead, Cancer,
Dr B Houghton, Clinical Lead, CHD,
Dr P Betts, Clinical Lead, Diabetic Care,
Community Nursing Services
Mrs G Ridgway, Director of Nursing & Quality, Western Community
Hospital, William Macleod Way, Millbrook, Southampton, SO16 4XE,
Tel.: 023 8090 2597
District Nursing
A Adams, Locality Manager, Western Community Hospital, William
Macleod Way, Southampton, Tel.: 023 8047 5410
A Robbins, Locality Manager, Moorgreen Hospital, Botley Road,
West End, Southampton, Tel.: 023 8047 2258
Family Planning Services
Mrs R Gurr, Manager, Contraception & Sexual Health Service, Quay
to Health, The Quays, 27 Harbour Parade, Southampton, Tel.: 023
8038 8916
Health Visitors
Mrs C Halcrow, Manager - Health Visitors, Central Health Clinic,
East Park Terrace, Southampton, Tel.: 023 8090 2500
Ms M Hanson, Health Visitor/School Nursing Liaison, Old Nurses
Home, Mailpoint 89, Southampton General Hospital, Tremona Road,
Southampton, SO16 6YD, Tel.: 023 8079 6868
HIV/AIDS
Ms L Breadner, HIV, Clinical Nurse Specialist, Newtown Health
Clinic, Lyon Street, Southampton, SO14 0LX, Tel.: 0238 090219
Ms K Humphrey, HIV, Specialist Nurse, Newtown Health Clinic, Lyon
Street, Southampton, SO14 0LX, Tel.: 0238 090219
Ms L Wilson, HIV CNS MH, Newtown Health Clinic, Lyon Street,
Southampton, SO14 0LX, Tel.: 0238 090219
Liaison Services
Ms M Hanson, Health Visitor/School Nursing Liaison, Old Nurses
Home, Mailpoint 89, Southampton General Hospital, Tremona Road,
Southampton, SO16 6YD, Tel.: 023 8079 6868
Mrs G W Nicholson, Patient Discharge Facilitator, Old Nurses Home
Mailpoint 89, Southampton General Hospital, Tremona Road,
Southampton, SO16 6YD, Tel.: 023 8079 6602
School Nursing
Mrs C Halcrow, Manager - School Nursing, Central Health Clinic,
East Park Terrace, Southampton, Tel.: 023 8090 2500
Ms M Hanson, Health Visitor/School Nursing Liaison, Old Nurses
Home, Mailpoint 89, Southampton General Hospital, Tremona Road,
Southampton, SO16 6YD, Tel.: 023 8079 6868
Specialist Nursing Services
Ms J Mitchell, Specialist Nurse, Diabetic Care, Diabaetes Resource
Centre, Royal South Hants Hospital, Tel.: 02380 825885
Ms D Privett, Clinical Nurse Specialist, Leg Ulcers, Newtown Clinic,
Lyon Street, Southampton, SO14 0LX, Tel.: 02380 900218
The Homeless/Travellers & Asylum Seekers
Ms P Campbell, Team Leader, Homeless, Asylum Seekers, 30
Cranbury Avenue, Southampton, SO14 0LT, Tel.: 023 8033 6991

Southampton University Hospitals NHS Trust
Trust Headquarters, Southampton General Hospital
Tremona Road, Shirley
SOUTHAMPTON
Hampshire
SO16 6YD
Tel.: 023 8077 7222
Fax.: 023 8079 4153

Community Midwifery
Miss K Baker, Associate Director, Midwifery & Nursing, Princess
Anne Hospital, Coxford Road, Shirley, Southampton, Hampshire,
SO16 5YA, Tel.: 023 8079 6021

South Central Strategic Health Authority

Vale of Aylesbury Primary Care Trust

Trust Headquarters, Verney House
Gatehouse Road
AYLESBURY
Bucks
HP19 8ET
Tel.: 01296 310000

Admin & Senior Management
Mrs L Lake-Stewart, Director of Clinical Services & Nursing, Verney House, Gatehouse Road, Aylesbury, Bucks, HP19 8ET, Tel.: 01296 310080

Child Health
Mrs E Coleridge-Smith, Assistant Director of Child & Family Services, c/o Sue Nicholls Centre, Manor House, Bierton Road, Aylesbury, HP20 1EG, Tel.: 01296 489951
Ms Y Marsh, Operational Manager, Sue Nicholls Centre, Manor House, Bierton Road, Aylesbury, HP20 1EG, Tel.: 01296 504230

Child Health Records
Ms Y Marsh, Operational Manager, Sue Nicholls Centre, Manor House, Bierton Road, Aylesbury, Bucks, HP20 1EG, Tel.: 01296 504230

Child Protection/Safeguarding Children
Mrs C Gregory, Looked After Children, Specialist Nurse, Sue Nicholls Centre, Manor House, Bierton Road, Aylesbury, Bucks, HP20 1EG, Tel.: 01296 504788
Mrs T Atcheson, Named Nurse, Child Protection, Sue Nicholls Centre, Manor House, Bierton Road, Aylesbury, Bucks, HP20 1EG, Tel.: 01296 504639

Clinical Leads (NSF)
Dr H Pegrum, Clinical Lead, Cancer, Florence Nightingale House, Stoke Mandeville Hospital, HP21 8AL, Tel.: 01296 394710
Ms L Lake-Stewart, Clinical Lead, Care of the Elderly, Verney House, Gatehouse Road, Aylesbury, Bucks, HP19 8ET, Tel.: 01296 310080
Dr J O'Grady, Clinical Lead, Diabetes, CHD, Verney House, Gatehouse Road, Aylesbury, Bucks, HP19 8ET, Tel.: 01296 310144
Ms E Coleridge-Smith, Clinical Lead, Children, Sue Nicholls Centre, Manor House, Bierton Road, Aylesbury, Bucks, HP20 1EG, Tel.: 01296 489951
Dr J O'Grady, Clinical Lead, Diabetes, Verney House, Gatehouse Road, Aylesbury, Bucks, HP19 8ET, Tel.: 01296 310144

Community Matrons
Mr C Butterworth, Respite Care, Community Matron, Paediatrics, Wing Unit, Manor House, Bierton Road, Aylesbury, HP20 1EG, Tel.: 01296 504476

Community Nursing Services
Aylesbury, Out of Hours Nursing Service 6pm-7am, Tel.: 01296 331511
Buckingham, Out of Hours Nursing Service, Tel.: 01280 824842
Thame, Out of Hours Nursing Service, Tel.: 01844 260926
Ms K Wheatley, Lead Nurse - Nursing Service 9am-6pm, Manor House, Bierton Road, Aylesbury, HP20 1EG, Tel.: 01296 339840

District Nursing
Ms A MacKellar, Clinical Manager - District Nursing, Manor House, Bierton Road, Aylesbury, HP20 1EG, Tel.: 01296 504460

Equipment Loan Services
Ms F Kent, Equipment Resource Nurse, Manor House, Bierton Road, Aylesbury, HP20 1EG, Tel.: 01296 504654
Ms F Kent, Equipment Resource Nurse, Manor House, Bierton Road, Aylesbury, HP20 1EG, Tel.: 01296 504354

Family Planning Services
Ms M Dennis, Senior Nurse, Sexual Health Service, Brookside Clinic, Station Way, Aylesbury, HP20 2SQ, Tel.: 01296 421722 x 249

Health Visitors
Ms V Pink, Clinical Manager - Health Visiting, Sue Nicholls Centre, Manor House, Bierton Road, Aylesbury, HP20 1EG, Tel.: 01296 504460

HIV/AIDS
Ms L Stephen, Senior Nurse/Sister, Sexual Health Service, Brookside Clinic, Station Way, Aylesbury, HP20 2SQ, Tel.: 01296 422150 x275

Liaison Services
Ms G Rennie, Paediatric Liaison, Community Paediatric Office, Stoke Mandeville Hospital, Aylesbury, HP21 8AL, Tel.: 01296 315142

Other Services
Ms S Gutteridge, Modern Matron, Thame Community Hospital, East Street, Thame, Oxon, OX9 3JL, Tel.: 01844 212727
Ms A Phelan, Modern Matron, Buckingham Community Hospital, High Street, Buckingham, MK18 1NU, Tel.: 01280 813243
Ms J Taptiklis, Assistant Director, Adult & Older Peoples Services, Manor House, Bierton Rd, Aylesbury, HP20 1EG, 01296 504363
Ms R Rowland, Rapid Access Strategic Lead, Intermediate Care, Intermediate Care Services, VAICS, Quainton Ward, Manor House, Bierton Road, Aylesbury, HP20 1EG, Tel.: 01296 504747

Pharmacy
Ms J Butterworth, Pharmaceutical Advisor, Verney House, Gatehouse Road, Aylesbury, HP19 8ET, Tel.: 01296 310097

School Nursing
Ms H Dickinson, Acting School Health Nurse Co-ordinator, Sue Nicholls Centre, Manor House, Bierton Road, Aylesbury, HP20 1EG, Tel.: 01296 504234

Specialist Nursing Services
Ms G Tucker, Project Lead, Community Matrons, Manor House, Bierton Road, Aylesbury, HP20 1EG, Tel.: 01296 504460
Ms S Douglas, Specialist Nurse Manager, Back Care, Manor House, Bierton Road, Aylesbury, HP20 1EG, Tel.: 01296 504722
Mrs T Stammers, Nurse Specialist, Breast Care, Chemo Day Unit, Stoke Mandeville Hospital, Aylesbury, HP21 8AL, Tel.: 01296 315127
Ms L Broad, Community Matron, Chronic Disease Management, Manor House, Bierton Road, Aylesbury, HP20 1EG, Tel.: 01296 504581
Clinical Nurse Specialist, Continence, Quainton Ward, Manor House, Bierton Road, Aylesbury, HP20 1EG, Tel.: 01296 504433
Ms C Finegan, Community Matron, COPD, Manor House, Bierton Road, Aylesbury, HP20 1EG, Tel.: 01296 504312/4316/4322
Ms E Haines, Community Matron, COPD, Manor House, Bierton Road, Aylesbury, HP20 1EG, Tel.: 01296 504312/4316/4322
Ms S Foster, Community Matron, Diabetes, Manor House, Bierton Road, Aylesbury, HP20 1EG, Tel.: 01296 504312/4316/4322
Ms M Harding, Clinical Nurse Specialist, Diabetic Care, Diabetes Centre, Stoke Mandeville Hospital, Aylesbury, HP21 8AL, Tel.: 01296 315530/1
Ms J Petzing, Clinical Nurse Specialist, Diabetic Care, Diabetes Centre, Stoke Mandeville Hospital, Aylesbury, HP21 8AL, Tel.: 01296 315530/1
Ms S Barton, Community, Clinical Nurse Specialist, Head Injury, Camborne Centre, Jansel Square, Aylesbury, HP21 7ET, Tel.: 01296 337760 x 204
Ms J Godden, Community Matron, Heart Failure, Manor House, Bierton Road, Aylesbury, HP20 1EG, Tel.: 01296 504312/4316/4322
Ms J McEwan, Community Matron, Heart Failure, Manor House, Bierton Road, Aylesbury, HP20 1EG, Tel.: 01296 504312/4316/4322
Ms A Brinklow, Specialist Practitioner, Multiple Sclerosis, Rayners Hedge, Croft Road, Aylesbury, HP21 7RD, Tel.: 01296 393319
Ms E Parry, Manager, Neuro-Rehabilitation, Rayners Hedge, Croft Road, Aylesbury, HP21 7RD, Tel.: 01296 393319
Ms D Pounds, Modern Matron, Neuro-Rehabilitation, Rayners Hedge, Croft Road, Aylesbury, HP21 7RD, Tel.: 01296 393319
Ms J Wilson, Care Nurse, Older People, Manor House, Bierton Road, Aylesbury, HP20 1EG, Tel.: 01296 504312/4316/4322
Ms K Henderson, Modern Matron, Palliative Care, Florence Nightingale House Hospice, Stoke Mandeville Hospital, Aylesbury, HP21 8AL, Tel.: 01296 394710

South Central Strategic Health Authority

Mr R Radley, Colo-Rectal, Specialist Nurse, Stoma Care, Stoke Mandeville Hospital, Aylesbury, HP21 8AL, Tel.: 01296 315121
Ms M Wood, Colo-Rectal, Specialist Nurse, Stoma Care, Stoke Mandeville Hospital, Aylesbury, HP21 8AL, Tel.: 01296 315121
Ms C Cheney, Community Co-ordinator, Stroke Care, Rayners Hedge, Croft Road, Aylesbury, HP21 7RD, Tel.: 01296 393319
Ms F Brockwell, Specialist Nurse, Tissue Viability, Manor House, Bierton Road, Aylesbury, HP20 1EG, Tel.: 01296 504581

West Hampshire NHS Trust

Trust Headquarters, Tatchbury Mount Hospital
Colmore
SOUTHAMPTON
SO40 2RZ
Tel.: 02380 874000

Learning Disabilities

Andover Team, Andover Health Centre, Andover, SP10 3LD, Tel.: 01264 324582
Mr D Barry, Senior, Winchester, Eastleigh & Andover, Nurse Manager, Highcroft, Romsey Road, Winchester, Hants, SO22 5DH, Tel.: 01962 893716
Eastleigh Team, Mount Hospital, Church Road, Eastleigh, SO50 6DR, Tel.: 023 8061 3866
Ms G Moulster, Lead Nurse, Tatchbury Mount, Calmore, Southampton, Tel.: 023 8087 4024
Mr J Stagg, Clinical Nurse Specialist, Hawthorn Lodge, Moorgreen Hospital, West End, Southampton, S030 3JB, Tel.: 023 8047 5150
Winchester Team, Highcroft, Romsey Road, Winchester, Hants, SO22 5DH, Tel.: 01962 893716

Winchester & Eastleigh Healthcare NHS Trust

Trust Headquarters, Royal Hampshire County Hospital
Romsey Road
WINCHESTER
Hampshire
SO22 5DG
Tel.: 01962 863535
Fax.: 01962 824826

Acute Specialist Nursing Services

Ms S Rushby, Clinical Nurse Specialist, Acute Pain,
Ms L Arkell, Clinical Nurse Specialist, Breast Care,
Ms L Booth, Clinical Nurse Specialist, Breast Care,
Ms L Britton, Clinical Nurse Specialist, Cardiac Rehabilitation,
Ms M Fitzgerald-Baron, Clinical Nurse Specialist, Cardiac Rehabilitation,
Ms S Airey, Clinical Nurse Specialist, Colorectal,
Ms J Lawrence, Clinical Nurse Specialist, Dermatology,
Ms S Grainger-Allen, Clinical Nurse Specialist, Diabetes,
Ms J Head, Clinical Nurse Specialist, Diabetes,
Ms M MacDonald, Clinical Nurse Specialist, Diabetes,
Mr D Bowman, Clinical Nurse Specialist, Endoscopy,
Ms J Kimble, Clinical Nurse Specialist, Gastroenterology,
Ms L McCabe, Clinical Nurse Specialist, IBD,
Ms S Dailly, Clinical Nurse Specialist, Infection Control,
Ms A Long, Clinical Nurse Specialist, Macmillan,
Ms K Rundle, Clinical Nurse Specialist, Macmillan,
Ms M Thomson, Clinical Nurse Specialist, Macmillan,
Ms C Best, Clinical Nurse Specialist, Nutrition,
Ms A Burch, Clinical Nurse Specialist, Rehabilitation, - Neuro,
Ms S Wolstenholme, Clinical Nurse Specialist, Respiratory,
Ms M Rees, Clinical Nurse Specialist, Sexual Health,
Ms E Blacker, Clinical Nurse Specialist, Stoma Care,
Ms E Holding, Clinical Nurse Specialist, Stoma Care,
Ms T Chambers, Clinical Nurse Specialist, Tissue Viability,
Ms L Jackson, Clinical Nurse Specialist, Vascular,

Admin & Senior Management

Ms R Buckley, Senior Nurse,
Mr J Dean, Senior Nurse,
Ms F Dekker, Senior Nurse,
Ms C Fielding, Senior Nurse,
Ms L Flower, Senior Nurse,
Ms H Hooper, Senior Nurse,
Ms K Horsefield, Senior Nurse,
Ms C Lakin, Senior Nurse,
Ms A MacDonald, Senior Nurse,
Ms F McCarthy, Senior Nurse,
Ms A McClarren, Senior Nurse,
Mr S O'Connor, Senior Nurse,
Ms J Pearman, Senior Nurse,
Mrs K Riley, Director of Nursing & Risk Management, Royal Hampshire County Hospital, Tel.: 01962 824733
Ms K Riley, Senior Nurse,
Ms P Shobbrook, Senior Nurse,
Ms S Skinner, Senior Nurse,
Ms C Williams, Senior Nurse,
Ms M Wright, Senior Nurse,
Ms H Young, Senior Nurse,

Child Health Records

Mrs J Iddiols, School Health Records, Child Health Info Dept, Highcroft, Romsey Road, Winchester, SO22 5DH, Tel.: 01962 863511 ext 405
Mr K Watkins, Pre-school Records, Child Health Info Dept, Highcroft, Romsey Road, Winchester, SO22 5DH, Tel.: 01962 863511 ext 220

Child Protection/Safeguarding Children

Ms B Derwent, Senior Nurse, Child Protection, Royal Hampshire County Hospital, Queens Road Offices, Winchester, SO22 5DG, Tel.: 01264 835247

Community Midwifery

Mrs J Barnes, Clinical Midwifery Manager - Eastleigh Community, The Mount Hospital, Tel.: 01962 825151
Ms L Collings, Midwifery, Clinical Nurse Specialist,
Mrs T Cooper, Clinical Midwifery Manager - Antenatal/Postnatal, Royal Hampshire County Hospital, Tel.: 01962 825580
Ms T Kemp, Midwifery, Clinical Nurse Specialist,
Mrs C Morris, Clinical Midwifery Manager - Winchester Community, Royal Hampshire County Hospital, Tel.: 01962 825151
Mrs J Pearman, Head of Midwifery, Florence Portal House, Royal Hampshire County Hospital, Tel.: 01962 824723
Mrs A White, Clinical Midwifery Manager - Andover Community, Andover Birth Centre, Andover War Memorial Hospital, Tel.: 01264 358811 ext 5210

Health Visitors

Ms V Rouse, Liaison Paediatric Health Visitor, Children's Community Nursing Office, Northbrook Ward, Royal Hampshire County Hospital, Tel.: 01962 824283

Liaison Services

Ms D Murray, Liaison Manager, Royal Hampshire County Hospital, Queens Road Offices, Winchester, SO22 5DG, Tel.: 01962 824212

Windsor, Ascot & Maidenhead Primary Care Trust

Trust Headquarters, King Edward V11 Hospital
St Leonards Road
WINDSOR
SL4 3DP
Tel.: 01753 621435

Admin & Senior Management

Mrs N Barber, Director of Nursing Services, King Edward VII Hospital, St Leonards Road, Windsor, SL4 3DP, Tel.: 01753 636802
Mr P Burgess, Chief Executive,

South Central Strategic Health Authority

Child Protection/Safeguarding Children
Miss S Hickson, Nurse for Looked After Children & Young People, Skimped Hill Health Centre, Market Place, Bracknell, RG12 1LH, Tel.: 01344 458136
Mrs J Irving, Nurse for Looked after Children & Young People, Looked After Children, Child Develop Centre, St Marks Hospital, St Marks Road, Maidenhead, SL6 6DU, Tel.: 01753 638687
Clinical Leads (NSF)
Ms P Lacey, Clinical Lead, Development Manager, Cancer, King Edward VII Hospital, Tel.: 01753 606845
Ms S Rogers, Clinical Lead, Care of the Elderly, King Edward VII Hospital, Tel.: 01753 606011
Community Nursing Services
Ms K Boyrangee, King Edward VII Hospital, Tel.: 01753 636500
District Nursing
Evening (District Nurses), (1900-2200), Tel.: 01753 859221/821441
Maidenhead, Community Services, St Mark's Hospital, Maidenhead, SL6 6DU, Tel.: 01753 638431
Ms S Parsons, District Nurses, King Edward VII Hospital, Tel.: 01753 638438
Windsor, King Edward VII Hospital, Tel.: 01753 860441
Health Visitors
Ms S Parsons, Health Visitors, King Edward VII Hospital, Tel.: 01753 638438

Wokingham Primary Care Trust
Trust Headquarters, Wokingham Hospital
Barkham Road
WOKINGHAM
RG41 2RE
Tel.: 0118 949 5000

Admin & Senior Management
Mrs H Mackenzie, Director of Clinical Development, Wokingham Community Hospital, Barkham Road, Wokingham, RG41 2RE, Tel.: 0118 949 5000
Child Health
Child Health Dept,
Ms W Vince, Child Health Service Manager, TVPCA, 7-9 Cremyll Road, Reading, RG1 8NQ, Tel.: 0118 918 3440
Child Health Records
Ms W Vince, Admin,
Child Protection/Safeguarding Children
Ms J Selim, Named Nurse, Child Protection, Wokingham Community Hospital, Tel.: 0118 949 2907
Clinical Leads (NSF)
Dr D Buckle, Clinical Lead, CHD & Diabetes, Tel.: 0118 9949 2915
District Nursing
Ms C Hogan, Community Nursing Manager,
Health Visitors
Ms T Curtis, Health Visitors - Nurse Facilitator, Wokingham Community Hospital, Tel.: 0118 949 5178
Learning Disabilities
Ms M Codling, Primary Care Liaison Nurse - Learning Disabilities, Wokingham Community Hospital, Tel.: 0118 949 2932
Liaison Services
Discharge Facilitators, Royal Berks & Battle Hospitals NHS Trust, Battle Hospital, Oxford Road, Reading, RG31 1AG, Tel.: 0118 987 5111
School Nursing
Ms T Holmes, School Nurses - Nurse Facilitator, Tel.: 0118 949 5070
Smoking Cessation
Mr R Toan, Manager, Tel.: 0118 949 3193
Specialist Nursing Services
Ms R Crowder, Professional Development Nurse, 57-59 Bath Road, Reading, RG30 2BA, Tel.: 0118 982 2895
Ms M Woods, Professional Development Nurse, 57-59 Bath Road, Reading, RG30 2BA, Tel.: 0118 982 2895

Ms P Pryn, Services Manager, Continence, Wokingham Community Hospital, Tel.: 0118 949 5148
Ms J Bliss, Head, Intermediate Care, Wokingham Community Hospital, Tel.: 0118 949 5087
Nurses, Macmillan, BA Macmillan House, Wokingham Hospital, Tel.: 0118 978 7843

Wycombe Primary Care Trust
Trust Headquarters, Rapid House
40 Oxford Road
HIGH WYCOMBE
HP11 2EE
Tel.: 01494 552200
Fax.: 01494 522046

Admin & Senior Management
Mr P Bennett, Chief Executive,
Ms J Dean, Director of Service Transformation, Tel.: 01494 552231
Child Health
Community Paediatric Dept, Wycombe Hospital, Tel.: 01494 426197
Child Health Records
As South Bucks NHS Trust,
Child Protection/Safeguarding Children
Ms J Davies, Tel.: 01494 734808
Clinical Leads (NSF)
Mr J Evans, Clinical Lead, Cancer,
Dr V Wadd, Clinical Lead, Diabetic Care,
Community Matrons
Ms J Petty,
Community Nursing Services
Ms O Vance, Director of Nursing, and Community Services, Tel.: 01494 734806
District Nursing
Ms A Barber, Tel.: 01494 537633
Ms F Croot, Tel.: 01494 537633
Ms M Paterson, Tel.: 01494 537633
Ms L Peer, Tel.: 01494 537633
Health Visitors
Ms H Dean, Tel.: 01494 552228
Ms D Smith, Tel.: 01494 552228
HIV/AIDS
Mr A Tippett, GUM, Wycombe General Hospital, Tel.: 01494 425430
Liaison Services
Ms P Collins, Neonatal, Sister, Wycombe General Hospital, Tel.: 01494 425126
Ms S Terry, Paediatric Liaison, Tel.: 01494 734809
School Nursing
Ms G Jeavons, Tel.: 01494 512687
Specialist Nursing Services
Mrs D Kelly, Children, Ward 11 Wycombe General Hospital, Tel.: 01494 425008
Ms S Hill, Continence, Marlow Health Clinic, Glade Road, Marlow, SL7 1DJ, Tel.: 01628 487439
Ms N Thompson, Continence, Marlow Health Clinic, Glade Road, Marlow, SL7 1DJ, Tel.: 01628 487439
Ms T Gill, Diabetic Care, Wycombe General Hospital, Tel.: 01494 425308

South East Coast Strategic Health Authority

with major towns and Primary Care Trust boundaries
Pop: 4,187,941

East of England

London

South Central

Dartford

Gillingham

Woking

Leatherhead

Sevenoaks

Aylesford

Sittingbourne

Whitstable

Farnham

Crawley

Redhill

Ashford

Dover

Horsham

Haywards Heath

Folkestone

Chichester

Lewes

Bexhill

Brighton

St. Leonard's

Worthing

Eastbourne

South East Coast Strategic Health Authority

South East Coast Strategic Health Authority

Adur Arun & Worthing Teaching Primary Care Trust

Trust Headquarters, 1 The Causeway
GORING BY SEA
West Sussex
BN12 6BT
Tel.: 01903 708400

Admin & Senior Management
Ms J Boyfield, Director, Adults & Older People's Services,
Mr B Deans, Deputy Chief Executive,
Mr S Phoenix, Chief Executive,
Ms A Wells, Acting Director, Children & Family Services,
Child Health
Ms A Donnelly, Specialist Health Visitor Childhood Accident Prevention, Unit L, Downlands Business Park, Lyons Way, Worthing, West Sussex, BN14 9LA, Tel.: 01903 846545/846547
Ms L Mulroney, Community Children's Nursing, Unit L, Downlands Business Park, Lyons Way, Worthing, West Sussex, BN14 9LA, Tel.: 01903 846548
Child Health Records
West Sussex Child Health Records, Child Health Bureau, PO Box 115, Chichester, PO19 4YT, Tel.: 01243 815400
Child Protection/Safeguarding Children
Ms S Cook, Child Protection, Children's Centre, Worthing Hospital, Park Road, Worthing, West Sussex, BN11 2DH, Tel.: 01903 286739
Clinical Leads (NSF)
Ms R Cottington, Clinical Lead, Children, Young People & Maternity Services,
Mr G Burgess, Clinical Lead, Cancer,
Mr B Deans, Clinical Lead, CHD,
Ms J Boyfield, Clinical Lead, Older People,
District Nursing
Ms L Card, Community Health Lead - Adur (including Shoreham & Lancing), Shoreham Health Centre, Pond Road, Shoreham, West Sussex, BN43 5US, Tel.: 01273 466040
Ms T Perris, Community Health Lead - Worthing, Unit L, Downlands Business Park, Lyons Way, Worthing, West Sussex, BN14 9LA, Tel.: 01903 846540
Ms T Streeter, Community Health Lead - Arun, Littlehampton Health Centre, Fitzalan Road, Littlehampton, West Sussex, BN17 5HG, Tel.: 01903 843600
Health Visitors
Ms L Gardner, Clinical Lead, Adur, Shoreham Health Centre, Pond Road, Shoreham, BN43 5US, Tel.: 01273 466074
Ms N Unwin, Clinical Lead, Worthing, Durrington Health Centre, Durrington Lane, Worthing, BN13 2RX, Tel.: 01903 843802
Ms S Van Der Vliet, Clinical Lead, Arun, Durrington Health Centre, Durrington Lane, Worthing, BN13 2RX, Tel.: 01903 843802
Ms G Walker, Children's Health Lead, The Causeway, Goring by Sea, West Sussex, BN12 6BT, Tel.: 01903 708504
HIV/AIDS
Ms M Wotherspoon, Unit L, Downlands Business Park, Lyons Way, Worthing, West Sussex, BN14 9LA, Tel.: 01903 846546
Liaison Services
Ms S Hutchby, Health Visiting Liaison, Worthing Hospital, Park Road, Worthing, West Sussex, BN11 2DH, Tel.: 01903 286769
Ms F Menzies, District Nursing Liaison, Worthing & Southlands Hospital, Homefield Road, Worthing, West Sussex, BN11 2DH, Tel.: 01903 205111 bleep 281
Ms K Walker, Health Visiting Liaison, Worthing Hospital, Park Road, Worthing, West Sussex, BN11 2DH, Tel.: 01903 286789

Other Services
Mrs P Lloyd, Matron, Salvington Lodge, Salvington Hill, Swandean, Worthing, BN13 3BW, Tel.: 01903 266399
Mrs L Squires-Early, Senior Nurse Manager, Zachery Merton Hospital, Glenville Road, Rustington, West Sussex, BN17 2EA, Tel.: 01903 858136
School Nursing
Ms M Walker, Community Health Lead, School Nursing service, Children's Centre, Worthing Hospital, Park Avenue, Worthing, BN11 2DH, Tel.: 01903 286742
Specialist Nursing Services
Ms J Mules, Continence, Unit L, Downlands Business Park, Lyons Way, Worthing, West Sussex, BN14 9LA, Tel.: 01903 846541
Ms B Holley, Card Team, Physical Disability, Northdown, Swandean, Arundel Road, Worthing, BN13 3EP, Tel.: 01903 843218
The Homeless/Travellers & Asylum Seekers
Health Visitor for Homeless, Unit L, Downlands Business Park, Lyons Way, Worthing, West Sussex, BN14 9LA, Tel.: 01903 846544

Ashford & St Peter's Hospital NHS Trust

Trust Headquarters, St Peter's Hospital
Guildford Road
CHERTSEY
KT16 0PZ
Tel.: 01932 872000

Community Midwifery
Community Midwifery Office, St Peter's Hospital, Tel.: 01932 722413
Labour Ward, Tel.: ext 2361
Mrs M Morris, General Manager Women's & Childrens Services, Head of Midwifery, The Croft, St Peter's Hospital, Tel.: 01932 723310
Ms T Spink, Community Midwifery Manager, St Peter's Hospital, Tel.: 01932 722413

Ashford Primary Care Trust

Trust Headquarters, Templar House
Tannery Lane
ASHFORD
Kent
TN23 1PL
Tel.: 01233 618330
Fax.: 01233 618378

Admin & Senior Management
Mr M Riley, Director of Service & Strategy, Templar House, Tannery Lane, Ashford, Kent, TN23 1PL, Tel.: 01233 618330
Child Health
East Kent Coastal PCT,
Child Protection/Safeguarding Children
Ms J Ward, East Kent Coastal PCT, Clinical Nurse Specialist,
Mrs W Everett, Named Nurse, Child Protection, Ashford Community Offices. Kings Avenue, Ashford, Kent, Tel.: 01233 204020
District Nursing
Mrs L Cameron, District Nursing & Intermediate Care, Ashford PCT, Tannery Lane, Ashford, Kent, Tel.: 01233 618353
Health Visitors
Mrs I Taylor, Community Nurse Manager (Health Visitors), Ashford Community Office, Kings Avenue, Ashford, TN23 1NT, Tel.: 01233 204009
Learning Disabilities
Ms V Bridges, Team Manager, Community LD Integrated with Social Services (Adults), KCC, Social Services, 70 Stour Street, Canterbury, Kent, CT1 2NW, Tel.: 01227 451741
Mr D Crothers, Head of Learning Disability Service, Eversley House, 19 Horn Street, Seabrook, Hythe, CT21 5SB, Tel.: 01303 717000
Mrs K Davies, Residential Services Manager/Clinical Nurse Specialist (East), Lanthorne Lodge, Lanthorne Road, Broadstairs, Kent, CT10 3PB, Tel.: 01843 602725

South East Coast Strategic Health Authority

Ms G Gregory, Team Manager, Community LD Integrated with Social Services (Adults), KCC, Social Services, Crispe House, Minnis Road, Birchington, Kent, CT7 9SF, Tel.: 01843 844648

Ms J Guntrip, Team Manager, Community LD Integrated with Social Services (Adults), KCC, Social Services, Civic Centre, Tannery Lane, Ashford, Kent, TN23 1PL, Tel.: 01223 205764/205747

Ms M Setterfield, Team Manager, Community LD Integrated with Social Services (Adults), Cairn Ryan, 101-103 London Road, Kearsney, Dover, Kent, CT16 3AA, Tel.: 01304 828555

Ms P Stevens, Residential Services Manager/Clinical Nurse Specialist (West), Eversley House, 19 Horn Street, Seabrook, Hythe, CT21 5SB, Tel.: 01303 717000

Ms T Stiff, Team Manager, Community LD Integrated with Social Services (Adults), Eversley House, 19 Horn Street, Seabrook, Hythe, CT21 5SB, Tel.: 01303 717000

Liaison Services
Ms S Vollans, William Harvey Hospital, Tel.: 01233 616157

Specialist Nursing Services
Hosted by Canterbury & Coastal PCT,

The Homeless/Travellers & Asylum Seekers
Ms P Cobb, Shepway, The Cottage, Asheton, Folkestone, CT19 5HL, Tel.: 01303 222363

Mrs I Taylor, Ashford, Ashford Community Office, Kings Avenue, Ashford, TN23 1NT, Tel.: 01233 204009

Bexhill & Rother Primary Care Trust

Trust Headquarters, Bexhill Hospital
Holliers Hill
BEXHILL-ON-SEA
East Sussex, TN40 2DZ
Tel.: 01424 735600

Admin & Senior Management
Ms D Parker, Director of Patient Services, Tel.: 01424 735600
Ms T Wilkinson, Chief Executive, Tel.: 01424 735600

Child Health Records
Child Health Services, Kipling Unit, Conquest Hospital, The Ridge, St Leonards-on-Sea, TN37 7RD, Tel.: 01424 755255

Child Protection/Safeguarding Children
Ms D Henderson, Looked After Children, Nurse Specialist, Oceon House, Floor 2, 87-89 London Road, St Leonards-on-Sea, TN37 6DH, Tel.: 01424 723002

Mrs D Barnes, Lead Nurse, Child Protection, Kipling Unit, Conquest Hospital, The Ridge, Hastings, TN37 7RD, Tel.: 01424 755470 x 8747/8477

Mrs K Miller, Lead Nurse, Child Protection, Kipling Unit, Conquest Hospital, The Ridge, Hastings, TN37 7RD, Tel.: 01424 755470 x 8747/8477

Clinical Leads (NSF)
Dr M Thomas, Clinical Lead, Cancer,
Dr J Rivett, Clinical Lead, CHD,
Mrs M Jones, Clinical Lead, Older People,

Community Nursing Services
Ms D Cooke, Head of Adult Services, Bexhill Health Centre, Holliers Hill, Bexhill on Sea, East Sussex, TN40 2DZ, Tel.: 01424 735600

District Nursing
Ms J Unicombe, Lead Nurse, District Nurses, Bexhill Health Centre, Holliers Hill, Bexhill on Sea, East Sussex, TN40 2DZ, Tel.: 01424 735612

Health Visitors
Ms J Kelham, Paediatric Liaison Health Visitor, Kipling Unit, Conquest Hospital, Tel.: 01424 755255
Ms D Pluckrose, Paediatric Liaison Health Visitor, Kipling Unit, Conquest Hospital, Tel.: 01424 755255
Ms A Singer, Head of Children's Services,

Other Services
Family Support Health Team, Eversfield Hospital, West Hill Road, St Leonards-on-Sea, TN38 0NG, Tel.: 01424 710105

Ms C Gillam, FRNC/Continuing Care Team, Based at Hastings & St Leonards PCT, Tel.: 01424 458227

School Nursing
Ms F Edmunds, Lead School Nurses & Lead on Public Health & Modernisation, Tel.: 01424 735600

Specialist Nursing Services
Ms S Whipps, Advanced Primary Practice, Nurse Consultant, Tel.: 01424 735312

Ms P Dickson, Advisor, Continence, Bexhill Hospital, Tel.: 01424 755255 ext 5332

Ms N Young, Nurse Consultant, Intermediate Care, Tel.: 01424 735312

Ms K Bontoft, Community Nurse, Macmillan, Oncology Dept, Conquest Hospital, The Ridge, St Leonards-on-Sea, TN37 7RD,

Ms J French, Community Nurse, Macmillan, Oncology Dept, Conquest Hospital, The Ridge, St Leonards-on-Sea, TN37 7RD,

Ms C Hood, Community Nurse, Macmillan, Oncology Dept, Conquest Hospital, The Ridge, St Leonards-on-Sea, TN37 7RD,

Brighton & Hove City Teaching Primary Care Trust

Trust Headquarters, 6th Floor, Vantage Point
New England Road
BRIGHTON
BN1 4GW
Tel.: 01273 295490

Admin & Senior Management
Mr T Blair-Stevens, Healthy City Manager/Public Health,
Ms M Eveleigh, Lead Nurse Primary Care,
Ms J Mellish, Assistant Director Service Improvement Directorate, Commissioner Older People Services,
Dr M Warburton, Director of Service Improvement,

Child Protection/Safeguarding Children
Ms P Lambert, Nurse Consultant, Child Protection, Southdowns Health NHS Trust, Clermont Child Protection, Unit 251, Preston Rd, Brighton, BN1 6SE, Tel.: 01273 295993

Clinical Leads (NSF)
Mr T Blair-Stevens, Clinical Lead, CHd & Diabetes,
Dr M Warburton, Clinical Lead, Cancer,
Ms J Mellish, Clinical Lead, Older People,

Community Midwifery
Ms C Drummond, Royal Sussex County Hospital, Eastern Road, Brighton, East Sussex, BN2 5BE, Tel.: 01273 696 955 x4373

Community Nursing Services
Ms J Heath, Lead Nurse Manager, Community Care Directorate, Brighton General Hospital, Elm Grove, Brighton, BN2 3EW, Tel.: 01273 696 011

District Nursing
Ms J Heath, Lead Nurse Manager (District Nurses), Community Care Directorate, Brighton General Hospital, Elm Grove, Brighton, BN2 3EW, Tel.: 01273 696 011

Equipment Loan Services
Ms J Gander, Acting Manager, The ICES Store, Belgrave Centre, Clarendon Place, Portslade, BN41 1DJ, Tel.: 01273 295 707

Family Planning Services
Ms S Ward, Morley Street Health Centre, Morley Street, Brighton, BN2 9RE, Tel.: 01273 696 011 x 3839

Health Visitors
Dr D Blincow, Children & Families Directorate (Health Visitors), Clinical Directorate, Brighton General Hospital, Elm Grove, Brighton, BN2 3EW, Tel.: 01273 696 011
Ms E Smith, Health Visitors Contact, Brighton General Hospital, Elm Grove, Brighton, BN2 3EW, Tel.: 01273 696 011

Learning Disabilities
Ms J Clark, Department of Specialist Services, Southdowns NHS Trust, Brighton General Hospital, Elm Grove, Brighton, BN2 3EW, Tel.: 01273 696 011

South East Coast Strategic Health Authority

Pharmacy
Ms J Moffatt, Head of Medicines Management, 6th Floor, Vantage Point, New England Road, Brighton, East Sussex, BN1 4GW,
School Nursing
Ms T Beer, Practice Manager for School Nursing, School Clinic, Morley Street, Brighton, BN2 9DH, Tel.: 01273 267 300
Ms H Hough, Practice Manager for School Nursing, School Clinic, Morley Street, Brighton, BN2 9DH, Tel.: 01273 267 300
Ms D O'Brien, Based at Hove, Conway Court, Clarendon Road, Hove, BN3 3WS,

Brighton and Sussex University Hospitals NHS Trust

Trust Headquarters, The Royal Sussex County Hospital
Eastern Road
BRIGHTON, BN2 5BE
Tel.: 01273 696955

Acute Specialist Nursing Services
Ms M Caufield, Breast Care, Tel.: 01273 6996955 ext 4111
Ms M Daultrey, Breast Care, Tel.: 01444 441881 ext 4930
Ms A Gibbins, Cardiac, Tel.: 01273 696955 ext 7249
Ms R-M Hurst, Cardiac, Tel.: 01444 441881 ext 4889
Ms C Kenny, Cardiac, Tel.: 01273 696955 ext 7249
Ms L Bordoli, Diabetic Care, Tel.: 01273 696933 ext 4205
Ms J Brown, Diabetic Care, Tel.: 01444 441881 ext 4436
Ms K Campbell, Diabetic Care, Tel.: 01273 696933 ext 4205
Ms S Daley, Diabetic Care, Tel.: 01273 696933 ext 4205
Ms B Duff, Diabetic Care, Tel.: 01444 441881 ext 4442
Ms S Jones, Diabetic Care, Tel.: 01273 696933 ext 4205
Ms C Ord, Diabetic Care, Tel.: 01273 696933 ext 4205
Ms C Spence, Diabetic Care, Tel.: 01273 328145 ext 2110
Mr J Veysey, Diabetic Care, Tel.: 01273 696933 ext 4205
Ms M Yusuf, Diabetic Care, Tel.: 01273 696933 ext 4205
Ms L Dyer, Digestive Diseases, Tel.: 01273 696955 ext 7877
Ms J Grant, Digestive Diseases, Tel.: 01273 696955 ext 7877
Ms L MacKay, Digestive Diseases, Tel.: 01273 696955 ext 4349
Ms S Parker, Digestive Diseases, Tel.: 01273 696933 ext 4349
Mr W Louden, Adult Services, Epilepsy, Tel.: 01273 696955 ext 7830
Ms J Whitty, Fertility, Tel.: 01273 696955 ext 7622
Ms N Worcester, Haematology, Tel.: 01273 696955 ext 7482
Ms J Powell, Head Injury, Tel.: 01444 441881 ext 4441
Ms S Loveridge, Infection Control, Tel.: 01273 696955 ext 4595
Ms S Loveridge, Infection Control, Tel.: 01273 696955 ext 4595
Mr M Still, Infection Control, Tel.: 01273 696955 ext 4595
Ms D Collier, IV Therapy, Tel.: 01273 696955 ext 4922
Ms G O'Sullivan, IV Therapy, Tel.: 01273 696955 ext 4787
Ms L Kidd, Multiple Sclerosis, Tel.: 01444 441881 ext 4540
Mrs A Adsett, Palliative Care, Tel.: 01273 664694 ext 4693
Ms S Evans, Palliative Care, - Urological, 012273 664455 ext 7800
Brother Francis, Palliative Care, Tel.: 01273 328145 ext 2110
Ms N Huxter, Palliative Care, Tel.: 01273 328145 ext 2182
Ms C Lansdell, Palliative Care, Tel.: 01444 441881 ext 4255
Ms L Pritchard, Palliative Care, - Gynaecology, Tel.: 012273 664455
Mr C Twomey, Palliative Care, Tel.: 01273 664693 ext 4693
Ms A Scutt, Parkinson's Disease, Tel.: 01444 441881 ext 4736
Ms J Bullen, Respiratory, Tel.: 01273 665191 ext 5191
Mr B Lowden, Respiratory, Tel.: 01273 665190 ext 5190
Ms A Pavitt, Respiratory, Tel.: 01444 441881 ext 4944
Mr R Pryor, Resuscitation Training, Tel.: 01273 696955 ext 4579
Ms V Watts, Resuscitation Training, Tel.: 01444 441881 ext 4774
Ms J O'Donovan, Rheumatology, Tel.: 01273 673466 ext 4354
Ms T Walker, Stoma Care, Tel.: 01444 441881 ext 4318
Ms C Martin, Clinical Nurse Specialist, Wound Care, Tel.: 01273 696955 ext 4175
Ms L Scarborough, Nurse Specialist, Wound Care, Tel.: 01273 696955 ext 4175

Child Health
Ms M Bunker, Cystic Fibrosis (Children) Services, Tel.: 01273 328145 ext 2213
Mr A Monaghan, Paediatric Critical Care Liaison Team, Tel.: 01273 328145 ext 2167
Ms C Warde, Cystic Fibrosis (Children) Services, Tel.: 01273 328145 ext 2213
Community Midwifery
Ms J Cleary, Clinical Midwifery Manager for Princess Royal Hospital & surrounding community, Princess Royal Hospital, Lewes Road, Haywards Heath, West Sussex, RH16 4EX, 01444 441881 ext 6073
Community Office Princess Royal Hospital, Princess Royal Hospital, Lewes Road, Haywards Heath, West Sussex, RH16 4EX, Tel.: 01444 441881 ext 4414/18
Community Office Royal Sussex County Hospital, Royal Sussex County Hospital, Eastern Road, Brighton, East Sussex, BN2 5BE, Tel.: 01273 664794
Ms C Drummond, Head of Midwifery, Royal Sussex County Hospital, Eastern Road, Brighton, BN2 5BE, Tel.: 01273 696955 ext 4375/78
Emergencies - Out of hours, Princess Royal Hospital Central Delivery Suite, Princess Royal Hospital, Lewes Road, Haywards Heath, West Sussex, RH16 4EX, Tel.: 01444 441881 ext 4484/85
Emergencies, Maternity Bleep Royal Sussex, Royal Sussex County Hospital, Eastern Road, Brighton, East Sussex, BN2 5BE, Tel.: 01273 696955
Ms H Rogerson, Clinical Midwifery Manager for Royal Sussex County Hospital & surrounding community, Royal Sussex County Hospital, Eastern Road, Brighton, East Sussex, BN2 5BE, Tel.: 01273 696955 ext 4385

Canterbury & Coastal Primary Care Trust

Trust Headquarters, Chestfield Medical Centre
Reeves Way, Chestfield
WHITSTABLE
CT5 3QU
Tel.: 01227 794777

Admin & Senior Management
Ms P Barber, Director of Clinical Services, Unit 118, John Wilson Business Park, Reeves Way, Chestfield, Whitstable, Kent, CT5 3QY, Tel.: 01227 795085
Mr D Grayson, Chief Executive, Chestfield Medical Centre, Reeves Way, Chestfield, Whitstable, CT5 3QU,
Child Protection/Safeguarding Children
Ms S Birbeck, Named Nurse, Child Protection, Faversham Health Centre, Bank Street, Faversham, Kent, Tel.: 01795 562080
Ms J Ward, Child Protection, Broadstairs Health Centre, Tel.: 01843 255320
Clinical Leads (NSF)
Dr P Garrod, Clinical Lead, Cancer,
Community Nursing Services
Mrs M Falconer, Community Nurse Manager, Faversham Health Centre, Tel.: 01795 562042
District Nursing
Miss H Gardiner, Team Manager, Whitstable Health Centre, Tel.: 01227 594444
Mrs C Mackenzie, Team Manager, Canterbury Health Centre, Tel.: 01227 597035
Equipment Loan Services
Ms J Clifford, Head of OT, EKPT, Littlebourne Road, Canterbury, Kent,
Liaison Services
Ms P Brown, Community Liaison Nurse, Kent & Canterbury Hospital, Tel.: 01227 766877 ext 73074
Ms J Castle, Community Liaison Nurse, Kent & Canterbury Hospital, Tel.: 01227 766877 ext 73074

South East Coast Strategic Health Authority

Ms J Holden, Community Liaison Nurse, Kent & Canterbury Hospital, Tel.: 01227 766877 ext 73074

Mrs G Wilmot, Liaison Sister, Kent & Canterbury Hospital, Tel.: 01227 766877 ext 73074

Ms J Wright, Community Liaison Nurse, Kent & Canterbury Hospital, Tel.: 01227 766877 ext 73074

School Nursing

Ms L Maidment, Manager for School Nurses, Protea House, Marine Parade, Dover, Tel.: 01304 227227

Specialist Nursing Services

Mrs S Barker, Specialist Nursing Services Manager, Queen Victoria Memorial Hospital, King Edward Avenue, Herne Bay, Kent, CT6 6EB, Tel.: 01227 594721

Ms J Thackwray, Nurse Specialist, Cardiac, Broadstairs Health Centre, The Broadway, Broadstairs, Kent, CT10 2AJ, Tel.: 01843 255318

Ms J Peto, Nurse Specialist, Continence, Whitstable & Tankerton Hospital, Northwood Road, Whitstable, Kent, CT5 2HN, Tel.: 01227 594612

Ms J Spanton, Team Leader, Nurse Specialist, Diabetic Care, Paula Carr Centre, William Harvey Hospital, Kennington Road, Willsborough, Ashford, Kent, TN24 0LZ, Tel.: 01233 633331

Ms T Truscoth, Nurse Specialist, Epilepsy, Whitstable & Tankerton Hospital, Northwood Road, Whitstable, Kent, CT5 2HN, Tel.: 01227 594628

Mrs J Rawlings, Team Leader, Specialist Nurse, Older People, Protea House, New Bridge, Marine Parade, Dover, CT17 9HQ, Tel.: 01304 222225

Ms M Jackson, Team Co-ordinator, Respiratory, Whitstable & Tankerton Hospital, Northwood Road, Whitstable, Kent, CT5 2HN, Tel.: 01227 594640

The Homeless/Travellers & Asylum Seekers

Ms P Church, Homeless, Nurse Specialist, Canterbury Open Day Centre, Tel.: 01227 464904

Crawley Primary Care Trust

Trust Headquarters, 5th Floor
Overline House, Station Way
CRAWLEY, RH10 1JA
Tel.: 01293 572100

Admin & Senior Management

Mrs S Baker, Director of Nursing, Overline House, Station Way, Crawley, RH10 1JA, Tel.: 01293 572156

Mrs B Merrington, Head of Community Services, Overline House, Station Way, Crawley, RH10 1JA, Tel.: 01293 572158

Child Health

Ms S Baker, Director of Operations, Trust Headquarters, Tel.: 01293 572156

Child Health Records

Child Health Bureau, Western Sussex PCT, Graylingwell, Chichester, Tel.: 01243 815226

Child Protection/Safeguarding Children

Child Protection Adviser, Crawley Clinic, Exchange Road, Crawley, Tel.: 01293 582130

Named Nurse, Tel.: 01293 582136

Ms L Smith, Consultant Nurse, Safeguarding Children, Tel.: 01293 582136

Clinical Leads (NSF)

Dr S Xerri, Clinical Lead, Cancer, Tel.: 01293 527114

Ms S Dando, Clinical Lead, Care of the Elderly, Tel.: 01737 768511

Dr Truter, Clinical Lead, CHD, Tel.: 01293 527114

Ms S Baker, Clinical Lead, Children,

Ms S White, Clinical Lead, Diabetic Care, Tel.: 01293 572100

Community Matrons

Ms J Cooper, Community Matron, Primary Care, Tel.: 01293 572100

Ms A Holman, Community Matron, Primary Care, Tel.: 01293 572100

Ms S White, Community Matron, Primary Care, Tel.: 01293 572100

Community Midwifery

Midwifery, East Surrey Hospital, Redhill,

Community Nursing Services

Ms S Baker, Director of Nursing, Tel.: 01293 572156

Mrs B Merrington, Head of Community Services, Overline House, Station Way, Crawley, RH10 1JA, Tel.: 01293 572158

Ms L Phair, Nurse Consultant for Older People, Overline House, Station Way, Crawley, RH10 1JA, Tel.: 01293 572100

District Nursing

Service Manager (Adults), Overline House, Station Way, Crawley, RH10 1JA, Tel.: 01293 582100

Equipment Loan Services

Ms P Keynton-Hook, Overline House, Station Way, Crawley, RH10 1JA, Tel.: 01293 572100

Family Planning Services

Family Planning Services, Crawley Clinic, Exchange Road, Crawley, Tel.: 01293 582130

Health Visitors

Mr C Hunt, Health Visitor Liaison - Child & Family, Crawley Hospital, Tel.: 01293 600300

Ms C Pickering, Service Manager (Children)/Prof. Lead Health Visitors, Overline House, Station Way, Crawley, Tel.: 01293 572100

Learning Disabilities

Mr S Williams, Director of Development, Overline House, Station Way, Crawley, Tel.: 01293 572100

Liaison Services

Ms F Bridgland, Liaison - Adult & Elderly, Crawley Hospital, Westgreen Drive, Crawley, Tel.: 01293 600300

Discharge Liaison Facilitator, East Surrey Hospital, Tel.: 01737 768511/01293 597607

Ms C Hunt, Liaison - Paediatric Health Vistor, Crawley Hospital, Westgreen Drive, Crawley, Tel.: 01293 600300

Other Services

Mr G Anstee, Service Manager Unscheduled Care, Tel.: 01293 597600

Ms S Aston, Team Leader, Unscheduled Care,

Ms N Leighton, Team Leader, Intermediate Care Beds, Crawley Hospital, West Green Drive, Crawley, Tel.: 01293 600300

Pharmacy

Mr M Salter, Overline House, Station Way, Crawley, RH10 1JA, Tel.: 01293 572100

School Nursing

Ms C Pickering, Professional Leader School Nurses, Overline House, Station Way, Crawley, Tel.: 01293 572100

School Nurses, The Birch Tree, Old Barn Road, Crawley, RH11 7XG, Tel.: 01293 846190

Specialist Nursing Services

Ms A Bradley-Ingle, Heart Disease Nurse Adviser, Coronary Care, Trust Headquarters, Tel.: 01293 572100

Ms A Price, Dermatology, Ravendene, Brighton Road, Crawley, Tel.: 01293 597600

Ms Sarosi, Infection Control, Overline House, Station Way, Crawley, RH10 1JA, Tel.: 01293 572158

Nurse, Respiratory, Crawley Hospital, West Green Drive, Crawley, Tel.: 01293 600300

Ms D Walters, Nurse, TB, Crawley Hospital, Tel.: 01293 600300

Ms S Fentiman, Nurse, Tissue Viability, Tel.: 01293 572100

Ms G Walford, Nurse, Tissue Viability, Tel.: 01293 572100

The Homeless/Travellers & Asylum Seekers

Ms A Cooksley, Homeless Persons Health Visitor, Crawley Clinic, Exchange Road, Crawley, Tel.: 01293 525687

Walk In Centres

Planned Treatment Centre, Ravendene Primary Care Centre, Brighton Road, Crawley, Tel.: 01293 597600

Walk in Centre, Crawley Hospital, Tel.: 01293 600300

South East Coast Strategic Health Authority

Dartford & Gravesham NHS Trust
Trust Headquarters, Darent Valley Hospital
Darenth Wood Road
DARTFORD, Kent, DA2 8DA
Tel.: 01322 428100

Acute Specialist Nursing Services
Ms P Sequeira, Acute Pain,
Ms H Smith, Anti-Coagulation,
Ms K Miles, Macmillan, Breast Care,
Ms S Deacon, Cardiac Rehabilitation,
Ms M Lawrence, Cardiac Rehabilitation,
Ms R Minton, Cardiology,
Mr C Johnson, Colorectal,
Mr L Norton, Diabetic Care,
Ms H Wanstall, Chief, Dietitian,
Ms V Langridge, G.U.M,
Ms C Mentor-Morris, G.U.M,
Ms C Chambers/Ms S Francis, Gynaecology, - Urological,
Ms I Smith, Infection Control,
Ms M Townsend, Lung Cancer,
Ms J Walsh, Older People,
Ms L Grennall, Palliative Care,
Ms C Hannay, Respiratory,
Ms C Lewis, Stomatherapy, Stoma Care,
Ms D Everitt, Tissue Viability,
Ms A Elliott, Urology,

Admin & Senior Management
Ms S Flanagan, Lead Cancer Nurse, Tel.: 01322 428332
Ms J Kay, Director of Nursing, Darent Valley Hosp 01322 428653

Child Health
Mr S Hanson, Paediatric Home Care,
Ms J Simister, Paediatric Home Care Team, Tel.: 01322 428550
Mr C Ticehurst, Paediatric Home Care,

Child Protection/Safeguarding Children
Ms L Brooks, Paediatrics, Senior Nurse, Child Protection, Willow Ward, Darent Valley Hospital, Tel.: 01322 428889

Community Midwifery
Community Liaison Office, Opening Hours 0900-1530 hrs excludng bank hols & weekends,
Miss D Johnston, General Manager, Head of Midwifery, Tel.: 01322 428769
Out of hours - Delivery Suite, Tel.: 01322 428280
Out of hours - Switchboard, Tel.: 01322 428100
Ms V Tate, 'Out-Patient' Midwifery Manager, 01322 428753 bleep 161

Family Planning Services
Ms V Archer, Tel.: 01322 428280

HIV/AIDS
Mr S Kumar, Health Advisor - GUM,

Liaison Services
Mrs S Hornshaw, PALS Officer, Darent Valley Hospital, Tel.: 01332 428166

Other Services
Sr Y Taylor, Orthopaedic Bridging Team, Tel.: 01322 428717
Mr D Tunstill, Occupational Health Services, Tel.: 01322 428451
Ms B Webb, Palliative Care (Ellenor Foundation), Tel.: 01322 428293
Ms G Williams, Diabetes Team, Tel.: 01322 428286

Smoking Cessation
Ms C Rawkins, Tel.: 01322 428100 ext 4817

Dartford, Gravesham & Swanley Primary Care Trust
Trust Headquarters, Top Floor, Livingstone Hospital
East Hill, DARTFORD
Kent, DA1 1SA
Tel.: 01322 622369

Admin & Senior Management
Ms A David, Director of Nursing, Livingstone Hospital, East Hill, Dartford, Kent, DA1 1SA, Tel.: 01322 622398
Ms S Jones, Director of Services, Livingstone Hospital, East Hill, Dartford, Kent, DA1 1SA, Tel.: 01322 622398
Ms S Stanwick, Chief Executive,

Child Health
Ms J Chant, Business Manager, Livingstone Hospital, East Hill, Dartford, DA1 1SA, Tel.: 01322 622222
Mr G Perrott, General Manager, Livingstone Hospital, Tel.: 01322 622362
Ms J Shepherd, Child & Family Health Nurse Lead, Livingstone Hospital, East Hill, Dartford, DA1 1SA, Tel.: 01322 622321

Child Health Records
Mrs S Jones, Director of Services, Livingstone Hospital, Tel.: 01322 622398
Ms T West, CHS, Livingstone Hospital, Tel.: 01322 622340

Child Protection/Safeguarding Children
Child & Family Health Nurse Lead, Livingstone Hospital, East Hill, Dartford, DA1 1SA, Tel.: 01322 622321
Ms W Thoroughgood, Named Nurse, Child Protection, Livingstone Hospital, East Hill, Dartford, DA1 1SA, Tel.: 01322 622379

District Nursing
Mrs D Corderoy, Head of Public Health Nursing, Livingstone Hospital, East Hill, Dartford, DA1 1SA, Tel.: 01322 622398
General Manager, Dartford, Swanley Areas, Livingstone Hospital, East Hill, Dartford, DA1 1SA, Tel.: 01322 622324
Ms D Kelly, General Manager, Gravesend Area, Rochester Road Clinic, 107 Rochester Road, Gravesend, DA12 2HU, Tel.: 01474 534795
Mrs J Owen, Head of Adult Health Nursing (District Nurses), Livingstone Hospital, East Hill, Dartford, DA1 1SA, Tel.: 01322 622398
Rochester Road Clinic, Gravesend Area, 107 Rochester Road, Gravesend, DA12 2HU, Tel.: 01474 534795

Family Planning Services
Mrs D Corderoy, Head of Public Health Nursing, Livingstone Hospital, East Hill, Dartford, DA1 1SA, Tel.: 01322 622398

Health Visitors
Ms J Shepherd, Child & Family Health Nurse Lead - Health Visitors, Livingstone Hospital, East Hill, Dartford, DA1 1SA, Tel.: 01322 622321

HIV/AIDS
Ms W Liddiard, Livingstone Hospital, Tel.: 01322 622370

Liaison Services
Ms C Balderson, Continuing Care Liaison, Gravesemd & North Kent Hospital, Tel.: 01474 574202
Ms D Rollings, Consultant Nurse Intermediate Care Services, Livingstone Hospital, East Hill, Dartford, DA1 1SA, Tel.: 01322 622398

Pharmacy
Mrs G Lewis, Head of Non Medical Prescribing,

East Elmbridge & Mid Surrey Primary Care Trust
Trust Headquarters, Cedar Court
Guildford Road
FETCHAM
Leatherhead, KT22 9RX
Tel.: 01372 227300
Fax.: 01372 227368

Admin & Senior Management
Mr P Chapman, Head of Professional Development (Nursing), Cedar Court, Guildford Road, Fetcham, Leatherhead, KT22 9RX, Tel.: 01372 227327
Mr A Kennedy, Chief Executive,

South East Coast Strategic Health Authority

Child Health Records
Child Health Records Office Co-ordinator, Child Health Records Dept, Ewell Court Clinic, Ewell Court Avenue, Ewell, Surrey, KT19 0DZ, Tel.: 0208 394 8150
Pre-School Immunisations, Child Health Records Dept, Ewell Court Clinic, Ewell Court Avenue, Ewell, Surrey, KT19 0DZ, Tel.: 0208 394 8152
Pre-School Transfer Clerk, Child Health Records Dept, Ewell Court Clinic, Ewell Court Avenue, Ewell, Surrey, KT19 0DZ, 0208 394 8151
School Health Team, Child Health Records Dept, Ewell Court Clinic, Ewell Court Avenue, Ewell, Surrey, KT19 0DZ, Tel.: 0208 394 8153/4/5/6
Ms J Strong, Co-ordinator, (excluding Dorking area), Ewell Court Clinic, Ewell Court Avenue, Ewell, KT19 0DZ, Tel.: 020 8393 1382
Ms C Tallo, (excluding Dorking area), Ewell Court Clinic, Ewell Court Avenue, Ewell, KT19 0DZ, Tel.: 020 8393 1382
Child Protection/Safeguarding Children
Named Nurse, Child Protection, Cedar Court, Guildford Road, Fetcham, Leatherhead, KT22 9RX, Tel.: 01372 227252
Clinical Leads (NSF)
Ms K Laws, Clinical Lead, Cancer,
Community Nursing Services
Ms S Bonynge, Locality Leader, Community Nursing Services, Cedar Court, Guildford Road, Fetcham, Leatherhead, KT22 9RX, Tel.: 01372 227300
Ms A Chapple, Locality Leader, Community Nursing Services, Cedar Court, Guildford Road, Fetcham, Leatherhead, KT22 9RX, Tel.: 01372 227300
Ms P Taylor, Locality Leader, Community Nursing Services, Cedar Court, Guildford Road, Fetcham, Leatherhead, KT22 9RX, Tel.: 01372 227300
District Nursing
Mrs S Bonynge, Operational Manager, Tel.: 01372 227346
Mrs A Chapple, Service Manager, Tel.: 0208 393 7707
Mrs P Taylor, Operational Manager, Tel.: 01372 227345
Family Planning Services
Mrs M Ingle, Lead Nurse, Family Planning Office, Leatherhead, Hospital, Poplar Road, Leatherhead, KT22 8SD, Tel.: 01372 384337
Health Visitors
Mrs S Bonynge, Operational Manager, Tel.: 01372 227346
Mrs A Chapple, Service Manager, Tel.: 0208 393 7707
Mrs P Taylor, Operational Manager, Tel.: 01372 227345
Other Services
Mrs J Brogan, Modern Matron, Leatherhead Hospital, Tel.: 01372 384344
Mrs V Dixon, Modern Matron, Molesey Hospital, Tel.: 0208 941 4481
Mrs S Grose, Modern Matron, New Epsom & Ewell Cottage Hospital, Tel.: 01372 734843
Mrs J Layzell, Modern Matron, Dorking Hospital, Tel.: 01737 768511 ext 1223
School Nursing
Mrs S Bonynge, Operational Manager, Tel.: 01372 227346
Mrs A Chapple, Service Manager, Tel.: 0208 393 7707
Mrs P Taylor, Operational Manager, Tel.: 01372 227345
Smoking Cessation
Ms J Carr, Smoking Cessation Co-ordinator, Cedar Court, Guildford Road, Fetcham, Leatherhead, KT22 9RX, Tel.: 01372 227387
Specialist Nursing Services
Ms A Strong, Advisor, Breast Feeding, Breast Care, Epsom General Hospital, Dorking Road, Epsom, Tel.: 01372 735367
Ms R Lavender, Senior Advisor, Continence, New Epsom & Ewell Cottage Hospital, Horton Lane, West Park, Epsom, KT19 8PB, Tel.: 01372 734841
Ms P French, Lead Nurse, S Funded Care, Continuing Care, Fitzalan House, 70 High Street, Ewell, Surrey, Tel.: 0208 393 8526
Mrs L Wilkinson, Specialist Nurse, Multiple Sclerosis, Poplar, New Epsom & Ewell Community Hospital, West Park Road, Horton Lane, Epsom, KT19 9PB, Tel.: 01372 734897

Ms S Gay, Nurse Specialist, Parkinson's Disease, Poplar, New Epsom & Ewell Community Hospital, West Park Road, Horton Lane, Epsom, KT19 9PB, Tel.: 01372 734897
Mrs J Davey, Specialist Nurse, Respiratory, Leatherhead Hospital, Poplar Road, Leatherhead, KT22 8SD, Tel.: 01372 384344

East Kent Coastal Primary Care Trust
Trust Headquarters, Protea House
New Bridge, Marine Parade
DOVER
CT17 9HQ
Tel.: 01304 227227

Admin & Senior Management
Mr D Grayson, Chief Executive,
Child Health
Mrs K-A Hatcher, Head of Community Childrens Nursing Service, The Children's Assessment Unit, Kent & Canterbury Hospital, Ethelbert Rd, Canterbury, Kent, CT1 3NG, Tel.: 01227 864125
Child Protection/Safeguarding Children
Mrs L Allan, Looked After Children, Designated Nurse, Queens House, Queen Street, Ramsgate, CT11 9DH, Tel.: 01843 255250 ext 5249
Ms J Downing, Thanet & Dover Areas, Named Nurse, Child Protection, c/o Protea House, New Bridge, Marine Parade, Dover, Kent, CT17 9HQ, Tel.: 01304 227227 ext 2244
Ms J Ward, Designated Nurse, Child Protection, Protea House, New Bridge, Marine Parade, Dover, Kent, CT17 9HQ, Tel.: 01304 227227 ext 2276
Clinical Leads (NSF)
Mr M Parks, Clinical Lead, Cancer,

East Kent Hospitals NHS Trust
Trust Headquarters, Kent & Canterbury Hospital
Ethelbert Road
CANTERBURY
Kent
CT1 3NG
Tel.: 01227 766877

Acute Specialist Nursing Services
Ms R Barnes, Breast Care, William Harvey Hospital, Kennington Road, Willesborough, Ashford, Kent, TN24 0LZ, Tel.: 01233 616657 x86657
Ms N Davies, Breast Care, Buckland Hospital/William Harvey Hospital, Tel.: 01233 616657
Ms S Fitzgerald, Breast Care, Kent & Canterbury Hospital, Ethelbert road, Canterbury, Kent, CT1 3NG, Tel.: 01227 766877 x 74494
Ms S Kum, Breast Care, QEQMH, St Peter's Road, Margate, Kent, CT9 4AN, Tel.: 01843 225544 x 62690
Ms P Price, Breast Care, Kent & Canterbury Hospital, Ethelbert road, Canterbury, Kent, CT1 3NG, Tel.: 01227 766877 x 74653
Ms L Parrish, Dermatology, QEQMH, St Peter's Road, Margate, Kent, CT9 4AN, Tel.: 01843 225544 x 62658
Ms J Barber, Diabetes, QEQMH, St Peter's Road, Margate, Kent, CT9 4AN, Tel.: 01843 234470
Ms P Hughes, Diabetes, William Harvey Hospital, Kennington Road, Willesborough, Ashford, Kent, TN24 0LZ, Tel.: 01233 616047
Ms S Kinnear, Diabetes, Kent & Canterbury Hospital, Ethelbert road, Canterbury, Kent, CT1 3NG, Tel.: 01227 864050
Ms J Muir, Diabetes, QEQMH, St Peter's Road, Margate, Kent, CT9 4AN, Tel.: 01843 234470
Ms J Sponton, Diabetes, William Harvey Hospital, Kennington Road, Willesborough, Ashford, Kent, TN24 0LZ, Tel.: 01233 616047
Ms L Pike, Epilepsy, William Harvey Hospital, Kennington Road, Willesborough, Ashford, Kent, TN24 0LZ, Tel.: 01233 633331
Ms L Dempster, Infection Control, William Harvey Hospital, Kennington Road, Willesborough, Ashford, Kent, TN24 0LZ, Tel.: 01233 633331 x 88079

South East Coast Strategic Health Authority

Ms S Roberts, Infection Control, QEQMH, St Peter's Road, Margate, Kent, CT9 4AN, Tel.: 01843 225544 x 62305

Ms D Weston, Infection Control, Kent & Canterbury Hospital, Ethelbert road, Canterbury, Kent, CT1 3NG, Tel.: 01227 766877 x 74270

Ms A Will, Paediatrics, QEQMH, St Peter's Road, Margate, Kent, CT9 4AN, Tel.: 01843 225544 x 62454

Ms L Frost, Palliative Care, QEQMH, St Peter's Road, Margate, Kent, CT9 4AN, Tel.: 01843 225544 x 65074

Ms T Neill, Palliative Care, William Harvey Hospital, Kennington Road, Willesborough, Ashford, Kent, TN24 0LZ, Tel.: 01233 633331 x 86024

Ms T Oliver, Palliative Care, William Harvey Hospital, Kennington Road, Willesborough, Ashford, Kent, TN24 0LZ, Tel.: 01233 633331 x 88352

Ms P Readl, Palliative Care, QEQMH, St Peter's Road, Margate, Kent, CT9 4AN, Tel.: 01843 225544 x 65074

Ms J Sellen, Palliative Care, Kent & Canterbury Hospital, Ethelbert road, Canterbury, Kent, CT1 3NG, Tel.: 01227 766877 x 73835

Ms T Shinglesten, Palliative Care, Kent & Canterbury Hospital, Ethelbert road, Canterbury, Kent, CT1 3NG, Tel.: 01227 766877 x 73835

Ms A Herbert, Respiratory, Tel.: 01304 865452

Ms J Bell, Stoma Care, William Harvey Hospital, Kennington Road, Willesborough, Ashford, Kent, TN24 0LZ, Tel.: 01233 616643

Ms M Cullerton, Stoma Care, William Harvey Hospital, Kennington Road, Willesborough, Ashford, Kent, TN24 0LZ, Tel.: 01233 633331 x 88648

Ms J Elliott, Tissue Viability, Kent & Canterbury Hospital, Ethelbert road, Canterbury, Kent, CT1 3NG, Tel.: 01227 766877 x 73793

Child Protection/Safeguarding Children
Ms P Jedrzejewski, Named Nurse, Child Protection,

Community Midwifery
Maternity Department, Kent & Canterbury Hospital, Ethelbert Road, Canterbury, Kent, CT1 3NG, Tel.: 01227 766877 ext 74597

Mrs S Moore, Head of Midwifery, Kingsgate Ward, Queen Elizabeth The Queen Mothers Hospital, St Peters Road, Margate, CT9 4AN, Tel.: 01843 225544 x 63084

Mrs L Stevens, Dover Family Birthing Centre, Midwifery Manager, Buckland Hospital, Coombe Valley Road, Dover, Kent, CT17 0HD, Tel.: 01233 633331 ext 86171

Ms L Stevens, Assistant Head of Midwifery, Buckland Hospital, Coombe Valley Road, Dover, Kent, CT17 0HD, Tel.: 01304 201624

HIV/AIDS
Ms B Mann, HIV, Clinical Nurse Specialist, William Harvey Hospital, Tel.: 01303 220018 x 84287

East Kent Partnerships NHS Trust

Trust Headquarters
Littlebourne Road
CANTERBURY
CT1 1AZ
Tel.: 01227 459371
Fax.: 01227 812268

Learning Disabilities
Adults - East, The Lodge, Lanthorne Court, Lanthorne Road, Broadstairs, CT10 8ND, Tel.: 01843 602725

Adults - East, Cairn Ryan, 101 London Road, Dover, Tel.: 01304 825555

Adults - West, Eversley House, 19 Horn Street, Hythe, CT21 5SB, Tel.: 01303 717000

Ashford, Adults West, Eversley House, 19 Horn Street, Hythe, CT21 5SB, Tel.: 01303 717030

Mr D Crothers, Service Manager, Learning Disability Services, Eversley House, 19 Horn Street, Hythe, Kent, CT21 5SB, Tel.: 01303 717000

Laurel House, 41 Old Dover Road, Canterbury, CT1 3HH, Tel.: 01227 597111

Shepway, Eversley House, 19 Horn Street, Hythe, CT21 5SB, Tel.: 01303 717000

Mr J Thomas, Operations Manager, East, The Lodge, Lanthorne Court, Lanthorne Road, Broadstairs, CT10 8ND,

Ms B Young, Manager, Children's Services, Queen House, Queens Street, Ramsgate, CT11 9DH, Tel.: 01843 255252

East Surrey Primary Care Trust

Trust Headquarters, St Johns Court
51 St Johns Road
REDHILL
RH1 6DS
Tel.: 01737 780209

Admin & Senior Management
Ms E Best, Chief Executive, St Johns Court, 51 St Johns Road, Redhill, RH1 6DS, Tel.: 01737 780209

Mr A Warren, Director of Health & Social Care Services, St Johns Court, 51 St Johns Road, Redhill, RH1 6DS, Tel.: 01737 214789

Mrs S Wilson, Director of Nursing, Children Young People & Families, St Johns Court, 51 St Johns Road, Redhill, RH1 6DS, Tel.: 01737 214872

Child Health
Childrens Home Care, Room 11, Maple Annexe, East Surrey Hospital, Canada Avenue, Redhill, RH1 5RH, Tel.: 01737 231797

Child Health Records
Child Health Records, Child Health, Maple House, East Surrey Hospital, Canada Avenue, Redhill, RH1 5RH, Tel.: 01737 231639

Child Protection/Safeguarding Children
Mrs A Boodhoo, Consultant Nurse Vulnerable Children, 47 Woodlands Road, Redhill, RH1 6HB, Tel.: 01737 214861

Mrs L Dawson, Specialist Health Visitor Post Natal Depression, St Johns Court, 51 St Johns Road, Redhill, RH1 6DS, Tel.: 01737 214765

Ms C Hawthornthwaite, Looked After Children, Specialist Nurse, 129 Farningham Road, Caterham, CR3 6LN, Tel.: 01737 737846

Community Matrons
Ms S Buss, Community Matron, Caterham Dene Hospital, Church Road, Caterham, Surrey, CR3 5RA, Tel.: 01883 837535

Ms C Thorn, Community Matron, Caterham Dene Hospital, Church Road, Caterham, Surrey, CR3 5RA, Tel.: 01883 837535

District Nursing
Mr L Davies, Team Leader for Health & Social Care - East Surrey, St Johns Court, 51 St Johns Road, Redhill, RH1 6DS, Tel.: 01737 214792

Mrs B Pink, Health & Social Care Service Manager - Tandridge, Nursing Lead for Joint Directorate, St Johns Court, 51 St John's Road, Redhill, RG1 6DS, Tel.: 01737 214794

Mrs L Savory, Team Leader for Health & Social Care - Tandridge, Caterham Dene Hospital, Church Road, Caterham, CR3 5RA, Tel.: 01883 837521

Family Planning Services
Family Planning Service, Maple House, East Surrey Hospital, Canada Avenue, Redhill, RH1 5RH, Tel.: 01737 768511 ext 6848

Health Visitors
Mrs S Ashfield, Senior Health Promotion Specialist Infant Nutrition, St Johns Court, 51 St Johns Road, Redhill, RH1 6DS, Tel.: 01737 214839

Mrs L Barker, Clinical Team Leader Public Health, St Johns Court, 51 St Johns Road, Redhill, RH1 6DS, Tel.: 01737 214853

Mrs H Bennett, Clinical Team Leader Public Health, St Johns Court, 51 St Johns Road, Redhill, RH1 6DS, Tel.: 01737 214845

Liaison Services
Mrs J Hopkins, Specialist Paediatric Liaison Nurse, Maple Annex, East Surrey Hospital, Canada Avenue, Redhill, RH1 5RH, Tel.: 01737 768511 ext 6858

South East Coast Strategic Health Authority

Other Services

Ms E Clark, Service Manager for 24 hr Care Services, St Johns Court, 51 St Johns Road, Redhill, RH1 6DS, Tel.: 01737 214846

Mrs J Don, Health & Social Care Service Manager, Intermediate Care & Hospital Services, St Johns Court, 51 St Johns Road, Redhill, RH1 6DS, Tel.: 01737 214844

Mrs C Hurman, Team Leader for Health & Social Care, Evening Service & Primary Care Centres, 47 Woodlands Road, Redhill, RH1 6HB, Tel.: 01737 214865

Ms C Jones, Modern Matron, Caterham Dene Hospital, Church Road, Caterham, Surrey, CR3 5RA, Tel.: 01883 837503

Mrs L Mouland, Consultant Nurse for Older Adults & Intermediate Care, St Johns Court, 51 St Johns Road, Redhill, RH1 6DS, Tel.: 01737 214821

Mrs J Philips, Team Leader for Health & Social Care, Intermediate Care Team, Maple Annexe, East Surrey Hospital, Canada Avenue, Redhill, RH1 5RH, Tel.: 01737 768511 ext 6880

School Nursing

Mrs L Litchfield, Childrens Homecare Team Manager, Room 11, Maple Annexe, East Surrey Hospital, Canada Avenue, Redhill, RH1 5RH, Tel.: 01737 231797

Mrs L Roberts, Clinical Team Leader Public Health, St Johns Court, 51 St Johns Road, Redhill, RH1 6DS, Tel.: 01737 214814

Ms L Roberts, Clinical Team Leader School Nursing, St Johns Court, 51 St Johns Road, Redhill, RH1 6DS, Tel.: 01737 214814

Smoking Cessation

Ms H Thurlow, Smoking Cessation Adviser, St Johns Court, 51 St Johns Road, Redhill, RH1 6DS, Tel.: 01737 214761

Specialist Nursing Services

Ms S Buxton, Clinical Governance Lead, Caterham Dene Hospital, Church Road, Caterham, Surrey, CR3 5RA, Tel.: 01883 837500

Mrs B McCormack, Advisor, Continence, 47 Woodland Road, Redhill, RH1 6HB, Tel.: 01737 214867

Ms D Hamdy, Liaison Nurse, Dermatology, St Johns Court, 51 St Johns Road, Redhill, RG1 6DS, Tel.: 01737 214769

Ms L Howell, Nurse Specialist, Infection Control, 47 Woodlands Road, Redhill, RH1 6HB, Tel.: 01737 214873

Ms C Wright, Nurse Specialist, Parkinson's Disease, 47 Woodlands Road, Redhill, RH1 6HB, Tel.: 01737 767608

The Homeless/Travellers & Asylum Seekers

Ms C Kinnard, Health Visitor for Homeless People, 47 Woodlands Road, Redhill, RH1 6HB, Tel.: 01737 214863

East Sussex County Healthcare NHS Trust

Trust Headquarters, Bowhill
The Drive, Hellingly
HAILSHAM, East Sussex
BN27 4ER
Tel.: 01323 440022

Learning Disabilities

Mr I Adenis, Senior Clinical Nurse, Old Mill House, Mill Lane, Uckfield, Tel.: 01825 744123

Mr A Bowman, Community Nurse, St Marys House, Eastbourne,

Ms S Button, Service Manager, Woodside, The Drive, Hellingly, Hailsham, East Sussex, BN27 4ER,

Mr K Goodsell, Community Nurse, Gambier House,

Mr M Green, Community Nurse, Old Mill House, Mill Lane, Uckfield,

Ms N Palmer, Community Nurse, Old Mill House, Mill Lane, Uckfield,

Ms C Searle, Community Nurse, St Marys House, Eastbourne,

Ms D Siggins, Community Nurse, Gambier House,

East Sussex Hospitals NHS Trust

Trust Headquarters, St Anne's House
The Ridge
ST LEONARDS-ON-SEA
East Sussex, TN37 7PT
Tel.: 01424 755255

Community Midwifery

Mrs C Cowling, Community Midwifery Manager, Conquest Hospital, The Ridge, St Leonards-on-Sea, East Sussex, TN37 7RD, Tel.: 01424 755255 ext 8940

Ms D Street, Community Midwifery Manager, Eastbourne District General Hospital, Kings Drive, Eastbourne, BN21 2UD, Tel.: 01323 417400 ext 4158

Smoking Cessation

Ms B Lynes O'Meara, Smoking Cessation, Community Midwives Office, Conquest Hospital, The Ridge, St Leonards,

Eastbourne Downs Primary Care Trust

Trust Headquarters, 1 St Anne's Road
EASTBOURNE
BN21 3UN
Tel.: 01323 417714

Admin & Senior Management

Ms G Brocklehurst, Chief Executive, 1 St Anne's Road, Eastbourne, BN21 3UN, Tel.: 01323 417714

Ms N Creasey, Associate Director, Corporate Affairs & Organisational Development, 1 St Anne's Road, Eastbourne, BN21 3UN, Tel.: 01323 417714

Mr C Hix, Director of Corporate Resources & Systems, 1 St Anne's Road, Eastbourne, BN21 3UN, Tel.: 01323 417714

Mr J Vesely, Director of Service Delivery, 1 St Anne's Road, Eastbourne, BN21 3UN, Tel.: 01323 417714

Child Health

Ms A Alexander, Avenue House, Eastbourne, Tel.: 01323 440022

Child Health Records

Child Health Records, Apex Centre, Hailsham,

Child Protection/Safeguarding Children

Ms C Evans, Looked After Children, Named Nurse, Centenary House, The Avenue, Eastbourne, BN21 3XY, Tel.: 01323 440022 ext 4109

Ms M Simon, Assistant Director Operations (Children), Avenue House, The Avenue, Eastbourne, BN21 3XY, Tel.: 01323 440022

Ms D Sampson, Designated Nurse, Child Protection, Hailsham Health Centre, Vicarage Field, Hailsham, East Sussex, BN27 1BE, Tel.: 01323 446992

Clinical Leads (NSF)

Dr M Barnes, GP Lead, Cardiovascular & Stroke, Seaford Health Centre, Dane Road, Seaford, BN25 1DH, Tel.: 01323 490022

Dr J Darwent, GP Lead, Sexual Health, The Medical Centre, 10 Richmond Road, Pevensey Bay, BN24 6AQ, Tel.: 01323 465100

Ms S Clark, Clinical Lead, (Commissioning), Cancer, 1 St Anne's Road, Eastbourne, BN21 3UN,

Dr H Thomas, GP Lead, Cancer, The Surgery, 6 College Road, Eastbourne, BN21 4HY, Tel.: 01323 735044

Mr P Trevethic, Clinical Lead, (Commissioning), CHD, 1 St Anne's Road, Eastbourne, BN21 3UN,

Dr J Andrews, GP Lead, Diabetic Care, Princes Park Health Centre, Wartling Road, Eastbourne, BN22 7PF, Tel.: 01323 744644

Ms C Heaps, Clinical Lead, Diabetic Care, Hailsham Health Centre, Vicarage Fields, Hailsham, East Sussex, BN27 1BE, Tel.: 01323 446992

Dr H Thomas, GP Lead, Palliative Care, The Surgery, 6 College Road, Eastbourne, BN21 4HY, Tel.: 01323 735044

Community Nursing Services

Ms

Ms A Webster, Assistant Director Operations - Adults, Avenue House, The Avenue, Eastbourne, BN21 3XY, Tel.: 01323 440022 ext 4076

District Nursing

Mrs P Bansel, Clinical Lead Practice Nurses, Centenary House, The Avenue, Eastbourne, BN21 3XY, Tel.: 01323 440022 ext 4022

Mr M Lawlor, Clinical Lead District Nurses, Centenary House, The Avenue, Eastbourne, BN21 3XY, Tel.: 01323 440022 ext 4109

South East Coast Strategic Health Authority

Ms R Stark, Practice Development Manager, Centenary House, The Avenue, Eastbourne, BN21 3XY, Tel.: 01323 440022 ext 4022

Ms C Tyler, Holiday Patient Referrals, Avenue House, The Avenue, Eastbourne, BN21 3XY, Tel.: 01323 440022

Family Planning Services

Family Planning Services, Avenue House, The Avenue, Eastbourne, BN21 3XY, Tel.: 01323 440165

Mr M Jones, Clinical Nurse Specialist/Co-ordinator (Sexual Health), Family Planning & Sexual Health, Tel.: 01323 444165

Health Visitors

Ms H Dutchman, Clinical Lead Health Visitors, Centenary House, The Avenue, Eastbourne, BN21 3XY, Tel.: 01323 440022 ext 4107

Liaison Services

Ms P Ertl, General Liaison, Eastbourne District General Hospital, Kings Drive, Eastbourne, BN21 3UD, Tel.: 01323 417100 ext 4196

Ms J Spashett, General Liaison, Eastbourne District General Hospital, Kings Drive, Eastbourne, BN21 3UD, Tel.: 01323 417100 ext 4196

Ms J Vanston, General Liaison, Eastbourne District General Hospital, Kings Drive, Eastbourne, BN21 3UD, Tel.: 01323 417100 ext 4196

School Nursing

Ms C Hobbs, Clinical Lead, School Nursing, Centenary House, The Avenue, Eastbourne, BN21 3XY, Tel.: 01323 444189

Smoking Cessation

Ms K Cooper, Co-ordinator, Centenary House, The Avenue, Eastbourne, BN21 3XY, Tel.: 01323 440022

Specialist Nursing Services

Mr N Cole, Substance Misuse Lead, Centenary House, The Avenue, Eastbourne, BN21 3XY, Tel.: 01323 418996

Ms J Piper, Manager, Intermediate Care, Firwood House, Brassey Avenue, Hamden Park, BN22 9QJ, Tel.: 01323 503758

Ms H Sayce, Terminal Care, Sister, Macmillan, Princes Park Health Centre, Wartling Road, Eastbourne, BN22 7PF,

Mr N Starley, Terminal Care, Sister, Macmillan, Princes Park Health Centre, Wartling Road, Eastbourne, BN22 7PF, Tel.: 01323 744644

Ms B Walding, Terminal Care, Sister, Macmillan, Princes Park Health Centre, Wartling Road, Eastbourne, BN22 7PF, Tel.: 01323 744644

Ms G Bennett, Nurse, Tissue Viability, Health Centre, Hamden Park, Eastbourne, BN22 9QJ, Tel.: 01323 503758

Ms K Bennett, Nurse, Tissue Viability, Health Centre, Hamden Park, Eastbourne, BN22 9QJ, Tel.: 01323 503758

Frimley Park Hospital NHS Trust

Trust Headquarters, Frimley Park Hospital
Portsmouth Road, Frimley
CAMBERLEY
Surrey
GU16 5UJ
Tel.: 01276 604604
Fax.: 01276 604148

Community Midwifery

Community Office, Direct Line 01276 604241, Tel.: ext 4241
Emergencies, Tel.: Mat Bleep 059
Mrs M Saker, Head of Midwifery, Tel.: 01276 604210

Guildford & Waverley Primary Care Trust

Trust Headquarters, Broadmede House
Farnham Business Park, Weydon Lane
FARNHAM
Surrey, GU9 8QT
Tel.: 01252 305700

Admin & Senior Management

Ms L Compton, Director of Operations, Broadmede House, Farnham Business Park, Weydon Lane, Farnham, GU9 8QT, Tel.: 01252 305700

Mrs J Thwaites, Associate Director, Community Nursing, Jarvis Centre, Stoughton Road, Guildford, GU1 1LJ, Tel.: 01483 783115

Child Health

Ms J Dalton, Community Nurse Manager, Jarvis Centre, Stoughton Road, Guildford, GU1 1LJ, Tel.: 01483 783273

Mrs J Thwaites, Associate Director, Community Nursing, Jarvis Centre, Stoughton Road, Guildford, GU1 1LJ, Tel.: 01483 783115

Child Health Records

Child Health Records, Jarvis Centre, Stoughton Road, Guildford, GU1 1LJ,

Child Protection/Safeguarding Children

Mrs S Curzon-Hope, Named Nurse, Child Protection, Jarvis Centre, Stoughton Road, Guildford, GU1 1LJ, Tel.: 01483 783142

Clinical Leads (NSF)

Ms W Panting, Clinical Lead, COPD,

Mrs E Rodgers, Clinical Lead, Unscheduled Care, Tel.: 01483 783273

Mrs J Thwaites, Clinical Lead, CHD & Diabetes, Jarvis Centre, Tel.: 01483 783115

Ms S Wardle, Clinical Lead, Care of the Elderly, Milford Hospital,

Ms J Dalton, Clinical Lead, Children,

Community Matrons

Community Matrons, Haslemere Health Centre, Church Lane, Haslemere, Surrey, Tel.: 01483 782376

Mrs W Panting, Community Nurse Manager, Jarvis Centre, Stoughton Road, Guildford, GU1 1LJ, Tel.: 01483 783273

District Nursing

Ms L Rodgers, Community Nurse Manager, Jarvis Centre, Stoughton Road, Guildford, GU1 1LJ, Tel.: 01483 783273

Mrs J Thwaites, Associate Director, Community Nursing, Jarvis Centre, Stoughton Road, Guildford, GU1 1LJ, Tel.: 01483 783115

Equipment Loan Services

Ms R Parry, Haslemere Hospital, Tel.: 01483 782330

Family Planning Services

Dr L Howard, Consultant GUM/Head of Family Planning, Farnham Road Hospital Site, Guildford, GU2 5LX, Tel.: 01483 576208

Health Visitors

Ms J Dalton, Community Nurse Manager, Jarvis Centre, Stoughton Road, Guildford, GU1 1LJ, Tel.: 01483 783273

HIV/AIDS

Ms F Oakley,

Learning Disabilities

Provided by Surrey Hampshire Borders Trust,

Liaison Services

Ms R Culley, Paediatric Liaison Health Visitor, Royal Surrey Hospital, Egerton Road, Guildford, GU2 5XX, Tel.: 01483 571122 ext 4911

Ms J Harber, Community Liaison, Royal Surrey Hospital, Egerton Road, Guildford, GU2 5XX, Tel.: 01483 464058/571122

Ms R Parry, Liaison Services, Haslemere Hospital, Tel.: 01483 782330

Pharmacy

Ms F Harris, Head Pharmacist, Broadmede House, Weydon Lane, Farnham, GU9 8QT, Tel.: 01252 305700

School Nursing

Ms J Dalton, Community Nurse Manager, Jarvis Centre, Stoughton Road, Guildford, GU1 1LJ, Tel.: 01483 783273

Smoking Cessation

Jarvis Centre, Stoughton Road, Guildford, GU1 1LJ,

Specialist Nursing Services

Ms J Holland, Associate Director, Cancer & Palliative Care Services, Beacon Centre, Royal Surrey County Hospital, Egerton Road, Guildford, Surrey, Tel.: 01483 783400

Advisory Service, Continence, Farnham Hospital, Farnham, Surrey, Tel.: 01483 782000

Ms B Ellis-Macey, Continence, Farnham Hospital, Farnham, Surrey, Tel.: 01483 782000

Services, COPD, Jarvis Centre, Tel.: 01483 571122 x 4677

South East Coast Strategic Health Authority

Mrs G Hall, Specialist Nurse, Diabetic Care, Haslemere Hospital, Tel.: 01483 783020

Ms J Patterson, Diabetic Care, St Luke's Wing, Royal Surrey County Hospital, Tel.: 01483 571122 ext 6959

Services, Diabetic Care, Haslemere Health Centre, Church Lane, Haslemere, Surrey, Tel.: 01483 783020

Mrs N Ward, Specialist Nurse, Diabetic Care, Haslemere Hospital, Tel.: 01483 783020

Team, Macmillan, The Beacon, Gill Avenue, Guildford, Tel.: 01483 783423

Mrs T Bennett, Parkinson's Disease, Farnham Hospital & Centre for Health, Farnham,

Mrs J Kaye, Parkinson's Disease, Florence Desmond Day Hospital, Royal Surrey County Hospital, Tel.: 01483 406727

Team, Parkinson's Disease, Royal Surrey County Hospital, Egerton Road, Guildford, Tel.: 01483 406727

The Homeless/Travellers & Asylum Seekers

Ms L Wright, Healthcare for the Homeless, Guildford Action, Leapale Road, Guildford, Tel.: 01483 449827

Walk In Centres

Guildford Walk in Centre, Egerton Road, Guildford, Tel.: 01483 402788

Hastings & St. Leonards Primary Care Trust

Trust Headquarters
PO Box 124
ST LEONARDS-ON-SEA
East Sussex
TN38 9WH
Tel.: 01424 457100

Admin & Senior Management

Mrs D Parker, Director of Patient Services, Trust Headquarters,

Ms T Wilkinson, Chief Executive,

Child Health Records

Ms E Frawley, Child Health Manager, Kipling Unit, Conquest Hospital, The Ridge, Hastings, TN37 7RD, Tel.: 01424 755255

Child Protection/Safeguarding Children

Ms F Edmunds, Child & Family Health Services Dev Nurse/Lead School Nurse, Bexhill Hospital, Holliers Hill, Bexhill on Sea, East Sussex, TN40 2DZ, Tel.: 01424 755255

Mrs D Barnes, Lead Nurse, Child Protection, Kipling Unit, Conquest Hospital, The Ridge, Hastings, TN37 7RD, Tel.: 01424 755470 x 8747/8477

Mrs K Miller, Lead Nurse, Child Protection, Kipling Unit, Conquest Hospital, The Ridge, Hastings, TN37 7RD, Tel.: 01424 755470 x 8747/8477

Clinical Leads (NSF)

Mr P Bryden, Clinical Lead, Cancer,

District Nursing

Ms D Cooke, District Nursing Manager, Trust Headquarters, Tel.: 01424 755470 x 5663

Health Visitors

Ms J Kellham, Paediatric Liaison Health Visitors, Kipling Unit, Conquest Hospital, The Ridge, Hastings, TN37 7RD, Tel.: 01424 755255

Ms D Pluckrose, Paediatric Liaison Health Visitors, Kipling Unit, Conquest Hospital, The Ridge, Hastings, TN37 7RD, Tel.: 01424 755255

Other Services

Ms K Dadswell, TB, Health Visitor, Old Town Surgery, 13 De La Warr Road, Bexhill, TN40 2GH, Tel.: 01424 217212

Ms J Paulin, TB, Health Visitor, Bexhill Health Centre, Holliers Hill, Bexhill-on-Sea, TN40 2DZ, Tel.: 01424 220077

School Nursing

Ms F Edmunds, School Nurse Manager, Trust Headquarters, Tel.: 01424 755470 x 5665

Specialist Nursing Services

Ms C Adkins, Lead Practice Nurse, Trust Headquarters, Tel.: 01424 457100

Ms J Tyler, Lead, Nurse Practitioner, Trust Headquarters, Tel.: 01424 735600

The Homeless/Travellers & Asylum Seekers

Ms R Day, Health Visitor, Silchester Mews, St Leonards, Tel.: 01424 717391

Horsham & Chanctonbury Primary Care Trust

Trust Headquarters, New Park House
North Street
HORSHAM
West Sussex
RH12 1RJ
Tel.: 01403 223202

Admin & Senior Management

Ms S Creamer, Director of Modernisation & Partnership, New Park House, North Street, Horsham, West Sussex, RH12 1RJ, Tel.: 01403 223283

Mrs S Giddings, Director of Nursing & Quality, New Park House, North Street, Horsham, West Sussex, RH12 1RJ, Tel.: 01403 223269

Mr G Howells, Deputy Director of Nursing & Quality, New Park House, North Street, Horsham, West Sussex, RH12 1RJ, Tel.: 01403 223273

Ms A Ugur, Chief Executive,

Child Health

Ms J Allport, Child Health Specialist Nurse, New Park House, North Street, Horsham, West Sussex, RH12 1RJ, Tel.: 01403 223217

Mr G Howells, Deputy Director of Nursing & Quality (School Nurses), New Park House, North Street, Horsham, West Sussex, RH12 1RJ, Tel.: 01403 223273

Ms F Lucas, PEC Nurse (Children & Young People), Steyning Health Centre, Tanyard Lane, Steyning, BN44 3RJ, Tel.: 01903 843400

Child Health Records

West Sussex Child Health Records, Child Health Bureau, PO Box 115, Chichester, PO19 6YT, Tel.: 01243 815400

Child Protection/Safeguarding Children

Ms J Allport, Child Health Advisor, New Park House, North Street, Horsham, West Sussex, RH12 1RJ, Tel.: 01403 223217

Clinical Leads (NSF)

Ms F Lucas, Clinical Lead, Children & Young People, Tel.: 01903 843400

Ms T Smith, Clinical Lead, Cancer, Tel.: 01403 782931

Dr A Rainbow, Clinical Lead, CHD, Tel.: 01903 843400

Dr D Howell, Clinical Lead, Diabetic Care, Tel.: 01403 223283

Ms S Giddings, Clinical Lead, Older People, Tel.: 01403 223269

Community Matrons

Mr S Cemm, New Park House, Horsham, Tel.: 01273 492255

Mrs A Harrison, New Park House, Horsham, Tel.: 01403 223270

Mrs S McGill, New Park House, Horsham, Tel.: 01403 223274

Mrs S Moody, New Park House, Horsham, Tel.: 01403 223213

Community Nursing Services

Mr G Howells, Deputy Director of Nursing & Quality, New Park House, North Street, Horsham, West Sussex, RH12 1RJ, Tel.: 01403 223273

District Nursing

Mr G Howells, Deputy Director of Nursing & Quality, New Park House, North Street, Horsham, West Sussex, RH12 1RJ, Tel.: 01403 223273

Equipment Loan Services

Mr G Howells, Deputy Director of Nursing & Quality, New Park House, North Street, Horsham, West Sussex, RH12 1RJ, Tel.: 01403 223273

South East Coast Strategic Health Authority

Health Visitors
Mr G Howells, Deputy Director of Nursing & Quality, New Park House, North Street, Horsham, West Sussex, RH12 1RJ, Tel.: 01403 223273
School Nursing
Mr G Howells, Deputy Director of Nursing & Quality, New Park House, North Street, Horsham, West Sussex, RH12 1RJ, Tel.: 01403 223273
Specialist Nursing Services
Dr A Rainbow, Doctor, CHD, Steyning Health Centre, Tanyard Lane, Steyning, BN44 3RJ,
Mr D Walters, Team Manager/Nurse Specialist, Continence, New Park House, North Street, Horsham, West Sussex, RH12 1RJ, Tel.: 01403 223222
Dr D Howell, Doctor, Diabetic Care, New Park House, North Street, Horsham, West Sussex, RH12 1RJ,
Ms P Stevens, Nurse Specialist, Vascular, New Park House, North Street, Horsham, West Sussex, RH12 1RJ, Tel.: 01403 223279

Maidstone & Tunbridge Wells NHS Trust

Trust Headquarters, Pembury Hospital
Tonbridge Road
PEMBURY
Kent
TN2 4QJ
Tel.: 01892 823535

Admin & Senior Management
Mr B Place, Director of Nursing, Pembury Hospital, Tonbridge Road, Pembury, Kent, TN2 4QJ, Tel.: 01892 823535 ext 3735
Child Protection/Safeguarding Children
Mrs F Young, Child Protection Lead, Monckton Ward, Maidstone Hospital, Hermitage Lane, Maidstone, Kent, ME16 9QQ, Tel.: 01622 224754 ext 4754
Community Midwifery
Mrs G Duffey, Head of Nursing & Midwifery for Women & Children's Services, Maidstone General Hospital, Hermitage Lane, Barming, Maidstone, Kent, ME16 9QQ, Tel.: 01622 224374
Emergencies - Out of hours, Maidstone General Hospital, Hermitage Lane, Barming, Maidstone, Kent, ME16 9QQ, Tel.: 01622 224426
Ms H Faloon, Community & Outpatient Services, Midwifery Manager, Tel.: 01892 633484
Ms H Thomas, Inpatient Services, Midwifery Manager, Tel.: 01622 224610
Liaison Services
Ms J Humphries, Discharge Liaison, Maidstone Hospital, Hermitage Lane, Maidstone, ME16 9QQ, Tel.: 01622 224892
Mrs M Kenward, Paediatric Liaison, Monckton Ward, Maidstone Hospital, Hermitage Lane, Maidstone, Kent, ME16 9QQ, Tel.: 01622 224754

Maidstone Weald Primary Care Trust

Trust Headquarters, Forstal Ward
Preston Hall
AYLESFORD
Kent
ME20 7NJ
Tel.: 01622 711250

Admin & Senior Management
Ms R Sparks, Acting Chief Executive,
Child Health Records
Ms H Missons, Manager, Cobtree Ward, Preston Hall, Tel.: 01622 885900
Child Protection/Safeguarding Children
Ms J Mercer, Lead Nurse, Child Protection, Tel.: 01622 795745
Ms J Gower, Designated Nurse, Looked After Children, Ditton Ward, Preston Hall, Aylesford, Kent, ME20 7NJ, Tel.: 01622 885916

Clinical Leads (NSF)
Dr P Lewis, Clinical Lead, CHD, Diabetes
Dr B Millar, Clinical Lead, Cancer,
Dr L Selman, Clinical Lead, Older People,
Community Nursing Services
Ms P Evans, Associate Director of Nursing, Tel.: 01622 795739
Ms S Fletcher, Head of Community Nursing, Tel.: 01622 795714
District Nursing
Ms P Brownbridge, Public Health, Lead Nurse, Tel.: 01580 714935
Liaison Services
Ms S Andrews, Training Liaison for Carers & Care Workers, Coxheath Centre, Tel.: 01622 225669
Ms M Bennett, Training Liaison for Carers & Care Workers, Coxheath Centre, Tel.: 01622 225669
Paediatric Liaison, Monckton Ward, Maidstone Hospital, Tel.: 01622 224754
Other Services
Ms T Edburah, Paediatric Audiology, Cobtree Ward,
Ms D Hallam, Community, Rehabilitation Team (Elderly), Coxhealth Centre, Heath Road, Coxheath, Maidstone, ME17 4AH, Tel.: 01622 225834
Ms G Holland, Stroke Co-ordinator, Coxhealth Centre, Heath Road, Coxheath, Maidstone, ME17 4AH, Tel.: 01622 225836
Mrs C Jones, Disability & Rehab Team (DART), Tel.: 01622 225671
Ms S Mobbs, Manager, Supportive Care Team (includes Rapid Response, Domocillary & Night Services), Farm Cottage, Maidstone Hospital, Tel.: 01622 224117
Ms S Schlig, Growth, Birling Ward, Tel.: 01622 225652
Ms V Winter, Elderly, Coxhealth Centre, Heath Road, Coxheath, Maidstone, ME17 4AH, Tel.: 01622 225838
School Nursing
Ms P Jones, School Nursing, Lead Nurse, Tel.: 01622 795729
Specialist Nursing Services
Ms S Jones, Continence, Ditton Ward, Preston Hall Hospital, Tel.: 01622 795716
Ms V Winter, Continuing Care, Coxheath Centre, Tel.: 01622 225840
Ms S Fielder, Infection Control, Preston Hall, Tel.: 01622 224038
Ms H Carter, Lead Nurse, Older People, Tel.: 01622 795729
The Homeless/Travellers & Asylum Seekers
Ms A King, Travellers, 14 Pelican Court, Wateringbury, ME18 5SS, Tel.: 01622 817686

Medway NHS Trust

Trust Headquarters, Medway Hospital
Windmill Road
GILLINGHAM
Kent
ME7 5NY
Tel.: 01634 830000

Acute Specialist Nursing Services
Ms L Boast, Macmillan Nurse, Breast Care, Tel.: 01634 825033
Ms W Emery, Surgical Care, Practitioner, Breast Care, Tel.: 5425
Ms J Hackney, Nurse Specialist, Cancer,
Ms L Houston, Nurse Specialist, Cancer,
Ms C Eastlake, Macmillan, Clinical Nurse Specialist, Colorectal, Tel.: 01634 825211
Ms K Taylor, Nurse Practitioner, Colorectal, - Advanced, Tel.: 01634 825211
Ms S Croney, Nurse Specialist, Dermatology, Tel.: ext 5016
Ms L Hutchinson, Nurse Specialist, Diabetes, Tel.: ext 3861
Ms H Jessop, Nurse Specialist, Diabetes, Tel.: ext 3861
Ms L Meth, Nurse Specialist, Genito Urinary, - Medicine, Tel.: ext 5005
Ms A Griffiths, Macmillan, Clinical Nurse Specialist, Gynae/Oncology, Tel.: 01634 825131
Ms S Bucknell, Macmillan, Clinical Nurse Specialist, Haematology-Oncology, Tel.: 01634 825186

Ms D Evans, Macmillan, Clinical Nurse Specialist, Head & Neck, Tel.: ext 5427

Ms F McKay, Macmillan, Clinical Nurse Specialist, Lung Cancer, Tel.: 01634 825212

Ms S Hurst, Nurse Specialist, Multiple Sclerosis, Tel.: ext 5003

Ms G Worcester, Nurse Specialist, Osteoporosis, Tel.: ext 3892

Ms C Harnett, Nurse Practitioner, Otorhinolaryngology, Tel.: ext 5052

Ms A Kitchingham, Macmillan, Clinical Nurse Specialist, Palliative Care, Tel.: 01634 833807

Ms J Pople, Macmillan, Clinical Nurse Specialist, Palliative Care, Tel.: 01634 833807

Ms S Rama, Macmillan, Clinical Nurse Specialist, Palliative Care, Tel.: 01634 833807

Ms J Kinchel, Nurse Specialist, Respiratory, Tel.: ext 5647

Ms S Pook, Nurse Specialist, Respiratory, Tel.: ext 5213

Ms S Reed, Nurse Specialist, Respiratory, Tel.: ext 5213

Ms L Blagden, Screening, Nurse Specialist, Retinal, Tel.: ext 3822

Ms W Pointer, Nurse Specialist, Rheumatology, Tel.: ext 3905

Ms L Ryan, Nurse Specialist, Rheumatology, Tel.: ext 3905

Ms F Anscomb, Nurse Specialist, Stoma Care, Tel.: bleep 738

Ms C Harvey, Nurse Specialist, Stoma Care, Tel.: bleep 485

Ms T Wells, Macmillan, Clinical Nurse Specialist, Upper GI, Tel.: 01634 828910

Ms R Felton, Nurse Practitioner, Urology, Tel.: ext 5428

Ms C Kelly, Nurse Practitioner, Urology, Tel.: bleep 526

Ms I Viera, Macmillan, Clinical Nurse Specialist, Urology, Tel.: 01634 838918

Child Health

Ms H Archdeacon, Neonatal Sister, Oliver Fisher Neonatal Unit, Medway Maritime Hospital, Tel.: 01634 825125

Ms S Davis, Child Home Care Team (incl Oncology), Magpies Centre, Medway Maritime Hospital, Tel.: 01634 830000 ext 5135/6

Ms P Fergusson, Child Home Care Team (incl Oncology), Magpies Centre, Medway Maritime Hospital, Tel.: 01634 830000 ext 5135/6

Ms L Leighton, Child Home Care Team (incl Oncology), Magpies Centre, Medway Maritime Hospital, Tel.: 01634 830000 ext 5135/6

Ms N White, Child Diabetes, Medway Maritime Hospital, Tel.: 01634 830000 ext 5209

Child Health Records

Ms L Powell, Centre Admin/Systems Manager - School Health Records, Sanderson CDC, Medway Maritime Hospital, Tel.: 01634 825190

Child Protection/Safeguarding Children

Ms S Winchester, Senior Nurse, Child Protection, Residence 13, Medway Maritime Hospital, Tel.: 01634 830000 ext 5166

Community Midwifery

Mr M Flynn, General Manager, Medway Maritime Hospital, Tel.: 01634 830000 ext 5208

Mrs K Taylor, Head of Midwifery, Level 3, Green Zone, Medway Maritime Hospital, Tel.: 01634 825157

Health Visitors

Paediatric Health Visitor, CDC, Medway Maritime Hospital, Tel.: 01634 830000 ext 5192

Learning Disabilities

Mrs S Brooker, Senior Nurse Manager, Residence 13, Medway Maritime Hospital, Windmill Road, Gillingham, Kent, ME7 5NY, Tel.: 01634 830000 ex 5533

School Nursing

School Health Dept,Rochester, Strood, Isle of Grain, Hoo Peninsular, Keystone Centre, Gun Lane, Strood, Tel.: 01634 717755 ext 217

School Health Dept, Sittingbourne, Sittingbourne Memorial Hospital, Bell Road, Sittingbourne, Tel.: 01795 418300

School Health Dept, Gillingham, Rainham, Rainham Health Centre, Holding Street, Rainham, Tel.: 01634 374047

School Health Dept, Chatham, Elm House Clinic, New Road, Chatham, Tel.: 01634 400123

School Health Dept, Minster, Sheppey, Sheerness, Preston Skreens, Minster Road, Minster, Sheppey, Tel.: 01795 870985

Medway Teaching Primary Care Trust

**Trust Headquarters, 7-8 Ambley Green
Bailey Drive
GILLINGHAM
Kent
ME8 0NJ**
Tel.: 01634 294654

Admin & Senior Management

Ms M Bullen, Director Workforce Development, Unit 7-8, Ambley Green, Bailey Drive, Gillingham, Kent, ME8 0NJ, Tel.: 01634 382777

Child Health

Ms E Byers, Paediatric Liaison Advisor, Residence 13, Medway Maritime Hospital, Windmill Road, Gillingham, Kent, ME7 5NY, Tel.: 01634 830000 ext 5304

Child Health Records

School Age Records, Medway NHS Trust,

Ms C Underwood, Medway & Swale PCT, New Court, 1 New Road, Rochester, Kent, ME1 1BD, Tel.: 01634 835021

Child Protection/Safeguarding Children

Ms C Hayward, Looked After Children's Named Nurse, Medway Maritime Hospital, Windmill Road, Gillingham, Kent, ME7 5NY, Tel.: 01634 838907

Ms C Ross, Designated/Named Nurse, Child Protection, Unit 2, Ambley Green, Bailey Drive, Gillingham, Kent, ME8 0NJ, Tel.: 01634 382888

Community Nursing Services

Community Nursing Services, Unit 2, Ambley Green, Bailey Drive, Gillingham, Kent, ME8 0NJ, Tel.: 01634 382888

District Nursing

Ms V Clark, Locality Director - Chatham, Lordswood, Lordswood Health Centre, Sultan Road, Lordswood, Kent, ME5 8TJ, Tel.: 01634 660441

Ms B Edwards, Lead District Nurse, Unit 2, Ambley Green, Bailey Drive, Gillingham, Kent, ME8 0NJ, Tel.: 01634 382888

Ms B Mead, Locality Director - Rochester, Strood, Keystone Centre, Gun Lane, Strood, Kent, ME2 4UL, Tel.: 01634 717755

Ms J Norton, Locality Director, Unit 7-8, Ambley Green, Bailey Drive, Gillingham, Kent, ME8 0NJ, Tel.: 01634 382777

Mr C Wilbur, Community Services Manager, Parkwood Health Centre, Long Catlis Road, Rainham, Kent, ME8 9PR, Tel.: 01634 234400

Ms A Winter, Rapid Response - Intermediate Care Services Manager, Unit 2, Ambley Green, Bailey Drive, Gillingham, Kent, ME8 0NJ, Tel.: 01634 382947

Health Visitors

Ms L Bailey, Lead, Health Visitor, Unit 2, Ambley Green, Bailey Drive, Gillingham, Kent, ME8 0NJ, Tel.: 01634 382888

Liaison Services

Discharge Liaison Nurse, St Barts Hospital, New Road, Rochester, Kent, ME1 1DS, Tel.: 810905

Other Services

Ms C Grainger, Clinical Lead, Unscheduled Care, Quayside House, Pembroke Rd, Chatham Maritime, Chatham, Kent, ME4 4UH also Medway Maritime Hospital, Tel.: 01634 830000

Ms H Martin, Professional Head, Integrated Working, Unit 2, Ambley Green, Bailey Drive, Gillingham, Kent, ME8 0NJ, Tel.: 01634 382888

Ms C Robson, Y.O.T./Counsellor, Family & Adolescent Centre, 67 Balfour Road, Chatham, Kent, ME4 6QX, Tel.: 01634 336251

Specialist Nursing Services

Ms D Gallagher, Hospice, Modern Matron, Wisdom Hospice, High Bank, Rochester, Kent, ME2 2NU, Tel.: 01634 830456

Ms P Haggarty, Domiciliary Team Leader, Wisdom Hospice, High Bank, Rochester, Kent, ME2 2NU, Tel.: 01634 830456

Ms C Rawson, Practice Nurse Advisors, 7-8 Ambley Green, Bailey Drive, Gillingham, Kent, ME8 0NJ, Tel.: 01634 38277

Ms M Kirk, Cardiac Rehabilitation, Unit 2, Ambley Green, Bailey Drive, Gillingham, Kent, ME8 0NJ, Tel.: 01634 382832

South East Coast Strategic Health Authority

Ms C Mould, Advisor, Continence, Unit 2, Ambley Green, Bailey Drive, Gillingham, Kent, ME8 0NJ, Tel.: 01634 382809

Ms J Manuel, Lead Nurse, Free Nursing Care, Continuing Care, Keystone Centre, Gun Lane, Strood, Kent, ME2 4UL, Tel.: 01634 295577

Ms A Mangan, Community, Specialist Nurse, Diabetic Care, Parkwood Health Centre, Long Catlis Road, Rainham, Kent, ME8 9PR, Tel.: 01634 238657

Ms S Larkin, Community, Nurse Specialist, Elderly Care, Unit 2, Ambley Green, Bailey Drive, Gillingham, Kent, ME8 0NJ, Tel.: 01634 382803

Ms W Bennett, Community Development Nurse, IV Therapy, Unit 2, Ambley Green, Bailey Drive, Gillingham, Kent, ME8 0NJ, Tel.: 01634 382805

Ms N Battle, Team, Respiratory, Unit 2, Ambley Green, Bailey Drive, Gillingham, Kent, ME8 0NJ, Tel.: 01634 382860

Ms C Parnell, Advisor, Tissue Viability, Unit 2, Ambley Green, Bailey Drive, Gillingham, Kent, ME8 0NJ, Tel.: 01634 382814

Mid Sussex Primary Care Trust

Trust Headquarters, Sheencroft House
10-12 Church Road
HAYWARDS HEATH
West Sussex, RH16 3SN
Tel.: 01444 475700
Fax.: 01444 475757

Admin & Senior Management
Mr R Hathaway, Acting Chief Executive, Mid Sussex PCT, Sheencroft House, 10-12 Church Road, Haywards Heath, West Sussex, RH16 3SN, Tel.: 01444 475700

Ms L Strong, Director of Community & Intermediate Care, Mid Sussex PCT, Sheencroft House, 10-12 Church Road, Haywards Heath, West Sussex, RH16 3SN, Tel.: 01444 475700

Child Health
Ms C Flowerdew, Children & Young Person's Services Manager (School Nurses), Mid Sussex PCT, Sheencroft House, 10-12 Church Road, Haywards Heath, West Sussex, RH16 3SN, Tel.: 01444 475700

Child Protection/Safeguarding Children
Ms G Fraher, Nurse Co-ordinator of Child & Adult Protection, Haywards Heath Health Centre, Heath Road, Haywards Heath, West Sussex, RH16 3BB, Tel.: 01444 414100

Clinical Leads (NSF)
Dr M Patel, Clinical Lead, CHD, Tel.: 01342 327555

District Nursing
Ms S Hyde, Clinical Team Leader - District Nursing, Mid Sussex PCT, Sheencroft House, 10-12 Church Road, Haywards Heath, West Sussex, RH16 3SN, Tel.: 01444 475700

Family Planning Services
Ms C Flowerdew, Children & Young Person's Services Manager, Mid Sussex PCT, Sheencroft House, 10-12 Church Road, Haywards Heath, West Sussex, RH16 3SN, Tel.: 01444 475700

Health Visitors
Ms C Flowerdew, (Health Visitors) - Children & Young Person's Services Manager, Mid Sussex PCT, Sheencroft House, 10-12 Church Road, Haywards Heath, West Sussex, RH16 3SN, Tel.: 01444 475700

Other Services
Ms C Bates, Intermediate Care Services Manager, Beechmont, The Princess Royal Hospital, Lewes Road, Haywards Heath, West Sussex, RH16 4EX, Tel.: 01444 441881

Mr K Davies, Specialist Services Manager (Funded Nursing Care, Continence), Sheencroft House, 10-12 Church Road, Haywards Heath, West Sussex, RH16 2AR, Tel.: 01444 475700

Ms D Hall, Head of Occupational Therapy, The Princess Royal Hospital, Lewes Road, Haywards Heath, West Sussex, RH16 4EX, Tel.: 01444 441881

Ms W McCarthy, Clinical Placements Facilitator, Sheencroft House, 10-12 Church Road, Haywards Heath, West Sussex, RH16 2AR, Tel.: 01444 475700

Ms D McGreevy, Health Promotion Manager, Sheencroft House, 10-12 Church Road, Haywards Heath, West Sussex, RH16 2AR, Tel.: 01444 47500

Ms C Payne, Speech & Language Therapy Services Manager, Horsham Hospital, Hurst Road, Horsham, West Sussex, RH12 2DR, Tel.: 01403 227000

Ms N Sullivan, Podiatry Services Manager, Sheencroft House, 10-12 Church Road, Haywards Heath, West Sussex, RH16 2AR, Tel.: 01444 47500

Ms A M Whent, Head of Long Term Conditions, Sheencroft House, 10-12 Church Road, Haywards Heath, West Sussex, RH16 2AR, Tel.: 01444 47500

Smoking Cessation
Ms D Balfour, Smoking Cessation & Tobacco Control Co-ordinator, Sheencroft House, 10-12 Church Road, Haywards Heath, West Sussex, RH16 3SN, Tel.: 01444 475700

Specialist Nursing Services
Ms S Brind, Clinical Team Leader - Practice Nurses, Meadows Surgery, Temple Grove, Gatehouse Lane, Burgess Hill, West Sussex, RH15 9XN, Tel.: 01444 242860

Ms L McEwan, Funded Nursing Care, Sheencroft House, 10-12 Church Road, Haywards Heath, West Sussex, RH16 3SN, Tel.: 01444 475700

Ms J Groom, Advisor, Continence, Sheencroft House, 10-12 Church Road, Haywards Heath, West Sussex, RH16 3SN, Tel.: 01444 475700

Ms S Loveridge, Nurse, Infection Control, Sheencroft House, 10-12 Church Road, Haywards Heath, West Sussex, RH16 3SN, Tel.: 01444 47500

Ms M Elliott, Clinical Specialist Falls, Osteoporosis, Sheencroft House, 10-12 Church Road, Haywards Heath, West Sussex, RH16 3SN, Tel.: 01444 475700

North Surrey Primary Care Trust

Trust Headquarters, Bournewood House
Guildford Road
CHERTSEY
Surrey
KT16 0QA
Tel.: 01932 722010
Fax.: 01932 875346

Admin & Senior Management
Ms C McGruer, Director of Nursing, Bournewood House, Guildford Road, Chertsey, Surrey, KT15 0QA, Tel.: 01932 722256

Child Health
Ms C Squire, Head of Children's Service, Chertsey Health Centre, Chertsey, Surrey, KT16 8HZ,

Child Health Records
Child Health Records, c/o Surrey Heath & Woking PCT, Goldsworth Park, Denton Way, Woking, Surrey, GU21 3LQ, Tel.: 01483 728201

Child Protection/Safeguarding Children
Ms C Robjohn, Named Nurse, Child Protection, Green Health Centre, Bond Street, Englefield Green, Surrey, TW20 0PF, Tel.: 01 784 437671

Clinical Leads (NSF)
Dr M Kanagasundaram, Clinical Lead, Prescribing,
Dr B Oberai, Clinical Lead, Clinical Governance,
Dr S Boghossian-Tighe, Clinical Lead, Cancer,
Dr J Pittard, Clinical Lead, CHD,

Community Matrons
Ms M Celinski, Community Matron, Weybourne House, St Peter's Hospital, Guildford Road, Chertsey, Surrey, Tel.: 01932 722915

Ms A Delacare, Community Matron, Weybourne House, St Peter's Hospital, Guildford Road, Chertsey, Surrey, Tel.: 01932 722915

South East Coast Strategic Health Authority

Mrs J Finney, Community Matron, Weybourne House, St Peter's Hospital, Guildford Road, Chertsey, Surrey, Tel.: 01932 722915

Ms S Perl, Community Matron, Weybourne House, St Peter's Hospital, Guildford Road, Chertsey, Surrey, Tel.: 01932 722915

Ms L Rabbidge, Community Matron, Weybourne House, St Peter's Hospital, Guildford Road, Chertsey, Surrey, Tel.: 01932 722915

Community Nursing Services

Ms C Harding, Head of Community Nursing, Ashford Clinic, 66 Stanwell Road, Ashford, TW15 3DU, Tel.: 01784 883698

District Nursing

Ms B Cornish, West Elmbridge Borough District Nurse Manager, Walton Health Centre, Rodney Road, Walton on Thames, Surrey, Tel.: 01932 414224

Ms D Potter, Spelthorne Borough District Nurse Manager, Ashford Clinic, 66 Stanwell Road, Ashford, Middlesex, TW15 3DU, Tel.: 01784 883703

Ms R Smith, Spelthorne Borough District Nurse Manager, Ashford Clinic, 66 Stanwell Road, Ashford, Middlesex, TW15 3DU, Tel.: 01784 883661

Ms C Thyer, Runnymede Borough District Nurse Manager/Lead Nurse for Adult Protection, Addlestone Health Centre, 45 Station Road, Addlestone, Surrey, KT15 2BH, Tel.: 01932 843585

Family Planning Services

Ms N Fitzgerald, Staines Health Centre, Burges Way, Knolwe Green, Staines, Middx, TW18 1XD, Tel.: 01 784 883793

Health Visitors

Health Visiting for Disabled Children, c/o Surrey heath & Woking Area PCT, Tel.: 01 483 728201

Ms L Jamison, Childrens Service Manager (Runnymede), Chertsey Health Centre, Stepgates, Chertsey, Surrey, KT16 8HZ, Tel.: 01 932 565655

Ms A Knock, Childrens Service Manager (Spelthorne), Lalenam Road, Sheppton, TW17 8EJ, Tel.: 01 784 883631

Ms J Selvey, Childrens Service Manager (West Elmbridge), Walton Health Centre, Rodney Road, Walton on Thames, Surrey, Tel.: 01 932 228999

HIV/AIDS

Ms N Fitzgerald, Ward 2, St Peter's Hospital, Tel.: 01 932 722373

Mr J Quirk, Sexual Health, Old Ward 2, St Peters Hospital, Tel.: 01 932 722373

Liaison Services

Intermediate Care Team & Community Night Nursing Service, The Ramp, St Peter's Hosp, Chertsey, Surrey, KT16 8HZ, 01 932 722537

Other Services

Mrs F Collins, Care Home Support Team, Sunbury Health Centre, Green Street, Sunbury on Thames, TW16 6RH,

Mr F Foreman, Stroke Co-ordinator, Administration, Walton Hospital, Tel.: 01 932 414189

Ms F Jones, Practice Development Facilitator, Tel.: 01 932 722010

Ms C Jordan, Practice Development Facilitator, Tel.: 01 932 722010

Ms S McMullen, Lead Nurse, Walk in Centre, Weybridge Community Hospital, Church Road, Weybridge, KT13 8DW, Tel.: 01 932 852931

Minor Injuries Unit & Treatment Centre, Walton Community Hospital, Rodney Road, Walton on Thames, KT12 3DL, Tel.: 01 932 220060

NHS Funded Health Care Team, The Mill, Abbey Mill Business Park, Eashing, Surrey, GU7 2QL, Tel.: 01 483 860038

Queen Elizabeth House, Torin Court, Englefield Green, TW20 0PJ, Tel.: 01 784 471452

Ms R Smith, Lead Nurse for Vulnerable Adults, Ashford Clinic, 66 Stanwell Road, Ashford, TW15 3DU, Tel.: 01 784 883661

Walton Community Hospital, Rodney Road, Walton on Thames, KT12 3DL, Tel.: 01 932 220060

Weybridge Community Hospital, Church Road, Weybridge, KT13 8DW, Tel.: 01 932 852931

School Nursing

Ms L Jamison, Childrens Service Manager (Runnymede), Chertsey Health Centre, Stepgates, Chertsey, Surrey, KT16 8HZ, Tel.: 01 932 565655

Ms A Knock, Childrens Service Manager (Spelthorne), Lalenam Road, Sheppton, TW17 8EJ, Tel.: 01 784 883631

Ms J Selvey, Childrens Service Manager (West Elmbridge), Walton Health Centre, Rodney Road, Walton on Thames, Surrey, Tel.: 01 932 228999

Smoking Cessation

Ms M Meredith, West Surrey Smoking Cessation Service, 60 Stoughton Road, Jarvis Centre, Guildford, Surrey, GU1 1LJ, Tel.: 01 483 532828

Specialist Nursing Services

Ms C Garner, Nurse Specialist, Continence, Old Ward 2, St Peters Hospital, Tel.: 01 932 722089

Ms S Whitmore, COPD, Hazel Ward, St Peters Hospital, Tel.: 01 932 723660

Ms T Bushell, Nurse Specialist, Diabetic Care, Old Ward 2, St Peters Hospital, Tel.: 01 932 723315

Ms R Neve, Nurse Specialist, Diabetic Care, Old Ward 2, St Peters Hospital, Tel.: 01 932 723315

Nurses, Runnymede & W Elmbridge, Macmillan, Weybridge Hospital, Tel.: 01 932 852931

Nurses, Spelthorne, Macmillan, The Princess Alice Community Nursing Team, Tel.: 01372 461804

Ms V Martin, Parkinson's Disease, Medical Directors Office, Villa 22, Tel.: 01 932 722920

Ms V Nicholls, Parkinson's Disease, Medical Directors Office, Villa 22, Tel.: 01 932 722920

Ms J Hardman, Nurse Specialist, Tissue Viability, c/o Hounslow PCT, Tel.: 020 8321 2435

Ms J Stevens, Nurse Specialist, Tissue Viability, c/o Hounslow PCT, Tel.: 020 8321 2435

North West Surrey Mental Health Partnership NHS Trust

Trust Headquarters, Abraham Cowley Unit
St Peters Hospital, Guilford Road
CHERTSEY
Surrey
KT16 0QA
Tel.: 01932 872010

Learning Disabilities

Ms K Atkinson, Service Co-ordinator, Specialist Learning Disabilities, Mayford Lodge, Guildford Road, Chertsey, KT16 0QA, Tel.: 01932 722088

Other Services

Ms C Bryan, Team Manager, Drug & Alcohol Services, Abraham Cowley Unit Windmill Team, Holloway Hill, Lyne, Chertsey, KT16 0AE, Tel.: 01932 723309

Mr R Corrie, Ward Manager, Drug & Alcohol Inpatient Services, Windmill House, Tel.: 01932 722096

Mr D Jones, Forensic Services Co-ordinator, Tel.: 01932 723188

Ms P Manley, Manager, Chrysalis Eating Disorders Services, Tel.: 01932 722681

Ms R Norman, Geesemere Day Services, Tel.: 01932 872954

Queen Victoria Hospital NHS Foundation Trust

Trust Headquarters, Holtye Road
EAST GRINSTEAD
West Sussex, RH19 3DZ
Tel.: 01342 414000

Acute Specialist Nursing Services

Ms T Simms, Nurse Specialist, Breast Care,

Ms J Kerr, Nurse Specialist, Head & Neck,

Ms K Taylor, Nurse Specialist, Infection Control,

Ms M Aylward, Nurse Specialist, Pain Management,

Ms J Oakley, Nurse Specialist, Parkinson's Disease,

South East Coast Strategic Health Authority

Admin & Senior Management
Mrs C Becher, Director of Nursing, Queen Victoria Hospital NHS Foundation Trust, Holtye Road, East Grinstead, West Sussex, RH19 3DZ, Tel.: 01342 414000
Ms L Falk, Assistant Director of Nursing,
Mr T Martin, Medical Director,
Mrs A Parke, Assistant Director of Nursing/CG,
Child Protection/Safeguarding Children
Ms C Becher, Trust Lead, Child Protection,
Ms D Yeoh, Nurse, Child Protection,
Discharge Co-ordinators
Ms L Malins, Matron, Duty,
Matrons/Modern Matrons
Ms A Parker, Modern Matron, Critical Care,
Ms L Malins, Modern Matron, Duty,
Ms T Oxley, Modern Matron, Family Health,
Ms A Sumner, Modern Matron, Surgical,

Royal Surrey County Hospital NHS Trust
Trust Headquarters, Royal Surrey County Hospital
Egerton Road
GUILDFORD
Surrey
GU2 7XX
Tel.: 01483 571122

Acute Specialist Nursing Services
Ms S Crossley, Specialist Nurse, Acute Pain, Tel.: ext 4453
Mr J Stones, Specialist Nurse, Acute Pain, Tel.: ext 4453
Ms H McKinnon, Specialist Nurse, Breast Care, Tel.: ext 6908
Ms S Merry, Specialist Nurse, Breast Care, Tel.: ext 6908
Ms P Wilgoose, Specialist Nurse, Breast Care, Tel.: 01483 406624
Ms C Johnson, Specialist Nurse, Cardiac, Tel.: ext 4526
Ms C Page, Specialist Nurse, Cardiac, Tel.: ext 4445
Ms T Quince, Specialist Nurse, Cardiac, Tel.: ext 4526
Ms A Bates, Specialist Nurse, Colorectal, Tel.: ext 4363
Ms R Maundrill, Specialist Nurse, Critical Care, Tel.: ext 2188
Ms M Maisey, Specialist Nurse, Diabetic Care, Tel.: ext 6959
Ms J Patterson, Specialist Nurse, Diabetic Care, Tel.: ext 6959
Ms D Perry, Nurse, Endoscopist, Tel.: ext 4171
Mr G Pinn, Specialist Nurse, GI, (Upper GI & HPB Cancers), Tel.: ext 6890
Ms M James, Specialist Nurse, Gynae/Oncology, Tel.: ext 4147
Ms E Toms, Specialist Nurse, Gynae/Oncology, Tel.: ext 4147
Ms W-R Mitchell, Specialist Nurse, Gynaecology, Tel.: ext 2094
Ms S Knowles, Allergy, Specialist Nurse, Immunology, Tel.: ext 6724
Ms M Ayton, Specialist Nurse, Infection Control, Tel.: 01483 464196
Ms A Walker, Specialist Nurse, Infection Control, Tel.: ext 4580
Ms P Brew, Specialist Nurse, Lung Cancer, Tel.: ext 4849
Ms J Brown, Specialist Nurse, Macmillan, Tel.: ext 4188
Ms H Holmes, Specialist Nurse, Macmillan, Tel.: ext 4188
Ms S Williams, Specialist Nurse, Macmillan, Tel.: ext 4188
Ms K Roberts, Specialist Nurse, Nutrition, Tel.: ext 6724
Ms D Tayar, Specialist Nurse, Ophthalmology, Tel.: ext 4934
Ms A Blake, Specialist Nurse, Orthopaedics, - Trauma, Tel.: ext 6940
Ms J Kaye, Specialist Nurse, Parkinson's Disease, Tel.: 01483 406727
Ms C Long, Specialist Nurse, Psychiatric, Tel.: 01483 464154
Ms A Miers, Specialist Nurse, Respiratory, Tel.: ext 4677
Ms M Briggs, Specialist Nurse, Resuscitation Training, Tel.: ext 4938
Ms J Evans, Specialist Nurse, Rheumatology, Tel.: 01483 464159
Ms S Caffarey, Specialist Nurse, Stoma Care, Tel.: ext 4363
Ms A Lovegrove, Specialist Nurse, Stoma Care, Tel.: ext 4363
Ms R McCaulisse, Specialist Nurse, Stoma Care, Tel.: ext 4363
Ms J McCormack, Specialist Nurse, Stroke Care, Tel.: ext 4893
Ms C Johnson, Specialist Nurse, Thrombolysis, Tel.: ext 4526
Ms S Briggs, Specialist Nurse, Tissue Viability, Tel.: ext 2040
Ms R Peers, Specialist Nurse, Transfusion, Tel.: ext 4482

Ms K Ewington, Specialist Nurse, Urology, Tel.: ext 4540
Ms D Higgins, Specialist Nurse, Urology, Brachytherapy, ext 2058
Ms S Langley, Specialist Nurse, Urology, Tel.: ext 4540
Ms B Lindsey, Specialist Nurse, Urology, Tel.: ext 4540
Ms M Pietrasik, Specialist Nurse, Urology, Tel.: ext 4540
Ms C Saunders, Specialist Nurse, Urology, Tel.: ext 4540
Ms Y Dawes, Specialist Nurse, Viral Hepatitis, Tel.: 01483 406873
Child Health
Ms V Rimmer, Paediatric, Nurse, Epilepsy, Tel.: ext 4635
Child Protection/Safeguarding Children
Ms J Hughes, Midwifery, Named Nurse, Child Protection, Royal Surrey County Hospital, Tel.: 01483 571122
Ms J James, Named Nurse, Child Protection, - Paediatrics, Royal Surrey County Hospital, Tel.: 01483 571122 ext 2043
Community Midwifery
Emergencies, Royal Surrey County Hospital, Tel.: bleep 0125
Emergencies - Delivery Suite, Royal Surrey County Hospital, Tel.: 01483 464133
Ms J Hughes, Head of Midwifery, Maternity Office, Level G, Royal Surrey County Hospital, Tel.: 01483 406725
Health Visitors
Ms R Culley, Liaison, Health Visitor, Tel.: ext 4911
Liaison Services
Ms D Gauntlett, Community, Liaison Nurse, Tel.: ext 4058
Ms J Harber, Community, Liaison Nurse, Tel.: ext 4058
Ms J Perkins, Community, Liaison Nurse, Tel.: ext 4058
Ms J Rosen, Community, Liaison Nurse, Tel.: ext 4058

Royal West Sussex NHS Trust
Trust Headquarters, St Richard's Hospital
Spitalfield Lane
CHICHESTER
West Sussex
PO19 6SE
Tel.: 01243 788122
Fax.: 01243 531269

Acute Specialist Nursing Services
Ms J Boxall, Hospital Macmillan, Nurse Specialist, Tel.: ext 2819 bleep 263
Ms M McCormick, Senior Clinical Nurse, A&E, Tel.: ext 3433 bleep 190
Ms E Thomas, Macmillan, Clinical Nurse Specialist, Breast Care, Tel.: ext 3310 bleep 167
Ms S White, Lead Macmillan, Clinical Nurse Specialist, Breast Care, Tel.: ext 3310 bleep 185
Mr T Hutson, Lead Nurse Manager, Cancer, - Palliative Care, Tel.: ext 2813/2508
Ms S Thornett, Acting Lead Cancer Nurse, Nurse Specialist, Cancer, Tel.: ext 2764 bleep 254
Ms S Moore, Research Nurse, Cardiac, Tel.: ext 5123
Ms L Beagley, British Heart Foundation, Nurse Specialist, Cardiac Rehabilitation, Tel.: ext 5124
Ms D Keeping, British Heart Foundation, Nurse Specialist, Cardiac Rehabilitation, Tel.: ext 5124
Ms J Day, Specialist Nurse, Colorectal, Tel.: ext 5235 bleep 346
Ms S Zanato-Robertson, Nurse Specialist, Dermatology, Tel.: ext 5384
Ms L Avery, Nurse Consultant, Diabetes, Tel.: ext 3743
Ms S Homeyard, Nurse Specialist, Diabetes, - Paediatrics, Tel.: ext 3748
Ms S Moore, Nurse Specialist, Diabetes, Tel.: ext 3744
Ms A Tier, Nurse Specialist, Diabetes, Tel.: ext 3749 bleep 049
Ms M Wilson, Nurse Specialist, Diabetes, Tel.: ext 3746
Ms S Rigby, Nurse Advisor, Gynae/Oncology, Tel.: ext 2969
Ms V Griffiths, Clinical Nurse Specialist, Haematology, ext 3597 bleep 054
Ms M Foster, Nurse, Heart Failure, Tel.: ext 5103 bleep 268

South East Coast Strategic Health Authority

Ms S Grant, Nurse, Infection Control, Tel.: ext 3674
Ms H Richards, Nurse Specialist, Infection Control, Tel.: ext 3674 bleep 067
Ms S Best, Clinical Nurse Specialist, Maxillofacial, Tel.: ext 3359 bleep 365
Ms M McIntyre, Lead Nurse, Medicine, Tel.: ext 5110 bleep 051
Ms K Fretter, Lead Nurse, Orthopaedics, - Surgical, Tel.: ext 5248 bleep 121
Ms C Meynell, Advisor, Infant Feeding, Paediatrics, Tel.: ext 2987
Ms T Hamilton-Shairp, Clinical Nurse Specialist, Pain Management, Tel.: ext 2413 bleep 125
Ms S Franks, Nurse, Parkinson's Disease, Tel.: ext 2202
Ms N Gohl, Nurse Specialist, Respiratory, Tel.: ext 2395 bleep 369
Ms F Haas, Nurse Specialist, Respiratory, Tel.: ext 2395 bleep 369
Ms M Russell, Senior, Nurse Specialist, Respiratory, Tel.: ext 2395 bleep 179
Mr T Eade, Officer, Resuscitation, Tel.: ext 3257 bleep 053
Ms S Heron, Nurse, Stoma Care, Tel.: ext 5255 bleep 066
Ms B Reed, Nurse, Stoma Care, Tel.: ext 5255 bleep 066
Ms J Ashworth, Clinical Nurse Specialist, Tissue Viability, Tel.: ext 2765 bleep 308
Ms R O'Donnell, Nurse Specialist, Transfusion, Tel.: ext 3583 bleep 152
Ms A Denyer, Nurse Specialist, Upper GI, Tel.: ext 2764
Ms M Harris, Specialist Nurse, Urology, Tel.: ext 3143 bleep 257
Admin & Senior Management
Ms J Whitakker, Lead Nurse & Deputy General Manager CTC, Tel.: ext 2549 bleep 370
Community Midwifery
Mrs H Parker, Head of Midwifery, Maternity Unit, St Richard's Hospital, Tel.: 01243 788122 ext 2966
HIV/AIDS
Ms B Hayman, HIV Nurse Specialist/Senior Health Advisor Sexual Health, Tel.: ext 3669

Shepway Primary Care Trust

Trust Headquarters
8 Radnor Park Avenue
FOLKESTONE
CT19 5BN
Tel.: 01303 222481

Admin & Senior Management
Ms A Sutton, Chief Executive,
Child Health
Dr Y Parks, Clinical Director, Children & Families Directorate, Temple Ward, St Martin's Hospital, Littlebourne Road, Canterbury, CT1 1TD, Tel.: 01227 459371
Ms O Windibank, Community Child Team Leader, George Turle House, London Road, Canterbury, CT2 8LF, Tel.: 01227 597051
Child Health Records
Child Health Records South Kent, South Kent Hospitals NHS Trust, Child Health Admin, 1 Radnor Park Road, Folkestone, CT19 5BW, Tel.: 01303 222413
Ms R Woodward, Child Health Records Canterbury & Thanet, Ash Eton, Radnor Park West, Folkestone, CT19 5HL, Tel.: 01303 222315
Child Protection/Safeguarding Children
Ms W Everett, Named Nurse, Child Protection, Ashford Community Offices, Kings Avenue, Ashford, Kent, Tel.: 01233 204020
Clinical Leads (NSF)
Ms J Stone, Clinical Lead, Cancer,
Community Nursing Services
Mrs P Campbell, Director, Littlebourne Road, Canterbury, Ct1 1AZ, Tel.: 01227 459371
Family Planning Services
Mrs V Dodds, Manager, Folkestone Health Centre, Dover Road, Folkestone, CT20 1JY, Tel.: 01303 228849

Health Visitors
Special Needs Health Visitor, Canterbury, Mary Sheridan Centre, 43 New Dover Road, Canterbury, CT1 3AT, Tel.: 01227 766877
Ms D Special Needs Health Visitor, Thanet, Kingfisher Children's Centre, Lanthorne Road, Broadstairs, Tel.: 01843 873700
Specialist Nursing Services
Ms L Pike, Multiple Sclerosis, Westbrook Centre, 150 Canterbury Road, Margate, CT9 5DD, Tel.: 01843 255429

South Downs Health NHS Trust

Trust Headquarters, J3, Brighton General Hospital
Elm Grove
BRIGHTON
BN2 3EW
Tel.: 01273 696011

Child Health Records
Ms M Russell, Child Health Records, The School Clinic, Morley Street, Brighton, BN2 9DH, Tel.: 01273 267300
Child Protection/Safeguarding Children
Ms V Wright, Looked After Children, Clermont Unit, 251 Preston Road, Brighton, BN1 6SE, Tel.: 01273 295467
Ms P Lambert, Nurse Consultant, Child Protection, Clermont Unit, 251 Preston Road, Brighton, BN1 6SE, Tel.: 01273 295993
Community Nursing Services
Ms J Heath, Brighton General Hospital, Tel.: 01273 696011 ext 3436
Family Planning Services
Ms S Ward, Morley Street Surgery, Morley Street Clinic, Ivory Place, Brighton, BN2 2RA, Tel.: 01273 385500 ext 3839
Health Visitors
Ms E Smith, Health Visitor, Aldrington House, 35 New Church Road, Hove, BN3 4AG, Tel.: 01273 778383
HIV/AIDS
Ms A Bamford, Hazel Cottage, Warren Road, Woodingdean, BN2 6DA, Tel.: 01273 605385
School Nursing
Ms A Garmston, School Nurse, Aldrington House, 35 New Church Road, Hove, BN3 4AG, Tel.: 01273 778383
The Homeless/Travellers & Asylum Seekers
Ms N House, Morley Street Surgery, Morley Street Clinic, Ivory Place, Brighton, BN2 2RA, Tel.: 01273 385500

South West Kent Primary Care Trust

Trust Headquarters, Wharf House
Medway Wharf Road
TONBRIDGE
Kent
TN9 1RE
Tel.: 01732 375200
Fax.: 01732 362525

Admin & Senior Management
Mr S Ford, Chief Executive, Sevenoaks Hospital, Hospital Road, Sevenoaks, TN13 3PG, Tel.: 01732 470200
Child Health Records
Mrs J Corfield, Administration, Homoeopathic Hospital, 41 Church Road, Tunbridge Wells, TN1 1JN, Tel.: 01892 539144
Mrs B Packman, Computer, Homoeopathic Hospital, 41 Church Road, Tunbridge Wells, TN1 1JN, Tel.: 01892 539144
Child Protection/Safeguarding Children
Mrs S Robinson, Child Protection, Homoeopathic Hospital, 41 Church Road, Tunbridge Wells, TN1 1JN, Tel.: 01892 539144 ext 4757/8
Ms P Seabrook, Child Protection, Homoeopathic Hospital, 41 Church Road, Tunbridge Wells, TN1 1JN, Tel.: 01892 539144 ext 4757/8
Clinical Leads (NSF)
Dr P Goozee, Clinical Lead, Cancer,
Dr P Goozee, Clinical Lead, CHD,

South East Coast Strategic Health Authority

Dr V Walker, Clinical Lead, Children,
Dr M Pauling, Clinical Lead, Older People,
District Nursing
Ms B Windess, Community Services Manager, The Bungalow, Tonbridge Cottage Hospital, Vauxhall Lane, Tonbridge, TN11 0NE, Tel.: 01732 360951
Family Planning Services
Mr K Anker, Manager, Allen Gardiner Cottage, Pembury Road, Tunbridge Wells, TN2 3QQ,
Dr J Cooke, Lead for Family Planning, Sexual Health,
Health Visitors
Ms P Seabrook, Paediatric Health Visitor, Homoeopathic Hospital, 41 Church Rd, Tunbridge Wells, TN1 1JN, 01892 539144 ext 4758
Liaison Services
Ms A Stetcher, Liaison, Continuing Care, The Bungalow, Tonbridge Cottage Hospital, Tel.: 01732 360951
Ms M Marshall, Liaison, Elderly Care, The Bungalow, Tonbridge Cottage Hospital, Tel.: 01732 360951
School Nursing
Mr K Anker, Manager, School Health/Nursing Service, Allen Gardiner Cottage, Pembury Road, Tunbridge Wells, TN2 3QQ,
School Nurses, Homoeopathic Hospital, 41 Church Road, Tunbridge Wells, TN1 1JN,
Specialist Nursing Services
Ms S Ingham, Continence, Tonbridge Cottage Hospital, Tel.: 01732 368929
Ms A Carroll, Infection Control, Tonbridge Cottage Hospital, Tel.: 1732 368929
Ms R Dury, Team Co-ordinator, Rapid Response, The Bungalow, Tonbridge Cottage Hospital, Tel.: 01732 360951

Surrey & Sussex Healthcare NHS Trust

Trust Headquarters, East Surrey Hospital
Maple House, Canada Avenue
REDHILL
Surrey
RH1 5RH
Tel.: 01737 768511

Community Midwifery
Mrs S Chapman, Head of Midwifery, Maternity Unit, East Surrey Hospital, Tel.: 01737 768511 ext 6819
Discharges, Transfers, Burstow Ward, Tel.: 01737 782917
Mrs C Tweddle, Clinical Community Manager, Maternity Unit, East Surrey Hospital, Tel.: 01737 768511 ext 6819

Surrey Hampshire Borders NHS Trust

Trust Headquarters, The Ridgewood Centre
Old Bisley Road
FRIMLEY, Surrey
GU16 9QE
Tel.: 01276 692919

Learning Disabilities
Mrs S Bunyan, Clinical Director, 65 Cranley Road, Guildford, Surrey, GU1 2JW, Tel.: 01483 532767

Surrey Heath & Woking Primary Care Trust

Trust Headquarters, West Byfleet Health Centre
Madeira Road
WEST BYFLEET, KT14 6DH
Tel.: 01932 356830

Admin & Senior Management
Ms J Dale, Chief Executive,
Dr J Omany, Medical Director, Woking Hospice, Hillview Road, Woking, GU22 7HW, Tel.: 01483 881750
Ms P Rogers, Chief Nurse, Goldsworth Park Health Centre, Woking, GU21 3LQ, Tel.: 01483 728201

Child Health
Mr C Mills, Childrens Services, Goldsworth Park Health Centre, Woking, GU21 3LQ, Tel.: 01483 728201
Child Health Records
Child Health Records, Goldsworth Park Centre, Woking, GU21 3LQ, Tel.: 01483 728201
Child Protection/Safeguarding Children
Mrs J Baker, Named Nurse, Child Protection, Goldsworth Park Centre, Woking, GU21 3LQ, Tel.: 01483 728201
Ms J Banks, Designated Nurse, Child Protection, (West Surrey), Goldsworth Park Centre, Woking, GU21 3LQ, Tel.: 01483 728201
Clinical Leads (NSF)
Dr R de Ferrars, Clinical Lead, Cancer,
Dr J Omany, Clinical Lead, Cancer,
Dr N Sellers, Clinical Lead, Diabetic Care,
Dr C Dunstan, Clinical Lead, Older People,
Community Matrons
Ms K Thurlby, Manager, West Byfleet Health Centre, Madeira Road, West Byfleet, KT14 6DH, Tel.: 01932 340411
District Nursing
Mrs Y Ryan, Hospital Manager, Woking Community Hospital, Heathside Road, Woking, GU22 7HS, Tel.: 01483 715911
Ms L Titheridge, District Nurse (Woking), West Byfleet Health Centre, Madeira Road, West Byfleet, KT14 6DH, Tel.: 01932 340411
Ms M Watts, Hospice Matron, Woking Hospice, Hillview Road, Woking, Surrey, GU22 7HW, Tel.: 01483 881750
Family Planning Services
Ms L Major, Team Leader, Family Planning, Woking Community Hospital, Heathside Road, Woking, Surrey, GU22 7HS, Tel.: 01483 715911
Health Visitors
Ms C Mulligan, Health Visitor (Woking Locality), St John's Health Centre, Hermitage Road, St Johns, Woking, GU21 1TD, Tel.: 01483 764871
Ms P Szuzman, Paediatric Liaison Health Visitor, Frimley Children's Centre, 12 Church Road, Frimley, Surrey, GU16 5UJ, Tel.: 01483 782800
Liaison Services
MacMillan Nurse, Tel.: 01483 881756
Paediatric Liaison, St Peter's Hospital, Guildford Road, Chertsey, Surrey, KT16 0PZ, Tel.: 01932 872000 ext 2359
Pharmacy
Mr T Dowdall, Chief Pharmacist, Woking Community Hospital, Heathside Road, Woking, Surrey, GU22 7HS, Tel.: 01483 715911
School Nursing
Ms W Checkley, Clinical Manager, Woking Community Hospital, Heathside Road, Woking, GU22 7HS, Tel.: 01483 715911

Surrey Oaklands NHS Trust

Trust Headquarters, Oakland House
Coulsdon Road
CATERHAM
Surrey
CR3 5YA
Tel.: 01883 383838

Learning Disabilities
Croydon North Community Outreach Team, Community Learning Disability Team, Rees House, 2 Morland Road, Croydon, CR0 6NA, Tel.: 020 8239 4441
Croydon South Community Outreach Team, 48B Chipstead Valley Road, Croydon, CR5 2RA, Tel.: 020 8405 6747
Dorking & Horley, Clarendon House, 28 West Street, Dorking, RH4 1QJ, Tel.: 01306 502401
Epsom, Old Town Hall, The Parade, Epsom, KT18 5BY, Tel.: 01372 204090
Mr P Kinsey, Director of Operations, Oaklands House, Coulsdon Road, Caterham, Surrey, CR3 5YA, Tel.: 01883 383544

South East Coast Strategic Health Authority

Ms N Morritt, Team Manager, Rees House, 2 Morland Road, Croydon, CR0 6NA, Tel.: 020 8239 4427

Redhill & Reigate, Kingsfield Centre, Philanthropic Road, Redhill, RH1 4DP, Tel.: 01737 288288

Mrs P Smyth, Director of Nursing, Learning Disability Services, Oaklands House, Coulsdon Road, Caterham, Surrey, CR3 5YA, Tel.: 01883 383634

Tandridge, Bracketts Resource Centre, 116/8 Station Road East, Oxted, RH8 0QA, Tel.: 01883 382387

Sussex Downs & Weald Primary Care Trust

Trust Headquarters
36-38 Friar's Walk
LEWES, BN7 2PB
Tel.: 01273 485300

Admin & Senior Management
Ms R Diggins, Director of Operations, 36-38 Friar's Walk, Lewes, East Sussex, BH7 2PB, Tel.: 01273 485300
Ms F Henniker, Chief Executive,
Child Health Records
Ms M Askew, Crowborough, Uckfield, Heathfield,
Ms M Russell, Lewes, Newhaven, Peacehaven, School Clinic, Morley Street, Brighton,
Child Protection/Safeguarding Children
Mr K O'Sullivan, Advisor, Child Protection, Orchard House, Neville Road, Lewes, BN7 1PF, Tel.: 01273 402508
District Nursing
Ms S Bromage, Uckfield & Heathfield Locality, Services Manager, Heathfield Community Centre, Sheepsetting Lane, Heathfield, TN21 0XG, Tel.: 01435 865811
Mr D Jones, Newhaven & Peacehaven Locality, Services Manager, Newhaven Rehab Centre, Church Hill, Newhaven, BN9 9HH, Tel.: 01273 513441
Mrs E Singfield, Crowborough Locality, Services Manager, Grove House, South View Road, Crowborough, TN6 1HB, Tel.: 01892 669393 ext 6164
Ms N Walker, Lewes Locality, Services Manager, Orchard House, Neville Road, Lewes, BN7 1PF, Tel.: 01273 402508
Family Planning Services
Crowborough Hospital, Southview Road, Crowborough, East Sussex, TN6 1HB, Tel.: 01892 603105
Peacehaven, c/o Joy Monroe, Morley Street Family Planning Clinic, Brighton, Tel.: 01273 696011 ext 3839
Uckfield Community Hospital, Framfield Road, Uckfield, East Sussex, TN22 5AW, Tel.: 01825 745060
Other Services
Ms J Brown, General Manager, Newhaven Rehabilitation Centre, Church Hill, Newhaven, BN9 9HH, Tel.: 01273 513441
Ms B Darking, General Manager, Lewes Victoria Hospital, Neville Road, Lewes, BN7 1PF, Tel.: 01273 474153
Mrs F Georgiou, General Manager, Crowborough Hospital, Southview Road, Crowborough, TN6 1HB, Tel.: 01892 652284 ext 6222
Miss E Trigg, General Manager, Uckfield Community Hospital, Frownfield Road, Uckfield, East Sussex, TN22 5AW, Tel.: 01825 769999
School Nursing
Ms S Bromage, Uckfield & Heathfield Locality School Nurses, Services Manager, Heathfield Community Centre, Sheepsetting Lane, Heathfield, TN21 0XG, Tel.: 01435 865811
Mr D Jones, Newhaven & Peacehaven Locality School Nurses, Services Manager, Newhaven Rehab Centre, Church Hill, Newhaven, BN9 9HH, Tel.: 01273 513441
Mrs E Singfield, Crowborough Locality School Nurses, Services Manager, Grove House, South View Road, Crowborough, TN6 1HB, Tel.: 01892 669393 ext 6164

Ms N Walker, Lewes Locality School Nurses, Services Manager, Orchard House, Neville Road, Lewes, BN7 1PF, Tel.: 01273 402508
Smoking Cessation
Ms J Dann, Uckfield Community Hospital, Fromfield Road, Uckfield, East Sussex, TN22 5AW, Tel.: 01825 769999 ext 5145
Specialist Nursing Services
Ms J Lucy, Advisor, Continence, Bow Hill, The Drive, Hellingly, BN27 4EP, Tel.: 01323 440022 ext 3517
Lead Nurse, Public Health, Grove House, The Grove, Southview Road, Crowborough, TN6 1HB, Tel.: 01892 603123

Swale Primary Care Trust

Trust Headquarters
Kent Science Park
200 Winch Road
SITTINGBOURNE
Kent
ME9 8EF
Tel.: 01795 416800
Fax.: 01795 416801

Admin & Senior Management
Mrs S Allum, Director of Professional Development, Kent Science Park, 200 Winch Road, Sittingbourne, Kent, ME9 8EF, Tel.: 01795 416807
Ms G Sainsbury, Community Hospitals Services Manager, Sittingbourne Memorial Hospital, Bell Road, Sittingbourne, Kent, Tel.: 01795 418300
Child Health Records
Ms C Underwood, Hawthorn Road Clinic, Strood, ME2 2HU, Tel.: 01634 294654
Child Protection/Safeguarding Children
Ms C Yates, Lead for Safeguarding Children, Swale PCT, Bramblefield Clinic, Grovehurst Road, Sittingbourne, ME10 2ST, Tel.: 01795 421386
Clinical Leads (NSF)
Ms H Medlock, Clinical Lead, CHD, Cancer, Tel.: 01795 416800
Mr A Scott-Clark, Clinical Lead, Diabetic Care, Tel.: 01795 416800
Ms M Parsons, Clinical Lead, Older People, Tel.: 01795 416800
Community Matrons
Ms T Lund, Community Hospital Matron, Sheppey Community Hospital, Plover Road, Off Barton Hill Drive, Minster, ME12 3LT, Tel.: 01795 879100
District Nursing
Ms R Norman, Clinical Nurse Manager, Bramblefields Clinic, Grovehurst Road, Sittingbourne, ME10 2ST, Tel.: 01795 421386
Family Planning Services
Ms H Morton, Sexual Health Services Manager, Medway Maritime Hospital, Windmill Road, Gillingham, ME7 5NY, Tel.: 01634 833779
Health Visitors
Ms S Clark, Lead Health Visitor, Swale PCT, Bramblefield Clinic, Grovehurst Road, Sittingbourne, ME10 2ST, Tel.: 01795 421386
Other Services
Ms B Simmons, Head of Frank Lloyd Home, Tel.: 01795 420044
School Nursing
Ms S Whiting, Lead School Nurse, Residence 13, Medway Hospital, Tel.: 01634 830000
Specialist Nursing Services
Ms M Rees, Lead Practice Nurse, Swale PCT, Kent Science Park, 200 Winch Road, Sittingbourne, ME9 8EF, Tel.: 01795 416816
Ms C Mould, Service Manager, Advisory, Continence, Bramblefields Clinic, Tel.: 01795 421442
Ms A Mangan, Nurse, Diabetic Care, Parkwood Health Centre, Tel.: 01634 238657
Ms C Kendall, Liaison Nurse, Discharges, St Bart's Hospital, Rochester, Kent, Tel.: 01634 810900

South East Coast Strategic Health Authority

West Kent NHS and Social Care Trust

Trust Headquarters
35 Kings Hill
WEST MALLING
Kent
ME19 4AX
Tel.: 01732 520400

Learning Disabilities
Community Services for Dartford, Gravesham & Medway, Archery House, Bow Arrow Lane, Dartford Kent, Tel.: 01322 622219
Dartford & Gravesham Team, Archery House, Bow Arrow Lane, Dartford, DA2 6PB, Tel.: 01322 622114
Hastings Services, High Glades, Hastings, Tel.: 01424 753696
Maidstone Services, The Courtyard, Pudding Lane, Maidstone, Kent, ME14 1PA, Tel.: 01622 776300
Medway Adult Support Team, Rochester Health Centre, Delce Road, Rocester, Kent, ME1 2EL, Tel.: 01634 813738
Tonbridge Team, Baltic Road Clinic, 2 Baltic Road, Tonbridge, Kent, TN9 2NA, Tel.: 01732 356522

West Sussex Health and Social Care Trust

Trust Headquarters, Swandean
Arundel Road
WORTHING
BN13 3EP
Tel.: 01903 843000

Admin & Senior Management
Ms H Greatorex, Director of Nursing,

Learning Disabilities
Ms A Abbott, Clinical, Chichester, Services Manager, 72 Stockbridge Road, Chichester, West Sussex, PO19 2QJ, Tel.: 01243 783067
Mr K Hollister, Deputy Director, 9 College Lane, Chichester, PO19 4PQ,
Mr M Kidgell, Head of Service, Martyn Long Centre, 78 Crawley Road, Horsham, West Sussex, RH12 4HN, Tel.: 01403 225100
Mr K C Lee, Learning Disabilities, Community Nurse Manager, 1 St Georges Road, Worthing, BN11 2DS, Tel.: 01903 843350
Mr B Taylor, Head of Service, 1 St Georges Road, Worthing, BN11 2DS, Tel.: 01903 843354

Western Sussex Primary Care Trust

Trust Headquarters, Bramber Building
9 College Lane
CHICHESTER
PO19 6FX
Tel.: 01243 770770

Admin & Senior Management
Ms C Holloway, Chief Executive,
Mrs J King, Director of Community & Intermediate Care, Amberley Building, 9 College Lane, Chichester, PO19 6FX, Tel.: 01243 534030

Child Health
Ms G Cunningham, Child Community Nurse, Tel.: 01243 815227
Ms J Evans, Child Community Nurse, Tel.: 01243 815227

Child Health Records
Ms S Price, Acting, Manager, Child Health Bureau, PO Box 115, Chichester, PO19 4YT, Tel.: 01243 815337

Child Protection/Safeguarding Children
Mrs R Blackmore, Named Nurse Secondee, Child Protection, Barnfield, 9 College Lane, Chichester, Tel.: 01243 815235
Mrs J Clarke, Named Nurse Secondee, Named Nurse, Child Protection, Barnfield, 9 College Lane, Chichester, Tel.: 01243 15235
Mrs C Harrison, Acting Named Nurse, Clinical Nurse Specialist, Child Protection, Barnfield, 9 College Lane, Chichester, Tel.: 01243 15235

Clinical Leads (NSF)
Ms S Dewar, Clinical Lead, Cancer, Parklands Surgery, 4 Parklands Road, Chichester, PO19 3DT, Tel.: 01243 782819
Ms H Horswell, Clinical Lead, Cancer, Parklands Surgery, 4 Parklands Road, Chichester, PO19 3DT, Tel.: 01243 782819
Ms S Barrett, Clinical Lead, Care of the Elderly, Riverbank Medical Centre, Dodsley Lane, Easebourne, Midhurst, Tel.: 01730 812121
Dr J Bosman, Clinical Lead, CHD, 8 Copper Beach Drive, Tangmere, Chichester, PO20 2HN, Tel.: 0771 512721

Community Nursing Services
Ms S Grant, Acting Head of Community Nursing, Amberley, 9 College Lane, Chichester, Tel.: 01243 815379

District Nursing
Single Point of Referral, District Nursing Services, 9 College Lane, Chichester, Tel.: 01243 815521

Family Planning Services
Mr K Hollister, Associate Director, Facilities Management & Child & Family Services, Amberley Building, 9 College Lane, Chichester, PO19 6FX,

Health Visitors
Mrs L McEntaggart, Head of Health Visiting, Amberley, 9 College Lane, Chichester, Tel.: 01243 815279

HIV/AIDS
Ms B Dawson, Aids Health Adviser, Tel.: 01903 708661

Liaison Services
Ms G Blunden-Codd, Community/Hospital Liaison Health Visitor, St Richard's Hospital, Spitalfield Lane, Chichester, PO19 4SE, Tel.: 01243 788122 ext 5178
Mrs L McEntaggart, Head of Liaison Health Visitor Service, Amberley Building, 9 College Lane, Chichester, Tel.: 01243 815279

Pharmacy
Mr D Phizackerley, Prescribing Team Manager, Primary Care & Public Involvement, Bramber Building, 9 College Lane, Chichester, PO19 6FX,

School Nursing
Mrs L McEntaggart, School Nursing, Amberley, 9 College Lane, Chichester, Tel.: 01243 815279

Specialist Nursing Services
Ms J Broadbridge, Continence, The Lodge, St Richard's Hospital, Tel.: 01243 831525
Ms J Day, Stoma Care, St Richard's Hospital, Tel.: 01243 788122 ext 3314

Worthing & Southlands Hospitals NHS Trust

Trust Headquarters, Worthing Hospital
Lyndhurst Road
WORTHING
West Sussex
BN11 2DH
Tel.: 01903 205111

Acute Specialist Nursing Services
Mr R Williams, Health Adviser, Tel.: ext 3681
Ms I Bateman, Clinical Nurse Specialist, Acute Pain, Tel.: 4990 or 5942
Ms L Morrice, Clinical Nurse Specialist, Anaesthetics, Tel.: ext 4990
Ms E Purser, Clinical Nurse Specialist, Blood Transfusion, ext 4167
Ms L Roe, Clinical Nurse Specialist, Blood Transfusion, ext 4167
Ms B Bird, Clinical Nurse Specialist, Breast Care, Tel.: ext 5068
Ms G Felton, Clinical Nurse Specialist, Breast Care, Tel.: ext 5068
Ms J Finley, Clinical Nurse Specialist, Breast Care, Tel.: ext 5068
Ms L Phippen, Clinical Nurse Specialist, Breast Care, Tel.: ext 5247
Ms J Scott, Clinical Nurse Specialist, Cardiac, Tel.: ext 5089
Ms C Steer, Specialist Nurse, Cardiac Rehabilitation, Tel.: ext 6816
Ms C Wrapson, Specialist Nurse, Cardiac Rehabilitation, ext 6816
Ms R Mitchell, Clinical Nurse Specialist, Chronic Pain, - Acute, Tel.: ext 3734

South East Coast Strategic Health Authority

Ms L Folkes, Clinical Nurse Specialist, Dermatology, Tel.: ext 3607
Ms H Brown, Clinical Nurse Specialist, Diabetes, Tel.: ext 5044
Ms S Da Costa, Clinical Nurse Specialist, Diabetes, Tel.: ext 5096
Ms K Davies, Clinical Nurse Specialist, Diabetes, Tel.: ext 5044
Ms C Dempsey, Clinical Nurse Specialist, Diabetes, Tel.: ext 5044
Ms A McHoy, Clinical Nurse Specialist, Diabetes, Tel.: ext 5539
Ms D Wamae, Clinical Nurse Specialist, Diabetes, Tel.: ext 5044
Ms J Williams, Clinical Nurse Specialist, Diabetes, Tel.: 01903 285096
Ms J Farrow, Nurse Specialist, Epo Link, Tel.: ext 5106
Ms N Booth, Macmillan, Women & Children, Clinical Nurse Specialist, Gynae/Oncology, Tel.: ext 4350
Ms S Thompson, Clinical Nurse Specialist, Haematology, Tel.: ext 5509/5266
Ms M Morley, Clinical Nurse Specialist, Head & Neck, Tel.: ext 4235
Ms L Ashton, Clinical Nurse Specialist, Infection Control, Tel.: ext 4271
Mr B Robinson, Clinical Nurse Specialist, Infection Control, Tel.: ext 4525
Ms J Stanley, Clinical Nurse Specialist, Lung Cancer, Tel.: ext 4339
Ms L Sobrido, Clinical Nurse Specialist, Lymphoedema, Tel.: 01903 285132
Ms R Bradley, Clinical Nurse Specialist, Neurology, Tel.: ext 5534
Mr C Kershaw, Clinical Nurse Specialist, Neurology, Tel.: ext 5534
Ms K White, Clinical Nurse Specialist, Neurology, Tel.: ext 4332
Ms A Blackwell, Clinical Nurse Specialist, Older People, Tel.: ext 5651
Ms J Hughes, Research Nurse, Oncology, Tel.: ext 4192
Ms K Melville-Brown, Clinical Nurse Specialist, Paediatrics, Tel.: ext 5166
Ms C Lynch, Clinical Nurse Specialist, Palliative Care, - Cancer, Tel.: ext 4804
Ms D Peters, Clinical Nurse Specialist, Palliative Care, - Cancer, Tel.: ext 4801
Ms M Brownson, Community Nurse, Respiratory, Tel.: ext 5859
Ms S Douglas, Clinical Nurse Specialist, Respiratory, Tel.: ext 5858
Ms K Folkes, Clinical Nurse Specialist, Respiratory, Tel.: ext 5858
Ms J Hardaker, Clinical Nurse Specialist, Respiratory, Tel.: ext 5865
Ms S Wickens, Community Liaison, Clinical Nurse Specialist, Respiratory, Tel.: ext 5859
Ms D Finney, Clinical Nurse Specialist, Rheumatology, Tel.: ext 5828
Ms S Webster, Clinical Nurse Specialist, Rheumatology, Tel.: ext 4083
Ms L Burgoyne, Clinical Nurse Specialist, Sleep Studies, Tel.: ext 5801
Ms A Alidina, Clinical Nurse Specialist, Stoma Care, Tel.: ext 5776
Ms J Myer, Clinical Nurse Specialist, Stoma Care, Tel.: ext 5494
Ms S Streatfield, Clinical Nurse Specialist, Stoma Care, Tel.: ext 5494
Ms D Walters, Medicine, Clinical Nurse Specialist, TB, Tel.: ext 5566
Ms J Slade, Clinical Nurse Specialist, TBC,
Ms C Brazier, Clinical Nurse Specialist, Theatres, Tel.: ext 5616
Ms S McDonald, Clinical Nurse Specialist, Urology, Tel.: ext 5494
Ms K Penhallow, Clinical Nurse Specialist, Wound Care, Tel.: ext 5560

Admin & Senior Management
Ms D Chaffer, Director of Nursing, Worthing Hospital, Lyndhurst Road, Worthing, West Sussex, BN11 2DH, Tel.: 01903 205111 ext 5058
Ms B Thorp, Associate Director of Nursing, Worthing Hospital, Lyndhurst Road, Worthing, West Sussex, BN11 2DH, Tel.: 01903 205111 ext 5086
Child Health
Ms K Melville-Brown, Community Children, Worthing Hospital, Lyndhurst Road, Worthing, West Sussex, BN11 2DH, Tel.: 01903 205111 ext 5166
Child Health Records
Child Development Centre, Tel.: 01903 286700

Child Protection/Safeguarding Children
Ms S Cook, Child Protection, Worthing Hospital, Tel.: 01903 286739
Community Midwifery
Mrs E Nolan, Head of Midwifery, Worthing Hospital, Lyndhurst Road, Worthing, West Sussex, BN11 2DH, Tel.: 01903 205111
Family Planning Services
Ms L Swalwell, Worthing Hospital, Lyndhurst Road, Worthing, West Sussex, BN11 2DH, Tel.: 01903 843502
Learning Disabilities
Learning Disabilities, St Georges Road, Tel.: 01903 843350
Liaison Services
Ms S Wood, Liaison Services, Worthing Hospital, Tel.: 01903 708442
Matrons/Modern Matrons
Ms L Clements, Tel.: ext 5435
Ms S Gallagher, Tel.: ext 4360
Mr A Ittoo, Tel.: ext 5635
Mr N Jarrett, Tel.: ext 5888
Mr D Lawson, Tel.: ext 5898
Mr M Lindo, Tel.: ext 4071
Ms E Nolan, Tel.: ext 5145
Ms H Rogers, Tel.: ext 4360
Ms H Tipa, Tel.: ext 4512
Ms P Woodcock, Tel.: ext 4558
School Nursing
Ms B Thorp, Assoc. Director of Nursing,
Smoking Cessation
Ms A Colbourne, Smoking Cessation, Worthing Hospital, Lyndhurst Road, Worthing, West Sussex, BN11 2DH, Tel.: 01903 205111 ext 5621
The Homeless/Travellers & Asylum Seekers
Ms C Barrett, The Homeless/Travellers, Worthing Hospital, Lyndhurst Road, Worthing, West Sussex, BN11 2DH, Tel.: 01903 846548

South West Strategic Health Authority

with major towns and Primary Care Trust boundaries
Pop: 3,922,301

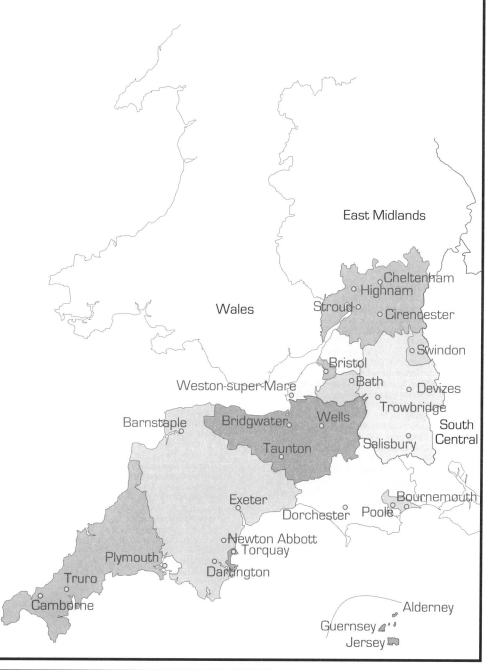

South West Strategic Health Authority

South West Strategic Health Authority

Avon & Wiltshire Mental Health Partnership NHS Trust

Trust Headquaraters, Bath NHS House
Newbridge Hill
BATH, BA1 3QE
Tel.: 01225 731731

Learning Disabilities
Mrs J Lund, Community, Nurse Manager, 1st Floor, Beaver House, 147-150 Victoria Road, Swindon, SN1 3BU, Tel.: 01793 644900
Mr M Naji, Director, Postern House, Cherry Orchard, Marlborough, SN8 4AS, Tel.: 01672 517600
Mrs H Rhodes, Team Leader, 44-46 Bedwin Street, Salisbury, Wiltshire, SP1 3UW, Tel.: 01722 410813
Ms G Ruddle, Deputy Director, Postern House, Cherry Orchard, Marlborough, SN8 4AS, Tel.: 01672 517600

Bath & North East Somerset Primary Care Trust

Trust Headquarters St Martin's Hospital
Midford Road
BATH
BA2 5RP
Tel.: 01225 831800

Admin & Senior Management
Ms D Renfrew, Director of Primary Care & Clinical Quality, St Martin's Hospital, Midford Road, Bath, BA2 5RP, Tel.: 01225 831800
Child Health
Ms S Andreson, Child Health Dept, Newbridge,
Mr M Bowden, Assistant Director, Children's Services,
Ms V Crough, Child Health Dept, Newbridge,
Ms M Lewis, Community Child Senior Nurse, Tel.: 01225 731624
Lifetime Service, Child Health Dept, Newbridge, Tel.: 01225 731624
Child Health Records
Ms J Ainley, Children's Services Manager, Bath NHS House, Child Health Dept, Newbridge Hill, Bath BA1 3QE, Tel.: 01225 731595
Child Protection/Safeguarding Children
Ms S Bailey, Advisor, Specialist Nurse, Child Protection, Bath NHS House, Child Health Dept, Newbridge Hill, Bath BA1 3QE, Tel.: 01225 731595
Clinical Leads (NSF)
Dr K Morgan, Clinical Lead, Cancer,
Ms A Thomas, Clinical Lead, CHD,
Mr M Bowden, Clinical Lead, Assistant Director, Children,
Ms A Thomas, Clinical Lead, Diabetes,
Ms C Chalmers, Clinical Lead, Assistant Director, Older People,
Community Midwifery
Ms J Griffith, Assistant Director,
Community Nursing Services
Ms J Griffith, Assistant Director,
District Nursing
Ms S Bailey, Bath City, Community Nurse Manager, Fairfield Park Health Centre, Tyning, Camden,
Ms J Griffith, Assistant Director of Primary Care Development,
Family Planning Services
Ms S Cole, Family Planning Services, St Martin's Hospital, Bath, BA2 5RP, Tel.: 01225 831593 ext 1593
Health Visitors
Ms J Griffith, Assistant Director,
Learning Disabilities
Ms D Cooper, Locality Manager, North Somerset, Tel.: 01934 418148

Mr M Hennessey, Service Manager, Westm 3rd Floor, Andil House, Court Street, Trowbridge, BA14 8BR, Tel.: 01224 760106
Mr M MacCallam, Locality Manager, Bridges Community Team, Tel.: 01225 831557
Mr G McBrian, General Manager, North & West Wiltshire County Council, County Hall, Bythesea Road, Trowbridge, BA14 8LE, Tel.: 01225 7761667
Ms A Phillips, Director,
Mr P Stevenson, Service Manager, North, 3/4 Burlands Road, Chippenham, SN15 3DF, Tel.: 01249 659197
Ms S Turner, Locality Manager, Bristol, Tel.: 0117 908 8390
Liaison Services
Ms A Morland, Manager,
Pharmacy
Ms R Grant,
Specialist Nursing Services
Ms A Boys, Lead Nurse, RNCC,
Ms S Parry, Lead Nurse, Continuing Health Care,
Ms E Whelan, Parkinson's Disease, St Martins Hospital, Tel.: 01225 831544
The Homeless/Travellers & Asylum Seekers
Mr K Morgan, Director of Public Health,

Bournemouth Primary Care Trust

Trust Headquarters, 11 Shelley Road
Boscombe
BOURNEMOUTH
BH1 4JQ
Tel.: 01202 443700

Admin & Senior Management
Ms D Fleming, Chief Executive,
Mrs A Swan, Director of Clinical Services, 11 Shelley Road, Boscombe, Bournemouth, Tel.: 01202 443726
Child Health
Ms G Wakely, Team Leader, Dorset Healthcare NHS Trust, Boscombe Clinic, 11 Shelley Road, Tel.: 01202 443035
Child Health Records
Child Health Records, Dorset Healthcare NHS Trust, 11 Shelley Road, Boscombe, Bournemouth, BH1 4JQ, Tel.: 01202 303400
Ms J Langford, Supervisor (Dorset Healthcare NHS Trust), 11 Shelley Road, Boscombe, Bournemouth, BH1 4JQ, Tel.: 01202 443142
Child Protection/Safeguarding Children
Ms M Tryska, Adviser, Child Protection, 11 Shelley Road, Tel.: 01202 443151
Ms J Waddingham, Co-ordinator, Child Protection, 11 Shelley Road, Tel.: 01202 443151
Clinical Leads (NSF)
Dr S Charles, Clinical Lead, CHD & Diabetes,
Dr J Foulkes, Clinical Lead, Cancer,
Community Nursing Services
Ms A Swan, Director of Community Services, Tel.: 01202 443726
District Nursing
District Nurses, 11 Shelley Road, Boscombe, Bournemouth, BH1 4JQ, Tel.: 01202 443042
Family Planning Services
Mr C Hilder, Clinical Team Leader - Contraceptive Health Services, Poole Clinic, Shaftesbury Road, Poole, BH15 2NT, Tel.: 01202 668453
Health Visitors
Health Visitors, 11 Shelley Road, Boscombe, Bournemouth, BH1 4JQ, Tel.: 01202 443042
Liaison Services
Ms R Day, Postpoint PC01, Royal Bournemouth Hospital, Castle Lane East, Bournemouth, BH7 7DW, Tel.: 01202 704223
Mr C Harris, Liaison, Discharge Co-ordinator, Royal Bournemouth Hospital,

South West Strategic Health Authority

Ms G Hill, Postpoint PC01, Royal Bournemouth Hospital, Castle Lane East, Bournemouth, BH7 7DW, Tel.: 01202 704223

Ms L Shaw, Postpoint PC01, Royal Bournemouth Hospital, Castle Lane East, Bournemouth, BH7 7DW, Tel.: 01202 704223

Ms M Simmonds, Staff Nurse, Christchurch Hospital, Postpoint x7, Fairmile Road, Christchurch, BH23 2JX, Tel.: 01202 705369

Other Services

Ms J Ainley, Physiotherapist - Community Assessment & Rehabilitation, Royal Bournemouth Hospital, Castle Lane East, Bournemouth, BH7 7DW, Tel.: 01202 704031

Ms V Fuller, Co-ordinator, Community Assessment & Rehabilitation, Royal Bournemouth Hospital, Castle Lane East, Bournemouth, BH7 7DW, Tel.: 01202 704031

Mr C Kilgore, Community Assessment & Rehabilitation, Charge Nurse, Royal Bournemouth Hospital, Castle Lane East, Bournemouth, BH7 7DW, Tel.: 01202 704031

Ms M Lands, Community Assessment & Rehabilitation, Staff Nurse, Royal Bournemouth Hospital, Castle Lane East, Bournemouth, BH7 7DW, Tel.: 01202 704031

Ms L Porch, Senior Staff Nurse - Community Assessment & Rehabilitation, Royal Bournemouth Hospital, Castle Lane East, Bournemouth, BH7 7DW, Tel.: 01202 704031

Ms K Silcock, Senior O/T - Community Assessment & Rehabilitation, Royal Bournemouth Hospital, Castle Lane East, Bournemouth, BH7 7DW, Tel.: 01202 704031

Ms L Simpson, Office Administrator - Community Assessment & Rehabilitation, Royal Bournemouth Hospital, Castle Lane East, Bournemouth, BH7 7DW, Tel.: 01202 704031

Ms S Tanner, Office Administrator - Community Assessment & Rehabilitation, Royal Bournemouth Hospital, Castle Lane East, Bournemouth, BH7 7DW, Tel.: 01202 704031

Ms H Tully, Senior O/T - Community Assessment & Rehabilitation, Royal Bournemouth Hospital, Castle Lane East, Bournemouth, BH7 7DW, Tel.: 01202 704031

Ms S Williams, Senior O/T - Community Assessment & Rehabilitation, Royal Bournemouth Hospital, Castle Lane East, Bournemouth, BH7 7DW, Tel.: 01202 704031

Specialist Nursing Services

Mr C Delaine, Continence, 11 Shelley Road, Tel.: 01202 443111

Ms M Gray, Continence, 11 Shelley Road, Tel.: 01202 443111

Mr G Padmore, Continence, 11 Shelley Road, Tel.: 01202 443111

Ms S Gooding, Advisor, Infection Control, South & East Dorset PCT, Victoria House, Princess Road, Ferndown, Dorset, BH22 9JA, Tel.: 01202 893000 ext 692

Ms V Douglas, Nurse Advisor, Leg Ulcers, Poole PCT, Rosemary Medical Centre, Rosemary Gardens, Parkstone, Poole, Dorset, BH12 3HP, Tel.: 01202 741300

Bristol North Teaching Primary Care Trust

Trust Headquarters, King Square House
King Square
BRISTOL
BS2 8EE
Tel.: 0117 9002692

Admin & Senior Management
Mr C Born, Chief Executive,

Child Health
Mr D Binfield, Looked After Children's Nurse, King Square House, King Square, Bristol, Bs2 8EE, Tel.: 0117 9002645

Via North Bristol NHS Trust,
Mrs P Young,

Child Health Records
Over 5s, Via North Bristol NHS Trust,
Under 5s, Child Health Dept, King Square House, King Square, Bristol, BS2 8EE, Tel.: 0117 9002692

Child Protection/Safeguarding Children
Mrs J Chart, Child Protection Supervisor,

Ms J Norman, Advisor, Child Protection, King Square House, King Square, Bristol, BS2 8EE, Tel.: 0117 9002347

Clinical Leads (NSF)
Dr A Wint, Clinical Lead, Cancer,
Ms J Shepherd, Clinical Lead, CHD,
Ms C McConnell, Clinical Lead, Children,
Ms B Coleman, Clinical Lead, Diabetic Care,
Mr T Wye, Clinical Lead, Older People,

Community Nursing Services
Ms H Lockett, Head of Operations & Nursing, King Square House, King Square, Bristol, BS2 8EE, Tel.: 0117 9002299

District Nursing
Mrs J Huckle, Professional Lead District Nurses, Eastville Health Centre, East Park, Eastville, Bristol, BS5 6YA, Tel.: 0117 9026762

Mrs S Lamb, Professional Lead Practice Nursing/Treatment Room Nursing, Dr Norman & Partners, Charlotte Keel Health Centre, Seymour Road, Easton, Bristol, BS5 0VA,

Mrs T Phillips, Professional Executive Committee Nurse Member, Lawrence Weston Clinic, Ridingleaze, Lawrence Weston, Bristol, BS11 0QE, Tel.: 0117 938 0293

Mrs M Richmond, Professional Executive Committee Nurse Member, Southmead Health Centre, Ullswater Road, Southmead, Bristol, Tel.: 0117 908 4651

Family Planning Services
Via North Bristol NHS Trust,

Health Visitors
Ms J Wrench, Assistant Professional Lead Health Visitors, Avonmouth Medical Centre, Collins Road, Avonmouth, Bristol, BS11 9JJ, Tel.: 0117 9824322

Smoking Cessation
Bristol North PCT Health Promotion, Child Protection, King Square House, King Square, Bristol, BS2 8EE, Tel.: 0117 9002481

Specialist Nursing Services
Ms A Hepplewhite, Nurse, Dermatology, St George Health Centre, Bellevue Road, St George, Bristol, BS5 7PH, Tel.: 0117 9612161

Ms P Pearce, Manager, Intermediate Care, Hazelbrook, 20 Ellsworth Road, Henbury, Bristol,

Ms A Fraser, Nurse Consultant, Older People, King Square House, King Square, Bristol, BS2 8EE, Tel.: 0117 9002251

Ms B Forbes, Sickle Cell & Thalassaemia, Central Health Clinic, Tower Hill, Bristol, BS2 0JD, Tel.: 0117 9227571

The Homeless/Travellers & Asylum Seekers
Ms G Burdis, The Haven c/o Montpeliar Health Centre, Bristol, BS6 5PT,

Ms C Jesudason, The Haven c/o Montpeliar Health Centre, Bristol, BS6 5PT,

Ms S Postlethwaite, Education Lead, Bristol North PCT, King Square House, King Square, Bristol, BS2 8EE, Tel.: 0117 900 2623

Bristol South & West Primary Care Trust

Trust Headquarters, King Square House
King Square
BRISTOL
BS2 8EE

Admin & Senior Management
Ms D Evans, Chief Executive, Tel.: 0117 900 3429

Ms S Field, Director of Nursing & Professional Development, Tel.: 0117 900 2613

Child Protection/Safeguarding Children
Ms S Field, Director of Nursing & Professional Development, Tel.: 0117 900 2613

Ms J Mathers, Child Protection Nurse Manager (Designated Nurse), Tel.: 0117 900 2670

Community Midwifery
This service is covered by United Bristol Healthcare NHS Trust,

South West Strategic Health Authority

Community Nursing Services
Ms A Davies, Operational Services Manager, Tel.: 0117 963 9603
Ms S Whitehead, Operational Services Manager, 0117 963 9603
District Nursing
Ms A Davies, Operational Services Manager, Tel.: 0117 963 9603
Ms H Stanford, Professional Lead - District Nursing, Tel.: 0117 900 2201
Ms S Whitehead, Operational Services Manager, 0117 963 9603
Family Planning Services
This service covered by United Bristol Healthcare NHS Trust,
Health Visitors
Ms C Bryant, Professional Lead - Health Visiting, Tel.: 0117 900 2314
Ms A Davies, Operational Services Manager, Tel.: 0117 963 9603
Ms J Leung, Professional Lead - Health Visiting, Tel.: 0117 900 2211
Ms H Stone, Professional Lead - Health Visiting, 0117 900 2208
Ms S Whitehead, Operational Services Manager, 0117 963 9603
Specialist Nursing Services
Ms S Field, Director of Nursing & Professional Development, Tel.: 0117 900 2613

Central Cornwall Primary Care Trust

Trust Headquarters, Sedgemoor Centre
Priory Road
ST AUSTELL, Cornwall
PL25 5AS
Tel.: 01726 77777
Fax.: 01726 71777

Admin & Senior Management
Mrs L Manuell, Chief Executive, Central Cornwall PCT, Sedgemoor Centre, Priory Road, St Austell, Cornwall, PL25 5AS, Tel.: 01726 627907
Ms C Williams, Director of Operational Services, Central Cornwall PCT, Sedgemoor Centre, Priory Road, St Austell, Cornwall, PL25 5AS, Tel.: 01726 627969
Child Health
Ms J Davidson, North, Threemilestone Nursing Centre, Tel.: 01872 354329
Ms J Duff, South, Falmouth Health Centre, Tel.: 01326 434783
Child Health Records
Child Health Records, Via Royal Cornwall Hospitals NHS Trust, Truro, TR1 3LJ, Tel.: 01872 250000
Clinical Leads (NSF)
Mr P Blackwell-Smyth, Clinical Lead, Cancer,
Dr H Dalal, Clinical Lead, CHD,
Dr G Matthews, Clinical Lead, CHD,
Dr P Merrin, Clinical Lead, Diabetic Care,
Dr M Ellis, Clinical Lead, Older People,
Community Nursing Services
Ms A Coston, Rapid Assessment Team Leader (Carrick), 1st Floor, Vivian House, Newham Road, Truro, TR1 2DP, Tel.: 01872 274371
Ms A Higginson, Rapid Assessment Team Leader (Restormel), St Austell Community Hospital, Porthpean Road, St Austell, Cornwall, Tel.: 01726 67274
District Nursing
Ms J Chamberlain, Lead District Nurse, Sedgemoor Centre, Priory Road, St Austell, Cornwall, PL25 5AS, Tel.: 01726 627874
District Nurses, The Surgery, Tregony Road, Probus, TR2 4JZ, Tel.: 01726 883809
District Nurses, The Health Centre, Trevaylor Road, Falmouth, TR11 2LH, Tel.: 01326 434771
District Nurses, Chacewater Health Centre, Chacewater, Truro, TR4 8QS, Tel.: 01872 561437
District Nurses, 27 Lemon Street, Truro, TR1 2LS, Tel.: 01872 354400
District Nurses, Penryn Surgery, Saracen Way, Penryn, TR10 8HX, Tel.: 01326 436938

District Nurses, Westover/Woodland Surgeries, Western Terrace, Falmouth, TR11 2LH, Tel.: 01326 211943
District Nurses, 18 Lemon Street, Truro, TR1 2LZ, Tel.: 01872 354314
District Nurses, Narrowcliff Surgery, Narrowcliff, Newquay, TR7 1QD, Tel.: 01637 893681
District Nurses, Newquay Hospital, Newquay, Tel.: 01637 893663
District Nurses, St Eval Community Nurses Office, St Eval, Cornwall, Tel.: 01841 540919
District Nurses, St Austell Community Hospital, Porthpean Road, St Austell, PL26 6AA, Tel.: 01726 291223
District Nurses, Par Health Centre, Par, St Austell, PL24 2AJ, Tel.: 01726 813431
District Nurses, The Clay Practices, Victoria Road, Roche, St Austell, Cornwall, Tel.: 01726 891998
District Nurses, Perranporth Healthy Living Centre, Perranporth, Truro, Tel.: 01872 573878
Health Visitors
Health Visitors, Westover Surgery, Western Terrace, Falmouth, TR11 4QJ, Tel.: 01326 436661
Health Visitors, Surgery, Trescobeas Road, Falmouth, TR11 2UN, Tel.: 01326 434886
Health Visitors, Saracen Way Surgery, Penryn, TR10 8HX, Tel.: 01326 436939
Health Visitors, Falmouth Health Centre, Trevaylor Road, Falmouth, TR11 2LH, Tel.: 01326 434782
Health Visitors, Chacewater Health Centre, Truro, TR4 8QS, Tel.: 01872 560073
Health Visitors, Surgery, Tregony Road, Probus, TR2 4JZ, Tel.: 01726 883951
Health Visitors, 27 Lemon Street Surgery, Truro, TR1 2LS, Tel.: 01872 354401
Health Visitors, Community Centre for Healthy Living, Perranporth, TR6 0EY, Tel.: 01872 571212
Health Visitors, including Portscatho, Threemilestone Nursing Centre, Pengelly Way, Truro, TR3 6DD, Tel.: 01872 354326
Matrons/Modern Matrons
Ms M Albury, Community Matron, The Perranporth Surgery, Perranporth, TR6 0PS, Tel.: 01872 572255
Ms S Aris, Community Matron, The Surgery, Tregony Road, Probus, Truro, TR2 4JZ, Tel.: 01726 882745
Ms S Aris, Community Matron, The Surgery, Gerrans Hill, Portscatho, TR2 5EE, Tel.: 01872 580345
Ms B Bromley, Community Matron, Multi Disciplinary Team Office, St Austell Community Hospital, Porthpean Road, St Austell, Tel.: 01726 291132
Ms N Burgess, Community Matron (job share), The Health Centre, Trevaylor Road, Falmouth, TR11 2LH, Tel.: 01326 210090
Ms C Coombes, Community Matron (job share), The Health Centre, Trevaylor Road, Falmouth, TR11 2LH, Tel.: 01326 210090
Ms C Coombes, Community Matron, The Surgery, Bissoe Road, Carnon Downs, TR3 6JD, Tel.: 01872 863221
Ms E Cotterill, Community Matron, The Surgery, River Street, Mevagissey, PL26 6UE, Tel.: 01726 843701
Ms T Hind, Community Matron, The Surgery, Penarth Road, St Agnes, TR5 0TN, Tel.: 01872 553881
Ms E James, Community Matron, The Penryn Surgery, Saracen Way, Penryn, TR10 8HX, Tel.: 01326 372502
Ms S Jockusch, Community Matron, Narrowcliff Surgery, Narrowcliff, Newquay, TR7 2QF, Tel.: 01637 873363
Ms H Lyndon, Lead Community Matron, Tel.: 07919 891065
Ms M Prior, Community Matron, The Surgery, Parka Road, St Columb Road, TR9 6PG, Tel.: 01726 860236/880359
Ms M Rowe, Community Matron, Park Medical Centre, 19 Bridge Road, St Austell, PL25 5HE, Tel.: 01726 73042
Ms J Spriggs, Community Matron, Trescobeas Surgery, Trescobeas Road, Falmouth, TR11 4UN, Tel.: 01326 315615

South West Strategic Health Authority

Cheltenham & Tewkesbury Primary Care Trust

Trust Headquarters, Unit 43, Central Way
Arle Road,
CHELTENHAM
Gloucestershire, GL51 8LX
Tel.: 01242 548800

Child Protection/Safeguarding Children
Mrs C Branagh, Acting Named Nurse,
Mrs A Fenton-Jones, Child Protection Supervisor,
Clinical Leads (NSF)
Dr J Moore, Clinical Lead, CHD,
Dr S Kinder, Clinical Lead, Children,
Dr G Wilson, Clinical Lead, Diabetic Care,
Dr J Kearlsey, Clinical Lead, Older People,
Community Nursing Services
Mrs V Wilcox, Assistant Director/Lead Nurse, Unit 43 Central Way, Arle Road, Cheltenham, Gloucestershire, GL51 8LX, Tel.: 01242 548800
District Nursing
Mrs C Carrington-Green, Acting Nurse Patch Manager - Head for Children & Family Services,
Mrs J Dexter, Acting Nurse Patch Manager - Head for Adults & Older Peoples Services,
Miss J Young, Acting Nurse Patch Manager - Clinical Governance (Community Nursing),
Specialist Nursing Services
Mrs M Altham, Practice Nurse Facilitator,
Mrs J Brown, Specialist Nurse, OOHs,
Mrs L Lowe, Health Care Advisor, Continuing Care,
Mrs K Elliott, Heart Disease Nurse, Coronary Care,
Mrs K Ullyart, Parkinson's Disease,

Cornwall Partnership NHS Trust

Trust Headquarters
Porthpean Road
ST AUSTELL, Cornwall
PL26 6AD
Tel.: 01726 291000

Learning Disabilities
Dr T McClatchey, Director of Services & Modernisation, 'Chy Govenek' Threemilestone Industrial Estate, Threemilestone, Truro, Cornwall, TR4 9LD, Tel.: 01872 358731

Cotswold & Vale Primary Care Trust

Trust Headquarters, Corrinium House
Cirencester Hospital, Tetbury Road
CIRENCESTER
GL7 1UX
Tel.: 01285 884694

Admin & Senior Management
Mr B Cope, Deputy Director, Nursing, Sandpits Clinic, Dursley, Gloucester, GL11 5QF, Tel.: 01453 549940
Mr R James, Chief Executive,
Ms M Stubbs, Director of Nursing, Sandpits Clinic, Dursley, Gloucester, GL11 5QF, Tel.: 01453 549940
Child Health
Ms A Melton, Sandpits Clinic, Dursley, Gloucestershire, GL11 5QF, Tel.: 01453 549940
Child Health Records
Ms C Bodkin, Health Centre, Rikenal, Gloucester, GL1 1LY, Tel.: 1452 5891015
Child Protection/Safeguarding Children
Ms V Livesey, Child Protection, 13 Park Road, Gloucester, GL1 1LY, Tel.: 01452 529781

Clinical Leads (NSF)
Dr S Cole, Clinical Lead, Cancer,
Dr C Morton, Clinical Lead, CHD,
Dr L West, Clinical Lead, Diabetic Care,
Dr C Nicholls, Clinical Lead, Older People,
Community Midwifery
Ms D Harison, Midwifery Manager, Stroud Maternity Hospital, Field Road, Stroud, Gloucestershire, GL5 2JB, Tel.: 01453 562150
Mrs M Poole, Head of Midwifery, Stroud Maternity Hospital, Field Road, Stroud, Gloucestershire, GL5 2JB, Tel.: 01453 562140
Community Nursing Services
Ms A Fletcher, Community Services Manager, Community Health Centre, Tetbury Road, Cirencester, GL7 1UY, Tel.: 01285 884666
Ms F Law, Community Services Manager, Beeches Green Health Centre, Stroud, GL5 4BH, Tel.: 01453 766331
District Nursing
Ms A Fletcher, Community Services Manager, Community Health Centre, Tetbury Road, Cirencester, GL7 1UY, Tel.: 01285 884666
Ms F Law, Community Services Manager, Beeches Green Health Centre, Stroud, GL5 4BH, Tel.: 01453 766331
Family Planning Services
GUM/Family Planning, Cheltenham General Hospital, Sandford Road, Cheltenham, GL53 7AN,
Ms D Harvey, Manager, Gloucester Royal Hospital, Great Western Road, Gloucester, Tel.: 08454 222222
HIV/AIDS
Mr M Bunting, County HIV Care Co-ordinator, Tel.: 01242 274285/01452 311744
Liaison Services
Ms R Sutters, District Nursing, Gloucester Acute Hospitals Trust, Tel.: 08454 222222
School Nursing
Ms C Barnes, Community Services Manager, School Health/Nursing Service, 13 Park Road, Gloucester, GL1 1LY, Tel.: 01452 529781
Specialist Nursing Services
Ms J Walton, Continence, Gloucestershire Hospitals NHS Trust, Tel.: 01285 884523
Ms J Lawrence, Infection Control, Gloucestershire Hospitals NHS Trust, Tel.: 08454 222222
Nurses, Cotswolds, Macmillan, Gloucestershire Hospitals NHS Trust, Tel.: 08454 222813
Nurses, Stroud Berkley Vale, Macmillan, Gloucestershire Hospitals NHS Trust, Tel.: 01452 371022
Ms S Kendall, Stoma Care, Gloucestershire Hospitals NHS Trust, Tel.: 08454 222222
Mr E Lewis, Stoma Care, Gloucestershire Hospitals NHS Trust, Tel.: 08454 222222

Devon Health & Social Care Partnership NHS Trust

Trust Headquarters, Wonford Hospital
Dryden Road
EXETER
EX2 5AF
Tel.: 01392 403433

Learning Disabilities
Mr G Baines, Locality Manager, Teignbridge, South Hams & West Devon, Lescase Building, Shinners Bridge, Dartington, Devon, Tel.: 01803 861819
Ms M Edwards, Locality Manager, Exeter & East Devon, Ashclyst Centre, Hospital Lane, Whipton, Exeter, Tel.: 01392 208356
Ms C Elliot, Locality Manager, Mid & North Devon, Newcombes CRC, Belle Parade, Crediton, EX17 2AB, Tel.: 01363 773746
Ms G Montgomery, Associate Director of Nursing, Wonford House Hospital, Dryden Road, Exeter, Tel.: 01392 208298
Mr S Newman, Head of Learning Disability Services, Trust Headquarters, Devon County Council, Tel.: 01392 383659

South West Strategic Health Authority

Dorset Healthcare NHS Trust

Trust Headquarters
11 Shelley Road
BOSCOMBE
Bournemouth
BH1 4JQ
Tel.: 01202 303400

Learning Disabilities
Miss L Bailey, Clinical, Adults - West, Nurse Specialist, The Cedars, 37 Recreation Road, Poole, BH12 2EA, Tel.: 01202 747689
Ms J Dickie, Children, Clinical Nurse Specialist, Castle Hill House, 65 Bournemouth Road, Poole, BH14 0EN, Tel.: 01202 747416
Mr J Flynn, Community Nurse, SS Dept, Jubilee Close, Jubilee Retail Park, Weymouth, DT4 7BG, Tel.: 01305 760139
Ms V Maniatt, Community Nurse, SS Dept, The Grove, Rax Lane, Bridport, DT6 3JL,
Ms P Moore, Community Nurse, SS Local Office, Bath Road, Sturminster Newton, DT10 1DR, Tel.: 01258 472652
Mrs C Pacey, Lead, Adults, Clinical Nurse Specialist, LDS, 1st Floor, Kings Park Hospital, Gloucester Road, Boscombe, Bournemouth, Dorset, BH7 6JE, Tel.: 01202 303757
Mrs M Young, LD Service (West Dorset), Clinical Nurse Specialist, Whitehouse Resource Centre, Coldharbour, Sherborne, Dorset, DT9 4HL, Tel.: 01935 816782

East Devon Primary Care Trust

Trust Headquarters, Unit 1
Exeter Airport International Business Park
EXETER
EX5 2HL
Tel.: 01392 356900

Admin & Senior Management
Mrs J Ingram, Head of Health & Social Care, Fairfield House, New Street, Honiton, EX14 1BS, Tel.: 01392 384488
Ms E Smith, Director of Nursing & HR, Unit 1 Exeter Airport International Business Park, Exeter, EX5 2HL, Tel.: 01392 207433
Child Health
Ms E Smith, Director of Nursing & HR, Unit 1 Exeter Airport International Business Park, Exeter, EX5 2HL, Tel.: 01392 356900
Ms J Winslade, Matron, Budleigh Satterton Hospital, Budleigh Satterton, EX9 6HF, Tel.: 01395 279684
Child Health Records
Mr A Pavey, Child Health Dept, Newcourt House, Old Rydon Lane, Exeter, EX2 7JU, Tel.: 01392 449823
Child Protection/Safeguarding Children
Ms M Thornberry, Named Nurse, Child Protection, Joint Agency Team, Fairfield House, New Street, Honiton, EX14 1BS, Tel.: 01392 384463
Community Midwifery
Ms E Smith, Director of Nursing & HR, Unit 1 Exeter Airport International Business Park, Exeter, EX5 2HL, Tel.: 01392 207433
District Nursing
Ms J Mitchell, Matron, Matrous Cottage, Exmouth Hospital, Claremont Grove, Exmouth, EX8 2JN, Tel.: 01395 279684
Ms E Smith, Director of Nursing & HR, Unit 1 Exeter Airport International Business Park, Exeter, EX5 2HL, Tel.: 01392 207433
Family Planning Services
Ms J Elworthy, Nurse Manager, 4 Barnfield Hill, Exeter, EX1 1SR, Tel.: 01392 276892
Pharmacy
Mr J Davey, Chief Pharmaceutical Advisor, Unit 1 Exeter Airport International Business Park, Exeter, EX5 2HL, Tel.: 01392 356900
Smoking Cessation
Ms L Palmer, Exmouth Hospital, Claremont Grove, Exmouth, EX8 2JN, Tel.: 01395 279684

East Somerset NHS Trust

Trust Headquarters, Yeovil District Hospital
Higher Kingston
YEOVIL
Somerset
BA21 4AT
Tel.: 01935 475122
Fax.: 01935 426850

Acute Specialist Nursing Services
Ms S Williams, Breast Care, Tel.: 01935 384352
Ms S Down, Diabetic Care, Tel.: 01935 384517
Ms V Smith, Haematology, Tel.: 01935 384528
Ms P Whelan, Co-ordinator, Osteoporosis, Tel.: 01935 384569
Ms A Crewes, Respiratory, Tel.: 01935 384574
Ms M Soulsby, Stoma Care, Tel.: 01935 384352
Admin & Senior Management
Miss A Moon, Director of Nursing & Clinical Governance, Yeovil District Hospital, Higher Kingston, Yeovil, Somerset, BA21 4AT, Tel.: 01935 384370
Child Health
Mr I Evans, Stroke Services, South Petherton Hospital, Hospital Lane, South Petherton, Somerset, TA13 5AR,
Ms A Hoorrocks, Viability/Vascular, Preston Road Clinic, Fiveways Roundabout, Yeovil, BA21 3AA, Tel.: 01935 423984
Ms A Stannett, Paediatric Oncology, Tel.: 01935 384558
Ms T Frost, Paediatrics, Tel.: 01935 384558
Ms J Hunt, Paediatrics, Tel.: 01935 384558
Child Protection/Safeguarding Children
Ms A Allen, Child Protection, Glenys Salisbury, Preston Road Clinic, Yeovil, BA21 3AA, Tel.: 01935 423981
Community Midwifery
Ms M Andrews, Maternity Manager, Women's Unit, Yeovil District Hospital, Higher Kingston, Yeovil, Somerset, BA21 4AT, Tel.: 01935 384442
Liaison Services
Mrs J Ingram, Health & Social Care Team, Level 4, Yeovil District Hospital, Higher Kingston, Yeovil, Somerset, BA21 4AT, Tel.: 01935 413119
Other Services
Miss C Lawson, Stroke Services, Yeovil District Hospital, Tel.: 01935 384826

Exeter Primary Care Trust

Trust Headquarters, Dean Clarke House
Southernhay East
EXETER
EX1 1PQ
Tel.: 01392 207522

Admin & Senior Management
Ms T Reeves, Director of Clinical Leadership & Quality, Dean Clarke House, Southernhay East, Exeter, EX1 1PQ, Tel.: 01392 687102
Mrs J Smith, Chief Executive, Dean Clarke House, Southernhay East, Exeter, EX1 1PQ,
Child Health
Ms J Rose, Lead Nurse, Franklyn House, Tel.: 01392 208472
Child Health Records
Over 5s, School Health Dept, Newcourt House, Old Rydon Lane, Exeter, EX2 7JU, Tel.: 01392 449830
Mr D Price, Manager, Newcourt House, Old Rydon Lane, Exeter, EX2 7JU, Tel.: 01392 449825
Under 5s, Child Health Dept, Newcourt House, Old Rydon Lane, Exeter, EX2 7JU, Tel.: 01392 449823
Child Protection/Safeguarding Children
Ms C Mitchell, Named Nurse, Child Protection, Royal Devon & Exeter Hospital (Heavitree), Theatres Corridor, Gladstone Road, Exeter, EX1 2ED, Tel.: 01392 405212

South West Strategic Health Authority

Clinical Leads (NSF)
Dr B Leger, Clinical Lead, Cancer,
Dr H Arshi, Clinical Lead, CHD,
Dr M Ramell, Clinical Lead, Diabetic Care,
Dr D White, Clinical Lead, Older People,
District Nursing
Ms D White, District Nurse Adviser, Franklyn House, Franklyn Drive,
St Thomas, Exeter, EX2 9HS, Tel.: 01392 208426
Family Planning Services
Ms J Elworthy, Nurse Manager, Contraception Service, c/o Walk-in-Centre, Sidwell Street, Exeter,
Health Visitors
Ms S Tancock, Service Development Manager - Health Visiting,
Franklyn House, Franklyn Drive, St Thomas, Exeter, EX2 9HS, Tel.: 01392 208426
Other Services
Ms H Back, Community Hospital Matron, Arlington Centre, Hospital Lane, Exeter, EX1 3RB, Tel.: 01392 208314
Ms S Robinson, Walk-in-Centre, Sidwell Street, Exeter, Tel.: 01392 284945
Smoking Cessation
Ms C Williams, Specialist Advisor, Dean Clarke House, Tel.: 01392 207469
Specialist Nursing Services
Ms D Yarde, Continence, Franklyn House, Tel.: 01392 208465
Ms J Prytherch, Tissue Viability, Franklyn House, Tel.: 01392 208463
The Homeless/Travellers & Asylum Seekers
Ms B Lyons, Clock Tower Surgery, 9 New North Road, Exeter, EC4 4HF, Tel.: 01392 208290

Gloucestershire Hospitals NHS Foundation Trust
Trust Headquarters, 1 College Lawn
CHELTENHAM
Gloucestershire
GL53 7AG
Tel.: 01242 222222
Fax.: 01242 221214
Community Midwifery
Miss P Morgan, Head of Midwifery, Gloucestershire Royal Hospital,
Great Western Road, Gloucester, GL1 3NN, Tel.: 01452 395528
Mrs V Mortimore, Head of Midwifery, St Pauls Wing, Cheltenham
General Hospital, Sandford Road, Cheltenham, Gloucestershire,
GL53 7AN, Tel.: 08454 222222 ext 2380
Ms J Richards, Clinical/Community Manager, Cheltenham General
Hospital, Sandford Road, Cheltenham, Gloucestershire, GL53 7AN,
Tel.: 08454 222222 ext 4364

Gloucestershire Partnership NHS Trust
Trust Headquarters
Rikenel, Montpellier
GLOUCESTER
GL1 1LY
Tel.: 01452 891000
Fax.: 01452 891001
Learning Disabilities
Ms M C Bater, Forest CLDT, Belle Vue Centre, Belle Vue Road,
Cinderford, Glos, GL14 2AB, Tel.: 01594 827771
Ms M Downey, Stroud CLDT, 1st Floor, Westridge, Horsemarling
Lane, Stonehouse, Glos, GL10 3HA, Tel.: 01453 827161
Ms H Johnstone, Cirencester CLDT, Chesterton Halt Resource &
Info Centre, Meadow Road, Cirencester, Glos, GL7 1YA, Tel.: 01285 648530
Mr K Keane, Cheltenham LDHQ, 1st Floor Delancey Hospital,
Charlton Lane, Cheltenham, Glos, GL53 9DU, Tel.: 01242 272184

Mr K Keane, Stroud CLDT, 1st Floor, Westridge, Horsemarling Lane,
Stonehouse, Glos, GL10 3HA, Tel.: 01453 827161
Mr K Keane, Forest CLDT, Belle Vue Centre, Belle Vue Road,
Cinderford, Glos, GL14 2AB, Tel.: 01594 827771
Mr K Keane, Cirencester CLDT, Chesterton Halt Resource & Info
Centre, Meadow Road, Cirencester, Glos, GL7 1YA, Tel.: 01285 648530
Mr K Keane, Gloucester CLDT, Acorn House, Horton Road,
Gloucester, GL1 3PX, Tel.: 01452 891363
Ms B Maxey, Gloucester CLDT, Acorn House, Horton Road,
Gloucester, GL1 3PX, Tel.: 01452 891363
Mr R Miller, Lead Nurse/Modern Matron, LDS, 1st Floor, Delancey
Hospital, Charlton Lane, Cheltenham, Glos, GL53 9DU, Tel.: 01242 272124
Mr T Quinn, Care Group Manager - Learning Disability Services, 1st
Floor, Delancey Hospital, Charlton Lane, Cheltenham, Glos, GL53
9DU, Tel.: 01242 27127
Ms S Stallard, Tewkesbury CLDT, Avon House, Green Lane
Business Park, Tewkesbury, Glos, GL20 8SJ, Tel.: 08454 223989
Ms R White, Forest CLDT, Belle Vue Centre, Belle Vue Road,
Cinderford, Glos, GL14 2AB, Tel.: 01594 827771

Kennet & North Wiltshire Primary Care Trust
Trust Headquarters, Southgate House
Pans Lane
DEVIZES
SN10 5EQ
Tel.: 01380 728899

Admin & Senior Management
Ms C Clarke, Chief Executive, Southgate House, Pans Lane,
Devizes, SN10 5EQ,
Child Health Records
Ms J Ainley, Manager, Child Health Department, Newbridge Hill,
Bath, BA1 3QE, Tel.: 01225 313640
Child Protection/Safeguarding Children
Ms K Larard, Child Protection, Melksham Community Hospital, Spa
Road, Melksham, SN12 7NZ, Tel.: 01225 701053
Clinical Leads (NSF)
Mr N Brown, Clinical Lead, Cancer, Rowden Surgery, Rowden Hill,
Chippenham, SN15 2SB,
Community Midwifery
Greenways Maternity Unit, Chippenham Community Hospital,
Rowden Hill, Chippenham, SN15 2AS, Tel.: 01249 456433
Maternity Unit, Trowbridge Community Hospital, Adcroft Street,
Trowbridge, BA14 8PH, Tel.: 01225 765840
Ms V Tinsley, Manager, Chippenham, Devizes, Malmesbury &
Trowbridge Hospitals,
District Nursing
Ms I Barker, District Nurse Lead, Southgate House, Pans Lane,
Devizes, SN10 5EQ, Tel.: 01380 733803
Equipment Loan Services
Mediquip, Redman Road, Portmarsh Industrial Estate, Calne, SN11
9PS, Tel.: 01249 815052
Family Planning Services
Ms S Elkins, Sexual Health, 51 Rowden Hill, Chippenham, SN15
2AN, Tel.: 01249 447100
Ms L Savill, Senior Health Promotion Officer, Southgate House,
Pans Lane, Devizes, Wiltshire, SN10 5EQ, Tel.: 01380 733808
Health Visitors
Ms A Batterbee, Health Visitor Manager, Rowden Surgery, Rowden
Hill, Chippenham, SN15 2SB, Tel.: 01249 448752
HIV/AIDS
Ms S Elkins, 51 Rowden Hill, Chippenham, SN15 2AN, Tel.: 01249 447100
Ms L Savill, Senior Health Promotion Officer, Southgate House,
Pans Lane, Devizes, SN10 5EQ, Tel.: 01380 733808

South West Strategic Health Authority

Learning Disabilities

Mr A Mogg, Team Leader, West Wiltshire CTPLD, Newbury House, Aintree Avenue, White Horse Business Park, Trowbridge, BA14 0XB, Tel.: 01225 760106

Mr D Proudfoot, Team Leader, Kennet CTPLD, Postern House, Cherry Orchard, Marlborough, SN8 4AS, Tel.: 01672 515637

Mr M Stewart, Team Leader, North Wiltshire CTPLD, Bewley House, Marshfield Road, Chippenham, SN15 1JW, Tel.: 01249 707900

Pharmacy

Mr J Campbell, Lead Prescribing Adviser, Southgate House, Pans Lane, Devizes, SN10 5EQ, Tel.: 01380 733787

School Nursing

Ms L Benke, School Nurse Lead,

Specialist Nursing Services

Ms J Wiscombe, Children's Continuing Care Co-ordinator, 51 Rowden Hill, Chippenham, SN15 1AJ, Tel.: 01249 456627

Mr M Ronan, Nurse Specialist, Children, Children's Disability Team, Lowbourne House, Lowbourne, Melksham, SN12 7DX, Tel.: 01225 709777

Ms J Woodman, Diabetes, Diabetic Services, The Halve Clinic, Trowbridge, BA14 8SA, Tel.: 01225 766161

Ms H Dawson, Nurse, Infection Control, Southgate House, Pans Lane, Devizes, SN10 5EQ,

Ms A Stephens, Nurse Specialist, Neurology, Chippenham Community Hospital, Rowden Hill, Chippenham, SN15 2AJ, Tel.: 01249 447100

Mrs G Wicks, Tissue Viability, Trowbridge Community Hospital, Adcroft Street, Trowbridge, BA14 8PH, Tel.: 01225 711300

Mendip Primary Care Trust

Trust Headquarters, Priory House
Priory Health Park, Glastonbury Road
WELLS, Somerset
BA5 1XL
Tel.: 01749 836500

Admin & Senior Management

Mr R Smith, Chief Executive,

Child Health Records

Child Health Records, Taunton Deane PCT, Wellspring Road, Taunton, TA2 7PQ, Tel.: 01823 333491

Child Protection/Safeguarding Children

Mrs J Parsons, Child Protection, Frome Victoria Hospital, Tel.: 01373 456637

Clinical Leads (NSF)

Dr C Absolon, Clinical Lead, Cancer,

Dr S Holmes, Clinical Lead, Diabetic Care,

Dr U Naumann, Clinical Lead, Older People,

Community Nursing Services

Mrs R Levenson, Director of Operatonal Services & AHP Lead, Mendip PCT, Priory House, Priory Health Park, Glastonbury Road, Wells, Somerset, BA5 1XL, Tel.: 01749 836542

District Nursing

Ms A Butcher, Community Service Manager (District Nursing), Mendip PCT, Priory House, Priory Health Park, Glastonbury Road, Wells, Somerset, BA5 1XL, Tel.: 01749 836500

Health Visitors

Ms D Low, Community Service Manager (Health Visiting), Mendip PCT, Priory House, Priory Health Park, Glastonbury Road, Wells, Somerset, BA5 1XL, Tel.: 01749 836500

School Nursing

Ms B Buckley, Community Services Manager, (School Health Advisors), Mendip PCT, Priory House, Priory Health Park, Glastonbury Road, Wells, Somerset, BA5 1XL, Tel.: 01749 836500

Specialist Nursing Services

Ms C Kennett, Cardiac Rehabilitation, Mendip PCT, Priory House, Priory Health Park, Glastonbury Road, Wells, Somerset, BA5 1XL, Tel.: 01749 836500

Mrs R Richardson, Continence, St Martin's Hospital, Midford Road, Bath, BA2 5RP, Tel.: 01225 831766

Mrs S Furze, Nurse Facilitator, Diabetic Care, Mendip PCT, Priory House, Priory Health Park, Glastonbury Road, Wells, Somerset, BA5 1XL, Tel.: 01749 836500

Mrs S Wise, Nurse Facilitator, Diabetic Care, Mendip PCT, Priory House, Priory Health Park, Glastonbury Road, Wells, Somerset, BA5 1XL, Tel.: 01749 836500

Ms S Jones, Liaison Nurse, Discharges, Shepton Mallet Community Hospital, Old Wells Road, Shepton Mallet, Somerset, BA4 4PG, Tel.: 01749 341121

Ms W Grey, Nurse, Infection Control, West Mendip Hospital, Old Wells Road, Glastonbury, Somerset, BA6 8JD, Tel.: 01448 836450

Ms E Ewens, Respiratory, Mendip PCT, Priory House, Priory Health Park, Glastonbury Road, Wells, Somerset, BA5 1XL, Tel.: 01749 836500

Ms C Andrews, Co-ordinator, Stroke Care, Shepton Mallet Community Hospital, Old Wells Road, Shepton Mallet, Somerset, BA4 4PG, Tel.: 01749 342931

Mid Devon Primary Care Trust

Trust Headquarters, Newcourt House
Old Rydon Lane
EXETER, EX2 7JU
Tel.: 01392 449700

Admin & Senior Management

Ms K Crompton, Director of Clinical Practice, Tel.: 01392 449829

Ms L Dunaway, Chief Executive,

Mr N McNeill, Director of Operations & HR, Newcourt House, Old Rydon Lane, Exeter, EX2 7JU, Tel.: 01392 449857

Child Health Records

Over 5s, School Health Department, Newcourt House, Old Rydon Lane, Exeter, EX2 7JU, Tel.: 01884 449830

Mr D Price, Manager, Newcourt House, Old Rydon Lane, Exeter, EX2 7JU, Tel.: 01392 449825

Under 5s, Child Health Department, Newcourt House, Old Rydon Lane, Exeter, EX2 7JU, Tel.: 01392 449823

Child Protection/Safeguarding Children

Mrs V Watkins, Child Protection, Tiverton & District Hospital, Tel.: 01884 2234708

Clinical Leads (NSF)

Ms P Anning,Clinical Lead, Cancer, Newcourt House, 01392 449700

Dr K Gillespie, Clinical Lead, CHD, Tel.: 01837 658051

Mrs J Jones, Clinical Lead, Diabetic Care, Okehampton Community Hospital, Tel.: 01837 658000

Ms R Thompson, Clinical Lead, Older People, Tiverton & District Hospital, Kennedyway, Tiverton, EX16 6AN, Tel.: 01884 235400

Community Nursing Services

Ms U Froggitt, Cullompton Health Centre, Exeter Hill, Cullompton, EX15 1EP, Tel.: 01884 33766

Other Services

Ms S Cunningham, Public Health Nursing (Health Visiting & School Nursing), Newcourt House, Old Rydon Lane, Exeter, EX2 7JU, Tel.: 01392 449790

Ms M Hamer, Discharge Co-ordinator - Elderly Care, Okehampton Community Hospital, Cavell Way, Okehampton, EX20 1PH, Tel.: 01837 658000

Mr J Hampshire, Discharge Co-ordinator - Elderly Care, Tiverton & District Hospital, William Street, Tiverton, EX16 6AN, Tel.: 01884 253251

Ms M Sutherland, Discharge Co-ordinator - Elderly Care, Crediton Hospital, Western Road, Crediton, EX17 3NH, Tel.: 01363 775588

Ms J Potter, Infection Control, RD&E Hospital Wonford, Barrack Road, Exeter, EX2 5DW, Tel.: 01392 411611

Pharmacy

Ms K Button, Advisor, Pharmaceutical, Raymond Penny House, Phoenix Lane, Tiverton, EX16 6LR, Tel.: 01884 234473

South West Strategic Health Authority

School Nursing
Ms J Rose, School Nurse Advisor, Franklyn House, Franklyn Drive, Exeter, Devon, Tel.: 01392 208472
Smoking Cessation
Ms P Temple, Advisor, Smoking Cessation, Raymond Penny House, Phoenix Lane, Tiverton, EX16 6LR, Tel.: 01884 234483
Specialist Nursing Services
Ms H O'Brien, Continence, Tiverton Clinic, Belmont Hospital, Tiverton, EX16 6QY, Tel.: 01884 253341
Ms J Jones, Diabetic Care, Okehampton Community Hospital, Cavell Way, Okehampton, EX20 1PN, Tel.: 01837 658000
Ms A Garrett, Nurse Specialist, Respiratory, RD&E Hospital Wonford, Barrack Road, Exeter, EX2 5DW, Tel.: 01392 411611

North & East Cornwall Primary Care Trust

Trust Headquarters, Lamellion Hospital
Station Road
LISKEARD, PL14 4DG
Tel.: 01579 335340

Child Health
Ms H Newson, Director of Operational Services, Liskeard Community Hospital, Clemo Road, Liskeard, PL14 3XA, Tel.: 01579 335200
Child Health Records
Community Clerk, Community Office, Liskeard Community Hospital, Clemo Road, Liskeard, PL14 3XA, Tel.: 01579 335200
Child Protection/Safeguarding Children
Ms T Davis, Clinical Manager, Liskeard Community Hospital, Clemo Road, Liskeard, PL14 3XA, Tel.: 01579 335215
Clinical Leads (NSF)
Ms L Kendall, Clinical Lead, All NSFs, Cancer,
Community Nursing Services
Ms H Newson, Director of Operational Services, Liskeard Community Hospital, Clemo Road, Liskeard, PL14 3XA, Tel.: 01579 335200
District Nursing
Ms H Newson, Director of Operational Services, Liskeard Community Hospital, Clemo Rd, Liskeard, PL14 3XA, 01579 335200

North Bristol NHS Trust

Trust Headquarters, Beckspool Road
Frenchay
BRISTOL, BS16 1JE
Tel.: 0117 970 1212

Acute Specialist Nursing Services
Ms H Cook, Paediatric Diabetes Nurse, Southmead Hospital, Bristol, Tel.: 0117 959 4945
Ms A Gunn, Paediatric Diabetes Nurse, Southmead Hospital, Bristol, Tel.: 0117 959 4945
Ms C Parsloe, Paediatric Diabetes Nurse, Southmead Hospital, Bristol, Tel.: 0117 959 4945
Child Protection/Safeguarding Children
Ms J Norman, North Bristol NHS Trust, Named Nurse, Child Protection, 1st Floor, King Square House, King Square, Bristol, BS2 8EE, Tel.: 0117 900 2347
Community Midwifery
Mrs R Fielding, Community Midwifery Manager, Midwifery Office, Southmead Hospital, Bristol, BS10 5NB, Tel.: 0117 959 5301
Ms A Remmers, Director of Midwifery, Midwifery Office, Southmead Hospital, Bristol, BS10 5NB, Tel.: 0117 959 5301
Community Nursing Services
Mr G Jones, Paediatric Community Nurse, Woodland Childrens' Unit, Southmead Hospital, Bristol, Tel.: 0117 959 5351
Discharge Co-ordinators
Ms D Porter, Head of Care Management, Trust Headquarters, Tel.: 0117 970 1212

Family Planning Services
Ms J Hughes, Head of Nursing Gynae, Fertility & Sexual Health, Southmead Hospital, Westbury-on-Trym, Bristol, 0117 959 5309
Ms T Masters, Family Planning, Nurse Consultant, Wendover, Downend Road, Downend, Bristol, Tel.: 0117 957 3206
Ms A Steele-Nicholson, Family Planning, Staff Nurse, Wendover, Downend Road, Downend, Bristol, Tel.: 0117 957 3206
Matrons/Modern Matrons
Ms H Burden, NICU, Modern Matron, Southmead Hospital, Westbury-on-Trym, Bristol, BS10 5NB, Tel.: 0117 950 5050 x5085
Ms R Fielding, Maternity, Modern Matron, Southmead Hospital, Westbury-on-Trym, Bristol, BS10 5NB, Tel.: 0117 950 5050
Ms R Jahans-Price, Plastic Surgery, Modern Matron, Frenchay Hospital, Beckspool Road, Bristol, BS16 1JE, Tel.: 0117 950 5050
Ms D McCrum, Modern Matron, C Ward, Southmead Hospital, Westbury-on-Trym, Bristol, BS10 5NB, Tel.: 0117 950 5050 x5060
Ms L Miller, Musculo-Skeletal, Modern Matron, Southmead Hospital, Westbury-on-Trym, Bristol, BS10 5NB, Tel.: 0117 950 5050 x5953
Ms S Withers, Maternity, Modern Matron, Southmead Hospital, Westbury-on-Trym, Bristol, BS10 5NB, Tel.: 0117 950 5050
Ms J Gillard, Modern Matron, Cardiology, Southmead Hospital, Westbury-on-Trym, Bristol, BS10 5NB, Tel.: 0117 950 5050 x5061
Ms J O'Neill, Modern Matron, Care of the Elderly, Frenchay Hospital, Beckspool Road, Bristol, BS16 1JE, Tel.: 0117 950 5050 x3107
Ms V McHugh, Modern Matron, Gynaecology, Cotswold Ward, Southmead Hospital, Westbury-on-Trym, Bristol, BS10 5NB, Tel.: 0117 950 5050 x5095
Ms H Nicholson, Modern Matron, Infectious Diseases, K Ward, Southmead Hospital, Westbury-on-Trym, Bristol, BS10 5NB, Tel.: 0117 950 5050 x5396
Ms J McIntyre, Modern Matron, Medicine, Southmead Hospital, Westbury-on-Trym, Bristol, BS10 5NB, Tel.: 0117 950 5050 x2389
Ms M Betts, Modern Matron, Paediatrics, Frenchay Hospital, Beckspool Road, Bristol, BS16 1JE, Tel.: 0117 950 5050
Ms F Wilkes, Modern Matron, Renal, Southmead Hospital, Westbury-on-Trym, Bristol, BS10 5NB, Tel.: 0117 950 5050
Ms V Bodkin, Modern Matron, Respiratory, G Ward, Outpatients, Southmead Hospital, Westbury-on-Trym, Bristol, BS10 5NB, Tel.: 0117 950 5062
Ms L Potter, Modern Matron, Stroke Care, Ward 1, Elgar House, Southmead Hospital, Westbury-on-Trym, Bristol, BS10 5NB, Tel.: 0117 950 5050 x5064
Ms J Vickery, Modern Matron, Surgery, Southmead Hospital, Westbury-on-Trym, Bristol, BS10 5NB, Tel.: 0117 950 5050 x2191

North Devon Primary Care Trust

Trust Headquarters
Crown Yealm House
Pathfields Business Park
SOUTH MOLTON
Devon, EX36 3LH
Tel.: 01769 575100
Fax.: 01769 573740

Admin & Senior Management
Mrs J Kelly, Chief Executive, Crown Yealm House, Pathfields Business Park, South Molton, Devon, EX36 3LH, Tel.: 01769 575100
Mrs N Kennelly, Acting Director of Operations, Crown Yealm House, Pathfields Business Park, South Molton, Devon, EX36 3LH, Tel.: 01769 575100
Mrs C Thomas, Associate Director of Professional Practice, Crown Yealm House, Pathfields Business Park, South Molton, Devon, EX36 3LH, Tel.: 01769 575100
Child Health Records
Ms A Lewis-Smith, Head of Children's Services, Crown Yealm House, Pathfields Business Park, South Molton, Devon, EX36 3LH, Tel.: 01769 575100

South West Strategic Health Authority

Child Protection/Safeguarding Children
Mrs A Allen, Child & Family Protection Advisor, Barnstaple Health Centre, Vicarage Street, Barnstaple, EX32 7BH, Tel.: 01271 371761 ext 204

Clinical Leads (NSF)
Mr M Warner, Clinical Lead, Cancer, Crown Yealm House, Pathfields Business Park, South Molton, Devon, EX36 3LH, Tel.: 01769 575100
Mr M Warner, Clinical Lead, CHD, Crown Yealm House, Pathfields Business Park, South Molton, Devon, EX36 3LH, Tel.: 01769 575100
Mr M Warner, Clinical Lead, Diabetic Care, Crown Yealm House, Pathfields Business Park, South Molton, Devon, EX36 3LH, Tel.: 01769 575100

District Nursing
Mrs C Thomas, Associate Director of Professional Practice, Crown Yealm House, Pathfields Business Park, South Molton, Devon, EX36 3LH, Tel.: 01769 575100

Family Planning Services
Ms L Bell, Barnstaple Health Centre, Vicarage Street, Barnstaple, EX32 7BH, Tel.: 01271 371761

Health Visitors
Ms A Lewis-Smith, Head of Children's Services, Crown Yealm House, Pathfields Business Park, South Molton, Devon, EX36 3LH, Tel.: 01769 575100

Learning Disabilities
Ms Y`Yvonne Lewis, Crown Yealm House, Pathfields Business Park, South Molton, Devon, EX36 3LH, Tel.: 01769 575100

Pharmacy
Mr R Croker, Head of Prescribing & Medicines Management, Crown Yealm House, Pathfields Business Park, South Molton, Devon, EX36 3LH, Tel.: 01769 575100

School Nursing
Ms A Lewis-Smith, Head of Children's Services, Crown Yealm House, Pathfields Business Park, South Molton, Devon, EX36 3LH, Tel.: 01769 575100

Specialist Nursing Services
Ms J Watson, Clinical Nurse Specialist, Cardiac Rehabilitation, 24 Castle Street, Barnstaple, Tel.: 01271 335402
Ms D Flynn, Clinical Nurse Specialist, Continence, Continence Department, Torrington Community Hospital, Torrington, North Devon, Tel.: 01805 625794
Ms J Smith, Physio Specialist, Continence, Continence Department, Torrington Community Hospital, Torrington, North Devon, Tel.: 01805 625794
Mr N Lawton, Clinical Nurse Specialist, Dermatology, Litchdon Medical Centre, Landkey Road, Barnstaple, EX32 9LL, Tel.: 01271 323443
Ms A Tithecott, Clinical Nurse Specialist, Heart Failure, Level 4, Coronary Care, North Devon District Hospital, Raleigh Park, Barnstaple, Tel.: 01271 322577
Ms C Himon, Clinical Nurse Specialist, Lymphoedema, 12 Boutport Street, Barnstaple,

North Dorset Primary Care Trust
Trust Headquarters, Forston Clinic
Charminster
DORCHESTER, DT2 9TB
Tel.: 01305 361300

Admin & Senior Management
Mr S Cole, General Manager, Community Hospitals, Forston Clinic, Tel.: 01305 361355
Ms S Hine, Professional & Clinical Services Manager, Forston Clinic, Tel.: 01305 361326
Ms B Merricks, Director of Primary Care & Community Services, Forston Clinic, Tel.: 01305 361242
Dr D Phillips, Director of Public Health, Forston Clinic, Tel.: 01305 361385
Ms J Ray, Public Health Manager, Forston Clinic, Tel.: 01305 361336

Child Protection/Safeguarding Children
Ms A Baker, Named Nurse, Child Protection, Forston Clinic, Tel.: 01305 361202

Community Nursing Services
Ms S Shead, Community Manager (Sherborne Locality), 1st Floor, Yeatman Hospital, Hospital Lane, Sherborne, Dorset, DT9 3JU, Tel.: 01305 361547
Ms D Stenner, Community Manager (North Dorset Locality), Westminster Memorial Hospital, Shaftesbury, Tel.: 01747 475275
Ms S Willgress, Community Manager (Blandford Locality), Blandford Hospital, Blandford, Tel.: 01305 361704

Family Planning Services
Ms V Latham, Manager, Contraception & Youth Advisory Services, 55 High West Street, Dorchester, DT1 1UT, Tel.: 01305 267141/269894

Other Services
Ms F Abbott-Hawkins, Manager Community Alcohol & Drug Advisory Service, 28 High West Street, Dorchester, Dorset, Tel.: 01305 265635
Ms J Kinsella, Head of Wheelchair Services, Blandford Hospital, Blandford, Tel.: 01305 361743

Pharmacy
Ms K Gough, Pharmaceutical Adviser, Forston Clinic, Tel.: 01305 361290

School Nursing
Ms C Bowyer, School Nurse Team Leader, Blandford Clinic, Blandford, Tel.: 01258 452949

Smoking Cessation
Ms L Ross, Smoking Cessation & Lifestyle Manager, Forston Clinic, Tel.: 01305 361255

Specialist Nursing Services
Ms L Woodward, Women's Health, Blandford Hospital, Milldown Road, Blandford, Dorset, DT11 7DD, Tel.: 01305 361700
Ms M Lambert, Manager/Specialist Nurse, Continence, 55 High West Street, Dorchester, DT1 1UT, Tel.: 01305 259978
Ms A Follett, Nurse Specialist, Diabetes, Forston Clinic, Charminster, Dorchester, DT2 9TB, Tel.: 01305 361291
Ms L Reed, Infection Prevention & Control, Specialist Nurse, Infection Control, Forston Clinic, Charminster, Dorchester, DT2 9TB, Tel.: 01305 361342
Ms M Rimley, Nurse Consultant, Minor injuries, Forston Clinic, Charminster, Dorchester, DT2 9TB, Tel.: 01305 361230
Ms J Smith, Nurse Specialist, Tissue Viability, Blandford Hospital, Milldown Road, Blandford, Dorset, DT11 7DD, Tel.: 01305 361704

North Somerset Primary Care Trust
Trust Headquarters, Waverley House
Old Church Road
CLEVEDON, BS21 6NN
Tel.: 01275 546770

Child Health Records
Child Health Records, King Square House, King Square, Bristol, Tel.: 0117 976 6600

Child Protection/Safeguarding Children
Ms P Richards, Named Nurse, Waverley House, Old Church Road, Clevedon, BS21 6NN, Tel.: 01275 546713

Clinical Leads (NSF)
Dr M Kammerling, Clinical Lead, CHD, Older People,
Dr M Kammerling, Clinical Lead, Cancer,
Dr M Taylor, Clinical Lead, Diabetic Care,

Community Nursing Services
Mrs G Blackshaw, Director of Nursing, Waverley House, Old Church Road, Clevedon, BS21 6NN, Tel.: 01275 546711

Family Planning Services
Ms J Korr, Teenage Pregnancy, c/o YMCA, Weston-Super-Mare, Over 21's Clinic, Weston General Hospital, Uphill, Weston-Super-Mare, Tel.: 01934 636363

South West Strategic Health Authority

Other Services
Ms K Harrington, Facilitator, Stroke Care, Worle Health Centre, High Street, Worle, Weston-super-Mare, BS22 6HB, Tel.: 01934 529523
Miss J Hudson, Allied Health Professional Lead, Waverley House, Old Church Road, Clevedon, Tel.: 01275 546715
Mr M Kammerling, Public Health, Director, Waverley House, Old Church Road, Clevedon, Tel.: 01275 546731
Smoking Cessation
Mr C Burton, Co-ordinator, Waverley House, Old Church Road, Clevedon, Bs21 6NN, Tel.: 01275 546743
Specialist Nursing Services
Ms J Towler, Free Nursing Care Lead, Waverley House, Old Church Road, Clevedon, BS21 6NN, Tel.: 01275 546712
Ms K Williams, Advisor, Continence, Weston General Hospital, Uphill, Weston-Super-Mare, Tel.: 01934 636363
Ms V Arthur, Specialist Nurse, Diabetic Care, - Paediatrics, Worle Health Centre, Weston-super-Mare, BS23 3NT, Tel.: 01934 635377/07775 778448
Ms A Barrett, Specialist Nurse, Diabetic Care, - Adults, Weston General Hosp, Uphill, Weston-super-Mare, 01934 636363 ext 3100
Ms L Davies, Lead, Tissue Viability, - Wound Care, Graham Road Surgery, 22 Graham Road, Weston-Super-Mare, Tel.: 01934 623638

Northern Devon Healthcare NHS Trust
Trust Headquarters, Northern Devon District Hospital
Raleigh Park, BARNSTAPLE
Devon, EX31 4JB
Tel.: 01271 322577

Admin & Senior Management
Ms R Brunt, Director of Nursing, Munro House, North Devon District Hospital, Raleigh Park, Barnstaple, EX31 4JB, Tel.: 01271 311603
Child Health Records
Child Health Records, Info Dept, Suite 5, Munro House, North Devon District Hospital, Tel.: 01271 311683
Community Midwifery
Mrs J Drury, Head of Midwifery, Maternity Services, North Devon District Hospital, Raleigh Park, Barnstaple, Devon, EX31 4JB, Tel.: 01271 322641
Mrs W Seddon, (ANC/Community Manager), Maternity Services, North Devon District Hospital, Raleigh Park, Barnstaple, Devon, EX31 4JB, Tel.: 01271 311589
Learning Disabilities
Mr D Jenkins, Forest Hill House, New Road, Bideford, EX39 5HB, Tel.: 01237 424330
Liaison Services
Ms A Adams, Hospital Discharge Facilitator, North Devon District Hospital, Tel.: 01271 322577

Plymouth Hospitals NHS Trust
Trust Headquarters, Derriford House
Derriford Road
PLYMOUTH
Devon
PL6 8DH
Tel.: 01752 777111
Fax.: 01752 768976

Child Health
Ms A Barker, CLIC Domic Care, Paediatric Outreach Office 3, Tel.: 01752 763457
Ms J Clarke, Child Community Team Leader, The Terraces, Mount Gould Hospital, Plymouth, PL4 7QD, Tel.: 01752 272322
Ms H McLindon, Paediatric Outreach Manager, Paediatric Outreach Office, Level 12, Derriford Hospital, Plymouth, PL6 8DH, Tel.: 01752 763477/8 or 777111
Child Health Records
Child Health Info Services, GA Building, Derriford, Plymouth, PL6 8DH, Tel.: 01752 763527

Child Protection/Safeguarding Children
Mrs C Reilly, Child Protection, Derriford House, Derriford Road, Plymouth, Devon, PL6 8DH, Tel.: 01803 866665
Community Midwifery
Emergencies, Tel.: 01752 517888
Maternity Reception, Tel.: 01752 763652
Mrs A Williams, Community Midwifery Manager, Level 5 Maternity Unit, Derriford Hospital, Plymouth, Devon, PL6 8DH, Tel.: 01752 763625
Mrs S Williams, Acting Head of Midwifery, Level 5 Maternity Unit, Derriford Hospital, Plymouth, Devon, PL6 8DH, Tel.: 01752 763655
Health Visitors
Mrs J Bassett, Health Visitor Special Needs, Tel.: 01752 550741 ext 3431
Liaison Services
Ms D Baumer, Paediatric Liaison, Paediatric Outreach Office, Level 12, Derriford Hospital, Plymouth, PL6 8DH, Tel.: 01752 763478
Ms J Brown, Paediatric Liaison, Paediatric Outreach Office, Level 12, Derriford Hospital, Plymouth, PL6 8DH, Tel.: 01752 763478
School Nursing
Mrs G Gilbert, School Nurse Special Needs, Tel.: 01752 550741 ext 3431

Plymouth Primary Care Trust
Trust Headquarters, Building One
Derriford Business Park, Brest Road
PLYMOUTH, Devon
PL6 5QZ
Tel.: 01752 315315

Admin & Senior Management
Dr P Hardy, PEC Chair, Building One, Derriford Business Park, Brest Road, Plymouth, Devon, PL6 5QZ,
Ms A James, Chief Executive, Building One, Derriford Business Park, Brest Road, Plymouth, Devon, PL6 5QZ,
Child Protection/Safeguarding Children
Mrs S Baldwin, Advisor, Child Protection, Admin Block, Mount Gould Hospital, Mount Gould Road, Plymouth, Devon, PL4 7QD, Tel.: 01752 272480
Community Nursing Services
Community Nursing Services, Cumberland Centre, Damerel Close, Plymouth, PL1 4JZ, Tel.: 01752 314616/314636
Family Planning Services
Mrs A Cope, Tel.: 01752 314632
Family Planning Service, Cumberland Centre, Tel.: 01752 314633
Learning Disabilities
Mr J Banks, Community, Services Manager, LD Services, Westbourne Scott Hospital, Beacon Park Road, Plymouth, PL2 2PQ, Tel.: 01752 314333
Liaison Services
Liaison - District Nurses Sisters, Based Derriford Hospital, Derriford, Plymouth, PL6 8DH, Tel.: 01752 792687
Specialist Nursing Services
Ms O Robertson, Continence, Cumberland Centre, Tel.: 01752 314631
Mrs L Shevlin, Co-ordinator, Macmillan, 1 Stamford Cottages, St Luke's Hospice, Stamford Road, Plymstock, PL9 9AX, Tel.: 01752 482384
Ms M Fear-Price, Tissue Viability, Cumberland Centre, Tel.: 01752 314652

Poole Hospital NHS Trust
Trust Headquarters, Poole Hospital
Longfleet Road
POOLE, Dorset
BH15 2JB
Tel.: 01202 665511
Fax.: 01202 442562

South West Strategic Health Authority

Acute Specialist Nursing Services
Ms L Green, Sister, Nurse Practitioner, A&E, Tel.: ext 2134
Ms M Chandrabose, Nurse Specialist, Anti-Coagulation, ext 8391
Ms G Gribben, Nurse Specialist, Anti-Coagulation, Tel.: ext 8391
Ms H Watkins, Practitioner, Blood Transfusion, Tel.: ext 8727
Ms T Acock, Macmillan, Nurse Specialist, Breast Care,
Ms M Pidgley, Macmillan Nurse, Breast Care, Tel.: ext 8671
Ms S Toomer, Macmillan, Nurse Specialist, Breast Care,
Ms L Everett, Senior Specialist Nurse, Cardiac Rehabilitation, Tel.: ext 2876
Ms V Tite, Senior Specialist Nurse, Cardiac Rehabilitation, ext 2876
Ms A Orchard, Nurse Specialist, Chemotherapy, Tel.: ext 2656/8319
Ms A Alexander, Nurse Specialist, Colorectal, - Oncology, ext 2968
Ms J Paisley, Nurse Co-ordinator, Colposcopy, Tel.: ext 2584/2329
Ms A McMahon, Lead Nurse, COPD,
Ms C Love, Nurse Specialist, Dermatology, Tel.: ext 8024
Mr J Abel, Nurse Specialist, Diabetes, Tel.: ext 8295
Ms D Clark, Nurse Specialist, Diabetes, Tel.: ext 8063
Ms S Klejdys, Nurse Specialist, Diabetes, Tel.: ext 8062
Ms B MacHugh, Childrens, Nurse, Diabetes, Tel.: ext 2662
Ms C McGregor, Childrens, Nurse, Diabetes, Tel.: ext 2662
Ms H Buckley, Deputy, Nurse Specialist, Gastroenterology, ext 8601
Ms S Surgenor, Nurse Specialist, Gastroenterology, Tel.: ext 8601
Ms D McBride, Macmillan, Nurse Specialist, Genetics,
Ms M Leach, Nurse Specialist, Gynae/Oncology, Tel.: ext 8261
Macmillan Nurse, Gynae/Oncology, Tel.: ext 8261
Ms S Morton, Nurse Specialist, Head & Neck, Tel.: bleep 0967
Ms H Trotman, Nurse Specialist, Head & Neck, Tel.: bleep 0967
Ms T Stoodley, Specialist Nurse, Heart Failure,
Ms L O'Shea, Nurse, Infection Control, Tel.: ext 2232
Ms G Walker, Senior Nurse, Infection Control, Tel.: ext 2232
Ms E Scott, Lecturer, Practitioner, ITU, Tel.: ext 2495
Ms L Cherrett, Nurse Specialist, Lung Care, Tel.: ext 8338
Ms J Barclay, Nurse Specialist, Lymphoedema,
Ms S Collins, Facilitator, Staff Development Med & Pharmacy Services, Medicine, Tel.: ext 2619
Ms C Chandler, Nurse Specialist, Multiple Sclerosis, Tel.: ext 2362/8824
Ms C King, Support Nurse, Multiple Sclerosis, Tel.: ext 2362
Ms C Ward, Nurse Specialist, Multiple Sclerosis, Tel.: ext 2362/8824
Ms F Cramb, Advanced, Nurse Practitioner, Neonatal, Tel.: ext 2330
Ms S Dower, Advanced, Nurse Practitioner, Neonatal, Tel.: ext 2330
Ms C Ingham, Advanced, Nurse Practitioner, Neonatal, ext 2330
Ms A Hillard, Menopausal, Nurse Specialist, Obstetrics,
Mr D Sheehy, Obstetrics, Tel.: ext 8217
Ms D Ford, Senior Nurse, Occupational Health, Tel.: ext 2035
Ms S Otter, Nurse, Occupational Health, Tel.: ext 2035
Ms C Balmer, Research, Sister, Oncology, Tel.: ext 2135
Ms A Iskender, Research Nurse, Oncology,
Ms T King, Lecturer, Practitioner, Oncology, Tel.: ext 8227
Ms J Christopher, Specialist Nurse, Osteoporosis, Tel.: ext 8658
Ms V Maiden, Educational Facilitator, Paediatrics, Tel.: ext 2238
Ms P Cameron, Pain Management,
Ms M Layzell, Nurse Specialist, Pain Management, Tel.: ext 8420
Ms E Mann, Nurse Consultant, Pain Management, Tel.: ext 2770
Mr C Algar, Macmillan, Specialist Nurse, Palliative Care, - Community, Tel.: ext 8101
Mr C Elgar, Clinical Nurse Specialist, Palliative Care, Tel.: 0788 7796784
Ms C Graham, Clinical Nurse Specialist, Palliative Care, ext 8101
Ms M Higgs, Macmillan, Specialist Nurse, Palliative Care, - Community, ext 8101
Mr C Hunt, Clinical Nurse Specialist, Palliative Care, Tel.: ext 8102
Mr A Stone, Clinical Nurse Specialist, Palliative Care, Tel.: ext 8102
Ms A Bush, Nurse Specialist, Parkinson's Disease, Tel.: ext 8012
Ms J Potter, Nurse Specialist, Parkinson's Disease, Tel.: ext 2401
Ms S Gallimore, Senior Radiographer, Radiology, Tel.: ext 2257
Ms L Clayton, Nurse Specialist, Respiratory, Tel.: ext 8336

Mr C Brown, Senior Officer, Resuscitation, Tel.: ext 8421
Ms E Kerr, Nurse Specialist, Resuscitation, Tel.: Bleep 0265
Ms J Kershaw, Nurse Specialist, Resuscitation, Tel.: ext 8421
Mr I McDougall, Officer, Resuscitation, Tel.: ext 8421
Ms T Cornell, Senior, Rheumatology, Tel.: ext 2849
Ms J Taylor, Research, Nurse Practitioner, Rheumatology,
Ms S Wright, Practitioner, Rheumatology,
Ms J Sheldon, Nurse, Stoma Care,
Ms C Snelgrove, Nurse, Stoma Care,
Ms L Stainer, Nurse Specialist, Surgery, Tel.: ext 8650
Ms H Walsgrove, Lecturer, Practitioner, Surgery, Tel.: ext 8650
Ms S Gibb, Early Pregnancy, Nurse Counsellor, Surgical, ext 8432
Ms A Graham, Nurse Specialist, Tissue Viability, Tel.: ext 2940
Ms H Currie, Neck of Femur, Nurse Practitioner, Trauma, ext 8457
Ms J Lockhart, Nurse Specialist, Trauma, Tel.: ext 8652
Ms E Rogers, Nurse Practitioner, Trauma, Tel.: ext 8457
Ms J Wilson, Trauma,
Ms J Lockhard, Lecturer, Practitioner, Trauma & Orthopaedics, Tel.: ext 8652
Ms A Moxham, Nurse Specialist, Upper GI, Tel.: ext 8739
Admin & Senior Management
Mr M Smits, Director of Nursing, Management Corridor, Poole Hospital,
Child Health
Ms P Jarvis, Associate Director of Operations for Womens & Childrens Health, Tel.: 01202 448286
Mr D Shortland, Clinical Director, Tel.: 01202 442039
Child Health Records
Ms B Peddie, Primary Care General Manager, Tel.: 01202 448651
Child Protection/Safeguarding Children
Dr J Kelsall, Child Protection, Tel.: 01202 448370
Ms K Roberts, Named Nurse, Child Protection, Poole Hospital, Longfleet Road, Poole, Dorset, BH15 2JB, Tel.: 01202 442861
Community Midwifery
Antenatal Screen Coordinator, Tel.: 01202 448608
Ms H Matthews, Bereavement Counsellor,
Mrs C Tickell, Child Protection Named Midwife, St Mary's Maternity Unit, Poole Hospital, Tel.: 01202 442190
Ms H Williams, Coordinating Supervisor of Midwives, Tel.: 01202 448577
Ms T Wise, Cranio Sacral Therapy Service, Tel.: 01202 442515
Equipment Loan Services
Mr A Mainstone, Manager, Tel.: 01202 442244
Matrons/Modern Matrons
Ms V Horn, Senior Manager for Directorate of Medicine & Elderly, Modern Matron, Poole Hospital NHS Trust, Longfleet Road, Poole, Dorset, BH15 2JB, Tel.: 01202 448692
Mr G Walker, Senior Manager for Cardiology & Medicine, Modern Matron, Poole Hospital NHS Trust, Longfleet Road, Poole, Dorset, BH15 2JB, Tel.: 01202 448757

Poole Primary Care Trust

Trust Headquarters, First Floor, Westover House
West Quay Road
POOLE, Dorset
Tel.: 01202 688880

Admin & Senior Management
Dr A Dawson, Acting Chief Executive,
Ms S Elliott, Director of Service Delivery, Parkstone Health Centre, Mansfield Road, Parkstone, Poole, Dorset, BH14 0DJ, Tel.: 01202 710234
Child Health Records
Child Health Records, 11 Shelley Road, Boscombe, Bournemouth, BH1 4JQ, Tel.: 01202 303400
Child Protection/Safeguarding Children
Mrs K Roberts, Advisor/Named Nurse, Poole PCT, 11 Shelley Road, Boscombe, Bournemouth, BH1 4JQ, Tel.: 01202 443151

South West Strategic Health Authority

Mrs M Tryska, Advisor/Named Nurse, SE Dorset PCT, 11 Shelley Road, Boscombe, Bournemouth, BH1 4JQ, Tel.: 01202 443151

Mrs G Walters, Advisor,

Clinical Leads (NSF)

Dr L Maxwell, Clinical Lead, Cancer,

Dr S Liddiard, Clinical Lead, CHD,

Dr R Benson, Clinical Lead, Diabetic Care,

Community Nursing Services

Ms S Elliott, Director of Service Delivery, Tel.: 01202 710234

District Nursing

Ms M Fox, Primary Care Matron District Nursing, Tel.: 01202 710234 Parkstone Health Centre, Tel.: 01202 711538

Ms M Willis, Primary Care Matron District Nursing, Tel.: 01202 710234

Health Visitors

Ms H Thomas, Primary Care Matron Health Visiting, 01202 710234

Ms K Vermeulen, Primary Care Matron Health Visiting, Tel.: 01202 710234

Liaison Services

Ms S Gale, Team Leader, Community Liaison, Room 37, Cornelia House, Poole Hospital, Longfleet Road, Poole, BH15 2JB, Tel.: 01202 448398

Ms M Kirkham, Team Leader, Community Liaison, Room 37, Cornelia House, Poole Hospital, Longfleet Road, Poole, BH15 2JB, Tel.: 01202 448398

School Nursing

Ms T Smith, Team Leader, School Nurse Manager, Parkstone Health Centre, Mansfield Road, Poole, Dorset, BH14 0DJ, Tel.: 01202 710234

Specialist Nursing Services

Ms S Ockenden, Palliative Care Team, Oncology, Canford Heath Clinic, Canford Heath, Poole, Tel.: 01202 602855

Royal Bournemouth & Christchurch Hospitals NHS Foundation Trust

Trust Headquarters, Royal Bournemouth Hospital
Castle Lane East
BOURNEMOUTH
Dorset, BH7 7DW
Tel.: 01202 303626
Fax.: 01202 704077

Acute Specialist Nursing Services

Ms N Vickery, Clinical Leader, Royal Bournemouth Hospital, Tel.: 01202 704773/4776

Ms D Potter, Nurse Specialist, Allergy, General Outpatients, Royal Bournemouth Hospital, Tel.: 01202 704820 bleep 2664

Ms I Batty, Nurse Practitioner, Breast Care, - Endocrine, Ward 17, Royal Bournemouth Hospital, Tel.: 01202 704676

Ms L Gifford, Macmillan, Clinical Nurse Specialist, Breast Care, Royal Bournemouth Hospital, Tel.: 01202 704524/704433

Ms T Longshaw, Nurse Practitioner, Breast Care, - Endocrine, Ward 17, Royal Bournemouth Hospital, Tel.: 01202 704676

Ms G Vipas, Macmillan, Clinical Nurse Specialist, Breast Care, Outpatients, Royal Bournemouth Hospital, Tel.: 01202 704524/704433

Ms C Weight, Macmillan, Clinical Nurse Specialist, Breast Care, Royal Bournemouth Hospital, Tel.: 01202 704524/704433

Ms N Young, Improvement Facilitator, Cancer, Royal Bournemouth Hospital, Tel.: 01202 704253

Ms G Evans, Arrhythmia, Nurse Specialist, Cardiac, Royal Bournemouth Hospital, Tel.: 01202 726154 bleep 2622

Ms A Jackson, Arrhythmia, Nurse Specialist, Cardiac, Royal Bournemouth Hospital, Tel.: 01202 726154 bleep 2616

Ms S O'Connor, Arrhythmia, Nurse Specialist, Cardiac, Royal Bournemouth Hospital, Tel.: 01202 726154 bleep 2621

Ms V Sievey, Sister, Cardiac, Royal Bournemouth Hospital, Tel.: 01202 704515

Ms E Gilder, Cardiac, Liaison Sister, Cardiac Rehabilitation, Cardiac Department, Royal Bournemouth Hospital, Tel.: 01202 704515

Ms J James, Co-ordinator, Cardiac Rehabilitation, Royal Bournemouth Hospital, Tel.: 01202 704515

Ms S Osborn, Nurse, Cardiac Rehabilitation, Royal Bournemouth Hospital, Tel.: 01202 704515

Ms D Barker, Specialist Nurse, Colorectal, Royal Bournemouth Hospital, Tel.: 01202 704611

Ms J Boot, Specialist Nurse, Colorectal, Royal Bournemouth Hospital, Tel.: 01202 704611

Ms S Pullinger, Nurse Practitioner, Colorectal, Ward 25, Royal Bournemouth Hospital, Tel.: 01202 704078

Ms S Tripcony, Nurse Practitioner, Colorectal, Ward 25, Royal Bournemouth Hospital, Tel.: 01202 704078

Ms J Paisley, Trainee Nurse, Colposcopy, HRT Specialist Nurse, Royal Bournemouth Hospital, Tel.: 01202 704672

Ms Y Thomas, Trainee Nurse, Colposcopy, HRT Specialist Nurse, Royal Bournemouth Hospital, Tel.: 01202 704672

Ms S Lester, Paediatric, Nurse Specialist, Dermatology, Christchurch Hospital, Tel.: 01202 705481

Ms J Everett, Nurse Specialist, Diabetes, Royal Bournemouth Hospital, Tel.: 01202 704888

Ms P Hamilton, In patients, Nurse Specialist, Diabetes, BDEC, Royal Bournemouth Hospital, Tel.: 01202 704061

Ms P Miles, Nurse Specialist, Diabetes, Royal Bournemouth Hospital, Tel.: 01202 704888

Ms H Nicholls, Nurse Specialist, Diabetes, Royal Bournemouth Hospital, Tel.: 01202 704888

Ms J Coleman, Sister, Fertility, Women's Health Unit, Royal Bournemouth Hospital, Tel.: 01202 704660

Ms P Wharton, Health Advisor, G.U.M, Royal Bournemouth Hospital, Tel.: 01202 704536

Ms S-A Palmer, Health Advisor, Genito Urinary, Royal Bournemouth Hospital, Tel.: 01202 704537

Ms S-A Palmer, Health Advisor, Genito Urinary, Royal Bournemouth Hospital, Tel.: 01202 704537 ext 4646

Ms A Cowling, Clinical Leader, GU Medicine, Royal Bournemouth Hospital, Tel.: 01202 704641

Ms J Brown, Nurse Specialist, Gynaecology, Women's Health Unit, Royal Bournemouth Hospital, Tel.: 01202 704938

Ms C Chapman, Specialist Nurse, Haematology, Pathology Dept, Royal Bournemouth Hospital, Tel.: 077852 80085

Ms J Campbell, Senior Nurse, Infection Control, Pathology Dept, Royal Bournemouth Hospital, Tel.: 01202 704842

Ms R Middlemass, Nurse, Infection Control, Pathology Dept, Royal Bournemouth Hospital, Tel.: 01202 704842

Ms M Munro, Nurse Specialist, Lung Care, Thoracic Dept, Royal Bournemouth Hospital, Tel.: 01202 704876/303626

Ms M O'Donoghue, Nurse Specialist, Lung Care, Thoracic Dept, Royal Bournemouth Hospital, Tel.: 01202 704876/303626

Ms H Rogers, Clinical Leader, Macmillan, Christchurch Hospital, Tel.: 01202 705237

Ms L Purandare, Clinical Nurse Specialist, Medical Oncology, Oncology Research Office, Royal Bournemouth Hospital, Tel.: 01202 726127

Mr J Devine, Nurse Practitioner, Orthopaedics, c/o Ward 8, Royal Bournemouth Hospital, Tel.: Bleep 2491

Ms C Russell, Nurse Practitioner, Orthopaedics, c/o Ward 8, Royal Bournemouth Hospital, Tel.: Bleep 2493

Ms M Trayler, Nurse Practitioner, Orthopaedics, c/o Ward 8, Royal Bournemouth Hospital, Tel.: Bleep 2443

Ms G Williamson, Nurse Practitioner, Orthopaedics, c/o Ward 8, Royal Bournemouth Hospital, Tel.: Bleep 2492

Ms A Fox, Nurse Specialist, Palliative Care, Ward 11, Royal Bournemouth Hospital, Tel.: 01202 726021

Ms C Lunn, Nurse, Palliative Care, Royal Bournemouth Hospital, Tel.: 01202 726021 bleep 2414

South West Strategic Health Authority

Ms C Thompson, Lead, Nurse Specialist, Parkinson's Disease, G3 Admin, Christchurch Hospital, Tel.: 01202 705320 bleep 2160
Ms B Gofton, Nurse Specialist, Respiratory, Royal Bournemouth Hospital, Tel.: 01202 704864
Ms M Townsend, Specialist Nurse, Respiratory, Dept Thoracic Medicine, Royal Bournemouth Hospital, Tel.: 01202 704568 bleep 2118
Ms H Killingback, Principal Officer, Resuscitation, Royal Bournemouth Hospital, Tel.: 01202 704664
Ms J Freak, Macmillan, Nurse Specialist, Skin Cancer, Royal Bournemouth Hospital, Tel.: 01202 704725 bleep 2656
Ms B Owles, Senior Clinical Leader, Stoma Care, Royal Bournemouth Hospital, Tel.: 01202 704813
Ms J Sheldon, Nurse Specialist, Stoma Care, Royal Bournemouth Hospital, Tel.: 01202 704813
Ms C Snelgrove, Nurse, Stoma Care, Royal Bournemouth Hospital, Tel.: 01202 704813
Mr D Thomas, Specialist Nurse, TB, DTM, Royal Bournemouth Hospital, Tel.: 01202 704560
Mr H Wilding, Nurse Specialist, TB, Thoracic Medicine Dept, Royal Bournemouth Hospital, Tel.: 01202 704560
Ms S Dillon, Nurse Practitioner, Upper GI, Ward 26, Royal Bournemouth Hospital, Tel.: 01202 704082
Mr M Goodman, Specialist Nurse, Upper GI, Royal Bournemouth Hospital, Tel.: 01202 704340 bleep 2298
Ms D Abbott, Specialist Nurse, Urodynamics, Women's Health Unit, Royal Bournemouth Hospital, Tel.: 01202 704675
Ms D Dew, Nurse Practitioner, Urology, Royal Bournemouth Hospital, Tel.: 01202 704871
Ms C Goldsmith, Nurse Practitioner, Urology, Royal Bournemouth Hospital, Tel.: 01202 704871
Ms S Laver, Nurse Practitioner, Urology, Royal Bournemouth Hospital, Tel.: 01202 704871
Ms B Morris, Nurse Practitioner, Urology, Royal Bournemouth Hospital, Tel.: 01202 704871
Ms J Parnell, Nurse Practitioner, Urology, Royal Bournemouth Hospital, Tel.: 01202 704871
Ms Y Webb, Nurse Practitioner, Urology, Royal Bournemouth Hospital, Tel.: 01202 704871
Ms A Cummins, Clinical Nurse Specialist, Urology/Oncology, Urology Unit, Wards 15/16, Royal Bournemouth Hospital, Tel.: 01202 704977 bleep 2415
Ms S Baker, Specialist Nurse, Vascular, Royal Bournemouth Hospital, Tel.: 01202 704188
Ms N Bennett, Nurse Practitioner, Vascular, Ward 14, Royal Bournemouth Hospital, Tel.: 01202 704425
Ms P Johnson, Nurse Practitioner, Vascular, Ward 14, Royal Bournemouth Hospital, Tel.: 01202 704425
Ms S Papworth, Nurse Practitioner, Vascular, Ward 14, Royal Bournemouth Hospital, Tel.: 01202 704425
Ms J Rasti, Nurse Practitioner, Vascular, Ward 14, Royal Bournemouth Hospital, Tel.: 01202 704425
Ms C Thompson, Nurse Practitioner, Vascular, Ward 14, Royal Bournemouth Hospital, Tel.: 01202 704425
Ms M Feltham, Lead, Specialist Nurse, Wound Care, General OPD, Royal Bournemouth Hospital, Tel.: 01202 704820/1
Ms S Lewis, Specialist Nurse, Wound Care, General Outpatients, Royal Bournemouth Hospital, Tel.: 01202 704820

Admin & Senior Management
Ms B Atkinson, Director of Nursing & Midwifery,
Child Protection/Safeguarding Children
Mrs G Wakely, Clinical Advisor, Bournemouth Primary Care Trust, Tel.: 01202 443151
Community Midwifery
Ms V Chappell, Clinical Lead, Twynham Group Practice, Maternity Unit, Royal Bournemouth Hospital, Tel.: 01202 704685
Mrs E Deane, Clinical Leader Compass Group Practice, Maternity Unit, Royal Bournemouth Hospital, Tel.: 01202 704685

Miss C Haken, Clinical Leader Rainbow Group Practice, Maternity Unit, Royal Bournemouth Hospital, Tel.: 01202 704685
Mrs P Knight, Senior Clinical Leader, Royal Bournemouth Hospital, Tel.: 01202 704685
Mr N Tomlin, Head of Midwifery, Royal Bournemouth Hospital, Tel.: 01202 704683
HIV/AIDS
Ms R Woodward, HIV, Clinical Nurse Specialist, Sexual Health, Royal Bournemouth Hospital, Tel.: 01202 704646

Royal Cornwall Hospitals NHS Trust

Trust Headquarters, Royal Cornwall Hospital
Treliske
TRURO
Cornwall
TR1 3LJ
Tel.: 01872 274242

Child Protection/Safeguarding Children
Ms A Reynolds, Looked After Children & Young People, Clinical Nurse Specialist, LAC YP Health Team, Child Health Dept, Pendragon House, Gloweth, Truro, TR1 3XQ, Tel.: 01872 254590/254515
Ms K Rowlands, Looked After Children & Young People, Clinical Nurse Specialist, LAC YP Health Team, Child Health Dept, Pendragon House, Gloweth, Truro, TR1 3XQ, Tel.: 01872 254590/254515
Ms R Hayes, Child Protection, Pendragon House, Royal Cornwall Hospital, Truro, TR1 3LS, Tel.: 01872 254549
Mr C Nash, Child Protection, Royal Cornwall Hospital, Treliske, Truro, Cornwall, TR1 3LJ, Tel.: 01726 291000
Liaison Services
Ms P Peacey, Continuing Care Liaison Nurse, West Cornwall Hospital, Penzance, TR18 2PF, Tel.: 01736 874171
Ms K Radcliffe, Continuing Care Liaison Nurse, Kynance House, Royal Cornwall Hospital, Treliske, Truro, TR1 3LJ, Tel.: 01872 252484
Ms B Savage, Continuing Care Liaison Nurse, Kynance House, Royal Cornwall Hospital, Treliske, Truro, TR1 3LJ, Tel.: 01872 252631

Royal Devon & Exeter Healthcare NHS Trust

Trust Headquarters, Royal Devon & Exeter
Barrack Road
EXETER
Devon
EX2 5DW
Tel.: 01392 411611

Community Midwifery
Community Midwives, Ansaphone 01392 405114, Royal Devon & Exeter Hospital (Wonford), Barrack Road, Exeter, EX2 5DW, Tel.: 01392 411611
Maternity Department, Exeter City, Royal Devon & Exeter Hospital (Heavitree), Gladstone Road, Exeter, EX1 2ED, Tel.: 01392 411611
Ms M Patterson, Matron Community Midwifery, Tel.: 01392 405041
Ms L Trevelyn, Head of Midwifery, Maternity Unit, Royal Devon & Exeter Hospital (Heavitree), Gladstone Road, Exeter, EX1 2ED, Tel.: 01392 405114

Royal National Hospital for Rheumatic Diseases

Trust Headquarters, Upper Borough Walls
BATH
BA1 1RL

Tel.: 01225 465941
Fax.: 01225 421202

Acute Specialist Nursing Services

Ms A Pacey, Clinical Nurse Specialist, Head Injury, - Neuro, Royal National Hospital for Rheumatic Diseases, Upper Borough Walls, Bath, BA1 1RL, Tel.: 01225 465941

Ms M Ricketts, Clinical Nurse Specialist, Pain Management, Royal National Hospital for Rheumatic Diseases, Upper Borough Walls, Bath, BA1 1RL, Tel.: 01225 465941

Ms S Brown, Clinical Nurse Specialist, Rheumatology, Royal National Hospital for Rheumatic Diseases, Upper Borough Walls, Bath, BA1 1RL, Tel.: 01225 465941

Ms C McCabe, Nurse Consultant, Rheumatology, Royal National Hospital for Rheumatic Diseases, Upper Borough Walls, Bath, BA1 1RL, Tel.: 01225 465941

Mr M Burgess, Clinical Nurse Specialist, Stroke Care, Royal National Hospital for Rheumatic Diseases, Upper Borough Walls, Bath, BA1 1RL, Tel.: 01225 465941

Admin & Senior Management
Ms Y Glenn, Service Development Manager, Royal National Hospital for Rheumatic Diseases, Upper Borough Walls, Bath, BA1 1RL, Tel.: 01225 465941

Child Protection/Safeguarding Children
Ms E Crawley, Consultant, Paediatrician, Tel.: 01225 473458

Discharge Co-ordinators
Ms C Gray, Tel.: 01225 473456

Ms D Morris, Admission Co-ordinator, Head Injury, Tel.: 01225 473458

Ms C Washbrook, Rheumatology, Tel.: 01225 465941 ext 299

Equipment Loan Services
Occupational Therapy (Neuro), Tel.: 01225 473450

Liaison Services
Ms C Gray, Tel.: 01225 473456

Ms D Morris, Admission Co-ordinator, Head Injury, Tel.: 01225 473458

Ms C Washbrook, Rheumatology, Tel.: 01225 465941 ext 299

Matrons/Modern Matrons
Modern Matron, Head Injury, Tel.: 01225 465941 ext 458

Modern Matron, Rheumatology, Tel.: 01225 465941 ext 299

Royal United Hospital NHS Trust

Trust Headquarters, Combe Park
BATH
Avon
BA1 3NG
Tel.: 01225 428331
Fax.: 01225 824304

Admin & Senior Management
Ms C Hall, Director of Nursing, Royal United Hospital NHS Trust, Combe Park, Bath, Avon, BA1 3NG, Tel.: 01225 428331

Salisbury Health Care NHS Trust

Trust Headquarters, Salisbury District Hospital
Oldstock Road
SALISBURY
Wiltshire
SP2 8BJ
Tel.: 01722 336262
Fax.: 01722 330221

Child Protection/Safeguarding Children
Ms C Ferguson, Named/Designated Nurse, Child Protection, Central Health Clinic, Tel.: 01722 329404

Community Midwifery
Community Midwifery Services, Non-Urgent Calls via Maternity Reception Monday-Saturday, Tel.: 01722 425178

Community Midwifery Services, Referrals & Supervision, Urgent Calls via SDH Switchboard, Tel.: 01722 336262

Mrs B Maddy, Head of Maternity & Neonatal Services, Tel.: 01722 425171

Somerset Coast Primary Care Trust

Trust Headquarters, 2nd Floor
Mallard Court, Express Park
BRIDGWATER, TA6 4RN
Tel.: 01278 432000

Admin & Senior Management
Mrs J Brown, Director of Service Delivery & Development,

Mr A Carpenter, Chief Executive,

Ms V Squire, Head of Community Nursing Services, 01278 432090

Child Health Records
Child Health Records, Taunton Deane PCT, Wellsprings Road, Taunton, TA2 7PQ, Tel.: 01823 333491

Child Protection/Safeguarding Children
Ms L Keedwell, c/o Peter Holmes Annex, Burnham-On-Sea Hospital, Burnham-On-Sea, Tel.: 01278 760983

Clinical Leads (NSF)
Dr G Tanner, Clinical Lead, Cancer,

Dr T Wright, Clinical Lead, CHD,

Mrs A Anderson, Clinical Lead, Children,

Community Midwifery
Mary Stanley Wing, Tel.: 01278 444517

Mrs M O'Sullivan, Head of Midwifery, Maternity Unit, Taunton Hospital, Taunton, TA1 5DA, Tel.: 01823 342567

Community Nursing Services
Ms V Squire, Head of Community Nursing Services, Tel.: 01278 432090

District Nursing
Ms V Squire, Professional Lead for District Nursing, Tel.: 01278 432075

Equipment Loan Services
Mediquip, Taunton, Somerset,

Health Visitors
Ms J Smith, Professional Lead for Health Visiting, Deputy Head of Community Nursing, Tel.: 01278 432075

Learning Disabilities
c/o Somerset Social Care Partnership, Barclay Street, Bridgewater, Somerset,

Liaison Services
Community Liaison Department, Taunton & Somerset Hospital, Tel.: 01823 333444 ext 2660/1

Pharmacy
Ms H Spry, Medicine Manager, c/o Somerset Coast PCT HQ, Tel.: 01278 432000

School Nursing
Ms J Healey, Professional Lead for School Nursing, Tel.: 01278 432075

Walk In Centres
Bridgwater Hospital, Tel.: 01278 436732

Burnham Hospital, Tel.: 01278 773121

Minehead Hospital, Tel.: 01643 707251 ext 238

Somerset Partnership NHS and Social Care Trust

Trust Headquarters, Broadway
Broadway Park, Barclay Street
BRIDGWATER
Somerset, TA6 5YA
Tel.: 01278 720200

Learning Disabilities
Dr S Frazer, Clinical Lead, Trust Headquarters, Broadway, Tel.: 01278 446151

Mrs D Rowe, Lead Director Learning Difficulties, Burton Place, Taunton, TA1 4HE, Tel.: 01823 423126

Mr M Sutherland, Lead Nurse, Learning Difficulties, Fiveways Resource Centre, Ilchester Road, Yeovil, BA21 3BB, Tel.: 01935 470600

South West Strategic Health Authority

South & East Dorset Primary Care Trust
Trust Headquarters, Victoria House
Princes Road, Ferndown
DORSET
BH22 9JR
Tel.: 01202 850600

Admin & Senior Management
Mr A Cawthron, Chief Executive, Tel.: 01202 850600
Ms S Rastrick, Director, Clinical Services, Tel.: 01202 850600
Child Health Records
Ms J Langford, Supervisor, Dorset Healthcare NHS Trust, 11 Shelley
Road, Boscombe, Bournemouth, BH1 4JQ, Tel.: 01202 443142
Child Protection/Safeguarding Children
Ms L Trehane, Advisor, Child Protection, 11 Shelley Road,
Boscombe, Bournemouth, BH1 4JQ, Tel.: 01202 443151
Ms M Tryska, Advisor, Child Protection, 11 Shelley Road,
Boscombe, Bournemouth, BH1 4JQ, Tel.: 01202 443151
Ms J Waddingham, Co-ordinator, Child Protection, 11 Shelley Road,
Boscombe, Bournemouth, BH1 4JQ, Tel.: 01202 443151
Clinical Leads (NSF)
Dr P Harker, Clinical Lead, CHD, Diabetes, Cancer,
Mrs A Salter, Clinical Lead, Children,
Mr R Webb, Clinical Lead, Older People,
Community Nursing Services
Mrs T Cole, Matron - Christchurch Locality, G3 Christchurch
Hospital, Fairmile Road, BH23 2JX, Tel.: 01202 705339
Mrs L Gardiner, Matron - East Dorset Locality, c/o St Leonards
Hospital, BH24 2RR, Tel.: 01202 584252
Mrs D Selwyn, Matron - Purbeck Locality, Wareham Clinic, Streche
Road, Wareham, BH20 4PG, Tel.: 01929 556855
Equipment Loan Services
Ms P Raylor, c/o Victoria House, Ferndown, BH22 9JR, Tel.: 01202
850600
Pharmacy
Ms S Martindale, Pharmacy Advisor, Victoria House, Ferndown,
BH22 9JR, Tel.: 01202 850600
School Nursing
Ms D Campbell, Team Leader, School Health/Nursing Service, Poole
PCT, St Leonards Hospital, Tel.: 01202 855644
Specialist Nursing Services
Mr S Trowbridge, Nurse Specialist, Diabetic Care, Victoria House,
Tel.: 01202 850600
Ms P Lesson, Nurse Specialist, Heart Failure, St Leonards
Community Hospital, BH24 2RR, Tel.: 01202 584217
Ms S Gooding, Infection Control, Victoria House, Tel.: 01202 850600
Walk In Centres
Local Treatment Centre, c/o Heather Smith, Matron, St Leonards
Hospital, Nr Kingwood, BH24 2RR,
Minor Injuries Unit, Swanage Hospital, BH19 2ES, Tel.: 01929
422282
Minor Injuries Unit, Victoria Hospital, Winbourne, BH21 1ER,

South Devon Healthcare NHS Trust
Trust Headquarters, Torbay Hospital
Lawes Bridge
TORQUAY
Devon
TQ2 7AA
Tel.: 01803 614567

Admin & Senior Management
Ms E Childs, Director of Nursing & Quality, Hengrave House, Torbay
Hospital, Lawes Bridge, Torquay, Devon, TQ2 7AA, Tel.: 01803
655707
Child Health Records
Child Health Records, Hengrave House, Torbay Hospital, Lawes
Bridge, Torquay, Devon, TQ2 7AA, Tel.: 01803 614567

Child Protection/Safeguarding Children
Ms C Cunningham, Child Protection, Torbay Hospital, Tel.: 01803
655720
Community Midwifery
Mrs L Leyshon, Directorate Manager, Head of Midwifery, Maternity
Unit, Torbay Hospital, Tel.: 01803 654657
Family Planning Services
Ms J Walsham, Manager, Torbay Hospital, Tel.: 01803 614567
Liaison Services
Mr S Newey, Community Liaison, Hengrave House, Torbay Hospital,
Tel.: 01803 614567
Ms C Payling, Community Liaison, Hengrave House, Torbay
Hospital, Tel.: 01803 614567
School Nursing
School Health, Vowden Hall, Torbay Hospital, Tel.: 01803 614567

South Gloucestershire Primary Care Trust
Trust Headquarters, Monarch Court
Emerald Park
EMERSON'S GREEN
South Gloucestershire
BS16 7FH
Tel.: 0117 330 2400
Fax.: 0117 330 2401

Child Health
Ms M Hennessy, Clinical Lead Manager Children & Family Services,
Monarch Court, Emerald Park, Emerson's Green, BS16 7FH, Tel.:
0117 330 2400
Child Health Records
Ms M Hennessy, Clinical Lead Manager Children & Family Services,
Monarch Court, Emerald Park, Emerson's Green, BS16 7FH, Tel.:
0117 330 2400
Child Protection/Safeguarding Children
Ms C Chesterman, Clinical Lead Manager for Safeguarding Children,
Monarch Court, Emerald Park, Emerson's Green, South
Gloucestershire, BS16 7FH, Tel.: 0117 330 2400
Clinical Leads (NSF)
Ms E Brown, Clinical Lead, Cancer, Tel.: 0117 330 2400
Dr C Payne, Clinical Lead, CHD, Tel.: 0117 330 2400
Mrs M Rogers, Clinical Lead, Diabetic Care, Tel.: 0117 330 2400
Community Matrons
Ms A Griffiths, Kingswood Locality, Community Matron, Downend
Clinic, Buckingham Gardens, Downend, Bristol, BS16 5TW, Tel.:
0117 330 2505
Ms R Julius, Severnvale Locality, Community Matron, Downend
Clinic, Buckingham Gardens, Downend, Bristol, BS16 5TW, Tel.:
0117 330 2505
Ms S Parris, Clinical Lead Manager for Adults, Older People & Long
Term Conditions, Monarch Court, Emerald Park, Emerson's Green,
BS16 7FH, Tel.: 01454 412636
Ms M Samson, Yate Locality, Community Matron, Downend Clinic,
Buckingham Gardens, Downend, Bristol, BS16 5TW, Tel.: 0117 330
2505
Community Midwifery
North Bristol NHS Trust,
Community Nursing Services
Ms A Wond, Nurse Executive, Monarch Court, Emerald Park,
Emerson's Green, BS16 7FH, Tel.: 0117 3302400
District Nursing
Ms S Parris, Clinical Lead Manager for Adults, Older People & Long
Term Conditions, Monarch Court, Emerald Park, Emerson's Green,
BS16 7FH, Tel.: 0117 330 2400
Equipment Loan Services
Ms S Ball, Community Equipment Co-ordinator, Cadbury Heath
Health Centre, Parkwall Road, Cadbury Heath, Bristol, BS30 8HS,
Tel.: 0117 980 5731 ext 220

South West Strategic Health Authority

Ms N Phillips, Clinical Lead Manager Clinical Effectiveness & Risk Management for Nursing, Monarch Court, Emerald Park, Emerson's Green, BS16 7FH, Tel.: 0117 330 2400
Family Planning Services
North Bristol NHS Trust,
Health Visitors
Ms M Hennessy, Clinical Lead Manager Children & Family Services, Monarch Court, Emerald Park, Emerson's Green, BS16 7FH, Tel.: 0117 330 2400
Learning Disabilities
Mrs K Mackay, Head of Service, South Gloucestershire Joint Learning Difficulties Service, Social Services Dept, St Luke's Close, Emerson's Way, Emerson's Green, S. Gloucestershire, BS16 7AL, Tel.: 01454 866343
Pharmacy
Ms S Mulvenna, Head of Medicines Management, Monarch Court, Emerald Park, Emerson's Green, BS16 7FH, Tel.: 0117 330 2400
School Nursing
North Bristol NHS Trust,
Specialist Nursing Services
Ms B Mason, Clinical Lead Manager for Emergency & Out of Hours Services, Frendoc, 12a High Street, Staple Hill, Bristol, BS16 5HP, Tel.: 0117 956 8820
Ms V Anderson, Nurse Specialist, Dermatology, Kennedy Way Surgery, Kennedy Way, Yate, Bristol, BS37 4AA,
Ms K Prout, Nurse Specialist, Parkinson's Disease, North Bristol NHS Trust, Frenchay Hospital, Tel.: 0117 970 1212
The Homeless/Travellers & Asylum Seekers
Ms M Hennessy, Travellers Health Visiting Service - Clinical Lead Manager Children & Family Services, Monarch Court, Emerald Park, Emerson's Green, BS16 7FH, Tel.: 0117 330 2400

South Hams & West Devon Primary Care Trust

Trust Headquarters, Lescaze Offices
Shinner's Bridge
DARTINGTON
Devon
TQ9 6JE
Tel.: 01803 866665
Fax.: 01803 867679

Admin & Senior Management
Ms K Grimshaw, Director of Professional Practice, Lescaze offices, Shinner's Bridge, Dartington, Devon, TQ9 6JE, Tel.: 01803 866665
Mr A Tibbenham, Chief Executive, Tel.: 01803 866665
Child Protection/Safeguarding Children
Mrs C Reilly, Advisor/Named Nurse Child Protection & Domestic Violence, Lescaze offices, Shinner's Bridge, Dartington, Devon, TQ9 6JE, Tel.: 01803 866665 ext 1926
Clinical Leads (NSF)
Mrs J Crang, Clinical Lead, Cancer,
Mr S Brown, Clinical Lead, CHD,
Dr M Loverock, Clinical Lead, Diabetic Care,
Ms D White, Clinical Lead, Older People,
Community Nursing Services
Mrs P Bridle, Locality Manager, Tavistock, Tavistock Hospital, Spring Hill, Tavistock, PL19 8LD, Tel.: 01822 612233
Ms I Clifford, Locality Manager, Ivybridge, Yealmpton, Yealm Medical Centre, Market Street, Yealmpton, PL8 2EA, Tel.: 01752 880567
Mr A Moore, Locality Manager, Totnes, Totnes Community Hospital, Coronation Road, TQ9 5GH, Tel.: 01803 862622
Mrs B Morrison, Locality Manager, Dartmouth, Dartmouth Hospital, Mansion House Street, Dartmouth, TQ6 9BD, Tel.: 01803 832255
Mrs J Warner, Locality Manager, Kingsbridge, South Hams Hospital, Plymouth Road, Kingsbridge, TQ7 1AT, Tel.: 01548 852349

Health Visitors
Mrs P Bridle, Locality Manager, Health Visitors - Tavistock, Tavistock Hospital, Spring Hill, Tavistock, PL19 8LD, Tel.: 01822 612233
Ms I Clifford, Locality Manager, Health Visitors - Ivybridge, Yealmpton, Yealm Medical Centre, Market Street, Yealmpton, PL8 2EA, Tel.: 01752 880567
Mr A Moore, Locality Manager, Health Visitors - Totnes, Totnes Community Hospital, Coronation Road, TQ9 5GH, Tel.: 01803 862622
Mrs B Morrison, Locality Manager, Health Visitors - Dartmouth, Dartmouth Hospital, Mansion House Street, Dartmouth, TQ6 9BD, Tel.: 01803 832255
Mrs J Warner, Locality Manager, Health Visitors - Kingsbridge, South Hams Hospital, Plymouth Road, Kingsbridge, TQ7 1AT, Tel.: 01548 852349

South Somerset Primary Care Trust

Trust Headquarters, Chataway House
Chard Business Park, Leach Road
CHARD
Somerset
TA20 1FR
Tel.: 01460 238600
Fax.: 01460 238699

Admin & Senior Management
Mrs M Monnington, Director of Nursing & Learning, Chataway House, Chard Business Park, Leach Road, Chard, Somerset, TA20 1FR, Tel.: 01460 238610
Dr V Pearson, Chief Executive,
Child Health
Ms B Cooke, Locality Manager, Charterhouse, Bartec 4, Watercombe Lane, Yeovil, BA20 2SU, Tel.: 01935 423981
Child Health Records
Ms S Barnett, Manager, Patient & Contracting Services, Taunton Deane PCT, Wellsprings Road, Taunton, Somerset, TA2 7PQ, Tel.: 01823 333491
Child Protection/Safeguarding Children
Mrs A Allen, Consultant Nurse for Somerset, Preston Road Clinic, Fiveways Roundabout, Preston Road, Yeovil, Somerset, BA21 3AA, Tel.: 01935 423981
Ms M Reid, Nurse, Child Protection, Preston Road Clinic, Fiveways Roundabout, Preston Road, Yeovil, Somerset, BA21 3AA, Tel.: 01935 423981
Mrs G Salisbury, Child Protection, Preston Road Clinic, Fiveways Roundabout, Preston Road, Yeovil, Somerset, BA21 3AA, Tel.: 01935 423981
Clinical Leads (NSF)
Dr P Scott, Clinical Lead, Cancer, Hamdon Medical Centre, Matts Lane, Stoke Sub Hamdon, Somerset, TA14 6QE, Tel.: 01460 822236
Dr L Smith, Clinical Lead, CHD, Westlake Surgery, High Street, West Coker, Somerset, BA22 9AH, Tel.: 01935 862212
Dr J Horne, Clinical Lead, Diabetic Care, Crewkerne Health Centre, Middle Path, Crewkerne, Somerset, TA18 8BX, Tel.: 01460 72435
Community Nursing Services
Ms M Crumb, Locality Manager, Charterhouse, Bartec 4, Watercombe Lane, Yeovil, BA20 2SU,
District Nursing
Ms M Crumb, Locality Manager, Charterhouse, Bartec 4, Watercombe Lane, Yeovil, BA20 2SU,
Pharmacy
Mr M Brindly, Pharmaceutical Advisor, Chataway House, Chard Business Park, Leach Road, Chard, Somerset, TA20 1FR, Tel.: 01460 238600
Ms K Holcombe, Pharmaceutical Advisor, Chataway House, Chard Business Park, Leach Road, Chard, Somerset, TA20 1FR, Tel.: 01460 238600

South West Strategic Health Authority

Smoking Cessation
Ms N Crocker, Smoking Cessation Specialist, Chataway House,
Chard Business Park, Leach Road, Chard, Somerset, TA20 1FR,
Tel.: 01460 238672
Specialist Nursing Services
Ms C Weller, Nurse Specialist, Continence, Preston Road Clinic,
Fiveways Roundabout, Preston Road, Yeovil, Somerset, BA21 3AA,
Tel.: 01935 423981
Ms S Down, Nurse Consultant, Diabetes, Charterhouse, Bartec 4,
Watercombe Lane, Yeovil, BA20 2SU,
Ms K Anderson, Senior Nurse, Infection Control, Charterhouse,
Bartec 4, Watercombe Lane, Yeovil, BA20 2SU,
Ms M Small, Specialist Nurse, Physical Disability, Preston Road
Clinic, Fiveways Roundabout, Preston Road, Yeovil, Somerset,
BA21 3AA, Tel.: 01935 423981
Mr I Evans, Nurse Consultant, Stroke Care, Charterhouse, Bartec 4,
Watercombe Lane, Yeovil, BA20 2SU,
Ms A Horrocks, Specialist Nurse, Tissue Viability, Preston Road
Clinic, Fiveways Roundabout, Preston Road, Yeovil, BA21 3AA,
The Homeless/Travellers & Asylum Seekers
Ms S Burton, Health Visitor, Penn Hill Surgery, St Nicholas Close,
Yeovil, Somerset, BA20 1SB, Tel.: 01935 474704

South West Dorset Primary Care Trust

Trust Headquarters, Hillfort House
Poundbury Road
DORCHESTER
Dorset, DT1 2PN
Tel.: 01305 368900

Admin & Senior Management
Mr I Brennan, Director of Community Health Services, Hillfort House,
Poundbury Road, Dorchester, Dorset, DT1 2PN, Tel.: 01305 368900
Child Protection/Safeguarding Children
Ms J Bowen, Children's Services & Vulnerable Adults, Specialist
Nurse, Hillfort House, Poundbury Road, Dorchester, Dorset, DT1
2PN, Tel.: 01305 368900
Clinical Leads (NSF)
Ms H Lawson, Clinical Lead, Cancer,
Dr F Watson, Clinical Lead, CHD,
Community Matrons
Ms R Cox, Community Matron, Hillfort House, Poundbury Road,
Dorcester, Dorset, DT1 2PN, Tel.: 01305 368940
Ms M Grant, Community Matron, Hillfort House, Poundbury Road,
Dorcester, Dorset, DT1 2PN, Tel.: 01305 368940
Ms A Stephens, Community Matron, Hillfort House, Poundbury
Road, Dorcester, Dorset, DT1 2PN, Tel.: 01305 368940
Ms J Tomlin, Community Matron, Hillfort House, Poundbury Road,
Dorcester, Dorset, DT1 2PN, Tel.: 01305 368940
Community Nursing Services
Ms L Moxom, Community Modern Matron, Senior Nurse, Hillfort
House, Poundbury Rd, Dorchester, Dorset, DT1 2PN, 01305 368945
Equipment Loan Services
Nottingham Rehab Services,
Health Visitors
Ms T Bradley, Community Services Manager - Health Visiting, Hillfort
House, Poundbury Road, Dorchester, Dorset, DT1 2PN, Tel.: 01305
368945
Specialist Nursing Services
Ms T Palmer, Nursing Home Co-ordinator, Continuing Care, Hillfort
House, Poundbury Rd, Dorchester, Dorset, DT1 2PN, 01305 368923

South Wiltshire Primary Care Trust

Trust Headquarters
Cross Keys House, Queen Street
SALISBURY, SP1 1EY
Tel.: 01722 345000
Fax.: 01722 345005

Child Health Records
Mrs C Chalk, Manager, Community Child Health Dept, Salisbury
District Hospital, Salisbury, SP2 8BJ, Tel.: 01722 336262 ext 2095
Child Protection/Safeguarding Children
Ms C Ferguson, Named/Designated Nurse, Child Protection, Central
Health Clinic, Tel.: 01722 329404
Clinical Leads (NSF)
Dr C Glaysher, Clinical Lead, Cancer,
Dr F Collins, Clinical Lead, CHD,
Dr M Moore, Clinical Lead, Diabetic Care,
Dr H McKeown, Clinical Lead, Older People,
Community Matrons
Ms V Wrixon, Community Matron,
District Nursing
District Nurses, Community Nursing Office, Central Health Clinic,
Tel.: 01722 329404
Nursing Referrals, (0800-1630 via Ambulance HQ), Tel.: 01249
651271
Health Visitors
Health Visitors, Community Nursing Office, Central Health Clinic,
Tel.: 01722 329404
School Nursing
Mrs J Wilson, School Nurse, Salisbury District Hospital, Tel.: 01722
336262
Specialist Nursing Services
Ms L Collings Wells, Continence, Central Health Clinic, Tel.: 01722
323196
Ms J Curtis, Continence, Central Health Clinic, Tel.: 01722 323196
Mrs J Oxenham, Diabetic Care, Salisbury District Hospital, Tel.:
01722 336262 ext 2176
Ms J Chamberlain, Parkinson's Disease, Nunton Day Hospital, Tel.:
ext 2146
Intensive Home Support, Community Team, Rehabilitation, Nunton
Day Hospital, Tel.: ext 4152/4330

Swindon & Marlborough NHS Trust

Trust Headquarters, The Great Western Hospital
Marlborough Road
SWINDON
Wiltshire
SN3 6BB
Tel.: 01793 604020
Fax.: 01793 604021

Acute Specialist Nursing Services
Ms S Rhodes, Anti-Coagulation, Tel.: 01793 604051
Ms M Taylor, Anti-Coagulation, Tel.: 01793 604051
Ms L Lark, Breast Screening, Breast Care, - Screening, Tel.: 01793
604237
Ms J O'Connell, Chemotherapy, Tel.: 01793 426996
Nurses, Dermatology, Tel.: 01793 604370/604362
Ms P Kirkman, Diabetes, Tel.: 01793 604308
Ms C Kirkman, Specialist Nurse, Diabetic Care, Tel.: 01793 604305
Ms M Olive, Diabetic Care, Tel.: 01793 604307
Ms B Guliet, Specialist Nurse, Epilepsy, Tel.: 01793 604020
Ms P Daly, Gastroenterology, Tel.: 01493 604128
Ms J Watson, Gastroenterology, Tel.: 01493 604128
Ms R Williams, Genetics, Tel.: 01793 604828
Ms H Forrest, Infection Control, Tel.: 01793 604551
Ms R Lockwood, Infection Control, Tel.: 01793 605562
Ms V Davey, Macmillan, Tel.: 01793 604339
Ms J Gray, Macmillan, Tel.: 01793 604351
Ms N Ockwell, Nutrition, Tel.: 01793 605149
Ms K Kyne, Occupational Health, 9 The Mall, Swindon, SN1 4JA,
Tel.: 01793 604475
Ms A Politt, Nurse Advisor, Occupational Health, 9 The Mall,
Swindon, SN1 4JA, Tel.: 01793 604475
Ms S Black, Oncology, - Adults, Tel.: 01793 604340

South West Strategic Health Authority

Ms A Koster, Oncology, - Adults, Tel.: 01793 604341

Ms A Robertson, Clinical Nurse Specialist, Oncology, Tel.: 01793 604020

Ms N Coggins, Link Nurse, Orthopaedics, Tel.: 01793 605867

Ms L Hocking, Link Nurse, Orthopaedics, Tel.: 01793 605867

Ms M Curtis, Pain Management, Tel.: 01793 604327

Ms D Denley, Specialist Nurse, Pain Management, Tel.: 01793 604020

Ms E Phipps, Specialist Nurse, Pain Management, Tel.: 01793 604020

Mr J Taylor, RTO, Resuscitation, Tel.: 01793 604535

Mr T Thompson, RTO, Resuscitation, Tel.: 01793 604535

Ms J Hanley, Stoma Care, Tel.: 01793 604147

Mr C Keen, (A&E), Thrombolysis, Tel.: 01793 604104

Ms A Roberts, Nurse Specialist, Vascular, Tel.: 01793 604020

Admin & Senior Management
Mrs F Thompson, Director of Nursing, Great Western Hospital, Marlborough Road, Swindon, Wiltshire, SN3 6BB, Tel.: 01793 604183

Child Health
Ms C Critchley, Community Children's Sister (Oncology), Childrens Ward, The Great Western Hospital, Marlborough Road, Swindon, Wilts, SN3 6BB, Tel.: 01793 604969

Ms S Facey, Community Children's Sister, Childrens Ward, The Great Western Hospital, Marlborough Road, Swindon, Wilts, SN3 6BB, Tel.: 01793 604969

Ms N Farthing, Community Children's Sister (Diabetes), Childrens Ward, The Great Western Hospital, Marlborough Road, Swindon, Wilts, SN3 6BB, Tel.: 01793 604969

Miss J Smith, Childrens Services, Senior Nurse, The Great Western Hospital, Marlborough Road, Swindon, Wilts, SN3 6BB, Tel.: 01793 604944

Ms R Townend, Community Childrens Nurse, Palliative Care Sister, The Great Western Hospital,

Ms F Twoney, Clinical Nurse Specialist, Marlborough House,

Ms L Winwood, Community Children's Sister, The Great Western Hospital, Tel.: 01793 604020

Child Protection/Safeguarding Children
Miss J Smith, Named Nurse, Child Protection, Children's Services, Great Western Hospital, Tel.: 01793 604944

Community Midwifery
Ms S Bailey, Community Midwifery Manager, Tel.: 01793 604829
Maternity Unit, bleep Midwife on duty, Tel.: 01793 604020
Ms C Rattigan, Head of Midwifery, Tel.: 01793 604953

Health Visitors
Ms J Asherson, Liaison Health Visitor, The Great Western Hospital, Tel.: 01793 604020/846729

Liaison Services
Ms J Asherson, Liaison Health Visitor, The Great Western Hospital, Tel.: 01793 604020/846729

Ms P Tomlinson, Discharge Liaison Sister, The Great Western Hospital, Tel.: 01793 605153

Swindon Primary Care Trust

Trust Headquarters
North Swindon District Centre, Thamesdown Drive
SWINDON
SN25 4AN
Tel.: 01793 708700

Admin & Senior Management
Mrs G May, Lead Nurse, Tel.: 01793 708700
Ms J Stubbings, Chief Executive,

Child Health
Ms L Campion, Head of Children, Young People & Family Services, North Swindon District Centre, Thamesdown Drive, Swindon, SN25 6AN, Tel.: 01793 708734

Child Health Records
Mr I Smart, Child Health Manager, Chatsworth House, 6 Bath Road, Swindon, SN1 4BP, Tel.: 01793 719001

Child Protection/Safeguarding Children
Mrs A Gray, Looked After Children, Specialist Nurse, Hut 8, Swindon Borough Council, Euclid Street, Swindon, SN1 2JH, Tel.: 01793 464334

Mrs A Grace, Designated Nurse, Child Protection, North Swindon District Centre, Thamesdown Drive, Swindon, Wilts, SN25 4AN, Tel.: 01793 708748

Mrs J Morrison, Named Nurse, Child Protection, Chatsworth House, 6 Bath Road, Old Town, Swindon, SN1 4BP, Tel.: 01793 716807

Clinical Leads (NSF)
Mr A Dancyger, Clinical Lead, Cancer,

District Nursing
Ms D Blake, Team Leader, N W Community Team (District Nurses), Pinehurst People's Centre, Beech Avenue, Swindon, SN2 1JT, Tel.: 01793 489530

Family Planning Services
Ms J Paterson, Manager, Contraceptive & Sexual Health Services, Swindon Health Centre, Carfax Street, Swindon, SN1 1ED, Tel.: 01793 486991

Health Visitors
Mrs N Edwards, Service Manager, Health Visitors, Eldene Health Centre, Swindon, Tel.: 01793 695151
Ms G Fitzgerald, Parenting Health Visitor, Priory Road Surgery, Park North, Swindon, Tel.: 01793 616240/613235

Learning Disabilities
Mr G Walker, Learning Disabilities Manager, Chatsworth House, 6 Bath Road, Old Town, Swindon, SN1 4BP, Tel.: 01793 644900

Liaison Services
Ms G Emberey, Discharge Liaison Nurse/Team Leader, Brunel Treatment Centre, Liden Suite, Great Western Hospital, Marlborough Road, Swindon, SN3 6BB, Tel.: 01793 646370 Bleep 8076
Mrs J Jenkins, Paediatric Liaison Health Visitor, Eldene Health Centre, Swindon, Wilts, Tel.: 01793 695151 Bleep 2628

Other Services
Swindon Intermediate Care Centre, (Community Hospitals), Downs Way, Swindon, SN3 6BW, Tel.: 01793 605530

School Nursing
Mrs J Lyons, School Nursing Team Leader, West Swindon Health Centre, Link Avenue, Swindon, SN5 7DL, Tel.: 01793 889440

Smoking Cessation
Mrs C Jones, Specialist Advisor, Trust Headquarters, North Swindon District Centre, Thamesdown Drive, Swindon, SN25 4AN, Tel.: 01793 708756

Specialist Nursing Services
Mrs G May, Team Leader, Specialist Nurses, Eldene Health Centre, Swindon, Tel.: 01793 695151
Ms L Salter, Continence, Independent Living Centre, Stratton Road, Swindon, SN1 2PN, Tel.: 01793 488502
Nurses, Macmillan, Prospect Foundation, Moormead Road, Wroughton, Swindon, Tel.: 01793 813355
Mrs J Cadogan, Nurse, Tissue Viability, SWICC, Marlborough Road, Swindon, SN3 6BB, Tel.: 01793 605592

The Homeless/Travellers & Asylum Seekers
Mrs A Nott, Swindon Health Centre, Carfax Street, Swindon, SN1 1ED, Tel.: 01793 428523

Walk In Centres
Mrs A Kinsella, Walk-in-Centre Manager, Swindon Health Centre, Cefax Street, Swindon,, Tel.: 01793 428524

Taunton & Somerset NHS Trust

Trust Headquarters, Taunton & Somerset Hospital
Musgrove Park
TAUNTON, Somerset
TA1 5DA
Tel.: 01823 333444

South West Strategic Health Authority

Acute Specialist Nursing Services
Ms E Hawden, Bereavement Officer, Tel.: ext 2106
Mrs A Dibble, Breast Care, Tel.: ext 2453
Ms Y Wells, Team Leader, Children, Tel.: 01823 342078
Ms J Connolly, Continence, Tel.: 01823 342111
Ms J Bailey, Coronary Care, Tel.: ext 2064
Ms J Taylor, Coronary Care, Tel.: ext 2064
Ms A Turner, Coronary Care, Tel.: ext 2064
Ms M Watkinson, Diabetic Care, Tel.: 01823 343434
Ms M James, Genetics, Tel.: 01823 342039
Ms K Smith, Genetics, Tel.: 01823 342039
Ms B Fuller, Haematology, Tel.: 01823 342296
Mr C Hold, Infection Control, Tel.: 01823 342611
Ms P Davey, Physical Disability,
Ms S Halford, Respiratory, Tel.: ext 3461
Mr S Reeves, Resuscitation Training, Tel.: bleep 2148
Mrs J Catto, Stoma Care,
Mrs L Vickery, Vascular, Tel.: ext 4004

Admin & Senior Management
Ms L Redfern, Director for Patient Care & Nursing, Taunton &
Somerset Hospital, Musgrove Park, Taunton, Somerset, TA1 5DA,
Tel.: 01823 342448

Child Health
Ms M Gardiner, Paediatric Diabetes, Tel.: 01823 343434

Child Protection/Safeguarding Children
Ms J Fowler, Child Protection, Tel.: 01823 343208

Community Midwifery
Mrs L Davy, Midwifery Matron, Tel.: 01823 343414
Director of Midwifery, Maternity Uhit, Taunton & Somerset Hospital,
Tel.: 01823 342567
Maternity Unit, Tel.: 01823 342059
Mrs S E Unsworth, Midwifery Matron, Tel.: 01823 344583

HIV/AIDS
Mrs S Crocker, AIDS, Taunton & Somerset Hospital, Tel.: 01823
289891

Liaison Services
Ms G Lerwill, Liaison Hospital/Comm Nurse Assessors, Musgrove
Park Hospital, Tel.: 01823 333444 ext 2660/1

Matrons/Modern Matrons
Ms S Gilbert, Modern Matron, Alfred Morris House, Tel.: 01823
342044
Ms N Monteiro, Modern Matron, A&E, Tel.: 01823 343892
Ms B Fuller, Modern Matron, Cancer, Tel.: 01823 344550
Ms J Huss, Modern Matron, CCU, Tel.: 01823 333444 bleep 2004
Ms S Pilkington, Modern Matron, Children, Tel.: 01823 342573
Ms S Matravers, Modern Matron, Elderly Care, Tel.: 01823 344147
Ms A Morgan, Modern Matron, General Surgery, Tel.: 01823 342004
Ms H Mattock, Modern Matron, Head & Neck, Tel.: 01823 344619
Ms C Panton, Modern Matron, ITU, Tel.: 01823 342153
Mr R Conway, Modern Matron, Medical Admissions, Tel.: 01823
343151
Ms C Dight, Modern Matron, Orthopaedics, Tel.: 01823 342654
Ms C Hoeller, Modern Matron, Outpatients, Tel.: 01823 342445
Ms M Dodwell, Day, Modern Matron, Surgery, Tel.: 01823 342762
Ms J Whelan, Modern Matron, Theatres, Tel.: 01823 342327

Taunton Deane Primary Care Trust

Trust Headquarters
Wellsprings Road
TAUNTON
TA2 7PQ
Tel.: 01823 344401

Admin & Senior Management
Mrs S Balcombe, Director of Nursing & Patient Services, Taunton
Deane PCT, Wellsprings Road, Taunton, TA2 7PQ, Tel.: 01823
344226
Mr E Colgan, Chief Executive,

Child Health Records
Ms S Barnett, Patient & Practitioner Services Manager, Taunton
Deane PCT, Wellsprings Road, Taunton, TA2 7PQ, Tel.: 01823
333491

Child Protection/Safeguarding Children
Miss C Blackmore, Named Nurse, Child Protection, Taunton Deane
PCT, Wellsprings Road, Taunton, TA2 7PQ, Tel.: 01823 344303

Clinical Leads (NSF)
Dr T Morkane, Clinical Lead, Diabetes, Cancer,
Dr T Morkane, Clinical Lead, CHD,
Dr L Pollock, Clinical Lead, Older People,

Community Nursing Services
Mrs S Balcombe, Director of Nursing & Patient Services, Taunton
Deane PCT, Wellsprings Road, Taunton, TA2 7PQ, Tel.: 01823
344226

District Nursing
Ms A Smith, District Nurse Professional Lead, Taunton Deane PCT,
Wellsprings Road, Taunton, TA2 7PQ, Tel.: 01823 344226

Equipment Loan Services
Ms S Phillipson, Occupational Therapy Team Leader, Taunton
Deane PCT, Wellsprings Road, Taunton, TA2 7PQ, Tel.: 01823
344226

Family Planning Services
Ms T Evans, Contraceptive & Sexual Health Services, Lead Nurse,

Pharmacy
Mr S Greene, Director of Pharmacy,

Teignbridge Primary Care Trust

Trust Headquarters, Bridge House
Collett Way, Brunel Industrial Estate
NEWTON ABBOT
Devon, TQ12 4PH
Tel.: 01626 357000

Admin & Senior Management
Ms L Cooney, Director of Professional Practice, Trust Headquarters,
Tel.: 01626 357000
Ms P Smith, Chief Executive, Trust Headquarters, Tel.: 01626
357023

Child Protection/Safeguarding Children
Ms C Cunningham, Child Protection, Child Health Directorate,
SDHCT, Torbay Hospital, Tel.: 01803 655801

Health Visitors
Ms J Slingsby, Health Visitors, Teignbridge PCT, Tel.: 01626 357000

Liaison Services
Ms C Cotter, Adult Protection, Link Nurse, Teignbridge PCT, Tel.:
01626 357003
Ms C Cotter, Service Development Co-ordinator (Adults),
Teignbridge PCT, Bridge House, Collette Way, Brunel Ind Estate,
Newton Abbot, TQ12 4PH, Tel.: 01626 357003
Ms J Monks, Lead Nurse, NHS Funded Care Co-ordinator, South &
West Devon Health Authority, Lescase Offices, Shinners Bridge,
Dartington, Tel.: 01803 866665
Ms M Weymouth, Specialist Nurse Assessor, Gateway Team, Tel.:
01626 357213

Matrons/Modern Matrons
Ms L Baxter, Community, Modern Matron, Tel.: 01626 354321
Ms A Bourne, Community, Modern Matron, Tel.: 01626 832279
Ms S Readman, Community, Modern Matron, Tel.: 01626 772161

Other Services
Ashburton & Buckfastleigh Hospital, Eastern Road, Ashburton, Tel.:
01364 652203
Bovey Tracey Hospital, Furzeleigh Lane, Bovey Tracey, Tel.: 01626
832279
Dawlish Community Hospital, Barton Terrace, Dawlish, Tel.: 01626
868500
Newton Abbot Hospital, East Street, Newton Abbot, Tel.: 01626
354321

South West Strategic Health Authority

Ms M O'Neil, Co-ordinator, Medical Admissions Team, SDHCT, Torbay Hospital, Tel.: 01803 655776

Teignmouth Hospital, Mill Lane, Teignmouth, Tel.: 01626 772161

Ms M Bell, Co-ordinator, Torbay Hospital Outreach Team, Respiratory, SDHCT, Torbay Hospital, Tel.: 01803 655199

School Nursing
Ms J Slingsby, Health Visitors, Teignbridge PCT, Tel.: 01626 357000

Smoking Cessation
Ms G House, Facilitator, Teignbridge PCT, Tel.: 01626 357039

Specialist Nursing Services
Ms R Archer, Specialist Nurse, Continence, Newton Abbot Hospital, East Street, Newton Abbot, Tel.: 01626 354321

Ms K Stocker, Specialist Nurse, Parkinson's Disease, Newton Abbot Hospital, East Street, Newton Abbot, Tel.: 01626 354321

Torbay Primary Care Trust

Trust Headquarters, Rainbow House
Avenue Road
TORQUAY
Devon
TQ2 5LS
Tel.: 01803 210910

Admin & Senior Management
Ms L Cooney,
Ms S Newman,
Ms S Newman, Lead Nurse, Nurse Board Member, Paignton Hospital, Church Street, Paignton, TQ3 3AG, Tel.: 01803 557425

Mr S Worswick, Chief Executive,

Child Protection/Safeguarding Children
Mrs C Cunningham, Child Protection, Torbay Hospital, Lawes Bridge, Torquay, TQ2 7AA, Tel.: 01803 655720

Clinical Leads (NSF)
Dr F Tolley, Clinical Lead, CHD, Children,
Dr F Tolley, Clinical Lead, Cancer,
Dr W Heale, Clinical Lead, Older People,

District Nursing
Mr R Anderson, Locality Manager, Paignton, Paignton Hospital, Tel.: 01803 557425

Ms L Cooney, District Nurse Adviser, Newton Abbot Hospital, 62 East Street, Newton Abbot, TQ12 4PT, Tel.: 01626 354321

Mr S Goodchild, Locality Manager, Torquay, Rainbow House, Tel.: 01803 210921

Ms A Redmayne, Locality Manager, Brixham, Brixham Hospital, Greenswood Road, Brixham, TQ5 9HW, Tel.: 01803 882153

Health Visitors
Ms S Newman, Health Visitor Adviser, Paignton Hospital, Tel.: 01803 557425

United Bristol Healthcare NHS Trust

Trust Headquarters, Marlborough Street
BRISTOL
BS1 3NU
Tel.: 0117 929 0666

Child Health
Ms J Berry, Jessie May Trust: Child Palliative Home Care, 35 Old School House, Kingswood Foundation Estate, Britannia Road, Kingswood, Bristol, BS15 8DB, Tel.: 0117 9582172

Ms J Bowman, Jessie May Trust: Child Palliative Home Care, 35 Old School House, Kingswood Foundation Estate, Britannia Road, Kingswood, Bristol, BS15 8DB, Tel.: 0117 9582172

Ms R Butcher, Jessie May Trust: Child Palliative Home Care, 35 Old School House, Kingswood Foundation Estate, Britannia Road, Kingswood, Bristol, BS15 8DB, Tel.: 0117 9582172

Ms E Lewington, Manager, Jessie May Trust: Child Palliative Home Care, 35 Old School House, Kingswood Foundation Estate, Britannia Road, Kingswood, Bristol, BS15 8DB, Tel.: 0117 9582172

Child Protection/Safeguarding Children
Mrs S Windfeld, Named Midwife, St Michael's Hospital, Southwell Street, Bristol, BS2 8EG, Tel.: 0117 928 5201

Community Midwifery
Ms L Damsell, Midwifery Matron, St Michael's Hospital, Tel.: 0117 928 5263

Ms J Ford, Midwifery Matron, St Michael's Hospital, Tel.: 0117 928 5296

Ms S O'Callaghan, Midwifery Matron, St Michael's Hospital, Tel.: 0117 928 5283

Ms A Tizzard, Midwifery Matron, St Michael's Hospital, Tel.: 0117 928 5211

Mrs S Windfeld, Head of Midwifery, St Michael's Hospital, Southwell Street, Bristol, BS2 8EG, Tel.: 0117 928 5201

Liaison Services
Ms W Rug, Drug Liaison Midwife, St Michael's Hospital, Southwell Street, Bristol, BS2 8EG, Tel.: 0117 928 5488

West Dorset General Hospitals NHS Trust

Trust Headquarters, Dorset County Hospital
Williams Avenue
DORCHESTER
Dorset
DT1 2JY
Tel.: 01305 251150
Fax.: 01305 254155

Acute Specialist Nursing Services
Ms L King, Nurse Co-ordinator, Early Pregnancy, Tel.: 01305 255760

Ms J Barrett, Nurse Specialist, Acute Pain, Tel.: ext 4228

Ms J Jackson, Nurse Practitioner, Advanced Neonatal, Tel.: 01305 254235 bleep 510

Ms M O'Flaherty, Inflammatory Disease, Nurse Specialist, Bowel, Tel.: 01305 255102

Ms S Phillips, Inflammatory Disease, Nurse Specialist, Bowel, Tel.: 01305 255102

Ms F Lambert, Lead, Nurse Specialist, Breast Care, Tel.: 01305 255160

Ms A Saunders, Lead, Nurse Specialist, Breast Care, Tel.: 01305 255160

Ms L Baldrey, Lead Nurse, Cancer, Tel.: 01305 255509 bleep 363

Ms E Jacknelle, Nurse, Cardiac Rehabilitation, Tel.: 01305 255707

Ms W Longley, Nurse, Cardiac Rehabilitation, Tel.: 01305 255707

Ms A Podmore, Nurse, Cardiac Rehabilitation, Tel.: 01305 255707

Mr S Porter, Nurse, Cardiac Rehabilitation, Tel.: 01305 255707

Ms E Tovell, Nurse, Cardiac Rehabilitation, Tel.: 01305 255707

Ms G Daubany Nun, Community Nurse, Children, Tel.: 01305 254279

Ms J Hopcraft, Community Nurse, Children, Tel.: 01305 254279

Ms J Meikle, Community Nurse, Children, Tel.: 01305 254279

Ms H Watson, Nurse Practitioner, Colorectal, Tel.: 01305 255273 bleep 375

Ms R Hill, Lead Nurse, Colposcopy, Tel.: ext 4143

Ms M Cooper, Specialist Nurse, Dermatology, Tel.: 01305 255118

Ms E Adams, Diabetes, Tel.: 01305 255342 bleep 439

Ms L Parker, Diabetes, Tel.: 01305 255342

Ms J Watson, Diabetes, Tel.: 01305 255342

Ms S O'Flannagan, Service Co-ordinator, Nurse Specialist, Fertility, Tel.: 01305 254141

Ms V Fletcher-Burnett, Specialist Nurse, Genito Urinary, - HIV, Tel.: 01305 762710

Ms L Newton, Nurse Specialist, Gynaecology, Tel.: 01305 255719

Ms A Wood, Nurse Specialist, Haematology, - Chemotherapy, Tel.: 01305 254359

Ms T Dare, Nurse, Heart Failure, Tel.: 01305 255610 bleep 569

Ms G Payne, Nurse Specialist, Infection Control, Tel.: 01305 254269 bleep 208

South West Strategic Health Authority

Mr A Hillcox-Smith, Nurse Specialist, Lung Cancer, Tel.: 01305 255289

Ms C Dart, Lymphoedema, Tel.: 01305 255370

Ms K Gibbons, Team Leader, Child & Adolescent, Nurse Therapist, MH, Tel.: 01305 255705

Ms J Handley, Nurse Specialist, Parkinson's Disease, Tel.: 01305 254789

Ms A Bolton, Chronic Failure, Nurse Specialist, Renal, Tel.: 01305 255372

Ms J Chaloner, Transplant, Nurse, Renal, Tel.: 01305 254546

Ms S Hanson, Staff Development, Sister, Renal, Tel.: 01305 255538

Ms C Smith, Specialist Nurse, Renal, - Anaemia, Tel.: 01305 255605

Ms K Gardiner, Specialist Nurse, Respiratory, Tel.: 01305 254238 bleep 351

Ms J Raleigh, Clinical Nurse Specialist, Rheumatology, Tel.: 01305 254789

Ms V Clothier, Stoma Care, Tel.: 01305 255152 bleep 316

Ms F Mortlock, Stoma Care, Tel.: 01305 255152 bleep 316

Ms D Ashton, Nurse Specialist, Stroke Care, Tel.: 01305 255557

Ms T Lloyd, Nurse Specialist, Tissue Viability, Tel.: 01305 762633

Ms J Wraight, Nurse Specialist, Upper GI, Tel.: 01305 255710

Ms A Lowndes, Nurse Specialist, Urology/Oncology, Tel.: 01305 255145 bleep 224

Child Health

Ms S Bond, Paediatric Diabetes, Dorset County Hospital,

Ms G Daubany-Nunn, Children's Community Nurse, Dorset County Hospital, Tel.: 01305 254279

Ms J Hopcraft, Children's Community Nurse, Dorset County Hospital, Tel.: 01305 254279

Ms S MacLeod, Children with Learning Disabilities, Senior Nurse, The Swifts, Digby Court, 33 Edward Road, Dorchester, DT1 2HL, Tel.: 01305 265616

Ms J Meikle, Children's Community Nurse, Dorset County Hospital, Tel.: 01305 254279

Child Health Records

Ms A True, Information Officer, Child Health Records, Children's Centre, Damers Road, Dorchester, DT1 2LB, Tel.: 01305 254729

Child Protection/Safeguarding Children

Ms A Ryder, Specialist Nurse, Child Protection, Children's Centre, Dorset County Hospital, Tel.: 01305 254708

Community Midwifery

Ms J Hall, Senior Midwife for Ante-Natal Care, Tel.: 01305 254229

Ms C Voce, Head of Midwifery, Maternity Unit, Dorset County Hospital, Tel.: 01305 254207

Mrs L Walters, Senior Midwife for Post Natal Care, Tel.: 01305 254229

West Gloucestershire Primary Care Trust

Trust Headquarters, Units 14 & 15
Highnam Business Centre
HIGHNAM, Gloucester
GL2 8DN
Tel.: 01452 389400

Admin & Senior Management
Mr S Colledge, Chief Executive,

Child Health Records
Mrs C Bodkin, Manager, Rikenel, Montpellier, Gloucester, GL1 1LY, Tel.: 01452 891000

Child Protection/Safeguarding Children
Ms L Thornton, Child Protection, Rikenel, Montpellier, Gloucester, GL1 1LY, Tel.: 01452 891098

Clinical Leads (NSF)
Dr H Annett, Clinical Lead, CHD, Diabetes,
Dr H Brown, Clinical Lead, Older People,

District Nursing
Mr B Cope, District Nurses, Community Hospitals, Nurse Advisor, 31 Park Road, Gloucester, GL1 1LH, Tel.: 01452 891492

Ms L Dibben, District Nurses, Community Nurse Manager, Unit 14 Highnam Business Centre, Tel.: 01452 389448

Ms M Getgood, Forest of Dean, Community Nurse Manager, Dilke Hospital, Cinderford, GL14 3HX, Tel.: 01594 598100

Ms F Law, Stroud, Community Nurse Manager, Stroud Maternity Hospital, Stroud, GL5 2JB, Tel.: 01453 562140

Family Planning Services
Dr P Allen, Manager, Hope Hospital, Gloucester Royal Hospital, Great Western Road, Gloucester, GL1 3NN, Tel.: 01452 395999

Health Visitors
Ms T Harbottle, Adviser Health Visitors, Rikenel, Montpellier, Gloucester, GL1 1LY, Tel.: 01452 891097

Ms K Morris Edwards, Acting, Health Visitor, 31 Park Road, Gloucester, GL1 1LH, Tel.: 01452 891487

Specialist Nursing Services
Nurses, Continence, Rikenel, Montpellier, Gloucester, GL1 1LY, Tel.: 01452 891000

Nurses, Macmillan, Wheatstone, North Upton Lane, Gloucester, Tel.: 01452 371022

Ms B Harding, Stoma Care, Quedgeley Clinic, St James, Quedgeley, GL2 4WD, Tel.: 01452 891400

Mr C Palmer, Tissue Viability, Collingwood House, Gloucester, Tel.: 01452 891240

The Homeless/Travellers & Asylum Seekers
Ms G Clay, Clinical Specialist Health & Homelessness, The Family Haven, 31 Spa Road, Gloucester, GL1 1UY, Tel.: 01452 500671

West of Cornwall Primary Care Trust

Trust Headquarters
Foundry Road
CAMBORNE, TR14 8DS
Tel.: 01209 888222
Fax.: 01209 886572

Admin & Senior Management
Mrs A Cook, Community & Primary Services Manager, West of Cornwall PCT, Camborne Health Office, Rectory Road, Camborne, Cornwall, TR14 7DL, Tel.: 01209 886500

Ms A Lejk, Chief Executive, Tel.: 01209 888222

Child Protection/Safeguarding Children
Ms C Nash, Lead Health Visitor, Child Protection, CC PCT Head Office, Sedgemoor Centre, Priory Road, St Austell, PL25 5AS, Tel.: 01726 627815

Clinical Leads (NSF)
Dr S Freegard, Clinical Lead, CHD,
Mr S Deeble, Lead, Older People,

Community Midwifery
Mrs C Joyce, Director of Midwifery, Central Cornwall PCT, Sedgemoor Centre, Priory Road, St Austell, PL25 5AE, Tel.: 01726 267930

Community Nursing Services
Acute Care at Home Team, Kernowdoc, Cudmore House, Treliske, Truro, TR1 2YZ,

Rapid Assessment Team (Kerrier), Camborne Redruth Community Hospital, Barncoose Terrace, Redruth, Cornwall, TR15 3ER, Tel.: 01209 881627

Rapid Assessment Team (Penwith), Penzance Social Services, Roscadghill Parc, Heamoor, Penzance, Cornwall, TR18 3QQ, Tel.: 01872 323392

District Nursing
Mrs A Cook, Community & Primary Services Manager, Kerrier, Camborne Health Office, Tel.: 01209 886531

District Nurses, Hayle Health Centre, Bodriggy Health Centre, Queensway, Hayle, Cornwall, TR27 4PB, Tel.: 01736 752056

District Nurses, Pool Health Centre, Station Road, Poole, Cornwall, TR15 3DU, Tel.: 01209 886571

District Nurses, Redruth Health Centre, Forth Noweth, Redruth, Cornwall, TR15 1AU, Tel.: 01209 881850

South West Strategic Health Authority

District Nurses, The Health Centre, St Mary's, Isles of Scilly, TR21 0HE, Tel.: 01720 422423

District Nurses, St Just Health Centre, Cape Cornwall, St Just, Penzance, Cornwall, TR19 7HX, Tel.: 01736 788866

District Nurses, St Ives Health Centre, Community Clinic, Stennack Hill, St Ives, Cornwall, TR26 1RU, Tel.: 01736 576130

District Nurses, St Keverne Health Centre, St Keverne, Nr Helston, Cornwall, TR12 6PB, Tel.: 01326 280767

District Nurses, Mullion Health Centre, Mullion, Nr Helston, Cornwall, TR12 7DQ, Tel.: 01326 240693

District Nurses, Camborne Health Office, Rectory Road, Camborne, Cornwall, TR14 7DL, Tel.: 01209 886500

District Nurses, Helston Community Hospital, Meneage Road, Helston, Cornwall, TR13 8DR, Tel.: 01326 435830

District Nurses, Marazion Health Centre, Gwallon Lane, Marazion, Penzance, Cornwall, TR17 0HW, Tel.: 01736 711566

District Nurses, Penzance Health Office, Bellair, Alverton, Penzance, Cornwall, TR18 4TA, Tel.: 01736 575500

Health Visitors

Health Visitors, St Ives Health Centre, Community Clinic, Stennack Hill, St Ives, Cornwall, TR26 1RU, Tel.: 01736 576130

Health Visitors, Camborne Health Office, Rectory Road, Camborne, Cornwall, TR14 7DL, Tel.: 01209 886500

Health Visitors, Pool Health Centre, Station Road, Poole, Cornwall, TR15 3DU, Tel.: 01209 886571

Health Visitors, St Just Health Centre, Cape Cornwall, St Just, Penzance, Cornwall, TR19 7HX, Tel.: 01736 788866

Health Visitors, Redruth Health Centre, Forth Noweth, Redruth, Cornwall, TR15 1AU, Tel.: 01209 881850

Health Visitors, Penzance Health Office, Bellair, Alverton, Penzance, Cornwall, TR18 4TA, Tel.: 01736 575500

Health Visitors, Helston Health Centre, Trengrouse Way, Helston, Cornwall, TR13 8AX, Tel.: 01326 435869

Health Visitors, St Keverne Health Centre, St Keverne, Nr Helston, Cornwall, TR12 6PB, Tel.: 01326 280767

Health Visitors, Marazion Health Centre, Gwallon Lane, Marazion, Penzance, Cornwall, TR17 0HW,

Health Visitors, Hayle Health Centre, Bodriggy Health Centre, Queensway, Hayle, Cornwall, TR27 4PB, Tel.: 01736 752056

Health Visitors, Mullion Health Centre, Mullion, Nr Helston, Cornwall, TR12 7DQ, Tel.: 01326 240693

Other Services

Ms L Day, Hospital Services Manager, Camborne Redruth Community Hospital, Barncoose Terrace, Redruth, Cornwall, TR15 3ER, Tel.: 01209 881600

Mr W Gummery-Richards, Matron, Camborne Redruth Community Hospital, Barncoose Terrace, Redruth, Cornwall, TR15 3ER, Tel.: 01209 881688

Ms G Head, Physiotherapy Services, Helston Hospital, Meneage Road, Helston, TR13 8DR,

Ms K Line, Podiatry Services, Camborne Redruth Hospital, Tel.: 01209 881762

Ms M Mallett, Matron, Helston Community Hospital, Meneage Road, Helston, Cornwall, TR13 8DR, Tel.: 01326 435800

Ms J Mitchell, Orthopaedic Triage Service, Camborne Redruth Hospital, Tel.: 01209 881658

Ms S Newman, Speech & Language, Unit 2, Harleigh Road, Bodmin, Tel.: 01208 256290

Poltair Hospital, Heamoor, Penzance, Cornwall, TR20 8SR, Tel.: 01736 575570

Ms K Roach, Therapy Manager, Camborne Redruth Hospital, Tel.: 01209 881780

Ms J Smith, Occupational Therapy Services, Poltair Hospital, Heamoor, Penzance, TR20 8SR, Tel.: 01726 575570

St Mary's Hospital, St Mary's, Isles of Scilly, TR21 0LE, Tel.: 01720 422392

School Nursing

School Nursing, Redruth Health Centre, Forth Noweth, Redruth, Cornwall, TR15 1AU, Tel.: 01209 881850

School Nursing, Camborne Health Office, Rectory Road, Camborne, Cornwall, TR14 7DL, Tel.: 01209 886500

School Nursing, Pool Health Centre, Station Road, Poole, Cornwall, TR15 3DU, Tel.: 01209 886571

School Nursing, Helston Health Centre, Trengrouse Way, Helston, Cornwall, TR13 8AX, Tel.: 01326 435869

School Nursing, Penzance Health Office, Bellair, Alverton, Penzance, Cornwall, TR18 4TA, Tel.: 01736 575500

Specialist Nursing Services

Ms D Hore, MIU - Minor Injuries, Nurse Consultant, St Aubyn Villa, Bodmin Community Hospital, Bodmin, Tel.: 01208 251412

Ms R Ryder, Community Practice Leader, Threemilestone Community Nurses Office, Threemilestone, Truro, Tel.: 01872 272266

Ms D Appleton, Specialist Nurse, Continence, Bodmin Community Hospital, Bodmin, Tel.: 01208 251499

Ms S Eustice, Nurse Consultant, Continence, Bodmin Community Hospital, Bodmin, Tel.: 01208 251333

Ms L Osborne, Nurse Consultant, Parkinson's Disease, Camborne/Redruth Community Hospital, Barncoose Terrace, Redruth, Tel.: 01209 881627

Ms D Denn, Specialist Nurse, Respiratory, Moorland Road Health Office, Moorland Road, St Austell, Tel.: 01726 291200

Ms J Waldron, Specialist Nurse, Respiratory, CPT Trust Headquarters, Porthpean Road, St Austell, Tel.: 01726 291012

Ms M Scott, Nurse Consultant, Stroke Care, Camborne/Redruth Community Hospital, Barncoose Terrace, Redruth, Tel.: 01209 881698

Ms N Kimpton, Lead Nurse, Community, Tissue Viability, Bodmin Community Hospital, Bodmin, Tel.: 01208 251499

Ms D O'Shea, Specialist Nurse, Tissue Viability, Bodmin Community Hospital, Bodmin, Tel.: 01208 251499

West Wiltshire Primary Care Trust

Trust Headquarters, Unit B, Valentines
Epsom Square
White Horse Business Park
TROWBRIDGE
Wiltshire
BA14 0XG
Tel.: 01225 754453

Admin & Senior Management
Mrs C Clarke, Chief Executive, Southgate House, Pans Lane, Devizes, SN10 5EQ,

Child Health Records
Ms J Ainley, Manager, Child Health Department, Newbridge Hill, Bath, BA1 3QE, Tel.: 01225 313640

Child Protection/Safeguarding Children
Ms K Lanard, Child Protection, Melksham Community Hospital, Tel.: 01225 701053

Clinical Leads (NSF)
Dr D Elliott, Clinical Lead, CHD, Diabetes,
Dr D Elliott, Clinical Lead, Cancer,
Dr H Fairfield, Clinical Lead, Children,
Dr S Major, Clinical Lead, Older People,

District Nursing
Ms I Barker, District Nurse Lead, Southgate House, Pans Lane, Devizes, SN10 5EQ,

Learning Disabilities
Mr M Hennessey, Service Manager, 3rd Floor, Andil House, Court Street, Trowbridge, BA14 8BR,

Learning Disability Team, 3rd Floor, Andil House, Court Street, Trowbridge, BA14 8BR, Tel.: 01225 760106

Mr G McBrien, General Manager, Wiltshire County Council, County Hall, Bythesea Road, Trowbridge, BA14 8LE, Tel.: 01225 771667

Liaison Services

Ms J Parfur, County Hall, Trowbridge, Tel.: 01225 773540

Specialist Nursing Services

Ms J Braithwaite, Diabetic Care, Trowbridge Health Centre, The Halve, Trowbridge, BA14 8SA, Tel.: 01225 766161

Ms M Cannock, Diabetic Care, Diabetes Centre, Royal United Hospital, Combe Park, Bath, BA1 3NG, Tel.: 01225 824173

Ms J Woodman, Diabetic Care, Trowbridge Health Centre, The Halve, Trowbridge, BA14 8SA, Tel.: 01225 766161

Weston Area Health NHS Trust

Trust Headquarters, Weston General Hospital
Grange Road
WESTON SUPER MARE
Somerset
BS23 4TQ
Tel.: 01934 636363

Admin & Senior Management

Ms R Slater, Director of Nursing & Operations, Weston General Hospital, Tel.: 01934 636363

Child Health

Mrs K Roberts, Divisional Manager for Children, Young People & Maternity Services, Drove House, Drove Road, Weston Super Mare, BS23 3NT, Tel.: 01934 635376

Ms A Shepherd, Childrens Services Manager, Childrens Services, Drove House, Drove Road, Weston Super Mare, BS23 3NT, Tel.: 01934 418804

Child Protection/Safeguarding Children

Ms P Richards, Senior Nurse, Child Protection, North Somerset PCT, Waverley House, Clevedon, BS21 6NN, Tel.: 01934 546770

Community Midwifery

Ms K Mayer, Community Midwifery Manager, Ashcombe Unit, Weston General Hospital, Tel.: 01934 647189

Mrs K Roberts, Head of Midwifery, Ashcombe Unit, Weston General Hospital, Tel.: 01934 647189

Mrs S Sheldon, Midwifery Manager, Ashcombe Unit, Weston General Hospital, Tel.: 01934 647189

Family Planning Services

Ms K Harper, Sexual Health Manager, W.I.S.H. Centre, Weston General Hospital, Tel.: 01934 881234

Ms K Roberts, Head of Midwifery, Ashcombe Unit, Weston General Hospital, Tel.: 01934 647189

West Midlands Strategic Health Authority

with major towns and Primary Care Trust boundaries

Pop: 5,334,006

North West

East Midlands

Newcastle-u-Lyne

○ Leek

○ Stoke on Trent

○ Stafford

○ Burton on Trent

○ Shrewsbury

○ Telford

Cannock ○

○ Lichfield

Wolverhampton ○

○ Walsall

West Bromwich

Birmingham

○ Nuneaton

Dudley ○

Sandwell ○

○ Aston

Stourbridge ○

○ Solihull

○ Rugby

○ Coventry

○ Kidderminster

Redditch

○ Warwick

○ Worcester

○ Hereford

Wales

South West

South Central

West Midlands Strategic Health Authority

West Midlands Strategic Health Authority

Birmingham Children's Hospital NHS Trust

Trust Headquarters, Diana, Princess of Wales Childrens Hospital
Steelhouse Lane
BIRMINGHAM
West Midlands
B4 6NH
Tel.: 0121 333 9999
Fax.: 0121 333 9998

Acute Specialist Nursing Services

Ms J Hardy, Inherited Metabolic Disorder, Nurse Specialist, ext 9962
Ms S Kearney, Urodynamics Sister, Tel.: ext 9222
Ms A Daniels, Advanced Nurse Practitioner, Cardiac, Tel.: ext 9404
Ms P Dewick, Liaison Sister, Cardiac, Tel.: ext 9449
Ms J Kidd, Liaison Sister, Cardiac, Tel.: ext 9449
Ms A Cole, Lead, Nurse Specialist, Cleft, Tel.: ext 8092
Ms J Tomlinson, Nurse Specialist, Cleft, Tel.: ext 8092
Ms B Wills, Nurse Specialist, Cleft, Tel.: ext 8092
Ms S Sanders, Nurse Specialist, Cystic Fibrosis, Tel.: ext 9248
Ms B Concannon, Nurse Specialist, Epilepsy, - Neuro, Tel.: ext 8184
Ms R Sandhu, Liaison Sister, Gastroenterology, Tel.: ext 8718
Ms K Ballard, Nurse Specialist, Macmillan, Tel.: ext 8682
Ms S Beardsmore, Nurse Specialist, Macmillan, Tel.: ext 8687
Ms C Davies, Nurse Specialist, Macmillan, Tel.: ext 8685
Ms N Fitzmaurice, Nurse Specialist, Macmillan, Tel.: ext 8687
Ms S Neilson, Nurse Specialist, Macmillan, Tel.: ext 8684
Ms L Fendick, Liaison Sister, Nephrology,- Transplantation, ext 9215
Mr C Bunford, Nurse Specialist, Nutrition, Tel.: ext 8042
Mr C Holden, Clinical Nurse Specialist, Nutrition, Tel.: ext 8042
Ms E Sexton, Clinical Nurse Specialist, Nutrition, Tel.: ext 8042
Ms M Bradwell, Nurse Specialist, Oncology, - Haematology, Tel.: ext 8245
Ms C Hitchott, Retinoblastoma, Nurse Specialist, Oncology, Tel.: ext 9277
Ms M McCalla, Paediatric, Nurse Specialist, Ophthalmology, Tel.: ext 9470
Ms C Thomas, Burns, Nurse Specialist, Paediatrics,
Ms D Jones, Nurse Specialist, Plastic Surgery, Tel.: ext 8117
Ms C Capelett, Community, Liaison Sister, Renal, Tel.: ext 9209
Ms F Gamston, Community, Liaison Sister, Renal, Tel.: ext 9209
Mr G Gordon, Nurse Team Leader Liver Unit, Renal, Tel.: ext 8272
Ms S Taylor, Community, Liaison Sister, Renal, Tel.: ext 9209
Ms S Frost, Nurse Specialist, Respiratory, Tel.: ext 9248
Ms M Tabberner, Nurse Specialist, Respiratory, Tel.: ext 9248
Ms J Sira, Paediatric, Nurse Specialist, Viral Hepatitis, Tel.: ext 8271

Admin & Senior Management

Ms E Morgan, Director of Nursing, Birmingham Children's Hospital NLHS Trust, Steelhouse Lane, Birmingham, West Midlands, B4 6NH, Tel.: 0121 333 8409

Child Health

Dealt with by South Birmingham PCT,

Child Protection/Safeguarding Children

Ms P Rees, Head of Child Protection Support Team, Child Protection, Steelhouse Lane, Birmingham, B4 6NH, Tel.: 0121 333 9999 x 8528
Ms A Knight, Nurse Specialist, Child Protection, Steelhouse Lane, Birmingham, B4 6NH, Tel.: 0121 333 9999 x 9534

Liaison Services

Ms A Bowen, Liaison Services, Manor Hospital, Moat Road, Walsall, West Midlands, Tel.: 01922 721172
Ms K Fowler, Liaison Services, Mosley Hall Hospital, Alcester Road, Birmingham, B13 8JL, Tel.: 0121 4425600

Birmingham Heartlands & Solihull NHS Trust

Trust Headquarters, Birmingham Heartlands Hospital
Bordesley Green East, Bordesley Green
BIRMINGHAM
West Midlands
B9 5SS
Tel.: 0121 424 2000
Fax.: 0121 424 2200

Acute Specialist Nursing Services

Mr R Adkins, CAPD, Clinical Nurse Specialist, Tel.: ext 43302
Ms J Gilks, Feeding Co-ordinator,
Ms T Manji, Training & Education, Nurse Specialist,
Ms J Patel, Discharge, Clinical Nurse Specialist,
Ms S Barnes, Clinical Nurse Specialist, Anaemia, Tel.: ext 43160
Ms D Hamilton, Clinical Nurse Specialist, Anti-Coagulation, Tel.: ext 41706
Ms J Sullivan, Clinical Nurse Specialist, Asthma, - Brittle, Tel.: ext 42437
Ms C Bate, Clinical Nurse Specialist, Breast Care, Tel.: ext 45306
Ms J Milward, Clinical Nurse Specialist, Breast Care,
Ms J Price, Clinical Nurse Specialist, Breast Care, Tel.: ext 45306
Ms L Abel, Nurse Practitioner (Triage), Cardiac, Tel.: ext 42685
Ms S Brace, Lead Nurse Practitioner (Triage), Cardiac, Tel.: ext 42685
Ms R Eggington, Rehabilitation, Clinical Nurse Specialist, Cardiac, Tel.: ext 42902
Ms C McIlduff, Lead Rehabilitation Nurse, Cardiac, Tel.: ext 43312
Ms G O'Regan, Rehabilitation (Phase 2), Cardiac, Tel.: ext 42902
Ms K Sanghera, Rehab (Asian Cardiac Education), Cardiac, Tel.: ext 43312
Ms J Barton-Rayner, Clinical Nurse Specialist, Cardiology, Tel.: ext 42901
Ms H Carolan, (Chest Pain Assessment Unit), Cardiology, Tel.: ext 42344
Ms J Conway, Nurse Specialist, Cardiology, Tel.: ext 42206
Ms K Creedon, Rehab, Cardiology, Tel.: ext 44286
Ms H Lane, Nurse Specialist, Cardiology, Tel.: ext 42206
Ms J Pitt, Lead Clinical Trials Co-ordinator, Cardiology,
Ms J Smith, Specialist Nurse, Cardiology, Tel.: ext 42206
Ms D Tidmarsh, Specialist Nurse, Cardiology, Tel.: ext 43566
Ms H Whitlam, Specialist Nurse, Cardiology, Tel.: ext 43416
Ms C Grimley, Clinical Nurse Specialist, Colorectal, Tel.: ext 43730
Ms S Murcott, Clinical Nurse Specialist, Colorectal, Tel.: ext 43740
Ms Y Higgins, Outreach, Clinical Nurse Specialist, Critical Care, Tel.: ext 41416
Ms S Quinton, Outreach, Critical Care, Tel.: ext 41416
Ms R Davies, Clinical Nurse Specialist, Cystic Fibrosis, Tel.: ext 43577
Ms C Evans, Clinical Nurse Specialist, Cystic Fibrosis, Tel.: ext 42515
Ms J Hussey, Clinical Nurse Specialist, Cystic Fibrosis, Tel.: ext 40579
Ms S Robbins, Clinical Nurse Specialist, Dermatology,
Ms N Getlevog, Paediatric, Clinical Nurse Specialist, Diabetic Care,
Ms J Hand, Clinical Nurse Specialist, Diabetic Care, Tel.: ext 41176
Ms E Keenan, Clinical Nurse Specialist, Diabetic Care,
Ms J McAleese, Clinical Nurse Specialist, Diabetic Care, Tel.: ext 45268
Ms S Mughal, Clinical Nurse Specialist, Diabetic Care, ext 40174
Ms M Patel, Clinical Nurse Specialist, Diabetic Care,
Ms A Dodds, Pre Dialysis, Clinical Nurse Specialist, Dialysis, Tel.: ext 42677
Ms S Handley, (Home Dialysis), Clinical Nurse Specialist, Dialysis,
Ms A Doyle, Clinical Nurse Specialist, Elderly Care,
Ms D Cash, Clinical Nurse Specialist, Endoscopy,

West Midlands Strategic Health Authority

Ms H Lodhi, Clinical Nurse Specialist, ENT Surgery,
Ms K Markham, Clinical Nurse Specialist, ENT Surgery,
Ms C Smith, Clinical Nurse Specialist, Fertility,
Ms R Gardiner, Clinical Nurse Specialist, Gastroenterology,
Ms E Roberts, Clinical Nurse Specialist, Gynaecology,
Mr C Bryan, Specialist Nurse, Heart Failure, Tel.: ext 41709
Ms N Buckley, Specialist Nurse, Heart Failure, Tel.: ext 44076
Ms C Kerrigan, Paediatric, Clinical Nurse Specialist, Immunology,
Mr K Baker, Clinical Nurse Specialist, Infection Control, Tel.: ext 42659
Ms S Beaupierre, Clinical Nurse Specialist, Infection Control, Tel.: ext 41137
Ms N Roberts, Clinical Nurse Specialist, Infection Control, Tel.: ext 41137
Ms J Room, Clinical Nurse Specialist, Infection Control, Tel.: ext 41137
Ms C Tweedale, Clinical Nurse Specialist, Infection Control,
Ms B Leung, Clinical Nurse Specialist, Lung Cancer,
Ms L Reaper, Clinical Nurse Specialist, Lung Cancer,
Ms D Silvey, Clinical Nurse Specialist, Lung Cancer, Tel.: ext 41433
Ms B Bennett, Clinical Nurse Specialist, Nutrition, Tel.: ext 41435
Ms K Pedwell, Clinical Nurse Specialist, Ophthalmology,
Ms S Abbott, Clinical Nurse Specialist, Pain Management,
Ms R Edgcumbe, Clinical Nurse Specialist, Pain Management,
Ms E Morrison, Clinical Nurse Specialist, Pain Management,
Ms S Tonks, Clinical Nurse Specialist, Pain Management,
Ms S Bonney, Clinical Nurse Specialist, Palliative Care,
Ms J Brittle, Clinical Nurse Specialist, Palliative Care,
Ms N Cordwell, Clinical Nurse Specialist, Palliative Care,
Ms A Dainty, Clinical Nurse Specialist, Palliative Care,
Ms M Handy, Clinical Nurse Specialist, Palliative Care,
Ms K MacKellar, Clinical Nurse Specialist, Palliative Care,
Ms D Terry, Clinical Nurse Specialist, Radiology, Tel.: ext 41278
Ms C Richardson, Nurse Specialist, Renal, Tel.: ext 42160
Ms C Murphy, Paediatric, Clinical Nurse Specialist, Respiratory,
Ms P Sweeney, Clinical Nurse Specialist, Respiratory, Tel.: ext 43314
Ms C Wogan, Paediatric, Respiratory, Tel.: ext 43825
Ms B Blackhall, Clinical Nurse Specialist, Rheumatology,
Ms D Lane, Clinical Nurse Specialist, Rheumatology,
Ms L Bowman, Clinical Nurse Specialist, Stoma Care, Tel.: ext 43730
Ms P Keane, Clinical Nurse Specialist, Stoma Care, Tel.: ext 43740
Mr P Carr, Clinical Nurse Specialist, Stroke Care, Tel.: ext 41231
Ms C Stone, Clinical Nurse Specialist, Transfusion, Tel.: ext 40614
Ms J Illsley, Clinical Nurse Specialist, Upper GI,
Ms J Bailey, Clinical Nurse Specialist, Urology, Tel.: ext 40093
Ms L Grinnell-Moore, Clinical Nurse Specialist, Urology, Tel.: ext 40093
Ms S Hesketh, Clinical Nurse Specialist, Urology, Tel.: ext 40093
Ms A Moore, Clinical Nurse Specialist, Urology,
Ms E Burke, Clinical Nurse Specialist, Vascular, Tel.: ext 40115
Ms Y Hall, Clinical Nurse Specialist, Vascular, Tel.: ext 40115

Community Midwifery
Community Clerk, Solihull Hospital, Lode Lane, Solihull, West Midlands, B91 2LJ, Tel.: 0121 709 0209
Mrs P East, Matron Low Risk, Birmingham Heartlands Hosp, Bordesley Green East, Bordesley Green, Birmingham, West Midlands, B9 5SS, Tel.: 0121 424 2726
Emergencies, Birmingham Heartlands Hosp, Bordesley Green East, Bordesley Green, Birmingham, West Midlands, B9 5SS, Tel.: 0121 773 6422
Emergencies, Solihull Hospital, Lode Lane, Solihull, West Midlands, B91 2LJ, Tel.: 0121 424 4051
Ms P Jordan, Midwifery Counsellor,
HIV/AIDS
Ms M Owen, HIV, Tel.: ext 40361

Liaison Services
Ms P Kimberly, Discharge Liaison,
Ms M McLaughlin, Discharge Liaison,
Ms C McNulty, Discharge Liaison,
Ms G Richards, Discharge Liaison,

Birmingham Women's Healthcare NHS Trust

Trust Headquarters, Metchley Park Road
Edgbaston
BIRMINGHAM
B15 2TG
Tel.: 0121 472 1377
Fax.: 0121 627 2602

Acute Specialist Nursing Services
Ms M Emery, Nurse Practitioner, Advanced Neonatal, Tel.: ext 2726
Ms R Marshall, Nurse Practitioner, Advanced Neonatal, Tel.: ext 2726
Ms C Rutherford, Nurse Practitioner, Advanced Neonatal, Tel.: ext 2726
Child Health
Ms J Owen, Director of Nursing & Midwifery, Tel.: 0121 472 1377 ext 2607
Child Health Records
Ms P E Salisbury, Inpatient Maternity Services, Matron, Tel.: 0121 472 1377 ext 4254
Child Protection/Safeguarding Children
Ms E Giles, Lead Nurse/Midwife for Safeguarding Children, Child Protection, Birmingham Womens' Hospital, Edgbaston, Birmingham, B15 2TG, Tel.: 0121 472 1377 ext 4532
Community Matrons
Mrs V R Johnson, Community Matron - Community & Birth Centre, Birmingham Womens' Hospital, Edgbaston, Birmingham, B15 2TG, Tel.: 0121 472 1377 ext 4123
Community Midwifery
Community enquiries during office hours, Birmingham Womens' Hospital, Edgbaston, Birmingham, West Midlands, B15 2TG, Tel.: 0121 627 2660
Community enquiries outside office hours/Bank Holidays/Weekends, Via First Response, Birmingham Womens' Hospital, Edgbaston, Birmingham, West Midlands, B15 2TG, Tel.: 01384 215666
Mrs V R Johnson, Matron for Community Midwifery Services & Birth Centre, Birmingham Womens' Hospital, Edgbaston, Birmingham, West Midlands, B15 2TG, Tel.: 0121 472 1377 ext 4123
Ms J Owen, Director of Nursing & Midwifery, Tel.: 0121 472 1377 ext 4023
Other Services
Dr M Hocking, Consultant Neonatologist, Tel.: 0121 472 1377 ext 2646

Burntwood, Lichfield & Tamworth Primary Care Trust

Trust Headquarters, Merlin House
Etchell Road, Bitterscote
TAMWORTH
B78 3HF
Tel.: 01827 306111

Child Health
Paediatric Community Nurses, Tamworth Health Centre, Upper Gungate, Tamworth, B79 7EA, Tel.: 01827 308810
Child Health Records
Child Health Department, St Michael's Hospital, Trent Valley Road, Lichfield, WS13 6EF, Tel.: 01543 414555
Child Protection/Safeguarding Children
Ms H Widdowson, Designated Nurse, Child Protection, Guardian House, Lichfield, WS13 6WA, Tel.: 01543 420433

West Midlands Strategic Health Authority

Clinical Leads (NSF)
Ms K Chapman, Clinical Lead, Cancer,
Dr Y Sawbridge, Clinical Lead, CHD,
Dr R Hawkes, Clinical Lead, Diabetic Care,
Dr J Barlow, Clinical Lead, Older People,
Community Nursing Services
Ms M Barrow, Locality Manager - Tamworth, Sir Robert Peel Hospital, Mile Oak, Tamworth, B78 3NG, Tel.: 01827 263815
Ms F Lee, Locality Manager - Burntwood & Lichfield, Victoria Hospital, Friary Road, Lichfield, Tel.: 01543 414555
Family Planning Services
Provided by South Staffordshire Healthcare Trust,
Learning Disabilities
Provided by South Staffordshire Healthcare Trust,
Other Services
Ms S Baines, Discharge Co-ordinator, Victoria, Lichfield,
Ms T Groom, Discharge Co-ordinator, Sir Robert Peel Hospital, Mile Oak, Tamworth, B78 3NG,
Specialist Nursing Services
Cardiac, Sir Robert Peel Hospital, Mile Oak, Tamworth, B78 3NG,
Continence, St Michael's Hospital, Trent Valley Road, Lichfield, WS13 6EF,
Diabetes, Guardian House, Lichfield, WS13 6WA,
Neuro/MS, Sir Robert Peel Hospital, Mile Oak, Tamworth, B78 3NG,
Rheumatology, Sir Robert Peel Hospital, Mile Oak, Tamworth, B78 3NG,
Stroke Co-ordinator, Sir Robert Peel Hospital, Mile Oak, Tamworth, B78 3NG,

Burton Hospitals NHS Trust
Trust Headquarters, Queen's Hospital
Belvedere Road
BURTON-ON-TRENT
Staffordshire
DE13 0RB
Tel.: 01283 566333

Community Midwifery
Ms L Bird, Community Midwifery Manager, Tel.: 01827 288495

Cannock Chase Primary Care Trust
Trust Headquarters, Block D
Beecroft Court, off Beecroft Road
CANNOCK
WS11 1JP
Tel.: 01543 465100
Fax.: 01543 465110

Admin & Senior Management
Mrs E Onions, Director of Nursing & Operational Services,
Mr J-P Parsons, Chief Executive,
Clinical Leads (NSF)
Dr V K Singh, Clinical Lead, CHD,
Mrs J Wright, Clinical Lead, Diabetic Care,
Mrs E Onions, Clinical Lead, Older People,
District Nursing
Mrs J Barratt, Head of Community Services, Beecroft Clinic, Crown House, Beecroft Road, Cannock, WS11 1JP, Tel.: 01543 500110
Family Planning Services
Dr A Kundu, Clinical Director, Sexual Health Service, White Lodge Community Unit, New Penkridge Road, Cannock, WS11 1HN, Tel.: 01543 469759
Liaison Services
Mrs L Jones, CHD, Liaison Nurse, Heath Hayes Health Centre, Goorsemoor Road, Heath Hayes, Cannock, Tel.: 01543 277933
Pharmacy
Mr M Seaton, Medicines Management Advisor, Block D, Beecroft Court, off Beecroft Road, Cannock, WS11 1JP, Tel.: 01543 465100

Specialist Nursing Services
Mrs L Smith, (Nursing Homes), Continence, West Chadsmoor Clinic, Clarion Way, Chadsmoor, Cannock, Tel.: 01543 879787
Mrs S Priddey, Heart Failure, Great Wyrley Health Centre, Wardles Lane, Great Wyrley, WS6 6JD, Tel.: 01922 415627
Mrs J Manzie, Consultant, Intermediate Care, Spring Meadow, Cannock Chase Hospital, Brunswick Road, Cannock, WS11 2SF, Tel.: 01543 576963

Coventry Teaching Primary Care Trust
Trust Headquarters, Christchurch House
Greyfriars Lane
COVENTRY
Warwickshire
CV1 2GQ
Tel.: 02476 552225

Admin & Senior Management
Mr M Attwood, Joint Chief Executive,
Mr S Jones, Joint Chief Executive,
Child Protection/Safeguarding Children
Ms A Burley, Designated Nurse, Child Protection, Tel.: 02476 246261
Mrs J Hill, Named Nurse, Child Protection,
Clinical Leads (NSF)
Ms V Robson, Clinical Lead, Cancer,
Dr P Barker, Clinical Lead, CHD,
Ms J Cryer, Clinical Lead, Older People,
Learning Disabilities
Mr A Bennett, General Manager, Learning Disability Services, River House, Gulson Hospital, Gulson Road, Coventry, CV1 2HR, Tel.: 024 7622 4055 ext 3154
Community Nurses, Logan Assessment Services, Logan Road, Henley Green, Coventry, CV2 1AG, Tel.: 024 7660 4608
Ms J Connell, Operational Manager, Learning Disability Service, River House, Gulson Hospital, Gulson Road, Coventry, CV1 2HR, Tel.: 024 7624 6238
Ms L Mutchell, Services Manager, Cashs Lane,
Ms M Whateley, Childrens Service Lead, Bridge House,

Dudley Beacon and Castle Primary Care Trust
Trust Headquarters
St Johns House, Union Street
DUDLEY
West Midlands
DY2 8PP
Tel.: 01384 366111

Admin & Senior Management
Ms B Ingram, Head of Primary Care/Lead Nurse, Trust Headquarters, St Johns House, Union Street, Dudley, DY2 8PP, Tel.: 01384 366111
Child Health Records
Ms E Flavell, General Service Manager, Paytons House, Ridge Hill, Brierley Hill Road, Stourbridge, DY8 5ST, Tel.: 01384 366126
District Nursing
Ms S Cooper, Locality General Manager, Trust Headquarters, St Johns House, Union Street, Dudley, DY2 8PP, Tel.: 01384 366111
Ms B Ingram, Head of Primary Care/Lead Nuse, Trust Headquarters, St Johns House, Union Street, Dudley, DY2 8PP, Tel.: 01384 366111
Family Planning Services
Ms L Johnson, Family Planning Manager, Central Clinic, Hall Street, Dudley, DY1 7BX, Tel.: 01384 366466
Health Visitors
Ms S Cooper, Locality General Manager, Trust Headquarters, St Johns House, Union Street, Dudley, DY2 8PP, Tel.: 01384 366111

West Midlands Strategic Health Authority

Ms B Ingram, Head of Primary Care/Lead Nuse, Trust Headquarters, St Johns House, Union Street, Dudley, DY2 8PP, Tel.: 01384 366111

Pharmacy
Ms A Tennant, Specialist in Pharmaceutical Health, St Johns House, Union Street, Dudley, DY2 8PP, Tel.: 01384 366632

Dudley Group of Hospitals NHS Trust

Trust Headquarters, C Block
Russells Hall Hospital
DUDLEY
DY1 2HQ
Tel.: 01384 456111
Fax.: 01384 244072

Acute Specialist Nursing Services
Ms H Flavell, Anti-Coagulation, Russells Hall Hospital, Dudley, DY1 2HQ, Tel.: 01384 456111
Ms D Gibb, Clinical Nurse Specialist, Breast Care, Russells Hall Hospital, Dudley, DY1 2HQ, Tel.: 01384 456111
Ms C Wilcox, Clinical Nurse Specialist, Breast Care, Russells Hall Hospital, Dudley, DY1 2HQ, Tel.: 01384 456111
Mrs R Willetts, Clinical Nurse Specialist, Breast Care, Russells Hall Hospital, Dudley, DY1 2HQ, Tel.: 01384 456111
Ms L Waldron, Matron, Cancer, Russells Hall Hospital, Dudley, DY1 2HQ, Tel.: 01384 456111
Mr G Dimmock, Co-ordinator, Discharges, Russells Hall Hospital, Dudley, DY1 2HQ, Tel.: 01384 456111
Ms K Fletcher, Co-ordinator, Discharges, Russells Hall Hospital, Dudley, DY1 2HQ, Tel.: 01384 456111
Ms N Howells, Co-ordinator, Discharges, Russells Hall Hospital, Dudley, DY1 2HQ, Tel.: 01384 456111
Ms L Ray Bould, Infection Control, Russells Hall Hospital, Dudley, DY1 2HQ, Tel.: 01384 456111
Ms F Chambers, Macmillan, Russells Hall Hospital, Dudley, DY1 2HQ, Tel.: 01384 456111
Mr J Gilde, Palliative Care, Russells Hall Hospital, Dudley, DY1 2HQ, Tel.: 01384 456111
Mrs H Hill, Clinical Nurse Specialist, Stoma Care, - Colorectal, Russells Hall Hospital, Dudley, DY1 2HQ, Tel.: 01384 456111
Mrs K Parry, Clinical Nurse Specialist, Stoma Care, - Colorectal, Russells Hall Hospital, Dudley, DY1 2HQ, Tel.: 01384 456111
Ms S Davis, Upper GI, Russells Hall Hospital, Dudley, DY1 2HQ, Tel.: 01384 456111
Mrs B Fairley, Upper GI, Russells Hall Hospital, Dudley, DY1 2HQ, Tel.: 01384 456111
Mrs N Whitehorse, Upper GI, Russells Hall Hospital, Dudley, DY1 2HQ, Tel.: 01384 456111

Admin & Senior Management
Ms A Close, Director of Nursing, Russells Hall Hospital, Dudley, DY1 2HQ, Tel.: 01384 244577

Community Midwifery
Community Midwives, Russells Hall Hospital, Tel.: 01384 456111 x 4358
Emergencies, Russells Hall Hospital, Tel.: 01384 456111
Ms Y Jones, Matron Maternity, Russells Hall Hospital, Tel.: 01384 456111 x 3066
Ms S Mansell, Head of Midwifery, Russells Hall Hospital, Tel.: 01384 456111 x 1513

Dudley South Primary Care Trust

Trust Headquarters,
Ridge Hill
Brierley Hill Road
STOURBRIDGE
West Midlands
DY8 5ST
Tel.: 01384 457373

Admin & Senior Management
Ms J Parker, Head of Professional Development, Tel.: 01384 244479
Mrs K Vilton, Director of Modernisation/Deputy Chief Executive/Lead Nurse, Ridge Hill Site, Brierley Hill Road, Stourbridge, DY8 5ST,

Child Health
Ms S Preston, General Manager, Paytons House, Brierley Hill Road, Stowbridge,

Child Health Records
Ms E Flowell-Bowen, General Services Manager, Child Health Services,

Child Protection/Safeguarding Children
Mrs M Reynolds, Senior Nurse, Child Protection, Cross Street Health Centre, Cross Street, Dudley, West Midlands, DY1 1RN, Tel.: 01384 366213

Clinical Leads (NSF)
Dr J Speakman, Clinical Lead, Cancer,

Learning Disabilities
Brierley Hill, Kingswinford, Gate Lodge, High Street, Ablecote, Stourbridge, DY8 4JB, Tel.: 01384 813930
Dudley, The Ladies Walk Centre, Sedgley, Dudley, DY3 3UA, Tel.: 01384 813363
Halesowen, Halesowen Health Centre, 14 Birmingham Street, Halesowen, B63 3HL, Tel.: 0121602 8833
Ms B Nicholls, Community, Development Manager, Ridge Hill, Brierley Hill Road, Wordsley, Stourbridge, DY8 5ST, Tel.: 01384 457373
Ms C Richardson, General Manager, Ridge Hill, Brierley Hill Road, Wordsley, Stourbridge, DY8 5ST, Tel.: 01384 244477
Sedgley/Coseley, The Ladies Walk Centre, Sedgley, Dudley, DY3 3UA, Tel.: 01384 813360
Stourbridge, Gate Lodge, High Street, Ablecote, Stourbridge, DY8 4JB, Tel.: 01384 813925

Liaison Services
Ms D Tolley, Liaison, Russells Hall Hospital, Dudley,

Pharmacy
Mr D Hervis, Community Pharmacist, Paytons House, Brierley Hill Road, Stourbridge,

Specialist Nursing Services
Ms J Maloney, Substance Misuse Team, Prof Developt Spec, Kinver Ward, Bushey Fields Hospital, Bushey Fields Road, Dudley, DY1 2LZ,
Ms G Davey, Continence, Tel.: 01384 271271

The Homeless/Travellers & Asylum Seekers
Ms P Owens, Travelling Families Lead, Cross Street Health Centre, Tel.: 01384 459500

East Staffordshire Primary Care Trust

Trust Headquarters, Edwin House
Second Avenue, Centrum 100
BURTON-ON-TRENT
DE14 2WF
Tel.: 01283 507100

Admin & Senior Management
Mr M Docherty, Director of Operations/Executive Nurse, Edwin House, Second Avenue, Centrum 100, Burton-on-Trent, DE14 2WF, Tel.: 01283 507100
Ms M Gill, Community Services Manager, Edwin House, Second Avenue, Centrum 100, Burton-on-Trent, DE14 2WF, Tel.: 01283 507100
Mr S Poyner, Chief Executive, Tel.: 01283 507100

Child Health
Via Trust Headquarters, Edwin House, Second Avenue, Centrum 100, Burton-on-Trent, DE14 2WF, Tel.: 01283 507100

Child Health Records
Ms C Farmer, Child Health Department, South Staffordshire Healthcare Trust, St Michaels Hospital, Lichfield, Tel.: 01543 414555

West Midlands Strategic Health Authority

Child Protection/Safeguarding Children
Dr L Light, Child Protection, South Staffordshire Healthcare Trust, St Michaels Hospital, Lichfield, Tel.: 01543 414555
Ms H Widdowson, Child Protection, South Staffordshire Healthcare Trust, St Michaels Hospital, Lichfield, Tel.: 01543 414555

Clinical Leads (NSF)
Ms V Mallows, Clinical Lead, Cancer, Trust Headquarters,
Ms M Freeman, Clinical Lead, Care of the Elderly, Trust HQ

Community Nursing Services
Via Trust Headquarters, Edwin House, Second Avenue, Centrum 100, Burton-on-Trent, DE14 2WF, Tel.: 01283 507100

District Nursing
Via Trust Headquarters, Edwin House, Second Avenue, Centrum 100, Burton-on-Trent, DE14 2WF, Tel.: 01283 507100

Family Planning Services
Dr Khundu, Child Health Department, South Staffordshire Healthcare Trust HQ, St George's Hospital, Stafford,

Liaison Services
Ms D Griffin, Queens Hospital, Burton-on-Trent, DE13 0RB,

Smoking Cessation
Ms N Winters, Edwin House, Second Avenue, Centrum 100, Burton-on-Trent, DE14 2WF, Tel.: 01283 507100

Eastern Birmingham Primary Care Trust

Trust Headquarters, Waterlinks House
Richard Street, Aston
BIRMINGHAM
B7 4AA
Tel.: 0121 333 4113

Admin & Senior Management
Ms S Christie, Chief Executive,

District Nursing
Ms M Crundwell, Nurse Manager, North East Area, Waterlinks House, Tel.: 0121 333 4133
Ms S Fitzpatrick, Clinical Nurse Leader - Greater Yardley Area,
Ms T Moghal, Clinical Nurse Leader - Greater Yardley Area,
Sheldon, Greater Yardley Area, Harvey Road Health Centre, Tel.: 0121 255 2820
Sheldon, Greater Yardley Area, Fox Team, Shirley Road Health Centre, Tel.: 0121 764 7400
Sheldon, Greater Yardley Area, Horrell Road Health Centre, Tel.: 0121 255 7700
Ms T Taylor, Nurse Manager, Hodge Hill Area, Harlequin Surgery, 160 Shard End Crescent, Shard End, B34 7BP, Tel.: 0121 747 2564
Ms L Thomas, Nurse Manager, Hodge Hill Area, Harlequin Surgery, 160 Shard End Crescent, Shard End, B34 7BP, Tel.: 0121 747 2564
Yardley, Greater Yardley Area, Park Medical Centre, Tel.: 0121 766 5594
Yardley, Greater Yardley Area, Stetchford Health Centre, Tel.: 0121 255 2840
Yardley, Greater Yardley Area, Yardley Green Medical Centre, Tel.: 0121 255 4215

George Eliot Hospital NHS Trust

Trust Headquarters, George Eliot Hospital
College Street
NUNEATON
Warwickshire
CV10 7DJ
Tel.: 024 7635 1351
Fax.: 024 7686 5058

Community Midwifery
Community Direct Line, ANC 1st Floor Maternity Building, Tel.: 024 7686 5022
Ms A Crompton, Community Midwifery Manager, Tel.: 024 765022
Emergencies - Labour Ward, Ground Floor Maternity Building, Tel.: 024 7686 5246

Mrs K Howker, Head of Midwifery, George Eliot Maternity Unit, College Street, Nuneaton, Tel.: 024 765197

Good Hope NHS Trust

Trust Headquarters, Good Hope Hospital
Rectory Road
SUTTON COLDFIELD
West Midlands
B75 7RR
Tel.: 0121 378 2211
Fax.: 0121 378 6029

Community Midwifery
Mrs M Coleman, Head of Midwifery, Tel.: 0121 378 2211 x 3203/3182
Community Midwifery Office, Fothergill Block, Good Hope Maternity Unit, Rectory Road, B75 7RR, Tel.: 0121 378 2211 ext 3214
Emergencies, Delivery Suite, Tel.: 0121 378 6032
Ms H Melville, Community Midwifery Manager, Tel.: 0121 378 2211 ext 3214
Stockland Green Health Centre, Tel.: 0121 465 2366

Liaison Services
Mr B McFadzean, Discharge Co-ordinator, Good Hope Hospital, Tel.: 0121 378 2211 ext 2025

Heart of Birmingham Teaching Primary Care Trust

Trust Headquarters, Bartholomew House
142 Hagley Road, Edgbaston
BIRMINGHAM
B16 9PA
Tel.: 0121 224 4600
Fax.: 0121 224 4601

Admin & Senior Management
Ms S Ali, Director of Nursing, Trust HQ, Bartholomew House, 142 Hagley Road, Edgbaston, Birmingham, B16 9PA, Tel.: 0121 224 4600
Mrs K Evans, Assistant Director of Nursing, Trust HQ, Bartholomew House, 142 Hagley Road, Edgbaston, Birmingham, B16 9PA, Tel.: 0121 224 4768
Mrs G Gerald, Nurse Education & Development Manager, Trust HQ, Bartholomew House, 142 Hagley Road, Edgbaston, Birmingham, B16 9PA, Tel.: 0121 224 4053

Child Protection/Safeguarding Children
R Kang, Safeguarding Children, Bartholomew House, 142 Hagley Road, Edgbaston, Birmingham, B16 9PA, Tel.: 0121 224 4600

Clinical Leads (NSF)
Dr N Ahmed, Locality Clinical Lead, Coventry Road Medical Centre, 448 Coventry Road, Small Heath, B10,
Dr V Bathla, Locality Clinical Lead, Handsworth Medical Centre, 143 Albert Road, Handsworth, B21 9LE,
Dr I Marok, Locality Clinical Lead,
Dr S Mukherjee, Locality Clinical Lead, Newtown Health Centre, Melbourne Avenue, Newtown, Birmingham,
Dr S Pandit, Locality Clinical Lead, 1 Brinklow Tower, Frank Street, Highgate,
Dr S Raghavan, Clinical Lead, CHD & Diabetes,
Dr N Rati, Locality Clinical Lead, Laurie Pike Health Centre, 91 Birchfield Road, Aston,
Dr R Muralidhar, Clinical Lead, Cancer,

Community Matrons
Ms V Foxall, Community Matron, Bartholomew House, 142 Hogley Road, Tel.: 0121 766 5550
Ms L Mukwedeya, Community Matron, Contact via Trust HQ,
Ms J Weston, Community Matron, Contact via Trust HQ,

Community Nursing Services
Ms J Conaty, Community Alcohol Nurse, Colston Health Centre, 10 Bath Row, Lee Bank, Birmingham, B15 1LZ, Tel.: 0121 255 7925

West Midlands Strategic Health Authority

Ms S McCutcheon, Community Alcohol Nurse, Colston Health Centre, 10 Bath Row, Lee Bank, Birmingham, B15 1LZ, Tel.: 0121 255 7925

Health Visitors

Ms G Mngaza, Health Visitor Development Post, Balsall Heath Health Centre, 43 Edward Road, Balsall Heath, Tel.: 0121 446 2300

Matrons/Modern Matrons

Ms M Balthazor, Sparkbrook Locality, Modern Matron, Centre for Community Health, St Patricks, Frank Street, Highgate, B12 0YA, Tel.: 0121 446 1102

Ms D Bennett, Perry Barr Locality, Modern Matron, St Stephens Centre, 171 Nivevah Road, Handsworth, B21 0SY, Tel.: 0121 465 4764

Ms P Beswick, Perry Barr Locality, Modern Matron, St Stephens Centre, 171 Nivevah Road, Handsworth, B21 0SY, Tel.: 0121 465 4764

Ms M Rutledge, Ladywood Locality, Modern Matron, Gee House, Holborn Hill Business Centre, Nechells, B7 5JE, Tel.: 0121 465 4872

Ms T Sheridan, Sparkbrook Locality, Modern Matron, Centre for Community Health, St Patricks, Frank Street, Highgate, B12 0YA, Tel.: 0121 446 1103

Ms C Wint, Ladywood Locality, Modern Matron, Gee House, Holborn Hill Business Centre, Nechells, B7 5JE, Tel.: 0121 465 4814

School Nursing

Ms J Savage, School Nurse Clinical Lead, Aston Health Centre, 175 Trinity Road, Birmingham, B6 6JA, Tel.: 0121 255 2200

Specialist Nursing Services

Ms G Dhaliwal, Nurse, CHD, Carnegie Centre, Hunters Road, Hockley, Birmingham, B19 1DR, Tel.: 0121 523 1863

Ms H Lawless, Nurse, CHD, Carnegie Centre, Hunters Road, Hockley, Birmingham, B19 1DR, Tel.: 0121 523 1864

Mrs B Cunningham, Nurse Specialist, Diabetic Care, Unit 3, Peel Place, 50 Carver Street, Hockley, Birmingham, B1 3AS, Tel.: 0121 262 6436

Mrs M Leo, Nurse Specialist, Diabetic Care, Unit 3, Peel Place, 50 Carver Street, Hockley, Birmingham, B1 3AS, Tel.: 0121 262 6436

Ms L Miller, Lead Nurse, Haemoglobinopathy, Ladywood Community Health Centre, St Vincents St West, Ladywood, B16 8RP,

Ms T Gallagher, Nurse: Health Visitor, PEC, Aston Health Centre, 175 Trinity Road, Birmingham, B6 6JA, Tel.: 0121 255 2200

Mr D Ladd, Nurse, PEC, Ladywood Community Health Centre, St Vincents Street West, Ladywood, B16 8RP, Tel.: 0121 465 4218

Ms J Panter, Nurse, PEC, Laurie Pike Health Centre, 91 Birchfield Road, Aston,

Ms M Cotter, Nurse, Respiratory, Lansdowne Health Centre, 34 Lansdowne Street, Birmingham, B18 7EE,

Ms K Jukes, Nurse, Respiratory, Lansdowne Health Centre, 34 Lansdowne Street, Birmingham, B18 7EE, Tel.: 0121 523 1862

Ms P Steward, Nurse, Respiratory, Lansdowne Health Centre, 34 Lansdowne Street, Birmingham, B18 7EE, Tel.: 0121 523 1860

Ms M Smith, Nurse Specialist, Tissue Viability, Lansdown Health Centre, 34 Lansowne Street, Birmingham, B18 7EE,

Ms J Stanton, Lead Nurse, Tissue Viability, Lansdown Health Centre, 34 Lansowne Street, Birmingham, B18 7EE,

The Homeless/Travellers & Asylum Seekers

Ms J Conaty, Community Nursing for the Homeless,

Ms J Davis, Travelling Families, Health Visitor, Balsall Heath Health Centre, 43 Edward Road, Balsall Heath, Birmingham, B12 9LP, Tel.: 121 446 2300

Ms M Evans, Team Co-ordinator, Birmingham Asylum Seeker Health Outreach Team, Health Visitor, Victoria Road Health Centre, Victoria Road, Aston, Birmingham, B6 5HP, Tel.: 0121 766 5550

Ms A Higgs, Birmingham Asylum Seeker Health Outreach Team, Health Visitor, Victoria Road Health Centre, Victoria road, Aston, Birmingham, B6 5HP, Tel.: 0121 327 8901

Ms S McCutcheon, Community Nursing for the Homeless, Health Exchange, William Booth Centre, William Booth Lane, off Constitution Hill, Birmingham, B4 6HA, Tel.: 0121 255 7925

Ms H Saimbi, Asylum Seeker & Refugee Centre for Health, Broadway Health Centre, Cope Street, Ladywood, Birmingham, B18 7BA, Tel.: 0121 456 1551

Hereford Hospitals NHS Trust

Trust Headquarters, Hereford County Hospital
Union Walk
HEREFORD
Herefordshire
HR1 2ER
Tel.: 01432 355444
Fax.: 01432 354310

Community Midwifery
Head of Midwifery, Tel.: 01432 355444/372953

Herefordshire Primary Care Trust

Trust Headquarters, Vaughan Building
Ruckhall Lane
Belmont
HEREFORD
Herefordshire
HR2 9RP
Tel.: 01432 344344

Admin & Senior Management

Ms T Jay, Director of Clinical Development - Lead Executive Nurse, Vaughan Building, Ruckhall Lane, Belmont, Hereford, HR2 9RP, Tel.: 01432 344344

Child Health

Ms C Norris, Paediatrics, 1 Ledbury Road, Hereford, HR1 2SX, Tel.: 01432 373940

Ms P Thomas, Paediatrics, 1 Ledbury Road, Hereford, HR1 2SX, Tel.: 01432 373940

Child Protection/Safeguarding Children

Ms L Renton, Designated Nurse, Child Protection, Belmont Abbey, Tel.: 01432 344344

Community Nursing Services

Mrs C Blackaby, Locality Manager, Ross-on-Wye, Ross Community Hospital, Ross-on-Wye, HR9 5LQ, Tel.: 01989 562100

Mrs C Blackaby, Locality Manager, Ledbury, Ledbury Community Hospital, Ledbury, HR7 4QN, Tel.: 01531 632488

Mrs C Blackaby, Locality Manager, Bromyard, Bromyard Community Hospital, Bromyard, HR7 4QN, Tel.: 01885 485700

Ms S Doheny, Locality Manager, Hereford City, Gaol Street Clinic, Hereford, HR1 2HU, Tel.: 01432 378910

Mr G Taylor, Locality Manager, Leominster, Kingston, Leominster Community Hospital, South Street, Leominster, HR6 8JH, Tel.: 01568 614211

District Nursing

Mrs C Blackaby, Locality Manager, Ledbury (District Nurses), Ledbury Community Hospital, Ledbury, HR7 4QN, Tel.: 01531 632488

Mrs C Blackaby, Locality Manager, Bromyard (District Nurses), Bromyard Community Hospital, Bromyard, HR7 4QN, Tel.: 01885 485700

Mrs C Blackaby, Locality Manager, Ross-on-Wye (District Nurses), Ross Community Hospital, Ross-on-Wye, HR9 5LQ, Tel.: 01989 562100

Ms S Doheny, Locality Manager, Hereford City (District Nurses), Gaol Street Clinic, Hereford, HR1 2HU, Tel.: 01432 378910 Emergencies (night), Tel.: 01432 355444

Mr G Taylor, Locality Manager, Leominster, Kingston (District Nurses), Leominster Community Hospital, South Street, Leominster, HR6 8JH, Tel.: 01568 614211

Family Planning Services

Ms M Bell, Administrator, Belmont Abbey, Belmont, Hereford, Herts, HR2 9RP, Tel.: 01432 344344

West Midlands Strategic Health Authority

Learning Disabilities
Children, Paediatric Therapy Team, Belmont Abbey, Belmont, Hereford, HR2 9RP, Tel.: 01432 344344
Hereford City & S Herefordshire, Herefordshire Integrated Community, Hillrise Resource Centre, 41 Southbank Road, Hereford, HR1 2TL, Tel.: 01432 373203
Mr B McAlinden, Operational Service Manager, Community Services, Herefordshire Integrated Community, Hillrise Resource Centre, 41 Southbank Road, Hereford, HR1 2TL, Tel.: 01432 373203
North Herefordshire, Office Suite 4, 5 Broad Street, Leominster, HR6 8BT, Tel.: 01568 616397

Specialist Nursing Services
Ms C Goodhead, Continence, Gaol Street Clinic, Tel.: 01432 378910
Nurses, Macmillan, St Michael's Hospice, Bartestree, Hereford, HR1 4HA, Tel.: 01432 853076
Ms C Evans, Clinical Nurse Specialist, Parkinson's Disease, Goal Street Clinic, Tel.: 01432 378910

The Homeless/Travellers & Asylum Seekers
Ms K Henson, Travellers, Liaison Nurse, Child Health Department, Belmont Abbey, Tel.: 01432 363938

Mid Staffordshire General Hospitals NHS Trust

Trust Headquarters, Staffordshire General Hospital
Weston Road
STAFFORD
ST16 3SA
Tel.: 01785 257731
Fax.: 01785 230538

Acute Specialist Nursing Services
Mr C Mackenzie, Clinical Nurse Specialist, Cardiology, Mid Staffs General Hospital, Tel.: 01785 257731 ext 4604
Ms J Holmes, Nurse Consultant, Continence, Cannock Chase Hospital, Tel.: 01543 572757 ext 6425
Ms P Tweed, Clinical Nurse Specialist, Dermatology, Cannock Chase Hospital, Tel.: 01543 572757 ext 6033
Ms K Anderson, Clinical Nurse Specialist, Diabetic Care, Cannock Chase Hospital, Tel.: 01543 572757 ext 6626
Ms G Green, Clinical Nurse Specialist, Diabetic Care, Mid Staffs General Hospital, Tel.: 01785 257731 ext 4223
Ms C Hill, Clinical Nurse Specialist, Diabetic Care, Mid Staffs General Hospital, Tel.: 01785 257731 ext 4224
Ms L Skelton, Clinical Nurse Specialist, Diabetic Care, Cannock Chase Hospital, Tel.: 01543 572757 ext 6626
Ms K Whitehead, Clinical Nurse Specialist, Diabetic Care, - Paediatrics, Mid Staffs General Hospital, Tel.: 01785 257731 ext 4017
Mr P Tittensor, Clinical Nurse Specialist, Epilepsy, Mid Staffs General Hospital, Tel.: 01785 257731 ext 4239
Ms K Pickstock, Clinical Nurse Specialist, Lung Cancer, Mid Staffs General Hospital, Tel.: 01785 257731 ext 2022
Ms A Logan, Clinical Nurse Specialist, Parkinson's Disease, Cannock Chase Hospital, Tel.: 01543 572757 ext 6018
Ms S Noble, Clinical Nurse Specialist, Rehabilitation, Cannock Chase Hospital, Tel.: 01543 572757 ext 6541
Ms J Smythe, Clinical Nurse Specialist, Respiratory, Mid Staffs General Hospital, Tel.: 01785 257731 ext 2024
Ms J Davenport, Clinical Nurse Specialist, Skin Cancer, Cannock Chase Hospital, Tel.: 01543 572757 ext 6032
Ms S Jackson, Clinical Nurse Specialist, Tissue Viability, Mid Staffs General Hospital, Tel.: 01785 257731 ext 4611

Child Health
Ms K Woolliscroft, Senior Nurse, Paediatrics, Tel.: 01785 257731 ext 4812

Child Protection/Safeguarding Children
Ms T Randell, Consultant Paediatrician, Child Protection,

Community Midwifery
Emergencies, Tel.: Bleep via Area
Mrs W Hayes, Community Midwifery Manager, Staffordshire General Hospital, Tel.: 01785 230483
Mrs G Landon, Head of Midwifery/Directorate Manager, Women & Childrens Directorate, Staffordshire General Hospital, Tel.: 01785 257731 ext 4817

Equipment Loan Services
Ms J Burke, Equipment Co-ordinator, Based at Cannock Chase Hospital but covers Mid Staffs also, Tel.: 01543 576416

Newcastle Under-Lyme Primary Care Trust

Trust Headquarters, Bradwell Hospital
Talke Road, Chesterton
NEWCASTLE-UNDER-LYME
ST5 7NJ
Tel.: 01782 425440
Fax.: 01782 425445

Admin & Senior Management
Mr I Ashbolt, PCT Chair,
Dr S Bridgman, Director of Public Health,
Mrs J Gallimore, Director of Operations & Clinical Services,
Dr M Griffiths, Executive Committee Chair,
Mr D Icke, Director of Finance,
Mr I Rogerson, Chief Executive,

Clinical Leads (NSF)
Dr S Bridgman, Clinical Lead, Cancer,
Dr S Bridgman, Clinical Lead, Children,
Dr J Edwards, Clinical Lead, Long Term Conditions,
Mrs J Gallimore, Lead, Palliative Care,

Community Matrons
Mrs S Forrester O'Neill, Community Matrons Manager,

Community Nursing Services
Mrs H Anderson, Assistant Director of Therapies,
Ms P Wheeler, Assistant Director of Nursing Services,

District Nursing
Mrs S Forrester O'Neill, District Nurse Lead,

Health Visitors
Mrs R Charles, Health Visitor Lead,

Liaison Services
Mrs J Elliott, Patient Advice Liaison Service Manager, Newcastle under Lyme Library, Ironmarket, Newcastle under Lyme, Tel.: 01782 427427

Pharmacy
Mrs J Butterworth, Head of Medicines Management & Prescribing,

North Birmingham Primary Care Trust

Trust Headquarters, Blakelands House
400 Aldridge Road, Perry Barr
BIRMINGHAM, B44 8BH
Tel.: 0121 332 1900
Fax.: 0121 332 1901

Child Protection/Safeguarding Children
Ms L Szaroleta, Modern Matron, Blakelands House, 400 Aldridge Road, Perry Bar, Birmingham, B44 8BH, Tel.: 0121 332 1900

Community Matrons
Ms S Gordon, Modern Matron, Blakelands House, 400 Aldridge Road, Perry Bar, Birmingham, B44 8BH, Tel.: 0121 332 1900
Ms L Malpass, Modern Matron, Blakelands House, 400 Aldridge Road, Perry Bar, Birmingham, B44 8BH, Tel.: 0121 332 1900
Ms K Parry, Modern Matron, Blakelands House, 400 Aldridge Road, Perry Bar, Birmingham, B44 8BH, Tel.: 0121 332 1900
Ms L Szaroleta, Modern Matron, Blakelands House, 400 Aldridge Road, Perry Bar, Birmingham, B44 8BH, Tel.: 0121 332 1900

District Nursing
Ms K Parry, Modern Matron, Blakelands House, 400 Aldridge Road, Perry Bar, Birmingham, B44 8BH, Tel.: 0121 332 1969

West Midlands Strategic Health Authority

School Nursing

Ms S Gordon, Modern Matron, Blakelands House, 400 Aldridge Road, Perry Bar, Birmingham, B44 8BH, Tel.: 0121 332 1900

North Staffordshire Combined Healthcare NHS Trust

Trust Headquarters, Bucknall Hospital
Eaves Lane, Bucknall
STOKE-ON-TRENT
Staffordshire
ST2 8LD
Tel.: 01782 273510

Acute Specialist Nursing Services

Ms L Craig, Continence, Stoke Health Centre, Tel.: 01782 425251/2

Ms J Fenton, Continence, Stoke Health Centre, Tel.: 01782 425251/2

Ms D Cooper, Diabetic Care, Hanford Health Centre, Tel.: 01782 421000

Ms K Woolley, Diabetic Care, Hanford Health Centre, Tel.: 01782 421000

District Nursing Team, Paediatrics, Hanford Health Centre, Tel.: 01782 421000

Ms S Booth, Palliative Care, Westcliffe Hospital, Turnhurst Road, Chell, Stoke on Trent,, Tel.: 01782 425892

Mrs A Yeung, Respiratory, Dept Respiratory Med, North Staffs Hosp NHS Trust, Newcastle Rd, Stoke on Trent, ST4 6QG, Tel.: 01782 715444

Ms D Latham, North Staffs Hospital NHS Trust, Stoma Care, NSPD, City General Hospital, Newcastle Road, Stoke on Trent, ST4 6QG, Tel.: 01782 552762

Ms J Rust, North Staffs Hospital NHS Trust, Stoma Care, NSPD, City General Hospital, Newcastle Road, Stoke on Trent, ST4 6QG, Tel.: 01782 553181

Ms S Hawkins, Tissue Viability, The Annex, Bucknall Hospital, Tel.: 01782 275130

Admin & Senior Management

Dr C Buttanshaw, Chief Executive, Bucknall Hospital, Eaves Lane, Bucknall, Stoke on Trent, Staffordshire, ST2 8LD, Tel.: 01782 273510

Mr D Pearson, Exec Director of Clinical Governance & Nursing, Bucknall Hospital, Eaves Lane, Bucknall, Stoke on Trent, Staffordshire, ST2 8LD, Tel.: 01782 275050

Child Health Records

Child Health Info Dept, Bucknall Hospital, Eaves Lane, Bucknall, Stoke on Trent, Staffordshire, ST2 8LD, Tel.: 01782 273510

School Health Records, Bedord House Clinic, Havelock Place, Stoke on Trent, ST1 4PR, Tel.: 01782 425000

Child Protection/Safeguarding Children

Ms F Manning, Child Protection, Werrington Clinic, Salters Close, Werrington, Stoke on Trent, ST9 0DB, Tel.: 01782 304411

Learning Disabilities

Mrs K Johnson, General Services Manager, Learning Disabilities Operating Unit, London House, Floor 3, Hide Street, Stoke-on-Trent, ST4 1NF, Tel.: 01782 427614

Mrs H Mycock, General Manager, Nurse Advisor, London House, Floor 3, Stoke on Trent, Tel.: 01782 427615

Ms M Prior, Senior Nurse/Modern Matron, Longton Cottage Hospital, Upper Belgrave Road, Longton, Stoke-on-Trent, ST3 4QX, Tel.: 1782 425637

Liaison Services

Mrs A Crutchley, Liaison Acute, Hanford Health Centre, New Inn Lane, Hanford, Stoke on Trent, ST4 8EX, Tel.: 01782 421000

Mrs M Malpass, Liaison Acute, Hanford Health Centre, New Inn Lane, Hanford, Stoke on Trent, ST4 8EX, Tel.: 01782 421000

Ms N Smith, Liaison Elderly, Stoke Health Centre, Honeywall, Stoke on Trent, ST4 2JB, Tel.: 01782 425220

Ms T Smith, Liaison Paediatric Health Visitor, Hanford Health Centre, New Inn Lane, Hanford, Stoke on Trent, ST4 8EX, Tel.: 01782 421000

Ms A Westbrook, Liaison Paediatric Health Visitor, Hanford Health Centre, New Inn Lane, Hanford, Stoke on Trent, ST4 8EX, Tel.: 01782 421000

School Nursing

Mrs C Scotton, School Nurse, Asthma, Stoke Health Centre, Tel.: 01782 425220

North Stoke Primary Care Trust

Trust Headquarters, Unit 3 Whittle Court
Town Road
HANLEY
Stoke-on-Trent
ST1 2QE
Tel.: 01782 227774

Admin & Senior Management

Mrs T Cookson, Director of Integrated Primary Care, Whittle Court, Town Road, Hanley, Stoke-on-Trent, ST1 2QE, Tel.: 01782 227700

Mr M Ridley, Interim Joint Chief Executive, Whittle Court, Town Road, Hanley, Stoke-on-Trent, ST1 2QE, Tel.: 01782 227700

Child Protection/Safeguarding Children

Ms P Carr, Named Nurse, Child Protection, Whittle Court, Town Road, Hanley, Stoke-on-Trent, ST1 2QE, Tel.: 01782 227773/227789

Clinical Leads (NSF)

Dr G Rajaratunam, Clinical Lead, CHD & Diabetes, Tel.: 01782 298000

Dr J Hapuarachchi, Clinical Lead, Cancer, Tel.: 01782 206866

Dr T Cookson, Clinical Lead, Care of the Elderly, Tel.: 01782 227700

Community Matrons

Ms A Fallows, Community Matron, Ward 2b, Westcliffe Hospital, Tel.: 01782 425825

Ms T Hall, Community Matron, Ward 2b, Westcliffe Hospital, Tel.: 01782 425825

Ms H Millington, Community Matron, Ward 2b, Westcliffe Hospital, Tel.: 01782 425825

Ms N Whieldon, Community Matron, Ward 2b, Westcliffe Hospital, Tel.: 01782 425825

Community Nursing Services

Ms A Brett, Locality Manager, Whittle Court, Town Road, Hanley, Stoke-on-Trent, ST1 2QE, Tel.: 01782 227700

Ms A Gething, Acting Locality Manager, Whittle Court, Town Road, Hanley, Stoke-on-Trent, ST1 2QE, Tel.: 01782 227700

Ms J Glynn, Clinical Development Manager, Whittle Court, Town Road, Hanley, Stoke-on-Trent, ST1 2QE, Tel.: 01782 227700

District Nursing

Ms M Ambrose, District Nurse, Smallthorne Health Centre, 2 Baden Road, Smallthorne, Stoke on Trent, ST6 1SA, Tel.: 01782 425764

Ms M Bourne, District Nurse, Moorcroft Medical Centre, Botteslow Street, Hanley, Stoke on Trent, ST1 3JN, Tel.: 01782 425061

Ms J Harrison, District Nurse, Abbey Hulton Clinic, Leek Road, Abbey Hulton, Stoke on Trent, ST2 8BP, Tel.: 01782 427903

Ms A Hooper, District Nurse, Hanley Health Centre, Upper Huntbach Street, Hanley, Stoke on Trent, ST1 2BN, Tel.: 01782 425125

Ms G Jervis, District Nurse, Eaton Park, Hoveringham Drive, Berryhill, Stoke on Trent, ST2 9PS, Tel.: 01782 425191

Ms C Kaminskas, District Nurse, Tunstall Health Centre, Dunning Street, Tunstall, Stoke on Trent, ST6 6BE, Tel.: 01782 425825

Ms L Massey, District Nurse, Hanley Health Centre, Upper Huntbach Street, Hanley, Stoke on Trent, ST1 2BN, Tel.: 01782 425125

Ms J Powell, Sister, Smallthorne Health Centre, 2 Baden Road, Smallthorne, Stoke on Trent, ST6 1SA, Tel.: 01782 425764

Ms G Shaw, District Nurse, Hanley Health Centre, Upper Huntbach Street, Hanley, Stoke on Trent, ST1 2BN, Tel.: 01782 425125

West Midlands Strategic Health Authority

Ms W Thornton, District Nurse, Eaton Park, Hoveringham Drive, Berryhill, Stoke on Trent, ST2 9PS, Tel.: 01782 425191

Ms B Trenchard, District Nursing Professional Advisor, Smallthorne Health Centre, 2 Baden Road, Smallthorne, Stoke on Trent, ST6 1SA, Tel.: 01782 425759

Ms P Walley, District Nurse, Knypersley Road Surgery, 117 Knypersley Rd, Norton, Stoke on Trent, ST6 8JA, 01782 541975

Ms S Williams, District Nurse, Burslem Health Centre, Chapel Lane, Burslem, Stoke on Trent, ST6 2AB, Tel.: 01782 425706

Ms P Wood, District Nurse, Tunstall Health Centre, Dunning Street, Tunstall, Stoke on Trent, ST6 6BE, Tel.: 01782 425825

Health Visitors

Ms E Bamford, Health Visitor, Bentilee Health Centre, Bargrave Road, Dreseden, Stoke on Trent, ST3 4LR, Tel.: 01782 425913

Ms K Brayford-West, Health Visitor, Hanley Health Centre, Upper Huntbach Street, Hanley, Stoke on Trent, ST1 2BN, Tel.: 01782 425127

Ms J Brindley, Health Visitor, Burslem Health Centre, Chapel Lane, Burslem, Stoke on Trent, ST6 2AB, Tel.: 01782 425712

Ms U Chadburn, Health Visitor Nurse Advisor, Whittle Court, Town Road, Hanley, Stoke-on-Trent, ST1 2QE, Tel.: 01782 227780

Ms C Cooper, Health Visitor, Bentilee Health Centre, Bargrave Road, Dreseden, Stoke on Trent, ST3 4LR, Tel.: 01782 425913

Ms F Cosgrove, Health Visitor, Moorcroft Medical Centre, Botteslow Street, Hanley, Stoke on Trent, ST1 3JN, Tel.: 01782 425062

Ms L Elliot, Health Visitor, Westcliffe Hospital, Turnhurst Road, Chell, Stoke on Trent, ST6 6LD, Tel.: 01782 425890

Ms J Frost, Health Visitor, Eaton Park, Hoveringham Drive, Berryhill, Stoke on Trent, ST2 9PS, Tel.: 01782 425190

Ms S Gammon, Health Visitor, Hanley Health Centre, Upper Huntbach Street, Hanley, Stoke on Trent, ST1 2BN, Tel.: 01782 425127

Ms J Harper, Health Visitor, Tunstall Health Centre, Dunning Street, Tunstall, ST6 6BE, Tel.: 01782 425809

Ms R Johnson, Health Visitor, Tunstall Health Centre, Dunning Street, Tunstall, Stoke on Trent, ST6 6BE, Tel.: 01782 425809

Mr J Lacy, Health Visitor, Burslem Health Centre, Chapel Lane, Burslem, Stoke on Trent, ST6 2AB, Tel.: 01782 425712

Ms J Latham, Health Visitor, Bentilee Health Centre, Bargrave Road, Dreseden, Stoke on Trent, ST3 4LR, Tel.: 01782 425913

Ms J Locke, Health Visitor, Cobridge Community Centre, Bursley Road, Grange Park, Cobridge, Stoke on Trent, Tel.: 01782 425893

Ms P Lownds, Health Visitor, Abbey Hulton Clinic, Leek Road, Abbey Hulton, Stoke on Trent, ST2 8BP, Tel.: 01782 427900

Ms J Mannion, Health Visitor, Hanley Health Centre, Upper Huntbach Street, Hanley, Stoke on Trent, ST1 2BN, Tel.: 01782 425127

Ms A Marsh, Health Visitor, Furlong Medical Centre, Furlong Road, Tunstall, Stoke on Trent, ST6 5UD, Tel.: 01782 425895

Ms C McGrath, Health Visitor, Tunstall Health Centre, Dunning Street, Tunstall, ST6 6BE, Tel.: 01782 425809

Ms J Myatt, Health Visitor, Moorcroft Medical Centre, Botteslow Street, Hanley, Stoke-on-Trent, ST1 3JN,

Ms L Purcell, Health Visitor, Smallthorne Health Centre, 2 Baden Road, Smallthorne, Stoke on Trent, ST6 1SA, Tel.: 01782 425766

Ms J Rhead, Health Visitor, Westcliffe Hospital, Turnhurst Road, Chell, Stoke on Trent, ST6 6LD, Tel.: 01782 425890

Ms J Rodger, Health Visitor, Smallthorne Health Centre, 2 Baden Road, Smallthorne, Stoke on Trent, ST6 1SA, Tel.: 01782 425766

Ms J Sargeant, Health Visitor, Furlong Medical Centre, Furlong Road, Tunstall, Stoke on Trent, ST6 5UD, Tel.: 01782 425895

Ms H Stair, Health Visitor, Eaton Park, Hoveringham Drive, Berryhill, Stoke on Trent, ST2 9PS, Tel.: 01782 425190

Ms J Tomkinson, Health Visitor, Westcliffe Hospital, Turnhurst Road, Chell, Stoke on Trent, ST6 6LD, Tel.: 01782 425890

Ms S Urquhart, Health Visitor, Hanley Health Centre, Upper Huntbach Street, Hanley, Stoke on Trent, ST1 2BN, Tel.: 01782 425127

Ms J Wardle, Health Visitor, Furlong Medical Centre, Furlong Road, Tunstall, Stoke on Trent, ST6 5UD, Tel.: 01782 425895

Ms A Weaver, Health Visitor, Abbey Hulton Clinic, Leek Road, Abbey Hulton, Stoke on Trent, ST2 8BP, Tel.: 01782 427900

Liaison Services

Ms J Gratty, Discharge Liaison Team Manager, University Hospital of North Staffordshire, Tel.: 01782 553122

Matrons/Modern Matrons

Mrs T Barker, Modern Matron, Westcliffe Hospital, Chell, Stoke-on-Trent, ST6 6LA,

Mrs A Cole, Modern Matron, Haywood Hospital, Tel.: 01782 556249

Pharmacy

Ms S Noyce, Whittle Court, Town Road, Hanley, Stoke-on-Trent, ST1 2QE, Tel.: 01782 227700

School Nursing

Miss H Cootes, School Nurse, Whitfield Valley Health Centre, Fegg Hayes, Stoke-on-Trent, ST6 6QR,

Ms B Cope, School Nurse Team Leader, Whittle Court, Town Road, Hanley, ST1 2QE, Tel.: 01782 425760

Ms S Coventry, School Nurse, Whitfield Valley Health Centre, Fegg Hayes Road, Fegg Hayes, Stoke on Trent, ST6 6QR, Tel.: 01782 425726

Ms C Davies, School Nurse, Bentilee Health Centre, Bargrave Road, Dreseden, Stoke on Trent, ST3 4LR, Tel.: 01782 425913

Ms J Heath, School Nurse, Burslem Health Centre, Chapel Lane, Burslem, Stoke on Trent, ST6 2AB, Tel.: 01782 425714

Ms A Hough, School Nurse, Tunstall Health Centre, Dunning Street, Tunstall, Stoke on Trent, ST6 6BE, Tel.: 01782 425808

Ms H Jones, School Nurse, Abbey Hulton Clinic, Leek Road, Abbey Hulton, Stoke on Trent, ST2 8BP, Tel.: 01782 427900

Ms S Murphy, School Nurse, Bentilee Health Centre, Bargrave Road, Dreseden, Stoke on Trent, ST3 4LR, Tel.: 01782 425913

Ms K Powell, School Nurse, Tunstall Health Centre, Dunning Street, Tunstall, Stoke on Trent, ST6 6BE, Tel.: 01782 425808

Ms C Skelton, School Nurse, Bentilee Health Centre, Bargrave Road, Dreseden, Stoke on Trent, ST3 4LR, Tel.: 01782 425913

Ms M Stevenson, School Nurse, Hanley Health Centre, Upper Huntbach Street, Hanley, Stoke on Trent, ST1 2BN, Tel.: 01782 425135

Specialist Nursing Services

Ms M Coxon, BME Ward 2b Westcliffe, Tel.: 01782 425346

Ms A Evans, Spirometry Specialist, Ward 26, Westcliffe Hospital, Tel.: 01782 425715

Ms D Bentley, CHD, Ward 2b, Westcliffe Hospital, Chell, Stoke on Trent, ST6 6LA, Tel.: 01782 425346

Ms Y Mawby, CHD, Ward 2b, Westcliffe Hospital, Chell, Stoke on Trent, ST6 6LA, Tel.: 01782 425715

Ms J Flexer, Diabetes, Support Ward 2b, Tel.: 01782 425346

Ms J Joynson, Diabetic Care, Ward 2b, Westcliffe Hospital, Chell, Stoke on Trent, ST6 6LA, Tel.: 01782 425346

Mrs A Twemolw, Lead Nurse, Osteoporosis, Haywood Hospital, Tel.: 01782 556147

Mrs J Matthews, Clinical Nurse Specialist, Rehabilitation, - Medicine, Haywood Hospital, Tel.: 01782 556166

Mrs L Sanderson, Discharge Co-ordinator, Rehabilitation, Haywood Hospital, Tel.: 01782 556307

Miss S Turner, Head Injury Co-ordinator, Rehabilitation, - Medicine, Haywood Hospital, Tel.: 01782 556211

Mrs A Brownfield, Clinical Nurse Specialist, Rheumatology, Haywood Hospital, Tel.: 01782 556208

Ms M Dishman, Community Sister, Rheumatology, Haywood Hospital, Tel.: 01782 556299

Mrs M Kirwan, Research Nurse, Rheumatology, Haywood Hospital, Tel.: 01782 556204

Mrs M Roxas, Research, Nurse Specialist, Rheumatology, Haywood Hospital, Tel.: 01782 556146

Dr S Ryan, Nurse Consultant, Rheumatology, Haywood Hospital, Tel.: 01782 556201

West Midlands Strategic Health Authority

Miss C Thwaites, Nurse Lecturer, Rheumatology, Haywood Hospital, Tel.: 01782 556201
Walk In Centres
Haywood Hospital Walk-in Centre, High Lane, Burslem, Stoke-on-Trent, Staffs, ST6 7AG,

North Warwickshire Primary Care Trust

Trust Headquarters
139 Earls Road
NUNEATON
Warwickshire
CV11 5HP
Tel.: 024 7664 2200
Fax.: 024 7635 14334

Admin & Senior Management
Mr D Allcock, Deputy Chief Executive/Director of Finance & Contracting, Tel.: 024 7664 2200
Mr J Callwood, Director of Workforce Development & Nursing, Tel.: 024 7664 2200
Mrs A Heckles, Chief Executive, Tel.: 024 7664 2200
Dr A Roy, Acting Medical Director, Tel.: 0121 3294927
Dr M Stern, Director of Public Health, Tel.: 024 7686 5625
Child Health
Ms A Robson, General Manager, Joint Children's Services, Tel.: 024 7686 5245
Mr D Widdas, Child with Complex Needs, Tel.: 024 7635 1333
Child Health Records
Child Health Records, Riversley Park Centre, Nuneaton, Tel.: 024 7637 8601
Child Protection/Safeguarding Children
Ms M Weeks, Specialist Nurse, Child Protection, St Nicholas Park Clinic, Tel.: 024 7637 8601
Community Matrons
Community Matrons, St Nicolas Clinic, Nuneaton, Tel.: 024 7632 9753
District Nursing
Ms W Hampshire, Rural North Area, Tel.: 024 7632 9753
Ms K Sheffield, Bedworth Area, Tel.: 024 7632 9753
Mrs L Watson, Nuneaton Area, Tel.: 024 7632 9753
Health Visitors
Ms W Hampshire, Rural North Area, Tel.: 024 7632 9753
Ms K Sheffield, Bedworth Area, Tel.: 024 7632 9753
Mrs L Watson, Nuneaton Area, Tel.: 024 7632 9753
Learning Disabilities
Ms K Phipps, Director of Mental Health & Learning Disability, Tel.: 024 7664 2200
Mr M Saunders, Associate Director of Learning Disability Services, Wolverley Services, Tel.: 01562 850461
Liaison Services
Mr S Crews, Director of Patient Liaison & Communication, Tel.: 024 7664 2200
Matrons/Modern Matrons
Ms W Walton, Modern Matron, Bramcote Hospital, Tel.: 024 7638 2200
School Nursing
Ms M Holden, School Nursing, Tel.: 024 7632 9753
Ms H Walmsley, Specialist School Nursing Services, Tel.: 01675 463590
Specialist Nursing Services
Ms H Goding, Nurse, Macmillan, Tel.: 01926 495321

Oldbury & Smethwick Primary Care Trust

Trust Headquarters, Kingston House
438 High Street
WEST BROMWICH
B70 9LD
Tel.: 0121 500 1500

Admin & Senior Management
Ms G Combes, Chief Executive,
Specialist Nursing Services
Ms S Basra, Nurse,
Ms D McAndrew, Nurse,

Redditch & Bromsgrove Primary Care Trust

Trust Headquarters
Crossgate House
Crossgate Road
REDDITCH
Worcs
B98 7SN
Tel.: 01527 507040

Admin & Senior Management
Ms J Abbey, Director of Clinical Services & Nursing,
Mr E Kelly, Chief Executive,
Child Health
Mrs J Leigh, Children with Special Needs, Church Hill Clinic, Tanhouse Lane, Church Hill, Redditch, Tel.: 01527 488750
Child Health Records
Mrs J Cole, Admin, Smallwood Health Centre, Tel.: 01527 488740
Child Protection/Safeguarding Children
Ms R Davis, Senior Nurse, Child Protection, Smallwood Health Centre, Tel.: 01527 488741
Ms J Harris, Redditch, Named Nurse, Child Protection, Smallwood Health Centre, Church Green West, Redditch, B97 4DJ, Tel.: 01527 488741
Ms L James, Bromsgrove, Named Nurse, Child Protection, Smallwood Health Centre, Church Green West, Redditch, B97 4DJ, Tel.: 01527 488741
Ms C Whiehouse, Nurse Consultant, Child Protection, Isaac Maddox House, Shrub Hill Road, Worcester, WR4 9RW, Tel.: 01905 681590
Clinical Leads (NSF)
Dr C Laxton, Clinical Lead, CHD,
Dr J Wells, Clinical Lead, CHD,
Dr M Leg, Clinical Lead, Diabetic Care,
District Nursing
Ms P Hall, Primary Care Manager, Bromsgrove, Princess of Wales Community Hospital, Bromsgrove, B61 0BB, Tel.: 01527 488059
Ms S Warner, Primary Care Manager, Redditch, Smallwood Health Centre, Church Garden West, Redditch, B97 4DJ, Tel.: 01527 488764
Liaison Services
Ms R Herbert, Liaison Care Co-ordinator Redditch, Prospect House, Redditch, Tel.: 01527 488678
Ms L Jeavons, Liaison Care Co-ordinator Redditch, Prospect House, Redditch, Tel.: 01527 488678
Ms L Ravenscroft, Liaison Care Co-ordinator Bromsgrove, Princess of Wales Community Hospital, Tel.: 01527 488037
Specialist Nursing Services
Miss T Palmer, Continence, Smallwood House, Tel.: 01527 488658
Mrs S Checketts, Diabetic Care, Diabetes Resource Centre, Smallwood House, Church Garden West, Redditch, B97 4BD, Tel.: 01527 488649
Ms M Burley, Macmillan, Prospect House, Tel.: 01527 488671
Ms R Williams, CONI, Paediatrics, Crabbs Cross Clinic, 1 Kenilworth Close, Crabbs Cross, Redditch, B97 5LE, Tel.: 01527 488773

Robert Jones & Agnes Hunt NHS Trust

Trust Headquarters
Gobowen
OSWESTRY
Shropshire
SY10 7AG
Tel.: 01691 404000

West Midlands Strategic Health Authority

Acute Specialist Nursing Services

Ms K Jenner, Nurse Practitioner, Arthroplasty, Robert Jones & Agnes Hunt, Tel.: 01691 404223

Ms N Leese, Nurse Practitioner, Arthroplasty, Robert Jones & Agnes Hunt, Tel.: 01691 404272

Mr C Chapman, Nurse Practitioner, Foot & Ankle, Robert Jones & Agnes Hunt, Tel.: 01691 404202

Ms C Evans, Nurse Consultant, Muscular Dystrophy, Robert Jones & Agnes Hunt, Tel.: 01691 404333

Ms L Barker, Nurse Specialist, Pain Management, Robert Jones & Agnes Hunt, Tel.: 01691 404215

Ms A Meadows, Nurse Specialist, Rheumatology, Robert Jones & Agnes Hunt, Tel.: 01691 404432

Ms A Lamb, Nurse Consultant, Spinal Injuries, Robert Jones & Agnes Hunt, Tel.: 01691 404109

Ms G Kanes, Nurse Practitioner, Sports, Robert Jones & Agnes Hunt, Tel.: 01691 404165

Ms C Pemberton, Nurse Specialist, Tumour, Robert Jones & Agnes Hunt, Tel.: 01691 404107

Admin & Senior Management

Ms S Byrom, Director of Nursing, Robert Jones & Agnes Hunt NHS Trust, Gobowen, Oswestry, Shropshire, SY10 7AG, Tel.: 01691 404000

Child Protection/Safeguarding Children

Ms S Marsden, Sister, Child Protection, Robert Jones & Agnes Hunt Orthopaedic Hospital NHS Trust, Oswestry, SY10 7AG, Tel.: 01691 404444

Discharge Co-ordinators

Ms S Duffy, Sister, Robert Jones & Agnes Hunt Orthopaedic Hospital NHS Trust, Oswestry, SY10 7AG, Tel.: 01691 404000 bleep 168

Liaison Services

Ms A Harper, P.A.L., Robert Jones & Agnes Hunt Orthopaedic Hospital NHS Trust, Oswestry, SY10 7AG, Tel.: 01691 404000

Matrons/Modern Matrons

Ms S Pugh, Modern Matron, Trauma & Orthopaedics, Robert Jones & Agnes Hunt Orthopaedic Hospital NHS Trust, Oswestry, SY10 7AG, Tel.: 01691 404000 bleep 134

Other Services

Ms C Evans, Physiotherapy Practitioner for the Spinal Unit, Tel.: 01691 404473

Ms G McArdle, Physiotherapy Practitioner for the Spinal Unit, Tel.: 01691 404464

Rowley Regis & Tipton Primary Care Trust

Trust Headquarters, Kingston House
438 High Street
WEST BROMWICH, B70 9LD
Tel.: 0121 500 1500

Admin & Senior Management

Mr G Griffiths, Chief Executive,

Clinical Leads (NSF)

Dr M Fairfield, Clinical Lead, CHD & Diabetes,

Dr C Browne, Clinical Lead, Cancer,

Dr C Molloy, Clinical Lead, Older People,

Specialist Nursing Services

Ms J Gunnell, Nurse,

Ms F Houghton, Nurse,

Royal Orthopaedic NHS Trust

Trust Headquarters, Royal Orthopaedic Hospital
Bristol Road South, Northfield
BIRMINGHAM, B31 2AP
Tel.: 0121 685 4000

Admin & Senior Management

Ms V Morris, Director of Nursing, Royal Orthopaedic NHS Trust, Bristol Road South, Northfield, Birmingham, B31 2AP, Tel.: 0121 685 4000

Royal Wolverhampton Hospitals NHS Trust

Trust Headquarters, New Cross Hospital
Wolverhampton Road
WOLVERHAMPTON
West Midlands
WV10 0QP
Tel.: 01902 307999

Admin & Senior Management

Ms D Bott, Director of Nursing, New Cross Hospital, Wolverhampton Road, Wolverhampton, West Midlands, WV10 0QP,

Child Protection/Safeguarding Children

Ms J Henry, Midwife, Child Protection, New Cross Hospital, Tel.: 01902 643019

Ms S Judge, Nurse, Child Protection, New Cross Hospital, Tel.: 01902 643019

Community Midwifery

Ms S Griggs, Head of Midwifery, Management Offices, Ward A3, New Cross Hospital, Tel.: 01902 643019

Ms J Henry, Senior Midwifery Manager, New Cross Hospital, Wolverhampton Road, Wolverhampton, WV10 0QP, Tel.: 01902 643011

Maternity Unit, New Cross Hospital, Wolverhampton Road, Wolverhampton, WV10 0QP, Tel.: 01902 643019

Liaison Services

Specialist Midwife Drugs Liaison, New Cross Hospital, Tel.: 01902 643011

Rugby Primary Care Trust

Trust Headquarters, Swift Park
Old Leicester Road
RUGBY, CV21 1DZ
Tel.: 01788 550860

Admin & Senior Management

Mrs J Freer, Director of Patient Services,

Mr P Maddock, Chief Executive,

Child Health Records

Child Health Records, Orchard Centre, Lower Hill Morton Road, Rugby, CV21 3SR, Tel.: 01788 555108

Child Protection/Safeguarding Children

Child Protection Team, Orchard Centre, Lower Hill Morton Road, Rugby, CV21 3SR, Tel.: 01788 555137

Clinical Leads (NSF)

Ms H Gammell, Clinical Lead, Cancer,

Ms H King, Clinical Lead, CHD,

Mrs J Freer, Clinical Lead, Children,

Community Nursing Services

Ms J Oliver, Head of Provider Services, Orchard Centre, Lower Hill Morton Road, Rugby, CV21 3SR, Tel.: 01788 555111

District Nursing

Mrs J Oliver, Head of Provider Services, Orchard Centre, Lower Hill Morton Road, Rugby, CV21 3SR, Tel.: 01788 551212

Health Visitors

Mrs C Davies, Clinical Lead, Health Visiting, Orchard Centre, Lower Hill Morton Road, Rugby, CV21 3SR, Tel.: 01788 555111

Liaison Services

Ms S Lee, Discharge Liaison, Swift House, Hospital of St Cross, Barby Road, Rugby, Tel.: 01788 545227

Ms A Neal, Discharge Liaison, Swift House, Hospital of St Cross, Barby Road, Rugby, Tel.: 01788 545227

School Nursing

Ms L Hitch, Team Leader, School Nurses, Orchard Centre, Lower Hill Morton Road, Rugby, CV21 3SR, Tel.: 01788 555111

Specialist Nursing Services

Ms J Shaw, Advisor, Continence, Orchard Centre for Community Health, Lower Hillmorton Road, Rugby, CV21 3SR, Tel.: 01788 555105

West Midlands Strategic Health Authority

Sandwell and West Birmingham Hospitals NHS Trust

Trust Headquarters, Birmingham City Hospital
Dudley Road
BIRMINGHAM
B18 7QH
Tel.: 0121 507 4847

Admin & Senior Management
Ms P Werhun, Director of Nursing, Birmingham City Hospital, Dudley Road, Birmingham, B18 7QH,
Community Midwifery
Ms M Bradley, Maternity Services Co-ordinator, City Hospital, Birmingham,
Ms J Freer, Women Services Manager, Sandwell Women Health Centre,
Ms K Guarnell, Head of Midwifery Services, City Hospital Maternity Unit, Dudley Road, Birmingham, B18 7QH,
Ms L Nieston, Midwifery Manager, Sandwell Women Health Centre,
Ms E Parchment, Community Midwifery Manager, City Hospital, Birmingham, Tel.: 0121 507 5328
Ms K Quarrell, Head of Midwifery Services, Sandwell Women Health Centre,
Liaison Services
Miss S Dwyer, Assessment & Discharge Planning, Sandwell General Hospital, Tel.: 0121 553 1831
Ms E Quarrell, Discharge Planning Paediatric, Sandwell General Hospital, Tel.: 0121 553 1831 ext 3326

Sandwell Mental Health NHS & Social Care Trust

Trust Headquarters
48 Lodge Road
WEST BROMWICH
West Midlands
B70 8NY
Tel.: 0121 553 7676
Fax.: 0121 607 3290

Learning Disabilities
Mr R Hall, Director of Care Governance, 48 Lodge Road, West Bromwich, West Midlands, B70 8NY, Tel.: 0121 553 7676
Learning Disability Team, Albert Street, Wednesbury, WS10 7EW, Tel.: 0121 505 3216

Shrewsbury & Telford Hospitals NHS Trust

Trust Headquarters, Mytton Oak Road
SHREWSBURY
Shropshire
SY3 8XQ
Tel.: 01743 261000
Fax.: 01743 261006

Community Midwifery
Mrs L J Adams, Telford & Wrekin Community, Senior Midwife, Tel.: 01952 222315
Miss S J Breslin, Womens Services Manager, Maternity Unit, Royal Shrewsbury Hospital, Tel.: 01743 261000
Mrs A Gregory-Page, Shrewsbury Community (Central & South), Senior Midwife, Tel.: 01743 261675
Mrs G E Williams, Head of Midwifery, Tel.: 01743 261000 ext 3630

Shropshire County Primary Care Trust

Trust Headquarters, Shelton Hospital
Bicton Heath, SHREWSBURY
Shropshire
SY3 8DN
Tel.: 01743 261000

Child Health
Ms D Williamson, Child Health, Senior Nurse, Berrington Suite, Shelton Hospital, Bicton Heath, Shrewsbury, Tel.: 01743 492258
Child Health Records
Ms J Bennett, Support Services Manager, Children & Young People, Longbow House, Harlescott Lane, Shrewsbury, Tel.: 01743 450800
Child Protection/Safeguarding Children
Ms S Cooke, Named Nurse, Child Protection, Berrington Suite, Shelton Hospital, Bicton Heath, Shrewsbury, Tel.: 01743 492258
Clinical Leads (NSF)
Dr C Bates, Clinical Lead, Cancer,
Dr L Sweeney, Clinical Lead, CHD,
Dr I Gillis, Clinical Lead, Diabetic Care,
Dr K Jackson, Clinical Lead, Older People,
Community Nursing Services
Ms M Reese, Area Senior Nurse - North, Tel.: 01691 652100
Mrs E Timmins, Lead Nurse, Primary Care & Senior Nurse South, The Health Centre, Easthope Road, Church Stretton, SY6 6BL, Tel.: 01694 724973
Ms D Williamson, Area Senior Nurse - Shrewsbury & Atcham, Berrington Suite, Shelton Hospital, Bicton Heath, Shrewsbury, Tel.: 01743 492258
District Nursing
Ms M Reese, P. Nursing Lead, Whitchurch Community Hospital, Whitchurch, Tel.: 01948 666292
Ms E Timmins, District Nurse Lead, Church Stretton Health Centre, Easthope Road, Church Stretton, Tel.: 01694 724973
Family Planning Services
Ms S Jones, Manager, Sexual Health, 3rd Floor, Princess House, The Square, Shrewsbury, Tel.: 01743 283382
Health Visitors
Ms D Williamson, Health Visitor Lead, Berrington Suite, Shelton Hospital, Bicton Heath, Shrewsbury, Tel.: 01743 492258
Learning Disabilities
Shropshire Team, Winston Churchill Buildings, Radbrook Road, Radbrook, Shrewsbury, SY3 9BL, Tel.: 01743 254080
Mrs M Stepien, Senior Community Nurse, Churchill Buildings, Radbrook Road, Radbrook, Shrewsbury, SY3 9BL, Tel.: 01743 254080
Liaison Services
Mr N Davies, Continuing Health Care Co-ordinator, Berrington Suite, Shelton Hospital, Bicton Heath, Shrewsbury, 01743 261000 x 63083
Other Services
Mr A Matthews, Hospital Manager, Whitchurch Community Hospital, Whitchurch, Shropshire, Tel.: 01948 666292
Mr C McLauchlan, Business Development Manager, Stone House Community Hospital, Union Street, Bishops Castle, Shropshire, Tel.: 01588 638220
Mr C McLauchlan, Hospital Manager, Ludlow Community Hospital, Gravel Hill, Ludlow, Shropshire, Tel.: 01584 872201
Mr K Moore, Hospital & Business Development Manager, Bridgnorth Hospital, Northgate, Bridgnorth, Shropshire, Tel.: 01746 762641
School Nursing
Ms T Smith, School Nurse Co-ordinator, Tel.: 01939 235277
Smoking Cessation
Dr K Lewis, Clinical Director, Smoking Cessation, William Farr House, Mytton Oak Road, Shrewsbury, Tel.: 01743 261300
Specialist Nursing Services
Ms J Round, Team Leader, Macmillan, Hadley Health Centre, High Street, Hadley, Telford, Tel.: 01952 222609

Solihull Primary Care Trust

Trust Headquarters
20 Union Road
SOLIHULL, West Midlands
B91 3EF
Tel.: 0121 711 7171
Fax.: 0121 711 7212

West Midlands Strategic Health Authority

Admin & Senior Management
Ms C Robertson, Deputy Director of Community Health Services, Trust Headquarters, Tel.: 0121 712 8483
Mr D Rosling, Deputy Director of Community Health Services, Trust Headquarters, Tel.: 0121 712 8546
Ms Y Sawbridge, Director of Nursing, Trust Headquarters, Tel.: 0121 711 7171
Ms H Woodburn, Director of Service Delivery, Trust Headquarters, Tel.: 0121 711 7171
Child Health
Community Children Nursing Team, Tel.: 01564 732802
Child Health Records
Mrs T McCulloch, Child Health Manager, 20 Union Road, Solihull, West Midlands, B91 3EF, Tel.: 0121 712 8535
Child Protection/Safeguarding Children
Ms K M Probert, Nurse Specialist, Safeguarding Children, Shirley Clinic, 276 Stratford Road, Shirley, Solihull, B90 3AD, Tel.: 0121 745 9109
Clinical Leads (NSF)
Dr I Morgan, Clinical Lead, Cancer,
Mrs J Gilroy, Clinical Lead, Diabetic Care, Tel.: 0121 770 4432
Community Matrons
Case Managers, Crabtree Drive, Chelmsley Wood, Birmingham, Tel.: 0121 329 0100
Community Nursing Services
Mrs A Barley, Clinical Lead - South, 20 Union Road, Solihull, West Midlands, B91 3EF, Tel.: 0121 712 8544
Mrs J Cove, Clinical Lead - Central, 20 Union Road, Solihull, West Midlands, B91 3EF, Tel.: 0121 712 8545
Mrs A Massey, Acting Lead Nurse, Evening & Night Nursing Service, Downing Close, Knowle, Tel.: 01564 732803
Mrs J Satterthwaite, Clinical Lead - North, 20 Union Road, Solihull, West Midlands, B91 3EF, Tel.: 0121 712 8543
Family Planning Services
Mrs P Nicholls, Co-ordinator, Sexual Health & Contraceptive Services, Tel.: 0121 705 8737
Learning Disabilities
Adult Team, Oliver House, 4 Ivy Lodge Close, Marston Green, Birmingham, B37 7HL, Tel.: 0121 779 5860
Liaison Services
Ms A Duncanson, Team Leader Liaison Services, Solihull Hospital, Lode Lane, Solihull, B91 2JL, Tel.: 0121 424 5100
Other Services
Ms S Dean, Team Leader, Intermediate Care Services, Arden Lee, Tel.: 0121 712 1873
Ms J Reed, Adult & Intermediate Care Services Manager, Tel.: 0121 424 4046
School Nursing
Mrs W Hall, Acting Clinical Leader School Nurses, 20 Union Road, Solihull, West Midlands, B91 3EF, Tel.: 0121 712 8524
Specialist Nursing Services
Mrs S Graham, Continence, Tel.: 0121 770 8205
Ms H Hannigan, Continence, Tel.: 0121 770 8205
Ms S Robbins, Nurse Specialist, Dermatology, Grove Road, Solihull, Tel.: 0121 705 3814
Clinical Nurse Specialist, Palliative Care, Tel.: 01564 732804
Ms F Trevelyan, Nurse Specialist, Tissue Viability, Crabtree Drive, Chelmsley Wood, Birmingham, Tel.: 0121 329 0100

South Birmingham Primary Care Trust

Trust Headquarters, Moseley Hall Hospital
Alcester Road
MOSELEY
Birmingham
B13 8JL
Tel.: 0121 442 5600

Admin & Senior Management
Ms C Fearns, Director, Service Modernisation & Primary Care, Moseley Hall Hospital, Alcester Road, Moseley, Birmingham, B13 8JL, Tel.: 0121 442 5622
Mrs P Hackett, Associate Director, Community Services, Windsor House, 11a High Street, Kings Heath, Birmingham, B14 7BB, Tel.: 0121 687 4652
Mr G Urwin, Chief Executive,
Child Health
Ms D Bolt, Community Childrens Services, Bloomsbury Health Centre, 63 Rupert Street, Nechells, Birmingham, B7 5BD,
Ms L Bretherton, Community Childrens Services, Harvey Ward, Good Hope Hospital, Rectory Road, Sutton Coldfield, West Midlands,
Ms L Bridges, Community Childrens Services, Barbara Hart Respite Unit, 132 Mary Hill Hall Road, Kings Norton, Birmingham, B30 3QJ,
Mr M Cooper, Community Childrens Services, Bloomsbury Health Centre, 63 Rupert Street, Nechells, Birmingham, B7 5BD,
Ms C Farrell, Community Childrens Services, Bloomsbury Health Centre, 63 Rupert Street, Nechells, Birmingham, B7 5BD,
Ms J Ferys, Community Childrens Services, Bloomsbury Health Centre, 63 Rupert Street, Nechells, Birmingham, B7 5BD,
Ms A Leask, Lead Nurse, School Nurses, Windsor House, 11a High Street, Kings Heath, Birmingham, B14 7BB,
Ms Y Malone, Community Childrens Services, Bloomsbury Health Centre, 63 Rupert Street, Nechells, Birmingham, B7 5BD,
Ms P McClenaghan, Community Childrens Services, Barbara Hart Respite Unit, 132 Mary Hill Hall Road, Kings Norton, Birmingham, B30 3QJ,
Mrs L Merris, Team Leader, Community Childrens Services (also Palliative Care Team), Bloomsbury Health Centre, 63 Rupert Street, Nechells, Birmingham, B7 5DT, Tel.: 0121 255 7138
Ms T Moore, Community Childrens Services, Harvey Ward, Good Hope Hospital, Rectory Road, Sutton Coldfield, West Midlands,
Ms J Newham, Community Childrens Services, Harvey Ward, Good Hope Hospital, Rectory Road, Sutton Coldfield, West Midlands,
Ms Z Noakes, Community Childrens Services, Barbara Hart Respite Unit, 132 Mary Hill Hall Road, Kings Norton, Birmingham, B30 3QJ,
Ms B Rush, Community Childrens Services, Barbara Hart Respite Unit, 132 Mary Hill Hall Road, Kings Norton, Birmingham, B30 3QJ,
Ms A Sims, Community Childrens Services, Barbara Hart Respite Unit, 132 Mary Hill Hall Road, Kings Norton, Birmingham, B30 3QJ,
Ms G Taylor, Community Childrens Services, Bloomsbury Health Centre, 63 Rupert Street, Nechells, Birmingham, B7 5BD,
Ms R Taylor Smith, Community Childrens Services, Bloomsbury Health Centre, 63 Rupert Street, Nechells, Birmingham, B7 5BD,
Ms B Timms, Community Childrens Services, Bloomsbury Health Centre, 63 Rupert Street, Nechells, Birmingham, B7 5BD,
Child Protection/Safeguarding Children
Ms C Edwards, Lead, Child Protection, Windsor House, 11a High Street, Kings Heath, Birmingham, B14 7BB,
Clinical Leads (NSF)
Dr A Enrequez-Puga, Clinical Lead, CHD,
Dr G Spurgin, Clinical Lead, Diabetic Care,
District Nursing
Ms K Birchley, Locality Lead Nurse (Edgbaston), Windsor House, 11A High Street, Birmingham, B14 7BD, Tel.: 0121 687 4600
Ms E Meredith, Operational Support Nurse, Windsor House, 11A High Street, Birmingham, B14 7BD, Tel.: 0121 687 4600
Mr J Nolan, Locality Lead Nurse (Northfield), Windsor House, 11A High Street, Birmingham, B14 7BD, Tel.: 0121 687 4600
Ms T Phillips, Training/Education Lead, Service Modernisation & Primary Care, 15 Katie Road, Selly Oak, B29 6J9, Tel.: 0121 687 4600
Ms C Thompson, Locality Lead Nurse (Selly Oak), Windsor House, 11A High Street, Birmingham, B14 7BD, Tel.: 0121 687 4600
Ms P Truman, Operational Support Nurse, Windsor House, 11A High Street, Birmingham, B14 7BD, Tel.: 0121 687 4600

West Midlands Strategic Health Authority

Learning Disabilities
Ms S Francis, Directorate Manager, Waterlinks House, 5th Floor, Richard Street, Nechells, B7 4AA, Tel.: 0121 255 7019
Ms S Harris, Nurse Development Manager, Waterlinks House, 5th Floor, Richard Street, Nechells, B7 4AA, Tel.: 0121 255 7019
Miss A Thompson, Director, Waterlinks House, 5th Floor, Richard Street, Nechells, B7 4AA, Tel.: 0121 255 7000
School Nursing
Ms A Leask, Lead Nurse, School Nursing, Windsor House, 11a High Street, Kings Heath, Birmingham, B14 7BB,

South Staffordshire Healthcare NHS Trust
Trust Headquarters, Corporation Street
STAFFORD
Staffordshire
ST16 3AG
Tel.: 01785 257888

Admin & Senior Management
Mr N Carr, Director of Nursing, South Staffs Healthcare NHS Trust, Corporation Street, Stafford, Staffordshire, ST16 3AG,
Child Protection/Safeguarding Children
Ms S Byrne, Looked after Children, Designated Nurse, 2nd Floor, Guardian House, Rotten Row, Lichfield, WS13 6JB, Tel.: 01543 420428/420429
Ms M Rawsell, Secretary, Looked after Children, 2nd Floor, Guardian House, Rotten Row, Lichfield, WS13 6JB, Tel.: 01543 420433
Ms H Widdowson, Child Protection, 2nd Floor, Guardian House, Rotten Row, Lichfield, WS13 6JB, Tel.: 01543 420433
Learning Disabilities
Burton & Uttoxeter, Margaret Stanhope Centre, Outwoods Site, Belvedere Road, Burton on Trent, DE13 0RB, Tel.: 01283 505330
Ms G Harper, Clinical, Co-ordinator, White Lodge Community Unit, New Penkridge Road, Cannock, WS11 1HN, Tel.: 01543 506356
Lichfield & Burntwood, David Parry Suite, St Michael's Hospital, Trent Valley Road, Lichfield, WS13 6EF, Tel.: 01543 442030
Mrs J Morris, Clinical Director, Crooked Bridge Road, Stafford, ST16 3NE, Tel.: 01785 222888 ext 5471
Ms P Pritchard, Clinical, Co-ordinator, New Burton House, Burton Bank Lane, Moss Pit, Stafford, ST17 9JW, Tel.: 01785 258178
Tamworth, Hockley Centre, 1-3 Beauchamp Road, Hockley, Tamworth, B77 5HP, Tel.: 01827 284407

South Stoke Primary Care Trust
Trust Headquarters, Heron House
120 Grove Road, Fenton
STOKE-ON-TRENT
ST4 4LX
Tel.: 01782 298000
Fax.: 01782 298298

Admin & Senior Management
Ms J Carnell, Director of Nursing & Operations, Tel.: 01782 298152
Mr M Ridley, Chief Executive,
Child Health Records
Child Health Records, Child Health Info Dept, Bucknall Hospital, Eaves Lane, Stoke on Trent, ST2 8LD, Tel.: 01782 273510
School Health Records, Bedford House Clinic, Havelock Place, Shelton, Stoke on Trent, ST1 4PR, Tel.: 01782 425000
Child Protection/Safeguarding Children
Ms P Carr, Named Nurse, Child Protection,
Clinical Leads (NSF)
Dr M McCarthy, Clinical Lead, Cancer,
Dr G Rajaratnam, Clinical Lead, CHD, - Diabetes,
District Nursing
Mr M Bristow, Trust Headquarters, Tel.: 01782 298010
Out of hours, Tel.: 01782 425230

Family Planning Services
Mrs A Taylor, Acting Senior Nurse Public Health Practice, Trust Headquarters, Tel.: 01782 298025
Other Services
CAST Team, Hanford Health Centre, Tel.: 01782 421000

South Warwickshire General Hospitals NHS Trust
Trust Headquarters, Warwick Hospital
Lakin Road, WARWICK
CV34 5BW
Tel.: 01926 495321
Fax.: 01926 482603

Community Midwifery
Mrs A Gough, Clinical Governance Midwife, Warwick Hospital, Lakin Road, Warwick, CV34 5BW, Tel.: 01926 495321
Mrs H Walton, Head of Midwifery, Warwick Hospital, Lakin Road, Warwick, CV34 5BW, Tel.: 01926 495321

South Warwickshire Primary Care Trust
Trust Headquarters, Westgate House
Market Square
WARWICK
CV34 4DE
Tel.: 01926 493491
Fax.: 01926 495074

Admin & Senior Management
Ms Y Diment, General Manager, Special Services, Royal Leamington Spa Rehabilitation Hospital, Heathcote Lane, Warwick, CV34 6SR, Tel.: 01926 317700
Ms T French, Chief Executive,
Ms M Mello, Director of Nursing & Quality, Westgate House, Market Street, Warwick, CV34 4DE, Tel.: 01926 493491
Child Health Records
Community Health Offices, Alcester Road, Stratford Upon Avon, Warks, CV37 6PW, Tel.: 01789 269264
Child Protection/Safeguarding Children
Ms M Durack, Child Protection/Looked After Children, Designated Nurse, Westgate House, Market Street, Warwick, CV34 4DE, Tel.: 01926 493491
Clinical Leads (NSF)
Ms B Thorpe, Clinical Lead, Cancer,
Dr R Lambert, Clinical Lead, CHD,
Dr S Inman, Clinical Lead, Older People,
Community Matrons
Mrs Y Wallsgrove, Stratford Localilty, Community Matron, Community Health Offices, Stratford upon Avon, CV37 6PW,
Community Nursing Services
Community Nursing Services, Westgate House, Market Street, Warwick, CV34 4DE, Tel.: 01926 493491
District Nursing
Mrs J Packer, District Nursing - Warwick Locality, Corrunna Court, Corrunna Road, Warwick, CV34 5XH, Tel.: 01926 475966
Ms B Thorpe, Senior Nurse, Prof Lead, District Nursing - Stratford Locality, Community Health Offices, Stratford Upon Avon, Warks, CV37 6PW, Tel.: 01789 269264
Family Planning Services
Ms B Du Bois, Clinical Lead, St Mary's Lodge, 12 St Mary's Road, Leamington Spa, Warks, CV31 1JN, Tel.: 01926 339261
Health Visitors
R Suchak, Health Visiting, Cape Road Clinic, Cape Road, Warwick, CV34 4JP, Tel.: 01926 400001
Learning Disabilities
Mrs C Ingham, Nursing Manager, Whitnash Lodge, Royal Leamington Spa Rehabilitation Hospital, Heathcote Lane, Warwick, CV34 6SR, Tel.: 01926 317746

West Midlands Strategic Health Authority

Liaison Services

Ms J Davis, Warwick Hospital, Lakin Road, Warwick, CV34 5BW, Tel.: 01926 495321

Ms B Sly, Liaison, Community Psychiatric Nursing, Yew Tree House, 87 Radford Road, Leamington Spa, Warks, CV31 1JQ, Tel.: 01926 450660

Smoking Cessation

Mr P Hooper, Westgate House, Market Street, Warwick, CV34 4DE, Tel.: 01926 493491

Specialist Nursing Services

Nurses, Continence, Whitnash Lodge, Royal Leamington Spa Rehabilitation Hospital, Heathcote Lane, Warwick, CV34 6SR, Tel.: 01926 317700

Ms J Davis, Lead Nurse, Continuing Care, Cape Road Clinic, Cape Road, Warwick, CV34 4JP, Tel.: 01926 408137

Ms H Airey, Co-ordinator, Discharges, Royal Leamington Spa Rehabilitation Hospital, Heathcote Lane, Warwick, CV34 6SR, Tel.: 01926 317700

Ms A Hyslop, Learning Disabilities, Nurse Specialist, Epilepsy, Royal Leamington Spa Rehabilitation Hospital, Heathcote Lane, Warwick, CV34 6SR, Tel.: 01926 317563

Ms C Talbot, Infection Control, Royal Leamington Spa Rehabilitation Hospital, Heathcote Lane, Warwick, CV34 6SR, Tel.: 01926 317700

The Homeless/Travellers & Asylum Seekers

Mr G Wells, Consultant in Public Health Medicine, Westgate House, Market Street, Warwick, CV34 4DE, Tel.: 01926 493491

South Western Staffordshire Primary Care Trust

Trust Headquarters, Mellor House
Corporation Street
STAFFORD
ST16 3SR
Tel.: 01785 220004
Fax.: 01785 221251

Admin & Senior Management

Ms C Adams, Deputy Director of Primary Care & Professional Development,

Ms S Fisher, Director of Finance & Performance,

Dr Z Iqbal, Director of Public Health & Partnership,

Mr W Price, Chief Executive,

Mrs J Warren, Director of Primary Care & Professional Development,

Child Health

Mrs G Dixon, Community Services Manager, Mellor House, Corporation Street, Stafford, ST16 3SR, Tel.: 01785 220004 ext 5936

Child Health Records

Ms T Davies, Stafford Central Clinic, North Walls, Stafford, ST16 3AE, Tel.: 01785 223099

Ms P Roberts, Stafford Central Clinic, North Walls, Stafford, ST16 3AE, Tel.: 01785 223099

Child Protection/Safeguarding Children

Ms J Arbon, Child Protection, Stafford Central Clinic, North Walls, Stafford, ST16 3AE, Tel.: 01785 223099

Clinical Leads (NSF)

Dr Z Iqbal, Clinical Lead, CHD,

Ms J Brown, Clinical Lead, Diabetic Care,

Dr G Dixon, Clinical Lead, Older People,

Community Nursing Services

Mrs B Clark, Community Services Manager, Trentside Clinic, Stafford Road, Stone, ST15 0HE, Tel.: 01785 816915

Mrs G Dixon, Community Services Manager, Mellor House, Corporation Street, Stafford, ST16 3SR, Tel.: 01785 220004 ext 5936

Mrs F Sutherland, Community Services Manager, Trentside Clinic, Stafford Road, Stone, ST15 0HE, Tel.: 01785 816915

District Nursing

Mrs B Clark, Community Services Manager, Trentside Clinic, Stafford Road, Stone, ST15 0HE, Tel.: 01785 816915

Ms B Clark, Community Services Manager, Codsall Clinic, Elliott's Lane, Codsall, Tel.: 01902 847676

Mrs G Dixon, Community Services Manager, Mellor House, Corporation Street, Stafford, ST16 3SR, Tel.: 01785 220004 ext 5936

Mrs F Sutherland, Community Services Manager, Trentside Clinic, Stafford Road, Stone, ST15 0HE, Tel.: 01785 816915

Equipment Loan Services

Ms J Nunn, Head of Occupational Therapy, Stone Rehabilitation Centre, Stafford Road, Stone, ST15 0HE, Tel.: 01785 816915

Liaison Services

Ms J Adams, Perton Clinic, Coleridge Drive, Perton, WV6 7QE, Tel.: 01902 758150

Ms J Hughes, Trentside Clinic, Stafford Road, Stone, ST15 0TT, Tel.: 01785 811471

Ms J Jones, Perton Clinic, Coleridge Drive, Perton, WV6 7QE, Tel.: 01902 758150

Ms A Lavelle, Trentside Clinic, Stafford Road, Stone, ST15 0TT, Tel.: 01785 811471

Ms J Roberts, Discharge Liaison, Mid Staffs General Hospital, Westonwood, Stafford, ST16 3SA,

Other Services

Ms J Brown, Dietetics, Stafford Central Clinic,

Ms J Nunn, Occupational Therapy, Stone Rehab Centre,

Ms C Ward, Physiotherapy Manager, Codsall Clinic, Elliotts Lane, Codsall, WV8 1PH, Tel.: 01902 847676

Pharmacy

Ms C Riley, Head of Medicines Management, Mellor House, Corporation Street, Stafford, ST16 3SR, Tel.: 01785 220004 ext 5181

Specialist Nursing Services

Ms B Clark, Services Manager, Codsall Clinic, Elliott's Lane, Codsall, Tel.: 01902 847676

Ms F Sutherland, Services Manager, Trentside Clinic, Stafford Road, Stone, ST15 0HE, Tel.: 01785 816915

Ms L Deavin, Lead, Cancer, - Diabetes, Mellor House, Corporation Street, Stafford, ST16 3SR, Tel.: 01785 220004 ext 5165

Ms C Astbury, Nurse Specialist, Continence, West Chadsmoor Clinic, Clarion Way, Cannock, WS11 2NJ, Tel.: 01543 879787

Ms S Collett, Nurse Specialist, Diabetic Care, Codsall Clinic, Elliotts Lane, Codsall, WV8 1PH, Tel.: 01902 847676

Ms A Birkett, Nurse Specialist, Macmillan, Trentside Clinic, Stafford Road, Stone, ST15 0TT, Tel.: 01785 811471

Ms D Lloyd, Nurse Specialist, Rheumatology, Cannock Chase Hospital, Brunswick Road, Cannock, WS11 5XY, Tel.: 01543 572757

Ms M Poole, Nurse Specialist, Wound Care, Stafford Central Clinic, North Walls, Stafford, ST16 3AE, Tel.: 01785 223099

South Worcestershire Primary Care Trust

Trust Headquarters, Isaac Maddox House
Shrub Hill Road
WORCESTER
WR4 9RW
Tel.: 01905 760026

Admin & Senior Management

Mr P Bates, Chief Executive, (Acting), Tel.: 01905 760026

Ms J Patel, Director of Clinical Services & Nursing,

Child Health

Child Health, Isaac Maddox House, Shrub Hill Road, Worcester, WR4 9RW, Tel.: 01905 681560

Dr A Mills, Community Consultant Paediatrician,

Ms J Stephens, Head of Specialist Children's Service,

West Midlands Strategic Health Authority

Child Health Records
Child Health Department, Isaac Maddox House, Tel.: 01905 681560
Child Protection/Safeguarding Children
Child Health/Child Protection, Isaac Maddox House, Shrub Hill Road, Worcester, WR4 9RW, Tel.: 01905 681560
Ms C Whiehouse, Nurse Consultant, Child Protection, Isaac Maddox House, Shrub Hill Road, Worcester, WR4 9RW, Tel.: 01905 681560
District Nursing
Mrs S Hulme, Assistant Director, Clinical Services & Nursing, Worcester City, Moor Street Clinic, Worcester, WR1 3DB, Tel.: 01905 681650/653
Mrs L Levy, Assistant Director, Clinical Services & Nursing, Wychavon, Pershore Health Centre, Priest Lane, Pershore, WR10 1RD, Tel.: 01386 502009
Mrs M McCurry, Assistant Director, Clinical Services & Nursing, Malvern Hills, Malvern Community Hospital, Lansdown Crescent, Malvaern, WR14 2AW, Tel.: 01684 612630
Family Planning Services
Clinical Director, Moor Street Clinic, Worcester, Tel.: 01905 681635
Learning Disabilities
Bromsgrove Team, Catshill Clinic, The Dock, Catshill, Bromsgrove, Tel.: 01527 488330
Droitwich Team, Droitwich Health Centre, Ombersley Street, Droitwich, Tel.: 01905 681020
Evesham Team, Evesham Health Centre, Merstow Green, Evesham, Tel.: 01386 502321
Ms J Large, Nurse Advisor, Evesham Health Centre, Merstow Green, Evesham, WR11 4BS, Tel.: 01386 502321
Malvern Team, Malvern Health Centre, Victoria Park Road, Malvern, Tel.: 01684 612795
Redditch Team, Smallwood House, Church Green West, Redditch, Tel.: 01527 488630
Mrs K Robinson, Service Manager, Smallwood House, Church Green West, Redditch, Worcestershire, B97 4BD, Tel.: 01527 488632
Ms L Troth, Team Leader, Smallwood House, Church Green West, Redditch, Worcestershire, B97 4BD, Tel.: 01527 488630
Worcester Team, St John's Clinic, 1 Bromyard Road, Worcester, Tel.: 01905 681902
School Nursing
Ms L Allen, School Nurse, Malvern Health Centre, Tel.: 01684 612669
Mrs C Ashforth, School Nurse, Droitwich Health Centre, Tel.: 01905 681033
Ms S Ballard, School Nurse, Henwick Halt, Tel.: 01905 681723
Ms A Black, School Nurse, Henwick Halt, Tel.: 01905 681611
Ms J Cahill, School Nurse, Henwick Halt, Tel.: 01905 681725
Ms S Coleman, School Nurse, Malvern Health Centre, Tel.: 01684 612671
Ms C Cooke, School Nurse, Henwick Halt, Tel.: 01905 681910
Mrs J Counter, School Nurse, Droitwich Health Centre, Tel.: 01905 681034
Mrs P Day, School Nurse, Evesham Health Centre, Tel.: 01386 502329
Ms C Eastwell, School Nurse, Henwick Halt, Tel.: 01905 681910
Ms P Edwards, School Nurse, Upton Clinic, Tel.: 01684 612803
Ms L Gallagher, School Nurse, Malvern Health Centre, Tel.: 01684 612814
Ms L Horne, School Nurse, Malvern Health Centre, Tel.: 01684 612669
Ms T Lovett, School Nurse, Pershore Health Centre, Tel.: 01386 502013
Ms C Nicholls, School Nurse, Evesham Health Centre, Tel.: 01386 502329
Ms T Owen, School Nurse, Henwick Halt, Tel.: 01905 681616
Ms H Robinson, School Nurse, Evesham Health Centre, Tel.: 01386 502330

Ms C Rogerson, School Nurse, Henwick Halt, Tel.: 01905 681909
Mr I Stevens, School Nurse, Malvern Health Centre, Tel.: 01684 612669
Ms J Thomas, School Nurse, Malvern Health Centre, Tel.: 01684 612663
Ms A Waldron, School Nurse, Pershore Health Centre, Tel.: 01386 502013
Ms A Williams, School Nurse, Pershore Health Centre, Tel.: 01386 502013
The Homeless/Travellers & Asylum Seekers
Mrs B Bryan, Health Visitor for Travellers, Evesham Health Centre, Tel.: 01386 502316

Staffordshire Moorlands Primary Care Trust
Trust Headquarters, Moorlands House
Stockwell Street
LEEK
Staffordshire
ST13 6HQ
Tel.: 01538 487234

Admin & Senior Management
Mr T Bruce, Chief Executive,
Mrs J Gibson, Director of Nursing, Moorlands House, Stockwell Street, Leek, Staffordshire, ST13 6HQ, Tel.: 01538 487243
Child Health
Mrs N Isteed, Diabetic Children Service, Hanford Health Centre, New Inn Lane, Hanford, Stoke on Trent, Tel.: 01782 421000
Mrs T Malkin, Team Leader, Children Community Nursing Team, Cheadle Hospital, Royal Walk, Cheadle, Stoke on Trent, ST10 1NS, Tel.: 01538 487500
Mrs A Willdigg, Senior Nurse Manager, Childrens Services, Leek Moorlands Hospital, Ashbourne Road, Leek, Staffs, ST13 5BQ, Tel.: 01538 487500
Child Health Records
Mrs S Clare, Bedford House Clinic, Havelock Place, Shelton, Stoke on Trent, Staffs, ST5 6PN, Tel.: 01782 425000
Child Protection/Safeguarding Children
Mrs A Willdigg, Senior Nurse Manager, Childrens Services, Leek Moorlands Hospital, Ashbourne Road, Leek, Staffs, ST13 5BQ, Tel.: 01538 487500
Clinical Leads (NSF)
Dr J Bell, Clinical Lead, Cancer, Moorlands House, Stockwell Street, Leek, ST13 6HQ,
Ms J Gibson, Clinical Lead, Care of the Elderly, Moorlands House, Stockwell Street, Leek, ST13 6HQ,
Ms S Cooper, Clinical Lead, CHD, Cheadle Hospital,
Ms D Clohesy, Clinical Lead, Diabetic Care, Leek Moorlands Hospital,
District Nursing
Ms S Cooper, District Nurses, Senior Nurse Manager, Adult Services, Cheadle Hospital, Royal Walk, Cheadle, Stoke on Trent, ST10 1NS, Tel.: 01538 487500
Health Visitors
Mrs A Willdigg, Health Visitors, Senior Nurse Manager, Childrens Services, Leek Moorlands Hospital, Ashbourne Road, Leek, Staffs, ST13 5BQ, Tel.: 01538 487500
Liaison Services
Ms L Johnson, PALS Officer,
Mrs T Smith, Hanford Health Centre, New inn Lane, Hanford, Stoke on Trent, ST4 8EX, Tel.: 01782 421000
Mrs A Willdigg, Senior Nurse Manager, Childrens Services, Leek Moorlands Hospital, Ashbourne Road, Leek, Staffs, ST13 5BQ, Tel.: 01538 487500
Specialist Nursing Services
Mrs D Clohesy, Diabetic Care, - Adults, Leek Moorlands Hospital, Ashbourne Road, Leek, Staffordshire, ST13 5BQ, Tel.: 01538 487100

West Midlands Strategic Health Authority

Telford & Wrekin Primary Care Trust

Trust Headquarters, Sommerfeld House
Sommerfeld Road, Trench Lock
TELFORD
Shropshire
TF1 5RY
Tel.: 01952 222322

Admin & Senior Management
Mrs P Bickley, Director of Nursing Development & Patient
Experience, Sommerfeld House, Sommerfeld Road, Trench Lock,
Telford, TF1 5RY, Tel.: 01952 265199
Child Health Records
Mrs J A Bennett, Services for Children & Young People, Longbow
House, Harlescott Lane, Shrewsbury, sy1 3AS, Tel.: 01743 450800
Child Protection/Safeguarding Children
Mrs P Bickley, Designated Nurse, Child Protection, Sommerfeld
House, Sommerfeld Road, Trench Lock, Telford, TF1 5RY, Tel.:
01952 265199
Clinical Leads (NSF)
Dr J Vaid, Clinical Lead, Consultant Paediatrician, Services for
Children & Young People, Longbow House, Longbow Close,
Harlescott Lane, Shrewsbury, SY1 3AS, Tel.: 01743 450800
Dr A Inglis, Clinical Lead, Renal, Sutton Hill Medical Practice,
Maythorne Close, Sutton Hill, Telford, TF7 4DH, Tel.: 01952 586471
Dr P Spencer, Clinical Lead, Renal, Dawley Medical Practice, Webb
House, King Street, Dawley, Telford, TF4 2AA, Tel.: 01952 630500
Community Nursing Services
Mrs S Dalebo, Community Neighbourhood Nurse Manager, 1st
Floor, Colliers Way, Old Park, Telford, TF3 4AW, Tel.: 01952 217400
Mrs A Davies, Community Neighbourhood Nurse Manager, 1st Floor,
Colliers Way, Old Park, Telford, TF3 4AW, Tel.: 01952 217400
Mrs L Randle, Community Neighbourhood Nurse Manager, 1st Floor,
Colliers Way, Old Park, Telford, TF3 4AW, Tel.: 01952 217400
Family Planning Services
Ms S Jones, Sexual Health Services Manager, Sexual Health
Services, 3rd Floor Princess House, The Square, Shrewsbury, SY1
1JX, Tel.: 01743 283382
Learning Disabilities
Mr S Dale, Team Manager, Joint Community Learning Disabilites
Team, 40 Taro Bank, Wellington, Telford, TF1 1HW, Tel.: 01743
202600
School Nursing
Mrs S Dalebo, School Nurses, Professional Lead HV's, 1st Floor,
Colliers Way, Old Park, Telford, TF3 4AW, Tel.: 01952 217400
Specialist Nursing Services
Mrs P Virdee, Asian Link Nurse, Cancer, Hadley Health Centre, High
Street, Hadley, Telford, TF1 4NG, Tel.: 01952 251498
Mrs C Mear, Team Leader, Advisor, Continence, 1st Floor, Colliers
Way, Old Park, Telford, TF3 4AW, Tel.: 01952 217400
Team, Intermediate Care, Ground Floor, Derby House, C Wing,
Lawn Central, Telford, TF3 4JA, Tel.: 01952 202953
Ms J Tickle, Nurse Specialist, Leg Ulcers, 1st Floor, Colliers Way,
Old Park, Telford, TF3 4AW, Tel.: 01952 217400
Team, Rapid Response, Ground Floor, Derby House, C Wing, Lawn
Central, Telford, TF3 4JA, Tel.: 01952 202850
Ms M Whiting, Nurse Specialist, Respiratory, c/o The Health Centre,
Wrekin Drive, Donnington, Telford, TF2 8EA, Tel.: 01952 272170

University Hospital Birmingham NHS Trust

Trust Headquarters, PO Box 9551, Maindrive
Queen Elizabeth Medical Centre
BIRMINGHAM
West Midlands
B15 2PR
Tel.: 0121 4323232

Admin & Senior Management
Dame C Elcoat, Director of Nursing, PO Box 9551, Maindrive, Queen
Elizabeth Medical Centre, Birmingham, B15 2PR, Tel.: 0121
4323232

University Hospital of North Staffordshire NHS Trust

Trust Headquarters, Royal Infirmary
Princess Road, Hartshill
STOKE-ON-TRENT
Staffordshire
ST4 7LN
Tel.: 01782 552405

Community Midwifery
Community Midwifery Services, Tel.: 01782 552405
Community Office, Tel.: 01782 552405
Mrs P Cornwall, Clinical Midwife Manager, Womens & Childrens
Division, Newcastle Road, Stoke-on-Trent, Staffordshire, ST4 6QG,
Tel.: 01782 552463
Mrs K Meadowcroft, Community Co-ordinator, Tel.: 01782 552422
Mrs D Sexton-Bradshaw, Directorate Manager, Head of Midwifery,
Womens & Childrens Division, Newcastle Road, Stoke-on-Trent,
Staffordshire, ST4 6QG, Tel.: 01782 552400
Trust Headquarters, Royal Infirmary
Princess Road, Hartshill
STOKE ON TRENT
Staffordshire
ST4 7LN
Tel.: 01782 552405

Community Midwifery
Community Midwifery Services, Tel.: 01782 552405
Mrs P Cornwall, Clinical Midwife Manager, Women & Childrens
Division, Newcastle Road, Stoke on Trent, Staffordshire, ST4 6QG,
Tel.: 01782 552463
Mrs K Meadowcroft, Community Co-ordinator, Tel.: 01782 552422
Mrs D Sexton-Bradshaw, Directorate Manager, Head of Midwifery,
Women & Childrens Division, Newcastle Road, Stoke on Trent,
Staffordshire, ST4 6QG, Tel.: 01782 552400

University Hospitals Coventry & Warwickshire NHS Trust

Trust Headquarters, Clifford Bridge Road
Walsgrave
COVENTRY
West Midlands
CV2 2DX
Tel.: 024 7660 2020

Child Protection/Safeguarding Children
Ms C Ellis, Named Nurse, Child Protection, Walsgrave Hospital,
Clifford Bridge Rd, Coventry, CV2 2DX, Tel.: 02476 602020 x 7007
Community Midwifery
Emergencies, Community Midwife on Call, Walsgrave Hospital,
Clifford Bridge Road, Walsgrave, Coventry, Warwickshire, CV2 2DX,
Tel.: 024 7660 2020
Mrs A O'Reilly, Community Midwifery Manager, Walsgrave Hospital,
Clifford Bridge Road, Walsgrave, Coventry, Warwickshire, CV2 2DX
Tel.: 024 7696 7425

Walsall Hospitals NHS Trust

Trust Headquarters, Manor Hospital
Moat Road
WALSALL, West Midlands
WS2 9PS
Tel.: 01922 721172
Fax.: 01922 656621

West Midlands Strategic Health Authority

Community Midwifery
Mrs E Fallon, General Manager, Women's & Children's Services, Walsall Hospitals NHS Trust, Moat Road, Walsall, WS2 9PS, Tel.: 01922 721172 ext 7733
Mrs L Gostling, Matron, Community Midwifery Service, Walsall Hospitals NHS Trust, Moat Road, Walsall, WS2 9PS, Tel.: 01922 721172 ext 6327

Walsall Teaching Primary Care Trust
Trust Headquarters, Jubilee House
Bloxwich Lane
WALSALL, WS2 7JL
Tel.: 01922 618388

Admin & Senior Management
Mr A Howie, Chief Executive,
Ms V Jones, Assistant Director of Nursing Services, Bloxwich Hospital, Reeves Street, Bloxwich, Walsall, WS3 2JJ, Tel.: 01922 858665
Mr T Mingay, Director of Health & Social Care Services, Tel.: 01922 858421
Ms K Parsons, Director of Primary Care,

Child Health
Ms S Archibald, Clinical Team Leader, Sycamore House, Tel.: 01922 858148
Ms D Smith, Paediatric Liaison Health Visitor/Home Care Team Manager, East Wing, Manor Hospital, Moat Road, Walsall, WS2 9PS, Tel.: 01922 721172 ext 7404
Mrs C Thompson, H'capping Conditions in Childhood Health Visitors, Walsall Child Assessment Unit, Coalheath Lane, Shelfield, WS4 1PL, Tel.: 01922 858729

Child Health Records
Short Heath Clinic, Tel.: 01922 858644

Child Protection/Safeguarding Children
Mrs D Bray, Named Nurse for Looked After Children, Room 107, Blakenall Village Centre, Thames Road, Blakenall, Walsall, WS3 1LZ, Tel.: 01922 443908
Mrs M Chaudhry, Health Co-ordinator for Looked After Children, Room 107, Blakenall Village Centre, Thames Road, Blakenall, Walsall, WS3 1LZ, Tel.: 01922 443909
Mrs L Albrighton, Named Nurse, Child Protection, Blakenall Village Centre, Thames Road, Blakenall, Walsall, WS3 1LZ, Tel.: 01922 443921
Mrs E Hurry, Designated Nurse, Child Protection, Blakenall Village Centre, Thames Road, Blakenall, Walsall, WS3 1LZ, Tel.: 01922 443920

Clinical Leads (NSF)
Dr P Giles, Clinical Lead, CHD & Diabetes,
Dr J Linnane, Clinical Lead, Cancer,
Dr T Skitt, Clinical Lead, Older People,

District Nursing
Ms A Bowen, Clinical Team Leader/Operations Manager District Nurses Rapid Assessment Team - South & West, Goscote Hospital, Goscote, Walsall, Tel.: 01922 494370
District Nursing Out of hours, Bank Holidays & Weekends & Evening Service, Dorothy Pattison Hospital, Alumwell Close, Walsall, WS2 9XH, Tel.: 01922 858000
District Nursing Referrals - East, Shelfield Clinic, Coalheath Lane, Shelfield, Walsall, WS4 1RL, Tel.: 01922 858717
District Nursing Referrals - North, Bloxwich Hospital, Tel.: 01922 858600
District Nursing Referrals - South, Dorothy Pattison Hospital, Alumwell Close, Walsall, WS2 9XH, Tel.: 01922 858095
District Nursing Referrals - West, Short Heath Clinic, Bloxwich Road North, Short Heath, Willenhall, Tel.: 01922 858652/3
Mr T O'Shaughnessy, District Nursing Clinical Team Leader - North & East, Beechdale Centre, Edison Road, Beechdale Estate, Walsall, WS2 7EZ, Tel.: 01922 775050

Family Planning Services
Ms M Pillinger, Clinical Team Leader, Hatherton Centre, Hatherton Street, Walsall, WS1 1YB, Tel.: 01922 775041

Health Visitors
Ms M Chaudhry, Clinical Lead, Health Visitors West, Short Heath Clinic, Tel.: 01922 858653
Ms K Cox, Clinical Lead, Health Visitors North, Beechdale Centre, Tel.: 01922 775050
Ms D Parker, Clinical Lead, Health Visitors East, Sycamore House, Tel.: 01922 858148
Ms J Richardson, Clinical Lead, Health Visitors South, Sycamore House, Tel.: 01922 858148
Ms D Smith, Paediatric Liaison Health Visitor/Home Care Team Manager, East Wing, Manor Hospital, Moat Road, Walsall, WS2 9PS, Tel.: 01922 721172 ext 7404

Learning Disabilities
Bloxwich, 5 Wightwick Close, Bloxwich, Walsall, Tel.: 01922 858674
Daisybank Community Unit, Fallowfield Road, Walsall, WS5 3DY, Tel.: 01922 775086
Great Barr, 1/2 Suttons Drive, Off Chapel Lane, Great Barr, Birmingham, Tel.: 0121 360 6453
Great Barr, 1 Lakeview Close, Queslett Road, Great Barr, Birmingham, Tel.: 0121 480 5931
Great Barr, 2 Lakeview Close, Queslett Road, Great Barr, Birmingham, Tel.: 0121 480 5928
Great Barr, 2/3 Handsworth Drive, Off Queslett Road, Great Barr, Birmingham, Tel.: 0121 325 0660
Orchard Hills, Fallowfield Road, Walsall, WS5 3DY, Tel.: 01922 775092
Springside Community Unit, 2 Spring Lane, Pelsall, Walsall, WS4 1AZ, Tel.: 01922 858700
Walsall, 164 Walker Road, Walsall, WS3 1BZ, Tel.: 01922 858677
Mr J Wright, Service Manager, Learning Disability Service, 5 Lake View Close, Queslett Road, Great Barr, Birmingham, B43 7EZ, Tel.: 0121 480 5945

Specialist Nursing Services
Ms D Lowe, Continence, Patient Support Centre, Units 8/9 Bentley Lane, Walsall, WS2 8TL, Tel.: 01922 632305
Team, Continuing Care, Little Bloxwich Day Hospice, Stoney Lane, Little Bloxwich, WS3 3DW, Tel.: 01922 858735
Mr J Myatt, Diabetic Care, E Wing, Manor Hospital, Moat Road, Walsall, WS2 9PS, Tel.: 01922 721172 ext 6543
Ms J Long, Physical Disability, - Adults, Beechdale Health Centre, Tel.: 01922 775053
Mrs M Craddock, Rehabilitation, Dartmouth House, Ryecroft Place, Ryecroft, WS3 1SW, Tel.: 01922 775095
Ms S Sandhu, TB, Moat Road Clinic, Moat Road, Walsall, WS2 2PS, Tel.: 01922 775077
Ms J Cave, Co-ordinator, Tissue Viability, Short Heath Clinic, Tel.: 01922 858671
Ms D Chaloner, Nurse, Tissue Viability, Short Heath Clinic, Tel.: 01922 858671

The Homeless/Travellers & Asylum Seekers
Ms D Falkener, Travelling Families Link Health Visitor, Brownhills Clinic, Pier Street, Brownhills, Tel.: 01543 372219

Wednesbury & West Bromwich Primary Care Trust
Trust Headquarters, Kingston House
438 High Street, WEST BROMWICH
B70 9LD
Tel.: 0121 500 1500

Admin & Senior Management
Mr G Griffiths, Chief Executive,

Child Health Records
Child Health Records, Sandwell & West Birmingham NHS Trust, Tel.: 0121 553 1831

West Midlands Strategic Health Authority

Child Protection/Safeguarding Children
Shared service supplied by Oldbury & Smethwick PCT, Tel.: 0121 543 3996

Clinical Leads (NSF)
Dr K Sidhu, Clinical Lead, Cancer,
Dr M Fairfield, Clinical Lead, CHD,
Dr E Clark, Clinical Lead, Diabetic Care,
Dr J Brown, Clinical Lead, Older People,

Community Nursing Services
Ms J Daly, Associate Director Clinical Quality (Nursing), Kingston House, 438 High Street, West Bromwich, B70 9LD, Tel.: 0121 500 1500

District Nursing
District Nursing message taking service, Tel.: 0121 607 3083

Equipment Loan Services
Joint Equipment Store, Crystal Drive, Smethwick, Tel.: 0121 569 3666

Family Planning Services
Ms D Partridge, Lead Nurse, Tel.: 0121 533 2820

Health Visitors
Health Visitors message taking service, Tel.: 0121 530 8008

Liaison Services
Lead Nurse Free Nursing Care, Tel.: 0121 533 2932
Wednesbury Discharge Planners, Tel.: 0121 505 5553
West Bromwich Discharge Planners, Tel.: 0121 607 3359

School Nursing
School Health Nurses message taking service, Tel.: 0121 533 2800

Specialist Nursing Services
Ms D Owen, Lead Nurse, Continence, Tel.: 0121 607 3575
Ms H Edwards, Nurse Specialist, Diabetic Care, Tel.: 0121 533 2800
Ms M Hems, Nurse Specialist, Heart Failure, Tel.: 0121 601 2208
Ms S Davidson, Nurse, Older People, Tel.: 0121 601 2208
Ms M Perry, Nurse Specialist, Respiratory, Tel.: 0121 601 2208

Wolverhampton City Primary Trust

Trust Headquarters, Coniston House
Chapel Ash
WOLVERHAMPTON
WV3 0XE
Tel.: 01902 444888

Admin & Senior Management
Mr J Crocket, Chief Executive,

Child Health
Ms S Rust, Community Child Nursing, Red Hill Street Health Centre, Tel.: 01902 444700
Ms J Wilding, General Manager, Child Health, Tel.: 01902 444306

Child Health Records
Child Health Records, Red Hill Street Health Centre, Wolverhampton, WV1 1NR, Tel.: 01902 444302

Child Protection/Safeguarding Children
Ms M Viggers, Child Protection, Red Hill Street Health Centre, Tel.: 01902 444348

Clinical Leads (NSF)
Dr M Epsley, Clinical Lead, Older People,
Dr A Phillips, Clinical Lead, Cancer,

Community Nursing Services
Ms J Wilding, Director of Nursing, 10/12 Tettenhall Road, Wolverhampton, WV1 4SA, Tel.: 01902 444306

District Nursing
Night Nursing Co-ordinator, Maltings Mobility Centre, The Maltings, Herbert Street, Wolverhampton, WV1 1NQ, Tel.: 01902 556000
Ms J Wilding, Director of Nursing, 10/12 Tettenhall Road, Wolverhampton, WV1 4SA, Tel.: 01902 444306

Health Visitors
Ms D Barzda, Paediatric Health Visitor, Red Hill Street Health Centre, Tel.: 01902 444700
Paediatric Health Visitor, New Cross Hospital, Wednesfield Road, Wolverhampton, WV10 0QP, Tel.: 01902 307999 ext 2462

HIV/AIDS
Mr J McLean, Snow Hill Centre, Contraception Services, Wolverhampton, Tel.: 01902 444448

School Nursing
Ms H Hawkins-Dady, School Health/Nursing Service, Specialist, Red Hill Street Health Centre, Tel.: 01902 444161

Specialist Nursing Services
Mrs R Morris, Continence, Steps to Health, Low Hill Community Health Centre, Showell Circus, Low Hill, Wolverhampton, WV10 9TH, Tel.: 01902 444604
Ms E Wilson, Co-ordinator, Diabetic Care, Diabetes Centre, New Cross Hospital, Tel.: 01902 642858
Nurses, Infection Control, New Cross Hospital, Tel.: 01902 307999 ext 3507
Nurses, Rapid Response, Stepping Stones, c/o Warstones Health Centre, Warstones Drive, Wolverhampton, Tel.: 01902 444897
Visitor Co-ordinator, TB, New Cross Hospital, Tel.: 01902 642947
Ms J Rainey, Tissue Viability, Pendeford Health Centre, Tel.: 01902 444025

The Homeless/Travellers & Asylum Seekers
Ms A James, Health Visitor Women's Hostels, Refuges, Red Hill Street Health Centre, Tel.: 01902 575238
Ms H Williams, Health Visitor Homeless, Travellers, Pendeford Health Centre, Whitburn Close, Wolverhampton, WV9 5NJ, Tel.: 01902 575237

Wolverhampton Health Care NHS Trust

Trust Headquarters, Cleveland/Leasowes
10/12 Tetterhall Road
WOLVERHAMPTON
WV1 4SA
Tel.: 01902 444446

Learning Disabilities
Mrs J Collier, General Manager, 44 Pond Lane, Parkfields, Wolverhampton, West Midlands, WV2 1HG, Tel.: 01902 444002

Worcester Mental Health NHS Trust

Trust Headquarters, Issac Maddox House
Shrub Hill Road
WORCESTER
WR4 9RW
Tel.: 01905 681511

Admin & Senior Management
Mr C Vines, Director of Clinical Services & Nursing, Issac Maddox House, Shrub Hill Road, Worcester, WR4 9RW, Tel.: 01905 681511

Worcestershire Acute Hospitals NHS Trust

Trust Headquarters, Worcester Royal Hospital
Charles Hastings Way, Newton Road
WORCESTER, WR5 1DD
Tel.: 01905 763333

Acute Specialist Nursing Services
Nurse Specialists, DVT, Anti-Coagulation, Worcestershire Royal, Tel.: 01905 763333 ext 30136
Nurse Specialists, Breast Care, Kidderminster, Tel.: 01562 823424 ext 53806
Nurse Specialists, Breast Care, Alexandra Hospital, Tel.: 01527 503030 ext 44625
Nurse Specialists, Breast Care, Worcestershire Royal, Tel.: 01905 760261
Nurse Specialists, Cardiac Rehabilitation, Kidderminster, Tel.: 01562 512315
Nurse Specialists, Cardiac Rehabilitation, Worcestershire Royal, Tel.: 01905 760868
Nurse Specialists, Cardiac Rehabilitation, Alexandra Hospital, Tel.: 01527 503882

Nurse Specialists, Cardiology, Alexandra Hospital, Tel.: 01527 507978

Nurse Specialists, Cardiology, Worcestershire Royal, Tel.: 01905 760591

Nurse Specialists, Colorectal, - Upper GI, Worcestershire Royal, Tel.: 01905 760643

Nurse Specialists, Colorectal, Alexandra Hospital, Tel.: 01527 512195/6

Nurse Specialists, Dermatology, Kidderminster, Tel.: 01562 823424 ext 55150

Nurse Specialists, Dermatology, Worcestershire Royal, Tel.: 01905 760275

Nurse Specialists, Diabetes, - Adults, Kidderminster, Tel.: 01562 512322

Nurse Specialists, Diabetes, Worcestershire Royal, Tel.: 01905 763333 ext 33846

Nurse Specialists, Gastroenterology, Worcestershire Royal, Tel.: 01905 760732

Nurse Specialists, Gynaecology, Kidderminster, Tel.: 01562 823424 ext 53579

Nurse Specialists, Macmillan, Gynaecology, Worcestershire Royal, Tel.: 01905 733257

Nurse Specialists, Uro, Gynaecology, Worcestershire Royal, Tel.: 01905 733254

Nurse Specialists, EPU, Gynaecology, Worcestershire Royal, Tel.: 01905 733060

Nurse Specialists, Gynaecology, Alexandra Hospital, Tel.: 01527 512000/16

Nurse Specialists, Haematology, Worcestershire Royal, Tel.: 01905 760695

Nurse Specialists, Haematology, Kidderminster, Tel.: 01562 823424 ext 53807

Nurse Specialists, Haematology, Alexandra Hospital, Tel.: 01527 503030 ext 44053

Nurse Specialists, Infection Control, Alexandra Hosp. 01527 512185

Nurse Specialists, Infection Control, Worcestershire Royal, Tel.: 01905 733092

Nurse Specialists, Infectious Diseases, Worcestershire Royal, Tel.: 01905 760383

Nurse Specialists, Oncology, Worcestershire Royal, Tel.: 01905 760876

Nurse Specialists, Oncology, Alexandra Hospital, Tel.: 01527 503030 ext 42092

Nurse Specialists, Paediatrics, Worcestershire Royal, Tel.: 01905 763333 ext 30408

Nurse Specialists, Pain Management, - Acute, Alexandra Hospital, Tel.: 01527 503030 ext 44416

Nurse Specialists, Pain Management, - Chronic Pain, Worcestershire Royal, Tel.: 01905 733313

Nurse Specialists, Pain Management, - Chronic Pain, Kidderminster, Tel.: 01562 512379

Nurse Specialists, Pain Management, - Acute, Worcestershire Royal, Tel.: 01905 763333 ext 30725

Macmillan Nurses, Palliative Care, Alexandra Hospital, Tel.: 01527 512085

Nurse Specialists, Macmillan, Palliative Care, Worcestershire Royal, Tel.: 01905 760758

Nurse Specialists, Respiratory, Kidderminster, Tel.: 01562 512316

Nurse Specialists, Respiratory, Alexandra Hospital, Tel.: 01527 503030 ext 44991

Nurse Specialists, Lung Cancer, Respiratory, Worcestershire Royal, Tel.: 01905 733053

Nurse Specialists, Sleep Support, Respiratory, Worcestershire Royal, Tel.: 01905 763333 ext 30325

Nurse Specialists, Non-malignant & Allergy, Respiratory, Worcestershire Royal, Tel.: 01905 760255

Nurse Specialists, Rheumatology, Worcestershire Royal, Tel.: 01905 763333 ext 33466

Nurse Specialists, Stoma Care, - Colorectal, Worcestershire Royal, Tel.: 01905 763333 ext 30354

Nurse Specialists, Stroke Care, Worcestershire Royal, Tel.: 01905 760285

Nurse Specialists, Tissue Viability, Alexandra Hospital, Tel.: 01527 503030 ext 44749

Nurse Specialists, Trauma & Orthopaedics, Alexandra Hospital, Tel.: 01527 503030 ext 44279

Nurse Specialists, Trauma & Orthopaedics, Worcestershire Royal, Tel.: 01905 733043/760266

Macmillan Nurses, Urology, Alexandra Hospital, Tel.: 01527 503030 ext 44150

Nurse Specialists, Urology, Alexandra Hospital, Tel.: 01527 503030

Nurse Specialists, Urology, Worcestershire Royal, Tel.: 01905 760875

Nurse Specialists, Urology/Oncology, Kidderminster, Tel.: 01562 512328

Nurse Specialists, Vascular, - Surgical, Worcestershire Royal, Tel.: 01905 763333 ext 39301

Nurse Specialists, Leg Ulcers, Vascular, Worcestershire Royal, Tel.: 01905 763333 ext 302060

Nurse Specialists, Vascular, Worcestershire Royal, Tel.: 01905 763333 ext 39301

Community Midwifery

Community Midwifery, Via Switchboard, Kidderminster Treatment Centre, Bewdley Road, Kidderminster, DY11 6RJ, Tel.: 01562 823424

Community Midwifery, Via Switchboard, Alexandra Hospital, Woodrow Drive, Redditch, B98 7UB, Tel.: 01527 503030

Community Midwifery, Via Switchboard, Worcestershire Royal Hospital, Charles Hastings Way, Newtown Road, Worcester, WR5 1DD, Tel.: 01905 763333

Discharge Co-ordinators

Community Care Co-ordinator, Alexandra Hospital, Tel.: 01527 503030 ext 44358

Community Care co-ordinator, Worcestershire Royal, Tel.: 01905 763333 ext 33066

Discharge Co-ordinator, Alexandra Hospital, Tel.: 01527 503030 ext 44413

Discharge Co-ordinators, Worcestershire Royal, Tel.: 01905 763333 ext 33065/7

Integrated discharge team, Worcestershire Royal, Tel.: 01905 763333 ext 33043

Matrons/Modern Matrons

Modern Matron, A&E, Bleep via Switchboard, Alexandra Hospital, Tel.: 01527 503030

Modern Matron, A&E, Bleep via Switchboard, Worcestershire Royal Hospital, Tel.: 01905 763333

Modern Matron, Assessment, - Medical, Bleep via Switchboard, Worcestershire Royal Hospital, Tel.: 01905 763333

Modern Matron, Cardiology, Bleep via Switchboard, Worcestershire Royal Hospital, Tel.: 01905 763333

Modern Matron, Elderly Care, - Medicine, Bleep via Switchboard, Worcestershire Royal Hospital, Tel.: 01905 763333

Modern Matron, Gynaecology, Bleep via Switchboard, Alexandra Hospital, Tel.: 01527 503030

Modern Matron, ICCU, Bleep via Switchboard, Worcestershire Royal Hospital, Tel.: 01905 763333

Modern Matron, ICCU, Bleep via Switchboard, Alexandra Hospital, Tel.: 01527 503030

Modern Matron, Medicine, Bleep via Switchboard, Worcestershire Royal Hospital, Tel.: 01905 763333

Modern Matron, Medicine, Bleep via Switchboard, Alexandra Hospital, Tel.: 01527 503030

Modern Matron, Minor injuries, Bleep via Switchboard, Kidderminster Treatment Centre, Tel.: 01562 823424

Modern Matron, Neonatal, Bleep via Switchboard, Worcestershire Royal Hospital, Tel.: 01905 763333

West Midlands Strategic Health Authority

Modern Matron, Outpatients, Bleep via Switchboard, Kidderminster Treatment Centre, Tel.: 01562 823424

Modern Matron, Outpatients, Bleep via Switchboard, Worcestershire Royal Hospital, Tel.: 01905 763333

Modern Matron, Paediatrics, Bleep via Switchboard, Worcestershire Royal Hospital, Tel.: 01905 763333

Modern Matron, Surgery, Bleep via Switchboard, Alexandra Hospital, Tel.: 01527 503030

Modern Matron, Surgery, Bleep via Switchboard, Worcestershire Royal Hospital, Tel.: 01905 763333

Modern Matron, Theatres, Bleep via Switchboard, Alexandra Hospital, Tel.: 01527 503030

Modern Matron, Theatres, Bleep via Switchboard, Worcestershire Royal Hospital, Tel.: 01905 763333

Modern Matron, Trauma & Orthopaedics, Bleep via Switchboard, Alexandra Hospital, Tel.: 01527 503030

Modern Matron, Trauma & Orthopaedics, Bleep via Switchboard, Worcestershire Royal Hospital, Tel.: 01905 763333

Wyre Forest Primary Care Trust

Trust Headquarters, 7th Floor, Brook House
Kidderminster Hospital, Bewdley Road
KIDDERMINSTER
Worcestershire, DY11 6RJ
Tel.: 01562 826329

Admin & Senior Management
Mrs S Dugan, Director of Clinical Services, 7th Floor, Brock House, Kidderminster Hospital, Bewdley Road, Kidderminster, DY11 6RJ, Tel.: 01562 826311

Mrs C E Ferguson, Nurse Development Manager, 6th Floor, Brock House, Kidderminster Hospital, Bewdley Road, Kidderminster, DY11 6RJ, Tel.: 01562 826381

Child Health
Ms L Smith, Children with Special Needs Team Leader, Kidderminster Health Centre, Bromsgrove Street, Kidderminster, DY10 1PG, Tel.: 01562 820091 ext 226

Child Health Records
Ms C Poole, Admin Manager - Worcester Community & Mental Health Trust, Kidderminster Health Centre, Bromsgrove Street, Kidderminster, DY10 1PG, Tel.: 01562 820091 ext 207

Child Protection/Safeguarding Children
Ms J Acton, Named Nurse, Child Protection, Kidderminster Health Centre, Bromsgrove Street, Kidderminster, DY10 1PG, Tel.: 01562 820091 ext 230

Ms C Whiehouse, Nurse Consultant, Child Protection, Isaac Maddox House, Shrub Hill Road, Worcester, WR4 9RW, Tel.: 01905 681590

Community Matrons
Ms J Hooper, Community Matron, Kidderminster Health Centre, Bromsgrove Street, Kidderminster, DY10 1PG, Tel.: 01562 820091

Ms J Jones, Community Matron, Bewdley Medical Centre, Dog Lane, Bewdley, Worcs, DY12 2EG, Tel.: 01299 403677

Ms A Price, Community Matron, Church Street Surgery, David Corbet House, Callows Lane, Kidderminster, DY10 2JG, Tel.: 01562 822501

District Nursing
District Nurses - Emergencies/Nights, (1800-2230), Tel.: 01562 823424

Mrs C E Ferguson, Nursing Development Manager, 6th Floor, Brock House, Kidderminster Hospital, Bewdley Road, Kidderminster, DY11 6RJ, Tel.: 01562 826381

Family Planning Services
Family Planning Service, B Block, Kidderminster Hospital, Bewdley Road, Kidderminster, DY11 6RJ, Tel.: 01562 823424

Health Visitors
Ms T Norris, Service Lead - Health Visitors, 6th Floor, Brock House, Kidderminster Hospital, Bewdley Road, Kidderminster, DY11 6RJ, Tel.: 01562 826384

Liaison Services
Ms B Green, Senior Primary Care Liaison Nurse, Discharge Support Centre, Worcestershire Royal Hospital, Charles Hastings Way, Worcester, WR5 1DD, Tel.: 01905 763333

Ms S Salisbury, Primary Care Liaison Nurse, Discharge Support Centre, Worcestershire Royal Hospital, Charles Hastings Way, Worcester, WR5 1DD, Tel.: 01905 763333

Pharmacy
Mrs A Kingham, Pharmaceutical Advisor, 6th Floor, Brock House, Kidderminster Hospital, Bewdley Road, Kidderminster, DY11 6RJ, Tel.: 01562 826325

School Nursing
Ms T Norris, Service Lead - School Nurses, 6th Floor, Brock House, Kidderminster Hospital, Bewdley Road, Kidderminster, DY11 6RJ, Tel.: 01562 826384

Smoking Cessation
Mrs M Calladine, Smoking Cessation Officer, 6th Floor, Brock House, Kidderminster Hospital, Bewdley Road, Kidderminster, DY11 6RJ,

Specialist Nursing Services
Ms L Hatch, Specialist Nurse, Continence, Brinton Suite, A Block, Kidderminster Hospital, Tel.: 01562 513265

Mrs R Mayall, Facilitator, Continuing Care, Brinton Suite, A Block, Kidderminster Hospital, Tel.: 01562 513264

Ms D Edwards, Specialist Nurse, Diabetic Care, A2, A Block, Kidderminster Hospital,

Ms G Ash, Macmillan, Stourport Health Centre, Worcester Street, Stourport on Severn, DY13 8EH, Tel.: 01299 827131

Mrs K Coles, Macmillan, Stourport Health Centre, Worcester Street, Stourport on Severn, DY13 8EH, Tel.: 01299 827131

Mrs J Griffiths, Macmillan, Stourport Health Centre, Worcester Street, Stourport on Severn, DY13 8EH, Tel.: 01299 827131

Mrs N Kelly, Specialist Nurse, Multiple Sclerosis,

Ms L Moseley, Specialist Nurse, Parkinson's Disease, Brinton Suite, A Block, Kidderminster Hospital, Tel.: 01562 823424 ext 3159

Ms C Rochelle, Specialist Nurse, Rheumatology, Brinton Suite, A Block, Kidderminster Hospital, Tel.: 01562 823424 ext 3159

Ms J Stephen-Haynes, Lecturer & Practitioner, Tissue Viability, Stourport Health Centre, Worcester Street, Stourport on Severn, DY13 8EH, Tel.: 01299 827131

Yorkshire & The Humber SHA

with major towns and Primary Care Trust boundaries
Pop: 5,038,849

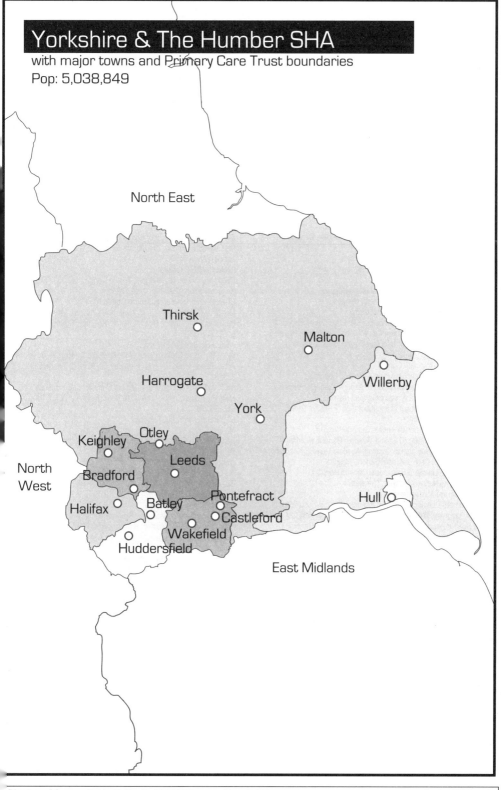

North East

Thirsk

Malton

Harrogate

Willerby

York

Keighley

Otley

North
West

Leeds

Bradford

Pontefract

Hull

Halifax

Batley

Castleford

Wakefield

Huddersfield

East Midlands

Yorkshire and The Humber SHA

Yorkshire and The Humber Strategic Health Authority

Airedale NHS Trust

Trust Headquarters, Airedale General Hospital
Skipton Road
KEIGHLEY
West Yorkshire
BD20 6TD
Tel.: 01535 652511

Acute Specialist Nursing Services
Ms J Isherwood, Acute Pain, Airedale General Hospital,
Ms L Green, Breast Care, Airedale General Hospital,
Ms D Parker, Breast Care, Airedale General Hospital,
Mrs S Brown, Rehabilitation, Cardiac,
Ms L Lomas, Colorectal, Airedale General Hospital,
Ms R Binks, Nurse Consultant, Critical Care, Airedale General Hospital,
Ms J Egerton, Nurse Specialist, Diabetic Care,
Mr P Gardner, Diabetic Care, Airedale General Hospital,
Mrs J Sunderland, Diabetic Care,
Ms C Vick, Diabetic Care, Airedale General Hospital,
Ms K Beckett, Fertility, Airedale General Hospital,
Mrs C Parkinson, Macmillan, Gynaecology,
Ms P Dyminski, Haematology-Oncology, Airedale General Hospital,
Ms A Choyce, Hospital, Infection Control, Airedale General Hospital,
Ms S McCarthy, Community, Infection Control, Airedale General Hospital,
Ms S Moorhouse, Infection Control,
Ms J Harrison, Lung Cancer, Airedale General Hospital,
Ms M Huit, Macmillan, Lymphoedema, Airedale General Hospital,
Ms K Sinclair, Macmillan, Airedale General Hospital,
Ms J Duerden, Lead Cancer Nurse/Macmillan, Palliative Care, Airedale General Hospital,
Ms L Greatley, Respiratory, Airedale General Hospital,
Mr M Harris, Resuscitation Training, Airedale General Hospital,
Mr M Wiseman, Resuscitation Training, Airedale General Hospital,
Ms J Ross, Stoma Care, Airedale General Hospital,
Ms J Anderson, Liaison, TB, Airedale General Hospital,
Mrs J Gailfoyle, Nurse Specialist, Transfusion,
Admin & Senior Management
Mrs M Hornett, Director of Nursing, Airedale General Hospital, Steeton, Keighley, West Yorkshire, BD20 6TD, Tel.: 01535 294014
Mrs J Scarrott, Assistant Director of Nursing, Airedale General Hospital, Steeton, Keighley, West Yorkshire, BD20 6TD, Tel.: 01535 294016
Child Health
Ms A Blackie, Paediatric Diabetes, Airedale General Hospital, Tel.: 01535 652511
Ms K Cooke, Children's Outreach, Airedale General Hospital, Tel.: 01535 652511
Child Health Records
Child Health Records, Skipton General Hospital, Keighley Road, Skipton, BD23 2RJ, Tel.: 01756 792233
Child Protection/Safeguarding Children
Ms B Cox, Named Nurse, Child Protection, Millennium Business Park, Steeton, Nr Keighley, BD20 6RB, Tel.: 01535 338747
Learning Disabilities
Managed by Bradford District Care Trust,
Liaison Services
Ms E Snee, Discharge Liaison, Airedale General Hospital,
School Nursing
Ms L Wilkinson, Child Health/School Nurses - Airedale PCT, Director of Nursing, Airedale House, 21A Mornington Street, Keighley, BD21 2EA, Tel.: 01535 690416

Smoking Cessation
Craven & Harrogate Rural District Trust (Chard),
Ms J Probert, Director of Nursing, The Hamlet, Hornbeam Park, Harrogate, HC2 8RE, Tel.: 01423 815150
Mrs S Wilson, CHARD, based at Airedale General Hospital,

Airedale Primary Care Trust

Trust Headquarters, Airedale House
21a Mornington Street
KEIGHLEY
West Yorkshire
BD21 2EA
Tel.: 01535 690416
Fax.: 01535 672639

Admin & Senior Management
Ms C Kirby, Assistant Director of Community Services, Millennium Business Park, Station Road, Steeton, Keighley, BD20 6RB, Tel.: 01535 338753
Ms L Wilkinson, Director of Community & Nursing Services, Airedale PCT, Airedale House, 21a Mornington Street, Keighley, BD21 2EA, Tel.: 01535 690416
Child Health Records
Child Health Records, Keighley Health Centre, Oakworth Road, Keighley, BD21 1SA, Tel.: 01535 295661
Child Protection/Safeguarding Children
Mrs B Cox, Nurse Consultant Vulnerable Children, Millennium Business Park, Station Road, Steeton, Keighley, BD20 6RB, Tel.: 01535 338748
Clinical Leads (NSF)
Mrs J Brosnan, Clinical Lead, CHD, Diabetes, Millennium Business Park, Station Road, Steeton, Keighley, BD20 6RB, Tel.: 01535 338731
Ms K Wilkinson, Clinical Lead, Nurse Consultant, Continence, Keighley Health Centre, Oakworth Road, Keighley, BD21 1SA, Tel.: 01535 295640
Community Nursing Services
Ms L Wilkinson, Director of Community & Nursing Services, Airedale PCT, Airedale House, 21a Mornington Street, Keighley, BD21 2EA, Tel.: 01535 690416
District Nursing
Ms L Oxborough, Nurse Consultant District Nursing, Millennium Business Park, Station Road, Steeton, Keighley, BD20 6RB, Tel.: 01535 338733
Family Planning Services
Ms L Paine, Service Manager, Sexual Health, Millennium Business Park, Station Road, Steeton, Keighley, BD20 6RB, Tel.: 01535 338732
Health Visitors
Ms L Paine, Service Manager, Health Visiting, Millennium Business Park, Station Road, Steeton, Keighley, BD20 6RB, Tel.: 01535 338732
Other Services
Ms L Barrett, Interpreting Services/Vulnerable People/ Hard to Reach Patients/Substance Misuses, Millennium Business Park, Station Road, Steeton, Keighley, BD20 6RB, Tel.: 01535 338734
Mrs J Brosnan, Practice Nurse Clinical Lead/Diabetes Lead & CHD, Millennium Business Park, Station Road, Steeton, Keighley, BD20 6RB, Tel.: 01535 338738
Mr N Hughes, PPI & Children's Services, Millennium Business Park, Station Road, Steeton, Keighley, BD20 6RB, Tel.: 01535 338734
Ms L Kershaw, Practice Development, Millennium Business Park, Station Road, Steeton, Keighley, BD20 6RB, Tel.: 01535 338724
Ms C Kirby, Podiatry Manager, Millennium Business Park, Station Road, Steeton, Keighley, BD20 6RB, Tel.: 01535 338724
Ms S Robinson, Clinical Director of Dental Services, Skipton General Hospital, Keighley Road, Skipton, North Yorkshire, Tel.: 01756 792233

Yorkshire and The Humber SHA

Mr M Warden, Community Health Team, Millennium Business Park, Station Road, Steeton, Keighley, BD20 6RB, Tel.: 01535 338760
Ms K Wilkinson, Nurse Consultant Continence Service, Keighley Health Centre, Oakworth Road, Keighley, BD21 1SA, Tel.: 01535 295640

Pharmacy
Mr J Pearse, Assistant Director/Pharmaceutical Advisor, 21a Mornington Street, Keighley,

School Nursing
Ms L Paine, Service Manager, Health Visiting, School Nurse, Millennium Business Park, Station Road, Steeton, Keighley, BD20 6RB, Tel.: 01535 338732

Smoking Cessation
Mrs J Brosnan, Practice Nurse Clinical Lead/Diabetes Lead & CHD, Millennium Business Park, Station Road, Steeton, Keighley, BD20 6RB, Tel.: 01535 338738

Specialist Nursing Services
Ms K Wilkinson, Nurse Consultant, Continence, Keighley Health Centre, Oakworth Road, Keighley, BD21 1SA, Tel.: 01535 295640
M Mitchell, Nurse Specialist, Palliative Care, Millennium Park, Station Road, Steeton, Tel.: 01535 338733
C Winterburn, Nurse, Rehabilitation, Millennium Park, Station Road, Steeton, Tel.: 01535 338751

The Homeless/Travellers & Asylum Seekers
Ms L Paine, Health Visiting, School Nurse & Sexual Health, Millennium Business Park, Station Road, Steeton, Keighley, BD20 6RB, Tel.: 01535 338732

Barnsley District General Hospital NHS Trust
Gawber Road
BARNSLEY
South Yorkshire
S75 2EP
Tel.: 01226 730000
Fax.: 01226 202859

Child Health
Ms J Bridson, Community Paediatrics Outreach Sister, Ward 37, Barnsley District General Hospital, Tel.: 01226 777987
Ms J Eaton, Paediatric Asthma, Ward 37, Barnsley District General Hospital, Tel.: 01226 777987
Ms C Edwards, Community Paediatrics Outreach Sister, Ward 37, Barnsley District General Hospital, Tel.: 01226 777987
Mrs D Gibson, Paediatric Diabetes, Ward 37, Barnsley District General Hospital, Tel.: 01226 777987
Ms M Kinsman, Paediatrics, Senior Nurse, Ward 38, Barnsley District General Hospital, Tel.: 01226 730000 ext 2518

Community Midwifery
Ms S Barnes, Clinical Midwife Specialist, Tel.: ext 2933 bleep 283
Emergencies - Delivery Suite, Tel.: ext 2249 or 01226 777902
Ms K Grigg, Child Protection Manager, Project Midwife, Tel.: ext 2092 bleep 217
Mrs J Scarfe, Head of Midwifery/Patient Services Manager, Tel.: 01226 730000
Clinical Management Team, Obstetrics, Tel.: 01226 730000

Barnsley Primary Care Trust
Trust Headquarters, Kendray Hospital
Doncaster Road
BARNSLEY, S70 3RD
Tel.: 01226 777811

Admin & Senior Management
Ms A Claire, Chief Executive,

Child Health Records
Over 5s, School Health Dept, New Street Health Centre, Tel.: 01226 777893
Under 5s, Child Health Dept, New Street Health Centre, Tel.: 01226 730000 x 3177/3181

Child Protection/Safeguarding Children
Ms M Sheffield, Designated Nurse, Child Protection, Safeguarding Children Dept, Lundwood Health Centre, Littleworth Lane, Lundwood, S71 5RG, Tel.: 01226 777844

Clinical Leads (NSF)
Dr G Lusty, Clinical Lead, Cancer,
Dr E Reilly, Clinical Lead, CHD,
Dr S Rayner, Clinical Lead, Children,
Dr M Gan, Clinical Lead, Diabetic Care,
Dr S Small, Clinical Lead, Older People,

Community Nursing Services
Community Service Manager, Locality 1, Mount Vernon Hospital, Mount Vernon Road, Barnsley, S70 4GP, Tel.: 01226 777845
Mr R Preston, Community Service Manager, Locality 2, Mount Vernon Hospital, Mount Vernon Road, Barnsley, S70 4GP, Tel.: 01226 777845
Mr D Ramsey, Community Service Manager, Locality 5, Mount Vernon Hospital, Mount Vernon Road, Barnsley, S70 4GP, Tel.: 01226 777845
Ms G Stansfield, Community Service Manager, Locality 4, Lundwood Health Centre, Littleworth Lane, Lundwood, S71 5RG, Tel.: 01226 777024
Ms S Wing, Community Service Manager, Locality 3, Mount Vernon Hospital, Mount Vernon Road, Barnsley, S70 4GP, Tel.: 01226 777845

District Nursing
Athersley Clinic, Tel.: 01226 777851
Cudworth Health Centre, Tel.: 01226 780773
Darton Health Centre, Tel.: 01226 390721
Dodworth Health Centre, Tel.: 01226 777852
Ms R Donoghue, Lead Nurse, District Nursing, Mount Vernon Hospital, Mount Vernon Road, Barnsley, Tel.: 01226 777864
Garland House, Tel.: 01226 759622
Goldthorpe Centre, Tel.: 01709 895124
Great Houghton Clinic, Tel.: 01226 340098
Grimethorpe Clinic, Tel.: 01226 780274
Hoyland Health Centre, Tel.: 01226 350222
Lundwood Health Centre, Tel.: 01226 777853
Macmillan Service, Tel.: 01226 777848
Mapplewell Health Centre, Tel.: 01226 390251
New Street Health Centre, Tel.: 01226 777849
Penistone Clinic, Tel.: 01226 763205
Royston Clinic, Tel.: 01226 700669
Silkstone Health Centre, Tel.: 01226 791036
Stairfoot Clinic, Tel.: 01226 777855
Thurnscoe Centre, Tel.: 01709 886462
Wombwell Clinic, Tel.: 01226 340220
Worsbrough Centre, Tel.: 01226 648019

Family Planning Services
Central Family Planning Clinic, Queens Road, Barnsley, Tel.: 01226 249949

Health Visitors
Athersley Clinic, Tel.: 01226 777851
Ms A Battye, Paediatric Health Visitor, Barnsley District General Hospital, Gawber Road, Barnsley, S75 2EP, Tel.: 01226 730000 ext 2618
Cudworth Health Centre, Tel.: 01226 780773
Darton Health Centre, Tel.: 01226 390721
Dodworth Health Centre, Tel.: 01226 777852
Garland House, Tel.: 01226 759622
Goldthorpe Centre, Tel.: 01709 895124
Great Houghton Clinic, Tel.: 01226 340098
Grimethorpe Clinic, Tel.: 01226 780274
Hoyland Health Centre, Tel.: 01226 350222
Ms L Johnson, Health Visitors, Royston Clinic, Tel.: 01226 700669
Lundwood Health Centre, Tel.: 01226 777853
Macmillan Service, Tel.: 01226 777848
Mapplewell Health Centre, Tel.: 01226 390251

Yorkshire and The Humber SHA

New Street Health Centre, Tel.: 01226 777849
Penistone Clinic, Tel.: 01226 763205
Royston Clinic, Tel.: 01226 700669
Silkstone Health Centre, Tel.: 01226 791036
Stairfoot Clinic, Tel.: 01226 777855
Thurnscoe Centre, Tel.: 01709 886462
Wombwell Clinic, Tel.: 01226 340220
Worsbrough Centre, Tel.: 01226 648019
Learning Disabilities
Mrs S Clarke, Senior Operations Manager, Learning Disability Service, Wellington House, 36 Wellington Street, S70 1AW, Tel.: 01226 775819
Learning Difficulties Team, Birk House, Calder Crescent, Kendray, Barnsley, Tel.: 01226 775377
Ms W Lowder, Operations Manager, (Senior), BMBC Social Services Dept, Wellington House, Barnsley, South Yorkshire, Tel.: 01226 772516
Ms S Moylan, Team Leader, Social Work, Birk House, Calder Crescent, Kendray, Barnsley, Tel.: 01226 775377
Ms J Price, Team Leader, Nursing, Birk House, Calder Crescent, Kendray, Barnsley, Tel.: 01226 775377
Liaison Services
Diabetes, Tel.: 01226 777772
School Nursing
School Health Service, New Street Health Centre, New Street, Barnsley, S70 1LP, Tel.: 01226 777893
Specialist Nursing Services
Ms J Brown, Practice Development, Nurse, Keresforth Centre, Off Broadway, Barnsley, S70 6RS, Tel.: 01226 777864
Ms S Baker-Hollinworth, Clinical Lead, Continence, - Urology, Lundwood Health Centre, Tel.: 01226 777023
Marie Curie
Marie Curie, Macmillan, Birdwell Clinic, Barnsley, S70 5TF, Tel.: 01226 777963
Ms E Higgins, Macmillan Team Leader Community, Palliative Care, Birdwell Clinic, Barnsley, S70 5TF, Tel.: 01226 777963
Ms C Nayeri, Unit Manager, Respite Unit & Community, Rehabilitation, Physical Disability & Sensory Impairment Service, Keresforth Centre, Off Broadway, Barnsley, S70 6RS, Tel.: 01226 777791
Ms L Hepworth, Tissue Viability, Mount Vernon Hospital, Mount Vernon Road, Barnsley, Tel.: 01226 730000 ext 3215

Bradford City Primary Care Trust
Trust Headquarters, Douglas Mills
Bowling Old Lane
BRADFORD
BD5 7JR
Tel.: 01274 237290
Fax.: 01274 237453

Admin & Senior Management
Mrs F Clark, Director, Nursing & Primary Care, Douglas Mills, Bowling Old Lane, Bradford, BD5 7JR, Tel.: 01274 237290
Mr S Kelsey, Clinical Governance Manager,
Ms K Leach, Deputy Director, Nursing & Locality Services,
Mrs L Longfield, Older People's Commissioning & Integrated Services Manager,
Ms S Simpson Prentis, Professional Development Unit Co-ordinator, Function Room, Douglas Mills, Bowling Old Lane, Bradford, BD5 7JR, Tel.: 01274 237290
Ms C Thatcher, Head of Primary Care,
Ms L Throp, Chief Executive,
Child Health
Ms S Bottomley, Specialist Service Manager (Children), Horton Park Centre, 99 Horton Park Avenue, Bradford, BD7 3EG,
Mrs F Clark, Director, Nursing & Primary Care, Douglas Mills, Bowling Old Lane, Bradford, BD5 7JR, Tel.: 01274 237290

Child Protection/Safeguarding Children
Mrs R Mulley, Senior Nurse Vulnerable Children, Leeds Road Hospital, Maudsley Street, Bradford, BD3 9LH, Tel.: 01274 363434
Clinical Leads (NSF)
Dr M Taylor, Clinical Lead, CHD & Diabetes,
Dr I Fenwick, Clinical Lead, Cancer,
Ms K Leach, Clinical Lead, Older People,
Community Nursing Services
Mrs F Clark, Director, Nursing & Primary Care, Douglas Mills, Bowling Old Lane, Bradford, BD5 7JR, Tel.: 01274 237290
District Nursing
Mrs F Clark, Director, Nursing & Primary Care, Douglas Mills, Bowling Old Lane, Bradford, BD5 7JR, Tel.: 01274 237290
Family Planning Services
Mrs F Clark, Director, Nursing & Primary Care, Douglas Mills, Bowling Old Lane, Bradford, BD5 7JR, Tel.: 01274 237290
Liaison Services
Mrs F Clark, Director, Nursing & Primary Care, Douglas Mills, Bowling Old Lane, Bradford, BD5 7JR, Tel.: 01274 237290
Specialist Nursing Services
Ms M Bannister, Nurse Consultant, Diabetic Care, Horton Park Centre, 99 Horton Park Avenue, Bradford, BD7 3EG, Tel.: 01274 228899
The Homeless/Travellers & Asylum Seekers
Ms L Barry, Specialist Services Manager, Douglas Mills, Bowling Old Lane, Bradford, BD5 7JR, Tel.: 01274 237290

Bradford District Care NHS Trust
Trust Headquarters, New Mill
Victoria Road, Saltaire
SHIPLEY
BD18 3LD
Tel.: 01274 494194

Admin & Senior Management
Mr S Bootland, Director of Nursing, New Mill, Victoria Road, Saltaire Shipley, BD18 3LD, Tel.: 01274 363507
Learning Disabilities
Mr L J Bebb, Nursing Services Manager, Waddiloves Health Centre, 44 Queens Road, Bradford, BD8 7BT, Tel.: 01274 481161
Mr S Bootland, Director of Nursing, New Mill, Victoria Road, Saltaire Shipley, BD18 3LD, Tel.: 01274 363882
Mr B Stanley, Director, Learning Disability Services, Waddiloves Health Centre, 44 Queens Road, Bradford, BD8 7BT, Tel.: 01274 481161

Bradford South & West Primary Care Trust
Trust Headquarters, Bryan-Sutherland House
Dunnock Avenue
Clayton Heights
BRADFORD
BD6 3XH
Tel.: 01274 321800
Fax.: 01274 321805

Admin & Senior Management
Ms L Allen, Assistant Director of Nursing/Head of Professional Development,
Ms P Corrigan, Director of Nursing & Operational Services,
Dr B Hakin, OBE, Chief Executive, Tel.: 01274 321800
Child Health
Ms C Woffendin, Locality Nurse Leader, Tel.: 01274 322590
Child Health Records
Ms C Woffendin, Locality Nurse Leader, Tel.: 01274 322590
Child Protection/Safeguarding Children
Ms R Mullay, Leeds Road Hospital, Maudsley Street, Bradford, BD3 9LH, Tel.: 01274 36343
Ms C Woffendin, Locality Nurse Leader, Tel.: 01274 322590

Yorkshire and The Humber SHA

Clinical Leads (NSF)
Dr S Wood, Clinical Lead, Children, Cancer,
Dr C Harris, Clinical Lead, CHD,
Dr P Atherton, Clinical Lead, Diabetic Care,
Community Matrons
Ms L Allen, Assistant Director of Nursing/Head of Professional
Development,
Community Nursing Services
Ms P Corrigan, Director of Nursing & Operational Services, Tel.:
01274 321800
Mr R O'Connell, Acting Head of Community Nursing
Services/Assistant Director of Nursing, Tel.: 01274 322330
District Nursing
Mr R O'Connell, Locality Nurse Leader, Holmewood Health Centre,
Dulverton Green, Holmewood Road, Holmewood, Bradford, BD4
9EE, Tel.: 01274 681103
Ms G Ryan, Locality Nurse Leader, Tel.: 01274 323687
Ms C Woffenden, Locality Nurse Leader, Tel.: 01274 322590
Health Visitors
Ms C Woffenden, Locality Nurse Leader, Tel.: 01274 322590
Learning Disabilities
Ms C Livens, Learning Disabilities Lead, Tel.: 01274 323373
School Nursing
Ms C Woffenden, Locality Nurse Leader (School Nurses), Tel.: 01274
322590
Specialist Nursing Services
Mrs D Adlard, Cancer Lead Nurse, Tel.: 01274 424202
Ms D Gibbons, Heart Failure Nurse, Tel.: 01274 322737
Mrs P Hubbard, Rehabilitation, Nurse Consultant, Older People, Tel.:
01274 322900
Ms Z Ridewood, Parkinson's Disease, Tel.: 01274 322744

Bradford Teaching Hospitals NHS Foundation Trust
Trust Headquarters, Bradford Royal Infirmary
Duckworth Lane
BRADFORD
West Yorkshire
BD9 6RJ
Tel.: 01274 542200
Fax.: 01274 364909
Community Midwifery
Mrs J Gerrard, Head of Midwifery/Service Nurse Midwife Manager,
Bradford Royal Infirmary Maternity Unit, Smith Lane, Bradford, BD9
6RJ, Tel.: 01274 364500
Mrs A Wilkinson, Community Midwifery Manager, Community Office,
Bradford Royal Infirmary Maternity Unit, Tel.: 01274 364533

Calderdale & Huddersfield NHS Trust
Trust Headquarters, The Calderdale Royal Hospital
Salterhebble
HALIFAX
West Yorkshire
HX3 0PW
Tel.: 01422 357171
Child Health
Child Health, Childrens Services, Princess Royal Community Health
Centre, Greenhead Rd, Huddersfield, HD1 4EW, Tel.: 01484 344000
Ms A Thomas, Children's Community Team Leader, Calderdale
Royal Hospital, Tel.: 01422 224164
Ms L Tweedale, Children's Specialist Needs Co-ordinator,
Calderdale Royal Hospital, Tel.: 01422 224206
Child Health Records
Child Health Records, Childrens Services, Princess Royal
Community Health Centre, Greenhead Road, Huddersfield, HD1
4EW, Tel.: 01484 344000

Community Midwifery
Mrs A Lovatt, Associate Director, Nursing & Midwifery, Women &
Children's Division, Huddersfield Royal Infirmary, Acre Street,
Lindley, Huddersfield, West Yorkshire, HD3 3EA, Tel.: 01484 342568
Mrs A Lovatt, Associate Director, Nursing & Midwifery, Calderdale
Royal Hospital, Salterhebble, Halifax, West Yorkshire, HX3 0PW,
Tel.: 01422 357171
Ms H McNair, Head of Midwifery, Huddersfield Royal Infirmary, Acre
Street, Lindley, Huddersfield, West Yorkshire, HD3 3EA,
Women & Children's Division, Calderdale Royal Hospital, Tel.: 01484
342568
Women & Children's Unit, Calderdale Royal Hospital, Tel.: 01422
224420
Mrs L Anderson, Nurse Specialist, Breast Care,
Learning Disabilities
Mr J B Markiewicz, Lead Manager, Learning Difficulties Service,
Hebden Bridge Health Centre, Hangingroyd Lane, Hebden Bridge,
HX7 6AG, Tel.: 01422 841123

Calderdale Primary Care Trust
Trust Headquarters, 4th Floor, F Mill
Dean Clough
HALIFAX
West Yorkshire
HX3 5AX
Tel.: 01422 281300

Admin & Senior Management
Mrs G Connor, Assistant Director/Head of Nursing, St John's Health
Centre, Lightowler Road, Halifax, HX1 5NB, Tel.: 01422 341611
Dr M Pritchard, Chief Executive, School House, 56 Hopwood Lane,
Halifax, HX1 5ER, Tel.: 01422 307300
Child Health
Ms D Catlow, Team Leader, Beechwood Community Health Centre,
Tel.: 01422 355626
Child Health Records
Mr I Wilkinson, Locality Support Manager, Brighouse Health Centre,
Lawson Road, Brighouse, HD6 1MZ, Tel.: 01484 712515
Child Protection/Safeguarding Children
Ms J Kaye, Looked After Children, Specialist Nurse, 4th Floor, Dean
Clough, Halifax, HX1 5AX, Tel.: 01422 281468
Ms H Smith, Looked After Children, Designated Nurse, 4th Floor,
Dean Clough, Halifax, HX1 5AX, Tel.: 01422 281468
Ms S Smith, Safeguarding Children, Nurse Consultant, 4th Floor,
Dean Clough, Halifax, HX1 5AX, Tel.: 01422 281468
Ms C Short, Named Nurse, Child Protection, 4th Floor, Dean Clough,
Halifax, HX1 5AX, Tel.: 01422 281468
Clinical Leads (NSF)
Dr B Kelsey, Clinical Lead, Cancer,
Dr P Butcher, Clinical Lead, CHD,
Dr S Rumbold, Clinical Lead, Children,
Dr G Scholefield, Clinical Lead, Diabetic Care,
Dr D Graham, Clinical Lead, Older People,
Community Nursing Services
Family & Community Management Team, Calderdale Royal Hospital,
Salterhebble, Halifax, HX3 0PW, Tel.: 01422 357171
District Nursing
Ms A Brier, Out of hours Team Co-ordinator,
Out of hours ansaphone, Tel.: 01484 347057
St John's Health Centre, Tel.: 01422 341611
Family Planning Services
Ms A Hodgson, Sexual Health Counsellor, Laura Mitchell Health
Centre, Tel.: 01422 363541
Ms K Jeffrey, Sexual Health Co-ordinator, Laura Mitchell Health
Centre, Tel.: 01422 363541
Health Visitors
Mrs C Marsh, Liaison, Health Visitor, TB, St John's Health Centre,
Tel.: 01422 341611

Yorkshire and The Humber SHA

HIV/AIDS
Ms K Wallis, Laura Mitchell Health Centre, Great Albion Street, Halifax, HX1 1DR, Tel.: 01422 305523

Liaison Services
Ms J Piatkowski, Discharge Liaison, Calderdale Royal Hospital, Salterhebble, Halifax, HX3 0PW, Tel.: 01422 357171 ext 2164/9

Specialist Nursing Services
Ms V Allinson, Breast Care, Jayne Garforth Cancer Support Centre, Free School Lane, Halifax, HX1 2YP, Tel.: 01422 357171 ext 2569
Mrs L Greenman, Continence, Allan House Clinic, Station Road, Sowerby Bridge, Halifax, HX6 3AD, Tel.: 01422 832063
Ms T Akroyd, Diabetic Care, Calderdale Royal Hospital, Tel.: 01422 357171 ext 2021/2
Mrs A Philips, Diabetic Care, Calderdale Royal Hospital, Tel.: 01422 357171 ext 2021/2
Mrs J Russell, Diabetic Care, Calderdale Royal Hospital, Tel.: 01422 357171 ext 2021/2
Ms A Gammon, Macmillan, Calderdale Royal Hospital, Tel.: 01422 357171
Ms M Kanniah, Macmillan, Calderdale Royal Hospital, Tel.: 01422 357171
Mrs T Adams, Stoma Care, Calderdale Royal Hospital, Tel.: 01422 357171
Ms J Collins, Tissue Viability, Calderdale Royal Hospital, Tel.: 01422 357171 ext 2529

Craven Harrogate & Rural District Primary Care Trust

Trust Headquarters, The Hamlet
Hornbeam Park
HARROGATE
North Yorkshire
HG2 8RE
Tel.: 01423 815150
Fax.: 01423 859600

Admin & Senior Management
Ms R Carter, Head of Unscheduled Care, The Hamlet, Hornbeam Park, Harrogate, North Yorkshire, HG2 8RE, Tel.: 01423 859605
Mrs A Woodhouse, Head of Community Development, The Hamlet, Hornbeam Park, Harrogate, HG2 8RE, Tel.: 01423 859633

Child Health
Ms J Dicks, Head of Children's Services, The Hamlet, Hornbeam Park, Harrogate, North Yorkshire, HG2 8RE, Tel.: 01423 859716

Child Health Records
Child Health Records, Harrogate District Hospital, Lancaster Park Road, Harrogate, HG2 7SX,

Child Protection/Safeguarding Children
Mrs E Curran, Senior Nurse, Child Protection, Jennyfields Health Centre, Grantley Drive, Harrogate, HG3 2XT, Tel.: 01423 558107

Clinical Leads (NSF)
Ms R Donaldson, Clinical Lead, Long Term Conditions, Iles Lane Clinic, Knaresborough, HG5 8DY, Tel.: 01423 544133
Mr A Clark, Clinical Lead, CHD, Cancer, The Hamlet, Hornbeam Park, Harrogate, HG2 8RE, Tel.: 01423 815150
Mr J Hancock, Clinical Lead, Care of the Elderly, The Hamlet, Hornbeam Park, Harrogate, HG2 8RE, Tel.: 01423 815150
Ms J Probert, Clinical Lead, Children, The Hamlet, Hornbeam Park, Harrogate, HG2 8RE, Tel.: 01423 815150
Mrs J Probert, Clinical Lead, Diabetic Care, The Hamlet, Hornbeam Park, Harrogate, HG2 8RE, Tel.: 01423 815150

Community Midwifery
Mrs L Harris, Head of Midwifery, Harrogate District Hospital, Lancaster Park Road, Harrogate, HG2 7SX,

Community Nursing Services
Mrs J Probert, Director of Nursing & Service Modernisation, The Hamlet, Hornbeam Park, Harrogate, HG2 8RE, Tel.: 01423 815150

District Nursing
Ms T Balderson, Locality Manager, The Hamlet, Hornbeam Park, Harrogate, HG2 8RE, Tel.: 01423 815150
Ms R Donaldson, Locality Manager, The Hamlet, Hornbeam Park, Harrogate, HG2 8RE, Tel.: 01423 815150
Mrs J James, Locality Manager, The Hamlet, Hornbeam Park, Harrogate, HG2 8RE, Tel.: 01423 815150

Equipment Loan Services
Ms T Balderson, Skipton Hospital, Keighley Road, Skipton, BD23 2RJ, Tel.: 01765 792233
Ms B Hood, Joint Equipment Store, Manager, Back The Parade, Harrogate, Tel.: 01423 508961

Family Planning Services
Ms L McCutcheon, Skipton Hospital,

Learning Disabilities
Mr K Millar, Head of Learning Disabilities, The Hamlet, Hornbeam Park, Harrogate, HG2 8RE, Tel.: 01423 859224

Pharmacy
Ms S Dale, Prescribing Advisor, Skipton Hospital, Keighley Road, Skipton, BD23 2RJ, Tel.: 01765 792233

Specialist Nursing Services
Ms D Shepherd, 1st Contact Care, Nurse Consultant, Jennyfields Health Centre, Grantley Drive, Harrogate, HG3 2XT, Tel.: 01423 558112

The Homeless/Travellers & Asylum Seekers
Ms E Wetton, The Homeless & Refugees, 54 Church Avenue, Harrogate, HG1 4HG, Tel.: 01423 557246

Doncaster & Bassetlaw Hospitals NHS Foundation Trust

Trust Headquarters, Doncaster Royal Infirmary
Armthorpe Road
DONCASTER
DN2 5LT
Tel.: 01302 366666
Fax.: 01302 320098

Acute Specialist Nursing Services
Ms L Robinson, Anaesthetics, Lead Nurse, Acute Pain, Doncaster Royal Infirmary, Tel.: ext 3099
Ms J Beevers, Nurse Practitioner, Arthroplasty, Doncaster Royal Infirmary, Tel.: ext 30030
Ms J Earl, Nurse Practitioner, Arthroplasty, Doncaster Royal Infirmary, Tel.: ext 3030
Ms L Carmichael, Nurse Specialist, Breast Care, Doncaster Royal Infirmary, Tel.: ext 3926
Ms S Crate, Clinical Nurse Specialist, Breast Care, Bassetlaw, Tel.: 01909 500990 ext 2328
Ms C Dyer, Clinical Nurse Specialist, Breast Care, Doncaster Royal Infirmary, Tel.: ext 3926
Ms B Langdale, Nurse Specialist, Breast Care, Doncaster Royal Infirmary, Tel.: ext 3926
Ms C Robinson, Clinical Nurse Specialist, Breast Care, Bassetlaw, Tel.: 01909 500990 ext 2328
Ms D Whitehead, Clinical Nurse Specialist, Breast Care, Bassetlaw/DRI, Tel.: 01909 500990 x 2328
Ms M Barrett, Clinical Nurse Specialist, Cardiac Rehabilitation, Doncaster Royal Infirmary, Tel.: bleep 460
Ms W Cook, Clinical Nurse Specialist, Cardiac Rehabilitation, Bassetlaw District General Hospital, Tel.: 01909 500990 ext 2944
Mr P Snell, Clinical Nurse Specialist, Cardiac Rehabilitation, Bassetlaw District General Hospital, Tel.: 01909 500990 ext 2944
Ms L Bagguley, Nurse Specialist, Chest Pain, Bassetlaw, Tel.: 01302 500990 bleep 475
Ms J Clarke, Nurse Specialist, Chest Pain, Doncaster Royal Infirmary, Tel.: bleep 976
Ms A Wilson, Nurse Specialist, Chest Pain, Doncaster Royal Infirmary, Tel.: bleep 973

Yorkshire and The Humber SHA

Ms C Brown, Nurse Specialist, Colorectal, Doncaster Royal Infirmary, Tel.: ext 3141

Ms F Darlington, Nurse Specialist, Colorectal, Doncaster Royal Infirmary, Tel.: ext 3141

Ms J Hughes, Nurse Specialist, Colorectal, Doncaster Royal Infirmary, Tel.: ext 3141

Ms D Knowles, Nurse Specialist, Colorectal, Doncaster Royal Infirmary, Tel.: ext 3141

Ms J Price, Nurse Specialist, Colorectal, Bassetlaw/Doncaster Royal Infirmary, Tel.: 01909 500990 ext 2742

Ms J Steers, Nurse Specialist, Colorectal, Doncaster Royal Infirmary, Tel.: ext 3141

Ms N Biggins, Advisor, Continence, Doncaster Royal Infirmary, Tel.: ext 3017

Ms B Lupton, Advisor, Continence, Doncaster Royal Infirmary, Tel.: ext 3017

Ms G Richardson, Clinical Nurse Specialist, Critical Care, Tel.: ext 4207

Ms S Veater, Clinical Nurse Specialist, Dermatology, Doncaster Royal Infirmary, Tel.: ext 4171/3830

Ms M Eggleston, Specialist Nurse, Diabetes, Doncaster Royal Infirmary, Tel.: 01302 366666 ext 4273

Ms G French, Nurse Specialist, Diabetes, Bassetlaw District General Hospital, Tel.: 01909 500990 ex 2647/2648

Ms A Johnson, Specialist Nurse, Diabetes, Doncaster Royal Infirmary, Tel.: 01302 366666 ext 4273

Ms H McMahon, Nurse Specialist, Diabetes, Bassetlaw District General Hospital, Tel.: 01909 500990 ex 2647/2648

Ms S Needle, Nurse Specialist, Diabetes, Bassetlaw District General Hospital, Tel.: 01909 500990 ex 2647/2648

Ms D Perks, Nurse Specialist, Diabetes, Bassetlaw District General Hospital, Tel.: 01909 500990 ex 2647/2648

Ms Y Severein, Specialist Nurse, Diabetes, Doncaster Royal Infirmary, Tel.: 01302 366666 ext 4273

Ms G Smout, Specialist Nurse, Diabetes, Doncaster Royal Infirmary, Tel.: 01302 366666 ext 4273

Mr C Nile, Facilitator - DRI/Bassetlaw, Discharges, Doncaster Royal Infirmary, Tel.: ext 4088

Ms L Bedford, Facilitator, Dynamic Case, Doncaster Royal Infirmary, Tel.: bleep 229

Ms G Meeghan, Facilitator, Dynamic Case, Doncaster Royal Infirmary, Tel.: bleep 910

Ms J Smith, Facilitator, Dynamic Case, Doncaster Royal Infirmary, Tel.: bleep 332

Ms A Stores, Facilitator, Dynamic Case, Doncaster Royal Infirmary, Tel.: bleep 635

Ms A Whitlam, Facilitator, Dynamic Case, Doncaster Royal Infirmary, Tel.: bleep 628

Ms C Doran, Clinical Nurse Specialist, Epilepsy, Tickhill Road Hospital, Tel.: 01302 796217

Mr A Perry, Clinical Nurse Specialist, Epilepsy, Tickhill Road Hospital, Tel.: 01302 796217

Ms B Chui, Clinical Nurse Specialist, Genito Urinary, - Medicine, Doncaster Royal Infirmary, Tel.: ext 3731

Ms J Hodkinson, Clinical Nurse Specialist, Gynae/Oncology, Doncaster Royal Infirmary, Tel.: ext 4673

Ms J Burman, Clinical Nurse Specialist, Haematology-Oncology, Doncaster Royal Infirmary, Tel.: ext 6111

Ms J Ryles, Clinical Nurse Specialist, Head & Neck, Doncaster Royal Infirmary, Tel.: ext 6331

Ms B Bacon, Clinical Nurse Specialist, Infection Control, Bassetlaw District General Hospital, Tel.: 01909 500990 ext 2357

Ms C Scholey, Clinical Nurse Specialist, Infection Control, Doncaster Royal Infirmary, Tel.: ext 3748

Ms A Swift, Clinical Nurse Specialist, Infection Control, Doncaster Royal Infirmary, Tel.: ext 3748

Ms L Young, Clinical Nurse Specialist, Infection Control, Doncaster Royal Infirmary, Tel.: ext 4602

Ms C Causer, Nurse Specialist, Lung Cancer, Doncaster Royal Infirmary, Tel.: ext 6185

Ms P Cook, Nurse Specialist, Lung Cancer, Doncaster Royal Infirmary, Tel.: ext 6185

Ms N Godfrey, Nurse Specialist, Lung Cancer, Doncaster Royal Infirmary, Tel.: ext 6185

Ms L Pollard, Nurse Specialist, Lung Cancer, Bassetlaw District General Hospital, Tel.: 01909 500990 ext 2982

Ms G Horne, Lead Nurse, Macmillan, Doncaster Royal Infirmary, Tel.: ext 3194

Mr J Reasbeck, Pre-assessment, Orthopaedics, Doncaster Royal Infirmary, Tel.: ext 4185

Mr S Yemm, Pre-assessment, Orthopaedics, Doncaster Royal Infirmary, Tel.: ext 4185

Ms J Kerrigan-Wain, Nurse Practitioner, Pain Management, Montagu, Tel.: 01709 321106 ext 5228

Mr G Payne, Nurse Practitioner, Pain Management, Montagu, Tel.: 01709 321106 ext 5228

Ms T Blenkinsop, Clinical Nurse Specialist, Palliative Care, Doncaster Royal Infirmary, Tel.: ext 3142

Ms J Boswell, Clinical Nurse Specialist, Palliative Care, Bassetlaw, Tel.: 01909 500990 ext 2946

Ms D Cordall, Clinical Nurse Specialist, Palliative Care, Bassetlaw District General Hospital, Tel.: 01909 500990 ext 2981

Ms L Jones, Clinical Nurse Specialist, Palliative Care, Bassetlaw, Tel.: 01909 500990 ext 2946

Ms S Salmon, Clinical Nurse Specialist, Palliative Care, Doncaster Royal Infirmary, Tel.: ext 3142

Ms L Bowskill, Clinical Nurse Specialist, Pre-assessment, Bassetlaw, Tel.: 01909 500990 ex 2260/2593

Ms J Dickinson, Clinical Nurse Specialist, Pre-assessment, Bassetlaw, Tel.: 01909 500990 ex 2260/2593

Ms L Gilfillin, Clinical Nurse Specialist, Pre-assessment, Bassetlaw, Tel.: 01909 500990 ex 2260/2593

Ms J Kinnell, Clinical Nurse Specialist, Pre-assessment, Bassetlaw, Tel.: 01909 500990 ex 2260/2593

Ms M Sloane, Clinical Nurse Specialist, Pre-assessment, Bassetlaw, Tel.: 01909 500990 ex 2260/2593

Ms M Jaffar, Clinical Nurse Specialist, Respiratory, Doncaster Royal Infirmary, Tel.: ext 3994

Ms R Marrison, Clinical Nurse Specialist, Respiratory, Doncaster Royal Infirmary, Tel.: ext 3994

Ms N Severein-Kirk, Clinical Nurse Specialist, Respiratory, Doncaster Royal Infirmary, Tel.: ext 3994

Ms E Mantle, Diabetic Screening, Retinal, Doncaster Royal Infirmary, Tel.: ext 4606

Ms A Stallard, Diabetic Screening, Retinal, Doncaster Royal Infirmary, Tel.: ext 4606

Ms I Thomasson, Diabetic Screening, Retinal, Doncaster Royal Infirmary, Tel.: ext 4606

Ms L Geddes, Clinical Nurse Specialist, Rheumatology, Doncaster Royal Infirmary, Tel.: ext 6181

Ms K Seymour, Clinical Nurse Specialist, Rheumatology, Doncaster Royal Infirmary, Tel.: ext 6181

Ms M Lester, Clinical Nurse Specialist, Tissue Viability, Bassetlaw District General Hospital, Tel.: 01909 500990 ext 2901

Ms T Vernon, Lead Nurse, Tissue Viability, Doncaster Royal Infirmary, Tel.: ext 3359

Ms Y Elmore, Specialist Nurse, Upper GI, Doncaster Royal Infirmary, Tel.: ext 4722

Ms T Hammond, Nurse Practitioner, Urology/Oncology, Bassetlaw, Tel.: 01909 500990 ext 2074

Ms J Horseman, Nurse Practitioner, Urology/Oncology, Doncaster Royal Infirmary, Tel.: ext 6122

Ms T Soar, Nurse Practitioner, Urology/Oncology, Doncaster Royal Infirmary, Tel.: ext 6122

Ms J Starr, Nurse Practitioner, Urology/Oncology, Bassetlaw, Tel.: 01909 500990 ext 2074

Ms S Johnson, Specialist, Wound Care, Doncaster Royal Infirmary, Tel.: ext 4723

Ms K Leake, Specialist, Wound Care, Doncaster Royal Infirmary, Tel.: ext 4723

Admin & Senior Management

Mrs H Bond, Director of Nursing, Doncaster Royal Infirmary, Tel.: 01302 553183

Child Health

Ms A Ash, Children's Community Nursing Services, Doncaster Royal Infirmary, Tel.: ext 3175

Ms A Ince, Children's Community Nursing Services, Doncaster Royal Infirmary, Tel.: ext 3175

Child Health Records

Ms J Hayton, Child Health Records, Doncaster Royal Infirmary, Tel.: 01302 366666 ext 4045

Ms J Needham, Child Health Records, Tickhill Road Hospital, Tel.: 01302 796309

Child Protection/Safeguarding Children

Ms J Brunt, Nurse Specialist, Child Protection, Bassetlaw District General Hospital, Tel.: 01909 500990 ext 2514

Ms M Corbett, Senior Nurse Advisor, Child Protection, Tickhill Road Hospital, Tel.: 01302 796000 ext 6236

Ms G Genders, Nurse Specialist, Child Protection, Doncaster Royal Infirmary, Tel.: ext 6468

Ms B Lupton, Advisor, Continence, Doncaster Royal Infirmary, Tel.: ext 3017

Ms C Scholey, Infection Control, Doncaster Royal Infirmary, Tel.: ext 3748

Ms A Swift, Infection Control, Doncaster Royal Infirmary, Tel.: ext 3748

Ms T Blenkinsop, Palliative Care, Doncaster Royal Infirmary, Tel.: ext 3142

Ms L Jones, Palliative Care, Doncaster Royal Infirmary, Tel.: ext 3142

Ms S Salmon, Palliative Care, Doncaster Royal Infirmary, Tel.: ext 3142

Ms R Marrison, Clinical Nurse Specialist, Respiratory, Doncaster Royal Infirmary, Tel.: 01302 366666 ext 3994

Ms N Severein Kirk, Clinical Nurse Specialist, Respiratory, Doncaster Royal Infirmary, Tel.: 01302 366666 ext 3994

Community Midwifery

Emergencies - Central Delivery Suite, Women's Hospital, Doncaster Royal Infirmary, Tel.: 01302 553165

Ms V S Knight, Community Midwifery Services, Women's Hospital, Doncaster Royal Infirmary, Tel.: 01302 366666 x 3269

Community Nursing Services

Ms A Ash, Children's Community Nursing, Doncaster Royal Infirmary, Tel.: 01302 553175

Ms E Clifford, Children's Community Nursing, Doncaster Royal Infirmary, Tel.: 01302 553175

Ms A Ince, Children's Community Nursing, Doncaster Royal Infirmary, Tel.: 01302 553175

Ms J Taylor, Children's Community Nursing, Doncaster Royal Infirmary, Tel.: 01302 553175

HIV/AIDS

Ms J Fennell, HIV/AIDS Specialist Nurse, Retford Hospital, Tel.: 01777 274400 ext 4489

Liaison Services

Ms J Bakewell, Community Liaison Nurse, Retford Hospital, Tel.: 01777 274439

Ms G Barlow, Community Liaison Nurse, Doncaster Royal Infirmary, Tel.: ext 3613/bleep 414

Ms C Jackson, Community Liaison Nurse, Doncaster Royal Infirmary, Tel.: ext 3613/bleep 122

Matrons/Modern Matrons

Ms L Ball, Medical Directorate, Matron, Tel.: ext 2184

Ms M Blank, Lead Nurse, Matron, Montagu, Tel.: ext 4114

Ms M Dalton, Women's Services, Matron, Tel.: ext 6344

Ms D Gardiner, Special Surgery, Matron, Tel.: ext 4336

Ms J McQuade, Medical Directorate Assistant, Matron, Tel.: ext 3759

Ms R Mews, Surgical Directorate, Matron, Tel.: ext 4284

Ms J Pack, Medical Directorate Assistant, Matron, Tel.: ext 4037

Ms K Wilson, Women's Services, Matron, Tel.: ext 2225

Ms G Newbold, Matron, A&E, Tel.: ext 3365

Ms V Colquhoun, Critical Care, Matron, Anaesthetics, Tel.: ext 6163

Ms I Bradbury, Matron, Children, Tel.: ext 3838

Ms J Blockley, Matron, Elderly Care, Tel.: 806811

Ms L Jones, Matron, Orthopaedics, Tel.: ext 4067

Ms Y Walley, Day Surgery, Matron, Theatres, Tel.: ext 3772

Doncaster & South Humber NHS Trust

Trust Headquarters, St Catherine's Hospital
Tickhill Road, Balby
DONCASTER
South Yorkshire
DN4 8QN
Tel.: 01302 796000

Learning Disabilities

Mr S Colgan, Nurse Manager, William Molsen Centre, Kent Street, Grimsby, DN32 7DJ, Tel.: 01472 325323

Mr G Higgins, Chief Executive, Deputy, St Catherines House, St Catherines Hospital, Balby, Doncaster, DN4 8QN, Tel.: 01302 796141

Learning Disability Team, Girton Lodge, Loversall Hospital, Weston Road, Balby, Doncaster, DN4 8NX, Tel.: 01302 796154/5

Mrs C Williams, Community Homes, Senior Nurse, Girton Lodge, Loversall Hospital, Weston Road, Balby, Doncaster, DN4 8NX, Tel.: 01302 796149

Doncaster Central Primary Care Trust

Trust Headquarters, White Rose House
Ten Pound Walk
DONCASTER, DN4 5DJ
Tel.: 01302 320111

Admin & Senior Management

Mrs L Kellett, Director of Integrated Clinical Services, White Rose House, Ten Pound Walk, Doncaster, DN4 5DJ, Tel.: 01302 320111 ext 3209

Mr S Morritt, Chief Executive,

Child Health

Child Health Department, Tickhill Road Hospital, Balby, Doncaster, DN4 8QL, Tel.: 01302 796249

Child Health Records

Child Health Department, Tickhill Road Hospital, Balby, Doncaster, DN4 8QL, Tel.: 01302 796249

Child Protection/Safeguarding Children

Ms A Hendley, Tickhill Road Hospital, Balby, Doncaster, DN4 8QL, Tel.: 01302 796235

Clinical Leads (NSF)

Ms H Marsh, Clinical Lead, Cancer,

Ms M Mayhew, Clinical Lead, CHD,

Dr A Graves, Clinical Lead, Diabetic Care,

Ms L Kellett, Clinical Lead, Older People,

Community Nursing Services

Mrs C Hill, Lead Nurse RNCC, Doncaster Central PCT, White Rose House, Ten Pound Walk, Doncaster, DN4 5DJ, Tel.: 01302 320111

District Nursing

Mrs C Hill, Head of Community Services, Doncaster Central PCT, White Rose House, Ten Pound Walk, Doncaster, DN4 5DJ, Tel.: 01302 320111

Other Services

Community Intervention Team, Tickhill Road Hospital, Weston Road, Balby, Doncaster, Tel.: 01302 796222

Mrs L Harvey, Head of Intermediate Care & Speciality Services, Tel.: 01302 796437

Yorkshire and The Humber SHA

Pharmacy
Mr S Davies, Head of Prescribing, White Rose House, Ten Pound Walk, Doncaster, DN4 5DJ, Tel.: 01302 320111
Smoking Cessation
Ms C Pougher, Manager, Sexual Health, White Rose House, Ten Pound Walk, Doncaster, DN4 5DJ, Tel.: 01302 320111
Specialist Nursing Services
Ms K Middleton, Team Manager, Dove Practice, Cavendish Court,
The Homeless/Travellers & Asylum Seekers
DOVE PMS, (Nurse lead practice offering general medical services to vulnerable groups), White Rose House, Ten Pound Walk, Doncaster, DN4 5DJ, Tel.: 01302 320111
Mrs J Webster, Acting Director of Strategic Dev & Commissioning, White Rose House, Ten Pound Walk, Doncaster, DN4 5DJ, Tel.: 01302 320111

Doncaster East Primary Care Trust

Trust Headquarters, White Rose House
Ten Pound Walk
DONCASTER, DN4 5DJ
Tel.: 01302 320111

Admin & Senior Management
Ms H E Beard, Director of Development,
Ms C Boswell, Chief Executive,
Ms S Rands, Director of Operational Services,
Child Health Records
Ms J Summerfield, Child Health, Tickhill Road Hospital, Balby, Doncaster, DN4 8QN, Tel.: 01302 796000
Child Protection/Safeguarding Children
Ms J Summerfield, Child Health, Tickhill Road Hospital, Balby, Doncaster, DN4 8QN, Tel.: 01302 796000
Community Matrons
Ms E Gascoigne, Community Matron, c/o Cantley Health Centre, Goodison Boulevard, Cantley, Doncaster, Tel.: 01302 534957
Ms M Holgate, Community Matron, c/o Cantley Health Centre, Goodison Boulevard, Cantley, Doncaster, Tel.: 01302 534957
Community Nursing Services
Ms C Prewett, Clinical Manager,
District Nursing
Ms S Blow, Health Visitor, c/o Cantley Health Centre, Goodison Boulevard, Cantley, Doncaster, Tel.: 01302 534957
Mr B Ross, Health Visitor, c/o Cantley Health Centre, Goodison Boulevard, Cantley, Doncaster, Tel.: 01302 534957
Health Visitors
Ms S Blow, Health Visitor, c/o Cantley Health Centre, Goodison Boulevard, Cantley, Doncaster, Tel.: 01302 534957
Mr B Ross, Health Visitor, c/o Cantley Health Centre, Goodison Boulevard, Cantley, Doncaster, Tel.: 01302 534957
Liaison Services
Ms E Carllidge, Paediatric Liaison Health Visitor, Children's Hospital, Doncaster Royal Infirmary, Armthorpe Road, Doncaster, DN2 5LT, Tel.: 01302 366666 ext 3014
School Nursing
C Prewett, Child Health, Tickhill Road Hospital, Balby, Doncaster, DN4 8QN, Tel.: 01302 796243
Specialist Nursing Services
Ms K Kemp, Advisor, Continence, Hollybush Health Centre, Church Balk, Edenthorpe, Doncaster, DN3 2PP, Tel.: 01302 890444
Ms M Eggleston, Nurse Specialist, Diabetes, Day Care Centre, Doncaster Royal Infirmary, Armthorpe Road, Doncaster, DN2 5LT, Tel.: 01302 738993
Ms A Johnson, Nurse Specialist, Diabetes, Day Care Centre, Doncaster Royal Infirmary, Armthorpe Road, Doncaster, DN2 5LT, Tel.: 01302 738993
Ms Y Severein, Nurse Specialist, Diabetes, Day Care Centre, Doncaster Royal Infirmary, Armthorpe Road, Doncaster, DN2 5LT, Tel.: 01302 738993

Ms G Smout, Nurse Specialist, Diabetes, Day Care Centre, Doncaster Royal Infirmary, Armthorpe Road, Doncaster, DN2 5LT, Tel.: 01302 738993
Ms C Doran, Nurse Specialist, Epilepsy, Admin Block, Tickhill Road Hospital, Balby, Doncaster, DN4 8QL, Tel.: 01302 796217
Ms A Perry, Nurse Specialist, Epilepsy, Admin Block, Tickhill Road Hospital, Balby, Doncaster, DN4 8QL, Tel.: 01302 796217
Ms A Burton, Nurse Specialist, Heart Failure, White Rose House, Ten Pound Walk, Doncaster, DN4 5DJ, Tel.: 01302 320111
Ms A Crundell, Nurse Specialist, Heart Failure, White Rose House, Ten Pound Walk, Doncaster, DN4 5DJ, Tel.: 01302 320111
Ms J Montero, Nurse Specialist, Heart Failure, White Rose House, Ten Pound Walk, Doncaster, DN4 5DJ, Tel.: 01302 320111
Mr M Casey, Nurse Specialist, Parkinson's Disease, Cantley Health Centre, Goodison Boulevard, Cantley, Doncaster, Tel.: 01302 379520
Ms M Dowie, Nurse Specialist, Respiratory, Admin Block, Tickhill Road Hospital, Balby, Doncaster, DN4 8QL, Tel.: 01302 796219
Ms R McCook, Nurse Specialist, Respiratory, Admin Block, Tickhill Road Hospital, Balby, Doncaster, DN4 8QL, Tel.: 01302 796219
Ms G Segust, Nurse Specialist, Respiratory, Admin Block, Tickhill Road Hospital, Balby, Doncaster, DN4 8QL, Tel.: 01302 796219

Doncaster West Primary Care Trust

Trust Headquarters, West Lodge
St Catherine's, Tickhill Road, Balby
DONCASTER
DN4 8QN
Tel.: 01302 796796

Admin & Senior Management
Mrs P Brooks Cordon, Director of Primary Care and Clinical Services, Tel.: 01302 796762
Mr M Potts, Chief Executive,
Mrs S Whitfield, Assistant Director of Clinical Services, Tel.: 01302 796767
Child Protection/Safeguarding Children
Ms A Ayari, Nurse Specialist, Child Protection,
Ms M Corbet, Senior Nurse, Child Protection,
Ms R Topping, Children's, Nurse Specialist, Child Protection,
District Nursing
District Nurses, Mexborough Health Centre, Adwick Road, Mexborough, South Yorkshire, S64 0BY, Tel.: 01709 570028
Family Planning Services
Ms S Cookson, Head of Sexual Health, East Laith Gate House, East Laith Gate, Doncaster, DN1 1JE,
Health Visitors
Health Visitors, Mexborough Health Centre, Adwick Road, Mexborough, South Yorkshire, S64 0BY, Tel.: 01709 570028
Other Services
Mr A Brankin, Head of Podiatry, East Laith Gate House, East Laith Gate, Doncaster, DN1 1JE,

East Leeds Primary Care Trust

Trust Headquarters, Oak Tree House
408 Oakwood Lane
LEEDS
LS8 3LG
Tel.: 0113 305 9521

Admin & Senior Management
Mr L Adams, Director of Public Health,
Ms S Cannon, Director of Nursing & Health Modernisation,
Mr L Hughes, Chief Executive,
Ms D Joseph, Director of Primary Care & Locality Services, East Leeds PCT, Oaktree House, 408 Oakwood Lane, Leeds, LS8 3LG, Tel.: 0113 3059521
Mr M Robinson, Director of Public Health,

Yorkshire and The Humber SHA

Child Health
Ms P Hill, Community Services Manager - Child Health, Child Health, Willow House, St Mary's Hospital, Greenhill Road, Leeds, Tel.: 0113 3055263
Child Protection/Safeguarding Children
Ms S Smith, Designated Nurse, North Wing, St Mary's House, St Marys Road, Leeds, Tel.: 0113 2952342
Clinical Leads (NSF)
Dr R Bell, Clinical Lead, Older People,
Dr Davis, Clinical Lead, Diabetes & CHD,
Dr Mossad, Clinical Lead, Cancer,
Community Nursing Services
Ms T Ali, Locality Manager, Harehills, Burmantofts Clinic, Cromwell Mount, Leeds, Tel.: 0113 2953330
Ms G Armstrong, Locality Manager, Kippax/Garforth, Garforth Clinic, Lidgett Lane, Garforth, Tel.: 0113 2863429
Ms A Robertson, Seacroft, Seacroft Clinic, Tel.: 0113 2951060
District Nursing
Ms M Bennett, Practice Nurse - Nursing Support & Dev Team, Halton Clinic, 2a Primrose Lane, Halton, Leeds, Tel.: 0113 295 1888
Ms S Medina, Nursing Support & Development Team, District Nurse, Halton Clinic, 2a Primrose Lane, Halton, Leeds, Tel.: 0113 295 1888
Family Planning Services
City Wide Service, Hosted by South Leeds PCT,
Health Visitors
Ms L Rodgers, Nursing Support & Development Team, Health Visitor, Halton Clinic, 2a Primrose Lane, Halton, Leeds, Tel.: 0113 295 1888
Other Services
Ms L Cady, Locality Planner - Harehills, Burmantofts Clinic, Tel.: 0113 295 3330
Ms S Gale, Team Leader, Intermediate Care Team, District Nurse, York Towers, York Road, Leeds, Tel.: 0113 295 3043
Mr Keith, Locality Planner - Seacroft, Seacroft Clinic, Tel.: 0113 295 1060
Ms C Mulrooney, Team Leader, Physiotherapist - Intermediate Care Team, York Towers, York Road, Leeds, Tel.: 0113 295 3043
Ms A North, Joint Care Management Team, York Towers, York Road, Leeds, Tel.: 0113 295 3042
Mr P See Smith, Co-ordinator, East Leeds Integrated Palliative Care Service, York Towers, York Road, Leeds, Tel.: 0113 295 3067
Ms Y Watson, Locality Planner - Kippax/Garforth, Garforth Clinic, Tel.: 0113 2863429
Smoking Cessation
Ms K Newboult, Co-ordinator, Smoking Cessation Advisors, Oaktree House, 408 Oakwood Lane, Leeds, LS8 3LG, Tel.: 0113 3059542
Specialist Nursing Services
Ms B Kingswood-Burke, NHS Funded Care (Residental & Nursing Homes), Lead Nurse, York Towers, York Road, Leeds,
Ms D Burke, Facilitator, CHD, Oaktree House, 408 Oakwood Lane, Leeds, LS8 3LG, Tel.: 0113 305 9542/43
Ms K Newboult, Facilitator, CHD, Oaktree House, 408 Oakwood Lane, Leeds, LS8 3LG, Tel.: 0113 305 9542/43
Ms D McCartney, Practice Nurse Facilitator, Oaktree House, 408 Oakwood Lane, Leeds, LS8 3LG, Tel.: 0113 3059540/41
Ms J Stocks, Practice Nurse Facilitator, Oaktree House, 408 Oakwood Lane, Leeds, LS8 3LG, Tel.: 0113 3059540/41
Ms V Walker, Nurse Specialist, Respiratory, York Towers, York Road, Leeds, Tel.: 0113 295 3498/99
The Homeless/Travellers & Asylum Seekers
Ms E Greer, Homeless/Travellers, Health Visitor, Health Access Team, Avenue Hill, Chapeltown, Leeds, Tel.: 0113 2951790
No Fixed Abode Team, 68 York Street, Leeds, Tel.: 0113 295 4840

East Yorkshire Primary Care Trust

Trust Headquarters, Health House
Grange Park Lane
WILLERBY

East Yorkshire
HU10 6DT
Tel.: 01482 650700

Admin & Senior Management
Ms D Collins, Modern Matron, Community Ward, Westwood Hospital, Beverley, HU17 8BU, Tel.: 01482 389156
Mr A Williams, Chief Executive,
Child Health
Ms G Hunter, Clinical Team Manager, Tel.: 01724 290055
Child Health Records
Pre-School Records, Tel.: 01482 617880
School Age, Tel.: 01482 617904
Ms M Syrett, Manager, Victoria House, Park Street, Hull, HU2 8TD, Tel.: 01482 617857
Child Protection/Safeguarding Children
Ms N Walker-Hall, Named Nurse, Child Protection, Health House, Grange Park Lane, Willerby, HU10 6DT, Tel.: 01482 672181
Clinical Leads (NSF)
Dr R Clarke, Clinical Lead, Cancer,
Community Nursing Services
Ms K Newsome, Professional Lead Practice Nursing, Health House, Grange Park Lane, Willerby, HU10 6DT, Tel.: 01482 650700
Ms M Such, Head of Community Services, Health House, Grange Park Lane, Willerby, HU10 6DT, Tel.: 01482 672051
Ms C Wood, Director of Quality & Clinical Services, Tel.: 01482 672175
District Nursing
Ms S Barker, Clinical Team Manager - Haltemprice Locality, Cottingham Clinic, King Street, Cottingham, HU16 5QJ, Tel.: 01482 335151
Ms G Hunter, Clinical Team Manager - Goole Locality, Hessle Health Centre, Hull Road, Hessle, HU13 9LZ, Tel.: 01724 290055
Family Planning Services
Provided via Community Trust,
Health Visitors
Ms A Lewis, Professional Lead Health Visiting, Tel.: 01482 672096
Liaison Services
Mr D Falcon, PALS co-ordinator, Health House, Grange Park Lane, Willerby, HU10 6DT, Tel.: 01482 672074 ext 2074
Specialist Nursing Services
Ms A Taylor, Facilitator, Specialist Nurse, Diabetic Care, Health House, Grange Park Lane, Willerby, HU10 6DT, Tel.: 01482 672181
Ms M Nicol, Macmillan, Batholomew Medical Centre, Batholomew Avenue, Goole, DN14 6AW, Tel.: 01405 721314
Ms D Riley, Nurse Specialist, Palliative Care, Batholomew Medical Centre, Batholomew Avenue, Goole, DN14 6AW, Tel.: 01405 721314

Eastern Hull Primary Care Trust

Trust Headquarters, Netherhall
1 Wawne Road , Sutton
HULL
HU7 4YG
Tel.: 01482 335400

Admin & Senior Management
Mr I McInnes, Chief Executive, Netherhall, 1 Wawne Road, Sutton, Hull, HU7 4YG,
Ms D Phillips, Director of Professional Development, Netherhall, 1 Wawne Road, Sutton, Hull, HU7 4YG, Tel.: 01482 335441
Child Health Records
Pre-School, Victoria House, Park Street, Hull, HU2 8TD, Tel.: 01482 617880
School Age, Victoria House, Park Street, Hull, HU2 8TD, Tel.: 01482 617904
Ms M Syrett, Manager, Victoria House, Park Street, Hull, HU2 8TD, Tel.: 01482 617857

Yorkshire and The Humber SHA

Child Protection/Safeguarding Children
Ms S Pierce, Victoria House, Park Street, Hull, HU2 8TD, Tel.: 01482 617839
Clinical Leads (NSF)
Dr N Abd-Marium, Clinical Lead, Cancer, Netherhall, Wawne Road, Sutton, Tel.: 01482 336543
Ms D Andrews, Clinical Lead, Care of the Elderly, Highfields, Netherhall, Wawne Road, Sutton, Tel.: 01482 336543
Mr P Davis, Clinical Lead, CHD, Netherhall, Wawne Road, Sutton,
Ms S Craven, Clinical Lead, Diabetic Care, Tel.: 01482 335400
District Nursing
Ms A Speak, Team Manager, District Nurses, Tel.: 01482 826788
Family Planning Services
Ms K Stainsbury, West Hull PCT, Brunswick House,
Health Visitors
Ms B Horner, Team Manager, Health Visitors, Tel.: 01482 831494
Learning Disabilities
Mr K Balcolmbe, West Hull PCT, Brunswick House,
Liaison Services
Provided by Hulll & East Riding Community Trust,
Pharmacy
Mr M Rymer, Netherhall, Wawne Road, Sutton, Hull,
School Nursing
Ms G Freeby, Child Health/School Nurses,
Ms S Oxton, Child Health/School Nurses,
Smoking Cessation
Mr P Brown, West Hull PCT, Brunswick House,
Specialist Nursing Services
Team, Cardiac Rehabilitation, Rank Ward, Princess Royal Hospital, Tel.: 01482 335480
Ms S Craven, Nurse Specialist, Diabetic Care, Netherhall, 1 Wawne Road, Sutton, Hull, HU7 4YG, Tel.: 01482 335408
Nurse, Endoscopy, Highlands Health Centre, Tel.: 01482 839494
Bransholme Health Centre, Macmillan, Tel.: 01482 826788
Unit, Minor injuries, Bransholme Health Centre, Tel.: 01482 826788
Ms N Parkinson, Team Manager, Palliative Care, Highfields, Wawne Road, Sutton, Tel.: 01482 336543
Mrs C Crone, Prison Health Care,
Ms K Dexter, Respiratory, Bransholme Health Centre, Tel.: 01482 826788
Ms H Lock, Substance Misuse, Highlands Health Centre, Tel.: 01482 339494

Eastern Wakefield Primary Care Trust

Trust Headquarters, Castleford, Normanton & District Hospital
Lumley Street, Hightown
CASTLEFORD
WF10 5LT
Tel.: 01977 605500
Fax.: 01977 605501

Admin & Senior Management
Ms V Barker, Director of Public Health, Tel.: 01977 665783
Ms C Briggs, Director of Finance & Commissioning, Tel.: 01977 665787
Ms G Galdins, Director of Corporate Development, Tel.: 01977 665786
Mr M Grady, Chief Executive, Tel.: 01977 665799
Mrs H Mortimer, Director of Quality & Operations (Chief Nurse), Tel.: 01977 665784
Ms W Pearson, Director of Primary Care, Tel.: 01977 665785
Child Health
Ms S Fox, Head of Children & Young People's Services, Tel.: 01977 665856
Ms M Powell, Children's Community Nursing Team, Tel.: 01977 665545
Child Health Records
Ms J Earnshaw, Tel.: 01977 665850

Child Protection/Safeguarding Children
Ms C Hall, Child Protection, Tel.: 01977 665577
Clinical Leads (NSF)
Dr P Dewhirst, Clinical Lead, Cancer,
Dr P Earnshaw, Clinical Lead, CHD,
Ms J Wilson, Clinical Lead, Diabetic Care,
Ms H Mortimer, Clinical Lead, Older People,
Community Nursing Services
Mr J Harwood, Head of Adult Services, Castleford, Normanton & District Hospital, Lumley Street, Hightown, Castleford, WF10 5LT, Tel.: 01977 665840
District Nursing
Ms A Smith, Modern Matron, Castleford, Normanton & District Hospital, Tel.: 01977 665855
Ms S Tinker, Single Point of Access, Tel.: 01977 665886
Health Visitors
Ms J Hartley, Modern Matron, Castleford, Normanton & District Hospital, Tel.: 01977 665855
Other Services
Intermediate Care Services, Friarwood Lane, Pontefract, WF8 1UA, Tel.: 01977 606025
School Nursing
Ms H Murphy, School Nurses, Castleford, Normanton & District Hospital, Tel.: 01977 662319
Smoking Cessation
Mr S Evans, Castleford, Normanton & District Hosp., 01977 665730
Specialist Nursing Services
Ms S Potter, Case Management, Tel.: 01924 465419
Ms A Wilkes, Liaison, Cardiac, Tel.: 01977 606009
Ms S Stoner, Continence, Castleford, Normanton & District Hospital, Tel.: 01977 603034
Ms A M Johnson, Coronary Heart Disease, Castleford, Normanton & District Hospital, Tel.: 01977 665754
Ms A Christensen, Dermatology, Castleford, Normanton & District Hospital, Tel.: 01977 665561
Ms S Ross, Infection Control, Castleford, Normanton & District Hospital, Tel.: 01977 665887
Ms L Priestley, Macmillan, Prince of Wales Hospice, Half Penny Lane, Pontefract, Tel.: 01977 708868
Ms P Hirst, Palliative Care, Prince of Wales Hospice, Half Penny Lane, Pontefract, Tel.: 01977 708868
Ms C Brown, Tissue Viability, ICES Building, Trinity Business Park, Waldorf Way, Wakefield, Tel.: 01924 465758
Ms J Newbold, Tissue Viability, ICES Building, Trinity Business Park, Waldorf Way, Wakefield, Tel.: 01924 465758

Hambleton & Richmondshire Primary Care Trust

Trust Headquarters, Station Road Business Park
Station Road
THIRSK, North Yorkshire
YO7 1PZ
Tel.: 01845 573800
Fax.: 01845 573805

Admin & Senior Management
Mr S Kirk, Chief Executive, Station Road Business Park, Station Road, Thirsk, North Yorkshire, YO7 1PZ, Tel.: 01845 573800
Child Health
Ms S Hainsworth, Head of Children & Family Services, Rutson Community Hospital, Front Offices, High Street, Northallerton, Tel.: 01609 751369
Child Health Records
Child Health Records Clerk, IM&T Dept, Suite 1, Mile House Business Park, Darlington Road, Northallerton, DL6 2NW, Tel.: 01609 751200
Corporate IM & T Manager, Trust Headquarters, Tel.: 01845 573800

Yorkshire and The Humber SHA

Child Protection/Safeguarding Children
Ms L Styles, Looked After Children, Specialist Nurse,
Ms K Hedgley, Advisor, Child Protection,
Ms E Wyllie, Senior Nurse, Child Protection, Front Offices, Rutson
Community Hospital, High Street, Northallerton, DL7 8EN, Tel.:
01609 764839

Clinical Leads (NSF)
Dr P Kirby, Clinical Lead, CHD, Diabetes & Children,
N Carlisle, Clinical Lead, Cancer,
E Rooney, Clinical Lead, Older People,

Community Nursing Services
Ms E Rooney, Rutson Community Hospital, High Street,
Northallerton, North Yorkshire, DL7 8EN,

District Nursing
Ms L Bone, Locality Practitioner, 12A Friarage Street, Northallerton,
DL7 1DP, Tel.: 01609 771841
Ms C McGee, Locality Practitioner, 12A Friarage Street,
Northallerton, DL7 1DP, Tel.: 01609 771841

Equipment Loan Services
Ms C Wright, Assistant Director of Community Services, Front
Offices, Rutson Community Hospital, High Street, Northallerton, N
Yorks, DL7 8EN,

Family Planning Services
Ms S Hainsworth, Head of Children & Family Services, Rutson
Community Hospital, Front Offices, High Street, Northallerton, Tel.:
01609 751369

Health Visitors
Ms S Hainsworth, Head of Children & Family Services, Rutson
Community Hospital, Front Offices, High Street, Northallerton, Tel.:
01609 751369
Ms S Carr, Liaison, Health Visitor, Paediatrics,

Learning Disabilities
Mr D Hendy, Nurse Advisor, Front Offices, Rutson Community
Hospital, High Street, Northallerton, DL7 8EN, Tel.: 01609 763926
Ms B Wilson, Nurse Advisor, Front Offices, Rutson Community
Hospital, High Street, Northallerton, DL7 8EN, Tel.: 01609 763926

Liaison Services
PALS Officer, Trust Headquarters, Station Road Business Park,
Station Road, Thirsk, N Yorkshire, Y07 1PZ, Tel.: 01845 573800

School Nursing
Ms R Wigin, School Nurse Advisor, Thirsk Health Centre, Chapel
Street, Thirsk, YO7 1LX, Tel.: 01845 521683

Smoking Cessation
J Abraham, Smoking Cessation Advisor, Trust Headquarters, Station
Road Business Park, Station Road, Thirsk, N Yorkshire, Y07 1PZ,
Tel.: 01845 573800

Specialist Nursing Services
Ms C McGee, Nurse Advisor, Continence, 12A Friarage Street,
Northallerton, North Yorkshire, Tel.: 01609 771841
Mr A Collyer, Nurse Advisor, Infection Control, Trust Headquarters,
Station Road Business Park, Station Road, Thirsk, N Yorkshire, Y07
1PZ, Tel.: 01845 573800
Ms C Ward, Nurse Consultant, Palliative Care, Front Offices, Rutson
Community Hospital, High Street, Northallerton, DL7 8EN, Tel.:
01609 762001
Ms J Parrington, Reach Nurse, Respiratory, Respiratory Dept,
Friarage Hospital, Northallerton, DL6 1JG, Tel.: 01609 764582
Ms A McGrath, Nurse, Tissue Viability, 12A Friarage Street,
Northallerton, North Yorkshire, Tel.: 01609 771841

Harrogate Health Care NHS Trust

Trust Headquarters, Strayside Wing
Harrogate District Hospital, Lancaster Park Road
HARROGATE
North Yorkshire
HG2 7SX
Tel.: 01423 885959

Admin & Senior Management
Ms A Monaghan, Director of Nursing, Harrogate Health Care NHS
Trust, Strayside Wing, Harrogate District Hospital, Lancaster Park
Road, Harrogate, HG2 7SX, Tel.: 01423 885959

Huddersfield Central Primary Care Trust

Trust Headquarters, St Lukes House
Blackmoorfoot Road, Crossland Moor
HUDDERSFIELD
HD4 5RH
Tel.: 01484 460000

Child Health
Ms S Dawson, Practice Nurse, PRCHC, Greenhead Road,
Huddersfield, HD1 4EW, Tel.: 01484 344000 ext 4328
Ms K Gomersall, Development, Nurse, PRCHC, Greenhead Road,
Huddersfield, HD1 4EW, Tel.: 01484 344000 ext 4328

Child Health Records
Child Health Records, CWS, Calderdale & Huddersfield NHS Trust,
Huddersfield Royal Infirmary, Acre Street, Huddersfield, Tel.: 01484
342000

Child Protection/Safeguarding Children
Ms P Hughes, Child Protection, MHHC, Dalton Green Lane, Dalton,
Huddersfield, HD5 9TS, Tel.: 01484 347854
Ms A Logue, Child Protection, MHHC, Dalton Green Lane, Dalton,
Huddersfield, HD5 9TS, Tel.: 01484 347854

Clinical Leads (NSF)
Dr S Bhatti, Clinical Lead, Cancer & Children,
Dr H Corder, Clinical Lead, CHD & Cancer,
Dr K Basnett, Clinical Lead, Older People,

Community Nursing Services
Mrs K Basnett, Director of Patient Experience, PRCHC, Greenhead
Road, Huddersfield, HD1 4EW, Tel.: 01484 344000 ext 4375
Mrs C Donaldson, Head of Operational Services, PRCHC,
Greenhead Road, Huddersfield, HD1 4EW, Tel.: 01484 344000 ext
4342

District Nursing
Mr C Hedgecox, Locality Manager, MHHC, Dalton Green Lane,
Dalton, Huddersfield, HD5 9TS, Tel.: 01484 347855
Ms P Owen, Locality Manager, Golcar Clinic, Scar Lane, Golcar,
Huddersfield, HD7 4AR, Tel.: 01484 347888
Ms T Schofield, Head of Professional Development, PRCHC,
Greenhead Road, Huddersfield, HD1 4EW, Tel.: 01484 344000

Family Planning Services
Family Planning Service, Calderdale & Huddersfield NHS Trust, Acre
Street, Lindley, Huddersfield, Tel.: 01484 342000

Health Visitors
Ms C Carty, Thalassemia, Health Visitor, PRCHC, Greenhead Road,
Huddersfield, HD1 4EW, Tel.: 01484 344321
Ms J Henderson, TB, Health Visitor, PRCHC, Greenhead Road,
Huddersfield, HD1 4EW, Tel.: 01484 344322

Learning Disabilities
Mr D Cromack, Team Manager, Greenhead Resource Unit, 24
Greenhead Road, Huddersfield, HD1 4EN, Tel.: 01484 347600
Mrs S Dent, Director, Learning Disabilities, St Lukes Hospital,
Blackmoorfoot Road, Crosland Moor, Huddersfield, Tel.: 01484
343207

Other Services
The Whitehouse, 23A New North Parade, Huddersfield, HD1 5JU,
Tel.: 01484 301911

Smoking Cessation
Ms P Hodgson, Manager, PRCHC, Greenhead Road, Huddersfield,
HD1 4EW, Tel.: 01484 344285

Specialist Nursing Services
Ms C Thompson, Sapphire Nurse, Calderdale & Huddersfield NHS
Trust, Huddersfield Royal Infirmary,
Ms J Livesey, Advisor, Continence, PRCHC, Greenhead Road,
Huddersfield, HD1 4EW, Tel.: 01484 344317

Ms E Davey, Nurse Specialist, Diabetic Care, PRCHC, Greenhead Road, Huddersfield, HD1 4EW, Tel.: 01484 344269

Ms D Lewis, Nurse Consultant, Elderly Care, Calderdale & Huddersfield NHS Trust, Huddersfield Royal Infirmary,

Ms L Readding, Nurse, Stoma Care, Calderdale & Huddersfield NHS Trust, Huddersfield Royal Infirmary,

Ms S Milburn, Nurse, Tissue Viability, Calderdale & Huddersfield NHS Trust, Huddersfield Royal Infirmary,

The Homeless/Travellers & Asylum Seekers

Ms D Farmer, The Whitehouse, 23A New North Parade, Huddersfield, HD1 5JU, Tel.: 01484 301911 ext 7713

Ms C Rhodes, The Whitehouse, 23A New North Parade, Huddersfield, HD1 5JU, Tel.: 01484 301911 ext 7713

Hull & East Yorkshire Hospitals NHS Trust

Trust Headquarters, Hull Royal Infirmary
Anlaby Road
HULL, East Yorkshire
HU3 2JZ
Tel.: 01482 328541

Child Protection/Safeguarding Children

Ms C Luckman, Midwife, Child Protection, Anlaby Suite, Craven Building, Hull Royal Infirmary, Tel.: 01482 675103

Ms C Turner, Senior Nurse, Child Protection, Anlaby Suite, Craven Building, Hull Royal Infirmary, Tel.: 01482 675103

Ms J Wollaston, Senior Nurse, Child Protection, Anlaby Suite, Craven Building, Hull Royal Infirmary, Tel.: 01482 675103

Community Midwifery

Mrs J Rowe, Community Midwifery Manager, Hull & East Yorkshire Women & Childrens Hospital, Hull (Anlaby Rd), Hull Royal Infirmary, HU3 2JZ, Tel.: 01482 672778

Mrs K Thirsk, Head of Midwifery, Hull & East Yorkshire Women & Childrens Hospital, Hull (Anlaby Rd), Hull Royal Infirmary, HU3 2JZ, Tel.: 01482 675246

Humber Mental Health Teaching NHS Trust

Trust Headquarters, West House
Westwood Hospital
BEVERLEY
East Yorkshire
HU17 8BU
Tel.: 01482 886600

Learning Disabilities

Mrs T Bailey, Operations Manager, Community Learning Disability Services & Assertive Outreach, 1st Floor, Townend Court, Cottingham Road, Hull, HU6 8QG, Tel.: 01482 343125

Mrs A Kent, Head of Profession, Learning Disability, Willerby Hill, Beverley Road, Willerby, HU10 6ED, Tel.: 01482 389239

Leeds Mental Health Services Teaching NHS Trust

Trust Headquarters, The Mansion
Tongue Lane
LEEDS
LS6 4QB
Tel.: 0113 275 8721

Learning Disabilities

Mr N Campbell, Clinical Lead, Sycamore House, St Mary's Hospital, Greenhill Road, Armley, Leeds, LS12 3QE, Tel.: 0113 305 5350

Ms J Cassidy, Clinical Leader, Willow House, St Mary's Hospital, Greenhill Road, Leeds, LS12 3QE, Tel.: 0113 305 5377

Mrs S Dunham, Associate Director, Learning Disability Services, Sycamore House, St Mary's Hospital, Greenhill Road, Armley, Leeds, LS12 3QY, Tel.: 0113 3055053

Ms S Kelly, Clinical Services Manager, Willow House, St Mary's Hospital, Greenhill Road, Leeds, LS12 3QE, Tel.: 0113 305 5377

Ms J Mason, Nurse Advisor, The Mansion, Tongue Lane, Meanwood, Leeds, LS6 4QB, Tel.: 0113 295 2874

Mrs Y Sessions, Clinical Services Manager, Sycamore House, St Mary's Hospital, Greenhill Road, Armley, Leeds, LS12 3QE, Tel.: 0113 305 5046

Mr B Wilks, Clinical Lead, Sycamore House, St Mary's Hospital, Greenhill Road, Armley, Leeds, LS12 3QE, Tel.: 0113 305 5053

Leeds North East Primary Care Trust

Trust Headquarters, Sycamore Lodge
7a Woodhouse Cliff
LEEDS
LS6 2HF
Tel.: 0113 305 9763
Fax.: 0113 305 9880

Admin & Senior Management

Ms J Bolus, Director of Clinical Development,

T Stein, Chief Executive,

Child Health Records

East Leeds PCT, Oaktree House, 408 Oakwood Lane, LS8 3LG, Tel.: 0113 305 9521

Child Protection/Safeguarding Children

Ms K Marshall, Child Protection, Stockdale House, 2nd Floor, Victoria Road, Headingley, Leeds, LS6 1WA, Tel.: 0113 203 3422

Community Matrons

Ms D Boyne, Sycamore Lodge, 7A Woodhouse Cliff, Leeds, LS6 2HF, Tel.: 0113 305 9838

Community Midwifery

Midwifery, Leeds General Infirmary, Great George Street, Leeds, LS1 3EX, Tel.: 0113 233 6202

District Nursing

Ms D Myers, Stockdale House, 2nd Floor, Victoria Road, Headingley, Leeds, LS6 1WA, Tel.: 0113 203 3423

Equipment Loan Services

Mr S Cluderay, Chapeltown Health Centre, Spencer Place, Leeds, LS7 4BB, Tel.: 0113 295 1052

Family Planning Services

South Leeds PCT, 1st Floor, Navigation House, 8 George Mann Road, Quayside Park, Leeds, LS10 1DJ, Tel.: 0113 305 9666

Health Visitors

Ms H Rowland, Stockdale House, 2nd Floor, Victoria Road, Headingley, Leeds, LS6 1WA, Tel.: 0113 203 3424

Learning Disabilities

Mr S Cluderay, Chapeltown Health Centre, Spencer Place, Leeds, LS7 4BB, Tel.: 0113 295 1052

Liaison Services

East Leeds PCT, Oaktree House, 408 Oakwood Lane, LS8 3LG, Tel.: 0113 305 9521

Pharmacy

Mr M Hossain, Stockdale House, 2nd Floor, Victoria Road, Headingley, Leeds, LS6 1WA, Tel.: 0113 203 3439

School Nursing

East Leeds PCT, Oaktree House, 408 Oakwood Lane, LS8 3LG, Tel.: 0113 305 9521

Specialist Nursing Services

Ms S Margerisen, CHD, HF, Leafield Clinic, Tel.: 0113 295 1901

Ms V Nicholson, Diabetes, Leafield Clinic, Tel.: 0113 295 3522

The Homeless/Travellers & Asylum Seekers

Mr S Cluderay, Chapeltown Health Centre, Spencer Place, Leeds, LS7 4BB, Tel.: 0113 295 1052

Leeds North West Primary Care Trust

Trust Headquarters, 2nd Floor
Mill House, Troy Road, Horsforth
LEEDS
LS18 5TN
Tel.: 0113 305 7120

Yorkshire and The Humber SHA

Admin & Senior Management
Ms J Coombs, Executive Lead Nurse,
Ms L Smith, Chief Executive,
Clinical Leads (NSF)
Dr C Cochrane, Clinical Lead, Children, Older People,
Dr P Selby, Clinical Lead, Cancer,
Dr S Hayes, Clinical Lead, CHD,
Dr P Dearing, Clinical Lead, Diabetic Care,

Leeds Teaching Hospitals NHS Trust
Trust Headquarters, Chief Executive's Office
1st Floor Trust HQ, St James Hospital
LEEDS, West Yorkshire
LS9 7TF
Tel.: 0113 243 3144
Fax.: 0113 243 6223

Acute Specialist Nursing Services
Ms K Kubie, Nurse, Asthma, - Paediatrics, Room 89B, A Floor,
Clarendon Wing, The Leeds General Infirmary,
Ms M Wray, Nurse Specialist, Cardiac, - Paediatrics, Ward 10, Leeds
General Infirmary, Great George Street, Leeds, LS1 3EX,
Ms D Beaumont, Specialist Nurse, Cleft Lip & Palate, - Paediatrics,
Northern & Yorkshire Cleft Lip & Palate Service, Room 200, A Floor,
Clarendon Wing, LGI,
Ms E Blair, Specialist Nurse, Cleft Lip & Palate, - Paediatrics,
Northern & Yorkshire Cleft Lip & Palate Service, Room 200, A Floor,
Clarendon Wing, LGI,
Ms S Esgate, Specialist Nurse, Cleft Lip & Palate, - Paediatrics,
Northern & Yorkshire Cleft Lip & Palate Service, Room 200, A Floor,
Clarendon Wing, LGI,
Ms D Phare, Specialist Nurse, Cleft Lip & Palate, - Paediatrics,
Northern & Yorkshire Cleft Lip & Palate Service, Room 200, A Floor,
Clarendon Wing, LGI,
Ms H Blythe, Nurse, Cystic Fibrosis, - Paediatrics, CF Unit,
Children's Day Hospital, St James's Hospital,
Ms A Dodds, Nurse, Cystic Fibrosis, - Paediatrics, CF Unit,
Children's Day Hospital, St James's Hospital,
Ms C A Bacon, Nurse Specialist, Diabetic Care, - Paediatrics, Room
165 Diabetes Nurse Office, Level 04 Gledhow Wing, St James's
Hospital,
Ms J Cropper, Nurse Specialist, Diabetic Care, - Paediatrics, Room
103, Ward 52 Clarendon Wing, The General Infirmary,
Ms J Exall, Nurse Specialist, Diabetic Care, - Paediatrics, Room 165
Diabetes Nurse Office, Level 04 Gledhow Wing, St James's Hospital,
Ms C Gelder, Nurse Specialist, Diabetic Care, - Paediatrics, Room
165 Diabetes Nurse Office, Level 04 Gledhow Wing, St James's
Hospital,
Ms M Hill, Nurse Specialist, Diabetic Care, - Paediatrics, Room 103,
c/o Wd 52, A Floor, Clarendon Wing, Belmont Grove, Leeds, LS2
9NS,
Ms W Sewell, Nurse Specialist, Diabetic Care, - Paediatrics, Room
99A Ward 52 A Floor, Clarendon Wing, The General Infirmary,
Belmont Grove, Leeds, LS2 9NS,
Ms J Walker, Nurse Specialist, Endocrine Surgery, - Paediatrics,
Room 89B, A Floor, Clarendon Wing, The General Infirmary,
Ms J Kellett, Nurse Specialist, Epilepsy, - Paediatrics, Room 125, B
Floor, Clarendon Wing, Leeds General Infirmary,
Ms A Westoby, Clinical Nurse Specialist, Haematology, - Paediatrics,
Regional Paediatric Oncology & Haematology Unit, Children's Day
Hospital, St James's University Hosp,
Ms K Kubie, Nurse Specialist, Immunology, - Paediatrics, c/o
Children's Day Care Unit, C Floor, Clarendon Wing, The General
Infirmary, Leeds,
Ms A Towers, Outreach, Neonatal, - Paediatrics, Neonatal Unit, St
James's University Hospital,
Ms A Wood, Outreach, Neonatal, - Paediatrics, Neonatal Unit, St
James's University Hospital,

Ms S Stanley, Nurse Practitioner, Nephrology, - Paediatrics, Renal
Ward, 12A St James's University Hospital,
Ms G Lazonby, Nurse, Nutrition, - Paediatrics, Room 169 A Floor,
Clarendon Wing, The General Infirmary, Belmont Grove, Leeds, LS2
9NS,
Ms D Highfield, Regional, Clinical Nurse Specialist, Oncology, -
Paediatrics, Regional Paediatric Oncology & Haematology Unit,
Children's Day Hospital, St James's University Hosp,
Ms G Dixon, Specialist Nurse, Pain Management, - Paediatrics, c/o
Dept of Anaesthetics, St James's University Hospital,
Ms E Lane, Sister, Pain Management, - Paediatrics, c/o Dept of
Anaesthetics, Leeds General Infirmary,
Ms T Latham, Sister, Pain Management, - Paediatrics, c/o Dept of
Anaesthetics, Leeds General Infirmary,
Ms C Scott, Clinical Nurse Specialist, Radiotherapy, - Paediatrics,
c/o Nightingale Ward, Cookridge Hospital, Hospital Lane, Cookridge,
Leeds, LS16 6QB,
Ms C Mosby, Nurse Specialist, Renal, - Paediatrics, Children's Renal
Services, St James's University Hospital,
Ms G Jackson, Nurse, Rheumatology, - Paediatrics, Children's
Outreach Office, A Floor, Clarendon Wing, Belmont Grove, Leeds,
LS2 9NS,
Ms C Thomas, Children's Bowel, Nurse Specialist, Stoma Care, -
Paediatrics, Room 169 A Floor, Clarendon Wing, The General
Infirmary, Belmont Grove, Leeds, LS2 9NS,
Ms M Whitaker, Surgical Outreach Nurse, Surgical Services, -
Paediatrics, Ward 27, St James's University Hospital,
Ms J Hodsman, Children's Surgical/Urology Outreach Nurse,
Urology, - Paediatrics, Ward 15, St James's University Hospital,
Mr C Taylor, Charge Nurse/Paediatric Surgical/Urology Outreach
Nurse, Urology, - Paediatrics, Ward 15, St James's University
Hospital,
Child Protection/Safeguarding Children
Ms N Pendris, Child Protection, Clarendon Wing, 0113 392 6754
Community Midwifery
Ms S Deighton, Team Leader, Leeds General Infirmary & St James's
University Hospital, Leeds General Infirmary, Great George Street,
Leeds, LS1 3EX, Tel.: 0113 392 3630
Deputy Chief Nurse/Head of Midwifery, Trust Headquarters, St
James Hospital, Beckett Street, Leeds, LS9 7TF, Tel.: 0113 206
7210
Emergencies, Leeds General Infirmary, Great George Street, Leeds,
LS1 3EX, Tel.: 0113 392 3830
Ms A McIntyre, Team Leader, Leeds General Infirmary & St James's
University Hospital, Leeds General Infirmary, Great George Street,
Leeds, LS1 3EX, Tel.: 0113 392 3630
Office Based at Clarendon Wing, General Infirmary, Belmont Grove,
Leeds, LS2 9NS, Tel.: 0113 392 2784/6735
Health Visitors
Ms B Durrans, Paediatric Health Visitor, Clarendon Wing, Leeds
General Infirmary, Belmont Grove, Leeds, LS2 9NS, Tel.: ext 23832
Liaison Services
Mrs A Rush, Paediatric Liaison Nurse A & E, A & E Dept, Jubilee
Wing, Leeds General Infirmary, Leeds, LS1 3EX, Tel.: 0113 3922523
Ms M Graham, Liaison Nurse, Asthma, - Paediatrics, CF Unit,
Children's Day Hospital, St James's University Hospital,
Ms W Dickson, Liaison Nurse - Babies/Young Children, Cardiac, -
Paediatrics, Ward 10 Leeds General Infirmary, Great George Street,
Leeds, LS1 3EX,
Mr M Fresson, Liaison Nurse - adolescents/young adults, Cardiac, -
Paediatrics, Ward 10 Leeds General Infirmary, Great George Street,
Leeds, LS1 3EX,
Ms E Lyles, Liaison Nurse, Macmillan, - Paediatrics, Regional
Paediatric Oncology & Haematology Unit, Children's Day Hospital, S
James's University Hosp,
Mr D Thomas, Liaison Nurse, Macmillan, - Paediatrics, Regional
Paediatric Oncology & Haematology Unit, Children's Day Hospital, S
James's University Hosp,

s P Seymour, Liaison Sister - Surgery, Neonatal, - Paediatrics, eonatal Surgical Unit, The Clarendon Wing, Leeds General irmary,
ther Services
s E Scanlon, Nurse Consultant, Tissue Viability, St James niversity Hospital, Beckett Street, Leeds, LS9 7TF, Tel.: 0113 65504

eeds West Primary Care Trust

ust Headquarters, Bremner House
hn Charles Way, Gelderd Business Park
EEDS, LS12 6QD
el.: 0113 305 9400

dmin & Senior Management
P Morrin, Director of Nursing & Health Care Development, emner House, John Charles Way, Gilderd Business Park, Leeds, 12 6QD, Tel.: 0113 3059400
hild Health
s S Norfolk, This service is provided locally but hosted by Leeds ast PCT, Tel.: 0113 2951550
hild Health Records
s S George, Managed centrally at St Mary's Hospital, Tel.: 0113 5 5000
hild Protection/Safeguarding Children
s C Fairhead, Child Protection,
s D Hampshire, Designated Nurse, Child Protection, St Mary's ouse, Tel.: 0113 295 2300
strict Nursing
s J Gare, Senior Nurse, Bremner House, John Charles Way, lderd Business Park, Leeds, LS12 6QD, Tel.: 0113 305 9400
s S Tchumak, Senior Nurse, Bremner House, John Charles Way, lderd Business Park, Leeds, LS12 6QD, Tel.: 0113 305 9400
ealth Visitors
s C Walker, Community Physical Disability, Health Visitor, The ommunity Rehabilitation Unit, St Mary's Hospital, Tel.: 0113 305 00
aison Services
s L Elwin, Physical Disabilities Community, Liaison Nurse, The ommunity Rehabilitation Unit, St Mary's Hospital, Tel.: 0113 305 00
s M Rowlands, Service Manager, Specialist Health Liaison Service, el.: 0113 305 9400
ther Services
rs E Padmore, Practice Placement Facilitator,
moking Cessation
J Fear, Director of Public Health, Tel.: 0113 305 9400

id Yorkshire Hospitals NHS Trust

ust Headquarters, Rowan House
nderfields General Hospital, Aberford Road,
AKEFIELD
F1 4EE
el.: 01924 213850

ommunity Midwifery
rs W Dodson, Community Midwifery Manager, Pontefract General irmary, Friarwood Lane, Pontefract, West Yorkshire, WF8 1PL, el.: 01977 606552
mergencies, Delivery Suite, Dewsbury & District Hospital, Tel.: 924 816250
rs S Schofield, Head of Midwifery, Dewsbury & District Hospital, alifax Road, Dewsbury, WF13 4HS, Tel.: 01924 512000
s A South, Matron, Dewsbury & District Hospital, Halifax Road, ewsbury, WF13 4HS, Tel.: 01924 512000
earning Disabilities
r B Ramruttun, General Manager, Learning Disability Service, esource Centre, Cullingworth Street, Dewsbury, WF13 4AN, Tel.: 924 816274

North Bradford Primary Care Trust

Trust Headquarters, New Mill
Victoria Road, Saltaire
BRADFORD
West Yorkshire
BD18 3LD
Tel.: 01274 366266
Fax.: 01274 366273

Admin & Senior Management
Ms L Hill, Acting Chief Executive,
Child Health Records
Bradford Health Informatics Service, Comm HQ, New Mill, Victoria Road, Saltaire, West Yorkshire, BD18 3LD,
Mrs J Greenwood, Information Systems Co-ordinator, Bradford Health Informatics Service, New Mill, Victoria Road, Saltaire, West Yorkshire, BD18 3LD, Tel.: 01274 366172
Ms D Hirst, Under 5's, Tel.: 01274 366151
Miss E Whiteley, Over 5's, Tel.: 01274 366168
Child Protection/Safeguarding Children
Ms L Chennells, Assistant Director of Commissioning, New Mill, Victoria Road, Saltaire, Bradford, BD18 3LD, Tel.: 01274 366034
Ms R Mulley, Child Protection, Leeds Road Hospital, Maudsley Street, Bradford, BD3 9LH, Tel.: 01274 363434
Clinical Leads (NSF)
Dr J O'Sullivan, Clinical Lead, Cancer,
Dr D McIvor, Clinical Lead, CHD,
Dr B Karet, Clinical Lead, Diabetic Care,
Community Nursing Services
Mrs S Ince, Director of Provider Services, New Mill, Victoria Road, Saltaire, Bradford, BD18 3LD, Tel.: 01274 366266 ext 6239
District Nursing
Ms K Line, Service Development Nurse, New Mill Level 2, Tel.: 01274 366244
Health Visitors
Ms P Corson, Service Development Nurse, New Mill Level 2, Tel.: 01274 366284
HIV/AIDS
Ms C Riddiough, Co-ordinator, HIV Prevention, New Mill, Victoria Road, Saltaire, Bradford, BD18 3LD, Tel.: 01274 366107
Liaison Services
Hospital/Community Elderley/Acute, St Luke's Hospital, Little Horton Lane, Bradford, BD5 0NA, Tel.: 01274 734744
Other Services
Ms L Kitson, Modern Matron, Shipley Hospital, 98 Kirkgate, Shipley, BD18 3LT, Tel.: 01274 227515
Ms L Twigger, Modern Matron, Eccleshill Community Hospital, 450 Harrogate Road, Eccleshill, B010 0JE, Tel.: 01274 323100
Specialist Nursing Services
Ms C Dodd, Drugs Team, Eccleshill Clinic, Tel.: 01274 322214
Ms J Warburton, Case Management Team, Eccleshill Clinic, Tel.: 01274 322283
Mr S Grant, Pharmacaeutical Advisor, Asthma, New Mill, Victoria Road, Saltaire, Bradford, BD18 3LD, Tel.: 01274 366266
Ms D McIvor, Cardiac Rehabilitation, Eccleshill Clinic, Tel.: 01274 322173
Ms E Hambling, Continence, Eccleshill Clinic, Tel.: 01274 322181
Ms L Chennells, Breast Care/Paediatric Stoma Care, Elderly Care, New Mill, Victoria Road, Saltaire, Bradford, BD18 3LD, Tel.: 01274 366034
Ms L Kitson, Elderly Care, Shipley Hospital, Shipley, BD18 3TL, Tel.: 01274 227515
Ms J Winterbottom, Assistant Director of Commissioning, Epilepsy, - Diabetes, New Mill, Victoria Road, Saltaire, Bradford, BD18 3LD, Tel.: 01274 366253
Mr R Longbottom, Assistant Director Commissioning, Genetics, New Mill, Victoria Road, Saltaire, Bradford, BD18 3LD, Tel.: 01274 366262

Yorkshire and The Humber SHA

Ms S Coleman, Clinical Governance Manager, Infection Control, New Mill, Victoria Road, Saltaire, Bradford, BD18 3LD, Tel.: 01274 366245

Ms D Crossland, Service Development Nurse, Palliative Care, New Mill, Victoria Road, Saltaire, Bradford, BD18 3LD, Tel.: 01274 366261

Team, Palliative Care, Daisy Bank, Duckworth Lane, Bradford, BD9 6RL, Tel.: 01274 363767

Ms A Clarkson, Tissue Viability, Eccleshill Clinic, Tel.: 01274 322191

North East Lincolnshire Primary Care Trust

Trust Headquarters, 1 Prince Albert Gardens
GRIMSBY
DN31 3HT
Tel.: 01472 302800

Child Health Records
Ms L Grice, Team Leader, Admin Services, Scartho Hall, Scartho Road, Grimsby, DN33 2BA, Tel.: 01472 875563
Mrs S Huckle, System Administrator Child Health, Scartho Hall, Scartho Road, Grimsby, DN33 2BA, Tel.: 01472 875208

Child Protection/Safeguarding Children
Mrs S Barrelle, Safeguarding Children Team, Specialist Nurse, Tel.: 01724 282282 ext 5443
Ms L Benefer, Facilitator, Northern Lincolnshire & Goole Hospitals NHS Trust, Safeguarding Children Team, Diana Princess of Wales Hospital, Scartho Road, Grimsby, DN33 2BA, Tel.: 01472 874111 ext 2942
Ms P Cherrell, Facilitator, Northern Lincolnshire & Goole Hospitals NHS Trust, Safeguarding Children Team, Diana Princess of Wales Hospital, Scartho Road, Grimsby, DN33 2BA, Tel.: 01472 874111 ext 1281
Mrs J Fell, Looked After Children Team, Specialist Nurse, Tel.: 01472 874111 ext 2731
Ms P Taylor, Northern Lincolnshire & Goole Hospitals NHS Trust, Specialist Nurse, Safeguarding Children Team, Diana Princess of Wales Hospital, Scartho Road, Grimsby, DN33 2BA, Tel.: 01472 874111 ext 7821

Clinical Leads (NSF)
Dr P Twomey, Clinical Lead, Cancer & CHD,

Community Nursing Services
Mrs L Poucher, Director of Clinical Services, 1 Prince Albert Gardens, Grimsby, DN31 3HT, Tel.: 01472 302850
Mrs L Revell, Assistant Director Clinical Services, 1 Prince Albert Gardens, Grimsby, DN31 3HT, Tel.: 01472 302850

District Nursing
Barton Practice, District Nurses, 33 Laceby Road, Tel.: 01472 278751
Cleethorpes Clinic, District Nurses, St Hughe's Avenue, Tel.: 01472 232235
Cleethorpes Medical Centre, District Nurses, 323 Grimsby Road, Tel.: 01472 200485
Collett Practice, District Nurses, 2 Littlefield Lane, Tel.: 01472 340425
Culshaw Practice, District Nurses, 17 Chantry Lane, Tel.: 01472 361181
Fieldhouse Medical Centre, District Nurses, 13 Dudley Street, Tel.: 01472 344146
Grimsby Community Clinic, Kingsley Grove, Tel.: 01472 875 373
Immingham, District Nurses, Tel.: 01469 510688
Lavin Practice, Cleethorpes - District Nurses, 32 Albert Road, Tel.: 01472 236558
Lawless Practice, District Nurses, 11 Dudley Street, Tel.: 01472 344120
Potter Practice, District Nurses, 31 Chantry Lane, Tel.: 01472 348936
Scartho Medical Centre, District Nurses, 26 Waltham Road, Scartho, Tel.: 01472 874260

Health Visitors
Barton Practice, Health Visitors, 33 Laceby Rd, Tel.: 01472 278752
Cleethorpes Clinic, Health Visitors, St Hughe's Avenue, Tel.: 01472 232233
Cleethorpes Medical Centre, Health Visitors, 323 Grimsby Road, Tel.: 01472 290119
Collett Practice, Health Visitors, 2 Littlefield Lane, 01472 269375
Culshaw Practice, Health Visitors, 17 Chantry Lane, Tel.: 01472 269750
Mrs A Darby, Specialist Health Visitor Substance Misuse, Olympia House, Saxon Court, Gilbey Road, Grimsby, Tel.: 01472 355220
Fieldhouse Medical Centre, Health Visitors, 13 Dudley Street, Tel.: 01472 347057
Ms K Henderson, Professional Lead for Health Visiting, Cleethorpe Clinic, St Hugh's Avenue, Cleethorpes, DN35 8ED, Tel.: 01472 232233
Hope Street Medical Centre, Health Visitors, Tel.: 01472 313400
Immingham, Health Visitors, Tel.: 01469 510680
Lavin Practice, Cleethorpes - Health Visitors, 32 Albert Road, Tel.: 01472 232260
Lawless Practice, Health Visitors, 11 Dudley Street, Tel.: 01472 269557
Potter Practice, Health Visitors, 31 Chantry Lane, Tel.: 01472 340932
Scartho Medical Centre, Health Visitors, 26 Waltham Road, Scartho Tel.: 01472 753662

Liaison Services
Ms J Lowe, Liaison, Medical, Rheumatology, Diana, Princess of Wales Hospital, Scartho Road, Grimsby, DN33 2BA, Tel.: 01472 874111 ext 7818
Ms H Pearce, Liaison, Surgical, Diana, Princess of Wales Hospital, Scartho Road, Grimsby, DN33 2BA, Tel.: 01472 874111 ext 7219

School Nursing
Ms P Holmes, Professional Lead for School Nursing, Cleethorpes Clinic, St Hugh's Avenue, Cleethorpes, DN35 8ED, Tel.: 01472 232247
School Health/Nursing Service, Cleethorpes, Cleethorpes Clinic, St Hugh's Avenue, Cleethorpes, DN35 8ED, Tel.: 01472 232233
School Health/Nursing Service, Grimsby, Grimsby Community Clini Kingsley Grove, Tel.: 01472 874111
School Health/Nursing Service, Grimsby, Cromwell Road Clinic, Te 01472 503353

Smoking Cessation
Mr D Hardy, Smoking Cessation, Co-ordinator, North Lincs Primary Care Trust, Scawby House, Health Place, Wrawby Road, Brigg, DN20 8GS, Tel.: 01742 276617

Specialist Nursing Services
Mrs J Smith, Moving & Handling Co-ordinator, Training & Development, Diana Princess of Wales Hospital, Grimsby, Tel.: 01472 874111 ext 2559
Ms P Robinson, Marie Curie, Cancer, Tel.: 01472 874111 ext 1262
Ms J Coombs, Nurse, Continence, 6 Dudley Street, Grimsby, Tel.: 01472 356973
Mrs A Burton, Diabetic Care, Cleethorpes Clinic, St Hugh's Avenue Cleethorpes, DN35 8ED, Tel.: 01472 232236
Mrs A Frejiszyn, Nurse Specialist, Infection Control, Scartho Hall, Scartho Road, Grimsby, DN33 2BA, Tel.: 01472 874111 ext 1030
Mrs C Lloyd, Nurse Consultant, Intermediate Care, Wilbus Respite Centre, Barnmouth Drive, Grimsby, DN37 9EJ, Tel.: 01472 326589
Ms L Foster, Macmillan, Palliative Care, St Andrew's Hospice, Peak Lane, Grimsby, Tel.: 01472 358757
Ms L Maloney, Macmillan, Palliative Care, St Andrew's Hospice, Peaks Lane, Grimsby, Tel.: 01472 358757
Ms V Revill, Lead Nurse, Palliative Care, St Andrew's Hospice, Peaks Lane, Grimsby, Tel.: 01472 358757
Mrs L Mapplebeck, Nurse, Tissue Viability, Cleethorpes Clinic, St Hugh's Avenue, Cleethorpes, DN35 8ED, Tel.: 01472 232237

The Homeless/Travellers & Asylum Seekers
Ms A Faulding, Health Visitor for Asylum Seekers & TB Contacts, Grimsby Clinic, Kingsley Grove, Grimsby, Tel.: 01472 875373

North Kirklees Primary Care Trust

Trust Headquarters, Beckside Court
Bradford Road
BATLEY, WF17 5PW
Tel.: 01924 351600

Admin & Senior Management
Mr P Sands, Chief Executive,
Child Health
Child Health Services, Beauford House, Serpentine Road, Cleckheaton, BD19 3HU, Tel.: 01274 852337
Child Protection/Safeguarding Children
Mrs K Hemsworth, Child Protection, Beckside Court, Bradford Road, Batley, WF17 5PW, Tel.: 01924 359504/359935
Community Nursing Services
Community Nurse Advisor, Dewsbury & District Hospital, Healds Road, Dewsbury, WF13 4HS, Tel.: 01924 512000
District Nursing
Mr R Flack, Central Arcade, 12 Central Arcade, Cleckheaton, BD19 5DN,
Ms L Hall-Bentley, Central Arcade, 12 Central Arcade, Cleckheaton, BD19 5DN,
Mr I Wightman, Central Arcade, 12 Central Arcade, Cleckheaton, BD19 5DN,
Family Planning Services
Mrs K Vasiljevs, Co-ordinator, Woodkirk House, Dewsbury & District Hospital, Tel.: 01924 512076
HIV/AIDS
Mrs M Hill, Health Adviser - STD, Dewsbury & District Hospital, Tel.: 01924 512000 ext 3384
Ms M Nichols, HIV Liaison Sister, Chadwick Clinic, Dewsbury & District Hospital, Tel.: 01924 816120
Liaison Services
Ms S Davison, Discharge Co-ordinator, Ward 21, Dewsbury & District Hospital, Tel.: 01924 512000 ext 3122
Mrs B Turner, TB Liaison, Dewsbury & District Hospital, Tel.: 01924 512160
Specialist Nursing Services
Ms L Newton, Breast Care, Dewsbury & District Hospital, Tel.: 01924 816182
Ms A Barker, Senior Nurse, Continence, Dewsbury & District Hospital, Tel.: 01924 512000 ext 3541
Ms P McManus, Diabetic Care, Dewsbury & District Hospital, Tel.: 01924 816097
Ms T Pickup, Diabetic Care, Dewsbury & District Hospital, Tel.: 01924 816097
Ms A Wisher, Diabetic Care, Dewsbury & District Hospital, Tel.: 01924 816097
Ms J O'Donnell, Infection Control, Dewsbury & District Hospital, Tel.: 01924 512159
Mr R Lane, Support Team, Palliative Care, Dewsbury & District Hospital, Tel.: 01924 512000 ext 3504
Miss J Edmond, Stoma Care, Dewsbury & District Hospital, Tel.: 01924 512000 ext 3268
The Homeless/Travellers & Asylum Seekers
Ms J Oliver, Homeless, Health Visitor, Woodkirk House, Dewsbury & District Hospital, Tel.: 01924 512158

North Lincolnshire Primary Care Trust

Trust Headquarters, Health Place
Wrawby Road
BRIGG, North Lincolnshire
DN20 8GS
Tel.: 01652 659659

Admin & Senior Management
Ms C Waters, Chief Executive, Tel.: 01652 601250
Child Health
Ms S May, Clinical Development Coordinator, Tel.: 01652 601232
Child Health Records
Ms C Childs, Manager, Monarch House, Queensway Business Park, Arkwright Way, Scunthorpe, DN16 1AL, Tel.: 01724 290606/7
Child Protection/Safeguarding Children
Ms S Glossop, Child Protection, Monarch House, Queensway Business Park, Arkwright Way, Scunthorpe, DN16 1AL, Tel.: 01724 290609
Clinical Leads (NSF)
Dr A Morris, Clinical Lead, Cancer,
Dr T Birtwhistle, Clinical Lead, Care of the Elderly,
Dr C Trueman, Clinical Lead, Diabetic Care,
Community Matrons
Ms A Kelly, Community Matron, Health Place, Wrawby Road, Brigg, DN20 8GS, Tel.: 01652 601239
Community Nursing Services
Cluster Co-ordinators, North Lincolnshire PCT, Health Place, Wrawby Road, Brigg, DN20 8GS, Tel.: 01652 659659
District Nursing
Mrs J Mason, Clinical Lead/District Nursing, Health Place, Wrawby Road, Brigg, North Lincs, DN20 8GS, Tel.: 01652 601213
Family Planning Services
Ms K Adlard, Family Planning Services For Young People Only, Tel.: 01724 290600
Health Visitors
Mr J Berry, Clinical Lead/Health Visiting, Health Place, Wrawby Road, Brigg, North Lincs, DN20 8GS, Tel.: 01652 601225
Learning Disabilities
Mr M Griffiths, Service Co-ordinator, Tel.: 01724 298222
Learning Disability Team, Tel.: 01724 298222
Liaison Services
Ms V Ferraby, Liaison - Discharge Planning Team, Scunthorpe General Hospital, Cliff Gardens, Scunthorpe, DN15 7BH, Tel.: 01724 282282 ext 2100
Ms T Smith, Liaison - Discharge Planning Team, Scunthorpe General Hospital, Cliff Gardens, Scunthorpe, DN15 7BH, Tel.: 01724 282282 ext 2100
School Nursing
Mrs K Adlard, Clinical Lead/School Nursing, Monarch House, Queensway Business Park, Arkwright Way, Scunthorpe, DN16 1AL, Tel.: 01724 290600
Specialist Nursing Services
Ms J Kent, Clinical Lead, Practice Nursing, Health Place, Wrawby Road, Brigg, DN20 8GS, Tel.: 01652 601225
Ms C Bunch, Breast Care, Scunthorpe General Hospital, Cliff Gardens, Scunthorpe, Tel.: 01724 282282 ext 5084
Ms A Day, Continence, The Cedars, Bigby Road, Brigg, DN20 8HH, Tel.: 01652 600102
Ms M Weston, Primary Care, Diabetes, Diabetes Centre, Scunthorpe General Hospital, Cliff Gardens, Scunthorpe, Tel.: 01724 282282 ext 2829
Ms C Day, Infection Control, Health Place, Wrawby Road, Brigg, DN20 8GS, Tel.: 01652 601185
Ms P Coleman, Liaison, Paediatrics, Disney Ward, Scunthorpe General Hospital, Cliff Gardens, Scunthorpe, Tel.: 01724 282282 ext 5692
Ms J Chester, Palliative Care, Health Place, Wrawby Road, Brigg, DN20 8GS, Tel.: 01652 601127
Ms C Marshall, Stoma Care, Health Place, Wrawby Road, Brigg, DN20 8GS, Tel.: 01652 601230
Ms M Knight, Tissue Viability, Health Place, Wrawby Road, Brigg, DN20 8GS, Tel.: 01652 601106
The Homeless/Travellers & Asylum Seekers
Ms S May, Clinical Development Coordinator, Health Place, Wrawby Road, Brigg, North Lincs, DN20 8GS, Tel.: 01652 601232

Yorkshire and The Humber SHA

North Sheffield Primary Care Trust

Trust Headquarters, Firth Park Clinic
North Quadrant, Firth Park
SHEFFIELD
S5 6NU
Tel.: 0114 226 4031

Admin & Senior Management
Mr A Buck, Chief Executive,
Mrs A Harrison, Director of Primary Care Nursing, Firth Park Clinic, North Quadrant, Firth Park, Sheffield, S5 6NU, Tel.: 0114 226 2368

Child Health Records
Ms A Ford, Team Leader, Centenary House, Heritage Park, 55 Albert Terrace Road, Sheffield, S6 3BR, Tel.: 0114 226 2091

Child Protection/Safeguarding Children
Liz Hughes Consultant Nurse Safeguarding Children Service , Centenary House Heritage Park, 55 Albert Terrace Road, Sheffield, S6 3BR, Tel.: 0114 226 2144 /2007

Clinical Leads (NSF)
Ms L Reid, Clinical Lead, CHD & Diabetes,
Mr H McCulloch, Clinical Lead, Cancer,
Dr E Birkby, Clinical Lead, CHD,
Mr H McCullough, Clinical Lead, Diabetic Care,
Mrs L Tully, Clinical Lead, Older People,

District Nursing
Mrs C Hardy, District Nursing, Development Manager, Firth Park Clinic, North Quadrant, Firth Park, Sheffield, S5 6NU,

Family Planning Services
Family Planning Service, Central Health Clinic, Mulberry Street, Sheffield, S1 2PJ, Tel.: 0114 271 6816

Health Visitors
Mrs A Wilcock, Health Visiting, Development Manager, Firth Park Clinic, North Quadrant, Firth Park, Sheffield, S5 6NU,

Liaison Services
Children's Hospitals, Tel.: 0114 271 7312
Jessop Wing Maternity, Tel.: 0114 226 8264
Northern General Hospital, Tel.: 0114 271 4731
Weston Park Hospital, Tel.: 0114 267 0222

School Nursing
Mrs M Tudor, School Nurse Manager, Centenary House, Heritage Park, 55 Albert Terrace Road, Sheffield, S6 3BR, Tel.: 0114 226 2148

Northern Lincolnshire & Goole Hospitals NHS Trust

Trust Headquarters, Diana, Princess of Wales Hospital
Scartho Road
GRIMSBY
DN33 2BA
Tel.: 01472 874111

Acute Specialist Nursing Services
Ms R Cubbison, Practitioner, Breast Care, - Advanced, Diana Princess of Wales Hospital, Tel.: 01472 874111 ext 2712
Ms A Andrews, Emergency, Nurse Practitioner, Cardiac, Diana Princess of Wales Hospital, Tel.: 01472 874111 ext 7626
Ms K Dunderdale, Nurse Specialist, Cardiac, Scunthorpe General Hospital, Tel.: 01724 282282 ext 2895
Mr J Loughborough, Specialist Nurse, Cardiac Rehabilitation, Diana Princess of Wales Hospital, Tel.: 01472 874111 ext 7626
Mr G Briggs, Macmillan, Specialist Nurse, Chemotherapy, Diana Princess of Wales Hospital, Tel.: 01472 874111 ext 2529
Ms K Smith, Macmillan, Nurse Practitioner, Chemotherapy, Diana Princess of Wales Hospital, Tel.: 01472 874111 ext 2529
Ms C Andrews, Specialist Nurse, Diabetes, Scunthorpe General Hospital, Tel.: 01724 282282 ext 2069
Ms C Briggs, Specialist Nurse, Diabetes, Scunthorpe General Hospital, Tel.: 01724 282282 ext 2069

Ms C Portogallo, Specialist Nurse, Diabetes, Scunthorpe General Hospital, Tel.: 01724 282282 ext 2069
Ms M Slimbwanyambe, Nurse Specialist, Diabetes, - Paediatrics, Diana Princess of Wales Hospital, Tel.: 01472 874111 ext 1283
Ms N Wright, Clinical Nurse Specialist, Gynae/Oncology, Scunthorp General Hospital, Tel.: 01724 282282 ext 5560
Ms H Carolan, Clinical Nurse Specialist, Haematology, Scunthorpe General Hospital, Tel.: 01724 282282 ext 5313
Ms J Brown, Nurse Specialist, IBD, Diana Princess of Wales Hospital, Tel.: 01472 874111 ext 7594
Ms J Tickle, Transfusion Specalist Practitioner, Immunology, Diana Princess of Wales Hospital, Tel.: 01472 874111 ext 7659
Ms J Girdham, Clinical Nurse Specialist, Infection Control, Scunthorpe General Hospital, Tel.: 01724 282282 ext 2517
Ms J Jones, Clinical Nurse Specialist, Infection Control, Diana Princess of Wales Hospital, Tel.: 01472 874111 ext 7658
Ms S Samways, Infection Control, Scunthorpe General Hospital, Tel.: 01724 282282 ext 2517
Ms J Fenwick, Clinical Nurse Specialist, Ophthalmology, Scunthorp General Hospital, Tel.: 01724 282282 ext 5427
Ms J Howitt, Clinical Nurse Specialist, Ophthalmology, Scunthorpe General Hospital, Tel.: 01724 282282 ext 5427
Ms E Nuttall, Clinical Nurse Specialist, Ophthalmology, Diana Princess of Wales Hospital, Tel.: 01472 874111 ext 1277
Ms L Southwell, Clinical Nurse Specialist, Ophthalmology, Diana Princess of Wales Hospital, Tel.: 01472 874111 ext 1277
Ms K Blanco, Nurse Specialist, Respiratory, Diana Princess of Wale Hospital, Tel.: 01472 874111 ext 7329
Ms L Jackson, Nurse Specialist, Respiratory, Scunthorpe General Hospital, Tel.: 01724 282282 ext 2739
Ms K Cherrell, Nurse Practitioner, Upper GI, Diana Princess of Wales Hospital, Tel.: 01472 874111 ext 2680
Ms A Eckersley, Clinical Nurse Specialist, Urology, Scunthorpe General Hospital, Tel.: 01724 282282 ext 2823

Child Health Records
Ms C Davies, Business Manager, Scunthorpe & Goole, Scunthorpe General Hospital, Tel.: 01724 282282 ext 5563
Ms C Hansen, Business Manager, Grimsby, Diana Princess of Wales Hospital, Tel.: 01472 874111 ext 1261

Child Protection/Safeguarding Children
Ms P Taylor, Safeguarding Children's Team Manager, Scunthorpe General Hospital & Diana Princess of Wales Hospital, Tel.: 01472 875215

Community Midwifery
Ms H Keane, Modern Matron, Scunthorpe General Hospital, Tel.: 01724 282282 ext 5466
Ms S Youssef, Modern Matron, Diana Princess of Wales Hospital, Tel.: 01472 874111 ext 7884

Discharge Co-ordinators
Ms J Algar, Co-ordinator, Modern Matron, Children, Scunthorpe General Hospital, Tel.: 01724 282282 ext 5304
Ms L Barker, Co-ordinator, Modern Matron, Children, Diana Princes of Wales Hospital, Tel.: 01472 874111 ext 2995
Ms H Keane, Co-ordinator, Modern Matron, Gynaecology, - Maternity, Scunthorpe General Hospital, Tel.: 01724 282282 ext 5466
Ms S Youssef, Co-ordinator, Modern Matron, Gynaecology, - Maternity, Diana Princess of Wales Hospital, Tel.: 01472 874111 ex 7884
Ms S Ainslie, Co-ordinator, Modern Matron, Sexual Health, Scunthorpe General Hospital & Diana Princess of Wales Hospital, Tel.: 01724 282282 ext 2136

Family Planning Services
Ms S Ainslie, NE Lincs, Scunthorpe General Hospital & Diana Princess of Wales Hospital, Tel.: 01724 282282 ext 2136

Matrons/Modern Matrons
Ms J Algar, Modern Matron, Children, Scunthorpe General Hospital Tel.: 01724 282282 ext 5304

s L Barker, Modern Matron, Children, Diana Princess of Wales
ospital, Tel.: 01472 874111 ext 2995

s S Ainslie, Modern Matron, Sexual Health, Scunthorpe General
ospital & Diana Princess of Wales Hospital, Tel.: 01724 282282 ext
136

Rotherham General Hospitals NHS Trust

rust Headquarters, Rotherham General Hospital
oorgate Road
ROTHERHAM, South Yorkshire
S60 2UD
el.: 01709 820000

Acute Specialist Nursing Services

s K Wakefield, Senior Nurse, Infection Control, Rotherham District
eneral Hospital, Tel.: 01709 304721

s D Askew, Officer, Resuscitation Training, Rotherham District
eneral Hospital, Tel.: 01709 304748

Admin & Senior Management

rs G Small, Deputy Director of Nursing & Quality, Rotherham
strict General Hospital, Moorgate Road, Rotherham, S60 2UD,
el.: 01709 820000

rs E Smith, Director of Nursing & Quality, Rotherham District
eneral Hospital, Moorgate Road, Rotherham, S60 2UD, Tel.: 01709
04503

Community Midwifery

mergencies, Labour Suite, Tel.: 01709 304491

s T Jenkinson, Community Midwifery Manager, Tel.: 01709 307253

rs J Lovett, Directorate Manager, Head of Midwifery, Tel.: 01709
04255

rs K Norton, General Manager, Tel.: 01709 304255

bstetrics Unit, Tel.: 01709 304058

Rotherham Primary Care Trust

rust Headquarters, Bevan House
akwood Hall Drive
ROTHERHAM
outh Yorkshire
S60 3AQ
el.: 01709 302001

Admin & Senior Management

r J McIvor, Chief Executive, Tel.: 01709 302012

Child Health

s K Abbott, Respite Nurse, Bramley House, Orchard Children's
entre, Tel.: 01709 304913

rs L Ballin, Nurse Co-ordinator, Child Development Centre,
otherham District General Hospital, Moorgate Road, Rotherham,
S60 2UD, Tel.: 01709 820000 ext 4430

s J Devine, Community Child Nurse, Wickersley Health Centre,
oplar Glade, Rotherham, S66 2JQ, Tel.: 01709 304913

s K Watson, Health Education Advisor Nurse, Tel.: 01709 304913

Child Protection/Safeguarding Children

rs L Bishop, Looked After Children's Nurse, Doncaster Gate
ospital, Doncaster Gate, Rotherham, S65 1DW, Tel.: 01709
4820

rs L Dakin, Nurse Advisor, Child Protection, Doncaster Gate
ospital, Doncaster Gate, Rotherham, S65 1DW, Tel.: 01709
4857

rs K Porteous, Senior Nurse Advisor, Child Protection, Doncaster
ate Hospital, Doncaster Gate, Rotherham, S65 1DW, Tel.: 01709
4857

Clinical Leads (NSF)

r R Cullen, Clinical Lead, Cancer,

rs J Abbott, Clinical Lead, CHD, Public Health Oak House,
oorhead Way, Bramley, Rotherham, S66 1YY, Tel.: 01709 302156

Community Matrons

s M Bunclark, Community Matron, Maltby Health Centre, Braithwell
oad, Maltby, Rotherham, S66 8JE,

Ms L Hatfield, Community Matron, Rother Valley Locality, Unit 1,
Nine Trees Trading Estate, Thurcroft, Rotherham, S66 9JG, Tel.:
01709 302651

Ms J Pearson, Community Matron, Ferham Clinic, Ferham Road,
Rotherham, S61 1EA, Tel.: 01709 302430

Ms K Shaw, Community Matron, Doncaster Gate Hospital,

Ms C Staniforth, Community Matron, Wentworth Locality, Unit 4,
Enterprise Court, Farfield Park, Manvers, Rotherham, S63 5DB, Tel.:
01709 302493

Community Nursing Services

Mrs T Daniel, Patient Safety, Senior Nurse, Oak House, Tel.: 01709
302069

Mrs K Henderson, Director of Provider Services, Oak House, Tel.:
01709 302038

Mrs G Mennell, Senior Clinical Manager, Adult Services, Doncaster
Gate Hospital, Tel.: 01709 304834

Mrs Y Weakley, Senior Clinical Manager, Children & Young People
Services, Doncaster Gate Hospital, Tel.: 01709 304913

District Nursing

Ms M Hutchinson, Team Leader, District Nurses, Doncaster Gate
Hospital, Tel.: 01709 304867

Ms J Smith, Team Leader, District Nurses, Doncaster Gate Hospital,
Tel.: 01709 304882

Ms A Tinker, Team Leader, District Nurses, Doncaster Gate
Hospital, Tel.: 01709 304933

Equipment Loan Services

Mr M Foster, Operational Manager, Rotherham Equip & Wheelchair
Service, Chesterton Road, Eastwood Trading Estate, Rotherham,
S65 1SX, Tel.: 01709 302270

Family Planning Services

Mrs S Wigglesworth, Co-ordinator, Nurse Manager, Doncaster Gate
Hospital, Tel.: 01709 820000

Health Visitors

Ms K Bell, Team Leader, Health Visitors, Central, Doncaster Gate
Hospital, Tel.: 01709 304934

Ms J Dickinson, Team Leader, Health Visitors, Doncaster Gate
Hospital, Tel.: 01709 304818

Ms C Herbert, Team Leader, Health Visitors, Doncaster Gate
Hospital, Tel.: 01709 304828

Ms P Wake, Liaison, Health Visitor, c/o Children's Ward 3,
Rotherham District General Hospital, Moorgate Road, Rotherham,
S60 2UD, Tel.: 01709 820000 ext 7208

Learning Disabilities

Ms A Baxter, Operations Manager, (Provision), Rotherham Learning
Disability Service, 220 Badsley Moor Lane, Rotherham, S60 2QU,
Tel.: 01709 302842

Ms M Daniels, Operations Manager, (Community), Rotherham
Learning Disability Service, 220 Badsley Moor Lane, Rotherham,
S60 2QU, Tel.: 01709 302843

Pharmacy

Ms S Paddock, Community Pharmacy Advisor, Oak House,
Moorhead Way, Rotherham, S66 1YY, Tel.: 01709 302047

School Nursing

Ms S Fearnely, Special School Nursing - Hilltop School, Tel.: 01709
304913

Ms E Lees, Special School Nursing - Newman School, Tel.: 01709
304913

Ms C Phillips, Special School Nursing - Kelford School, Tel.: 01709
304913

Specialist Nursing Services

Ms L Cartlidge, Hospice at Home, Rotherham Hospice, Broom
Road, Rotherham, S60 2SW, Tel.: 01709 829900

Mrs L Mills, Aural Care, Primary Ear Care Centre, Doncaster Gate
Hospital, Tel.: 01709 304987

Mrs S Beard, Nurse Specialist, Breast Care, - Cancer, Ward B4/B5,
Rotherham District General Hospital, Moorgate Road, Rotherham,
S60 2UD, Tel.: 01709 304725

Yorkshire and The Humber SHA

Mrs J Mangnall, Nurse Advisor, Continence, Urology Suite, Rotherham District General Hospital, Tel.: 01709 304588

Mrs L Astbury, Specialist Nurse, Diabetic Care, Diabetes Centre, Rotherham District General Hospital, Tel.: 01709 307910

Mrs A Bird, Specialist Nurse, Diabetic Care, Diabetes Centre, Rotherham District General Hospital, Tel.: 01709 307921

Mrs S Gamble, Nurse Specialist, Diabetic Care, - Paediatrics, Diabetes Centre, Rotherham District General Hospital, Tel.: 01709 307921

Mrs M Hurley, Specialist Nurse, Diabetic Care, Diabetes Centre, Rotherham District General Hospital, Tel.: 01709 307910

Mrs F Smith, Clinical Nurse Specialist, Diabetic Care, Diabetes Centre, Rotherham District General Hospital, Tel.: 01709 307910

Ms A Billings, Nurse Specialist, Infection Control, Rotherham District General Hospital, Tel.: 01709 304721

Mrs M Collinson, Service Lead, Lymphoedema, Rotherham Hospice, Tel.: 01709 829900

Miss K Jones, Nurse, Macmillan, Rotherham Hospice, Tel.: 01709 829900

Mr T Lawton, Nurse, Macmillan, Rotherham Hospice, Tel.: 01709 829900

Mrs B Lund, Nurse, Macmillan, Rotherham Hospice, Tel.: 01709 829900

Mrs L Mason, Nurse, Macmillan, Rotherham Hospice, Tel.: 01709 829900

Mrs S Ripley, Nurse, Macmillan, Rotherham Hospice, Tel.: 01709 829900

Miss B Young, Nurse, Macmillan, Rotherham Hospice, Tel.: 01709 829900

Mrs K Potts, Hospice Matron, Palliative Care, Rotherham Hospice, Tel.: 01709 829900

Ms T Turton, Nurse Specialist, TB, Doncaster Gate Hospital, Tel.: 01709 304921

Mrs T Green, Nurse Specialist, Tissue Viability, Doncaster Gate Hospital, Tel.: 01709 304948

The Homeless/Travellers & Asylum Seekers

Ms J McVann, Health Worker for Young People & Homelessness, The Gate Surgery, Chatham Street, Rotherham, S65 1DT, Tel.: 01709 302660

Scarborough & N E Yorks Healthcare NHS Trust

Trust Headquarters, Scarborough Hospital
Woodlands Drive
SCARBOROUGH
North Yorkshire, YO12 6QL
Tel.: 01723 368111
Fax.: 01723 377223

Acute Specialist Nursing Services

Ms S Clarke, Colonoscopy Nurse, Scarborough Hospital, Tel.: 01723 385106

Ms P Strickland, Nurse Specialist, Acute Pain, Scarborough Hospital, Tel.: 01723 368111

Ms S Barker, Nurse Specialist, Breast Care, Scarborough Hospital, Tel.: 01723 368111 ext 2446

Ms S Ledden, Nurse Specialist, Breast Care, Scarborough Hospital, Tel.: 01723 368111 ext 2446

Ms A Ward, Nurse Specialist, Breast Care, Scarborough Hospital, Tel.: 01723 368111 ext 2446

Ms C Pye, Nurse Specialist, Chemotherapy, Scarborough Hospital, Tel.: 01723 368111 ext 2446

Ms V Tyson, Nurse Specialist, Chemotherapy, Scarborough Hospital, Tel.: 01723 368111 ext 2446

Ms L Jones, Nurse Specialist, Discharges, Scarborough Hospital, Tel.: 01723 342593

Ms S Bacon, Nurse Specialist, DVT, Scarborough Hospital, Tel.: 01723 385079

Ms K Barron, Nurse Specialist, Infection Control, Scarborough Hospital, Tel.: 01723 342484

Ms S Marquis, Nurse Specialist, Infection Control, Scarborough Hospital, Tel.: 01723 342395

Ms D Winter, Nurse Specialist, Infection Control, Scarborough Hospital, Tel.: 01723 342484

Mr G Beadle, Nurse Specialist, Palliative Care, Scarborough Hospital, Tel.: 01723 368111 ext 2446

Ms C Wilson, Nurse Specialist, Palliative Care, Scarborough Hospital, Tel.: 01723 368111 ext 2446

Ms G Almack, Nurse Specialist, Respiratory, Scarborough Hospital, Tel.: 01723 342037

Ms H Kavanagh, Nurse Specialist, Respiratory, Scarborough Hospital, Tel.: 01723 342037

Ms T Lee, Nurse, Resuscitation Training, Scarborough Hospital, Tel.: 01723 342498

Ms S Kingscott, Nurse Specialist, Rheumatology, Scarborough Hospital, Tel.: 01723 385058

Ms J Campbell, Nurse Specialist, Stoma Care, Scarborough Hospital, Tel.: 01723 368111 ext 2446

Ms A Rowe, Nurse Specialist, Stoma Care, Scarborough Hospital, Tel.: 01723 368111 ext 2446

Ms S Haigh, Nurse Specialist, Tissue Viability, Scarborough Hospital, Tel.: 01723 368111 ext 2455

Admin & Senior Management

Mrs S Harrison, Acute Services, Nurse Manager, Scarborough Hospital, Tel.: 01723 342473

Mrs H Woodward, Acute Services, Nurse Manager, Scarborough Hospital, Tel.: 01723 368111

Child Protection/Safeguarding Children

Ms S Ward, Looked After Children Nurse, Northway Cllinic, Northway, Scarborough, YO12 7AF, Tel.: 01723 342714

Ms A Kershaw, Named Nurse, Child Protection, Northway Cllinic, Northway, Scarborough, YO12 7AF, Tel.: 01723 342714

Community Midwifery

Ms M Carlin, Midwife Specialist, Early Pregnancy Assessment Unit,

Ms H Gerraughty, Labour Ward Manager, Tel.: 01723 342124

Mrs S Precious, Antenatal Screen Co-ordinator,

Ms Y Webster, SCBU Neonatal Nursing Service, Head of Midwifery, Maternity Unit, Scarborough Hospital, Tel.: 01723 342341

Matrons/Modern Matrons

Mr M Grant, Modern Matron, Acute Medicine, A & E, Tel.: 01723 368111

Mr A Mooraby, Modern Matron, Acute Medicine, Tel.: 01723 368111

Ms P Norman, Modern Matron, Acute Medicine, Tel.: 01723 368111

Ms L Gaskill, Modern Matron, Acute Surgery, Tel.: 01723 368111

Ms P Haywood Sampson, Modern Matron, Acute Surgery, Tel.: 01723 368111

Ms S Thompson, Modern Matron, Acute Surgery, Tel.: 01723 368111

Ms A Wood, Modern Matron, Acute Surgery, Tel.: 01723 368111

Ms B Young, Modern Matron, Paediatrics, Tel.: 01723 368111

Scarborough, Whitby & Ryedale Primary Care Trust

Trust Headquarters
13 Yorkersgate
MALTON
North Yorkshire
YO17 7AA
Tel.: 01653 602900
Fax.: 01653 690804

Admin & Senior Management

Mrs P Greenwood, Head of Nursing & Community Hospitals, Whitby Hospital, Spring Hill, Whitby, North Yorkshire, YO21 1DP, Tel.: 01947 824344

Child Health
Ms J Doe, Locality Manager, Northway Clinic, Scarborough, North Yorkshire, Tel.: 01723 342716
Ms J Fambely, Children In Need, Nurse Specialist, Pickering Clinic, Train Lane, Pickering, N Yorks, YO18 8DX, Tel.: 01751 472652
Child Health Records
Ms E Houlton, Head of Children & Family Services, Talbot House, 13 Queen Street, Scarborough, North Yorkshire, YO11 1HA, Tel.: 01723 508206
Child Protection/Safeguarding Children
Ms J Fambely, Children in Need Nurse Specialist, Pickering Clinic, Train Lane, Pickering, North Yorkshire, YO18 8DX, Tel.: 01751 472652
Ms A Kershaw, Child Protection Nurse Specialist, Northway Clinic, Scarborough, North Yorkshire, Tel.: 01723 342714
Ms S Ward, Child Protection & Looked After Children Nurse Specialist, Northway Clinic, Scarborough, North Yorkshire, Tel.: 01723 342747
Clinical Leads (NSF)
Ms E Houlton, Clinical Lead, Childrens Services, Talbot House, 13 Queen Street, Scarborough, North Yorkshire, YO11 1HA, Tel.: 01723 508206
Dr T McCormack, Clinical Lead, CHD, Whitby Group Practice, Whitby, Tel.: 01947 820888
Dr D Humphries, Clinical Lead, Diabetic Care, Scarborough & North East Yorkshire NHS Trust,
Mr A Lovett, Clinical Lead, Older People, SWR PCT, 13 Yorkersgate, Malton, YO17 7AA, Tel.: 01653 602900
Community Nursing Services
Mrs A Beedle, Locality Manager, Whitby Hospital, Spring Hill, Whitby, YO21 1DP, Tel.: 01947 824205
Ms J Doe, Locality Manager, Northway Clinic, Scarborough, Tel.: 01723 342716
Mrs M Stevens, Locality Manager, Malton & Norton District Hospital, Middlecave Road, Malton, Tel.: 01653 693041
District Nursing
Mrs A Beedle, Locality Manager, Whitby Hospital, Spring Hill, Whitby, YO21 1DP, Tel.: 01947 824205
Ms J Doe, Locality Manager, Northway Clinic, Scarborough, Tel.: 01723 342716
Mrs M Stevens, Locality Manager, Malton & Norton District Hospital, Middlecave Road, Malton, Tel.: 01653 693041
Equipment Loan Services
Ms S Gould, SWR PCT, Swinton Grange, Malton, YO17 6QR, Tel.: 01653 604625
Family Planning Services
Ms E Houlton, Head of Children & Family Services, Talbot House, 13 Queen Street, Scarborough, North Yorkshire, YO11 1HA, Tel.: 01723 508206
Learning Disabilities
Ms J Cleary, Locality Manager, LD, North Yorkshire House, 442-444 Scalby Road, Scarborough, YO12 6ZY, Tel.: 01723 508711
Pharmacy
Mr M Randerson, Head of Medicines Managements, SWR PCT, Swinton Grange, Malton, YO17 6QR, Tel.: 01653 604617
Smoking Cessation
Ms S Briggs, Specialist Smoking Advisor, Scarborough General Hospital, Tel.: 01723 362685
Specialist Nursing Services
Ms S Baker, Specialist Nurse, Breast Care, Scarborough General Hospital, Tel.: 01723 368111
Ms A Hollingsworth, Continence, Scarborough General Hospital, Tel.: 01723 342483
Ms M Brown, Nurse Specialist, Diabetic Care, Scarborough General Hospital, Tel.: 01723 342274
Ms M Foster, Nurse Specialist, Diabetic Care, Scarborough General Hospital, Tel.: 01723 342274

Ms S Young, Nurse Specialist, Diabetic Care, Scarborough General Hospital, Tel.: 01723 342274
Ms M Jenkins, Specialist Nurse, Infection Control, Scarborough General Hospital, Tel.: 01723 368111
Mrs J M Calvert, Community, Nurse Specialist, Macmillan, St Catherine's Hospice, High Farm, Throxenby Lane, Newby, Scarborough, YO12 5RE, Tel.: 01723 356043
Ms R Harley, Community, Nurse Specialist, Macmillan, St Catherine's Hospice, High Farm, Throxenby Lane, Newby, Scarborough, YO12 5RE, Tel.: 01723 356043
Mrs J Josey, Community, Nurse Specialist, Macmillan, St Catherine's Hospice, High Farm, Throxenby Lane, Newby, Scarborough, YO12 5RE, Tel.: 01723 356043
Mrs K Sartain, Community, Nurse Specialist, Macmillan, St Catherine's Hospice, High Farm, Throxenby Lane, Newby, Scarborough, YO12 5RE, Tel.: 01723 356043
Mr S Smart, Community, Nurse Specialist, Macmillan, St Catherine's Hospice, High Farm, Throxenby Lane, Newby, Scarborough, YO12 5RE, Tel.: 01723 356043
Mrs Jenkins, Specialist Nurse, Stoma Care, Scarborough General Hospital, Tel.: 01723 368111
Mrs U Adderley, Specialist Nurse, Tissue Viability, Malton & Norton District Hospital, Tel.: 01653 693041
The Homeless/Travellers & Asylum Seekers
Ms C Bushnaq, Care of the Homeless, 13 Queen Street, Scarborough, North Yorkshire, YO11 1HA, Tel.: 01723 508212
Ms S Stow, Care of the Homeless, 13 Queen Street, Scarborough, North Yorkshire, YO11 1HA, Tel.: 01723 508212

Selby and York Primary Care Trust

Trust Headquarters, Sovereign House
Kettlestring Lane, Clifton Moor
YORK
North Yorkshire
YO30 4GQ
Tel.: 01904 825110
Fax.: 01904 825125

Admin & Senior Management
Mr G Hardman, Lead Nurse, Sovereign House, Tel.: 01904 825125
Dr S Ross, Chief Executive, Tel.: 01904 825110
Child Health
Mr D Clark, Head of Children & Family Services, 37 Monkgate, York, YO31 7PB, Tel.: 01904 724016
Child Health Records
Pre School (East/South/West), Raincliffe Street Clinic, Selby, YO8 0AN,
Pre School (North), Easingwold Health Centre, Crabmill Lane, Easingwold, York, YO61 3BU,
School Health Records, Park Cottage, Bootham Park Hospital, York, YO30 7BT, Tel.: 01904 454880
Child Protection/Safeguarding Children
Ms B Metcalfe-Green, Looked After Children's Nurse, Tadcaster Health Centre, Crab Garth, Tadcaster, LS24 8HD, Tel.: 079040 14402
Ms S Rees, Senior Nurse Child Protection, Community Services, Tadcaster Health Centre, Crab Garth, Tadcaster, LS24 8HD, Tel.: 01937 832407
Ms S Roughton, Designated Nurse, Child Protection, Tadcaster Health Centre, Crab Garth, Tadcaster, LS24 8HD, Tel.: 01937 832407
Clinical Leads (NSF)
Dr R Markham, Clinical Lead, Cancer,
Mr A Bucklee, Clinical Lead, Care of the Elderly,
Dr K Griffith, Clinical Lead, CHD,
Mr J Khombattee, Clinical Lead, Diabetic Care,
Dr J Reid, Clinical Lead, Diabetic Care,
Mrs H Rice, Clinical Lead, Older People,

Yorkshire and The Humber SHA

Community Midwifery
Ms J Aspinall, Head of Care Services, Health & Social Care, 37 Monkgate, York, YO31 7PB, Tel.: 01904 724115

Community Nursing Services
Mrs J Aspinall, Head of Care Services, 37 Monkgate, York, YO31 7PB, Tel.: 01904 724115
Support Managers, Clementhorpe Health Centre, Cherry Street, York, YO23 1AP, Tel.: 01904 670888

District Nursing
Mrs J Aspinall, Head of Care Services, 37 Monkgate, York, YO31 7PB, Tel.: 01904 724115
District Nurses - Central, Monkgate Health Centre, 31 Monkgate, York, YO31 7WA, Tel.: 01904 724440
Ms P Keaney, District Nurses - South, Raincliffe Street Clinic, Selby, YO8 0AN, Tel.: 01757 706136
Ms V Simpson, District Nurses - North, Haxby/Wigginton Health Centre, Tel.: 01904 765982

Equipment Loan Services
Mr C Ryan, Unit 3-4, Geraldis Court, Phoenix Business Park, Hazel Court, James Street, York, YO10 3DQ, Tel.: 01904 551068

Family Planning Services
Family Planning Service, Monkgate Health Centre, 31-35 Monkgate, York, YO3 7PB, Tel.: 01904 725432
Monkgate Family Planning Clinic, Monkgate Health Centre, Monkgate, York, YO31 7WA, Tel.: 01904 630352
Personal Medical Service, Monkgate Health Centre, 31-35 Monkgate, York, YO3 7PB, Tel.: 01904 725400
Walk in Centre, Monkgate Health Centre, 31-35 Monkgate, York, YO3 7PB, Tel.: 01904 725402

Health Visitors
Health Visitors - Central, Monkgate Health Centre, 31 Monkgate, York, YO31 7WA, Tel.: 01904 724440
Ms P Keaney, Health Visitors - South, Raincliffe Street Clinic, Selby, YO8 0AN, Tel.: 01757 706136
Ms V Simpson, Health Visitors - North, Haxby/Wigginton Health Centre, Tel.: 01904 765982

Learning Disabilities
Mr J Hoult, Nurse Manager, Systems House, Amy Johnson Way, York, YO30 4GW, Tel.: 01904 724152
Ms R Jenkinson, Nurse Co-ordinator ICSS, Systems House, Amy Johnson Way, York, YO30 4GW, Tel.: 01904 724159
Mr G Terry, Head of Learning Disability Service, 37 Monkgate, York, YO31 7PB, Tel.: 01904 724098
York Team, Acomb Health Centre, 1 Beech Garden, Acomb, York, YO26 5LD, Tel.: 01904 727587

Liaison Services
Ms P Sloss, Head of User & Patient Access, Strategic Partners & Localities, 37 Monkgate, York, YO31 7PB, Tel.: 01904 724108

Specialist Nursing Services
Ms S Beckett, Head of Therapeutic & Specialist Services, 37 Monkgate, York, YO31 7PB, Tel.: 01904 724141
Ms R Horseman, Continence, Clifton Health Centre, Water Lane, Clifton, York, YO30 6PS, Tel.: 01904 727582
Nurses, Macmillan, Tadcaster Clinic, Crab Garth, Tadcaster, Tel.: 01904 724476

The Homeless/Travellers & Asylum Seekers
Mrs J Aspinall, Head of Care Services, Health & Social Care, 37 Monkgate, York, YO31 7PB, Tel.: 01904 724115

Walk In Centres
York NHS Walk-in Centre, Monkgate Health Centre, 31 Monkgate, York, YO31 7PB, Tel.: 01904 674557

Sheffield Care Trust

Trust Headquarters, Fulwood House
Old Fulwood Road
SHEFFIELD
S10 3TH
Tel.: 0114 271 6310

Admin & Senior Management
Mr T Flatley, Lead Professional (Nursing),
Ms K Green, Lead Prof. (Social Work & Social Care) The Yews,
Dr K Kendall, Lead Consultant Psychiatrist, Forest Lodge,
Dr R Warner, Lead Consultant Psychiatrist, Argyll House,

Liaison Services
Liaison Psychiatry, Longley Centre, Norwood Grange Drive, S5 7JT, Tel.: 0114 226 1621

The Homeless/Travellers & Asylum Seekers
Mr R David, Homeless Assessment & Support Team (MH), Hanover Medical Centre, William Street, Tel.: 0114 226 2525

Sheffield Children's NHS Trust

Trust Headquarters, Western Bank
SHEFFIELD
S10 2TH
Tel.: 0114 271 7000

Acute Specialist Nursing Services
Mr J Pagdin, Limb Reconstruction Service, Tel.: 0114 271 7575
Ms T Urquhart, Clinical Nurse Specialist, Late Effects, Tel.: 0114 271 7000 bleep 209
Ms L Mangle, Nurse Specialist, ADHD, Ryegate Children's Centre, Tel.: 0114 271 7640
Ms J Warburton, Nurse Specialist, ADHD, Ryegate Children's Centre, Tel.: 0114 271 7640
Ms K Holmes, Specialist Nurse, Continence, - Urology, Tel.: 0114 2260502
Ms J Searles, Specialist Nurse, Continence, - Urology, Tel.: 0114 2260502
Ms H Woodcock, Specialist Nurse, Continence, - Urology, Tel.: 0114 2260502
Ms S Bott, Specialist Nurse, Cystic Fibrosis, Tel.: 0114 271 7375
Ms J Carr, Specialist Nurse, Dermatology, Tel.: 0114 2717580
Ms C Longton, Specialist Nurse, Dermatology, Tel.: 0114 2717580
Mr M Denial, Specialist Nurse, Diabetic Care, Tel.: 0114 271 7320
Ms N Rogers, Specialist Nurse, Diabetic Care, Tel.: 0114 271 7320
Ms E Walker, Metabolic Bone, Disease, Tel.: 0114 271 7890
Ms S Carney, Specialist Nurse, Endocrine Surgery, Tel.: 0114 2717815
Ms P Hall, Specialist Nurse, Epilepsy, Tel.: 0114 271 7621
Mrs B Warden, Liaison Nurse, Epilepsy, Ryegate Children's Centre, Tel.: 0114 271 7620
Ms S Hawnt, Specialist Nurse, Gastroenterology, Tel.: 0114 2717111
Ms A Bradbury, Specialist Nurse, Genetics, Tel.: 0114 271 7032
Ms N Crawford, Specialist Nurse, Genetics, Tel.: 0114 271 7027
Ms H Fairlough, Specialist Nurse, Genetics, Tel.: 0114 271 7027
Ms V Vidler, Nurse Consultant, Haematology, Tel.: 0114 271 7329
Ms J Hobbs, Specialist Nurse, Immunology, Tel.: 0114 271 7223
Ms J Austin, Specialist Nurse, Infection Control, Tel.: 0114 271 7413
Ms J Cuffling, Specialist Nurse, Infection Control, 0114 271 7413
Mr A Beddow, Specialist Nurse, Macmillan, Tel.: 0114 271 7588
Ms L Charlish, Specialist Nurse, Oncology, Tel.: 0114 271 7588
Ms R Ducker, Specialist Nurse, Oncology, Tel.: 0114 271 7588
Mrs R Reaney, Specialist Nurse, Pain Management, Tel.: 0114 271 7000 bleep 139
Ms L Wood, Specialist Nurse, Pain Management, Tel.: 0114 271 7000 bleep 139
Ms S Carney, Auxology, Specialist Nurse, Research, Tel.: 0114 2717815
Ms H Abernathy, Specialist Nurse, Respiratory, Tel.: 0114 271 7414
Ms N Butler, Specialist Nurse, Respiratory, Tel.: 0114 271 7414
Ms A Critchlow, Specialist Nurse, Respiratory, Tel.: 0114 271 7414
Ms A Jackson, Specialist Nurse, Resuscitation Training, Tel.: 0114 271 7494
Ms T Ralph, Specialist Nurse, Resuscitation Training, 0114 271 7494
Ms S Rush, Bone Marrow, Specialist Nurse, Transplant, Tel.: 0114 271 7472

Child Protection/Safeguarding Children
Ms J Axe, Nurse Specialist, Child Protection, Child Assessment Unit, Tel.: 0114 2717675
Ms D Richardson, Nurse Specialist, Child Protection, Child Assessment Unit, Tel.: 0114 2717675
Community Nursing Services
Ms S Hubbert, Community Outreach, Specialist Nurse, Tel.: 0114 271 7435
Mr L Richardson, Community Outreach, Specialist Nurse, Tel.: 0114 271 7435
Ms S Stevens, Community Outreach, Specialist Nurse, Tel.: 0114 271 7435
Liaison Services
Liaison Health Visitor, Sheffield Children's Hospital, Western Bank, Sheffield, S10 2TH, Tel.: 0114 271 7312

Sheffield South West Primary Care Trust
Trust Headquarters, Fulwood House
5 Old Fulwood Road
SHEFFIELD
S10 3TG
Tel.: 0114 271 1100

Admin & Senior Management
Dr J Soo-Chung, Chief Executive,
Mrs J Thornton, Head of Nursing, Fulwood House, 5 Old Fulwood Road, Sheffield, S10 3TG, Tel.: 0114 271 1183
Child Health
Ms M Tudor, Service Manager, Centenary House, Heritage Park, 55 Albert Terrace Road, Sheffield, S6 3BR, Tel.: 0114 226 2010
Child Health Records
Centenary House, Tel.: 0114 226 2006
Child Protection/Safeguarding Children
Ms M Palawan, Child Protection, Centenary House, Tel.: 0114 226 2007
Clinical Leads (NSF)
Dr A Gore, Clinical Lead, Cancer,
Dr S Bradford, Clinical Lead, CHD,
Community Matrons
Ms E Darley, Community Matron, Unit E, Old Station Drive, Tel.: 114 2264100
Ms M Glaves, Community Matron, Unit E, Old Station Drive, Tel.: 114 2264100
Ms N Peterson, Community Matron, Unit E, Old Station Drive, Tel.: 114 2264100
Ms L Tilsley, Community Matron, Unit E, Old Station Drive, Tel.: 114 2264100
District Nursing
Referral Office, District Nurses, Tel.: 0114 226 4100
Equipment Loan Services
Provided by Sheffield Care Trust,
Family Planning Services
Central Health Clinic, Mulberry Street, Sheffield, S1 2PJ, Tel.: 0114 271 6816
South East Sheffield Primary Care Trust,
Health Visitors
Central Contact, Health Visitors, Tel.: 0114 226 4100
Learning Disabilities
This is covered by Sheffield Care Trust,
Liaison Services
Children's Hospital, Tel.: 0114 271 7312
Jessop Wing, Tel.: 0114 226 8264
Northern General Hospital, Tel.: 0114 271 4730/4974
Weston Park Hospital, Tel.: 0114 267 0222 ext 5306
Pharmacy
Ms L Miller, Pharmacy, Fulwood House, Fulwood, Sheffield, S10 3TG,

Specialist Nursing Services
Ms S Stainrod, Continence, 7 Edmund Road, Sheffield, S2 4EA, Tel.: 0114 271 6837
Ms B King, Tissue Viability, Manor Clinic, 18 Ridgeway Road, Sheffield, S12 2ST, Tel.: 0114 271 6416
The Homeless/Travellers & Asylum Seekers
This is covered by South East Sheffield PCT,

Sheffield Teaching Hospitals NHS Foundation Trust
Trust Headquarters
8 Beech Hill Road
SHEFFIELD
S10 2SB
Tel.: 0114 271 2251

Acute Specialist Nursing Services
Ms J Grant, PEG, Royal Hallamshire Hospital, Tel.: 0114 271 1900 ext 14014
Ms P Mark, TNF, Clinical Nurse Specialist, Royal Hallamshire Hospital, Tel.: 0114 271 1900 ext 13814
Ms J McDaid, HPB, Nurse Specialist, Royal Hallamshire Hospital,
Ms E McFarlane, Hepatology, Royal Hallamshire Hospital, Tel.: 0114 271 1900 bleep 808
Mrs J Williams, Clinical Nurse Specialist, Acute Pain, Northern General Hospital, Tel.: 0114 2434343 ext 14630
Ms B Wright, Acute Pain, Royal Hallamshire Hospital, Tel.: 0114 271 1900 ext 11659
Ms C Powell, Latex, Allergy, Royal Hallamshire Hospital, Tel.: 0114 271 1900 ext 6368
Ms L Carver, Anti-Coagulation, - Oral, Royal Hallamshire Hospital, Tel.: 0114 271 1900 ext 13820
Mr S Rollings, Anti-Coagulation, - Oral, Royal Hallamshire Hospital, Tel.: 0114 271 1900 ext 13820
Ms B Selvon, Nurse Specialist, Arthroplasty, Northern General Hospital, Tel.: 0114 226 6229 bleep 131
Ms A Thorpe, Nurse Specialist, Arthroplasty, Northern General Hospital, Tel.: 0114 226 6229 bleep 131
Ms M Henson, Asthma, Royal Hallamshire Hospital, Tel.: 0114 271 1900 ext 12879
Mrs F Armitage, Clinical Nurse Specialist, Breast Care, Royal Hallamshire Hospital, Tel.: 0114 271 3311
Ms J Beauman, Macmillan, Clinical Nurse Specialist, Breast Care, Weston Park Hospital, Tel.: 0114 226 5328
Ms K Flint, Breast Care, Royal Hallamshire Hospital, Tel.: 0114 271 1900 ext 13311
Mrs A Gray, Clinical Nurse Specialist, Breast Care, Royal Hallamshire Hospital, Tel.: 0114 271 3311
Ms S Thompson, Breast Care, Royal Hallamshire Hospital, Tel.: 0114 271 1900 ext 14211
Ms J Ashworth, Cardiac, Royal Hallamshire Hospital, Tel.: 0114 271 1900 ext 15395
Ms Y Davenport, Co-ordinator, Cardiac, Royal Hallamshire Hospital, Tel.: 0114 271 1900 ext 15598
Ms T Thompson, Support, Cardiac, Royal Hallamshire Hospital, Tel.: 0114 271 1900 ext 15395
Mr S Nicol, Co-ordinator, Chronic Pain, Northern General Hospital, Tel.: 0114 2434343 ext 15218
Ms D Poole, Chronic Pain, Royal Hallamshire Hospital, Tel.: 0114 271 1900 ext 13648
Ms J Dean, Nurse Consultant, Colorectal, Northern General Hospital, Tel.: 0114 226 6182
Ms S Alcock, Continence, Royal Hallamshire Hospital, Tel.: 0114 271 1900 ext 14187
Ms R Simmons, Continence, Royal Hallamshire Hospital, Tel.: 0114 271 1900 ext 11774

Yorkshire and The Humber SHA

Ms A Humphrey, Macmillan, Continuing Care, Northern General Hospital, Tel.: 0114 271 1900 ext 14940

Ms L Hewitt, COPD, Royal Hallamshire Hospital, Tel.: 0114 271 1900 ext 66388

Ms J Higgs, COPD, Royal Hallamshire Hospital, Tel.: 0114 271 1900 ext 66388

Ms T Ingle, COPD, Royal Hallamshire Hospital, Tel.: 0114 271 1900 ext 12979

Ms T Ward, COPD, Royal Hallamshire Hospital, Tel.: 0114 271 1900 ext 12979

Ms P Field, Rehabilitation, Coronary Care, Royal Hallamshire Hospital, Tel.: 0114 271 1900 ext 14588

Ms M Sharpe, Rehab, Coronary Care, Royal Hallamshire Hospital, Tel.: 0114 271 1900 ext 14588

Ms S Murray, Cystic Fibrosis, Royal Hallamshire Hospital, Tel.: 0114 271 1900 bleep 658

Ms A Percival, Cystic Fibrosis, Royal Hallamshire Hospital, Tel.: 0114 271 1900 ext 66281

Ms L Butler, Dermatology, Royal Hallamshire Hospital, Tel.: 0114 271 1900 ext 13795

Ms S Beverdige, Diabetic Care, Royal Hallamshire Hospital, Tel.: 0114 271 1900 ext 14445

Ms V Scott, Diabetic Care, Royal Hallamshire Hospital, Tel.: 0114 271 1900 ext 15620

Ms M Sutton, Diabetic Care, Royal Hallamshire Hospital, Tel.: 0114 271 1900 ext 13481

Ms C Taylor, Diabetic Care, Royal Hallamshire Hospital, Tel.: 0114 271 1900 ext 13481

Ms K Towse, Diabetic Care, Royal Hallamshire Hospital, Tel.: 0114 271 1900 ext 13481

Ms J Everard, Gest. Trophoblastic, Clinical Nurse Specialist, Disease, Weston Park Hospital, Tel.: 0114 2265000 ext 65205

Ms K Dunkley, Endocrine Surgery, Royal Hallamshire Hospital, Tel.: 0114 271 1900 ext 13714

Ms V Ibbotson, Endocrine Surgery, Royal Hallamshire Hospital, Tel.: 0114 271 1900 ext 15412

Ms B Roberts, Endocrine Surgery, Royal Hallamshire Hospital, Tel.: 0114 271 1900 ext 13714

Ms J Kelly, Endoscopy, Royal Hallamshire Hospital, Tel.: 0114 271 1900 ext

Ms L Winship, Endoscopy, Royal Hallamshire Hospital, Tel.: 0114 271 1900 ext 12166

Ms J Collins, Epilepsy, Royal Hallamshire Hospital, Tel.: 0114 271 1900 ext 12186

Ms S A Collins, Epilepsy, Royal Hallamshire Hospital, Tel.: 0114 271 1900 ext 12186

Ms J Gore, Epilepsy, Royal Hallamshire Hospital, Tel.: 0114 271 1900 ext 12186

Ms S Kuc, Epilepsy, Royal Hallamshire Hospital, Tel.: 0114 271 1900 ext 12186

Ms C McMulkin, Epilepsy, Royal Hallamshire Hospital, Tel.: 0114 271 1900 ext 12186

Ms C Wilson, Epilepsy, Royal Hallamshire Hospital, Tel.: 0114 271 1900 ext 12186

Ms S Buckton, Gastroenterology, Royal Hallamshire Hospital, Tel.: 0114 271 1900 ext 12209

Ms R Colllins, Gastroenterology, Royal Hallamshire Hospital, Tel.: 0114 271 1900 ext 12209

Ms B Furniss, Macmillan, GI, Royal Hallamshire Hospital, Tel.: 0114 271 1900 ext 66072

Mrs P Hutson, Nurse Practitioner, GI, Northern General Hospital, Tel.: 0114 271 5117

Mrs K Smith, Nurse Consultant, GI, - Endoscopy, Northern General Hospital, Tel.: 0114 271 5117

Ms T Slater, Gynaecology, Royal Hallamshire Hospital, Tel.: 0114 271 1900 ext 68315

Ms V Fairley, Clinical Nurse Specialist, Haematology, Royal Hallamshire Hospital, Tel.: 0114 271 1900 ext 12075

Ms J Farnsworth, Haematology, Royal Hallamshire Hospital, Tel.: 0114 271 1900 ext 13211

Ms A Foster, Macmillan, Haematology, Royal Hallamshire Hospital, Tel.: 0114 271 1900 ext 12075

Ms F Marry, Macmillan, Haematology, Royal Hallamshire Hospital, Tel.: 0114 271 1900 ext 12075

Ms M Ward, Macmillan Nurse, Haematology, Royal Hallamshire Hospital, Tel.: 0114 271 1900 ext 13629

Ms T White, Clinical Nurse Specialist, Head & Neck, Royal Hallamshire Hospital, Tel.: 0114 226 8776

Ms F Ashworth, Immunology, Northern General, Tel.: 0114 271 1900 ext 66964

Ms P Hempshall, Infection Control, Royal Hallamshire Hospital, Tel.: 0114 271 1900 ext 13120

Ms J Linskill, Infection Control, Royal Hallamshire Hospital, Tel.: 0114 271 1900 ext 13120

Ms W Smith, Infection Control, Royal Hallamshire Hospital, Tel.: 0114 271 1900 ext 14569

Ms L Young, Infection Control, Royal Hallamshire Hospital, Tel.: 0114 271 1900 ext 14569

Ms S Naylor, Clinical Nurse Specialist, Infectious Diseases, - HIV, Royal Hallamshire Hospital, Tel.: 0114 271 1900 ext 12884

Mr R Poll, Nurse Consultant, Infectious Diseases, - Hepatitis, Royal Hallamshire Hospital, Tel.: 0114 271 1900 ext 11776

Ms M Vincent, Nurse Specialist, Limb Reconstruction, Northern General Hospital, Tel.: 0114 2266 bleep 507

Ms A Clegg, Nurse Specialist, Lung Cancer, Northern General Hospital, Tel.: 0114 226 6956

Ms P Munro, Nurse Specialist, Lung Cancer, Northern General Hospital, Tel.: 0114 226 6956

Ms A Sorsby, Nurse Specialist, Lung Cancer, Weston Park Hospital, Tel.: 0114 226 5000 bleep 356

Ms H Stanley, Nurse Specialist, Lung Cancer, Royal Hallamshire Hospital, Tel.: 0114 226 1499 ext 61499

Mr P Saunders, Macmillan, Northern General Hospital, Tel.: 0114 271 1900 ext 14940

Ms V Edwards, Metabolic, Medicine, Northern General Hospital, Tel. 0114 271 1900 ext 66546

Ms E Cam, Multiple Sclerosis, Royal Hallamshire Hospital, Tel.: 0114 271 1900 ext 12302

Ms A Cox, Multiple Sclerosis, Royal Hallamshire Hospital, Tel.: 0114 271 1900 ext 12302

Ms K Kay, Multiple Sclerosis, Royal Hallamshire Hospital, Tel.: 0114 271 1900 ext 12302

Ms D Watts, Multiple Sclerosis, Royal Hallamshire Hospital, Tel.: 0114 271 1900 ext 12302

Ms H Nixon, Neuromuscular, Neurology, Royal Hallamshire Hospital Tel.: 0114 271 1900 ext 12186

Ms J Rowney, Neuro Support, Neurology, Royal Hallamshire Hospital, Tel.: 0114 271 1900 ext 12690

Ms S Ryles, Neuromuscular, Neurology, Royal Hallamshire Hospital Tel.: 0114 271 1900 ext 12186

Ms T Walsh, Neuromuscular, Neurology, Royal Hallamshire Hospita Tel.: 0114 271 1900 ext 13431

Mrs H Lee, Macmillan, Neuro-oncology, Royal Hallamshire Hospital, Tel.: 0114 271 1900 ext 12019

Ms J Genge, Neurosurgery, Royal Hallamshire Hospital, Tel.: 0114 271 1900

Mrs L Gunn, Neurosurgery, Royal Hallamshire Hospital, Tel.: 0114 271 1900

Ms K Maden, IV, Nutrition, Royal Hallamshire Hospital, Tel.: 0114 271 1900 ext 3135

Ms R Jacques, Ophthalmology, Royal Hallamshire Hospital, Tel.: 0114 271 1900 ext 12422

Ms T Lingard, Infant Feeding Support, Paediatrics, Royal Hallamshire Hospital, Tel.: 0114 271 1900 ext 68249

Ms J Newell, Macmillan, Clinical Nurse Specialist, Palliative Care, Central Campus, Royal Hallamshire Hospital, Tel.: 0114 271 2307

Yorkshire and The Humber SHA

Ms S Richardson, Macmillan, Clinical Nurse Specialist, Palliative Care, Central Campus, Royal Hallamshire Hospital, Tel.: 0114 271 2307

Ms D Saunby, Macmillan, Clinical Nurse Specialist, Palliative Care, Central Campus, Royal Hallamshire Hospital, Tel.: 0114 271 2307

Ms J Siddall, Clinical Nurse Specialist, Palliative Care, Central Campus, Weston Park Hospital, Tel.: 0114 226 5000 bleep 318

Ms A Franks, Parkinson's Disease, Royal Hallamshire Hospital, Tel.: 0114 271 1900 ext 11704

Ms L Nelson, Parkinson's Disease, Royal Hallamshire Hospital, Tel.: 0114 271 1900 ext 11704

Ms R Berry, Plastics & Reconstructive Surg Support, Plastic Surgery, Royal Hallamshire Hospital, Tel.: 0114 271 1900 ext 14708

Ms S Bratley, Nurse Practitioner, Pre-Operative, Northern General Hospital, Tel.: 0114 226 6369

Ms E Carrington, Nurse Practitioner, Pre-Operative, Northern General Hospital, Tel.: 0114 226 6369

Ms J Hitchens, Nurse Practitioner, Pre-Operative, Northern General Hospital, Tel.: 0114 226 6369

Ms N Stoford, Nurse Practitioner, Pre-Operative, Northern General Hospital, Tel.: 0114 226 6369

Ms M Walker, Nurse Practitioner, Pre-Operative, Northern General Hospital, Tel.: 0114 226 6369

Mr I Armstrong, Pulmonary Hypertension, Pulmonary Disorder, Royal Hallamshire Hospital, Tel.: 0114 271 1900 ext 11719

Ms L Tann, Hypertension, Pulmonary Disorder, Royal Hallamshire Hospital, Tel.: 0114 271 1900 ext 11719

Ms A Cooper, General, Rehabilitation, Royal Hallamshire Hospital, Tel.: 0114 271 1900 ext 11770

Community Team, Renal, Royal Hallamshire Hospital, Tel.: 0114 271 1900 ext 15143

Ms J Hine, Specialist Counsellor, Renal, Royal Hallamshire Hospital, Tel.: 0114 271 1900 ext 15325

Ms D Kendray, Pre Treatment Advisor, Renal, Royal Hallamshire Hospital, Tel.: 0114 271 1900 ext 15438

Ms K Ambler, Nurse, Research, Tel.: 0114 271 5887

Ms C Daniel, Respiratory, Royal Hallamshire Hospital, Tel.: 0114 271 1900 ext 14668

Ms H Till, Resuscitation Training, Royal Hallamshire Hospital, Tel.: 0114 271 1900 ext 14668

Ms K Bruce, Clinical Nurse Specialist, Rheumatology, Royal Hallamshire Hospital, Tel.: 0114 271 1900 ext 11958

Ms N Nasell, Clinical Nurse Specialist, Rheumatology, Royal Hallamshire Hospital, Tel.: 0114 271 1900 ext 13806

Ms N Newell, Clinical Nurse Specialist, Rheumatology, Royal Hallamshire Hospital, Tel.: 0114 271 1900 ext 13086

Ms G Bell, Nurse Consultant, Sexual Health, - GUM, Royal Hallamshire Hospital, Tel.: 0114 271 1900 ext 13526

Ms P Muter, Neurogenic Bladder Specialist, Spinal Injuries, Northern General Hospital, Tel.: 0114 271 1900 ext 15624

Ms L Wright, Neurogenic Bladder Specialist, Spinal Injuries, Northern General Hospital, Tel.: 0114 271 1900 ext 15624

Ms V Goodfellow, Clinical Nurse Specialist, Stoma Care, Northern General Hospital, Tel.: 0114 226 9197

Mr A Tappe, Clinical Nurse Specialist, Stoma Care, Royal Hallamshire Hospital, Tel.: 0114 271 2056

Mrs K Totty, Clinical Nurse Specialist, Stoma Care, Northern General Hospital, Tel.: 0114 226 9261

Ms E Atkin, Co-ordinator, Stroke Care, Royal Hallamshire Hospital, Tel.: 0114 271 1900

Ms S Barnston, Liaison, Stroke Care, Royal Hallamshire Hospital, Tel.: 0114 271 1900 ext 11834

Ms C Doyle, Stroke Care, Royal Hallamshire Hospital, Tel.: 0114 271 900 ext 12186

Ms C Kamara, Stroke Care, Royal Hallamshire Hospital, Tel.: 0114 271 1900 ext 61222

Ms H Knight, Co-ordinator, Stroke Care, Royal Hallamshire Hospital, Tel.: 0114 271 1900 bleep 742

Ms F Purdy, Co-ordinator, Stroke Care, Royal Hallamshire Hospital, Tel.: 0114 271 1900 ext 15180

Ms K Parker, Tissue Viability, Royal Hallamshire Hospital, Tel.: 0114 271 1900 ext 12489

Ms C Charley, Bone Marrow Co-ordinator, Transplant, Royal Hallamshire Hospital, Tel.: 0114 271 1900 ext 12263

Ms H Jessop, Bone Marrow Co-ordinator, Transplant, Royal Hallamshire Hospital, Tel.: 0114 271 1900 ext 12263

Ms V Lennon, Regional Co-ordinator, Transplant, Royal Hallamshire Hospital, Tel.: 0114 271 1900 ext 15138

Ms S Siddall, Regional Co-ordinator, Transplant, Royal Hallamshire Hospital, Tel.: 0114 271 1900 ext 15138

Ms J Bickerstaff, Nurse Specialist, Upper GI, - Pancreatic, Royal Hallamshire Hospital, Tel.: 0114 266 8755

Ms P Allen, Urology, Royal Hallamshire Hospital, Tel.: 0114 271 1900 ext 12498

Ms R Lochiel, Vascular, Royal Hallamshire Hospital, Tel.: 0114 271 1900 ext 14688

Ms H Trender, Vascular, Royal Hallamshire Hospital, Tel.: 0114 271 1900 ext 14688

Ms M Yates, Vascular, Royal Hallamshire Hospital, Tel.: 0114 271 1900 ext 14688

Admin & Senior Management

Mrs H Drabble, Chief Nurse, Chief Nurse's Office, 8 Beech Hill Road, Sheffield, S10 2SB, Tel.: 0114 271 2251

Ms A Smith, Deputy Chief Nurse, Chief Nurse's Office, 8 Beech Hill Road, Sheffield, S10 2SB, Tel.: 0114 226 1459

Child Protection/Safeguarding Children

Ms S Clarke, Matron, Child Protection, Jessop Wing, Royal Hallamshire Hospital, Tree Root Walk, Sheffield, S10 2SF, Tel.: 0114 226 8147

Mrs H Goodison, Midwife, Child Protection, Jessop Wing, Royal Hallamshire Hospital, Tree Root Walk, Sheffield, S10 2SF, Tel.: 0114 226 8453

Community Midwifery

Community Midwifery Liaison Office, 0800-1630 hours, Tel.: 0114 226 8301

Duty Matron, Jessop Wing, Royal Hallamshire Hospital, Tree Root Walk, Sheffield, S10 2SF, Tel.: 0114 271 1900 bleep 902

Miss D Watkins, Nurse Director, Head of Midwifery, Jessop Wing, Royal Hallamshire Hospital, Tree Root Walk, Sheffield, S10 2SF, Tel.: 0114 226 8295

Discharge Co-ordinators

Ms M Kent, Admission & Discharge, Neurosurgery, Royal Hallamshire, Tel.: 0114 271 1900 ext 68839

Liaison Services

Ms L Browell, Co-ordinator - Discharge, Northern General Hospital, Herries Road, Sheffield, S5 7AU, Tel.: 0114 243 4343 ext 14368

Ms J Buchanan, Community Liaison Sister, Weston Park Hospital, Whitham Road, Sheffield, S10 2SJ, Tel.: 0114 226 5306

Ms M Dudley, Discharge Specialist, Royal Hallamshire Hospital, Glossop Road, Sheffield, S10 2JF, Tel.: 0114 271 1900 ext 13464

Ms N Furniss, Discharge Specialist, Royal Hallamshire Hospital, Glossop Road, Sheffield, S10 2JF, Tel.: 0114 271 1900 ext 13464

Ms A Hall, Rehab, Northern General Hospital, Herries Road, Sheffield, S5 7AU, Tel.: 0114 243 4343 ext 14757

Ms Y Matthews, Intermediate Care, Northern General Hospital, Herries Road, Sheffield, S5 7AU, Tel.: 0114 243 4343 ext 14757

Mrs M Norfolk, Maternity Liaison Service, Jessop Wing, Royal Hallamshire Hospital, Tree Root Walk, S10 2SF, Tel.: 0114 226 8301

Ms R Sykes, Discharge Specialist, Royal Hallamshire Hospital, Glossop Road, Sheffield, S10 2JF, Tel.: 0114 271 1900 ext 13464

Matrons/Modern Matrons

Ms J Barnes, Modern Matron, Tel.: 0114 271 2681

Ms C Jameson, Modern Matron, Tel.: 0114 271 3693

Mrs A Edis, Bone Surgery, Metabolic Bone Unit, Northern General Hospital, Tel.: 0114 271 1900 ext 6148

Yorkshire and The Humber SHA

Ms M J Coates, Modern Matron, General Surgery, Royal Hallamshire Hospital, Tel.: 0114 271 2904

Mrs K Gott, Modern Matron, General Surgery, Northern General Hospital, Tel.: 0114 271 4600

Mrs D Driscoll, GU Medicine, Royal Hallamshire Hospital, Tel.: 0114 271 1900 ext 13541

Mr M Salt, Haematology, Royal Hallamshire Hospital, Tel.: 0114 271 1900 ext 13629

Mr M Salt, Immunology, - Palliative Care, Northern General Hospital, Tel.: 0114 271 1900 ext 13629

Mrs J Clohessy, Infectious Diseases, Royal Hallamshire Hospital, Tel.: 0114 271 1900 ext 13545

Mrs J Marsden, Infectious Diseases, Royal Hallamshire Hospital, Tel.: 0114 271 1900 ext 13545

Ms S Wesley, Modern Matron, Neurosurgery, Royal Hallamshire Hospital, Tel.: 0114 271 1900 ext 13610

Ms A Jarvis, Modern Matron, Orthopaedics, Out-Patients Department, Northern General Hospital, Tel.: 0114 226 6227

Ms K Stone, Modern Matron, Orthopaedics, Northern General Hospital, Tel.: 0114 271 4486

Mrs A Edis, Rheumatology, - Dermatology, Royal Hallamshire Hospital, Tel.: 0114 271 1900 ext 6148

Mrs S Browton, Spinal Injuries, M & SRC Unit, Northern General Hospital, Tel.: 0114 271 1900 ext 15655

Other Services

Ms M Martin, Substance Misuse Midwife, Jessop Wing, Royal Hallamshire Hospital, Tree Root Walk, Sheffield, S10 2SF, Tel.: 0114 271 1900 ext 68114

Sheffield West Primary Care Trust

Trust Headquarters, West Court
Hillsborough Barracks, Langsett Road
SHEFFIELD, S6 2LR
Tel.: 0114 226 4600

Admin & Senior Management
Mr S Gilby, Chief Executive, West Court, Hillsborough Barracks, Langsett Road, Sheffield, S6 2LR, Tel.: 0114 2264600

Child Protection/Safeguarding Children
Ms K Devlin, Child Protection, Centenary House, Heritage Park, Albert Terrace Road, Sheffield, S6 3BR, Tel.: 0114 226 2007

Community Matrons
Mrs J Morgan, Director of Operations, West Court, Hillsborough Barracks, Langsett Road, Sheffield, S6 2LR, Tel.: 0114 2264654

District Nursing
Mrs J Morgan, Director of Operations, West Court, Hillsborough Barracks, Langsett Road, Sheffield, S6 2LR, Tel.: 0114 2264654

Health Visitors
Mrs J Morgan, Director of Operations, West Court, Hillsborough Barracks, Langsett Road, Sheffield, S6 2LR, Tel.: 0114 2264654

South East Sheffield Primary Care Trust

Trust Headquarters, 9 Orgreave Road
Handsworth
SHEFFIELD, S13 9LQ
Tel.: 0114 226 4050
Fax.: 0114 226 4051

Admin & Senior Management
Ms J Mason, Director of Clinical Services, SE PCT, 9 Orgreave Road, Handsworth, Sheffield, S13 9LQ, Tel.: 0114 226 2421

Ms S Nutbrown, Acting Lead Nurse, Mosborough Health Centre, 34 Queen Street, Sheffield, S20 5BQ, Tel.: 0114-08451 222 423

Child Protection/Safeguarding Children
Ms F Cunnin, Acting Director of Public Health, SE PCT, 9 Orgreave Road, Handsworth, Sheffield, S13 9LQ, Tel.: 0114 226 2455

Ms J Palmer, Child Protection Advisor, Centenary House, Heritage Park, 55 Albert Terrace Road, Sheffield, S6 3BR, Tel.: 0114 226 2141

Clinical Leads (NSF)
Dr P Hodgkin, Clinical Lead, Cancer, Richmond Medical Centre, 462 Richmond Road, Sheffield, S13 8NA, Tel.: 0114-08451 252 531

Dr B J Hopkins, Clinical Lead, CHD, Whitehouse Surgery, 189 Prince of Wales Road, Sheffield, S2 1FA, Tel.: 0114-08451 227 587

Dr D Judge, Clinical Lead, Diabetic Care, SE PCT, 9 Orgeave Road, Handsworth, Sheffield, S13 9LQ, Tel.: 0114 226 2429

Ms J Watson, Clinical Lead, Older People, Charnock Health Centre, 203 White Lane, Sheffield, S12 3GG, Tel.: 0114 226 2832

District Nursing
Ms E Wragg, Manor Clinic, 18 Ridgeway Road, Sheffield, S12 2ST, Tel.: 0114 2716403

Family Planning Services
Dr H King, Consultant Family Planning & Sexual Health Services, Central Health Clinic, 1 Mulberry Street, Sheffield, S1 2PJ, Tel.: 0114 271 8851

Health Visitors
Ms B Long, Liaison, Health Visitor, Jessop Wing, Royal Hallamshire Hospital, Glossop Road, Sheffield, S10 2JF, Tel.: 0114 271 1900

Pharmacy
Ms C Nash, Chief Practice Pharmacist, SE PCT, 9 Orgreave Road, Handsworth, Sheffield, S13 9LQ, Tel.: 0114 226 4062

School Nursing
Ms M Tudor, Service Manager, School Nursing, Centenary House, Hertiage Park, 55 Albert Terrace Rd, Sheffield, S6 3BR, Tel.: 0114 226 2148

Smoking Cessation
Ms J Carter, Lead Development Nurse, SE PCT, 9 Orgreave Road, Handsworth, Sheffield, S13 9LQ, Tel.: 0114 226 4061

Ms S Plant, Stop Smoking Specialist, SE PCT, 9 Orgreave Road, Handsworth, Sheffield, S13 9LQ, Tel.: 0114 226 2402

The Homeless/Travellers & Asylum Seekers
Ms K Crapper, Traveller Health, Central Health Clinic, 1 Mulberry Street, Sheffield, S1 2PJ, Tel.: 0114 226 1741

Ms S Givans, Homeless Assessment Support Team (HAST), Hanover Medical Centre, 100 William Street, Sheffield, S10 2EB, Tel.: 0114 226 2527

South Huddersfield Primary Care Trust

Trust Headquarters, St Luke's House
Blackmoorfoot Road
Crosland Moor
HUDDERSFIELD
HD4 5RH
Tel.: 01484 466000

Admin & Senior Management
Ms D Campbell, Deputy Director of Primary Care, St Luke's House, Tel.: 01484 466000

Ms S Greig, Deputy Director of Public Health, St Luke's House, Tel.: 01484 466000

Mr K Holder, Chief Executive, St Luke's House,

Ms G Ruddlesdin, Deputy Director of Primary Care, St Luke's House Tel.: 01484 466000

Child Health Records
Ms G Ruddlesdin, Deputy Director of Primary Care, St Luke's House Tel.: 01484 466000

Child Protection/Safeguarding Children
Ms P Hughes, Child Protection, Mill Hill Health Centre, Tel.: 01484 347854

Ms A Logue, Child Protection, Mill Hill Health Centre, Tel.: 01484 347854

Clinical Leads (NSF)
Dr S Bhatti, Director of Public Health,
Ms D Campbell, Programme Manager - Sure Start,
Ms D Lewis, Clinical Lead, HRI,
Ms C McKenna, Director of Commissioning & Service Dev.,

District Nursing
Ms G Ruddlesdin, Deputy Director of Primary Care, St Luke's House, Blackmoorfoot Road, Crosland Moor, Huddersfield, HD4 5RH, Tel.: 01484 466000

Family Planning Services
Ms G Ruddlesdin, Deputy Director of Primary Care, St Luke's House, Blackmoorfoot Road, Crosland Moor, Huddersfield, HD4 5RH, Tel.: 01484 345602

Health Visitors
Mrs J Henderson, TB Specialist Nurse, Health Visitor, Princess Royal Community Health Centre, Greenhead Road, Huddersfield, HD1 4EW, Tel.: 01484 344322

Mrs J Martland, STD, Health Visitor, GUM Clinic, Princess Royal Community Health Centre, Greenhead Road, Huddersfield, HD1 4EW, Tel.: 01484 344311

Mrs J Worth, STD, Health Visitor, GUM Clinic, Princess Royal Community Health Centre, Greenhead Road, Huddersfield, HD1 4EW, Tel.: 01484 344311

HIV/AIDS
Ms H Horton, Assistant Director Commissionng & Service Development, St Luke's House, Tel.: 01484 344311

Liaison Services
Liaison - Elderly, Huddersfield Royal Infirmary, Acre Street, Lindley, Huddersfield, HD3 3EA, Tel.: 01484 342000

Other Services
Mrs D Lewis, Practice Development Unit, St Luke's Hospital, Crosland Moor, Huddersfield, HD4 5RQ, Tel.: 01484 343000 ext 3630

Specialist Nursing Services
Ms V Walker, Breast Care, Huddersfield Royal Infirmary, Tel.: 01484 342000 ext 2827

Ms J Whiteley, Continence, Fartown Health Centre, Spaines Road, Fartown, HD2 2QA,

Ms E Jobes, Specialist Nurse, Diabetic Care, Princess Royal Community Health Centre, Greenhead Road, Huddersfield, HD1 4EW, Tel.: 01484 344269

Ms L Redding, Nurse, Stoma Care, Huddersfield Royal Infirmary, Tel.: 01484 342000 ext 2607

Ms S Milburn, Nurse, Tissue Viability, Huddersfield Royal Infirmary, Tel.: 01484 342000 ext 2102

The Homeless/Travellers & Asylum Seekers
Ms D Farmer, The Whitehouse, 23A New North Parade, Huddersfield, HD1 5JU, Tel.: 01484 301911 ext 7713

South Leeds Primary Care Trust
Trust Headquarters, Navigation House
George Mann Road, Quayside Business Park
LEEDS
LS10 1DJ
Tel.: 0113 3059 666

Admin & Senior Management
Miss T Cannell, Director of Clinical Services, Navigation House, 8 George Mann Road, Quayside Business Park, Leeds, LS10 1DJ, Tel.: 0113 3059 740

Mrs S Sinclair, Director of Nursing & Professional Development, Navigation House, 8 George Mann Road, Quayside Business Park, Leeds, LS10 1DJ, Tel.: 0113 305 9688

Child Health
Hosted by East Leeds PCT,

Child Protection/Safeguarding Children
Hosted by East Leeds PCT,

Clinical Leads (NSF)
Miss L Hollingsworth, Clinical Lead, Cancer,
Miss P Andrewartha, Clinical Lead, Care of the Elderly,
Miss K Naylor, Clinical Lead, CHD,
Miss S Lunn, Clinical Lead, Diabetic Care,

Community Nursing Services
Ms H Childs, Assistant Director - Service Delivery, St Georges Centre, St Georges Way, Middleton, Leeds, LS10 4UZ, Tel.: 0113 392 9877

District Nursing
Ms H Childs, Assistant Director - Service Delivery, St Georges Centre, St Georges Way, Middleton, Leeds, LS10 4UZ, Tel.: 0113 392 9877

Family Planning Services
Mr N Fittock, Head of Service, James Reed House, Beeston Village Medical Centre, Tel.: 0113 295 3359

Learning Disabilities
Ms K Padgett, Locality Manager, Beeston Community Clinic, Tel.: 0113 295 4900

Other Services
Ms D Atherton, Intermediate Care, Morley Health Centre, Tel.: 0113 295 4600

Pharmacy
Mr A Hutchinson, Head of Medicines Management, Tel.: 0113 305 9712

Specialist Nursing Services
Ms K Naylor, BHF, Nurse, CHD, Navigation House, 8 George Mann Road, Quayside Business Park, Leeds, LS10 1DJ, Tel.: 0113 3059 666

Ms J Sutcliffe, Nurse, COPD, Hunslet Health Centre, Tel.: 0113 277 1811

The Homeless/Travellers & Asylum Seekers
Dr R Turner, Director of Public Health, Navigation House, 8 George Mann Road, Quayside Business Park, Leeds, LS10 1DJ, Tel.: 0113 305 9705

South West Yorkshire Mental Health NHS Trust
Trust Headquarters, Fernbank
3-5 St John's North
WAKEFIELD
West Yorkshire
WF1 3QD
Tel.: 01924 814814

Learning Disabilities
Ms C Buchanan, Unit Manager, Greenhead Resource Unit, 24 Greenhead Road, Huddersfield, HD1 4EN, Tel.: 01484 347600

Ms S Eccles, Learning Difficulties Team, Community Nurse, Tel.: 01422 841123 or 393773

Mr J Markiewicz, Clinical Director, Calder Valley Team, Hebden Bridge Health Centre, Hangingroyd Lane, Hebden Bridge, West Yorkshire, HX7 6AG, Tel.: 01422 841123

Mrs J Smith, Clinical Nurse Manager, Dewsbury Learning Disability Team, The Resource Centre, Cullingworth Street, Dewsbury, WF13 4AN, Tel.: 01924 816275

Mr T Whelan, Services Manager, Ackworth Villa, Fieldhead Hospital, Wakefield, Tel.: 01924 327481

Wakefield West Primary Care Trust
Trust Headquarters, White Rose House
West Parade
WAKEFIELD, WF1 1LT
Tel.: 01924 213050
Fax.: 01924 213157

Admin & Senior Management
Mr A Geldart, Chief Executive, Tel.: 01924 213136

Mrs A Robinson, Director of Nursing & Operational Services, Tel.: 01924 213021

Child Health Records
Child Health Dept, Castleford & Normanton District Hospital, Hightown, Castleford, WF10 5LT, Tel.: 01977 605519/605555

Yorkshire and The Humber SHA

Child Protection/Safeguarding Children
Mr C Hall, Safeguarding Children, Nurse Consultant, Castleford &
Normanton District Hospital, Tel.: 01977 605577
Clinical Leads (NSF)
Dr J Lawn, Clinical Lead, CHD,
Dr J Wilson, Clinical Lead, Older People,
District Nursing
Ms B Crawford, Assistant Director, Children & Family Services,
Health Visitors, Tel.: 01924 213205
Ms A Gill, Assistant Director Adult Services, District Nurses, Tel.:
01924 213232
Mrs A Robinson, Director of Nursing & Operational Services, Tel.:
01924 213021
Family Planning Services
Margaret Street Clinic, Wakefield, WF1 2DQ, Tel.: 01924 327586
Health Visitors
Ms B Crawford, Assistant Director, Health Visitors, Children & Family
Services, Tel.: 01924 213205
Specialist Nursing Services
Ms M Burt, Modern Matron, White Rose House, West Parade,
Wakefield, WF1 1LT, Tel.: 01924 213022
Ms J Wilson, Matron, Continuing Care, Pinderfields Hospital, Tel.:
01924 213800
Ms T Cragis, Matron, Intermediate Care, Trinity Business Park, Tel.:
01924 398068
Nurses, Palliative Care, Pinderfields General Hospital, Aberford
Road, Wakefield, WF1 4DG, Tel.: 01924 213658
Ms T Cooper, Community Matron, Physical Disability, Community
Equipment Services, Trinity Business Park, Tel.: 01924 327198
Ms A Ogilrie, Nurse Practitioner, Practice Development, White Rose
House, West Parade, Wakefield, WF1 1LT, Tel.: 01924 213162
Ms F Stainthorpe, Facilitator, Practice Development, White Rose
House, West Parade, Wakefield, WF1 1LT, Tel.: 01924 213174
Ms L Williamson, Community Matron, Rehabilitation, Trinity Business
Park, Tel.: 01924 398068
Ms L Shyman, Nurse Specialist, TB, Community Equipment
Services, Trinity Business Park,
Ms C Brown, Tissue Viability, Elm Bank, Wakefield, WF1 4LH, Tel.:
01924 327112
Ms J Newbold, Tissue Viability, Elm Bank, Wakefield, WF1 4LH, Tel.:
01924 327112

West Hull Primary Care Trust

Trust Headquarters,
Brunswick House
Strand Close
HULL
HU2 9DB
Tel.: 01482 317000

Admin & Senior Management
Mr A Burnell, Director of Primary Health Care Services, Brunswick
House, Strand Close, Hull, HU2 9DB, Tel.: 01482 317031
Mr M Douggan, Head of -S/A PR. Care Services, Orchard Park
Health Centre, Ellerburn Avenue, Hull, Tel.: 01482 857191
Mrs Y Edwards, Head of Primary Care Services, Marmaduke Street
Health Centre, Marmaduke Street, Hull, HU3 3BH, Tel.: 01482
223675
Mrs L Whincup, Head of Prof/Prac. Development, Westbourne NHS
Centre, Westbourne Avenue, Hull, Tel.: 01482 35500
Child Health
Mrs S Bell, Senior Practitioner for Childrens Services & Partnerships,
Boothferry Clinic, Bethune Avenue, Hull, Tel.: 01482 336604
Mr D Parks, Paediatric Asthma, Nurse Facilitator, 147 Ellerburn
Avenue, Hull, HU6 9RG, Tel.: 01482 335240
Child Health Records
Pre-School, Victoria House, Park Street, Hull, HU2 8TD, Tel.: 01482
617880

School Age, Victoria House, Park Street, Hull, HU2 8TD, Tel.: 01482
617904
Ms M Syrett, Manager, Tel.: 01482 617857
Child Protection/Safeguarding Children
Ms J McDermott, Named Nurse, Child Protection, 147 Eccerburn
Avenue, Hull, HU6 9RG, Tel.: 01482 335240
Ms B Smith, Family Support Services, Child Protection, Victoria
House, Park Street, Hull, HU2 8TD, Tel.: 01482 617839
Clinical Leads (NSF)
Mr A Burnell, Director of Primary Healthcare Services, WHPCT,
Brunswick House, Strand Close, Hull, HU2 9DB, Tel.: 01482 317031
Mr H Jones, Director of Commissioning & Partnerships, WHPCT,
Brunswick House, Strand Close, Hull, HU2 9DB, Tel.: 01482 317044
Dr W Richardson, Clinical Lead, Director of Public Health, Cancer,
WHPCT, Brunswick House, Strand Close, Hull, HU2 9DB, Tel.:
01482 317030
Community Matrons
Mrs H Lagopolous, Community Matron, Age Concern, Porter Street,
Hull, Tel.: 01482 591538
Miss W Maude, Community Matron, Age Concern, Porter Street,
Hull, Tel.: 01482 591538
Mrs A St Paul, Community Matron, Age Concern, Porter Street, Hull,
Tel.: 01482 591538
Community Nursing Services
Ms S Pender, Palliative Care Out of Hours Nursing Service,
Westbourne Centre, Westbourne Avenue, Hull, Tel.: 01482 335498
Ms J Robson, Palliative Care Out of Hours Nursing Service,
Westbourne Centre, Westbourne Avenue, Hull, Tel.: 01482 335498
District Nursing
Mrs A Horton, Modern Matron, Marmaduke Street Health Centre,
Marmaduke Street, Hull, HU3 3BH, Tel.: 01482 223675
Mrs T Kingdom, Modern Matron, Clarendon Health Centre,
Clarendon Street, Hull, HU2 8GD, Tel.: 01482 617883
Family Planning Services
Mrs Y Richardson, Head of Sexual and Reproductive Health, Conife
House, Prospect Street, Hull, HU2 8PX, Tel.: 01482 336399
Other Services
Ms D McIntyre, Continuing Care Team, Westbourne Centre,
Westbourne Avenue, Hull, HU5 3HP, Tel.: 01482 335511
Ms J Paddison, Continuing Care Team, Westbourne Centre,
Westbourne Avenue, Hull, HU5 3HP, Tel.: 01482 335511
Pharmacy
Mrs A Wilson, Pharmaceutical Advisor, Brunswick House, Strand
Close, Hull, HU2 9DB, Tel.: 01482 317018
Smoking Cessation
Specialist Health Promotion Unit, Victoria House, Park Street, Hull,
HU2 8TD, Tel.: 01482 223191
Specialist Nursing Services
Mrs D Parks, Nurse Facilitator, Asthma, - Paediatrics, 147 Ellerburn
Avenue, Hull, HU6 9RG, Tel.: 01482 335240
Mrs M Fletcher, Senior Nurse Facilitator, Long Term Conditions
Team, Disease, Age Concern, Bradbury House, Porter Street, Hull,
Tel.: 01482 591538
Mrs K Cartlich, Nurse Liaison (Team Leader - Long Term
Conditions), TB, c/o Chest Clinic, Hull Royall Infirmary, Anlaby Roa
Hull, Tel.: 01482 674366
The Homeless/Travellers & Asylum Seekers
Mr L Latham, Modern Matron, The Quays, Myton Street, Hull, HU1
2PS, Tel.: 01482 335335

York Hospitals NHS Trust

Trust Headquarters, Bootham Park
YORK
North Yorkshire
YO30 7BY
Tel.: 01904 631313

Yorkshire and The Humber SHA

Child Health Records
Ms P Keany, South - Child Health Records, School Health Dept, Raincliffe Street Clinic, Selby, YO8 4AN, Tel.: 01757 706136
Ms V Simpson, North - Child Health Records, Haxby & Wiggington Health Centre, 2 The Village, Wiggongton, York, YO32 2LL, Tel.: 01904 765982

Child Protection/Safeguarding Children
Dr R Ball, Designated & Named Doctor Paediatric Consultant, York Hospital, Wigginton Road, York, YO31 8HE, Tel.: 01904 631313
Mrs M Jackson, Named Midwife, Antenatal Dept, York Hospital, Wigginton Road, York, North Yorkshire, YO31 8HE, Tel.: 01904 726729 Bleep 739
Ms J Martin, Named Nurse Child Protection & Paediatric Liaison, Child Assessment Unit, York Hospital, Wigginton Road, York, YO31 8HE, Tel.: 01904 726647

Community Midwifery
Mrs M Jackson, Named Midwife, Antenatal Dept, York Hospital, Wigginton Road, York, YO31 8HE, Tel.: 01904 726729 Bleep 739
Ms K Thompson, Clinical Midwifery Manager, Maternity Unit, York Hospital, Tel.: 01904 726723

Family Planning Services
Mrs R Millman, Clinic Manager, Family Planning Clinic, Monkgate Health Centre, York, YO31 7WA, Tel.: 01904 630352

Health Visitors
Paediatric Health Visitors, York District Hospital, Tel.: 01904 453684

Liaison Services
Ms C Burke, Adult Hospital/Community Discharge, Sister, Ward 21, York District Hospital, Wigginton Road, York, YO31 8HE, Tel.: 01904 631313
Ms D Hosie, Adult Hospital/Community Discharge, Sister, Ward 21, York District Hospital, Wigginton Road, York, YO31 8HE, Tel.: 01904 631313
Ms J Lewis, Adult Hospital/Community Discharge, Sister, Ward 21, York District Hospital, Wigginton Road, York, YO31 8HE, Tel.: 01904 631313
Ms C Lockie, Adult Hospital/Community Discharge, Sister, Ward 21, York District Hospital, Wigginton Road, York, YO31 8HE, Tel.: 01904 631313
Ms K Partington, Adult Hospital/Community Discharge, Sister, Ward 1, York District Hospital, Wigginton Road, York, YO31 8HE, Tel.: 1904 631313

Matrons/Modern Matrons
Ms J Crampton, Child Health, Children's Assessment Unit, York Hospital, Wigginton Road, York, YO31 8HE, Tel.: 01904 726117

School Nursing
Ms S Burn, School Health Administration Manager, Child Development Centre, York District Hospital, Tel.: 01904 726539
Ms V Smith, School Nurses, Park Cottage, The Main Drive, Bootham Park, York, YO30 7BT, Tel.: 01904 725331

Yorkshire Wolds & Coast Primary Care Trust

Trust Headquarters, Four Winds
Market Weighton Road
DRIFFIELD
YO25 9LH
Tel.: 01377 253000

Admin & Senior Management
Ms G Poole, Head of Community Services/Lead Nurse, Tel.: 01482 36675
Mr A Smith, Chief Executive,

Child Health Records
Pre-School Records, Victoria House, Park Street, Hull, HU2 8TD, Tel.: 01482 617880
School Age Records, Victoria House, Park Street, Hull, HU2 8TD, Tel.: 01482 617904
Ms M Syrett, Manager, Tel.: 01482 617857

Clinical Leads (NSF)
Dr T Allison, Clinical Lead, Children,
Dr D Ross, Clinical Lead, Cancer,
Dr D Ross, Clinical Lead, CHD,
Dr D Wigglesworth, Clinical Lead, Diabetic Care,

District Nursing
Mr A Hood, District Nurses, Tel.: 07711 223619
Ms C Peak, District Nurses, Tel.: 07876 591443
Ms R Scott, District Nurses, Tel.: 07876 591952

Health Visitors
Mr A Hood, Health Visitors, Tel.: 07711 223619
Ms C Peak, Health Visitors, Tel.: 07876 591443
Ms R Scott, Health Visitors, Tel.: 07876 591952

Specialist Nursing Services
Ms M Meldrum, Diabetic Care, Bridlington & District Hospital, Bessingby Road, Bridlington, YO16 4QP, Tel.: 01262 423154
Ms J Smith, Diabetic Care, Bridlington & District Hospital, Bessingby Road, Bridlington, YO16 4QP, Tel.: 01262 423154

Wales

with major towns and Primary Care Trust boundaries

Llangefni

Colwyn Bay

St. Asaph

Mold

North West

Caernarfon

Wrexham

North Wales

West Midlands

Mid & West Wales

Lampeter

Brecon

Merthyr Tydfil

Llanelli

Abertillery

Neath

South East Wales

Chepstowe

Swansea

Pontypridd

Newport

Caerphilly

Bridgend

Cardiff

Penarth

South West

Wales

Mid & West Wales Region

Bridgend LHB

LHB Headquarters, North Court
David Street, Bridgend Industrial Estate
BRIDGEND
CF31 3TP
Tel.: 01656 754400

Admin & Senior Management
Ms M Cooksley, Deputy Nurse Director,
Ms N Joyce, Practice Nurse Facilitator,
Mrs L Lewis, Nurse Assessor NHS Funded Care,
Ms S Morgan, Director of Nursing/Director of Modernisation,
Mr G Owen, Head of Service Modernisation,
Mrs S Roberts, Senior Nurse Assessor NHS Funded Care,
Ms R Ward, Senior Nurse Advisor, Continuing NHS Health Care,
Community Nursing Services
Commission community services from Bro Morgannwg NHS Trust,
Specialist Nursing Services
Specialist & Liaison Nurses, Employed by Bro Morgannwg NHS Trust,

Bro Morgannwg NHS Trust

Trust Headquarters
71 Quarella Road
BRIDGEND, Mid Glamorgan
CF31 1YE
Tel.: 01656 752752

Child Health Records
Child Health Records, Neath, Port Talbot, Central Clinic, 21 Orchard Street, Swansea, SA1 5AT, Tel.: 01792 651501
Child Health Records, Bridgend, Community Health Office, 71 Quarella Road, Bridgend, Mid Glamorgan, CF31 1YE, Tel.: 01639 762398
Child Protection/Safeguarding Children
Ms S Mason, Bridgend Child Protection, Ward 4, Glanrhyd Hospital, Bridgend, CF31 4LN, Tel.: 01656 753873
Ms J Rees, Neath Child Protection, Tel.: 01639 762372
Ms K Lewis, Child Protection, Tel.: 01639 683164
Community Midwifery
Mrs C Dowling, Head of Midwifery, Directorate of Women & Childrens Services, Tel.: 01656 752307
Maternity Unit, Tel.: 01639 762020
Ms C Williams, Assistant, Head of Midwifery, Neath Hospital, Tel.: 01656 752752
Community Nursing Services
Ms B Gough, Head of Community Nursing, Community Health Office, 71 Quarella Road, Bridgend, Mid Glamorgan, CF31 1YE, Tel.: 01639 762398
Ms L Panes, Directorate Manager, Community Health Office, 71 Quarella Road, Bridgend, Mid Glamorgan, CF31 1YE, Tel.: 01639 762009
District Nursing
Ms B Gough, Head of Community Nursing, Community Health Office, 71 Quarella Road, Bridgend, Mid Glamorgan, CF31 1YE, Tel.: 01639 762398
Health Visitors
Health Visitor - Paediatrics, Princess of Wales Hospital, Coity Road, Bridgend, CF31 1RQ,
Ms A Cook, Health Visitor, Cardiac Rehabilitation, Health Clinic, Bryncwils, Sarn, Bridgend, Tel.: 01656 725529
Learning Disabilities
Mr R Edwards, Community Response Team - Llwyneryr Unit, Community Nurse, Tel.: 01792 771262
Ms A English, Taff Ely, Clinical Nurse Specialist, Heddan, Elan Valley, Rhydyfelin, Pontypridd, CF37 5PN, Tel.: 01443 668800

Ms J Evans, Children's CBT, Community Nurse, Facing the Challenge, Gwerneinon House, 224 Derwen Fawr Road, Derwen Fawr, Swansea, Tel.: 01792 297101
Mr I Ferris, General Manager, Head of Nursing, LD Directorate, Hensol, Pontyclun, CF72 8YS, Tel.: 01656 753403
Ms A Giordano, Merthyr, Clinical Nurse Specialist, Cae'r Wern, Ynysfach, Merthyr Tydfil, CF48 1AD, Tel.: 01685 383723
Mr C Griffiths, Cardiff South East, Clinical Nurse Specialist, 30 Richmond Road, Roath, CF2 3AS, Tel.: 029 2046 2466
Mr C Griffiths, Cardiff North East, Clinical Nurse Specialist, 35 Ty Gwyn Road, Penylan, CF2 5JG, Tel.: 029 2048 5570
Mr B Hayward, Cardiff South West, Clinical Nurse Specialist, 30 Riverside Terrace, Ely, CF5 5AS, Tel.: 029 2055 1184
Mr B Hayward, Cardiff North West, Clinical Nurse Specialist, 10 Penlline Road, Whitchurch, CF4 2AD, Tel.: 029 2061 0711
Ms K Hopkins, Community Support Team North, Community Nurse, 151 Clasemont Road, Tel.: 01792 701343
Mr T Humphrey, Swansea, Senior Nurse, Llwyneryr Unit, 151 Clasemont Road, Morriston, Swansea, SA6 6AH, Tel.: 01792 771262
Mr R Jones, Bridgend, Clinical Nurse Specialist, Celtic Court, Tremains Road, Bridgend, CF31 1TZ, Tel.: 01656 650290
Mr M Lloyd, Cynon, Clinical Nurse Specialist, Old YMCA Buildings, Gas Works Road, Aberaman, Aberdare, CF44 6RS, Tel.: 01685 881404/879896
Ms M Marshallsay, Community, Nurse Manager, Tresedar Way, Caerau, Ely, CF5 5XE, Tel.: 029 2056 9491
Mr P Price, Community Support Team South, Community Nurse, Cefn Coed Hospital, Cockett, Swansea, SA2 0GH, Tel.: 01792 587749
Mr J Racickis, Community Support Team East, Community Nurse, Civic Centre, Neath, SA12 3QZ, Tel.: 01639 764612
Mr S Wade, Director, LD Service, Hensol Hospital, Miskin, Pontyclun,
Mr K Whittington, Barry, Clinical Nurse Specialist, 26 Newlands Street, Barry, Vale of Glamorgan, CF62 8EA, Tel.: 01446 732434
Mr G Williams, Rhondda, Clinical Nurse Specialist, Old Town Hall, 15 Dewinton Street, Tonypandy, Tel.: 01443 431513
Liaison Services
Mrs G Bizby, Bridgend Liaison, Princess of Wales Hospital, Coity Road, Bridgend, CF31 1RQ, Tel.: 01656 752752
Ms D E M Harries, Bridgend Liaison, Princess of Wales Hospital, Coity Road, Bridgend, CF31 1RQ, Tel.: 01656 752752
Ms M Price, Neath Liaison, Neath General Hospital, Briton Ferry Road, Neath, SALL 2LQ, Tel.: 01639 641161
Mrs M Tidball, Bridgend Liaison, Princess of Wales Hospital, Coity Road, Bridgend, CF31 1RQ, Tel.: 01656 752752
Specialist Nursing Services
Ms P Griffiths, Breast Care, Princess of Wales Hospital, Tel.: 01656 752752
Ms R Kendall, Breast Care, Princess of Wales Hospital, Tel.: 01656 752752
Ms M Feeney, Colorectal, Princess of Wales Hospital, 01656 752752
Mr K Ridler, Neath, Port Talbot, Continence, Neath General Hospital, Tel.: 01639 762224
Mrs B Smith, Bridgend, Continence, Tel.: 01656 752924
Ms C Beaverstock, Diabetic Care, Neath General Hospital, Tel.: 01639 762255
Ms P Price, Diabetic Care, Princess of Wales Hospital, Coity Road, Bridgend, CF31 1RQ, Tel.: 01656 752752
Mrs J Jones, Bridgend, Macmillan, Y Bwthyn Newydd, Princess of Wales Hospital, Tel.: 01656 752752
Mrs P Lewis, Bridgend, Macmillan, Y Bwthyn Newydd, Princess of Wales Hospital, Tel.: 01656 752752
Mrs S Owen, Bridgend, Macmillan, Y Bwthyn Newydd, Princess of Wales Hospital, Tel.: 01656 752752
Ms L Sheridan, Neath, Port Talbot, Palliative Care, Y Rhosyn, Neath General Hospital, Tel.: 01639 641161

Wales

Carmarthenshire LHB

LHB Headquarters, Unit 5, Parc Dafen
Heol Cropin
LLANELLI
Carmarthenshire
SA14 8QW
Tel.: 01554 744400
Fax.: 01554 744401

Admin & Senior Management
Ms L John, Assistant Nurse Director, Unit 5, Parc Dafen, Heol Cropin, Llanelli, Carmarthenshire, SA14 8QW, Tel.: 01554 744400
Miss J Paterson, Nurse Director, Unit 5, Parc Dafen, Heol Cropin, Llanelli, Carmarthenshire, SA14 8QW, Tel.: 01554 744400

Child Protection/Safeguarding Children
Mrs J Morgan, Co-ordinator, Child Protection,

Clinical Leads (NSF)
Dr T Davies, Clinical Lead, Diabetic Care,

Family Planning Services
Ms L Cox, Youth Liaison Nurse,
Ms N Morgan, Youth Liaison Nurse,
Ms A Parry, Youth Liaison Nurse,

Other Services
Mrs J Cox, Practice Nurse Adviser,
Mrs A Evans, Practice Nurse Adviser,

Pharmacy
Mrs K Haines, Manager, Pharmacy,

Specialist Nursing Services
Mrs B Martin, Integrated Care Manager, Unit 5, Parc Dafen, Heol Cropin, Llanelli, Carmarthenshire, SA14 8QW, Tel.: 01554 744400
Ms R Davies, Specialist Nurse, CDM, Unit 5, Parc Dafen, Heol Cropin, Llanelli, Carmarthenshire, SA14 8QW, Tel.: 01554 744400
Ms C Hurlin, Co-ordinator, CDM, Tel.: 01554 744400
Ms A Downing, Specialist Nurse, CHD, Unit 5, Parc Dafen, Heol Cropin, Llanelli, Carmarthenshire, SA14 8QW, Tel.: 01554 744400
Ms H Rees, Nurse Specialist, COPD, Tel.: 01554 744400
Ms J Willey, Nurse Specialist, COPD, Tel.: 01554 744400
Ms C Cottrell, Nurse Specialist, Diabetes, Tel.: 01554 744400
Ms H Green, Nurse Specialist, Diabetes, Tel.: 01554 744400
Ms L Thomas, Nurse Specialist, Diabetes,
Ms W Churchaise, Nurse Specialist, Heart Failure,
Ms R Davies, Nurse Specialist, Heart Failure,
Ms H Llewellyn Griffiths, Nurse Specialist, Heart Failure,

Carmarthenshire NHS Trust

Trust Headquarters, Glangwili Hospital
CARMARTHEN
SA31 2AF
Tel.: 01267 235151

Admin & Senior Management
Dr G Owen, Director, Family Health Services - Carmarthenshire, West Wales General Hospital, Tel.: 01267 235151 ext 2415
Mr K Tribble, General Manager - Carmarthenshire, West Wales General Hospital, Tel.: 01267 235151 ext 2415
Ms J Waktins, Directorate Nurse Intermediate & Palliative Care - Carmarthenshire, Myndd Mawr Hospital, Tumble, Llanelli, SA14 6BU, Tel.: 01554 756567 ext 3851

Child Health
Ms M Brooker, Community Paediatric Team - Carmarthenshire, West Wales General Hospital, Carmarthen, SA31 2AF, Tel.: 01267 235151
Mrs N Davies, Family Support Service - Carmarthenshire, Jobs Well House, Jobs Well Road, Johnstown, Carmarthen, SA31 3HG, Tel.: 01267 234987
Family Health Services, West Wales General Hospital, Carmarthen, SA31 2AF, Tel.: 01267 235151
Ms R Jones, Paediatric Oncology - Carmarthenshire, West Wales General Hospital, Carmarthen, SA31 2AF, Tel.: 01267 235151

Ms B Williams, Community Paediatric Team - Carmarthenshire, West Wales General Hospital, Carmarthen, SA31 2AF, Tel.: 01267 235151

Child Health Records
Mrs M James, Child Health Services, West Wales General Hospital, Carmarthen, SA31 2AF, Tel.: 01267 227908

Child Protection/Safeguarding Children
Mrs K Toohey, Carmarthenshire, Senior Nurse, Child Protection, West Wales General Hospital, Carmarthen, SA31 2AF, Tel.: 01267 227056

Community Midwifery
Mrs C Bell, Director of Midwifery Services (Acting), West Wales General Hospital, Dolgwili Road, Glangwili, Carmarthen, SA31 2AF, Tel.: 01267 227956

District Nursing
Ms R Keil, Directorate Nurse, District Nursing & Sexual Health, Myndd Mawr Hospital, Tumble, Llanelli, SA14 6BU, Tel.: 01554 756567 ext 3855

Family Planning Services
Dr A Cattell, Manager, Carmarthen Locality, Tel.: 01267 225001

Health Visitors
Ms R Marks, Head of Health Visiting Services, West Wales General Hospital, Carmarthen, SA31 2AF, Tel.: 01267 235151 ext 2957

Liaison Services
Family Health Services, West Wales General Hospital, Carmarthen, SA31 2AF, Tel.: 01267 235151

School Nursing
Ms R Marks, Head of School Nursing Services, West Wales General Hospital, Carmarthen, SA31 2AF, Tel.: 01267 227957

Specialist Nursing Services
Mr F Aitken, Disability Resource Team - Llanelli/Dinefwr Locality, Myndd Mawr Hospital, Tel.: 01554 756567
Ms J Hickey, Co-ordinator, Bereavement Services, Ty Cynorth, Carmarthen,
Ms M James, Dare Care Manager - Llanelli/Dinefwr Locality, Ty Bryngwyn, Tel.: 01554 756567 ext 6613
Ms L Walters, Llanelli/Dinefwr Locality, Continence, Myndd Mawr Hospital, Tel.: 01554 756567 ext 3856
Ms J Young, Discharge Planning Carmarthenshire, Continuing Care, Prince Phillip Hospital, Llanelli, Tel.: 01554 756567 ext 3702
Ms J Thomas, Carmarthen Locality, Diabetic Care, West Wales General Hospital, Tel.: 01267 235151
Mrs S Evans, Llanelli/Dinefwr Locality, Elderly Care, Myndd Mawr Hospital, Tel.: 01554 756567 ext 3702
Ms S Evans, Carmarthen Locality, Infection Control, West Wales General Hospital, Tel.: 01267 235151
Ms S Meecham, Ty Cymorth, Team Leader, Carmarthen Locality, Macmillan, West Wales General Hospital, Carmarthen, SA31 2AF, Tel.: 01267 235151ext 2655
Ms A Samuel, Llanelli/Dinefwr Locality, Macmillan, Ty Bryngwyn Palliative Care Day Centre, Tel.: 01554 756567
Mr J Annandale, Llanelli/Dinefwr Locality, Respiratory, Prince Philip Hospital,
Ms I Williams, Carmarthen Locality, Stoma Care, West Wales General Hospital, Carmarthen, SA31 2AF, Tel.: 01267 235151

Ceredigion & Mid Wales NHS Trust

Trust Headquarters, Bronglais General Hospital
Caradog Road, ABERYSTWYTH
Ceredigion, SY23 1ER
Tel.: 01970 635304

Child Health
Ms E Bray, Specialist Needs Children, Family Support Team, 9 Market Street, Aberystwyth, SY23 1DL, Tel.: 01970 627016

Child Health Records
Child Health Records, Bronglais Hospital, Caradoc Road, Aberystwyth, Ceredigion, SY23 1ER, Tel.: 01970 623131

Wales

Child Protection/Safeguarding Children
Ms R Harrison, Child Protection, Bronglais Hospital, Tel.: 01970 635794

Community Midwifery
Mrs C Cotter, Head of Midwifery, Bronglais Hospital, Caradog Road, Aberystwyth, Dyfed, SY23 1ER, Tel.: 01970 635317

Community Nursing Services
Mr S Griffiths, Director of Nursing & Patient Services, Bronglais Hospital, Tel.: 01970 635771

District Nursing
Mr S Griffiths, Director of Nursing & Patient Services, Bronglais Hospital, Tel.: 01970 635771

Family Planning Services
Mrs L Jones, Family Planning Service, Cardigan Hospital, Cardigan, SA43 1EB, Tel.: 01239 612214

Learning Disabilities
Services administered by Pembrokeshire & Derwen NHS Trust,

Liaison Services
Ms J Williams, Discharge Liaison Nurse, Bronglais Hospital, Tel.: 01970 635979

School Nursing
School Health/Nursing Service, Bronglais General Hospital, Tel.: 01970 635317

Specialist Nursing Services
Mrs D Richards, Breast Care, Bronglais Hospital, Tel.: 01970 623131
Mrs D Lewis, Cardio vascular, Bronglais Hospital, Tel.: 01970 623131
Mrs P Miller, Continence, Bronglais Hospital, Tel.: 01970 623131
Ms S Oliver, Diabetic Care, Bronglais Hospital, Tel.: 01970 635750
Mrs J Cuttress, Palliative Care, Bronglais Hospital, Tel.: 01970 623131
Mrs C Stevens, Palliative Care, Bronglais Hospital, Tel.: 01970 623131
Mrs B Lewis, Parkinson's Disease, Bronglais Hospital, Tel.: 01970 623131
Mrs S Pugh, Respiratory, Bronglais Hospital, Tel.: 01970 623131
Mrs M Platt, Stoma Care, Bronglais Hospital, Tel.: 01970 623131

Ceredigion LHB
LHB Headquarters, The Bryn
North Road, LAMPETER
SA48 7HA
Tel.: 01570 424100

Admin & Senior Management
Ms H Williams, Nurse Director, Ceredigion LHB, The Bryn, North Road, Lampeter, SA48 7HA,

Clinical Leads (NSF)
Dr S Griffiths, Medical Director, All NSFs Lead,
Mrs C Tofts, Clinical Governance,

Neath Port Talbot LHB
Suite A
Brittanic House, Llandarcy
NEATH, West Glamorgan
SA10 6JQ
Tel.: 01792 326500
Fax.: 01792 326501

Admin & Senior Management
Mrs G Atkinson, Continuing Care Co-ordinator, LHB Headquarters, Tel.: 01792 326548
Mrs T Evans, Nurse Assessor,
Mrs J Hill, Nurse Director, LHB Headquarters, Tel.: 01792 316510
Mr D Morgan, Deputy Nurse Director, LHB Headquarters, Tel.: 01792 326535
Mrs B Reynolds, Long Term Illness Assessor & Practice Nurse Facilitator, LHB Headquarters, Tel.: 01792 326543
Mrs N Reynolds, Senior Nurse Assessor,

Clinical Leads (NSF)
Ms K Jones, NSF Facilitator,
Mr G Lyth, NSF Project Manager,

District Nursing
Ms L Fitchett, Nurse Member/Health Visitor, Queens Road Medical Centre, Skewen, Neath,

Pembrokeshire & Derwen NHS Trust
Trust Headquarters, Withybush General Hospital
Fishguard Road
HAVERFORDWEST
Pembrokeshire, SA61 2PZ
Tel.: 01437 764545

Admin & Senior Management
Mrs C Hayes, Head of Nursing & Quality, Acute & Community Division, Withybush General Hospital, Tel.: 01437 773118
Mrs C Oakley, Director of Nursing, Tel.: 01437 773777

Child Health
Mr D Morrissey, Paediatrics & Child Health, Senior Nurse, Withybush General Hospital, Tel.: 01437 773858

Child Protection/Safeguarding Children
Mrs J Hughes, Named Nurse, Child Protection, Child Health Dept, Withybush General Hospital, Tel.: 01437 773851
Ms S Edwards, Specialist Nurse, Looked After Children, Child Health Dept, Withybush General Hospital, Tel.: 01437 772341

Community Midwifery
Mrs G Evans, Acting General Manager, Maternity Dept, Withybush General Hospital, Tel.: 01437 764545
Ms K Isherwood, Senior Midwife, Ante Natal Clinic, Withybush General Hospital, Tel.: ext 3206

District Nursing
Ms S Hay, Service Manager, Community & Rehabilitation, Pembroke Dock Health Care Centre, Water Street, Penbroke Dock, SA72 6DW, Tel.: 01646 682635
Ms C Leslie, District Nurse/Acute Care at Home Co-ordinator, c/o ACAH, Withybush Hospital, Tel.: 01437 773022

Family Planning Services
Ms J Clark, Sexual Health Advisor, Withybush General Hospital,
Ms M Power, Lead Nurse, Family Planning, Winch Lane Health Centre, Haverfordwest, Tel.: 01437 767801
Mrs G Evans, Acting General Manager, Gynaecology, Withybush General Hospital, Tel.: 01437 773291

HIV/AIDS
Ms J Rees, HIV/AIDS, Blood-borne Viruses, Withybush General Hospital, Tel.: 01437 773125

Learning Disabilities
Mr T Farley, Community Nurse, Havefordia House, Winch Lane, Haverfordwest, Tel.: 01437 776619
Ms J Harris, Ty Llewellyn, West Wales General Hospital, Carmarthen, SA31 2AF, Tel.: 01267 227034
Ms C Lockett, Community, Services Manager, Havefordia House, Winch Lane, Haverfordwest, Tel.: 01437 776445
Ms P Sani, Team Manager, Canolfan Felinfach, Lampeter, SA48 8AF, Tel.: 01545 572735/6/7
Ms C Tweedale, Community Services Manager, 5/6 Queen Street, Carmarthen, Tel.: 01267 222456
Ms C Tweedale, Learning Disabilities, Community Services Manager, 1 Penlan, Penlan Road, Carmarthen, SA31 1DM, Tel.: 01267 244410

Specialist Nursing Services
Ms L Dawson, Manual Handling Trainer, Withybush General Hospital,
Ms S Horsley, Pregnancy Loss, Clinical Nurse Specialist, Ward 2, Withybush General Hospital,
Ms J Hughes, Contining Care Nurse, Withybush General Hospital,
Ms S Morgan, Clinical Nurse Specialist, Ward 10, Withybush General Hospital,

Wales

Mr P Stace, Medical Devices Co-ordinator, Withybush General Hospital,

Ms T Thomas, Nurse Practitioner, Chemotherapy Day Unit, Ward 10, Withybush General Hospital,

Ms R Swinglehurst, Specialist Nurse, Acute Pain, Main Theatre, Withybush General Hospital,

Ms F Jenkins, Clinical Nurse Specialist, Anti-Coagulation, Withybush General Hospital,

Mrs N Powell, Specialist Nurse, Breast Care, Withybush General Hospital,

Ms P Emery, Liaison, Specialist Nurse, Cardiac, Winch Lane Medical Centre, Haverfordwest, Tel.: 01437 767801

Ms K Nur, Specialist Nurse, Chronic Pain, Withybush General Hospital,

Ms J Bowen, Clinical Nurse Specialist, Continence, Winch Lane Medical Centre, Tel.: 01437 767801

Ms L Atherton, Clinical Nurse Specialist, Diabetic Care, Withybush General Hospital,

Ms P Davies, Clinical Nurse Specialist, Diabetic Care, - Paediatrics, Withybush General Hospital,

Ms C Phillips, Co-ordinator, Discharges, Withybush General Hospital,

Ms K Johns, Clinical Nurse Specialist, Gastroenterology, Withybush General Hospital,

Ms S Owen, Clinical Nurse Specialist, Genetics, Yorke Street, Milford Haven,

Ms S Richards, Senior Nurse, Infection Control, Withybush General Hospital,

Mrs L Doyle, Clinical Nurse Specialist, Macmillan, Winch Lane Health Centre, Haverfordwest, Tel.: 01437 767801

Ms J Griffiths, Clinical Nurse Specialist, Macmillan, The New Tenby Cottage Hospital, Gas Lane, The Norton, Tenby, Pembs, SA70 8AG, Tel.: 01834 840071

Ms N Lewis, Nurse, Occupational Health, Withybush General Hospital,

Ms E Williams, Clinical Nurse Specialist, Parkinson's Disease, Winch Lane Health Centre, Haverfordwest, Tel.: 01437 767801

Ms Y Phillips, Clinical Nurse Specialist, Rehabilitation, Ward 14, Withybush General Hospital,

Ms J Evans, Clinical Nurse Specialist, Respiratory, Withybush General Hospital,

Ms C Hobson, Trainer - Clinical Skills, Resuscitation, Withybush General Hospital,

Ms S Morris, Clinical Nurse Specialist, Rheumatology, Withybush General Hospital,

Ms J Calvert, Clinical Nurse Specialist, Stoma Care, Withybush General Hospital,

Ms L Coombes, Clinical Nurse Specialist, Stroke Care, Ward 14, Withybush General Hospital,

Ms J Cole, Clinical Nurse Specialist, Surgery, c/o Ward 3, Withybush General Hospital,

Ms B Andrews, Clinical Nurse Specialist, Tissue Viability, Withybush General Hospital,

Ms S Gulliver, Liaison Nurse, Trauma, Orthopaedic Dept, Withybush General Hospital,

Ms J Rees, Blood Borne, Clinical Nurse Specialist, Viruses, Withybush General Hospital,

Pembrokeshire LHB

LHB Headquarters, Unit 4, Merlins Court
Winch Lane
HAVERFORDWEST
SA61 1SB
Tel.: 01437 771220

Admin & Senior Management
Mrs J Bowen, Director of Nursing, LHB Headquarters, Tel.: 01437 771220

Child Protection/Safeguarding Children
Mrs J Evans, Designated Nurse, Child Protection, PO Box 13, St Davids Hospital, Carmarthen, SA31 3YH, Tel.: 01267 225018/225074

Clinical Leads (NSF)
Mrs K Charles, Clinical Lead, CHD & Diabetes, Pembrokeshire LHB, Unit 4, Merlins Court, Winch Lane, Haverfordwest, SA61 1SB, Tel.: 01437 771220

Specialist Nursing Services
Ms A Bury, Nurse Assessor, NHS Funded Nursing Care, LHB Headquarters, Tel.: 01437 771220

Ms A Edwards, Integrated Care Manager, Continuing Care & Individual Patient Commissioning, LHB Headquarters, Tel.: 01437 771220

Powys LHB

LHB Headquarters, Mansion House
Bronllys
BRECON
Powys
LD3 0LU
Tel.: 01874 711661

Admin & Senior Management
Mr H George, Director of Finance, LHB Headquarters, Tel.: 01874 712713

Ms J Meighan Davies, Head of District Nursing, Specialist Nursing Services & Professional Lead for Practice Nurses, Builth Wells Hospital, Builth Wells, LD2 3HE, Tel.: 01982 554339

Ms S Penny, Director of Human Resources, LHB Headquarters, Tel.: 01874 712548

Ms J Roberts, Director of Nursing, LHB Headquarters, Tel.: 01874 712652

Child Health
Mr K Roche, Community Paediatrics Nursing Co-ordinator, The Annexe, Llandrindod Wells Hospital, Llandrindod Wells, LD1 5HF, Tel.: 01597 828710

Child Health Records
Mr V Ness, Head of Women & Child Health, c/o Brecon Children's Centre, Brecon Hospital, Powys, Tel.: 01874 615681

Ms C Stanley, Senior Administrator Child Health, Ynys-y-Plant, Newtown, Powys, Tel.: 01686 617452

Child Protection/Safeguarding Children
Mrs P Galliuccio, Head of Child Protection & Looked After Children, Named Nurse, c/o Ynys-y-Plant, Newtown Powys, Tel.: 01686 617443

Community Midwifery
Miss J Richards, Head of Midwifery, Builth Community Hospital, Tel.: 01982 552221

Community Nursing Services
Ms M Baker, Lead Community Nurse for Mid Powys, Llandrindod Wells Hospital, Llandrindod Wells, Tel.: 01597 828791

Ms L Gethin, Lead Community Nurse for North Powys, Newtown Hospital, Newtown, Tel.: 01686 617232

Mrs J Meighan Davies, Head of District Nursing, Specialist Nursing Services & Professional Lead for Practice Nurses, Builth Wells Hospital, Builth Wells, LD2 3HE, Tel.: 01982 554339

Ms J Smalley, Lead Community Nurse for South Powys, Brecon War Memorial Hospital, Brecon, Tel.: 01874 625624

Health Visitors
Mrs S Jones, Head of Health Visiting, Ystradgynlais Community Hospital, Tel.: 01639 846429

Learning Disabilities
Dr M Browning, Team Leader, North, Newtown, Tel.: 01686 617700

Mr S Crayden, South, Clinical Nurse Specialist, Brecon, Tel.: 01874 623741

Ms G Griffiths, Team Member, South, Llandrindod Wells Social Services Department, Tel.: 01597 827102

Wales

Mr P Hartley, Team Member, South, Brecon Social Services Department, Tel.: 01874 623741

Mr J O'Shaughnessy, North, Clinical Nurse Specialist, Welshpool Social Services Department, Tel.: 01938 552017

School Nursing

Mrs S Jones, Head of School Nurses, Ystradgyngais Community Hospital, Tel.: 01639 846429

Specialist Nursing Services

Ms H Rees-Harris, Clinical Nurse Specialist, Cardiac, Brecon Hospital, Tel.: 01874 625780

Mr D Wright, Nurse Specialist Cardiac, Newtown Hosp., SY16 2DW,

Ms J Davies, Cardiac Rehabilitation, Brecon Hospital, Brecon, Powys, LD3 7NB, Tel.: 01874 625780

Mr C Backhouse, Lead Nurse, Chronic Disease Management, Builth Wells Hospital, LD2 3HE,

Ms K Pearce, Head, Continence, Newtown Hospital, Newtown, Powys, SY16 2DW, Tel.: 01686 617237

Ms S Powell, Clinical Nurse Specialist, Continence, Bronllys Hospital, Tel.: 01874 712436

Ms P Pritchard, Specialist Nurse, Diabetes, Mid Powys, Builth Wells Hospital,

Ms J Jarvis, Clinical Nurse Specialist, Diabetic Care, Brecon Health Centre, Tel.: 01874 622121

Ms S A Jones, Clinical Nurse Specialist, Diabetic Care, Newtown Health Centre, Tel.: 01686 623396

Ms K Jennings, Liaison Nurse, Discharges, Welshpool Health Centre, Tel.: 01938 556429

Ms L Mead, Liaison Nurse, Discharges, Builth Wells Hospital, Tel.: 01982 554302

Ms K Rogers, Liaison Nurse, Discharges, Machynlleth Hospital, Tel.: 01654 705250

Ms A Whitelaw, Liaison Nurse, Discharges, Brecon Hospital, Tel.: 01874 615637

Ms R Alves, Nurse, Infection Control, Mansion House, Bronllys, Brecon, Powys, LD3 0LU, Tel.: 01874 712636

Ms S Cartwright, Nurse, Macmillan, Park Street Clinic, Newtown, Tel.: 01686 617374

Ms G Davies, Nurse, Macmillan, Park Street Clinic, Newtown, Tel.: 01686 617374

Ms E Rhodes, Nurse, Macmillan, Ystradgynlais Hospital, Tel.: 01639 346478

Ms S Wheeler, Macmillan, Llandrindod Wells Hospital, Powys, LD1 5HF, Tel.: 01597 828793

Ms A Price, Nurse, Occupational Health, Hilfa Unit, Bronllys, LD3 0LU, Tel.: 01874 712599

Ms V Davies, Clinical Nurse Specialist, Pain Management, Bronllys Hospital, Bronllys, Brecon, LD3 0LU, Tel.: 01874 712503

Ms J Price, Nurse, Parkinson's Disease, Hilfa Unit, Bronllys Hospital, Bronllys, Brecon, LD3 0LU, Tel.: 01874 712595

Ms H Rawlins, Facilitator for Practice Nursing, Primary Care, Brecon Hospital, Tel.: 01874 712533

Ms P Garner, Clinical Nurse Specialist, Respiratory, Ystradgynlais Hospital, Tel.: 01639 730942

Ms L Bowen, Clinical Nurse Specialist, Tissue Viability, Builth Wells Hospital, Tel.: 01982 554342

Ms J Griffin, Clinical Nurse Specialist, Tissue Viability, Newtown Health Centre, Tel.: 01686 629249

Swansea LHB

**LHB Headquarters, Kidwelly House
Charter Court, Phoenix Way
LLANSAMLET, SA7 9FS**
Tel.: 01792 784800

Admin & Senior Management

Ms J Worthing, Nurse Director/Nursing & Childrens' Lead, Swansea LHB, Kidwelly House, Charter Court, Phoenix Way, Llansamlet, SA7 9FS, Tel.: 01792 326500

Clinical Leads (NSF)

Dr Hilliard, Clinical Lead, Cancer,

Dr J Hilliard, Clinical Lead, CHD,

Dr B Lloyd, Clinical Lead, Diabetic Care,

Dr J Vincent, Clinical Lead, Diabetic Care,

District Nursing

Mrs G Haram, Head of District Nursing, Cwmbwrla Clinic, Caebricks Road, Tel.: 01792 458839

Ms J Skiffins, Nurse, Swansea LHB, Kidwelly House, Charter Court, Phoenix Way, Llansamlet, SA7 9FS,

Specialist Nursing Services

Out of Hours/Weekends, Tel.: 01792 561155

Ms P Barker, Co-ordinator, Palliative Care, S.P.I.C.E., Bonymaen Clinic, Caernarvon Way, Swansea, SA1 7HL, Tel.: 01792 480066

Swansea NHS Trust

**Trust Headquarters, Central Clinic
Trinity Buildings, 21 Orchard Street
SWANSEA
West Glamorgan
SA1 5AT**
Tel.: 01792 651501

Admin & Senior Management

Mrs C Burns, Community Nurse Manager, Central Clinic, Orchard Street, Swansea, SA1 5AT, Tel.: 01792 517090

Mr T Webb, Community Services Manager, Central Clinic, Orchard Street, Swansea, SA1 5AT, Tel.: 01792 651501

Child Health

Mrs J Lane, Clinical Service Manager, Health Visiting, Central Clinic, Orchard Street, Swansea, SA1 5AT, Tel.: 01792 517987

Child Health Records

Central Health Records, Central Clinic, Tel.: 01792 651501 ext 7810

Miss A E Evans, Appointment Manager,

Child Protection/Safeguarding Children

Mrs P Davies, Protection of Vulnerable Adults, Clinical Nurse Specialist, Central Clinic, Orchard Street, Swansea, SA1 5AT, Tel.: 01792 517099

Mrs J Israel, Looked After Children's Health Visitor, Gorseinon Clinic, Princess Street, Gorseinon, Swansea, Tel.: 01792 896543

Mrs R Beaumont-Wood, Clinical Nurse Specialist, Child Protection, Central Clinic, Orchard Street, Swansea, SA1 5AT, Tel.: 01792 517926

Mrs J Rees, Named Nurse, Child Protection, Central Clinic, Orchard Street, Swansea, SA1 5AT, Tel.: 01792 517913

Community Midwifery

Ms S Passey, Senior Community Midwife, Singleton Hospital, Sketty, Swansea, SA2 8QA, Tel.: 01792 285052

Ms J Payne, Head of Midwifery/Supervisor of Midwives, Division of Women & Child Health, Singleton Hospital, Tel.: 01792 285465

District Nursing

Miss J Hopkins, Clinical Service Manager, District Nursing, Central Clinic, Orchard Street, Swansea, SA1 5AT, Tel.: 01792 517991

Health Visitors

Mrs J Lane, Clinical Service Manager, Health Visiting, Central Clinic, Orchard Street, Swansea, SA1 5AT, Tel.: 01792 458839/475110

Mrs J Morris, Health Visitor Disability Team, Lakeside, Swansea, Tel.: 01792 517987

Liaison Services

Miss J Hopkins, Continuing Care Clinical Service Manager, District Nursing, Central Clinic, Orchard Street, Swansea, SA1 5AT, Tel.: 01792 517991

Other Services

Mrs C Koukos, Sure Start Manager, Gorseinon Hospital, Gorseinon, Swansea, SA4 4UU, Tel.: 01792 895940

Specialist Nursing Services

Mrs B Powell, Advisor, Continence, Central Clinic, Orchard Street, Swansea, SA1 5AT, Tel.: 01792 517852

Wales

Mrs H Mogford, Clinical Nurse Specialist, Diabetic Care, Singleton Hospital, Tel.: 01792 205666 ext 5167

Mrs F Purchase, Diabetic Care, Singleton Hospital, Tel.: 01792 205666 ext 5167

Mrs A Appleton, Discharge Liaison, Elderly Care, Morriston Hospital, Tel.: 01792 703299/703272

Ms S Gwynne, Discharge Liaison, Elderly Care, Morriston Hospital, Tel.: 01792 703299/703272

Ms H Thomas, Discharge Liaison, Elderly Care, Morriston Hospital, Tel.: 01792 703299/703272

Mrs D Davies, Lead Nurse, Infection Control, Morriston Hospital, Tel.: 01792 702222

Mrs S Coles, Colorectal, Stoma Care, Singleton Hospital, Tel.: 01792 205666 ext 5367

Ms C Greenway, Colorectal, Stoma Care, Singleton Hospital, Tel.: 01792 205666 ext 5367

Ms G Griffiths, Colorectal, Stoma Care, Singleton Hospital, Tel.: 01792 205666 ext 5367

The Homeless/Travellers & Asylum Seekers
Ms L Reid-Jones, Homeless Outreach, Youth Homeless, Swansea Youth Homeless Team, 32-36 High Street, Swansea, SA1 1LF, Tel.: 01792 455105

Mrs J Saunders, Asylum Seekers Health Team, Central Clinic, Orchard Street, Swansea, SA1 5AT, Tel.: 01792 517882

Mrs G Smith, Health Visitor for Travellers, Port Tennant Surgery, 125 Port Tennant Road, Port Tennant, Swansea, SA1 8JN, Tel.: 01792 468935

North Wales Region

Anglesey LHB

LHB Headquarters, 17 High Street
Llangefni, ANGLESEY
LL77 7LT
Tel.: 01248 751229

Admin & Senior Management
Ms S Roberts, Nurse Director, 17 High Street, Llangefni, Anglesey, LL77 7LT,

Mrs M Walmsley, Practice Development, Nurse, Tel.: 01248 751229
Clinical Leads (NSF)
Ms P Mowll, Clinical Lead, Cancer, CHD, Diabetes, Anglesey LHB,
Ms S Roberts, Clinical Lead, Care of the Elderly, Anglesey LHB,
Community Nursing Services
Provided by North West Wales NHS Trust,

Conwy and Denbighshire NHS Trust

Trust Headquarters, Ysbyty Glan Clwyd
Bodelwyddan
RHYL, Denbighshire
LL18 5UJ
Tel.: 01745 583910

Admin & Senior Management
Mr I R Bellingham, Executive Director of Operations,
Miss H Young, Director of Nursing,
Child Health
Ms J Douglas, Diana Community Childrens Nurse, Paediatrics, Top Floor, Royal Alexander Hospital, Marine Drive, Rhyl, LL18 3AS, Tel.: 01745 443245 x 3245
Mrs R Shaw, Head of Child & Adolescent Nursing, Paediatric Out Patients Department, Tel.: 01745 534338
Child Health Records
Child Health Department, Royal Alexandra Hospital, Tel.: 01745 443000
Child Protection/Safeguarding Children
Mr A Ingledew, Denbighshire, Child Protection, Royal Alexandra Hospital, Tel.: 01745 443186

Mr L Owen, Conwy, Child Protection, Health Premises, Argyll Road, Llandudno, LL30 1DF, Tel.: 01492 862018
Community Midwifery
Maternity Office, Tel.: 01745 583910
Mrs J Riley, Head of Midwifery, Ysbyty Glan Clwyd, Tel.: 01745 534647
Community Nursing Services
Community Directorate Headquarters, Royal Alexandra Hospital, Marine Drive, Rhyl, Denbighshire, LL18 3AS, Tel.: 01745 443000
Ms E Morgan, General Manager, Head of Nursing, Tel.: 01745 443179
District Nursing
Mrs H Kerr, Denbighshire, Tel.: 01824 704702
Ms L Prior, Community Services Manager, Conwy, Colwyn Bay Hospital, Colwyn Bay, LL29 8AY, Tel.: 01492 515218
Ms R Shaw, Child & Adolescent Health Directorate, Glan Clwyd Hospital, Tel.: 01745 583910
Family Planning Services
Dr K Jain, Consultant, Royal Alexandra Hospital, Tel.: 01745 443301
Ms E Stafford, Nurse Co-ordinator, Royal Alexandra Hospital, Tel.: 01745 443301
Learning Disabilities
Mr P Hosker, Clinical Nurse Manager Denbighshire Team, Henllan Centre, Henllan, Denbigh, LL16 5YA, Tel.: 01745 813871
Mr G McDonald, Clinical Nurse Manager Conwy Team, Civic Offices, Glan y Don, Abergele Road, Colwyn Bay, LL29 8AR, Tel.: 01492 575374
Mr D Williams, Service Manager, Learning Disability, Denbigh Infirmary Clinic, Ruthin Road, Denbigh, LL16 3ES, Tel.: 01745 818124
Specialist Nursing Services
Mrs G Baker, Continence, Royal Alexandra Hospital, Tel.: 01745 443000
Ms A Steen, Dermatology, Glan Clwyd Hospital, Tel.: 01745 583910 Bleep 4085
Mr D Casey, Nurse Manager, Infection Control, Glan Clwyd Hospital, Tel.: 01745 583910 ext 4796
Mrs M Cooper, Macmillan, Colwyn Bay Hospital, Tel.: 01492 515218
Mrs A Howarth, Macmillan, Prestatyn Hospital, Tel.: 01745 853487
Ms M Lindsey, Macmillan, Denbigh Infirmary, Denbigh, LL16 3ES, Tel.: 01745 812624
Mr T Shea, Macmillan, Cancer Centre, Glan Clwyd Hospital, Tel.: 01745 583910
Mrs J Weatherhead, Macmillan, Colwyn Bay Hospital, Tel.: 01492 515218
Ms B Cooledge, Pain Management, Anaesthetic Dept, Glan Clwyd Hospital, Tel.: 01745 583910 ext 4993
Ms S Meyers, Pain Management, Anaesthetic Dept, Glan Clwyd Hospital, Tel.: 01745 583910 ext 4993
Mrs F Whitehirst, Tissue Viability, Royal Alexandra Hospital, Tel.: 01745 443000

Conwy LHB

LHB Headquarters, Glyn Colwyn
Nant-y-Glyn, COLWYN BAY
LL29 7PU
Tel.: 01492 536586

Admin & Senior Management
Ms S Owen, Nurse Director,
Mr W Thomas, General Manager,

Denbighshire LHB

LHB Headquarters, Ty Livingstone
HM Stanley Hospital
ST ASAPH, Denbighshire
LL17 0RS
Tel.: 01745 589601

Wales

Admin & Senior Management
Ms A Carroll, Senior Nurse Manager/Support to Nurse Executive, Denbighshire LHB Headquarters, Tel.: 01745 589601

Mrs C McEvoy, Lead Nurse Assessor - General,

Ms L Morgan, General Manager/Head of Nursing, The Royal Alexander Hospital, Marine Drive, Rhyl, LL18 3AS, Tel.: 01745 443183

Ms S Morris, Continuing Care Co-ordinator,

Ms H Nicholas, Public & Patient Liaison Manager, Denbighshire LHB Headquarters,

Mrs S Staveley, Continuing Care Facilitator - Children,

Mrs J Trowman, Director/Nursing Executive, Denbighshire LHB Headquarters, Tel.: 01745 589601

Child Health Records
Ms M Drakes, Child Health Administrator, Royal Alexander Hospital, Tel.: 01745 443000 ext 3168

Child Protection/Safeguarding Children
Mrs A Ingledew, Safeguarding Children, Senior Nurse, Argyll Road, Llandudno, Tel.: 01492 862020

Mrs C Mason, Deputy Senior Nurse Safeguarding Children, Argyll Road, Llandudno, Tel.: 01492 862032

District Nursing
Ms H Kerr, Manager, District Nurses, Ruthin, Mount Street, Ruthin, Tel.: 01824 704702

Family Planning Services
Family Planning, The Royal Alexandra Hospital, Marine Drive, Rhyl, Tel.: 01745 443301

Health Visitors
Ms L Fletcher, Senior Nurse Manager Public Health - Health Visitors, Royal Alexander Hospital, Rhyl, Denbighshire, LL18 3AS, Tel.: 01745 443000 ext 3343

Mrs Williams, Health Visitor Team Leader, Royal Alexander Hospital, Rhyl, Denbighshire, LL18 3AS, Tel.: 01745 443186

Learning Disabilities
Mr R Holden, General Manager, The Royal Alexander Hospital, Marine Drive, Rhyl, Tel.: 01745 443244

Liaison Services
Ms J Davies, Discharge Liaison Nurse, Tel.: 01745 534913

Mrs C Nosworthy, Community Discharge Liaison, Tel.: 01745 534913

Other Services
Ms E Edwards, Hospital Manager, Denbigh Infirmary, Llangollen Hospital & Ruthin Community Hospital,

Ms H Kerr, Denbighshire Community Services Manager, Tel.: 01824 704702

Ms L Prior, Conwy Community Services Manager, Tel.: 01492 507548

Mrs M Whittam, Clinical Gov Lead - Community,

Pharmacy
Mr W Duffield, Head of Prescribing Advice, Matthew House, St Asaph Business Park, St Asaph, Tel.: 01745 582721

School Nursing
Ms L Fletcher, Senior Nurse Manager Public Health - Child Health/School Nurses, Royal Alexander Hospital, Rhyl, Denbighshire, LL18 3AS, Tel.: 01745 443000 ext 3343

Smoking Cessation
Ms C A Jones, Smoking Cessation Specialist, Matthew House, St Asaph Business Park, St Asaph, Tel.: 01745 582721

Specialist Nursing Services
Mr J Heron, Nurse Specialist, Cardiac Rehabilitation, Tel.: 01745 534923

Ms N Wivell, Nurse Specialist, Cardiac Rehabilitation, Tel.: 01745 534923

Ms M Goodwin, Cardioversion Nurse, Cardiology, Tel.: 01745 583910 ext 6584

Ms J Baker, Advisor, Continence, Tel.: 01745 443128

Ms R Hunter, Practitioner, Continence, Royal Alexandra Hospital, Tel.: 01745 443128

Ms P Jones, Practitioner, Continence, Royal Alexandra Hospital, Tel.: 01745 443128

Ms V Loftus, Nurse Specialist, Dermatology, Tel.: Bleep 4085

Ms A Steen, Nurse Specialist, Dermatology, Tel.: Bleep 4085

Ms E Alcock, Nurse Specialist, Diabetic Care, Tel.: 01745 534911

Ms J Lewis, Nurse Specialist, Diabetic Care, Tel.: 01745 534911

Ms N Lewis, Nurse Specialist, Diabetic Care, Tel.: 01745 534911

Ms J Roberts, Nurse Specialist, Diabetic Care, Tel.: 01745 534911

Ms J Colcough, Nurse Specialist, DVT, Tel.: Bleep 4471

Ms H Stephens, Assessment Team, Elderly Care, Tel.: 01745 823429

Ms S Stavely, Nurse Specialist, G.U.M, Tel.: 01745 534709

Mr A Bennett, Nurse Specialist, Heart Failure, Tel.: Bleep 4555

Ms J Weatherhead, Nurse Specialist, Lung Cancer, Tel.: 01745 583910 ext 6588

Ms R Wyn Davies, Specialist Practitioner, Lymphoedema, Tel.: 01745 445169

Ms A Ellis, Community, Clinical Nurse Specialist, Macmillan, Colwyn Bay Community Hospital, Tel.: 01492 807530

Ms S Hughes, Community, Clinical Nurse Specialist, Macmillan, Colwyn Bay Community Hospital, Tel.: 01492 807700

Ms I Logan, Hospital, Clinical Nurse Specialist, Macmillan, North Wales Cancer Treatment Centre, Tel.: 01745 445168

Ms S Looker, Community, Clinical Nurse Specialist, Macmillan, Prestatyn Community Hospital, Tel.: 01745 853746

Ms C Roberts, Community, Clinical Nurse Specialist, Macmillan, Denbigh Infirmary Clinic, Tel.: 01745 818123

Ms Y Rose, Hospital, Clinical Nurse Specialist, Macmillan, North Wales Cancer Treatment Centre, Tel.: 01745 445147

Ms G Sullivan, Community, Clinical Nurse Specialist, Macmillan, Colwyn Bay Community Hospital, Tel.: 01492 807700

Mr M Hall, Specialist Senior Occupation Therapist, Occupational Health, Denbigh Infirmary Clinic, Tel.: 01745 818123

Ms J Pottle, Occupational Therapist, Occupational Health, Colwyn Bay Community Hospital, Tel.: 01492 807575

Mr T Shea, Macmillan, Services Manager, Palliative Care, North Wales Cancer Treatment Centre, Tel.: 01745 445172

Ms S Roberts, Nurse Specialist, Parkinson's Disease, Tel.: 01745 534847

Ms L Jones, Pulmonary Outreach Rehab Team, Pulmonary Disorder, Bleep 4552/4553, Tel.: 01745 534878

Ms L Tadgell, Pulmonary Outreach Rehab Team, Pulmonary Disorder, Bleep 4552/4553, Tel.: 01745 534878

Ms Y Bredow, Nurse Specialist, Respiratory, Tel.: 01445 583910 ext 6588

Ms R Glynn, Nurse Specialist Rheumatology, 01745 583910 xt 3478

Ms D Hudson, Nurse, Stroke Care, Tel.: Bleep 4215

Ms S Ostenak, Nurse, Stroke Care, Tel.: Bleep 4215

Ms J Wray, Nurse Specialist, Stroke Care, 01745 534961 bleep 3643

Ms R Kirkham, Nurse Specialist, Thrombolysis, Tel.: Bleep 4022

Ms E Gittins, Seconded, Nurse, Tissue Viability, Tel.: 01745 443116

Ms F Whitehurst, Nurse, Tissue Viability, Tel.: 01745 443116

Ms S Hall, Nurse Specialist, Upper GI, Tel.: 01745 445298

Flintshire LHB
LHB Headquarters, Preswylfa
Hendy Road
MOLD, CH7 1PZ
Tel.: 01352 744103

Admin & Senior Management
Ms N Rees, Director of Nursing, Flintshire LHB, Preswylfa, Hendy Road, Mold, CH7 1PZ,

Child Protection/Safeguarding Children
Ms A Owen, Specialist Health Practitioner - Looked After Children & Care Leavers, Tel.: 01352 701040

Clinical Leads (NSF)
Ms M Popplewell, Clinical Lead, Diabetic Care,

Wales

Gwynedd LHB
LHB Headquarters, Eryldon
Campbell Road
CAERNARFON, Gwynedd
LL55 1HU
Tel.: 01286 672451

Admin & Senior Management
Mr M Davidson, Assistant Director Vulnerable Groups, Tel.: 01286 674240
Ms N Horne, Practice Development Nurse Manager/Diabetic Lead/Nurse Reviewer, Tel.: 01286 674216
Ms E Hugheston-Roberts, Assistant Nurse Director/Intermediate Care Lead, Tel.: 01286 674271
Mr P Liptrot, Executive Nurse Director, Gwynedd LHB, Eryldon, Campbell Road, Caernarfon, LL55 1HU, Tel.: 01286 672451
Mr S Owen, Practice Development Nurse Manager/CHD Lead, Tel.: 01286 674268
Child Health
Ms H Liptrot, Children's Reviewer/NSF Lead, Tel.: 01286 674264
Other Services
Ms V Hughes, Out of Hours Nurse Practitioner, Tel.: 01286 674277
Ms R Lewis, Out of Hours Nurse Practitioner, Tel.: 01286 674277
Mr A Parry, Out of Hours Nurse Practitioner, Tel.: 01286 674277
Mr A Parry, Out of Hours Nurse Practitioner, Tel.: 01286 674277
Specialist Nursing Services
Ms N Hughes, Nurse Reviewer/, Nurse, Cardiac Rehabilitation, Tel.: 01286 674297
Ms M Maloney, Nurse, Cardiac Rehabilitation, Tel.: 01286 674214
Ms N Smits, Nurse, Cardiac Rehabilitation, Tel.: 01286 674214
Mr R Jones, Manager, Continuing Care, Tel.: 01286 674237
Ms S Wyn Jones, Deputy Manager, Continuing Care, Tel.: 01286 674201
Ms F Bareham, Nurse, Practice Development, (Nursing Homes), Tel.: 01286 674266
Ms K Pritchard, Nurse, Practice Development, (Nursing Homes), Tel.: 01286 674265

North East Wales NHS Trust
Trust Headquarters, Wrexham Maelor Hospital
Croesnewydd Road
WREXHAM, Clwyd
LL13 7TD
Tel.: 01978 291100

Admin & Senior Management
Mrs Y Harding, Head of Nursing, Catherine Gladstone House, Hawarden Way, Mancot, Deeside, Flintshire, CH5 2EP, Tel.: 01244 538883
Child Health
Ms K Swale, Assistant Community Services Manager, Catherine Gladstone House, Hawarden Way, Mancot, Deeside, Flintshire, CH5 2EP, Tel.: 01244 538883
Child Health Records
Child Health Records, Child Health Dept, Wrexham Child Health Centre, PO Box 2073, Croesnewydd Road, Wrexham, LL13 7ZA, Tel.: 01978 725153
Ms A Tudor, Manager, Catherine Gladstone House, Hawarden Way, Mancot, Deeside, Flintshire, CH5 2EP, Tel.: 01244 538883
Child Protection/Safeguarding Children
Senior Nurse Wrexham, Wrexham Child Health Centre, Tel.: 01978 727021
Ms M Denwood, Senior/Named Nurse, Child Protection, Catherine Gladstone House, Hawarden Way, Mancot, Deeside, Flintshire, CH5 2EP, Tel.: 01244 538883
Mrs J Williams, Designated Nurse, Child Protection, Preswylfa, Hendy Road, Mold, North Wales, CH7 1PZ, Tel.: 01352 700227 ext 4097

Community Midwifery
Mrs D Cooper, Head of Midwifery, Wrexham Maelor Hospital, Tel.: 01978 725021
Mrs C Evans, Community Clerk, Wrexham Maelor Hospital, Tel.: 01978 725323
Ms S Jones, Deputy, Head of Midwifery, Wrexham Maelor Hospital, Tel.: 01978 725096
Learning Disabilities
Mr A Bell, Community Services Manager, 6th Floor, Entrance 3, County Hall, Mold, Flintshire, CH7 6NN, Tel.: 01352 704390
Liaison Services
Ms E Bedford, Connah's Quay Clinic, Connah's Quay, CH5 4HA, Tel.: 01244 813486
Ms M Jones Hughes, Community Sister, Ty Mawddach, Wrexham Maelor Hospital, Tel.: 01978 362478
Specialist Nursing Services
Ms Y Lush, Breast Care, Clwydian House, Tel.: 01978 727297
Ms K Hodgeson, Cardiac Rehabilitation, Tel.: 01978 727294
Ms C Bailey, Continence, Trinity House, Wrexham,
Ms C Monks, Diabetic Care, Wrexham Maelor Hospital, Tel.: 01978 727111
Ms G Ward, Diabetic Care, Wrexham Maelor Hospital, Tel.: 01978 727111
Ms R Evans, Genetics, Wrexham Maelor Hospital, Tel.: 01978 725065
Ms C Owen, Genetics, Wrexham Maelor Hospital, Tel.: 01978 725065
Ms C Gardner, Infection Control, Wrexham Maelor Hospital, Tel.: 01978 291100 bleep 5203
Ms J Purton, Infection Control, Maelor Hospital, Tel.: 01978 725203
Mrs c Davies, Macmillan, Wrexham Maelor Hospital, Tel.: 01978 291100
Mrs A Howarth, Macmillan, Greenfield Clinic, Tel.: 01352 712468
Mrs H King, Macmillan, Wrexham Maelor Hospital, Tel.: 01978 291100
Nurses, Macmillan, Buckley Health Centre, Tel.: 01244 545277
Ms P Lloyd, Respiratory, Clwydian House, Wrexham Maelor Hospital, Tel.: 01978 727294
Ms J Murray, Stoma Care, Wrexham Maelor Hospital, Tel.: 01978 291100 ext 7298
Ms C Williams, Tissue Viability, Clwydian House, Tel.: 01978 727444
Ms C Williams, Wound Care, Wrexham Maelor Hospital, Tel.: 01978 291100
The Homeless/Travellers & Asylum Seekers
Ms A Dunbabin, Refugees, Trinity House, Trinity Street, Wrexham, Tel.: 0773 2415 679
Ms J Harvey, Travellers, Queensferry Clinic, Queensferry, Tel.: 01244 813383
Ms A Roberts, Travellers, Hightown Clinic, Bryncabaau Road, Hightown, Wrexham, Tel.: 01978 364081
Ms J Williams, Refugees, Trinity House, Trinity Street, Wrexham, Tel.: 0773 2840 716

North West Wales NHS Trust
Trust Headquarters
Ysbyty Gwynedd
BANGOR
Gwynedd
LL57 2PW
Tel.: 01248 384384

Admin & Senior Management
Mr R A Jones, Executive Nursing Director, Ysbyty Gwynedd, LL57 2PW, Tel.: 01248 384212
Ms G Roberts, Women & Families Directorate General Manager, Tel.: 01248 384999
Ms S Thomas, Head of Nursing & Maternity Services, Tel.: 01248 384998

Wales

Child Health
Ms A Al Barazi, Children with Complex Needs/Palliative Care, Bodwrdda, St David's Road, Caernaefon, LL55 1EL, Community Childrens Nurses, Tel.: 01286 684019
Ms A Naylor, Lead Nurse, Specialist Skills in Behaviour Management/Disabilities, Child Development Team, Holyhead Road, Bangor, Tel.: 01248 364700
Ms E Vaughan Rowlands, Children's Oncology Nurse, Children's Unit, Ysbyty Gwynedd, Penrhosgarnedd, Gwynedd, LL57 2PW, Tel.: 01248 354384
Ms M Williams, Children with Complex Needs/Palliative Care, Bodwrdda, St David's Road, Caernaefon, LL55 1EL,
Ms M Michael, Paediatric, Diabetic Care, Ysbyty Gwynedd, Tel.: 01286 384520

Child Health Records
Child Health Records, Bodwrdda, Tel.: 01286 684000

Child Protection/Safeguarding Children
Mrs S A Thomas, Named Nurse, Child Protection, Ysbyty Gwynedd, Bangor, Tel.: 01248 384998

Community Midwifery
Mrs G Black, Community Midwifery Manager Women & Families Services, Tel.: 01248 385014
Mrs H Jones, Professional Lead for Midwifery, Ysbyty Gwynedd, Tel.: 01248 384110
Mrs K Kardtomeikel, Antenatal Screening Midwife, Ysbyty Gwynedd,

Community Nursing Services
Mr
Mr M J Jones, Head of Nursing, Community Hospitals & Rehabilitation Directorate, Bodfan, Eryri Hospital, Caernarfon, LL55 2YE, Tel.: 01286 662715

District Nursing
Arfon, District Nurses, Bodfan, Eryri Hospital, Caernarfon, LL55 2YE, Tel.: 01286 662780
Dwyfor, Meirionnydd, District Nurses, Community Office, Bron-y-Garth Hospital, Penrhyndeudraeth, LL48 6HE, Tel.: 01766 772136
Emergencies - Senior Manager On Call, District Nurses, Ysbyty Gwynedd Switchboard, Tel.: 01248 384384
Mrs S M Jones, Senior District Nurse Mon, District Nursing Office, Social Services Dept, Anglesey County Council, Llangefni, Anglesey, Tel.: 01248 751847
Mon, District Nurses, District Nursing Office, Social Services Dept, Anglesey County Council, Llangefni, Anglesey, Tel.: 01248 753110
Mrs M Owen, Senior District Nursing Dwyfor, Meirionnydd, District Nursing Office, Bron y Garth Hospital, Penrhynddeudraeth, Tel.: 01766 772136
Mrs D Roberts, Senior District Nurse Arfon, District Nursing Office, Bodfan, Eryri Hospital, Tel.: 01286 662739

Family Planning Services
Mrs K Thomas, Bodwrdda, St David's Road, Caernarfon, LL55 1EL, Tel.: 01286 684013

Health Visitors
Health Visitors, Gwynedd, Tel.: 01286 684009
Health Visitors, Ynys Mon, Tel.: 01248 753134

HIV/AIDS
Holyhead Clinic, Ysbyty Penrhos Stanley, Penrhos Beach Road, Holyhead, Anglesey, LL65 2QA, Tel.: 01407 766000
Llandudno Clinic, Llandudno General Hospital, Hospital Road, Llandudno, Conwy, LL30 1LB, Tel.: 01492 860066
Pwllheli Clinic, Ala Road, Pwllheli, Gwynedd, LL53 5BL, Tel.: 01758 701000
Telephone Number for all Clinic times, Tel.: 01248 370376
Ysbyty Gwynedd Clinic, Penrhosgarnedd, Gwynedd, LL57 2PW, Tel.: 01248 384384

Learning Disabilities
Mr P Baker, Challenging Behaviour Service Manager (LD), Bryn y Neuadd, Llanfairfechan, Conwy, LL33 OHH, Tel.: 01248 682560
Mr O Evans, Team Leader, Arfon, 2nd Floor, Penrallt, Caernarfon, LL55 1BN, Tel.: 01286 682754/682763

Mr S Hughes, Service Manager, Head of Nursing, Directorate HQ, Bryn y Neuadd, Llanfairfechan, Conwy, LL33 0HH, Tel.: 01278 682613
Mr S McGuinness, Team Leader, Meirionnydd, Bristol House, Fos y Felin, Dolgellau, Meirionnydd, LL40 1AA also based at Bryn y Neuadd, Tel.: 01341 422012/01248 682834
Ms D Roberts, Team Leader, Ynys Mon, Shire Hall, Glanhwfa Road, Llangefni, Ynys Mon, LL77 7TS, Tel.: 01248 752718
Ms A Rowlands, Team Leader, Dwyfor, Dwyfor Council Offices, Embankment Road, Pwllheli, Tel.: 01758 704145

Liaison Services
Ms V Birch, Bed Manager, Ysbyty Gwynedd, Tel.: 01248 384334
Ms L Hughes, Discharge Co-ordinator, Ysbyty Gwynedd, Tel.: 01248 384334
Ms D Richards, Continuing Care Facilitator, Beechwood House, Dolgellau, LL40 1AU, Tel.: 01341 421412

Other Services
Ms A Bentley, Transplant Co-ordinator, Ysbyty Gwynedd, Tel.: 01248 384448
Mr L Williams, Mon & Arfon Rapid Response Team Co-ordinator, Bodfan, Tel.: 01286 662765

School Nursing
Mrs J Roberts, School Nursing, Senior Nurse, Ffestiniog Memorial Hospital, Tel.: 01766 831281/01286 684014

Specialist Nursing Services
Ms L Hall, Colposcopy, Ysbyty Gwynedd, Tel.: 01248 385003
Ms N Rosser Hughes, Tenovus, Specialist Nurse, Ysbyty Gwynedd, Tel.: 01248 384431
Ms M Evans, Breast Care, Llandudno General Hospital, Tel.: 01492 862397
Ms E Hughes, Breast Care, Ysbyty Gwynedd, Tel.: 01248 384674
Ms M Williams, Breast Care, Ysbyty Gwynedd, Tel.: 01248 384674
Mr D Macey, Specialist Nurse, Cardiology, Ysbyty Gwynedd, Tel.: 01248 384482
Ms L Hughes, Colorectal, - Stoma, Ysbyty Gwynedd, Tel.: 01248 384671
Ms L Jones, Specialist Nurse, Colorectal, - Stoma, Ysbyty Gwynedd, Tel.: 01248 384671
Mr D Roberts, Specialist Nurse, Colorectal, - Stoma, Ysbyty Gwynedd, Tel.: 01248 384671
Ms A Barnsley, Continence, Bryn y Neuadd Hospital, Llanfairfechan, LL33 0HH, Tel.: 01248 682552
Ms E Pritchard, Continence, Ysbyty Gwynedd, Tel.: 01248 384672
Ms C Graham, Cystic Fibrosis, Ysbyty Gwynedd, Tel.: 01248 385111
Ms Y Stone, Cystic Fibrosis, Ysbyty Gwynedd, Tel.: 01248 385111
Ms J Everden, Dermatology, Ysbyty Gwynedd, Tel.: 01248 385369 bleep 055
Ms D Fisher, Diabetic Care, Ysbyty Gwynedd, Tel.: 01248 384082
Ms D Hughes, Diabetic Care, Ysbyty Gwynedd, Tel.: 01248 384082
Ms R Sherrington, Diabetic Care, Ysbyty Gwynedd, Tel.: 01248 384082
Ms Y Harding, Nurses Co-ordinator, Diana, Catherine Gladstone House, Hawarden, Mancot, Deeside, Tel.: 01244 538883
Ms I Thomas, Gastroenterology, Ysbyty Gwynedd, Tel.: 01248 384923
Ms C Owen, Counsellor, Genetics, Ysbyty Gwynedd, Tel.: 01248 384079
Ms S Carter, Infection Control, Ysbyty Gwynedd, Tel.: 01248 384060
Mr G Porter-Jones, Public Health, Infection Control, Ysbyty Gwynedd, Tel.: 01248 384598
Ms J Emsley, Macmillan, Bodfan, Tel.: 01286 662775
Ms A Jones, Macmillan, Bodfan, Tel.: 01286 662775
Ms L Minto, Macmillan, Ysbyty Gwynedd, Tel.: 01248 385121
Ms C Muskatt, Oncology, Ysbyty Gwynedd, Tel.: 01248 385121
Ms V Monaghan, Pulmonary Disorder, Ysbyty Gwynedd, Tel.: 01248 384785
Mr M Nash, Head, Pulmonary Disorder, Ysbyty Gwynedd, Tel.: 01248 384785

Wales

Ms E English, Specialist Nurse, Respiratory, Ysbyty Gwynedd, Tel.: 01248 384178/5145

Ms S Jones, Specialist Nurse, Respiratory, Ysbyty Gwynedd, Tel.: 01248 384178/5145

Ms A Breslin, Rheumatology, Ysbyty Gwynedd, Tel.: 01248 384682

Ms A Whitlow, Specialist Nurse, Stroke Care, Ysbyty Gwynedd, Tel.: 01248 384373

Ms R Griffiths, Thrombolysis, Ysbyty Gwynedd, Tel.: 01248 384663

Ms S Hughes, Thrombolysis, Ysbyty Gwynedd, Tel.: 01248 384663/384097

Ms J Mercer-Edwards, Specialist Nurse, Thrombolysis, Ysbyty Gwynedd, Tel.: 01248 384335 bleep 800

Ms S Stubbs, Genito Urinary, Urology, Ysbyty Gwynedd, Tel.: 01248 384053

Ms L Poulton, Urology/Oncology, Ysbyty Gwynedd, Tel.: 01248 384673

Ms F Evans, Vascular, Ysbyty Gwynedd, Tel.: 01248 384309

Ms M Lloyd Jones, Wound Care, Beechwood House, Tel.: 01341 421412

Wrexham LHB

LHB Headquarters, Technology Park
Rhyd Broughton Lane
WREXHAM, LL13 7YP
Tel.: 01978 346500

Admin & Senior Management

Ms L Burdge, Practice Development Nurse, Wrexham LHB, Technology Park, Rhyd Broughton Lane, Wrexham, LL13 7YP, Tel.: 01978 346500

Mr P Foster, Nurse Practitioner, Caia Park Health Project, Tel.: 01978 346500

Ms C Girvan, Case Manager Long Term Illness, Tel.: 01978 346500

Mrs G Latham, Community Services Manager, Chirk Community Hospital, Chirk, LL14 5LN, Tel.: 01691 772430

Mrs S Roden, Community Services Manager, Grove Road Health Centre, Wrexham, LL11 1DY, Tel.: 01978 350193

Mrs S Willis, Director of Nursing, Wrexham LHB, Technology Park, Rhyd Broughton Lane, Wrexham, LL13 7YP, Tel.: 01978 346500

Child Health

Ms K Czerniak, Children's Ward Specialist Nurse, Wrexham Maelor Hospital, Tel.: 01978 291100

Child Health Records

Ms K Swale, Assistant Community Services Manager,

Ms A Tudor, Manager, Catherine Gladstone House, Hawarden Way, Deeside, CH5 2EP, Tel.: 01244 538883

Child Protection/Safeguarding Children

Child Protection, Catherine Gladstone House, Hawarden Way, Mancot, Flintshire, CH5 2EP, Tel.: 01244 538883

Ms C O'Grady, Looked After Children, Kelso House, 13 Grosvenor Road, Wrexham, Tel.: 267174

Ms J Snelling, Senior Nurse Wrexham, Wrexham Child Health Centre, Tel.: 01978 727021

Clinical Leads (NSF)

Ms L Ward, Contact for all NSFs,

Community Nursing Services

Ms J Atkin, Community Nurse, Grove Road Health Centre, Wrexham, LL11 1DY, Tel.: 01978 263006

Mr E Bennell, Community Nurse, Grove Road Health Centre, Wrexham, LL11 1DY, Tel.: 01978 262477

Ms E Binns, Community Nurse, Elspeth Binns, Plas Y Byrn Surgery, Chapel Street, Wrexham, LL13 7DD, Tel.: 01978 290157

Ms A Byrne, Community Nurse, Chirk Clinic, Station Avenue, Chirk, Wrexham, LL14 5LS, Tel.: 01691 774225

Ms A Davies, Community Nurse, Elspeth Binns, Plas Y Byrn Surgery, Chapel Street, Wrexham, LL13 7DD, Tel.: 01978 290157

Ms J Davies, Community Nurse, Gresford Health Centre, Poplar Avenue, Gresford, Wrexham, Tel.: 01978 856559

Ms J Edwards, Community Nurse, Penley Clinic, Maelor School, Penley, Wrexham, LL13 0LU, Tel.: 01948 830135

Ms K Evans, Community Nurse, Chirk Clinic, Station Avenue, Chirk, Wrexham, LL14 5LS, Tel.: 01691 774225

Ms D Griffiths, Community Nurse, Pen-Y-Maes Health Centre, Beech Street, Summerhill, Wrexham, LL11 4UF, Tel.: 01978 752818

Ms N Jenkins-Jones, Community Nurse, Plas Madoc Clinic, Acrefair, Wrexham, LL14 3HE, Tel.: 01978 812163

Ms M Jones, Community Nurse, Grove Road Health Centre, Wrexham, LL11 1DY, Tel.: 01978 263006

Ms L Jones-Tattum, Community Nurse, Plas Madoc Clinic, Acrefair, Wrexham, LL14 3HE, Tel.: 01978 812163

Ms B Lewis, Community Nurse, Brynteg Clinic, Darby Road, Southsea, Wrexham, LL11 6RN, Tel.: 01978 752869

Ms B Matthias, Community Nurse, Coedpoeth Health Centre, Smithy Road, Coedpoeth, Wrexham, LL11 3NS, Tel.: 01978 754053

Ms E Nott, Community Nurse, Rhostyllen Clinic, James Street, Rhostyllen, LL14 4AW, Tel.: 01978 311496

Ms J Roberts, Community Nurse, Coedpoeth Health Centre, Smithy Road, Coedpoeth, Wrexham, LL11 3NS, Tel.: 01978 754053

Ms J Sankey, Community Nurse, Rhos Health Centre, Broad Street, Rhos, Wrexham, LL14 1AA, Tel.: 01978 846776

Mr K Wells, Community Nurse, Grove Road Health Centre, Wrexham, LL11 1DY, Tel.: 01978 262477

District Nursing

Ms J Bellis, Strathmore, District Nurse, Grove Road Health Centre, Grove Road, Wrexham, LL11 1DY, Tel.: 01978 263006

Ms S Bellis, Strathmore, District Nurse, Grove Road Health Centre, Grove Road, Wrexham, LL11 1DY, Tel.: 01978 263006

Ms A Berry, District Nurse, Gresford Health Centre, Poplar Avenue, Gresford, Wrexham, LL12 8EP, Tel.: 01978 856559

Ms M Blackburn, District Nurse, Plas Y Byrn Surgery, Wrexham, LL13 7DD, Tel.: 01978 290157

Ms M Browne, District Nurse, Plas Madoc Clinic, Acrefair, Wrexham, LL14 3HE, Tel.: 01978 812163

Ms J Clark, District Nurse, Rhos Health Centre, Broad Street, Rhos, Wrexham, LL14 1AA, Tel.: 01978 846776

Mr C Cripps, District Nurse, Grove Road Health Centre, Wrexham, LL11 1DY, Tel.: 01978 262477

Ms M Davies, Strathmore, District Nurse, Grove Road Health Centre, Grove Road, Wrexham, LL11 1DY, Tel.: 01978 263006

Ms L Edwards, District Nurse, Chirk Clinic, Station Avenue, Chirk, Wrexham, LL14 5LS, Tel.: 01691 774225

Ms L Edwards, District Nurse, Rhostyllen Clinic, James Street, Rhostyllen, LL14 4AW, Tel.: 01978 311496

Ms S Edwards, District Nurse, Rhos Health Centre, Broad Street, Rhos, Wrexham, LL14 1AA, Tel.: 01978 846776

Ms A Evans, District Nurse, Rhos Health Centre, Broad Street, Rhos, Wrexham, LL14 1AA, Tel.: 01978 846776

Ms C Evans, District Nurse, Grove Road Health Centre, Wrexham, LL11 1DY, Tel.: 01978 262477

Ms R Garner, District Nurse, Gresford Health Centre, Poplar Avenue, Gresford, Wrexham, LL12 8EP, Tel.: 01978 856559

Mr C Griffiths, District Nurse, Gresford Health Centre, Poplar Avenue, Gresford, Wrexham, LL12 8EP, Tel.: 01978 856559

Ms P Howell, District Nurse, Pen-Y-Maes Health Centre, Beech Street, Summerhill, Wrexham, LL11 4UF, Tel.: 01978 752818

Ms T Hughes, District Nurse, Chirk Clinic, Station Avenue, Chirk, Wrexham, LL14 5LS, Tel.: 01691 774225

Ms W Hughes, District Nurse, Plas Y Byrn Surgery, Wrexham, LL13 7DD, Tel.: 01978 290157

Ms H Jones, District Nurse, Plas Madoc Clinic, Acrefair, Wrexham, LL14 3HE, Tel.: 01978 812163

Ms J Jones, District Nurse, Penley Clinic, Maelor School, Penley, Wrexham, LL13 0LU, Tel.: 01948 830135

Ms J Jones, District Nurse, Grove Road Health Centre, Wrexham, LL11 1DY, Tel.: 01978 262477

Wales

Ms J Jones, Strathmore, District Nurse, Grove Road Health Centre, Grove Road, Wrexham, LL11 1DY, Tel.: 01978 263006

Ms L Jones, District Nurse, Pen-Y-Maes Health Centre, Beech Street, Summerhill, Wrexham, LL11 4UF, Tel.: 01978 752818

Ms V Jones, District Nurse, Rhostyllen Clinic, James Street, Rhostyllen, LL14 4AW, Tel.: 01978 311496

Ms C Kane, District Nurse, Grove Road Health Centre, Wrexham, LL11 1DY, Tel.: 01978 262477

Ms J Lloyd, District Nurse, Coedpoeth Health Centre, Smithy Road, Coedpoeth, Wrexham, LL11 3NS, Tel.: 01978 754053

Ms G Lloyd Jones, Evening Nursing Service, District Nurse, Out of Hours GP Co-Operative, Pendine Park, Summerhill, Wrexham, Tel.: 01978 759832

Ms C Morris, District Nurse, Coedpoeth Health Centre, Smithy Road, Coedpoeth, Wrexham, LL11 3NS, Tel.: 01978 754053

Ms L Morris, Strathmore, District Nurse, Grove Road Health Centre, Grove Road, Wrexham, LL11 1DY, Tel.: 01978 263006

Ms K Norman, District Nurse, Coedpoeth Health Centre, Smithy Road, Coedpoeth, Wrexham, LL11 3NS, Tel.: 01978 754053

Ms A Overthrow, District Nurse, Rhos Health Centre, Broad Street, Rhos, Wrexham, LL14 1AA, Tel.: 01978 846776

Ms R Overthrow, District Nurse, Brynteg Clinic, Derby Road, Southsea, Wrexham, LL11 6RN, Tel.: 01978 752869

Ms L Owen, District Nurse, Coedpoeth Health Centre, Smithy Road, Coedpoeth, Wrexham, LL11 3NS, Tel.: 01978 754053

Ms S Parry, District Nurse, Chirk Clinic, Station Avenue, Chirk, Wrexham, LL14 5LS, Tel.: 01691 774225

Ms M Pirie, Evening Nursing Service, District Nurse, Out of Hours GP Co-Operative, Pendine Park, Summerhill, Wrexham, Tel.: 01978 759832

Ms A Price, District Nurse, Brynteg Clinic, Derby Road, Southsea, Wrexham, LL11 6RN, Tel.: 01978 752869

Ms A Roberts, District Nurse, Plas Madoc Clinic, Acrefair, Wrexham, LL14 3HE, Tel.: 01978 812163

Ms C Roberts, District Nurse, Brynteg Clinic, Derby Road, Southsea, Wrexham, LL11 6RN, Tel.: 01978 752869

Ms J Roberts, District Nurse, Plas Madoc Clinic, Acrefair, Wrexham, LL14 3HE, Tel.: 01978 812163

Ms J Roberts, District Nurse, Plas Y Byrn Surgery, Wrexham, LL13 7DD, Tel.: 01978 290157

Ms J Roscoe, District Nurse, Pen-Y-Maes Health Centre, Beech Street, Summerhill, Wrexham, LL11 4UF, Tel.: 01978 752818

Ms J Ross, District Nurse, Gresford Health Centre, Poplar Avenue, Gresford, Wrexham, LL12 8EP, Tel.: 01978 856559

Ms D Salisbury, Evening Nursing Service, District Nurse, Out of Hours GP Co-Operative, Pendine Park, Summerhill, Wrexham, Tel.: 01978 759832

Ms L Sangar, District Nurse, Brynteg Clinic, Derby Road, Southsea, Wrexham, LL11 6RN, Tel.: 01978 752869

Ms Z Scott, District Nurse, Penley Clinic, Maelor School, Penley, Wrexham, LL13 0LU, Tel.: 01948 830135

Ms J Skelson, District Nurse, Chirk Clinic, Station Avenue, Chirk, Wrexham, LL14 5LS, Tel.: 01691 774225

Ms M Stanley, District Nurse, Rhostyllen Clinic, James Street, Rhostyllen, LL14 4AW, Tel.: 01978 311496

Ms J Steele, Evening Nursing Service, District Nurse, Out of Hours GP Co-Operative, Pendine Park, Summerhill, Wrexham, Tel.: 01978 759832

Ms P Whilding, District Nurse, Plas Madoc Clinic, Acrefair, Wrexham, LL14 3HE, Tel.: 01978 812163

Ms J Williams, District Nurse, Plas Y Byrn Surgery, Chapel Street, Wrexham, LL13 7DD, Tel.: 01978 290157

Ms E Wilson, District Nurse, Plas Madoc Clinic, Acrefair, Wrexham, LL14 3HE, Tel.: 01978 812163

Ms K Wilson, District Nurse, Chirk Clinic, Station Avenue, Chirk, Wrexham, LL14 5LS, Tel.: 01691 774225

Ms M Wynne, District Nurse, Pen-Y-Maes Health Centre, Beech Street, Summerhill, Wrexham, LL11 4UF, Tel.: 01978 752818

Family Planning Services

Ms S Padmore, Sexual Health Advisor, Wrexham Maelor Hospital, Tel.: 01978 291100

Health Visitors

Mr C Baker, Health Visitor, Prince Charles Road, Queens Park, Tel.: 01978 262191

Ms M Bowler, Health Visitor, Gwersyllt Health Centre, Beech Street, Gwersyllt, Tel.: 01978 750193

Ms M Bowler, Specialist Practice Mentor - health visiting, Gwersylut Clinic, Beech Street, Gwersyut, Tel.: 01978 364081

Ms O Bowyer, Health Visitor, Penley Clinic, Maelor School, Penley, Wrexham, LL13 0LU, Tel.: 01948 830284

Ms A Dunbabin, Health Visitor, Strathmore Surgery, Chester Road, Wrexham, Tel.: Wxm 290968

Ms S Edwards, Health Visitor, Plas Madoc Clinic, Acrefair, Wrexham, LL14 3HE, Tel.: 01978 822192

Ms J Fieldhouse, Health Visitor, Brynteg Clinic, Derby Road, Southsea, Wrexham, LL11 6RN, Tel.: 01978 757546

Ms B Gough, Health Visitor, Plas Madoc Clinic, Acrefair, Wrexham, LL14 3HE, Tel.: 01978 822192

Ms J Graham, Health Visitor, Rhos Health Centre, Broad Street, Rhos, Wrexham, LL14 1AA, Tel.: 01978 840151

Ms C Gudgeon, Health Visitor, Coedpoeth Health Centre, Smithy Road, Coedpoeth, Wrexham, LL11 3NS, Tel.: 01978 752776

Ms D Hall, Health Visitor, Hightown, Brynycabanau Road, Hightown, Tel.: 01978 364081

Ms L Hallett, Health Visitor, Chirk Clinic, Station Avenue, Chirk, Wrexham, LL14 5LS, Tel.: 01691 773581

Ms D Hodson, Paediatric Liaison, Health Visitor, Maelor Children's Centre, Maelor Hospital, Wrexham, Tel.: 725601

Ms J Hughes, Health Visitor, Chirk Clinic, Station Avenue, Chirk, Wrexham, LL14 5LS, Tel.: 01691 773581

Ms P Hughes, Health Visitor, Gwersyllt Health Centre, Beech Street, Gwersyllt, Tel.: 01978 750193

Ms S Hughes, Health Visitor, Rhos Health Centre, Broad Street, Rhos, Wrexham, LL14 1AA, Tel.: 01978 840151

Mr C Hulme, Health Visitor, Prince Charles Road, Queens Park, Tel.: 01978 262191

Ms C Humphreys, Health Visitor, Cefn Mawr Clinic, Well Street, Cefn M, Wrexham, Tel.: Wxm 824756

Ms K Jones, Health Visitor, School Road, Llay, Tel.: 01978 856749

Ms S Jones, Health Visitor, Ruabon Clinic, High Street, Ruabon, Tel.: 01978 821204

Ms E Lloyd, Health Visitor, Rhostyllen Clinic, James Street, Rhostyllen, LL14 4AW, Tel.: 01978 357151

Ms J Lloyd, Practice Development, Health Visitor, Rossett Clinic, The Green, Rosset, Tel.: 01244 571158

Ms J Lloyd, Health Visitor, Coedpoeth Health Centre, Smithy Road, Coedpoeth, Wrexham, LL11 3NS, Tel.: 01978 752776

Ms J Lloyd, Health Visitor, Rossett Clinic, The Green, Rossett, Tel.: 01244 570409

Ms D McLeod, Health Visitor, Brynteg Clinic, Derby Road, Southsea, Wrexham, LL11 6RN, Tel.: 01978 757546

Ms A Parry, Health Visitor, Llangollen Health Centre, Regent Street, Llangollen, Tel.: 01978 861247

Ms L Pusey, Health Visitor, Prince Charles Road, Queens Park, Tel.: 01978 262191

Ms A Roberts, Health Visitor, Hightown, Brynycabanau Road, Hightown, Tel.: 01978 364081

Ms A Roberts, Specialist Practice Mentor - health visiting, Hightown Clinic, Wrexham, Tel.: 01978 364081

Ms R Roberts, Health Visitor, Brynteg Clinic, Derby Road, Southsea, Wrexham, LL11 6RN, Tel.: 01978 757546

Ms R Rogers, Health Visitor, Grove Road Health Centre, Grove Road, Wrexham, Tel.: 01978 362510

Ms S Rowan, Health Visitor, Grove Road Health Centre, Grove Road, Wrexham, Tel.: 01978 362510

Wales

Ms J Sankey, Health Visitor, Gresford Health Centre, Poplar Avenue, Gresford, Wrexham, LL12 8EP, Tel.: 01978 853439

Ms R Thompson, Health Visitor, Rossett Clinic, The Green, Rossett, Tel.: 01244 570409

Ms A Williams, Health Visitor, Rhos Health Centre, Broad Street, Rhos, Wrexham, LL14 1AA, Tel.: 01978 840151

Ms J Williams, Health Visitor, Strathmore Surgery, Chester Road, Wrexham, Tel.: Wxm 290968

Ms J Wort, Health Visitor, Prince Charles Road, Queens Park, Tel.: 01978 262191

Liaison Services

Ms J Cliff, Liaison, BHF Cardiac Nurse, Clwydian House, Wrexham Maelor Hospital, Tel.: 01978 291100

Ms M Jones-Hughes, Liaison, District Nursing, Ty Mawddach, Maelor Hospital, Wrexham, Tel.: 01978 362478

Other Services

Mrs J Edwards, Reviewer - Continuing Care,

Mrs D Griffiths, Continuing Care Manager (Wrexham & Flintshire), LHB Headquarters, Tel.: 01978 346500

Mrs S Howard, Reviewer - Continuing Care,

Miss E Thompson, Reviewer - Continuing Care,

School Nursing

Ms J Hill, Specialist Practice Mentors - School Nursing, Coedpoeth Clinic, Smithy Road, Wrexham, Tel.: 01978 752776

Ms L Taylor, Practice Development, School Nurse, Rossett Clinic, The Green, Rossett, Tel.: 01244 571158

Smoking Cessation

Ms J Rogers, Smoking Cessation Officer - North Wales Service, Tel.: 01352 755543

Specialist Nursing Services

Ms Y Lush, Macmillan, Nurse Specialist, Breast Care, Clwydian House, Wrexham Maelor Hospital, Tel.: 01978 727297

Ms J Renshaw, Macmillan, Nurse Specialist, Breast Care, Clwydian House, Wrexham Maelor Hospital, Tel.: 01978 727297

Ms K Hodgeson, Clinical Nurse Specialist, Cardiac Rehabilitation, Clwydian House, Wrexham Maelor Hospital, Tel.: 01978 727294

Ms A Roberts, Clinical Nurse Specialist, Colorectal, Clwydian House, Wrexham Maelor Hospital, Tel.: 01978 291100

Ms C Bailey, Advisor, Continence, Trinity House, Wrexham, Tel.: 01978 290071

Ms S Darlington, Practitioner, Continence, Trinity House, Wrexham, Tel.: 01978 290071

Ms K Bate, Clinical Nurse Specialist, Dermatology, Wrexham Maelor Hospital, Tel.: 01978 291100

Ms A Owen, Nurse Specialist, Diabetes, Tel.: 01978 346500

Ms C Monks, Clinical Nurse Specialist, Diabetic Care, Gillian Ward, Wrexham Maelor Hospital, Tel.: 01978 727111

Ms G Ward, Clinical Nurse Specialist, Diabetic Care, Wrexham Maelor Hospital,

Ms L Cropper, Peritoneal, Clinical Nurse Specialist, Dialysis, Renal Unit, Wrexham Maelor Hospital, Tel.: 01978 291100

Ms S Lewis, Specialist Nurse, Epilepsy, ECG Department, Wrexham Maelor Hospital, Tel.: 01978 291100

Mr R Evans, Clinical Nurse Specialist, Genetics, Ante-Natal, Wrexham Maelor Hospital, Tel.: 01978 725065

Ms C Owen, Ante-Natal, Clinical Nurse Specialist, Genetics, Wrexham Maelor Hospital, Tel.: 01978 291100

Ms J Samuel, Clinical Nurse Specialist, Haematology, Clwydian House, Wrexham Maelor Hospital, Tel.: 01978 291100

Ms J Welstand, Nurse Specialist, Heart Failure, Clwydian House, Wrexham Maelor Hospital, Tel.: 01978 291100

Ms L Bradford, Clinical Nurse Specialist, Infection Control, Ty Elaine, Wrexham Maelor Hospital, Tel.: 01978 725203

Ms J Purton, Advisor, Infection Control, Ty Elaine, Wrexham Maelor Hospital, Tel.: 01978 725203

Ms C Roberts, Public Health/Community, Infection Control, Wrexham Maelor Hospital, Tel.: 01978 291100

Ms A Gostage, Nurse Specialist, Lung Cancer, Clwydian House, Wrexham Maelor Hospital, Tel.: 01978 291100

Ms E Lund, Specialist Nurse, Lymphoedema, Nightingale House Hospice, Chester Road, Wrexham,

Mrs C Davies, Macmillan, Wrexham Maelor Hospital, Tel.: 01978 291100

Ms A Foster, Nursing Service Advisor, Macmillan, Nightingale House Hospice, Chester Road, Wrexham,

Ms P Edwards, Clinical Nurse Specialist, Nutrition, Clwydian House, Wrexham Maelor Hospital, Tel.: 01978 291100

Ms J Wykes, Clinical Nurse Specialist, Nutrition, Clwydian House, Wrexham Maelor Hospital, Tel.: 01978 291100

Ms K Cooper, Nurse Specialist, Respiratory, Tel.: 01978 346500

Ms P Lloyd, Clinical Nurse Specialist, Respiratory, Clwydian House, Wrexham Maelor Hospital, Tel.: 01978 727294

Ms G Johnson, Clinical Nurse Specialist, Rheumatology, Clwydian House, Wrexham Maelor Hospital, Tel.: 01978 291100

Ms J Murray, Clinical Nurse Specialist, Stoma Care, Clwydian House, Wrexham Maelor Hospital, Tel.: 01978 727444 ext 7298

Miss J Timmins, Nurse Consultant, Substance Misuse, Swn Y Coed, Grove Road, Wrexham,

Ms B Pritchard, Clinical Nurse Specialist, Tissue Viability, Clwydian House, Wrexham Maelor Hospital, Tel.: 01978 727444

Ms C Williams, Advisor, Tissue Viability, Clwydian House, Wrexham Maelor Hospital, Tel.: 01978 727444

Ms A Camps, Macmillan, Nurse Specialist, Upper GI, Clwydian House, Wrexham Maelor Hospital, Tel.: 01978 291100

Ms A Giddins, Clinical Nurse Specialist, Urology, Glyndwr Ward, Wrexham Maelor Hospital, Tel.: 01978 291100

The Homeless/Travellers & Asylum Seekers

Ms J Adkins, Project Health Worker - Travellers Project, Clwydian House, Wrexham, Tel.: 01978 352880

Ms A Dunbabin, Asylum Seekers, Health Visitor, Trinity House, Trinity Street, Wrexham, Tel.: 07732 415679

Ms J Williams, Asylum Seekers, Health Visitor, Trinity House, Trinity Street, Wrexham, Tel.: 07732 415679

South East Wales Region

Blaenau Gwent LHB

LHB Headquarters, Station Hill
ABERTILLERY, NP13 1UJ
Tel.: 01495 325400

Admin & Senior Management
Mr B Bolt, Nurse Director,
Clinical Leads (NSF)
Mr B Bolt, Contact for all NSF,

Caerphilly LHB

LHB Headquarters, Ystrad Mynach Hospital
Caerphilly Road, Hengoed
CAERPHILLY, CF82 7XU
Tel.: 01443 862056

Admin & Senior Management
Mrs C Hayes, Director of Nursing, Ystrad Mynach Hospital, Caerphilly Road, Hengoed, Caerphilly, CF82 7XU, Tel.: 01443 815103

Child Health
Mrs S Jones, Senior Nurse, Ystrad Mynach Hosp., 01443 862056

Child Protection/Safeguarding Children
Mrs S Jones, Senior Nurse, Child Protection, Ystrad Mynach Hospital, Tel.: 01443 862056

Clinical Leads (NSF)
Dr K Gully, Clinical Lead, CHD & Diabetes,

Mrs C Hayes, Clinical Lead, Cancer & Care of the Elderly, Ystrad Mynach Hospital, Caerphilly Road, Hengoed, Caerphilly, CF82 7XU, Tel.: 01443 862056

Community Midwifery
Mrs C Hayes, Director of Nursing, Ystrad Mynach Hospital, Caerphilly Road, Hengoed, Caerphilly, CF82 7XU, Tel.: 01443 862056

Community Nursing Services
Mrs D Francis, Senior Nurse for Community & Partnerships, Ystrad Mynach Hospital, Tel.: 01443 862056

District Nursing
Mrs C Hayes, Director of Nursing, Ystrad Mynach Hospital, Caerphilly Road, Hengoed, Caerphilly, CF82 7XU, Tel.: 01443 862056

Learning Disabilities
Mr C Edmonds,

Pharmacy
Ms C Jones, Head of Primary Care,

Specialist Nursing Services
Ms M Burgham-Malin, Practice Nurse Facilitator, Ystrad Mynach Hospital,
Mrs D Francis, Senior Nurse for Community & Partnerships, Ystrad Mynach Hospital, Tel.: 01443 862056
Ms S Sroczynska, CHD, Ystrad Mynach Hospital,
Ms J Challenger, Nurse Consultant, Older People, Ystrad Mynach Hospital,

Cardiff & Vale NHS Trust

Trust Headquarters, Univ Hospital of Wales
Heath Park
CARDIFF
CF14 4XW
Tel.: 029 2074 7747

Admin & Senior Management
Miss S Gregory, Nurse Director,
Miss S Revell, General Manager, Llandough Hospital, Penlan road, Penarth, Vale of Glamorgan, CF64 2XX, Tel.: 029 2071 1711

Child Health
Ms R Bentley, Paediatric Oncology - Vale of Glamorgan Area, Llandough Hospital, Tel.: 029 2071 1711
Ms S Coffey, Paediatric Oncology - Vale of Glamorgan Area, Llandough Hospital, Tel.: 029 2071 1711
Hospital/Community, Paediatrics, Lansdowne Hospital, Sanatorium Road, Canton, Cardiff, CF1 8UL, Tel.: 029 2037 2451
Ms L Lowes, Paediatric Diabetes Cardiff Area, Child Health Department, University Hospital of Wales, Tel.: 029 2074 5435
Ms J Menon, Paediatric Oncology - Vale of Glamorgan Area, Llandough Hospital, Tel.: 029 2071 1711
Ms E Spear, Paediatric Respiratory - Vale of Glamorgan Area, Llandough Hospital, Tel.: 029 2071 1711

Child Health Records
Child Health Department, Lansdowne Hospital, Sanatorium Road, Canton, Cardiff, CF1 8UL, Tel.: 029 2037 2451

Child Protection/Safeguarding Children
Ms K Ellaway, Named Nurse, Child Protection, Lansdowne Hospital, Sanitorium Road, Cardiff, CF11 8PL, Tel.: 02920 932645 ext 2645

Community Midwifery
Directorate of Obs & Gynaecological, University Hospital of Wales, Heath Park, Cardiff, South Glamorgan, CF4 4XW, Tel.: 029 2074 3238
Emergencies, University Hospital of Wales, Heath Park, Cardiff, South Glamorgan, CF4 4XW, Tel.: 029 2071 6001
Mrs B Rees, Head of Midwifery, University Hospital of Wales, Heath Park, Cardiff, South Glamorgan, CF4 4XW, Tel.: 029 2074 3238

Community Nursing Services
Ms J Theed, Director of Nursing, Lansdowne Hospital, Sanatorium Road, Canton, Cardiff, CF1 8UL, Tel.: 029 2037 2451

District Nursing
District Nurses, (0830-1700 Mon-Fri), Tel.: 029 2049 5816
Emergencies/Night, Tel.: 029 2049 5816
Nursing Control, Tel.: 029 2056 7370 (24hrs)

Liaison Services
Liaison - Hospital/Community, Paediatrics, Lansdowne Hospital, Sanatorium Road, Canton, Cardiff, CF1 8UL, Tel.: 029 2037 2451

Specialist Nursing Services
Ms B Smith, Accident Prevention Cardiff Area, Lansdowne Hospital, Tel.: 029 2037 2451
Ms K Doyle, Tenovus - Vale of Glamorgan Area, Breast Care, Llandough Hospital, Tel.: 029 2071 1711
Ms H McGarrigle, Vale of Glamorgan Area, Breast Care, Llandough Hospital, Tel.: 029 2071 1711
Ms Y Perston, Vale of Glamorgan Area, Colorectal, Llandough Hospital, Tel.: 029 2071 1711
Ms A Yates, Cardiff Area, Continence, Lansdowne Hospital, Tel.: 029 2037 2451
Ms C Davies, Vale of Glamorgan Area, Cystic Fibrosis, Llandough Hospital, Tel.: 029 2071 1711
Ms J Jenkins, Vale of Glamorgan Area, Cystic Fibrosis, Llandough Hospital, Tel.: 029 2071 1711
Ms H Smith, Vale of Glamorgan Area, Diabetic Care, Llandough Hospital, Tel.: 029 2071 1711
Ms S Coodye, Vale of Glamorgan Area, Infection Control, Llandough Hospital, Tel.: 029 2071 1711
Ms I Foster, Cardiff Area, Infection Control, Lansdowne Hospital, Tel.: 029 2037 2451
Ms J Baker, Macmillan, Vale of Glamorgan Area, Lung Cancer, Llandough Hospital, Tel.: 029 2071 1711
Ms K Cracknell, Vale of Glamorgan Area, Nutrition, Llandough Hospital, Tel.: 029 2071 1711
Ms A Jones, Cardiff Area, Palliative Care, Lansdowne Hospital, Tel.: 029 2037 2451
Ms M Lewis, Vale of Glamorgan Area, Palliative Care, Llandough Hospital, Tel.: 029 2071 1711
Ms S Jones, Vale of Glamorgan Area, Respiratory, Llandough Hospital, Tel.: 029 2071 1711
Ms P Stevens, Vale of Glamorgan Area, TB, Llandough Hospital, Tel.: 029 2071 1711
Ms Y Orrell, Vale of Glamorgan Area, Tissue Viability, Llandough Hospital, Tel.: 029 2071 1711
Ms Y Orrell, Cardiff Area, Tissue Viability, Lansdowne Hospital, Tel.: 029 2037 2451

Cardiff LHB

LHB Headquarters
Trenewydd, Fairwater Road
LLADAFF
Cardiff
CF5 2LD
Tel.: 029 2055 2212

Admin & Senior Management
Ms A Hogie, Assistant Nurse Director,
Mrs J Theed, Nurse Director,

Community Nursing Services
All posts employed by Cardiff & Vale NHS Trust, Tel.: 029 2074 7747

Gwent Healthcare NHS Trust

Llanfrechfa Grange
CWMBRAN
Gwent
NP44 8YN
Tel.: 01633 623623

Admin & Senior Management
Mr D Hopkins, Divisional Lead Nurse/Borough Manager - Caerphilly Community Services, Ystrad Mynach Hospital, Tel.: 01443 811373

Wales

Mrs C Hucker, Clinical Governance Facilitator - Community Division, County Hospital, Tel.: 01495 765799

Mrs R Jones, Acting General Manager Community Division, County Hospital, Coed y-Gric Road, Griffithstown, Pontypool, Torfaen, NP4 5YA, Tel.: 01495 768755

Mrs R Jones, Divisional Professional Lead Nurse/Borough Manager, County Hospital, Coed y Gric Road, Griffithstown, Pontypool, Torfaen, NP4 5YA, Tel.: 01495 768751

Dr P Khanna, Consultant/Chief of Staff for Community & Care of Elderley Services, Nevill Hall Hospital, Tel.: 01873 732162

Mr C Phillpott, Borough Manager, Monmouthshire Community Services, Chepstow Community Hospital, Tel.: 01291 636633

Ms J Reader, Head of Nurse Education & Training, Llanfrechfa Grange Hospital, Tel.: 01633 623636

Mrs K Smith, Temporary Borough Manager, Newport Community Services, St Woolos Hospital, Tel.: 01633 656393

Ms K Smith, Borough Manager, Newport Community Services, St Woolos Hospital, Tel.: 01633 656393

Mrs J Sweeting, Borough Manager, Blaenau Gwent Community Services & Directorate Manager Sexual & Reproductive Health, Ebbw Vale Health Centre, Tel.: 01495 353007

Miss L Trounce, Development Manager - Community, County Hospital, Coed-Y-Gric Road, Griffithstown, Tel.: 01495 768763

Mrs L Walbeoff, Clinical Services Manager/Lead Nurse, Gwent GP Out of Hours Service, Mamhilad, Tel.: 01495 765244

Mrs W Warren, Nurse Director,

Child Health

Ms K Coldridge, Borough Manager, Community Children's Nursing, Caerphilly/Blaenau Gwent, Tel.: 01633 618020

Ms C Crocker, Community Childrens Nursing Directorate Manager, Women, Child & Family Division, Block 9, Royal Gwent Hospital, Tel.: 01633 238026

Ms T Davis, Borough Manager, Community Children's Nursing, Torfaen, Tel.: 01633 618020

Ms J Field, Community Children's Nursing, Senior Nurse, Risca Health Centre, Tel.: 01633 618020

Ms J Marie, Borough Manager, Community Children's Nursing, Newport, Tel.: 01633 618020

Ms L McMahon, Enteral Feeding Specialist Nurse, Community Children's Service, Tel.: 01633 618020

Ms O O'Meara, Lead Nurse, Community Children's Service, Palliative Care, Risca Health Centre, Tel.: 01633 618020

Ms R Richardson, Borough Manager, Community Children's Nursing, Monmouth, Tel.: 01633 618020

Child Health Records

Blaenau Gwent Child Health Records, Ebbw Vale Health Centre, Tel.: 01495 303013

Blaenau Gwent Child Health Records, Risca Health Centre, Risca, NP1 6YE, Tel.: 01633 618000

Caerphilly Child Health Records, Ystrad Mynach Hospital, Tel.: 01443 811411

Gwent - Child & Adolescent Health Service, Ty Bryn Unit, St Cadoc's Hospital, Caerleon, Tel.: 01633 436831/33

Ms S Hall, Borough Manager - Child & Adolescent Health Service, Monmouthshire Child Health Records, Oakfield House, Llanfrechfa Grange, Tel.: 01633 623509

Newport Child Health Records, Clytha Clinic, 27 Clytha Park Road, Newport, NP9 4PA, Tel.: 01633 435900

Torfaen Child Health Records, Oakfield House, Llanfrechfa Grange, Tel.: 01633 623516

Child Protection/Safeguarding Children

Mrs L Brown, Grange House, Llanfrechfa Grange, 01633 623802

Ms J Barrell, Lead Midwife, Child Protection, Tel.: 07946 578278

Community Midwifery

Community Office, Nevill Hall Hospital, Brecon Road, Abergaveny, Gwent, NP7 7EG, Tel.: 01873 732137

Emergencies (out of hours), Royal Gwent Hospital, Cardiff Road, Newport, Gwent, NP9 2UB, Tel.: 01633 234949

Mrs A McHugh, Community Midwifery Manager, Royal Gwent Hospital, Cardiff Road, Newport, Gwent, NP9 2UB, Tel.: 01633 234763

Mrs T Mudd, Manager, Nevil Hall Hospital, Brecon Road, Abergaveny, Gwent, NP7 7EG, Tel.: 01873 732117

Out of hours (after 5pm), Labour Ward, Nevill Hall Hospital, Brecon Road, Abergaveny, Gwent, NP7 7EG, Tel.: 01873 732120

Mrs G Ratcliffe, Midwifery Manager, Caerphilly Birth Centre,Caerphilly District Miner's Hospital, St Martin's Road, Caerphilly, CF83 2WW, Tel.: 029 2080 7233

Mrs G Thomas, Consultant Midwife, Caerphilly Birth Centre,Caerphilly District Miner's Hospital, St Martin's Road, Caerphilly, CF83 2WW, Tel.: 029 2080 7342

Community Nursing Services

Mrs P Evans, Senior Nurse (adults), Torfaen Borough Community Hospitals, County Hospital, Tel.: 01495 768638

Mrs M Hopkins, Senior Nurse (adults), Monmouthshire Borough Community Hospitals, Chepstow Community Hospital, Tel.: 01291 636599

Mrs R Lee, Senior Nurse (adults), Newport Borough Community Hospitals, St Woolos Hospital, Tel.: 01633 238303

Mrs T Newell, Senior Nurse (adults), Blaenau Gwent Borough Community Hospitals, Ebbw Vale Health Centre, Tel.: 01495 353034

Mrs J Woods, Senior Nurse (adults), Caerphilly Borough Community Nursing Service, Ystrad Mynach Hospital, Tel.: 01443 811320

District Nursing

Mrs J Chivers, Senior Nurse, Caerphilly Borough District Nursing Service, Ystrad Mynach Hospital, Tel.: 01443 811441

Mrs G Heslop, Intermediate Care Team Leader, Blaenau Gwent Reablement Team, Top Floor Flat, Blaina Hospital, Tel.: 01495 293302

Mrs T Hinnem, Senior Nurse, Newport Borough District Nursing Service, St Woolos Hospital, Tel.: 01633 656394

Mrs S Pinkstone, Senior Nurse, Blaenau Gwent Borough District Nursing Service, Ebbw Vale Health Centre, Tel.: 01495 353009

Mrs A Roberts, Intermediate Care Team Leader, Blaenau Gwent Rapid Response Team, Top Floor Flat, Blaina Hospital, Tel.: 01495 294183

Mrs E Takel, Senior Nurse, Monmouthshire Borough District Nursing Service, Chepstow Community Hospital, Tel.: 01291 636632

Mrs A Wilson, Senior Nurse, Torfaen Borough District Nursing Service, County Hospital, Tel.: 01495 768622

Family/Sexual Health

Dr C Fleming, Clinical Director, Directorate of Sexual & Reproductive Health, Llanfrechfa Grange Hospital, Gwent, Tel.: 01633 623623

Mrs J Jones, Senior Nurse for Community Gynaecology & Sexual Health, Llanfrechfa Grange Hospital, Gwent, Tel.: 01633 623722

Mrs K Kibble, HIV Specialist Nurse, GUM Dept, Royal Gwent Hospital, Tel.: 01633 234555

Mrs J Maynard, Specialist Nurse, GUM, Royal Gwent Hospital, Tel.: 01633 234555

Mrs J Payne, Admin. Manager for Gynaecology, Llanfrechfa Grange Hospital, Gwent, Tel.: 01633 623721

Health Visitors

Ms A Davies, Caerphilly Health Visitor Borough Manager, Caerphilly, Tel.: 01633 618000

Ms C Overs, Head of Health Visiting, Oakfield House, Llanfrechfa, Cwmbran, Tel.: 01633 623623/01633 618000

Mr C Phillips, Health Visitor Borough Manager, Blaenau Gwent & Monmouth, Tel.: 01633 618000

Ms G Powell, Health Visitor Borough Manager, Newport & Torfaen, Tel.: 01633 618000

Ms M Swidenbank, Health Visitor Borough Manager, Caerphilly, Tel. 01633 618000

HIV/AIDS

Mrs J Jones, HIV Nurse - GUM Dept, Royal Gwent Hospital, Tel.: 01633 236372

Learning Disabilities

Ms K Halford, Team Manager, Newport CLDT, Royal Chambers, 3rd Floor, High Street, Newport, Tel.: 01633 235234

Mr S Harris, Team Leader, Torfaen CLDT, Alders House, Llanfrechfa Grange, Cwmbran, Gwent, Tel.: 01633 623559

Mr A Hopkins, Clinical Services Manager, Alders House, Llanfrechfa Grange, Cwmbran, Gwent, Tel.: 01633 623554

Dr R Jacques, Clinical Director, Learning Disabilities, Alders House, Llanfrechfa Grange, Cwmbran, Gwent, Tel.: 01633 623615

Ms N Jenkins, General Manager, St Cadoc's Hospital, Caerleon, Gwent, Tel.: 01633 436778

Ms L Marshall, Team Leader, Monmouth CLDT, Leven House, Lion Street, Abergavenny, Gwent, Tel.: 01873 852729

Dr C O'Connor, Head of Psychology, Alders House, Llanfrechfa Grange, Cwmbran, Gwent, Tel.: 01633 623563

Ms S Price, Clinical Lead, Speech & Language Therapy, Alders House, Llanfrechfa Grange, Cwmbran, Gwent, Tel.: 01633 623563

Dr Sundari, Team Leader, Children's Service, Alders House, Llanfrechfa Grange, Cwmbran, Gwent, Tel.: 01633 623549

Ms H Thomas, Head Occupational Therapist, Caerphilly LD Team, Lansing Linde Office Block, Newbridge Road Ind Estate, Blackwood, Tel.: 01495 233221

Ms H Thomas, Team Leader, Caerphilly CLDT, Nurse Specialist, Lansing Linde, Newbridge Industrial Estate, Pontllanfraith, Blackwood, Tel.: 01495 233233

Ms S Williams, Team Leader, Blaenau Gwent CLDT, Nurse Specialist, The Bridge Centre, Foundry Bridge, Abertillery, Gwent, Tel.: 01495 322660

Liaison Services

Mrs S Baldwin, Liaison Nurse, Intermediate Care, Blaina Hospital, Hospital Road, Nantyglo, Blaenau Gwent, Tel.: 01495 293293

Mrs L Barnes, Liaison Nurse, Intermediate Care, Blaina Hospital, Hospital Road, Nantyglo, Blaenau Gwent, Tel.: 01495 293293

Ms N Beerenbrock, Discharge Liaison Team, St Woolos Hospital, Stow Hill, Newport, NP20 4SZ, Tel.: 01633 238285

Mrs W Davies, Discharge Liaison Team, St Woolos Hospital, Stow Hill, Newport, NP20 4SZ, Tel.: 01633 238285

Ms C Green, Research Liaison Nurse, St Woolos Hospital, ext 8967

Mrs A Lewis, Case Manager Liaison Services, Ystrad Mynach Hospital, Caerphilly Road, Ystrad Mynach, Hengoed, CF82 7XU, Tel.: 01443 811312

Mrs J Llewellyn, Case Manager Liaison Services, Ystrad Mynach Hospital, Caerphilly Road, Ystrad Mynach, Hengoed, CF82 7XU, Tel.: 07900 682895

Mrs F Mallett, Discharge Liaison Nurse, County Hospital, Coed Y Gric Road, Griffithstown, Pontypool, Torfaen, NP4 5YA, Tel.: 01495 768760

Mrs S Price, Discharge Liaison Nurse, Monmouthshire, Tel.: 01600 775100

Mrs S Thomas, Case Manager Liaison Services, Ystrad Mynach Hospital, Caerphilly Road, Ystrad Mynach, Hengoed, CF82 7XU, Tel.: 07748 110800

Mrs J Turner, Discharge Liaison Nurse, Monmouthshire, Tel.: 01291 435666

Other Services

Miss J Davies, Home Enteral Feeding Clinical Specialist Dietitian, Dietetic Portacabin, LGH, Tel.: 01633 623778

Medical Loans Service, Llanfrecha Grange Hospital, Torfaen, Tel.: 01633 623446

Mrs L Owen, Home Enteral Feeding Clinical Specialist Dietitian, Dietetic Portacabin, LGH, Tel.: 01633 623622

Speech & Language Therapy, Llanyravon House, Llanfrechfa Grange, Cwmbran, NP44 8YN, Tel.: 01633 623740

Mrs M Vacara, Divisional Head Occupational Therapy, St Cadoc's Hospital, Lodge Road, Caerleon, Tel.: 01633 436838

School Nursing

Ms L Berry, School Health Nursing Team Leader, Torfaen, Tel.: 01633 618003

Ms P Davies, School Health Nursing Team Leader, Newport, Tel.: 01633 618003

Ms J Peaple, School Health Nursing Team Leader, Blaenau Gwent, Tel.: 01633 618003

Ms A Phillips, School Health Nursing Team Leader, Caerphilly, Tel.: 01633 618003

Ms S Stevens, School Health Nursing Team Leader, Monmouth, Tel.: 01633 618003

Mrs J Williams, Senior Nurse, School Health Nursing, Risca Health Centre, Tel.: 01633 618003

Specialist Nursing Services

Mrs H Ford, Medical Loans Service, Nurse Manager, Medical Loans Dept, Llanfrecha Grange, Torfaen, Tel.: 01633 623815

Mrs L Law, Senior Nurse Manager, Continence, Llanfrechfa Grange Hospital, Llanfrechfa, Cwmbran, Torfaen, NP44 8YN,

Mrs K Logan, Nurse Consultant, Continence, Llanfrechfa Grange Hospital, Llanfrechfa, Cwmbran, Torfaen, NP44 8YN,

Ms V Prichard, Community Team Leader, Infection Control, St Cadocs Hospital, Lodge Road, Caerleon, NP18 3XQ, Tel.: 01633 436781

Mrs C Rees, Nurse Specialist, Leg Ulcers, Blaina Hospital, Tel.: 01495 293293

Ms K Phillips, Lead Midwife, Substance Misuse, Royal Gwent Hospital, Tel.: ext 4763

Ms C Green, Wound Healing, Research Nurse, Wound Care, Tel.: 07789390244

Women, Child & Family Division

Dr I Bowler, Chief of Staff, Child & Family Directorates, Women, Child & Family Division, Royal Gwent Hospital, Cardiff Road, Newport, NP20 2UB,

Ms B Cannito, Divisional Partnership Manager, Women, Child & Family Division, Block 9, Royal Gwent Hospital, Tel.: 01633 436792

Ms S Crane, General Manager, Women, Child & Family Division, Block 9, Royal Gwent Hospital, Cardiff Road, Newport, NP20 2UB, Tel.: 01633 238905

Mr A Cresswell, Directorate Manager, Child & Family Psychological Health, St Cadocs Hospital, Caerleon, NP18 3XQ, Tel.: 01633 436831

Ms C Crocker, Divisional Lead Nurse/Community Nursing Directorate Manager, Women, Child & Family Division, Block 9, Royal Gwent Hospital, Tel.: 01633 238026

Miss H Denman, Directorate Manager, Child Health, Women, Child & Family Division, Block 9, Royal Gwent Hospital, Tel.: 01633 234257

Mrs C Garrick, Divisional Lead Nurse - Midwifery & Directorate Manager, Obstetrics, Women, Child & Family Div, Nevill Hall Hospital, Brecon Road, Abergaveny, Gwent, NP7 7EG, Tel.: 01873 732084

Ms N Kelly, Divisional Performance & Improvement Manager, Women, Child & Family Division, Block 9, Royal Gwent Hospital, Tel.: 01633 656043

Mrs V Lawrence, Directorate Manager, Gynaecology - Women, Child & Family Div, Conference Centre, Nevill Hall Hospital, Abergavenny, Gwent, NP7 7EG, Tel.: 01873 732038

Mr I Stokes, Chief of Staff, Women's Services, Women, Child & Family Division, Neville Hall Hospital, Abergavenny, NP7 7EG,

Merthyr Tydfil LHB

LHB Headquarters, The Business Centre
Triangle Business Park
MERTHYR TYDFIL
CF48 4TQ
Tel.: 01685 358500

Admin & Senior Management

Mrs L Lewis, Clinical Governance Development Manager, Tel.: 01685 358500

Mrs M Thomas, Nurse Director, Tel.: 01685 358580

Child Protection/Safeguarding Children

Ms C Duffin-Jones, GPS, Tel.: 01685 358500

Wales

Clinical Leads (NSF)
Ms L Bolderson, Clinical Lead, CHD, Tel.: 01685 358500
Ms P Clinical Lead, Children,
Mr S Davies, Clinical Lead, Diabetes,
Community Nursing Services
No Direct Service Provision Provided,
Other Services
Mrs K Davies, Continuing Care Reviewer, Tel.: 01685 358500
Mrs S Evans, NHS Funded Care Assessor, Tel.: 01685 358500
Pharmacy
Ms S Evans, Head of Pharmacy, Tel.: 01685 358500
Specialist Nursing Services
Ms L Bolderson, Nurse Facilitator, CHD, Tel.: 01685 358500
Ms J Griffiths, Nurse, CHD, Tel.: 01685 358500
Ms J Williams, Practice Nurse with special interest, Respiratory
Medicine, Tel.: 01685 358500

Monmouthshire LHB
LHB Headquarters,
Chepstow Community Hospital
Tempest Way
CHEPSTOW
NP16 5YX
Tel.: 01291 636400

Admin & Senior Management
Ms J Thomas, Director of Nursing, Monmouthshire LHB, Chepstow
Community Hospital, Tempest Way, Chepstow, NP16 5YX,

National Public Health Service for Wales
Unit 1, Charnwood Court
Heol Billingsley
Parc Nantgarw
CARDIFF
CF15 7QZ
Tel.: 01443 824163
Fax: 01443 824161

Admin & Senior Management
Dr C Rogers, National Director, Unit 1, Charnwood Court, Heol
Billingsley, Parc Nantgarw, Cardiff, CF15 7QZ, Tel.: 01443 824163
Child Health
Mrs R Myles, Children & Young People Team Leader,
Child Protection/Safeguarding Children
Mrs D Calder, Designated Nurse Child Protection & Looked After
Children, on behalf of Bridgend, Neath & Port Talbot & Swansea
LHBs, Tel.: 01792 607536
Mrs J Evans, Designated Nurse Child Protection & Looked After
Children, on behalf of Carmarthenshire, Ceredigion, Pembrokeshire
& Powys LHB's, Tel.: 01267 225018
Mrs C Jones, Designated Nurse Child Protection & Looked After
Children, on behalf of Cardiff, Merthyr Tydfil, Rhondda Cynon Taff &
Vale of Glamorgan LHB's, Tel.: 029 2040 2498
Mrs L Slater, Designated Nurse Child Protection & Looked After
Children, on behalf of Blaenau Gwent, Caerphilly, Monmouthshire,
Newport & Torfaen LHB's, Tel.: 01495 765112
Mrs J Williams, Designated Nurse Child Protection & Looked After
Children, on behalf of Ynys Mon (Anglesey), Conwy, Denbighshire,
Flintshire, Gwynedd & Wrexham LHB's, Tel.: 01352 700227
Mrs R Myles, Team Coordinator, Child Protection, Tel.: 029 2040
2480

Newport LHB
LHB Headquarters, Wentwood Suite
St Cadocs Hospital, Caerleon
NEWPORT
NP18 3XQ
Tel.: 01633 436200

Admin & Senior Management
Ms E Elias, Director of Nursing, Newport LHB,

North Glamorgan NHS Trust
Trust Headquarters
Prince Charles Hospital
METHYR TYDFIL
CF47 9DT
Tel.: 01685 721721

Admin & Senior Management
Ms M Thomas, Deputy of Nursing Services, Tel.: 01685 728732
Mrs R J Walker, Executive Director of Nursing,
Child Health
Mrs S Evans, Children with Special Needs, Clinical Nurse Specialist,
Kenshole Children's Centre, Aberdare Hospital, Tel.: 01685 872411
ext 4681
Child Health Records
Child Health Records, Community Offices, Aberdare General
Hospital, Tel.: 01685 872411
Mr C Moulds, Admin Manager, Prince Charles Hospital, Tel.: 01685
728714
Child Protection/Safeguarding Children
Mr C Parsons, Child Protection, Community Offices, Aberdare
General Hospital, Tel.: 01685 872411 ext 4711
Community Midwifery
Ms J Davies, Head of Midwifery, Based at Prince Charles Hospital,
Merthyr Tydfil, CF47 9DT, Tel.: 01685 721721
Ms L Edwards, Community Midwifery Manager, Based at Prince
Charles Hospital, Merthyr Tydfil, CF47 9DT, Tel.: 01685 728895
Community Nursing Services
Community Nursing Services, Community Offices, Aberdare General
Hospital, Aberdare, CF44 0RF, Tel.: 01685 872411
District Nursing
Ms S Jones, District Nurses, Senior Nurse, Community Offices,
Aberdare General Hospital, Tel.: 01685 872411 ext 4712
Health Visitors
Mrs A Roberts, Head of Health Visiting, Community Offices,
Aberdare General Hospital, Tel.: 01685 872411 ext 4710
Learning Disabilities
Services administered by Bro Morgannwg NHS Trust,
Mrs R Walker, Director of Nursing/Patient Services, Tel.: 01685
721721
Liaison Services
Ms S Evans, Discharge Liaison, Prince Charles Hospital, Tel.: 01685
721721 ext 8341
Ms L Estebanez, Liaison, Paediatrics, Hollies Health Centre, Merthyl
Tydfil, CF47 8ET, Tel.: 01685 384023 ext 240
School Nursing
Mrs A Roberts, Head of School Nursing, Community Offices,
Aberdare General Hospital, Tel.: 01685 872411 ext 4710
School Health/Nursing Service, Community Offices, Aberdare
General Hospital, Tel.: 01685 872411
Specialist Nursing Services
Ms M Davies, MDTU, Acute Pain, Prince Charles Hospital, Tel.:
01685 721721 ext 8344
Mrs D Jehu, Breast Care, Prince Charles Hospital, Tel.: 01685
721721 ext 8205
Ms A Allen, Medical Directorate, Cardiac Rehabilitation, Prince
Charles Hospital, Tel.: 01685 721721 ext 8304
Ms E Crook, Medical Directorate, Cardiac Rehabilitation, Prince
Charles Hospital, Tel.: 01685 721721 ext 8304
Ms A Brown, Diabetic Care, Prince Charles Hospital, Tel.: 01685
728490
Ms R Evans, Diabetic Care, Prince Charles Hospital, Tel.: 01685
728490
Ms J Harlow, Diabetic Care, Prince Charles Hospital, Tel.: 01685
728490

Nurses, Genetics, Glenys Hill, Hollies Health Centre, Tel.: 01685 884023

Ms C Harris, Community, Infection Control, Prince Charles Hospital, Tel.: 01685 728495

Ms L James, Specialist, Infection Control, Prince Charles Hospital, Tel.: 01685 721721

Mrs L Carless, Macmillan, Aberdare Hospital, Tel.: 01685 872411

Mrs S Fosterjohn, Macmillan, Aberdare Hospital, Tel.: 01685 872411

Mrs A Litchfield, Macmillan, Aberdare Hospital, Tel.: 01685 872411

Mrs J Pocknell, Macmillan, Aberdare Hospital, Tel.: 01685 872411

Mrs Y Rees, Co-ordinator, Palliative Care, Prince Charles Hospital, Tel.: 01685 721721

Ms B Woods, Respiratory, Prince Charles Hospital, Tel.: 01685 721721 ext 8495

Mrs M A Goodwin, Stoma Care, Prince Charles Hospital, Tel.: 01685 721721

Ms C Duffy, Day Care, Surgery, Prince Charles Hospital, Tel.: 01685 721721

Mr M Ogonovsky, Tissue Viability, - Urological, Prince Charles Hospital, Tel.: 01685 721721 ext 8223

Pontypridd & Rhondda NHS Trust

Trust Headquarters, Dewi Sant Hospital
Albert Road
PONTYPRIDD
Mid Glamorgan
CF37 1LB
Tel.: 01443 492464

Child Health
Mrs L Booker, Specialist Nurse Co-ordinator Children with Special Needs, Community Health Office, Dewi Sant Hospital, Pontypridd, CF37 1LB, Tel.: 01443 443785

Mrs P Pritchard, Specialist Health Visitor for Children with Behavioural Problems, Children's Assessment Centre, Royal Glamorgan Hospital, Tel.: 01443 443443 ext 3383

Child Health Records
Child Health Records, Community Health Office, Dewi Sant Hospital, Albert Road, Pontypridd, CF37 1LB, Tel.: 01443 492464

Child Protection/Safeguarding Children
Mrs C Ellis, Clinical Nurse Specialist, Child Protection, Unit 2, Fairway Court, Treforest, CF37 5UA, Tel.: 01443 827354

Mrs J Randell, Named Nurse, Child Protection, Unit 2, Fairway Court, Freforest, CF37 5UA, Tel.: 01443 827353

Community Nursing Services
Mrs J E Harries, Directorate Manager, Womanm Child & Family Directorate (Community), Community Health Offices, Dewi Sant Hospital, Pontypridd, CF37 1LB, Tel.: 01443 443755

District Nursing
Mrs M Harris, Head of District Nursing, Community Health Office, Albert Road, Pontypridd, CF37 1LB, Tel.: 01443 443787

Mrs J Powell, Professional Support (District Nursing), Community Health Office, Dewi Sant Hospital, Pontypridd, CF37 1LB, Tel.: 01443 443814

Family Planning Services
Mrs S Doran-Hughes, Family Planning Nurse Practitioner, Community Health Office, Dewi Sant Hospital, Pontypridd, CF37 1LB, Tel.: 01443 443770

Health Visitors
Mrs S Bushnell, Professional Support (Children's Services), Community Health Offices, Dewi Sant Hospital, Pontypridd, CF37 1LB, Tel.: 01443 443774

Mrs T Cameron, Paediatric Health Visitor, Children's Assessment, Royal Glamorgan Hospital, Tel.: 01443 443443 ext 4024

Mrs E Edwards, On Track Health Visitor, Ashfield House, East Road, Thorstown, RCT, Tel.: 01443 757055

Families First Health Visitor, Engine House, Depot Road, Aberdare, CF44 8DL, Tel.: 01685 880097

Mrs M Gibb, Sure Start Health Visitor, Ynyscynon Nursery, Trealaw, Rhondda Cynon Taff, Tel.: 01443 424905

Mrs L Hannington, Community Manager (Children's Services), Community Health Offices, Dewi Sant Hospital, Pontypridd, CF37 1LB, Tel.: 01443 443754

Mrs O Jones, Sure Start Health Visitor, Ynyscynon Nursery, Trealaw, Rhondda Cynon Taff, Tel.: 01443 424905

Mrs S Saunders, Children with Special Needs, Health Visitor, Children's Assessment, Royal Glamorgan Hospital, Tel.: 01443 443443 ext 3384

Specialist Nursing Services
Mrs G Hughes, Breast Care, Royal Glamorgan Hospital, Tel.: 01443 443056

Mrs R Batten, Cardiac Rehabilitation, Royal Glamorgan Hospital, Tel.: 01443 443386

Mrs S Foulkes, Continence, Community Health Office, Admin Block, Dewi Sant Hospital, Pontypridd, CF37 1LB, Tel.: 01443 492464

Ms H Husband, Diabetic Care, Royal Glamorgan Hospital, Tel.: 01443 443443

Mrs S Cole, South, Macmillan, Y Bwythyn, Pontypridd District Hospital, Pontypridd, CF37 4AL, Tel.: 01443 486144

Mrs E Davies, North, Macmillan, Llwynypia Hospital, Tel.: 01443 440440 ext 5504

Mrs K Kirwan, South, Macmillan, Y Bwythyn, Pontypridd District Hospital, Pontypridd, CF37 4AL, Tel.: 01443 486144

Mrs S O'Brien, North, Macmillan, Llwynypia Hospital, Tel.: 01443 440440 ext 5504

Ms S Jones, Stoma Care, Royal Glamorgan Hospital, Tel.: 01443 443053

Mrs K Bevan, Tissue Viability, Community Health Office, Dewi Sant Hospital, Tel.: 01443 443770

Rhondda Cynon Taff LHB

LHB Headquarters, Units 16-18
Centre Court, Treforest Industrial Estate
PONTYPRIDD
CF37 5YR
Tel.: 01443 824400

Admin & Senior Management
Mrs L Williams, Nurse Director, Unit 16, Centre Court, Treforest Ind Estate, Treforest, Pontypridd, Tel.: 01443 824408

Child Health Records
Child Health Records, North Glamorgan NHS Trust, Prince Charles Hospital, Merthyr Tydfil, Mid Glamorgan, CF47 9DT, Tel.: 01685 721721

Child Health Records, Pontypridd & Rhondda NHS Trust, Royal Glamorgan Hospital, Ynys Maerdy, Llantrisant, CF72 8XR, Tel.: 01443 443443

Child Protection/Safeguarding Children
Mrs L Williams, Nurse Director, Unit 16-18 Centre Court, Treforest Ind Estate, Treforest, Pontypridd, CF37 5YR, Tel.: 01443 824400 x 408

Community Nursing Services
Community Nursing Staff, Employed by Pontypridd & Rhondda & North Glamorgan NHS Trusts,

Pharmacy
Mr B Hawkins, Head of Medicine Management,

Specialist Nursing Services
Ms E Howlett, Facilitator, Asthma, Llwynypia Hospital, Rhondda,,

Mr A Bray, Facilitator, Diabetic Care, Diabetes Resource Unit, Royal Glamorgan Hospital, Talbot Green,

Ms C Jones, Facilitator, Cynon Valley, Diabetic Care, Primary Care Support Unit, Aberdare,

Wales

Torfaen LHB

LHB Headquarters, Block C, Mamhilad House
Mamhilad Park Estate
PONTYPOOL
NP4 0YP
Tel.: 01495 745868

Admin & Senior Management
Ms V Warner, Nurse Director, LHB Headquarters,
Community Nursing Services
Community Nursing Services, These services are provided by Gwent
Healthcare NHS Trust,
District Nursing
District Nursing, Tel.: 01633 623636
Out of Hours nurses, Tel.: 07971549361
Rapid Response, Tel.: 01633 623636
Liaison Services
Hospital Discharge, Tel.: 01633 238311
Other Services
Blaenavon Healthcare Unit, Tel.: 01495 790236
Continuing Care, Tel.: 01495 768644
County Hospital, Tel.: 01495 768768
Hospital Social Work Dept, Tel.: 01495 768611
Specialist Nursing Services
Mr C Backhouse, Facilitator, CHD, Mamhilad House, Mamhilad Park,
Pontypool,

Vale of Glamorgan LHB

LHB Headquarters, 2 Stanwell Road
PENARTH
CF64 3EA
Tel.: 029 2035 0600

Admin & Senior Management
Mrs K Bergmanski, Director of Nursing,

Velindre NHS Trust

Trust Headquarters, 2 Charnwood Court
Heol Billngsley, Parc Nantgarw
CARDIFF
CF15 7QZ
Tel.: 029 2031 6916

Admin & Senior Management
Ms D Smith, Director of Nursing, Velindre NHS Trust, 2 Charnwood
Court, Heol Billingsley, Parc Nantgarw, Cardiff, CF15 7QZ, Tel.: 029
2031 6916

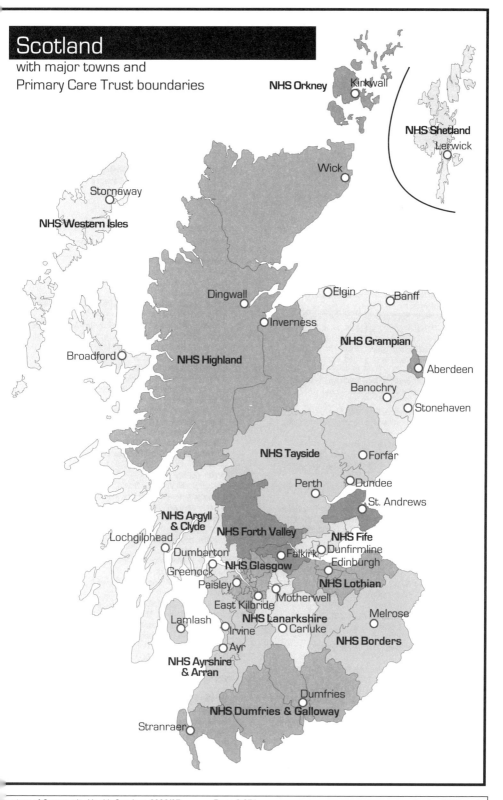

Scotland

with major towns and
Primary Care Trust boundaries

NHS Orkney Kirkwall

NHS Shetland Lerwick

Wick

Stornaway

NHS Western Isles

Dingwall · Elgin · Banff

Inverness

NHS Grampian

Broadford

NHS Highland Aberdeen

Banochry

Stonehaven

NHS Tayside Forfar

Perth · Dundee

St. Andrews

NHS Argyll & Clyde

Lochgilphead **NHS Forth Valley** **NHS Fife**

Dumbarton Falkirk · Dunfirmline

Greenock **NHS Glasgow** Edinburgh

Paisley **NHS Lothian**

East Kilbride Motherwell

Lamlash Melrose

Irvine **NHS Lanarkshire** Carluke

Ayr **NHS Borders**

NHS Ayrshire & Arran

Dumfries

NHS Dumfries & Galloway

Stranraer

Scotland

NHS Ayrshire & Arran

Ayrshire & Arran Primary Care Division
Eglinton House
Ailsa Hospital, Dalmellington Road
AYR
KA6 6AB
Tel.: 01292 513600

Child Health
Ms A M Bannatyne, Community Children's Nursing Service, Rainbow House, Ayrshire Central Hospital, Irvine, KA12 8SS, Tel.: 01284 323071
Ms M Bell, Child Health, Dept Child Health, Ayrshire Central Hospital, Irvine, KA12 8SS, Tel.: 01294 323431
Ms K Brennen, Rainbow House Nursing Dept, Rainbow House, Ayrshire Central Hospital, Irvine, KA12 8SS, Tel.: 01294 323070
Child Health Records
Child & School Health Records Dept, East Ayrshire: School, Ayrshire Central Hospital, Kilwinning Road, Irvine, KA12 8SS, Tel.: 01294 323427
Child & School Health Records Dept, North Ayrshire: Pre-School, Ayrshire Central Hospital, Kilwinning Road, Irvine, KA12 8SS, Tel.: 01294 323432
Child & School Health Records Dept, North Ayrshire: School, Ayrshire Central Hospital, Kilwinning Road, Irvine, KA12 8SS, Tel.: 01294 323428
Child & School Health Records Dept, South Ayrshire: School, Ayrshire Central Hospital, Kilwinning Road, Irvine, KA12 8SS, Tel.: 01294 323426
Child & School Health Records Dept, South Ayrshire: Pre-School, Ayrshire Central Hospital, Kilwinning Road, Irvine, KA12 8SS, Tel.: 01294 323427
Child & School Health Records Dept, East Ayrshire: Pre-School, Ayrshire Central Hospital, Kilwinning Road, Irvine, KA12 8SS, Tel.: 01294 323433
Child Protection/Safeguarding Children
Ms M Bell, Designated Nurse, Child Protection, Dept Child Health, Ayrshire Central Hospital, Irvine, KA12 8SS, Tel.: 01294 323431
District Nursing
Ms L Moore, Director of Nursing, Eglinton House, Ailsa Hospital,
Learning Disabilities
Mr J Begbie, Patient/Primary Care Manager, Arrol Park Resource Centre, Doonfoot Road, Ayr, KA7 4DW, Tel.: 01292 614901
East Team, Cumnock Health Centre, 2 Tanyard, Cumnock, KA18 1BF, Tel.: 01290 424790
East Team, Strathlea Resource Centre, Holmes Road, Kilmarnock, KA1 1TR, Tel.: 01563 571591
Ms J McCreath, Co-ordinator, East Teams, Tel.: 01563 571591
Mr A Middleton, Co-ordinator, South Team, Tel.: 01292 614903
North Team, 3 Town Resource Centre, Nelson Road, Saltcoats, Tel.: 01294 607123
Mr J Smith, Co-ordinator, North Team, Tel.: 01294 607123
South Team, Arrol Park Resource Centre, Doonfoot Road, Ayr, KA7 4DW, Tel.: 01292 614910
Mr T Stevenson, Nurse Advisor, Tel.: 01292 614973
Liaison Services
Ms W Jess, Liaison, Sister, Kirklandside Hospital, Kilmarnock, KA1 5LH, Tel.: 01563 575400
Ms J Jobes, Liaison, TB, Nurse, Tel.: 01294 323525
Liaison Services, Biggart Hospital, Biggart Road, Prestwick, KA9 2HQ, Tel.: 01292 470611
Ms A McLellan, Liaison, Sister, Maybole Day Hospital, Maybole, KA19 7BY, Tel.: 01655 884019
Specialist Nursing Services
Ms M Brown, Practice Development Nurse, Tel.: 01294 323 461
Ms K Percival, Practice Development Nurse, Tel.: 01294 323 457

Mr C Rodden, Clinical Trainer, Tel.: 01292 513283
Ms J Campbell, Nurse Advisor, Continence, Tel.: 01292 513947
Ms P Macrae, (SAFE Project Coordinator), Elderly Care, North Ayr Health Centre, Glenmuir Place, Ayr, KA8 9RS, Tel.: 01294885554
Ms E M Cubbins, Nurse Specialist, Epilepsy, Tel.: 01294 323362
Mr B Wilson, Nurse Specialist, Infection Control, Tel.: 01563 577 484
Ms J Neilly, Nurse Advisor, Palliative Care, 1a Hunters Avenue, Ayr, Tel.: 01292 513616
Ms E McMath, Nurse, Tissue Viability, 1a Hunters Avenue, Ayr, Tel.: 01292 513623

East Ayrshire Community Health Partnership
CHP Headquarters, Strathlea Cottages
Holmes Road
KILMARNOCK, KA1 1TW
Tel.: 01563 549680

Admin & Senior Management
Ms M Currie, General Manager, Strathlea Cottages, Holmes Road, Kilmarnock, KA1 1TW, Tel.: 01563 549680
Community Nursing Services
Mrs B Brown, Professional, Nurse Advisor, West Lodge, Ailsa Hospital, Tel.: 01292 289564
District Nursing
J Benson, District Sister, Dr Lau & Partners, Maybole Health Centre, 6 High Street, Maybole,
G Brown, District Sister, Drs McCulloch/Barr/Anderson, The Health Centre, 109a Henrietta Street, Girvan,
A Deighton, District Sister, Drs McMaster & Moore, The Health Centre, 109a Henrietta Street, Girvan,
S Grimmer, District Sister, Dr Scobie & Partners, Maybole Health Centre, 6 High Street, Maybole,
B McMaster, District Sister, Dr McNichol & Partners, 36 Mongomerie Street, Tarbolton,
S McQuilken, District Sister, Dr Dowell, Mill O Shield Road, Drongan,
J Piper, District Sister, Dr McNichol & Partners, 36 Mongomerie Street, Tarbolton,
A Sillars, District Sister, Dr Dowell, Mill O Shield Road, Drongan,
S Stewart, District Sister, Dr Maxwell & Sloan, Church Street, Ballantrae,
Health Visitors
M Allan, Health Visitor, Dr Dowell, Mill O Shield Road, Drongan,
A Davidson, Health Visitor, Dr A Ferguson, 33 Main Street, Dalmellington, KA6 7QL,
M Elder, Health Visitor, Dr McNichol & Partners, 36 Mongomerie Street, Tarbolton,
A Goldie, Health Visitor, Dr McNichol & Partners, 36 Mongomerie Street, Tarbolton,
S Green, Health Visitor, Drs McMaster & Moore, The Health Centre, 109a Henrietta Street, Girvan,
P McCallum, Health Visitor, Dr Maxwell & Sloan, Church Street, Ballantrae,
J McMillan, Health Visitor, Dr Lau & Partners, Maybole Health Centre, 6 High Street, Maybole,
L Pettigrew, Health Visitor, Drs McCulloch/Barr/Anderson, The Health Centre, 109a Henrietta Street, Girvan,
J Rosie, Health Visitor, Dr Malloch & Partners, "Columba" Dailly,
L Rush, Health Visitor, Dr Dowell, Mill O Shield Road, Drongan,
E Turner, Health Visitor, Dr A Ferguson, 33 Main Street, Dalmellington, KA6 7QL,

NHS Ayrshire & Arran
Boswell House
Hawkhead Road
PAISLEY
PA2 7BN
Tel.: 0141 842 7200
Fax.: 0141 848 1414

Scotland

Admin & Senior Management
Mrs F McQueen, Director of Nursing, Boswell House, Hawkhead Road, Paisley, PA2 7BN, Tel.: 0141 842 7200
Child Health
Ms E Bishop, Paediatric Outreach, Tel.: 01563 521133 ext 2806
Mrs A Hoyle, Neonatal Homecare Team, Tel.: 01294 323349
Community Midwifery
Miss A Cunningham, Senior Nurse/Midwife Manager, Ayrshire Central Hospital, Kilwinning Road, Irvine, Ayrshire, KA12 8SS, Tel.: 01294 323390
Emergencies, Ayrshire Central Hospital, Kilwinning Road, Irvine, Ayrshire, KA12 8SS, Tel.: 01294 274191
Maternity Area, Ayrshire Central Hospital, Kilwinning Road, Irvine, Ayrshire, KA12 8SS, Tel.: 01294 271852
Ms A Porter, Senior, Midwife, Ayrshire Central Hospital, Kilwinning Road, Irvine, Ayrshire, KA12 8SS,
Ms M Rodger, Senior, Midwife, Ayrshire Central Hospital, Kilwinning Road, Irvine, Ayrshire, KA12 8SS,
Specialist Nursing Services
Ms S McPhee, Ayr Hospital, Dalmellington Road, Ayr, Tel.: ext 4494
Ms V Kerr, Nurse, Breast Care, Crosshouse Hospital, Kilmarnock, KA2 0BE, Tel.: 01563 521133 ext 2895
Ms A Roy, Nurse, Colorectal, Crosshouse Hospital, Kilmarnock, KA2 0BE, Tel.: 01563 521133 ext 2567
Ms M Jamieson, Lead Nurse, Dermatology, Crosshouse Hospital, Kilmarnock, KA2 0BE, Tel.: 01563 521133 ext 2923
Ms M Nicol, Liaison Nurse, Dermatology, Heathfield Clinic, Prestwick, Tel.: 01292 610557 ext 3504
Ms C Rennie, Nurse, Head & Neck, Crosshouse Hospital, Kilmarnock, KA2 0BE, Tel.: 01563 521133 ext 3806
Ms P Beattie, Specialist, Lung Cancer, Crosshouse Hospital, Kilmarnock, KA2 0BE, Tel.: 01563 521133 ext 2911
Ms J McNeil, Multiple Sclerosis, Ayrshire Central Hospital, Irvine, Tel.: 01294 274191 ext 3029
Ms A Bunce, Liaison, Respiratory, Crosshouse Hospital, Kilmarnock, KA2 0BE, Tel.: 01563 521133 ext 2517
Ms C Harvey, Specialist, Tissue Viability, Crosshouse Hospital, Kilmarnock, KA2 0BE, Tel.: 01563 521133 ext 3877

North Ayrshire Community Health Partnership
Pavilion 8
Ayrshire Central Hospital, Kilwinning Road
IRVINE
KA12 8SS
Tel.: 01294 323579

Admin & Senior Management
Ms L Boyd, General Manager, Pavilion 8, Ayrshire Central Hospital, Irvine, Tel.: 01294 323514
Mr A Stout, Arran Manager, Arran War Memorial Hospital, Lamlash, Isle of Arran, KA27 8EP, Tel.: 01770 600522
Community Nursing Services
Ms P Campbell, Community Nursing Sister, Arran War Memorial Hospital, Tel.: 01770 600080
Ms V Ransome, Community Nursing Sister, Arran War Memorial Hospital, Tel.: 01770 600080
Health Visitors
Ms M Millar, Health Visitor, Arran War Memorial Hospital, Tel.: 01770 600570
Other Services
Ms J Fowler, Senior Occupational Therapist, Arran War Memorial Hospital, Tel.: 01770 600551
Ms A Keir, Senior Physiotherapist, Arran War Memorial Hospital, Tel.: 01770 600551
Specialist Nursing Services
Ms K Stout, Emergency Nurse Practitioner, Arran War Memorial Hospital, Tel.: 01770 600777

Ms C Weir, Hospital Charge Nurse/Senior Midwife, Arran War Memorial Hospital, Tel.: 01770 600777
Ms I MacDonald, Nurse, Public Health, Arran War Memorial Hospital, Tel.: 01770 600570

South Ayrshire Community Health Partnership
Heathfield House
Heathfield Road
AYR
KA8 9DX
Tel.: 01292 513892

Admin & Senior Management
Mrs J Atkinson, General Manager, South Ayrshire LHCC/CHP, Heathfield House, Heathfield Road, Ayr, KA8 9DX, Tel.: 01292 513862
Child Protection/Safeguarding Children
Ms L Pettigrew, Child Protection Advisor, Heathfield House, Heathfield Road, Ayr, KA8 9DX, Tel.: 01292 513872
Community Midwifery
Ms A Porter, Senior Midwife, North Ayr Health Centre, Glenmuir Place, Ayr, Tel.: 01292 885500
District Nursing
Mr A Brown, Professional Nurse Advisor, Heathfield House, Heathfield Road, Ayr, KA8 9DX, Tel.: 01292 513870
Ms B Brown, Professional Nurse Advisor, Heathfield House, Heathfield Road, Ayr, KA8 9DX, Tel.: 01292 513871
Other Services
Ms S Johnston, Public Health Practitioner, Heathfield House, Heathfield Road, Ayr, KA8 9DX, Tel.: 01292 513866
Ms K McGuire, CHP Implementation Manager, Heathfield House, Heathfield Road, Ayr, KA8 9DX, Tel.: 01292 513892
Ms A Sinclair, Operational Manager, Tel.: 01292 513863
Ms E Smith, Public Health Practitioner, Heathfield House, Heathfield Road, Ayr, KA8 9DX, Tel.: 01292 513866
Pharmacy
Ms D Lamprell, Community Development Pharmacist, Heathfield House, Heathfield Road, Ayr, KA8 9DX, Tel.: 01292 513883
School Nursing
Ms J Milne, Public Health School Nurse, Heathfield House, Heathfield Road, Ayr, KA8 9DX, Tel.: 01292 513868
Specialist Nursing Services
Ms K Frater, Nurse Practice Facilitator, Tel.: 01292 513875
Ms K Wilson, Practice Education Facilitator, Tel.: 01292 513874
Ms A Milliken, Nurse, Heart Failure, Tel.: 01292 513873
Ms P Macrae, Co-ordinator, Older People, Tel.: 01292 513867
The Homeless/Travellers & Asylum Seekers
Ms D Sinclair, Public Health Facilitator for Homeless Clients, Heathfield House, Heathfield Road, Ayr, KA8 9DX, Tel.: 01292 513889

NHS Borders

Borders Community Health Partnership
Newstead
MELROSE
Roxburghshire, TD6 9DB
Tel.: 01896 825508
Fax.: 01896 825577

Admin & Senior Management
Mr R Roberts, Borders CHP, Newstead, Melrose, Roxburghshire, TD6 9DB, Tel.: 01896 825508
Child Health
Ms J Mitchell, Lead Nurse, NHS Borders, Newstead, Melrose, TD9 9DB, Tel.: 01896 825503

Scotland

Ms D Moss, Child Health, Nurse Consultant, Ward 15, Borders General Hospital, Melrose, TD6 6BS, Tel.: 01896 826692
Mrs C Wise, Community Children's Nurse, Tel.: 01573 223001
Child Health Records
Ms M Grzybowski, Community Paediatrics, NHS Borders, Borders General Hospital, Melrose, TD6 9BS, Tel.: 01896 826000
Child Protection/Safeguarding Children
Mrs E Kerr, Senior Nurse, Child Protection, Child Protection Review Unit, Council Chambers, Albert Place, Galashiels, TD1 3DL, Tel.: 01896 662762
Community Nursing Services
Ms J Mitchell, Lead Nurse, NHS Borders, Newstead, Melrose, TD9 9DB, Tel.: 01896 825503
Ms J Romanes, Community Hospitals Lead Nurse, NHS Borders, 4 Nurses Houses, Dingleton Road, Melrose, TD6 9QN, Tel.: 01896 823493
District Nursing
Ms J Mitchell, Lead Nurse, NHS Borders, Newstead, Melrose, TD9 9DB, Tel.: 01896 825503
Learning Disabilities
Ms K Haughey, Community Charge Nurse (Special Interest Autism), 1 Dingleton Cottages, Dingleton Road, Melrose, TD6 9HR, Tel.: 01896 823682
Mr S Russell, Community Charge Nurse (Special Interest Epilepsy), 1 Dingleton Cottages, Dingleton Road, Melrose, TD6 9HR, Tel.: 01896 823682
Mrs J Seymour, Community Charge Nurse, 1 Dingleton Cottages, Dingleton Road, Melrose, TD6 9HR, Tel.: 01896 823682
Liaison Services
Ms G Black, Children Liaison Nurse, Ambulatory Care Unit, Ward 15, Borders General Hospital, Melrose, TD6 6BS, Tel.: 01896 826082
Ms C Gordon, Children Liaison Nurse, Ambulatory Care Unit, Ward 15, Borders General Hospital, Melrose, TD6 6BS, 01896 826082
Specialist Nursing Services
Ms G Donaldson, Specialist Nurse, Cardiac, Tel.: 01896 826650
Mrs D Edgar, Specialist Nurse, Cardiac, Borders General Hospital, Melrose, TD6 9BS, Tel.: 01896 826205
Ms J Elliot, Officer, Cardiac Rehabilitation, Tel.: 01896 826650
Ms H Clark, Nurse Specialist, Diabetic Care, Borders General Hospital, Melrose, TD6 9BS, Tel.: 01896 826580
Ms M Low, Nurse Specialist, Diabetic Care, Tel.: 01896 826580
Ms E Oliver, Nurse Specialist, Diabetic Care, Borders General Hospital, Melrose, TD6 9BS, Tel.: 01896 826658
Ms S Robertson, Nurse Specialist, Diabetic Care, Borders General Hospital, Melrose, TD6 9BS, Tel.: 01896 826580
Ms M Bowers, Acting, Nurse Specialist, Dialysis, Borders General Hospital, Melrose, TD6 9BS, Tel.: 01896 826637
Mrs E Howie, Specialist Nurse, GI, Tel.: 01896 826454
Mrs S Rumming, Clinical Service Manager, Medicine, DME/Medicine, Borders General Hospital, Melrose, TD9 6BS, Tel.: 01896 826656
Ms R Johnstone, Nurse Specialist, Oncology, Borders General Hospital, Melrose, TD6 9BS, Tel.: 01896 826832
Mrs J Kilshaw, Nurse Specialist, Oncology, Borders General Hospital, Melrose, TD6 9BS, Tel.: 01896 826830
Ms J Smith, Nurse Specialist, Oncology, Borders General Hospital, Melrose, TD6 9BS, Tel.: 01896 826831
Ms K Brackenbridge, Nurse Specialist, Palliative Care, Borders General Hospital, Melrose, TD6 9BS, Tel.: 01896 826829
Ms E Ferguson, Nurse Specialist, Palliative Care, Borders General Hospital, Melrose, TD6 9BS, Tel.: 01896 826635
Ms P MacMahon, Nurse Specialist, Palliative Care, Borders General Hospital, Melrose, TD6 9BS, Tel.: 01896 826828
Mr L Tucker, Nurse Specialist, Palliative Care, Borders General Hospital, Melrose, TD6 9BS, Tel.: 01896 826815
Ms L Bell, Nurse Specialist, Respiratory, Borders General Hospital, Melrose, TD6 9BS, Tel.: 01896 826635
Mrs E Dodds, Nurse Specialist, Respiratory, Tel.: 01896 826635

Mrs P Cannon, Specialist Nurse, Rheumatology,
Mrs S Gollock, Nurse, Stoma Care, Tel.: 01896 826568
Ms S Haines, Co-ordinator, Stroke Care, Tel.: 01896 826096

NHS Dumfries & Galloway

Annandale & Eskdale Community Health Partnership
Lockerbie Health Centre
Victoria Gardens
LOCKERBIE
Tel.: 01387 811743

Admin & Senior Management
Mrs B Roxburgh, Nurse Manager, Lockerbie Health Centre, Victoria Gardens, Lockerbie, Tel.: 01576 205520
Child Health Records
Child Health Records, Lockerbie Health Centre, Victoria Gardens, Lockerbie, Tel.: 01576 205541
School Health Records, Lockerbie Health Centre, Victoria Gardens, Lockerbie, Tel.: 01576 205541
Child Protection/Safeguarding Children
Child Protection, Locality Offices, Nithbank Hospital, 01387 244000
District Nursing
Annan District Nurses, Tel.: 01461 207696/207697
Ecclefechan District Nurses, Tel.: 01576 300694
Gretna District Nurses, Tel.: 01461 339240
Langholm District Nurses, Tel.: 013873 80212
Lochmaben District Nurses, Tel.: 01387 811745
Lockerbie District Nurses, Tel.: 01576 205534
Moffat District Nurses, Tel.: 01683 220555
Family Planning Services
Family Planning Services, Nithbank Hospital, Tel.: 01387 244000
Health Visitors
Annan Health Visitors, Tel.: 01461 201210/207695
Gretna Health Visitors, Tel.: 01461 339242
Langholm Health Visitors, Tel.: 013873 80212
Lochmaben Health Visitors, Tel.: 01387 811748
Lockerbie Health Visitors, Tel.: 01576 205531
Moffat Health Visitors, Tel.: 01683 221531
Liaison Services
Ms B Scott, Liaison, Dumfries & Galloway, Social Services Dept, Dumfries & Galloway Royal Infirmary, Bankend Road, Dumfries, DG1 4AP, Tel.: 01387 246246
Pharmacy
Community Pharmacy Advisor, Lockerbie Health Centre, Victoria Gardens, Lockerbie, Tel.: 01576 205529
School Nursing
School Nurses, Lockerbie Health Centre, Victoria Gardens, Lockerbie, Tel.: 01576 205538
Specialist Nursing Services
Ms G Bell, Specialist Nurse, Diabetes, Annan, Green Croft House, Tel.: 01461 206991

Dumfries & Nithsdale Local Health Partnership
LHP Headquarters
Nithbank
DUMFRIES
DG1 2SD
Tel.: 01387 244657
Fax.: 01387 244403

Admin & Senior Management
Mrs M Anderson, Nurse Manager, Tel.: 01387 244415
Mr S Oliphant, LHCC Manager,
Mr S Oliphant, General Manager, Tel.: 01387 244657

Child Protection/Safeguarding Children
Ms E Brodie, Health Visitor, Child Protection,
Community Nursing Services
Community Nursing Services, Locality Management Offices, Nithbank, Dumfries, DG1 2SD, Tel.: 01387 244448
District Nursing
District Nurses, Upper Nithsdale, Health Centre, Thornhill, Tel.: 01848 330208
District Nurses, Nithsdale - Dumfries, Nithbank, Tel.: 01387 244448
Health Visitors
Health Visitors, Upper Nithsdale, Health Centre, Thornhill, Tel.: 01848 330208
Health Visitors, Nithsdale - Dumfries, Nithbank, Tel.: 01387 244448

Stewartry Community Health Partnership
67 Queen Street
CASTLE DOUGLAS
DG7 1EG
Tel.: 01556 502386
Fax.: 01556 502490

Admin & Senior Management
Mrs M Houston, Nurse Manager,
Ms J White, General Manager,
Child Protection/Safeguarding Children
Ms T Gillespie, Stewartry LHCC & Wigtownshire LHCC, Health Visitor, Child Protection, Tel.: 0773 6955493
Community Midwifery
Ms K Hamblin, Midwife,
District Nursing
District Nurses, LHCC Offices, 67 Queen Street, Castle Douglas, DG7 1EG, Tel.: 01556 502386
Health Visitors
Health Visitors, LHCC Offices, 67 Queen Street, Castle Douglas, DG7 1EG, Tel.: 01556 502386
Pharmacy
Ms A Mason,
School Nursing
School Health/Nursing Services, LHCC Offices, 67 Queen Street, Castle Douglas, DG7 1EG, Tel.: 01556 502386
Smoking Cessation
Ms T Grierson,

Wigtownshire Community Health Partnership
Victoria Place
STRANRAER
DG9 7HX
Tel.: 01776 706900

Child Health
Ms E Keery, Newton Stewart Health Centre, Newton Stewart, Tel.: 01671 402504
Ms A McCurry, Waverley Medical Centre, Stranraer, Tel.: 01776 706900
Child Health Records
Pre-School Records, Child Health Directorate, Nithbank, Dumfries, DG1 2SD, Tel.: 01387 244000 ext 4562
School Records, Child Health Directorate, Nithbank, Dumfries, DG1 2SD, Tel.: 01387 244000 ext 4561
Child Protection/Safeguarding Children
Ms E Brodie, Annandale & Eskdale LHP & Dumfries & Upper Nithsdale LHP, Nurse Advisor, Child Protection, Tel.: 0773 6955512
Ms T Gillespie, Nurse Consultant, Child Protection, NHS Dumfries & Galloway, Child Health, Nithbank, Dumfries, DG1 8DS, Tel.: 01387 244572
Nurse Advisor, Stewartry LHP & Wigtownshire LHP, Child Protection, Tel.: 0773 6955493

Community Nursing Services
Mrs K Wallace, Community Nurse Manager, Locality Office, Victoria Place, Stranraer, DG9 7HX, Tel.: 01776 706900 ext 4002
District Nursing
Ms E Barton, District Nurse, Waverley Medical Centre, Dalrymple Street, Stranraer, Tel.: 01776 889412
Ms D Dillon, District Nurse, Waverley Medical Centre, Dalrymple Street, Stranraer, Tel.: 01776 889412
Ms B Dunn, District Nurse, Waverley Medical Centre, Dalrymple Street, Stranraer, Tel.: 01776 889412
Ms J Greenwood, District Nurse, Health Centre, Newton Stewart, Tel.: 01671 403744
Ms I Hunter, District Nurse, Waverley Medical Centre, Dalrymple Street, Stranraer, Tel.: 01776 889412
Mrs A MacDonald, District Nurse, Wigtown Surgery, 01988 402649
Ms C Makepeace, District Nurse, Whithorn Clinic, Tel.: 01988 500811
Ms A Wilson, District Nurse, Waverley Medical Centre, Dalrymple Street, Stranraer, Tel.: 01776 889412
Health Visitors
Ms N Aitchison, Team Leader, Public Health Nurse Team, Waverley Medical Centre, Dalrymple Street, Stranraer, Tel.: 01776 705763
Ms A Bate, Health Visitor, Waverley Medical Centre, Dalrymple Street, Stranraer, Tel.: 01776 705763
Ms H Dodds, Health Visitor, Waverley Medical Centre, Dalrymple Street, Stranraer, Tel.: 01776 705763
Health Visitor, Waverley Medical Centre, Dalrymple Street, Stranraer, Tel.: 01776 705763
Ms B Jennings, Health Visitor, Wigtown Surgery, Tel.: 01988 402649
Ms Y Lhamo, Health Visitor, Health Centre, Newton Stewart, Tel.: 01671 403068
Ms N McVicar, Health Visitor, Waverley Medical Centre, Dalrymple Street, Stranraer, Tel.: 01776 705763
Ms D Roe, Health Visitor, Whithorn Clinic, Tel.: 01988 500411
Ms S Rogers, Health Visitor, Health Centre, Newton Stewart, Tel.: 01671 403068
Mrs C Sellers, Health Visitor, Waverley Medical Centre, Dalrymple Street, Stranraer, Tel.: 01776 705763

NHS Fife

Dunfermline & West Fife Community Health Partnership
Admin Block, Lynebank Hospital
Halbeath Road
DUNFERMLINE
KY11 4UW
Tel.: 01383 565380
Fax.: 01383 565324

Admin & Senior Management
Ms R Brown, Dunfermline Locality, Lead Nurse, Admin Block, Lynebank, Tel.: 01383 565458
Ms S Dempsey, Locality Manager, (West Fife), Admin Block, Lynebank, Tel.: 01383 565339
Ms L Eydmann, Locality Manager, (Dunfermline), Admin Block, Lynebank, Tel.: 01383 565465
Ms V Hatch, Service Development Manager, Admin Block, Lynebank, Tel.: 01383 565455
Ms S Manion, General Manager, Admin Block, Lynebank, Tel.: 01383 565330
Dr A McGovern, Clinical Director, Dunfermline Locality, Admin Block, Lynebank, Tel.: 01383 565247
Ms L Mitchell, West Fife Locality, Lead Nurse, Admin Block, Lynebank, Tel.: 01383 565327
Dr G Robson, Clinical Director, West Life Locality, Admin Block, Lynebank, Tel.: 01383 565336

Scotland

Child Health
Ms K Duhre, Paediatric Home Care Manager, Lynebank Hospital,
Ms M Paris, Acting Clinical Services Facilitator - Child Health, Admin Block, Lynebank, Tel.: 01383 565320
Health Visitors
Ms P Binny, Health Visitor, Ward 5, Lynebank, Tel.: 01383 565331
Learning Disabilities
Mrs P Colville, Lynebank Hospital, Tel.: 01383 565230
Other Services
Dr F Baty, Psychology, Lynebank Hospital,
Dr K Cheshire, Psychology, Lynebank Hospital,
Pharmacy
Mrs E McPhail, Chief Pharmacist, Pentland Flats, Lynebank,
Specialist Nursing Services
Ms A McEwan, Nurse, Cardio vascular, Carnegie Clinic, Dunfermline, Tel.: 01383 729911
Ms F Mitchell, PMS Nurse, Cardio vascular, Rosewell Registry, Tel.: 01592 861962
Ms L Williams, Nurse, Cardio vascular, Rosewell Registry, Tel.: 01592 861962
Ms C Davidson, Support Nurse, Clinical Development, Admin Block, Lynebank, Tel.: 01383 565328
Ms M Mateos, Support Nurse, Clinical Development, Admin Block, Lynebank, Tel.: 01383 565328
Ms P Miller, Advisor, Continence, Rosewell Registry, Tel.: 01592 861962
Mrs C Carson, Community, Nurse Specialist, Diabetes, Carnegie Clinic, Tel.: 01383 729911
Ms H York, PMS Nurse, Diabetes, Rosewell Registry, Tel.: 01592 861962

Fife Acute Hospitals Operating Division

Trust Headquarters, Hayfield House
Hayfield Road
KIRKCALDY
KY2 5AH
Tel.: 01592 643355
Child Health
Ms N Anderson, Neonatal Sister - Preterm Babies - Home Care, Forth Park Hospital, 30 Bennochy Road, Kirkcaldy, Fife, KY2 5RA,
Ms P Cobain, Breastfeeding Support Midwife,
Ms I Fenske, Breastfeeding Support Midwife,
Ms E Ireland, Parenthood/Health Promotion Midwife,
Mr K Macormack, Neonatal Practitioner,
Ms M McGill, Ambulatory Paediatric Care, Staff Nurse,
Ms L Robertson, Paediatric, Diabetic Care, Victoria Hospital, Hayfield Road, Kirkcaldy, KY2 5AH, Tel.: 01592 643355 ext 8364
Community Midwifery
Mrs C Cummings, Midwifery Nurse Manager, Forth Park Hospital, Bennochy Road, Kirkcaldy, KY2 5RA, Tel.: 01592 643355 ext 2756
Ms J Leggate, Co-ordinator for Community Midwifery Services, Forth Park Hospital, Bennochy Road, Kirkcaldy, KY2 5RA, Tel.: 01592 643355 ext 2756
Liaison Services
Mrs J Tinlin, Diabetic, Liaison Nurse, Queen Margaret Hospital, Whitefield Road, Dunfermline, KY12 0SU, Tel.: 01383 623623 ext 3728
Ms B Page, Liaison, Dermatology, Queen Margaret Hospital, Whitefield Road, Dunfermline, KY12 0SU, 01383 623623 ext 2982
Ms S Robertson, Liaison, Dermatology, Victoria Hospital, Hayfield Road, Kirkcaldy, KY2 5AH, Tel.: 01592 643355 ext 8057
Other Services
Ms J Ogden, Opthalmology, Queen Margaret Hospital, Whitefield Road, Dunfermline, KY12 0SU, Tel.: 01383 623623 ext 4130
Ms H Paterson, Low Vision, Queen Margaret Hospital, Whitefield Road, Dunfermline, KY12 0SU, Tel.: 01383 623623 ext 4130
Ms R Robertson, Opthalmology, Queen Margaret Hospital, Whitefield Road, Dunfermline, KY12 0SU, 01383 623623 ext 4130

Ms R Stuart, Clinical Research, Queen Margaret Hospital, Whitefield Road, Dunfermline, KY12 0SU, Tel.: 01383 623623 ext 3228
Specialist Nursing Services
Ms W Chrystal, Menopause Nurse, Forth Park Hospital, Bennochy Road, Kirkaldy, KY2 5RA, Tel.: 01592 643355 ext 2824
Ms E Graham, Upper Limb Nurse, Queen Margaret Hospital, Whitefield Road, Dunfermline, KY12 0SW, Tel.: 01383 623623 ext 4348
Ms V Nicholson, Clinical Research, Victoria Hospital, Tel.: 01592 643355 ext 8223
Ms M Pheely, Infertility, Victoria Hospital, Tel.: 01592 643355 bleep 8407
Ms J Croft, Acute Pain, Based at Queen Margaret Hospital & Victoria Hospital,
Ms A McKean, Asthma, - Paediatrics, Based at Queen Margaret Hospital & Victoria Hospital,
Ms S Jamieson, Breast Care, Queen Margaret Hospital, Tel.: 01383 623623 ext 5536
Ms M Malloch, Breast Care, Queen Margaret Hospital, Tel.: 01383 623623 ext 5536
Ms S Lamond, Specialist Nurse, Cardiac, Queen Margaret Hospital, Tel.: 01383 623623 ext 7028
Ms P Rodger, Specialist Nurse, Cardiac, Queen Margaret Hospital, Tel.: 01383 623623 ext 7028
Ms S Pearson, Cardiac Rehabilitation, Victoria Hospital, Tel.: 01592 643355 ext 8561
Ms M Traill, Cardiac Rehabilitation, Queen Margaret Hosp, Tel.: 01383 623623 ext 2622
Mr D Sandeman, Specialist Nurse, Chest Pain, Based at Victoria Hospital, Tel.: 01592 643355
Ms M Urquhart, Colorectal, - Oncology, Based at Queen Margaret Hospital & Victoria Hospital,
Ms H Ogg, Specialist Nurse, Dermatology, Victoria Hospital, Tel.: 01592 648180
Mrs F Jamieson, Specialist Nurse, Diabetic Care, Based at Victoria Hospital, Tel.: 01592 643355 ext 8365
Mrs M Martin, Specialist Nurse, Diabetic Care, Based at Victoria Hospital, Tel.: 01592 643355 ext 8365
Ms J Penman, Diabetic Care, Queen Margaret Hospital, Tel.: 01383 623623 ext 3232
Ms J Tinlin, Diabetic Care, Queen Margaret Hospital, Tel.: 01383 623623 ext 3728
Ms K Thompson, Blood Borne, Disease, Based at Queen Margaret Hospital & Victoria Hospital,
Ms M Crawford, G.U.M, Based at Queen Margaret Hospital & Victoria Hospital,
Ms S Paxton, Nurse Practitioner, G.U.M, Victoria Hospital, Tel.: 01592 643355 ext 8377
Ms H Smith, Advisor, G.U.M, Victoria Hospital, Tel.: 01592 643355 ext 8377
Ms E Brash, Gastroenterology, Queen Margaret Hospital, Tel.: 01383 623623 ext 3232
Ms S Dewar, Gastroenterology, Victoria Hospital, Hayfield Road, Kirkcaldy, KY2 5AH, Tel.: 01592 643355 ext 8566
Ms A MacDonald, Gastroenterology, Victoria Hospital, Tel.: 01592 643355 ext 1566
Ms J McCafferty, Gynae/Oncology (pager 07623608397), Gynae/Oncology, Forth Park Hospital, Tel.: 01592 643355 ext 273`
Ms I Russell, Gynaecology, - Urology, Based at Queen Margaret Hospital & Victoria Hospital,
Ms J Martin, Haematology, Queen Margaret Hospital, Tel.: 01383 623623 xt 2421/3858
Ms G Wilson, Haematology, Victoria Hospital, Tel.: 01592 643355 ext 8526
Ms J Philip, Head & Neck, - Oncology, Based at Queen Margaret Hospital & Victoria Hospital,
Ms P Hope, Infection Control, Queen Margaret Hospital, Tel.: 0138 623623 x2509

Scotland

Mrs M Selbie, Nurse, Infection Control, Victoria Hospital, Tel.: 01592 643355 ext 8563

Ms H Preston, Lung Cancer, Based at Queen Margaret Hospital & Victoria Hospital,

Ms G Sandeman, Lung Cancer, Victoria Hospital, Tel.: 01592 643355 ext 8552

Ms M Shaw, Nutrition, Queen Margaret Hospital, Tel.: 01383 623623

Ms B Grant, Ophthalmology, Based at Queen Margaret Hospital & Victoria Hospital,

Ms L Gordon, Osteoporosis, Based at Queen Margaret Hospital & Victoria Hospital,

Ms F Proctor, Pain Management, Queen Margaret Hospital, Tel.: 01383 623623 ext 3703

Ms J Malecki, Palliative Care, Victoria Hosp. 01592 643355 ext 8878

Ms E O'Donnell, Palliative Care, Queen Margaret Hospital, Tel.: 01383 623623 ext 7064

Mrs J Reid, Specialist Nurse, Parkinson's Disease, Based at Victoria Hospital, Tel.: 01592 643355 ext 8834

Ms L Coyne, Plastic Surgery, Queen Margaret Hospital, Tel.: 01383 623623 ext 5537

Ms G Black, Respiratory, Based at Queen Margaret Hospital & Victoria Hospital,

Ms O Lamont, Nurse, Respiratory, Queen Margaret Hospital, Tel.: 01383 623623 ext 4237

Ms H Smith, Respiratory, Victoria Hospital, Tel.: 01592 643355 ext 8168

Ms B Wilson, Officer, Resuscitation Training, Queen Margaret Hospital, Whitefield Road, Dunfermline, KY12 0SW, Tel.: 01383 623623 ext 2649

Ms J Zinkiewicz, Officer, Resuscitation Training, Victoria Hospital, Hayfield Road, Kirkcaldy, KY2 5AH, Tel.: 01592 643355 ext 8297

Ms J Hamilton, Stoma Care, Queen Margaret Hospital, Tel.: 01383 623623 ext 6328

Ms V Ness, Stoma Care, Based at Queen Margaret Hospital & Victoria Hospital,

Ms A Cassells, Specialist Nurse, Stroke Care, Based at Queen Margaret Hospital, Tel.: 01383 623623

Ms H Fraser, Co-ordinator, Stroke Care, Based at Queen Margaret Hospital, Tel.: 01383 623623 ext 2406

Ms A Wilson, Tissue Viability, Based at Queen Margaret Hospital & Victoria Hospital,

Ms R Cameron, Urology, Queen Margaret Hospital, Tel.: 01383 623623 ext 2626

Ms L Drummond, Urology, Based at Queen Margaret Hospital & Victoria Hospital,

Ms L Frew, Urology/Oncology, Based at Queen Margaret Hospital & Victoria Hospital,

Ms R Robbins, Vascular, Queen Margaret Hospital, Tel.: 01383 623623 ext 5537

Fife Primary Care Division

Cameron House
Cameron Bridge
LEVEN, Fife
KY8 5RG
Tel.: 01592 712812

Admin & Senior Management

Ms I Souter, Director of Nursing and Quality, Cameron House, Cameron Bridge, Leven, KY8 5RG, Tel.: 01592 712812

Child Health

Ms J Adams, Community Children's Nursing, Tel.: 01383 565357

Ms M Aitken, Community Children's Nursing, Tel.: 01383 565358

Ms K Duhre, Lead, Community Children's Nursing, Tel.: 01383 565373

Ms H Fernie, Manager, Child Health, Ward 12, Cameron Hospital, Windygates, KY8 5RG, Tel.: 01592 712472

Ms L Mushet, Community Children's Nursing, Tel.: 01383 565362

Child Health Records

Child Health Department, Cameron Hospital, Cameron Bridge, Leven, KY8 5RR, Tel.: 01592 712472

Child Protection/Safeguarding Children

Mrs B A Rowland, Nurse Advisor, Child Protection, Greenfield Clinic, Flat 2, Campsie, Lynebank Hospital, Halbeath Rd, Dunfermline, Fife, KY11 4UW, Tel.: 01383 565395

District Nursing

Ms I Souter, Director of Nursing and Quality, Cameron House, Cameron Bridge, Leven, KY8 5RG, Tel.: 01592 712812

Family Planning Services

Family Planning Services, c/o Mary Hendry, Carnegie Clinic, Dunfermline, Tel.: 01383 722911

Health Visitors

Ms J Gemmel, Breast Feeding Liaison Health Visitor, Carnegie Clinic, Dunfermline, Tel.: 01383 722911

Learning Disabilities

Mr M Gordon, Community Nurse Manager, Lynebank Hospital, Halbeath Road, Dunfermline, KY11 4UW, Tel.: 01383 623623

Ms I Soutar, Director of Nursing, Cameron House, Cameron Bridge, Leven, KY8 5RG, Tel.: 01592 712762

Liaison Services

Mrs D Cattanach, Women's Aid Comm. Staff Nurse Liaison, New Park Surgery, 163 Robertson Road, Dunfermline, KY11 4JW, Tel.: 01383 728944

Ms A Lambie, Encopresis Liaison Health Visitor, Rosyth Health Centre, Park Road, Rosyth, KY11 2SE, Tel.: 01383 416181

Ms J Munro, Encopresis Liaison Health Visitor, Millhill Surgery, 87 Woodmill Street, Dunfermline, KY11 4JW, Tel.: 01383 621222

Ms C Rainbow, Liaison, District Nurse, Continence, Bellyeoman Surgery, Bellyeoman Road, Dunfermline, KY12 0AE, Tel.: 01383 721266

Mrs L Lewis, Liaison, Paediatrics, Nethertown Surgery, Tel.: 01383 623516

Other Services

Mrs J Gemmell, Public Health Practitioner, Carnegie Clinic, Inglis Street, Dunfermline, Tel.: 01383 722911

Ms A Hatton, Clinical Co-ordinator, Carnegie Clinic, Inglis Street, Dunfermline, Tel.: 01383 722911

Specialist Nursing Services

Miss S Jamieson, Breast Care, Queen Margaret Hospital, Whitefield Road, Dunfermline, KY12 0SU, Tel.: 01383 623623

Ms M Malloch, Breast Care, Queen Margaret Hospital, Whitefield Road, Dunfermline, KY12 0SU, Tel.: 01383 623623

Mrs P Millar, Continence, Rosewell Clinic, 2 Ballingry Road, Lochore, Fife, KY5 8ET, Tel.: 01592 869924

Mrs L Carruthers, Infection Control, Cameron Hospital, Tel.: 01592 712472

Nurses, Macmillan, Cedar House, Willow Drive, Kirkcaldy, KY1 2LF, Tel.: 01592 205452

Ms A Donaldson, Multiple Sclerosis, SGSU, Tel.: 01592 712472

Ms D McCallion, Multiple Sclerosis, SGSU, Tel.: 01592 712472

Ms M Steel, Brain Injury Outreach, Neurology, SGSU, Tel.: 01592 712472

Mr B Sutherland, Rehabilitation, SGSU, Tel.: 01592 712472

Ms F Lovegrove, Rheumatology, Sir George Sharp Unit, Cameron Hospital, Tel.: 01592 712472

Ms C Malcolm, Rheumatology, Sir George Sharp Unit, Cameron Hospital, Tel.: 01592 712472

Ms N Thomson, Rheumatology, Sir George Sharp Unit, Cameron Hospital, Tel.: 01592 712472

Ms A McEwan, Cardio, Vascular, Carnegie Clinic, Tel.: 01383 722911

The Homeless/Travellers & Asylum Seekers

Mrs J Caldwell, Health Visitor for Travellers, Auchtermuchty Health Centre, Auchtermuchty, KY14 7AW, Tel.: 01337 826633

Scotland

Glenrothes & North East Fife Community Health Partnership

St Andrews Memorial Hospital
Abbey Walk
GLENROTHES
KY16 9LG
Tel.: 01334 468684

Admin & Senior Management
Ms L Ronalson, Lead Nurse, Glenrothes Hospital, Lodge Rise, Glenrothes, KY7 5TG, Tel.: 01592 743505
Child Protection/Safeguarding Children
Ms B Rowland, Child Protection, Kinghorn Health Centre, Rossland Place, Kinghorn, Tel.: 01592 891614
Clinical Leads (NSF)
Ms M McDonald, Clinical Lead, Cancer, Victoria Hospital, Kirkcaldy, Tel.: 01592 643355
District Nursing
Cos Lane Surgery, Woodside Road, Glenrothes, Tel.: 01592 610769
Glenrothes Hospital, District Nurses, Lodge Rise, Glenrothes, Tel.: 01592 743302
Glenwood Health Centre, Napier Road, Glenrothes, Tel.: 01592 756631
Leslie Clinic, Anderson Drive, Leslie, Tel.: 01592 743388
Markinch Health Centre, Markinch, Tel.: 01592 761087
Pitteuchar Health Centre, Glamis Centre, Glenrothes, Tel.: 01592 773507
Family Planning Services
Family Planning Services, Dovecot Clinic, Russell Drive, Glenrothes, Tel.: 01592 753566
Health Visitors
Glenrothes Hospital, Health Visitors, Lodge Rise, Glenrothes, Tel.: 01592 745931
School Nursing
Ms F Anderson, School Nurse, Dovecot Clinic, Russell Drive, Glenrothes, Tel.: 01592 753566
Ms S Lindsay, School Nurse, Dovecot Clinic, Russell Drive, Glenrothes, Tel.: 01592 753566
Ms F Mathewson, School Nurse, Glenwood Health Centre, Napier Road, Glenrothes, Tel.: 01592 756631
Ms J Pow, School Nurse, Dovecot Clinic, Russell Drive, Glenrothes, Tel.: 01592 753566
Ms J Todd, School Nurse, Glenwood Health Centre, Napier Road, Glenrothes, Tel.: 01592 756631
Smoking Cessation
Ms E King, Markinch Health Centre, High Street, Markinch, Tel.: 01592 761087
Ms K Lindsay, Cos Lane Surgery, Glenrothes, Tel.: 01592 610769
Ms G Stewart, Glenrothes Hospital, Lodge Rise, Glenrothes, Tel.: 01592 745931
Specialist Nursing Services
Ms H Lawrie, Elderly Care, Glenrothes Hospital, Lodge Rise, Glenrothes, Tel.: 01592 743505
Ms D Morgan, Practitioner, Public Health, Glenrothes House, North Street, Glenrothes, Tel.: 01592 769090

Kirkcaldy & Levenmouth Community Health Partnership

CHP Headquarters
Cameron Hospital, Cameron Bridge
WINDYGATE
Fife, KY8 5RR
Tel.: 01592 226708
Fax.: 01592 226899

Admin & Senior Management
Dr J Clark, Community Lead,
Mr G Cunningham, General Manager,

Dr J Duncan, Community Lead,
Community Nursing Services
Ms N Connor, Community Nursing Representative,
Mrs C Greig, Senior Nurse,
Ms F Leslie, Community Nursing Representative,
Ms S Redman, Community Nursing Representative,
Health Visitors
Ms M Campbell, Health Visitor,

NHS Forth Valley

Clackmannanshire Community Health Partnership

RSNH, Old Denny Road
LARBERT, FK5 4SD
Tel.: 01324 404085

Admin & Senior Management
Ms K O'Neill, General Manager,

Falkirk Community Health Partnership

Old Denny Road
LARBERT
FK5 4SD
Tel.: 01324 404133

Admin & Senior Management
Ms S Dow, General Manager,
Mr G Melrose, Director of Nursing, Tel.: 01324 570700
Ms R Warner, Deputy, Director of Nursing, Tel.: 01324 404023
Child Health Records
Child Health Records, Stirling Royal Infirmary, Livilands, Stirling, FK8 2AU, Tel.: 01786 434000
Child Protection/Safeguarding Children
Ms J Brown, Child Protection, Camelon Clinic, 1 Baird Street, Camelon, Tel.: 01324 627942
District Nursing
District Nurses, Old Denny Road, Larbert, Falkirk, FK5 4SD, Tel.: 01324 570700
Ms E Rodger, South LHCC, Nurse Advisor, Tel.: 01324 404438
Health Visitors
Ms D Budd, Special Needs, Health Visitor, St Ninians Health Centre, Mayfield Road, Stirling, FK7 0BS, Tel.: 01786 479555
Health Visitors, Old Denny Road, Larbert, Falkirk, FK5 4SD, Tel.: 01324 570700
Specialist Nursing Services
Ms L Roe, Lead Nurse, Cancer, Bonnybridge Health Centre, Bonnybridge, FK4 1ED, Tel.: 01324 815105
Ms R McDade, Continence, Bonnybridge Health Centre, Bonnybridge, FK4 1ED, Tel.: 01324 815105
Ms D Anderson, Infection Control, Trust Headquarters, Tel.: 01324 404430
Dr J Boothe, Nurse Consultant, Older People, Bo'ness Hospital, Dean Road, Bo'ness, EH51 0DH, Tel.: 01506 829580
Ms J O'Hare, Tissue Viability, Bonnybridge Health Centre, Bonnybridge, FK4 1ED, Tel.: 01324 814685
The Homeless/Travellers & Asylum Seekers
Ms F Turner, Specialist Worker to the Homeless, Council Advice Shop, 23/25 High Street, Falkirk, Tel.: 01324 501418

Forth Valley Acute Hospitals Division

Westburn Avenue
FALKIRK
FK1 5ST
Tel.: 01324 624000

Child Health
Ms H Bauld, Team Leader, Paediatric Outreach Service,
Ms G Boyle, Paediatric Outreach, Tel.: 01786 434000 ext 4328

Scotland

Ms S McDermid, Paediatric Outreach, Tel.: 01324 616058 ext 5777
Ms J Paterson, Community Liaison Sister, Stirling Royal Infirmary, Livilands, Stirling, FK8 2AU, Tel.: 01786 434000 ext 4569
Ms N Thomson, Paediatric Diabetic Liaison, Stirling Royal Infirmary, Livilands, Stirling, FK8 2AU, Tel.: 01786 434667

Community Midwifery
Miss L Donaldson, General Manager, Head of Midwifery, Falkirk & District Royal Infirmary, Majors Loan, Falkirk, Lothian, FK1 5QE, Tel.: 01324 624000 ext 5614
Ms B Seaman, Nurse Manager, Stirling Royal Infirmary, Livilands, Stirling, Lothian, FK8 2AU, Tel.: 01324 624000

Liaison Services
Mrs A Bytheway, Liaison, Elderly, Falkirk & District Royal Infirmary, Major's Loan, Falkirk, FK1 5QE, Tel.: 01324 624000 ext 5775
Ms D Coulter, Liaison, Surgery, Medical & Day Surgery, Falkirk & District Royal Infirmary, Major's Loan, Falkirk, FK1 5QE, Tel.: 01324 624000 ext 5776
Ms A Kinghorn, Paediatric Diabetic Liaison, Stirling Royal Infirmary, Livilands, Stirling, FK8 2AU, Tel.: 01786 434667
Ms S Milne, Liaison, Paediatrics, Falkirk & District Royal Infirmary, Major's Loan, Falkirk, FK1 5QE, Tel.: 01324 616093
Ms D Wilkinson, Liaison, Respiratory, Falkirk & District Royal Infirmary, Major's Loan, Falkirk, FK1 5QE, Tel.: 01324 624000 ext 5774

Other Services
Ms J Burrage, Sub-Fertility, Falkirk & District Royal Infirmary, Tel.: 01324 624000 ext 5140
Ms F Dick, Nurse Co-ordinator, Stroke Team, Stirling Royal Infirmary, Tel.: 01786 434000 ext 4666
Mr G Ramage, Resuscitation Training Officer, Stirling Royal Infirmary, Tel.: 01786 434000 ext 4663

Specialist Nursing Services
Ms S McNaughton, Macmillan, Breast Care, Stirling Royal Infirmary, Tel.: 01786 434000 ext 4086
Ms J Currie, Diabetic Care, Falkirk & District Royal Infirmary, Tel.: 01324 624000 ext 5746
Ms J Harrower, Diabetic Care, Stirling Royal Infirmary, Tel.: 01786 434472
Miss M Bar, Infection Control, Falkirk & District Royal Infirmary, Tel.: 01324 624000 ext 5773
Ms S Stevenson, Infection Control, Stirling Royal Infirmary, Tel.: 01786 434000 ext 4666
Ms V Duncan, Leg Ulcers, Falkirk & District Royal Infirmary, Major's Loan, Falkirk, FK1 5QE, Tel.: 01324 624000 ext 5771
Miss L McMillan, Macmillan, Falkirk & District Royal Infirmary, Tel.: 01324 624000 ext 5772
Ms N McIndoe, Multiple Sclerosis, Stirling Royal Infirmary, Tel.: 01786 434000 ext 4759
Ms E Cairney, Macmillan, Oncology, Stirling Royal Infirmary, Tel.: 01786 434000 ext 4560
Ms K Mair, Parkinson's Disease, Falkirk & District Royal Infirmary, Tel.: 01324 624000 ext 5639
Ms K Booth, Stoma Care, Stirling Royal Infirmary, Tel.: 01786 434000 ext 4243
Ms S Young, Stoma Care, - Breast, Falkirk & District Royal Infirmary, Tel.: 01324 624000 ext 5770
Ms J McCall, Stroke Care, Falkirk & District Royal Infirmary, Tel.: 01324 624000 ext 5140
Ms M Hamill, Urology, Falkirk & District Royal Infirmary, Tel.: 01324 434000 ext 5294
Ms L Malone, Urology, Stirling Royal Infirmary, Tel.: 01786 434000 ext 4448

orth Valley Primary Care Division
Old Denny Road
LARBERT
Falkirk, FK5 4SD
Tel.: 01324 570700

Admin & Senior Management
Ms R Warner, Interim, Director of Nursing, Tel.: 01324 404023
Child Health Records
Child Health Records, Stirling Royal Infirmary, Livilands, Stirling, FK8 2AU, Tel.: 01786 434000
Child Protection/Safeguarding Children
Mrs M Berry, Nurse Advisor, Child Protection, Ward 5, Sauchie Hospital, Parkhead, Sauchie, FK10 3BW, Tel.: 01259 728582
Mrs D Morgan, Nurse Advisor, Child Protection, Ward 5, Sauchie Hospital, Parkhead, Sauchie, FK10 3BW, Tel.: 01259 728582
District Nursing
Ms M Govern, Night Service, Carer Support, Tel.: 01324 611711
Ms T McLean, North LHCC, Tel.: 01324 404228
Ms E Rodger, South LHCC, Tel.: 01324 404438
Learning Disabilities
North Team, Orchard House Health Centre, Union Street, Stirling, FK8 1PH, Tel.: 01786 849705
South Team, Red Lodge, Old Denny Road, Larbert, FK5 4SD, Tel.: 01324 552664
Specialist Nursing Services
Mrs L Wright, Bonybridge Hospital, Bonnybridge, FK4 1BD, Tel.: 01324 814685
Ms L Roe, Lead Nurse, Cancer, Falkirk Infirmary, Tel.: 01324 678504
Ms R McDade, Continence, Bonnybridge Health Centre, Bonnybridge, FK4 1ED, Tel.: 01324 815105
Ms D Anderson, Infection Control, Trust Headquarters, Tel.: 01324 404430
The Homeless/Travellers & Asylum Seekers
Ms F Turner, Specialist Worker to the Homeless, Council Advice Shop, 23/25 High Street, Falkirk, Tel.: 01324 501418

Stirling Community Health Partnership
Old Denny Road
LARBERT, FK5 4SD
Tel.: 01324 404155
Admin & Senior Management
Mr E MacDonald, General Manager,
Ms R Warner, Interim, Director of Nursing, Tel.: 01324 404023
Child Health Records
Ms K Harrower, Child Health Records, Stirling Royal Infirmary, Livilands, Stirling, FK8 2AU, Tel.: 01786 434000
Child Protection/Safeguarding Children
Ms C Pickles, Nurse for Looked After Children, SRI,
Ms M Berry, Child Protection, Camelon Clinic, 1 Baird Street, Camelon, Tel.: 01324 627942
Community Nursing Services
Ms T McLean,
District Nursing
Ms M Govern, Night Service, Carer Support, Tel.: 01324 611711
Ms T McLean, North LHCC, Nurse Advisor, Tel.: 01324 404228
Ms L Raukin, District Nurses, Old Denny Road, Larbert, Falkirk, FK5 4SD, Tel.: 01324 570700
Family Planning Services
Ms E Rodger,
Health Visitors
Ms L Raukin, Health Visitors, Old Denny Road, Larbert, Falkirk, FK5 4SD, Tel.: 01324 570700
Learning Disabilities
Ms McMullen, Ms L Orr, Ms I Tannabutt
Liaison Services
Ms C Crevar, D/N Discharge Co-ordinator,
Pharmacy
Ms K Kilpatrick,
School Nursing
Ms B Craig, Public Health Nurse - Schools,
Ms K Harrower, Child Health/School Nurses,
Ms S Lynn, Public Health Nurse - Schools,

Scotland

Specialist Nursing Services
Ms D Anderson, Trust Headquarters, Tel.: 01324 404430
Ms L Wadalell, Sensory Impairment, RSWH,
Ms L Roe, Lead Nurse, Cancer, Trust Headquarters,
Ms L Walker, Nurse, Cancer, Falkirk Royal Infirmary,
Ms R McDade, Continence, Bonnybridge Health Centre,
Bonnybridge, FK4 1ED, Tel.: 01324 815105
Ms C Creanar, Co-ordinator, Discharges, SRI,
Ms L Wright, Lymphoedema, Bonnybridge Health Centre,
Ms J O'Hare, Tissue Viability, Bonnybridge Health Centre,
Bonnybridge, FK4 1ED, Tel.: 01324 814685
The Homeless/Travellers & Asylum Seekers
Specialist Worker to the Homeless, Council Advice Shop, 23/25 High
Street, Falkirk, Tel.: 01324 501418

NHS Grampian

Aberdeen City Community Health Partnership
Summerfield House
2 Eday Road
ABERDEEN, AB15 6RE
Tel.: 01224 558644
Fax.: 01224 558726

Admin & Senior Management
Ms H Kelman, General Manager,
Community Nursing Services
Mrs H Hardisty, Senior Service Manager, Summerfield House, 2
Eday Road, Aberdeen, AB16 5RE, Tel.: 01224 558407
District Nursing
Ms J McNutt, Service Manager, Torry Neighbourhood Centre, Oscar
Road, Torry, Aberdeen, Tel.: 01224 530281
Family Planning Services
Family Planning Services, 13 Golden Square, Aberdeen, AB1 1RH,
Tel.: 01224 642711
Health Visitors
Mrs R Eunson, Service Manager, Foresterhill Health Centre,
Westburn Road, Aberdeen, Tel.: 01224 553982
Mr G Poon, Lead Nurse, Summerfield House, 2 Eday Road,
Aberdeen, AB16 5RE, Tel.: 01224 558526
Liaison Services
Mrs F Dunne, Service Manager, Summerfield House, 2 Eday Road,
Aberdeen, AB16 5RE, Tel.: 01224 558571
The Homeless/Travellers & Asylum Seekers
Ms J MCNutt, Service Manager, Torry Neighbourhood Centre, Oscar
Road, Torry, Aberdeen, Tel.: 01224 530281

Aberdeenshire Community Health Partnership
Inverurie Hospital
Upperboat Road
INVERURIE, AB51 3UL
Tel.: 01467 622840
Fax.: 01467 672705

Admin & Senior Management
Mr J Stuart, General Manager, Aberdeenshire CHP, Inverurie
Hospital, Upperboat Road, Inverurie, AB51 3UL, Tel.: 01467 672723
Child Health Records
Community Child Health Records Dept, Royal Cornhill Hospital,
Aberdeen,
Child Protection/Safeguarding Children
Ms P Smart, Senior Nurse, Child Protection, 3rd Floor, Royal
Aberdeen Childrens Hospital, Westburn Road, Aberdeen, AB25
2ZG, Tel.: 01224 559529

Community Midwifery
Ms L Taylor, Lead Nurse, NALCHP, Chalmers Hospital, Clunie
Street, Banff, AB45 1JA, Tel.: 01261 819048
Community Nursing Services
Ms E Chisholm, Lead Nurse, KLCHP, Arduthie Lodge, Kincardine
Community Hospital, Stonehaven, Tel.: 01569 792063
Ms L Taylor, Lead Nurse, NALCHP, Chalmers Hospital, Clunie
Street, Banff, AB45 1JA, Tel.: 01261 819048
District Nursing
Ms E Chisholm, Lead Nurse, KLCHP, Arduthie Lodge, Kincardine
Community Hospital, Stonehaven, Tel.: 01569 792063
Ms L Taylor, Lead Nurse, NALCHP, Chalmers Hospital, Clunie
Street, Banff, AB45 1JA, Tel.: 01261 819048
Family Planning Services
Family Planning, 13 Golden Square, Aberdeen, AB1 1RH, Tel.:
01224 642711
Health Visitors
Ms L Taylor, Lead Nurse, NALCHP, Chalmers Hospital, Clunie
Street, Banff, AB45 1JA, Tel.: 01261 819048
Pharmacy
Ms E Neil, Pharmacist, North Aberdeenshire LCHP, Medicines Dept,
Westholme, Woodend Hospital, Aberdeen,

Grampian University Hospitals Division
Foresterhill House
Ashgrove Road West, ABERDEEN
AB25 2ZB
Tel.: 01224 681818

Admin & Senior Management
Mrs U Lyon, Acting Assistant Director of Nursing, Clinical Services B
Basement, Main Theatre Suite, Aberdeen Royal Infirmary, Aberdeen
AB25 2ZB, Tel.: 01224 553999
Child Health
Ms C Cameron, Community Children's Nurse Specialist, Royal
Aberdeen Children's Hospital, Cornhill Road, Aberdeen, AB25 2ZG,
Tel.: 01224 552724
Ms A Mill, Cystic Fibrosis Specialist Nurse, Royal Aberdeen
Children's Hospital, Cornhill Road, Aberdeen, AB25 2ZG, Tel.: 0122
551140
Nurse Manager, Child Health, Royal Aberdeen Children's Hospital,
Westburn Road, Aberdeen, AB25 2ZG, Tel.: 01224 551708
Ms C Reid, Community Children's Nurse Specialist, Royal Aberdeen
Children's Hospital, Cornhill Road, Aberdeen, AB25 2ZG, Tel.: 0122
552724
Ms J Reid, Paediatric Growth & Endocrine Nurse Specialist, Royal
Aberdeen Children's Hospital, Cornhill Road, Aberdeen, AB25 2ZG,
Tel.: 01224 552799
Ms A Rennie, Community Children's Nurse, Inverurie Health Centre
Inverurie, AB51 4SU, Tel.: 01467 621265
Ms L Riach, Paediatric Specialist Renal Nurse, Royal Aberdeen
Children's Hospital, Cornhill Road, Aberdeen, AB25 2ZG, Tel.: 0122
553055
Ms P Stephen, Paediatric Oncology, Royal Aberdeen Children's
Hospital, Cornhill Road, Aberdeen, AB25 2ZG, Tel.: 01224 554650
Child Health Records
Pre-School Records, Community Child Health Records Dept, Argyll
House, Cornhill Road, Aberdeen, AB25 2ZR, Tel.: 01224 553335
School Records, Community Child Health Records Dept, Argyll
House, Cornhill Road, Aberdeen, AB25 2ZR, Tel.: 01224 552665
Child Protection/Safeguarding Children
Ms P Smart, Nurse Consultant, Child Protection, Community Child
Health, Royal Aberdeen Children's Hospital, Cornhill Road,
Aberdeen, AB25 5DG, Tel.: 01224 559529
Community Midwifery
Mrs L Campbell, Midwifery Services Manager, Dr Gray's Hospital,
Elgin, IV30 1SN, Tel.: 01343 558369

Miss J Milne, Assistant Director of Nursing, GUHT, Aberdeen Maternity Hospital, Cornhill Road, Aberdeen, AB25 2ZL, Tel.: 01224 554903

Ms K Polson, Clinical Manager, Community Midwives, Aberdeen Maternity Hospital, Tel.: 01224 552701

Health Visitors

Ms J Garden, Specialist Health Visitor Children with Special Needs, Raeden Centre, Midstocket Rd, AB15 5PD, 01224 321381 ext 72235

Ms M Mcjannett, Health Visitor (Medical Genetics), Royal Aberdeen Children's Hospital, Cornhill Road, Aberdeen, AB25 2ZG, Tel.: 01224 552882

Ms S Munro, Specialist Health Visitor Children with Special Needs, Woodlands School, Craigton Road, AB15 9PR, Tel.: 01224 551603

Ms C Simmonds, Specialist Health Visitor Children with Special Needs, Beechwood School, Midstocket Road, AB15 5LQ, Tel.: 01224 323405

Ms C Smith, Paediatric Liaison Health Visitor, Royal Aberdeen Children's Hospital, Cornhill Road, Aberdeen, AB25 2ZG, Tel.: 01224 552725

Liaison Services

Mr C Farquharson, Alcohol Liaison,

Ms A Swaffield, Paediatric Diabetes Liaison Nurse, Royal Aberdeen Children's Hosp., Cornhill Rd, Aberdeen, AB25 2ZG, 01224 552734

Ms K McLewan, Liaison, Diabetic Care,

Ms A Swaffield, Liaison, Diabetic Care,

Other Services

Ms D Barber, Nutritional Support, Specialist Nurse,

Ms S Bevan, Epilepsy Field Worker,

Ms R Cooper, Hospital Supportive Care Team, Specialist Nurse,

Ms H Hailey, Co-ordinator, Neurofibromatosis,

Ms H Hailey, Co-ordinator, Neurofibromatosis,

Ms M McJannett, Genetics Health Visitor,

Ms M McKenzie, Early Supported Discharge,

Ms F O'Dea, Hospital Supportive Care Team, Specialist Nurse,

Ms S Sutherland, Hospital Supportive Care Team, Specialist Nurse,

Specialist Nursing Services

Ms S Alexander, Menopause, Specialist Nurse,

Ms P Dundas, Hep C, Specialist Nurse,

Ms D Fraser, Motor Neurone, Specialist Nurse,

Ms A Mill, CF, Specialist Nurse,

Ms C Purdie, Dystonia, Specialist Nurse,

Ms E Benton, Screening, Specialist Nurse, Colorectal,

Ms K Copp, Macmillan Nurse, Colorectal,

Ms K Griffiths, Specialist Nurse, Cystic Fibrosis,

Ms J Reid, Specialist Nurse, Endocrine Surgery,

Ms J Rae, Specialist Nurse, Haemophilia,

Ms H Fryer, Specialist Nurse, Infection Control,

Ms D Pacitti, Specialist Nurse, Infection Control,

Ms A Smith, Specialist Nurse, Infection Control,

Ms F Geddes, Specialist Nurse, IV Therapy, - Chemotherapy,

Ms J Horne, Specialist Nurse, IV Therapy, - Chemotherapy,

Ms T Learmouth, Specialist Nurse, IV Therapy, - Chemotherapy,

Ms L Brown, Specialist Nurse, Lung Cancer,

Ms Z Taylor, Nurse, Multiple Sclerosis,

Ms M Ritchie, Specialist Nurse, Neuro-oncology,

Ms M Dwan, Specialist Nurse, Nutrition,

Ms P Stephen, Specialist Nurse, Oncology,

Ms L Caie, Specialist Nurse, Parkinson's Disease,

Ms A Robertson, Sister, Respiratory,

Ms J Davis, Specialist Nurse, Stroke Care,

Ms J Thain, Specialist Nurse, Stroke Care,

Ms A Campbell, Specialist Nurse, Urology,

Moray Community Health Partnership

Dr Gray's Hospital
ELGIN
IV30 1SN
Tel.: 01343 543131

Admin & Senior Management

Mr A Fowlie, General Manager, Morray CHP, Dr Gray's Hospital, Elgin, IV30 1SN, Tel.: 01343 543131

Ms H Robbins, Lead Nurse, Morray CHP, Dr Gray's Hospital, Elgin, IV30 1SN, Tel.: 01343 567834

Clinical Leads (NSF)

Ms C Galletly, Clinical Lead, Cancer, Dr Grays Hospital, Elgin, Tel.: 01343 543131

Mr J Laverty, Clinical Lead, Diabetic Care, Dr Grays Hospital, Elgin, Tel.: 01343 543131

Community Nursing Services

Ms H Robbins, Lead Nurse, Morray CHP, Dr Gray's Hospital, Elgin, IV30 1SN, Tel.: 01343 567834

Specialist Nursing Services

Ms S Shearer, Nurse Specialist, Continence, Admin Block, Dr Gray's Hospital, Elgin, Tel.: 01343 567423

Ms J Stewart, Nurse Specialist, Infection Control, Maryhill House, 317 High Street, Elgin, Tel.: 01343 567571

NHS Grampian

Summerfield House
Eday Road
ABERDEEN
AB25 2ZH
Tel.: 01224 558565

Admin & Senior Management

Mr D Benton, Nursing Director, Summerfield House, Eday Road, Aberdeen, AB15 6RE, Tel.: 01224 558565

Mrs H Robbins, Nurse Facilitator/Lead Nurse, Moray Community Health & Social Care Part, Dr Gray's Hospital, Elgin, IV30 1SN, Tel.: 01343 567832

HIV/AIDS

Ms J McKay, HIV/Aids/Sexual Health,

Ms A McKenzie, HIV/Aids/Sexual Health,

Ms E McKenzie, HIV/Aids/Sexual Health,

Ms R Taylor, HIV/Aids/Sexual Health,

Learning Disabilities

Ms S Carr, Service Manager, Community Nurses - Aberdeenshire, Woodlands Hospital, Craigton Road, Cults, Aberdeen, AB15 9PR, Tel.: 01224 663123 ext 71340

Ms S Conlin, Service Manager, Community Nurses - Moray, Highfield House, Northfield Terrace, Elgin, IV30 1NE, Tel.: 01343 562111

Mr K Milne, Team Leader, Specialist Heatlth Visitors/Specialist Schools, Community Division, Royal Cornhill Hospital, Aberdeen, AB25 2ZH, Tel.: 01224 276834

Ms F Parley, Service Manager, Community Nurses - Aberdeen, Nurse Advisor, Woodlands Hospital, Craigton Road, Cults, Aberdeen, AB15 9PR, Tel.: 01224 663123 ext 51566

Other Services

Mr R Stuart, Dentistry, Dr Gray's Hospital, Elgin, Tel.: 01343 567205

School Nursing

Ms A Work, School Nurse, Child Health Dept, Dr Gray's Hospital, Elgin, Tel.: 01343 567265

Specialist Nursing Services

Ms V Bain, Nurse Specialist, Breast Care,

Ms S Ingram, Nurse Specialist, Breast Care,

Ms L McLennan, Nurse Specialist, Breast Care,

Ms C Reid, Nurse Specialist, Breast Care,

Ms K Copp, Macmillan Nurse, Colorectal,

Mrs S Shearer, Nurse Specialist, Continence,

Ms R Amin, Specialist Nurse, Diabetic Care, Woolmanhill Hospital, Aberdeen, Tel.: 01224 555471 ext 55471

Ms I Hill, Specialist Nurse, Diabetic Care, Woolmanhill Hospital, Aberdeen, Tel.: 01224 555527 ext 55527

Mr J Laverty, Nurse Specialist, Diabetic Care, Dr Grays Hospital, Elgin,

Scotland

Ms I Stead, Specialist Nurse, Diabetic Care, Woolmanhill Hospital, Aberdeen, Tel.: 01224 555481 ext 55481
Mr R Browning, Nurse Specialist, Infection Control,
Mrs J Stewart, Nurse Specialist, Infection Control,
Ms B Beaton, Nurse, Macmillan,
Ms A Collier, Nurse, Macmillan,
Mr K Ferguson, Nurse, Macmillan, The Oaks Hospice, Morriston Road, Elgin,
Ms C Galletly, Nurse, Macmillan, The Oaks Hospice, Morriston Road, Elgin,
Ms H Kidd, Nurse, Macmillan,
Ms J Sim, Nurse,Macmillan, The Oaks Hospice, Morriston Rd, Elgin,
Ms C Cameron, Community, Nurse Specialist, Paediatrics,
Ms C Craig, Community, Nurse Specialist, Paediatrics,
Ms C Findlay, Nurse Specialist, Stoma Care,
Ms A Patterson, Nurse Specialist, Stoma Care,
Ms J Sim, Nurse Specialist, Stoma Care, The Oaks Hospice, Morriston Road, Elgin,
Ms M Strachan, Nurse Specialist, Stoma Care,
The Homeless/Travellers & Asylum Seekers
Ms K Campbell, Homeless, Health Visitor,
Mr R Knight, Homeless, Health Visitor,

NHS Greater Glasgow

East Dunbartonshire Community Health Partnership

Tel.: 0141 777 6090

Admin & Senior Management
Mr K Redpath, Tel.: 0141 777 6090

East Glasgow Community Health Partnership
85 Milngavie Road
Bearsden, GLASGOW
G61 2DN
Tel.: 0141 531 6281

Admin & Senior Management
Ms L Cameron, Practice Manager, Anniesland Medical Centre, 778 Crow Road, Glasgow, Tel.: 0141 954 8860
Mr R Peat, General Manager, 85 Milngavie Road, Bearsden, Glasgow, G61 2DN, Tel.: 0141 531 6281
Child Protection/Safeguarding Children
Ms F McManus, West House, Gartnavel Royal Hospital, Tel.: 0141 211 3756
Family Planning Services
Ms M Lamont, Family Planning & Reproductive Health Care, Senior Nurse, Sandyford Initiative, 2-6 Sandyford Place, Glasgow, G3 7NB, Tel.: 0141 211 8130

East Renfrewshire Community Health Partnership

Tel.: 0141 300 1229

Admin & Senior Management
Mr T Eltringham, Tel.: 0141 300 1229

Greater Glasgow Primary Care Division
Divisional Headquarters, Gartnavel Royal Hospital
1055 Great Western Road
GLASGOW
G12 0XH
Tel.: 0141 211 3600
Fax.: 0141 211 0307

Admin & Senior Management
Ms J Arroll, Director of Allied Health Professions, Tel.: 0141 211 0251
Ms I Colvin, General Manager, Addictions Services, Tel.: 0141 420 5638
Ms R Crocket, Director of Nursing, Tel.: 0141 211 3712
Mr A Maclean, General Manager, Support Services, Tel.: 0141 211 3500
Dr J Mitchell, Clinical Director, North/East Sector, Tel.: 0141 531 3256
Mr I Smith, Glasgow Drug Problem Services Clinical Director/Lead, Tel.: 0141 531 9254
Mr I Smith, Drugs & Alcohol Clinical Director/Lead, Tel.: 0141 531 9254
Dr J Taylor, Clinical Director, South Sector, Tel.: 0141 429 8278
Dr A Wilson, Clinical Director, West Sector, Tel.: 0141 211 3201
Child Health
Adolescent Services - Gartnavel Royal Directorate Team, Top Floor Left, West House, Gartnavel Royal Hospital, Tel.: 0141 211 0231
East Glasgow Adolescent Team, 90-92 Kerr Street, Bridgeton, Glasgow, G40 2QP, Tel.: 0141 531 3300
Forensic Adolescent Team West, Tel.: 0141 211 9059
Gartnavel Royal Adolescent Unit, 1055 Great Western Road, Glasgow, G12 0XH, Tel.: 0141 211 3589/0622
North Glasgow Adolescent Team, Possilpark Health Centre, 85 Denmark Street, Glasgow, G22 5DG, Tel.: 0141 531 6107
South Glasgow Adolescent Team, 5th Floor, Old Mill Studios, 187 Old Rutherglen Road, Glasgow, G5 0RE, Tel.: 0141 300 6300
West Glasgow Adolescent Team, Knightswood Clinic, 192 Knightswood Road, Glasgow, G13 2XJ, Tel.: 0141 211 9069
Child Protection/Safeguarding Children
Ms J Brown, Child Protection Unit, Yorkhill Hospital, 2nd Floor Medical Records Building, Dalnair Street, Galsgow, G3 8SJ, Tel.: 0141 201 9253/201 3756
Family Planning Services
Dr A Bigrigg, Director, Sexual Health Services, The Sandyford Initiative, 2 Sandyford Place, Sauchiehall Street, Glasgow, G3 7NB, Tel.: 0141 211 8130
Ms R Ilet, Associate Director for Health Inequalities (Sexual Health), Tel.: 0141 211 6700
Mr R Nandwani, Genito-Urinary Medicine Associate Director for External Affairs, Tel.: 0141 211 8601
Learning Disabilities
Adolescent Learning Disabilities East Glasgow Team, 90-92 Kerr Street, Bridgeton, Glasgow, G40 2QP, Tel.: 0141 531 3300
Mr M Feinmann, Joint General Manager, Glasgow Learning Disability Partnership, Killearn Resource Centre, 29 Shakespeare Street, Maryhill, Glasgow, G20 8TH, Tel.: 0141 287 8227
Mr M McClements, Commissioning Manager, Killearn Resource Centre, 29 Shakespeare Street, Maryhill, Glasgow, G20 8TH, Tel.: 0141 276 3600
Mr M McCue, Complex Needs Services Manager/Head of Professio (Nursing), Killearn Resource Centre, 29 Shakespeare Street, Maryhill, Glasgow, G20 8TH, Tel.: 0141 276 3600
Mr T Quinn, Personnel Manager, Killearn Resource Centre, 29 Shakespeare Street, Maryhill, Glasgow, G20 8TH, Tel.: 0141 276 3600
Dr N Simpson, Glasgow Learning Disability Partnership Clinical Director/Lead, Tel.: 0141 211 3527
Mr E Steel, Locality Services Manager, Killearn Resource Centre, 2 Shakespeare Street, Maryhill, Glasgow, G20 8TH, 0141 276 3600
Dr L Watt, Divisional Medical Director Learning Disabilities, Tel.: 0141 211 3869
Liaison Services
Heart Failure Liaison Nursing Service, Level 4 - Western Infirmary, Dumbarton Road, Glasgow, G11 6NT, Tel.: 0141 211 6302
Ms A Taylor, Multicultural Outreach Liaison Nurse, Tel.: 0141 211 3898

Scotland

Other Services

Ms J Alexander, Clinical Director, Physical Disability Teams, Tel.: 0141 435 7714

Continence Service, Cambuslang Clinic, Johnson Drive, Glasgow, G72 8JR, Tel.: 0141 641 8423

Dr H Dobson, Clinical Director, West of Scotland Breast Screening Service, Stock Exchange Court, Nelson Mandela Place, Glasgow, G2 1QY, Tel.: 0141 572 5800

Glasgow Drug Problem Service, Woodside Health Centre, 20 Barr Street, Glasgow, G20 7LR, Tel.: 0141 531 9257

Ms D Kersell, Clinical Director, Community Treatment Centre for Brain Injury, 70 Commerical Road, Gobals, Glasgow, G5 0QZ, Tel.: 0141 300 6313

Pharmacy
Pharmacy enquiries, Tel.: 0141 211 3766

Mr D Thomson, Director of Pharmacy, Tel.: 0141 211 0255

The Homeless/Travellers & Asylum Seekers
Ms K Benson, Primary Care Homeless Service Manager, Tel.: 0141 553 2808

Ms A Docherty, Glasgow Homelessness Partnership (Head of Profession), Tel.: 0141 302 2705

Mr J Goldie, Team Leader - Homeless Addiction Team, Tel.: 0141 552 9287

Learning Disability Homeless Team, Homelessness Health & Resources Services, 55 Hunter Street, Glasgow, G4 2801, Tel.: 0141 553 2801

Ms A McDonald, Refugee Nurse Co-ordinator, Tel.: 0131 531 6719

Ms G Munroe, Team Leader - Homeless Families, Tel.: 0141 287 1845

Inverclyde Community Health Partnership
(was part of NHS Argyll & Clyde)
Greenock Health Centre
20 Duncan Street
GREENOCK
PA15 4LY
Tel.: 01475 724477

Child Health
Foxbar Clinic, Morar Drive, Paisley, PA2 9QR, Tel.: 01505 813119
Gourock Health Centre, Shore Street, Gourock, PA19 1AQ,
Port Glasgow Health Centre, 2 Bay Street, Port Glasgow, PA14 EW,

Child Health Records
Ms A Aitken, Clerical Officer, Greenock Health Centre, Tel.: 01475 24477

Child Protection/Safeguarding Children
Ms I Mgugan, Child Protection Advisor,

Community Nursing Services
Ardgowan Medical Centre, Nelson Street, Greenock, PA16 8HW,
Boglestone Clinic, Port Glasgow, PA14 5UA,
Gourock Health Centre, Shore Street, Gourock, PA19 1AQ,
Greenock Health Centre, 20 Duncan Street, Greenock, PA15 4LY,
Mrs A MacDougall, Associate Lead Nurse, Greenock Health Centre, 20 Duncan Street, Greenock, PA15 4LY, Tel.: 01475 724477
Port Glasgow Health Centre, 2 Bay Street, Port Glasgow, PA14 EW,
Ms F Van Der Meer, Lead Nurse, Inverclyde LHCC, Greenock Health Centre, 20 Duncan Street, Greenock, Inverclyde, Tel.: 01475 24477

District Nursing
Gourock Health Centre, Shore Street, Gourock, PA19 1AQ,
Greenock Health Centre, 20 Duncan Street, Greenock, PA15 4LY,
Port Glasgow Health Centre, 2 Bay Street, Port Glasgow, PA14 EW,

Family Planning Services
Ms M Smith, Boglestone Clinic, Port Glasgow, Tel.: 01475 701058

Liaison Services
Ms M Irvine, Elderly Liaison, Greenock Health Centre, 20 Duncan Street, Greenock, PA15 4LY, Tel.: 01475 724477

Smoking Cessation
Ms L Coyle, Smoking Cessation Advisor, Greenock Health Centre,

Specialist Nursing Services
Ms A Johnstone, Specialist, Continence, Boglestone Clinic, Port Glasgow, PA14 5UA, Tel.: 01475 701058

The Homeless/Travellers & Asylum Seekers
Ms F Van Der Meer, Lead Nurse, Greenock Health Centre, Tel.: 01475 724477

Levern Valley Community Health Partnership
(was part of NHS Argyll & Clyde)
Barrhead Health Centre
201 Main Street
BARRHEAD
G78 1SA
Tel.: 0141 880 6161

Admin & Senior Management
Ms F Downer, Lead Nurse,
Mr G Oliver, General Manager,

Child Health Records
Child Health Records, Hollybush, Dykebar Hospital, Grahamston Road, Paisley, PA2 7DE, Tel.: 0141 884 9099

Child Protection/Safeguarding Children
Ms I McGugan, Child Protection, Foxbar Clinic, Morar Drive, Paisley, PA2 9QR, Tel.: 01505 813119

District Nursing
Evenings District Nurses, Tel.: 0141 886 3604

Ms A Thompson, Head of Nursing, Hollybush, Dykebar Hospital, Grahamston Road, Paisley, PA2 7DE, Tel.: 0141 884 9099

Family Planning Services
Ms S Mason, Co-ordinator, Russell Institute, Causeyside Street, Paisley, PA1 1UR, Tel.: 0141 889 8701

Liaison Services
Ms M Berekis, Liaison, Child with Special Needs, Panda Centre, Hawkhead Hospital, Paisley, PA2 7BL, Tel.: 0141 889 8151

Miss E Blain, Liaison, Geriatrics, Foxbar Clinic, Morar Drive, Foxbar, Paisley, PA2 9QR, Tel.: 01505 813119

Ms A McMillan, Liaison, General District Nurse, Foxbar Clinic, Morar Drive, Foxbar, Paisley, PA2 9QR, Tel.: 01505 813119/812248

Ms K Sinclair, Liaison, Paediatric Specialist, Foxbar Clinic, Morar Drive, Foxbar, Paisley, PA2 9QR, Tel.: 01505 813119

Ms S Dickie, Liaison, Breast Care, Foxbar Clinic, Morar Drive, Foxbar, Paisley, PA2 9QR, Tel.: 01505 813119

School Nursing
Ms A Thompson, Head of Nursing, School Health/Nursing Service, Hollybush, Dykebar Hospital, Grahamston Road, Paisley, PA2 7DE, Tel.: 0141 884 9099

Specialist Nursing Services
Ms M Hay, Diabetic Care, Royal Alexandra Hospital, Corsebar Road, Paisley, PA2 9PN, Tel.: 0141 887 9111

Ms M Stride, Infection Control, Room 7, Admin, Hawkhead Hospital, Tel.: 0141 889 8151

Mrs C McIntyre, Macmillan, ACCORD Premises, Ward 6, Hawkhead Hospital, Paisley, PA2 7BL, Tel.: 0141 581 2000

Ms R Miller, Macmillan, ACCORD Premises, Ward 6, Hawkhead Hospital, Paisley, PA2 7BL, Tel.: 0141 581 2000

Ms M Moore, Macmillan, ACCORD Premises, Ward 6, Hawkhead Hospital, Paisley, PA2 7BL, Tel.: 0141 581 2000

Ms M Rodger, Macmillan, ACCORD Premises, Ward 6, Hawkhead Hospital, Paisley, PA2 7BL, Tel.: 0141 581 2000

Ms F Ross, Respiratory, Russell Institute, Tel.: 0141 889 8701

Ms H O'Donnell, Blood Borne, Viruses, Public Health Department, NHS Argyll & Clyde, Ross House, Hawkhead Road, Paisley, PA2 7BN, Tel.: 0141 842 7203

Scotland

The Homeless/Travellers & Asylum Seekers
Ms M Armstrong, Health Visitor for Travellers, Foxbar Clinic, Morar Drive, Foxbar, Paisley, PA2 9QR, Tel.: 01505 813119

Lomond & Argyll Primary Care Division

(was part of NHS Argyll & Clyde)
Trust Headquarters
Aros
LOCHGILPHEAD
PA31 8LD
Tel.: 01546 606600

Child Health
Ms N Cummins, Team Leader, Community Children's Nursing Service, Acorn Centre, Tel.: 01389 754121 ext 3685
Ms G Currie, Lochgilphead, Mid-Argyll-Kintyre & Islay, Tel.: 01369 704341
Ms A Hair, Community Children's Nursing Service, Tel.: 01389 754121
Ms S Henderson, Oban Community Children's Nursing Service, Tel.: 01631 567500
Ms B Oliphant, Dunoon & Bute Community Children's Nursing Service, Tel.: 01369 704341
Ms J Young, Argyll Community Children's Nursing Service,
Community Midwifery
Mrs B Adair, Midwifery Manager, Vale of Leven Hospital, North Main Street, Alexandria, G83 0UA, Tel.: ext 3285
Mrs C Dreghorn, Team Leader, Campbeltown Hospital, Ralston Road, Campbeltown, PA28 6LE,
Ms F Hood, Team Leader, Victoria Hospital, Isle of Bute, High Street, Rothesay, PA20 9JJ,
Midwifery Manager, Dunoon & District General Hospital, Sandbank Road, Dunoon, PA23 7RL, Tel.: ext 238
Mrs J Thorp, Senior Midwife, Mid Argyll Hospital, Blarbuie Road, Lochgilphead, Argyll, PA31 8JZ, Tel.: 01546 602449
District Nursing
Mrs E Campbell, District Nurses/Midwives, Tel.: 01369 860 562
Health Visitors
Mrs E Campbell, Health Visitors, Tel.: 01369 860 562
Learning Disabilities
Mr R Bain, Community Nurse, Beardmore Centre, Clydebank, Tel.: 0141 562 2326
Ms A-L Dickie, Clinical Nurse Manager,
Ms J Fitzpatrick, Clinical Nurse Specialist, Beardmore Business Centre, 9 Beardmore Street, Dalmuir, Clydebank, G81 4HA, Tel.: 0141 562 2333
Mr R Macfarlane, Clinical Nurse Specialist,
Ms L Radcliffe, Community Advocate, Dumbarton Joint Hospital, Tel.: 01389 607339
Mrs C Wallis, Development Manager, Main Building, Victoria Infirmary, East King Street, Helensburgh,

North Glasgow Community Health Partnership

Woodside Health Centre
Barr Street
GLASGOW
G20 7LR
Tel.: 0141 531 9507

Admin & Senior Management
Mr M Currie, General Manager,
Mr I Macdonald, Practice Manager,
Ms F Mackenzie, Development Nurse,
Ms L McMenemy, Development Nurse,
Ms E Morrison, Lead Nurse,
Ms E O'Neill, Professional Nurse Advisor,

Clinical Leads (NSF)
Dr D Spence, Clinical Lead, CHD,
Dr J Mackenzie, Clinical Lead, Diabetic Care,

North Glasgow University General Hospital Division

Division HQ, 300 Balgrayhill Road
GLASGOW
G21 3UR
Tel.: 0141 201 4200
Fax.: 0141 201 4201

Admin & Senior Management
Ms T Crawford, Associate Director of Nursing, Tel.: 0141 211 51461
Ms M Smith, Director of Nursing,
Child Health
Ms E Callandar, Vulnerable Infant Project, Princess Royal Maternity Unit, Alexandra Parade, Glasgow, Tel.: 0141 211 5400
Community Midwifery
Miss M McGinley, Divisional Nurse, Head of Midwifery, Medical Block, Glasgow Royal Infirmary, Tel.: 0141 211 4304
Mrs S Smith, Clinical Midwifery Manager, Level 2, Princess Royal Maternity, 16 Alexandra Parade, Glasgow, G31 2ER, Tel.: 0141 211 5343
Liaison Services
Ms B Stuart, Neonatal Liaison, Princess Royal Maternity Unit, Alexandra Parade, Glasgow, Tel.: 0141 211 5400

Paisley Community Health Partnership

(was part of NHS Argyll & Clyde)
Larchgrove
Dykebar Hospital
PAISLEY
PA2 7DE
Tel.: 0141 884 9027

Admin & Senior Management
Mrs E McGarrigle, Acting Directorate Nurse Lead, Paisley PC Services, Sir James Clark Building, Abbey Mill Business Centre, Seephill, Paisley PA1 1TJ,
Mrs M McGhee, Assistant Director of Nursing, Merchiston Hospital, By Johnstone, Tel.: 01505 328261
Mrs J Still, Directorate General Manager, Tel.: 0141 842 4842
Child Health
Ms M Berekis, Children with Special Needs, Panda Centre, Hawkhead Hospital, Paisley, PA2 7BL, Tel.: 0141 889 8151
Ms K Sinclair, Liaison, Paediatric Specialist, Foxbar Clinic, Morar Drive, Foxbar, Paisley, PA2 9QR, Tel.: 01505 813119
Child Health Records
Child Health Records, Hollybush, Dykebar Hospital, Grahamston Road, Paisley, PA2 7DE, Tel.: 0141 884 9099
Child Protection/Safeguarding Children
Child Protection, Foxbar Clinic, Morar Drive, Foxbar, Paisley, PA2 9QR, Tel.: 01505 813119
District Nursing
Evenings, Tel.: 0141 886 3604
Ms A Thompson, Head of Nursing, Hollybush, Dykebar Hospital, Grahamston Road, Paisley, PA2 7DE, Tel.: 0141 884 9099
Family Planning Services
Ms S Mason, Co-ordinator, Russell Institute, Causeyside Street, Paisley, PA1 1UR, Tel.: 0141 889 8701
Liaison Services
Miss E Blain, Liaison, Geriatrics, Match Room, Royal Alexandra Hospital, Corse Bar Road, Paisley, Tel.: 0141 887 9111
Ms A McMillan, General Liaison, District Nurse, Match Room, Royal Alexandra Hospital, Corse Bar Road, Paisley, Tel.: 0141 887 9111

Scotland

Specialist Nursing Services
Ms M Docherty, Diabetic Care, Royal Alexandra Hospital, Corsebar Road, Paisley, PA2 9PN, Tel.: 0141 887 9111
Ms M Stride, Infection Control, Johnstone Hospital, Tel.: 0141 889 8151
Mrs C McIntyre, Macmillan, Renfrew Health Centre, Paisley Road, Renfrew, Tel.: 0141 886 5921
Ms R Miller, Macmillan, Renfrew Health Centre, Paisley Road, Renfrew, Tel.: 0141 886 5921
Ms M Moore, Macmillan, Renfrew Health Centre, Paisley Road, Renfrew, Tel.: 0141 886 5921
Ms M Rodger, Macmillan, ACCORD Premises, Ward 6, Hawkhead Hospital, Paisley, PA2 7BL, Tel.: 0141 581 2000
Mr F Ross, Respiratory, Russell Institute, Tel.: 0141 889 8701
Ms H O'Donnell, Blood Borne, Viruses, Public Health Department, NHS Argyll & Clyde, Ross House, Hawkhead Road, Paisley, PA2 7BN, Tel.: 0141 842 7203

The Homeless/Travellers & Asylum Seekers
Ms M Armstrong, Health Visitor for Travellers, Foxbar Clinic, Morar Drive, Foxbar, Paisley, PA2 9QR, Tel.: 01505 813119

Renfrewshire & Inverclyde Primary Care Division
(was part of NHS Argyll & Clyde)
Dykebar Hospital
Grahamston Road
PAISLEY, Strathclyde
PA2 7DE
Tel.: 0141 884 5122

Admin & Senior Management
Ms L Smith, Director of Nursing & Quality, Merchiston Hospital, Brookfield by Johnstone, PA5 8TY, Tel.: 01505 384027

Child Health
Gourock Health Centre, 181 Shore Street, Gourock, PA19 1AQ, Tel.: 01475 634617 (0830-1700)
Greenock Health Centre, Greenock Health Centre, Tel.: 01475 724477 (0830-1700)
Ms L Guinea, Community Children's Nursing Service, Skylark Centre, Inverclyde Hospital, Tel.: 01475 656310
Ms H McLean, Community Children's Nursing Service, Tel.: 0141 889 8151 ext 247
Pt Glasgow Health Centre, Bay Street, Pt Glasgow, PA14 5ED, Tel.: 01475 745321 (0830-1700)
Ms K Sinclair, Community Children's Nursing Service, Tel.: 0141 889 8151 ext 247

Child Health Records
Child Health Records, Gourock Health Centre, 181 Shore Street, Gourock, PA19 1AQ, Tel.: 01475 634617 (0830-1700)
Child Health Records, Greenock Health Centre, Greenock Health Centre, Tel.: 01475 724477 (0830-1700)
Child Health Records, Pt Glasgow Health Centre, Bay Street, Pt Glasgow, PA14 5ED, Tel.: 01475 745321 (0830-1700)

Child Protection/Safeguarding Children
Ms I McGugan, Child Protection, Foxbar Clinic, Morar Drive, Paisley, PA2 9QR, Tel.: 01505 813119

Community Nursing Services
Community Nursing Services, Greenock Health Centre, 20 Duncan Street, Greenock, PA15 4LY, Tel.: 01475 724477
Ms A Thompson, Head of Nursing, Hollybush, Dykebar Hospital, Grahamston Road, Paisley, PA2 7DE, Tel.: 0141 884 9099

District Nursing
Emergencies, Night, Tel.: 01475 720995
Gourock Health Centre, 181 Shore Street, Gourock, PA19 1AQ, Tel.: 01475 634617 (0830-1700)
Pt Glasgow Health Centre, Bay Street, Pt Glasgow, PA14 5ED, Tel.: 01475 745321 (0830-1700)

Ms F Vandermeer, Lead Nurse, Greenock Health Centre, Tel.: 01475 724477 (0830-1700)

Family Planning Services
Family Planning Service, Greenock Health Centre, Greenock Health Centre, Tel.: 01475 724477 (0830-1700)
Mrs M Smith, STD, Greenock Health Centre, Greenock Health Centre, Tel.: 01475 724477

Learning Disabilities
Ms F A Boyle, Clinical Nurse Manager, Old Johnstone Clinic, 1 Ludovic Square, Johnstone, PA5 8EE, Tel.: 01505 325703
Community Team, Elizabeth Martin Clinic, 1 Burns Square, Greenock, PA16 0NT, Tel.: 01475 650529

Liaison Services
Mrs B Buchanan, Liaison : Inverclyde Royal Hospital/Community, Inverclyde Royal Hospital, Larkfield Road, Greenock, PA16 0XN, Tel.: 01475 633777
Ms M Irvine, Geriatics, Greenock Health Centre, Greenock Health Centre, Tel.: 01475 724477

Specialist Nursing Services
Ms S Stratton, Diabetic Care, Inverclyde Royal Hospital, Tel.: 01475 633777
Nurses, Macmillan, Ardgowan Hospice, Greenock, Tel.: 01475 726830

Renfrewshire Community Health Partnership
(was part of NHS Argyll & Clyde)
Health Centre
103 Paisley Road
RENFREW
PA4 8LH
Tel.: 0141 886 2012

Admin & Senior Management
Ms E McGarrigle, Lead Nurse,
Ms L Miller, Community Nurse Lead,

Child Health
Ms M Berekis, Children with Special Needs, Panda Centre, Hawkhead Hospital, Paisley, PA2 7BL, Tel.: 0141 889 8151
Ms K Sinclair, Liaison, Paediatric Specialist, Foxbar Clinic, Morar Drive, Foxbar, Paisley, PA2 9QR, Tel.: 01505 813119

Child Health Records
Child Health Records, Hollybush, Dykebar Hospital, Grahamston Road, Paisley, PA2 7DE, Tel.: 0141 884 9099

Child Protection/Safeguarding Children
Ms I McGugan, Child Protection, Foxbar Clinic, Morar Drive, Foxbar, Paisley, PA2 9QR, Tel.: 01505 813119

District Nursing
Evenings, Tel.: 0141 886 3604
Ms A Thompson, Head of Nursing, Hollybush, Dykebar Hospital, Grahamston Road, Paisley, PA2 7DE, Tel.: 0141 884 9099

Family Planning Services
Ms S Mason, Co-ordinator, Russell Institute, Causeyside Street, Paisley, PA1 1UR, Tel.: 0141 889 8701

Liaison Services
Miss E Blain, Liaison, Geriatrics, Foxbar Clinic, Morar Drive, Foxbar, Paisley, PA2 9QR, Tel.: 01505 813119
Ms A McMillan, General Liaison, District Nurse, Foxbar Clinic, Morar Drive, Foxbar, Paisley, PA2 9QR, Tel.: 01505 813119/812248
Ms S Dickie, Liaison, Breast Care, Foxbar Clinic, Morar Drive, Foxbar, Paisley, PA2 9QR, Tel.: 01505 813119

School Nursing
Ms A Thompson, Head of Nursing, School Health/Nursing Service, Hollybush, Dykebar Hospital, Grahamston Road, Paisley, PA2 7DE, Tel.: 0141 884 9099

Specialist Nursing Services
Ms M Hay, Diabetic Care, Royal Alexandra Hospital, Corsebar Road, Paisley, PA2 9PN, Tel.: 0141 887 9111

Scotland

Ms M Stride, Infection Control, Room 7, Admin, Hawkhead Hospital, Tel.: 0141 889 8151
Mrs C McIntyre, Macmillan, ACCORD Premises, Ward 6, Hawkhead Hospital, Paisley, PA2 7BL, Tel.: 0141 581 2000
Ms R Miller, Macmillan, ACCORD Premises, Ward 6, Hawkhead Hospital, Paisley, PA2 7BL, Tel.: 0141 581 2000
Ms M Moore, Macmillan, ACCORD Premises, Ward 6, Hawkhead Hospital, Paisley, PA2 7BL, Tel.: 0141 581 2000
Ms M Rodger, Macmillan, ACCORD Premises, Ward 6, Hawkhead Hospital, Paisley, PA2 7BL, Tel.: 0141 581 2000
Mr F Ross, Respiratory, Russell Institute, Tel.: 0141 889 8701
Ms H O'Donnell, Blood Borne, Viruses, Public Health Department, NHS Argyll & Clyde, Ross House, Hawkhead Road, Paisley, PA2 7BN, Tel.: 0141 842 7203

The Homeless/Travellers & Asylum Seekers
Ms M Armstrong, Health Visitor for Travellers, Foxbar Clinic, Morar Drive, Foxbar, Paisley, PA2 9QR, Tel.: 01505 813119

South East Glasgow Community Health Partnership
Govanhill Health Centre
233 Calder Street
GLASGOW
G42 7DR
Tel.: 0141 531 8303

Admin & Senior Management
Mrs M Farrell, General Manager, Govanhill Health Centre, Tel.: 0141 531 8303
Community Nursing Services
Ms A M Carr, Lead Nurse, Govanhill health Centre, Tel.: 0141 531 8336
District Nursing
Ms A M Carr, Lead Nurse, Govanhill Health Centre, 0141 531 8336
Smoking Cessation
Ms M Lynch, Public Health Practitioner, Govanhill Work Space, 69 Dixon Road, Glasgow, G42 8AT, Tel.: 0141 433 4938
The Homeless/Travellers & Asylum Seekers
Ms S Tees, Asylum Team, Health Visitor, Gorbals Health Centre, 45 Pine Place, Glasgow, G5 0BQ, Tel.: 0141 531 8293
Ms J Wright, Asylum Team, Health Visitor, Gorbals Health Centre, 45 Pine Place, Glasgow, G5 0BQ, Tel.: 0141 531 8293

South Glasgow University Hospitals Division
Southern General Hospital
1345 Govan Road
GLASGOW
G51 4TF
Tel.: 0141 201 1100
Fax.: 0141 201 2999

Admin & Senior Management
Ms M Henderson, Director of Nursing, Management Offices, Southern General Hospital, 1345 Govan Road, Glasgow, G51 4TF, Tel.: 0141 201 1100
Child Protection/Safeguarding Children
Ms M C Corr, Castlemilic Health Centre, Tel.: 0141 531 8500
Ms M Livingstone, Child Protection, Govanhill Health Centre, Tel.: 0141 531 8300
Ms M Marshall, Child Protection, Gorbals Health Centre, Tel.: 0141 531 8200
Community Midwifery
Team Base of Midwives, Geographically based teams in both community & hopsital, Southern General Hospital, Tel.: 0141 201 2256
Ms L Wojciechowska, Senior Midwifery Manager, Southern General Hospital, Tel.: 0141 201 2230

Community Nursing Services
Ms E Love, Lead Nurse, Govanhill Health Centre, 233 Calder Street, Glasgow, G42 7DR, Tel.: 0141 531 8336
Smoking Cessation
Ms M Lynch, Govanhill Work Place, 69 Dixon Road, Glasgow, G42 8AT, Tel.: 0141 433 4938
The Homeless/Travellers & Asylum Seekers
Ms S Quinn, Asylum Team Health Visitors, Gorbals Health Centre, 45 Pine Place, Glasgow G5 0BQ,
Ms S Tees, Asylum Team Health Visitors, Gorbals Health Centre, 45 Pine Place, Glasgow G5 0BQ,
Ms C Whitelaw, Asylum Team Health Visitors, Gorbals Health Centre, 45 Pine Place, Glasgow G5 0BQ,

South West Glasgow Community Health Partnership
1st Floor
Clutha House, 120 Cornwall Street South
GLASGOW, G41 1AD
Tel.: 0141 427 8276

Admin & Senior Management
Miss C McNeill, General Manager, Tel.: 0141 427 8276
Community Nursing Services
Ms L Young, Lead Nurse, Tel.: 0141 427 8272

West Dunbartonshire Community Health Partnership
Hartfield Clinic
Latta Street
DUMBARTON
G82 2DS
Tel.: 01389 604532

Admin & Senior Management
Mrs E Hudson, Lead Nurse, Hartfield Clinic, Tel.: 01389 604540
Child Health
Pre School, Victoria Infirmary, Helensburgh, G84 7BU, Tel.: 01436 655007
School, Victoria Infirmary, Helensburgh, G84 7BU, Tel.: 01436 655012
Child Health Records
Pre School, Victoria Infirmary, Helensburgh, G84 7BU, Tel.: 01436 655007
School, Victoria Infirmary, Helensburgh, G84 7BU, Tel.: 01436 655012
Clinical Leads (NSF)
Dr A Woodburn, Clinical Lead, Cancer,
Community Nursing Services
Ms K Eastwood, Director of Nursing, Hartfield Clinic, Latta Street, Dumbarton, G82 2DS, Tel.: 01389 604549
Hartfield Clinic, Latta Street, Dumbarton, G82 2DS, Tel.: 01389 604540
District Nursing
Bank Street Clinic, 46-48 Bank Street, Alexandria, G83 0LS, Tel.: 01389 759774
Community Nursing Service, Medical Centre, 12 East King Street, Helensburgh, G84 7QL,
Dr Calder Practice, District Nurses, Tel.: 01436 679630
Dr Robin Practice, District Nurses, Tel.: 01436 672277
Dumbarton Health Centre, Station Road, Dumbarton, G82 1PU, Tel.: 01389 763111
Health Visitors
Dr Calder Practice, Health Visitors, Tel.: 01436 679633
Dr Robin Practice, Health Visitors, Tel.: 01436 678142
Liaison Services
Vale of Leven District General Hospital, Alexandria, G83 0UA, Tel.: 01389 754121

Scotland

Other Services

Ms S Aird, Resuscitation Officer, Hartfield Clinic, Tel.: 01389 604542
Mr D A Ross, Complaints Clinical Risk Manager, Hartfield Clinic, Tel.: 01389 604534

West Glasgow Community Health Partnership

Tel.: 0141 211 1433

Admin & Senior Management
Mr G Breslin, Tel.: 0141 420 2403
Ms L Nicol, Tel.: 0141 211 1433

West Renfrewshire Community Health Partnership

(was part of NHS Argyll & Clyde)
Ross House
Hawkhead Road
PAISLEY
PA2 7BN
Tel.: 0141 842 7200

Admin & Senior Management
Ms L Smith, Director of Nursing & Quality, Merchiston Hospital, By Brookfield, Johnstone,

Child Health Records
Child Health Records, Hollybush, Dykebar Hospital, Grahamston Road, Paisley, PA2 7DE, Tel.: 0141 884 9099

Child Protection/Safeguarding Children
Ms I McGugan, Foxbar Clinic, Morar Drive, Paisley, PA2 9QR, Tel.: 01505 813119

Community Nursing Services
Mrs D Duffy, Lead Nurse, Banchory Cottage, By Brookfield, Johnstone, PA5 8TY, Tel.: 01505 384027

District Nursing
District Nurses, Hollybush, Dykebar Hospital, Grahamston Road, Paisley, PA2 7DE, Tel.: 0141 884 9099

Family Planning Services
Ms S Mason, Co-ordinator, Russell Institute, Causeyside Street, Paisley, PA1 1UR, Tel.: 0141 889 8701

Yorkhill Division

Dalnair Street
Yorkhill
GLASGOW, G3 8SJ
Tel.: 0141 201 0000

Admin & Senior Management
Ms E Daniels, Senior Nurse Community Development, Ward 5B, Tel.: 0141 201 0715
Ms L Robertson, Community Services Manager, Tel.: 0141 201 0324

Child Health
Ms J Belmore, Paediatric Oncology Outreach Nurse, Schiehallion Day Care Unit, Dalnair Street, Glasgow, G3 8SJ, 0141 201 9314
Mr D Fraser, Child & Family Psychiatry Community Nurse Therapy, Tel.: 0141 201 0730
Ms A Freeland, Community Children's Nursing Team, 0141 201 0007
Ms C Haggerty, Paediatric Renal Liaison Team, Ward 6A Renal Ward, Dalnair Street, Glasgow, G3 8SJ, Tel.: 0141 201 0120
Ms S Hay, Community Children's Nursing Team, 0141 201 0007
Ms S Kennedy, Liaison Aftercare Children with Tracheostomies, Tel.: 0141 201 0846
Ms D King, Paediatric Renal Liaison Team, Ward 6A Renal Ward, Dalnair Street, Glasgow, G3 8SJ, Tel.: 0141 201 0120
Ms C Lewis, Community Children's Nursing Team, 0141 201 0007
Ms S McRea, Attention Deficit Disorder, Tel.: 0141 201 0220
Ms R Robinson, Community Neonatal Liaison, Tel.: 0141 201 0529/30

Child Health Records
School Health Records, Southbank Child Centre, Tel.: 0141 201 0912/0936

Child Protection/Safeguarding Children
Ms E Greaves, Looked After & Accommodated Children, LAAC Team, Springburn Health Centre, 200 Springburn Way, Glasgow, G21 1TR, Tel.: 0141 232 9105
Ms C Kean, Looked After & Accommodated Children, Pathways to Health, 115 Wellington Street, Glasgow, G2 2XT, Tel.: 0141 302 2681
Ms A Knox, Child Protection - Yorkhill, Tel.: 0141 201 0000
Ms E Daniels, Child Protection, Ward 5B, Royal Hospital for Sick Children, Yorkhill, Glasgow, G3 8SJ, Tel.: 0141 201 0715

Community Midwifery
Community Midwifery Manager, Page No 2110, Queen Mother's Hospital, Yorkhill, Glasgow, G3 8SH, Tel.: 0141 201 0550
Emergencies, Page No 2503, Queen Mother's Hospital, Yorkhill, Glasgow, G3 8SH, Tel.: 0141 201 0550
Ms E Stenhouse, Directorate Manager, Queen Mother's Hospital, Yorkhill, Glasgow, G3 8SH, Tel.: 0141 201 0552/1

Health Visitors
Ms A M Forde, Special Needs Health Visitor, Glenfarg Suite, Possilpark Health Centre, Tel.: 0141 531 6191
Ms A Ingram, Special Needs Health Visitor, Achamore Child Centre, Tel.: 0141 211 6150
Ms A Kennedy, Special Needs Health Visitor, Southbank Child Centre, 207 Old Rutherglen Road, Glasgow, G5 0RE, Tel.: 0141 201 0949
Ms L Kilby, Special Needs Health Visitor, Bridgeton Child Development Centre, Tel.: 0141 531 6550
Ms I McArthur, Neurology, Health Visitor, Royal Hospital for Sick Children, Yorkhill, Glasgow, G3 8SJ, Tel.: 0141 201 0660/0713
Ms J Reilley, Liaison Health Visitor, Royal Hospital for Sick Children, Tel.: 0141 201 0172
Ms A Tausney, Special Needs Health Visitor, Southbank Child Centre, 207 Old Rutherglen Rd, Glasgow, G5 ORE, Tel.: 0141 201 0925

Liaison Services
Ms A Freeland, Liaison, District Nurse, Royal Hospital for Sick Children, Yorkhill, Glasgow, G3 8SJ, Tel.: 0141 201 6910
Ms S Kennedy, Liaison Aftercare for Children with Tracheostomies, Tel.: 0141 201 0846
Ms J Reilly, Specialist Liaison Paediatric Health Visitor Medical, Surgery, Acute, Royal Hospital for Sick Children, Yorkhill, Glasgow, G3 8SJ, Tel.: 0141 201 0172
Ms R Robinson, Community Neonatal Liaison, Tel.: 0141 201 0529/30

Other Services
Ms A Crawford, Cleft Lip & Palate, Royal Hospital for Sick Children, Yorkhill, Glasgow, G3 8SJ, Tel.: 0141 201 9286
Ms K Trower, Pain Control, Royal Hospital for Sick Children, Yorkhill, Glasgow, G3 8SJ, Tel.: 0141 201 0449
Ms S Wallace, Cleft Lip & Palate, Royal Hospital for Sick Children, Yorkhill, Glasgow, G3 8SJ, Tel.: 0141 201 9286

School Nursing
Ms E Anderson, Child Health/School Nurses, Possilpark Health Centre, 85 Denmark Street, Glasgow G22, Tel.: 0141 531 6196
Ms M Bell, Specialist Nurse - Child Health/School Nurses, Southbank Child Centre, 207 Old Rutherglen Road, Glasgow, G5 0RE, Tel.: 0141 201 0901
Ms C Coleman, Special Schools - Child Health/School Nurses, Plean Street Clinic, 18 Plean Street, Glasgow, G14, Tel.: 0141 232 4710
Ms L Daniels, Community Senior Nurse - School Nursing, Tel.: 0141 201 0715
Ms B Dryden, Child Health/School Nurses, Braidfield High School, Queen Mary Avenue, Clydebank, G81, Tel.: 0141 951 8140
Ms R Duff, Child Health/School Nurses, Southbank Child Centre, 207 Old Rutherglen Road, Glasgow, G5 0RE, Tel.: 0141 201 0901

Scotland

Ms S Fotheringham, Child Health/School Nurses, Castlemilk Health Centre, 71 Dougrie Drive, Glasgow, G45, Tel.: 0141 531 8555

Ms I Hoskins, Child Health/School Nurses, Plean Street Clinic, 18 Plean Street, Glasgow G14, Tel.: 0141 232 4703

Ms S Kayes, Child Health/School Nurses, Cathkin High School, Western Road, Cambuslang, G72 8YS, Tel.: 0141 641 8569

Ms J McAlister, Child Health/School Nurses, Parkhead Health Centre, Salamanca Street, Glasgow, Tel.: 0141 531 9045

Ms P McKay, Child Health/School Nurses, Cardonald Clinic, Berryknowes Road, Cardonald, Tel.: 0141 883 8393

Ms G Wilson, Specialist Nurse - Child Health/School Nurses, Southbank Child Centre, 207 Old Rutherglen Road, Glasgow, G5 0RE, Tel.: 0141 201 0937

Ms L Wright, Child Health/School Nurses, Brookwood Villa, 166 Drymen Road, Glasgow, G61, Tel.: 0141 570 2306

Specialist Nursing Services

Ms D Brownlee, React Community Nurse, Royal Hospital for Sick Children, Yorkhill, Glasgow, G3 8SJ, Tel.: 0141 201 0330

Ms D Campbell, Team Leader, Ventilation Services, 5th Floor, Royal Hospital for Sick Children, Yorkhill, Glasgow, G3 8SJ,

Ms M Henderson, UTI Sister, 6th Floor, Royal Hospital for Sick Children, Yorkhill, Glasgow, G3 8SJ, Tel.: 0141 201 0205

Ms K Leitch, UTI Sister, 6th Floor, Royal Hospital for Sick Children, Yorkhill, Glasgow, G3 8SJ, Tel.: 0141 201 0205

Ms E Morton, Allergy, Royal Hospital for Sick Children, Yorkhill, Glasgow, G3 8SJ, Tel.: 0141 201 0408

Ms E Jardine, Asthma, Royal Hospital for Sick Children, Yorkhill, Glasgow, G3 8SJ, Tel.: 0141 201 0670

Ms S Kennedy, Tracheostomy, Surgical Neonates, Cardio vascular, Royal Hospital for Sick Children, Yorkhill, Glasgow, G3 8SJ, Tel.: 0141 201 0846

Ms L Cassidy, Cystic Fibrosis, Royal Hospital for Sick Children, Yorkhill, Glasgow, G3 8SJ, Tel.: 0141 201 0316

Ms F Lomas, Cystic Fibrosis, Royal Hospital for Sick Children, Yorkhill, Glasgow, G3 8SJ, Tel.: 0141 201 0316

Ms L Mason, Cystic Fibrosis, Royal Hospital for Sick Children, Yorkhill, Glasgow, G3 8SJ, Tel.: 0141 201 0316

Ms L McInnes, Dermatology, Royal Hospital for Sick Children, Yorkhill, Glasgow, G3 8SJ, Tel.: 0141 201 0408

Ms A Spiers, Dermatology, Royal Hospital for Sick Children, Yorkhill, Glasgow, G3 8SJ, Tel.: 0141 201 0408

Mr G Allison, Diabetic Care, Royal Hospital for Sick Children, Yorkhill, Glasgow, G3 8SJ, Tel.: 0141 201 0331

Mr M Fergusson, Diabetic Care, Royal Hospital for Sick Children, Yorkhill, Glasgow, G3 8SJ, Tel.: 0141 201 0331

Ms A Johnston, Diabetic Care, Royal Hospital for Sick Children, Yorkhill, Glasgow, G3 8SJ, Tel.: 0141 201 0331

Ms F Lamb, Diabetic Care, Royal Hospital for Sick Children, Yorkhill, Glasgow, G3 8SJ, Tel.: 0141 201 0331

Ms E McNeill, Nurse Specialist, Endocrine Surgery, 0141 201 0245

Ms S McCartney, Sister, Enuresis, 6th Floor, Royal Hospital for Sick Children, Yorkhill, Glasgow, G3 8SJ, Tel.: 0141 201 0127

Ms M Wilson, Epilepsy, - Neuro, Royal Hospital for Sick Children, Yorkhill, Glasgow, G3 8SJ, Tel.: 0141 201 0145

Ms A Smith, Gastrostomy, Gastroenterology, Royal Hospital for Sick Children, Yorkhill, Glasgow, G3 8SJ, Tel.: 0141 201 0192

Ms E McKirdy, Haemophilia, Royal Hospital for Sick Children, Yorkhill, Glasgow, G3 8SJ, Tel.: 0141 201 9305

Ms J Belmore, Macmillan, Royal Hospital for Sick Children, Yorkhill, Glasgow, G3 8SJ, Tel.: 0141 201 9313

Ms L Russell, Neurology, Royal Hospital for Sick Children, Yorkhill, Glasgow, G3 8SJ, Tel.: 0141 201 0660/0173

Ms C McGuckin, Sister, Nutrition, 5th Floor, Royal Hospital for Sick Children, Yorkhill, Glasgow, G3 8SJ, Tel.: 0141 201 9343

Ms E Brewis, Outreach, Oncology, Royal Hospital for Sick Children, Yorkhill, Glasgow, G3 8SJ, Tel.: 0141 201 9314

Ms A Clarkin, Outreach, Oncology, Royal Hospital for Sick Children, Yorkhill, Glasgow, G3 8SJ, Tel.: 0141 201 9313

Ms E Loomes, Orthopaedics, Royal Hospital for Sick Children, Yorkhill, Glasgow, G3 8SJ, Tel.: 0141 201 9216

Ms K Parker, Orthopaedics, Royal Hospital for Sick Children, Yorkhill, Glasgow, G3 8SJ, Tel.: 0141 201 9216

Ms D King, Outreach, Renal, Royal Hospital for Sick Children, Yorkhill, Glasgow, G3 8SJ, Tel.: 0141 201 0120

Ms Y Bennett, Stoma Care, Royal Hospital for Sick Children, Yorkhill, Glasgow, G3 8SJ, Tel.: 0141 201 6929

NHS Highland

Argyll & Bute Community Health Partnership
(transferred from NHS Argyll & Clyde)
CHP Headquarters
Aros, LOCHGILPHEAD
PA31 8LB
Tel.: 01546 606600

Child Health Records
Transfer of Child Health Records, Lorn & Islands District General Hospital, Glengallan Road, Oban, PA34 4HH, Tel.: 01631 567500

District Nursing
Ms J Bett, Locality Manager, Mid Argyll, Mid Argyll Hospital, Lochgilphead, PA31 8JZ, Tel.: 01546 604911

Community Nursing Kintyre, Kintyre, Health Centre, Stewart Road, Campbeltown, PA28 6AT, Tel.: 01586 552224

Ms M Davidson, Nurse Manager, Cowal, Dunoon & District General Hospital, 360 Argyll Street, Dunoon, PA23 8HU, Tel.: 01369 704341

Mr J Dreghorn, Locality Manager, Islay Community Nursing Services, Islay Hospital, Bowmore, Isle of Islay, PA43 7JD, Tel.: 01496 301000

Ms S Drummond, Locality Manager, Kintyre, Campbeltown Hospital, Ralston Road, Campbeltown, PA28 6LE, Tel.: 01586 552224

Islay District Nurses, Bowmore Surgery, Main Street, Bowmore, Isle of Islay, Tel.: 01496 810204

Ms L Macintyre, Bute Acting, Nurse Manager, Victoria Annexe, Rothesay, Isle of Bute, PA20 9JH, Tel.: 01700 502943

Ms J McDowall, Bute Acting, Nurse Manager, Victoria Annexe, Rothesay, Isle of Bute, PA20 9JH, Tel.: 01700 502943

Ms M Newiss, Locality Manager, North Argyll, The Surgery, Connel, Oban, PA37 1PH, Tel.: 01631 710065

Family Planning Services
Family Planning Service, The Surgery, Connel, Oban, PA37 1PH, Tel.: 01631 710065

Learning Disabilities
Mr R MacFarlane, Clinical Nurse Specialist, Victoria Infirmary, Tel.: 01436 655022

Liaison Services
Ms F Carmichael, Diabetes Liaison Islay, Islay Hospital, Tel.: 01496 301000

Ms H Crawford-Patterson, Cardiac Liaison Mid Argyll, Mid Argyll Hospital, Tel.: 01546 602449/606487

Ms M Moss, Cowal Elderly, Liaison Sister, Dunoon General Hospital, Tel.: 01369 704341 ext 272

Ms M Thomson, Diabetes Liaison Kintyre, Campbeltown Hospital, Tel.: 01586 552224

Other Services
Ms A Campbell, Public Health Practitioner, Lorn Medical Centre, Soroba Road, Oban, PA34 4HE, Tel.: 01631 570082

Ms M Clark, Cowal Stroke, Rehab, Dunoon General Hospital, Tel.: 01369 704341 ext 251

School Nursing
Ms J Bett, Locality Manager, Mid Argyll School Health/Nursing Service, Mid Argyll Hospital, Lochgilphead, PA31 8JZ, Tel.: 01546 604911

Community Nursing Kintyre, Kintyre School Health/Nursing Service, Health Centre, Stewart Road, Campbeltown, PA28 6AT, Tel.: 01586 552224

Scotland

Ms M Davidson, Nurse Manager, Cowal School Health/Nursing Service, Dunoon & District General Hospital, 360 Argyll Street, Dunoon, PA23 8HU, Tel.: 01369 704341

Mr J Dreghorn, Locality Manager, Islay School Health/Nursing Service, Islay Hospital, Bowmore, Isle of Islay, PA43 7JD, Tel.: 01496 301000

Ms S Drummond, Locality Manager, Kintyre School Health/Nursing Service, Campbeltown Hospital, Ralston Road, Campbeltown, PA28 6LE, Tel.: 01586 552224

Ms S Henderson, Community Children North Argyll, Lorn & Island District General Hospital, Tel.: 01631 567500 ext 612

Ms L Macintyre, Bute Acting School Health/Nursing Service, Nurse Manager, Victoria Annexe, Rothesay, Isle of Bute, PA20 9JH, Tel.: 01700 502943

Ms J McDowall, Bute Acting School Health/Nursing Service, Nurse Manager, Victoria Annexe, Rothesay, Isle of Bute, PA20 9JH, Tel.: 01700 502943

Ms M Newiss, Locality Manager, North Argyll School Health/Nursing Service, The Surgery, Connel, Oban, PA37 1PH, Tel.: 01631 710065

Specialist Nursing Services

Ms C Robertson, Kintyre, Continence, Campbeltown Hospital, Tel.: 01586 552224

Ms W Musson, Mid Argyll, Clinical Nurse Specialist, Elderly Care, Care of Elderly Unit, Mid Argyll Hospital, Tel.: 01546 602323

Ms J Aitcheson, Islay, Macmillan, Islay Hospital, Tel.: 01496 301000

Ms H Brown, North Argyll, Macmillan, Lorn & Islands District General Hospital, Tel.: 01631 567523

Ms M Donald, Bute, Macmillan, Victoria Hospital, Rothesay, Tel.: 01700 503938

Ms M MacLeod, Mid Argyll, Macmillan, Mid Argyll Hospital, Tel.: 01546 602323

Ms T Morrison, Cowal, Macmillan, Cowal Hospice, Dunoon General Hospital, Tel.: 01369 707732

Ms M Mitchell, Kintyre, Palliative Care, Campbeltown Hospital, Tel.: 01586 552224

Mr P Gay, Kintyre, Stoma Care, Campbeltown Hospital, Tel.: 01586 552224

Ms G Wotherspoon, North Argyll, Stoma Care, Lorn & Islands District Generall Hospital, Tel.: 01631 567573

Mid Highland Community Health Partnership

Ross Memorial Hospital
Ferry Road
DINGWALL, IV15 9QS
Tel.: 01349 863313
Fax.: 01349 865852

Admin & Senior Management
Dr J Douglas, Clinical Lead,
Ms G McVicar, General Manager, Tel.: 01349 863313
Child Health
Mr S Mackay, Children's Services Manager,

NHS Highland

Highland Acute Division, Raigmore Hospital
INVERNESS
IV2 3UJ
Tel.: 01463 704000

Admin & Senior Management
Ms H Spratt, Director of Nursing, Tel.: 01463 704630
Child Health
Ms J Baird, Local Services Manager Inverness Town & Community, Community Offices, Royal Northern Infirmary, Tel.: 01463 704622
Ms H Johnston, Community Paediatrician - Skye & Lochalsh, Tel.: 01471 822062
Mrs G Keel, Local Services Manager Skye & Lochalsh, Dr Mackinnon Memorial Hospital, Broadford, Isle of Skye, Tel.: 01471 822137

Locality Manager, Lochaber, Belford Hospital, Fort William, PH33 6BS, Tel.: 01397 702481

Mr G MacDonald, Local Services Manager Nairn, Badenoch, Strathspey, Town & County Hospital, Nairn, IV12 5EE, Tel.: 01667 452101

Mr G MacVicar, Local Services Manager Ross & Cromarty, Maywood, Ferry Road, Dingwall, IV15 9QS, Tel.: 01349 863313

Ms J McKelvie, Local Services Manager Sutherland, Lawson Memorial Hospital, Golspie, Sutherland, KW10 6SS, Tel.: 01408 633293

Mr K Oliver, Children's Services Manager, Terrapin Building, Raigmore Hospital, Tel.: 01463 701342

Ms A Phimister, Local Services Manager Caithness, Caithness General Hospital, Bankhead Road, Wick, KW1 5NS, Tel.: 01955 605050

Ms P Rankine, Highland Community Children's Nurse Team, Tel.: 01463 705320

Ms A Rennie, Highland Community Children's Nurse Team, Tel.: 01463 705320

Child Health Records
Child Health Records, Children's Services, Room 12, Terrapin Building, Raigmore Hospital, Inverness, Tel.: 01463 701318
Child Protection/Safeguarding Children
Ms G Pincock, Skye & Lochalsh, Child Protection, Admin Office, Dr Mackinnon Memorial Hospital, Broadford, Isle of Skye, Tel.: 0770 8043720
Ms S Young, Child Protection, Terrapin Building, Raigmore Hospital, Tel.: 01463 701309
Community Midwifery
Ms H Bryers, Link Supervisor/LSA Officer NHS Highland, Senior Midwife, Raigmore Hopsital, Inverness, IV2 3UJ, Tel.: 01463 704000 ext 5373
Ms S McLeod, Midwifery Team Leader, Midwifery Led Unit, Belford Hospital, Fort William, PH33 6BS, Tel.: 01397 700371
Midwifery - Broadford, Tel.: 01471 822790
Midwifery - Portree, Tel.: 01478 611924
Ms R Scott, Lead Midwife - Skye & Lochalsh, Dr Mackinnon Memorial Hospital, Broadford, Isle of Skye, Tel.: 01471 820219
Mrs A Watt, Acting Senior Midwife, First Floor Maternity Unit, Raigmore Hospital, Inverness, IV2 3UJ, Tel.: 01463 705373
Community Nursing Services
Ms K Earnshaw, Clinical Co-ordinator - Skye & Lochalsh, Admin Office, Dr Mackinnon Memorial Hospital, Boradford, Isle of Skye, Tel.: 01471 822137
District Nursing
Ms J Baird, Local Services Manager Inverness Town & Community, Community Offices, Royal Northern Infirmary, Tel.: 01463 704622
District Nurse - Carbost, Tel.: 01478 640210
District Nurse - Staffin, Tel.: 01470 562205
Emergencies, Ross & Cromarty, Maywood, Ferry Road, Dingwall, IV15 9QS, Tel.: 01349 862220
Emergencies, Caithness, Caithness General Hospital, Bankhead Road, Wick, KW1 5NS, Tel.: 01955 605050
Emergencies & Nights (24 hrs), Lochaber, Belford Hospital, Fort William, PH33 6BS, Tel.: 01397 702481
Emergencies & Nights (ansaphone 24 hrs), Inverness Town & Community, Community Offices, Royal Northern Infirmary, Tel.: 01463 230850
Emergencies (24 hrs), Skye & Lochalsh, Dr Mackinnon Memorial Hospital, Broadford, Isle of Skye, Tel.: 01478 613200
Ms M Ferguson, District Nurse - Raasay, Tel.: 01478 660204
Mrs G Keel, Local Services Manager Skye & Lochalsh, Dr Mackinnon Memorial Hospital, Broadford, Isle of Skye, Tel.: 01471 822137
Ms R Keppie, District Nurse - Dunvegan, Tel.: 01470 521216
Mr G MacDonald, Local Services Manager Nairn, Badenoch, Strathspey, Town & County Hospital, Nairn, IV12 5EE, Tel.: 01667 452101

Scotland

Ms S MacKay, District Nurse - Broadford/Kyleakin, Tel.: 01471 822762

Ms F MacLeod, District Nurse - Gleneig, Tel.: 01599 522284

Ms J MacRae, District Nurse - Sleat, Tel.: 01471 844 221

Mr G MacVicar, Local Services Manager Ross & Cromarty, Maywood, Ferry Road, Dingwall, IV15 9QS, Tel.: 01349 863313

Ms P Matheson, District Nurse - Portree, Tel.: 01478 612590

Ms J McKelvie, Local Services Manager Sutherland, Lawson Memorial Hospital, Golspie, Sutherland, KW10 6SS, Tel.: 01408 633293

Ms A Phimister, Local Services Manager Caithness, Caithness General Hospital, Bankhead Road, Wick, KW1 5NS, Tel.: 01955 605050

Mr P Short, Local Services Manager Lochaber, Belford Hospital, Fort William, PH33 6BS, Tel.: 01397 702481

Ms A Stoddart, District Nurse - Kyle, Tel.: 01599 534302

Family Planning Services
Dingwall, Tel.: 01349 863313

Fort William, Caol Clinic, Caol, Fort William, Tel.: 01397 702258

Inverness Town, Tel.: 01463 704622

Thurso, Tel.: 01847 893442

Wick, Tel.: 01955 605050

Health Visitors
Broadford Health Visitor, Tel.: 01471 822656

Caithness - Thurso, Tel.: 01847 893442

Caithness - Wick, Caithness - Wick, Tel.: 01955 604134

Dunvegan Health Visitor, Tel.: 01470 521776

Ms A Hudson, Gleneig Health Visitor, Tel.: 01599 522331

Ms M Hyslop, Sleat Health Visitor, Tel.: 01471 844212

Ms J MacKenzie, Portree Health Visitor, Tel.: 01478 612817

Ms F MacLean, Portree Health Visitor, Tel.: 01478 612817

Ms M Quinn, Kyle Health Visitor, Tel.: 01599 530172

Ms A Taylor, Portree Health Visitor, Tel.: 01478 612817

Learning Disabilities
Ms E Alexander, Inverness, Community Nurse, The Corbett Centre, Coronation Road, Inverness, IV3 8AD, Tel.: 01463 712342

Ms B Andrews, Wester Ross, Community Nurse, The Nurses Home, Poolewe, IV22 2JU, Tel.: 01455 781288

Ms M Barnes, Lochaber, Community Nurse, Community Clinic, Glen Nevis Place, Fort William, PH33 6DA, Tel.: 01397 709855

Ms F Campbell, Caithness, Community Nurse, Dunbar Hospital, Ormlie Road, Thurso, KW14 7XE, Tel.: 01847 893263 ext 244

Mr A Caswell, Professional, Inverness, Lead Nurse, Royal Northern Infirmary, Ness Walk, Inverness, Tel.: 01463 706946

Ms J Duncan, Badenoch & Strathspey, Community Nurse, CMHT, Badenoch & Strathspey, Grants Garage, 62 Grampian Road, Aviemore, PH22 1PD, Tel.: 01479 810957

Mr P Finley, Caithness, Community Nurse, Dunbar Hospital, Ormlie Road, Thurso, KW14 7XE, Tel.: 01847 893263 ext 244

Mr R Goodison, Learning Disabilities Nurse, Community Team, Old Health Centre, Golspie, KW10 6TL,

Ms L Grant, Nairn, Staff Nurse, Town & County Hospital, Cawdor Road, Nairn, IV12 5ED, Tel.: 01667 452914

Mr D Harper, Lochaber, Community Nurse, Community Clinic, Glen Nevis Place, Fort William, PH33 6DA, Tel.: 01397 709855

Ms M Hughes, Lochaber, Staff Nurse, Community Clinic, Glen Nevis Place, Fort William, PH33 6DA, Tel.: 01397 709855

Ms S Jones, Caithness, Senior Nurse, Dunbar Hospital, Ormlie Road, Thurso, KW14 7XE, Tel.: 01847 893263 ext 244

Lead Nurse, Learning Disabilities, New Craigs Hospital, Leachkin Road, Inverness, IV3 8NP, Tel.: 01463 242860 ext 2508

Ms M MacArthur, Inverness, Community Nurse, The Corbett Centre, Coronation Road, Inverness, IV3 8AD, Tel.: 01463 712342

Ms M Macdonald, Inverness, Community Nurse, The Corbett Centre, Coronation Road, Inverness, IV3 8AD, Tel.: 01463 712342

Ms J MacKay, Ross-Shire, Senior Nurse, Glenorrin, High Street, Dingwall, IV15 9TF, Tel.: 01349 867915

Mr D MacKintosh, Ross-Shire, Community Nurse, Glenorrin, High Street, Dingwall, IV15 9TF, Tel.: 01349 867915

Ms T MacRitchie, Skye & Lochalsh, Community Nurse, Broadford Hospital, Broadford, Isle of Skye, IV49 9AA, Tel.: 01471 822303

Ms A Murray, Inverness, Community Nurse, The Corbett Centre, Coronation Road, Inverness, IV3 8AD, Tel.: 01463 712342

Mr I Ward, Ross-Shire, Community Nurse, Glenorrin, High Street, Dingwall, IV15 9TF, Tel.: 01349 867915

Liaison Services
Mrs P Antonios, Medical/Geriatrics, Medical Centre, Martha Terrace, Wick, Tel.: 01955 603784

Mrs P Kidd, Elderly, Royal Northern Infirmary, Tel.: 01463 704626

Miss S Sangster, Obstetrics Clerical Liaison Officer, Raigmore Hospital, Inverness, IV2 3UJ, Tel.: 01463 704000 ext 4342

Mrs A Stewart, Caithness & Sunderland Surgical, Medical Centre, Martha Terrace, Wick, Tel.: 01955 603784

School Nursing
Ms H Gilpin, School Nurse - Portree, Tel.: 01478 613484

Ms J MacKenzie, School Nurse - Kyle, Tel.: 01599 534878

Specialist Nursing Services
Mrs A Liddell, Sutherland West, Lawson Memorial Hospital, Tel.: 01408 664063

Mrs M MacKay, Sutherland East, Lawson Memorial Hospital, Tel.: 01408 664063

Mr S Moorehead, Cardiac Rehabilitation, Caithness General Hospital, Tel.: 01955 605050

Ms L Randall, Continence, Royal Northern Infirmary, Tel.: 01463 242860 ext 3208

Mr E Wisemanin, Infection Control, Osprey House, Tel.: 01463 242860 ext 4026

Ms N MacAskill, Skye & Lochalsh, Nurse, Macmillan, Tel.: 01471 822913

Ms B MacDonald, Skye & Lochalsh, Nurse, Macmillan, Tel.: 01471 822913

Nurses, Macmillan, Royal Northern Infirmary, Tel.: 01463 242860 ext 3468

Ms L Phillips, Skye & Lochalsh, Nurse, Macmillan, Tel.: 01471 822913

Ms L Shakespeare, Caithness Area, Macmillan, Caithness General Hospital, Tel.: 01955 605050 ext 397

Ms J Laird-Measures, Community Nurse - Skye & Lochalsh, Paediatrics, Tel.: 01478 613772

Ms M MacLeod, Community Nurse - Skye & Lochalsh, Paediatrics, Tel.: 01478 613772

Ms M Ralston, Community Nurse - Skye & Lochalsh, Paediatrics, Tel.: 01478 613772

Mr A Randle, Community Nurse - Skye & Lochalsh, Paediatrics, Tel. 01478 613772

Ms J MacDonald, Co-ordinator, Palliative Care, Tel.: 01471 822194

North Highland Community Health Partnership
Caithness General Hospital
Bankhead Road
WICK
KW1 5NS
Tel.: 01955 880300

Admin & Senior Management
Ms D Bell, Lead Nurse,

Ms S Craig, General Manager,

Mrs G Haire, Assistant General Manager East Sutherland, Lawson Memorial Hospital, Tel.: 01408 633293

Mr A Robertson, Nurse,

Child Health
Ms J Livingstone, Lawson Hospital, Golspie, Sutherland, Tel.: 01408 633157

Scotland

Child Health Records
Ms K Morison, Community Nursing Admin. Lawson Hospital, Golspie, Sutherland, Tel.: 01408 633293
Pre-School, East Sutherland, Nursing Administration, Lawson Memorial Hospital, Tel.: 01408 633293
Ms A Thom, School Age East Sutherland, Lawson Memorial Hospital, Tel.: 01408 664023

Child Protection/Safeguarding Children
Mrs K Otter, Child Protection, Assynt Health Centre, Lochinver, IV27 4JZ, Tel.: 01571 844749

Community Midwifery
Mrs S McInnes, Supervisor of Midwives, Health Centre, Brora, KW9 6QJ, Tel.: 01408 622778

Community Nursing Services
Clinical Nurse Manager, Lawson Hospital, Golspie, Sutherland, KW14 1OSS, Tel.: 01408 633293

District Nursing
Ms J Bishop, Nurses House, Gordon Terrace, Bettyhill, Sutherland, KW14 7SX, Tel.: 01641 521832

Health Visitors
Ms M McFadyen, Health Visitor, Health Centre, Kinlochbervie, IV27 4SX, Tel.: 01971 521758
Ms K Otter, Health Visitor, Assynt Medical Practice, Lochinver, IV27 4JZ, Tel.: 01571 844749

Learning Disabilities
Ms S Jones, The Old Health Centre, Golspie, Sutherland, KW10 6TL,

Other Services
Community Rehab Team, Physiotherapy, Nurse's House, Melvich, KW14 7YJ, Tel.: 01641 531356
Occupational Therapy & Speech Language Therapy, Nurse's House, Bervie Road, Kinlochbervie, IV27 4RY, Tel.: 01971 521114

School Nursing
Ms J Bishop, Child Health/School Nurses, Nurse's House, Bettyhill, By Thurso, KW14 7SS, Tel.: 01641 521832
Ms J Livingstone, School Nurse East Sutherland, Lawson Memorial Hospital, Tel.: 01408 664058
Ms M McFadyen, Child Health/School Nurses, Health Centre, Kinlochbervie, IV27 4SX, Tel.: 01971 521758

Specialist Nursing Services
Ms A Liddell, Nurse, Macmillan, Health Centre, Lairg, IV27 4DD, Tel.: 01549 402556
Ms M Mackay, Nurse, Macmillan, Lawson Memorial Hospital, Tel.: 01408 664063

South East Highland Community Health Partnership
CHP Headquarters, St Vincents Hospital
KINGUSSIE
PE1 1ET
Tel.: 01540 661219

Admin & Senior Management
Ms J Baird, Director of Community Care, John Dewar Building, Inverness Business & Retail Pk, Highlander Way, Inverness, IV2 GE, Tel.: 01463 706805
Ms P McClelland, Community Care Manager, Social Work Dept, School House, Milton Park, Aviemore, PH22 1RR, Tel.: 01479 810251

Community Midwifery
Mrs K Bell, Nursing/Midwifery, Aviemore Health Centre, Grampian Road, Aviemore, PH22 1PF, Tel.: 01479 810640
Mrs C Cameron-Mackintosh, Nursing/Midwifery, 1 Old Mill Road, Tomatin, IV2 4UA, Tel.: 01808 511202
Mrs J Craven, Nursing/Midwifery, Foyers Medical Centre, Lower Foyers, IV2 6XU, Tel.: 01456 486412
Mrs J Dick, Nursing/Midwifery, 1 Old Mill Road, Tomatin, IV2 4UA, Tel.: 01808 511202

Mrs A Graham, Nursing/Midwifery, Aviemore Health Centre, Grampian Road, Aviemore, PH22 1PF, Tel.: 01479 810640
Mrs B Hewlett, Nursing/Midwifery, Ian Charles Hospital, Castle Road, Grantown on Spey, PH26 3HR, Tel.: 01479 873835
Mrs D Kinnaird, Team Leader/Nursing/Midwifery, Ian Charles Hospital, Castle Road, Grantown on Spey, PH26 3HR, Tel.: 01479 873835
Mrs E Mackenzie, Health Visiting/Midwifery, 1 Old Mill Road, Tomatin, IV2 4UA, Tel.: 01808 511202
Mrs S McCulloch, Nursing/Midwifery, Ian Charles Hospital, Castle Road, Grantown on Spey, PH26 3HR, Tel.: 01479 873835
Mrs M Oswald, Nursing/Midwifery, Medical Practice, Ardvonie Park, Gynack Road, Kingussie, PH21 1ET, Tel.: 01540 661293

Community Nursing Services
Mrs K Carson, Community Staff Nurse, Foyers Medical Centre, Lower Foyers, IV2 6XU, Tel.: 01456 486412
Mrs K Carson, Community Staff Nurse, 1 Old Mill Road, Tomatin, IV2 4UA, Tel.: 01808 511202
Mrs B Hay, Community Staff Nurse, Aviemore Health Centre, Grampian Road, Aviemore, PH22 1PF, Tel.: 01479 810640
Mrs A MacAllum, Community Staff Nurse, Ian Charles Hospital, Castle Road, Grantown on Spey, PH26 3HR, Tel.: 01479 873835
Mrs L Nelson, Community Staff Nurse, Medical Practice, Ardvonie Park, Gynack Road, Kingussie, PH21 1ET, Tel.: 01540 661293
Mrs S Telfer, Community Staff Nurse, Aviemore Health Centre, Grampian Road, Aviemore, PH22 1PF, Tel.: 01479 810640

Health Visitors
Mrs M Bentley, Health Visitor, Medical Practice, Ardvonie Park, Gynack Road, Kingussie, PH21 1ET, Tel.: 01540 662064
Mrs B Black, Health Visitor, Ian Charles Hospital, Castle Road, Grantown on Spey, PH26 3HR, Tel.: 01479 873837
Mrs E Mackenzie, Health Visiting/Midwifery, 1 Old Mill Road, Tomatin, IV2 4UA, Tel.: 01808 511202

Learning Disabilities
Ms J Duncan, Learning Disabilities, Grants Garage, 62 Grampian Road, Aviemore, PH22 1PD, Tel.: 01479 810957

School Nursing
Mrs B Black, School Nurse, Ian Charles Hospital, Castle Road, Grantown on Spey, PH26 3HR, Tel.: 01479 873837
Mrs J Johnson, School Nurse, Medical Practice, Ardvonie Park, Gynack Road, Kingussie, PH21 1ET, Tel.: 01540 662065

NHS Lanarkshire

Airdrie Community Health Partnership
Wester Moffat Hospital
Tower Road
AIRDRIE, ML6 8LW
Tel.: 01236 771053

Admin & Senior Management
Mr T Bryce, General Manager, Wester Moffat Hospital, Tel.: 01236 771058
Mr J Glennie, Clinical Services Manager, Wester Moffat Hospital,

Child Health Records
Over 5s, Adam Avenue Clinic, Tel.: 01236 769291 ext 139
Under 5s, Condorrat Health Centre, Tel.: 01236 723383

Child Protection/Safeguarding Children
Ms A Neilson, Child Protection, Roadmeetings Hospital, Tel.: 01555 772271

District Nursing
Adam Avenue Medical Centre, South Nimmo Street, Airdrie, Tel.: 01236 769291
Ms A Agnew, District Nurse,
Airdrie Health Centre, Monkscourt Avenue, Airdrie, ML6 0JU, Tel.: 01236 769388
Ms M Frances McLusky, District Nurse,
Ms J Goodwill, District Nurse,

Scotland

Ms M Lamb, District Nurse,
Ms C Ward, District Nurse,
Ms K Watters, District Nurse, Tel.: 01236 769291 x170
Ms I Wightman, District Nurse,
Ms J Wilson, District Nurse,
Other Services
Mrs H Henderson, Resusc Training Officer, Strathclyde Hospital,
Tel.: 01698 245000 ext 4025
Mrs A Lee, Breast Feeding Co-ordinator, Health Promotion
Department, Strathclyde Hospital, Tel.: 01698 258788
Mrs D McCormack, Research, Advanced Nurse Practitioner, Udston
Hospital, Tel.: 01698 245000
Mr T Wales, Resusc Training Officer, Strathclyde Hospital, Tel.:
01698 245000 ext 4025
Specialist Nursing Services
Mrs A Allington, Diana Nurses, Coathill Hospital, Tel.: 01236 421266
Mrs M Robertson, Diana Nurses, Coathill Hospital, Tel.: 01236
421266
Mrs J Close, Continence, Townhead Clinic, Lomond Road,
Coatbridge, ML3 2JN, Tel.: 01236 710256
Mrs G Queen, Continence, Townhead Clinic, Lomond Road,
Coatbridge, ML3 2JN, Tel.: 01236 710256
Mrs D Sneddon, Continence, Townhead Clinic, Lomond Road,
Coatbridge, ML3 2JN, Tel.: 01236 710256
Mrs J Kerr, Community, Infection Control, Clinical Services Dept,
Cleland Hospital, Tel.: 01698 863215
Mrs J McIntyre, Infection Control, Clinical Services Dept, Cleland
Hospital, Tel.: 01698 863215
Mr J White, Infection Control, Clinical Services Dept, Cleland
Hospital, Tel.: 01698 863215
Mrs K Wilson, Co-ordinator, Macmillan, Beckford Lodge, Tel.: 01698
285828
Ms C Weir, TB, Clinical Services Dept, Cleland Hospital, Tel.: 01698
863215
Mrs J Chalmers, Tissue Viability, Clinical Services Dept, Cleland
Hospital, Tel.: 01698 863215
Mrs L Jack, Tissue Viability, Clinical Services Dept, Cleland Hospital,
Tel.: 01698 863215
The Homeless/Travellers & Asylum Seekers
Mrs R Robertson, Nurse Co-ordinator, Homeless, Udston Hospital,
Tel.: 01698 245000

Clydesdale Community Health Partnership

Roadmeetings Hospital
Goremire Road
CARLUKE
ML8 4PS
Tel.: 01555 772271

Admin & Senior Management
Mrs M Aitken, General Manager, Roadmeetings Hospital, Tel.:
01555 772271
Mrs V Mackintosh, Clinical Development Manager, Roadmeetings
Hospital, Tel.: 01555 772271
Child Health Records
Child Health Records, Community Services Dept, Cleland Hospital,
Bellside Road, Cleland, Motherwell, ML1 5NR, Tel.: 01698 861095
District Nursing
Biggar Health Centre, Southcroft Road, Biggar, ML12 6AF, Tel.:
01899 220383
Braeside Clinic, 4 Braeside Terrace, Kirkmuirhill, ML11 9SD, Tel.:
01555 890413
Carluke Health Centre, Market Place, Carluke, ML8 4BP, Tel.: 01555
770635
Carnwath Health Centre, 7 Biggar Road, Carnwath, ML11 8HJ, Tel.:
01555 840775
Carstairs Surgery, School Road, Carstairs, Tel.: 01555 870512
Douglas Cottage, Douglas, ML11 0RE, Tel.: 01555 851446

Forth Clinic, Main Street, Forth, Tel.: 01555 811476
Lanark Health Centre, Woodstock Road, Lanark, ML11 7DH, Tel.:
01555 667150
Smoking Cessation
Mrs R Henderson, Smoking Cessation Co-ordinator, Roadmeetings
Hospital, Tel.: 01555 772271
Specialist Nursing Services
Mrs J Close, Continence, Townhead Clinic, Lomond Road,
Coatbridge, ML3 2JN, Tel.: 01236 710256
Mrs G Queen, Continence, Townhead Clinic, Lomond Road,
Coatbridge, ML3 2JN, Tel.: 01236 710256
Mrs D Sneddon, Continence, Townhead Clinic, Lomond Road,
Coatbridge, ML3 2JN, Tel.: 01236 710256
Mrs A Allington, Nurse, Diana, Coathill Hospital, Tel.: 01236 421266
Mrs M Robertson, Nurse, Diana, Coathill Hospital, Tel.: 01236
421266
Mrs J Kerr, Community, Infection Control, Clinical Services Dept,
Cleland Hospital, Tel.: 01698 863215
Mrs J McIntyre, Infection Control, Clinical Services Dept, Cleland
Hospital, Tel.: 01698 863215
Mr J White, Infection Control, Clinical Services Dept, Cleland
Hospital, Tel.: 01698 863215
Mrs K Wilson, Co-ordinator, Macmillan, Beckford Lodge, Tel.: 01698
285828
Ms C Weir, TB, Clinical Services Dept, Cleland Hospital, Tel.: 01698
863215
Mrs J Chalmers, Tissue Viability, Clinical Services Dept, Cleland
Hospital, Tel.: 01698 863215
Mrs L Jack, Tissue Viability, Clinical Services Dept, Cleland Hospital,
Tel.: 01698 863215

Coatbridge Community Health Partnership

Coathill Hospital
Hospital Street
COATBRIDGE
ML5 4DN
Tel.: 01236 707702

Admin & Senior Management
Mrs J Longford, Clinical Service Manager, Coathill Hospital, Hospital
Street, Coatbridge, ML5 4DN, Tel.: 01236 707706
Mr J Wright, General Manager, Coathill Hospital, Hospital Street,
Coatbridge, ML5 4DN, Tel.: 01236 707702
Child Health
Ms P Currie, 'Reach Out' Specialist Children's Service Co-ordinator,
Coathill Hospital, Hospital Street, Coatbridge, ML5 4DN, Tel.: 01236
707760
Mr M McGonigle, Youth Health Services Co-ordinator, Coatbridge
Health Centre, 1 Centre Park Court, Coatbridge, ML5 3AP, Tel.:
01236 432200
Child Health Records
Child Health Records, Adam Avenue Clinic, Adam Avenue, Airdrie,
ML6 6DN,
Child Protection/Safeguarding Children
Child Protection Service, Roadmeetings Hospital, Goremire Road,
Carlluke, Lanarkshire, ML8 4PS,
District Nursing
District Nurses, Coatbridge Health Centre, 1 Centre Park Court,
Coatbridge, ML5 3AP, Tel.: 01236 432200
Family Planning Services
Family Planning Service, Coatbridge Health Centre, 1 Centre Park
Court, Coatbridge, ML5 3AP, Tel.: 01236 432200
Health Visitors
Health Visitors, Coatbridge Health Centre, 1 Centre Park Court,
Coatbridge, ML5 3AP, Tel.: 01236 432200
Other Services
Ms L Brown, Clinical Governance Co-ordinator, Coathill Hospital,
Tel.: 01236 707757

Scotland

Mr P Campbell, Public Health Practitioner, Coathill Hospital, Tel.: 01236 707778

School Nursing
School Health/Nursing Service, Coatbridge Health Centre, 1 Centre Park Court, Coatbridge, ML5 3AP, Tel.: 01236 432200

Smoking Cessation
Co-ordinator, Smoking Cessation Service, Coathill Hospital, Hospital Street, Coatbridge, ML5 4DN, Tel.: 01236 707714

Specialist Nursing Services
Ms I McGonnigle, Nurse, CHD, Coathill Hospital, Hospital Street, Coatbridge, ML5 4DN, Tel.: 01236 707702

East Kilbride Community Health Partnership
Hunter Health Centre
Andrew Street
EAST KILBRIDE
G74 1AD
Tel.: 01355 906009

Admin & Senior Management
Mr C Cunningham, Locality General Manager, East Kilbride Locality, Red Deer Day Centre, Alberta Avenue, East Kilbride, Tel.: 01355 906009

Mrs S Dorrens, Public Health Practitioner, Hunter Health Centre, Andrew Street, East Kilbride,

Dr C Mackintosh, Lead Clinician, Hunter Health Centre, Andrew Street, East Kilbride,

Mr M O'Boyle, Management Accountant, NHS Lanarkshire, Strathclyde Hospital, Motherwell,

Mrs L Smith, Service Development Manager Long Term Conditions, Hunter Health Centre, Andrew Street, East Kilbride,

Ms K Todd, Service Development Manager Public Health, Hunter Health Centre, Andrew Street, East Kilbride,

Child Health Records
Child Health Records, Community Health Dept, Udston Hospital, Tel.: 01698 826770

District Nursing
Greenhills Health Centre, Tel.: 01335 234325

Hunter Health Centre, Andrew Street, East Kilbride, G74 1AD, Tel.: 01355 239111

Family Planning Services
Greenhills Health Centre, Family Planning, Tel.: 01335 234325

Hunter Health Centre, Family Planning, Andrew Street, East Kilbride, G74 1AD, Tel.: 01355 239111

Pharmacy
Mrs F Penny, Pharmacist, Greenhills Health Centre, 20 Greenhills Square, East Kilbride,

Hamilton/Blantyre/Larkhall Community Health Partnership
Udston Hospital
Farm Road
BURNBANK, ML3 9LA
Tel.: 01698 723230

Admin & Senior Management
Mrs M Brown, Clinical Development Manager, Udston Hospital, Farm Road, Burnbank, ML3 9LA, Tel.: 01698 723231

Mr G Sage, General Manager, Udston Hospital, Farm Road, Burnbank, ML3 9LA, Tel.: 01698 723230

Child Health
Blantyre Health Centre, 64 Victoria Road, Blantyre,

Larkhall Health Institute, Low Pleasance, Larkhall,

Child Health Records
Ms C Brown, Child Health Dept, Udston Hospital, Burnbank,

Child Protection/Safeguarding Children
Ms A Neilson, Child Protection, Roadmeetings Hospital, Goremire Road, Carluke,

Community Nursing Services
Ms K Wilson, Community Nurse Co-ordinator, Udston Hospital, Farm Road, Burnbank, ML3 9LA, Tel.: 01698 723215

District Nursing
Beckford Lodge, District Nurse Teams, Caird Street, Hamilton, ML8 0AL,

Blantyre Health Centre, District Nurse Teams, 64 Victoria Street, Blantyre,

Larkhall Health Institute, District Nurse Teams, Low Pleasance, Larkhall,

Viewpark Health Centre, District Nurse Teams, 119 Burnhead Road, Viewpark,

Family Planning Services
Ms C Courtney, Family Planning Service, Western Moffat Hospital, Airdrie,

Health Visitors
Beckford Lodge, Health Visitors, Caird Street, Hamilton, ML8 0AL,

Blantyre Health Centre, Health Visitors, 64 Victoria Street, Blantyre,

Larkhall Health Institute, Health Visitors, Low Pleasance, Larkhall,

Viewpark Health Centre, Health Visitors, 119 Burnhead Road, Viewpark,

Liaison Services
Health Discharge Manager, Hairmyres Hospital, East Kilbride,

Other Services
Ms J Aitken, Bereavement Service, Beckford Lodge, Tel.: 01698 285828

Smoking Cessation
Ms N Barr, Blantyre Health Partnership, 1 Station Road, Blantyre, Tel.: 01698 711820

Specialist Nursing Services
Mr M Wotherspoon, Macmillan, Beckford Lodge, Tel.: 01698 285828

The Homeless/Travellers & Asylum Seekers
Ms R Robertson, Health & Homeless Service, Udston Hospital, Tel.: 01698 72325

Lanarkshire Acute Hospitals Division
Centrum Park
Hagmill Road
COATBRIDGE
ML5 4TD
Tel.: 01236 438100

Admin & Senior Management
Mr P Wilson, Director of Nursing,

Community Midwifery
Mrs Y Bronsky, Service Manager - Women & Children's Directorate, Wishaw General Hospital, 50 Netherton Street, Wishaw, ML2 0DP, Tel.: 01698 366363

Ms N Kent, Deputy Service Manager, Wishaw General Hospital, 50 Netherton Street, Wishaw, ML2 0DP, Tel.: 01698 366354

Liaison Services
Ms F Kettles, Liaison, Law Hospital : Discharge Co-ordinator, Law Hospital, Carluke, ML8 5ER, Tel.: 01698 361100 ext 6649

Mrs I McIlwraith, Liaison, Hairmyres Hospital: General Community/Hospital Acute Sister, Hairmyres Hospital, East Kilbride, G75 8RG, Tel.: 01355 220292 ext 5349/534

Ms J McSheffrey, Liaison, Law Hospital : Discharge Co-ordinator, Law Hospital, Carluke, ML8 5ER, Tel.: 01698 361100 ext 6649

Mr T Miller, Liaison, Hairmyres Hospital: General Community/Hospital Acute Sister, Hairmyres Hospital, East Kilbride, G75 8RG, Tel.: 01355 220292 ext 5349/534

Ms M Thorn, Liaison, Law Hospital : Discharge Co-ordinator, Law Hospital, Carluke, ML8 5ER, Tel.: 01698 361100 ext 6649

Specialist Nursing Services
Mrs J Blue, Breast Care, Hairmyres Hospital, Tel.: 01355 220292

Mrs F Irvine, Breast Care, Hairmyres Hospital, Tel.: 01355 220292

Mrs P McKenna, Colorectal, Hairmyres Hospital, Tel.: 01355 220292

Scotland

Ms A Cummings, Diabetic Care, Hairmyres Hospital, Tel.: 01355 220292
Ms A Galbraith, Diabetic Care, Stonehouse Hospital, Stonehouse, Larkhall, ML9 3NT, Tel.: 01698 794019
Ms C Mitchell, Infection Control, Hairmyres Hospital, Tel.: 01355 220292
Mrs J Barrie, Pain Management, Hairmyres Hospital, Tel.: 01355 220292
Ms G Muir, Palliative Care, Hairmyres Hospital, Tel.: 01355 220292
Ms J Wright, Palliative Care, Hairmyres Hospital, Tel.: 01355 220292
Mr E Currie, Respiratory, Hairmyres Hospital, Tel.: 01355 220292
Mrs L Gibson, Respiratory, Hairmyres Hospital, Tel.: 01355 220292
Miss K Mearns, Respiratory, Hairmyres Hospital, Tel.: 01355 220292
Ms D Mitchell, Stoma Care, Hairmyres Hospital, Tel.: 01355 220292
Mrs A McFarlane, Tissue Viability, Hairmyres Hospital, Tel.: 01355 220292
Mrs F Sexton, Urology, Hairmyres Hospital, Tel.: 01355 220292

Lanarkshire Primary Care Division
Strathclyde Hospital
Airbles Road
MOTHERWELL
ML1 3BW
Tel.: 01698 245000

Admin & Senior Management
Mrs A Armstrong, Director of Nursing,
Ms M Forsyth, Clinical Development Manager, Udston Hospital, Farm Road, Burnbank, ML3 9LA, Tel.: 01698 723231
Mrs A Mackintosh, Clinical Development Manager/Head of Community Nursing Services, Roadmeetings Hospital, Goremire Road, Carluke, ML8 4PS, Tel.: 01555 772271
Mr M McAlpine, Operational Support Manager, Roadmeetings Hospital, Tel.: 01555 772271
Mr G Sage, Head of Specialist Nursing Services, Udston Hospital, Farm Road, Burnbank, ML3 9LA, Tel.: 01968 723230
Ms K Wilson, Community Nurse Co-ordinator, Udston Hospital, Farm Road, Burnbank, ML3 9LA, Tel.: 01698 723231

Child Health
Ms A Allington, Community Children's Nursing Service, Tel.: 01236 707712
Ms C McGunnigal, Community Children's Nursing Service, Tel.: 01235 707751
Ms M Robertson, Lead, Community Children's Nursing Service, Tel.: 01236 707712
Ms E Tonner, Community Children's Nursing Service, Tel.: 01236 707751

Child Health Records
Child Health Records, Motherwell, Wishaw, Clydesdale, Forth Clinic, Main Street, Forth, Tel.: 01555 811476
Child Health Records, Motherwell, Wishaw, Clydesdale, Community Services Dept, Cleland Hospital, Bellside Road, Cleland, Motherwell, ML1 5NR, Tel.: 01698 861095
Child Health Records, Hamilton & East Kilbride, Community Health Department, Udston Hospital, Tel.: 01698 826770
Over 5s, Airdrie, Coatbridge & Cumbernauld, Adam Avenue Clinic, Tel.: 01236 769291 ext 139
Under 5s, Airdrie, Coatbridge & Cumbernauld, Condorrat Health Centre, 16 Airdrie Road, Cumbernauld, G67 4JN, Tel.: 01236 723383

Child Protection/Safeguarding Children
Ms A Neilson, Child Protection & Vulnerable Children, Nurse Consultant, Roadmeetings Hospital, Goremire Road, Carluke, ML8 4PS, Tel.: 01555 772271 ext 220

Community Midwifery
Ms Y Bronsky, Supervisor of Midwives, Abronhill Health Centre, Pine Road, Abronhill, Cumbernauld, G67 3BE, Tel.: 01236 731881

District Nursing
Airdrie, Airdrie Health Centre, Monkscourt Avenue, Airdrie, ML6 0JU, Tel.: 01236 769388
Airdrie, Adam Avenue Medical Centre, South Nimmo Street, Airdrie, Tel.: 01236 769291
Clydesdale, Lanark Health Centre, Woodstock Road, Lanark, ML11 7DH, Tel.: 01555 667150
Clydesdale, Carluke Health Centre, Market Place, Carluke, ML8 4BP, Tel.: 01555 770635
Clydesdale, Biggar Health Centre, Southcroft Road, Biggar, ML12 6AF, Tel.: 01899 220383
Coatbridge, Coatbridge Health Centre, Centre Park Court, Coatbridge, ML5 3AP, Tel.: 01236 432200
Ms A Coia, Clinical Development Manager, Strathcyde Hospital, Motherwell LHCC, Aibles Rd, Motherwell, ML1 3BW, Tel.: 01698 254601ext 278
Cumbernauld, Kilsyth Health Centre, Burngreen Park, Kilsyth, G65 0HU, Tel.: 01236 822151
Cumbernauld, Condorrat Health Centre, Airdrie Road, Cumbernauld, G67 4HS, Tel.: 01236 723383
Cumbernauld, Kildrum Health Centre, Afton Road, Cumbernauld, g67 2EU, Tel.: 01236 731711
Cumbernauld, Central Health Centre, Cumbernauld, Tel.: 01236 731771
Cumbernauld, Abronhill Health Centre, Pine Road, Cumbernauld, G67 3BE, Tel.: 01236 731881
East Kilbride, Strathaven Health Centre, The Ward, Strathaven, ML10 6AS, Tel.: 01357 522993
East Kilbride, Greenhills Health Centre, Tel.: 01355 234325
East Kilbride, Hunter Health Centre, Andrew Street, East Kilbride, G74 1AD, Tel.: 01355 239111
Hamilton, Larkhall Health Institute, Low Pleasance, Larkhall, Tel.: 01698 884731
Hamilton, Blantyre Health Centre, Victoria Street, Blantyre, G72 0BS, Tel.: 01698 823583
Hamilton, Carnwath Health Centre, Carnwath, ML11 8HJ, Tel.: 01555 840775
Hamilton, Viewpark Health Centre, Burnhead Street, Viewpark, G71 5RR, Tel.: 01698 810171
Motherwell, Motherwell Health Centre, Tel.: 01698 254601
Motherwell, Bellshill Clinic, Main Street, Bellshill, ML4 1AB, Tel.: 01698 747572
Wishaw, Newmains Health Centre, Tel.: 01698 381006
Wishaw, Shotts Health Centre, Station Road, Shotts, ML7 4BA, Tel.: 01501 820519
Wishaw, Harthill Health Centre, Victoria Road, Harthill, ML7 5QB, Tel.: 01501 751795
Wishaw, Wishaw Health Centre, Kenilworth Avenue, Wishaw, ML2 7BQ, Tel.: 01698 355511

Family Planning Services
Ms C Courtney, Family Planning Services, Western Moffat Hospital, Airdrie,

Learning Disabilities
Mr M McGuigan, Senior Health Care Co-ordinator, Kirklands Hospital, Fallside Road, Bothwell, G71 8BB, Tel.: 01698 861570
Ms J Miller, General Manager, Kirklands Hospital, Fallside Road, Bothwell, G71 8BB, Tel.: 01698 245000
North Lanarkshire Team, Cleland Hospital, Bellside Road, Cleland, Lanarkshire, ML1 5NR, Tel.: 01698 861570
North Lanarkshire Team, Kirklands Hospital, Fallside Road, Bothwell, G71 8BB, Tel.: 01698 855530
South Lanarkshire Team, 45 John Street, Blantyre, G72 0JG, Tel.: 01698 417400
South Lanarkshire Team, Social Work Resources, South Vennel, Lanark, ML11 7JT, Tel.: 01555 673000

Liaison Services
Liaison Services, Health Discharge Manager, Hairmyres Hospital, East Kilbride,

Scotland

Other Services

Ms J Aitken, Bereavement Service, Beckford Lodge, Tel.: 01698 285828

Mrs M Aitken, General Manager, Clydesdale LHCC, Roadmeetings Hospital, Goremire Road, Carluke, ML8 4PS, Tel.: 01555 772271

Mrs J Brown, General Manager, Wishaw LHCC, Newmains Health Centre, Manse Road, Newmains, ML2 9AY, Tel.: 01698 381006

Mr T Bryce, General Manager, Airdrie LHCC, Wester Moffatt Hospital, Tower Road, Airdrie, Tel.: 01236 771058

Mr C Cunningham, General Manager, Motherwell LHCC, Motherwell Health Centre, Windmillhill Street, Motherwell, ML1 1TB, Tel.: 01698 254601

Mr J Loudon, General Manager, East Kilbride LHCC, Greenhills Health Centre, 20 Greenhills Square, East Kilbride, G75 8TA, Tel.: 01355 234325

Mr G Sage, General Manager, Hamilton LHCC, Udston Hospital, Burnbank, Hamilton, ML3 9LA, Tel.: 01698 823255

Mr C Sloey, General Manager, Cumbernauld LHCC, Central Health Centre, North Carbrain Road, Cumbernauld, G67 1EU, Tel.: 01236 731771

Mr J Wright, General Manager, Coatbridge LHCC, Coathill Hospital, Coatbridge, ML5 4DN, Tel.: 01236 421266

Smoking Cessation

Ms N Barr, Blantyre Health Partnership, 1 Station Road, Blantyre, Tel.: 01698 711820

Specialist Nursing Services

Mrs A Lee, Breast Feeding Co-ordinator, Strathclyde Hospital, Tel.: 01698 258788

Mrs D McCormack, Advanced Nurse Practitioner (Research), Udston Hospital, Tel.: 01698 245000

Mrs J Close, Continence, Townhead Clinic, Lomond Road, Coatbridge, ML3 2JN, Tel.: 01236 710256

Mrs G Queen, Continence, Townhead Clinic, Lomond Road, Coatbridge, ML3 2JN, Tel.: 01236 710256

Mrs D Sneddon, Continence, Townhead Clinic, Lomond Road, Coatbridge, ML3 2JN, Tel.: 01236 710256

Mrs A Allington, Nurse, Diana, Coathill Hospital, Tel.: 01236 421266

Mrs M Robertson, Nurse, Diana, Coathill Hospital, Tel.: 01236 421266

Mrs J Kerr, Community, Infection Control, Clinical Services Dept, Cleland Hospital, Tel.: 01698 863215

Mrs J McIntyre, Infection Control, Clinical Services Dept, Cleland Hospital, Tel.: 01698 863215

Mr J White, Infection Control, Clinical Services Dept, Cleland Hospital, Tel.: 01698 863215

Mr M Wotherspoon, Co-ordinator, Macmillan, Beckford Lodge, Tel.: 01698 285828

Mrs H Henderson, Officer, Resuscitation Training, Strathclyde Hospital, Tel.: 01698 245000 ext 4025

Mr T Wales, Officer, Resuscitation Training, Strathclyde Hospital, Tel.: 01698 245000 ext 4025

Ms C Weir, TB, Clinical Services Dept, Cleland Hospital, Tel.: 01698 863215

Mrs J Chalmers, Tissue Viability, Clinical Services Dept, Cleland Hospital, Tel.: 01698 863215

Mrs L Jack, Tissue Viability, Clinical Services Dept, Cleland Hospital, Tel.: 01698 863215

The Homeless/Travellers & Asylum Seekers

Mrs R Robertson, Homeless Nurse Co-ordinator, Udston Hospital, Tel.: 01698 245000

Motherwell Community Health Partnership

Strathclyde Hospital
Airbles Road
MOTHERWELL
ML1 3BW
Tel.: 01698 245083

Admin & Senior Management

Mrs E Wilson, General Manager, Motherwell CHP, Strathclyde Hospital, Tel.: 01698 245083

Child Health Records

Child Health Records, Community Services Dept, Cleland Hospital, Bellside Road, Cleland, Motherwell, ML1 5NR, Tel.: 01698 861095

Community Nursing Services

Bellshill Clinic, Main Street, Bellshill, Tel.: 01698 747572

Motherwell Health Centre, 138-144 Windmill Hill Street, Motherwell, Tel.: 01698 242610

Viewpark, 119 Burnhead Road, Viewpark, Uddingston, Tel.: 01698 810171

District Nursing

Bellshill Clinic, District Nurses, Main Street, Bellshill, Tel.: 01698 747572

Ms A Coia, Service Development Manager, Motherwell Health Centre, Tel.: 01698 245085

Motherwell Health Centre, District Nurse, 138-144 Windmill Hill Street, Motherwell, Tel.: 01698 242610

Mr J Murray, Service Development Manager, Motherwell Health Centre, Tel.: 01698 245085

Viewpark, District Nurses, 119 Burnhead Road, Viewpark, Uddingston, Tel.: 01698 810171

Health Visitors

Bellshill Clinic, Health Visitors, Main Street, Bellshill, Tel.: 01698 747572

Motherwell Health Centre, Health Visitors, 138-144 Windmill Hill Street, Motherwell, Tel.: 01698 242610

Viewpark, Health Visitors, 119 Burnhead Road, Viewpark, Uddingston, Tel.: 01698 810171

Liaison Services

Care Home Liaison Nurses, Strathclyde Hospital, 01698 245000

Smoking Cessation

Bellshill Clinic, Tuesdays 6.30-9pm, Main Street, Bellshill, Tel.: 01698 747572

Motherwell Health Centre, Thursdays 6.30-9pm, 138-144 Windmill Hill Street, Motherwell, Tel.: 01698 242610

Viewpark, Mondays 6.30-9pm, 119 Burnhead Road, Viewpark, Uddingston, Tel.: 01698 810171

North Lanarkshire Community Health Partnership

Central Health Centre
North Carbrain Road
CUMBERNAULD, G67 1BJ
Tel.: 01236 731771

Admin & Senior Management

Mr J Glennie, Service Development Manager, Public Health, Central Health Centre, North Carbrain Road, Cumbernauld, G67 1BJ, Tel.: 01236 731771

Mr S Kerr, General Manager, Central Health Centre, North Carbrain Road, Cumbernauld, G67 1BJ, Tel.: 01236 731771

Ms R McGuffie, Health Promotion Officer, Kildrum Health Centre, Lochlea Road, Cumbernauld, G67 1EU, Tel.: 01236 794104

Ms E O'Keefe, Public Health Practitioner, Kildrum Health Centre, Lochlea Road, Cumbernauld, G67 1EU, Tel.: 01236 794101

Mrs G Queen, Service Development Manager, Long Term Conditions, Central Health Centre, North Carbrain Road, Cumbernauld, G67 1BJ, Tel.: 01236 731771

Ms M Rattray, Operational Support Manager, Central Health Centre, North Carbrain Road, Cumbernauld, G67 1BJ, Tel.: 01236 731771

Child Health

Dr A Kay, Child Health, Central Health Centre, North Carbrain Road, Cumbernauld, G67 1BJ, Tel.: 01236 731771

Child Protection/Safeguarding Children

Mrs S Clark, Health Visitor, Child Protection, Kenilworth Medical Centre, Greenfaulds, Cumbernauld, G67, Tel.: 01236 451805

Scotland

District Nursing

Abronhill Health Centre, Pine Court, Cumbernauld, G67, Tel.: 01236 731881

Central Health Centre, North Carbrain Road, Cumbernauld, G67 1BJ, Tel.: 01236 731771

Condorrat Health Centre, Airdrie Road, Cumbernauld, G67, Tel.: 01236 723383

Kenilworth Medical Centre, Greenfaulds, Cumbernauld, G67, Tel.: 01236 451805

Kildrum Health Centre, Lochlea Road, Cumbernauld, G67 1EU, Tel.: 01236 731711

Kilsyth Health Centre, Burngreen, Kilsyth, G65 0HU, Tel.: 01236 822151

Liaison Services

Liaison Nurses, c/o Lanarkshire Primary Care Operations Division Headquarters, Strathclyde Hospital, Airbles Road, Motherwell, ML1 3BW, Tel.: 01698 245000

School Nursing

School Nurses, Condorrat Health Centre, Airdrie Road, Condorrat, Cumbernauld, G67 4HS, Tel.: 01236 723383

Smoking Cessation

Mrs A MacDonald, Co-ordinator, Abronhill Health Centre, Pine Court, Abronhill, Cumbernauld, G67, Tel.: 01236 731881

Specialist Nursing Services

Other Specialist Nurses, c/o Lanarkshire Primary Care Operations Division Headquarters, Strathclyde Hospital, Airbles Road, Motherwell, ML1 3BW, Tel.: 01698 245000

Ms E O'Keefe, Care of the Elderly, - Diabetes, Public Health Practitioner, Kildrum Health Centre, Cumbernauld, G67 1EU, Tel.: 01236 794101

Ms K Hunter, Nurse, Chronic Disease Management, Condorrat Health Centre, Airdrie Road, Cumbernauld, G67 4HS, Tel.: 01236 723383

Ms K Little, Nurse, Chronic Disease Management, Condorrat Health Centre, Airdrie Road, Cumbernauld, G67 4HS, Tel.: 01236 723383

Wishaw Newmains Shotts Harthill Community Health Partnership

Cleland Hospital
Bellside Road
CLELAND
ML1 5NR
Tel.: 01698 863235

Admin & Senior Management

Mr O Watters, General Manager,

Child Health Records

Ms L Russell, Operational Co-ordinator,

Community Nursing Services

Mr M Jamieson, Clinical Development Manager, Cleland Hospital, Bellside Road, Cleland, ML1 5NR, Tel.: 01698 863225

District Nursing

Ms N Jackson, District Nurse,

Ms S Kelly, District Nurse,

Ms I McMillan, District Nurse,

Health Visitors

Ms C Johnstone, Health Visitor,

Liaison Services

Care Home Liaison Nurses, Strathclyde Hospital, Airbles Road, Motherwell, Tel.: 01698 245000

School Nursing

Ms L Cullen, Public Health Nurse - School Nursing,

Smoking Cessation

Ms K McGhee, Co-ordinator, Smoking Cessation,

Specialist Nursing Services

Mrs M Hogg, Nurse, CHD,

NHS Lothian

East Lothian Community Health Partnership

Edenhall Hospital
Pinkieburn, MUSSELBURGH
EH21 7TZ
Tel.: 0131 536 8002

Admin & Senior Management

Mr D White, General Manager, Edenhall Hospital, Musselburgh, Tel.: 0131 536 8003

Child Health Records

Child Health Records, Community Child Health, Edenhall Hospital, Pinkieburn, Musselburgh, EH21 7TZ, Tel.: 0131 536 8000

Child Protection/Safeguarding Children

Mrs R Boyd, Lead Practitioner, Edenhall Hospital, Musselburgh, Tel.: 0131 536 8013

District Nursing

Mrs E Silence, Nurse Manager, 1st Floor, East Fortune House, Roodlands Hospital, Haddington, EH41 3PF, Tel.: 0131 536 8306

Family Planning Services

Family Planning, Roodlands Hospital, Tel.: 0131 536 8300

Health Visitors

Mrs R Boyd, Lead Practitioner, Edenhall Hospital, Musselburgh, Tel.: 0131 536 8013

Pharmacy

Ms C Lumsden, Prescribing Advisor,

Specialist Nursing Services

Ms F Bayait, Continence, Liberton Hospital, Lasswade Road, Edinburgh, EH16 6UB, Tel.: 0131 536 7800

Ms M Brown, Services Manager, Continence, Allander House, Leith Walk, Edinburgh, Tel.: 0131 537 4567

Ms H Wright, Continence, Liberton Hospital, Lasswade Road, Edinburgh, EH16 6UB, Tel.: 0131 536 7800

Mr G Whiting, Diabetic Care, East Fortune House, Roodlands Hospital, Tel.: 0131 536 8300 ext 58316

Ms C Horsburgh, Infection Control, Dept of Nursing & Quality, Edenhall Hospital, Tel.: 0131 536 8000

Nurses, Macmillan, Roodlands Hospital, Tel.: 0131 536 8300

Ms A Gardiner, Macmillan Nurse, Palliative Care, Roodlands Hospital, Haddington, Tel.: 0131 536 8332

Ms J Maltman, Macmillan Nurse, Palliative Care, Roodlands Hospital, Haddington, Tel.: 0131 536 8332

Mr T McInnes, Macmillan Nurse, Palliative Care, Roodlands Hospital, Haddington, Tel.: 0131 536 8332

Mr J Boyce, Practitioner, Public Health, Edenhall Hospital, Musselburgh, Tel.: 0131 536 8106

Ms L Primmer, Nurse, Tissue Viability, Allander House, Leith Walk, Edinburgh, Tel.: 0131 537 4565

Lothian Primary Care Division

Trust Headquarters, St Roque
Astley Ainslie Hospital, 133 Grange Loan
EDINBURGH
EH9 2HL
Tel.: 0131 537 9000

Admin & Senior Management

Mr M Duncanson, Chief Executive, St Roque, Astley Ainslie Hospital, Tel.: 0131 537 9000

Community Nursing Services

Dr L Pollock, Director of Nursing, St Roque, Astley Ainslie Hospital, Tel.: 0131 537 9510

Learning Disabilities

East Lothian Team, Dunpender, Herdmanflat Hospital, Aberlady Road, Haddington, EH42 3BU, Tel.: 0131 536 8547/8

Scotland

Mr A Littlejohn, Clinical Service Development Manager - Edinburgh, Mid & West Lothian, 65 Morningside Drive, Edinburgh, EH10 5NQ, Tel.: 0131 446 6808

Dr R Lyall, Clinical Director, 65 Morningside Drive, Edinburgh, EH10 5NQ, Tel.: 0131 446 6802

Midlothian Team, CLDT, Suite 7, 2 Lamb's Pend, Penicuik, Midlothian, EH26 8HR, Tel.: 01968 670697

Lothian University Hospitals Division
Trust Headquarters, 51 Little France Crescent
EDINBURGH
EH16 4SA
Tel.: 0131 536 1000
Fax.: 0131 536 1001

Admin & Senior Management
Mr P Campbell, Medicine & Critical Care, Clinical Nurse Manager, Royal Hospital for Sick Children, Edinburgh, EH9 1LF, Tel.: 0131 536 0738

Mrs D Hanley, Surgery & Theatres, Clinical Nurse Manager, Royal Hospital for Sick Children, Edinburgh, EH9 1LF, Tel.: 0131 536 2670

Ms J MacKenzie, Chief Nurse, Royal Hospital for Sick Children, Edinburgh, EH9 1LF, Tel.: 0131 536 0003

Ms J McGill, Community Child Health, Clinical Nurse Manager, Royal Hospital for Sick Children, Edinburgh, EH9 1LF, Tel.: 0131 536 0021

Child Health
Ms C Magennis, Community Children's Nurse, Royal Hosp for Sick Children, 14 Rillbank Terrace, Edinburgh, EH9 1LF, Tel.: 0131 536 0370

Ms R Oliver, Community Children's Nurse, Royal Hosp for Sick Children, 14 Rillbank Terrace, Edinburgh, EH9 1LF, Tel.: 0131 536 0378

Ms P Reid, Community Children's Nurse, Royal Hosp for Sick Children, 14 Rillbank Terrace, Edinburgh, EH9 1LF, Tel.: 0131 536 0367

Ms A Reilly, Staff Nurse, Royal Hosp for Sick Children, 14 Rillbank Terrace, Edinburgh, EH9 1LF, Tel.: 0131 536 0372

Ms C Ridley, Care Co-ordination Facilitator, Royal Hosp for Sick Children, 1Rillbank Terrace, Edinburgh, EH9 1LF, Tel.: 0131 536 0159

Ms C Thompson, Community Children's Nurse, Royal Hosp for Sick Children, 14 Rillbank Terrace, Edinburgh, EH9 1LF,

Ms J Young, Community Children's Nurse, Royal Hosp for Sick Children, 14 Rillbank Terrace, Edinburgh, EH9 1LF,

Community Midwifery
Ms Y Clark, Clinical Manager for Intrapartum & Inpatient Services, Royal Infirmary of Edinburgh, Tel.: 0131 242 2539

Community Midwifery Team - East Lothian, Roodlands Hospital, Haddington, Tel.: 0131 536 8304

Community Midwifery Team - Mid Lothian, Dalkeith Medical Centre, Tel.: 0131 561 5533

Community Midwifery Team - North East Edinburgh, Leith Community Treatment Centre, Tel.: 0131 536 6450

Community Midwifery Team - North West Edinburgh, Corstorphine Hospital for Stockbridge, Murrayfield areas, Tel.: 0131 459 7259

Community Midwifery Team - North West Edinburgh, Pennywell Resource Centre for Great Pilton & Blackhall areas, Tel.: 0131 537 0251

Community Midwifery Team - South Central Edinburgh, Tollcross Health Centre, Tel.: 0131 537 9847

Community Midwifery Team - South East Edinburgh, Craigmillar Medical Centre, Tel.: 0131 536 9630

Community Midwifery Team - South West Edinburgh, Sighthill Health Centre, Tel.: 0131 537 716

Community Midwifery Team - West Lothian Area, South Queensferry Health Centre, Tel.: 0131 537 4465

Community Midwifery Team - West Lothian Area, Armadale Medical Centre, Tel.: 01501 730339

Community Midwifery Team - West Lothian Area, Pentlands Medical Centre, Tel.: 0131 449 8615

Ms I Gardiner, Clinical Manager for Community, Outpatient & Day Assessment Services, Royal Infirmary of Edinburgh, 0131 242 2641

Ms L Kerr, Clinical Manager for Neonatal Services, Royal Infirmary of Edinburgh, Tel.: 0131 242 2585

Ms M Wilson, Chief Midwife, Royal Infirmary of Edinburgh, Tel.: 0131 242 2543

School Nursing
Ms L Heriot, Complex Needs Schools, Graysmill School, Redhall House Drive, Edinburgh, EH14 1JE, Tel.: 0131 443 8096

Specialist Nursing Services
Ms H Sharpe, Royal Hospital for Sick Children, Edinburgh, EH9 1LF, Tel.: 0131 536 0719

Ms A McMurray, Nurse Specialist, Asthma, Royal Hospital for Sick Children, Edinburgh, EH9 1LF, Tel.: 0131 536 0773

Ms O Duncan, Nurse Specialist, Cleft Lip & Palate, Royal Hospital for Sick Children, Edinburgh, EH9 1LF, Tel.: 0131 536 0743

Ms C Smith, Caseload Manager, Continence, - Stoma, Royal Hospital for Sick Children, Edinburgh, EH9 1LF, Tel.: 0131 536 0373

Ms I Boyd, Nurse Specialist, Cystic Fibrosis, Royal Hospital for Sick Children, Edinburgh, EH9 1LF, Tel.: 0131 536 0374

Ms A Malinson, Senior, Nurse Specialist, Cystic Fibrosis, Royal Hospital for Sick Children, Edinburgh, EH9 1LF, Tel.: 0131 536 0362

Ms L Marshall, Nurse Specialist, Diabetic Care, Royal Hospital for Sick Children, Edinburgh, EH9 1LF, Tel.: 0131 536 0735

Ms C O'Brien, Nurse Specialist, Diabetic Care, - Adolescent, Royal Hospital for Sick Children, Edinburgh, EH9 1LF, Tel.: 0131 536 0610

Ms H Richardson, Nurse Specialist, Diabetic Care, Royal Hospital for Sick Children, Edinburgh, EH9 1LF, Tel.: 0131 536 0735

Planning Nurse, Discharges, Royal Hospital for Sick Children, Edinburgh, EH9 1LF, Tel.: 0131 536 0062

Ms J Roach, Support Nurse, Endocrine Surgery, Royal Hospital for Sick Children, Edinburgh, EH9 1LF, Tel.: 0131 536 0807

Ms B Wardhaugh, Nurse Specialist, Endocrine Surgery, Royal Hospital for Sick Children, Edinburgh, EH9 1LF, Tel.: 0131 536 0807

Ms C Brand, Nurse Specialist, Epilepsy, Royal Hospital for Sick Children, Edinburgh, EH9 1LF, Tel.: 0131 536 0767

Ms P Rogers, Nurse Specialist, Gastroenterology, Royal Hospital for Sick Children, Edinburgh, EH9 1LF, Tel.: 0131 536 0797

Ms C Paxton, Nurse Specialist, Nutrition, Royal Hospital for Sick Children, Edinburgh, EH9 1LF, Tel.: 0131 536 0612

Ms C Lyons, Paediatric Outreach Nurse Specialist, Oncology, Royal Hospital for Sick Children, Sciennes Road, Edinburgh, EH9 1LF, Tel.: 0131 536 0427

Ms V McGarry, Co-ordinator, Outreach, Royal Hospital for Sick Children, Edinburgh, EH9 1LF, Tel.: 0131 536 0190

Ms L Cameron, Outreach Nurse Specialist, Paediatrics, - Oncology, Royal Hospital for Sick Children, 17 Millerfield Place, Edinburgh, Tel.: 0131 536 0427

Ms S Smyth, Nurse Specialist, Palliative Care, Royal Hospital for Sick Children, 14 Rillbank Terrace, Edinburgh, EH9 1LF, Tel.: 0131 536 0277

Ms T McGregor, Nurse Specialist, Renal, Royal Hospital for Sick Children, Edinburgh, EH9 1LF, Tel.: 0131 536 0731

Ms L McCarthy, Nurse Specialist, Respiratory, Royal Hospital for Sick Children, Edinburgh, EH9 1LF, Tel.: 0131 536 0000

Ms I Kelly, Nurse Specialist, Rheumatology, Royal Hospital for Sick Children, Edinburgh, EH9 1LF, Tel.: 0131 536 0979

Ms P Emsley, Nurse, Tissue Viability, Royal Hospital for Sick Children, Ward 3, Edinburgh, EH9 1LF, Tel.: 0131 536 0743

Mid Lothian Community Health Partnership
Dalkeith Health Centre
24/26 St Andrew Street
DALKEITH
EH22 1AP
Tel.: 0131 561 5531

Scotland

Admin & Senior Management

Ms M McMillan, Clinical Service Development Manager, Dalkeith Medical Centre, 24 St Andrews Street, Dalkeith, EH22 1AP, Tel.: 0131 561 5538

Mr D White, General Manager, Dalkeith Health Centre, Tel.: 0131 561 5531

Child Health

Ms L Cregan, Clinical Service Development Manager (School Nursing), 10 Chalmers Street, Edinburgh, Tel.: 0131 536 0270

Child Health Records

Ms L Kerr, Manager Child Health Records, Community Child Health, Edenhall Hospital, Pinkieburn, Musselburgh, EH21 7TZ, Tel.: 0131 536 8000

Child Protection/Safeguarding Children

Ms I Beyer, Link Nurse Child Protection, Gorebridge Health Centre, Tel.: 01875 820251

Ms J Ramchurn, Child Protection Adviser, Craigroyston Health Centre, Edinburgh, Tel.: 0131 315 2234

Community Midwifery

Ms M Miller, Team Leader, Community Midwifery, Dalkeith Medical Centre, Tel.: 0131 561 5533

Community Nursing Services

Ms M McMillan, Clinical Service Development Manager, Dalkeith Medical Centre, 24 St Andrews Street, Dalkeith, Tel.: 0131 561 5538

District Nursing

Ms M McMillan, Clinical Service Development Manager, Dalkeith Medical Centre, 24 St Andrews Street, Dalkeith, Tel.: 0131 561 5538

Family Planning Services

Ms L Green, Team Leader, Family Planning & Well Woman Services, Dean Terrace, Edinburgh, Tel.: 0131 315 4827

Learning Disabilities

Ms C Williams, Link Nurse, Cherry Road Resource Centre, Bonnyrigg, Tel.: 0131 663 2239

Liaison Services

Ms S Hardie, Discharge Liaison Nurse, Loanhead Social Work, Tel.: 0131 271 3925

Pharmacy

Ms D Bray, Primary Care Pharmacist, Dalkeith Medical Centre, Tel.: 0131 561 5528

Smoking Cessation

Ms F Doig, Smoking Cessation Co-ordinator, Rosslynlee Hospital, Midlothian, Tel.: 0131 536 7600

Specialist Nursing Services

Ms A McDiarmid, Link Nurse, Cancer, Roslin Surgery, Main Street, Roslin, Tel.: 0131 440 2043

Ms F Bayait, Continence, Liberton Hospital, Lasswade Road, Edinburgh, EH16 6UB, Tel.: 0131 536 7800

Ms H Wright, Continence, Liberton Hospital, Lasswade Road, Edinburgh, EH16 6UB, Tel.: 0131 536 7800

Mr G Whiting, Diabetic Care, East Fortune House, Roodlands Hospital, Tel.: 0131 536 8300 ext 58316

Ms C Horsburgh, Infection Control, Dept of Nursing & Quality, Edenhall Hospital, Tel.: 0131 536 8000

Nurses, Macmillan, Roodlands Hospital, Tel.: 0131 536 8300

Ms L Marr, Practitioner, Public Health, 1 Eskdail Court, Dalkeith, Tel.: 0131 271 3452

Ms S Baird, Link Nurse, Wound Care, Penicuik Health Centre, 37 Imrie Place, Penicuik, Tel.: 01968 671535

Ms A Lyall, Link Nurse, Wound Care, Penicuik Health Centre, 37 Imrie Place, Penicuik, Tel.: 01968 671535

North Edinburgh Community Health Partnership

Corstorphine Hospital
136 Corstorphine Road
EDINBURGH, EH12 6TT
Tel.: 0131 537 9532

Admin & Senior Management

Ms L Cowie, Lead Health Visitor,

Ms F Mitchell, General Manager, Corstorphine Hospital, 136 Corstorphine Road, Edinburgh, EH12 6TT, Tel.: 0131 334 5472

Child Health Records

Child Health Records, 25 Hatton Place, Edinburgh, EH9 1UB, Tel.: 0131 536 0461

Over 5s, Tel.: 0131 536 0286

Under 5s, Tel.: 0131 536 0284

Child Protection/Safeguarding Children

Ms J Ramchurn, Child Protection, Craigroyston Health Clinic, 1b Pennywell Road, Edinburgh, EH4 4PH, Tel.: 0131 315 2121

Community Midwifery

Ms I Gardiner, Community Midwifery Manager,

District Nursing

District Nurses, North West, Corstorphine Hospital, 136 Corstorphine Road, Edinburgh, EH12 6TT, Tel.: 0131 334 5472

District Nurses, North East, Mill Lane Clinic, 5 Mill Lane, Leith, EH6 6TJ, Tel.: 0131 536 8800

Ms H Elliott, North East, District Nurse, Emergencies/Night, (Ansaphone), Tel.: 0131 334 3490

Equipment Loan Services

Ms J Black, NA Home Equipment, Allander House, Leith Walk, Edinburgh, EH6 8NS, Tel.: 0131 537 4576

Family Planning Services

STD Health Advisers, Dept GUM, Royal Infirmary, Lauriston Place, Edinburgh, EH3 9YW, Tel.: 0131 536 2103/4

Health Visitors

Ms L Fraser, Health Visitor,

Health Visitors, Corstorphine Hospital, 136 Corstorphine Road, Edinburgh, EH12 6TT, Tel.: 0131 334 5472

Health Visitors, Mill Lane Clinic, 5 Mill Lane, Leith, EH6 6TJ, Tel.: 0131 536 8800

Other Services

Mr J Shanley, Harm Reduction Team, 22-24 Spittal Street, Edinburgh, EH3 9DU, Tel.: 0131 229 5686

Specialist Nursing Services

Ms J Black, NA Home Equipment, Allander House, Leith Walk, Edinburgh, EH6 8NS, Tel.: 0131 537 4576

Mr J Shanley, Harm Reduction Team, 22-24 Spittal Street, Edinburgh, EH3 9DU, Tel.: 0131 229 5686

Ms S Fife, Specialist Care Co-ordinator, Cancer, Springwell House, Ardmillan Terrace, Edinburgh, EH11 2JL, Tel.: 0131 537 7552

Ms M Brown, Continence, Allander House, Leith Walk, Edinburgh, EH6 8NS, Tel.: 0131 537 4567

Ms L Morrow, Continence, Allander House, Leith Walk, Edinburgh, EH6 8NS, Tel.: 0131 537 4567

Ms M Scott, Facilitator, Diabetic Care, Metabolic Unit, Western General Hospital, EH4 2XU, Tel.: 0131 537 3074

Mr I Forbes, Infection Control, Royal Edinburgh Hospital, Morningside Place, Edinburgh, EH10 5HF, Tel.: 0131 537 6000

Ms S Wilson, Infection Control, Astley Ainslie Hospital, Admin Block, Tel.: 0131 537 9000

South Edinburgh Community Health Partnership

Blackford Pavilion
Astley Ainslie Hospital, 133 Grange Loan
EDINBURGH, EH9 2HL
Tel.: 0131 537 9388

Admin & Senior Management

Mr C Beveridge, General Manager, South West Edinburgh, Sighthill Medical Centre, 380 Calder Road, Edinburgh, EH11 4AU, Tel.: 0131 537 7161

Mr T Montgomery, General Manager, South East Edinburgh, Craigmillar Medical Centre, 106 Niddrie Mains Road, Edinburgh, Tel.: 0131 536 9671

Scotland

Ms F Murphy, General Manager, South Central, Blackford Pavilion, Astley Ainslie Hospital, 133 Grange Loan, Edinburgh, EH9 2HL, Tel.: 0131 537 9388

Child Health Records
Child Health Records, 25 Hatton Place, Edinburgh, EH9 1UB, Tel.: 0131 536 0461
Over 5s, Tel.: 0131 536 0286
Under 5s, Tel.: 0131 536 0284

Child Protection/Safeguarding Children
Ms J Ramchurn, Child Protection, Craigroyston Health Clinic, 1b Pennywell Road, Edinburgh, EH4 4PH, Tel.: 0131 315 2121

District Nursing
District Nurses, South West, Sighthill Medical Centre, 380 Calder Road, Edinburgh, EH11 4AU, Tel.: 0131 537 7161
District Nurses, South east, Craigmillar Medical Centre, 106 Niddrie Mains Road, Edinburgh, Tel.: 0131 536 9671
Emergencies/Night, (Ansaphone), or Tel 0131 459 7230, Tel.: 0131 334 3490
Lead - District Nurses/Health Visitors, South Central, Blackford Pavilion, Astley Ainslie Hospital, 133 Grange Loan, Edinburgh, EH9 2HL, Tel.: 0131 537 9388

Family Planning Services
STD Health Advisers, Dept GUM, Royal Infirmary, Lauriston Place, Edinburgh, EH3 9YW, Tel.: 0131 536 2103/4

Health Visitors
Health Visitors, South East Edinburgh, Craigmillar Medical Centre, 106 Niddrie Mains Road, Edinburgh, Tel.: 0131 536 9671
Health Visitors, South West Edinburgh, Sighthill Medical Centre, 380 Calder Road, Edinburgh, EH11 4AU, Tel.: 0131 537 7161

Other Services
Ms J Munro, Joint Equipment Store South Central, 1(B) Slateford Road, Edinburgh, EH11 1NX, Tel.: 0131 313 2435
Ms J O'Rourke, N/A Home Equipment South East, Joint Equipment Store, Slakeford Road, Edinburgh, Tel.: 0131 537 4576
Mr J Shanley, Harm Reduction Team, 22-24 Spittal Street, Edinburgh, EH3 9DU, Tel.: 0131 229 5686

Specialist Nursing Services
Ms S Fife, Specialist Care Co-ordinator, Cancer, Springwell House, Ardmillan Terrace, Edinburgh, EH11 2JL, Tel.: 0131 537 7552
Ms M Brown, Continence, Allander House, Leith Walk, Edinburgh, EH6 8NS, Tel.: 0131 537 4567
Ms L Morrow, Continence, Allander House, Leith Walk, Edinburgh, EH6 8NS, Tel.: 0131 537 4567
Ms M Scott, Facilitator, Diabetic Care, Metabolic Unit, Western General Hospital, EH4 2XU, Tel.: 0131 537 3074
Mr I Forbes, Infection Control, Royal Edinburgh Hospital, Morningside Place, Edinburgh, EH10 5HF, Tel.: 0131 537 6000
Ms S Wilson, Infection Control, Astley Ainsley Hospital, Admin Block, Tel.: 0131 537 9000

West Lothian Community Health Partnership

Admin & Senior Management
General Manager,

West Lothian Primary Care Division

Trust Headquarters, Primary Care Directorate
Bangour Village Hospital
BROXBURN
EH52 6LW
Tel.: 01506 419666

Admin & Senior Management
Miss E M Campbell, Director of Nursing, St Johns Hospital at Howden, Tel.: 01506 419666
Mr D Small, General Manager,

Child Health
Mrs S McGill, Community Children's Nurse Service, St Johns Hospital at Howden, Tel.: 01506 419666

Mrs P McLean, Community Children's Nurse Service, St Johns Hospital at Howden, Tel.: 01506 419666
Ms D Trainor, Lead Nurse for Community Child & Health, Strathbrock Partnership Centre, 189a West Main Street, Broxburn, EH52 5LH, Tel.: 01506 771841/3

Child Health Records
Dr H Hammond, Consultant Community Paediatrician, St Johns Hospital at Howden, Tel.: 01506 419666

Child Protection/Safeguarding Children
Ms D Trainor, Child Protection, Strathbrock Partnership Centre, 189a West Main Street, Broxburn, EH52 5LH, Tel.: 01506 771841/3

Community Midwifery
Community Midwifery Services, Maternity Unit, St Johns Hospital, EH54 6PP, Tel.: 01506 419666
Mrs S McDonald, Women & Children's Services Manager, St Johns Hospital at Howden. Howden Road West, Livingston, EH54 6PP, Tel.: 01506 419666 ext 2072
Ms F McGuire, Community Midwifery Manager, Bathgate Primary Care Centre, Whitburn Rd, Bathgate, EH48 2SS, Tel.: 01506 651839
Ms S Smith, Clinical Midwifery Specialist, St Johns Hospital at Howden,
Ms S Stewart, Assistant Women & Children, Services Manager, St Johns Hospital at Howden, Tel.: 01506 419666

District Nursing
Ms C Bebbington, Locality Manager, West, Bathgate Primary Care Centre, Whitburn Road, Bathgate, EH48 2SS, Tel.: 01506 651824
Ms G Cottrell, Locality Manager, Central, Howden Health Centre, Livingston, EH54 6TP, Tel.: 01506 423873
Ms D Trainor, Locality Manager, East, Strathbrock Partnership Centre, 189a West Main Street, Broxburn, EH52 5LH, Tel.: 01506 771841/3

Family Planning Services
Ms G Cottrell, Howden Health Centre, Livingston, EH54 6TP, Tel.: 01506 423873

HIV/AIDS
Mr M Ogilvie, Dedridge Health Centre, Livingston, Tel.: 01506 414586

Liaison Services
Ms J Cooper, Howden Health Centre, Livingston, EH54 6TP, Tel.: 01506 418518
Ms M Melrose, Howden Health Centre, Livingston, EH54 6TP, Tel.: 01506 418518

Other Services
Ms G Cottrell, Locality Drug Clinic, Howden Health Clinic, Livingston, Tel.: 01506 423873
Ms L Maguire, Manual Handling, St Johns Hospital at Howden, Tel.: 01506 419666
Ms L Middlemist, Public Health Practitioner, Strathbrock Partnership Centre, Broxburn, Tel.: 01506 771849

School Nursing
Dr H Hammond, Consultant Paediatrician - School Health Service, St John's Hospital, Tel.: 01506 419666 ext 2783

Smoking Cessation
Ms H Connelly, Howden Health Centre, Livingston, EH54 6TP, Tel.: 01506 419666

Specialist Nursing Services
Ms S Black, Asthma, - Respiratory, St Johns Hospital at Howden, Tel.: 01506 419666
Ms M Smith, Asthma, - Respiratory, St Johns Hospital at Howden, Tel.: 01506 419666
Ms R Small, Breast Care, St Johns Hospital at Howden, Tel.: 01506 419666
Ms F Divers, Cardiac Rehabilitation, St Johns Hospital at Howden, Tel.: 01506 419666
Ms J MacCallum, Continence, Strathbrock Partnership Centre, 189a West Main Street, Broxburn, EH52 5LH, Tel.: 01506 771865
Ms L Young, Continence, Strathbrock Partnership Centre, 189a West Main Street, Broxburn, EH52 5LH, Tel.: 01506 771865

Scotland

Ms R Early, Diabetic Care, St Johns Hospital at Howden, Tel.: 01506 419666

Ms H Whitty, Diabetic Care, St Johns Hospital at Howden, Tel.: 01506 419666

Ms C Calder, Infection Control, St Johns Hospital at Howden, Tel.: 01506 419666

Ms D Harris, Infection Control, St Johns Hospital at Howden, Tel.: 01506 419666

Ms D Bennett, Palliative Care, c/o Dedridge Health Centre, Livingston, EH54 6QQ, Tel.: 01506 414586

Ms S Rae, Palliative Care, c/o Dedridge Health Centre, Livingston, EH54 6QQ, Tel.: 01506 414586

Ms A Simpson, Stoma Care, St Johns Hospital at Howden, Tel.: 01506 419666

Ms R Ropier, Tissue Viability, St Johns Hospital at Howden, Tel.: 01506 419666

The Homeless/Travellers & Asylum Seekers
Ms D Loughlin, St Johns Hospital at Howden, Tel.: 01506 419666

NHS Orkney

NHS Orkney
Community Nursing Dept
The Health Centre
New Scapa Road
KIRKWALL
Orkney
KW15 1BQ
Tel.: 01856 885400

Admin & Senior Management
Ms K Bree, Director of Nursing,
Child Health Records
Child Health Records, Health Centre, New Scapa Road, Kirkwall, KW15 1BQ, Tel.: 01856 888041
Child Protection/Safeguarding Children
Ms K Bree, Director of Nursing, Child Protection, Garden House, New Scapa Road, Kirkwall, Tel.: 01856 888288
Clinical Leads (NSF)
Ms M Mackie, Lead, Maternity Unit, Balfour Hospital, New Scapa Road, Kirkwall, Tel.: 01856 888002
Ms R Wood, Lead, Acute Services, Balfour Hospital, New Scapa Road, Kirkwall,
Mr K Farrer, Clinical Lead, Cancer, Balfour Hospital, New Scapa Road, Kirkwall, Tel.: 01856 888294
Ms H Tait, Clinical Lead, Care of the Elderly, Balfour Hospital, New Scapa Road, Kirkwall, Tel.: 01856 888046
Ms J Groundwater, Clinical Lead, CHD, Balfour Hospital, New Scapa Road, Kirkwall, Tel.: 01856 888195
Community Midwifery
Mrs M Mackie, Team Leader, Head of Midwifery, Balfour Hospital, New Scapa Road, Kirkwall, Orkney Isles, KW15 1BH, Tel.: 01856 888238
Community Nursing Services
Ms L Croy, Team Leader, Community Nursing Department, The Health Centre, New Scapa Road, Kirkwall, KW15 1BQ, Tel.: 01856 888191
Ms M O'Sullivan, Team Leader, Community Nursing Department, The Health Centre, New Scapa Road, Kirkwall, KW15 1BQ, Tel.: 01856 888155
Ms S Wan, Team Leader, Community Nursing Department, The Health Centre, New Scapa Road, Kirkwall, KW15 1BQ, Tel.: 01856 888041
District Nursing
District Nurses, Health Centre, New Scapa Road, Kirkwall, KW15 1BQ, Tel.: 01856 888041
Family Planning Services
Family Planning Service, Service provided by GP's,

Health Visitors
Health Visitors, Health Centre, New Scapa Road, Kirkwall, KW15 1BQ, Tel.: 01856 888041
Learning Disabilities
Mrs L Croy, Team Leader, Service Provided by Multidisciplinary Team, Tel.: 01856 888155
Liaison Services
Ms M Graham, Liaison/Discharge Co-ordinators, Balfour Hospital, New Scapa Road, Kirkwall, KW15 1BX, Tel.: 01856 888280
Pharmacy
Ms F Scott, Pharmacy Facilitator, Pharmacy Department, Balfour Hospital, Kirkwall, KW15 1BX, Tel.: 01856 888015
School Nursing
School Health/Nursing Services, Health Centre, New Scapa Road, Kirkwall, KW15 1BQ, Tel.: 01856 888262
Ms M Swannie, School Nursing, Health Centre, New Scapa Road, Kirkwall, KW15 1BQ, Tel.: 01856 888262
Smoking Cessation
Ms A Laird, Smoking Cessation Officer, Health Promotion Dept, Victoria Street, Kirkwall, KW15 1BQ, Tel.: 01856 879810
Specialist Nursing Services
Mr D Sinclair, Dementia, Health Centre, New Scapa Road, Kirkwall, KW15 1BQ, Tel.: 01856 852121
Mr K Farrer, Cancer, - Palliative Care, Balfour Hospital, New Scapa Road, Kirkwall, KW15 1BX, Tel.: 01856 888294
Ms M O'Sullivan, Team Leader, Continence, Health Centre, New Scapa Road, Kirkwall, KW15 1BQ, Tel.: 01856 888155
Ms C Page, Diabetic Care, Health Centre, New Scapa Road, Kirkwall, KW15 1BQ, Tel.: 01856 888218
Mr G Wharton, Public Health, Senior Nurse, Infection Control, Balfour Hospital, Tel.: 01856 888059
Ms A Rae, Oncology, Macmillan House, Balfour Hospital, New Scapa Road, Kirkwall, KW15 1BX, Tel.: 01856 888120

NHS Shetland

NHS Shetland
Headquarters, Brevik House
South Road
LERWICK
Shetland
ZE1 0RB
Tel.: 01595 743060

Admin & Senior Management
Miss S Laurenson, Chief Executive, Brevik House, Lerwick, Shetland, ZE1 0RB, Tel.: 01595 743063
Child Health
Ms J Kidson, Child & Adolescent Community Psychiatric Nursing Service, Tel.: 01595 743006
Ms K Anderson, Community Children's Nurse, Paediatrics, Tel.: 01595 743362
Child Protection/Safeguarding Children
Ms A Edge, Senior Nurse, Lerwick Health Centre, South Road, Lerwick, ZE1 0TB, Tel.: 01595 743096
Community Midwifery
Ms A M Edge, Community Senior Nurse, Lerwick Health Centre, South Road, Lerwick, ZE1 0TB, Tel.: 01595 743096
Community Nursing Services
Ms A Edge, Senior Nurse, Lerwick Health Centre, South Road, Lerwick, ZE1 0TB, Tel.: 01595 743339
District Nursing
Based at all 10 Health Centres throughout Shetland, Central Contact No 01595 743339,
Learning Disabilities
Ms A Holmes, Learning Disability Nurse, Lerwick Health Centre, South Road, Lerwick, Shetland, ZE1 0RB, Tel.: 01595 743330

Scotland

School Nursing
School Health/Nursing Services, Gilbert Bain Hospital, Lerwick, Shetland, Tel.: 01595 743076
Specialist Nursing Services
Mrs C Tonge, Health Visitor, Elderly Care, Tel.: 01595 743329
Ms L Cliff, Palliative Care, Tel.: 01595 743092

NHS Tayside

Angus Community Health Partnership
County Buildings
Forfar
ANGUS
DD8 3WS
Tel.: 01307 473197

Admin & Senior Management
Ms C Douglas, Acting Locality Manager, Tel.: 01241 822540
Mr R MacLeod, Associate Director of Nursing, Tayside Primary Care, Murray Royal Hospital, Perth, Tel.: 01738 564247
Miss S Wilson, General Manager,
Child Health Records
Child Health Records, Whitehills Health & Community Care Centre, Station Road, Forfar, DD8 3DY, Tel.: 01307 475259
Child Protection/Safeguarding Children
Mr J Whamond, Child Protection, Whitehills Health & Community Care Centre, Station Road, Forfar, DD8 3DY, Tel.: 01307 475259
Clinical Leads (NSF)
Dr L Murdoch, Clinical Lead, Learning Disabilities,
Dr R Wheater, Clinical Lead, CHD,
Dr G Kramer, Clinical Lead, Diabetic Care,
Community Nursing Services
Community Nursing Services, Whitehills Health & Community Care Centre, Station Road, Forfar, DD8 3DY, Tel.: 01307 475246
District Nursing
District Nurses/Health Visitors, Whitehills Health & Community Care Centre, Station Road, Forfar, DD8 3DY, Tel.: 01307 475246
Mrs E Wilson, District Nursing Service, Tayside PCT Trust Headquarters, Ashludie Hospital, Monifieth, Angus, DD5 4HQ, Tel.: 1382 527804
Family Planning Services
Family Planning Service, Whitehills Health & Community Care Centre, Station Road, Forfar, DD8 3DY, Tel.: 01307 475266
Other Services
Ms L Hamilton, Family Therapy, Abbey Health Centre, East Abbey Street, Arbroath, DD11 1EN, Tel.: 01241 430303
School Nursing
School Health/Nursing Service, Whitehills Health & Community Care Centre, Station Road, Forfar, DD8 3DY, Tel.: 01307 475259
Specialist Nursing Services
Mrs N Craig, Continence, Whitehills Health & Community Care Centre, Station Road, Forfar, DD8 3DY, Tel.: 01307 468383
Ms C Anderson, Diabetic Care, Abbey Health Centre, Tel.: 01241 430303
Ms A MacDonald, Diabetic Care, Abbey Health Centre, Tel.: 01241 430303
Mrs K Craig, Infection Control, Stracathro Hospital, Brechin, DD9 7QA, Tel.: 01356 647291
Mrs G Collie, Macmillan, Macmillan Day Care Centre, Stracathro Hospital, Tel.: 01356 647291
Mrs K Hunter, Macmillan, Macmillan Day Care Centre, Stracathro Hospital, Tel.: 01356 647291
Mrs A Petrie, Macmillan, Macmillan Day Care Centre, Stracathro Hospital, Tel.: 01356 647291
Mrs E Dale, Stoma Care, Stracathro Hospital, Brechin, DD9 7QA, Tel.: 01356 647291

Dundee Community Health Partnership
King's Cross
Ward 3, Clepington Road
DUNDEE
DD3 8EA
Tel.: 01382 424149

Admin & Senior Management
Mr D Lynch, General Manager,
Ms S Macfarlane, Practice Nurse,
Child Health
Ms C Foote, Nurse Co-ordinator, Wallacetown Health Centre, Lyon Street, Dundee, DD4 6RB, Tel.: 01382 459608
Miss S Murray, Project Manager - Child Information Services, Community Child Health Information Services, Ashludie Hospital, Monifieth, Dundee, DD5 4HP, Tel.: 01382 527523
Ms V Samson, PC Link Nurse Children, Westgate Health Centre, Charleston Drive, Dundee, Tel.: 01382 566313
Child Health Records
Miss S Murray, Records Officer, Community Child Health Records, Strathmartine Hospital, Dundee, DD3 0PG, Tel.: 01382 858334
Child Protection/Safeguarding Children
Ms A Burgham, Child Protection, Ryehill Health Centre, 1 Peter Street, Dundee, DD1 4JH, Tel.: 01382 668842
Clinical Leads (NSF)
Dr D Shaw, Clinical Lead, Cancer,
District Nursing
District Nurses Ansaphones, Central & East, Tel.: 01382 450711
District Nurses Ansaphones, West, Tel.: 01382 566842
Ms C Foote, Nurse Co-ordinator, Wallacetown Health Centre, Lyon Street, Dundee, DD4 6RB, Tel.: 01382 459608
Ms K Gibson, District Nurse,
Family Planning Services
Ms C Foote, Nurse Co-ordinator, Wallacetown Health Centre, Lyon Street, Dundee, DD4 6RB, Tel.: 01382 459608
Health Visitors
Ms H McGregor, Health Visitor,
HIV/AIDS
Aids/HIV, Tel.: 01382 204506
Liaison Services
Mr S Kane, Liaison, Mental Health, Wedderburn House, 1 Edward Street, Dundee, DD2 4TW, Tel.: 01382 346050 ext 30012
Smoking Cessation
Ms M Manzie, Co-ordinator, Health Promotion Centre, Kings Cross Hospital, Clepington Road, Dundee, DD3 8EA, Tel.: 01382 818479/424063
Specialist Nursing Services
Ms B James, Multicultural Health, Ryehill Health Centre, Tel.: 01382 666745
Ms W Reid, PC Link Nurses: Adult, Whitfield Health Centre, Tel.: 01382 501189
Ms L Blair, Continence, Wallacetown Health Centre, Tel.: 01382 459608
Ms A Faman, Diabetic Care, Diabetes Centre, Ninewells Hospital, Dundee, DD1 9SY, Tel.: 01382 632293
Ms M Robertson, Diabetic Care, Diabetes Centre, Ninewells Hospital, Dundee, DD1 9SY, Tel.: 01382 632293
Ms D Voigt, Diabetic Care, Diabetes Centre, Ninewells Hospital, Dundee, DD1 9SY, Tel.: 01382 632293
Ms A Norman, Epilepsy, - Adults, Ryehill Health Centre, Tel.: 01382 669392
Nurses, Macmillan, Tel.: 01382 660111

Perth & Kinross Community Health Partnership
Perth Royal Infirmary
PERTH, PH1 1NX
Tel.: 01738 473537

Scotland

Admin & Senior Management
Mr B Nicoll, General Manager, CHP Offices, Perth Royal Infirmary, Perth, PH1 1NX, Tel.: 01738 473537
Child Health Records
Child Health Records, Drumhar Health Centre, North Methven Street, Perth, PH1 5PD, Tel.: 01738 621181
Child Protection/Safeguarding Children
Ms G Proctor, Health Visitor, Child Protection, Drumhar Health Centre, North Methven Street, Perth, PH1 5PD, Tel.: 01738 564295
Community Nursing Services
Community Nursing Services, Drumhar Health Centre, North Methven Street, Perth, PH1 5PD, Tel.: 01738 621181
District Nursing
District Nursing, Drumhar Health Centre, North Methven Street, Perth, PH1 5PD, Tel.: 01738 621181
Health Visitors
Health Visitors, Drumhar Health Centre, North Methven Street, Perth, PH1 5PD, Tel.: 01738 621181
Liaison Services
Paediatric Liaison Nurse, Paediatrics, Drumhar Health Centre, Tel.: 01738 621181
Specialist Nursing Services
Ms W Latham, Practice Nurse Adviser, Drumhar Health Centre, Tel.: 01738 564232
Ms S Aitken, Macmillan,
Ms F Hamilton, Macmillan,
Ms J Potter, Macmillan,
Ms A Gourlay, Co-ordinator, Palliative Care,
The Homeless/Travellers & Asylum Seekers
Ms D Caldwell, Team Leader, Drumhar Health Centre,

Tayside University Hospitals Division
Ninewells Hospital
DUNDEE
DD1 1SY
Tel.: 01382 660111

Child Health
Respiratory Nurse Specialist, Paediatric Unit, Ninewells Hospital & Medical School, Dundee, DD1 9SY, Tel.: 01382 632947
Ms C Don,Community Childrens Nursel, Tel.: 01738 473287
Ms J Fitzgerald, Senior Paediatric Nurse Acute, Tel.: 01382 633647
Ms K Lawrence, Paediatric Epilepsy Nurse Specialist, Paediatric Unit, Ninewells Hospital & Medical School, Dundee, DD1 9SY, Tel.: 01382 636241
Ms K McIntyre, Paediatric Gastroenterology, Tel.: 01382 632949
Ms K McIntyre, Paediatric Oncology CLIC Nurse Specialist, Paediatric Unit, Ninewells Hospital & Medical School, Dundee, DD1 9SY, Tel.: 01382 632934
Ms G Milne, Paediatric Cystic Fibrosis Nurse Specialist, Paediatric Unit, Ninewells Hospital & Medical School, Dundee, DD1 9SY, Tel.: 01382 636584
Ms J Milne, Paediatric Outreach, Tel.: 01382 632949
Paediatric & Child Health Team, Ninewells Hospital, Dundee, DD1 9SY, Tel.: 01382 660111
Ms S Russell, Paediatric Outreach, Tel.: 01382 632949
Ms G Steel, Paediatric Oncology CLIC Nurse Specialist, Paediatric Unit, Ninewells Hospital & Medical School, Dundee, DD1 9SY, Tel.: 01382 632934
Ms L Wiggin, Clinical Team Manager/Head of Paediatric Nursing, Tel.: 01382 632971
Ms A Wright, Lead Paediatric Nurse Neonates, Tel.: 01382 633840
Child Protection
Tayside Child Protection Nurse 01738 473455 Mob. 0799 091 2448
Community Midwifery
Perth City & Kinross Area, Midwife, Perth Royal Infirmary, Taymount Terrace, Perth, Tayside, PH1 1NX, Tel.: 01738 473420
Directorate of Women & Child Health, Ninewells Hospital & Medical

School, Dundee, Tayside, DD1 9SY, Tel.: 01382 660111 ext 32812
Emergencies, Ninewells Hospital & Medical School, Dundee, Tayside, DD1 9SY, Tel.: 01382 660111 ext 32141
Team Manager, Women & Child Health, Tayside University Teaching Hospital, Dundee, Tel.: 01382 633114
Miss M Meldrum, Co-ordinator, Ninewells Hospital & Medical School, Dundee, Tayside, DD1 9SY, Tel.: 01382 632812
Ms K Smeaton, Lead Midwife, ANC, Level 7, Ninewells Hospital, Dundee, DD1 9SY, Tel.: 01382 632017
Paediatric Outreach /Community Services
Jeanette Fitzgerald Senior Paediatric Nurse 01382 660111 Ext 33797
Complex Needs Co ordnators Perth & Kinross 01738 564 601
Mob.0779 091 3291
Dundee 01382 435103
Angus 01307 475271 Mob. 0790 987 6735

Community Nurses for Children & Young People (Primary Care)
Perth& Kinross 01738 Mob. 0778 634 4900
Dundee & Angus 01382 451262 Mob. 0790 987 6735

Home Care Co-ordinator
Tayside 01382 632949 Mob.07884 441 452

Neo Natal Services
Case Manager Tayside & N E Fife 01382 660111

Nursing Team Perth &Kinross 01738 473287 Mob.0779 526 6744
Nursing Team Dundee & Angus 01382 632949 Mob. 0788 444 1452

School Nursing
Ms S McLauchlan, School Health, Tel.: 01738 473340

Specialist Nursing Services
Cystic Fibrosis Tayside and N E Fife: 01382 496584 Mobile 0790 417 4011 Bleep 5069
Diabetes Tayside and N E Fife Tel 01382 632981 /632725 Mobiles 0776 993 5525 0788 444 1463 0776 993 5525
Epilepsy Tayside and NE Fife 01382 496241 Mob.07795266744
Oncology / Haematology / Gastroenterology Tayside and N E Fife 01382 632934 Mob.0774 093 7100
Respiritory Tayside 01382 632947 / 01738 473782 Mob. 0779 526 6764

NHS Western Isles

Western Isles Community Health Partnership
Trust Headquarters, Health Board Office
37 South Beach Street
STORNOWAY
Isle of Lewis
HS1 2BN
Tel.: 01851 702997

Admin & Senior Management
Mr M Cook, Community Manager, Western Isles Health Board Offices, Isle of Lewis, Tel.: 01851 702997
Ms S Macleod, Community Liaison Secretary (for info in Lewis & Harris), Health Centre, Stornoway, HS1 2PS, Tel.: 01851 703545/702671
Ms C Morrison, Senior Nurse Community, Health Centre, Stornoway, Isle of Lewis, Tel.: 01851 703545
Ms F Morrison, Community Manager, Western Isles Health Board Offices, Isle of Lewis, Tel.: 01851 702997
Ms I Pritchard, Community Liaison Secretary (for info regarding Uist & Benbecula), Balivanich Clinic, Benbecula, HS7 5LA,
Child Health
Dr D Mathews, Child Health, Western Isles Hospital, Macaulay

Scotland

Road, Stornoway, HS1 2AF, Tel.: 01851 704704
Child Health Records
Ms J Macsween, Child Health Records, Western Isles Health Board
Offices, Isle of Lewis, Tel.: 01851 702997
Child Protection/Safeguarding Children
Mrs A McVie, Health Visitor, Child Protection, Ballivanich Clinic,
Balivanich, Isle of Benbecula, HS7 5LA, Tel.: 01870 602266
Community Midwifery
Ms C MacDonald, Senior Midwife, Western Isles Hospital, Macaulay
Road, Stornaway, Isle of Lewis, HS1 2AF, Tel.: 01851 704704
Community Nursing Services
Ms S Campbell, Team Leader/Family Health Nurse, Habost Clinic,
Ness, Isle of Lewis, Tel.: 01851 810468
Ms A Finlayson, Staff Nurse, Health Centre, Stornoway, Isle of
Lewis, Tel.: 01851 704888
Ms A Fraser, Family Health Nurse/Midwife, Uig/Bernera Medical
Practice, Isle of Lewis, Tel.: 01851 672283
Ms J Macarthur, Team Leader/Family Health Nurse, Carloway
Medical Practice, Isle of Lewis, Tel.: 01851 643333
Ms D Macdonald, Staff Nurse - Lochs, Leurbost Clinic, Lochs, Isle of
Lewis, Tel.: 01851 860471
Ms M Macdonald, Staff Nurse/Midwife - North Harris, North Harris
Medical Practice, Tarbert, Isle of Harris, Tel.: 01859 520421
Ms M Maciver, Team Leader, Uig/Bernera Medical Practice, Isle of
Lewis, Tel.: 01851 672283
Ms M Mackenzie, North Harris Team Leader/Midwife, North Harris
Medical Practice, Isle of Harris, Tel.: 01859 502421
Ms D M Maclean, Team Leader/Midwife - South Harris, Leverburgh
Medical Practice, Isle of Harris, Tel.: 01859 520384
Ms M Maclennan, South Harris, Staff Nurse, Leverburgh Clinic,
South Harris, Isle of Harris, Tel.: 01859 520384
Ms C Macleod, Team Leader, Family Health Nurse Group Medical
Practice, Health Centre Stornoway, Isle of Lewis, Tel.: 01851 703145
Ms J MacLeod, Group Medical Practice, Staff Nurse, Health Centre
Stornoway, Isle of Lewis, Tel.: 01851 703145
Ms M Macritchie, Team Leader, Borve Medical Practice, Isle of
Lewis, Tel.: 01851 850282
Ms R Macrtichie, Broadbay Medical Practice, Staff Nurse, Health
Centre, Stornoway, Isle of Lewis, Tel.: 01851 704888
Ms K McCulloch, Family Health Nurse, Health Centre, Stornoway,
Isle of Lewis, Tel.: 01851 704888
Ms M Montgomery, Lochs, Staff Nurse, Leurbost Clinic, Lochs, Isle
of Lewis, Tel.: 01851 860471
Ms A Morrison, Staff Nurse, Borve Medical Practice, Isle of Lewis,
Tel.: 01851 850282
Ms B Morrison, Staff Nurse, Carloway Medical Practice, Isle of
Lewis, Tel.: 01851 643333
Ms C Morrison, Staff Nurse, Health Centre, Stornoway, Isle of Lewis,
Tel.: 01851 703145
Ms K Morrison, Team Leader - Lochs, Leurbost Clinic, Lochs, Isle of
Lewis, Tel.: 01851 860471
Ms M Murray, Team Leader, Broadbay Medical Practice, Health
Centre Stornoway, Isle of Lewis, Tel.: 01851 704888
Ms P Murray, Staff Nurse, Habost/Group Medical Practice, Harbost
Clinic, Ness, Isle of Lewis, Tel.: 01851 810468
Ms M Smith, Family Health Nurse, Borve Medical Practice, Isle of
Lewis, Tel.: 01851 850282
Ms B Stewart, Staff Nurse, Carloway Medical Practice, Isle of Lewis,
Tel.: 01851 643333
Equipment Loan Services
Mr D Nicholson, Equipment Loan/Provider, Marybank Store,
Stornoway, Isle of Lewis, Tel.: 07811179380
Family Planning Services
Dr R Al-Kamil, Family Planning Clinic, Western Isles Hospital,
Macaulay Road, Stornoway, HS1 2AF, Tel.: 01851 704704
Health Visitors
Ms C Anderson (Trainee), FT, Health Visitor, Stornoway Health
Centre, Isle of Lewis, Tel.: 01851 703545

Ms A Jamieson, PT, Health Visitor, Stornoway Health Centre, Isle of
Lewis, Tel.: 01851 703545
Ms D Macdonald, PT, Health Visitor, Stornoway Health Centre, Isle
of Lewis, Tel.: 01851 703545
Ms S Mavicar, FT, Health Visitor, North Harris Medical Practice,
Tarbert, Isle of Harris, Tel.: 01859 502421
Ms M Munro, FT, Health Visitor, Stornoway Health Centre, Isle of
Lewis, Tel.: 01851 703545
Ms C Smith, PT, Health Visitor, Stornoway Health Centre, Isle of
Lewis, Tel.: 01851 703545
Ms S Wilson, FT, Health Visitor, Stornoway Health Centre, Isle of
Lewis, Tel.: 01851 703545
Learning Disabilities
Ms F Daniels, Learning Disability Nurse, Ardseileach Centre,
MacDonald Road, Stornoway, Isle of Lewis, HS1 2YT, Tel.: 01851
700341
Mr C Hill, Learning Disability Nurse, Ardseileach Centre, MacDonald
Road, Stornoway, Isle of Lewis, HS1 2YT, Tel.: 01851 700341

Dr J Tittmar, Manager Learning Disability, North Harris Medical
Practice, Tarbert, Isle of Harris, HS3 3BG, Tel.: 01859 502421
School Nursing
Mrs C B Macdonald, Health Centre, Stornoway, Isle of Lewis, Tel.:
01851 703545
Specialist Nursing Services
Ms M Graham, Audiology, Co-ordinator, Health Centre, Stornoway,
Isle of Lewis, Tel.: 01851 703545
Ms J Mackenzie, Patient Journey Facilitator, Western Isles Hospital,
Isle of Lewis, Tel.: 01851 704704
Mrs H Hebditch, Breast Care, - Stoma, Western Isles Hospital, Isle of
Lewis, Tel.: 01851 704704
Ms D Wilson, Nurse, Infection Control, Western Isles Hospital, Tel.:
01851 704704
Ms D Parkes, Nurse, Macmillan, Western Isles Hospital, Isle of
Lewis, Tel.: 01851 704704
Ms L Rogers, Nurse, Macmillan, Western Isles Hospital, Isle of
Lewis, Tel.: 01851 704704
Ms C Masson, Liaison Nurse, Stroke Care, Health Centre,
Stornoway, Isle of Lewis, Tel.: 01851 703545
Ms I Maciver, Nurse, Tissue Viability, Health Centre, Stornoway, Isle
of Lewis, Tel.: 01851 703545

Northern Ireland

with major towns and
Primary Care Trust boundaries

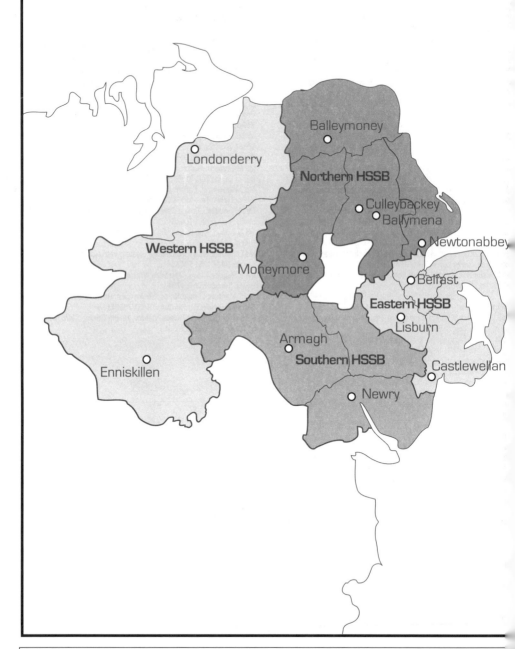

Northern Ireland

Eastern HSSB

Ards LHSCG
Ards Hospital
Church Street, Newtownards
BELFAST
BT23 4AS
Tel.: 028 9151 0222

Admin & Senior Management
Mr B Arthurs, Community Representative,
Ms I Foster, Community Trust Nurse,
Mr A Morris, Community Turst Social Services Rep,
Mr R Morton, General Manager,
Pharmacy
Ms P Finnegan, Pharmacist,

Belfast City Hospital HSS Trust
1 Lisburn Road
BELFAST
Co Antrim
BT9 7AB
Tel.: 028 9032 9241

Admin & Senior Management
Ms E Hayes, Director of Nursing, Belfast City Hospital HSS Trust, 51
Lisburn Road, Belfast, BT9 7AB, Tel.: 028 9032 9241
Child Health
Ms L Boyd, Peripatetic Paediatric ENT, Belfast City Hospital, Tel.:
028 9032 9241 ext 2170
Specialist Nursing Services
Ms E Aughey, Macmillan Oncology Nurse Practitioner, Belvoir Park
Hospital, Tel.: 028 9069 9069 ext 5247
Ms A Bradley, Genetics Nurse/Counsellor, Tel.: 028 902 63555
Ms M A Breen, TB Nurse Specialist, Belfast City Hospital, Tel.: 028
9026 3740 ext 2342
Ms J Buchanan, Senior Infection Control Nurse, Belfast City
Hospital, Tel.: 028 9032 9241 ext 2060
Ms S Cambridge, Diabetes Specialist Nurse, Belfast City Hospital,
Tel.: 028 9032 9241 ext 2555
Ms L Charlton, Cardiology Patient Support Nurse, Belfast City
Hospital, Tel.: 028 9032 9241 ext 2374
Ms B Conway, Macmillan Palliative Care Nurse, Belfast City
Hospital, Tel.: 028 9026 3934
Ms T Coyne, Gynaecology/Oncology Specialist Nurse, Belfast City
Hospital, Tel.: 028 9032 9241 ext 2982
Ms M Daly, Continence Manager (Nursing), Belfast City Hospital,
Tel.: 028 9026 3723
Ms M Devlin, Diabetes Specialist Nurse, Belfast City Hospital, Tel.:
028 9032 9241 ext 2555
Ms B Doherty, Community Renal Nurse, Tel.: 028 9026 3547/3544
Ms Z Doherty, Pre-Dialysis Nurse, Belfast City Hospital, Tel.: 028
9032 9241 ext 3222
Ms G Dunne, Wound Management Nurse, Belfast City Hospital, Tel.:
028 9032 9241 ext 3414
Ms A Finn, Macmillan Palliative Care Nurse, Belfast City Hospital,
Tel.: 028 9032 9241 ext 2015
Ms E J Gray, Breast Care Specialist, Belfast City Hospital, Tel.: 028
9032 9241
Ms C Gregg, Breast Care Specialist, Belfast City Hospital, Tel.: 028
9032 9241
Ms P Hanna, Anticoagulant Nurse, Belfast City Hospital, Tel.: 028
9026 3802 ext 3802
Ms R Hanna, Bronchiectasis Nurse (Respiratory), Belfast City
Hospital, Tel.: 028 9032 9241 ext 2043
Ms H Henderson, Chronic Pain Nurse, Belfast City Hospital, Tel.:
028 9032 9241 ext 3084

Ms K Hughes, Osteoporosis Nurse, Belfast City Hospital, Tel.: 028
9032 9241 ext 2114
Ms G Hutchinson, Heart Failure Nurse Specialist, Belfast City
Hospital, Tel.: 028 9032 9241 ext 2374
Ms L Jeffers, Macmillan Cancer Genetics Nurse, Tel.: 028 9026
3866
Ms K Johnston, Urology Nurse Specialist, Belfast City Hospital, Tel.:
028 9032 9241 ext 2117
Ms S Kane, Cardiac Rehabilitation Nurse, Belfast City Hospital, Tel.:
028 9026 3826
Ms J Kapur, Respiratory Nurse, Belfast City Hospital, Tel.: 028 9032
9241 ext 2076
Ms J Kelly, Urology Nurse Specialist (Action Cancer), Belfast City
Hospital, Tel.: 028 9026 3859
Ms V Keys, Heart Failure Nurse, Belfast City Hospital, Tel.: 028 9032
9241 ext 3724
Ms F Madden, Macmillan Palliative Care Nurse, Belvoir Park
Hospital, Tel.: 028 9069 9069
Ms S Mason, Parkinson Disease Nurse Specialist, Tel.: 028 9026
3920
Ms I McCormack, Dermatology Nurse Practitioner, Belfast City
Hospital, Tel.: 028 9032 9241
Ms K McCoy, Osteoporosis Nurse, Belfast City Hospital, Tel.: 028
9032 9241 ext 2114
Ms J McDonnell, TB Liaison Nurse, Belfast City Hospital, Tel.: 028
9032 9241 ext 2904
Ms M McFadden, Stroke Nurse Specialist, Belfast City Hospital, Tel.:
028 9032 9241
Ms L McFaul, Research Nurse - Breast Services, Belfast City
Hospital, Tel.: 028 9032 9241 ext 3027
Ms K McGuigan, Vascular Nurse Specialist, Belfast City Hospital,
Tel.: 028 9032 9241 ext 2038
Ms D McVey, Acute Pain Nurse, Belfast City Hospital, Tel.: 028 9032
9241 ext 3461
Ms M Mooney, Cardiac Rehabilitation Nurse, Belfast City Hospital,
Tel.: 028 9026 3826
Mr P Mulholland, Heart Failure Nurse Specialist, Belfast City
Hospital, Tel.: 028 9032 9241 ext 2374
Ms P O'Connor, Macmillan Palliative Care Nurse, Belvoir Park
Hospital, Tel.: 028 9069 9069
Ms B O'Kane, Breast Care Specialist, Belfast City Hospital, Tel.: 028
9032 9241
Ms S Parker, Nutritional Nurse Specialist, Belfast City Hospital, Tel.:
028 9032 9241 ext 3084
Ms B Patterson, Cardiac Rehabilitation Nurse, Belfast City Hospital,
Tel.: 028 9026 3826
Ms S Rafferty, COPD Nurse (Respiratory), Belfast City Hospital, Tel.:
028 9032 9241 ext 2904
Ms A Robinson, Lung Cancer Nurse Specialist, Belfast City Hospital,
Tel.: 028 9032 9241
Ms J Rogan, Tissue Viability Nurse, Belfast City Hospital, Tel.: 028
9032 9241 ext 2513
Ms L Rutherfore, Lung Cancer Nurse Specialist, Belfast City
Hospital, Tel.: 028 9032 9241
Ms N Stirling, Tissue Viability Nurse, Belfast City Hospital, Tel.: 028
9032 9241 ext 2513
Ms G Thompson, Nurse Colposcopist Clinical Services, Belfast City
Hospital, Tel.: 028 9026 3901
Ms E Wilson, Macmillan Palliative Care Nurse, Belvoir Park Hospital,
Tel.: 028 9069 9069
Ms C Stewart, Nurse, Respiratory, Belfast City Hospital, Tel.: 028
9032 9241 ext 2342
Ms D Doran, Specialist Nurse, Stoma Care, Belfast City Hospital,
Tel.: 028 9032 9241 ext 3837
Ms R Gilchrist, Specialist Nurse, Stoma Care, Belfast City Hospital,
Tel.: 028 9032 9241 ext 3837

Northern Ireland

Down LHSCG
Corncarane Building
Lower Square
CASTLEWELLAN
BT31 9DX
Tel.: 028 4377 2082

Admin & Senior Management
Ms E McEneaney, Trust Community Nursing Representative,
Ms B Mongan, Social Work Rep,
Mr G Moore, Nursing Representative,
Mr P Turley, Manager,

Down, Lisburn HSS Trust
Trust Headquarters, Lisburn Health Centre
25 Linenhall Street
LISBURN, Co Antrim
BT28 1BH
Tel.: 028 9266 5181

Admin & Senior Management
Mrs M Devlin, Principal Community Nurse/Operations Manager,
Lisburn Health Centre, BT28 1LU, Tel.: 028 92 665181
Mr A Finn, Director of Nursing & Acute Services, Lagan Side House,
Lagan Valley Hospital, Lisburn, Tel.: 028 9250 1200
Child Health
Ms J Chambers, Paediatrics : Down, Pound Lane Clinic,
Downpatrick, BT30 6HY, Tel.: 028 4461 3811
Ms M Duffy, Paediatrics : Lisburn, Hillsborough Health Centre, 29
Ballynahinch Street, Hillsborough, BT26 6AW, Tel.: 028 9268 3609
Mrs E McEneaney, Community Services Manager, Childrens,
Lisburn Health Centre, Linenhall Street, Lisburn, BT28 1LU, Tel.: 028
92 665181
Child Health Records
Child Health Office, 81 Market Street, Downpatrick, BT30 6LZ, Tel.:
028 4461 3511
Child Health Office, Lisburn Health Centre, Tel.: 028 9266 5181 ext
4472
Child Protection/Safeguarding Children
Mrs J McLaughlin, Nurse Advisor, Child Protection, Lisburn Health
Centre, Lisburn, Tel.: 028 9266 5181
Community Midwifery
Ms Z Borrland, Ward Manager, Maternity Services, Lagan Valley
Hospital, 39 Hillsborough Road, Lisburn, Co Antrim, BT28 1JP, Tel.:
02892 665141 ext 2128
Ms R Hood, Senior Principal Nurse/Maternity Services Manager,
Lagan Valley Hospital, 39 Hillsborough Road, Lisburn, Co Antrim,
BT28 1JP, Tel.: 02892 665141 ext 2579
Community Nursing Services
Ms M Devlin, Principal Community Nurse, Lisburn Health Centre,
Linenhall Street, Lisburn, BT28 1LU, Tel.: 028 9266 5181 ext 4511
District Nursing
Ms L Campbell, Community Services Manager, Community
Services, 29 Ballynahinch Street, Hillsborough, BT26 6AW, Tel.: 028
9268 3609
Mr L Clarke, Community Services Manager, Down, Community
Services, Pound Lane, Downpatrick, BT30 6HY, Tel.: 028 4461 3811
Ms J Colligan, Community Services Manager, Lisburn Health Centre,
Tel.: 028 9266 5181
Mrs M Doherty, Primary Care Manager, Newcastle Community
Services, Park Avenue, Newcastle, Co Down, BT33 0DY, Tel.: 028
4372 3346
Mrs M O'Neill, Patient/Primary Care Manager, Down, Community
Services, Park Avenue, Newcastle. Co Down, BT33 0DY, Tel.: 028
4372 3346
Ms M Robertson, Community Services Manager, Dunmurry Health
Centre, 19-21 Upper Dunmurry Lane, Dunmurry, Belfast, BT17 0AA,
Tel.: 028 9030 1029

Family Planning Services
Community Services, Main Street, Ballynahinch, BT24 8TN, Tel.:
028 9756 5456
Downe Hospital, Downpatrick, BT30 6HY, Tel.: 028 4461 3311
Dunmurry Health Centre, 19-21 Upper Dunmurry Lane, Dunmurry,
Belfast, BT17 0AA, Tel.: 028 9030 1029
Lisburn Health Centre, Tel.: 028 9266 5181
Stewartstown Road Health Centre, Belfast, BT17 0FB, Tel.: 028
9060 2705
HIV/AIDS
Ms S Liddle, Market House, The Square, Ballynahinch, BT24 8AE,
Learning Disabilities
Mr G Moore, Senior Nurse, Disability Resource Centre, Downshire
Hospital, Ardglass Road, Downpatrick, BT30 6RA, Tel.: 028 4461
6915
Liaison Services
Mrs E Quinn, Liaison, Lisburn, Lagan Valley Hospital, Lisburn, BT28
1JP, Tel.: 028 9266 5141
Specialist Nursing Services
Ms M McClements, Health Promotion, Market House, The Square,
Ballynahinch, BT24 8AE,
Ms J Morton, Breast Feeding, Market House, The Square,
Ballynahinch, BT24 8AE,
Ms B Murphy, Community Development, Stewartstown Road Health
Centre, Tel.: 028 9060 2705
Ms C Templeton, Domestic Care Scheme, Lagan Valley Hospital,
Tel.: 028 9266 5141
Mrs N Rice, Advisor, Continence, Lisburn Health Centre, Tel.: 028
9266 5181 ext 4432
Mrs H Francey, Lisburn, Diabetic Care, Lisburn Health Centre,
Lisburn, Tel.: 028 9266 5181
Ms A O'Reilly, Down, Diabetic Care, Newcastle Community Services
Park Avenue, Newcastle, BT33 0DY, Tel.: 028 4372 3346
Mrs F Lynch, Tissue Viability, Hillsborough Health Centre, 29
Ballynahinch Street, Hillsborough, BT26 6AW,

Lisburn LHSCG
Lisburn Square House
1-4 Haslems Lane
LISBURN
BT28 1TW
Tel.: 028 9267 7272

Admin & Senior Management
Ms S Browne, Community Trust Social Services,
Ms M Devlin, Community Trust Nursing,
Ms R Dougherty, Social Worker,
Mr S Gibson, Manager,
Ms C Goan, Nursing Manager,

North & West Belfast HSS Trust
Trust Headquarters, Glendinning House
6 Murray Street
BELFAST
BT1 6DP
Tel.: 028 9032 7156
Fax.: 028 9024 9109

Admin & Senior Management
Ms B Connolly, Director of Nursing, HSS Headquarters, Tel.: 028
9032 7156
Child Health Records
Child Health Records, Cupar Street Clinic, 91 Cupar Street, Belfast
BT13 2LJ, Tel.: 028 9032 7613
Child Health Records, Lancaster Street Clinic, 43 Lancaster Street,
Belfast, BT15 1EZ, Tel.: 028 9043 8401
Child Protection/Safeguarding Children
Ms H Tomb, Adviser, Child Protection, Lawther Buildings, Cupar
Street, Belfast, BT13 2LJ, Tel.: 028 9032 0840

Community Nursing Services
Ms A McLernon, Assistant, Director of Nursing, HSS Headquarters, Tel.: 028 9032 7156

District Nursing
Ms S Barr, Primary Care Co-ordinator - District Nurses, 89 Durham Street, Tel.: 028 9027 8822
Ms K Beck, 24 hour Nursing Team Co-ordinator - District Nurses, Tel.: 028 9024 6619
Ms B Denver, Primary Care Co-ordinator - District Nurses, Lancaster Street Clinic, 43 Lancaster Street, Belfast, BT15 1EZ, Tel.: 028 9043 8401

Family Planning Services
Mrs K McCabe, Manager, Lancaster Street Clinic, 43 Lancaster Street, Belfast, BT15 1EZ, Tel.: 028 9043 8401

Health Visitors
Mrs J M McBrinn, Primary Care Co-ordinator - Health Visitors, 89 Durham Street, Tel.: 028 9027 8822
Mrs K McCabe, Primary Care Co-ordinator - Health Visitors, Lancaster Street Clinic, 43 Lancaster Street, Belfast, BT15 1EZ, Tel.: 028 9043 8401

Learning Disabilities
Mrs A Campbell, Co-ordinator, Nursing & Theraputic Services, Everton Complex, 2 Ardoyne Road, Belfast, BT14 7AW, Tel.: 028 9056 6034

Other Services
Ms C Doherty, Ethnic Minorities, Cupar Street Clinic, Belfast, BT13 2LJ, Tel.: 028 9032 7613

School Nursing
Ms A Mulholland, School Nursing Team Leader, Lancaster Street Clinic, 45 Lancaster Street, Belfast, BT15 1EZ, Tel.: 028 9043 8401

Specialist Nursing Services
Ms S McKenna, Lancaster Street Clinic, 43 Lancaster Street, Belfast, BT15 1EZ, Tel.: 028 9043 8401
Ms M McCartan, Continence, Whiterock Health Centre, Whiterock Gardens, Belfast, BT12 7RQ, Tel.: 028 9032 3153
Ms P Woods, Diabetic Care, Lancaster Street Clinic, 43 Lancaster Street, Belfast, BT15 1EZ, Tel.: 028 9043 8401
Ms U McCaffrey, Nurse, Respiratory, Cupar Street Clinic, 91 Cupar Street, Belfast, BT13 2LJ, Tel.: 028 9032 7613

The Homeless/Travellers & Asylum Seekers
Ms S Semple, Lancaster Street Clinic, 43 Lancaster Street, Belfast, BT15 1EZ, Tel.: 028 9043 8401

North & West Belfast LHSCG
Howard Building, Twin Spires Centre
155 Northumberland Street
BELFAST
BT13 2JF
Tel.: 028 9024 4500

Admin & Senior Management
Ms P Cullen, General Manager,
Ms B Liddy, Community Representative,
Ms J McBrinn, Nursing Representative,
Mr T McQuillan, Community Representative,

North Down LHSCG
Bangor Community Hospital
Castle Street
BANGOR
BT20 4TA
Tel.: 028 9147 5109

Admin & Senior Management
Mr W Graham, Manager,
Ms L Johnston, Social Worker Rep,
Ms C Kane, Nursing Rep,
Mr E Munn, Community Rep,

Royal Group of Hospitals & Dental Hospital HSS Trust
Trust Headquarters
274 Grosvenor Road
BELFAST
BT12 6BA
Tel.: 028 9024 0503

Community Midwifery
Mrs E Bannon, Maternity Services Manager, Royal Jubilee Maternity, Grosvenor Road, BT12 6BB, Tel.: 028 9063 5539
Community Midwifery Services North Belfast, Shankill Health Centre, Shankill Parade, Belfast, BT13 1DS, Tel.: 028 9024 2199
Community Midwifery Services South Belfast, 83 Lisburn Road, Belfast, BT9 7AF, Tel.: 028 9026 3530
Community Midwifery Services West Belfast, Ballyowen Health Centre, Andersonstown Road, Belfast, BT11 9BY, Tel.: 028 9060 4151
Mrs C Holt, Clinical Midwifery Manager, Outpatient & Community Services, Royal Jubilee Maternity, Grosvenor Road, Belfast, BT12 6BB, Tel.: 028 90 633802

South & East Belfast HSS Trust
Trust Headquarters, Knockbracken Healthcare Park
Saintfield Road
BELFAST
BT8 8BH
Tel.: 028 9056 5555

Admin & Senior Management
Mr S O'Brien, Head of Adult Services, HSS Headquarters, Tel.: 028 9056 5675
Mr J Veitch, Head of Children's Services, HSS Headquarters, Tel.: 028 9056 5555

Child Health
Ms M McAroe, Manager, Child Health Services, Knockbracken Healthcare Park, Tel.: 028 9056 5656

Child Health Records
Child Health, Child Health Dept, Inver Villa, Knockbracken Healthcare Park, Saintfield Road, Belfast, BT8 8BH, Tel.: 028 9056 5907
School Health, School Health Dept, Inver Villa, Knockbracken Healthcare Park, Saintfield Road, Belfast, BT8 8BH, Tel.: 028 9056 5907

Child Protection/Safeguarding Children
Ms N C Toner, Nurse Manager, Central, Cregagh Clinic, 331 Cregagh Road, Belfast, BT6 0LE, Tel.: 028 9092 4773
Mrs M Kelly, Nurse Manager, South, Child Protection, Dunluce Health Centre, Tel.: 028 9024 0884
Ms D Webb, Nurse Manager, East, Child Protection, Holywood Arches Health Centre, Tel.: 028 9056 3300

Community Nursing Services
Mrs R Campbell, Primary Health Services Manager, Glen Villa, Knockbracken HealthCare Park, Tel.: 028 9056 4954

District Nursing
Mrs K Kane, Nurse Manager, South & East, Holywood Arches Health Centre, Westminster Avenue, Belfast, BT4 1NS, Tel.: 028 9056 3280

Health Visitors
Mrs M Kelly, Nurse Manager, South - Health Visitors, Dunluce Health Centre, Tel.: 028 9024 0884
Ms D Webb, Nurse Manager, East - Health Visitors, Holywood Arches Health Centre, Tel.: 028 9056 3300
Ms W Johnston, Health Visitor, Genetics, Floor A, West Podium Extension, Tower Block, Belfast City Hospital, Tel.: 028 9026 3555

HIV/AIDS
Mrs K Kane, Nurse Manager, Holywood Arches Health Centre, Westminster Avenue, Belfast, BT4 1NS, Tel.: 028 9056 3315

Northern Ireland

Learning Disabilities
Mr N Kelly, Team Manager, 8-10 Edgecumbe Gardens, Belfast, BT4 2EG, Tel.: 02890 204622

School Nursing
School Health/Nursing Service, Dunluce Health Centre, Tel.: 028 9024 0884

Specialist Nursing Services
Ms D Bosanko, Continence, Holywood Arches Health Centre, Westminster Avenue, Belfast, BT4 1NS, Tel.: 028 9056 3370
Ms E Breslin, Diabetic Care, Belvoir Clinic, Drumart Square, Belvoir Park, Belfast, BT8 4DL, Tel.: 028 9056 3370
Mrs T Getgood, Palliative Care, Marie Curie Centre, Kensington Road, Belfast, BT5 6NF, Tel.: 028 9088 2024
Mrs C Graham, Tissue Viability, Holywood Arches Health Centre, Westminster Avenue, Belfast, BT4 1NS, Tel.: 028 9056 3370

South & East Belfast LHSCG

1 Cromac Quay
Gas Works, Ormeau Road
BELFAST
BT7 2JD
Tel.: 028 9043 4004

Admin & Senior Management
Mrs N Bleakney, AHP,
Mr P Bohill, Nurse,
Mr C Bradley, Acute Rep,
Mr M Briggs, Community Rep,
Ms R Campbell, Nurse,
Mr P Gibson, Social Worker,
Ms S Green, Community Rep,
Miss P Harries, Acute Rep,
Mrs V Larmour, AHP,
Ms M Maguire, Manager,
Ms L McDowell, Social Worker,
Mr P McLaughlin, Board Rep,
Dr G Rankin, Community Trust Rep,
Clinical Leads (NSF)
Mr P Gibson, Clinical Lead, Care of the Elderly,
Dr G Rankin, Clinical Lead, Diabetic Care,
Pharmacy
Mr M Ball, Community Pharmacist,

Ulster Community & Hospitals HSS Trust

Trust Headquarters, Health & Care Centre
39 Regent Street
NEWTOWNARDS
Co. Down
BT23 4AD
Tel.: 028 9181 6666

Admin & Senior Management
Mrs I Foster, Deputy Director of Nursing, HSS Headquarters, Tel.: 028 9181 6666
Mrs V Jackson, Director of Nursing Quality & Clinical Effectiveness, Ulster Hospital, Upper Newtownards Road, Dundonald, Tel.: 028 9055 0484
Mrs A Milligan, General Manager, 3 Church Street, Newtonwards, BT23 4AN, Tel.: 028 9151 2168
Mrs L Paul, Director of Primary Care & Community Hospitals, HSS Headquarters, Tel.: 028 9181 6666
Child Health
Ms M Bunting, Child Health, Scrabo Children's Centre, Ards Hospital, Church Street, Newtownards, BT23 4AS, Tel.: 028 9151 0233
Ms J Kirkpatrick, Nurse Specialist, Paediatrics, Scrabo Children's Centre, Ards Hospital, Church Street, Newtownards, BT23 4AS, Tel.: 028 91 510190
Child Health Records
Ms H Patterson, Child Health/School Health Records, Scrabo

Children's Centre, Ards Hospital, Church Street, Newtownards, BT23 4AS, Tel.: 028 9151 0190
Child Protection/Safeguarding Children
Ms I McCready, Child Protection, Donaghadee Health Centre, 1-5 Killaughey Road, Donaghadee, BT21 0BL, Tel.: 028 9188 1176
Mrs J Todd, Child Protection, Donaghadee Health Centre, 1-5 Killaughey Road, Donaghadee, BT21 0BL, Tel.: 028 9188 1176
Community Midwifery
Mrs J Coffey, North Down & Ards Midwifery Service, Kircubbin Health Centre, Kircubbin, Newtownards, BT22 2SQ, Tel.: 028 4273 8974
Mrs A Coulter, North Down & Ards Midwifery Service, Donaghadee Health Centre, 1-5 Killaughey Road, Donaghadee, BT21 0BL, Tel.: 028 9048 4511 ext 2405
Mrs E Hylands, North Down & Ards Midwifery Service, Hollywood Health & Care Centre, Priory Surgery, 28 High Street, Holywood, Co Down, BT18 9AD, Tel.: 028 942 6881
Mrs E McElkerney, Directorate Manager, Woman & Child Health Directorate, Ulster Hospital, Dundonald, Belfast, BT16 1RH, Tel.: 028 9055 0496
Midwifery Service East Belfast, Holywood Arches Health Centre, Westminster Avenue, Belfast, BT4 1NS, Tel.: 028 9056 3371
Mrs J Newberry, Community Midwifery Manager, Ulster Hospital, Dundonald, Belfast, BT16 1RH, Tel.: 028 9048 4511
Mrs E Scott, North Down & Ards Midwifery Service, Old Mill Surgery, Ards Hospital, Church Street, Newtownards, BT23 4AS, Tel.: 028 9181 8518
Ms C Wylie, North Down & Ards Midwifery Service, Comber Health Centre, 5 Newtownards Road, Comber, BT23 5BA, Tel.: 028 9181 8518
Community Nursing Services
Mrs A Milligan, General Manager Primary Care - Health Visiting Lead, 3 Church Street, Newtonwards, Co Down, BT23 4AN, Tel.: 028 91 512168
Mr R Moore, Central Primary Services Manager (Specialist Nursing & Clinical Governance), HSCG Nursing Rep, Primary Care Office, 3 Church Street, Newtownards, Co Down, BT23 4AN, Tel.: 028 9181 6666
Ms A Rankin, Primary Services Manager (North Down Zone) - District Nursing, Prof Ld HSCG Nurs Rep, Bangor Admin, Newtownards Road, Bangor, Co Down, BT20 4LB or Holywood Health, Tel.: 028 91 468521
Mrs A Rankin, Primary Services Manager (Ards & Peninsula Zone) - District Nursing Lead, James Street FRC, James Street, Newtownards, Co Down, BT23 4EP, Tel.: 028 9181 8518
District Nursing
Ms H Finlay, Patient Services Manager - District Nursing, Bangor Administration, Newtownards Road, Bangor, BT20 4LB, Tel.: 028 9146 8521
Mrs A Rankin, Patient Services Manager - District Nursing, James Street FRC, James Street, Newtownards, BT23 4EP, Tel.: 028 9181 6666
Ms A Wightman, Nurse Manager - District Nursing, FRC James Street, Newtownards, Co Down, BT23 4EP, Tel.: 028 9181 8518
Ms B Wilson, Nurse Manager - District Nursing, Bangor Administration, Newtownards Road, Bangor, Co Down, BT20 4LB, Tel.: 028 9146 8521
Family Planning Services
Provided by North & West Belfast Trust, Clinics held at Bangor HC, Holywood Health & Care Centre & Regent Street Health & Care Centre,
Health Visitors
Ms M F McManus, Services Manager - Health Visiting, Donaghadee Health Centre, 1-5 Killaughey Road, Donaghadee, Co Down, BT21 0BL, Tel.: 028 9188 3775
Ms M McMurray, Nurse Manager - Health Visiting, Donaghadee Health Centre, 1-5 Killaughey Road, Donaghadee, Co Down, BT21 0BL, Tel.: 028 9188 3775

Learning Disabilities

Mr D Bradley, Programme Head, Health & Care Centre, Regent Street, Newtownards, BT23 4AL, Tel.: 028 9147 9657

Mr D Bradley, Programme Manager, Ards Community Hospital, Church Street, Newtownards, BT23 4AS, Tel.: 028 9181 2661

Community Team, 11-13 Ballyholme Road, Bangor, BT20 5JH, Tel.: 028 9147 9657

Mrs V Jackson, Director of Nursing Quality & Clinical Effectiveness, Ulster Hospital, Upper Newtownards Road, Dundonald, Tel.: 028 9055 0484

Mr G Murray, Lead Nurse Learning Disability, 11-13 Ballyholme Road, Bangor, BT20 5JH, Tel.: 028 9147 9657

Liaison Services

Mr R Moore, Liaison Services - Ethnic Minorities, 3 Church Street, Newtownards, BT23 4AN, Tel.: 028 9181 6666

Other Services

Ms C Sibbald, Behaviour Management, Health Visitor, James Street FRC, James Street, Newtownards, BT23 4EP, Tel.: 028 9181 8518

Ms J Taylor, Health Visitor for Public Health, Dept of Public Health Development, Ards Hospital, Tel.: 028 9181 2661

School Nursing

Ms M Bunting, School Nurses, Scrabo Children's Centre, Ards Hospital, Church Street, Newtownards, BT23 4AS, 028 9151 0233

Smoking Cessation

Ms T Brown, Health Promotion Department, Ards Hospital, Church Street, Newtownards, BT23 4AS, Tel.: 028 9181 2661

Specialist Nursing Services

Ms R Patterson, Nurse, Diabetic Care, Frederick Street Health Centre, 17 Frederick Street, Newtownards, BT23 4LR, Tel.: 028 9181 8518

Ms C Reilly, Nurse, Diabetic Care, Bangor Administration, Newtownards Road, Bangor, BT20 4LB, Tel.: 028 9146 8521

Ms J Sinnerton, Nurse Specialist, Respiratory, Bangor Administration, Newtownards Road, Bangor, BT20 4LB, Tel.: 028 9046 8521

Ms S Henderson, Nurse Specialist, Stoma Care, Holywood Health & Care Centre, 28 High Street, Holywood, BT16 9AD, Tel.: 028 9042 4881

Ms I Bradley, Nurse Specialist, Tissue Viability, Comber Health Centre, 5 Newtownards Road, Comber, BT23 5AU, Tel.: 028 9187 4820

The Homeless/Travellers & Asylum Seekers

Mr R Moore, Liaison, Travellers & Refugees, 3 Church Street, Newtownards, BT23 4AN, Tel.: 028 9151 2167

Northern HSSB

Antrim & Ballymena LHSCG

Unit 17 & 18 Galgorm Courtyard
BALLYMENA, BT42 1HL
Tel.: 028 2563 6740

Admin & Senior Management

Ms E Allen, Primary Care Development,

Ms L McNabney, Chairman of Board,

Causeway HSS Trust

Trust Headquarters
8E Coleraine Road
BALLYMONEY
Co Antrim, N Ireland
BT53 6BP
Tel.: 028 2766 6600

Admin & Senior Management

Mrs P Craig, Assistant Director Community Care & Nursing, Tel.: 028 2766 1325

Mrs M Gordon, Director Primary Care, Elder Care, Nursing & Quality, Tel.: 028 2766 1438

Mr J Toner, Acting Director Childrens Services, Tel.: 028 2766 1337

Child Health

Mrs A Hume, Senior Nurse Manager, 7a Castlerock Road, Coleraine, Co Londonderry, BT51 3HP, Tel.: 028 7034 4831

Ms S Johnston, Paediatric Team Co-ordinator, Child Development Centre, Robinson Hospital, Newal Road, Ballymoney, BT53 6HH, Tel.: 028 2766 0330 ext 4338

Ms S Johnston, Senior Nurse Manager, Child Development Centre, Robinson Hospital, Newal Road, Ballymoney, Tel.: 028 2766 0330

Child Health Records

Ms M Holmes, Manager, Child & School Health Records Dept, Armour Complex, Newal Road, Ballymoney, BT53 6HD, Tel.: 028 2766 1805

Child Protection/Safeguarding Children

Ms A Maybin, Senior Nurse Advisor, Child Protection, Ballymoney Health Centre, Newal Road, Ballymoney, Tel.: 028 2766 0313

Community Midwifery

Mrs V Wallance, Head of Midwifery, Maternity Ward, Causeway Hospital, 4 Newbridge Road, Coleraine, Tel.: 028 7034 6121

Community Nursing Services

Mrs J Elliott, Senior Nurse Manager, 7a Castlerock Road, Coleraine, Co Londonderry, BT51 3HP, Tel.: 028 7034 4831

Mrs M Senior, Senior Nurse Manager, Trust HQ, 8E Coleraine Road, Ballymoney, BT53 6BP, Tel.: 028 2766 1457

Learning Disabilities

Miss R Patterson, Senior Nurse Manager, Community Team, Mountfern Resource Centre, Rugby Avenue, Coleraine, BT52 1JL, Tel.: 028 7034 4700

Liaison Services

Mrs D Hanna, Cardiac Liaison Nurse, Coronary Care Unit, Causeway Hospital, Newbridge Road, Coleraine, 028 7034 6226

Other Services

Mrs C Skeet, Team Co-ordinator, Rapid Response Nursing Team, 8E Coleraine Road, Ballymoney, BT53 6BP, Tel.: 028 2766 1500

School Nursing

Mrs C Anderson, School Nursing Team Leader, Armour Complex, Newal Road, Ballymoney, Tel.: 028 2766 4101

Specialist Nursing Services

Causeway Local Health & Social Care Group, 9 Newal Road, Ballymoney, BT53 6HB, Tel.: 028 2766 8370

Mrs R Reilly, Paediatric Nurse, Continence, Coleraine Community Clinics, 7a Castlerock Road, Coleraine, Tel.: 028 7034 4831

Mrs M Glass, Nurse Specialist, Diabetic Care, Causeway Hospital, 4 Newbridge Road, Coleraine, BT52, Tel.: 028 7034 6265

Mrs D Campbell, Infection Control, Causeway Laboratory, 2 Newbridge Road, Coleraine, BT52 1TP, Tel.: 028 7032 7032

Mr T McVeigh, Nurse Specialist, Macmillan, Robinson Hospital, Newal Road, Ballymoney, Tel.: 028 2766 0322

Nurse Specialist, Multiple Sclerosis, MS Unit, Dalriada Hospital, 1a Coleraine Road, Ballycastle, BT54 6EY, Tel.: 028 2076 1522

Mrs M Kane, Nurse Specialist, Stoma Care, Out Patients Department, Causeway Hospital, 4 Newbridge Road, Coleraine, BT52, Tel.: 028 7034 6264

Mrs S Bellingham, Nurse, Tissue Viability, Trust HQ, 8e Coleraine Road, Ballymoney, Co Antrim, BT53 6BP, Tel.: 028 2766 1284

Causeway LHSCG

9 Newal Road
BALLYMONEY, BT53 6HB
Tel.: 028 2766 8370

Admin & Senior Management

Ms M Gordon, Nurse,

Ms K Lambe, Nurse,

Ms L Lee, Social Worker,

Mr J McCaughan, Community Pharmacist,

Ms F Surgeoner, Manager,

Mr S Vallelly, Social Worker,

Northern Ireland

East Antrim LHSCG

Bungalow 8, Whiteabbey Hospital Site
Doagh Road
NEWTOWNABBEY
BT37 9RH
Tel.: 02890 552242

Admin & Senior Management

Mrs S Blair, Allied Health Professions Rep,
Mr G Gibson, Social Services Rep,
Mr D Johnston, Nursing NHSSB Rep,
Ms T Kennedy, General Manager,
Mr S Logan, Social Work NHSSB Rep,
Ms C McCambridge, Social Services Rep,
Ms K Moore, Community Liaison Lead/Community Rep,
Mrs G Nelson, Nursing Rep,
Mrs L Patton, Nursing Acute Trust Rep,
Mrs R Simpson, Service User Rep,
Mrs H Winning, Community Trust Rep,
Ms L Gracey, Pharmacist,

Homefirst Community HSS Trust

Trust Headquarters, The Cottage
5 Greenmount Avenue
BALLYMENA
Co Antrim
BT43 6DA
Tel.: 028 2563 3700

Admin & Senior Management

Ms E Campbell, Acting Principal Officer, Spruce House, Braid Valley Hospital Site, Cushendall Road, Ballymena, BT43 6HL, Tel.: 028 2563 5543
Mrs U Cunning, Assistant Director Nursing, Spruce House, Braid Valley Hospital Site, Cushendall Road, Ballymena, BT43 6HL, Tel.: 028 2563 5684
Mrs E Graham, Principal Officer, The Surgery, Toome House, 55 Main Street, Toome, BT41 3TF, Tel.: 028 7965 9147
Mrs W Magowan, Senior Nurse Special Projects & Proff Development, Spruce House, Braid Valley Hospital Site, Cushendall Road, Ballymena, BT43 6HL, Tel.: 028 2563 5543
Mrs G Nelson, Principal Officer, Inniscoole Day Centre, Innis Avenue, Rathcoole, Newtownabbey, Tel.: 028 9085 1101

Child Health

Ms M Boyle, Community Childrens Nursing Specialist, 44 King Street, Tel.: 028 7963 1031
Ms S Dennison, Community Children Nursing Specialist, 44 King Street, Tel.: 028 7963 1031
Mrs G Edge, Senior, Childrens Community, Nurse Practitioner, CDC, Ferrard Site, Station Road, Antrim, Tel.: 028 9441 5737
Ms A Hughes, Community Children Nursing Specialist, Glengormley Health Centre, Tel.: 028 9034 2151
Ms P Johnston, Community Childrens Nursing Specialist, Carrickfergus Health Centre, Tel.: 028 9331 5824
Mrs C McCallum, Community Children's Nurse, CDC, Ferrard Site, Station Road, Antrim, Tel.: 028 9441 5742
Mrs H McKenna, Community Childrens Nursing Specialist, Carrickfergus Health Centre, Tel.: 028 9331 5824
Ms S Montgomery, Community Childrens Nursing Specialist, CDC, Ferrard Site, Station Road, Antrim, Tel.: 028 9441 5745
Mrs L Rogers, Team Leader, Community Children's Nurse/Acute Team, Ballymena Health Centre, Cushendall Road, Ballymena, Tel.: 028 2531 3156

Child Health Records

Miss R Johnston, Child Health Department, Homefirst Trust, Briad Valley Site, Cushendall Road, Ballymena, BT43 6HN, Tel.: 028 2563 5409

Child Protection/Safeguarding Children

Mrs D Kerr, Nurse Specialist, Child Protection, Maghera CSC, 3 Church Street, Maghera, Tel.: 028 7954 7471
Ms J Lees, Team Leader, Child Protection, Gurteen House, Holywell Hospital, Steeple Road, Antrim, Tel.: 028 9441 3155
Mrs A McLoughlin, Nurse Specialist, Child Protection, Glengormley CSC, 40 Carnmoney Road, Newtownabbey, BT36 4HR, Tel.: 028 9083 1432

Community Nursing Services

Co-ordinator Nursing Services, Inniscoole Day Centre, Innis Avenue, Rathcoole, Newtownabbey, Tel.: 028 9085 1101
Mrs P McDade, Nurse Manager, The Surgery, Toome House, 55 Main Street, Toome, BT41 3TF, Tel.: 028 7965 9147
Mrs H McKay, Nurse Manager, Spruce House, Braid Valley Hospital Site, Cushendall Road, Ballymena, BT43 6HL, Tel.: 028 2563 5543

District Nursing

Mrs F Brown, Health Visitors, Nurse Manager, Ballymena Health Centre, Cushendall Road, Ballymena, BT43 6HQ, Tel.: 028 2531 3150
Mrs K Elwood, Health Visitors, Nurse Manager, Carrickfergus Health Centre, Taylors Avenue, Carrickfergus, Tel.: 028 9331 5821
Mrs J Foster, Acting Nurse Manager - District Nurses, Station Road, Antrim, BT41 4BS, Tel.: 028 9441 3980
Mrs S Gault, Health Visitors, Nurse Manager, Slemish CSC, Cushendall Road, Ballymena, Tel.: 028 2563 5683
Mrs B Lowry, District Nurses, Nurse Manager, Inniscoole Day Centre, Innis Avenue, Rathcoole, Tel.: 028 9085 1101
Mrs P McDade, District Nurses, Nurse Manager, The Surgery, Toome House, 55 Main Street, Toome, BT41 3TF, Tel.: 028 7965 9147
Mrs M McGuigan, Health Visitors, Nurse Manager, The Diamond Centre, Market Square, Magherafelt, Tel.: 028 7936 1040
Mrs H McKay, District Nurses, Nurse Manager, Slemish Community Services Centre, Braid Valley Hospital Site, Cushendall Road, Ballymena, BT43 6PS, Tel.: 028 2563 5657
Mrs H Morrison, District Nurses, Nurse Manager, Carrickfergus Health Centre, Taylors Avenue, Carrickfergus, BT38 7HT, Tel.: 028 9331 5895

Health Visitors

Ms S Angel, Family Centre, Health Visitor, NSPCC Ballymena Family Support Team, 17-18 Tower Centre, Lower Mill Street, Ballymena, BT43 6AB, Tel.: 028 2564 7999
Ms C Davis, Family Centre, Health Visitor, Newtownabbey Family Centre,, Tel.: 028 9085 4231
Ms S McDade, Family Centre, Health Visitor, Westland Road, Cookstown, Tel.: 028 8672 3933
Ms A Pollock, Family Centre, Health Visitor, Antrim Family Centre, 411-413 Firmount Drive, Greystone Road, Antrim, BT41 1JL, Tel.: 028 9442 8715

Learning Disabilities

Mrs D Morgan, Nurse Manager, Toome House, 55 Main Street, Toome, Tel.: 028 7965 9147

Other Services

Mrs C Barr, HPSS Payments Specialist, Oak Cottage, Braid Valley Hospital Site, Cushendall Road, Ballymena, BT43 6HL, Tel.: 028 2563 5250
Mrs C Bateson, Team Leader Crisis Response, Greystone Offices, Unit 1, Rathenraw Ind Estate, 56 Greystone Road, Antrim, BT41 2SJ, Tel.: 028 9442 7900
Ms M Beare, Principal Officer (Old Age Psychiatry), Noble House, Holywell Hospital, 60 Steeple Road, Antrim, BT41 2RJ, Tel.: 028 9446 5211
Mrs M Irons, Nursing Services Manager, Holywell Hospital, 60 Steeple Road, Antrim, BT41 2RJ, Tel.: 028 9446 5211
Mr T McCabe, Nursing Services Manager, Noble House, Holywell Hospital, 60 Steeple Road, Antrim, BT41 2RJ, Tel.: 028 9446 5211
Ms B Mooney, Co-ordinator - Acute Care at Home, 1 Old Steeple Road, Antrim, BT41 1AF, Tel.: 028 9446 9832

Northern Ireland

Mrs H Morrison, Casefinder Co-ordinator, Antrim Health Centre, Station Road, Antrim, Tel.: 028 9441 3979

Mr C Reilly, Team Leader Community Outreach, Greystone Offices, Unit 1, Rathenraw Ind Estate, 56 Greystone Road, Antrim, BT41 2SJ, Tel.: 028 9442 7920

Mrs E Woolsey, Nursing Services Manager, Noble House, Holywell Hospital, 60 Steeple Road, Antrim, BT41 2RJ, Tel.: 028 9446 5211

School Nursing

Mrs M Coyles, CCN & School Nursing, Nurse Manager, Slemish CSC, Cushendall Road, Ballymena, Tel.: 028 2563 5694

Specialist Nursing Services

Mrs M Laverty, Orthogeriatric Co-ordinator, Community Services Centre, Whiteabbey Hospital, 95 Doagh Road, Newtownabbey, Tel.: 07951 779018

Ms A Laverty, Co-ordinator, Cardiac Rehabilitation, Rockfield Medical Centre, 73 Doury Road, Ballymena, BT43 6JD, Tel.: 028 2563 4437

Mrs K Lowry, Advisor, Continence, Spruce House, Briad Valley Hospital Site, Cushendall Road, Ballymena, BT43 6HL, Tel.: 028 2563 5278

Mrs R Megaw, Diabetic Care, Rockfield Medical Centre, 73 Doury Road, Ballymena, BT43 6JD, Tel.: 028 2565 4437

Mrs S McCann, Nurse Specialist, Epilepsy, Toome House, 55 Main Street, Toomebridge, Tel.: 028 7965 9147

Ms A Casey, Nurse Specialist, Heart Failure, Rockfield Medical Centre, 73 Doury Road, Ballymena, BT43 6JD, Tel.: 028 2563 4437

Ms F Gilmore, Co-ordinator, Palliative Care, Toome House, 55 Main Street, Toomebridge, Tel.: 028 7965 9147

Mrs C Speedy, Nurse Specialist, Respiratory, Rockfield Medical Centre, 73 Doury Road, Ballymena, BT43 6JD, Tel.: 028 2565 4437

Mrs R McSwiggan, Nurse Specialist, Tissue Viability, Toome House, 55 Main Street, Toomebridge, Tel.: 028 7965 9147

Mid-Ulster LHSCG

Manor House
High Street, MONEYMORE
BT45 7PB
Tel.: 028 8674 8761

Admin & Senior Management

Mr J Conlon, Community Rep,
Ms E Graham, Trust Nursing Rep,
Mr J McGrath, Manager,
Mr K McLaughlin, Community Rep,
Ms M Murphy, Social Work Rep,

United Hospitals HSS Trust

Trust Headquarters, Bush House
Bush Road
ANTRIM
Ireland
BT41 2QB
Tel.: 028 9442 4000

Admin & Senior Management

Mrs L Martin, Nursing Services Manager, Mid-Ulster Hospital, 59 Hospital Road, Magherafelt, BT45 5EX, Tel.: 028 796 31031 ext 2213

Child Protection/Safeguarding Children

Ms D Kerr, Acting, Nurse Specialist, Child Protection, Acute Hospital Trust, Antrim Family Centre, 411-413 Firmount Drive, Greystone, Antrim, BT41 1JL, Tel.: 028 944 28715

Community Midwifery

Ms M Maxwell, Community Midwifery Manager, Antrim Area Hospital, 45 Bush Road, Antrim, N Ireland, BT41 2RL, Tel.: 028 25 45427

Specialist Nursing Services

Ms M Carlin, Nurse, Macmillan, Mid-Ulster Hospital, 59 Hospital Road, Magherafelt, BT45 5EX, Tel.: 028 796 31031 ext 2397

Southern HSSB

Armagh & Dungannon HSS Trust

Trust Headquarters, St Luke's Hospital
Loughall Road
ARMAGH, BT61 7NQ
Tel.: 028 3752 2381

Child Health

Ms M Rafferty, Child Health, C Floor, South Tyrone Hospital, Corland Road, Dungannon, Tel.: 028 8772 2821

Child Health Records

Over 5s, Dungannon, Dungannon Health Clinic, 38 Thomas Street, Dungannon, Co Tyrone, BT70 1HS, Tel.: 028 8772 3101

Over 5s, Armagh, Victoria House, Tower Hill, Armagh, Tel.: 028 3752 2381

Under 5s, Armagh & Dungannon, Hill Building, St Luke's Hospital, Tel.: 028 3752 2381

Child Protection/Safeguarding Children

Ms M Rafferty, Child Protection, C Floor, South Tyrone Hospital, Corland Road, Dungannon, Tel.: 028 8772 2821

Community Midwifery

Mrs A McElroy, Team Leader, Community Midwives, Level 2, Mullinure Hospital, Loughall Road, Armagh, BT61 7NQ, Tel.: 028 3752 2381 ext 2353

Community Nursing Services

Armagh & Dungannon Community Nursing Services, CN Office, St Luke's Hospital, Armagh, BT61 7NQ, Tel.: 028 3752 2381 ext 2371

District Nursing

Armagh Community Nursing Services, CN Office, St Luke's Hospital, Armagh, BT61 7NQ, Tel.: 028 3752 2381

Dungannon Community Services, C Floor, South Tyrone Hospital, Corland Road, Dungannon, Tel.: 028 8772 2821

Family Planning Services

Mrs C Sutton, Dungannon Health Clinic, 38 Thomas Street, Dungannon, BT70 1HS, Tel.: 028 8772 3101

Health Visitors

Mrs D Graham, Asthma Health Visitor, Armagh Health Centre, Tel.: 028 3752 3165

Learning Disabilities

Mr T Doran, Head of Service, St Lukes Hospital, Armagh, BT61 7NQ, Tel.: 028 3752 2381

Mr A Rush, Team Leader, South Tyrone Hospital, Corland Road, Dungannon, Tel.: 028 8772 2821

Other Services

Mrs F Doran, Macmillan Home Care, Moy Health Centre, Charlemont Street, Moy, BT71 7SL, Tel.: 028 8778 9479

Mrs E Gaillard, Macmillan Home Care, Moy Health Centre, Charlemont Street, Moy, BT71 7SL, Tel.: 028 8778 9479

Mr P Moore, Family Support, Commercial Health Office, 3 The Square, Moy, BT71 7SG, Tel.: 028 8778 9648

Specialist Nursing Services

Ms A McConville, Continence, Commercial Health Office, 3 The Square, Moy, BT71 7SG, Tel.: 028 8778 9649

Ms M Brock, Diabetic Care, F Floor, South Tyrone Hospital, Tel.: 028 8772 2821

Mrs K Lelly, Infection Control, South Tyrone Hospital, Dungannon, BT71 4AU, Tel.: 028 8772 2821

Ms M Donnelly, Sister, Leg Ulcers, Dungannon Clinic, 028 8772 3101

Ms C Doyle, Sister, Leg Ulcers, Mullinure Hospital, Loughall Road, Armagh, Tel.: 028 3752 2381

Ms S McKinstry, Sister, Leg Ulcers, Mullinure Hospital, Loughall Road, Armagh, Tel.: 028 3752 2381

The Homeless/Travellers & Asylum Seekers

Miss C Donnelly, Health Visitor for Travellers, Dr Garvin's Surgery, Barrack Street, Coalisland, Co Tyrone, Tel.: 028 8774 0049

Mrs M McKenna, Armagh Health Centre, Tel.: 028 3752 3165

Northern Ireland

Armagh & Dungannon LHSCG
South Tyrone Hospital Site
Carland Road
DUNGANNON
BT71 4AU
Tel.: 028 8771 3680

Admin & Senior Management
Mr R Cummings, Community Rep,
Ms A Mallon, Community Rep,
Mr J Swail, Pharmacy Rep,
Ms J Toner, Nursing Rep,
Ms D Tunney, General Manager,

Craigavon & Banbridge Community HSS Trust
Trust Headquarters, Bannvale House
10 Moyallen Road
GILFORD
Co Down
BT63 5JX
Tel.: 028 3883 1983

Admin & Senior Management
Mrs R Burns, Director of Elderly & Primary Care/Executive Nurse Director, Bannvale House, 10 Moyallen Road, Gilford, Co Armagh, Tel.: 028 3883 3242
Mrs G Maguire, Assistant Director of Primary Care, Edenderry House, Gilford Road, Portadown, Tel.: 028 3839 8340
Child Health Records
Ms V Doyle, Lurgan Health & Social Services Centre, 100 Sloan Street, Lurgan, Tel.: 028 3832 7824
Child Protection/Safeguarding Children
Mrs U Turbitt, Team Manager, Nurse Specialist, Child Protection, 3 Orchard Business Park, Carn Offices, Portadown, Tel.: 028 3839 8282
Community Midwifery
Mrs M O'Dowd, Midwifery Team Manager, Brownlow Health & Social Services Centre, Legahory, Craigavon, Tel.: 028 3834 1431
District Nursing
Mrs G Caldwell, District Nurse Team Manager, Portadown Health & Social Services Centre, Tavanagh Avenue, Portadown, BT62 3AJ, Tel.: 028 3833 4400
Mrs D Campbell, District Nurse Team Manager, Lurgan Health & Social Services Centre, 100 Sloan Street, Lurgan, BT66 8NX, Tel.: 028 3832 7824
Mrs J Davidson, District Nurse Team Manager, Banbridge Health & Social Services Centre, Scarva Street, Banbridge, BT32 3AD, Tel.: 028 4066 8266
Family Planning Services
Ms S Malumphy, Health Visiting/Family Planning Team Manager, Banbridge Health & Social Services Centre, Scarva Street, Banbridge, Co Down, Tel.: 028 4066 8266
Health Visitors
Mrs S Malumphy, Health Visiting Team Manager (Acting), Banbridge Health & Social Services Centre, Scarva Street, Banbridge, BT32 3AD, Tel.: 028 4066 2866
Mrs M Norris, Health Visiting Team Manager, Portadown Health & Social Services Centre, Tavanagh Avenue, Portadown, BT62 3AJ, Tel.: 028 3833 4400
Mrs B Shields, Health Visiting Team Manager (Acting), Lurgan Health & Social Services Centre, 100 Sloan Street, Lurgan, BT66 8NX, Tel.: 028 3832 7824
Learning Disabilities
Mr P Rooney, Assistant Director of Disability Services, Rosedale, Bannvale House, 10 Moyallen Road, Gilford, Tel.: 028 3883 3248
Mr I Sutherland, Director Learning Disability Services, C&BHSST, Bannvale House, 10 Moyallen Road, Gilford, Tel.: 028 3883 3240

Mrs J Walsh, Community Nursing Team Manager, Moylinn House, Legahory Centre, Craigavon, Tel.: 028 3834 8811
Other Services
Ms F Wright, Clinical & Social Governance Facilitator, 2b Newry Road, Banbridge, Tel.: 028 4062 1700
School Nursing
Mrs R Toner, Specialist Nurse/Health Promotion Manager, 3 Orchard Business Park, Carn Offices, Carn, Portadown, Tel.: 028 3839 8282
Specialist Nursing Services
Ms M Redman, Behaviour Management/ADHD Nurse Specialist, Carn Offices, Orchard Business Park, Carn, Portadown, Tel.: 028 3839 8282
Ms A Ross, Nurse Team Leader, Children, Carn Offices, Orchard Business Park, Carn, Portadown, Tel.: 028 3839 8282
Ms M Thompson, Nurse Team Leader, Continence, Carn Offices, Orchard Business Park, Carn, Portadown, Tel.: 028 3839 8282
Ms F Murphy, Nurse Specialist, Diabetic Care, Carn Offices, Orchard Business Park, Carn, Portadown, Tel.: 028 3839 8282
Ms R Toner, Specialist Nurse/Health Promotion Manager, Macmillan, Carn Offices, Orchard Business Park, Carn, Portadown, Tel.: 028 3839 8282
Ms D McDonagh, Nurse Specialist, Tissue Viability, - Infection Control, Edenderry House, Gilford Road, Portadown, Tel.: 028 3839 8340
The Homeless/Travellers & Asylum Seekers
Ms G Hamilton, Black & Ethnic Minority Health Visitor, Brownlow Health & Social Services Centre, Legahory, Craigavon, Tel.: 028 3834 1431

Craigavon & Banbridge LHSCG
80-82 High Street
LURGAN
BT66 8BB
Tel.: 028 3834 3869

Admin & Senior Management
Ms J Baird, Community Rep,
Ms P Clarke, General Manager,
Ms G Maguire, Nurse Rep,
Mr G Maguire, Social Work Rep,
Mr R Anderson, Pharmacist,

Craigavon Area Hospital Group HSS Trust
Trust Headquarters, 68 Lurgan Road
Portadown
CRAIGAVON
Co. Armagh
BT63 5QQ
Tel.: 028 3833 4444
Fax.: 028 3861 2471

Admin & Senior Management
Mr J Mone, Director of Nursing & Quality, 68 Lurgan Road, Portadown, Craigavon, Co. Armagh, BT63 5QQ, Tel.: 028 3861 2430
Community Midwifery
Community Midwives, Brownlow HSS Centre, Legahorey, Craigavon, BT65 5BE, Tel.: 028 3834 1210
Ms M O'Dowd, Team Leader, Brownlow HSS Centre, Legahorey, Craigavon, BT65 5BE, Tel.: 028 3834 1431
Liaison Services
Ms A Hanna, Hospital Community Liaison Sister, Craigavon Area Hospital, 68 Lurgan Road, Portadown, BT63 5QQ,
Ms D McCuallagh, Liaison Sister, Craigavon Area Hospital, 68 Lurgan Road, Portadown, BT63 5QQ,
Mrs M McNally, Hospital Community Liaison Sister, Craigavon Area Hospital, 68 Lurgan Road, Portadown, BT63 5QQ,
Ms M Morris, Community Liaison Officer, Care of Older People, Lurgan Hospital, 100 Sloan Street, Lurgan, Tel.: 028 3861 3099

Other Services

Mrs S McCloskey, Area Bereavement, Co-ordinator, Craigavon Area Hospital, 68 Lurgan Road, Portadown, Co Armagh, BT63 5QQ, Tel.: 028 3861 3861

Specialist Nursing Services

Ms P Fearon, Nurse Specialist, Breast Care, Craigavon Area Hospital, Macmillan Building, 68 Lurgan Road, Portadown, Co Armagh, BT63 5QQ, Tel.: 028 3861 2086

Ms P Reavey, Nurse Specialist, Breast Care, Craigavon Area Hospital, Macmillan Building, 68 Lurgan Road, Portadown, Co Armagh, BT63 5QQ, Tel.: 028 3861 2086

Mrs A Trainor, Nurse Specialist, Breast Care, Craigavon Area Hospital, Macmillan Building, 68 Lurgan Road, Portadown, Co Armagh, BT63 5QQ, Tel.: 028 3861 2086

Mr S Cartmill, Co-ordinator, Cardiac Rehabilitation, Ward 1 North, CAHGT, Tel.: 028 3861 2911

Ms M J Thompson, Nurse, Coloproctology, Craigavon Area Hospital, 4 North, 68 Lurgan Road, Portadown, Co Armagh, BT63 5QQ, Tel.: 028 3861 2721

Ms B Trainor, Nurse, Coloproctology, Craigavon Area Hospital, 4 North, 68 Lurgan Road, Portadown, Co Armagh, BT63 5QQ, Tel.: 028 3861 2721

Mrs L Irwin, Specialist Nurse, Diabetic Care, Outpatients Dept, CAHGT, Tel.: 028 3861 2022

Mrs D Richardson, Nurse Specialist, DVT, Craigavon Area Hospital, 68 Lurgan Road, Portadown, Co Armagh, BT63 5QQ, Tel.: 028 3861 2796

Ms J Frazer, Nurse Specialist, Palliative Care, Craigavon Area Hospital, Macmillan Building, 68 Lurgan Road, Portadown, Co Armagh, BT63 5QQ, Tel.: 028 3861 3647

Ms R Hutcheson, Nurse Specialist, Palliative Care, Craigavon Area Hospital, Macmillan Building, 68 Lurgan Road, Portadown, Co Armagh, BT63 5QQ, Tel.: 028 3861 3647

Miss S Neil, Macmillan, Nurse Specialist, Palliative Care, Craigavon Area Hospital, 68 Lurgan Road, Portadown, BT63 5QQ,

Ms C Nelson, Nurse Specialist, Palliative Care, Craigavon Area Hospital, Macmillan Building, 68 Lurgan Road, Portadown, Co Armagh, BT63 5QQ, Tel.: 028 3861 3647

Ms R Dickson, Nurse Specialist, Respiratory, Nursing & Quality, CAHGT, Tel.: 028 3861 2966

Mrs B O'Connor, Officer, Resuscitation Training, Nursing & Quality, CAHGT, Tel.: 028 3861 2472

Ms A McMullan, Nurse Specialist, Rheumatology, Nursing & Quality, CAHGT, Tel.: 028 3861 2951

Mrs J McMahon, Nurse Specialist, Urology, Craigavon Area Hospital, 68 Lurgan Road, Portadown, Co Armagh, BT63 5QQ, Tel.: 028 3861 3840

Mrs K O'Neill, Nurse Specialist, Urology, Craigavon Area Hospital, 68 Lurgan Road, Portadown, Co Armagh, BT63 5QQ, Tel.: 028 3861 3840

Newry & Mourne HSS Trust

Trust Headquarters
Daisy Hill Hospital
5 Hospital Road
NEWRY
Co Down
BT35 8DR

Admin & Senior Management

Ms J O'Hagan, Director of Nursing & Community Health, Tel.: 028 3083 5056

Child Health Records

Child Health Records, John Mitchel Place, Newry, BT34 2BU, Tel.: 028 3083 4200

Over 5s, School Health Department,

Under 5s, Infant Health Department,

Child Protection/Safeguarding Children

Ms J Toner, Health Visitor, Child Protection, Drumalane House, Drumalane Road, Newry, Tel.: 028 3082 5077

Community Midwifery

Mrs K Donnelly, Team Leader, Ring of Gullion,

Ms H McAleavey, Acting Midwifery Manager, Nursing Administration, Daisy Hill Hospital, Newry, BT35 8DR, Tel.: 028 3083 5000 ext 2291

Mrs C McAlinden, Team Leader, Newry Team,

Mrs C Murphy, Head of Midwifery, Nursing Administration, Daisy Hill Hospital, Newry, BT35 8DR, Tel.: 028 3083 5000 ext 2291

Mrs A O'Hanlow, Team Leader, Mourne Team,

Community Nursing Services

Ms M McAllister, Assistant Director of Nursing, Adult & Older People, John Mitchel Place, Newry, BT34 2BU, Tel.: 028 3083 4200

Ms C Murphy, Assistant Director of Nursing, Child Health, John Mitchel Place, Newry, BT34 2BU, Tel.: 028 3083 4200

District Nursing

District Nurses, John Mitchel Place, Newry, BT34 2BU, Tel.: 028 3083 4200

Emergencies District Nurses, Tel.: 028 3083 5000

Family Planning Services

Ms C Murphy, Assistant Director of Nursing - Child Health, John Mitchel Place, Newry, BT34 2BU, Tel.: 028 3083 4200

Learning Disabilities

Mrs M Loughran, Team Leader, Health Centre, John Mitchell Place, Newry, Co Down, BT34 2BU, Tel.: 028 308 34205

School Nursing

School Health/Nursing Service, John Mitchel Place, Newry, BT34 2BU, Tel.: 028 3083 4200

Specialist Nursing Services

Mr B Trainor, Daisy Hill Hospital, Tel.: 028 3083 5000

Ms C McAnerney, Asthma, - Respiratory, Children's Ward, Daisy Hill Hospital, Tel.: 028 3083 5000

Ms S Russell, Asthma, - Respiratory, Rathfriland Health Centre, Rathfriland, BT34 5QH, Tel.: 028 4063 0666

Ms A McConville, Continence, Gate Lodge, Drumalane Road, Newry, BT35 8AP, Tel.: 028 3026 7335

Mrs M Corrigan, Coronary Care, Daisy Hill Hospital, Tel.: 028 3083 5000

Ms S Griffin, Diabetic Care, Clanrye Surgery, Newry Health Village, Monaghan Street, Newry, BT35 6BW, Tel.: 028 3026 7639

Ms S Lynch, Macmillan, Nurses Home, Daisy Hill Hospital, Newry, BT35 8DR, Tel.: 028 3083 5000

Ms A McKeever, Macmillan, Nurses Home, Daisy Hill Hospital, Newry, BT35 8DR, Tel.: 028 3083 5000

The Homeless/Travellers & Asylum Seekers

Ms F Adamson, Travellers Health Visitor, John Mitchel Place, Tel.: 028 3083 4200

Newry & Mourne LHSCG

Win Business Park
Canal Quay
NEWRY
BT35 6PH
Tel.: 028 3026 6875

Admin & Senior Management

Ms P Buckley, Community Rep,

Ms J Clarke, Nursing Rep,

Mr M Crilley, General Manager,

Ms H Daly, Community Rep,

Mr B Dornan, Social Services Rep,

Ms J O'Hagan, Nursing Rep,

Mr S Strain, Community Pharmacist,

Northern Ireland

Western HSSB

Altnagelvin Hospitals HSS Trust
Trust Headquarters, Altnagelvin Hospital
Glenshane Road
LONDONDERRY
BT47 6SB
Tel.: 028 7134 5171
Fax.: 028 7161 1222

Admin & Senior Management
Ms I Duddy, Director of Nursing,
Community Midwifery
Mrs M Beattie, Clinical, Midwife Specialist, Great James Street Health Centre, Londonderry, BT48 7DH, Tel.: 028 7136 5177
Mrs K McDaid, Directorate Manager, Women & Children's Directorate, Altnagelvin Hospital, Glenshane Road, Londonderry, BT47 6SB, Tel.: 028 7134 5171ext 3507

Foyle HSS Trust
Trust Headquarters, Riverview House
Abercorn Road
LONDONDERRY
BT48 6SB
Tel.: 028 7126 6111

Admin & Senior Management
Mr T Cassidy, Programme Manager, Family & Child Care, Riverview House, Abercorn Road, Londonderry, BT48 6SB, Tel.: 028 7126 6111
Mrs G Hillick, Programme Manager, (Acting) Community Health Care & Physical & Sensory Disability, Riverview House, Abercorn Road, Londonderry, BT48 6SB, Tel.: 028 7126 6111
Mr C MacElhatton, (Acting) Assistant Programme Manager Health Care, Woodview, Gransha Park, Clooney Road, Londonderry, BT47 6TF, Tel.: 028 7186 5157
Ms D Mahon, Programme Manager, Older People, Riverview House, Abercorn Road, Londonderry, BT48 6SB, Tel.: 028 7126 6111
Mrs P Mahon, Director of Health Care, Riverview House, Abercorn Road, Londonderry, BT48 6SB, Tel.: 028 7126 6111
Mrs M McNicholl, Assistant Programme Manager Disability, Woodview, Gransha Park, Clooney Road, Londonderry, BT47 6TF, Tel.: 028 7186 5157
Child Health
Mr C MacElhatton, (Acting) Assistant Programme Manager Health Care, Woodview, Gransha Park, Clooney Road, Londonderry, BT47 6TF, Tel.: 028 7186 5157
Miss P McSwiggan, Paediatric Liaison, Great James Health Centre, Tel.: 028 7136 5177
Child Health Records
Mrs T Conaghan, Manager, Information & Records, Bridgeview House, Gransha Park, Clooney Road, Londonderry, BT47 1TG, Tel.: 028 7186 5125
Over 5s, Tel.: 028 7186 5125
Pre-school, Tel.: 028 7186 5108
Child Protection/Safeguarding Children
Mrs L Crumlish, Child Protection, Gt James Street Health Centre, Londonderry, Tel.: 028 7136 5177
District Nursing
Ms G Brown, Assistant Programme Manager, Dawson House, Gransha Park, Londonderry, Tel.: 028 7186 0261
Mrs M Curran, Community Nurse Co-ordinator, Shantallow Health Centre, Racecourse Road, Londonderry, BT48 8NL, Tel.: 028 7135 1350
Mrs B Michaelides, Community, District Nursing, Nurse Manager, Woodview, Gransha Park, Londonderry, Tel.: 028 7186 5157
Health Visitors
Mrs M Hutton, Community, Health Visiting, Nurse Manager, Great

James Street Health Centre, Great James Street, Londonderry, Tel.: 028 7136 5177
Mrs K Jackson, Community, Health Visiting, Nurse Manager, Waterside Health Centre, Glendermott Road, Londonderry, Tel.: 028 7132 0100
Learning Disabilities
Mr R Boyle, Hospital Manager, Lakeview, Gransha Park, Clooney Road, Derry, BT47 6WJ, Tel.: 02871 65210
Mrs B Dooher, Community Nurse Co-ordinator, Rossabbey, 98 William Street, Derry, BT48 9AD, Tel.: 02871 272950
Mr J McEleney, Assistant Programme Manager, Lakeview, Gransha Park, Clooney Road, Derry, BT47 6WJ, Tel.: 02871 864363
Mr M McLaughlin, Assistant Programme Manager, Lakeview, Gransha Park, Clooney Road, Derry, BT47 6WJ, Tel.: 02871 864363
Mr P McLaughlin, Senior Social Worker, Rossabbey, 98 William Street, Derry, BT48 9AD, Tel.: 02871 272950
Mr P McLoone, APSW, Lakeview, Gransha Park, Clooney Road, Derry, BT47 6WJ, Tel.: 02871 864362
Mr T Millar, Programme Manager, Riverview House, Abercorn Road, Londonderry, BT48 6SB, Tel.: 02871 266111
Specialist Nursing Services
Mrs M McGinley, Advisor, Continence, Rectory Field, 19b Limavady Road, Londonderry, BT47 6JU, Tel.: 028 7134 9355
Ms L Willilams, Specialist, Diabetic Care, Strabane Health Centre, Upper Main Street, Strabane, Tel.: 028 7188 4534
Advisor, Infection Control, Maple Villa, Gransha Park, Londonderry, BT47 6TF, Tel.: 028 7186 4337
Mrs M Brown, Specialist, Intermediate Care, Maple Villa, Gransha Park, Londonderry, BT47 6TF, Tel.: 028 7186 4342
Ms C Mason, Specialist, Parkinson's Disease, Linavady Health Centre, Londonderry, Tel.: 777 61100
Mrs A McQuaide, Specialist, Stoma Care, Maple Villa, Gransha Park, Londonderry, BT47 6TF, Tel.: 028 7186 4365
Mrs F Curry, Specialist, Tissue Viability, Maple Villa, Gransha Park, Londonderry, BT47 6TF, Tel.: 028 7186 4375

Northern LHSCG
23a Bishop Street
DERRY
BT48 6PR
Tel.: 02871 369500
Fax.: 02871 273679

Admin & Senior Management
Ms Y Boyle, Social Services,
Mr P Cavanagh, Manager,
Mr S Heaney, Nursing Rep,
Ms M McGinley, Nursing Rep,
Mr E O'Kane, Community User Rep,

Sperrin Lakeland HSS Trust
Trust Headquarters, Strathdene House
Tyrone & Fermanagh
OMAGH
Co Tyrone
BT79 0NS
Tel.: 028 8283 5285

Admin & Senior Management
Mr E Fee, Director of Acute Services, Tyrone County Hospital, Omagh, BT79 0AP, Tel.: 028 8228 33588
Mr H S Mills, Chief Executive,
Mr V Ryan, Director of Community Care, Erne Hospital, Enniskillen, Co Fermanagh, BT74 6AY, Tel.: 028 6632 4711
Child Health
Mrs F Gilmore, Sperrin - Paediatrics, Omagh Health Centre, Tel.: 028 8224 3521
Ms F McDonnell, Manager, Sperrin, Tyrone & Fermanagh Hospital, Tel.: 028 8225 5117

Northern Ireland

Child Health Records
Lakeland Child Health Records, Erne Health Centre, Tel.: 028 6632 4711
Sperrin Child Health Records, Community Health Dept, Tyrone & Fermanagh Hospital, Tel.: 028 8224 5211

Child Protection/Safeguarding Children
Ms F McDonnell, Sperrin, Child Protection, Omagh Health Centre, Tel.: 028 8224 3521
Ms M Murphy, Lakeland, Child Protection, Tel.: 028 6638 2168

Community Midwifery
Community Midwifery Manager, Bridge Centre, 5A Holmview Avenue, Campsie, Omagh, Co Tyrone, BT79 0AQ, Tel.: 02882 254473
Community Midwives Fernagah, Health Centre, Church Street, Irvinestown, Co Fermanagh,
Community Midwives Fernagah, Health Centre, Erne Hospital, Enniskillen, Co Fermanagh,
Community Midwives Fernagah, Health Centre, Drumhaw, Lesnaskea, Co Fermanagh,
Community Midwives Omagh, Health Centre, Mountjoy Road, Omagh, Tel.: 028 8243/5564
Mrs L Moore, Community Midwifery Manager, Bridge Centre, 5A Holmview Avenue, Campsie, Omagh, Co Tyrone, BT79 0AQ, Tel.: 028 82254473

District Nursing
Emergencies, Sperrin District Nurses, Tel.: 028 8224 5211
Emergencies/Night, Lakeland District Nurses, Tel.: 028 6632 4711
Ms A McMenamin, Nurse Manager, Lakeland District Nurses, Erne Health Centre, Cornagrade Road, Enniskillen, BT74 6AY, Tel.: 028 6632 4711
Mrs B McQuade, Nurse Manager, Sperrin District Nurses, Cedar Villa, Tyrone & Fermanagh Hospital, Tel.: 028 8225 5117

Health Visitors
Mr B Cadogan, Lakeland - Sure Start Health Visitor, ARC Health Living Centre, 116-122 Sallyswood, Irvinestown, Tel.: 028 6862 1970
Ms F McDonnell, Nurse Manager, Sperrin Health Visitors, Cedar Villa, Tyrone & Fermanagh Hospital, Tel.: 028 8225 5117
Ms M Murphy, Nurse Manager, Lakeland Health Visitors, Erne Health Centre, Cornagrade Road, Enniskillen, BT74 6AY, Tel.: 028 6638 2168

HIV/AIDS
Ms P Charlton, Lakeland, Erne Health Centre, Tel.: 028 6638 2173
Miss N Conway, Lakeland, Erne Health Centre, Tel.: 028 6638 2170
Ms A Irvine, Lakeland, Lisnaskea Health Centre, Tel.: 028 6772 1566
Mrs H Kerr, Sperrin, Health Visitor, Carrickmore Health Centre, Tel.: 028 8076 1242
Mrs B O'Neill, Sperrin, Health Visitor, Omagh Health Centre, Tel.: 028 8224 3521
Mrs M Quinn, Sperrin, District Nurse, Omagh Health Centre, Tel.: 028 8224 3521

Learning Disabilities
Mrs J Boyd, Fermanagh Community Nurse, 15 Elliot Place, Enniskillen,
Mrs R Breen, Omagh Community Nurse, Omagh Health Centre, Omagh, Tel.: 02882 243521
Mr K Downey, Community Services Manager, Abbey House, 12 Abbey Street, Tel.: 02882 254514
Mrs R McIvor, Omagh Community Nurse, Omagh Health Centre, Omagh, Tel.: 02882 243521
Mrs P McLaughlin, Castlederg/Newtownstewart Community Nurse, trabaner, Tel.: 02871 382950
Mr M O'Neill, Dromore Community Nurse Co-ordinator, Main Street, Dromore,

Liaison Services
Mrs D I Armstrong, Lakeland - Paediatrics, Erne Hospital, Tel.: 028 6638 2172
Ms L Brennan, Lakeland - Hospital Discharge Co-ordinator, Erne Hospital, Tel.: 028 6632 4711 ext 2158

Mrs E Gilmour, Sperrin - Elderly, Omagh Health Centre, Tel.: 028 8224 3521
Ms C Mulholland, Lakeland - Elderly Health Visitor, Erne Health Centre, Tel.: 028 6638 2173
Mrs C Travers, Sperrin - General Hospital, Omagh Health Centre, Tel.: 028 8224 3521
Ms P Charlton, Lakeland, Coronary Care, Erne Health Centre, Tel.: 028 6638 2173
Ms M Doherty, Lakeland - Health Visitor, Diabetic Care, Erne Health Centre, Tel.: 028 6638 2173

Other Services
Mrs K Boles, Women's Refuge - Sperrin, Omagh Health Centre, Tel.: 028 8224 3521
Mrs U Canavan, Sperrin - Bereavement Support, Carrickmore Health Centre, Tel.: 028 8076 1242
Ms B Solon, Lakeland - Bereavement Support, Lisnaskea Health Centre, Tel.: 028 6772 1566
Ms J Thompson, Lakeland - Health Promotion Co-ordinator, Erne Health Centre, Tel.: 028 6638 2171

School Nursing
School Health/Nursing Service, Sperrin, Omagh Health Centre, Mountjoy Road, Omagh, BT78 2LB, Tel.: 028 8224 3521
School Health/Nursing Service, Lakeland, Erne Health Centre, Tel.: 028 6638 2168
School Health/Nursing Service, Sperrin, Tyrone & Fermanagh Hospital, Tel.: 028 8225 5392

Specialist Nursing Services
Mrs F J Gilmore, Sperrin - Pre Menstrual/Postal Natal Depression, Omagh Health Centre, Tel.: 028 8224 3521
Mrs J Loughran, Sperrin - Pre Menstrual/Postal Natal Depression, Omagh Health Centre, Tel.: 028 8224 3521
Ms S Donaldson, Lakeland, Asthma, Erne Health Centre, Tel.: 028 6632 4711
Ms V Nemuth, Lakeland, Asthma, Irvinestown Health Centre, Church Street, Irvinestown, Tel.: 028 6862 1212
Ms P Kearny, Sperrin, Breast Care, Tyrone County Hospital, Tel.: 028 8224 5211
Ms S McCrystal, Sperrin & Lakeland, Continence, Tel.: 028 8225 5067
Ms M Gallen, Sperrin, Diabetic Care, Outpatients Department, Tyrone County Hospital, Tel.: 028 8283 3266
Ms B Donnelly, Lakeland, Enuresis, Tel.: 028 6772 1566
Ms C McMahon, Lakeland, Enuresis, Tel.: 028 6772 1566
Ms J Donald, Sperrin, Infection Control, Gortin Medical Centre, Tel.: 028 6634 8275
Ms S Mulligan, Sperrin, Infection Control, Gortin Medical Centre, Tel.: 028 8164 8216
Mrs M Doody, Sperrin, Lactation, Omagh Health Centre, Tel.: 028 8224 3521
Mrs H Kerr, Sperrin, Lactation, Carrickmore Health Centre, Tel.: 028 8076 1242
Ms A McCrea, Lakeland - Human Milk Bank, Lactation, Irvinestown Health Centre, Tel.: 028 6862 1212
Mrs B McLaughlin, Sperrin, Lactation, Omagh Health Centre, Tel.: 028 8224 3521
Mrs K Menagh, Sperrin, Lactation, Omagh Health Centre, Tel.: 028 8224 3521
Ms A Fox, Sperrin, Leg Ulcers, Gortin Medical Centre, Tel.: 028 8164 8216
Ms H Ogle, Lakeland, Leg Ulcers, Erne Health Centre, Tel.: 028 6632 4711 ext 3509
Ms H Ogle, Sperrin, Leg Ulcers, Gortin Medical Centre, Tel.: 028 6634 8275
Mrs E King, Sperrin, Macmillan, Tyrone County Hospital, Tel.: 028 8224 5211
Mrs G Patterson, Sperrin, Macmillan, Tyrone County Hospital, Tel.: 028 8224 5211
Ms M Ruthledge, Stoma Care,

Mrs E Doherty, Sperrin, Terminal Care, Castlederg Health Clinic, Castlederg, Tel.: 028 8167 1406

Ms J Donald, Lakeland, Terminal Care, Tel.: 028 8284 1233

Mrs A Fox, Sperrin, Terminal Care, Omagh Health Centre, Tel.: 028 8224 3521

Mrs R Kelly, Sperrin, Terminal Care, Carrickmore Health Centre, Tel.: 028 8076 1242

Mrs U McCusker, Sperrin, Terminal Care, Omagh Health Centre, Tel.: 028 8224 3521

Ms P McGovern, Lakeland, Terminal Care, Rathmore Clinic, Tel.: 028 6665 8381

Ms H Moore, Lakeland, Terminal Care, Erne Health Centre, Tel.: 028 6632 4711

Ms V Quinn, Lakeland, Terminal Care, Roslea/NTB, Tel.: 028 6775 1366

The Homeless/Travellers & Asylum Seekers

Ms C McMahon, Sperrin - Travellers, Health Visitor, Omagh Health Centre, Tel.: 028 8224 3521

Strule & Erne LHSCG

Trillick Enterprise Centre
71-73 Main Street
TRILLICK
BT78 3ST
Tel.: 028 8956 1989

Admin & Senior Management

Mr P Dolan, General Manager,

Ms C Ferguson, Community Rep,

Ms C McGrenaghan, Social Work Rep,

Ms A Smyth, Nurse Rep,

Offshore

with major towns and
Primary Care Trust boundaries

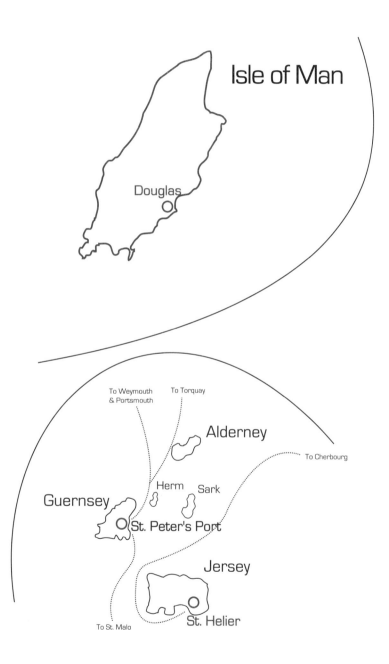

Isle of Man

Douglas

To Weymouth
& Portsmouth

To Torquay

Alderney

To Cherbourg

Herm

Sark

Guernsey

St. Peter's Port

Jersey

St. Helier

To St. Malo

Offshore

Isle of Man Department of Health & Social Security

Isle of Man Dept of Health & Social Security
Headquarters, Markwell House
Market Street
DOUGLAS
Isle of Man
IM1 2RZ
Tel.: 01624 685685

Child Health
Children's Ward, Nobles Hospital, Tel.: 01624 642285
School Clinic, Crookall House, Demesne Road, Douglas, IM1 3QA,
Tel.: 01624 642603
Child Health Records
Over 5s, School Clinic, Crookall House, Demesne Road, Douglas,
IM1 3QA, Tel.: 01624 642630
Under 5s, Crookall House, Demesne Road, Douglas, IM1 3QA, Tel.:
01624 642650
Child Protection/Safeguarding Children
Mrs C A Quilliam, Designated Nurse, Child Protection, Crookall
House, Tel.: 01624 642643
Community Midwifery
Mrs J Sloane, Head of Midwifery, Nobles Hospital, The Strang,
Braddan, IM4 4RJ, Tel.: 01624 650030
Ms J Williams, Lead Midwife Public Health, Nobles Hospital, The
Strang, Braddan, IM4 4RJ,
Community Nursing Services
Community Nursing Service, Crookall House, Demesne Road,
Douglas, IM1 3QA, Tel.: 01624 642650
Ms F Hampton, Community Nurse, Crookall House, Demesne Road,
Douglas, IM1 3QA, Tel.: 01624 642450
Dr I MacLean, Chief Admin Medical Officer, Crookall House,
Demesne Road, Douglas, IM1 3QA, Tel.: 01624 642645
Ms L Ryan, Community Nurse, Crookall House, Demesne Road,
Douglas, IM1 3QA, Tel.: 01624 642450
District Nursing
Miss A F Quilleash, Nurse Manager, Community Nurse Manager -
District Nurses, Crookall House, Demesne Road, Douglas, IM1 3QA,
Tel.: 01624 642644
Family Planning Services
Mrs S Porter, Service Manager, Crookall House, Demesne Road,
Douglas, IM1 3QA, Tel.: 01624 642678
Health Visitors
Mrs S Porter, Service Manager, Health Visiting & School Nursing,
Crookall House, Demesne Road, Douglas, IM1 3QA, Tel.: 01624
642678
Liaison Services
Nobles Hospital, Tel.: 01624 642642 ext 2406/212
School Nursing
Mrs S Porter, Service Manager, Health Visiting & School Nursing,
Crookall House, Demesne Road, Douglas, IM1 3QA, Tel.: 01624
642678
Specialist Nursing Services
Mrs D Quaye, Transfer of Care Co-ordinator, Tel.: mobile 425146
Mrs M Swindlehurst, Practice Development Facilitator, District
Nurses, Crookall House, Demesne Road, Douglas, IM1 3QA, Tel.:
01624 642105
Mrs M Coles, Aromatherapy, St Bridget's Hospice, Dorothy Pantin
House, Kensington Road, Douglas, IM1 3PE, Tel.: 01624 626530
Ms L Mitchell, Aromatherapy, St Bridget's Hospice, Dorothy Pantin
House, Kensington Road, Douglas, IM1 3PE, Tel.: 01624 626530
Mrs A Taylor, Aromatherapy, St Bridget's Hospice, Dorothy Pantin
House, Kensington Road, Douglas, IM1 3PE, Tel.: 01624 626530
Mrs V Johnson, Continence, 28 Derby Square, Douglas, Tel.: 01624
693551

Ms P Kermode, Communicable, Disease,
Ms P McClure, Hospital, Infection Control, Nobles Hospital,
Westmoreland Road, Douglas, IM1 4QA, Tel.: 01624 642240 bleep
161
Mrs M Green, Home Care Team, Macmillan, St Bridget's Hospice,
Dorothy Pantin House, Kensington Road, Douglas, IM1 3PE, Tel.:
01624 626530
Miss A Kewley, Home Care Team, Macmillan, St Bridget's Hospice,
Dorothy Pantin House, Kensington Road, Douglas, IM1 3PE, Tel.:
01624 626530
Miss M Lister, Home Care Team, Macmillan, St Bridget's Hospice,
Dorothy Pantin House, Kensington Road, Douglas, IM1 3PE, Tel.:
01624 626530
Mrs C Luck, Home Care Team, Macmillan, St Bridget's Hospice,
Dorothy Pantin House, Kensington Road, Douglas, IM1 3PE, Tel.:
01624 626530
Mrs S Lawley, Parkinson's Disease, Derby House, Derby Square,
Douglas, Isle of Man, Tel.: 01624 628462
Mrs S Ardern, Stoma Care, Nobles Hospital, Tel.: 01624 642376

States of Guernsey Board of Health

Guernsey Board of Health
Trust Headquarters, Princess Elizabeth Hospital
La Vauquiedor, St Martin
GUERNSEY
Channel Islands
GY4 6UU
Tel.: 01481 725241

Acute Specialist Nursing Services
Ms A Friend, Activities Manager, KEVII Hospital,
Ms L Laine, Clinic Sister, Castel Hospital,
Ms C Maxwell, Quality Manager, Lukis House,
Ms M Shaw, Lead Cancer Nurse,
Ms G Trump, Phlebotomist, Princess Elizabeth Hospital,
Ms K Leach, Clinical Nurse Specialist, Breast Care, - Screening,
Princess Elizabeth Hospital,
Mr P Herve, Clinical Nurse Specialist, Continence, Lukis House,
Ms P McDermott, Clinical Nurse Specialist, Continence, Lukis
House,
Ms A Kinch, Nurse Consultant, Diabetic Care, Princess Elizabeth
Hospital,
Mr P Cororan, Nurse Specialist, Elderly Care, Castel Hospital,
Mr M McSwiggan, Clinical Nurse Specialist, Elderly Care, Castel
Hospital,
Ms K Bull, Nurse, Infection Control, Princess Elizabeth Hospital,
Ms E Burgess, Lead Nurse, Infection Control,
Ms S Freestone, Nurse, Oncology,
Ms H Samman, Nurse, Oncology,
Ms J Welbourne, Clinical Nurse Specialist, Osteoporosis, Princess
Elizabeth Hospital,
Ms J Lynch, Clinical Nurse Specialist, Pain Management, Princess
Elizabeth Hospital,
Ms L Dorey, Sister, Palliative Care, - Oncology, Bulstrode House,
Ms K Gibbs, Sister, Palliative Care, - Oncology, Bulstrode House,
Ms A Inder, Nurse, Palliative Care,
Ms S Adam, Clinical Nurse Specialist, Parkinson's Disease,
Ms L Coggan, Nurse, Research,
Ms R Sherrington, Clinical Nurse Specialist, Respiratory,
Ms L Sarre, Nurse, Stoma Care, Surgical Unit/Princess Elizabeth
Hospital,
Mr A Cooke, Clinical Nurse Specialist, Substance Misuse, - Alcohol
Castel Hospital,
Ms S McGuigan, Dependency Project Co-ordinator, Substance
Misuse,
Ms A Mullin, Clinical Nurse Specialist, Tissue Viability, Lukis House

Admin & Senior Management
Mrs S Fleming, Deputy Director Continuing & Community Care, Castel Hospital, Castel, GY5 7NJ, Tel.: 01481 725241
Mrs J Gallienne, Senior Manager Community & Maternity Services, Mrs T Poxon, Director of Continuing & Community Care Services, Princess Elizabeth Hospital, Le Vauquiedor, St Martins, Guernsey, Tel.: 01481 725241 ext 4272

Child Health
Mrs J Gallienne, Senior Manager (Childrens Nursing Services), Lukis House, The Grange, St Peter Port, GY1 2QG, Tel.: 01481 725241
Ms S Mead, Child & Adolescent Services, Clinical Nurse Specialist, Bell House,

Child Health Records
Mr D Cade, Lukis House, The Grange, St Peter Port, GY1 2QG, Tel.: 01481 725241

Child Protection/Safeguarding Children
Mrs J Gallienne, Child Protection Services, Tel.: 01481 729021
Mrs D Pittman, Manager Health Visiting Child Protection Services, Tel.: 01481 725241 ext 5247

Community Midwifery
Ms H Kelso, Senior Manager, Maternity Services, Tel.: 01481 725241

Community Nursing Services
Mrs S Bourne, Community Team Manager (District Nursing), Lukis House, The Grange, St Peter Port, GY1 2QG, Tel.: 01481 725241 ext 5254
Mrs S Spaven, Community Team Manager (Home Care Services), Tel.: 01481 725241 ext 5255
Mrs K Sykes, Community Team Manager (Social Work), Tel.: 01481 725241 ext 3313

Family Planning Services
Mrs S Le Page, 7 Le Pollet, St Peter Port, GY1 1WQ, Tel.: 01481 714954

Learning Disabilities
Mr J Ashby, Head of Service, The Old Stables, Oberlands, St Martins, GY4 6UU, Tel.: 01481 725241

Liaison Services
Ms J Guezo, Quality Liaison, KEVII Hospital,
Mr A Moriarty, Access Manager, Princess Elizabeth Hospital, St Martins, GY4 6UU, Tel.: 01481 725241

Other Services
Mr G Ayres, Lecturer Practitioner, Castel Hospital,

Pharmacy
Mr E Freestone, Chief Pharmacist, Princess Elizabeth Hospital, St Martins, GY4 6UU, Tel.: 01481 725241

Smoking Cessation
Mrs G Le Roy, Health Promotion Unit, Princess Elizabeth Hospital, St Martins, GY4 6UU, Tel.: 01481 725241

Child Health Records
Child Health Records, Public Health, Le Bas Centre, St Saviour's Road, St Helier, Jersey, JE2 4RP, Tel.: 01534 623780
School Health Records, Public Health Dept, Le Bas Centre, St Saviour's Road, St Helier, Jersey, JE2 4RP, Tel.: 01534 623780

Child Protection/Safeguarding Children
Mr B A Bell, Child Protection, Family Nursing & Home Care, Le Bas Centre, St Saviour's Road, St Helier, Jersey, JE2 4RP, Tel.: 01534 623643

Community Midwifery
Mrs E Torrance, Modern Matron, Maternity, Tel.: 01534 622441

Community Nursing Services
Ms K Huchet, Director, Family Nursing & Home Care, Le Bas Centre, St Saviour's Road, St Helier, Jersey, JE2 4RP, Tel.: 01534 789950

District Nursing
District Nurses, Family Nursing & Home Care, Le Bas Centre, St Saviour's Road, St Helier, Jersey, JE2 4RP, Tel.: 01534 789950
Twilight, Tel.: 01534 622000 (1800-2200)

Family Planning Services
Family Planning Service, Community Health Dept, Le Bas Centre, St Saviour's Road, St Helier, Jersey, JE2 4RP, Tel.: 01534 789933

Health Visitors
Mrs A De Fretas, Health Visitor Secretary West,
Mrs H de Lucchi, Special Needs Health Visitor, Tel.: 01534 789950
Mrs C Wheelan, Health Visitor Secretary East,

HIV/AIDS
Ms I Morley, Community Co-ordinator, Family Nursing & Home Care, Le Bas Centre, St Saviour's Road, St Helier, Jersey, JE2 4RP, Tel.: 01534 789950

Learning Disabilities
Ms M Baudains, Directorate Manager, Social Services, Maison Le Pape, The Parade, St Helier, JE2 3PU, Tel.: 01534 623522

Liaison Services
Ms J Foley, Liaison, District Nurse Specialist/Hospital, Family Nursing & Home Care, Le Bas Centre, St Saviour's Road, St Helier, Jersey, JE2 4RP, Tel.: 01534 789950

School Nursing
School Health/Nursing Service, Community Health Dept, Le Bas Centre, St Saviour's Road, St Helier, Jersey, JE2 4RP, Tel.: 01534 623780

Specialist Nursing Services
Health Care Advisers, Tel.: 01534 789950
Ms M White, Stoma Care, Tel.: 01534 789950

States of Jersey

Jersey Health & Social Services Department

Jersey General Hospital
Gloucester Street
ST HELIER
Jersey
JE1 3QS
Tel.: 01534 622000

Child Health
Mrs J Buist, Community Paediatric Team, Family Nursing & Home Care, Le Bas Centre, St Saviour's Road, St Helier, Jersey, JE2 4RP, Tel.: 01534 623623
Mrs S Foster, Senior Clinical Medical Officer, Community Health Dept, Le Bas Centre, St Saviour's Road, St Helier, Jersey, JE2 4RP, Tel.: 01534 623703

Directory of Community Health Services 2006/07
ORDER FORM

Note: payment with order please, unless enclosing an official order

Please send..........copy/copies at £................each of the *Directory of Community Health Services 2006/07*, (see below for quantity discounts).

No of copies	1 - 9	10+
Unit prices (£) for NHS health professionals, booksellers, charities	29.95	19.95
Unit price (£) for others	49.95	34.95

Name...

Job description/Title...

Place of work...

Delivery address..

....

....

....Postcode..

Daytime Telephone No...

Email Address..

Order Ref No... Fax No..

I enclose a cheque for the sum of £.................made payable to **PMH Publications**

Credit Card Payments

Please debit my Visa/Mastercard/Delta (please delete as applicable)

Card No. _ _ _ _   _ _ _ _   _ _ _ _   _ _ _ _   Security code. _ _ _

Expiry date _ _ / _ _   for the sum of £...

Name and address of credit card holder (if different to above)

....

....Postcode..

OR: I HAVE ENCLOSED AN OFFICIAL PURCHASE ORDER – PLEASE INVOICE ME ☐

Signature.. Date..

From time to time PMH Publications and other companies may wish to send details of other products and offers to you. If you do not wish to receive these communications, please tick box ☐

Section 3: Indexing

England

East Midlands SHA	2.3
East of England SHA	2.24
London SHA	2.53
North East SHA	2.89
North West SHA	2.103
South Central SHA	2.138
South East Coast SHA	2.156
South West SHA	2.177
West Midlands SHA	2.201
Yorkshire and The Humber SHA	2.223

Wales

Mid & West Wales Region	2.253
North Wales Region	2.258
South East Wales Region	2.264

Scotland

NHS Ayrshire & Arran	2.272
NHS Borders	2.273
NHS Dumfries & Galloway	2.274
NHS Fife	2.275
NHS Forth Valley	2.278
NHS Grampian	2.280
NHS Greater Glasgow	2.282
NHS Highland	2.288
NHS Lanarkshire	2.291
NHS Lothian	2.296
NHS Orkney	2.300
NHS Shetland	2.300
NHS Tayside	2.301
NHS Western Isles	2.302

HSSBs Northern Ireland

Eastern HSSB	2.305
Northern HSSB	2.309
Southern HSSB	2.311
Western HSSB	2.314

Offshore

Isle of Man Department of Health & Social Security	2.318
States of Guernsey Board of Health	2.318
States of Jersey	2.319

Index: Trusts, PCTs, LHBs & CHPs

Index: Trusts, PCTs, LHBs & CHPs

Index: Trusts, PCTs, LHBs & CHPs

Index: Trusts, PCTs, LHBs & CHPs

Index: Trusts, PCTs, LHBs & CHPs

Index: Trusts, PCTs, LHBs & CHPs

ndex: Trusts, PCTs, LHBs & CHPs

Index: Towns

Index: Towns

Index: Towns

Index: Towns

Index: Towns

Index: Towns

Index: Towns

Index: Towns

Index: Towns

Index: Towns

Index: Towns

Index: Towns

Index: Towns

Index: Towns

Index: Towns

Index: Towns

Index: Towns

Index: Towns

Index: Towns

Index: Towns

Index: Towns

Index: Towns

Index: Towns

Index: Towns

Index: Towns

Index: Towns

Index: Towns

Index: Towns by Trust

Index: Towns by Trust

Index: Towns by Trust

Index: Towns by Trust

Index: Towns by Trust

Index: Towns by Trust

Index: Towns by Trust

Index: Towns by Trust

Index: Towns by Trust

Index: Towns by Trust

Index: Towns by Trust

Index: Towns by Trust

Index: Towns by Trust

Index: Towns by Trust

Index: Towns by Trust

Index: Towns by Trust

Index: Towns by Trust

Index: London Postcodes

Index: Advertisers